Handbook of Comparative and Development Public Administration

PUBLIC ADMINISTRATION AND PUBLIC POLICY

A Comprehensive Publication Program

Executive Editor

JACK RABIN
Professor of Public Administration and Public Policy
School of Public Affairs
The Capital College
The Pennsylvania State University—Harrisburg
Middletown, Pennsylvania

ANNALS OF PUBLIC ADMINISTRATION

Handbook of Comparative and Development Public Administration

Second Edition, Revised and Expanded

edited by

Ali Farazmand

Florida Atlantic University
Fort Lauderdale, Florida

MARCEL DEKKER, INC.   NEW YORK · BASEL

ISBN: 0-8247-0436-3

This book is printed on acid-free paper.

Headquarters
Marcel Dekker, Inc.
270 Madison Avenue, New York, NY 10016
tel: 212-696-9000; fax: 212-685-4540

Eastern Hemisphere Distribution
Marcel Dekker AG
Hutgasse 4, Postfach 812, CH-4001 Basel, Switzerland
tel: 41-61-261-8482; fax: 41-61-261-8896

World Wide Web
http://www.dekker.com

The publisher offers discounts on this book when ordered in bulk quantities. For more information, write to
Special Sales/Professional Marketing at the headquarters address above.

Current printing (last digit):
10 9 8 7 6 5 4 3 2 1

PRINTED IN THE UNITED STATES OF AMERICA

To my son, Cyrus

Foreword

For the last decade, this collection of essays on topics in comparative and development public administration has been a basic source of information for academics, practitioners, and students around the world.

Professor Ali Farazmand of Florida Atlantic University has now planned, organized, and edited this revised and expanded Second Edition, which updates and enhances the value of the original publication. Although a large majority of the chapters have been retained, most of them have been revised taking into account recent developments.

More than 20 new chapters have been added, increasing the collection to 76 chapters and making it even more comprehensive and current. Most parts of the volume contain new contributions. The contents are organized in two main units, the first treating a variety of elements in the study of comparative and development administration and the second dealing more specifically with administrative performance and political responsibility. There are two major alterations in the format, one in each unit. The first is a new group of four essays on historical bases of public administration and bureaucracy, dealing with ancient Persia; Greece, Rome, and Byzantium; India; and the Aztecs, Incas, and Mayas. The second is the deletion of a brief section on bureaucratic behavior and public policy, although one of the two articles in it has been shifted elsewhere in the volume.

As before, the authors represent an impressive array of expertise for many countries, but their contributions do not advocate any particular approach to comparative analysis. The result is a collection valuable enough to serve the differing needs of a variety of users.

This is a welcome addition to the literature available in our field at the opening of a new century.

Ferrel Heady
Professor Emeritus
Public Administration and Political Science
University of New Mexico
Albuquerque, New Mexico

Prologue

Public Administration always involves both processes and tools: the processes of implementing public policy and the tools of public office. Officials bear the responsibility for turning goals into realties—without them, policies remain only promises. In this context, development has two faces: it may refer to policies that affect a society's ability to achieve public goals, or to the capacity of government agencies to implement these purposes. I think of the first as the administration of development, and the latter as the development of administration. Of course, both need to be viewed in a comparative perspective in order to reach valid conclusions. Analyses based on just one case or country cannot discover what has general and theoretical significance and what is better is explained by unique circumstances.

This second edition of the *Handbook of Comparative and Development Public Administration* is a greatly expanded version of a work that has already established itself as a prime source of knowledge in this field. It is divided into two parts: the first dealing more with the administrative processes involved in development (both economic growth and bureaucratic capabilities) and the second part focuses on bureaucracy as a crucial instrumentality for these processes. Although the work emphasizes development in less developed countries, it does not neglect the experience of more developed countries: each sheds light on the other. Moreover, although the focus is on contemporary conditions, the book includes chapters on historical antecedents that put current conditions into a deeper context. Whatever happens today needs to be understood by looking into the past and this perspective also paves the way for anticipating the future more clearly.

The bureaucratic role in development is always complementary with non-bureaucratic roles. Within governance as a broad process, the agenda or goals of development are normally set outside the bureaucracy which is then charged with special responsibility for implementing public policies set by others. The private sector, including entrepreneurs working for profit in market systems and civic groups working for a wide diversity of principled concerns, is a partner in this process in that they both support and constrain public officials. Public policy depends heavily on their cooperation and initiatives to achieve its goals. Thus, both administration and bureaucracy must always be seen as elements in a complex, as parts of a much larger system.

Nevertheless, the processes of policy implementation and the interest of bureaucrats as citizens and subjects of a state inevitably help shape outcomes. We need to see these forces at work in the making of policy, where bureaucratic interests play a role, as well as in the implementing of policy where the capabilities and constraints experienced by officials help shape outcomes. In short, the divide between politics and administration is always amorphous and fluctuating. In some respects, we may even say that administration is just a form of politics. The chapters that follow shed light on these phenomena in many ways, at different levels, places, and times. They do not necessarily agree with each other or present a unified message. Rather, just as our world is a manifold inviting multiple perspectives on complex phenomena, so this handbook offers the reader a wide variety of points of view and insights. Editor Ali Farazmand has performed a remarkable service by bringing them all together and presenting them in a coherent pattern.

Fred W. Riggs
University of Hawaii
Honolulu, Hawaii

Preface

The second edition of this encyclopedic handbook is a major update—a revised and expanded version of the first edition, published a decade ago. The first edition was an overwhelming success as the only comprehensive handbook ever published that covered the twin fields of comparative and development public administration plus the field of bureaucratic politics and administrative theory. It was well received, readily adopted by key scholars, teachers, and trainers at universities and institutes around the world. Due to its overwhelming success, the first edition was reprinted several times during the 1990s, a decade of historical changes that included the fall of the USSR, sweeping privatization and governmental reforms around the world, and accelerating globalization of capital with significant implications—both positive and negative—for governance, public administration, and national self-determination.

The second edition of this encyclopedic handbook reflects these global changes with new discussions of historical roots of governance and public administration traced in the ancient civilizations, as well as original materials on ethics and accountability issues in modern public administration. Contemporary changes of significance demanded substantial revision of the first edition, plus significant updates that reflect currency in the fields of comparative and development public administration, as well as bureaucratic politics and administrative behavior worldwide. Addition of the historical materials as well as new treatments of ethical dimensions contributed to the expansion of the handbook from the 55 chapters of the first edition to 76 chapters, plus major revision and expansion of the chapters carried over from the first edition. The breadth, scope, issues, and coverage of materials in the new edition take the readers well beyond the horizon of the triple fields through their intellectual/conceptual foundations, development, and applications around the world.

The purpose of this edition remains the same as that of the first: to bring together essays that analyze basic issues and major aspects of the fields of comparative and development public administration, and comparative bureaucratic politics and public policy. Aspects of each field include a wide range of sectoral issues of industrial, urban, rural, agriculture, education, and other aspects of development and administration. The major concerns of students of comparative and development public administration as well as of policy makers include issues of changes, modernization, dependency and independence, government reorganization, administrative reform and development, privatization, globalization, political economy of reform, ethics and accountability, professionalism, and historical roots of modern public administration in the ancient and medieval civilizations and philosophical grounds of both the East and the West.

Additionally, a focus on bureaucracy, bureaucratic politics, and political regime maintenance, as well as alternatives to bureaucratic administration, can be chosen for comparative analysis of administrative performance and political functions. Alternatives to bureaucratic administration have gained global currency. Much of this global trend in government and public administration reforms has embraced sweeping privatization, which must be understood in the much broader context of the globalization of capitalism.

This book covers these aspects and approaches, as well as a wide range of functions and related issues. These include budgeting and financial management, planning and development, personnel administration, public management, public enterprise management, policy analysis, organization and reorganization, local and intergovernmental administration, globalization and regionalization, civil service politicization, bureaucratic politics, administrative efficiency and effectiveness, representation, corruption, ethics and accountability, civilization and administration, change and revolution, democracy, and more.

Such a comprehensive treatment has never been attempted before. Although smaller collections are available in the fields, they are narrowly conceived and have not gone beyond certain specific areas of the world. Most of these works either are grossly outdated or serve only a limited audience. The new edition of Ferrel Heady's *Public Administration: A Comparative Perspective* is, of course, a powerful textbook and is well adopted, but it is neither a handbook nor an encyclopedia. The worldwide adoption of the first edition of this handbook as a primary textbook as well as a reference book provided a strong impetus for publication of the second edition. The result is a comprehensive and up-to-date volume of original materials on governance, public administration, comparative and development administration, and comparative bureaucratic politics administrative theory and behavior that could have easily been published in two volumes but is offered in a single volume for adoption as a primary textbook as well as an encyclopedic reference book.

The book is divided into two major units, followed by a comprehensive index. The first unit, which is very broadly focused, is organized into 10 parts and 56 chapters It covers a wide range of issues and aspects of public administration and public policy in developed and developing nations of the world. Part I examines comparative and development administration in the temporal context of past, present, and future perspectives, followed by a discussion of the problems and organizational aspects of development and comparative administration. Part II presents a comprehensive discussion of ancient civilizations and administration, with original chapters on the administrative legacies of Persia, Greece, Rome, Byzantium, India, early native America, and later European traditions that shaped the modern enterprise of public administration. Part III presents 11 chapters on public administration in more developed nations of the West (North America and Europe), the East (Japan), and Australia. Of these, five chapters are entirely new, while others have been revised and updated. Part IV offers impressive material on public administration and governance issues in the former Soviet Union and eastern and southern Europe. Part V presents nine chapters on various aspects and issues of public administration and governance in Asia and Africa, with the most chapters focusing on Asia—covering countries from China, Thailand, and Korea in East Asia to India. Kenya, Nigeria, and southern Africa are covered by three other chapters.

Part VI covers various aspects of public administration in developing nations of the Near and Middle East, Latin America, and the Caribbean; seven chapters—three new and four revised and updated—analyze such issues as state and public administration traditions in Iran from ancient times as well as contemporary reform in that country, bureaucracy and reform in the Middle East and Latin America, local government in authoritarian Chile, and state administration in socialist Cuba. Part VII presents two chapters examining the issues of dependency, independence, and governance and administration of small states in a comparative perspective, with the latter being a new chapter in the volume. The four chapters in Part VIII are on public administration and public policy, with a focus on change, administrative reform and reorganization, democracy, ethics and accountability, development, and environmental policy in the Balkans. Two chapters are new; the other two are either revised or reprinted. Part IX presents four chapters on central issues and problems in comparative and development administration, with a focus on policy implementation and development, superoptimal policy choices across continents, executive personnel development, the role of the state in society, and government bureaucracies and their alternatives around the world. Part X offers five chapters—four of them new—on corruption, public service ethics and accountability, professionalism, and ethical issues in Internet application and healthcare administration.

The second unit of the book focuses on bureaucratic politics and administrative theory. The major themes of this unit are the political role of public bureaucracy (for example, system maintenance, regime enhancement, public policy, bureaucratization, social control, and bureaucratism) and the administrative role of bureaucracy in terms of performance, efficiency, achievement, public management, policy implementation, management of change, and development administration. Here, bureaucracy's role is analyzed both theoretically and empirically. The emphasis is on the comparative performance of public bureaucracies across nations, ideologies, and political systems. Commonalities as well as differences are explored in order to draw some generalizations from administrative and political theories, and for policy making.

Thus, this unit, like the first one, is an original contribution to the fields of comparative public administration, comparative politics, bureaucratic politics, and administrative theory. It is divided into six parts and 20 chapters. Part I provides a theoretical foundation for comparative bureaucratic politics and administrative theory. Three updated chapters analyze the bureaucratic link between administration and politics, the strategic environment of public managers in developing countries, and management of unforseen consequences due to potential achievement crises often experienced in development administration and in public bureaucracies across the world. Part II presents six major chapters on the use and abuse of bureaucratic power for administrative performance and political regime/system maintenance across the world. Theoretical and empirical analyses put these two broad thematic issues in perspectives. Here, new and revised chapters present empirical data on the role of bureaucracies in implementing social change and transformation, in promoting equity and bridging gender gaps, in managing change and development, in public administration, and in political system maintenance and regime enhancement in the United States, Europe, and Iran.

Part III offers two additional empirical chapter materials on the administrative and political roles of public bureaucracies of Europe: Greece and France. Discussions in Parts IV and V present six chapters with empirical data on the political and administrative roles of bureaucracies in developing nations of Asia, Africa, the Near and Middle East, and Central and Latin America. Here, individual country studies and comparative analysis across nations and regions shed light on the important role of bureaucracy as a powerful institution of power in social change—both positive and negative—and political order in three continents. Finally, Part VI presents three empirical chapters on the complex relationship among bureaucracy, change, and revolution. Drawing on specific cases of Iran, the Philippines, and some African nations, these chapters put into perspective the central issue of bureaucracy and revolution and examine significant implications of political and administrative theories of change, development, and revolution.

Like the first edition, this encyclopedic handbook is intended to serve students and instructors of comparative and development public administration, as well as those of comparative politics and policy, as a unique and comprehensive textbook at graduate and upper-undergraduate levels. It is also a most comprehensive reference source for researchers and policy makers in the areas concerned. The contributors and I hope that this book will fill a major gap in comparative and development public administration, in response to the need felt by many for a long time.

This project could not have been accomplished without the assistance and cooperation of those involved. I would like to thank all the contributors, who, despite their heavy research agenda, always responded promptly to my inquiries, demands, and memos. I am sure they will all be pleased with the finished volume. I would also like to acknowledge the assistance of former doctoral student and research assistant, Jack Pinkowski, who helped me in the early stages of the project. My special thanks also go to Jack Rabin, the series editor, whose cooperation throughout the project was much appreciated and to the production editor, Elizabeth Curione, at Marcel Dekker, Inc. Elizabeth must be commended for her hard work, patience, and professionalism in taking this huge project from the beginning to the end. She also worked with me on the almost equal-sized encyclopedic handbook *Crisis and Emergency Management*, which is being published simultaneously. I also extend thanks to Professors Ferrel Heady and Fred Riggs for reviewing the project and providing endorsing support via the Foreword and Prologue. Finally, I am indebted to my son, Cyrus, whose quality time with his father suffered by my concentration on this project. The book is dedicated to him.

Ali Farazmand

Contents

UNIT ONE   COMPARATIVE AND DEVELOPMENT ADMINISTRATION

Part I   Comparative and Development Administration as Fields of Study: History, Methods, Concepts, Problems, and Issues

Part II   Historical Bases of Public Administration and Bureaucracy

Part V   Public Administration in Developing Nations: Asia and Africa

**Part VI   Public Administration in Developing Nations: The Near and
Middle East, Latin America, and the Caribbean**

Part VII   Public Administration and Development, Dependency, and Independence: Theoretical and Empirical Aspects

Part VIII   Comparative Public Administration and Public Policy: Administrative Reform, Change, and Development

Part IX   Some Central Issues/Problems in Comparative and Development Administration

Contributors

Yaser M. Adwan, Ph.D. Social Security Corporation, Amman, Jordan

Adnan A. Alshiha, Ph.D. College of Architecture and Planning, King Faisal University, Damman, Eastern Province, Saudi Arabia

Greg Andranovich, Ph.D. Department of Political Science, California State University, Los Angeles, California

Demetrios Argyriades, Ph.D. R. F. Wagner Graduate School of Public Service, New York University, New York, New York

J. Norman Baldwin, Ph.D. Department of Political Science, University of Alabama, Tuscaloosa, Alabama

Bidhya Bowornwathana, Ph.D. Department of Political Science, Chulalongkorn University, Bangkok, Thailand

Gerald E. Caiden, B.Sc.(Econ.), Ph.D. School of Policy, Planning, and Development, The University of Southern California, Los Angeles, California

Ledivina V. Cariño, Ph.D. College of Public Administration, University of the Philippines, Quezon City, Philippines

John Carroll, AB.D., M.P.A. School of Public Administration, Florida Atlantic University, Fort Lauderdale, Florida

King W. Chow Department of Political Sciences, The University of Hong Kong, Hong Kong, China

Jeanne-Marie Col Department of Economic and Social Affairs, The United Nations, New York, New York

Robert B. Cunningham, Ph.D.   Department of Political Science, University of Tennessee, Knoxville, Tennessee

Andrew C. Danopoulos   College of Social Sciences, University of California at Davis, Davis, California

Constantine P. Danopoulos, Ph.D.   Department of Political Science, San Jose State University, San Jose, California

David L. Dillman, Ph.D.   Department of Political Science, Abilene Christian University, Abilene, Texas

Joseph W. Eaton   Economic and Social Development, Graduate School of Public and International Affairs, University of Pittsburgh, Pittsburgh, Pennsylvania

Milton J. Esman, Ph.D.   Department of Government, Cornell University, Ithaca, New York

Ali Farazmand, Ph.D.   School of Public Administration, Florida Atlantic University, Fort Lauderdale, Florida

Quinton A. Farley, M.P.A., J.D.   Office of Regional Counsel, Environmental Protection Agency, Dallas, Texas

Lon S. Felker, M.A., A.B., Ph.D.   Department of Economics, Finance, and Urban Studies, East Tennessee State University, Johnson City, Tennessee

Jean-Claude Garcia-Zamor, B.A., M.A., M.P.A., Ph.D.   School of Policy and Management, Florida International University, North Miami, Florida

David J. Gould[†]   Graduate School of Public and International Affairs, University of Pittsburgh, Pittsburgh, Pennsylvania

Lawrence S. Graham, B.A. , M.A., Ph.D.   Department of Government, University of Texas at Austin, Austin, Texas

John A. Halligan   Centre for Research in Public Sector Management, University of Canberra, Canberra, Australia

George L. Hanbury II, M.P.A.   President's Office, Nova Southeastern University, Fort Lauderdale, Florida

Keith M. Henderson, D.P.A.   Department of Political Science, State University College of New York at Buffalo, Buffalo, New York

Metin Heper, Ph.D.   Department of Political Science, Bilkent University, Ankara, Turkey

---

[†] Professor Emeritus, Deceased

Jack W. Hopkins, Ph.D.   School of Public and Environmental Affairs, and Center for Latin American and Caribbean Studies, Indiana University, Bloomington, Indiana

Lee-Jinn Hwa   College of Law, National Chengchi University, Taipei, Taiwan, Republic of China

Jamil E. Jreisat, Ph.D.   Department of Government and International Affairs, Public Administration Program, University of South Florida, Tampa, Florida

Carole L. Jurkiewicz, Ph.D.   Public Administration Institute, Lousiana State University, Baton Rouge, Lousiana

Behrooz Kalantari, Ph.D.   Public Administration Program, Savannah State University, Savannah, Georgia

Mohammad Mohabbat Khan, Ph.D.   Bangladesh Public Service Commission, Dhaka, Bangladesh

Peter H. Koehn, Ph.D.   Department of Political Science, University of Montana, Missoula, Montana

Filip Kovacevic   Department of Political Science, University of Missouri–Columbia, Columbia, Missouri

Steven G. Koven, Ph.D.   Department of Urban and Public Affairs, University of Louisville, Louisville, Kentucky

Kálmán Kulcsár   Academy of Sciences, Budapest, Hungary

William Kurtz   Department of Political Science, The University of Tennessee, Knoxville, Tennessee

Jae Eun Lee, Ph.D.   Social Science Research Institute, Yonsei University, Seoul, South Korea

Jerome S. Legge, Jr., Ph.D.   Department of Political Science, University of Georgia, Athens, Georgia

Sheryl L. Lutjens, Ph.D.   Political Science Department, Northern Arizona University, Flagstaff, Arizona

Earl Frank Mathers, M.P.A.   International Institute, USDA Graduate School, Washington, D.C.

Dhipavadee Meksawan   Office of the Civil Service Commission, Royal Government of Thailand, Bangkok, Thailand

John G. Merriam, Ph.D.   Department of Political Science, Bowling Green State University, Bowling Green, Ohio

Abbas Monavvarian, Ph.D.   Department of Public Administration, State Management Training Centre, Tehran, Iran

Anil Kumar Monga, M.A., M.Phil., Ph.D.   Department of Evening Studies, Panjab University, Chandigarh, India

John D. Montgomery, Ph.D.   John F. Kennedy School of Government, Harvard University, Cambridge, Massachusetts

Antony Moussios, D.P.A.   Department of Political Science, University of Georgia, Athens, Georgia

Stuart S. Nagel, Ph.D.   Department of Political Science, University of Illinois at Urbana–Champaign, Urbana, Illinois

Olatunde J. B. Ojo, Ph.D.   Department of Political and Administrative Studies, University of Port Harcourt, Port Harcourt, Nigeria

B. Guy Peters   Department of Political Science, University of Pittsburgh, Pittsburgh, Pennsylvania

John Power   Centre for Research in Public Sector Management, University of Canberra, Canberra, Australia

Alfredo J. Rehren, Ph.D.   Instituto Ciencia Política, Universidad Catolica de Chile, Santiago, Chile

Margaret F. Reid, Ph.D.   Department of Political Science, University of Arkansas, Fayetteville, Arkansas

Fred W. Riggs, Ph.D.   Professor Emeritus, Department of Political Science, University of Hawaii at Mano, Honolulu, Hawaii

Platon N. Rigos, B.A., M.A., Ph.D.   Department of Government and International Affairs, University of South Florida, Tampa, Florida

Gerry Riposa, Ph.D.   Department of Political Science, California State University–Long Beach, Long Beach, California

Karen Ruffing-Hilliard   U.S. Agency for International Development, Cairo, Egypt

Olof K. Ruin, Ph.D.   Department of Political Science, University of Stockholm, Stockholm, Sweden

Masaru Sakamoto   Faculty of Law, Ryukoku University, Kyoto, Japan

Frank P. Sherwood   Department of Public Administration, Florida State University, Tallahassee, Florida

Renata Wanda Siemienska, M.A., Ph.D.   Institute of Sociology, Warsaw University, Warsaw, Poland

William J. Siffin[†]   Department of Political Science and Public Affairs, Indiana University, Bloomington, Indiana

Alf Sjöström   Swedish Gallup, Stockholm, Sweden

Orapin Sopchokchai, Ph.D.   Department of Social Development, Thailand Development Research Institute, Bangkok, Thailand

V. Subramaniam, Ph.D.   Department of Political Science, Carleton University, Ottawa, Canada

Itoko Suzuki   Ritsumeikan Asia Pacific University, Beppu, Japan

Janice L. Thomas   Department of Justice and Risk Administration, Virginia Commonwealth University, Richmond, Virginia

Ian Thynne, Ph.D.   Department of Politics and Public Administration, University of Hong Kong, Hong Kong

Paul C. Trogen, B.A., M.A., Ph.D.   Department of Economics, Finance, and Urban Studies, East Tennessee State University, Johnson City, Tennessee

Krishna K. Tummala, Ph.D.   Department of Political Science, Kansas State University, Manhattan, Kansas

Ogwo J. Umeh, Ph.D.   Department of Public Administration, California State University, Hayward, California

Roger Wettenhall, Ph.D.   Centre for Research in Public Sector Management, University of Canberra, Canberra, Australia

David Wilsford, Ph.D.   Institute for American Universities, Aix-en-Provence, France

Lois Recascino Wise, Ph.D.   School of Public and Environmental Affairs, Indiana University, Bloomington, Indiana

Jong-Hae Yoo, Ph.D.   Department of Public Administration, Myongji University, Seoul, South Korea

Habib M. Zafarullah, Ph.D.   School of Social Science, University of New England, Armidale, New South Wales, Australia

---

[†] Deceased

1

Problem of Development Administration

William J. Siffin[†]   *Department of Political Science and Public Affairs, Indiana University, Bloomington, Indiana*

I. BUSINESS OF THEORY AND PARADIGMS

Some years ago two Americans were visiting agricultural universities in India looking for lessons from the creation of those rather novel Indian institutions. As they traveled, their conversations ranged. The subject of institution building came up. The political scientist observed that the institution-building perspective popular at the time was bad social science—an a priori theory containing a number of implicit and untested assumptions about causal relations but lacking rigorous rules for applying its contents to real-world situations.

"Maybe so," said his colleague, an agricultural economist with an earthy background of experience in farm management, "but I've found some helpful ideas in that stuff. In fact, if I'd known about that linkage business in the institution-building theory when I was running a project in Sierra Leone, I'd have done certain things differently, and probably better."

(The theory posited that "linkages" were important to institution building and that an organization had to establish certain kinds of connections with its environment to survive and thrive. In grand general terms, this claim was sensible enough, although it was not anchored in systematic evidence nor reinforced by precise specification of how to establish and evaluate the appropriate linkages.)

A light came on within the recesses of the political scientist's mind! He had been fretting about the subject of institution building for some time, bothered by the inadequacies of the dominant model of the day; in the rigorous sense of idealized social science it just wasn't good theory. It fit Anatole Rapoport's description of a theory with "explanatory appeal" but without much explanatory power. Yet here was an experienced and canny colleague affirming the practical utility of some features of that theory.

The point of the matter: ideas don't have to be theoretically rigorous and powerful to be useful in the uncertain and confusing world of pragmatic action. Messy and imprecise semiconcepts, or concepts that do not neatly transfer into clear, sharp applications in the real world, can be useful in the hands or minds of discerning practitioners. They are tools of thought and judgment for dealing with matters that "do not compute." "A little bit of knowledge can be either a dangerous thing or a useful thing, depending upon the circumstances" (Wilson 1987:59). Good theory reduces the danger of error, but it is not always available.

To some persons this claim is heresy, or at least a debasement of the Noble Principles of the social sciences, which hold that Theory is our credo and a Paradigm is our proper God. Not just

---

[†]Deceased.

any theory, of course, but *systematic* theory, grounded in a combination of evidence and logic, articulated in a form both objective and operational. The concerns of the world, however, do not limit themselves to matters covered by such theory, and the quest for it quite often diverts inquiry from utility, clothing naked truth in false, beguiling garments.

Now as in the 1960s, some scholars wrestle with the theory of institution building while others argue that there is no such thing—that institutions evolve in ways not entirely susceptible to human direction. Both views are of course couched in theoretical terms, but the theories involved are of variable quality, just as the terms used within them range from primitive to rigorously conceptual. "Bad theory" and fuzzy conceptualizing are what we use when we haven't anything better (or when we don't know any better). The trick is to avoid using "bad theory" badly, to remain constantly aware of the problems of conceptualization, and to abjure the impulse to emulate physical science when it comes to paradigms. If Thomas Kuhn has enhanced our methodological awareness with his influential argument about paradigms, he has also stimulated pathologies—misplaced quests for paradigms in messy domains identified on the basis of interest and desire, and lacking well-established defining characteristics (cf. Landau 1979, especially Chapter 2).

II. EMERGENCE OF DEVELOPMENT ADMINISTRATION

The institution-building situation mentioned above has its parallel in the so-called field of development administration. It, like the public administration of which it is a part, is "a subject matter in search of a discipline" (Swerdlow 1975:324). There is no embracing theory of development administration or of institution building. Indeed, the term "development administration" is not conceptualized in any precise and generally accepted fashion. The label identifies a loosely sensed "interest," which exists because some people deem it important. Its significance does not depend on a paradigm or a systematic array of theoretical knowledge. True, many of our particular concerns with public administration drive quests for good theory. It is equally true that there is no widespread agreement on the theoretical center and boundaries of the "field." There is more agreement on the premise that "development administration" is part of the subject matter of public administration. Both draw upon clusters of concepts and theory, some quite powerful and others not much more than useful conventions by which we try to order some of the booming, buzzing chaos of the world.

The intellectual context within which development administration emerged was rooted in a fortunate set of pragmatic concerns. Woodrow Wilson's benchmark essay of more than 100 years ago was inspired by a problem and an insight—the problem of integrity and effectiveness in American public administration. This led him to consider the possibility of mating a model—and some of the reality—of Prussian bureaucracy with the theory and practice of Constitutional government. Some decades later Leonard D. White produced the first widely used American textbook in the field. Writing well before Max Weber was discovered in the United States, White followed the Wilsonian perspective in his claim that "the study of administration should start from the base of management rather than the foundation of law" (Swerdlow 1975:325). This viewpoint laid a base for the developments of the past half century, during which public administration assimilated and absorbed achievements of the social sciences and confronted the issues of philosophical theory posed by such scholars as Vincent Ostrom (1973).

Development administration came along in the 1950s.

> Egbert de Vries, a prominent Dutch economist, and I learned in discussions with each other that each of us had started to use the term "development administration" in 1955 or 1956. I used it to conceptualize the nature of the administrative research and training program contemplated

for the Academy of Rural Development established subsequently at Comilla in East Pakistan (now Bangladesh) and for the academy at Peshawar in West Pakistan . . . (Gant 1979:xi).

The aim of the term was "to distinguish the focus of administration on the support and management of development . . . from the administration of law and order" (Gant 1979:19–20). Gant went on to claim, "The function of development administration is to assure that an appropriately congenial environment and effective administration support are provided for delivery of capital, materials, and services where needed in the productive process—whether in public, private, or mixed economies" (Gant 1979:xi).

He envisioned a subject matter parallel to "development economics," and was not at all troubled by the conceptual, theoretical, and empirical differences between administration and economics. Nor have been most of the scholars and practitioners who since 1955 have labored in the towers and vineyards of "development administration." If there is some grand problem of development administration, it is not the problem of failure to achieve a paradigm, or to cloak the "field" in the shining garb of systematic, comprehensive theory.

When it comes to the establishment of a field grounded in sound and powerful theory, it appears that George Gant was not far off the mark in drawing a parallel between development administration and development economics. The latter has achieved less than a distinguished record. Theory aplenty has been produced, presented, and applied, but it remains about as true in 2000 as it was in 1945 that "the most important feature of our experience of development . . . is its unpredictability" (Toye 1987:18).

The author of this conclusion argues that "giving more attention to the analysis of uncertainty can help theorists of development to move beyond the (in any case poorly defined) boundaries of the conventional classification of development economics schools. Such a move . . . has the further interesting property of building bridges towards disciplines other than economics" (Toye 1987:18). We are not alone in our lack of a good and comprehensive grounding of our attempts to examine and prescribe.

III. EVIDENCE OF RICHARD W. RYAN

If we lack a theoretical foundation, do we at least have a pervasive sense of order and agreement in our dealings with the subject of development administration? Under the auspices of the National Association of Schools of Public Affairs and Administration (NASPAA) and the U.S. Agency for International Development, Professor Richard W. Ryan analyzed the contents of about 40 courses on development administration and comparative administration offered at 27 American universities during the 1980s (Ryan 1986). His findings are instructive.

These courses display no compelling coherence. Among them, "development administration" is most often treated as a facet of comparative administration. Ferrel Heady's *Public Administration: A Comparative Perspective* (1984) is the most widely used text. The focus of this urbane book is public bureaucracy as it exists within different types of political systems. Heady briefly sketches five general features of public administration in developing countries, and carefully examines the interplay of bureaucracy and politics. His book is broad in scope and structural in orientation, a synthesis of two intellectual traditions: the grand approach to institutional comparison epitomized by Herman Finer, and Max Weber's view of bureaucracy. The work, like the courses in which it is used, emphasizes teaching more than practitioner training (Ryan 1986:9).

A number of other courses examined by Ryan use Coralie Bryant and Louise White's *Managing Developing in the Third World* (1982) as their base. Whether they begin with Heady, Bryant and White, or something else, the impressive feature of these courses is their diversity. Ryan's analysis of 36 syllabi found some commonality of content, notably attention to "bureaucratic and professional influences," politics, and conceptions and models of development. Twenty of the courses addressed the topic of project design and management. Surprisingly little attention was given to planning and budgeting. What are the implications of all this disparity?

1. Some hundreds of college students are taking courses in development administration and comparative administration every year. Do they as a consequence have a common lexicon and sh ared perspective? Are they parties to a pool of professional, technical, and intellectual know-how? The answer is, "Not much."

2. Of course, the academic offerings summed and assessed by Richard Ryan do not mirror the full content of "development administration." Enormous amounts of activity have occurred in training establishments, in developing countries, all of it labeled by reference to development administration. Here is where one finds attention to practical skills, in addition to the technical training found in professional academic programs. Much of the latter consists of courses in budgeting, accounting, planning, programming, decision making, organization theory, personnel administration, strategic management, and other theoretical and technical topics typical of professional school programs. Here one finds much of the substance of what is implied by the label "development administration."

The problem of development administration, if indeed there really is one, lies in some of the implications of this situation.

IV. PROBLEM OF DEVELOPMENT ADMINISTRATION

It can be argued that there really isn't much of a problem, inasmuch as there isn't much of a field. Development administration is a term that implies a question: "How can the ideas and mechanisms of public administration be used as instruments of social and economic development?"

This question excludes little, if anything, of the fuzzy domain of public administration, despite George Gant's effort to draw a boundary between "law and order" and "administration as the tool of change"—if only because certain kinds of order are an underlying imperative of managed change. Perhaps the idea of "development administration" as a distinctive subject matter is something of an absurdity.

But there *are* important and relatively distinctive problems of induced development that involve the intelligent application (or avoidance) of administrative arrangements. Some of them actually leap across the fuzzy boundaries of public administration; they are large questions about choices between deliberate, organized programming and reliance upon indirect action (such as indicative planning or recourse to the automatic working of the marketplace).

"Privatization" was a powerful buzzword in the 1980s and 1990s. If its use is sometimes intended to placate a dominating political bias, there can still be good sense in considering mechanisms that do not require elaborate public bureaucracies and effective policies for their working, in countries whose bureaucracies are limited in prowess and integrity. Of course, privatization implies a degree of regulation and an adequate infrastructure. These requirements can stimulate the imaginations of development programmers, enabling them to generate projects in the service of antiproject ends.

The general form of the question (when to choose or avoid an administrative arrangement or program) is significant. We are not overloaded with utilitarian answers. We lack a theory offering both a general line of response *and* concrete rules of action. Yet the problem to some extent is being attacked, with cases and lessons that seep into the awareness of analysts and decision makers.

If this type of problem spills beyond the conventional contents of public and development administration, many others lie somewhat more clearly within them. These are essentially "how-to" problems. They have been with us for decades. How to plan and budget? How to transform an existing bureaucracy, or some of its central elements, such as the arrangements for accounting and financial administration? During the 1970s "administrative reform" was an influential catchword; much was said and written, most of it more exhortative than instructive. "Administrative reform," like "development administration," labeled vast concerns. Sometimes the labels have been preface to perceptive and intelligent problem definitions.

Development administration in fact *is* the indicative but imprecise label for a set, or at least a potential batch, of problems. They possess some common properties—they involve questions about organizations and organizing, for example—but the actual things that interest us are also in vital ways unique in their locations and their contexts and in other ways.

By reference to their common attributes, we can speak or write generally about these things—this concern and the multitude of problems it embraces. When we do so, we are beginning to categorize (Landau 1979:179). But, as the above evidence indicates, the "we" involved has not proceeded very far in a common, consensual direction. Conceivably, following Landau's line of reasoning, "we" might be able to achieve a genuine field of development administration, but the record to this point is not assuring, suggesting that the effort to do so ought not to dominate our interests nor provoke contention. Our concern is essentially *practical*, and there is much to be said in favor of intelligent practical inquiry and action. We won't have a science, but we can draw to the fullest extent of our desires and abilities upon the fruits of pertinent scientific inquiry. As powerful concepts and elements of theory emerge within the intellectual context of our concerns we can exploit them to expand our knowledge, insofar as reality allows. What we have at this point is a vaguely stated concern and a variable bunch of problems. The manner in which some of those problems are addressed will affect the lives and prospects of large numbers of persons—the intended beneficiaries, and not infrequent victims, of "development." Under the circumstances, one central item on the messy agenda of development administration should be attention to the business of sound and careful problem definition.

V. DEFINING PROBLEMS

In the grandest sense possible, the problem of development administration is that of *designing organized arrangements that work to serve auspicious aims.* The term "problem" is not quite a synonym for "design," because designing arrangements of various kinds is one of the most ubiquitous human activities, some of which have become highly specialized within the domains of engineering and architecture. Yet the idea of "design" illuminates the concerns of development administration, and somewhat sets them apart within the entire enterprise we call public administration. The idea of "design" implies the idea of "problem." *A problem is an artificial analytical/normative construct*, a thing that exists only in the minds of humans, for there are no problems in nature. Nature *is*.

We regularly address familiar problems without thinking about their underlying properties. Yet a problem can be an exquisitely subtle and elusive thing. It involves, first of all, the comprehension of a situation—including knowledge of the causal factors that make that situation what it is. A problem also involves a judgment that this situation is undesirable—and that there is a known and preferable alternative to it, one that can be specified, legitimated, and implemented with assessable results.

The term problem has acquired the properties of a concept. Familiarly used as a primitive term whose meaning is specified by some empirical referent at hand, it can also be treated as an idea comprehending the essential attributes of a class or logical species, as in the above definition. The class can be disaggregated into two analytically distinctive subsets: simple problems (Landau labeled them "system maintenance problems"), and messy problems. The latter are problems of systems design under conditions of high uncertainty. And these are the problems typical of development.

Empirically, such problems display many, sometimes all, of these qualities: The causal characteristics of initial state conditions are not clearly comprehended. The properties and effects of an intervention are not well understood. And there is less than concurrence in the judgment of (1) what is wrong, and (2) what is better—that is, what constitutes a proper solution.

In such circumstances optimization is not the appropriate ideal. At best, a sensible quest will seek satisficing solutions. It may, in fact, be difficult or impossible to know precisely when such a kind of problem has been "solved."

The intransigence of such problems does not keep people from trying to define and attack them. It is, however, a splendid impulse to suboptimizing and misperception. Typically these two misperceptions are embedded in premature programming. This consists of defining the problem by the summary selection of a solution—usually through invoking the means at hand.

As the secretary general of agriculture in a West African country once said to me, "If the World Bank sends a livestock man, we shall have a livestock project. If the Bank sends a cotton specialist, we shall have a cotton project." Reportedly the Bank sent both, so the problems of agricultural development became livestock and cotton.

Facing imponderable challenges and commanding a variety of technologies, messy problems of development and development administration are often defined by quick reference to a sense of what can be done. If this is not altogether bad, it is not invariably good, because errors not only waste resources, they may cause harm to those least able to bear its consequences—the very people whose plight justifies the intervention.

One obvious implication of this situation—this application of a conscious concept of problems to the empirical concerns of development—is a need for the most auspicious possible definition of those problems. For "development administration" this means serious attention to defining problems to which administration is, or may be, an inherent part of the answer.

It means, as John Toye argued, systematic attention to the implications of uncertainty. In the case of development planning Toye observes:

> A major implication of substantial uncertainty for policy-makers is that the policy tools forged in the 1970s now seem too information-intensive to be used as they were designed. This appears to be so not only for developing countries . . . but even for . . . international organizations. . . . This places the design of cruder, but more serviceable, decision-making tools on the development policy agenda (Toye 1987:35–36).

If there is to be a subject matter called development administration, it ought to focus as fully as possible upon prospective problems related to the familiar subject matter of administration and to an abiding question: How do things seem to work within supposedly developmental settings?

One classic point of departure into this sort of inquiry is A.O. Hirschman's *Development Projects Observed* (1967). Hirschman analyzed a set of development projects, all of them confronted by significant uncertainties. To explain why some of these ventures worked better than others he posited the idea of the "hiding hand," a set of potentials that sometimes came into play to overcome the impediments of unanticipated circumstances. He argued that "the attempt to eliminate totally one particular kind of uncertainty may therefore not only be futile but counterproductive (Hirschman 1967:84–85).

Experts have argued over Hirschman's view. Toye sums the contentions. The underlying question persists: How can intelligent interventions be designed and implemented under conditions of uncertainty—that is, in the face of messy problems? Insofar as these interventions involve administrative arrangements, the question is an important item on the agenda of development administration.

VI. SO WHAT ABOUT THE SUBJECT MATTER?

The argument at this point holds that the informing focus for an agenda of development administration ought to be a very general question: How do administrative things work, under conditions of uncertainty, when the objective is to foster some sort of development?

The quest for answers to that question, informed by awareness of the nature of messy problems, can draw widely from knowledge of the subject matter of public administration. It will have to reconsider some of that knowledge from the perspective of would-be developmental environments. A benchmark example is Naomi Caiden and Aaron Wildavsky's *Planning and Budgeting in Poor Countries* (1974).

There is more, because development administration is committed to involvement in matters outside the boundaries of conventional public administration. There is, for example, the business of planning and managing rural development, a subject whose large and varied literature (e.g., Cohen 1987; Honadle and Klaus 1979; Korten and Alfonso 1981; Lele 1975; Moris, 1981) demonstrates the entwinement of administrative knowledge with applied science and information about particular socioeconomic environments. There are also health delivery, family planning and population control, environmental protection, transportation and communications, and other matters of infrastructure development and maintenance. Administration is intrinsic to all of these fields, in addition to the old standbys of budgeting, personnel, and management. What a fascinating mess, all of it present (or absent) in a congeries of cultural and political settings!

An alternative way to impose some order upon this enormity of concerns would be simply to adopt the Public Policy perspective. Then we could forget about development administration and build an agenda around the "process" framework, which is influential in the nondiscipline of Public Policy. In any case, the eclecticism of that subject matter area offers a model to think about.

Another alternative is to somewhat order the concerns that have given rise to our professed subject by attention to the questions and the concept noted above, attention informed by the methodological imperatives that should govern their analysis. In this case, a proper introduction would include the work of such scholars as Robert Chambers, A.O. Hirschman, Martin Landau, Charles Lindblom, and Herbert Simon, plus a good dose of attention to some empirical would-be problems.

The aim would be to equip clients with suitable tools of analysis—a bag of tools informed by awareness of the elemental difference between *methods* and *methodology.*

The result might be an inspired elaboration of what we now have—a subject matter lacking clear boundaries and crisp disciplinary rigor, addressing pragmatic problems with such analytic skill and talent as we can muster. Nothing more appears to be available.

REFERENCES

Bryant, C., and White, L. (1982). *Managing Development in the Third World.* Boulder, CO: Westview Press.

Caiden, N., and Wildavsky A. (1974). *Planning and Budgeting in Poor Countries.* New York: Wiley.

Chambers, R. (1985). *Managing Rural Development: Ideas and Experience from East Africa.* West Hartford, CT. Kumarian Press.

Cohen, J.M. (1987). *Integrated Rural Development.* Uppsala, Sweden: Scandinavian Institute of African Studies.

Gant, G.F. (1979). *Development Administration: Concepts, Goals, Methods.* Madison: University of Wisconsin.

Heady, F. (1984). *Public Administration: A Comparative Perspective.* New York: Marcel Dekker, 3d ed.

Hirschman, A.O. (1967). *Development Projects Observed.* Washington: Brookings Institution.

Honadle, G., and Klauss, R. (1979). *International Development Administration: Implementation Analysis for Development Projects.* New York: Praeger.

Korten, D., and Alfonso, F., eds. (1981). *Bureaucracy and the Poor: Closing the Gap.* New York: McGraw-Hill.

Landau, M. (1979). *Political Theory and Political Science: Studies in the Methodology of Political Inquiry,* Passaic, NJ: Humanities Press.

Lele, U. (1975). *The Design of Rural Development: Lessons from Africa.* Baltimore: Johns Hopkins University Press.

Moris, J. (1981). *Managing Induced Rural Development.* Bloomington: International Development Institute, Indiana University.

Ostrom, V. (1973). *The Intellectual Crisis in American Public Administration.* Tuscaloosa: University of Alabama.

Ryan, R.W. (1986). *Teaching Comparative-Development Administration at U.S. Universities: A Collection and Analysis of Syllabi.* West Hartford, CT: Kumarian Press.

Swerdlow, I. (1975). *The Public Administration of Economic Development.* New York: Praeger.

Toye, J. (1987). Development theory and the experience of development: issues for the future. In L. Emmering (ed.), *Development Policies and the Crisis of the 1980s.* Paris: OECD.

Wilson, J.Q. (1987). Social science and public policy: a personal note. In L.L. Lynn Jr. (ed.), *Knowledge and Policy: The Uncertain Connection.* Washington: National Academy of Sciences.

2

Comparative and Development Public Administration

Past, Present, and Future

Ali Farazmand   *School of Public Administration, Florida Atlantic University, Fort Lauderdale, Florida*

I. INTRODUCTION

Public administration is as old as civilization. The two have existed side by side, contributing to each other's development and decline. Public administration has heavily involved "development" since the earliest time, for almost all massive public works projects implemented by city states and empires were developmental in nature. Also, the concepts of government and public administration have been subjects of discussion for several millennia and both comparative governance and developmental administration components have shaped the early foundations of modern public administration. Philosophers and experts on governance and administration wrote on the nature of states and advised rulers on proper and efficient conduct of public affairs while administrative systems of the major empires and city states of the ancient world performed gigantic tasks of developmental projects through their bureaucracies and ad hoc organizations managed by the state (Farazmand 1991a, forthcoming; Gladden 1972; Nash 1969). In fact, development administration has always been a thriving field of practice in the history of public administration.

However, systematic study of comparative and development administration has been a recent phenomenon. These twin fields of public administration have gone through several ups and downs since the beginning of comparative studies in government, economics, policy, politics, and administration. These are, of course, primarily the Western traditions and are exported to developing nations. Comparative studies of politics and administration are mainly a twentieth-century academic development although studies of "other" nations or politics and administration were conducted in Europe as early as the nineteenth century. However, comparative studies proliferated after World War II. Of these, the fields of comparative politics and economics have been the dominant ones.

The fields of comparative and development public administration began to develop after World War II and comparative administration in particular gained momentum immediately after the war (Heady 1996). A number of factors contributed to this growing development: postwar occupation of nations by the United States and other leading powers; the need for extension of range and scope in public administration as a discipline; wartime experience of scholars and practitioners abroad; overseas technical assistance assignments; growth of the comparative politics section of the American Political Science Association as well as the comparative section of the American Society for Public Administration; and the increasing opportunities in the 1950s and 1960s for those interested in pursuing comparative public administration research and scholarship.

Initially, the comparative aspect was dominant in the studies but, as time passed, other elements changed the direction toward the developmental aspects of these studies. Money, ideology, and politics were among the main factors. The traditional focus on law and order, institutions and institution-building, and general functional areas of government administration gave way to the modified orientations of development, general systems model building, and middle-range theory formulations from the 1960s on (Heady 1996; Farazmand, forthcoming; Nash 1969; Waldo 1992).

While the comparative component of the studies had gained significance, especially through comparative politics and administration, the development administration component gained momentum on a variety of grounds: tremendous interest on the part of the multi-national corporations in developing and underdeveloped countries; their resources and markets; the superpower ideological, economic, military, and political competition between the United States and Western countries on the one hand and the USSR on the other in the developing nations; the collapse of colonial rule in Asia, Africa, and the Middle East, leaving behind their administrative, military, political, and economic legacies of dependency; and the consequences of postcolonial needs for a continued relationship between North and South countries, including the need for an efficient and effective administrative system for both nation-building and implementation of national development plans and goals (Huntington 1968; Heady 1996; Esman 1991; Blase 1973; Siffin 1976; Gant 1971; Riggs 1970, 1976).

This article presents (1) the early origin of modern comparative and development administration; (2) the modern profile of the twin fields of the movement from comparative to development administration; (3) the achievements and failures of the Comparative Administration Group (CAG) and the overall academic enterprise of the fields; (4) the challenges and trends in the study of comparative and development administration; and (5) the future trends and developments including the shape of the two components of public administration as a self-conscious enterprise in the approaching new millennium. A short conclusion will follow with some theoretical generalizations.

II. ORIGINS

Contrary to the established tradition that traces the study of public administration to Woodrow Wilson's writings at the end of the 19th century and the rise of the American administrative state, public administration as a field of study and practice has an origin in the earliest time of human civilization. Indeed, administration and civilization have existed side by side and nourished each other. Both were integral parts of human progress. Civilization promoted administration and administration made civilizational achievements possible (Waldo 1992; Nash 1969; Farazmand, forthcoming). Both have contributed to the development of each other for "civilization and administration always have been and still are intricately joined" (Waldo 1992:1).

A look at human history clearly reveals the significance of public administration and bureaucracy in contributing to the growth and development of civilization and their achievements around the globe. The Sumerians and Elamites (early Iranians) developed urban design and planning as well as the first prototype written scripts or languages which gave humans the tools to record history. These earliest languages served the bureaucracies and administrative systems of many empires that followed. The Egyptians, Assyrians, Greeks, Babylonians, Elamites, Medes, Persians, Chinese, Romans developed significant administrative systems on a large scale and founded the prototypes of the modern administrative state. At the heart of all these civilizational administrative systems was the concept of "development." In fact, it may be argued that development was a constant variable in all major civilizational powers and others because all strived for improvement in human conditions in governance, military, the economy, and society.

Massive public works projects were undertaken in the ancient empires by constructing bridges, roads, canals, monuments, temples, palaces, communication, and other enterprises. Egyptians built the Pyramids and developed medicine. Babylonians shielded themselves with fortified walls against outsiders and developed written administrative records. Chinese built the defensive walls and contributed to civil service examination systems. Greeks developed art, philosophy, governance theory, and the ship-building profession. Persians built the first universal empire with the largest administrative state on earth (with about 10 million to 12 million state-paid personnel) legged on a centralized, professional bureaucracy famous for its efficiency and effectiveness. Through that administrative state, they built the long Royal Roads, developed efficient postal/communication systems, improved taxation, and legal systems, built the gigantic underground irrigation canals or *qanats* thousands of miles long bringing water from highland areas to the desert and lower level fields turning arid lands into cultivabled ones as well as building the Suez Canal connecting the Red Sea to the Mediterranean Sea and the Athos canal hundred miles long in Eastern Europe (Farazmand 1991; Olmstead 1948; Herodotus 1954; Frye 1975).

Romans performed numerous public works projects and promoted the legal profession, administrative system, and legislative democracy. Others had similar contributions to human civilization. These massive public administration activities were "developmental" in nature, all contributing to the changing conditions of human societies and promoted the governing elites that operated the empires (Farazmand, forthcoming; Waldo 1992; Nash 1969; Gladden 1972).

Therefore, the origin of development administration is found in the ancient time just as the origin of public administration is rooted in the ancient world. Public administration was also studied seriously as a professional career in ancient time in Persia from the Achaemenid World-State Empire to the Sasanid period (559 B.C. to 651 A.D.) (Farazmand 1991a; Frye 1963, 1975; Olmstead 1948; Ghirshman 1954), in China (Chow 1990), and in Rome (Daley 1997). Obviously, Greek philosophers—Plato, Aristotle, and Exenophon—discussed in detail different forms of governance in search of the ideal state, society, and, by implication, public administration (Argyriades 1997; Argyle 1994).

Similarly, comparative study of public administration is rooted at least in ancient Greece where Athenian philosophers, especially Plato and Xenophon, discussed comparative governments. "The Greek was almost forced to think of what would now be called comparative government . . . found a great variety of political institutions, all indeed of the city-state type" (Sabine 1961:21). Plato devoted special attention to this matter in his writings on state, law, justice, and ideal government in theory (Sabine 1961) while Xenophon's analysis focused empirically on the existing "ideal ruler" in his major book, *Cyropaedia-Education of Cyrus*, on the benevolent and liberal king, Cyrus the Great, as the founder of the Persian Empire (Nadon 1996). With the death of Aristotle, the city-state as a form of democratic governance also died and led to absolute monarchy under the Macedonians (Sabine 1961).

All these philosophers as well as the father of history, Herodotus (1954), studied and wrote in a time full of diversity of governmental systems, from those of the Greek city-state to that of the major empires, particularly the stable and prosperous Achaemenid World-State Persian Empire (559–330 B.C.). After the death of Cyrus the Great and his son Cambyses, the Seven Persian Noblemen discussed "the relative merits of monarchy, aristocracy, and democracy" (Sabine 1961:22) to adopt for Persia (for details, see Herodouts 1954:28–241).

Persia and Greece presented models of governance and administration, the latter with political systems of governance and the former with a large-scale administrative system legged on a notoriously efficient and professional bureaucracy which has survived all political changes to the present day (Farazmand 1994a, 1997; Frye, 1963, 1975; Olmstead 1948). Thus, like development administration, comparative public administration has its roots in ancient time, the former being on practical grounds while the latter on theoretical basis. However, systematic study of development and comparative administration appears to be a more recent enterprise.

III. COMPARATIVE AND DEVELOPMENT ADMINISTRATION

The study of comparative and development administration as the twin fields of public administration is directly linked to the multidisciplinary fields of political science, economics, and cultural anthropology. The linkage began to develop sometimes before World War II, but it was after the war that such studies became fashionable.

The postwar developing nations, including the former colonies, adopted development plans for their national economies but many lacked institutional and administrative capacities to carry out those plans. Therefore, there developed fertile grounds for experts in public administration from the United States and other Western European countries in providing administrative know-how as well as technology to the developing nations (Heady 1996). The result was a tremendous interest in and growth of development administration as a field of study and practice.

The growing interest in development administration as a major component of comparative administration prompted many scholars in the general field of public administration to praise the academic expansion of development administration for both methodological and conceptual reasons. Methodologically, the field of development was wide open for rigorous academic studies and, conceptually, for producing new ideas and generalizations about human history and civilization development. Dwight Waldo was a leading praiser. As he noted, a concentration on the theme of development might "help to bring into useful association various clusters and types of activity that are now more or less separate and help clarify some methodological problems" (1964:27) even though he found it "impossible to define development."

By the 1960s the growth of development administration as a field of study and practice was well institutionalized. The most notable aspect of this development in the Western world was the emergence of the CAG. Founded under the auspices of the Ford Foundation in 1962, CAG was formed and headed by Fred Riggs, a leading scholar in the field. Under Riggs, a large number of studies were conducted around the world and funded by the Ford Foundation which showed interest in developmental aspects of developing nations. Grants from U.S. government agencies as well as other donors made it possible for the expanding field of study to proliferate and for the scholars who saw a shifted area of interest, for corporations and governments (Heady 1996; Waldo 1992).

Therefore, the focus on development administration as part of comparative administration was a reflection of financial reality. Follow the areas where money was available for it. The development administration focus was based on (1) the developmental needs, mainly economic; (2) the difference in needs of developing and developed nations; (3) the possibility of administering development; (4) transferability of development know-how; (5) the changeability or alterability of the political, social, economic, and cultural conditions of less developed countries; and (6) the developed nations of the industrial West as a model to adopt for achieving developmental goals by the developing nations with the desired goal to become like the Western nations.

The idea was an elitist one, designed by the Western governmental elites, as a planned intervention approach to change and transform developing countries into a market-based, elite-controlled, and closely tied with and conducive to the promotion of the Western values of economy politics, and culture. Prominent spokesmen of CAG, such as Esman, recommended further empowerment of the administrative elites. This elitist intervention plan was also aimed at creating and supporting local elites in developing nations to promote such a grand strategic design and to enhance the system in power. The masses of those nations were given little attention, however. The context was the cold war and the idea was to export American public administration to the third-world nations (Waldo 1992). "Experts in public administration, not only from the United States but from numerous European countries as well, were scattered around the world, engaged in similar projects to export administrative technology, largely from American experience, to a multitude of developing countries" (Heady 1996:21).

As Waldo (1992) points out, the elitist development administration as a field of study was exciting and encouraging for *development* as a concept and process carried positive connotation, reflecting progress in human conditions. The entire plan was devised by President Truman after his election in 1948 to extend the Marshall Plan to developing nations as well. It was "Point Four of his message to Congress" and was in (Waldo 1992:121):

> . . . the context of the developing Cold War. The Soviet Union and its communism must be contained; countries new, weak and poor were easy conquests or converts; a "Marshall Plan" for the emerging countries would help insure their independence and their evolution in the direction of liberal democracy. Dollars in quantity—and dollars then were very large—began to flow.

The whole plan was an American dream. As one expert of the time, Garth Jones (1976:99–100), describes it: "[T]he 1950s was a wonderful period. The 'American Dream' was the 'World Dream'—and the best and quickest way to bring the dream into reality was through the mechanism of public administration" (also quoted in Heady 1996:21). The desired goal was to modernize developing nations through the "developmental power of administrative tools devised in the West" (Siffin 1976:61).

The CAG under Riggs, who had done monumental work in the fields of comparative and development public administration, was praised for its major achievements (more of this below). However, it was not without criticisms. It was criticized for its major failures, including the production of many studies viewed as culturally biased, for favoring the dominant powers of the West against the developing nations, and indeed for being responsible for making conditions for the mass peoples in the developing countries worse by supporting and promoting the repressive governments of the Shah of Iran, Samoza of Nicaragua, and Marcos of the Philippines. It was further criticized for the studies and training programs that resulted in actual "antidevelopment" (for details of these criticisms of CAG, see Sigelman 1976; Henderson 1969; Jreisat 1976; Loveman 1976; Jun 1976; Peters 1988).

After the Iranian revolution of 1978–79 and the fall of the Shah's regime, known as "America's Shah" (Cottam, 1979), several experts with extensive experience in Iran and elsewhere looked back and provided assessments of the failures of the interventionist development programs, published in a special issue of *Public Administration Review* (1980:40; articles by Seitz, Sherwood, Siffin, and others; Heady 1996:31–32;). Loveman (1976) has made one of the strongest attacks on the CAG and its "anti-developmental" impacts. Loveman (1976:618–619) called the CAG movement and its leaders too elitist, with little concern for the masses in developing nations, and linked with the U.S. governmental technical assistance officials. As Heady (1996:33) points out, Loveman claimed that the aim of "the CAG and United States policy-makers turned to programs intended to build up administrative elites, often military elites."

Loveman and other critics attacked the CAG and the whole development administration movement for their contributions to the promotion of antidemocratic regimes in repressing their peoples and to making the conditions of poor developing countries worse. Peters (1988) had leveled the strongest criticisms against the comparative administration on academic research grounds, particularly on methodology. His criticism points to the major deficiencies, causes, and consequences of the comparative public administration for its lagging "behind other areas in political science in progress toward meeting tests of scientific rigor as measured by canons of social science" (Heady 1996:53). Peters offers "middle-range institutional theories" with bureaucracies as focuses of comparison in comparative and development public administration.

This is a good message to Heady (1996) who has been focusing on bureaucracy as the most important institutional base for comparative studies of public administration. This author concurs with both Heady and Peters on the use of bureaucracy as a focus of comparison, but would also add that nonbureaucratic, nongovernmental, grass-roots organizations as well as cultural and other indigenous factors unique to certain societies must be taken into account in the study and practice of public administration. The Western models of bureaucracy and administration are often too problematic to many societies of developing nations and often have assumptions that do not fit with developing nations and their peculiarities. The result of any elitist, top-down approach to development administration is the generation of more negative consequences than positive ones.

As the funding institutions and agencies lost their interest in supporting development and comparative administration research and training projects in the 1970s, so declined the academic interest in pursuing such studies. The result was a major decline in the twin fields of administration and the once popular *Journal of Comparative Administration* went out of publication. Although it was renamed with a different focus, *Administration & Society*, the journal no longer reflected the earlier themes and literature.

However, some European traditions have until today continued to produce studies in the fields, particularly in development administration. Examples include the British royal *Journal of Public Administration and Development* which has a development focus and the *International Journal of Administrative Science* which publishes articles on comparative and development administration and on developed as well as developing countries. In the United States, the key journals in the fields include *International Journal of Public Administration* and *Public Budgeting and Financial Management: An International Journal*.

IV. ACHIEVEMENTS AND FAILURES

The achievements and failures of the CAG and the academic development of comparative and development administration in the past are thoroughly analyzed by a prominent expert, Ferrel Heady, in his classic book *Public Administration: A Comparative Perspective* (1999). In a nutshell, the twin subfields of comparative and development administration have contributed significantly to the general field of public administration over the last four and one-half decades, since the end of World War II. More than anything else, development administration was concerned primarily with the preoccupation of the dominant Western capitalist powers with countering the spread of socialism and the Soviet influence on developing and underdeveloped nations of Asia, Africa, the Middle East, and Latin America.

This was a global concern for the capitalist superpowers of the West, especially the United States, against the superpower of the East. The socialist ideas of sharing wealth, leveling inequality, eliminating homelessness, and providing for the basic needs such as health, food, and shelter to all citizens were appealing to many peoples in the poor developing countries that were long suppressed and exploited by colonial and imperialist powers (Waldo 1992). "Noncapitalist-path to development" was a global strategy promoted by the former USSR and Eastern Europe and was adopted not only by the revolutionary socialist regimes such as Cuba, North Korea, Vietnam, and China, but also by some regimes pursuing mixed economies such as Egypt under Nasser, Tanzania under Nyerere, Mozanbique, and Angola, to name a few. At the heart of this developmental approach were issues of equitable distribution of national income, improvement in the welfare of the masses, economic justice, and elimination of human exploitations.

Countering this approach, the Western financial and administrative assistance to developing countries grew dramatically to strengthen their political and ruling elites and the regimes they operated and to alleviate some of the hardships such as absolute poverty, hunger, and disasters the masses suffered. This was done particularly under the direction of the United Nations Development Programs, U.S.-AID, and World Bank technical assistance programs. The result has been mixed so far.

Thus, development administration as a focus of comparative public administration was both intentionally designed and practical oriented in terms of scholarly interest for the flow of dollars was strong and continuous (Waldo 1992). Political and personal convictions in promoting certain governmental policies were also contributing factors in the growing interests among scholars in the field. The academic proliferation of studies in development administration contributed significantly to the field of comparative public administration and politics, but many of these studies were fragmented, diverse with case studies, without cohesive theoretical conclusions or generalizations. The relative decline of interest in comparative and development administration resulted in the exclusion from the curricula of the graduate public administration programs in the universities and colleges and in the funding supports for such studies. Since the 1980s, few university public administration programs in the United States have been offering courses in comparative or development administration.

Nevertheless, despite this instructional decline, the number of recent studies conducted and the books published in the twin fields have been impressive, making major contributions to the field of public administration (see, for example, Rowat 1988; Subramaniam 1990; Dwivedi and Henderson 1990; Farazmand 1991, 1994; 1997; 1999; Garcia-Zamor and Khator 1994; Esman 1991; Baker 1994; Heady 1996). This occurred despite the lack of any significant funding support from governmental or private organizations. One major explanation for this no-support productivity may be the special interest of certain scholars and experts who continue to produce in the fields. Their motivations may include personal growth, knowledge contribution, as well as the conditions of the people in the developing countries.

Other reasons may include renewed organizationally funded research, UN-sponsored studies aimed at improving human conditions in poor nations, World Bank, and other donor organizations promoting specific and purpose-oriented studies such as privatization of government enterprises, marketization of socialist nations, and U.S.-AID sponsored studies abroad (Farazmand 1996; 2000).

A remarkable continuity observed in the studies of comparative and development administration has been their focus on public bureaucracy as a major institutional arrangement for all governments around the world; it has supplied a sound, institutional framework for comparison in those studies (see the references cited above). Ferrel Heady has made a solid contribution to the twin fields by continuously revising and updating his classic book with such a focus on bureaucracy as a framework for comparison.

V.   CHALLENGES AND PROBLEMS

One of the major problems the fields of comparative and development administration have faced, and the challenge that has not yet been overcome, has been the problem of definition. Aside from the methodologoical problems in comparative administration studies, the term "development administration" has been confusing and never clearly defined (Heady 1996; Waldo 1992). The lack of consensus in defining what is meant by the term has led to major confusions reflected in various studies in the field.

Nevertheless, based on the overall literature, the concept of development administration is generally referred to as the two broad subsets of "administrative development" and "development administration" (Riggs 1976; Siffin 1991; Waldo 1992). The first refers to the development and enhancement of the administrative capacity and the skills in such areas as personnel, finance, accounting, management, taxation, and organizational development for carrying out development plans and achieving development goals in rural and urban areas. Institution-building and management training programs were key focuses of this trend in the 1950s and 1960s.

The second concept, development administration, was concerned with the administration of national development plans and achievements of their goals and objectives. Both reinforced each other and both were considered to be important. Riggs himself was generally clear on these two aspects of development administration definition. The distinction is more clear when we note that "administrative development" includes activities aimed at improving the traditional functions of governments such as maintenance of law and order, while the term "development administration" is exclusively focused on development functions of governments (Gant 1971; Heady 1996; Waldo 1964; Siffin 1992; Riggs 1975, 1976, for details).

Reviewing the intellectual aspects of public administration in general and development administration in particular, Siffin (1991:6) addresses the problem of the field very specifically. "There is no embracing theory of development administration, or of institution-building. Indeed, the term 'development administration' is not conceptualized in any precise and generally accepted fashion." According to Siffin (1991:8):

> [D]evelopment administration is a term that implies a question: "How can the ideas and mechanisms of public administration be used as instruments of social and economic development?" This question excludes little, if anything, of the fuzzy domain of public administration, despite George Gant's effort to draw a boundary between "law and order" and "administration as a tool of change"—if only because certain kinds of order are an underlying imperative of managed change. Perhaps the idea of "development administration" as a distinctive subject matter is something of an absurdity.

Another problem faced by researchers was the instability of many regimes in developing countries making sustainable development programs and projects difficult if not impossible. This problem was further marked by the mixed or negative results of the elitist-designed training programs conducted by the U.S.-AID, World Bank, and other sponsoring institutions far from the real problems faced by poor countries (Siffin 1991:10). Siffin describes this problem from his conversation with a West African government official:

> As the Secretary general of Agriculture in a West African country once said to me, "If the World Bank sends a livestock man, we shall have a livestock project. If the Bank sends a cotton specialist, we shall have a cotton project. Repeatedly the Bank sends both, so the problems of agricultural development became livestock and cotton."

Consequently, studies of development administration have often produced inconclusive, poor, and sometimes opposite generalizations. Despite this and other problems in the field, the opportunities in the areas of comparative and development administration are only beginning to expand, not shrink, due to the recent trends of globalism, globalization, privatization, structural readjustment, redefinition of public-private sector boundaries, growing gaps between the developed and developing nations, global environmental problems, and other developments outlined below.

VI. THE TWIN FIELDS IN THE FUTURE

The twin fields of comparative and development administration appear to be facing a number of challenges and opportunities in the future. Several trends have already emerged out of these developments, while others will likely emerge in the next few years.

1.   The New World Order has replaced the old order with major consequences, primarily for developing nations. Until the collapse of the USSR, there was a polarity in world order in which both the socialist and capitalist superpowers divided the world system, checked each other, and provided shields of protection for their allies in developed and developing countries. In that globally divided world system, political and administrative behaviors were generally predictable and developing nations had alternative superpowers available to choose from. Under the New World Order, such a choice is eliminated and many developing nations are subject to elite manipulation and possible repression without a chance of alternative political or social systems to choose from since the only social system considered acceptable is capitalism and the market system in which corporatism and bureaucratic-economic elites reign (Farazmand 1994c). The gap between the elite and the masses will likely grow larger not smaller. Consequently, the field of public administration will likely be reduced even more to system maintenance and regime enhancement around the developing world. These roles have already been a dominant feature of the larger superpowers as well, such as the United States under the neo-conservative era of the 1980s and 1990s. Public administration will be more like administration and enhancement of the powerful private interests/elites as opposed to the administration of societal affairs in promoting the general and public interests. This is especially true in regard to the multinational corporations and the role of comparative and development administration in promoting their interests (Farazmand 1994c; Korten 1980, 1990).

2.   There is more attention to indigenous cultural values, norms, and strengths of nations and people. This is important for the purpose of cultural integration through diversity.

3.   There is the democratization and the rising expectations among people in the developing world with the consequence of peoples demanding more human rights and resisting repression.

4.   There is more education and there are more women in the areas of politics and administration, both contributing to the changes in the traditional patterns of administration and both contributing to the increasing demands of citizens in society.

5.   There are more accommodations by the power elites in organizations of government, in business, and in administration while the masses are kept content or under control and there is the unpredictability in changing events around the globe; we are living in "the age of unreason" (Handy in Daft 1995:93).

6.   There has been a decline and collapse of some authoritarian regimes (e.g., Iran, Nicaragua, South Africa, and the Philippines).

7.   There is more diversity and inclusion rather than exclusion through globalization and global interactions.

8.   There is the growing role of the United Nations as an instrument of superpower domination in developing countries and the global bureaucracy, both visible and invisible, with the leadership roles played by Washington, London, and possibly some of the European nations such as Germany and France or the European Community as a whole.

9.   There is centralization and decentralization: centralization of corporate and international political military powers and the technologies at their disposal, and decentralization through further parcelization of nations based on ethnic, religious, cultural, and other factors for the purpose of easier control and domination in the international politics.

10.   There are Westernization and Americanization of the developing world.

11.   There are globalization of America and Americanization of the world and the consequently concomitant changes in the administration systems, values, and functions around the world.

12.   There is cultural convergence and global organizational reconfiguration of public-private sectors of administrative functions and of internalization by indigenous peoples of the American cultural values.

13.   There are increasing global mandates through the UN programs on global health, environment, population, energy, education, and the like, all producing opportunities for comparative and development administration to grow (Khator 1998).

14.   There are increasing demands for professionalization of bureaucracies and public services and of organizations in nonprofit and profit sectors, producing a more advanced cadre of managerial and administrative elites and, at the same time, promoting more advanced managerial capacity for development purposes.

15.   There are increasing interdependence and joint-venture operations, promoting opportunity and, concurrently, constraint and dependencies for developing countries.

16.   There is expansion of the Western-led market system and marketization around the developing nations and in socialist countries.

17.   There is increasing sophistication in development public administration, administrative development, policy planning and administration, contract administration development projects, privatization-mess clean-ups, and more.

18.   There is increasing pressures for serving the clients a market-like function of public organizations and public administration though it is not clear who the client is and will be (Peters 1998).

19.   There is expansion of computer use as a major tool of technology in communication, data processing, and administration around the world.

20.   There is increasing comparative research in public administration, global problem solving, strategy, cross-national analysis and development, corporate-government coordination, and associated issues.

21.   There is perhaps less American parochialism and ethnocentrism in public administration theory and practice, as more and more global information penetrates the American traditions of culture, administration, and citizenship. Such a global interaction will likely influence the American public administration which has been long held parochially and ethnocentrically (Riggs 1998). Americans will also have to adjust to the changing global conditions and such global movements as those on environment, health, peace, women's rights, and others. And with the changing technology and Internet computer and television sattlelite systems, it will be more difficult to keep Americans uninformed about the events around the globe, a phenomenon that has so far been effectively maintained by the elite-oriented media networks as well as by the government. By the year 2000 more millions of people around the globe will likely share information and more people will likely demand accountability and responsiveness on the part of their governments. In this process, public administration in the year 2000 will have to be more efficient, more effective, and more responsive and democratic than expected; at least, these will be the expected values and behaviors of public administration in the new, globally integrated world system (Farazmand 1994c).

22.   A related and important development that has emerged and will possibly become a new paradigm in the global study and practice of public administration is the concept of "sustainable development" which by various definitions refers to "global equilibrium," "environmental sustainability" by all governments, peoples, and institutions around the world and a holistic approach to sustainable development in the global village in which the developed nations as well as the developing have both interest in and responsibility for maintaining a balance for survival and growth needs of both advanced and non-advanced peoples and nations. In short, an ecosystem

is envisioned in development administration which calls for a global self-sustenance and this calls on the developed nations to contribute to the developing nations if they desire to remain developed and grow in the global ecosystem (Khator 1998; Riggs 1998; Farazmand 1998).

23.   There is increasing pressure for revolutionary changes in the developing nations and in some developed countries in the governmental and administrative systems. This trend seems to have already taken a surge in the forms of massive citizen participation in politics and in their demands for alternative systems to bureaucratic designs in public service delivery. Religious as well as secular models of public administration, including Islamic public administration (Farazmand 1998; Kalantari 1998) are increasingly being adopted as alternatives to the traditional models.

24.   There is growing pressure for adoption of nongovernmental and grass-roots organizations for development administration among the developing, and some developed, nations.

25.   There is a growing understanding that development administration is not exclusively related to developing nations. Rather, development is a universal phenomenon and all countries, including advanced ones, are engaged in development administration in a variety of areas. As Waldo (1992:133) points out, "**All** countries are developing, we now realize." Similarly, public administration as a field of study will be both "global and comparative" (Farazmand 1994c; Riggs forthcoming).

26.   In the New World Order, the American scholars, experts, government officials, and administrators are playing leadership roles around the world. If played negatively and for domination and exploitation, the natural results will likely be a more negative consequence against the U.S. government and its administrative values in the long run. Consequently, the long-term effectiveness of the U.S. public administration will likely diminish significantly among the peoples around the globe. American public administration is not and has never been an indigenous invention; it has been borrowed from thousands of years of experience gained since the dawn of human civilization. To be more effective, American public administration will need to be more globally cultured rather than ethnocentrically molded. Its ethnocentric values have produced arrogance among the experts and the common people around the globe will likely question such values and will likely resist. There will be mutual influences at global level.

27.   Another development will be the disappearance of the dichotomy myth between politics and administration and between policy and management. These dichotomies have caused more harm than benefit to public administration as a field of study or profession. A related development will be a continued focus on bureaucracy as a framework for comparison in comparative and development administration. As the most important and rational institution of administration, bureaucracy has been a focus of comparative analysis for thousands of years (Eisenstadt 1963).

28.   A further interest will also likely develop around the concept of organizational elite theory and administrative elite development. This will have a twofold consequence: enhancing the power of the elite, on the one hand, and increasing education of the masses concerning the elite power and its possible abuse of that power through administrative and organizational elites, on the other. This will likely result in a mass resistance to, and possible revolution against, such elite-power dominance; hence, a positive development although elite circularity will likely prevail again.

VII. CONCLUSION

The twin fields of comparative and development administration have roots in ancient time. As major components of modern public administration, comparative and development administration have struggled in their attempts to develop conceptually and practically since their inception after World War II. The post-war proliferation of interest and studies in both fields has resulted in a large number of publications which have contributed to the knowledge in public administration as a whole.

However, this knowledge has been a subject of criticism from various sources and on different grounds, ranging from the fragmentation of studies to the problems of definition and methodological and scientific rigor. Also, there was a major shift to "development administration" and away from "comparative administration" in post-1950s resulting in both achievements and failures—achievements in the impressive number of studies published and failures for the contributions by CAG to "antidevelopment" and making the conditions of the masses worse while beefing up dictatorial regimes and the elites that operate them. While the elitist comparative and development administration movement of the 1960s and 1970s failed and resulted in the decline of interest in the study of both subfields of public administration, the number of independently produced scholarly works in the twin fields is impressively increasing.

This article has reviewed the past and present of the twin fields of comparative and development administration and has outlined a number of trends and challenges that will face public administration in general and comparative and development administration in particular under the New World Order. In the future, public administration will be both global and comparative and development administration will be an integral part of this global public administration for all countries are developing at different levels.

REFERENCES

Argyle, Nolan (1994). "Public Administration, Administrative Thought and the Emergence of the Nation State," in Ali Farazmand (ed.). *Handbook of Bureaucracy*. New York: Marcel Dekker.

Argyriades, Demetrios (1997). "Administrative Legacies of Greece, Rome, and Byzantium." *International Journal of Public Administration* 20(12) December.

Baker, Randall (ed.) (1994). *Comparative Public Management: Putting U.S. Public policy and Implementation in Context*. Westport, CT: Praeger.

Blase, W. (1973). *Institute Building: A Source Book*. Beverly Hills: Sage.

Chow, King (1990). "Bureaucratic Problems in Ancient China: Causes and Implications." Paper presented at the 1990 Conference of the American Society for Public Administration, Los Angeles.

Cottam, Richard (1979), "Goodbye to America's Shah." *Foreign Policy* No. 34.

Daft, Richard (1995). *Organization Theory and Design*, 5th ed. New York: West Publishing.

Daley, Dennis (1997). "The Decline and Fall of the Roman Empire: Lessons for Management." *International Journal of Public Administration* 20(12) December.

Dwivedi, O.P. and K. Henderson (eds.). *Public Administration in World Perspective*. Iowa City: Iowa State University Press.

Eisenstadt, S.N. (1963). *The Political Systems of Empires*. New York: Free Press.

Esman, Milton (1991). *Management Dimensions of Development: Perspectives and Strategies*. West Hartford, CT: Kumarian Press.

Farazmand, Ali (1991a). "State Tradition and Public Administration in Iran in Ancient and Contemporary Perspective," in Ali Farazmand (ed.). *Handbook of Comparative and Development Public Administration*. New York: Marcel Dekker.

Farazmand, Ali (ed.) (1991b). *Handbook of Comparative and Development Public Administration*. New York: Marcel Dekker.

Farazmand, Ali (1994a). "Bureaucracy, Bureaucratization, and Debureaucratization in Ancient and Modern Iran," in Ali Farazmand (ed.). *Handbook of Bureaucracy*. New York: Marcel Dekker.

Farazmand, Ali (ed.) (1994b). *Handbook of Bureaucracy*. New York: Marcel Dekker.

Farazmand, Ali (1994c). "The New World Order and Global Public Administration," in Jean-Claude Gar-cia-

Zamor and Renu Khator (eds.). *Public Administration in the Global Village*. Westport, CN: Praeger.

Farazmand, Ali (1996). "Introduction: The Comparative State of Public Enterprise Management," in Ali Farazmand (ed.). *Public Enterprise Management*. Westport, CT: Greenwood Press.

Farazmand, Ali (1977a). "Professionalism, Bureaucracy, and Modern Governance: A Comparative Analysis," in Ali Farazmand (ed.). *Bureaucrats and Politicians in Modern Systems of Governance*. Thousand Oaks, CA: Sage.

Farazmand, Ali (1997b). "Administration of the Achaemenid World-State Persian Empire: Contributions to the Modern Administrative State and Public Administration." *International Journal of Public Administration* December.

Farazmand, Ali (1998). "Comparative and Development Administration 2000: A Symposium. *International Journal of Public Administration*, 21(12):1661–1666.

Farazmand, Ali (1999). "Globalization and Public Administration," *Public Administration Review* 59 (6) Nov./Dec.: 521–522.

———— ed; (2000). *Privatization or Public Enterprise Reform: Implications for Public Management* Westport, CT: Greenwood Press.

Frye, Richard (1963). *The Heritage of Persia*. New York: World Publishing.

Frye, Richard (1975). *The Golden Era of Persia*. New York: Harper & Row.

Gant, George (1971). *Development Administration: Concepts, Goals, and Methods*. Madison, WI: University of Wisconsin Press.

Garcia-Zamor, Jean-Claude and Renu Khator (eds.). *Public Administration in the Global Village*. Westport, CN: Praeger.

Ghirshman, R. (1954). *Iran: From the Earliest Time to the Islamic Conquest*. New York: Penguin Books.

Gladden, E.N. (1972). *History of Public Administration*. London: Frank Kass.

Heady, Ferrel (1996). *Public Administration: A Comparative Perspective*. New York: Marcel Dekker.

Henderson, Keith (1969). "Comparative Public Administration: The Identity Crisis." *Journal of Comparative Administration* 1 (May):65–84.

Herodotus (1954, 1984). *Histories*. New York: Penguin Books.

Huntington, Samuel (1968). *Political Order in Changing Society*. New York: St. Martin's.

Jones, Gart (1976). "Frontiersman in Search for the 'Lost Horizon': The State of Development Administration in the 1960s." *Public Administration Review* 36(1):99–110.

Jreisat, Jamil (1975). "Synthesis and Relevance in Comparative Public Administration." *Public Administration Review* 35(6):663–71.

Jun, Jong (1976). "Renewing the Study of Comparative Administration: Some Reflections of the Current Possibilities." *Public Administration Review* (Nov./Dec.):641–647.

Kalantari, Behrooz (1998). "In Search of a Public Administration Paradigm: Is There Anything to be Learned from Islamic Public Administration?" *International Journal of Public Administration*, 21(12):1821–1862.

Khator, Renu (1998). "The New Paradigm: From Development Administration to Sustainable Development Administration." *International Journal of Public Administration*, 21(12):1777–1802.

Korten, David (1990). *Getting to the 21st Century: Voluntary Action and the Global Agenda*. West Hartford, CT. Kumarian Press,

Loveman, Brian (1996). "The Comparative Administration Group, Development and Antidevelopment." *Public Administration Review* (Nov./Dec.):361–374.

Nash, Gerald (1969). *Perspectives on Administration: The Vistas of History*. Berkeley: Institute of Governmental Studies, University of California.

Olmstead, A.T. (1948). *History of the Persian Empire: The Achaemenid Period*. Chicago: University of Chicago Press.

Peters, Guy (1988). *Comparing Public Bureaucracies: Problems of Theory and Method*. Tuscaloosa: University of Alabama Press.

Peters, Guy (1998). "Administration in the Year 2000: Serving the Client." *International Journal of Public Administration*, 21(12):1759–1776.

Riggs, Fred (1970). *Frontiers of Development Administration*. Durham: Duke University Press.

Riggs, Fred (1976). "The Group and the Movement: Notes on Comparative and Development Administration." *Public Administration Review* (Nov./Dec.):648–654.

Riggs, Fred (1998). "Public Administration: A Futuristic Vision." *International Journal of Public Administration*, 21(12):1667–1758.

Rowat, Donald (ed.) (1988). *Public Administration in Developed Democracies*. New York: Marcel Dekker.

Sabine, George (1961). *A History of Political Theory*, 3rd ed. New York: Holt, Rinehart and Winston.

Sherwood, Frank (1980). "Learning from the Iranian Experience." *Public Administration Review* 40: 413–421.

Siffin, William (1976). "Two Decades of Public Administration in Developing Countries." *Public Administration Review* 36 (Jan./Feb.):61–71.

———— (1991). "The Problem of Development Administration," in Ali Farazmand (ed.) *Handbook of Comparative and Development Public Administration*. New York: Marcel Dekker.

Sigelman, Lee (1976). "In Search of Comparative Administration." *Public Administration Review* (Nov./Dec.):621–625.

Subramaniam, V. (1997). "Administrative Legacy of Ancient India." *International Journal of Public Administration*.

Waldo, Dwight (1964). *Comparative Public Administration: Prologue, Problems, and Promise*. Chicago: Comparative Administration Group, American Society for Public Administration.

———— (1992). *The Enterprise of Public Administration*. Novato, CA: Chandler and Sharp.

3
Organizational Perspective in Comparative and Development Administration

Jamil E. Jreisat   *Public Administration Program, University of South Florida, Tampa, Florida*

I. INTRODUCTION

A major thrust of comparative public administration research has always been geared to discovering administrative patterns and regularities over time and place. As a result, the comparativists devoted considerable attention to identification of environmental factors that affect administrative performance (Jreisat 1997). Comparative research often appeared perpetually searching for relevant variables, their range of variations, and the consequences of those variations in determining critical administrative issues (Thompson et al. 1959). The expectation has been that the search will ultimately advance the twin objectives of theory building and utility. Hence, the comparative administration project included a variety of research efforts to define, analyze, and explain similarities and differences of processes of management and organization crossnationally.

During almost five decades of studies, an extensive literature has been produced, as illustrated by Ferrel Heady's review (1996). Appraisal of progress made in achieving the objectives of the comparative movement, however, is inconclusive at best. The celebrated intellectual productivity has not been balanced with profound movement toward syntheses and cumulativeness of information, let alone the issue of practical relevance. Debates that ensued have often been tinged with criticisms, even occasional disenchantment among the most committed students of the field (see Tummala 1998; Heady 1996; Henderson 1982; Honadle and Klaus 1979; Jreisat 1975; Ilchman 1971).

Critical assessments also came from outside the field of public administration. Crossnational policy researchers (Antal et al. 1987:18) find that "two major consequences for the development of cross-national policy research stem from the public administration root." One echoes what many comparativists have recognized long time ago; namely, bridging the gap between theory and practice has not been easy and lack of theory and acceptable general frameworks has hindered cumulation of research results. The second is that the comparative approach is not central to the tradition of public administration research. "Such research tends by nature to be ethnocentric and parochial in its problem-solving orientation" (Antal et al. 1987:18). Realizing this situation, early comparative administration studies advanced perspectives that focus on contextual connections and particularly underscore the decisive impact of politics and culture on bureaucratic behavior (Jreisat 1997; Heady 1996; Riggs 1961, 1962). In fact, during the formative phase, the comparative movement was closely associated with comparative politics, and many scholars identified with both schools of thought.

Irrespective of varying opinions on the value of the comparative scholarship over time, some critical questions still need answers: Does administrative performance vary across cultures, and if so, how much of the observed difference can be attributed to cultural determinants? Similarly, does administrative performance vary with politics, and how much of the observed difference can be attributed to the political context? Apparently, results of the comparative studies often enhanced knowledge of politics and culture more than illuminated administrators and administration. Also, the "add-on" concern with development administration seems to have been confounded by complications and assumptions not sufficiently taking into account important differences in the social, political, and cultural contexts.

Although administration is a singular determinant of development, public administration is not development itself. Lack of conceptual clarity on what is administration and what is development, for example, only deepens theoretical fragmentation and hinders the cultivation of effective frameworks. In a significant way, diffusion of the subject matter prevents full appreciation of the complexities of development and reduces the scope and value of administrative variables, particularly in the delivery of traditional public services.

In the final analysis, reversal of the conceptual diffusion and other theoretical and practical problems discussed here will materialize only when the two major shortcomings of comparative studies (convergence and cumulativeness of research findings) are settled. A definition of the *unit of analysis* is a basic step in the efforts toward convergence (synthesis) as well as cumulativeness of results. The unit of analysis is crucial for defining relevant issues and problems; it often serves like a street sign or a road map that directs traffic movement and regulates its conditions. In many ways, the unit of analysis sets the boundaries of research, influences the selection of tools of research, and systematizes the collection of data—essential functions for developing integrated conceptual schemes for comparative crosscultural analysis. For these reasons, three units are differentiated: the individual, the organization, and the national bureaucracy.

A. The Individual

The main purpose of this perspective is to discover patterns of administrative behavior and to explain causes and influences shaping such behavior. This is the microlevel of administrative theory and process, presupposing a preference for small-scale phenomena—the human personality—before venturing into the larger ones. The problem of "why people behave the way they do" became central to this research, dominated by psychology. "Traditionally, the domain of psychology has been the individual and the quest to uncover the essential properties and universal features of the typical human being" (Nord and Fox 1996:148). The major areas of knowledge resulting from psychology have been personality, motivation, attitudes, and learning. These elements also have been core components of the Human Relations perspective as found in works of leading scholars in this area such as Rensis Likert, Chris Argyris, Douglas McGregor, and others.

Human resources management as well has been directly influenced by psychological studies, particularly issues of motivation, perception, learning, job satisfaction, attitudes, individual needs, and so forth (Eddy 1981). However, after reviewing major developments about psychologic factors and processes in organizational studies, W.R. Nord and S. Fox (1996:149) conclude that "emphasis has shifted from viewing individuals independently of context to consideration of the interplay between individuals and their contexts." Thus, the recent growth in attention to context and the "clear decline in the centrality of individual role" (1996:149) have rekindled awareness of the contextual relationships and, thus, underlined the significance of the organizational focus.

B. The Organization

Choosing the organization as the unit of analysis often is an implicit acceptance of the notion that the most meaningful administrative actions take place in the context of formal organizations. Organizations coordinate and facilitate individual efforts, converting them into sustained collective actions that accomplish or serve goals, above and beyond the capacity of any individual.

From a methodological perspective, the organization is recognized as a superior unit for comparative analysis because of its durable and measurable characteristics. Typically, organizations have specific purposes, concrete structures, determinable boundaries, defined communication channels, and central coordinative systems (March and Simon 1958:2–9). Also, organizations may be conceived as organisms that develop and grow, contract, change, and even die (J.D. Thompson 1967; G. Morgan 1986). No realistic view of the organization is possible without recognition of its dependence on or interchange with a larger system for its input of resources and technology and for discharging its output of goods and services.

Comparative organizational analysis treats the organization as a whole system, even while examining its components. "A number of crossnational comparative analysis studies have been done in the past 15 years, several of which show that structure differs across cultures regardless of technology" (Roberts and Grabowski 1996:415). Restructuring organizations is a global phenomenon and many conceptual insights are derived from international experiences in Europe and Japan as well as developing countries. Related is the growing interest in contextual or environmental constraints that influence organizational actions. Studies of public organizations have been specially conscious of these political, economic, and social constraints which limit the attainment of organizational goals (Jreisat 1997:49).

C. The National Bureaucracy

The focus on the national administrative system as the unit of analysis tends to concentrate on bureaucracy as a national institution and its relations with the environment, particularly the political authority. This is the macro level of administration, which exhibits interest in the overall characteristics that affect the performance of traditional public services. Aspects of this category of studies often overlap with comparative politics (see Rowat 1988). In fact, the early works in this area are totally preoccupied with reflection on political institutions in a handful of Western countries and a scattering of developing countries (Heady 1996). The recent emergence of many third world countries, however, brought forward issues and problems of management and nation building that heretofore were neglected or unfamiliar to scholars of Western comparative politics.

Nevertheless, certain models claim universal applicability to developed and developing countries alike. For example, Almond and Coleman's functional approach (1960) claims to offer a theoretical framework that makes possible the comparison of political systems of any type. While the basic premise of universal structures performing universal functions is arguable, a more serious difficulty with such works is the ancillary treatment of the administrative process as merely "rule application."

Another important orientation of comparative national studies is a commitment to determining how much of the differences in organizational management are caused by attributes of national culture. Findings of such research are often conveyed in terms of the impact of culture on managerial attitudes, beliefs, and behavior (Graves 1972; Hofstede 1980), with the other organizational variables either implied or neglected. Also, "in both single-culture and comparative studies, nation and culture have been used as if they were synonymous, with national boundaries separating one cultural group from another" (Adler et al. 1986:298). The difficulty in equating nation and culture is readily demonstrable in many developing countries with politically or militarily drawn boundaries as in Africa, the Middle East, or the Indian subcontinent.

Although comparative cultural studies of management are replete with variations and complexities, one conclusion is clear. There is no agreement on the importance of cultural influence on organization and management. In fact, results are often contradictory. One approach argues that culture determines managerial practices and culture is "the collective programming of the mind which distinguishes the members of one human group from another" (Hofstede 1980:25). Another perspective concludes that organizational variance is less dependent on culture than other contingencies such as technological development, interdependence with other organizations, market considerations (Child and Tayeb 1983), and type of political authority in the case of public organizations. Yet, no adequate explanation in crosscultural studies of human behavior and psychology is attainable to the finding that people behave in one way with members of their own culture and differently with members of foreign cultures. Reports indicate, for example, that Japanese and American businesspeople modify their within-culture styles when negotiating internationally (Graham 1985; Adler et al. 1986:303).

Crossnational analysis often tracks the political dimensions to produce classification schemes and characterizations of the political and administrative systems. But these classifications of regimes and paradigmatic debates of political factors usually are more informative about regime politics than about organization and management. Few of these distinctions are primarily focused on bureaucratic structures and functions as in Merle Fainsod's classification (quoted in Heady 1996:312). Fainsod's five bureaucracies flowing from political authority are (1) ruler-dominated bureaucracies, (2) military-dominated bureaucracies, (3) ruling bureaucracies, (4) representative bureaucracies, and (5) party-state bureaucracies.

II.   COMPARATIVE ORGANIZATIONAL ANALYSIS

Separation of the three units of analysis generally used (or confused) in comparative administration research is not to be applied rigidly or unalterably. The fact is that administered organizations are integral parts of a larger system with which they continually interact. In the 1930s, Chester Barnard established such a relationship by emphasizing that "the survival of an organization depends upon the maintenance of an equilibrium of complex character in a continuously fluctuating environment" (Barnard 1938:6). Thus, the organization regularly readjusts its internal operations according to environmental requirements. Max Weber, too, correlated the types of administrative staffs and the types of authority systems already developed; hence, bureaucracy is not a neutral tool but reflects conditions existing in the polity and the society (Diamant 1962:87). Classic theories of public administration, particularly those of the 1940s and 1950s, usually assumed these connections. Although the "ecology" of administration has been accepted as a valuable explanatory concept (see Riggs 1961), the implementation has often reflected a selective perception of the elements constituting this ecology. The assumption of traditional research has been that bureaucracy is subordinate to an executive "who exercises authority over a polity" (Riggs 1969).

In reality, therefore, a considerable weaving of mutual adjustments and reciprocal exchanges take place among the individual, the formal organization, and the national administrative system. Intersection and networking among the three units is commonly acknowledged even if hardly evaluated in a systematic manner (V.A. Thompson, 1965:9). Some exceptions are found as in Robert Merton's (1957) work on bureaucratic structure and personality, Chris Argyris (1957) on personality and organization, and Michel Crozier (1964) on the bureaucratic organization and its relations with the social and cultural systems of society. David McClelland (1961), in his study of organizational success in different cultures, seeks to discover whether social class origin influences the managers and their motivations.

Environmental and psychological factors are significant when related to organizational characteristics and performance. Preoccupation with individualistic psychology per se, as Victor Thompson (1965:7) points out, "tends to hide the institutional bases of events." Naturally, the study of organizations is concerned with individual personality and behavior, but only in those aspects that are determined by organizational structure. In fact, Thompson argues (1965:8, 9), the general standard personality assumed by organization theory fits most people; otherwise, organizations would have to be managed from top to bottom by psychiatrists.

Macrolevel frameworks that deal with national-political or cultural systems also tend to reduce the administrative issues. For researchers, bureaucracy becomes either a monolithic seeker of power and self-interest or an atomized collection of behaviors from which to infer the secrets of their motivation, satisfaction, compliance, or whatever is salient at the time.

In all this, the organization is not considered an autonomous, self-contained unit of analysis but as interdependent, interacting with other societal attributes. In these multiple connections with its context, the organization is not totally propelled by the force of technology that drives the world toward what Levitt (1983) calls "converging commonality." The organization has to follow a rational imperative, calculated to advance its chances of operating at a level of performance sufficient to ensure its survival within changing culture and political orders (Child and Tayeb 1983:27). Organizational rationality, attempting to produce desired outcomes by balancing input activities and technology, is thwarted by prescriptions that politicize the process or explain corruption as a corollary to rapid social and economic modernization (Huntington 1968:59).

In summary, while no unit of analysis can satisfy all comparative research interests, the formal organization, perhaps, is the most appropriate unit of analysis for achieving better integration of findings. The comparative organizational perspective can build on a strong foundation of theoretical and applied knowledge about organizations and their structures, behavior, and performance. Also, organizational analysis provides language, variables, criteria of verification, systematic collection of data, and rigorous, tested methodologies. We have good bases and rich materials waiting to be verified and integrated into coherent conceptual schemes and usable techniques before their application in various settings. Comparative organizational analysis serves such objectives and furthers the expansion and convergence of administrative knowledge to serve the environments of developing countries.

Following this path, we may compare total organizations or certain aspects of them in one or in several cultures. However, when we compare limited aspects (variables) of organizations crossculturally, such as employee satisfaction or training, we have not contributed much to administrative knowledge and skills unless the research results are related to the organization itself and its performance. Obviously, we could not have applied such seemingly restrictive criteria of comparative research in the 1950s or 1960s, because of scarce empirical information about other societies.

Today, after more than five decades of research productivity, theoretical integration and practical relevance are more pressing concerns in assessing the contributions of comparative and development administration. Satisfaction of these criteria requires informed application of conceptual frameworks to the real administrative processes and their effects on organizational performance. Conceptual frameworks of comparative organizational analysis have received considerable attention when they specified numerous variables or categories of variables for investigation. These models actually reveal a relatively high level of agreement on the main dependent variables such as organizational structure, leadership and power, the internal processes, and goals. Environment is the independent variable. Environmental influences are subdivided into variables or categories of variables that encompass political, social, economic, and cultural elements.

Questions of power, productivity, organizational form, role congruence, system mainte-nance, and adaptation are not novel to organization research. As a result, overlapping is evident in definitions and magnitude. But convergence requires some agreement among scholars about basic concepts and terms in the first place. As Ilchman (1971:12) points out, "The critical concerns of those in comparative administration" are directly or indirectly incorporated in the dependent vari-ables of the various models. Consider these examples:

1. M. Crozier's framework (1964)

Unit of analysis is the bureaucratic organization.
Independent variables are the social and cultural system, including values, attitudes toward authority, social control, and ascriptive achievement orientation.
Dependent variables are power, structure, decision processes, nature of task, internal rela-tionships, and rules.

2. M. Esman's model (1972)

Unit of analysis is the institution.
Independent variables are environment linkages: enabling, functional, normative, and dif-fused.
Dependent variables are leadership, doctrine, program, resources, and internal structure.

3. J.D. Thompson's framework (1967)

Unit of analysis is the organization.
Independent variable is the environment (uncertainty, criteria of rationality).
Dependent variables are power, structure, technology, and task.

True, empirical comparative organizational studies with frameworks such as those by Crozier, Esman, or Thompson are exceptional and demanding. But, except for Esman's (1972) institutional framework, the absence of political linkages and the general orientation of most available models to Western systems—mainly commercial enterprises—detract from their utility to comparative and development public administration. Reactions to these limitations have not been to extend and adapt but to extol the advantages of alternative conceptual schemes to improve the standing of the field with academicians and practitioners.

As a result, some recommendations proposed substitutes (policy analysis) or suggested improvements through subsets as project development and program management. Consultants, practitioners, and foreign aid advisers, pressed for immediate and applied administrative skills in dealing with the challenges of national development, are not satisfied with the slow and arduous advancement of comparative knowledge. Their interests usually are narrower and less abstract. Thus, the development project was presented to provide immediate focus on development con-cerns (Honadle and Klaus 1979; Paul 1983; Morgan 1983). Details about cases of project devel-opment and implementation have been conveyed in support of certain managerial conclusions (Paul 1983). A study of six successful cases of project management defines the "preconditions" essential for success as political commitment, resources efficiently utilized, and leadership (Paul 1983:75). These preconditions and a "set of mutually reinforcing management interventions" consistent with their environment achieved the successful results of the six development programs selected from among various third world countries (Paul 1983:76).

If project management appears to be a way to avoid imprecise and impractical literature on development administration, it, too, is being criticized for similar failures. Philip Morgan (1983:330) points out that "project means different things to different users." He recognizes that when ill-defined problems are segregated into discrete tasks, important elements are being ignored. Project management, for example, fails to identify important characteristics of labor force, the quality of institutional support, or impact on population.

Only more empirical evidence will resolve these issues. However, it is important to recognize that forming a disciplined, focused conceptualization of project management and targeting resources for project implementation cannot be equated with having autonomous project authority. Generally, projects are organizations or parts of organizations. Therefore, project management is consistent with organization management, and the competence of one contributes to the competence of the other. This compatibility is useful for dealing with the question of whether the very analytic tools implicit in the "project orthodoxy" can ever accommodate the expanded agenda of today's project goals (Morgan 1983:332).

Another escape from the current state of affairs in public administration (or what is perceived as its limitations and failures) is the area of policy analysis. Involvement of comparative administration in policy analysis is natural and fundamental. The more recent comparative policy research reflects the immediate influence of public administration and other fields of social sciences (Deutsch 1987:17). The primary influence of public administration on comparative policy research is felt in the problem orientation and the interest in applicability of such research. Thus comparative policy research is expanding beyond traditional political interest to achieve a multidisciplinarity in which public administration has a prominent role (Nagel 1984).

Comparative policy research may provide a dimension of realism to public administration but will not supply what comparative public administration is lacking at the present, despite optimistic claims. In fact, traditional policy analysis exhibits conspicuous neglect of administrative issues in its analyses. Deprived of knowledge of organizational processes, this research tradition often fluctuates between statistical reformulations of traditional decision-making frameworks and quantifiable rationalization of political and economic choices at various levels of government. Nevertheless, comparative policy research and comparative management share basic research interests that are better served through mutual and interdependent efforts.

III. CONCLUSION

Comparative and development administration offers a rich heritage of scholarly contributions that include studies of numerous countries, cultures, organizations, and groups. Public administration as a field of study is in the forefront of advocacy of values of participation, equality, and justice in dispensing public policies and outputs to the society. The emphasis on problem-solving orientations, applicability of knowledge, and development of techniques and skills gave public administration greater versatility as "the cutting edge of government," regardless of criticisms.

The current comparative and development administration faces the challenges of diffuseness and lack of cumulativeness of concepts and findings, common problems to social sciences. These challenges are different from the hopeful notion that in the future "public administration" theories or conclusions would be based on studies in various countries, not just in the United States (Riggs 1991:474). Nor are these difficulties related to familiar complaints that public administration "gets no respect" from political science (Tummala 1998:21). The suggestion in this study is that defining the unit of analysis is necessary for achieving higher levels of convergence and aggregation of research findings.

Three units of analysis are discussed and evaluated in terms of their attributes. Contributions and the greater promise of the comparative organizational perspective, however, are emphasized. At this level of "middle-range" conceptualization is the potential for meeting current needs of administrative development. Ultimately, the decisive factors in differentiating weaker from more powerful theories of administration are established by critical appraisals and with support of empirical evidence (Jreisat 1997a). Also, comparative public administration has to move beyond the descriptive to the analytical in anticipation of achieving more cumulativeness of knowledge and greater integration of concepts.

Finally, accepting comparative organizational analysis is not succumbing to a form of conceptual determinism or regulation. Instead, it is utilizing an existing vehicle to solve the basic problem of designating a unit of analysis deemed most suitable for crosscultural research. This important preliminary step should be followed by systematic attention to the selection of organizations and contexts for comparisons. If research is limited to a particular subset of countries, that is, industrial or Western, convergence will be limited and so will any claims to universality of theory. More than anything else, concepts of comparative administration need validation and integration. The quality and reliability of information generated through comparative organizational analysis is of greater promise to advance administrative theory and practice than all others.

REFERENCES

Adler, N.J., Doktor, R., and Redding, S.G. (1986). From the Atlantic to the Pacific century: cross-cultural management reviewed. *Yearly Review of Management of the Journal of Management 12*(2).

Almond, G.A., and Coleman, J.S. (1960). *The Politics of the Developing Areas.* Princeton, NJ: Princeton University Press.

Antal, A.B., Dierkes, M., and Weiler, H.N. (1987). Cross-national policy research: traditions, achievements and challenges. In Dierkes, Weiler, and Antal (eds.), *Comparative Policy Research: Learning from Experience.* New York: St. Martin's Press.

Argyris, C. (1957). *Personality and Organization.* New York: Harper & Row.

Barnard, C.I. (1938). *The Functions of the Executive.* Cambridge, MA: Harvard University Press.

Child, J., and Tayeb, M. (1983). Theoretical perspectives in cross-national organizational research. *International Studies of Management and Organization 7*(1):3–34.

Crozier, M. (1984). *The Bureaucratic Phenomenon.* Chicago: University of Chicago Press.

Deutsch, K.W. (1987). Prologue: achievement and challenges in 2000 years of comparative research. In M. Dierkes, H.N. Weiler, and A.B. Antal (eds.), *Comparative Policy Research.* New York: St. Martin's Press.

Diamant, A. (1962). The bureaucratic model: Max Weber rejected, rediscovered, reformed. In F. Heady and S.L. Stokes (eds.), *Papers in Comparative Public Administration.* Ann Arbor: University of Michigan.

Eddy, W.B. (1981). *Public Organization Behavior and Development.* Cambridge, MA: Winthrop Publishing.

Esman, M.J. (1972). The elements of institution building. In J. Eaton (ed.), *Institution Building and Development.* Beverly Hills, CA: Sage.

Graham, J.L. (1985). Cross-cultural marketing negotiations: a laboratory experiment. *Marketing Science 4*(2):130–146.

Graves, D. (1972). The impact of culture upon managerial attitudes, beliefs and behavior in England and France. *Journal of Management Studies 10*(1):40–56.

Heady, F. (1996). *Public Administration: A Comparative Perspective*, 5th ed. New York: Marcel Dekker.

Henderson, K.M. (1982). Comparative public administration: the United States view in international perspective. *Public Administration and Development 2*:169–183.

Hofstede, G. (1980). *Culture's Consequences: International Differences in Work-Related Values.* Beverly Hills, CA: Sage.

Honadle, G., and Klaus, R. (eds.) (1979). *International Development Administration: Implementation Analysis for Development Projects.* New York: Praeger.

Huntington, S.P. (1968). *Political Order in Changing Societies.* New Haven, CT: Yale University Press.

Ilchman, W.E. (1971). *Comparative Public Administration and Conventional Wisdom.* A Beverly Hills, CA: Sage.

Jreisat, J.E. (1997a). *Politics Without Process: Administering Development in the Arab World.* Boulder, CO: Lynne Reinner Publishers.

Jreisat, J.E. (1997b). *Public Organization Management: The Development of Theory and Process.* Westport, CT: Quorum Books.

Jreisat, J.E. (1975). Synthesis and relevance in comparative public administration. *Public Administration Review 35*(6).

Levitt, T. (1983). The globalization of markets. *Harvard Business Review 83*(2).

March, J.G., and Simon, H.A. (1958). *Organizations.* New York: John Wiley.

McClelland, D.C. (1961). *The Achieving Society.* New York: Van Nostrand Reinhold.

Merton, R.K. (1957). *Social Theory and Social Structure*, rev. ed. New York: Free Press.

Morgan, E.P. (1983). The project orthodoxy in development: re-evaluating the cutting edge. *Public Administration and Development 3*: 329–339.

Morgan, G. (1986). *Images of Organization.* Beverly Hills, CA: Sage.

Nagel, S. (1984). *Contemporary Public Policy Analysis.* Tuscaloosa: University of Alabama Press.

Nord, W.R. and Fox, S. (1996). The individual in organizational studies: the great disappearing act? In S.R. Clegg, C. Hardy, and W.R. Nord (eds.), *Handbook of Organization Studies.* Thousand Oaks, CA: Sage.

Paul, S. (1983). The strategic management of development programs: evidence from an international study. *International Review of Administrative Sciences XLIX*(1):71–86.

Riggs, F.W. (1991). Public administration: a comparativist framework. *Public Administration Review 51*(6).

Riggs, F.W. (1969). The structure of government and administrative reform. In R. Braibanti (ed.), *Political and Administration Development.* Durham, NC: Duke University Press.

Riggs, F.W. (1961). *The Ecology of Public Administration.* New York: Asia Publishing House.

Roberts, K.R., and Grabowski, M. (1996). Organizations, technology and structuring. In *Handbook of Organization Studies.* Thousand Oaks, CA: Sage.

Rowat, D.C. (ed.) (1988). *Public Administration in Developed Democracies: A Comparative Study.* New York: Marcel Dekker.

Thompson, J.D. (1967). *Organizations in Action.* New York: McGraw-Hill.

Thompson, J.D., Hammond, P.B., Hawkes, R.W., Junker, B.H., and Tuden, A. (1959). *Comparative Studies in Administration.* Pittsburgh, PA: University of Pittsburgh Press.

Thompson, V.A. (1965). *Modern Organization.* New York: Alfred A. Knopf.

Tummala, K.K. (1998). Comparative study and SICA. *Public Administration Review 58*(1).

4

Learning From Ancient Persia

Administration of the Persian Achaemenid World-State Empire

Ali Farazmand   *School of Public Administration, Florida Atlantic University, Fort Lauderdale, Florida*

I. INTRODUCTION

Iran, formerly Persia, has one of the longest and richest traditions of public administration and civilization in the world. With a global reputation of being "excellent administrators," Persians have in the past made significant contributions to the global theory and practice of governance and public administration. Beginning around 8000 years ago, Iranian bureaucracy and public administration grew first in the city state of Susa—one of the oldest sites of ancient civilization contemporary to Sumer—and then as the major institution of governance under the powerful Elamite, the Median, and the three Persian empires of Achaemenid, Parthia, and Sasanid (6000 B.C.–651 A.D.). When the Sasanid Persian Empire fell to the Islamic Arab forces in 651, it had already achieved the highest level of state and administrative traditions. Its advanced cultural, state, and administrative heritage was passed on to the Islamic Caliphate who adopted the Persian state and administration almost totally in governing the new empire led by the bedouin Arabs. That heritage is alive even today despite the centuries of foreign invasions of and influence on Iran, for Iranians have always found ways to restore and continue their past traditions and national character of independence.

The bureaucracy of the Persian Empire was a formidable institution of administration and governance, and it was both effective and efficient. The organizational and administrative principles developed under the Persian Achaemenid Empire had significant influence on the Roman administration and were adopted almost totally by the Islamic, the Ottoman, and later the Iranian Safavid rulers. Evidence of the influence of these principles can even be found in almost every contemporary government in the Middle/Near East, as the Persian Achaemenid legacy affected the entire region. The Persian administrative system, however, began to decline during the eighteenth and nineteenth centuries. Public administration in modern Iran is, therefore, a product of both the indigenous ancient tradition and modern concepts of organization and management borrowed from the West. Despite the declining nature of the Iranian administrative legacy, it is worth studying the once glorious traditions of public administration and bureaucracy that affected the whole known world.

This article highlights some of the Iranian traditions of administration, governance, and bureaucracy from the beginning, around 6000 B.C. to the end of the Persian Achaemenid world-state Empire in 330 B.C., when the conqueror Alexander burned its capital, Persepolis. While the political and administrative history of Iran under the Elamite, Median, and Persian Achaemenid empires is covered here, the central focus of the article is on the Persian Achaemenid period. Due to space limitations, therefore, the decentralized Parthian and the advanced centralized Sasanian administrative systems are not discussed here.

This essay attempts to introduce some of the Iranian contributions to the history of public administration and human civilization, for the two have been developed together.

While much is known about the Greek and Roman contributions to modern political and administrative systems, little is known in the West about the rich Persian or Iranian traditions of state, culture, and administration and the contributions they have made to the rest of the world. Iranians have made significant contributions both directly and indirectly to the Islamic and Western world and their administrative systems. While the city states of Athens and Sparta were busy discussing alternative forms of political systems, Persians were already administering with high managerial efficiency the largest and mightiest empire the ancient world had ever seen.

The purpose here is fourfold: (1) to present the Iranian historical traditions of governance and administration; (2) to present some key features of the Persian bureaucracy and administrative system under the world-state Achaemenid Empire; (3) to discuss some of the contributions the Persians have made directly or indirectly to the history of public administration; and (4) to draw some lessons/implications or applications for the modern administrative state and public administration in both developed and developing nations. The article is drawn mainly from my recently published as well as forthcoming works on Persian bureaucracy and public administration.[1] Numerous other historical sources have also been consulted, though some are not referenced here.

II.   ADMINISTRATION OF SUSA AND THE FEDERAL ELAM

As one of the oldest sites of ancient civilization, Susa (in the present southwest Iran) began political life around 6000 B.C., first as a city state rivaling Sumer in Mesopotamia, then as the capital of one of the oldest empires of antiquity, Elam, around 3000 B.C. Therefore, the earliest experience of state tradition and administrative functions on a massive scale in Iran began around 6000 B.C. The main instrument of public administration and governance under the long history of the federal state of Elam was the bureaucracy, which also played a powerful role under the Median and the Persian Empires.[2]

Unlike the small city-state of Sumer, the Elamite empire was formed and administered on a massive scale and governed a large territory comprising present Iran and a major part of the Near East including at times Babylonia and Assyria. Its occupation of Babylon for 500 years was undone by any other force until the Babylonian conquest by Cyrus the Great in the sixth century B.C. The bureaucracy and administrative system of the federated state of Elam—a federation of five major kingdoms (Kassite, Guti, Lullubi, Susiana, and Elam) under the overlordship of the Elamite king—were developed and experienced. Their bureaucratic contacts with the Assyrians and Babylonians gave them insights which they found useful. But, as a rival to Sumer, Babylon, and Assyria, the Elamite federal government developed the first Iranian tradition of public administration on a massive scale, though that tradition originated much earlier in the great city state of Susa.

While internal independence of the federated states was maintained, intergovernmental relations among them were regulated by numerous administrative rules and ordinances. Public administration flourished under the Elamites, who made significant contributions to both Iranian and world civilizations and their administrative traditions.

The federal structure of the Elamite empire was organized into three administrative layers of governance: the various provinces were ruled over by (1) the "governors" (*Halmenik*), who were under the control of (2) a "Viceroy" (*Sakanakkun*), who was subject to (3) the actual king of Elam (*Zunkir*). The kings had used two capitals: one in the lowland city of present Dizful and the other in Susa, the oldest civilized center of politics, trade, communication, and administration between the East and West.[3]

Religion strongly flourished in ancient Elam, where the female Great Goddess was in high power and equal to the male God. Certain kings of Elam were also elevated to the "Messenger of God," "regent," and ruler on earth.[4] It also appears that Elamites had some conceptions of an "after-life, in which various burial gifts would be of use."[5] Administration of Elam was developed and reflected both secular and religious aspects of law, politics, and government.

A remarkable achievement and legacy of the ancient Elamites was the "development of their own script, the proto-Elamite script—the designation applied to the earliest pictographic stage in contrast with the later Elamite linear script."[6] The Elamite written language was used as the official language in the bureaucracy for a long time, rivaling the Sumerian and Akkadian languages even later during the old Persian Empire of the Achaemenids.

Other major administrative achievements of the Elamites included the development and use of a binary weight system, which had a major influence on the fraction systems of the whole Mesopotamia; a massive number of administrative and business documents; major architectural works; the development and management of a gigantic system of underground canals (*Qanat*), for irrigation, an Iranian invention that turned the arid land into an agricultural land; the construction and maintenance of numerous public works and enterprises such as roads, bridges, cities and towns, communication centers, and economic and commercial centers; and the development and use of an advanced legal system—Elamite Penal Law, Civil Law, and Administrative Law. Also original to Elamites was the role of witnesses in the elaborate judicial proceedings with an "ordeal trial."[7]

Numerous administrative and business documents reveal evidence of extensive Elamite intergovernmental relations (IGR) among the federated kingdoms, hence development of an active intergovernmental management. In the cities, thriving activities reigned where, along with the villages, various professions of all kinds flourished, showing clear evidence of variety and stratification of professional and, hence, social classes in ancient Elam.[8]

III. ADMINISTRATION OF THE MEDIAN EMPIRE

The arrival of the Aryans, a people of Indo-European origin, on the Iranian plateau during their second wave of migration from central Asia around 1000 B.C. changed the composition of the population and the political power in Iran and the whole Near East. This group of young pastoral people was destined to change the history of mankind by conquering the known world in a single generation. They established a world-state empire with a largess heretofore unknown, and with an administrative system that was politically effective and managerially efficient. Of the two major branches of the Aryan people, the Medes succeeded first in establishing a formidable empire state rivaling Babylon, Lydia, Egypt, and Assyria. Centered in Ecbatana, or "place of assembly," in modern Hamadan in central Iran, the Median empire mastered the statecraft of both military and civil administration by the seventh century B.C. By capturing Nineveh, the capital of Assyria, the Medes finished off that world power forever in 612 B.C., and by totally absorbing Elam by 600 B.C., they set the stage for annexing Babylonia.[9]

Thus, the first half of the first millennium B.C. was "a turning point in human history," for the "center of the world 'politics' of the age shifted, from the watered valleys of the Nile and the

Mesopotamia to the less climatically favored region of the north and Iran."[10] Therefore, among the main players of the time, the Iranians emerged as the most victorious and were destined to dominate world politics for the next millennium.[11] This was accomplished by Persians, of course, under Cyrus the Great, who conquered the known world of antiquity and established the first world-state empire in political history.

The Medes left several major legacies in administration and governance, as well as a huge empire they built, which included all territories of the former Assyrian empire and almost all Asia, in a very short period of time. They were a young, vigorous people with great military ambitions, and with refined skills in government and administration. They, for the first time in history, adopted the concept of "state" and turned that idea into practice. Under the brilliant military leader Cyaxares King, they were also "the first who organized the Asiatic armies by uniting them into separate units—spearmen, archers, and cavalry."[12] The Medes sought to regularize relations among peoples in society, and all citizens would have access to and deal with a unified entity, the Median state. The military officials and civil bureaucrats of the state were all considered servants of the state, at the head of which stood the king. The state concept promoted impartiality among citizens dealing with the administrative state of the empire.

The Medes also adopted a federated system of governance and administration, and a system of collective decision-making. They established a strict administration of justice, particularly since the time of King Dioceses, a just arbitrator with high reputation who was chosen by the Median Assemblymen as their king. He established the monarchy, organized the sovereign domain with utmost efficiency and effectiveness, and united the diverse peoples of the large Median empire.[13] The federal system of government allowed for great flexibility among non-Median peoples or nations under the supreme authority of the Median king. The Magian priests played a major role in the state and administration of the empire.[14]

The second major legacy of the Medes was their development of an administrative system based on a trained bureaucracy with high expertise and prestige. They mastered statecraft and bureaucratic administration, not the kind that Assyrians practiced uprooting the subject peoples with utmost brutality, but a system with high efficiency and effectiveness while maintaining respect for local peoples' inputs. The bureaucracy under the Medes was professionalized by two principles: (1) elaborate training and apprenticeship for administrative positions; and (2) systematic experience in office characterized by role specialization, organizational hierarchy, and a unity of command system. No doubt, they learned considerably from the Elamite administration and from the Assyrian bureaucratic empire through long military and administrative encounters with them.

Many bureaucrats came from the nobility and from the Magies who played a formidable role in the Median government and society, but they also came from the class of common men who had great ability and aspired to join the ranks of the "men of pen" to serve the state and the king. The formation of a professional association by the bureaucrats led to the creation of a guild system, which was closed to nonbureaucrats. This professional association served its members as well as the state. In short, the Medes gained for Iranians, for the first time in history, a reputation as "excellent administrators."

IV.   THE WORLD-STATE PERSIAN ACHAEMENID EMPIRE

The Median empire was at its zenith of military power and was prepared to annex the rest of Mesopotamia and Babylonia, while the other branch of the Aryans, the Persians, were already emerging as a powerful kingdom in their base in Parsa (modern Fars) on the plains of south Iran. Their forces under Cyrus II, the Persian king, defeated the Median army in a battle commanded by the Median overlord Astyages, who had summoned Cyrus and was to punish him for refusing to denounce a tactical alliance with the last Babylonian prince Nabunaid. The mighty Median empire fell to Cyrus in 559 B.C., and thus emerged as one of the most brilliant military and political leaders of antiquity Cyrus the Great at the age of 40 who led the young and vigorous Persians (and Medes) in their "turn on the conquest of the world."[15]

The Achaemenid Persian Empire, founded by Cyrus the Great in 559 B.C., was the largest and the mightiest empire the ancient world had ever known. The traditional infrastructure in military, politics, governance, administration, culture, and economics that the Persians established has had a longlasting effect on not only Iran but also the entire Near/Middle Eastern government and their administrative systems. The Persian influence on European governance and administrative systems should also be mentioned, hence leaving a legacy found even in the modern administrative state of the West, including the United States.

How was such a huge empire with far extended territories and multinational diversity administered? What are some of the key features of the Achaemenid administrative system, and what can be learned about the efficiency and effectiveness of its notorious bureaucracy operating in every corner of the realm? What contributions did the Persian Achaemenids make to the theory and practice of governance and public administration, and what can be learned from the Persian administrative system for the modern administrative state? The following is an attempt to answer some of these and other related questions.

First, background is given on the founding father, Cyrus the Great, who established the empire and laid the constitutional foundation of the largest empire the ancient world had ever seen. The background also covers a discussion of Darius the Administrator, who reorganized, reformed, and stabilized the empire with a sound administrative system. Second, the organization and administrative system of the empire is discussed in some details outlining the position and status of (1) the Great King and the central government; (2) the famous *satrapy* system of governance, the institutional mechanisms of control over the *satrapal* administration and the adminitrative policy toward subject peoples; and (3) the Persian bureaucracy. Third, the discussion of the Persian bureaucracy includes the environment in which it operated, the positions and function of the bureaucratic elite, the structure and processes of the bureaucracy and administration, professionalization of the bureaucracy, and bureaucracy and public management. Fourth, the administrative reforms of Darius the Great are discussed with a focus on roads and communication systems, economic reforms and financial management, legal reform and justice administration, and local government reform. Finally, a conclusion is provided with an analysis of the nature of the Persian Empire, and with some of the implications for modern public administration and governance.

This article covers the pre-Aryan Iranian traditions of state, governance, and public administration in the ancient city state of Susa and then under the Elamite empire, the Median empire, and the world-state Persian Achaemenid Empire (6000 B.C. to 330 B.C.), when the latter was conquered by Alexander. No discussion will be made of the later Parthian decentralized administration, nor of the Sasanian advanced state and centralized administration.

A. Cyrus the Great as the Founding Father

Cyrus the Great was the founding father of the Persian Empire and of the new Iranian monarchy and its new constitution. In less than 30 years, Cyrus the Great expanded the Persian Empire from Asia in the East to Eastern Europe and North Africa, including Egypt and most of the Greek territory, in the West. More than 47 empires, kingdoms, and nations were incorporated into the Empire, forming a truly multinational, multiracial, and multicultural realm with a high diversity of ethnic and religious backgrounds. Only part of Greece, namely Athens and Sparta, escaped—

at times—the expansion of this mighty empire. But even these nations were both directly and indirectly influenced by the Persian gold, the threat of the Persian might, and the Great King's Peace, with the conditions attached.[16]

Like the Medes, the Persians under Cyrus the Great adopted the concept of "state" and formed the global world state empire of the Achaemenids. The Persian army was formidable. So was the Persian gold which, along with the Persian diplomacy, influenced nations and peoples of resistance, including those of the Athenians and Spartans, changing their policies and helping favored officials to gain positions of power. Persian gold often accomplished what the army could not, such as where it was not suitable to be deployed.

Cyrus was a military genius and a brilliant political leader with grand ambitions, a macromanagerial approach, and global perspectives. He was also a man of great energy and talents. But he was a man of wisdom and tolerance. His charismatic leadership transcended all boundaries of races, colors, religions, and nationalities. He was highly regarded by Persians and many non-Persians in all corners of the far-extended empire. Persians called him the Father, Greeks and Babylonians called him the Law-Giver, and Jews called him the Saver or Deliverer.[17]

Under Cyrus the Great, a universal liberal policy of tolerance toward and respect for the local traditions, customs, and religions of the diverse peoples in the Empire was adopted and institutionalized for the next two centuries, with modifications adopted by his successors later. That policy was also adopted under the Parthians and Sasanians for the next millennium, and so internalized a trait that has remained a major aspect of Iranian national character. Cyrus founded a democratic government based on freedom of religion, association, race, and color, and this was the first experience in the ancient world and indeed in political history. He outlawed slavery, and, unlike other empires, slavery was not a general practice under the Achaemenid Empire.[18] According to Herodotus, "No race is so ready to adopt foreign ways as the Persian," but "themselves they consider in every way superior to everyone else in the world, and allow other nations a share of good qualities."[19]

Cyrus was very conscious of the settled civilizations of some of the conquered peoples, and, as part of his global design, sought to create "a synthesis of ancient civilizations" aimed at uniting all the human world. His idea of a global state ruled by Persians, was put into practice for the first time in history, but his administrative policy was far more noble and just than any other in ancient civilization. For that same good reason, Cyrus the Great has been since remembered as a noble, liberal democrat and a "humane" leader[20] with many great legacies for his fellow Iranians and non-Iranians in the next two millennia. In decision making, he consulted with experts, key generals, members of the nobility, and high level administrators, and he relied on consensus. Cyrus never developed an elaborate royal court system, though his administrative establishment served him well; therefore, the corruption so characteristic of most royal courts in history was not an issue or a challenge to his empire. Nor did he have time enough to spend in Persia proper to devote to details of administration and his government. He adopted in principle the administrative system of the Medes and to an extent the Assyrian organization, but he departed from any previous systems of governance.

In kingship, Cyrus organized his expanding empire on the basis of a *satrapy* system and appointed his own governors. The former system of vassal-king used under the Medes and Assyrians disappeared in the Persian tradition of governance (more on this below). As a restless conqueror and a charismatic, skilled statesman, at the age of 70 he was still in expanding campaigns. He died in 530 B.C. three days after receiving a mortal wound in a battle he won in the far northeast. Persians lost a father, and the empire began to experience a short period of turmoil over the succession issue. Cyrus was a founding father and a world conqueror, leaving behind many legacies for Iranians and non-Iranians alike.

B.   Darius the Administrator

Cyrus's designated successor Prince Cambyses was the viceroy and king of Babylon and had already conquered Egypt, where he had adopted also the Pharaoh's title, ruled Egypt many years as their king, and observed the local traditions to an extent as he did in Babylon. He was a relatively experienced governor and a trained fighter, but also a tyrant. Cambyses's seven years of rule characterized a critical decade of the Persian Empire. He expanded the realm but was a harsh ruler. Until his conspicuous death in 522 B.C., he spent considerable time in structuring the Empire, under both his father's and his own rule. His death, on his way back to Persia from Egypt, resulted in a major debate among the so-called Great Seven Persian leaders who met secretly to depose a powerful magi who had falsely claimed himself as Cyrus's son Bardiya, and therefore his successor, and to decide on a constitution for the Empire. The real Bardiya—*satrap* of the northeast region of the realm—was in fact murdered by Cambyses's order earlier, while Cambyses was still in Egypt, and the pretender magi had gained popularity. Representing the noble aristocracy and aware of the facts, the seven paladins (Otanes, Gobryas, Darius, Ardumanish [Aspathines], and their seconds Intaphernes, Hydarnes, and Megabyxus), first exposed and killed the usurper, then debated the future form of government for Persia.

According to Herodotus,[21] the main arguments were about the forms of government Persia should adopt. While all agreed that no one could ever replace Cyrus as a leader in history, it was proper to debate the three forms of government to be adopted: democracy and government by people, oligarchy and rule by a council of nobles or aristocratic council, and monarchy and rule by the king with a professional bureaucracy—civil and military. Otanes opted for the democracy, Megabyxus was for the oligarchy, while Darius prevailed in persuading the uncommitted ones in favor of monarchy. Subsequently, all six had agreed to monarchy and chose Darius as the Great King, while Otanes "then withdrew on condition that he and his descendants should not be subject to any man,"[22] a condition that was granted.

Thus, Darius became the Great King on October 5, 522 B.C. Like many great Persians, Darius was of high birth, well trained as a noble, and had a powerful personality. He had gained status under Cyrus, namely as the king's spear-bearer (however, different accounts are presented by historians on Darius's position under Cyrus). Darius was also a great military leader. He was very young, in his twenties, when he assumed the kingship. From the beginning, he took serious steps to document his major achievements. As Cook points out, "Darius laid great stress on the fact that he fought nineteen battles and took captive nine kings in one and the same year." It was his *annus mirbilis.*[23]

In a few years, Darius expanded the Empire further into Asia in the east, including India, and to the west, taking over most of the Greek territories. The Achaemenid Persian Empire reached its largest size under Darius, it prospered economically and politically, and its stability and maturity provided the ruling Persians and all subject peoples with a harmony of relationship and opportunity for personal and professional development. Darius's achievements are too many to count, but he had a personality characterized by an ability to control his temper, persuasive communication ability, decisiveness in decision making, and mental and physical strength. But a most important characteristic feature of Darius was his great interest in micro-management and the details of government.

While Cyrus was a great conqueror and a genius military-political leader, Darius was a great political-administrative leader. Cyrus was a father to Persians and a savior or deliverer to Jews, while Darius was a law-giver to all subject peoples, but because of his interest in details of administration with an efficient financial management, he was also labeled a shopkeeper. While Cyrus never had time to build an elaborate administrative and royal capitol for his mighty empire, Darius spent considerable time doing so, and, therefore, the foundations of the royal-ceremonial megacity Persepolis—the wonder of the East and the richest city on earth—were laid, and the three capital cities of Susa, Pasargade, and Ecbatana continued to have significant importance as they did under the Medes and Elamites. During Darius's rule Persians reached their height of glory in military, administrative, political, economic, sociocultural, and religious aspects. The court became elaborate with more palaces, with kingship well institutionalized and powerful.

Founded by Cyrus the Great, the Persian Empire was further expanded and developed, consolidated, and stabilized under King Darius, who reorganized it and implemented a comprehensive program of reforms in administration and bureaucracy, government, economics, finance, law and justice, and communication systems. These reforms have had longlasting impacts on Persia with legacies in public administration traditions around the world for the next two millennia up to the present day, particularly in the Near/Middle East.

Under Darius, the Persian administration became more bureaucratic, the army became omnipotent, and the distance between the King and subjects increased, but he always kept faith with the great nobility. "He exerted power. He thought big, and what he did was a matter of urgency."[24] As Darius expressed it himself, "what was said to them by me, night and day it was done."[25] He was an outstanding organizational and administrative strategist, and strategic public management was a key feature of his reformed administrative system.

While Cyrus's style of governance was based on "rule of consent," Darius made his own decisions after hearing the opinions of his numerous advisors. He was a benevolent autocrat,[26] but he maintained a balance with the great nobility and never betrayed their interests. The court under him became elaborate, and, unlike Cyrus the Great or any other Achaemenid Kings after him who had only one wife, Darius married six wives and had numerous legitimate children, all placed in commanding positions of the army or *satrapy* or both. Darius died in November 486 B.C., after 37 years of reign. He had one military setback in his expedition against the nomadic Scythians or barbarians of north-central Asia. Although he did not destroy them, they never again became a problem for the Empire. Darius built many palaces and actively engaged in massive public work projects, leaving behind remarkable legacies in governance and public administration, as he did in other areas such as economics, arts, and architecture.

Darius was succeeded by his son Xerxes, whose pomp and power as the Great King of Persia surpassed that of any other. Under Xerxes, the Empire did not expand—its Western expansion was checked by a setback he experienced in the war against Greeks, but his setback was balanced by his taking Athens and by making Greeks accept the King's Peace with conditions. Under Xerxes the construction of Persepolis was completed, and Persia reached its highest glory of organization, military force, and cultural and ceremonial extravaganza. The Persian Royal Court was the most elaborate; the number of foreign exiles, professionals, and mercenaries at the service of the King increased tremendously. Xerxes displayed the glorious power and status of Persia in the world while Darius was a great king, a great organizer and administrator, and a conquerer. But no king ever reached the status of Cyrus the Great.

V.   ORGANIZATION AND ADMINISTRATIVE SYSTEM OF THE EMPIRE

The organization and administrative system of the Achaemenid Empire manifest unique features unknown before, with contributions to the modern administrative state. Although the Median administrative and court systems were adopted by Cyrus the Great, and some features of the Assyrian organizational structure were used in principle, the magnitude of the empire he had founded required a far more effective organization and administration. The vast Persian Empire was organized based on a powerful central government, a strong *satrapy* system, a highly effective and efficient administrative system legged on a professionalized bureaucracy, a liberal governance policy, and a formidable army commanded by the great aristocratic nobility.

A. The Great King and the Central Government

A five-level hierarchical structure formed the refined systems of governance and administration of the empire, with an organizational authority flowing from the Great King and central government to the *satrapal* and local governments. This hierarchical structure may be divided into two general levels: central and *satrapal*. At the top of the pyramid was the Great King, his court, and the central government armed with an efficient, professional bureaucracy and the army; next was the *satrap* and his court establishment, followed by the sub-*satraps* in charge of the provincial and local administrative districts.

The state was headed by a hereditary monarchy. The king was the supreme sovereign, enjoying a religious sanction: "By the grace of Ahura-Mazda I am king; Ahura-Mazda gave me the kingdom" are the words of Darius in the Behistun inscription. So speak Xerxes and Artaxerxes in their inscriptions of Ahura-Mazda, the Persian God, "who made Xerxes (Artaxerxes) king."[27] As the Empire grew larger and incorporated the previous empires, the Persian kings "sought and obtained the sanction of the religion of these countries," nationalities, and peoples for their sovereignty.[28] Cyrus the Great was called to rule Babylonians by their god Marduk, and Darius and Xerxes adopted names relating to the Egyptian god Re.

The Persian King had supreme authority and recognized "no equal on earth."[29] His titles, Great King and King of Kings, had unique meanings to his kingship, for there were no other kings under the Persian King.[30] The Greeks called him *Basileus,* "the one and only real king in the world."[31] Cambyses was made king of Babylon—an exception—but only in subordination to Cyrus, who was the "king of lands." Like his successors, Darius claims that he is "one king of many, one lord of many; the great king, king of kings, king of the countries possessing all kinds of peoples, king of this great earth far and wide."[32] The succession from Cyrus the Great to Darius and all the following kings was based on the Achaemenid blood, and Darius's succession was based on the virtue of "his being the oldest surviving line of the hereditary royal family." Xerxes succeeded him because of his mother Atossa, the daughter of Cyrus.[33]

The king's will as expressed in words was law. His word, however, was based on consultation with various sources, including the Persian nobles, the official experts of the bureaucracy (a custom required of the king), the Council of Advisors, the Council of Cabinet Ministers, and the regard for the countries and peoples of the *satrapies* concerned.[34] "The king of Persia might do whatsoever he desires," yet, in practice, he generally had regard to law and custom, and indeed "in certain respects, he was practically limited by the privileges enjoyed by the Persian nobles,"[35] including but not limited to the six prominent families associated with Darius in the overthrow of Gaumata the Magi. These families enjoyed unannounced access to the King, and only from these families could he take his wives.[36] Therefore, the King's supreme authority was limited by custom, tradition, and the nobility.

Second, after the Great King, the court played a formidable role in politics and administration of the Empire, for it was the central government. The centrality of the court is explained by the concentration of various powerful institutions, officials, and personalities. Clearly, the professional bureaucracy was the key institution of the central government (more on this later). Such key officials as the *arstibara* (spear-bearer), the *vacabara* (bow-bearer), *databara* (law-bearers or royal judges), *hazarapati* (commander in chief of armed forces and the Immortals, the Ten Thousand permanent bodyguards of the King, or the Kingsmen), the Grand-Vizir or prime minister as the cabinet secretary, and *ganzabara* (the treasurer) as well as many VIPs were powerful forces in the court, accompanied by the harem later in the Empire.[37]

Third, the strategic elite of the central government in Susa were the main governing power—after the King himself; the empire and its administrative system were based on it. Of this, the treasury as well as the legal and military elites constituted the most powerful administrators (more on the bureaucracy later). The above three powerful institutions formed the central government and the first levels of hierarchy in the *satrapal* administration of the Empire.

B.   The *Satrapy* System

A *Satrapy* was an enormous territory, which included several nations, kingdoms, and peoples and was headed by a *Satrap* or governor appointed by the Great King from the capital city of Susa, the central government. Cyrus the Great adopted in principle the general organization of the Median and Assyrian empires, but the *satrapal* system of governance and administration that he established was a Persian innovation with distinct characteristics. The Assyrians and Medians had tried a similar system on a smaller scale, and had divided their territories based on vassal-kingship and provinces, territories that were much smaller than *satrapies* in size and importance. In contrast, the vast Achaemenid Empire was divided into major *satrapies*—20 under Cyrus, 22 under Darius, and 23 or more under Xerxes—which was maintained for most of the duration of the 230 years of the empire. For example, several *satrapies* included Egypt and Libya, Babylon, Syria and beyond the river, Asia Minor, Macedonia with several islands, India, Parthia, Media, and Bactria. The Greek islands were also grouped into three to four *satrapies*, including Lydia with the strategic city of Sardis, a major *satrapal* power center in the west and the end of the Royal Road.

The *satrapal* system in the united state of Persia was based on several organizational principles and institutions of political and legal control. These principles included (1) tolerant governance; (2) centralization combined with a sufficient degree of decentralization; (3) a multiplicity of institutional controls; (4) relative equality before the law; (5) the divine kingship—the Great King as the sovereign, supreme authority, and also the head of the State; (6) the standardization of the state functions and administrative processes, based on (7) a centralized, professionalized, and powerful bureaucracy.

Below the Great King and his central government was the *satrap*, the governor of an enormous territory with tremendous power in civil, judicial, and military administration. Appointed from Susa by the King, the *satraps* were almost always recruited from the Persian nobility, although initially this position was also assigned to exceptional non-Persians, and later to a woman. At the district level, great flexibility was exercised by the recruitment and appointment of non-Persian local leaders as well as Persian administrators and governors. Local peoples were also allowed to choose their own leaders. As will be seen below, the tolerant liberal policy of the system founded by Cyrus the Great allowed the diverse peoples and nations of the Empire to practice their local customs and traditions as long as they did not pose a challenge to the central authority of the sovereign and his protector of the realm, the *satrap*.[38]

The *satrap* was granted a broad range of authorities, powers, functions, and responsibilities. His ruling establishment was modeled after the central government and the Great King's court. He ruled a vast territory covering different nations and peoples, even monarchies, and was surrounded by a miniature court of his own. He was the highest judicial authority and the head of the state administration in the *satrapy*. His discretionary power was wide in policy and administrative affairs, but in major policy issues he had to defer decisions to Susa.[39]

The functions and responsibilities of a *satrap* included maintenance of law and order; oversight of general administration; supervision in collection of taxes and tributes, as well as mobilization and supply of military forces and material resources for wars and defense; maintenance of the universal roads, and postal and communication routes; maintenance of the canals and other waterways such as Darius's Suez Canal in Egypt and Xerxes's Athos Canal in Europe, building and maintenance of public works; managing intergovernmental affairs with both the central government and other *satrapies;* and dealing with the neighboring *satrapies* on political and military affairs.

The fifth level in the hierarchy of the Persian governance and administrative system from the central government was the sub-*satrap* or provincial governor, an official recruited from both the ruling Persian or Median race and non-Persian local leaders. Thus, each *satrapy* was also divided into sub-*satrapies* or provinces headed by a sub-*satrap* or governor, totally responsible to the *satrap,* although provincial officials and peoples were not without direct access to the central government. The provincial or sub-*satrapies* were further divided into administrative districts headed by district administrators or political leaders of the local communities. For example, the *satrapy* of "Beyond the River" was divided into various provinces and local administrative districts, including Syria, Palestine, Phoenicia, Samaria, Judea, and Arabia.

There were of course strong *satrapies* and weak ones, but generally the *satraps* were powerful figures. And, in some *satrapies*, for example, Beyond the River, certain provinces were allowed some degree of local self-governance, such as the Phoenician city states which voluntarily joined the Empire and proved their continued loyalty to the united state of Persia.[40] Babylon lost its special status after a revolt that was put down under Xerxes, who then ordered its reduction into a part of the Beyond the River *satrapy.* That was the end of Babylon as a special *satrapy* or even as an important name.

C. Central Control of the *Satrapies*

Several institutional mechanisms established by the central government served as checks and balances in the satrapy system. This was essential for the administrative system to (1) maintain central control over the entire empire; (2) forestall any possible independence, disaffection, and revolt; (3) prevent abuse of authority and power by the *satraps*; (4) prevent corruption and decay in the system; (5) protect the diverse subject peoples in the multinational united state of Persia; and (6) maintain the territorial integrity of the empire.

First, there was a separation of civil from military administration in the *satrapy.* While in charge of civil administration with wide discretion, the *satraps* lacked the command of the military, which was given to an independent commander appointed by the central government and confirmed by the Great King. However, at times and based on personality, geographical, and kingship considerations, overlapping civil and military functions and authorities were also granted to certain *satraps*. Therefore, towards the end of the Empire, it is evident that some *satraps* assumed the both military and civil administration. The separation of military-civil administration denied the *satraps* the ability to amass both powers and to possibly challenge the central authority. The military commander kept the *satraps* under check and control of the central administration and of the king from afar. What was the chance of a conspiracy and joint revolt? Very slim.

Second, the independent commander-in-chief of the armed forces had enormous power, was close to the king, and was in control of the Persian army across the empire. Given the rapid communication system in place, the commander was able to monitor any changes of situations in *satrapies,* and the central government was swift to respond to challenges or revolts in any part of the united state.

The third institutional control of the *satrapy* was the presence in the *satrapal* courts of the "eyes of the king," an official appointed by the king who performed as a state attorney in legal matters. Fourth was the inspector general of the state, the "ears of the king," appointed and removed by the central government. The latter institution was highly admired by monarchs of the ancient world and was adopted by Charlemagne, the first holy emperor of Rome, to secure "cohesion between the various parts of his empire" more than a thousand years later.[41] The fifth institution of control was the periodic "examiners" of the state or representatives of the Great King who gave unexpected visits to *satraps* and their administrators and reported any corruptions and misman-agement in the *satrapies* to the central government.

The final institutional control over the *satrapal* position was the "King's secretary, an offi-cer who forms part of every governor's [*satrap*] establishment" in the *satrapy*.[42] Appointed by and reporting to the central administration, this powerful official served as (1) an independent liaison between the king and his *satrap*, (2) a monitor to check the *satrapal* court and his administration, (3) the powerful agent of the bureaucracy and the king, and (4) a model bureaucrat for the *satra-pal* and provincial administrations. He was the key officer-confidant who would read the king's letters and instructions to the *satrap*.

An example of how this official was instrumental to the effective central control over the *satrapal* power is the case of Oroetes, the powerful *satrap* of Phrygia, Lydia, and Ionia, who had a thousand Persians as his bodyguards. To remove and punish him for many crimes he had com-mitted and for his defiance of the central authority, Darius "called a meeting of the leading men in the country" for consultation to decide on the appropriate method of stopping him. Thirty of the company who were present competed so hotly for the privilege of undertaking this service that Darius was forced to make them draw lots. The winner at once carried the king's instructions and order to Oroetes's court, "opened the papers one by one, handing them to the king's secretary" with the instruction to read them aloud, ordering the guards to refuse to serve Oroetes. The instruc-tion also included the words: "King Darius commands the Persians in Sardis to kill Oroetes," an order which was carried out at once.[43]

Thus, powerful as the *satraps* were in their large territories, significant institutional mecha-nisms of control were exercised over them by the central administration of the united state of the Persian empire. Some of the above institutions of checks and balances were added to the system by Darius in his major administrative reforms discussed below.

D. Administrative Policy Toward Subject Peoples

A most important feature of the Persian system of governance and administration of the Empire was a universally applied liberal organizational policy of "tolerance and respect for subject peo-ples" throughout the far-extended territories of the realm. "The Persian was a tolerant govern-ment,"[44] with an administration characterized by both centralization and decentralization.[45] As a founder of the vast Empire with multinational peoples, Cyrus was very conscious of the settled civilizations, and he sought to create a united world-state with all diversities. He then adopted the liberal organizational policy of tolerant government. The traditional lives and customs of the many diverse peoples—indeed hundreds, even over a thousand—gathered into the vast empire were allowed to continue at local and even provincial levels, as long as their local practices did not con-flict with the centralized principles of administration and bureaucracy that were applied in carry-ing out the will of the king and in managing the political and economic policies of the realm. Administration of such a vast empire had to be flexible with respect to local governance.

Cyrus never abandoned—neither did his successors—the tolerant administrative policy towards the subject peoples, even when he had to deal with a subsequent revolt in Sardis, where he had appointed a Lydian in charge of the treasury. In Babylon, he at first tried a local leader as governor for three years, with his eldest son, Cambyses, as the viceroy and king's representative there, adopting the local conditions of governance and administration. Then Gobryas—the con-quering army leader in Babylon—was appointed as the *satrap*. When Cyrus conquered Babylo-nia, a large number of Jews in captivity were freed and sent to Palestine in 538 B.C., where he ordered their temple be rebuilt at the expense of the royal treasury. He sent to Jerusalem "Shesh-bazzar as governor with the store of gold and silver vessels that Nebuchadnezzar [the last Baby-lonian ruler] had removed."[46]

The centralized system of administration was based on various governmental, political, military, and bureaucratic institutions as well as on some traditions. Centralization was the key to effective and efficient administration of the vast empire—effective for political control, and efficient for organizational and managerial performance. But decentralization also served the system in two ways: (1) it was a central component of the "tolerant governance" policy, allowing for local and provincial leadership and respect for traditions of the subject peoples; and (2) it provided the administrative system with maximum opportunity for flexibility and efficiency. Both organizational principles of centralization and decentralization complemented each other toward the effective administration of the empire.

Unlike the Assyrians before and the Romans later who reduced subject peoples to slavery and obliterated their customs and traditions, the Persians, from Cyrus the Great on, maintained the universal policy of tolerant governance and administration. Not only were the Persians tolerant of the various traditions, customs, and religions in their realm; they took further steps and "actively supported the temple-worship of the gods of their subjects, or contributed to the building of their temples, and conferred on the priesthood and religious institutions special privileges. Cyrus and Darius not only permitted the rebuilding of the Jewish temples at Jerusalem, but laid the cost of it on the royal treasury."[47]

The administration of the "Beyond the River" *satrapy* with Damascus as its capital was, for example, conditioned by two principles: (1) the "diversity of ethnic and national groups, exhibiting various patterns of relationship vis-à-vis the Persian authority, and (2) considerations of administrative efficiency, with allowance for the interests of the local groups."[48] "Beyond the River," with the territories of Syria and Palestine, was initially organized together with Babylonia as "Babylonia and Beyond the River," implying more significance of the former. It was soon separated, perhaps under Darius, into two *satrapies*, an organizational restructuring that was reversed, this time signifying the latter. Under Xerxes, Babylon was punished for the revolt and reduced to a province of the Beyond the River *satrapy*; its previous status was never recovered again.[49]

Two types of organizational subdivision were adopted in the *satrapies:* (1) the administrative units for managerial efficiency and administrative purposes, and (2) the division based on ethnic, religious, and racial groupings in accordance with the tolerant governance policy. While the administrative subdivisions could expand or contract at different times, the ethnic grouping was generally unchanged. This dual system of administrative organization was one of the major innovations the Persians introduced to the governance system.[50] Both types of administrative subdivision along with the organizational principles of centralization and decentralization were integrated in the professionalized bureaucracy of the empire.

E. The Persian Bureaucracy

After the king and the noble-led army, the bureaucracy was the most powerful institution of the Persian world-state empire. It was the most efficient and most effective organizational instrument of governance and administration along with the Persian army. Its high efficiency was manifest in various managerial functions and processes, while its effectiveness was demonstrated in its performance as an instrument of political and administrative control throughout the far-extended empire.

The Persian bureaucracy was gigantic, centralized, and professionalized. Its size, functions, and performance surpassed any of the bureaucracies in ancient times. It was omnipresent and omnipotent in every corner of the realm. "Everywhere the armies of the Great King went, there the Achaemenid bureaucracy was planted with all of the comitants of administration—military, financial, and judicial—and communication with other provinces and [*satrapies*] was insured by the official language."[51]

F. The Environment of the Bureaucracy

The Persian bureaucracy operated in an environment that was both vast and diverse, stable and peaceful. The economy of the empire was prosperous, as the vastness and diversity of climate and natural resources of the empire provided an abundance of revenues for the treasury. The Achaemenid government recognized the significance of a sound economy for the maintenance and enhancement of the empire and its world-state scale of operations. Through various economic and financial reforms and with a sound judicial system in place, the Persian economy throughout the realm developed with a monetary system, leading to the growth of early capitalism, mercantilism, and free trade.

Capitalism grew along with the feudal system of economy and social relations, where aristocracy maintained the ruling status, but the society was court-oriented and court-guided. Silver coins and other precious metals were used as major instruments of exchange; gold, which was plentiful, was used primarily for royal, political, and military purposes. Taxation was also based on kind goods and services, as well as on money and precious metals. An advanced weight measuring system was adopted, fixed and variable property taxes collected with efficiency. The diversity of the economic system in the extended territories from east to west, with all their climatic differences, provided the Empire with a sound and flexible economy. No doubt, the peasantry carried the burden of taxation, particularly toward the end of the Empire when overtaxation and bureaucratic abuse became major problems and contributing factors to its vulnerability to external challenges. But, overall, the economy flourished under the powerful and stable Persian Empire.[52]

The prosperous economic environment throughout the Empire—with the exception of some areas and the drought years, of course—was conducive to the growth and development of professional middle class bureaucrats engaged in various activities of public administration. Rewards for government performance were available, and patronage appointments were numerous. Taxation was a major basis for revenue collection, but other ways of filling the treasury were unlimitedly available also.[53]

Similarly, the political environment was highly favorable to the development and empowerment of the Persian bureaucracy. The Persian bureaucrat was in a dominant position vis-à-vis the subject peoples, but their power was not unchecked for fairness and administrative efficiency. Generally, the Empire enjoyed stability and peace for over two centuries, a period long enough to produce a politically conducive environment for administrative as well as socioeconomic activities. The central and *satrapal* governments provided the key bases of political support for the bureaucrats, but bureaucrats also enjoyed political support from the military and from the economic and political elites at all levels. Further, their expertise served them as a formidable basis of power and politics.

The peaceful political environment attracted a large number of Greeks—politicians, exiled rulers, and professionals—who found the the Persian realm a suitable place to live and excel. The 30-year war between Athens and Sparta caused a decay in both nations, drained their resources and energy, and drove innumerable Greeks of high significance to Persia, where they all were welcomed and supported by the Persian administration. They excelled in their areas of interest, and the Achaemenid Persia provided them the opportunity to promote their Hellenic values and traditions. Persia enabled them to make contributions to the modern traditions of culture, science, politics, and government.

The religious environment was also favorable, as freedom of religion was recognized and respected by the authority. So was the respect for cultural and ethnic diversity. This allowed the Persian bureaucracy to operate in a fluid cultural and religious environment characterized by extreme diversities and tolerance for such diversity. Since Persians carried the burden of supplying the Empire with the leadership cadre in military and civil administrations, they were encouraged to have larger families and were rewarded for having more sons, for there was a perception of strength in numbers. As Herodotus notes, "those who have most sons receive an annual present from the king on the principle that there is strength in number."[54]

The Persian boys were educated from the age of five to 20, and along with some writing and reading they were taught three things: "to ride, to use the bow, and to speak the truth."[55] Physical education was emphasized and would start at dawn almost every day, and children of the nobility went through an even more rigorous program of training. Cadet schools had been set up since Darius's time to train Persian boys for appointments to the army, the court offices, and administrative posts. Persians were also taught not to pollute rivers, to respect their elders, and to have mercy on the weak. "They have a profound reverence for rivers: they never pelt a river with urine or spittle, or even wash their hands in one, or allow anyone else to do so."[56] Persians were further taught to balance faults against the good deeds in judgment. As Herodotus reports,

> I admire also the custom which forbids even the king himself to put a man to death for a single offence, and any Persian under similar circumstances to punish a servant by an irreparable injury. Their way is to balance faults against services, and then, if the faults are greater and more numerous, anger may take its course. . . . What they are forbidden to do, they are forbidden also to mention.[57]

One of the central cultural characteristics of all Persians was telling the truth and avoiding lies, for lying was considered a crime and subject to severe punishment, a key national cultural feature of Iranians throughout millennia to the present day. Other cultural features included a belief in "good thought, good talk, and good deed." Herodotus reports again: "They consider telling lies more disgraceful than anything else, and next to that, owing money. There are many reasons for their horror of debt, but the chief is their conviction that a man who owes money is bound also to tell lies."[58] While telling the truth was rewarded by society, the Persian judges and their justice administration were harsh on individuals who committed the crime of telling lies. These cultural values shaped the Persian administrative values and affected the bureaucratic behavior of the system.

The legal environment was similarly supportive, as the administrative-legal reforms of Darius (more on this later) provided a universal legal environment in which equality before law was strictly observed. The Royal Judges and the process of jurisprudence would not have mercy on violators and abusers of the system.[59] In short, the Persian bureaucracy operated in a generally stable environment, where law and order were maintained well.

G. The Bureaucratic Elite

Persians were the ruling elite in both civil and military administration, although local elites were allowed to function as traditional leaders as long as they did not question the legitimacy of the sovereign King and the Persian authority. Persians, however, formed the formidable strategic elite in bureaucracy and public administration, as they did in the military. With few exceptions, only the Persians and Medes served as the major military commanders.

The strategic position of the bureaucratic elite was based on the economic privileges they possessed for belonging to the nobility. The nobility, therefore, provided the major cadre of the strategic bureaucratic elite in both civil and military administrations. This put pressures on the nobility for supplying the commanding manpower to the Empire. The operational bureaucratic elite were recruited from all peoples throughout the entire realm. The central administration, however, maintained effective control over the huge bureaucracy through both strategic and operational elites. Strategic management was a central feature of the Persian bureaucracy and administration across the Empire. So was emergency management, for the Persian bureaucracy was forced to be prepared for all kinds of natural and manmade emergencies. Nothing should stop the operation of the Persian administration. Persian bureaucracy was not without red tape, particularly concerning major policy questions that had to be addressed to the central administration in Susa and Persepolis. But the greater overall efficiency of the administrative system often overshadowed any redtape that was expected in a gigantic bureaucracy.[60]

H.   Structure and Process of the Bureaucracy

The Persian bureaucracy was gigantic, with an organizational domain beyond imagination. Expectedly, the local and regional bureaucracies had limited direct contact with their counterparts in other regions or areas of administration, for the eastern and western extremities of the empire made it extremely difficult or impossible for such interorganizational communication. But such interorganizational communication was not uncommon among the bureaucracies of the neighboring *satrapies*. For example, the Babylonian bureaucrats had frequent communication with their counterparts in Media and Beyond the River, or the bureaucrats of the latter *satrapy* with their counterparts in Egypt. Nevertheless, no local or regional bureaucracy could escape the control of the central administration.

The bureaucracy was divided into several great departments, each with a huge number of patronage and career appointees. The departments of treasury and finance, communication and transportation and roads, public works, justice administration, and internal law and order formed the most important organizational structure of the Persian bureaucracy. There were also a huge number of public or state enterprises managing various public authorities operating like private business. Taxes and tolls were collected at waterways, communication points, city entrances, roads, bridges, harbors, ports and forts, transportation facilities, etc. Public enterprises also managed production factories and service industries.

The royal court at both the central and *satrapal* centers were the largest of all bureaucratic establishments. Temples of all religions also served as major institutional bases for the bureaucracy throughout the Empire. Although no clear statistical figure is reported by historians on the size of the Persian bureaucracy, a cursory estimation of the number of the personnel—patronage and career bureaucrats—performing a wide range of duties and functions indicate a bureaucracy of well over three million. This would include a range of functionaries from petty officers, informers, foot carriers, and workers in the courts to high officials in middle and strategic positions.

Persians never used slavery as a system of social and economic organization, but they benefited from an abundant number of mercenaries and contractual functionaries serving the bureaucracy, as well as from the conquered peoples obligated to provide various services to the united state of the empire. Periodic services performed by subject peoples need also to be included in the overall size of the bureaucracy. Adding the above to the formal size of the bureaucracy, we may come up with a large figure of 6 to 8 million employees working in the Persian bureaucracy. Management of such a huge bureaucracy with a remote control was a gigantic task, particularly in the absence of the communication technologies available in modern times.

As mentioned earlier, the Persian bureaucracy combined a dual organizational principle of centralization and decentralization. While the central administration was in absolute command of the bureaucracy, the *satrapal* system provided adequate flexibility in the administration of provincial and district/local territories. The latter were allowed to exercise a great deal of decentralization while conforming to the overall centralized policies of the administrative system based in Susa and Persepolis.

The administrative functions and processes of personnel, finance, communication, organizational coordination, and justice were facilitated by various systems employing the most efficient methods and tools the ancient time could offer. Recruitment was based on both patronage and merit, as the professionalized bureaucracy grew on a merit basis, whereas patronage and personally based recruitment were both common and considered important for political purposes. The treasury department was always the busiest organization in disbursing monetary compensations and rewards to those serving the state and the Great King.[61]

I. Professionalization of the Bureaucracy

Elevation of the bureaucracy and bureaucrats under the Median Empire had laid the foundation for professionalization of the Persian bureaucracy. The Medes were masters of statecraft, and they left behind an excellent administrative structure with exceptional organizational qualities. Further professionalization of the bureaucracy took place under the Achaemenid Empire with various principles which seemed to have remained significant throughout the duration of the Persians' rule. These included (1) recruitment based on merit and knowledge, (2) prior experience, (3) long-term apprenticeship training, (4) adherence to certain professional rules set by the establishment, (5) constant eagerness and attempts to improve personal performance and achieve excellence, and (6) acceptance by the professional association or "guild system," which was highly protective and closed to nonbureaucrats. The bureaucrats as "men of pen" were highly regarded and enjoyed prestige, power, and privileges in society.

Professionalization of the bureaucracy also led to the formation of a strong civil service system based on examination, merit performance, and pay system. While patronage played a major role in the bureaucracy, professional civil servants thrived in the Persian administration. The professional civil servants provided the continuity of office and performance in the implementation of the official policies issued from the central and *satrapal* administrations.

While Persians as the ruling elite enjoyed a superior position in the empire, followed by Medes, the privileges of a professional bureaucracy were by no means diminished for non-Persian bureaucrats around the vast Empire. Bureaucrats all over the realm were rewarded for good performance and for their professional qualifications regardless of their national, racial, or religious backgrounds. In fact, evidence clearly indicates that semi-slaves, mercenaries, and individuals of low social background were highly rewarded for their good service in the bureaucracy both at the central and *satrapal* administrations and were promoted to high positions. Jews, Greeks, Lydians, Egyptians, and other nationalities with slave-like backgrounds were able to rise to high positions in the court bureaucracy, then to governorship positions of provinces and administrative districts. Nehemiah is one example, who served as an eunuch in the royal court, who through both performance and loyalty was elevated to high position in the central bureaucracy as "cup-bearer of the Great King Artaxerxes [440 B.C.] at Susa." Hearing bad news about his city Jerusalem, he "gained the ear of the King—and of the queen: harem rule prevailed in Persia. Leave was granted him to return and rebuild Jerusalem."[62] Ezra, "a priest and scribe," was also elevated and granted royal permission accompanied by a body of priestly, temple and lay followers, with rich gift for the temple, and extensive powers to inquire the religious conditions, to instruct people, and to appoint judges for all the Jews 'Beyond the River.' "[63]

The professionalized bureaucracy was central to the government of the vast territory, with vast diversity of culture, ethnicity, climatic conditions, and geographical extremities. It was heavily relied upon by the central government for continuity and stability of the united state; it was a uniting institution with a common official language and with a common goal of serving the state and the Great King. The Persian bureaucrat enjoyed power, prestige, and high esteem in society and in the government. While the professional bureaucracy provided the state with stability and continuity of functions, patronage played a formidable role for political system-maintenance and enhancement of the Empire and its values. There were innumerable patronage officers who served the state and the king at level and each district.[64]

There were both harmony and conflict between the career, professional bureaucrats who were held in high esteem and prestige in society, on the one hand, and the numerous patronage appointees who also held influential positions in government, on the other. The strategic political appointees were, obviously, entrusted in high authority and tasks of leadership. But their relationship with the professional bureaucrats was characterized by harmony, not hostility. It was not uncommon for the patronage appointees to lose in a conflict to the entrusted professional administrators who had proven their loyalty and competence to the state and the Great King.[65]

Professionalization of the bureaucracy, however, led increasingly to such a high position in society that it was transformed gradually into a power contender, not vis-à-vis the Great King to whom it was loyal and subordinate, of course, but in general. As time passed, during the second century of the empire, the excessive bureaucratization led to increasing possibilities for bureaucratism and abuse of power. This problem was compounded by overtaxation and resulted in a general public disaffection with the administration's bureaucracy. Eventually, it took its toll on the empire, for the political and popular attitudes had already changed the perception of power among the peoples in the realm and made the empire susceptible to the serious invading challengers like Alexander, who had never abandoned his idea of invading Persia but whose challenge Persians did not take seriously and did not make adequate preparation to meet his assault.[66]

The administrative capital of the Empire was Susa, and the religious, ceremonial, or dynastic center was Persepolis, while Ecbatana (modern Hamadan), Babylon, and other major cities also served as commercial, strategic, and provincial capitals. Ecbatana also served as a major treasury center, and hence an administrative capital. Pasargade was also an early capital of the government. Some of the major *satrapal* capitals included Memphis in Egypt, Sardis in Lydia, and Babylon in Beyond the River. The official languages of the bureaucracy and administration of the Empire included Elamite, Akkadian or Aramaic, and the Old Persian of cuneiform script written on clay tablets. But Elamite and Aramaic continued to dominate the bureaucracy while the Old Persian served mainly royal purposes. The bureaucracy's effectiveness was also due to official languages of Elamite and Aramaic, which were used universally throughout the extended corners of the empire. The twin languages served as a unifying communication force to connect all peoples of the multinational empire.

J. Bureaucracy and Public Management

A central feature of the Persian Achaemenid bureaucracy was its ability to perform huge public management projects. These projects were of several kinds: capital project management, maintenance public management, operational management, organizational management, and development public management. Much can be learned from the Persian bureaucracy in the above areas, particularly in development management and capital management, the former for developing nations and the latter for the developed countries. The Persians relied heavily on team management, a system which was alive in Iran up to the 1960s, particularly in the rural/agricultural systems.

Team management has been a long historical tradition of Iranian public management, only to lose its application this century. The Persian bureaucracy managed massive projects of public works such as building and maintaining long roads to the far corners of the empire, building and maintaining huge communication and transportation systems, building dams and underground irrigation systems stretching thousands of miles away from the water origin, and the like. Strategic management was a key feature of the bureaucracy. The Persian administrative system became even more efficient since the reign of Darius the Great who launched major reforms in the economy, administration, justice, and management of the Empire.

The administrative reforms of Darius had several organizational and managerial themes that laid the foundation for a sound management system so necessary for the effective administration of a world-state empire. These organizational and managerial themes included: (1) the legitimacy of the Persian administrative state or bureaucracy; (2) the stability and favorability of the environment in which the bureaucracy and public management operated; (3) the sound leadership provided by the Persian administrative elite; (4) the professionalization and standardization of the bureaucracy; (5) the application of the Universal Law of Darius; (6) the liberal administrative policy of tolerant governance introduced by Cyrus the Great; (7) the antiwaste and anticorruption policies; (8) the expediency in organizational communication and managerial performance; and (9) strategic and emergency management.

K.   Administrative Reforms of Darius

The administrative reforms Darius launched were comprehensive, with far-reaching consequences. While Cyrus the Great founded the empire, Darius reorganized and reformed it, with great interest in micromanagement and details of its administration. During his reign, the Persian Empire reached its height, with a sound administrative system to maintain and manage its united world-state. The reforms of Darius focused on areas of governance in general and administration in particular. His governance policy did not depart from Cyrus's but simply reinforced it, whereas his organizational and administrative policies and programs extended far beyond what Cyrus had originally perceived.

Darius's administrative reforms covered the main areas of postal service and communication, taxation, economic management and financial administration, legal affairs and justice administration, and local government.

L.   Roads and Communication

The communication system was highly developed to facilitate the dissemination of information necessary for the administration of the state and for keeping the central government informed of all events throughout the realm and to keep in constant touch with the *satrapies*. Various forms of formal and informal channels of communication constituted the core of the system for information dissemination. An efficient system of roads and postal services was founded under Cyrus the Great and was expanded under Darius, which linked all parts of the empire to Susa and Persepolis. As Herodotus describes it, the road system was "excellently maintained and secured."[67] Roads were measured in *parasangs* (3.75 miles). All corners of the Empire were connected with major roads to the capital Susa and Persepolis.

The most famous of these roads was the royal highroad connecting Susa to Sardis in Europe, which, like other roads, had posting stations at regular intervals with well-maintained inns and caravanserais, and with garrisons at various stations. The other famous road was the road connecting Bacteria, the capital of the northcentral region of central Asia, to Susa. These and all other roads also served the riding postal services, a pony express, which was a Persian innovation. Although the riding postal system was used primarily for royal and administrative purposes, commercial use was not uncommon. The riding messengers were ready on all stations, where by day and night and under any weather conditions they rode swift horses and delivered messages. While normal travelers took about 90 days to travel the Sardis-Susa road, the riding messengers passed it in five days. All couriers were salaried employees of the state. Transportation on these roads was advanced to the level of excellence, and only Romans achieved similar excellence some 800 years later.[68]

In addition to the developed land communication network, sea transportation has been extensively used since Darius's time, when the world's first and largest oceanic navigation was carried out from the Hindus to the African shores and the Mediterranean via the Red Sea and the Suez Canal, which was built under Darius. Sea transportation from the Persian Gulf to the Mediterranean through the Suez Canal was a major achievement in ancient time, for it facilitated the commercial as well as military navigation on the high seas, connecting the western and eastern ends of the Empire and shortening transportation time.[69]

M. Economic Reforms and Financial Management

Rarely among ancient monarchs do we find rulers like Darius, "who so thoroughly understood that the successful state must rest on a sound economic foundation."[70] Darius's economic reforms were wide in scope and included the three sectors of government corporations or state enterprises, private sector (both urban and rural), and public sector. All three sectors flourished under his economic reforms, reinforcing each other. Although the feudal aristocracy dominated, commercial and mercantilistic economy prospered. The economic reform also included the major tax reforms with fiscal and monetary reforms as its backbone, affecting the tax structure, public finance, the price system, and the banking and financial institutions throughout the united state of the empire.

For the first time in the ancient world a fixed taxation was administered and stabilized, and the weights and measures were standardized with great details and specifications. Lands were carefully surveyed and various taxes—individual, collective, property, import-export, and excise—were collected, as well as a wide range of other taxes and tributes. These included municipal and public enterprise taxes, tolls on major roads and waterways, taxes on harbors and marketplaces, animal taxes, property taxes, and the like. In addition to various taxes, tributes were fixed on conquered peoples, except Persians. Persians never paid fixed taxes, but they paid the heavy blood tax, as they provided the empire with manpower for commanding military and administrative positions in the bureaucracy. The monetary policy of the state also affected the price and interest rate systems and, along with other financial measures, stabilized the flourishing economy.[71]

The monetary reform included an established universal coinage system, which along with the increasing urbanization, promoted a monetary economy, replacing the barter system to a great extent. Gold and silver coins were minted and used mainly for military, political, and administrative purposes, while copper and other precious metal coins were used for various economic and commercial activities. While gold was rare, and gold coins (*darics*) could be coined only by the Great King, silver and other coins could be minted by *satraps* for payment to soldiers and mercenaries and for commercial and public management purposes. The general term for tax was the old Persian *baji,* the tax collector was *bajikara.* The central treasury was located in Susa, Ecbatana, and Persepolis. Accountants (*hamarakaras*) and treasurers (*ganzabaraz*) were carefully selected and well paid. While the free enterprise system was promoted, state regulations were used to monitor and stabilize the economy.[72]

Banking activities expanded for the first time in the ancient world, and the number of banking institutions proliferated. The two most famous banking houses Egibi and Marashu and Sons operating in Babylon were but two examples; they were contracted out by the state for tax collection and financial management. Despite the prosperous and stabilized economy, the peasantry throughout the empire experienced hardship, for they paid the heavy price of taxation and supply of labor. The urban working class shared that hardship too, but they had the advantage of mobility, whereas the peasantry was mostly confined to the land under the aristocratic nobility, who both suppressed and protected the peasantry. This benevolent behavior of the feudal nobility has been a major structural aspect of the Iranian land tenure and rural-agrarian society well into the middle of the twentieth century.[73] Taxes of all kinds were collected with efficiency, and pay for services was a common financial management practice, particularly in urban areas. Public managers rarely had cash flow problems, for the treasury system had a constant flow of revenues coming in. The Persepolis treasury was the largest in the recorded history of the ancient world.[74]

N. Legal Reforms and Justice Administration

Darius's legal and judicial reforms were probably among the most famous and recognized elements of his administrative reform package. Like the universal coinage and standardization of weights and measures and comparative values of prices in the economy, Darius's Universal Ordinance of Laws and codes were significant measures that were applied equally throughout the empire. The Universal Law of Darius recognized no status or favoritism and was enforced by the Persian administration and Persian judges who, according to Herodotus and other sources, never failed to serve universal justice.[75] And as stated in the Bible, "The law of the Medes and Persians does not change."[76]

Darius borrowed from the Babylonian law of Hamurabi, but his universal law was distinctive in several ways: Unlike any previous laws, Darius's laws were both comprehensive and universal; they covered almost every aspect of political, social, economic, legal, military, and administrative systems, and the laws were applied throughout the entire empire. Whereas the Hamurabi law was confined to the royal court of Babylon, the Universal Law of Darius was enforced in far extended districts of the realm. The Old Persian terms of *data* and *data-bara* were used for law and judges respectively, and local judges, *dayyan*, were also used in local court trials. Ordeal trials were used with witnesses necessary for delivery of the verdict. Use of trial attorneys was allowed, and judges and court procedures were inspected periodically by the royal representatives from the central administration of justice. Cyrus the Great established, and Darius's reform reinforced, a universal policy of fairness and justice as a foundation of state stability. Darius also ordered the collection and study of Egyptian and Elamite legal codes for consideration in his legal reform. Thus, administration of justice constituted an essential component of Darius's administrative reforms. But injustice and repression were not uncommon from time to time after Darius, particularly during the second century of the Empire.[77]

O. Local Government Reform

The administrative structure of the local governments in the *satrapies* was modeled after the central administration, with variations reflecting diversity of geographical, ethnic, and cultural regions. Variation in local government administration was also a reflection of the universal policy of tolerance by the Persian administrative state toward the subject peoples. Such flexibility in local administrative leadership and governance served the united state of Persia, but it also presented potential for possible abuse of privilege. But the functions of the local governments did not change, as they all performed similar tasks of the bureaucracy. And the bureaucracy was the unifying institution of power and administration for the central government in Susa and Persepolis.

Darius's reform changed certain conditions in the local government, all aimed at better coordination between the local and central administrations. Direct local-central contacts were allowed for the first time between the two levels of government. This provided opportunity for the central government to check on the provincial and *satrapal* government, but it also added tension to the local-provincial-*satrapal* relationships. Second, increasing professinalization of the bureaucracy led to the further standardization of tasks in the administrative functions, therefore facilitating the centralized administrative control, particularly through auditing and other forms of achieving accountability. Uniformity and standardization of administrative processes contributed to further bureaucratic efficiency and effectiveness, while at the same time flexibility in local government leadership was maintained. Local traditions and customs were preserved, but the bureaucracy maintained its firm institutional mechanisms of control over the local government administration. However, the professionalization of the well-entrenched bureaucracy developed a tendency toward increasing bureaucratism and abuse of bureaucratic power, particularly during the last fifty years of the empire.

The gradual convergence of local conditions with the dominant Persian cultural values and traditions—whether naturally or by coercion or both—eventually replaced the local traditions with the ruling cultural values. But, the Persians also adapted to the local conditions they had settled in. By the second century, Persian colonies and their gradual integration with local peoples had already become a reality; Persians were everywhere. Somehow, both the ruling Persians and the local peoples found themselves in most places having a common interest of living together and sharing a common civilization. It was the overtaxation and increasing corruption in the court harems which, along with the resting mindset among Persians—a peaceful mindset that the Empire was too strong and invulnerable—that gradually weakened the Empire from within, making it susceptible for external invasion.[78]

The resting mindset, along with the engagement in luxury life among the ruling elite, prevented the empire from continuing the earlier traditions the Persians so dearly maintained. They never took Alexander's quest seriously, and they never made adequate preparation to meet such an onslaught, nor did they send adequate forces to stop his advances.[79] Nothing had happened in the last half century of the empire "to show that Persia was too weak to resist a serious invasion, especially if anything should arouse Iranian national sentiment."[80]

VI. CONCLUSION: IMPLICATIONS FOR MODERN PUBLIC ADMINISTRATION

The Persian tradition of public administration dates back as early as 6000 B.C., when the first experiences in state building and administration began in the Near East. As a city state and one of the earliest sites of human civilization, Susa in Iran began political life around 6000 B.C., leading to the first Iranian tradition of administration on a mass scale. As a contemporary power to Sumer, Babylon, and Assyria, Susa expanded its political life as the capital of the federated Elamite empire for over 2500 years, then the capital of the mightiest empire on earth, the Persian Achaemenid Empire.

The Iranian experience in state building and public administration, therefore, continued to dominate the entire Near/Middle East, Asia, and major parts of Europe, though Iran also received initial influence from the settled civilization of the Mesopotamia. For well over 2500 years of rule with a federal system of government, the Elamites left behind many traditions of government, politics, administration, law, and civilization; their legacies included the Elamite language, used as an official language of the Elamite and Persian bureaucracies for over 3000 years. Elamite contributions to art, religion, politics, and public management were considerable; their public management achieved a remarkable innovation in developing a gigantic underground irrigation system stretching thousands of miles, turning an arid land into a fertile one.

The arrival of the Aryans on the Iranian plateau during their second wave of migration at the turn of the first millennium resulted in a major change in the political life of the entire Middle/Near East and Asia. In a single generation, the Medes captured the entire area and by 600 B.C. were preparing to annex Babylonia, the remainder of the Mesopotamia, to their vast empire territory. But they fell to the emerging Persians, who were destined to turn the history of the ancient world around. By conquering virtually the entire known world, the Persians under Cyrus the Great founded the mightiest and largest empires the history of mankind had seen, and the vast territories of the Persian Achaemenid Empire—covering Asia, the Near/Middle East, Africa, and a major part of Europe—provided for over 230 years a peaceful and prosperous environment most suitable for the development and growth of economy, commerce, art, religion, civilization, politics, and administration.

Begun by the Medes, the Persian administrative traditions flourished so greatly that their legacies and impacts have been felt not only in Iran and in the region but also in many parts of the modern West. Iranians gained a universal reputation of "excellent administrators," and the Persian bureaucracy was famous for its high efficiency in public management and effectiveness in administering the largest empire on earth, covering virtually the entire known world (except Athens and

Sparta, which were also directly and indirectly influenced by the Persian gold, which bought favored party politicians in Athens and rulers in Sparta, and by the King's Peace which set the conditions for intergovernmental relations). The conqueror of the empire, Alexander, found the Persian systems of governance and administration so superior that he adopted the whole systems with little or no change for his entire domain, and this tradition was followed by the following Parthian and Sasanian Empires for the next millennium.

The fall of the Persian Empire to the Islamic Arabs in 651 A.D. did not result in the demise of Persian administrative excellence. On the contrary. The superior Persian traditions of state, culture, and administration captured the conqueror once again, and the bedouin Arabs adopted almost entirely the Sasanian state and administrative state systems. The Persian bureaucracy continued its long tradition with its own language and culture, and the Persians once again managed to display their national character of independence, high culture, and administrative excellence. This happened particularly during the Abased Caliphate which was totally Persianized and under Persian control.

The Persian administrative tradition continued to improve during the revived period of the Safavid Empire (1500–1700) in which the bureaucracy and administration had achieved high marks in public management and public service, particularly in public works and enterprise management. But this historical tradition began to decline during a prolonged period of relentless invasions by barbaric Monguls and Turks, and later during the 18th and 19th centuries of weak, despotic Qajar rule, inviting all kinds of foreign interference in Iranian politics and administration.

The modern Iranian public administration is based on the ancient traditions of Persian bureaucracy and administration on the one hand, and the modern concepts of management and organization borrowed from the West, on the other. This historical essay has outlined the traditions of state and public administration under the Persian Empire and before, but the focus has been on the Achaemenid Empire (559–330 B.C.), and no discussion has been made on the Parthian and Sasanian administrative systems. The latter empire had achieved a high level of advancement in theory and practice of organization, state, and administration, and discussion of its administrative legacy requires separate, lengthy treatment.

The section below focuses on the following questions: What can we learn from the administrative system of the Persian Achaemenid Empire? What are some of the implications of the Persian bureaucracy for the modern theory and practice of organization, public management, and the administrative state? The Persian Empire was both gigantic and multinational, with high diversity in languages, cultures, customs, traditions, and regions. It was managed by an administrative system that was politically effective and managerially efficient. Are there any implications from this administrative system for managing large administrative states or powerful countries like the United States in modern and postmodern times? The following is an outline of possible answers to the above questions.

1. A major lesson to be learned from the administrative system of the Persian Achaemenid Empire is the gigantic size of the bureaucracy and administrative state which covered multinational and multiracial territories, with extreme diversities and complexities. That huge bureaucracy was managed with such a high efficiency that no geographical area in the empire could escape the machinery of the central government.

2. A related implication is that the Persian bureaucracy and administrative system were both centralized and decentralized. Its centralization enabled the central government to maintain its firm control over the entire realm, while decentralization at local and provincial levels allowed adequate flexibility to adapt to the local conditions for the purposes of governance and administration. Even self-governance was allowed in some localities. In fact, for the first time in history, Persians put into practice the concept of "partnership in governance," a practice which was unique in ancient times, though the Medes and Elamites practiced a federated system of governance

before them and the Greeks did it in their island states. But the nature of the governance partnership practiced by Persians was unique with implications for modern governance.

3.   Another related lesson to be learned is the consistent liberal policy of government and administrative tolerance that the founding father Cyrus the Great established as part of the constitution of the vast empire. The universal liberal policy of government tolerance was a humane insurance policy against abuses and devastation of subject peoples, a tragedy that was so common under the previous and following empires in the region. The Persian liberal theory and practice of tolerant governance and administration were new phenomena never tried before. The Persian Achaemenids

> did rule their empire in a new way. Calculated frightfulness was not their practice. Deportations were relatively few. Tolerance of local forms of religion, social organization and even government was policy. Documented and orderly provincial government was an imperial goal (witness the treasury system). And many peoples of the empire were involved in its governance and functioning: Elamites and Babylonian scribes, Iranian and non-Iranian priests, Jewish and Greek mercenaries, Babylonian bankers and real estate dealers, Ionian tyrants and democrats, and Spartan and Athenian exiles—to name a few.[81]

The Persian empire was generally a peaceful empire, and such policies and actions of tolerance and partnership in governance and administration were integrative, and they were "something new in the history of Near Eastern attempts to create polities which transcend ethnic and national boundaries. *The* polity in this case was the Persian empire."[82] The peoples, the *dahyava*,

> were not to be seen as separate nations held enslaved by one nation, but as integral parts of the empire, the one real polity, over which the King and the Persians admittedly ruled. . . . Darius and his successors ruled a large land mass containing a bewildering variety of ethnic groups for almost two hundred years. They did it with very little violence and without the need for almost annual military activity characteristic of the smaller Assyrian empire. Rebellions were comparatively rare, and most involved political and dynastic party efforts to grab power at the center of government rather than attempts by parts of the empire to break away from the centre. Thus, Persian imperial philosophy . . . was effective. The conqueror of the empire, Alexander, incorporated much of this new thinking into his own idealistic vision of empire, and thus the Achaemenids made a direct contribution to the political and social concepts of the Hellenistic world.[83]

The liberal administrative/governance policies of the empire rejected discrimination based on race, color, religion, or party affiliation. These basic human rights were preserved and protected by not only the formal policy, but also the legal procedures of the Universal Law of Darius applied throughout the realm. There is a great deal to be learned from these Persian administrative policies and practices for the modern administrative systems, particularly in the United States with major ethnic, color, racial, and national diversity. The dual characteristics of the administrative system—centralization and decentralization—can also be an important application or lesson for the modern administrative systems around the world.

4.   Still other implications are the federalism and intergovernmental relations, so characteristic of the Elamite and Median empires. Therefore, the Iranian contribution to modern political and administrative systems should also be noted, in that perhaps Iran was the original developer of the federal system of governance in the world. Obviously the Greeks also borrowed from the earlier Elamites and passed this heritage on to the modern Western political theory, just as the Achaemenids made direct contributions to the Hellenistic world under the Selucid rule of Alexander. Achaemenid contributions to politics and administration of the modern world, therefore, were both direct and indirect through the Hellenic channels.

5.   The Elamite language was a major contribution to the world political history, civilization, and administration. The Elamites first, and Persians later, were the innovators in developing and managing gigantic underground irrigation systems turning arid lands into workable lands, and this system has been used for thousands of years in the entire Near/Middle East. This was a major achievement in managing water treatment, natural resources management, and efficient distribution of scarce resources, a managerial achievement that has direct applications for development management today.

6.   The Aryans—Medians and Persians—were the first in political history to develop the concept of "state" and to turn that concept into an operational reality. The empire was considered a state, and the Achaemenid empire was hence a world-state empire. The state was everything in the realm, and nations, peoples, and officials served the united state, which represented the Great King, the sovereign authority, who recognized no equal on earth, a devout worshipper of Ahura Mazda, and "who contained within his person and his office the welfare of the empire."[84]

7.   Another lesson to be learned is the professionalization of the bureaucracy, leading to the development of a caste-like guild system formed by the scribal bureaucrats enjoying privileges, prestige, power, and high esteem in government and society. The Persian bureaucrat was both efficient and effective, managerially, politically, and administratively. The guild was closed to outsiders, but qualifying entrance to the profession was welcomed. Apprenticeship training was key to joining the profession, but so was general education. Since Darius's time, there were colleges attached to major temples and military centers, where cadets and civil servants were trained for civil and military services, and where priestly and cult-requirements and medicine were studied.[85] "Important alike for appointment to the army, the court offices, and to administrative posts in the provinces, was the existence of something like cadet schools." At the courts, "all the boys of the foremost Persians," as Xenophon phrases it, were educated.[86]

Professionalization of the bureaucracy also resulted in the formation of a civil service system based on examination, training, stable pay system, and merit performance. The professional civil servants were held in high esteem in society, and they provided the administrative state with continuity in policy implementation and managerial efficiency. Therefore, the concept of civil service is not unique to the modern West; much has been learned, and more can be learned, from the ancient Persian administration, as well as from others.

8.   The administrative reforms of King Darius were major contributions to the following generations of empires and states. The taxation reforms and the financial systems operational in the Empire gained the Persians a major reputation of running a huge empire with a sound economic system and financial stability, leading to all kinds of economic, professional, artistic, cultural, and administrative prosperity. The stable and peaceful empire promoted all aspects of human civilization, passing legacies on to the following generations for the next two millennia. A direct lesson to be learned here is that administrative reforms, if genuine and implemented seriously, can have significant impacts in the management of the economy and society and in a more effective administration of government. If Persians did it 2500 years ago, it can be done in modern times too.

9.   Still another important aspect of the Persian administration was its excellent "emergency management" system, prepared for all kinds of natural and manmade disasters. The Persian military and civil administrations were well prepared and guarded against possible emergencies. It was a central policy of the government that the Empire must be prepared to meet all kinds of human and natural emergencies. Therefore, the Persian administration was skilled in emergency management. It was also an administrative ideology that the Persian army and bureaucracy should experience no setbacks in the face of crisis emergencies. The treasury, of course, was always ready to finance projects and activities for such a purpose. The effectiveness of the emergency management was mainly based on the "strategic management" philosophy and ideology characteristic of

the Persian administrative system. The Persian bureaucratic elite mapped out long-term strategic as well as short-term operational plans for expanding and maintaining organizational domains and for efficient management of acquired human, natural, and financial resources of the empire.

10.   Still another implication is the multimechanisms of institutional control over the *satrapal* governance and administration by the central government under the Persian Achaemenid Empire. Chief among these institutional checks and balances were the "ears and eyes of the king" and the special secretary of the king in the *satrapal* courts, plus the unannounced royal judges and inspectors who would give surprise visits to provincial and local bureaucrats and governors. Reporting directly to the central government, these independent visitors could make significant contributions to the overall checks and balances system of the government and to the achievement of effective accountability in bureaucracy and public administration.

11.   The dual systems of administrative division of the empire territory based on ethnic, cultural, and religious purposes of local self-governance, on the one hand, and the administrative division of the *satrapies*, provinces, and local geographical districts for political effectiveness and managerial efficiency, on the other, can have potential benefit for governing nations with diversity in race, culture, ethnicity, and religions.

12.   The huge public works of the Persian administration must also be mentioned. The bureaucracy, both civil and military, was heavily involved in major public works development projects. And development management was efficient. Roads, public baths, caravanserais, inns, communication centers, commercial and trade centers, underground irrigation systems, bridges, waterways and canals, and the like were built, developed, and maintained. Building and maintaining extensive roads and waterway canals were gigantic projects which required massive manpower with tremendous organizational coordination and managerial supervision. Huge numbers of mercenaries and half-slaves were employed in the enormous public works projects that were carried out with maximum efficiency. Public enterprise management was a major function of the Persian public administration under the Achaemenid Empire. The Persians relied heavily on team management and teamwork as basic organizational forms to manage small and large public works. This ancient Persian tradition was continued as part of Iranian public and private management up to the middle of the twentieth century, particularly in rural/agrarian Iran, but was gradually abandoned in the face of rural bureaucratization under the Shah in the 1960s. Team management has already become a global strategy to improve organizational performance in both public and private sectors.

13.   The successful administrative reforms of King Darius had several organizational and managerial themes that bear major implications or lessons for modern public administration. Later on, Romans adopted them and passed them on to the modern system of management. These included (1) the legitimacy of the Persian administrative state or bureaucracy; (2) the stability of the administrative environment; (3) the sound organizational leadership provided by the Persian administrative elite; (4) the professionalization of the bureaucracy; (5) application of the Universal Law of Darius; (6) the liberal administrative policy; (7) the antiwaste and antibureaucratic policies; and (8) the expediency in organizational communication and managerial performance.

14.   Finally, the stable and peaceful world-state empire of Achaemenid Persia attracted large numbers of Greek people—politicians, professionals, scientists, and paid mercenaries— who were driven out by the long period of war between Athens and Sparta. Persia harbored them and supported them, and it was through this peaceful state that the Hellenic values of politics and government were promoted, and Greeks' contributions to modern public service were facilitated.

The above is a short listing of some of the features of the Persian administrative systems that can have potential lessons and implications for modern public administration in both developed and developing countries. Further research is needed to shed more light on the Persian administrative contributions to modern public administration and government.

ENDNOTES

1. Farazmand, Ali. "State Tradition and Public Administration in Iran in Ancient and Contemporary Perspectives," in Farazmand, Ali (ed.). *Handbook of Comparative and Development Public Administration*, Marcel Dekker, New York, 1991, chapter 19, pp. 255–270; "Bureaucracy, Bureaucratization, and Debureaucratization in Ancient and Modern Iran," in Farazmand, Ali (ed.). *Handbook of Bureaucracy*, Marcel Dekker, Inc., New York, 1994, chapter 43, pp. 675–686; "Professionalism, Bureaucracy, and Modern Governance: A Comparative Perspective," in Farazmand, Ali (ed.). *Bureaucrats and Politicians in Modern Systems of Governance* (Thousand Oaks, CA: Sage, 1997), chapter 2; *State and Bureaucracy in Persia (Iran): 8000 Years of Public Administration*, Praeger, Westport, CT, forthcoming.

2. Cameron, G. G. *History of Early Iran*, Greenwood Press, New York, 1968; Ghirshman, R. *Iran: From the Earliest Times to the Islamic Conquest*, Penguin Books, New York, 1954.

3. *The Cambridge Ancient History*, Vol. I, Part II, Cambridge University Press, Cambridge, 1971, p. 648.

4. *Ibid.*, pp. 662–672.

5. *Ibid.*, p. 680.

6. *Ibid.*, p. 675.

7. *Ibid.*, also see *The Cambridge Ancient History*, vol. II, part 1, Cambridge University Press, Cambridge, 1973, pp. 271–288.

8. *Ibid.*, p. 680.

9. Dhalla, M.N. *Zoroastrian Civilization*, AMS Press, New York, 1977; Frye, Richard. *The Heritage of Persia*, The World Publishing Co., New York, 1963; Frye, Richard. *The Golden Age of Persia*, Harper and Row, New York, 1975; Olmstead, A.T. *History of the Persian Empire: The Achaemenid Period*, University of Chicago Press, Chicago, 1948.

10. Ghirshman, *op. cit.*, p. 75.

11. *Ibid.*

12. Herodotus, *The Histories*, Translated by Aubrey de Selincourt Penguin Books, New York, 1984, pp. 83–84.

13. *Ibid.*, p. 83.

14. *Ibid.*, p. 97.

15. Ghirshman, *op. cit.*, p. 113.

16. *The Cambridge Ancient History*, Vol. VI, Cambridge University Press, Cambridge, 1953.

17. Cook, J. M. *The Persian Empire*, Schocken Books, New York, 1983; Herodotus *op. cit.*; Olmstead, *op. cit.*

18. *Ibid.* Cook; Olmstead, *op. cit.*

19. Herodotus, *ibid.*, p. 97.

20. *Ibid.*

21 *Ibid.*, pp. 234–241.

22. Cook, *op. cit.*, p. 55.

23. *Ibid.*, p. 56.

24. *Ibid.*, p. 76.

25. Quoted in *ibid.*, p. 55.

26. *Ibid.*

27. Quoted in *The Cambridge Ancient History*, Vol. IV, Cambridge University Press, Cambridge, 1960, p. 185.

28. *Ibid.*

29. Herodotus, *op. cit.*; Cook, *op. cit.*

30. *The Cambridge Ancient History*, Vol. IV, 1960, p. 185.

31. *Ibid.*

32. *Ibid.*

33. *Ibid.*; see also Cook, *op. cit.*; Farazmand, "State Traditions," see p. 72; Frye, "Heritage or Golden Ages," also pp. 50, 51, 68.

34. *Ibid.* See also *The Cambridge Ancient History*, Vol. IV, 2nd edition, 1988, pp. 82–83.

35. *The Cambridge Ancient History*, Vol. IV, 1960, p. 186.
36. *Ibid.*
37. *Ibid.*
38. Farazmand, "State Tradition"; Cook, *op. cit.*; Olmstead, *op. cit.*
39. *Ibid.*; *The Cambridge Ancient History*, Vol. IV, 1960.
40. *Ibid.*
41. Ghirshman, *op. cit.*, p. 144.
42. Herodotus, *op. cit.*, p. 256.
43. *Ibid.*
44. *The Cambridge Ancient History*, Vol. IV, 1960, p. 187.
45. *Ibid.*; Cook, *op. cit.*; Ghirshman, *op. cit*; Farazmand, "State Tradition."
46. Cook, *op. cit.*, p. 41; *The Cambridge Ancient History*, Vol. VI, 1953, pp. 176–179.
47. *The Cambridge Ancient History*, Vol. IV, 1960, p. 188.
48. *The Cambridge Ancient History*, Vol. IV, 2nd edition, 1988, p. 147.
49. *Ibid.*; Cook, *op. cit.*
50. *Ibid.*; Frye, *The Heritage of Persia*; Olmstead, *op. cit.*
51. Frye, *ibid.*, p. 97.
52. *The Cambridge Ancient History*, Vol. IV, 1960; Vol. VI, 1953.
53. *Ibid.*
54. Herodotus, *op. cit.*, p. 98.
55. *Ibid.*
56. *Ibid.*
57. *Ibid.*
58. *Ibid.*
59. *Ibid.*
60. *The Cambridge Ancient History*, Vol. IV, 1960.
61. *Ibid.*; Cook, *op. cit.*; Frye, *The Golden Age of Persia*; Herodotus, *op. cit.*; Olmstead, *op. cit.*
62. *The Cambridge Ancient History*, Vol. VI, 1953, p. 169.
63. *Ibid.*, p. 168.
64. Farazmand, Ali. "Professionalism, Bureaucracy, and Modern Governance: A Comparative Perspective," paper presented at the 1993 Conference of the American Political Science Association, Washington, DC, September 1–4, 1993.
65. *Ibid.*
66. *Ibid.*; Cook, *op. cit.*; Olmstead, *op. cit.*
67. Herodotus, *op. cit.*
68. Ghirshman, *op. cit.*; Frye, *op. cit.*; Olmstead, *op. cit.*; *The Cambridge Ancient History*, Vol. IV, 1960, p. 193.
69. *Ibid.*; Cook, *op. cit.*
70. Olmstead, *op. cit.*, p. 185.
71. *Ibid.*, pp. 185–194; Frye, *The Heritage of Persia*; Ghirshman, *op. cit.*; Olmstead, *op. cit.*
75. Herodotus, *op. cit.*
76. Frye, *The Heritage of Persia*, pp. 98–103.
77. *Ibid.*
78. *Ibid.*
79. *Ibid.*
80. *The Cambridge Ancient History*, Vol. VI, 1953, p. 24.
81. *The Cambridge Ancient History*, Vol. IV, 2nd edition, 1988, p. 111.
82. *Ibid.*
83. *Ibid.*
84. *Ibid.*, p. 110.
85. Cook, *op. cit.*, p. 71.
86. Xenophon, Anabasis, I, 9. as quoted in *The Cambridge Ancient History*, Vol. IV, 1960, p. 191.

5

Administrative Legacies of Greece, Rome, and Byzantium

Demetrios Argyriades   *R. F. Wagner Graduate School of Public Service,*
New York University, New York, New York

I. THE ANCIENT CITY-STATE

If Orwell had been alive in 1984, he might have voiced relief because his dire predictions on global political trends had not come to pass. Events have since moved swiftly, but still further away from his prophetic vision of brave new worlds. No doubt it is too early to announce the triumph of freedom and the demise of tyranny. Indeed, the sudden widespread resurgence of religious and ethnic fundamentalism is anything but reassuring, and if we have learned something during the past six years it is, without a doubt, never to be surprised. We live, as Drucker put it, in an "age of discontinuity" when change—no less abrupt because it often comes without violence or bloodshed—is difficult to forecast. It is hard to predict the future course of events. But what is so arresting about recent developments in East and Central Europe is the massive and decisive delegitimization of "democratic centralism," the ne plus ultra of bureaucratic administration. Indeed one might well wonder to what extent those trends might not signal the end of an era, the last days of a model and management ideology, born in the Age of Reason although their antecedents hark far back all the way to the days of Byzantium and the Roman Empire.

The bureaucratic model was very much the product of 18th-century thought, the creation of a period which also saw the rise of industrialization, a quantum leap in science, advances in technology, and population growth. The outcome of reforms, whose intellectual origins were rooted in the doctrines of the European Enlightenment, the bureaucratic model posited both efficiency and the rule of law as its ultimate goals. Economy and integrity were equally its objectives. Nourished by the liberal humanitarian doctrines of the French Revolution and the nationalist tide which it carried in its wake, the bureaucratic state pressed on in the direction of centralization until the very forces that aided its beginnings now seemed to turn against it.

The manifest decline of bureaucratic centralism and its loss of credibility, vitality, and effectiveness add interest and relevance to the exploration and rediscovery of old administrative legacies, as part of an ongoing quest for alternative models of state organization. In this chapter I compare and contrast the administrative legacies produced under two sharply differing types of environment and political cultures: those of the ancient city-state (mostly Athens and Rome), and those of the empire—Roman and Byzantine.

A. Beginnings of Political-Governmental Self Awareness[1]

> We Europeans are the children of Hellas. Our civilization, which has its roots in the brilliant
> city life of the eastern Aegean has never lost the traces of its origins and stamps us with a char-
> acter by which we are distinguished from other great civilizations of the human family.—
> Fisher.[2]

There can be little doubt that from the soil of Greece—and I may add Judea—spring all the basic
concepts and values that have shaped our social institutions our ideas on government and public
life in general. It is also in Greece and Rome that politics, philosophy, and law first developed as
systematic inquiries into the nature, purposes, methods, and manifestations of social life and governance. Yet it was not the cradle of our civilization—neither Periclean Athens nor Cicero's
Rome—that saw the birth of an administrative culture. Rather that culture and structures of the
type which we associate with our contemporary world first saw the light of day in the Alexandrian era and in the Roman Empire, largely as a result of pressures generated by a vast expansion of
the scale and increase in the complexity of government activity.

Long before Sophocles praised the glory and the pitfalls of man, to him the Crown of Creation, the Iliad and the Odyssey had opened for mankind a mine of information and psychological insight into human behavior. Like the Bible for the Hebrews, Homer's epics served as a primary
source for the education and socialization of successive generations of citizens in Ancient Greece.

From Homer, Pindar, and Hesiod, the three great epic poets of pre-Classical Greece, the
Greeks derived the lessons that shaped the social values of the ancient city-state. Foremost among
those values, the practice of humility and moderation is linked to the beginnings of the cult of
Apollo at Delphi. Two maxims, in particular, *Meden Agan* and *Gnothi Seauton*,[3] preached the
importance of self-knowledge; they warned against the dangers of hubris and excess. Revulsion
against tyranny, dislike of arbitrariness and violence by one man were parallelled by fear of mob
rule. Both in fact, were seen as departures from the golden rule of temperance in the life of social
groups.

> Lust breeds the tyrant man. Lust, when fed and puffed with vanity on what disaccords with the
> time's advantage, clambering the sheer height goes over the drop, where nothing breaks his
> fall, where no firm foothold serves longer.—Sophocles, *Oedipus.*

Pervasive in Greek literature, suspicion of unreason and fear of all excess is also a major
theme of classical political and social theory, adding substance to the quest for a balanced constitution and safeguards against abuse of prerogative power.

It was Socrates and Plato, in a break with past tradition—a break which, incidentally, the
German philospher Nietzsche described as the beginning of the decline of Greece—who shifted
the focus decisively from the material world, the object of attention of pre-Socratic philosophers,
to man and his social environment. The break, which coincided with a profound political crisis in
all of Greece, also marked the inception of systematic enquiry in politics, philosophy, and ethics.
Significantly, however, neither law nor administration emerged as a distinct discipline until much
later.

In his classic "Ancient Law," Sir Henry Maine offered this explanation for this seeming
paradox:

> Few things are more impressive than the fact that no Greek-speaking people has ever felt itself
> seriously perplexed by the . . . questions of Free-will and Necessity . . . (or) ever showed the
> smallest capacity for producing a philosophy of Law. Legal science is a Roman creation and
> the problem of Free-will arises when we contemplate a metaphysical conception under a legal
> aspect. How came it to be a question whether invariable sequence was identical with necessary
> connection? I can only say that the tendency in Roman law, which became stronger as it

advanced, was to look upon legal consequences as united to legal causes by an inexorable necessity, a tendency most markedly exemplified in the definition of Obligation (as) *Juris vinculum quo necesitate adstringimur alicujus solvendae rei.*[4]

This development, however, as Sir Henry explained, was the product of a slow evolution which took many centuries to mature. It followed the decline of the ancient city-state—both Hellenic and Roman—and was marked by the rise of Christianity, whose division of the realm of the spirit from that of the state decisively transformed perceptions of the nature of citizenship on the one hand and the foundations of political discourse on the other.

"A rule-of-law state has no room for dictatorship by any class and even less so for the power of a management bureaucracy," proclaimed the draft platform that the Central Committee of the Soviet Communist Party approved in early February (*New York Times*, Feb. 19, 1990:A8). This startling rediscovery of the *état de droit* in the wake of *perestroika* only served to underscore the importance and fragility of this unique accomplishment of European political thought. Its antecedents may indeed lie way back, most probably in the days of Rome and the Roman Republic. However, as a theoretical construct with contemporary institutional applications, the *état de droit* (or *Rechtsstaat*, in German) is essentially the outcome of the intellectual ferment in 18th-century Europe, a product of the Enlightenment. In fact, it represents the logical conclusion of social contract theories, a cross between the view of the state and of civil society as artifacts, of man as a free agent, and of positive law as essentially the expression of the general will.

Of course, none of those concepts could have taken root in the days of ancient Greece and Rome. Nothing was more alien to the classical mind than (1) the separation, indeed contradistinction, between the state and citizen, and (2) the view of law as an instrumentality, a tool—in other words, of government administration.

In spite of many centuries of secularization, the laws retained in the Greece of Pericles, as well in as in the heyday of Cicero's Roman Republic, the aura and the majesty of their putative divine origins. The laws hold forth in *Crito*, interrogating Socrates, not as particular statutes of limited intent, but rather as Right Order divinely ordained, whose intentional violation was no less than transgression of morality and propriety.

> Then the laws will say: "Consider Socrates if this is true that in your present attempt you are going to do us wrong. For after having brought you into the world and nurtured and educated you and given you . . . a share in every good . . . we further . . . give the right to every Athenian that, if he does not like us when he has come of age . . . that he may go where he pleases and take the goods with him.[5]

This is hardly, you might say, the language one would use speaking of laws today, when acts of legislation are more often perceived as the products of dubious compromises between competing interests than as the embodiments of moral imperatives.

In ancient times, however, not only in Greece and Rome, but more so in Judaea, law was inseparable from religion. Like Moses, such early legislators as Minos or Lycurgus were uniformly held to have been divinely inspired: the former by Zeus; the latter by Apollo. The origins of laws were likewise often set in the far distant past, believed to be the legacy of mythical lawgivers, coeval, in most cases, with the foundation stones and ramparts of the city. Of many a city founder it was said that *moresque viris et moenia ponit.*[6]

The oldest codes of Athens and Rome alike consisted of an uneven mixture of ethical precepts, canons on ritual observance and organizational principles. However, subsequent important statutory enactments displayed the same confusion. For Solon as for Cicero, the laws were rules pertaining no less to ancestral worship and the upkeep of temples than to the mundane questions of adjudication of disputes and debt settlement. Even the rapid progress of secularization of government administration in post-Periclean Athens did not change this situation substantially. To

Greeks and Romans alike, the laws remained in essence those fundamental precepts which molded public attitudes and guided private citizens in almost every facet of their daily lives. One of the greatest orators of ancient Greece, Demosthenes, expressed this point of view:

> The whole life of men, O Athenians, whether they inhabit a great city or a small one, is governed by nature and by laws. Of these, nature is a thing irregular, unequal and peculiar to the individual possessor; laws are regular, common and the same for all. Nature, if it be depraved, has often vicious desires. . . . Laws desire what is just and honourable and useful . . . and that is law which all men ought to obey for many reasons and especially because every law is an invention and a gift of the Gods . . . a corrective of errors . . . a compact of the whole state, according to which all who belong to the state ought to live.[7]

The laws as correctives of Nature: that was surely a far cry from the position taken, some two millenia later, by the French philosopher Jean-Jacques Rousseau, for whom legal enactments were only at best attempts to replicate, reflect, and give free expression to an ideal order observable in Nature. The idealization of Nature was, of course, nothing new to the prophets of the Enlightenment, or indeed the Founding Fathers of the United States. Its origins go back a long way to the Stoics—from Zeno to Marcus Aurelius—and the decline of the ancient city-state. They coincide, in fact, with the disintegration of the Polis and *res publica* as focal points of loyalty and central frame of reference for the intense communal activity which citizens' self-rule implied. All these were largely lost in the indeterminancy of vast heterogeneous empires, whose bounds in the days of Jesus, roughly the dawn of our era, were seen as coextensive with mankind.

B.   Quest for the Good Life and Democratization

At the height of its development, the city-state in Greece and Rome alike was viewed as the ideal setting for the "good life" (*to eu zein*). It should not be overlooked that the ancient city-state was itself, in many cases, the product of slow evolution. It resulted from the merger or coalescence of families, of fratries and tribes initially for reasons of self-defense, later for other purposes. Rome was born of the coming together of Latin and Sabine villages established on its hills. The union of several tribes (*ethne*) brought Athens into being. A true confederation,[8] the ancient city-state was a military and religious organization long before it took on added economic and industrial dimensions. Thus in Rome the *campus martius* and *comitium* were distinguished from the *forum*, which had been set apart for commercial transactions. Likewise, the *agora* remained in ancient Athens the center of political and intellectual ferment long after it became a marketplace.

The origins and nature of the ancient city-state left an indelible mark on the classical concept and ideal of citizenship. In Greek and Latin alike, the definition of virtue (*arete*) for long conveyed the primacy of manliness and courage in the ancient scale of values. Aristotle, who defined happiness (*Eudaemonia*) not as a state of mind but rather as activity, indeed as purposeful action, considered that the quest for what was good for Man was none other than the object of the science of Politics.[9] According to Aristotle, not only was the *polis* "a creation of nature"[10] and man a political animal, but also, on that account, the *polis* represented an ideal environment for human self-fulfillment. It formed the best laboratory for both personal growth and the exercise of virtue because, in city-states that were properly structured (*poleis*), unlike despotic empires, men learned to command as well as to obey. They practiced rule and self-rule.

For Cicero also reason was the highest gift that Nature had bestowed on mankind. It inspired man "with a relish for his own kind" and reminded him that, as Plato put in in his letter to Archytos, a man is not born for self alone, "but for country and for kindred, claims that leave but a small part of him for himself."[11] Like Demosthenes the Athenian, the Roman Cicero exemplified the virtues of good citizenship: lifelong participation in the affairs of state and readiness for office, but also for the likelihood of adverse political fortune. Plutarch relates that long after his death, when

Octavian, his adversary, had become the emperor Augustus, he found one of his grandnephews reading a book by Cicero. The boy tried to conceal it, but Augustus took it from him, studied it carefully, and said: "An eloquent man, my child, and a great lover of his country."[12]

Love of country was highly praised in Greece and Rome alike. In both it was equated with respect for and obedience to the laws of the city-state. The view that men as citizens were creatures of the laws of the particular city to which they had been born is nowhere more eloquently expressed than in Plato's *Crito*.

As a belief, however, its currency was widespread throughout the ancient world. It meant more than compliance for fear of retribution. In some ways it came close to adherence to the precepts of a religious faith. Most men belonged to a city because they were born into a *gens*, much as today most people are born into a religion and carry its basic precepts throughout their lives no matter where they live. Nothing more clearly shows how alien the modern concepts of citizenship and territorial jurisdiction were to the ancient mind than the fact that, at the height of the Hellenistic period, despite the rise of strong homogenizing trends and cosmopolitan tendencies, the Greeks could live dispersed throughout the Near East, as far as Bactria and Upper Egypt, but always subject to their respective *politeumata* (i.e., legal systems).[13]

Indeed, the multiplicity of diverse legal systems was doubtlessly a factor in forcing recognition of "a common law of the Hellenes,"[14] already in the fourth century B.C.E. Analogous in origin although of much greater moment was the development in Rome of the *jus gentium*. Unable or reluctant to apply to foreign litigants either the *jus civile*, proper for Romans only, or the particular laws of the several cities from which those litigants hailed, the Romans chose instead to gradually compile a "law common to all nations"—i.e., a body of principles and customs observable in most of the Italian tribes with which they came into contact. The growth of the *jus gentium* and subsequent development of the *jus naturale* resulted from imperial expansion and the influence of Stoicism after the incorporation of Greece into the Roman realm. Originally, however, the low prestige accorded to the *jus gentium* reflected the low status of trade-related activities to which it mostly applied.

In Greece and Rome alike, production-oriented and economic concerns enjoyed rather low prestige. It is hardly accidental that many of those activities were carried out by slaves, who in several city-states vastly outnumbered the citizens. In sharp contrast to practices in our contemporary world, the law and administration of ancient times took very little notice of economic activity. Even in Athens, a major trading center during its golden age, Plato could take the view that business transactions and the collection of customs in the harbor and the market did not require the attention of city legislators in a well-ordered state. Likewise, they formed no part of the education of the future guardian elite.

Also for Aristotle a proper education (*paedeia*) formed an important part of the preparation for citizenship in the ideal state. It included, in particular, gymnastics, rhetoric, and music, but no economics or management. This was consistent with the belief that excessive preoccupation with business concerns was really incompatible with active participation in the affairs of state which, in well-ordered cities, was indistinguishable from the pursuit of the good life (*to eu zein*).

This pattern is familiar, vaguely reminiscent, in fact, of 19th-century England before the tide of reforms, beginning with the seminal Northcote and Trevelyan Report, transformed the administrative system and set the country firmly on the road to bureaucratization. The administrative system of the ancient city-state was decidedly preindustrial and prebureaucratic, marked by extensive devolution of administrative functions to the constituent units of the *polis* and dependent for the regular and effective discharge of those functions on voluntary service by unpaid members of the local gentry.

The practice of rotation of many a prominent post, in preference to elections, further lessened the distinction between government and governed, which the awesome scale and complexities of the modern megastate have made inevitable. In fact, it is noteworthy that the progress of democracy in the golden age of Greece was closely associated with the introduction of pay for service to the state. Ostensibly, the reason was one of social justice and political equality. In Pericles' words, reported by Thucydides, "In regard to poverty, if a man is able to benefit the city, he is not debarred by his position."[15]

The measure represented a milestone in the progress of democratization and the gradual shift of power from the wealthy few to the many. Perhaps no single change so deeply impressed the minds of Plato and Aristotle and influenced the direction of their thought. It marked their quest for measures to arrest what they considered as perilous decline to anarchy and mob rule. But even as dispassionate and measured an observer as the historian Thucydides viewed the passage to democracy as hardly an unmixed blessing. He saw it as accompanied by factionalism, greed, and what Montalembert, a critic of reform in both England and France, decried in the early 19th century as the "vénalité de charges."[16]

Payment for public service was introduced as an attempt to deal with the encrusted position of local oligarchies.[17] It should be emphasized, however, that rates of pay were low; 2 to 3 obols a day.[18] This hardly represented more than a meager subsistence allowance. The reaction which the practice of making such payments evoked must rather be seen in the light of the traditional concept of citizenship with its heavy stress on service, both military and political, and the lack of clear distinction in the ancient way of thinking between government and governed, on the one hand; between the public and private domains on the other.

This fusion of the roles of government and governed was soon put to the test with the tremendous expansion of public business which followed the transition, in Athens and Rome in particular, from chiefly agrarian polities to large commercial centers, the hubs of industrial activity and the mighty *metropoleis* of far-flung empires.

Even so, a strong tradition of voluntary service persisted for a long time, enabling city-states to tap both wealth and talent for public purposes. Especially noteworthy, and arguably a precursor of contemporary rules on tax deductions, was the institution of "liturgies" which, in extracting money to pay for public services, afforded the rich an occasion to show their civic spirit and also rise to prominence.

Ostensibly an alternative for state-provided services, those *leitourgiae* supported a wide range of activities, essentially of a cultural and educational nature. Financing the production of a theatrical play and training of a chorus (*choregia*) were typical of such activities. But even the construction and maintainance of warships (*trierarchia*) afforded their rich sponsors not merely an alternative to heavy taxation of wealth, but also the opportunity to build their reputation and curry favor with legislative bodies and courts of law alike.

Compelling civic virtue as often as they encouraged it, the *leitourgiai* did not for very long prove adequate to meet the needs for public revenue. Those needs, expanding rapidly with democratization, were partly met by means of annual tributes levied on subjugated cities. They mostly entailed, however, the imposition of taxes on citizens and strangers. The latter were divided into two categories: the transients (*xenoi*), and the settlers (*metoikoi*). Together with the slaves, they formed a major segment of the city population, often surpassing in numbers its native inhabitants. Especially significant was the economic role of immigrant settlers (*metoikoi*). Debarred from owning land, they were compelled to apply their talents and their wealth to other productive pursuits. In Athens, about whose *metoikoi* a fair amount is known, their part in the development of commerce and culture was certainly considerable. They shared in the obligations, but not in all the privileges, of citizenship. Many became renowned as bankers or industrialists: for example, Pasion and Phormion, two former slaves, and Cephalus, whose house provided the setting for Plato's famous dialogue *The Republic*. Perhaps best known of all were Aristotle of Stagira and Zenon, a native of Cyprus and the founder of Stoicism.

The prevalence and status of *metoikoi* and slaves in the ancient world sheds an interesting light on a particular concept of citizenship, common to Greece and Rome, whose tenacity through centuries of rapid social change is nothing less than remarkable. Neither the availability of manumition of slaves nor the absence of discrimination against resident aliens could modify this concept, to which the very notion of "naturalization" remained essentially alien. Citizenship was seen as birthright until the transformation, which made of Rome the center of a vast multinational empire, changed that.

On the benefit side, one of the salient features of this conception of citizenship was the intensity of feeling and commitment it contributed to the life of the community and the running of public affairs. On the minus side, however, it must be held responsible for the low place accorded to business, production, and manual labor, especially in the hierarchy of values. Hence Plato and Aristotle both sought to exclude the class of artisans and craftsmen from active participation in the affairs of state.[19] Keeping the body of citizens from growing uncontrollably was generally viewed as one sure way of safeguarding the welfare and good management of the city state, as well as its capacity for the good life.[20]

For Plato and Aristotle, but even for the leader of democratic Athens, Pericles, as far as we can gather from Thucydides' report of his Funeral Oration,[21] active citizenship required considerable leisure. At best, it was a life of undifferentiated concern for the affairs of state and active participation in public policy making. Like the Oxford-educated senior government official in pre–World War II Britain, the citizen of Athens was expected to turn his attention to a broad variety of issues, political or military, and contribute to decisions on a wide range of court cases.

The results were not always encouraging—not for Plato, at any rate. In fact, it was his quest for remedies against the perceived ill effects of this "jack-of-all-trade" concept of public mangement, that guided the *Discourse on Justice—the Republic.* It was by redefining the role and scope of citizenship that Plato came to grips with some of the foundations and basic characteristics of bureaucratic systems: hierarchy, specialization, and, most important of all, education and training for public office. For Plato and Aristotle, moral and philosophical considerations may have been paramount in fashioning their model of the ideal *polis.* There can be little doubt, however, that what they were addressing were the mounting problems of cities in disarray—the crisis precipitated by problems of complexity and scale. The growing inability of the ancient city-state to resolve those problems satisfactorily would soon lead to its demise and incorporation in the large empires of the Hellenistic and, later, Roman periods.

II. THE EMPIRE

Devolution and self-government, the marks of public management in the ancient city-state, did not completely vanish under the imperial rule established in the wake of the Alexandrian conquests and Caesar's march on Rome. However, they sustained a certain loss of relevance. This reflected the decline of public institutions through which they had been practiced but, still more fundamentally, a profound transformation in the nature and purpose of government. The arms of city government did not atrophy. They lost their former vigor and vitality, and their role was overshadowed by the superposition of a new and often alien superstructure. The ensuing friction became manifest as early as 167 B.C.E. in the Maccabean Revolt. Such incidents of struggle against external rule and foreign hegemony would later multiply, becoming a regular feature of life in the Roman Empire.

The drive for domination replaced traditional values as a formative influence in shaping new institutions. If, according to Thucydides, the Athenians soon discovered that the practice of democracy was not easily compatible with imperial expansion abroad,[22] the effect on Roman government of territorial conquests corroborated this finding. The German philosopher Hegel described in graphic terms this passage from republican to imperial rule:

> The first thing to be remarked respecting the imperial rule is that the Roman government was so abstracted from interest, that the great transition to that rule hardly changed anything in the constitution. The popular assemblies alone were unsuited to the new state of things, and disappeared. The emperor was *princeps senatus*, Censor, Consul, Tribune: he united all their nominally continuing offices in himself; and the military power—here the most essentially important—was exclusively in his hands. The constitution was an utterly unsubstantial form, from which all vitality, consequently all might and power, had departed; and the only means of maintaining its existence were the legions which the Emperor constantly kept in the vicinity of Rome. Public business was indeed brought before the Senate, and the Emperor appeared simply as one of its members; but the Senate was obliged to obey, and whoever ventured to gainsay his will was punished with death, and his property confiscated.[23]

Of course, as Hegel added, such personalization of public power could prove highly unstable for, as he prointed out:

> The Emperor rested on the army, and the Pretorian bodyguard which surrounded him. But the legions, and especially the Pretorians, soon became conscious of their importance, and arrogated to themselves the disposal of the imperial throne. At first they continued to show some respect for the family of Caesar Augustus, but subsequently the legions chose their own generals; such, vis., as had gained their good will and favor, partly by courage and intelligence, partly also by bribes and indulgence in the administration of military discipline.[24]

A. Quest for Domination and Emergence of New Structures

A novel superstructure emerges very gradually under those new conditions. Not surprisingly, it displays some of the salient features of modern bureaucratic organizations. Its principal components could be described as follows:

1. A framework for the conquest and control of vast and widely divers peoples and territories from the Danube and the Rhine to the Libyan and Arabian deserts.

2. A central systems maintainance and central control apparatus designed to keep the reins of power firmly in the hands of the Emperor and his entourage. Monopolization of power through centralization is the mark of the new system. A high authority structure will thus be fashioned gradually, with the emperor as its apex. In theory and in practice, decision-making power is vested in the hands of the Emperor alone and its legitimacy is sought chiefly through his deification. Turned into state religion, the worship of the incumbent of the imperial throne henceforth provides for the acts, pronouncements, and structures of government the aura and authority which, in the city-state, laws had derived from their putative divine origin.

The Empire was subdivided into regions of descending order of magnitude and importance. The province constituted the smallest unit and basic circumscription for purposes of territorial administration. It was headed by a provincial governor whose functions were wide ranging, not unlike, in some respects, those of the district commissioner in the days of the British Empire. The dispensation of justice and the collection of revenue stood out as his foremost tasks. The governor combined the functions of chief magistrate and principal tax collector for the region under his command. Both were demanding tasks considering the volume of litigation, the growing need for revenue, and the emperor's insistence—a truly Roman legacy—that law be applied correctly and uniformly throughout. Besides the money taxes, a motley of requisitions had to be levied in kind.

On matters of litigation, governors were forced, despite imperial admonitions to the contrary, to delegate their functions to appointed judges (*judices pedanei*) who decided on disputes. The governors however were required to pronounce themselves on the issues of law. They combined that responsibility with onerous administrative tasks, ranging from road repair and public works in general to the oversight of city councils and the keeping of the peace. Considering the number of townships in each province and their important role as source of public revenue, it is small wonder that governors often found themselves vulnerable to pressures from local interest groups and were forced to yield supervision of the task of tax collection to local functionaries appointed for that purpose.

The provinces were grouped into *dioceses*, a Greek term for administration. Dioceses were placed under the control of superintendents entitled vice agents of the pretorial prefects (*vices agentes praefectorum praetorio*) or *vicarii*, for short.[25]

The institution of the vicars in charge of dioceses was the outcome of reforms carried out by Diocletian, who reigned from 284 to 305 C.E. Twelve vicars were appointed in as many dioceses equally divided between the eastern and western hemispheres of the empire. This pattern underwent little change in the following centuries. The size and the number of provinces varied widely and so did the relative weight which they carried with the central administration. The functions and the fortunes of the vicars also oscillated greatly. In theory, they acted partly as appellate judges and partly as supervisors of the provincial governors. In practice, however, their authority was frequently ignored both by provincial governors and by pretorian prefects, who tended to bypass them in matters of taxation and litigation. Among the former, for instance, the proconsuls of Africa and Asia not only claimed exemption from this chain of command as a constitutional prerogative but, for that very reason, considered it their right to address themselves to the emperor directly.

The cities of Rome and, after 359, Constantinople the eastern capital, also represented exceptions to the general scheme of things. Both were governed by prefects, who were equal in rank to the pretorian prefects. However in both cases the emperor felt free to circumvent the hierarchy at will. He thus issued instructions even to minor officials on a wide range of matters. While this might be understandable in Rome and Constantinople by reason of proximity and the particularities of metropolitan government, disregard for the chain of command was so generalized as to take on a different meaning and an altogether singular complexion. It reflected, in a way, the nature of absolute power and the very human reluctance of all those that possess it to be bound by limitations—jurisdictional or other—to its exercise. It also reflected, however, the rapid, piecemeal growth of a new set of structures untouched by the formative influence of legislative control and subject to the pulls of territorial expansion as well as the pressures arising from security considerations in this vast, heterogeneous empire.

In theory and in practice, the administrative structures thus evolved were conduits first and foremost of the imperial power. They had no raison d'être other than to project and to enforce the emperor's sovereign will. In contrast to earlier times, law was par excellence the expression of his will which knew no outward bounds. As sole source of authority, the emperor could establish rules and abrogate old laws at pleasure. The often quoted principle, which the emperor Justinian had borrowed from Ulpian, aptly described the new situation: *Quod principi placuit, legis habet vigorem* (May what pleases the prince have the force of law).

The exercise of power knew no constitutional bounds. The notion of separation or division of functions was equally alien. The emperor was lawmaker. He was also commander in chief. He conducted foreign policy, concluded international treaties, and made war and peace, at will. He enjoyed complete control on all domestic matters including inland revenue and public expenditure. His was the right to appoint to all posts, both civil and military—indeed, the right of life and death on all his subjects. Faint echoes of the past occasionally reaffirmed the primacy of law and the force of tradition, but only in the guise of self-imposed limitations on a boundless sovereign power. Valentinian III (429 C.E.) was explicit on this point:

It is a pronouncement worthy of the majesty of the ruler that the emperor should declare himself bound by the laws so much as does our authority depend on the authority of law. To submit our imperial office to the law is in truth a greater thing than our imperial sovereignty.[26]

The primacy of the law, one of the core components of constitutional doctrine in the ancient city-state and a major part of the legacy of the Roman Republic, continued to exercise a substantial measure of influence centuries after its death. Thus Gregory the Great (540–604 C.E.) was to all intents and purposes paraphrasing Aristotle when he declared, "This is the difference between barbarian kings and Roman emperors, that barbarian kings are lords of slaves, but the Roman emperor is the lord of free men."[27]

Though tempered by tradition, imperial absolutism, the tight centralization and vast concentration of powers which it brought in trail could not have been conducive to good government. It seldom produced the efficiency with which it has been credited. We learn from extant sources that many of the practitioners of statecraft in those days took a rather dim view of the system which they were asked to apply. Its principal defects, as seen from their perspective, were partly poor division of functions among posts and partly poor selection and guidance of the incumbents. Complaints about the latter were particularly prevalent and clearly articulated as, for instance, in the following message addressed to Valentinian II by one of his subordinates:

My loyalty to you and my care for the common weal compel me, your majesty, not to conceal what requires reform. While the supreme charge of the affairs of the city belongs to the urban prefecture, certain parts of it are entrusted to minor offices, to govern which hardworking men of tried character ought to be appointed, that each may conduct his department smoothly and faultlessly. The public weal demands such men now from your majesty's judgment. But I do not wish to criticise the present holders, since it will satisfy my anxiety if you entrust the offices of the city to better men. As it is the whole weight of affairs falls on my shoulders, since the others, whom your clemency amidst your multifarious occupations cannot have tested, shirk their duties. In this happy age there are worthier men, the vein of good men is prolific. You will in future do better for your city if you choose those who do not wish to hold office.[28]

The notion that an office was a reward for loyalty rather than a repository of functions and responsibilities was aptly expressed by the terms *dignitas* and *honor*, which were applied in preference to *administratio*. It can be safely assumed that this view of an office could not invite the quest or systematic inquiry into the preconditions for the efficient discharge of its functions. True, competence and specialized knowledge were not altogether unappreciated. If this had been the case, why would the selection of Cyrus, a man of whom it was said "he understood nothing but poery," be criticized when that person was appointed to the prefecture of Constantinople?

That some criteria of competence for office did exist, seems certain, though they were mostly implicit and seldom fully thought out. Certainly loyalty and obedience to the emperor ranked high in the scale of values. So did probity and integrity, partly on account of the relative importance of judicial and revenue tasks in provincial administration, but partly also because of the potential for abuse. Influence peddling (*suffragium*), office trading, and extortion must have been quite common, if one judges from the frequency of attempts to regulate and circumscribe their practice.

Corruption and venality were doubtless as prevalent as they were a source of concern. However, attention was focused more on their effects on discipline than on their dysfunctional aspects. The concepts of efficiency, economy, and effectiveness remained at a nebulous stage during the period in question, and so did any notion that knowledge, skills, and training were linked to productivity. Some preference for lawyers was shown, establishing a pattern which with few interruptions continues to our day. However, no requirements or professional qualifications were laid down even for technical posts.

As in the golden age of Greece and the Roman Republic, rhetoric, mathematics, and possibly astronomy were viewed as sine qua non accomplishments of a gentleman and preparation for public office. However, as in England before World War II, the prevalent assumption was that administration required no special talents—none other, to be sure, than what a normal person of average ability and preferably "good breeding" would possess. Noble birth was highly valued, especially as an attribute toward civilian posts. The scions of good families enjoyed a certain advantage. They could move up the ladder much faster. If they did not escape the drudgery of lowly tasks altogether, they could reasonably expect to be placed on a "fast career track" in most cases.

However, notwithstanding a certain predilection for noble birth whose origins are traceable far back in ancient history, the imperial public service, in both Rome and Byzantium, displayed some of the attributes of a *carrière ouverte aux talents*. This was especially true of the army, where for obvious reasons, appointments and promotions depended very largely on military ability, experience, and, most of all, loyalty. Low birth was not a barrier, nor for that matter was membership in a barbarian sect or foreign ethnic group. The imperial public service was drawn from diverse segments of the population. It furthered the professional but also the social advancement of its members. The imperial civil service became in this regard a very early example of what centuries later the European bureaucracies would try, ever so slowly, to approximate: an avenue of mobility and tool of social change.

The later Roman Empire begins to exemplify some of the salient features of bureaucratic systems: a paid career officialdom, hierarchically structured and bound by vows of loyalty to their imperial masters. Such paid career officials will see devolve upon them increasingly wide-ranging and vital responsibilities which previously belonged to citizens elected or otherwise selected to carry out. They assisted in the drafting of ordinances and laws and in the formulation and implementation of policy. Last but not least, they played a vital role in the maintenance and operation of a system of taxation, an army organization, and public infrastructure of dimensions and complexity never previously known.

While for those very reasons the gradual evolution of bureaucratic structures could be viewed as a response to the challenge of changed circumstances, it should be emphasized that, in important ways, the system that developed was far from bureaucratic—in the Weberian sense, at any rate.[29] "Precision, speed, unambiguity . . . continuity and discretion" hailed by Weber as the virtues of bureaucracy could hardly be regarded as descriptive of the imperial Roman system. Overlapping jurisdictions and the ensuing confusion or friction went often hand in hand with poor division of labor, absence of specialization, and a certain inconsistency in administrative practice. There was broadly based recruitment, but no true meritocracy. Most of all, the separation between personal pursuits and public office, which Weber recognized as the hallmark of bureaucracy, had yet to strike roots deep into the conscience of the Roman imperial officialdom.

Throughout its long development, from its Roman beginnings into the Byzantine phase, the administrative system of the empire wavered between conflicting tendencies: on the one hand, the pulls arising from complexity and scale asserted themselves, forcing the grudging acceptance of some delegation of power, notably at the level of the pretorial prefects. On the other hand, the fear of grass-roots disaffection or personal intrigues often coupled with the need to stem the abuse of power further accentuated the centripetal forces inherent in the nature of autocratic government.

Overall, it would appear that the centralizing pressures grew progressively stronger with results whose dysfunctional aspects were compounded by the effects of geographical distance and the rapid turnover of people in the most senior posts. Characteristically, it is reported that a document dispatched from Milan to Rome required anywhere from 12 days to three weeks to reach its destination. Understandably, under those circumstances, a law signed by Constantine on 25 July did not reach Hispalis, Spain, until April the following year.[30]

One is tempted to speculate on the nature and the causes of this tight centralization, which so obviously ran counter to the requirements of efficiency and sound administration. It extended to decisions on appointments and promotions, taxation and finance, and the domains of law enforcement and justice. Although praetorian prefects enjoyed a measure of discretion in fixing the rates of taxation, this was strictly circumscribed and could be delegated to the provincial governor in emergencies only. However, most decisions required the imperial signature which, given the emperor's frequent travels, compounded the delays.

Excessive centralization and rapid turnover of cadres encouraged two parallel tendencies: on the one hand, propensity to interfere with the work of subordinates and, on the other hand, the practice of referring decisions to higher authorities. Often this was mandated, as in Constantine's requirement of the provincial governors that they submit all their court records to their praetorian prefects for scrutiny every six months; or Zeno's order that all military appointments be made not by the *duces*, as in the past, but only by "our divinity."

In most cases such extremes of centralization caused congestion at the top. They also illustrated the relatively low degree of institutionalization of authority, at least in the early centuries. Power was centralized; authority was personalized and dependent for legitimacy on the cult of the emperor. Curiously, such sacralization of power and the deification of the emperor did not completely obliterate the notion that all power was, in the last analysis, derived from the will of the people. Significantly also, the imperial office in Rome did not become hereditary nor was its exercise ever made contingent upon birth—not, in fact, until the shift of power to Constantinople and the emergence of Byzantium as the eastern Roman Empire.

B.   The Triumph of Christianity and The Byzantine Empire

The triumph of Christianity and its consolidation under Constantine the Great (306–337 C.E.) and his sucessors as the official state religion brought about some change. Worship of the emperor continued unabated, notwithstanding the distinction of the realm of the sacred from that of the profane, of God and of the world, and the consequent division of the spheres of church and state. Although no longer accorded divinity, the emperor was treated as the divinely appointed vice-regent of God. He was the Chosen of God, the Annointed of the Lord, and His Lieutenant, when he led the imperial armies into battle, as John Comnenus put it.[31] An equal of the apostles (*isapostolos*), he championed God on earth and ruled by divine inspiration. Henceforth all wars become crusades against the infidel or for the repression of heresy. All acts of disobedience are treated as a sacrilege.

True, the Greco-Roman concept of the primacy of the law did not subside. It survived chiefly in the fiction that power belonged to the people who gave it to the emperor. Justinian, in the *Lex de Imperio*, expressly made that point.[32] It also lingered in the method of conferring authority to rulers. In theory, the senate, the army, and the people had to cooperate in the election of the emperor. To these the church was added, in due course. In practice, however, the senate had dwindled to a small number of senior court officials; the army's acclamation and popular consent were normally received in ceremonial fashion from limited groups in each case acting on behalf of the whole body.

Last but not least, the doctrine of popular sovereignty survived in what Mommsen has called "the legal right of revolution."[33] This right was sometimes invoked by the patriarch as a warning and indeed on a few occasions was translated into action.[34] There can be little doubt, however, that such limiting factors, mostly rooted in the past, did not seriously reduce the substantial power of the emperor or significantly affect the manner of its exercise. Everything around the throne conspired to emphasize its splendor and transcendency. The accounterments of office—an elaborate court ceremonial, codified in the 10th century, and an array of titles, first in Latin and then in

Greek, which became the official language—reinforced the claims to invincibility, the majesty of the office, and its quasisacred nature. "The beauty of ceremonial," wrote Constantine Porphyrogenitus (944–959), "renders imperial power more splendid, more glorious and compels the admiration of both foreigners and subjects."[35]

Of the tangible symbols of power, none surpassed the crown and scepter in meaning and importance. In this and in the choice of most other accounterments and manifestations of sovereignty, the Sassanid Empire became the major source of inspiration. As the Persian kings were crowned by the Magian high priest, so in Constantinople coronation was adopted as the method of investiture, after the reign of Leo I in 457. Its importance grew with time, and from the seventh century it came to be performed in the Church of St. Sophia by the patriarch himself. Coronation symbolized the sacred nature and mission of the imperial office. It gave concrete expression to the belief that the emperor's authority as God's viceroy on earth was boundless; that his jurisdiction, moreover, extended well beyond the frontiers of the realm to the whole world. However, in sharp contrast to the western Empire, where the papacy arrogated to itself the major role in the act of coronation, the patriarch's participation was not considered necessary and sometimes was dispensed with; in cases of investiture of coemperors especially, the existing emperor performed it himself.

In theory, there was no limit to the number of coemperors, though under Constantine IV (668–685) the Christian example of the Trinity suggested a ceiling of three. Only one was deemed to be *Autocrator basileus* (i.e., emperor and king), but the practice of coopting smoothed the process of succession before the hereditary principle was established as the norm for legal accession to the throne.

The triumph of Christianity, complete by the time of the reign of Theodosius the Great (379–395), brought its own distinctive input to the subsequent development of the administrative framework which the pagan Roman Empire had gradually put into place. One of the major issues which confronted the new faith as the official state religion was the question of authority or power legitimation and the related crisis which the disintegration of intense traditional loyalties had precipitated. The problem was compounded by the barbarian invasions, which periodically wrested vast domains from central control.

An answer to this problem consisted in the attempt to represent the government of the Empire as a direct emanation from the divine power. According to this theory, which sought support in history and law, the Almighty had conferred upon the Roman people the right to rule the world. They had in turn conceded that power to Augustus and his successors.[36] Analogous in its effect was the doctrine of the Church, according to which Peter had been vested with authority by Jesus Christ and transmitted that authority to his successors in perpetuity. Both theories laid stress on the importance of succession and both enjoined obedience to the powers that be, because they were God willed.

The quest of legitimacy accounts, to a large extent, for the persistent claims to unity and continuity advanced by both Byzantium and Rome despite their growing differences. Such differences were intensified after Justinian's reign (527–565) momentarily restored the empire to its former grandeur and cohesion. The parting of the ways, occasioned by doctrinal disputes and the tensions generated by successive barbarian invasions, culminated in the year 800 when, Charlemagne received from Pope Leo III the crown of the empire. The rupture became final with the schism in 1054, which irrevocably severed the two branches of Christianity. The resulting cleavage influenced the political and broader institutional development of both East and Western Europe in ways that proved as lasting as they have been decisive.

Still, notwithstanding this division, it is possible to find important commonalities and a measure of continuity in the midst of rapid change. In both Rome and Byzantium, imperial institutions of public administration long remained emanations of the person of the emperor and their acts manifestations of his sovereign will. So pronounced was its personal nature and so pressing the dictates of military requirements that imperial administration will lack for many centuries a stable headquarters location. Instead, the core civil service migrated with the Emperor wherever foreign wars or other expeditions rendered his presence necessary.

Sedentarization came only very gradually during the later stages of the Byzantine Empire. It carried in its trail a sharper differentiation of the respective roles of centre and periphery, of military and civilian personnel, of public service management and court administration. It also opened the way towards the consolidation of stable pyramidal structures, which could be said to exemplify some of the salient features of public bureaucratic organizations.

Hierarchy and some measure of specialization had not been unknown before, under the Roman Empire. Now, however, they were heightened entailing, in Byzantium, a stricter separation of post from its incumbent and also, as a result, a measure of continuity in the discharge of functions which had not previously been possible. Appointments and promotions were only conferred by the Emperor. Although the threat of war and frequent barbarian invasions soon led to the progressive militarization of provincial government, the central administration remained civilian in character and composition. It was principally run by two major categories of officials: the *Kritai* and the *Secretikoi* (mostly financial ministers). Of the former, most important was the *Eparchos*, or prefect, of the City of Constantinople.

The wide range of his functions, set out in a 10th-century handbook, attested to the extent of state control over the social, religious, commercial, and economic activities of the city and the country at large. Regulation of wages and prices, the licensing of shops, import and export controls, strict enforcement of Sunday observance, and weekly working hours, as well as supervision of a wide range of services including social welfare, famine relief, poorhouses, hospitals, and orphanages give the nature and the measure of government initiative which approximate the scope and functions of bureaucracies in modern welfare states.

Considering its size and the oscillating fortunes of the empire, the Byzantine bureaucracy played an important role in keeping the country together and in projecting a culture which made of Constantinople a great metropolis and, almost until the end, one of the world's leading centres of learning, commerce, and the arts. Professionalism contributed to the efficiency of the Byzantine public service, which at the peaks of its greatness, first under Justinian (527–565), then Leo III (717–740), and finally under Basil and the Macedonian dynasty (867–1059), is said to have been high.[37] Another factor was openness to merit and the high educational standards of its members. Legal training instituted by Justinian declined to some extent under his successors. The longstanding practice, however, of granting financial support to students attested to the importance which the Byzantine Empire accorded the staffing of its public service with capable administrators.

An accident of birth could neither bar nor favor access to public office. Avoidance, on the contrary, of situations leading to hereditary claims prompted extensive use of eunuchs in positions of special trust and power. Only toward the end, the dispossessed members of the landed aristocracy became a hereditary civil service, and the list of public offices provided in *De Officiis* included many posts which had become empty titles.

The Byzantine Empire collapsed in 1453. To what extent its legacy was influential in shaping the administrative structures and public institutions of its Ottoman successor is a subject which deserves more attention than it has received. The Byzantine diaspora, which broadly coincided with the fall of Constantinople, added a potent impetus to the Renaissance in the West.

From Domenico Theotocopuli, El Greco, to Chryssoloras, a scholar, and Laskaris, a pioneer in printing, scores of Greek-speaking Byzantines flooded the Western centers of learning in Italy and Spain. As refugees, they helped revive the study of law and classical literature in much the way that scholars fleeing the Nazis in the 1930s contributed to the development of science and research in the United States.

The Renaissance in Italy and Reformation later gave a new lease of life to the concepts of local autonomy and urban self-rule. Progressively emasculated, the Holy Roman Empire was yet able to add to the legacy it inherited, the notion of *dominium* (as distinct from that of *imperium*), from which the modern concept of territorial jurisdiction of states hails.

Bueaucratic administration was certainly not born in 18th-centruty Europe. It was fashioned piecemeal in Byzantium and in Imperial Rome. What the prophets of the Enlightenment sought and contrived to accomplish was to infuse bureaucratic structures, hitherto control oriented, with respect for rationality, efficiency, objectivity, accountability, and justice.

Still tenous at best in many parts of the world, bureaucracy animated by respect for the rule of law is yet a noble legacy of the European Enlightenment. Paternalist at heart, protectionist at best such rule-of-law oriented administration could and did erect barriers against the abuse of power and the violation of human rights. What it has been unable to satisfy is the universal demand in advanced, heterogeneous, post-industrial societies for the measure of autonomy, degree of commitment to and level of participation in the administration of common concerns (*ta koina*), which remain the shining legacy of the ancient city state, the Greek polis and the Roman Res publica.

ENDNOTES

1. Term borrowed from Dwight Waldo, "A theory of public administration means in our time and theory of politics also," in *Public Administration: The State of the Discipline.* Edited by Naomi B. Lynn and Aaron Wildavsky. Chatham, NJ. Chatham Publishers, 1990:79.
2. H.A.L. Fisher. *A History of Europe.* London: Edward Arnold, 1949:1.
3. Literally, "Nothing too much," and "Know thyself."
4. Sir Henry Maine. *Ancient Law.* London: Oxford University Press, 1950:294–295.
5. Plato. *Crito.* Translated by Benjamin Jowett. New York: P.F. Collier and Son, 1937:40.
6. Fustel de Coulanges. *La Cité Antique.* Paris: Librairie Hachette, 1895:220.
7. Demosthenes, quoted by G. Lowes Dickinson, *The Greek View of Life.* London: Methuen, 1949:75.
8. F. de Coulanges, *op. cit.*, p. 144. See also Max Weber, *The City.* New York: Free Press, Macmillan, 1958:145.
9. "Since politics uses the rest of the sciences and since again it legislates as to what we are to abstain from, the end of this science must include those of the others, so that this end must be the good of man." *The Nicomachean Ethics of Aristotle*, translated and introduced by Sir David Ross. London: Oxford University Press, 1954.
10. *Aristotle's Politics*, translated by Benjamin Jowett. Oxford: Clarendon Press, 1945.
11. Cicero. "De Finibus" II, XIV. Translated by H. Rackham, in *Voices from the Past: A Classical Anthology for the Modern Reader* by J. & J. Maclean Todd. New York: E.P. Dulton, 1955:319.
12. *Ibid.*
13. F.W. Walbank. *The Hellenistic World.* Cambridge, MA: Harvard University Press, 1982:118. Significantly, it was in remote areas of Greece, like Aetolia and Achaea, where city-states did not develop a strong tradition of separatism and independence, that important federal states (*sympoliteiai*) arose.
14. *Ibid.*, p. 153.
15. Quoted from John A. Fine, *The Ancient Greeks: A Critical History.* Cambridge, MA: Harvard University Press, p. 392.
16. *De l'Avenir Politique de l'Angeleterre*, Paris 1856. Quoted in the course of the debate on Admission to the Civil Service London, Hansard, April 24, 1856, Cols. 1419–1423.
17. See Aristotle, *The Athenian Constitution*, translated by P.J. Rhodes. New York: Penguin Classics, 1984:66 et seq.
18. 3 obols, half a drachma, represented half a day's pay in late 5th-century Athens. See John A. Fine, *The Ancient Greeks, op. cit.*, p. 393.
19. Aristotle's *Politics, op. cit.*, Book VII, cc 4–12.

20. *Ibid.*
21. See M.I. Finley (ed.). *The Portable Greek Historians.* New York: Penguin Books, 1984:265–273.
22. Thucydides. *The Peloponnesian War*, Book III, 37 (the Mytilenian Debate).
23. G.W.F. Hegel. *The Philosophy of History.* New York: Dover, p. 314.
24. *Ibid.*
25. For details see A.H.M. Jones, *The Later Roman Empire 284–602*, Vol. 1. Baltimore: John Hopkins University Press, 1986.
26. Quoted from A.H.M. Jones, *The Later Roman Empire 284–602*, Vol. I, *op. cit.*, p. 321.
27. *Ibid.*
28. *Ibid.*, p. 383.
29. On the Weberian model see D. Argyriades, "Reconsidering Bureaucracy as Ideology" in G.E. Caiden and H. Siedentopf *Strategies for Administrative Reform.* Lexington MA D.C. Heath, (eds.) 1982:42 et seq.
30. A.H.M. Jones. *The Later Roman Empire 284–602*, *op. cit.*, p. 403.
31. Charles Diehl. *Byzantium: Greatness and Decline.* New Brunswick, NJ: Rutgers University Press, 1957:29.
32. Steven Runciman. *Byzantine Civilization.* London: E. Arnold, 1966:62.
33. Quoted from Steven Runciman, *Byzantine Civilization*, *op. cit.*, p. 62.
34. *Ibid.*
35. Charles Diehl. *Byzantium: Greatness and Decline*, *op. cit.*, pp. 30–31.
36. *Populus ei et in eum omne suum imperium et potestatem concessit*, quoted from James Bryce, *The Holy Roman Empire.* London: Macmillan, 1904: 256.
37. See Bryce and Runciman, *op. cit.*, *passim.* See also N.H. Baynes and H. St. L.B. Moss (eds.), Byzantium: *An Introduction to East Roman Civilization.* London: Oxford University Press, 1948, chapters 3 and 10.

6
Indian Legacy of Administration

V. Subramaniam   *Department of Political Science, Carleton University, Ottawa, Canada*

I. INTRODUCTION

Karl Marx and Max Weber were more or less in agreement about the irrelevance of ancient imperial bureaucracies to the modern industrial world. Max Weber in his famous essay on bureaucracy
dismissed them as patrimonial or prebendal with a few asides. (1) Marx, according to one interpretation of the "Asiatic Mode of Production," (2) regarded them as the cause of centurieslong stagnation of the process of economic evolution and was happy that British colonialism in India would
set in motion fundamental changes. (3) Their views were at least partly responsible for the lack of
sociological interest in ancient bureaucracies for sometime. Attention was focused on them in the
first instance in a revivalist manner by nationalist historians of India, China, or Iran, who proudly
unravelled the structures and processes of administration of their countries in ancient times. Since
then, some comparisons have been made: Etienne Balazs (4) felt that the study of eternally bureaucratized China will help in understanding bureaucratized communist regimes; Eisenstadt (5)
regarded bureaucracy as a power group in rivalry with other groups including the sovereign—and
others have challenged and criticized Weber's concept of patrimonial bureaucracy. Marxists and
neo-Marxists have produced volumes on AMP, but with no real interest in bureaucracy as such.
But the subject deserves a lot more investigation, comparison, and analysis in its own right.

Of the three fully developed ancient bureaucracies of India, China, and Iran, the Indian legacy has made the strongest and most widespread contribution to modern public administration in
the third world mainly through the agency of the British Empire. This happened because the
British had no precedents, experience, or ideas available in their own domestic nonbureaucratic
arrangements for applying to their new Indian possessions in the late 18th century and hence they
picked up, polished, and adapted the relevant practices of Indian administration to their immediate needs. As their empire expanded onto Southeast Asia and Africa, they simply transplanted
these onto their new possessions thus spreading the Indian legacy over large areas of the globe. For
this reason alone, the administrative legacy of ancient India is worth careful study.

This paper is a preliminary exploration of that legacy in terms of its modern relevance from
a sociological angle and falls naturally into four parts. In the first part, we discuss briefly the evolution of a tentacular imperial bureaucracy about the fourth century before Christ and its socioeconomic context. In the second part, we analyze how and why the goal of imperial unity through
imperial conquest and imperial bureaucratization was given up through a lack of that collusion
between the literati and the rulers which was established in China through a neo-Confucian synthesis—and how diluted administrative practices interlaced with feudalism were transmitted in

India through centuries of political division and foreign conquest. The third part explains how the main remnant of the tradition, the district overlord-coordinator, was taken over and modernized by the British East India Company at the right time and spread all over their Afro-Asian Empire. In the fourth part, we take a brief critical look at Marxist and Weberian attitudes to pre-British bureaucracies in India.

II. EVOLUTION OF IMPERIAL BUREAUCRACY

Early Hindu political institutions were not imperial; there were several democratic republics on one side and several monarchies with some ethical and institutional controls on power. Most republics were conquered and absorbed by neighboring kingdoms, but the Indian republican tradition is preserved for us not only in the writings of Greek scholars, but in the republican conciliar constitution of the Buddhist Sangha. (6) For quite a long while, the monarchs fought each other according to well known rules without absorbing and integrating rival kingdoms into a larger empire, being satisfied with proclaiming a vague paramountcy. The Rajasuya sacrifice performed by victorious monarchs, just confirmed and acknowledged this paramountcy. This arrangement gave way to imperial conquest and territorial absorption by the fifth century B.C. when the Nanda dynasty founded an empire in the Gangetic valley—which was soon after expanded and consolidated by Chandragupta Maurya into the famous Mauryan Empire, a little earlier to the first empire of Shi Huang Ti in China, and contemporaneous with the Achaemenid Empire in Iran. The three world states or empires thus took shape within a few years of each other—and in all the three cases, the powerholders opted for some form of bureaucracy to integrate their conquests and preserve their hold. In other words, the occasion and provocation for ancient bureaucracy was the need to knit and rule a new empire of sizeable area. The logic behind this is worked out in the structure of the famous contemporary work *Kautilya's Arthasastra*. (7) The first six "books" or sections describe in great detail a centralized bureaucracy while the next nine discuss the ways of acquiring other lands by war and diplomacy to build an empire. The order seems reversed; the acquisition of empire coming after the details of its administration, but their mutual relationship is clear.

    The options for an empire builder were few and clear. In a small kingdom or republic, a flexible mode of governing without elaborate formal structures was the norm. But with a large empire, the options were letting the old rulers continue as tributaries, or creating a new feudal order of nobles with full local power or structuring a new bureaucracy of paid loyal officials. The bureaucratic option was chosen as the best way to consolidate power with loyal officers without their own power-base. The logic behind this comes out clearly in Chapters X and XII of first book of *Arthasastra* dealing with the testing of ministers and officials with various temptations and the ruthless manner in which "thorns" (traitors) were to be dealt with. The bureaucracy was to be based not on birth or relationship, but on merit and loyalty alone without which the bureaucratic option to entrench power and hold an empire together would not work.

    We have a very detailed account of the structure and functions of Mauryan imperial bureaucracy in both *Kautilya's Arthasastra* and from the inscriptions of emperor Asoka. (8) The first source is important as it formed a prescriptive model for not only the contemporaneous Mauryan administration, but for generations of authors and for later empires and even smaller kingdoms. The second source provides an account of the practical details of administration in the Mauryan Empire at the time of Asoka.

    Arthasastra's first six "books" form probably the most detailed manual of monarchical administration in the ancient or medieval world, though more scholarly attention has been devoted to the last nine books on war, diplomacy, and international relations. The instructions on administration cover all areas and functions with brutal detail and clarity.

Indeed, the second book, with its 38 chapters, is the most specifically detailed account of imperial administration anywhere in the ancient world. Thus Chapter X on royal writs discusses all grammatical and stylistic nuances and Chapter XI on gems and gifts is a virtual catalogue of all contemporary products. Other chapters elaborate central administration, provincial, regional, field and village administration, municipal administration, financial and resource administration, justice and military administration. In fact, the titles of chapters in this second book illustrate the tentacular nature of Mauryan bureaucracy.

Formation of Villages
Division of Land
Construction of Forts
Buildings Within the Forts
Duties of the Chamberlain
Business of the Collection of Revenue by the Collector-General
Business of Keeping up Accounts in the Office of Accountants
Detection of What is Embezzled by Government Servants out of State Revenue
Examination of the Conduct of Government Servants
Procedure of Forming Royal Writs
Examination of Gems That Are to Be Entered into the Treasury
Conducting Mining Operations and Manufacture
Superintendent of Gold in the Goldsmiths' Office
Duties of the State Goldsmith in the High Road
Superintendent of Commerce
Superintendent of Forest Produce
Superintendent of the Armory
Superintendent of Weights and Measures
Measurement of Space and Time
Superintendent of Tolls
Regulation of Toll Dues
Superintendent of Weaving
Superintendent of Agriculture
Superintendent of Liquor
Superintendent of Slaughterhouse
Superintendent of Prostitutes
Superintendent of Ships
Superintendent of Cows
Superintendent of Horses
Superintendent of Elephants
Training of Elephants
Superintendent of Chariots
Superintendent of Infantry
Duties of the Commander-in-Chief
Superintendent of Passports
Superintendent of Pasture Lands
Duty of Revenue Collectors; Spies Under the Guise of Householders, Merchants, and Ascetics
Duty of a City Superintendent

It is impossible to discuss such a wealth of detail in a brief paper, but some important points may be noted. Kautilya glides lightly over contractual theories of kingship, assumes that a high concentration of power is necessary for civilized society to carry on, and advises the King against all sorts of stratagems, to be strong and diligent. At the same time, no man can run a state single-handed; one needs a central team of advisers and a large team of field executives. Kautilya implicitly bypasses the options of feudalist power-sharing and patrimonial delegation—and advises the monarch to choose all advisers and officers by various tests for loyalty and merit. The testing against "allurements" and particularly "religious allurement" in Chapter VII of the first book implies a separation of religion from politics and a sharp focus on ability and loyalty in the choice of ministers and officials.

The structure of central administration is given in great detail both in *Kautilya's Arthasastra* and in the Asokan inscriptions. (9) They agree about two or three top levels in central administration; a minister or ministers called Mantrin (Kautilya) or Mahamatra (Asoka); a council of ministers at the next level (Mantri parishad), and many top officers and public servants variously called Amatyas or Sachivas, in a clear hierarchy. These three levels were retained with slightly changed names in the later Gupta Empire in the fifth century A.D. and under Harsha in the seventh century. The general of the army was also a *Mantri* of equal status, as were the viceroys or *Kumaras* of the four large regions or provinces of the Mauryan Empire. Their high and equal status is borne out by the high annual salary of 48,000 panas assigned to them. The members of the council were either part-time or consultative and drew 12,000, but the public servants "amatyas" drew 24,000 panas, or half of the top Mantrins.

The army administration was separately organized as was accounting and financial administration through separate hierarchies. The office of Collector General (Samahartri) and the Accountant General (Akshapataladhyaksha) were separate and each had its own hierarchy. Chapter VI of Book II on the former goes into detail about the distinctions between current receipts and last balance, and between necessary and profitable expenditure while Chapter VII on accounts details various types of accounting deceptions and their punishment, and a separate long Chapter VII focused on embezzlement. Kautilya goes into minute detail about everything, but even more so in regard to finance. Thus Chapter XXI of Book II, on tolls, details various punishments for various offences relating to toll evasion and Chapter XVI on commerce discusses government monopolies of local produce and imports in detail and suitable ways of increasing profit. Two detailed chapters are again assigned to gold and currency.

The central administrative structure was generally replicated in the regions or provinces governed by viceroys. These were subdivided into divisions and districts. The district has continued to be the nerve center of field administration today. (10) The district officer then called Pradeshtri or Sthanika seems to have been much the same as his present day counterpart. He combined revenue collecting and magisterial duties and supervised the work of other technical or clerical officials (Yuktas) as well as village government under the Gopa. The Asokan inscriptions as well as Kautilya's work generally agree in most regards. As a great Buddhist emperor, Asoka of course appointed Dharma mahamatras or ethical superintendents to elevate the moral tone of society.

How was such an elaborate tentacular bureaucracy sustained in loyalty and efficiency in those days of difficult communication. It was achieved essentially through three factors: an elaborate system of internal spying and inspection, the hard work and vigilance of the emperor and his cohorts, and thirdly through a skeletal monetary economy with cash payments.

This bureaucratic system founded by Kautilya, Chandragupta, and Asoka was adopted by the successor empires of the Guptas, and of Harsha with minor changes in name and substance. (11) Thus we find an officer for war and peace, Sandhivigraha, another officer Uparika associated with provincial administration, Kumaramatyas or experienced officials, and Dandanayaka standing for a police or an army officer. The Guptas in the North and the Cholas in the South made a sophisticated system of village self-government an integral part of the administrative system. But the overall structures of central and provincial administration were essentially modifications of the Arthasastra-Asoka model.

Imperial unity did not, however, last in India as it did in China. The Mauryan Empire declined after Asoka and was replaced by the Sunga dynasty ruling over a smaller area. India was divided into a number of fairly sizeable independent states with the border areas being occupied by Greeks and Persian satraps. The Indianized Kushan Empire after straddling a good part of North India and areas of Central Asia lasted for a century after Christ spreading Buddhist culture.

This was followed by another period of border incursions and independent states until the Guptas in the fourth century welded a good part of India into an empire after subduing the Saka invaders. The empire declined due to Hun invasions and other disintegrative factors, giving way to several independent kingdoms. The empire of Harsha in the seventh century covering North India up to the Narmada River, a loose-knit federal empire was the swansong of the Hindu imperial tradition. After four centuries of smaller empires and some independent kingdoms, the Muslim invaders established a sultanate in Delhi from the late twelfth century. While their rule covered a good part of North India, it was checkered by change of dynasties, assassinations, intrigues, and rebellions and was not characterized by steady patterns of administration. The exception was Sher Shah in the late fifteenth century, whose revenue administration formed a model for the Mughals.

The Moghul Empire in the sixteenth and seventeenth centuries provided a steady pattern of administration, but its decline in the eighteenth century was followed by total anarchy in large parts of North India, when the British East India Company began its career or gradual conquest. Throughout the long period from the thirteenth to the eighteenth century, South India witnessed the rise and fall of the Vijayanagar Empire, the Bahmani Kingdom, the Muslim sultanates of Bijapur and Golconda largely under their Hindu ministers, the rise and fall of Mahratta power, and several smaller viceroyalties and kingdoms. This extremely cursory historical account underscores the point that India had no imperial administrative continuity as China had under the Mandarinate. Some administrative ideas, however, survived in modified or resuscitated forms. Let us investigate the causes of discontinuity in India and the nature of the modified continuity.

III. DEMISE OF GOAL OF IMPERIAL UNITY

The central fact of Indian history is that unified empires did not last long and for a good part of her history, India was politically divided. We suggest that the basic explanation for this contrast with China cannot be derived from Wittfogel's hydraulic despotism but is to be sought in the ambivalent attitude of Brahmins in particular and intellectuals in general to the state. The Wittfogel explanation based on hydraulic despotism gets nowhere as both India and China had large rivers and needed to control them for substantial food production. We know for a fact that India and Sri Lanka (and Southeast Asia to a lesser extent) evolved the decentralized caste-oriented self-sufficient village under similar conditions while China evolved a tightly organized bureaucracy. It follows that organized control of flowing water could not have been the compulsive reason; rather it was the way that the whole problem of social and political control was viewed by the princely and intellectual elites—collectively and functionally—that seems to have been the governing factor. The most significant fact is that the mainstream of Hindu intellectual thinking in regard to social control was based on the *Dharma Sastras* dealing mostly with social and caste duties and rituals, with "Rajaniti" or politics as a marginal part of it, in contrast to the Chinese literati's commitment to state service. I have analyzed and discussed the contrast in detail elsewhere (12) and will just summarize the argument briefly here.

It is well established that the durable relation between the literati and a unified empire in China was not decreed by nature but was achieved by a deliberate historical process substantially different from anywhere else in the world. About six or seven centuries before Christ, Europe, India, and China were all divided into many small political units, i.e. kingdoms, tribal republics, and city states. A little later a process of unification by conquest began in all of them, through the Roman Empire in Europe, the Mauryan Empire in India, and the Chin dynasty in China—and this was followed in all the three by a period of imperial disintegration. After that however, their paths diverged. In Europe, the regional kingdoms faced the united continental Catholic Church of scholar priests and both the state and the Church together were confronted with conquering and encircling Islam—giving rise to medieval feudalism, and church-state rivalry and a chain reaction leading to the nation-state and capitalism. In India, the imperial tradition disappeared and reappeared without real continuity. In China, however, the Han Empire succeeded the Chin after a period of disintegration and created an enduring imperial tradition of unity through the cooperation of scholars with a unified Chinese Empire which brought the country back to "harmony" after each period of disintegration. It was thus an enduring collective human contrivance, originally opposed by the very literati who became its pillars later.

The China of Confucius was a "feudal" country of many kingdoms and the gentleman-scholar of the Confucian School was expected to take service with different princes according to his free choice. Shih Huang Ti, then unified China by conquest, virtually exterminated the feudal aristocracy, almost destroyed Confucian literature, unified the script, and centralized the empire as far as possible in those times. The Confucian scholars or Chiint-su however were the implacable opponents of the imperial regime as described by the emperor's adviser Li Ssu thus (13):

> In the past the empire was troubled and divided. No one could succeed in uniting it. Thus the princes reigned simultaneously. In their discussions the scholars speak of ancient times in order to decry the present. They use false examples to stir up confusion in the actual state of affairs, they proclaim the excellence of the doctrines they have studied to abuse what your Majesty has established.

On Li Ssu's advice, Confucian classics were burned and the feudal nobility killed or transported to Shensi. While the old feudalism was destroyed, the centralized tyranny was resented so much that there were risings all over China in his son's time. Finally two leaders emerged after years of civil war, and Liu Pang, founder of the Han Dynasty defeated his rival and unified the country. After some infructuous efforts to resuscitate a facade of feudalism, the Hans settled for a compromise with the Chiintsu. The old books were "recovered," i.e., rewritten to legitimize the collaboration of the literati with the empire as loyal administrators. The Han emperor's supreme achievement was to persuade the new scholar class to whom the feudal age was personally unknown to accept as Confucian ideal, obedience to the emperor.

> By this clever distortion of the ancient feudal idea, the Han emperors made the doctrine of Confucius the strongest support of the centralized autocratic monarchy which the Sage had never known and which his followers formerly opposed to the last gasp. (14)

This "first great revolution" in Chinese history perpetuated the twin institutions of unified empire and scholar officialdom in mutual support. The scholars characterized every period of division as a temporary deviation from the harmony of unified empire which legend was as much its lifeblood as the scholars' services. Thus the confusion following the Han period was ended by the short lived Sui Dynasty, which restored the unified empire and the Mandarinate, followed by the Tang Dynasty which finalized the recruitment process by examination of scholar officials—which lasted along with the unified empire right until the first decade of this century.

By contrast, the Hindu Sastras and the epics with their long passages and even chapters (e.g., Santiparva of *Mahabharata*) on statecraft do not elevate it above Dharma. Kautilya was the only exception who placed imperial statecraft above all else in his *Artha Sastra* in the sixth century B.C. and thus legitimized the successful emergence of the centralized Mauryan Empire. But Hindu Dharma Sastras and Puranas began gradually undermining his extreme state-worship. Kautilya staked too much on a powerful state—with powers to disrobe monks, tax the rich merchants into abject submission, and even keep the Brahmins in their place. Any such ideology required the continuous support of a vested interest other than that of the king and his household.

This was created out of "a hitherto irreconcilably reactionary class," the Chi'in tzu, by converting them into an aristocracy of educated scholar-officials into supporting a centralized monarchy so that "the ideal of a centralized state became closely associated with the scholar class and the followers of the Confucian school". (15) There was no such evolution in India, where developments took in fact the opposite path but unfortunately Indian as well as western scholarship has often mistaken Kautilya's ideal as representing Indian reality for the best part of Indian history. The fact is that the Brahmin scholars, even while they took service under various kings, were never organized into the support of a centralized state, and generally stuck to the theory that Dharma rules and protects the king only so long as he upholds it. Some went out of their way to tear to pieces Kautilya's thinking which was akin to that of Li Ssu in China, a century later. The Kautilyan ideology withered away in its crucial aspects in regard to a centralized empire though his more mundane teachings in regard to day-to-day administration were preserved and practiced by smaller kingdoms—in contrast to the continuing collusion of scholars for centuries with a centralized empire in China. This resulted in the strangest paradox of Asian political history.

The Chinese scholars followed Kautilya's advice of establishing a tentacular bureaucracy for a centralized empire without having heard of him while the Brahmins followed Confucius' advice of taking service rather independently with competing princes in a divided India. *It was an ironic consummation of Confucian Brahmins for India and Kautilyan Mandarins for China.*

The Brahmin-Kshatriya rivalry is fully attested by Puranic and epic stories. (16) Summing up the rather confusing evidence in Puranas and reading between the lines, the Brahmins generally exercised the rights of coronation, legitimation, and advice, but their intellectual abilities and sacramental monopolies were challenged by Kshatriyas—particularly those following Buddhist and Jain religions from time to time, but not consistently. It is possible that Brahmin power was somewhat reduced during the period of Buddhist dominance of Emperor Asoka but only relatively. It is quite likely that the great Hindu reassertion during the period of the Gupta Empire and of Puranic compositions—saw Brahmin sacramental and legitimizing rights fully restored. Simultaneously they were extended to South India and Southeast Asia in a big way. At the same time, a continuing debate on the intellectual and social fronts was joined between Buddhism and Hinduism leading to the absorption of the former by the latter by the ninth or 10th century.

Throughout this long seesaw, there were only one or two definite occasions when Brahmins could have been roped into a permanent alliance of service to a unified Indian Empire namely, the formation of the Mauryan Empire, when Brahmin Kautilya advocated a centralized empire or Chakravarti -Kshetra—before Asoka's time of Buddhist dominance—or later when the Gupta Empire was established with a Brahminical bias. But it did not happen as in Han China for any number of unknown reasons. The Brahmins were lukewarm but not implacably opposed, but by the Gupta period the threshold of active collusion could not be reached due to the increasing dominance of Dharma Sastras. We can never really say whether Brahmin intellectuals were lukewarm because imperial political unification seemed difficult or it became difficult because of the non-cooperation of intellectuals.

Our main thesis may be rephrased thus. A rigidly structured institution like rational-functional bureaucracy required the total collusion of the intellectual elite (who staffed it) and the imperial power elite (who used it) over centuries in precapitalist gemeinschaft agricultural societies. China achieved it in several stages, but India in spite of producing the best blueprint for it in Kautilya's Arthasastra did not, for reasons discussed earlier. Instead, the intellectual elite built up a form of cultural integration which lasted until the advent of the British and which formed the basis of the Indian educated middle class.

There was some continuity of the Kautilyan bureaucratic model in other ways. Successive generations of scholars writing on statecraft replicated his ideas in a redefined adaptive manner keeping alive the same ideas of proper administration. Secondly, the general imperial administrative structure of Kautilya was adaptable for smaller empires after the 7th century, of the Vakatakas, Pratiharas, and Palas and they were also borrowed by the Mughal Empire later. But they could not be sustained in their fullness in a gemeinschaft society, without the total commitment of the intellectual elite. They underwent serious erosion in several ways. The later empires, including even Harsha's empire were loose—and ultimately local power centers of a feudal tributary nature grew up. In fact post-seventh-century Hindu administration in North or South Indian empires was essentially a combination of feudalism, bureaucracy, and village self-government. This combination had the advantage of avoiding anarchy when central power weakened.

Mughal administration, however, fashioned more of a centralized militarized prebendal bureaucracy. (17) The Mansabdhar in charge of an area was essentially commander of a certain number of horses and an executive who was helped in revenue administration by lower level bureaucrats. This office was only for life and his family was divested of all perks and official possessions on his death. It was thus a strange mixture—neither feudal nor bureaucratic. The Mansabdhar had no local roots in this apparently centralized bureaucracy—and this led to total anarchy in large areas when the empire declined.

To sum up, the Kautilyan heritage, lived on in terms of scholarly books on statecraft, and in a diluted feudalized form in Hindu states, while the Mughal centralization with a militarized bureaucracy left large areas a prey to anarchy when it disintegrated. But the Hindu literati, suppressed and ignored in this system came into their own with the advent of English education in the mid-19th century, forming the new derivative middle class which took over government and bureaucracy after India's independence. (18) Their revivalist pride in Hindu India's achievement, particularly of the Arthasastra Asoka bureaucracy forms an obvious romantic intellectual link apart from the continuing use of the district overlord in administration.

IV. BRITISH EAST INDIA COMPANY

The institution of the district overlord had survived in some weak form during the anarchy following the break up of the Mughal Empire in the 18th century. When the East India Company acquired the Diwani of Bengal (revenue collecting rights) from the Mughal emperor they did not take over this institution straight away. There was a horrendous interregnum of wholesale plunder, leasing of revenue to rapacious tax collectors and a man-made famine. Ultimately, under Warren Hastings as governor-general, a full-time officer called collector was appointed to collect land revenue and later he was progressively clothed with responsibility for law and order, agriculture, roads, education, indeed almost all aspects of administration, thus replicating the traditional Indian district overlord. (19) The institution was first justified by governors-general like Sir John Shore—on the need to present a united authority figure to the Orientals. In this century, it was justified by the Simon Commission as the need to bring face to face the common man with a complaint and an officer combining authority to settle it. Indeed British viceroys and statesmen were never tired of singing its praises. When the British organized their administration in Southeast Asia and in Africa later, they replicated this institution.

The adoption and export of this ancient Indian administrative institution to all the Afro-Asian possessions of the British Empire was initiated and facilitated by two major factors. In the first place when the British came to India, they had nothing in their own domestic administrative arrangements which they could transplant or replicate in India. After the Glorious Revolution of

1688, the British landed aristocrats including country squires governed the country on a voluntaristic pattern based on the gentleman-amateur ethic. (20) In the late 18th and early 19th centuries, British intellectuals and politicians reviled 'bureaucracy' as a continental disease of France and Prussia. They had nothing in their own administrative repertoire as the French had, for governing their Indian acquisitions. They were happy to revive and use the traditional Indian idea of the district overlord in the late 18th century.

The second factor was the strong influence of utilitarian philosophy on Indian administrators in combination with their own paternalism in the mid-19th century. (21) James Mill and John Stuart Mill, T. B. Macaulay, James Stephen, and Charles Trevelyan were all imbued with the utilitarian spirit of reform which they could not fully implement in their own homeland against traditionalist critics but in India, they had a free hand. The district overlord was to be recruited not ascriptively, but by a modern performance test, i.e., a competitive examination designed by Macaulay and to be armed with thoroughly streamlined legal codes bettering Code Napoleon. Thus the Indian district collector—the scion of the Mauryan Empire, revived and modernized by the British rulers in India bestrode the empire for a century—and is still around somewhat politicized—as the district coordinator and the hope of district development in India, Malaysia, and Africa.

V. MARXIST AND WEBERIAN ATTITUDES

Our analysis of ancient Indian bureaucracy as such seems self-sufficient in terms of our parameters. But a brief side glance at Weber's and Marx's ideas in this regard may be attempted cautiously. The first difficulty in this is that there is no agreement among competing Marxists and non-Marxists as to what is meant by Marx's Asiatic Mode of Production (AMP for short) or Precapitalist Mode of Production. (22) Secondly, several scholars have pointed out, the meager undeveloped European orientalist sources from which Weber and Marx drew. (23) Without bothering to study that debate we can look at the question afresh in our own way.

We may assume that Weber's characterization of modern legal rational bureaucracy involves (1) the mutual complementarity of these characteristics, and (2) assumes that a market and monetary economy was essential for these characteristics to be sustained. It then follows that ancient bureaucracies having only some of the characteristics and not being based on a monetary economy could not continue as legal-rational bureaucracies. We can argue that this mode of dismissing them is arbitrary. The Mauryan bureaucracy in India or the Han and Tang bureaucracies in China certainly exhibited the main characteristics of the Weberian list, of hierarchy, rules and regulations, division of labor, and career orientation in a sustained manner for long periods, in an economy which was at least partly monetary though predominantly barter and exchange based. There is thus no need to lump them under some pejorative labels like patrimonial or prebendal for nonstudy. The real argument for a sharper identification of modern legal-rational bureaucracy away from ancient bureaucracies was never spelled out precisely by Weber himself though it may be inferred by the second remove by marrying the general approach of Weber to that of his great contemporaries Tonnies and Durkheim. These two were more preoccupied with the emerging reorganization of Western society from all-purpose natural groups into functional artificial associations—a development which Tocqueville had noticed already in America, which artists and poets bewailed, and which Frazer had noted by contrast in his *Golden Bough*. Tonnies dealt with this development as such in detail while Durkheim was more concerned with its consequence "anomie" and the "organic" mode of integrating the emerging social units. Weber was aware of their work and its close relation to his own, but for unknown personal reasons, these three contemporaries would not draw sustenance from each other's work.

It is, however, clear to us that relating them gives us better explanation of the strength and weakness of ancient bureaucracies than Weber was inclined to inquire. Thus the impersonal legal-rational characteristics of modern bureaucracy—are sustained by a gesellschaft society that is itself organized into partly impersonal functional associations. This correspondence, makes it easy for bureaucracy's recruitment of personnel from society and its smooth interactions with society just as a monetary economy makes a bureaucratic career dependent on job performance with bureaucracy as a vocation—unlike in feudalistic, prebendal, or other modes of remuneration. To the extent to which bureaucracy's impersonal characteristics were divorced from that of a gemeinschaft society, it was vulnerable either to continuous dilution by contact or ineffectiveness by isolation. The lapses of bureaucratic into feudal structures in ancient India developed partly because of this. A similar development also overtook even Tudor bureaucracy in England after Elizabeth because it was evolved during a period of limited transport and communications and had fulfilled its main purpose of unifying the country.

It was an enlightened landed aristocracy that took power in the Glorious Revolution of 1688 and ran the country on a voluntaristic basis without much bureaucracy for a century and a half while bureaucracy took shape later in Louis XIV's France and Frederick the Great's Prussia when feudalism was in its death throes and a *gesellschaft* society was evolving along with faster communications. (24) It was this harmonious simultaneous evolution of society into *gesellschaft* and bureaucracy that sustained both in the 19th century and later. It was the isolation of bureaucracy in a *gemeinschaft* society that diluted it sooner or later.

Marx's AMP has been interpreted differently by Marxists themselves, but let us assume for the sake of argument that it meant bureaucratically controlled state monopolies in production without private property. It is doubtful if that picture obtained in India in its fullness during any period. In fact, during the late 18th century, when the East India Company was just entering India, it did not obtain at all: There was some state controlled production by Kharkhanas under the Mughals at one end, a substantial accumulation of capital for investment at another end, and a large surplus of privately manufactured cotton goods for export—a strange combination indeed. The firm establishment of British rule, far from generating an outburst of local capitalism as Marx might have expected, killed the textile industry, diverted Indian capital into money-lending and gold ornament manufacture, and created a purely salaried and professional bourgeoisie. Later Marxists like Kusinen have explained this as an alliance of monopoly capitalism in its imperial phase with the traditional elite (Degras). Whatever the merits of the original or refurbished AMP concept, it is clear that it gives no insights into the role of ancient or medieval Indian bureaucracy in the context of society at that time and Wittfogel's modified theory relating hydraulic society and bureaucratic control (which theory is disowned by several Marxists) does no better as we have already argued. In short, one purpose of this paper is to argue that neither Marx nor Weber have all that much to offer in understanding ancient bureaucracies and to suggest a really fresh look at them without rigid Weberian or Marxist commitments.

REFERENCES

1. Gerth, H.H., and Mills, C. Wright. *From Max Weber: Essays in Sociology*, Routledge and Kegan Paul, London, 1946; and Weber, Max. *Economy and Society*, Bedminster Press, New York, 1968.
2. Marx, Karl. *A Contribution to the Critique of Political Economy*, Penguin, Hammondsworth, 1973.
3. Feur, L. *Marx and Engels, Basic Writings on Politics and Philosophy*, Fontana Library, London, 1969.
4. Balazs, Etienne. *Chinese Civilization and Bureaucracy: Variations on a Theme*, Yale University Press, New Haven, 1964.
5. Eisenstadt, S.N. *Political Systems of Empires*, Free Press, New York, 1967. 6. Prasad, Beni. *State and Government in Ancient India*, Motilal Benarsidas, Delhi, 1958.
7. Sastry, Shama R. *Kautilya's Arthasastra*, Mysore Printing and Publishing House, Mysore, 1967.

8. Puri, B. N. *History of Indian Administration*, Vol. I, *Ancient Period*, Bharatiya Vidya Bhavan, Bombay, 1968, Chapter III.

9. *Ibid.*, Chapter III.

10. *Ibid.*, Chapter III.

11. *Ibid.*, Chapter V.

12. Subramaniam, V. *Cultural Integration in India*, Ashish Publishing House, New Delhi, 1979, Chapter II.

13. Fitzgerald, C.P. "China" in *A Short Cultural History*, Praeger, New York, 1961, Chapter IV.

14. *Ibid.*

15. *Ibid.*

16. Subramaniam, *op. cit.*

17. Puri, B.N. *History of Indian Administration*, Vol. II, *Medieval Period*, Bharatiya Vidya Bhavan, Bombay, 1975, Chapter VI.

18. Subramaniam, V. *Transplanted Indo-British Administration*, Ashish Publishing House, New Delhi, 1977; Subramaniam, V. (ed.). *Public Administration in the Third World*, Greenwood Publishing Group, Westport, 1990, Appendix II.

19. Subramaniam, 1977, *ibid.*, Chapter 7.

20. *Ibid.*, Chapters 6 and 10.

21. Misra, B.B. *The Indian Middle Classes*, Oxford University Press, Oxford, 1963; and Sen, Amartya Kumar and Williams, Bernard. *Utilitarianism and Beyond*, Cambridge University Press, Cambridge, England, 1982.

22. Krader, L. *The Asiatic Mode of Production*, Van Gorcum, Assen, 1975; Anderson, P. *Lineages of the Absolutist State*, New Left Book, New York, 1974; and Lichtheim, G. *Marx and the Asiatic Mode of Production*. St. Anthony's Papers 14, Oxford.

23. Turner, B. *For Weber: Essays on the Sociology of Fate*, Routledge and Kegan Paul, London, 1981, pp. 278–284.

24. Subramaniam, V. "British Administrative Institutions: Paradoxes of Acceptance, Adaptation and Rejection." *The Round Table*, London, 1983.

7

Development Administration in the Early Americas

Aztecs, Incas, and Mayas

Jean-Claude Garcia-Zamor　*School of Policy and Management, Florida International University, North Miami, Florida*

I. INTRODUCTION

The ancient civilizations had many features that were superior to those that existed and still exist in some Western countries. But their feudal social structures belong to an archaic world. Therefore, although much can be learned from them, many of their practices are unacceptable in modern times. Developing countries will need to apply the same caution they use when dealing with Western models, like the Weberian one, in borrowing from these ancient civilizations the lessons that could be valuable for them.

This paper will review the process of development administration in the ancient civilizations of the Americas and will draw some lessons that might enrich that process in the countries that are now carrying it out. A study of development administration in the setting of ancient times is unique because these early civilizations were not preoccupied with such a policy. Nevertheless, the practice of development administration was as present in those days as it is in the modern industrialized countries where it is not openly recognized.

It would be impractical to look at the ancient civilizations' policies and practices reviewed in this paper as a model to be applied as such to present-day developing countries. But national models could be inspired by the rational administrative systems of the Aztecs, the Mayas, and the Incas. Their bureaucratic tasks were not only of technical competence but of attitudes and behavioral approaches that were, for their time and place, humane.

II. WHAT IS DEVELOPMENT ADMINISTRATION?

Development administration is the organization and supervision of civil servants to define and achieve specific social and economic objectives. It is the human participation in the modernization process. Most developing countries are heavily involved in the formulation and implementation of development policies and programs. These activities are usually the main tasks of their bureaucracies. In industrialized societies where a substantial level of the development has already been effectuated, the main tasks of the bureaucracy are more diversified and seem to evolve around the preservation of the status quo.

In the context of the contemporary social and political important conditions in many countries, their administrators must play an increasingly important role in promoting social and economic change. They cannot be totally aloof from the conditions of the people. The Weberian concepts of impersonalized decision-making is not valid in those countries.[1] The administration of development activities implies the close involvement of the community, which must participate in achieving the objectives of development. Such public participation is presently viewed as indispensable if development projects have to succeed.[2]

The term development administration is used instead of public administration to emphasize that in developing countries the focus of attention is on the building and improvement of a public administration system as part of the total effort of national development. It covers both the administration of development (i.e., public administration as an instrument of national development) and the development of administration (i.e., measures to enhance the administrative capacity for development).

The development administration process in the Third World is often inspired and stimulated by donor organizations such as the World Bank, the International Monetary Fund, the U.S. Agency for International Development (USAID) and others, that view the lack of managerial skills as one of the main reasons for the wasting of foreign assistance funds. Since the early 1960s when approximately two thirds of the member countries of the United Nations began to gain their independence, billions of dollars have been invested for the development of Africa, Latin America, and Asia. While several of the Asian countries are emerging from underdevelopment, most African countries still lack any basic economic infrastructure. Foreign donors have faced the specter of pouring money into a bottomless pit when they attempt to aid Africa.

Because of the heavy involvement of foreign donors in all development activities in Africa and Latin America, the dependency on outside assistance has become a major characteristic of development administration. This trait is also present whenever the process of development administration is taking place in industrialized societies. In contrast to the third world, where it is focused in the activities of the national bureaucracies, in the more advance countries development administration can be found primarily in poor municipal and county governments. In both situations, the struggling bureaucracy finds itself dependent on external technical assistance and financing to develop projects and programs and to deliver services. While in the developing countries such external assistance is provided by international donor countries and institutions, in the municipal and county governments of the United States for example, the dependency is on state and federal assistance. In both cases the recipient governments are subjected to an array of restrictions that often limit the capacity of their bureaucracies to give priority to the urgent needs of their communities. However, one thing is quite clear—the tasks of these bureaucracies to promote development would not have been possible without outside assistance.[3]

In addition to that dependency on outside assistance, there are several characteristics that are almost always present in countries that are undergoing a process of development administration. Although the following list is not all inclusive, it includes the five of the most pronounced characteristics.

1. Unorganized and inefficient bureaucracy
2. Inadequate and unfair tax collection system
3. Nugatory agricultural practices
4. Warped judicial order
5. Poor educational system

One might question the validity of using an ancient civilization's model to find solutions to

20th-century problems.[4] But a review of the literature reveals numerous instances where the Western model is suggested for the bureaucracies of the third world.[5] It is not proven that such model can work better than the ancient civilizations model in the developing countries. Furthermore, the ancient civilizations had many features that were superior to those that existed and often still exist in some Western countries. For example, corruption was practically unknown in the Inca empire, a fact that really impressed the Spaniards. For good reason: the Spaniards' own political system, and those of all Europe at the time, could make no such claim.[6] During the height of Aztec civilization in Mexico, the Aztecs had running water and a sanitary system in their homes while the Europeans lived in squalor and filth, rarely bathing for fear of death. Enriched by the loot of a hundred triumphant campaigns, Tenochtitlan acquired at one point a splendor which was never duplicated in Europe. The diffusion and preservation of knowledge by an excellent universal educational system compared favorably with that in Europe at the time.[7] Without question the ancient civilizations of Latin America lacked many inventions crucial in the Old World. There were no iron and steel tools, no beasts of burden, no keystone arches or domes. Nevertheless, indigenous Americans constructed huge buildings, devised accurate calendars and speculated about the solar system. One of the many enigmas of the Mayas, for example, is that they managed to achieve what few major civilizations have done, supporting a complex society and large population on the thin soil and dispersed resources of tropical forests. Exactly how this was accomplished is still poorly understood.[8]

III. ADMINISTRATIVE LEGACIES OF THE ANCIENT CIVILIZATIONS

Although the civilizations of the Aztecs, Incas, and Mayas were not preoccupied with the process of development as a vital instrument for their survival, their own notions of "nation building" and "institutions building" were not very different from those of present day developing nations. They were able to develop some monumental projects without the assistance of the outside world.[9] This paper will review the five major characteristics that were previously mentioned as being present where the process of development administration is taking place and will point out how the ancient civilizations coped with them. Although the three civilizations considered here extended for several centuries and therefore had different priority policies and activities at different stages of their respective development, sufficient evidence of extended administrative practices is available to justify such an exercise.

A. Unorganized and Inefficient Bureaucracy

Good administration, like development, should be defined differently for each country and for each time period. Any definition of good and efficient administration should include the achievement of specific objectives through the management of a bureaucracy. Although the objectives of the rulers of the ancient civilizations were sometimes different from those of contemporary governments, these rulers managed their bureaucracies effectively often using democratic and despotic methods no longer acceptable. A brief review of their administrative machineries follows.

1. Aztecs

The main objective of Aztec public policy was to make alliances and form and administer an empire. The Aztecs excelled in civil administration. Their growing empire was governed more efficiently than many contemporary nations. The social system made each person feel that he or she played a vital part. Most questions of life or death were answered for the commoner by a combination of priests, warriors, statesmen, scientists, and teachers that could handle any eventuality.[10] The tasks of service delivery of the Aztec bureaucracy was simplified by grouping families within the tribes to form "divisions" for the purposes of land distribution and exploitation. No one was permitted to own land. In addition to deciding when the land should be cultivated and on which days the crops were to be reaped, these "divisions" had higher administrative and military duties. Each was an organization having its own headman and council.[11] Women held no office in this male-dominated society. Nevertheless, they advised their husband and sons, and so were able to exert a considerable unofficial pressure.[12]

2. Mayas

The ancient Maya was not a theocracy or primitive democracy, but rather a class society with strong political power concentrated in a hereditary elite. The Mayas had an excellent method of formalized territorial organization. Eventually some of the larger centers achieved a status approaching urban cities. For example, at Tikal, hundreds of structures believed to be residences of persons other than peasant farmers were mapped within the city's central precincts. No doubt the existence of this diversified social organization also brought about complex administrative problems necessitating a host of civil servants (magistrates, tribute collectors, law enforcers, etc.) who—along with the artists, craftsmen, merchants—almost surely constituted the equivalent of a "middle class."[13]

There is abundant evidence that the Mayan bureaucrats combined religious with civil functions. Religion was of central importance in Mayan life, and authority was exercised by a closely co-operating group of priests, each of whom acted equally as a leader over a particular geographical area. Some formal method of control must be assumed to account for the stable and orderly character of Mayan civilization over so wide an area and for so long a period of time.[14] The "official" image which emerges from Mayan documents is one of a static, caste-bound society; it is a world of the ruling classes, whom the people support and maintain in exchange for a completely abstract prosperity, made up of prophecies, mysteries, and collective mysticism. Very little social tension existed: only religious activity and great building enterprises.[15]

3. Incas

The Incas were masters of organization. They turned conquest into empire. In a land where for geographical, topographical, hydrographical and economic reasons, tight planning of resources was required, the Incas were extremely efficient. Their bureaucracy excelled in service delivery. The production and distribution of food, clothing and services, including road and canal building, were all functions of the state.

The Incas had an effective way of securing a loyal civil service. It was provided by a sort of formalized and licit nepotism. They also created an administrative machine capable of dealing with the vast territory under their control.[16] Provincial governors were carefully selected and their positions were appointments by merit, not by heredity as in the civil service. Thus, the Incas did not merely conquer foreign tribes and kingdoms with their armies; their administrative leadership peacefully integrated these people into one cohesive and viable political unit. A magnificent system of Incan-built roads linked the heart of the empire, Cusco, with the most distant provinces.[17] An extraordinary efficient postal service permitted dispatches to circulate rapidly. Messengers were stationed on major roads. They lived in groups of four or six in two thatched huts located about a mile from each other. The messengers were all young men who were especially good runners, and it was their duty to keep permanent watch of the road in order to catch sight of messengers from the other relays, and hurry out to meet them. To enable them to do this, these huts were built on high ground, in sight of one another.[18]

Bureaucrats were required to furnish their superiors with a record of births and deaths that had occurred in the territories they administered. Thanks to this constant census of his subjects, which was carried out kingdom by kingdom and province by province, the Inca ruler was able to make a judicious distribution of the tasks necessary to the public welfare. He also prepared an annual report on what each province produced in the way of goods. This was in order to learn what provisions would be required to come to the assistance of his vassals in the event they were to suffer from shortages or had a poor harvest, including what quantities of wool and cotton that would be needed to clothe them.[19]

B.   Inadequate and Unfair Tax Collection System

Most developing countries lack an adequate and fair tax collection system.[20] State revenues based on tax collection are low because even when a collection system exists, there are no serious consequences for those who evade payment. Government of most developing countries continue to base their development plans on expected foreign assistance and put little energy into generating internal revenues. These governments can learn in this area from the ancient civilizations. All of them had very efficient tax collection systems and the revenue collected (in the form of consumer goods since they had no money economy) was judiciously used to promote the welfare of their people.

1.   Aztecs

Montezuma's empire comprised approximately thirty provinces, each with a central town for collecting tribute, and many with governors imposed to facilitate exploitation. The tribute exacted from these provinces sustained the government, the officials, the educational system, state granaries for emergencies, and rewards for deserving warriors. Power was concentrated at the top. The Aztecs had a dictatorship and a political centralization based on an imperial type of hierarchy. Their tribute system was administered by an autocratic bureaucracy.[21] Continuity of payment was enforced by tax-gathering officials in key places; if their demands were not met, a military expedition was undertaken and the exactions greatly increased.[22] At the time of the Spanish Conquest the annual tribute collected by the ruler included no less than 52,000 tons of foodstuffs, 123,400 cotton garments, and 33,860 bundles of feathers. This tribute in kind was only a part of what the provinces contributed. In addition, services were extracted in the form of labor to build Montezuma's pyramid and other buildings. The frontier areas where supplies were provided for war were often exempted from paying taxes.[23]

2.   Mayas

It would have been difficult for such a compact and well organized society as the Maya to flourish without a strong social hierarchy battering upon it. Each Mayan village or settlement came under the control of a Lord, to whom taxes were payable. These taxes were twofold: on produce, and in personal service. A portion of all crops harvested had to be paid over to the state. These crops were stored in warehouses and later distributed to the non-productive members of society.[24] As with the Aztecs, the tribute also included produce, a kind of woven cotton cloth called *pati*, domesticated fowls, salt, dried fish, and all kinds of game and birds. It also included cacao, copal for incense, honey and wax, strings of jade and coral beads, and shells.[25]

3.   Incas

The Incas used personal service as a form of taxation and agricultural work became the economic basis of the system. Each family cultivated not only its own plot of land, but also worked on the fields assigned to the state, the produce from which supported the political superstructure.[26] In return for their fixed and reasonable share of the national product, the Inca upper caste provided sound and reliable administration, justice, welfare services, military services, and religious services. Everyone was provided with clothing, shoes, food, and all that is necessary in life, and it may be said there was no poor man or beggar throughout the empire. But while there were no poor, there were no rich either, since everyone had what was necessary without living in luxury.[27] It is safe to say that a high proportion of the architectural and technological constructions built in the Incaic period—temples, storehouse, roads, *tambos* (inns), bridges, fortresses, reservoirs, irrigation ditches, agricultural terraces, etc.—was dedicated to the direct or indirect benefit of the people rather than to the selfish vanity of the rulers.[28]

C. Nugatory Agricultural Practices

In most developing countries agriculture is the main source for accumulating savings. Agricultural practices are thus vital for the overall development process. Public efforts to advance the agricultural progress in the developing countries in Asia and the Far East are noticeable. However, in most Latin American and African countries the relationship between agricultural development and the total development process has not been clearly recognized. Despite rapid urbanization, the population in most developing areas is still concentrated in rural areas or small towns. Archaic political structures and outlooks tend to prevail in the rural areas, resisting changes which could raise production and permit broader distribution of benefits. An industrialization strategy is almost an inevitable phenomenon in the developing countries because their bureaucracies view it as the most reliable way toward development. However, instead of using the agricultural sector to provide raw materials for their new industries, they often fail to integrate that sector in their industrialization strategy. Furthermore, economic development usually brings a relative, if not an absolute, decline in the agricultural labor force.

The following brief review of agricultural practices in the ancient civilizations of Latin America shows that one key factor in the successful utilization of the land was the rulers' ability to mount major agricultural works programs to whose implementation the entire peasantry was fully committed. These agricultural works programs transformed traditional practices into "modern" ones in order to increase production.

1. Aztecs

As mentioned earlier, the most important duty of *Calpulli* was the redistribution of land which occurred at least every four years (see Ref. 11). The cultivated area, which had been worked until there were signs of declining yield, was burnt over. The other areas which had been left uncultivated for some eight years were then divided. The plots allocated to families were scattered about in the whole section of land. This was a wise provision, because it meant that everyone had an equal chance of farming a plot or richer land.[29]

After receiving the land, they began the spring sowing. The women and the children usually helped in this task. Very few Aztecs practiced any kind of irrigation, although they did fertilize their fields. The result of this system of land distribution and exploitation was that everyone accumulated a basic store of food which could probably see the entire society through difficult times. The farmer was thus the support of the nation.[30]

2. Mayas

Fundamental to the great achievements of the Maya people was the rare quality of knowing how to organize themselves to work as a team. Rarely in his life did a Maya act on his own or only for himself. This was particularly true in agriculture. The nature of the terrain was such that teams of peasants were needed to open up clearings in the forest, to cut down trees, to burn roots, and to keep clear the soil which had been son so laboriously.[31] Like the Aztecs, the Mayans depended on farmers. Rulers collected and distributed food surpluses. On occasion, political leaders extended their influence into the sphere of agriculture, particularly in the Late Classic period.[32] With increased specialization, administrative intervention was sometimes necessary to avoid the collapse of fragile economic systems in the face of crop failure or problems with the surplus of raw materials.[33]

Some scholars believe that the Maya were diligent farmers of swamps. What they have done was piling up the much from the *bajos* (seasonal swamps) and creating raise gardens surrounded by culverts and drainage ditches. The muck from the swamp and ditches would then become fertile soil.[34]

Recently a group of archaeologists working in Guatemala discovered a largely overlooked, until now, clever network of reservoirs and dams, stone-paved storm sewers and clay-lined drainage ditches that may have helped the Maya survive brutal bouts of seasonal drought. The management of water, the researchers say, could have been crucial in the creation of the powerful and advanced Maya nation-state.[35]

3.   Incas

For administrative purposes the Incas divided the lands of the empire into three categories: the lands of the sun god, the lands belonging to the Incan emperor and his imperial circles, and the lands that remained the communal property of the people. The people themselves were clustered into groups.[36] A method was developed to rotate labor. Under this system the commoners worked in turn the fields of the sun, the fields of the emperor, and the peasants' communal lands. The agricultural products of these communal lands were distributed among the commoners' households. The products yielded by the fields of the emperor and by the fields of the sun maintained the imperial court and the royal officials, fed and clothed those drafted into the Incan armies or into labor groups engaged in public works, and supported the priests and virgins consecrated to the cult of the sun. The surplus was stored in royal ganaries and warehouses to be distributed among the people in case of need.[37]

The key factor in their success in agriculture was their skill in water use. Despite the height of the Andes and the absence of electricity, steam engines, dynamite and iron, they were able to build great reservoirs where the water was collected and released slowly into miles of canals constructed through the mountains. As soon as the Incas conquered a new province they immediately sent engineers there to build canals for irrigation. The management of irrigation water and the immense works associated with it must have required a special administrative department.

When the highland farmers ran short of arable land, they invented terracing, which not only gave them more room but checked erosion and runoff. In time every valley was a spectacle of tier upon tier of terraces, with those at the float being perhaps a mile wide and those at the top a few feet, and the range of crops varying in kind from the temperate-zone cultigens at the top down to the tropical-zone plants at the lower levels.[38] This system is still being used in most developing countries to fight the erosion caused by intense deforestation and is the direct result of lessons already learned from ancient civilizations.

D.   Warped Judicial Order

The laws and their enforcement by judicial, quasijudicial and administrative hierarchies have important implications with regard to administrative capabilities for economic and social development on the one hand, and for human rights and welfare on the other. In the developing countries, the judicial systems generally have serious deficiencies. For example, the laws on important subjects may be deficient or inadequate; people may not understand the laws; legal processes may be slow and ineffective; legal services may be out of the reach of some persons; and privileged individuals may see themselves above any law of the land.

Unfortunately, the judicial system has not often been seen as a relevant factor when dealing with economic development. However, it has great capacity for facilitating change in many areas of the economy and the social order. Most particularly, a fair judicial system can provide a degree of certainty and predictability in economic relationships among individuals and, more importantly between governments and individuals.

A review of the judicial systems of the ancient civilizations of Latin America will follow. It will indicate how rulers were able to promote the development and welfare of their subjects using a legal framework that can still inspire progressive reforms in the judicial systems of developing countries.

1.   Aztecs

The administration of justice in the Aztec empire was something about which any nation could proudly boast, although the punishments were savage and vengeful. Because a criminal was liable not only to the society but to his gods as well, he was punished doubly. The laws of the Aztecs were an integral part of their life, reflecting their culture and mentality. Laws were equally applicable to high and low levels of society. However, the nobility and other privileged classes were judged by separate courts, and received private but more severe punishment.[39]

It should be pointed out that under Montezuma's rule, lawgiving was by no means confined to court etiquette and sumptuary rules; he promulgated, in addition, a new legal code governing such general matters as education, religious practices and festivities, while not ignoring such detailed questions as the treatment of adulterers, who were to be stoned and then thrown into a river. Drunkenness was another capital offense. This provision was applied even more strictly to nobles than to commoners; the former were to be killed for a first offense, while the latter were given a second chance before being executed.[40]

2.   Mayas

There are no records of a Mayan system of justice that was as disciplined as the Aztecs' one. For one thing the method of any kind of law enforcement would have faced the problem of the huge area to be regimented. A major deterrent from the use of repressive government methods was the scattered nature of the population. This remarkably smooth running yet informal style of government must have depended upon a placid and well adjusted citizenry, who held a notable unanimous opinion as to proper behavior. Two authors, after observing this, quoted Lord Moulton as saying in a different context; "the measure of civilization is the extent of man's obedience to the unenforceable." In this criterion, they added, the Maya must have measured high.[41]

3.   Incas

The leader of the smallest group of heads of households (usually numbering ten families) had two principal responsibilities. One, more or less that of an attorney, or representative, consisted in diligently and earnestly soliciting the help of the higher authorities, on behalf of those under his jurisdiction who were in any sort of difficulty. The second responsibility, which was of a judicial nature, consisted in reporting to his superiors all misdemeanors that occurred inside his group of ten.[42]

Law among the Incas was deliberately discriminatory. The higher a person's status in the hierarchy, the more law-respecting he was expected to be. As in the Aztec's system of justice, punishment was more severe for nobles than for the ordinary commoner committing the same crime.

Adultery, for example, earned the commoner, or the commoner's wife, a nasty session of torture. A member of the nobility caught in adultery was condemned to death. Crime seems to have been infrequent. There was little motivation for it and punishment was certain.[43]

E. Poor Educational System

Developing countries need effective education systems to provide them with manpower for public and business administration, technical posts in agriculture and industry, and research and teaching. Such investment in human resources is a first priority for development. Economists long regarded education as a simple "final consumption" and manpower as a "factor of production." The experience and setbacks encountered in implementing certain development programs and plans gradually led economists to recognize that education had an essential role, not only in the success of short term programs but also in the effective achievement of long term development. It is interesting to note that the ancient civilizations of Latin America had developed educational programs more advanced than those in existence in many modern-day nations.

1. Aztecs

Aztec society's concern with education was singular for its time—school was compulsory for children. They were two main types of schools, and attendance at one or the other determined social and economic status. The children of the nobility usually attended a school run by scholarly priests, in preparation for the priesthood or some high office in the state. Occasionally a talented son of a commoner gained entrance. To prepare students for future responsibilities, discipline was very strict and hours of study were long. In a vigorous intellectual regimen young boys studied religion, astronomy, philosophy, history, poetry, rhetoric, and oratory, among other disciplines. Although the spoken language was rich and expressive and lent itself to fine subtleties, the picture writing was limited. History was passed on by oral traditions committed to memory.[44]

Most of the other children attended one of the commoners' schools where they found a more relaxed, less intellectual atmosphere. Boys and girls were given practical instruction in basic subjects. Boys learned the rudiments of warfare, and those who excelled in the profession of arms could do very well for themselves; others had to be content with learning trades or lesser skills. Girls were instructed in the responsibilities of the household and motherhood. They were taught modesty, courtesy, and conformity.[45]

2. Mayas

The Mayas' civilization was clearly the greatest to flourish in pre-Columbian America. They studied the heavens to devise precise calendars, created a true writing system and built imposing cities. However, progress in deciphering Mayan writings has been slow. Their complex hieroglyphics once were thought to be incomprehensible. Not much is known about the educational system that existed within the Mayan empire.

As in almost all the early civilizations, it is extremely difficult to separate the Mayans' primitive scientific knowledge from its ritual context. The Mayas had evolved a considerable body of empirically derived information about the natural world. Arithmetic and astronomy had reached a level comparable to that achieved by the ancient Babylonians and surpassing in some respects that of the Egyptians. But science in the modern sense was not present. In its place there was, as with the Mesopotamian civilizations, a combination of fairly accurate astronomical data with what can only be called numerology, developed by Mayan intellectuals for religious purposes.[46]

3.   Incas

The school system of the Incas seems to be similar to that of the Aztecs. The sons of the Incan nobility were educated in the imperial schools where they learned Incan history, law and religion. A body of scholars lived in Cuzco, supported by the emperor and dedicated to the education of youth. These scholars were regarded with high esteem and dedicated to the education of youth. These scholars were regarded with high esteem among the Incas, and their teaching duties were considered to be of the utmost importance to the welfare of the nation. The education given by these scholars was more humanistic than pragmatic, and the development of well-rounded men seems to have been of greater importance than the training of specialists. Besides history, law, and religion, students learned music, poetry, philosophy, and the art of governing. The scholars guided their students to become more urbane, skillful, and humane and taught them oratory skills.

IV.   WHY ANCIENT CIVILIZATION MODEL?

The bureaucracies of the ancient civilizations seem to have faced the very same problems confronted by the bureaucracies of the developing countries. Despite the very different political framework of these ancient civilizations, their administrative practices can still guide the process of development administration in the developing countries. Economic development policies of the Aztecs, Mayas, and Incas have integrated the territories of these empires in a way that has never been accomplished in Africa, Asia, and Latin America. Even post–World War II Europe was geographically delineated in ways that required some careful integration policies within the new nations. The present situation in Yugoslavia is an extreme example of the problem.

In Africa, one of the major problems in the development of the continent is posed by the frontiers of the African states, a legacy of the colonial phase of their history. They were established without regard to linguistic and ethnic affiliations and often included nonrelated groups, some of whom did not even recognize colonial frontiers Beyond the boundaries of practically every state are people seeking to be re-united with those within. However, as legacies of the colonial regime, they are both resented and ardently defended. These disputes can last for years, if not decades, and affect the relations between neighboring countries. Asia and Latin America had a similar experience.

When the Incas captured new provinces for example, every effort was made to continue the previous local rulers in office. But the sons of these rulers were taken as hostages to Cuzco where they received the formal upper-class education. They were encouraged to marry Incan girls from the nobility before returning home in order to assure their loyalty and alliance. The Incans imposed their sun worship religion and the Quechua language on the new subjects.[47] The spread of Quechua was vital to the process of Incan assimilation. It filtered down even to the lowest strata of society. The community of language undoubtedly created a community of minds, and Quechua played in the Incan empire a role similar to that of Latin in the Roman Empire.

Another means of creating an organic unity among the subjects of the Incan empire was the state-planned movements of population. By imperial decree, colonies of Incas were moved to the fringes of the empire or to rebellious unassimilated regions within its boundaries. They were given lands, granted tax exemptions, honored with other privileges, and entrusted with the task of colonizing the natives and bringing them into the mainstream of Incan life. These massive movements of peoples were not exceptional, but a common policy that in a few generations altered the patterns of population settlements within the empire. These friendly assimilations helped to create a climate of unity and a common culture.[48] The Incas had a great knowledge of the way to conquer and how to bring the new subjects into the empire by good management. The need for countries to find integration formulas to stimulate their economics and broaden their markets has become obvious over the past decades, especially in Latin America and Africa. However, the integration models have been putting more emphasis in dynamic growth of regional and national gross products than in stimulating greater social progress.

Some of the policies and practices of the ancient civilizations of the Aztecs, Incas, and Mayas reviewed in this paper are inadequate as a model for development in modern time. The feodal social structures of these ancient civilizations belong to an archaic world. Therefore, although much can be learned from their rational administrative systems, many of their practices are unacceptable at the present. Developing countries will need to apply the same caution they use when dealing with Western models like the Weberian one, in borrowing from these ancient civilizations the lessons that could be valuable for them.

ENDNOTES

1. Garcia-Zamor, J. C. "The Application of Max Weber's Model in Non-Western Public Bureaucracies," in Ramesh K. Arora (ed.). *Politics and Administration in Changing Societies. Essays in Honor of Professor Fred W. Riggs*, Associated Publishing House, New Delhi, India, 1992.
2. Garcia-Zamor, J. C. *Public Participation in Development Planning and Management. Cases from Africa and Asia*, Westview Press, Boulder, CO, 1985.
3. Some of the earlier theories developed by the author of this paper dealt with the inner work of development administration (Garcia-Zamor, 1972, 1973, 1990, 1992). The dependency of development administration on outside assistance in both the developing and developed countries is discussed in a chapter entitled "Neoteric Theories for Development Administration in the New World Order," in J. C. Garcia-Zamor and R. Khator (eds.). *Public Administration in the Global Village*, Greenwood Press, Westport, CT, 1994.
4. A recently published article argued that public administrators can learn from studying Sophocles' *Antigone*. The author regards the ancient Greek play as a fruitful source of opportunities to reflect upon the ethical challenges facing modern public administration. Marini, Frank. "The Uses of Literature in the Exploration of Public Administration Ethics: The Example of Antigone." *Public Administration Review* 52 (September/October 1992) 420–426.
5. Garcia-Zamor, 1992, *op. cit.*
6. Karen, R. *The Inca: Empire Builders of the Americas*, Four Winds Press, New York, 1975.
7. Peterson, F. A. *Ancient Mexico*, Paragon Press, New York, 1979.
8. Wilford, J. N. "Did Warfare Doom Mayas' Ecology?" *The Miami Herald* (December 22 1992): 7L.
9. This self-reliance could have been the result of difficulties of communications or distrust of often hostile outsiders, but it was not typical only of the Aztecs, Incas, and Mayas. Recent advances in genetic technology have indicated that early settlers in a 8000-year-old site in Florida had little contact with outsiders over the village's 1000-year history. This conclusion has been reached by medical researchers who examined 8000-year-old tissue samples of numerous remains in a burial ground. The early results indicated these people changed very little genetically from generation to generation meaning that they likely had little or no contact with outside populations [*The Miami Herald* (January 23 1992): 5B].
10. Peterson, *op. cit.*, p. 104.
11. These "divisions" were named *Calpulli*. Their most important duty was the redistribution of land which occurred, at most, once every four years.
12. Burland, C., and Forman, W. *The Aztecs. Gods and Fate in Ancient Mexico*, Orbis, London, 1985.
13. Gallenkamp, C. Maya. *The Riddle and Rediscovery of a Lost Civilization*, David McKay Company, New York, 1976. Occasionally peasants might have been employed in the lower levels of this bureaucracy or filled certain posts on a rotating basis with positions of authority periodically changing, allowing adult males to work their way up a hierarchical ladder by holding a series of increasingly prestigious offices.

14. Morley, S. G., and Brainerd, G. W. *The Ancient Maya*, 4th edition. Revised by Robert J. Sharer, Stanford University Press, Stanford, CA, 1983.

15. Calvani, V. *The World of the Maya*, Editions Minerva, Geneva, 1976.

16. The Incas tried to have provinces correspond as much as possible to the native kingdoms they had added to the empire, or to tribal groups. However, when these were too small to fit the Inca notion of administrative efficiency, they combined two or three of them to constitute a province. To the Incas, a province was a certain number of taxpayers, neatly fitted into a decimal system. The top taxpaying unit consisted of 10,000 persons and, to be recognized as a province, a territory had to have at least one such unit. Most provinces had between two and four such units (Karen, 1975, p. 97).

17. Martin, L. *The Kingdom of the Sun. A Short History of Peru*, Charles Scribner's Sons, New York, p. 10. Through the matchlessly logical administrative hierarchy which, since the days of the earlier Incas, had gradually grown to amazing efficacy, society was firmly welded vertically to the person of the ruler. The gravest lack of the Incaic system lay in the complete absence of horizontal bonds linking officials of equal rank. The flow of authority was ever from the top down through the orderly sequence of ranks to the lowest officials (Means, 1964, pp. 10–11).

18. Vega, G. *The Incas. The Royal Commentaries of the Incas*, Orion Press, New York, 1961, p. 157.

19. *Ibid.*, p. 22.

20. A fair tax would be one that treats equally people in equal economic circumstances. This is known as horizontal equity. But a fair tax should also treats people in unequal economic situation unequally. This is refer to as vertical equity. The ideal is that taxes should be distributed among taxpayers in relation to their ability to pay.

21. Peterson, *op. cit.*, p. 116.

22. Davies, N. *The Aztecs: A History*, G. P. Putnam's Sons, New York, 1973, p. 110.

23. Vega, *op. cit.*, p. 112.

24. Whitlock, R. *Everyday Life of the Maya*, G. P. Putnam's Sons, New York, 1976, p. 67. To assist in governing outlying villages, magistrates known as *batab* (axe bearers) were selected. Essentially they functioned as provincial mayors, keeping a close rein on local government, judicial matters, and overseeing the collection of tributes paid by the peasants to the hierarchy.

25. Morley and Brainerd, *op. cit.*, p. 218.

26. Bennett, W. C. and Bird, B. B. *Andean Culture History*, Lancaster Press, New York, 1949, p. 221.

27. Vega, *op. cit.*, p. 125.

28. Mans, P. G. *Fall of the Inca Empire*, Gardian Press, Inc., New York, 1964, p. 11. Money was unknown and the myriad evils—avarice, corruption, cruelty, and oppression—which follows in its train were less present. Value alone was known, value in the form of flocks, utensils, apparel, food, drink, shelter, materials for handicrafts, and these came in abundance to all who would work for them diligently (Means, *Ibid.*, p. 11).

29. Burland and Forman, *op. cit.*, pp. 73–74.

30. *Ibid.*, p. 75.

31. Calvani, *op. cit.*, p. 59.

32. In what is now called the Classic Period, from 250 to 900 A.D., the Mayas built some 200 cities in southern Mexico, Guatemala, Belize and parts of Honduras and El Salvador. Places like Palenque, Tikal and Copan, with their soaring pyramids, represent the splendors of the period—though more recent discoveries have revealed that the civilization was prospering in the southern low lands of Guatemala even centuries before.

33. Henderson, J. S. *The World of the Ancient Maya*, Cornell University Press, Ithaca, NY, 1981, p. 152.

34. Booth, W. "Did Maya Tap Water for Power: Reservoir Network May Explain Success of Ancient Civilization." *The Washington Post* (February 18, 1991): A3. The ability to manage water lies at the center of vigorous debate over the rise and fall of the Maya. In much the same way that aggressive water management drew large populations to the arid landscape of Los Angeles and Phoenix, the Maya elite may have constructed elaborate systems to collect and store rainwater to draw settlers to their ceremonial centers.

35. Booth, *ibid.*, p. A3.

36. The Incas clustered the heads of families into groups of 10, 100, 500, 1000, and 10,000 men and placed

them under the direct authority of an Incan official whose rank in the Incan hierarchy depended on the number of individuals in his command. For example, a provincial governor had authority over 40,000 family heads. Imperial representatives, carefully instructed at court, periodically inspected all the subdivisions of the empire to audit accounts, revise policies, administer justice, and implement the emperor's directives (Martin, 1974, p. 14).

37. Martin, *op. cit.*, p. 14.
38. Hymans, E. and Ordish, G. *The Last of the Incas: The Rise and Fall of an American Empire*, Simon & Schuster, New York, 1963, p. 25.
39. Peterson, *op. cit.*, pp. 118–121.
40. Davies, *op. cit.*, p. 109.
41. Morley and Brainerd, *op. cit.*, p. 218.
42. Vega, *op. cit.*, p. 19.
43. Karen, *op. cit.*, pp. 101–104.
44. Meyer, C., and Gallenkamp, C. *The Mystery of the Ancient Maya*, Atheneum, New York, p. 76.
45. Meyer and Gallenkamp, *ibid.*, pp. 76–77.
46. Coe, M. D. *The Maya*, Thames & Hudson, New York, 1987, p. 130. Knowledge of Mayan thought represents only a tiny fraction of the whole picture. Out of thousands of books in which the full extent of their learning and ritual was recorded, only four have survived to modern times (three of them are prayer books). These are written on long strips of bark paper folded like screens and covered with gesso (Coe, 1987, p. 130).
47. Bennett and Bird, *op. cit.*, p. 220.
48. Martin, *op. cit.*, p. 12–13.

8

Roots to Branches

Tracing the Foundations of American Public Administration in Medieval England

John Carroll   *School of Public Administration, Florida Atlantic University, Fort Lauderdale, Florida*

I. INTRODUCTION

There are common assumptions in the field of public administration. It is often concluded that public administration is uniquely American in origin and design, with no substantial writings before 1880 (Argyle 1994a; Martin 1989). This notion is carried further when the first intellectual (Shafritz and Hyde 1992) or conscious (Stillman 1991) time line on American public administration begins with Woodrow Wilson's politics/administration dichotomy in his 1887 essay, "The Study of Administration" (Argyle 1994b; Henry 1992; Siffin 1991; Stillman 1991; Martin 1989). Neither belief is true. Argyle, Martin, Shafritz, and Hyde, as well as Waldo (1980) and Farazmand (1994), acknowledge that public administration is as old as civilization itself. The so-called "Seven Wonders of the Ancient World" may have been built by laborers, but they were also administered and managed by government authorities. France and Spain administered colonies in America long before Wilson's essay (Hopkins 1994).

The intent of this paper is to present evidence from an historical perspective that the American system of public administration and government can clearly trace its beginnings to the English system of government. The paper will put forward the notion that public administration is evolutionary, and many centuries of development and experiences existed prior to the establishment of the American constitutional system. It will begin with an essayed review of general public administration history, through to the beginnings of the American experience. The paper will then trace four periods of English history, using Humby's (1970) time line, to demonstrate the development of a public administration model. Many aspects of this model would later be adopted in America.

A. History of Public Administration

In the United States, we have a uniquely Western view of history and the world. We routinely trace the development of "history" back to the Renaissance, then medieval Europe, the Roman Empire, and ancient Greece. This is inaccurate, since we know that cities flourished along the Nile, Tigris and Euphrates, Yellow, and Indus rivers, not to mention the rainforests of Central and South America, the plains of what is now Iran, and in other locations. There were certainly people who administered those ancient cities, either through direct rule or as advisers to those who ruled.

Another Western misconception should be laid to rest. Civilization did not cease to exist when the Roman Empire fell in the fifth century of the Common Era. It continued to flourish and grow in China and the Far East, on the Indian subcontinent, in Africa, Australia, the Americas, and throughout the Middle East under Islamic rule. Aboriginal peoples built great pyramids and cities throughout the southwestern portions of North America, as well as in Central and South America. Complex societal structures existed in the Americas long before the arrival of the first colonial explorers and conquerors in the 16th century.

Except in areas that were geographically separated, like Australia and the Americas, ideas were able to flow throughout the ancient world. Cities, city-states, and nation-states established forms of governance. The ancients built roads, bridges, water transportation systems, and other public works projects. Ample physical evidence of their work can be found throughout Europe, North Africa, and the Middle East. They collected taxes and raised armies. Simply put, public administration existed. Methods of administration were passed along between different forms of government, communication through either conquest or trade, and generations of dynastic rulers.

We now know that philosophers such as Aristotle, Socrates, and Plato wrote about government. Their writings had implications for public administration. Many of their writings were translated to Latin and Arabic. Their ideas have been taught and adopted through the ages. When the great universities of Paris and Bologna were in their formative stages during the Middle Ages, a wealth of knowledge about ancient philosophers came from Arabic translations, brought to Spain by the Moors. Advisers to royalty in Islamic, Eastern, and Western nations would come to depend on university-educated men to manage their governments.

Religion has also had a heavy influence on public administration since ancient times. Monotheism was observed by Hebrews and Persians, long before the beginning of the Common Era. Worship in the system of multiple deities in Greece, Rome, Egypt, and India were integral to government operations. Christianity and Islam would also play important roles in public administration. Specifically, the Catholic Church was integral to the early development of Western monarchical governments (Bettenson 1963; Deansley 1969). During the Renaissance, reaction to the teachings of the Catholic Church would inspire Rationalist thinkers and the Protestant movement. The Communist movements of the 20th century repressed religious expression because of its perceived influence on those governed. In many respects today, religion continues to be influential in many national governments.

Indeed, public administration has a rich and ancient history. Throughout history, there have been contributions from various thinkers, each leaving his individual mark on the cumulative body of public administration.

B.   The American Experience

American public administration can clearly trace its start beyond the Founding Fathers to the Rationalist thinkers of the 17th and 18th centuries. Americans were colonial subjects of Great Britain, and replicated much of the British form of government. France exercised control over some Canadian and Louisiana territories, and Spain over areas such as the Florida peninsula. France and Spain are not considered in this context, although they also produced developmental administrative histories (Hopkins 1994; Stillman 1991). The system used by the British developed over a number of centuries, which can be traced back to the original Roman occupation. The Roman form of government was credited to Julius Caesar, who himself was heavily influenced by the Persian tradition of kingship and administration (Farazmand 1994). Vago (1991) traces the development of law along this same line.

Although government in America was relatively small until the turn of the past century, the

American style of public administration did not spring forth from its government overnight. It certainly did not suddenly evolve after Wilson's essay in 1887. At the time of the American Revolution, the colonies were basically a homogeneous society of English descent. The colonies adopted the English form of governing, from the local (municipal) to county (shire) levels almost in its entirety. Before the American constitutional system was established, the colonies considered themselves separate entities. When they severed ties to Great Britain in the Declaration of Independence, it was as 13 independent states. Each had its own form of government that resembled, in varying degrees, the English system. This exclusive independence was safeguarded in the Articles of Confederation and in the peace treaty signed with Britain ending the American Revolution (Berger 1987). When the Constitution replaced the Articles of Confederation, ideas borrowed from English thinkers continued to inspire the Founding Fathers. The unique model of federalism set down in the late 18th century by Americans developed into the styles of government and public administration we recognize today.

The men who would become known in America as the Founding Fathers were aware of the history that preceded them. For example, about one-half of the delegates to the Constitutional Convention were lawyers (Diamond 1981), considering themselves learned men. Those who helped form the American system were educated men who had served in either elective or administrative government roles from the end of the colonial period. Even though the Constitution does not mention the word "administration," the Founding Fathers anticipated that federal institutions would have to be established (Beach et al. 1997). The Founding Fathers were themselves administrators in local, state, and national government, or had experience serving in government. Many, from the signing of the Declaration of Independence on, would serve in positions through the Constitutional Convention and beyond. The founders knew they had to have administration (Beach et al. 1997).

In addition to the concepts of separate presidential and judicial branches, the American Constitution created a legislative branch that was further divided into two houses. Early bicameral legislatures, like the Roman senate, were supposed to counterbalance the popular will as expressed through other governing organs. In practice, the Roman senate was selected by the aristocratic patricians; that is, it represented a social and economic class. The upper house in the English system, the Lords, functioned similarly. It was hereditary noble body counterbalancing the commoners (Diamond 1981:96). The American federal legislative system of a lower chamber (House of Representatives) and an upper chamber (Senate) was similarly designed.

The earlier systems presupposed an aristocratic society, divided into different classes, with the divided houses mirroring this societal structure (Diamond 1981). A bicameral legislative system was part of the ancient idea of the mixed regime. The theory was that the best practical government was one that blended the three pure forms of monarchy, aristocracy, and democracy. A king would superintend the general interests of society, separate bodies would represent the aristocracy and general citizenry, and the three would be checks upon the others (Diamond 1981:96). A similar system in choosing U.S. senators existed until the 17th Amendment to the Constitution in 1913, which permitted direct election instead of selection by respective state legislatures. One could probably argue that today's body of U.S. senators more closely resembles its predecessors in the English House of Lords and the Roman senate as an aristocratic noble class, rather than representative of the "commoners" as it is purported.

II. "ROOTS TO BRANCHES": EVOLUTION OF GOVERNMENT AND PUBLIC ADMINISTRATION IN ENGLAND

Any discussion of the government of England in medieval times must begin with the king because he was its heart and driving force. Government was *his* government. It was conducted in his name and he personally made many of its decisions (Brown 1989). The English system of government and its public administration developed over centuries, borrowing from the Roman system that was later reinforced by the Christian church. As England grew in size and complexity, so did its government. This section will trace (in linear fashion) from the post-Roman days to the fully formed Parliament of 1461. Since the actions of English government were so closely identified with the ruler of the time, the time line of rulers (Table 1) has been provided to assist tracking the periods being reviewed. All years are considered to fall within the Common Era, unless otherwise mentioned.

A. Post–Roman/Anglo-Saxon Period (802–1066)

The history of Roman Britain stretched back beyond the invasion of Julius Caesar, to the time when Roman traders first exchanged small quantities of prestige goods with Celtic tribal chiefs. Shortly after the fall of Rome, sub-Roman communities were conquered by the ascendant Anglo-Saxon tribes (Hodges 1989:34). The concept of "kingship" was created on the eve of the first Christian missions to England (Bettenson 1963; Deansley 1969; Hodges 1989:41–42), reinforcing the ancient Roman system before it. More often than not, polities were short-lived, lineage chiefs were murdered, and there was little opportunity to create a sociopolitical system in which kinsmen and tribesmen walked in the chief's footprints (Hodges 1989:70–71). The Church provided the apparatus by which tribal leaders could mobilize labor for public works and military duties. Among the packages of ideas introduced by the Church were the notion of time itself, writing, and the invention of languages (Bettenson 1963; Deansley 1969; Hodges, 1989:190). The introduction, survival, and diffusion of English dialects, supplanting Celtic and Latin, could well be a consequence of the aboriginal circumstances of the fifth century, the cultural homogeneity of

Table 1 Kings of England, 802–1066

Reign	Monarch
802–839	Ecgberth
839–855	Aethelwulf
855–860	Aethelbald
860–866	Aethelberht
866–871	Aethelred I
871–899	Aelfred (the Great)
899–925	Eadward (the Elder)
925–939	Aethelstan (first monarch of all England)
940–946	Eadmund I (the Magnificent)
946–955	Eadred
955–959	Eadwy (the Fair)
959–975	Edgar
975–979	Eadward II (the Martyr)
979–1016	Aethelred II (the Unready)
1016	Eadmund II (Ironside)
1017–1035	Cnut I
1035–1040	Harold I
1040–1042	Cnut II
1042–1066	Edward the Confessor
	Harold II

Source: Humby (1970).

the community, and the powerful need to create a past for political purposes after about 600 (Hodges 1989:191).

Of course, England was by no means unified. Until the Viking invasions of the 860s there were many territories that owed their origins to postcolonial days. Anglo-Saxon England consisted of 30 or more kingdoms and groupings at this time. Peer-polity interaction (political competition and emulation among these territories) was indisputably a mechanism for unequal change and development between 600 and 900 (Hodges 1989:191). The English identity was born in the peculiar circumstances of the fifth and sixth centuries, and in the absence of the Church. The competition between these forces fueled the evolution of both, building upon fundamental social attributes originating in the fifth century. This powerful meshing of political and tribal aspirations must have stimulated the competition between the great kingdoms of England over the following century. By this time, England was also well advanced in the evolution of individual rights (Hodges 1989:200–201). Historians are now stressing the existence of basic administrative and social growth from late Saxon to Norman times. Central power was fully exercised in conjunction with local freedoms through shire (county) courts (Hodges 1989:201).

Divisions of government and responsibilities of officials were evident in this period. The highest official under the king was the *ealdorman*. The retention of the title *high-reeve* in the North may suggest that in early times *gerefa* had a wider application and was not used only of officials inferior to the ealdorman. In the 11th century the word *ealdorman* became *earl* (Whitelock 1955:63–64). His jurisdiction seems to have been the shire. From the second half of the 10th century, it was common for an ealdorman to have more than a single shire under him (Whitelock 1955:64). Like the king, the ealdorman had some rights over lands held by others, which had to be bought out by those who wished for immunity (Whitelock 1955:65).

The title *sheriff* is used in Cnut's (1017–1035) reign, and a *shire-man*, which represents the same official, occurs in documents between 964 and 988. The term *sheriff* is believed to be a derivative of *shire-reeve*. Some of the references to the king's *reeve* may refer to a sheriff, but it is a more general term and includes men in charge of royal estates, whose duties included the exercise of justice as well as the management of the royal estate and the collection of the king's farm. The reeve presided at a popular court (called a *hundred court* from the mid-10th century, or, in the Danelaw, a *wapentake*) at which suits were judged and to which traders brought the men they were taking into the country. The reeve collected the fines and took possession of forfeited property. The reeve arranged the execution of a convicted criminal. The reeve had many other duties. It was a busy life that was full of temptation and opportunities for corruption (Whitelock 1955:66).

Edward the Confessor (1042–1066), like his predecessors, governed in consultation with his *magnates*, or advisore, and the Anglo-Saxon Chronicle gives many indications of the meeting of his *witan*, or council. The composition of the witan in the earlier half of the 11th century differed little from what it had been in the 10th. It normally consisted of three classes of persons: great ecclesiastics, great lay nobles, and lesser men who attended either as officials of the royal household or for some special reason at the king's command. The witan might be consulted by the king on any act of government, on the promulgation of laws, on the levying of taxes, on diplomacy or defense, or in connection with the solemn ratification of grants of land or privilege. Its function was in the simplest sense to counsel the king (Douglas and Greenaway 1953:50). The witan would eventually develop into the parliament and bureaucracy of English government.

B.   Norman Conquest/Angevin Rulers (1066–1199)

In 1066, when Edward the Confessor died childless, the Anglo-Danish realm had an open choice of claimants to the throne (Warren 1985:7). Unfortunately for King Harold (1066), the kingdom of England was too tempting a prize for those who thought they had a better claim. Duke William of Normandy thought that the wealth of England could buy him enough knights to make Normandy the dominant power in northern France (Warren 1985:8). The Battle of Hastings gave Duke William the crown (1066–1087), but it did not give him the kingdom. The Norman conquest of England did not take place suddenly in 1066, but bitterly between 1068 and 1075 (Warren 1985:8). See Table 2 for reigning monarchs from 1066 to 1199.

The Norman Conquest had brought many changes to England, not least of which were the introduction of a French-speaking aristocracy in church and state. This French connection was reinforced in 1154 when Henry I's (1100–1135) grandson, Henry of Anjou (1154–1189), succeeded Stephen (1135–1154) as king and so linked England and Normandy with extensive territories in the west and southwest of France, thus creating the Angevin Empire (Duggan 1985:25). The feudal organization which was set up by the Norman kings marked the opening of a new era in English government. The lower ranks of society were less affected than their superiors by the events of 1066–1070. There remained in England a strong tradition of local administration which had already been crystallized into institutions. It was indeed a characteristic achievement in the Norman aristocracy to utilize existing organs of local government, and it was an essential part of the political genius of William the Conqueror, not only to respect local custom, but to develop the institutions of monarchy which he found existing in the land he conquered (Douglas and Greenaway 1953:49).

The essence of government was personal monarchy: The king governed the realm and summoned to his assistance those men who he thought could best help him in his work. In this sense the nucleus of the *curia* was the king's household, where his most intimate and trusted servants were found. The chancellor took his place alongside the king's huntsmen, and prominent officials included stewards, chamberlains, and butlers. Throughout this period the holders of the chief household offices, designated by humble title, were among the most important men in the land, and among the most influential members of the king's council (Douglas and Greenaway 1953:52–53).

William was therefore fortunate in succeeding to a monarchy that had been able to create a system of tax collection which had been regularly used to raise the *gelds*, and more particularly the Danegelds. When such a geld was levied, its total amount was decided in the king's council, and this was partitioned in a defined proportion among the various shires. Even the mechanism of tax collecting changed little. The Norman practice of allowing the sheriff to "farm" his shire (paying the king an agreed sum for the shire and later recouping from what he could actually raise from its inhabitants) was almost certainly in operation in the time of Edward the Confessor. The king had his Treasury at Winchester, and decisions relating to financial policy were decided by the king in

Table 2   Kings of England, 1066–1199

Reign	Monarch
1066–1087	William I (the Conqueror)
1087–1100	William II (Rufus the Red)
1100–1135	Henry I
1135–1154	Stephen
1154–1189	Henry II
1189–1199	Richard I

Source: Humby (1970).

consultation with his whole court. There was as yet no separate financial organization (Douglas and Greenaway 1953:54).

A hierarchical structure of public administration had already existed in most of England at the time of the Norman Conquest. England had been divided into *hundreds* (in the south) and *wapentakes* (in the north). These were grouped into shires under the authority of sheriffs, and shires were in turn grouped into regional governorships under the authority of earls. The Conquest had altered this structure in several ways: hundreds, wapentakes, and shires were retained, but the earldoms were swept away in their old form, the title "earl" with different powers being preserved for a few favored individuals. Into the basic structure were inserted two more specialized kinds of government agents: those who held the newly built castles for the king, and the officials appointed to look after newly created hunting reserves. (Green 1986).

Not until the reign of Henry I can there be discerned the beginnings of those changes which in time were to produce the English exchequer. By the accession of Henry II, the transformation was far advanced, and before his death, the organization created for the control of royal finance was contained in the *Dialogue of the Exchequer.* The Lower Exchequer counted the receipt and payment of money. The work of the lower exchequer was supervised by deputies of the treasurer and the chamberlains. The upper exchequer was the court supervisor of financial policy and passed judgment on all questions relating to royal finance. The upper exchequer was where the king himself might preside, if his place was not taken by his justiciar. In this court would be the great officers of the king's household: the chancellor, the marshall, the chamberlains, and other members of the curia as the king might summon for this purpose (Douglas and Greenaway, 1953:54–55).

Medieval kings had little time, even if they had the inclination or capacity, for routine administrative matters: Kingship was about much more than totting up accounts. Henry I spent much of his public life in military campaigning or in governmental activity in a wider sense, moving about his dominions, presiding over councils, dispensing patronage, and receiving emissaries. Yet his court was in a very real sense the center of government as well as of political life, and the knights of his household formed the nucleus of his army. The king personally presided over the hearing of important legal cases. He confirmed charters, issued new ones, or directed a course of action to be taken in individual disputes. Though the need for delegation was growing, it was still the king who gave the orders. He must have known his servants personally, and their high caliber was a direct reflection of his own ability to choose men who would serve him well. At every stage, therefore, administration could not help but be shaped by the king's personality and his style of kingship (Green 1986).

In other areas of law the Norman Conquest had far-reaching effects. The crown greatly enlarged its criminal jurisdiction and swept away the old compensatory tariffs. Old English law had made a basic distinction between those few heinous offenses for which no compensation could be paid, and the rest, for which compensation could be paid in due measure to the kin, the lord, or the king. The most serious offenses were now called *felonies.* The remainder were termed *misdemeanors*, offenses against the king which placed property and sometimes also land at the king's mercy. Thus the crown had not only increased the range of offenses subject to its jurisdiction but had also kept profits from the penalties imposed (Green 1986).

The growth of the judicial power of the king is perhaps the most important of all the English constitutional developments of these years (Douglas and Greenaway, 1953:57). It became the practice for the king's justice to use a jury to help ascertain the truth regarding facts that were under dispute, and the collective verdict given by selected men upon oath rapidly became a normal feature of such royal pleas. It is very possible that the employment of this device owed something to earlier English practice, particularly in the Danelaw, but its use certainly became much more common in the early Norman period, and it then became specifically associated with the royal administration (Douglas and Greenaway 1953:58).

The two centuries from 1050 to 1250 were a period of general resurgence in all aspects of European life—intellectual, religious, aesthetic, and political—in an environment of urban renewal and economic expansion characterized by an internationalism, a confidence, and a dynamism unknown since the fall of the Roman Empire (Duggan 1985:31). Most English scholars who returned home from the continental universities took influential positions in church and state. From the 1130s onwards, they formed a distinct professional elite, conscious of their status, and careful to record their educational achievement by retaining the title of *magister* (master), which they had acquired in the schools. The kings, from Henry I onward, systematically recruited magistri to staff their expanding administration, so that by 1200 the English monarchy was far in advance of the French in its employment of *schoolmen* (Duggan 1985:33). The "abbot's petition" establishes links between the growth of scholasticism in the 12th century (usually treated as intellectual and cultural history) and the bureaucratic government of 13th-century England (usually treated as legal and constitutional history) (Clanchy 1975:671). By 1200, law had become the dominant and indispensable subject in the schools, superior to the seven liberal arts and acknowledging no equal, except divinity (Clanchy 1975:671).

An important part of the process of professionalization of government under Henry II and his sons was an increasing use of written records. This reliance upon the written word can be seen in the royal courts with their plea rolls, the feet of fines, and judicial writs (Turner 1976:454). The great records of the time, such as *Domesday Book* and the early *Geld Rolls*, are themselves the outcome of a government which exercised control over all the departments of administration. The financial records of the 12th century such as the *Pipe Rolls* are at once a product and an illustration of the practice of the Exchequer whose operations are described with such fidelity in the *Dialogue of the Exchequer* (Douglas and Greenaway 1953:393). Casting accounts in Roman numerals necessitated mastering the complexities of the abacus. As feudal services began to be commuted to money payments, and as the king's exchequer started cumulative and systematic record keeping, every lord of knights in England needed a clerk and accountant who could make a formal record (Clanchy 1975:685).

This influx of trained men into public administration helped the establishment of stable bureaucratic institutions (exchequer, chancery, and judiciary) to support and implement royal government. Under Henry I, the exchequer was organized as an efficient accounting office, with an annual audit of royal income drawn up each year at Michaelmas (29 September) and recorded on the *Treasurer's Roll*, called the *Great Roll of the Pipe*. The earliest surviving *Pipe Roll* (1129–1130) shows a mature financial office in operation. By the end of the 12th century the English government was one of the most advanced and professional bureaucracies of the West, staffed by trained men and producing three main categories of written public records: (1) the *Exchequer Rolls* for finance; (2) the *Curia Regis Rolls* for recording the judgments of the royal courts; and (3) the *Chancery Rolls* for recording the charters and directives issued by the royal chancery (Duggan 1985:36).

Service in the royal government likewise provided a measure of economic security and held out the possibility of advancement. The demand for competent, professional administrators in all phases of royal and baronial administration had grown over the preceding century (Waugh 1980:855). In these years, national and local politics reflected the symbiotic relationship of patronage: The king and magnates needed as many loyal supporters as possible to confront one another and express their will, while landowners needed the protection of powerful patrons for their disputes (Waugh 1980:863). Royal patronage was the surest way to ascend the social ladder in the Middle Ages, so that fortunate men of humble origin might rise to spectacular heights, if they attracted the king's attention (Turner 1976:453).

Table 3   Kings of England, 1199–1272

Reign	Monarch
1199–1216	John
1216–1272	Henry III

Source: Humby (1970).

C.   Magna Carta/Forest Charter (1199–1272)

In 1215, a powerful group of English barons rose in rebellion against King John (1199–1216) at Runnymede and forced him to set his seal to Magna Carta—the most famous document in English history (Gillingham 1985:41). There had also been rebellions against William I, William II (1087–1100), Henry I, Stephen, Henry II, and Richard (1189–1199)—in other words, against every king since the Norman Conquest (Gillingham 1985:41). Yet in 1215, Magna Carta was an abysmal failure. It was meant to be a peace treaty, a formula that would put an end to the conflict between king and barons. In fact, civil war broke out again within three months of the meeting at Runnymede (Gillingham 1985:42). It was during this period that the Angevin Empire would collapse.

The rebels of 1215 were following a path marked out, not by former rebels, but by kings. Kings had granted charters before to individuals and to communities—ecclesiastical communities and urban communities. Then there were the communities of the shire. From the 1190s onward, Richard and then John began to grant rights and privileges to shire communities. From here it was a natural progression to conceive of the whole realm as a community, a corporate body capable of possessing rights and liberties. More than a century earlier indeed, in the year 1100, Henry I had granted a charter "to all his barons and faithful men." By the winter of 1214, Johns's opponents had resurrected this charter and were using it as a frame around which they could formulate their own demands. They were helped in this by some of the grievances which were uppermost in their minds that had also been dealt with in Henry I's charter, particularly abuses of royal patronage (Gillingham 1985:45–46).

The liberties granted by the king to his vassals, as in Magna Carta, were to be passed on to their men. Insofar as they governed by virtue of their franchises, lords would have found themselves under pressure from their tenants to grant political liberties. Restrictions on the number and the activities of *serjeants* of the peace, and others appointed or elected to enforce the laws, was a common concession by lords to their men. Yet liberties granted by charter remained by definition privileges, even when the recipients were communities. They were not the rights of individual citizens (Harding 1980:433–434).

The Forest Charter of 1217 established the administrators of forest laws. The royal forests were put under the direction of two justices of the forest. Below these officials was a *warden* for each forest who administered forest law at the local level, hearing and determining lesser offenses (trespasses of grazing animals, cutting brush, killing lesser game) than taking venison or oak trees. The latter were reserved for forest *eyres*. Foresters, both riding and walking, did most of the daily patrolling along with their assistants, called *garcons*. Their job was to arrest those caught in the act of poaching or find evidence for an attachment (arrest) when a poaching had obviously occurred. Foresters were normally appointees of the warden, but some held their positions by heredity and were called *foresters-in-fee*. In addition, foresters usually had four *verderers* elected to office in the county court. These men were selected from among the men of standing who had lands within the forest. The verderers were a part of the process of *attaching* (arresting or summoning) suspects in the local forest court and also presented a roll of attachments to the justices in eyre. The forest eyre justices made infrequent visits, but the population hated them no less for it, probably because the continued surveillance of the various forest officials kept the enforcement very visible (Hanawalt 1988:178–179).

Hunting was an integral part of aristocratic culture. It was the most esteemed pastime among peers and gentlemen, and for many of them it was also the most time-consuming. Hunting, both lawful and unlawful, retained an aura of danger and adventure. Indeed, hunting was not only a preparation for war, it was also a symbolic substitute for war (Manning 1992:185). The forest laws created the first officers who had a regular patrolling function and territory that was their beat (Hanawalt 1988:176). William the Conqueror established the royal forest in England (Hanawalt 1988:177). The subjects perceived the new forest laws as brutal, arbitrary, and an infringement on their long-established custom of using the forests for various products to supplement their economy or providing a sport requiring special skills (Hanawalt 1988:177).

By the 13th century roughly one-fourth of the land in England was turned over to royal forest, and in the process of creating homes for the king's deer, human dwellings were destroyed and people cleared from the land. Furthermore, forest administration required a set of laws and a judicial machinery that developed alongside common law but apart from it. Because the king mandated it rather than letting it evolve, as did common law, it always contained an arbitrary element. Abuses of the forest law were common among kings and their officials (Hanawalt 1988:178).

Despite this, the Magna Carta and the Forest Charter which grew out of it (also referred to as "the Charters") became synonyms for good government. Oaths and charters were the most binding things men knew. The sanction clause of Magna Carta 1215 was dropped from reissues because it may have gone too far against royalty. Still, Magna Carta was a public act, in charter form because no better was known, partaking of law, and given the publicity of law from the outset. It became the basis of efforts to secure government acceptable to the governed (Rothwell 1975:32–33). Early failures aside, Magna Carta would become the cornerstone of rights and freedoms in England.

D. Parliament and the Bureaucracy (1272–1461)

By 1272, England had a long history of ordered, literate royal government. Regular provision for writing the king's letters and handling his revenues had begun in late Anglo-Saxon times and by 1200 had developed into the highly organized offices of chancery and exchequer. During the Middle Ages, their workload and their records expanded further and two additional writing-offices, the *Privy Seal* and the *Signet*, were created. This was a true bureaucracy, bound to established proce-

Table 4   Kings of England, 1272–1461

Reign	Monarch
1272–1307	Edward I
1307–1327	Edward II
1327–1377	Edward III
1377–1399	Richard II
1399–1413	Henry IV
1413–1422	Henry V
1422–1461	Henry VI

Source: Humby (1970).

dures and proper warrants, keeping files, enrolling copies and served by career clerks. Westminster was their normal place of work and by the 14th century was the administrative capital (Brown 1989).

A medieval king had two main sources of income: First, his profits from land and lordship—what might be termed his traditional revenues; and secondly, taxation. In theory, a feudal king had no right to impose general taxation on his people. In other words, he needed to establish his right to tax all his subjects, and since in theory he had no right to take taxes, he had no option but to obtain consent for them (Given-Wilson 1985:55). To win consent for general taxation, the king had to prove that he needed the money. So gradually a compromise evolved: The king's requests for taxation would be based on a plea of national emergency, and in practice this almost invariably meant a military emergency. It might be defensive, the threat of foreign invasion, for example; or it might be offensive, such as the need to send an army abroad. Thus, the king claimed it was in the national interest to deal with a threat to the nation, that a tax should be granted. Public money must be raised to be spent in the public interest (Given-Wilson 1985:56–57).

It was in order to finance warfare that taxation was granted, and it was largely in order to get consent for taxation that parliaments were summoned. But the equation is not quite as simple as that. The word *parliament* first appears in England in the 1240s, and at this time it was an extended meeting of the king's council. In the very beginnings of parliament, taxation did not play an important role. Parliament comes from the French verb *parler*—to talk. The earliest parliaments were essentially discussion meetings. They provided an opportunity for the king to gather information, to issue ordinances, to dispense justice. Henry III (1216–1272) held about 17 parliaments, which were considered disorganized affairs. Their composition varied enormously, their functions were ill-defined, and they had no rules for procedure (Given-Wilson 1985:59–60).

The 30 or 40 years after the death of Edward I (1272–1307) saw a rapid change in parliament. From an ill-recorded and ill-defined assembly, parliament became a consistent, almost regular composition, developing procedures and the beginnings of recognized rights. Parliament became absolutely distinct from any other assembly. The lords were summoned as individuals. The "representative" knights, townsmen, and lower clergy also attended to make it a recognized assembly of the whole community. By midcentury, parliament possessed a number of the classic features of the English parliament (Brown 1989). By the 1330s, membership was largely defined by custom and practice, not by enactment. The members of parliament fell into two groups, those summoned individually—the lay and spiritual lords, justices, councillors, and clerks; and those chosen locally to represent their communities—the county knights, citizens and burgesses, barons, and representatives of the lower clergy. In 1272, there was little established custom, but by 1461 there were firm customs which lasted for centuries. There was a remarkable regularization of membership between the 1290s and the 1330s. From the 1370s on, there was a striking growth of interest in parliament among the political community (Brown 1989).

The late Middle Ages saw the creation not merely of a House of Lords but also of the concept of an hereditary peerage with several grades and privileges. In 1272, there were only two grades of lords: a small number of earls whose titles were hereditary, and a large number of military tenants of the crown called "barons," who did not form a coherent group and whose numbers were uncertain. By 1461, there were five grades of peer: dukes, marquesses, earls, viscounts, and a modest number of barons who had the title "lord." All were normally summoned to parliament, and passed the privilege to their heirs (Brown 1989).

Taxation was important in the origins of parliament because it gave shape, and permanence, and ultimately, power to original gatherings. By the middle of the 14th century, it was laid down by statute that only parliaments (in practice, the House of Commons) could grant the king taxation. The composition of parliament was also well established, and there were clear procedural guidelines. Parliament had become an institution (Given-Wilson 1985:68).

III. A NOTION OF EVOLUTIONARY DEVELOPMENT

Taking a longer perspective of English government, one might conclude that a constantly evolving form of government can be traced from Roman colonial era to the later Middle Ages (Hodges 1989:201). For centuries, England had the most professionally trained bureaucracy in Europe. By 1400, England had a fully formed government with branches of executive (king), judiciary (courts and assizes), legislative (parliament), and bureaucracy (chancery and exchequer).

The period 1189 to 1327 is best known for its constitutional history. It could be said that it was the 14th century, not the 13th, that was decisive for constitutional development. The real achievement of 1189–1327 was administrative and legal monarchy, but not limited monarchy. This period saw the further development of common law (Rothwell 1975:27) and individual rights. The marked expansion in royal government continued a development begun in the 12th century. As we know, Henry I organized the exchequer for accounting and called for the annual audit at Michaelmas, on 29 September of each year. This is coincidentally almost the same day that marks the end of the fiscal year in the United States government, as well as numerous state and local governments (30 September each year).

Development in English public administration continued over the centuries. By 1200, both the chancery and the exchequer were established offices and keeping elaborate records. By 1300, both had finally cast off their connection with the Household. By 1400, they were busier, more highly departmentalized, and more independent offices. The quantity of their records is evidence of the growing amount of government. By the mid-14th century the number of letters issued in the king's name by chancery and the other offices and courts was probably in excess of 100,000 a year. There was more government, more record of government, and more than growth in quantity (Brown 1989)—there was a true bureaucracy and a divided system of governing prior to the Renaissance.

By the 15th century, many English provincial towns had been accumulating liberties and privileges from the royal government for over three hundred years (Attreed 1992:207). By the later Middle Ages, the influence of biblical writings and those of Aristotle and Aquinas had inculcated basic concepts of positive law, custom, and the role of the monarch in assuring justice for his subjects (Attreed 1992:208). Moreover, the English had lived long enough with the courts and assizes in which such philosophies found expression and application, that royal responsibility for doing justice, keeping the peace and providing a venue for settlement was commonplace (Attreed 1992:208). Later, the American system of justice would be almost entirely copied from the English system. Sheriffs, bailiffs, circuit court judges, the concepts of felonies and misdemeanors, common law, and many other terms are in use today. All of these would become the cornerstone of a system carried to America.

The English system of currency developed in the 11th century survived intact until 1971. The English system of judiciary and the courts, developed in the 12th century, remained intact until 1971. The chancery and exchequer exist as cabinet posts under the prime minister. The British monarchy survives, although in a very different form. It retains much of its tradition and ceremonial functions. Parliament in its present form is almost identical to its 15th-century version, although its responsibilities have changed as it accumulated power over the centuries.

The popular notion is that the period of history commonly referred to as the "Middle Ages" was one of steady decline and that no positive accomplishments came forth until the "rebirth" during the Renaissance. I believe this paper demonstrates this notion to be incorrect. A clear line in both the present-day systems of Great Britain and the United States can be traced to the post–Roman colonial era (Waldo 1980). Government, its attendant bureaucracy, and a system of rights and liberties in England developed over a period of centuries. A key here is the surviving documents of the time. Those documents exist in abundance. The fact that the English took to writing down their activities contributed greatly to the overall development of their government.

While remnants of the Forest Laws remain in England, they may be loosely compared with the National Parks system in America. Magna Carta is now revered as one of the most sacred secular documents of the Western world, though it failed miserably at the time it was written. Many of its components can be found in the Constitution of the United States, particularly within the Bill of Rights. In an age when countries rise and fall within a lifetime, and technology changes constantly, the system of government that developed during the Middle Ages in England took over 1000 years. Even after it developed into a form we can clearly recognize by 1461, it continued to change and evolve.

Within 30 years of the death of Henry VI in 1461, Christopher Columbus would make his first voyage to the new world. The coming Renaissance period would bring more changes, and the Age of Enlightenment would add great thinkers into the English debate over government. Stillman (1991:24) notes that the Founding Fathers had over "six centuries of British constitutional history and a century and a half of colonial self government that contained ample numbers of good and bad models for government."

Just over 300 years later, England's prize colonies in North America would break away for the very same reasons the barons of 1215 revolted against King John. In fact, England's history is replete with examples of civil war and rebellion against the king on the basis of taxes and rights, from the time of William the Conqueror until the "glorious revolution" of 1688. America's "Magna Carta" to King George III would be the Declaration of Independence; its "Runnymede," the city of Philadelphia. Stillman (1991) states that Americans followed the Tudor style of governance, which itself was firmly grounded in medieval routes, and that the Revolution against Britain came only after the colonies believed this style was corrupted by the 18th-century English (Germanic descent) monarchs. He points out that the Declaration of Independence was a list of grievances against British administrative abuses.

A clear path from the present to the past has been established. The "branches" of American public administration had their "roots" in England's medieval times. Further investigation could trace those roots to the ancients, which were certainly studied during the Middle Ages. As we know, European universities of the time translated Arabic, Greek, and Roman-era Latin into documents for students to study. University graduates became the foundation of medieval English bureaucracy. It is probably safe to presume these first professionally educated public administrators in England were influenced by the ancients. The path, therefore, may go back much further.

"With all due respect to the Constitution, the history of republican governance in America did not begin with the formation of the national government in 1789. Most of the institutional structure of contemporary American public administration is at levels where history stretches back many years before that time" (Beach et al. 1997:512).

IV. A CONCLUSIONARY NOTE FROM LUTHER GULICK

In a commentary on the state of American public administration written in 1990, Luther Gulick reflected on the strength of the American system of government as

> . . . the greatest gamble of history, a comprehensive written constitution (was enacted), providing for a federal system with a national government of limited powers and a tripartite division of these into executive, legislative, and judicial arms designed to restrict the power of any one branch to act unilaterally. The Constitution proved adaptable to historical demands over time and through great social and technological change. It was soon amended to include the Bill of Rights, initiating the amendment process that would over the years (together with judi-

cial interpretation) broaden citizenship after abolition of slavery and the Civil War, extend voting and other rights to women and to all citizens, and gradually establish equality under law (Gulick 1990:599).

While we borrowed heavily from the structures and ideas of the English system, the American contribution is unique. Unlike the English, we chose to codify our system in a written Constitution after our initial experiment at confederation failed. From the time prior to the Declaration of Independence and since, Americans have openly debated their path. We chose a form of government that resembled many aspects the England system from which we evolved. Luther Gulick spoke for the sentiments of many when he praised the American system. However, we should not overlook that public administration and government have existed since the dawn of civilization, which makes the American story a relatively new addition to that history.

REFERENCES

Argyle, N.J. (1994a). Public administration, administrative thought, and the emergence of the nation state. In A. Farazmand (ed.), *Handbook of Bureaucracy*, 1–16. New York: Marcel Dekker.

Argyle, N.J. (1994b). The emergence of the American administrative state: the intellectual origins. In A. Farazmand (ed.), *Handbook of Bureaucracy*, 385–398. New York: Marcel Dekker.

Attreed, L. (1992). Arbitration and the growth of urban liberties in late medieval England. *Journal of British Studies 31*(3), 205–235.

Beach, J.C., Carter, E.D., Dede, M.J., Goodsell, C.T., Guigard, R.M., Haraway, W.M., Kumar, M., Morgan, B.N., and Sweet, V.K. (1997). State administration and the founding fathers during the critical period. *Administration and Society 28*, 511–530.

Bean, J.M.W. (1989). *From Lord to Patron: Lordship in Late Medieval England.* Philadelphia: University of Pennsylvania Press.

Beardwood, A. (1950). Royal mints and exchanges. In J. Willard, W. Morris, and W. Dunham (eds.), *The English Government at Work, 1327–1336*, Vol. III: *Local Administration and Justice*, 35–66. Cambridge, MA: Medieval Academy of America.

Berger, R. (1987). *Federalism: The Founders' Design.* Norman, OK: University of Oklahoma Press.

Bettenson, H. (1963). *Documents of the Christian Church* (2nd ed.). New York: Oxford University Press.

Bowers, R.H. (1983). From rolls to riches: king's clerks and money lending in thirteenth century england. *Speculum 58*(1), 60–71.

Brieght, C.C. (1989). Duelling ceremonies: the strange case of William Hackett, Elizabethan Messiah. *Journal of Medieval and Renaissance Studies 19*(1), 35–67.

Brown, A.L. (1989). *The Governance of Late Medieval England: 1272–1461.* Stanford, CA: Stanford University Press.

Carpenter, D.A. (1985). King, magnates, and society: the personal rule of King Henry III, 1234–1258. *Speculum 60*(1), 39–70.

Carpenter, D.A. (1985). Working the land. In L. Smith (eds.), *The Making of Britain: The Middle Ages*, 87–100. New York: Schocken Books.

Clanchy, M.T. (1975). *Moderni* in education and government in England. *Speculum 50*(4), 671–688.

Clanchy, M.T. (1985). The written word: from Domesday Book to Caxton. In L. Smith (ed.), *The Making of Britain: The Middle Ages*, 163–177. New York: Schocken Books.

Deansley, M. (1969). *A History of the Medieval Church: 590–1500* (9th ed.). Cambridge: Cambridge University Press.

Diamond, M. (1981). *The Founding of the Democratic Republic.* Itasca, IL: F.E. Peacock.

Douglas, D.C., and Greenaway, G.W. (1953). *English Historical Documents: c. 1042–1189.* New York: Oxford University Press.

Duggan, A. (1985). The new Europeans. In L. Smith (ed.), *The Making of Britain: The Middle Ages*, 23–40. New York: Schocken Books.

Dunham, W.H. (1980). "The Books of Parliament" and "The Old Record," 1396–1504. *Speculum 55*(5), 694–712.

Dyer, C. (1994). The English medieval village community and its decline. *Journal of British Studies 33*(4), 407–429.

Farazmand, A. (1994). Bureaucracy, bureaucratization, and debureaucratization in ancient and modern Iran. In A. Farazmand (ed.), *Handbook of Bureaucracy*, 675–686. New York: Marcel Dekker.

Farazmand, A., and Carroll, J.J. (March 1997). Teaching conceptual foundations in public administration. In B. Woolridge (chair), *Teaching Ethics.* 20th Annual Conference on Teaching Public Administration, Virginia Commonwealth University, Richmond.

Gillingham, J. (1985). Magna Carta and royal government. In L. Smith (ed.), *The Making of Britain: The Middle Ages*, 41–54. New York: Schocken Books.

Given-Wilson, C. (1985). War, politics, and parliament. In L. Smith (ed.), *The Making of Britain: The Middle Ages*, 55–70. New York: Schocken Books.

Green, J.A. (1986). *The Government of England Under Henry I.* Cambridge: Cambridge University Press.

Gulick, L.H. (1990). Reflections on public administration, past and present. *Public Administration Review 50*, 599–603.

Hanawalt, B.A. (1988). Men's games, king's deer: poaching in medieval England. *Journal of Medieval and Renaissance Studies 18*(2), 175–193.

Harding, A. (1980). Political liberty in the Middle Ages. *Speculum 55*(3), 423–443.

Henry, N. (1992). *Public Administration and Public Affairs*, (5th ed.). Englewood Cliffs, NJ: Prentice Hall.

Hodges, R. (1989). *The Anglo-Saxon Achievement: Archeology & the Beginnings of English Society.* Ithaca, NY: Cornell University Press.

Hopkins, J.W. (1994). Administration of the Spanish Empire in the Americas. In A. Farazmand (ed.), *Handbook of Bureaucracy*, 17–28. New York: Marcel Dekker.

Humby, C.L. (1970). *Kings and Queens of England.* London: Caroline Humby Designs.

Manning, R.B. (1992). Poaching as a symbolic substitute for war in Tudor and early Stuart England. *Journal of Medieval and Renaissance Studies 22*(2), 185–210.

Martin, D.W. (1989). *The Guide to the Foundations of Public Administration.* New York: Marcel Dekker.

McRee, B.R. (1992). Religious guilds and civic order: the case of Norwich in the late Middle Ages. *Speculum 67*(1), 69–97.

Meyer, E.T. (1950). Boroughs. In J. Willard, W. Morris, and W. Dunham (eds.), *The English Government at Work, 1327–1336*, Vol. III: *Local Administration and Justice*, 105–141. Cambridge, MA: Medieval Academy of America.

Morris, W.A. (1940). Prelude: complexity and basic phases of administrative control. In J. Willard and W. Morris (eds.), *The English Government at Work, 1327–1336*, Vol. I: *Central and Prerogative Administration*, 3–81. Cambridge, MA: Medieval Academy of America.

Nederman, C.J., and Feldwick, A. (1991). To the court and back again: the origins and dating of the *Entheticus de Dognate Philosophorum* of John of Salisbury. *Journal of Medieval and Renaissance Studies 21*(1), 129–145.

Neilson, N. (1940). The forests. In J. Willard and W. Morris (eds.), *The English Government at Work, 1327–1336*, Vol. I: *Central & Prerogative Administration*, 394–467. Cambridge, MA: Medieval Academy of America.

Osber, R. (1986). The Jesse Tree in the 1432 London entry of Henry VI: messianic kingship and the rule of justice. *Journal of Medieval and Renaissance Studies 16*(2), 213–232.

Plucknett, T.F.T. (1940). Parliament. In J. Willard and W. Morris (eds.), *The English Government at Work, 1327–1336*, Vol. I: *Central & Prerogative Administration*, 81–128. Cambridge, MA: Medieval Academy of America.

Post, J. (1985). The king's peace. In L. Smith (ed.), *The Making of Britain: The Middle Ages*, 149–162. New York: Schocken Books.

Rothwell, H. (1975). *English Historical Documents: c. 1189–1327.* New York: Oxford University Press.

Rutgers, M.R. (1997). Beyond Woodrow Wilson: the identity of the study of public administration in historical perspective. *Administration and Society 29*, 276–300.

Shafritz, J.M., and Hyde, A.C. (1992). Early voices. In J. Shafritz and A. Hyde (eds.), *Classics of Public Administration*, 1–10. Belmont, CA: Wadsworth Publishing.

Siffin, W.J. (1991). The problem of development administration. In A. Farazmand (ed.), *Handbook of Comparative and Development Public Administration*, 5–14. New York: Marcel Dekker.

Stillman, R.J. II (1991). *Preface to Public Administration: A Search for Themes and Direction.* New York: St. Martin's Press.

Turner, R.V. (1976). The judges of King John: their background and training. *Speculum 51*(1), 447–461.

Vago, S. (1991). *Law and Society* (3rd ed.). Englewood Cliffs, NJ: Prentice Hall.

Waldo, D. (1980). *The Enterprise of Public Administration.* Novato, CA: Chandler & Sharp.

Warren, W.L. (1985). The outer edge of the Earth. In L. Smith (ed.), *The Making of Britain: The Middle Ages,* 7–22. New York: Schocken Books.

Waugh, S.L. (1980). The profits of violence: the minor gentry in the rebellion of 1321–1322 in Gloucestershire and Herefordshire. *Speculum 55*(4), 843–869.

Waugh, S.L. (1983). Reluctant knights and jurors: respites, exemptions, and public obligations in the reign of Henry III. *Speculum 58*(4), 937–986.

Whitelock, D. (1955). *English Historical Documents: c. 500–1042.* New York: Oxford University Press.

9

Comparing the Public and Private Sectors in the United States

A Review of the Empirical Research

J. Norman Baldwin   *Department of Political Science, University of Alabama,
Tuscaloosa, Alabama*

Quinton A. Farley   *Office of Regional Counsel, Environmental Protection Agency,
Dallas, Texas*

I. INTRODUCTION

Comparing the public and private sectors in the United States has been a favorite pastime of scholars and practitioners of public administration. Almost every introductory text in American public administration devotes a section to establishing the distinguishing features of each sector and justifying the study of public administration. Throughout this literature eight themes recur that appear to comprise the most fundamentally agreed upon distinguishing features of the public sector. These distinguishing features include:

1. Activities highly constrained by laws, rules, regulations, and procedures (i.e., red tape).
2. Fragmentation of authority, or multiple formal accountabilities (e.g., to one's agency, clientele, legislative bodies, courts, chief executives, regulatory agencies, citizen groups).
3. Activities highly scrutinized and constrained by informal, political influences (e.g., media, political parties, public opinion, elected officials, interest groups).
4. *Political* goals or ends (multiple goals evolving from the compromise of pluralistic interests, not simply profits or efficiency goals).
5. Vague or unclear goals that are often difficult to measure (e.g., "establish justice," "promote the general welfare," "educate the children").
6. A monopolistic provision of goods and services that is not subject to market influences.
7. Frequent leadership turnover (i.e., elected and appointed officials).
8. Objectives, powers, and activities that have very broad and profound impacts on people and society (e.g., national defense, public education, taxation, incarceration).

In addition to academic accounts of the fundamental distinctions of the public sector, the media and laymen consistently iterate four characteristics of government and public servants: (1) government is wasteful and inefficient; (2) public servants are insensitive, unmotivated "bureaucrats"; (3) public organizations provide excessive job security for their employees; and (4) one will never get ahead financially in a government job. Generally accompanying these criticisms are explicit and implicit assumptions that these problems are either unique to government or not as extreme in the private sector.

Despite this pervasive descriptive literature asserting the differences between the sectors, no one has endeavored a recent comprehensive review of the empirical research in order to determine whether the sectors differ as markedly as the descriptive accounts would lead us to believe.[1] This chapter therefore presents this review. From an academic viewpoint, such a review allows us to test the fundamental assumptions upon which the discipline of public administration is built. In so doing, it contributes insight into the traditional question of whether there ought to be an independent study of public administration or a generic study of management. A preponderance of empirically supported public-private differences would enhance the legitimacy of the discipline of public administration, whereas a paucity of empirically supported differences might fuel skepticism concerning further development of the discipline.

From an academic viewpoint, such as review also contributes to the theory-building process in public administration. The most commonly noted distinguishing features of the public sector explored in this review are not a set of propositions linked together in a theoretical perspective such as rationalism, political economy, democratic administration, or public choice. Nor does this review intend to support or propose a theory of public administration. Instead, this review explores the validity of common plausible assumptions concerning the differences between the sectors in an inductive test of the broader theory that the public and private sectors are different.

Finally, from a practical viewpoint, such a review endeavors to help determine the legitimacy of privatizing the provision of governmental services. If certain characteristics of the private sector are in fact unique and bring about a more efficient provision of goods and services, then privatization is a credible alternative as long as efficiency demands predominate political sentiments. If certain private-sector characteristics are not unique or do not bring about enhanced efficiency, then privatization potentially impedes the allocation of a variety of goods and values typically accomplished by the provision of goods and services in the public sector—for example, the accomplishment of equity in the provision of goods and services, due process rights of employees, political responsiveness, and representative bureaucracy.

II. METHOD

To simplify a review of 93 studies and hundreds of findings, we grouped the studies into seven major categories. The categories were initially determined by grouping studies that investigated the same variable. They were expanded by including studies that investigated variables that were very similar or at least indirectly related to the core variable in the category. As a consequence, the three most common themes emerging as a basis for the categories were (1) compensation, (2) organizational performance (e.g., efficiency, effectiveness, and productivity), and (3) employee characteristics. Three additional themes emerging were (1) job security, (2) effects of the work environment on employees (e.g., job satisfaction and need fulfillment), and (3) external appeal of the sectors. A final category included the remaining studies, which were too diverse or too few in numbers to constitute an independent category with at least five studies.

III. FINDINGS

A. Compensation

The findings from 26 comparative compensation studies indicate fairly consistently that public employees enjoy better compensation than private employees. Moreover, several-studies (Bellante and Long 1981; Long 1982; Smith and Nock 1980; Smith 1976a, 1978) indicate that public employees earn more than private employees when adjusting or controlling for such factors as work responsibilities; employee education, training, and productivity; fringe benefits; and unemployment probabilities. In short, public employees earn more than private employees with comparable jobs, education, training, and productivity. They also earn more than private employees, considering the financial value of fringe benefits and job security (Fogel and Lewin 1974).

Despite these findings, the findings from several studies and subsamples of studies indicate the opposite. The most significant of these studies (Smith 1976b) found that male state and local government employees earn less than their private-sector counterparts. Although their samples of employee wages were substantially more narrow than Smith's, Quinn (1979) and Porter and Keller (1981) also found that local government employees earn less than private employees.

Surprisingly, almost all the studies evaluating public and private compensation according to employee perceptions of compensation and self-report measures of satisfaction with compensation indicate that public compensation is not as substantial or satisfying as private compensation. The two most impressive studies (Kilpatrick et al. 1964; Lawler 1965), however, were conducted before the Federal Pay Comparability Act of 1970 was enacted, and the remaining studies (Barton and Waldron 1978; Newstrom et al. 1976; Nowlin 1982) are so narrow in scope that it would be difficult to generalize from their findings.

Overall, in contrast to the other studies reviewed in this chapter, the compensation studies are quite sophisticated. There are many studies, the cross section of employees' wages surveyed is broad, the samples are large, the data are predominantly nonperceptual, and the data analysis is fairly sophisticated (e.g., multiple regression, analysis of variance). Generalizations concerning public versus private compensation, however, often mask the wide variations which exist between different classes and types of jobs (Havemann and Lanouette 1978). For example, while the majority of federal employees may fare better in compensation than their private-sector counterparts, the salaries of political appointments and high-level career executives cannot come close to the six- and seven-digit salaries of their equivalents in corporate America. Generalizations about public versus private compensation can also mask wide variations that exist from state to state and locality to locality.

B. Organizational Performance

The 57 studies that compare public and private efficiency, effectiveness, productivity, and other outcomes indicate inconsistent findings, but generally reflect more favorably on private organizations. The four studies of school systems (Bryan and Smiley 1983; Coleman et al. 1982; Murname 1983; Oates 1981) generally suggest that students in private schools attain higher achievement test scores than students in public schools. Two studies comparing the efficiency of water utilities (Bruggink 1982; Crain and Zardkoohi 1978) yield contradictory findings. Eight studies comparing the efficiency of electric utilities (Hellman 1972; Meyer 1975; Moore 1970; Neuberg 1977; Peltzman 1971; Spann 1977; Wallace and Junk 1970; Yunker 1975) also yield contradictory findings, but generally reflect more positively on the performance of public utilities. Finally, four of five studies of refuse collection systems (Hirsch 1965; Pier et al. 1974; Savas 1977, 1980; Savas and Brettler 1977; Stevens 1984) indicate that public systems exceed the performance of private systems.

Four organizational performance studies identified investigate a diversity of public and private organizations. In a comparison of 10 public and 11 private organizations providing a variety of goods and services, the National Center for Productivity and Quality of Working Life (NCPQ) (1978) concluded that the private sector is more "effective" than the public sector. They base their conclusion, however, on findings from an aggregation of studies that was not designed to systematically compare public- and private-sector effectiveness (e.g., the studies utilized different questionnaires with different measures). Golembiewski et al. (1982), in turn, concluded that organization development interventions are equally successful in both sectors. Although they also base their conclusion on findings from an aggregation of studies, given the 574 cases of organization development interventions investigated, their conclusion is more generalizable across public and private organizations than the NCPQ's. Stevens (1984), in turn, compared 20 southern California cities and found that municipal provision of services was more expensive than private contracting in seven of eight service areas. Finally, Bruce et al. (1985) compared 29 private and 16 public organizations and found no significant differences in organization responsiveness to clientele.

In addition to the performance studies reviewed here, Perry (1984) identified 13 studies that compare the performance of public and private transit systems. Six indicate that private transit systems are more efficient, four indicate the opposite, and three indicate no difference in sector performance. Savas (1982), in turn, identified nine studies that compare the performance of public and private health-care systems, including nursing homes, general hospitals, and health insurance providers. Eight findings from these studies reflect more positively on the private sector, two on the public sector, and six reflect no difference in sector health-care provision. He also identified four studies that compare the cost of public and private education and found public education to be more costly than private education.

Isolated comparative performance studies also exist in service areas ranging from fire protection and day care to legal aid and tree trimming (Ahlbrandt 1973; Bennett and Johnson 1980; City of San Francisco 1972; Hayes 1977; Hermann et al. 1977; Krashinsky 1978; Patton 1973). Moreover, public-private performance comparisons are frequently reported in newspaper articles and Congressional testimonies (see Savas 1982:89–117). Both of these systematic studies and secondary sources generally indicate that private organizations outperform public organizations and that private contracting is a more cost-efficient means of service delivery than governmental provision of services.

Overall, relative to the other public-private comparative studies, there are a large number of organizational performance studies. And almost all of these studies base their findings on nonperceptual data and fairly sophisticated statistical analysis.

C. Employee Characteristics

Relative to the other studies reviewed, there are also numerous studies comparing public and private employee characteristics. Although these studies investigate a broad cross section of employees, they investigate such a diversity of employee characteristics without replication that it is somewhat difficult to draw strong conclusions concerning how public and private employees differ. However, the studies do indicate that public and private employees are more different than similar. They also indicate that public employees are perceived as possessing more positive characteristics (e.g., empathy, subscription to duty, advanced degrees) than private employees.

A loosely define area of focus of several studies in this category is worker motivation and occupational involvement. Three studies (Guyot 1960; Kilpatrick et al. 1964; U.S. Office of Personnel Management 1979) indicate that public employees are more motivated and involved than private employees; two studies (Buchannan 1974, 1975) indicate the opposite; and one study (Baldwin 1984) indicates no difference between public and private employee motivation.

In conclusion, the employee characteristics studies investigate a diversity of employees and organizations, large samples of employees, and a wide variety of employee characteristics. Since their data, however, are typically generated through surveys in which respondents provide self-assessments of their personalities, their findings are more subjective and impugnable than the findings from the compensation and organizational performance studies.

D. Job Security

The studies assessing public- and private-sector job security suggest fairly consistently that public employees enjoy greater job security than private employees. Fifteen of 22 findings support this conclusion, including those from three significantly large studies (Baldwin 1987; Kilpatrick et al. 1964; Long 1982). Many of these studies, however, investigate variables that are indirectly related to job security—for example, satisfaction and dissatisfaction with job security; the value, need, and importance placed on job security; and risk aversion. In drawing conclusions we assumed that employees who were more satisfied with their job security probably enjoyed more job security and that employees who place a higher value on job security and were more risk averse were probably attracted to the sector that provided the most job security.

Several variables indirectly related to job security—turnover, unemployment, layoff, and "quit" probabilities—were also included in this category. We further assumed that the degree of job security offered by various organizations would be partially reflected in these probabilities and that organizations providing greater job security might experience lower unemployment, turnover, layoff, and quit probabilities.[2]

In conclusion, the job security studies investigate a fairly large number of individuals, occupational levels, and organizations. Although many studies assess job security through perceptual measures, they are complemented by the studies that measure unemployment, turnover, layoffs, and quits.

E. Effects of the Work Environment on Employees

The 11 comparative studies that address the effects of the work environment on employees generally focus on job and need satisfaction. The four studies addressing "needs" (Newstrom et al. 1976; Paine et al. 1966; Porter and Mitchell 1967; Rhinehart et al. 1969) compare the extent to which public and private employees are capable of satisfying five Maslowian needs—physiological, security, social, esteem, and self-actualization—through their work environments.

The preponderance of the studies in this category indicate that public employees experience less job satisfaction than private employees and that the public sector is a less need-satisfying environment than the private sector. However, two studies (Kilpatrick et al. 1964; NCPQ 1978) with large employee and organization samples indicate that public and private employees experience equivalent job satisfaction, and one study (Grupp and Richards 1975) indicates that state-appointed officials are more satisfied with their jobs than private-sector executives.

Although there are not as many studies in this category as those previously reviewed, they permit sharper conclusions. The agencies and firms investigated are more varied than those in the organizational performance category, and the variables investigated are more focused than those in the employee characteristics category. This category also includes several studies with an impressive number and breadth of employees and organizations surveyed. The primary limitation of this category, however, is that *all* of the findings are based on self-assessments of job and need satisfaction ascertained through questionnaire measures—not observable, countable measures. Although questionnaires may be the most practical instrument for measuring job and need satisfaction, methodological purists will probably always question the validity of the findings from these studies.

F. Appeal of the Sectors

The comparative studies of the appeal of the sectors generally investigate the attractiveness of the sectors for individuals *outside* the public or private sectors. Four of the five studies (Avirgan 1967; Frederickson 1967; Graham and Renwick 1972; Sheard 1970) focus on the appeal of the sectors for college students. Although each of these studies is fairly narrow in scope, their findings are fairly consistent—the private sector is a more appealing work environment for college students than the public sector.

The Kilpatrick et al. (1964) study, however, is an especially significant study, which overshadows the others in this category. It is such an in-depth study of the relative appeal of the sectors that we present only the major findings. The findings generally indicate that a variety of federal employees always find federal employment more appealing, while a variety of "non-federal" employees always find private business more appealing. However, the appeal of federal employment for federal employees is greater than the appeal of private business for nonfederal employees, and the difference in the appeal of federal and business employment for federal employees is greater than the difference in the appeal of private business and federal employment for nonfederal employees. Finally, the findings indicate that high school, college, and graduate students find federal and private employment equally appealing.

Although the Kilpatrick et al. study must be given considerable weight relative to the other studies in this category, it is over 35 years old. Moreover, given the paucity of studies in this category and the narrowness of their focus, providing a generalization about the relative appeal of the sectors would not be responsible. Even if the Kilpatrick et al. findings are still valid, there is a substantial need for investigations of the appeal of state and local government relative to private-sector employment.

G. Remaining Findings

The findings associated with the variables that could not be applied to the preceding categories are so diverse that they permit only two broad generalizations. First, they indicate that the public and private sectors are more different than similar. Second, the findings from the studies with large samples, broad units of analysis, and wide ranges of agencies (Brown and Erie 1981; Buchanan 1974; Kilpatrick et al. 1964; Long 1975; NCPQ 1978; Rainey 1979; U.S. OPM 1979) generally indicate that the private organizations investigated possess more positive organizational characteristics (e.g., "first-year job challenge," "chance of being really successful," "competency of supervisors") than the public organizations investigated.

The findings from several studies in this category, however, relate directly or indirectly to several of the most commonly noted differences between the sectors. Buchanan (1975), for example, investigated four public and four private organizations and found that the *private* organizations experience more red tape ("structural salience") than the public organizations. Rainey (1977), in turn, found somewhat the opposite in his comparison of five government agencies and four business enterprises. He found that the government agencies experience greater "formalization" and less "flexibility of personnel procedures" than the business enterprises. In the same study Rainey also compared the clarity of public and private sector goals and found *no* significant differences between the two. De Allesi (1974), in turn, compared executive leadership turnover in 200 publicly and privately owned electric utilities and found that the *private* executives turn over more frequently than the public executives. Finally, Baldwin (1987) investigated 50 public and 12 private organizations and found that the public organizations experience greater leadership turnover and less goal clarity than the private organizations.

IV. DISCUSSION

A. Fundamental Differences and Common Criticisms

Of the eight most commonly noted fundamental differences between the sectors, only three are the focus of empirical investigations. The studies addressing these differences, however, are so few in number or so limited in scope that their findings are not generalizable. As a consequence, the foundation for establishing the most fundamental differences between the sectors, and therefore the field of public administration, largely rests on descriptive, *not* empirical accounts. Given the frequency with which the eight fundamental differences are repeated in the literature, one might be quite safe in assuming that these accounts are fairly accurate. This literature should be respected. The absence of empirical verification, however, does permit an element of doubt that lends potential credibility to a body of literature (e.g., Buchanan 1975; Mainzer 1973; Murray 1975; Weiss 1974) that argues against several of the fundamental differences.

The four common criticisms of the public sector relative to the private sector, in turn, have *all* been empirically investigated. Two of the four criticisms are substantiated by the research. The studies indicate that public employees generally enjoy greater job security than private employees, and the data could be interpreted as indicating that public employees enjoy excessive job security. They also indicate, with mixed consistency, that private organizations are more efficient than public organizations. However, they do *not* indicate that public employees are underpaid and unmotivated. They consequently indicate that the public sector may be suffering a somewhat unjustifiable or exaggerated negative image, a problem reflected in the negative findings from several "appeal of the sector" studies.

B. Public Administration or Generic Management?

In addition to an abundance of sector differences, the authors found that the public-private comparative research generally fails to address a very significant issue—whether the differences between the sectors *really make a difference.* For example, the research does not address whether more secure public employees work less hard, whether less satisfied public employees produce less, and whether more highly compensated public employees turnover less frequently. With few exceptions (e.g., Buchanan 1974; Rainey 1977), the empirical literature does not consider whether the variables in which the two sectors differ have a significant impact on variables relevant to the effective operation of public and private organizations. As a consequence, a narrow to broad range of descriptive and empirical public-private comparative literature may be trivial.

The potential triviality of many public-private differences coupled with the fact that the most fundamental differences between the sectors have generally not been empirically verified provide a potential field day for those partial to the generic study of management. Yet the findings from this review do not provide conclusive evidence in favor of the generic study of management, nor do they deprecate the value of our impressions of the differences between the sectors. Instead, they identify a need for further research to investigate the assumptions of a pervasive descriptive literature that is fundamental to the discipline of public administration. In harmony with the reviews of Garson and Overman (1983), McCurdy and Cleary (1984), Perry and Kraemer (1986), and White (1986a,b), they indicate a need for more rigorous theory building in public administration.[3]

Although the public-private research generally does not investigate the most commonly noted differences and their impacts, it still indicates a preponderance of differences between the sectors. Arguing against the independent study of public administration is consequently difficult. However, considering that this research typically investigates hypothesized *differences* between the sectors, the preponderance of differences may be understandable. Had the body of research focused on theoretically sound hypothesized *similarities* between the sectors, a majority of the findings might have reflected public-private similarities. What appears to be the critical practical issue is therefore not just the quantity of public-private differences or similarities, but again, whether the differences or similarities have a substantial impact on public organizations. To the extent that impacts are currently unknown, it is difficult to argue *conclusively* in favor of or against the independent study of public administration.[4]

C. Privatization

Although the organizational performance studies indicate that the private sector generally performs better than the public sector, it is also difficult to argue conclusively in favor of the *general* trend toward privatization. The success of the private sector is not quite consistent enough, and advocating privatization on the basis of sector performance comparisons can be misleading. If we are willing to abandon the values inherent in the multiple accountabilities of the public sector, or if multiple accountabilities are sufficiently built into private-sector provision of services, then public-private comparisons are relevant. Otherwise, the red tape brought about by multiple accountabilities unfairly disadvantages the public sector in such comparisons. The existing performance studies, however, indicate that the choice of sectors usually impacts the provision of services, that the impact of each sector often varies by service area, and that private contracting is a very credible alternative for the provision of public services, especially if efficiency values predominate public sentiments.

V. SUMMARY AND CONCLUSION

The quality of the public-private comparative studies varies substantially. Given their nonperceptual measures, large samples, and large number of studies, the compensation and organizational performance studies are the most internally and externally valid. Although the studies in the remaining categories are not as consistently valid, they address variables that are more difficult to gather data on and measure. Consequently, they typically utilize perceptual measures and compare very few organizations. Many of these studies, however, reflect state-of-the-art methodologies and should be lauded for investigating very large samples of employees.

   The studies reviewed also date between 1962 and 1987, with few reported in the 1960s and a fairly even distribution reported throughout the 1970s and 1980s. The general finding from each category therefore reflects the average nature of each sector in the United States primarily during a 17-year period, not the *changing* nature of each sector.[5] Keeping in mind this and the preceding methodological limitations, the findings from this review can be summarized as follows:

1. Public employees, especially federal employees, enjoy greater compensation and job security than private employees.
2. Private organizations are frequently, but not consistently, more cost-efficient and more productive than public organizations.
3. Public and private employees are different, with public employees possessing more positive characteristics than private employees.
4. Private employees enjoy greater job satisfaction and need fulfillment than public employees.
5. Inconsistent findings and study limitations prevent a generalization as to which sector is the most appealing.
6. Overall, the public and private sectors are *different.*

The findings further do not support contemporary criticisms concerning *unmotivated, underpaid* public employees. The comparative studies also generally do not investigate the most commonly noted differences between the sectors and their impact on public and private organizations. As a consequence, despite the volume and richness of the research reviewed in this chapter, sector comparisons remain fertile grounds for future empirical investigations in the United States.

ACKNOWLEDGMENT

Special thanks to Tina Leeds, Harold Martin, Jerry Perkins, Alan Saltzstein, and Stuart Miller.

NOTES

1. In 1976 Rainey et al. provided a fairly comprehensive review of the descriptive and empirical comparative literature. Since then the comparative empirical studies have doubled.
2. These rates are also explained on the basis of public-private differences in wages, fringe benefits, and firm size.
3. To indict the entire body of public-private comparative research for nontheoretical tendencies would be misleading. Much of the body is a collection of studies from diverse disciplines, and many studies provide building blocks for theory within their respective disciplines, *not* the discipline of public administration. Moreover, the comparative compensation research is a particularly impressive cumulation of studies that often build on one another and utilize advanced methodologies.
4. Determining the relative impact of the public-private differences is often difficult for two reasons: (1) vague public-sector goals often prevent the establishment of valid measures of productivity, efficiency, and effectiveness, and (2) comparable measures of public- and private-sector performance often do not exist.
5. Changes in public demands, party in power, laws, economic conditions, organization structure, etc. cause the differences and similarities between the sectors to change. Although sector changes over time are not a focus of this review, the sectors can change during a depression, Viet Nam War, Watergate, or Iranscam era.

REFERENCES

Ahlbrandt, R.S. (1973). *Municipal Fire Protection Services: Comparison of Alternative Organizational Forms.* Beverly Hills, CA: Sage.

Avirgan, A.L. (1967). Report on a conference of college recruitment problems. *Personnel Journal 46,* 272–281.

Baldwin, J.N. (1984). Are we really lazy? *Review of Public Personnel Administration 4,* 80–89.

Baldwin, J.N. (1987). Public versus private: not that different, not that consequential. *Public Personnel Management 16,* 181–193.

Barton, M.F., and Waldron, D.G. (1978). Differences in risk preferences between the public and private sectors. *Human Resource Management 17,* 2–4.

Bellante, D., and Long, J. (1981). The political economy of rent-seeking society: the case of public employees and their unions. *Journal of Labor Research 2,* 1–14.

Bennett, J.T., and Johnson, M.J. (1980). *Federal Government Growth, 1957–78: Theory and Empirical Evidence.* New York: International Center for Economic Policy Studies.

Brown, M.K., and Erie, S.P. (1981). Blacks and the legacy of the Great Society: the economic and political impact of federal social policy. *Public Policy 29,* 299–320.

Bruce, W., Blackburn, J.W., and Spelsberg, M. (1985). Bureaucratic responsiveness: an empirical study. *Public Personnel Management Journal 14,* 1–14.

Bruggink, T.H. (1982). Public versus private regulated enterprise in the municipal water industry: a comparison of operating costs. *Quarterly Review of Economics and Business 22*, 111–125.

Bryan, T., and Smiley, A. (1983). Learning disabled boys' performance and self-assessment on physical fitness tests. *Perceptual and Motor Skills 56*, 443–450.

Buchanan, B. II (1974). Government managers, business executives and organization commitment. *Public Administration Review 35*, 339–347.

Buchanan, B., II (1975). Red tape and the service ethic: some unexpected differences between public and private managers. *Administration and Society 6*, 423–428.

City of San Francisco Contracts Out Budget Bureau Services and Saves $$ (1972). *Newsletter, Municipal Finance Officers Association 54*, 2.

Coleman, J., Hoffer, T., and Kilgore, S. (1982). Cognitive outcomes of public and private schools. *Sociology of Education 55*, 65–76.

Crain, W.M., and Zardkoohi, A. (1978). A test of the property-rights theory of the firm: water utilities in the United States. *Journal of Law and Economics 21*, 395–408.

De Alessi, L. (1974). Managerial tenure under private and government ownership in the electric power industry. *Journal of Political Economy 82*, 645–653.

Fogel, W., and Lewin, D. (1974). Wage determination in the public sector. *Industrial and Labor Relations Review 27*, 410–431.

Frederickson, H.G. (1967). Understanding attitudes toward public employment. *Public Administration Review 27*, 411–422.

Garson, D.G., and Overman, S.E. (1983). *Public Management Research in the United States.* New York: Praeger.

Golembiewski, R.T., Proehl, C.W., and Sink, D. (1982). Estimating the success of OD applications. *Teaching and Training Development Journal 36*, 86–95.

Graham, W.K., and Renwick, P.A. (1972). Expected need deficiency and preference for three types of organizations. *Journal of Psychology 82*, 21–26.

Grupp, F.W., and Richards, A.R. (1975). Job satisfaction among state executives in the U.S. *Public Personnel Management 4*, 104–109.

Guyot, J.F. (1960). Government bureaucrats are different. *Public Administration Review 29*, 195–202.

Hayes, F.O'R. (1977). *Productivity in Local Government.* Lexington, MA: Lexington Books.

Havemann, J., and Lanouette, W.J. (1978). The comparability factor in federal employees' pay. *National Journal* (Sept. 30), 1552–1555.

Hellman, R. (1972). *Government Competition in the Electric Utility Industry.* New York: Praeger.

Hermann, R., Single, E., and Boston, J. (1977). *Counsel for the Poor: Criminal Defense in Urban America.* Lexington, MA: Lexington Books.

Hirsch, W.Z. (1965). Cost of an urban government service: refuse collection. *Review of Economics and Statistics* (Feb.), 87–92.

Kilpatrick, F.P., Cummings, M.C., and Jennings, M.K. (1964). *Source Book of a Study of Occupational Values and the Image of the Federal Service.* Washington: Brookings Institution.

Krashinsky, M. (1978). The cost of day care in public programs. *National Tax Journal 31*, 363–372.

Lawler, E.E. (1965). Managers' perceptions of their subordinates' pay and their superiors' pay. *Personnel Psychology 18*, 413–422.

Long, G.E. (1975). Public-private sectoral differences in employment discrimination. *Southern Economic Journal 42*, 89–96.

Long, G.E. (1982). Are government workers overpaid: alternative evidence? *Journal of Human Resources 17*, 123–131.

Mainzer, L. (1973). *Political Bureaucracy.* Glenview, IL: Scott, Foresman.

McCurdy, H.E., and Cleary, R. (1984). Why can't we resolve the research issue in public administration? *Public Administration Review 44*, 49–55.

Meyer, R.A. (1975). Publically owned versus privately owned utilities—a policy choice. *Review of Economics and Statistics 57*, 391–399.

Moore, T.G. (1970). The effectiveness of regulation of electric utility prices. *Southern Economic Journal 36*, 365–375.

Murname, R.J. (1983). How client characteristics affect organization performance: lessons for education. *Journal of Policy Analysis and Management 2*, 403–417.

Murray, M. (1975). Comparing public and private management: an exploratory essay. *Public Administration Review 34*, 364–371.

National Center for Productivity and Quality of Working Life. (1978). *Employee Attitudes and Productivity Differences Between the Public and Private Sectors.* Washington: National Center for Productivity and Quality of Working Life.

Neuberg, L.G. (1977). Two issues in the municipal ownership of electric power distribution. *Bell Journal of Economics 8*, 303–323.

Newstrom, J.W., Reif, W.E., and Monckza, R.M. (1976). Motivating the public employee: fact vs. fiction. *Public Personnel Management 5*, 67–72.

Nowlin, W.A. (1982). Factors that motivate public and private sector managers: a comparison. *Public Personnel Management 11*, 224–227.

Oates, W.A. (1981). Independent schools: landscape and learning. *Daedalus 110*, 1–16.

Paine, F.T., Carroll, S.J. Jr., and Leete, B.A. (1966). Need satisfactions of managerial personnel in a government agency. *Journal of Applied Psychology 50*, 247–249.

Patton, D.K. (1973). *Economic Development Administration.* City of New York, letter report dated June 21.

Peltzman, S. (1971). Pricing in public and private enterprises: electric utilities in the United States. *Journal of Law and Economics 14*, 109–148.

Perry, J.L. (1984). *Organization Form and Transit Performance: A Research Review and Empirical Analysis.* Washington: United States Department of Transportation.

Perry, J.L., and Kraemer, K.L. (1986). Research methodology in the *Public Administration Review. Public Administration Review 46*, 215–226.

Pier, W.J., Vernon, R.B., and Wicks, J.H. (1974). An empirical comparison of government and private production efficiency. *National Tax Journal 27*, 653–656.

Porter, F., and Keller, R.L. (1981). Public and private pay levels: a comparison in large labor markets. *Monthly Labor Review 104*, 22–26.

Porter, L.W., and Mitchell, V.F. (1967). Comparative study of need satisfactions in military and business hierarchies. *Journal of Applied Psychology 51*, 139–144.

Quinn, J.F. (1979). Wage differentials among older workers in the public and private sectors. *Journal of Human Resource Management 14*, 41–62.

Rainey, H.G. (1977). Comparing Public and Private: Conceptual and Empirical Analysis of Incentives and Motivation Among Government and Business Managers. Unpublished doctoral dissertation, Ohio State University.

Rainey, H.G. (1979). Perceptions of incentives in business and government: implications for civil service reform. *Public Administration Review 39*, 440–448.

Rhinehart, J.B., Barrell, R.P., De Wolfe, A.S., Griffin, J.E., and Spaner, F.E. (1969). Comparative study of need satisfactions in government and business hierarchies. *Journal of Applied Psychology 53*, 230–235.

Savas, E.S. (1977). An empirical study of competition in municipal service delivery. *Public Administration Review 37*, 717–724.

Savas, E.S. (1980). Public vs. private in the garbage game. *Wharton Magazine* (Spring), 58–63.

Savas, E.S. (1982). *Privatizing the Public Sector.* Chatham, NJ: Chatham House.

Savas, E.S., and Brettler, E.M. Sr. (1977). Management and financial alternatives for the delivery of a local government service in the United States: a case of solid waste collection. *Local Finance 6*, 17–31.

Sheard, J.L. (1970). College student preferences for types of work organizations. *Personnel Journal* (April), 299–304.

Smith, M.P., and Nock, S.L. (1980). Social class and the quality of working life in public and private organizations. *Journal of Social Issues 36*, 59–75.

Smith, S.P. (1976a). Pay differentials between federal government and private sector workers. *Industrial and Labor Relations Review 29*, 179–197.

Smith, S.P. (1976b). Government wage differential by sex. *Journal of Human Resources 11*, 185–189.

Smith, S.P. (1978). Federal pay scales: how much is too much? *Federal Reserve Bank of New York Quarterly Review 3*, 7–15.

Spann, R.M. (1977). Public versus private provision of governmental services. In *Budgets and Bureaucrats: The Sources of Governmental Growth* (T.E. Bocherding, ed.). Durham, NC: Duke University Press.

Stevens, B.J. (1984). Comparing public and private sector productive efficiency: an analysis of eight activities. *National Productivity Review 3*, 395–406.

U.S. Office of Personnel Management. (1979). *Federal Employee's Attitude Survey.* Washington: U.S. Office of Personnel Management.

Wallace, R.L., and Junk, P.E. (1970). Economic efficiency of small municipal electric generating systems. *Land Economics 46*, 98–104.

Weiss, H.L. (1974). Why business and government exchange executives. *Harvard Business Review* (July/Aug.), 129–140.

White, J.D. (1986a). On the growth of knowledge in public administration. *Public Administration Review 46*, 15–24.

White, J.D. (1986b). Dissertations and publications in public administration. *Public Administration Review 46*, 227–234.

Yunker, J.A. (1975). Economic performance of public and private enterprise: the case of U.S. electric utilities. *Journal of Economics and Business 28*, 60–67.

10
Alternative to Privatization

A Case Study from Fort Lauderdale, Florida

George L. Hanbury II   *President's Office, Nova Southeastern University,*
Fort Lauderdale, Florida

I. INTRODUCTION

During the late 1980s, just before the "craze for privatization," the city manager of Fort Lauderdale initiated extensive "team" training efforts following Florida Power and Light's (FPL) Total Quality Management (TQM) training. Since then, both FPL and the city have dismantled most of the formal processes. What went wrong with TQM? Is TQM still a valid practice in Fort Lauderdale city government? What theories were practiced, and how were their principles tested?

Governments at all levels are emphasizing and implementing the concept of privatization and "reinventing government." Privatization means different things to different people, but the common denominator is the removal, or sharing, of government's hand from some important activity conducted in the public interest. We are in the process of privatizing everything from the post office to schools, prisons, and airports. In this trend for the public sector a fad or the way of the future?

In recent years, local governments have witnessed market-based competition entering industries that have typically been their protected monopolies. Can market-based competition bring financial benefits to the taxpayer? What does the future hold for local governments that refuse to compete? Will municipalities be reduced to "contract organizations" as the word "privatization" conjures? Are the concepts taught and practiced in TQM a paradox to the "downsizing," "rightsizing," and "entrepreneurial spirit" of "reinventing government?" Or, are they essential tools for the beleaguered bureaucrat to sharpen his or her competitive edge in an "entrepreneurial world"?

This chapter, presented as a case study from my perspective as the former city manager of Fort Lauderdale, will answer the questions posed, and offer a new alternative to privatization, and to those who aspire to quality and continuous improvement in the delivery of public service.

> Effective executives, no matter how high they rise remain inquisitive, curious about everything. They read, go around, look, explore, wonder, make connections, always know that their company is not the whole, but only part of it. They are by nature restless (Bennis 1989:92).

II. TOTAL QUALITY MANAGEMENT

In the 1920s, Walter Shewhart first introduced statistical process control (SPC) charts to monitor quality in mass production manufacturing. During the 1930s, Shewhart and his colleagues including a young Ph.D. in statistics, E. Edwards Deming, expanded these techniques at the Western Electric Bell Labs (Milakovich 1995:13).

General Douglas MacArthur invited Deming to teach statistical process control (SPC) techniques to the Japanese during the occupation after World War II. Since then, quality and customer service have taken on revolutionary meanings. His influence on management and the imposition of Total Quality Management (TQM) on Japanese industries such as automobiles, electronics, and steel are legendary. Since the early 1950s, the Japanese have symbolically honored the American who taught them how to manage quality and improve productivity by presenting the Deming Prize. The *Deming Prize* has become the internationally recognized symbol of business excellence (Milakovich 1995:103).

Connie Hoffman, city manager of Fort Lauderdale (1981–1989), an effective executive who brought innovation and strategic planning to a city government with no plan for organizational development, let alone a mission, by turning to a program initiated by Florida Power and Light (FPL) in 1981, emulating the Deming model. The program initiated by Hoffman was entitled TEAM, an acronym for Together Everyone Accomplishes More (C. Hoffman, personal communication, Dec. 5, 1995).

Milakovich emphasizes that "Four principles of quality underlie FPL's Quality Improvement Program: (1) customer satisfaction—quality is customer satisfaction; (2) plan-do-check-act cycle as professed by Deming and Shewart; (3) management by fact—collecting data for evaluation; (4) respect for people—creative thought for all employees" (Milakovich 1995:106). Hoffman and her management team embraced these principles.

FPL's mission statement read, "During the next decade, we want to become the best managed electric utility in the United States and an excellent company overall, and be recognized as such." CEOs of major corporations had recognized FPL as the benchmark of quality; however, as a testimonial to substantiate their claims, and to give even greater credibility to their commitment to quality, in 1988, FPL was awarded the Edison Electric Institute Award for Quality Improvement in a utility, and in 1989, they received the prestigious Japanese *Deming Prize*. Finally, the bastion of business reporting, the Wall Street Journal, reported that its subscribers recognized FPL as the nation's *best managed public utility* (Milakovich 1995:106–110).

III. BEST CITY BY 1994

Fort Lauderdale's mission statement read, "To be the best city of its size by 1994, and recognized as such" (Fort Lauderdale Mission Statement 1984). Desiring to emulate FPL's success and commitment to quality, the city manager initiated total quality leadership training for employees in 1986, and a new spirit was born in the city.

Through a positive public information campaign, the voters approved a bond referendum for $44.7 million. The bond issue was one way to work toward the mission statement and see tangible improvements. Funds approved were for parks, Riverwalk, beach revitalization, international swimming Hall of Fame, and the Museum of Science and Discovery.

Everyone (citizens and employees) echoed the theme of Best City by 1994. Billboards, bus benches, and city stationery all proclaimed the goal, and focused the vision of a practically undefinable phrase to be "real" in everyone's eye, depending on their perspective. In fact, the slogan is what attracted me to respond to the invitation to apply for city manager early in 1990, after Connie Hoffman's retirement from public service.

When the City Commission employed me in June of that year, my job was to see that the projects approved by the voters were finished, and aggressive economic development efforts undertaken. Although much planning and discussion through citizen committees, and employee teams had occurred, they had actually undertaken little construction. I embraced the concept of TEAM training and encouraged its concepts; however, by 1992, and at the height of a national economic recession, I had deemphasized TEAM, just as the new president of FPL dismantled the TQM program in 1990, the year after they won the *Deming Prize.*

IV. PROBLEM STATEMENT AND LITERATURE REVIEW

What happened to TEAM and to Quality Improvement initiated by the president of FPL and the city manager of Fort Lauderdale? Did the privatization effort of the 1990s kill what seemed like a productive program? Or, was it the political atmosphere, and the economic malaise that permeated the country at that time?

The parallels of TQM, in the city, and FPL are similar. Both organizations had quality improvement teams (QIT) that reported successful stories, and were broken into four categories: (1) functional teams—members were all volunteers from the same unit; (2) cross-functional teams—members dealt with problems that cut across organizational barriers; (3) task teams—members appointed from one or more organizational units to work on specific problems; (4) lead teams—members served on steering committees to guide other teams and were lead by management.

Information central (IC) kept files and stories on each team. The stories consisted of seven steps: reason for improvement; current situations; analysis; countermeasures; results; standardization and plans. In both cases, the QI story format specified participation by the work force, but its rigid methodology had the opposite effect.

Unfortunately, they inappropriately applied this seven-step process to too many processes and functions. The paper work was horrendous. It actually discouraged many hard-working employees who wanted to decide on behalf of the customer, but were frustrated by having to apply the standard format to each decision. Many employees resented taking time to participate in the rigorous exercises necessary to come to what they thought was a logical conclusion (L. Shatas, personal communication, Dec. 5, 1995). In addition, some of the first requests I heard from department heads, and employees, as their new city manager, was to discontinue the voluminous reports that seemingly answered nothing, and pay for extra effort and time necessary to learn the methods of TEAM.

Milakovich confirms these observations, "This centralized approach later stigmatized the QIP as rigid and designed to maintain separate quality bureaucracies" (1995:109). Just as with employees of the city, the amount of uncompensated extra effort required to learn the statistical methodology demanded of the TQC approach, frustrated employees of FPL. Others felt they devoted too much effort to winning the *Deming Prize* and not enough to employee empowerment. (Milakovich 1995:109). They felt they did not have the authority and resources to serve their customers.

Warren Bennis writes, "Empowerment is the collective effect of leadership, evident in five themes: people feel significant; learning and competence matter; failure is an event not a person; people are part of a community or family; work is exciting, stimulating, challenging, fascinating and fun" (1989:30). From comments made, FPL and Fort Lauderdale employees were going through the TQM motions, but not satisfying Bennis's criteria!

FPL and Fort Lauderdale tried to follow Deming's (1993:23) Fourteen Points for Management. Deming felt that "deadly diseases" created by American managers, could be overcome through the following practices:

1.   Create constancy of purpose toward improvement of product and service, with the aim to become competitive and stay in business.

2.   Adopt the new philosophy. We are in a new economic age. Western management must awaken to the challenge.

3.   Cease dependence on inspection to achieve quality. Eliminate the need for inspection on a mass basis by building quality into the product in the first place.

4.   End the practice of awarding business on the basis of price tag. Instead minimize total cost. Move toward a single supplier for any one item, on a long-term relationship of loyalty and trust.

5.   Improve constantly and forever the system of production and service to improve quality and productivity, and thus constantly decrease costs.

6.   Institute training on the job.

7.   Institute leadership.

8.   Drive out fear, so that everyone may work effectively for the company.

9.   Break down barriers between departments.

10.   Eliminate slogans, exhortations, and targets for the work force such as zero defects and new levels of productivity.

11a.   Eliminate work standards on the factory floor.

11b.   Eliminate management by objective. Eliminate management by numbers, numerical goals. Substitute leadership.

12a.   Remove barriers that rob the hourly worker of his right to pride of workmanship.

12b.   Remove barriers that rob people in management and in engineering of their right to pride for workmanship. Abolish the annual or merit rating and management by objective.

13.   Institute a vigorous program of education and self improvement.

14.   Put everybody in the company to work to accomplish the transformation. The transformation is everybody's job.

FPL and the City of Fort Lauderdale found out that the Fourteen Points were easier said than done. Following the rules of procedure became a substitute for management. FPL obviously got lost in the process and seemed to lose sight of a basic tenet of management and the needs of the organization as professed by the "original scientific management guru," Frederick W. Taylor (1911:15): "secure the maximum prosperity for the employer coupled with maximum prosperity for each employee."

Despite the approach of a major recession, FPL continued, like an uncontrolled locomotive approaching a washed out bridge, to create cycles of special bureaucracies and added layers of analysis which greatly increased unnecessary expenses. In desperation, after it was too late to curb expenses, FPL not only dismantled its TQ program, it began a series of layoffs that continued for years (Wall Street Journal 1993). The recession of the 1990s had officially taken its toll. Likewise, the citizens and employees of the City of Fort Lauderdale were about to successfully confront one of its greatest economic challenges since the Great Depression.

V.   RECESSION AND FORT LAUDERDALE CITY GOVERNMENT

If either organization could have withstood the rigid rules and procedures of TQM, the influence of the economic woes of the 1990s would have definitely resulted in its demise. By 1992, after two years of fiscal stress without any end in sight, the recession took its toll. Labor contracts negotiated during the solid growth years of the late 1980s in Fort Lauderdale could not be financially met and keep the same number of workers. Drastic changes needed to be made, and all the labor unions gave concessions with hopes that the economic downturn was temporary. Though unions gave concessions to preserve jobs, jobs eventually were reduced. Emotional levels were high, and budget hearings became acerbic and antagonistic. Three unions represent 80% of Fort Lauderdale's work force. They did not want to hear about TQM. They wanted jobs! Unfortunately, that was the beginning of five long years of reductions in force that were the most difficult for me as a manager of 30 years.

Also, during this period of time, "running government like a business," became the admonition of those either in elected office or running for an elected position. Privatization became a standard operating procedure for a cure of the ills of the city, and local governments were going to have to "tighten their belts" just as the private sector was doing.

VI. PRIVATIZATION

Osborne and Gaebler (1992:61) state:

> When the government contracts out a public service, it retains its funding responsibility but hires a private company to provide the service. The primary motivation for contracting out is to cut government costs by employing more economically efficient private vendors. Contracting out also allows public agencies to exploit the efficiency and specialized skills offered by the private sector that may be unavailable within government.

According to Savas (1994:404), "Privatization means relying more on private institutions and less on government to satisfy societal needs." Likewise, Butler defines privatization as the "shifting of a function, either in whole or in part, from the public sector to the private sector" (cited in Gormley 1994:215).

Savas (1994:404) reasons that overwhelming support of privatization comes from negative feelings about government in general. "It derives from the widespread feeling that government has become too big, too powerful, too costly, too inefficient, and overly intrusive and dominant in daily life." Such was the economic and political atmosphere in Fort Lauderdale in 1992. Most of the employees, including management, however, professed the feelings of Miller and Simmons (1998:529): "The act of privatizing is an act of simulation. . . . Much in evidence is visceral thrill-seeking, fake imagery, and supercilious bureaucrat-bashing.

Robert W. Bailey points out that when words become political weapons, they often lose their clarity. Privatization is no exception. According to Bailey (1987:148–151), at least 10 issues should be considered before policy makers and public managers agree to privatize.

1. *Hidden monopolies.* Hidden monopolies mitigate the efficiencies expected from the breakup of a public monopoly. These monopolies could be in labor or in available vendors who might contract to deliver a service.

2. *Availability of a vendor.* Many advocates of privatization assume that a vendor will always be available to purchase a government asset or to contract the services needed to be delivered.

3. *Continuing need to regulate.* Government will still need to regulate a delivered service though it has been privatized. Privatizing a service does not leave the government without *responsibilities* or *accountability*.

4. *Transition costs.* The theoretical literature on which privatization is based assumes perfect knowledge and mobility, and individuals will seek Pareto-optimality. Transition costs are rarely mentioned. The public manager must face the costs of disruption associated with transition, potential labor problems, vendors' failure to deliver, vulnerability to litigation caused by tort actions in transition, or poor management.

5. *Loss of economies of scale.* Economies of scale may be lost if the operations of a government monopoly were transferred to many smaller private operating companies. The argument

for small is efficiency through competition; the argument for large is economy of scale. The answer is better management.

6. *Problem of estimating market value.* If a public organization is to privatize some of its assets, how does it establish the price? If the price is not at a maximum yield, what has been gained by privatizing?

7. *Contract compliance.* There will be auditing requirements, program evaluation, and investigatory needs if corruption or criminal activity is to be discouraged, reduced, or eliminated. As a practical matter, contract compliance will require a managerial unit to oversee vendor actions—another hidden cost.

8. *Lost opportunities.* In privatizing a service or an asset, the government may lose opportunities to affect better service or to act more efficiently.

9. *Costs of failure.* It is possible that many private actors who wish to take over public services will fail either from lack of quality, or bankruptcy, leaving clients without services. In either event, the public sector must provide the service as before privatization or bear the transition costs as the service is transferred to another private actor.

10. *Limits of governance.* Privatization redefines the relationship between what is public and what is private, what is of the commons and what is not. If the private actors are community-based, intermediate organizations, the outcome may be socially beneficial. If not, a sense of public legitimacy will have been squandered for marginal productivity enhancement—a trade off that not only is unquantifiable but is even more dangerous to effective governance.

In addition, Kettl (1993) reports that market competition may poses significant problems such as corruption. Corruption, and conflicts of interest, can occur throughout the contracting process. The implication of corruption, and the fertilization of corruption through inefficient or inadequate monitoring of contracted services should be of concern to all. From my perspective, initiatives that sprung out of the Progressive movement such as civil service and the council manager form of government were initiated, and their concepts sustained, in the name of efficiency and effectiveness but most of all ethical administration of public services. It must be disheartening to those that have worked hard to maintain ethical public practices, to see the insidious nature of corruption and spoils return in the guise of "contracting out."

Services provided by private contractors can also be disrupted if the contractor does not do well, if equipment breaks down, or if the contractor suffers its own labor problems or goes bankrupt. Contractors may be less flexible than governments. For instance, New York City switches its garbage trucks to snow plow duty when bad weather occurs. Such options might not be available if a community becomes dependent on private garbage haulers who do not own snow plows (Kettl 1993:164–165).

VII. LABORATORIES FOR PRIVATIZATION

In spite of these cautions, state and local governments in the United States, more than anywhere else in the world, are serving as laboratories for privatization. Virtually every type of service provided by governments—ranging from ambulances to zoning—is being provided privately in one form or another somewhere in the United States (Fixler and Poole 1987:164). Fixler and Poole note that our decentralized American federal system is the reason for such experimentations. It is precisely the 50-state, thousand-city system that has allowed the freedom to experiment with various forms of private service delivery. It has, moreover, given the economist and political scientists the diversity of examples and multiplicity of data points needed to draw empirical conclusions. Fixler and Poole (1987:177) believe that "those empirical conclusions again and again point to the superior flexibility, responsiveness, and cost-effectiveness of privatization."

I do not share Fixler and Poole's opinion. I admit that competitive efforts have been financially beneficial for the taxpayer; however, I believe public employees, when given the opportunity, can be just as responsive and cost-effective. I believe, we should remember that privatization only adds another instrument to the tools of the policy maker; it is not a panacea. If fully aware of the hidden costs, the potential for failure, and the inadequate guarantees for obtaining the efficiencies that theory suggests will accrue, policy makers may then decide to privatize—certainly not sooner, as been done by many.

VIII.   PUBLIC MANAGER'S ROLE IN PRIVATIZATION

For the public manager, however, it should not be just a matter of informed judgment based on experience in public management and on policy analyses more exacting than is currently presented by advocates of privatization (Bailey 1987:151). Decisions by the public manager should also be weighed that are based on a moral "belief in, the American regime values; and, second, a sense of extensive benevolence for the people of the nation" (Frederickson and Hart 1985:551).

Public employees fear that privatization will mean either the loss of their jobs or at least a reduction in pay and fringe benefits (Fixler and Poole 1987:175). Privatization to many public employees means "privateering." The word privateer is akin to the word privatization; both are derived from the word private. A privateer is defined in Webster's New Collegiate Dictionary as "an armed private ship licensed to attack enemy shipping." Savas confirms this conception by pointing out that the word privatization "summons opponents to the battlements, and therefore the Regan administration, for instance, found a less inflammatory banner, 'productivity enhancement through competition,' under which to encourage consideration of contracting out."

Likewise, Donald F. Kettl (1993:158) states that not only is virtually every service imaginable contracted out, but contracting out has become a near-universal phenomenon. According to the Mercer Group, which conducted a survey of privatization in 1990, "Virtually all local governments surveyed contracted out at least one service to a private company." Though everyone contracts out something, and almost everything can be contracted out, there is little consensus among local governments about what services to contract out.

According to the International City Management Association (ICMA), more than half the 1681 local governments surveyed during the mid-1980s contracted out only two services—vehicle towing and storage and legal services. Most of the nearly 75 goods and services identified by ICMA were contracted out by fewer than a third of all the governments surveyed. Kettl, 1993:158

The Mercer Group survey found that local governments were most likely to contract out engineering, management and maintenance of parking garages, landscaping and grounds maintenance, human resources, food and medical services, service for the aging, consulting, landfill, data processing and wastewater services (p. 158).

Martin (1996:2–8) identifies ten mayor considerations that can be grouped into four main categories as "potentially important" to local governments in selecting services for public-private competition. The first group, Martin refers to as "service considerations." Service considerations and their criteria for favorable consideration for public-private competition are:

1.   Core versus ancillary services: Ancillary services refer to "support or housekeeping services." Core services refer to police, fire, and land use planning. *Criterion 1: Ancillary services are preferable to core services.*

2.   Hard versus soft services: Soft services call for "significant exercise of the contractors'

discretion." Hard services call for services that require significant discretion, and adherence to professional standards of performance and behavior. *Criterion 2: Hard services are preferable to soft services.*

3.   Stand-alone versus interrelated services: Stand-alone services are essentially self-contained systems. Interrelated services are major components of a larger service delivery system. *Criterion 3: Stand-alone services are preferable to interrelated services.*

4.   Service segmentation: Service segmentation refers to the ability of a service to be subdivided either geographically or by the task. *Criterion 4: Services that can be segmented are attractive for competition.*

5.   Service precedents: *Criterion 5: Services that have previously been contracted out or targeted successfully for public-private competition.*

The second through fourth groups are identified as "external market considerations, internal market considerations, and political resistance."

From my personal observation, the last grouping, political resistance, may be the most important yet least discussed aspect, in making the final decision. For instance, if the interest in the private sector is considerable, and profit is the motive, there will be considerable lobbying for the service. Conversely, if the service is heavily unionized and exercises considerable political "clout," there may be substantial political resistance to privatizing. Martin, almost prophetically, states, "The previous points will be used to justify the latter" (1996:2–8).

Kettl, likewise, reports "Local governments are least likely to contract out programs at the core of their missions. Prisons, police, fire, water and sewage treatment, and emergency communications are all fundamental programs that protect the public health and safety" (1993: 160). Some governments, like Scottsdale, Arizona, have contracted out such services as fire; however, for both programmatic and political reasons, most local governments have been reluctant to turn such basic responsibilities over to the private sector. The costs of service disruptions could be high, and political fallout from problems with services such as police and fire could be fatal.

According to Kettl (1993:161), private contractors reduce costs through three principal techniques. First, because they are free of government rules and civil service requirements, they have more flexibility than public agencies. They use incentive pay systems and have greater freedom to hire and fire workers. They employ more part-time workers, have less absenteeism, and use employees for more than one task. Second, private contractors tend to pay lower wages than government agencies. Third and most important, contractors tend to pay their workers much lower fringe benefits, especially retirement benefits. The difference in fringe benefits is "the largest difference between the government and the private contractor," according to the National Commission for Employment Policy.

From my own perspective, thirty years ago, public employees made less than their private sector colleagues; however, their pension was sound and stable. Today, however, because of competitive wage studies and strong union contracts; not only are pension costs higher than the private sector, wages are very competitive, and in some cases higher than the private sector. This fact will continue to place great strains on all services offered by the public sector.

Gormley restates Kettl's (1994:224) position that "government agencies hire (and reward) front-line bureaucrats trained to manage contracts." Indeed, from my experience, as governments have privatized more, public administrators have metamorphosed into contract administrators. The front-line bureaucrat becomes the contract administrator for the provision of the service instead of the supervisor of a crew of employees to perform the work. Unfortunately, as he also emphasizes, many localities have not prepared, or trained their middle managers for such complexities. This neglect has resulted in the audit of the service performed left to the private party which could result in either positive action or waste and additional cost (Sun-Sentinel 1999).

IX. ASSUAGING NEGATIVE ASPECTS OF PRIVATIZATION

To assuage some negative aspects of privatization and diffuse employee opposition, public sector managers in many jurisdictions have developed many techniques. Such techniques compose three basic approaches: helping those who go to the private sector, helping those who stay in the public sector, and easing the personal-adjustment process (Fixler and Poole 1987:175).

One of the most important examples of the first approach is for the governmental unit that is contracting out a service to require the contractor to give the current government employees the right of first refusal for most or all of the jobs under the contract. A newer technique is to help public employees in forming companies to take over work previously done in-house. Another important way of reducing employee fear and opposition is to adopt a no-layoff policy, if possible. In such cases, the city government may decide that any net reductions in staffing levels due to privatization will be dealt with via attrition and transfers to other departments, rather than via layoffs. However, as privatization continues to expand into other services, or the economy worsens, this option may not be possible. Other options include using some money saved during the first year of privatization, either for one-time redundancy payments to the displaced employees or to pay for their retraining for other jobs. Another possibility is to provide incentives for early retirement, and finally severance pay (Fixler and Poole 1987:175–176).

Too much privatization will cause a loss of the critical mass of the organization to make such absorptions, and may even reduce the local government to no more than a contract agency, unable to provide smaller services normally expected of municipalities.

Because of years of demands from elected officials for downsizing, rightsizing, privatizing, and load shedding, our institutions are indeed weak. Middle managers' positions have been decimated, and like a weak gazelle on the African plains, public administration becomes vulnerable for attack. The more vulnerable and weaker public administration becomes, the more we hear the "need for strong leadership" from those that are attacking.

Frederickson (1997) points out that ever since Osborne and Gaebler reported "this is a book about governance, not politics" the term governance has been the "politically correct term" to attack bureaucracy, and distinguish between those who "steer" (positive), and those who "row" (negative). To me, euphemisms, all too often, attempt to make contradictory statements, in reality they do not. As a politician in the recent impeachment hearings said, "When people say this is not about sex, it's about perjury—it is about sex!"

I concur with Frederickson's proclamation: "Governance implies importance. Governance implies legitimacy. Governance implies a dignified, positive contribution to the achievement of public purposes" (1997:8). He continues, "Public administration has always been about governance, not merely management" (1997:93). Its commitment to effectiveness and efficiency is exceeded only by a genuine moral commitment to serve a greater collective good. In short, as Frederickson reports, "The spirit of public administration is dependent on a moral base of benevolence to all citizens" (1997:234).

Frederickson cautions, however, that regardless of the techniques used, "Can even the best management (some may be inclined to say Total Quality Management) overcome the problems of flawed policy?. . . . We should insist that we cannot solve the problems of contradictory, incoherent, and intentionally vague policy by better management alone" (1997:229).

X. FORT LAUDERDALE REVISITED

To exercise governance and give leadership in a political world demanding "government to be run more like a business," it was the intention of Fort Lauderdale employees and management to be competitive. Even more important, the evidence shows that what matters most to taxpayers is not who does government services but how they are performed. A policy analyst, John D. Donahue of Harvard University, observed that "public versus private matters, but competitive versus noncompetitive usually matters more." One study, for example, found, that in communities where there was competition to provide electric service, costs were reduced by 11%, despite whether the service provider was government or a private concern. Large private monopolies, however, are just as subject to inefficiencies as is the government monopoly. Donahue continues, "It is the presence of competition, not the locus of power, that matters." (Kettl, 1993:162)

Public administrators today are encouraged to be entrepreneurial. Indeed, the mantra of public administration in the last decade has been to maximize public services and benefits in the presence of reduced or limited resources through such phrases as "reinventing," "downsizing," "innovative leadership," and "entrepreneurship." Everyone knows that entrepreneurs take risks. Are public officials encouraged to take risks with public funds? In my opinion, no. Therefore, in an effort to be innovative, "entrepreneurial," and competitive, yet ethically responsible, in Fort Lauderdale, privatization became known as "public-private competition."

Necessity became the mother of invention in Fort Lauderdale. With my full endorsement, and the support of the top executive staff, as well as the leadership of the AFSCME union president, Cathy Dunn, and the labor relations manager, Scott Milinski, a new acronym for sharpening our competitive tools was born—CALM (Cooperative Association of Labor and Management).

Through negotiations, the labor unions agreed to the creation of and participation in labor-management committees in order to save jobs and face competition with the private sector. Though there had been years of TEAM leadership training, it had not involved the union leadership. The union leadership looked with suspicion on such programs. Now, with privatization at our doorsteps, we had the union leadership agreeing to teams, but the TEAM concept had been formally dismantled, and its primary coordinator laid off because of the recession.

The answer was to initiate the TQM training received during the TEAM years in order to combat the threat of privatization, or the more widely used euphemism "public-private competition." The new name of this tool for competition—CALM.

XI. CALM

The ultimate goal of CALM was to empower each employee with the confidence and knowledge to meet or exceed citizen (customer) requirements (AFSCME 1995). Sound familiar? The guidelines of CALM were:

1. Unwavering commitment to the citizen (customer).
2. Recognition by management of quality and a willingness to accept responsibility for well-being and improvement of the system by leaderless team groups.
3. Accepting the crucial role of education and self-improvement in accomplishing the change.
4. Implementing a team approach to cross-functional management and breaking down internal barriers to cooperation, and flattening the organization.
5. Using communication channels rather than relying on regulation or inspection to overcome obstacles, improve the system, and achieve quality.
6. Thinking systemically and using appropriate statistical tools to measure and control variation.

As stated by Steven Cohen and William Eimicke (1994:450):

Total Quality Management is a simple but revolutionary way of performing work. Total means applying to every aspect of work from identifying customer needs to aggressively evaluating whether the customer is satisfied. Quality means meeting and exceeding customer expectations. Management means developing and maintaining the organizational capacity to constantly improve quality.

In spite of Deming's warning of slogans, CALM not only created welcomed halcyon days with the AFSCME union, it also allowed the reestablishment of many positive ideas and precepts of TQM by another name.

The employees' participation and enthusiasm became greater when managers allowed decisions made through this "bottom-up" process. They were now becoming more efficient, more customer service oriented, and effective, not for the city, but to save their jobs. During the process, however, I believe we all rediscovered the true meaning of public service we seemed to have possibly forgotten during the acerbic public budget hearings, and ill feelings among employees caused by layoffs.

For example, Fort Lauderdale employees competitively bid, and won contracts for bulk trash collection, operations of the city jail, and utility pipe installation. These competitive projects allowed the taxpayer to save $6 million. Conversely, city employees lost contracts through competitive bidding in areas of vehicle maintenance, water meter reading, and bridge tending saving $600,000 in the budget.

On December 5, 1995, the City Commission of Fort Lauderdale was presented a systematic plan, created by employees and management, outlining what city employees will do to provide continuous improvement of the city's delivery of services. The plan called for the establishment of internal management systems that set quality standards, defined customers' requirements, and monitored them accurately while providing continuous statistical feedback (Hanbury 1995).

Fort Lauderdale employees have made a commitment to validate, monitor, and refine, in order to have continuous improvement and be competitive with the private sector. The recognition and acceptance of such activities in local government, today, would not have been possible without the early training of TQM.

Today in Fort Lauderdale city government, although you won't hear TQM or TEAM, you will hear expressed by members of the labor unions as well as management phrases such as *total quality*, *customer-driven*, and *continuous improvement*. Challenges such as these make management today much more exciting and yet ambiguous.

"Bottom-up" management with empowerment requires new thoughts and acceptance by management. Some managers find such "productivity enhancement through competition," hard to accept (Savas 1994:404–412). It is far more demanding to be a facilitator and broker instead of a hierarchal leader. As stated by John Nalbandian (1991:56), "Meeting these challenges requires substantial technical expertise that extends to an understanding of the political, economic and social dimensions of the challenges. The city manager must balance the expectations that the governing body has of the manager with the expectations of an increasingly professional staff."

XII. CONCLUSION

Given society's demands and the growing complexity of the nation's problems, public-private ties are inevitable, necessary, and desirable. The days when the government could assemble the world's best experts on every conceivable subject are long gone. Careful public management thus requires meticulous attention to the variations of administrative problems, and to the enduring core issues. It also requires zealous public oversight, particularly of the public-private relationships that are most likely to be troublesome—the relationships with the greatest market imperfections.

Regardless of the creativity of the public manager, because of the demands placed on governments by legislators and their constituents, privatization is not a fad, but the way of the future. I believe its concepts will be with public officials long into the 21st century. It will place added challenges on the public manager, and require his further education and push his leadership skills to the limit. Successful public managers will have to approach their work with a high level of managerial skill, problem solving ability, interpersonal sensitivity, tolerance for ambiguity, a willingness to accept responsibility, and the capability to convince his or her employees to have a competitive spirit while maintaining an ethically moral base.

Group dynamic exercises similar to CALM and other TQM disciplines enhance the opportunity for public employees to stretch their minds, challenge them to think, and allow new thoughts and ideas to be built into systems. Such management practices, in Fort Lauderdale, have enabled proposed tax rates to be stable, employees to be empowered, motivated and productive while generating efficient practices.

Most of all, it has established systems that enable the Fort Lauderdale public employee to be competitive with the private sector, and prepare themselves for "the armed private ship licensed to attack enemy shipping." Finally, its teachings have created a sense of customer service in Fort Lauderdale employees that I believe is exemplary. In my opinion, it is the *effective* alternative to privatization for the *effective* executive.

Such is the case for Fort Lauderdale. Obviously, TQM is not dead, but it may go by another name, just as it does in the private sector. "Indeed, many companies that have successfully adopted TQM don't even use the phrase 'total quality' anymore; it has simply become a way of doing business" (Jacob 1993:66).

In the search for public-private competition, seeking the public interest is paramount, and should never be forgotten. The government, after all, is not just another principal dealing with just another agent. In most markets, the search for compromise between buyer and seller is the central activity. The government is more than an automobile manufacture buying steel and glass or a corporation buying a new computer or telephone system. "It is representative of the public and its goals must represent public goals as embodied in law. Pursuing those goals—and the sense of the public interest that lies behind them—is the central task of government" (Kettl 1993:39–40).

Recognizing that such pursuits are paramount, it is hoped that the reader realizes from this case study that TQM as an alternative to privatization is not a paradox for the truly "effective executive." The perceived paradox of "privatization and TQM" are indeed just perceptions. When TQM is introduced, and embraced, by the public manager, the operations of the public agency are improved, and its competitive edge is sharpened. Its introduction has enabled reform, and has forced public managers to be "effective executives" who *"read, go around, look, explore, wonder, make connections, always know that their company is not the whole, but only part of it. They are by nature restless"* (Bennis 1989:92).

With such admonitions, I finish this chapter with the reality of Osborne and Gaebler's (1992:107) summation:

> Competition is here to stay, regardless of what our governments do. In today's fast-moving marketplace, the private sector is rapidly taking market share away from public organizations. We can ignore this trend and continue with business as usual watching fewer and fewer people use public institutions. . . . Or we can wake up and embrace competition as a tool to revitalize our public institutions.

REFERENCES

American Federation of State, County and Municipal Employees. (1995). Redesigning government/Partners for change. AFSCME Sept/Oct:20–21.

Bailey, R. (1987). Uses and misuses of privatization. In S. Hanke (ed.), *Prospects for Privatization*, 138–152. New York: Academy of Political Science.

Bennis, W. (1989). *Why Leaders Can't Lead: The Unconscious Conspiracy Continues.* San Francisco: Jossey Bass.

Caudle, S. (1994). *Reengineering for Results: Keys to Success from Government Experience.* Washington: National Academy of Public Administration

City of Fort Lauderdale. *1984 Mission Statement.* Fort Lauderdale, FL.

Cohen, S., and Eimicke, W. (1994). Focused total quality management in the New York City Department of Parks and Recreation. *Public Administration Review 54*(5).

Deming, W. (1993). *Out of the Crisis.* Cambridge: MA. Massachusetts Institute of Technology.

FPL stepping up restructuring. (1991, July 29). *Wall Street Journal*, p. C12.

FPL group trims to work force as part of cost cutting plans. (1993, Oct. 25). *Wall Street Journal*, p. C12.

Fixler, P. Jr., and Poole, R. Jr. (1987). Status of state and local privatization. In S. Hanke (ed.), *Prospects for Privatization*, 164–178. New York: Academy of Political Science.

Frederickson, G. (1997). *The Spirit of Public Administration.* San Francisco: Jossey-Bass.

Frederickson, G., and Hart, D. (1985). The public service and the patriotism of benevolence. *Public Administration Review 45*(5), 547–553.

Gormley, W. Jr. (1994). Privatization revisited. *Policy Studies Review*, Autumn/Winter:215–233.

Hanbury, G. (1995, Dec. 5). Productivity improvement: Report to City Commission.

Hanbury, G., Bryant, S., and Brogsdorf, D. (1996, Nov. 22). Privatization: local government competing with the private sector. In B. Havlick (Producer), *A Satellite TeleVideo Training Event.* Tampa, FL: Innovation Groups.

Jacob, R. (1993, Oct. 18). Managing: TQM: more than a dying fad. Yes, the movement has its critics. But applied properly, principles of Total Quality Management can still deliver big payoffs. Here's how. *Fortune*, 66.

Kettl, D. (1993). *Sharing Power: Public Governance and Private Markets.* Washington: Brookings Institution.

Martin. L. (1996). Evaluating service contracting. *MIS Report 28*(3). Washington: ICMA.

Martin. L. (1998). Circular A-76: Privatization or Public-Private Competition? *Public Manager (Fall).*

Milakovich, M. (1995). *Improving Service Quality Achieving High Performance in the Public and Private Sector.* Delray Beach, FL: St. Lucie Press.

Miller, H., and Simmons, J. (1998). The irony of privatization. *Administration and Society 30*(5).

Nalbandian, J. (1991). *Professionalism in Local Government: Transformations in the Roles, Responsibilities and Values of City Managers.* San Francisco: Jossey-Bass.

Osborne, D., and Gaebler, T. (1992). *Reinventing Government: How the Entrepreneurial Spirit Is Transforming the Public Sector.* Reading, MA: Addison-Wesley.

Perlmutter, F., and Cnaan, R. (1995). Entrepreneurship in the public sector. The horns of a dilemma. *Public Administration Review 55*(1).

Savas, E. (1994). On privatization. In F. Lane (ed.), *Current Issues in Public Administration*, 5th ed., 404–413. New York: St. Martin's Press.

Taylor, F. (1911). *Principles of Scientific Management.* New York: W.W. Norton.

11

Implementing the Denationalization Option

Great Britain and the United States

Antony Moussios and Jerome S. Legge, Jr.   *Department of Political Science, University of Georgia, Athens, Georgia*

I. INTRODUCTION

The sale of state assets to the private sector has gained much momentum in capitalist systems. Hardly any public enterprise is exempt from being considered for such transactions. Founded on public choice critiques of public management (Butler and Moore 1988:8) and on market reform theories restricting the extent of government intervention (Fraser Institute 1980:155), privatization initiatives are incorporated in public policies formulated by highly developed Western democracies. In addition, other countries interested in privatization include developing nations, such as Turkey, Malaysia, and the Philippines. Although the literature on privatization is bountiful in debating the merit and rationale of this policy option, it relegates considerably less attention to implementation problems. More importantly for our purposes, besides casual references to privatization experiences in other nations, the literature fails to provide a comprehensive examination of the manner in which policies are formulated and executed across nations. A comparative approach to privatization revealing the differences and similarities of policy reasoning, purpose, and strategy across various governments benefits understanding of the scope and the substance of the concept. This chapter attempts to register comparisons in the conception and implementation of the privatization option by two national governments, the United States and the United Kingdom.

Because of common institutional roots found in these two northern Atlantic democracies, a comparative analysis can be facilitated. Both nations demonstrate a high degree of industrialization and economic development. Both economies are "mixed," although national traditions place limits on government intervention, and value economic individuality and self-reliance. Similarly, the bureaucracy in both nations is both well developed and entrenched (Peters 1984:42). In addition, in recent years, the two nations have placed considerable stock in privatization as a policy instrument for improving the ability of national governments to come to terms with financial straits. The high budgetary deficit and the heavy public-sector borrowing requirements of nationalized industries respectively evident in the United States and United Kingdom have induced the adoption of privatization. Finally, the ideological kinship between the two governing parties in the 1980s accounts for the simultaneous emphasis allocated to privatization.

II. CONCEPT OF PRIVATIZATION

Privatization is a generic concept utilized to describe several institutional arrangements that exist to allocate collective goods and services (Savas 1982; Butler 1985). Their production and distribution require a form of collective action, remedial of their joint consumption and nonexcludable characteristics. In mixed economies, governments have traditionally demonstrated a commitment to the undertaking of collective action to assure the availability of collective goods and services. However, collective action is not necessarily synonymous with government action, particularly where, through the decentralization of the allocative process and the voluntary participation of consumers, collective goods are financed, produced, and distributed by collective organizations, small in size, and composed of members with common values and interests. The provision of fire or police protection in American cities provides a relevant illustration. Recently, government growth is observed in public supply of noncollective goods. With less frequency in the United States, the public sector has intervened in the provision of toll goods, otherwise supplied by the marketplace. Although exclusion of toll goods benefits is readily obtainable, monopoly charges toward private-sector producers of such goods preceded government involvement, in the form of regulation, or ownership. State regulation of corporations in the transportation, communication, and utility industries exemplify such an involvement. The privatization option reverses these trends by using four basic methods, which utilize the private sector in some capacity to replace the government's role.

In the case of "contracting out," government finances the delivery of goods and services by private firms and nonprofit organizations. This type of privatization is preferred by municipalities in the supply of local services. Privatization also involves the use of vouchers, a direct government subsidy to the consumer of a public service. This method enhances the consumer's freedom of choice. Food stamp, housing, and education programs primarily avail themselves to voucher usage. A third form of privatization is deregulation. In this case, government removes restrictions previously imposed on private-sector behavior, which have resulted in the removal of competition. Deregulation, particularly in the United States, took place within the airline, trucking, and telecommunications industries. The final, and more relevant to this chapter, method of privatization is state asset sales. The government actually sells public corporations to the private sector, which continues the provision of goods and services to the public. The sale of CONRAIL in the United States and the denationalization program executed in Britain, France, and elsewhere illustrate this method. Privatization hardly implies the demise of the government. Simply, the government recognizes the private sector's contribution to the most effective and efficient allocation of certain public services (Rushefsky 1984:221).

III. HYPOTHESIS

This chapter intends to analyze the implementation of denationalization in two distinct, but comparable, national contexts. More emphatically, it argues that although the implementation of the denationalization programs was achieved in a more timely and less controversial fashion in the United Kingdom, it accomplished more ambitious and substantial objectives in the United States. In Britain, the hierarchial nature of Westminster, in conjunction with adherence to incremental policy development, eliminated many implementation problems associated with the execution of denationalization (Campbell 1983:12–22). The dominance of the British Treasury in economic, industrial, and budgetary policy-making authority disallows any centrifugal tendencies, which could precipitate objections to the deliverance of new and substantial policy objectives. The Treasury's central role is further fostered by the secrecy that characterizes consultations between the ministry and interest groups, and with other government agencies, and also by the strong camaraderie that pervades bureaucratic relationships in Britain. Party discipline, still the prevailing force in determining the MP's voting behavior, assures the government of nonconditional approval of its policy objectives. Similarly, neutrality of the British civil service preserves the expressed intentions of the political executive during the implementation stage. The British government generally is seeking to introduce private capital into the industries through the creation of hybrid companies, in which the state retains a holding, ranging from a very small minority stake to just over 50%.

In contrast, the implementation of privatization in the Untied States endures considerable obstacles. The fragmentation of political authority provides the major impediment to an expedient execution of policy. Involvement by numerous actors capable of vetoing unfavorable policy outcomes often frustrates attempts to deliver programmatic objectives. The openness and wide availability of access points in the policy process allow pluralist forces to diffuse executive will, and to tolerate the promotion of private agendas with regard to policy priorities. As the ensuing discussion of the CONRAIL sale reveals, subgovernments constitute the primary forum in which delivery arrangements of policies are agreed upon.

IV. PATH TO DENATIONALIZATION

In the United States, sale of state assets to the private sector has rarely occurred, simply because few public enterprises exist. The CONRAIL sale is the focal point of the privatization program introduced by the Reagan administration. The story of CONRAIL begins on April 1, 1976, when Congress created the Consolidated Rail Corp., amalgamating the bankrupt Penn Central Railroad and five other smaller railway lines in the Northeast. The federal government owned 85% of the company stock (the remaining 15% is owned by CONRAIL employees) and subsidized the maintenance of a freight and commuter rail system in the region by investing $7.7 billion over a period of 10 years. The employees, through wage concessions at 12% below the average wage in the railroad industry, also contributed to the firm's continual operations. CONRAIL was competing against two large railroads, the Norfolk Southern (NS) and the CSX Corporation, and several smaller ones. The first privatization proposals emerged in 1980 (U.S.R.A. 1981:77), by then Secretary of Transportation Drew Lewis, but were speedily dismissed by Congress. By late 1983, when indications appeared that CONRAIL could operate profitably, a tentative agreement was reached between the Department of Transportation (DOT) and Congress to sell the government's share of ownership to the private sector. However, starting in mid-1984, the method of transferring the company to the private sector became the focal point of conflict between the Administration and Congress. The DOT preferred a negotiated sale to a single buyer (the NS). However, the U.S. House of Representatives, articulating the concerns of CONRAIL's labor, management, and shippers and of other railroads, favored the public offering of CONRAIL's stock, to maintain the competitive structure and the availability of rail services in the Northeast. After a 3-year period of intense negotiations, in September 1986 the DOT accepted the sales bill, proposed by the Senate-House Conference Committee of Transportation, that legislated the largest ever initial public offering in the United States, in the amount of $1.65 billion. First indications acclaimed this offering a resounding success (Heidenheimer et al. 1983:140).

In Britain, the wide nationalization of resources is a postwar phenomenon. Reflecting the perilous state of several industries, the central government resolved the problem by recourse to public ownership. Later, Britain's dependence upon foreign supplies of strategic resources, the misuse of private monopoly power, the emphasis on central economic planning and rationalization, and welfare policies were echoed in explanations given for the expansion of the public sector (Curwen 1986:31–35). In the mid-1970s, voter disillusionment with the performance of public enterprises became more evident, and culminated with the electoral victory of the Conservative party in 1979.

The sale of British TELECOM in 1984 concluded the largest denationalization program to date. TELECOM the principal supplier of telecommunication services in the United Kingdom, became autonomous from the post office in July 1981. The same Telecommunications Act that incorporated TELECOM addressed the issue of deregulation of the telecommunications industry. A private consortium called "Mercury" was licensed to compete with TELECOM in the corporate-business segment of the long-distance communications market. In spite of this competition, British TELECOM commanded the lion's share of the British telecommunications market. The Conservative government decided on the 51% denationalization of British TELECOM in 1982 after considering the huge sums of public sector borrowing required by all nationalized industries (Heald 1985:13). The danger from transferring TELECOM to the private sector as a monopoly resulted in the formation of a regulatory agency. This was proposed in the form of the Office of Telecommunications (OFTEL) (Newman 1986:18). The first Telecommunications Bill included some clauses that placed British TELECOM in a position of licensing its own competitors. However, the bill was halted by the dissolution of Parliament for the 1983 election. A subsequent transportation bill that reduced TELECOM's regulatory authority was introduced in July 1983, and received the Royal Assent on April 12, 1984. British TELECOM remains a hybrid corporation that dominates the telecommunications market, although some indications exist that foreign investments will be allowed in the industry.

V. COMPLEX THEORY OF DENATIONALIZATION

Generally, the more complexity that underlies the theoretical disposition and the causal relationships operative in denationalization, the more taxing the implementation of such a program (on importance of basic theoretical conception of policy implementation; see Bardach 1977:250). Proponents of denationalization often ignore the critical sale procedures, or conditions, required for producing the expected benefits, and assume that denationalization can work under a variety of circumstances.

The sale of public enterprises to the private sector enhances the freedom of consumer choices in a bimodal way. The subsidization of public enterprises with public income forces the taxpayers to assume "implied shareholdings" in these enterprises, and allocation of capital resources that these individuals might not choose privately. In addition, public enterprises often enjoy statutory monopoly powers, or utilize their market strength to compete "unfairly" (Heald and Steel 1982:337). Denationalization of such enterprises may benefit consumer choices by facilitating the entry of private operators and the availability of a greater array of services. In the CONRAIL sale, the administration's plan to negotiate a merger with the NS, a direct competitor, only partially alleviated the prior restrictions placed on consumer choices. Taxpayers received little return on their "implied shareholdings" of CONRAIL, since the sale's price tag fell short of the government investment. Moreover, the proposed sale to the NS would further limit the number of potential providers of railroad services in the Northeast. Without question, competitive market pressures certainly would be minimal as a consequence of such transaction. Similarly, the extent of permissible competition with the British TELECOM after denationalization is the focal point of the program theory debate. The liberalization program in 1981 failed to produce adequate competition. Even the government's response in creating a regulatory agency to maintain some control over the private monopoly seems rather inadequate in light of the American experience about the capture of regulatory agencies by the subject industries. Such quasi-judicial institutional building is uncommon and ineffective in Britain, where the lack of any formal separation of powers enables the ministers to exert pressure on regulators to conform to government policy.

The second argument in favor of denationalization concerns efficiency (Heald and Steel

1982:339). Public enterprises are viewed axiomatically as less efficient than private enterprises, because they are insulated from market fluctuations. For both sectors, the lack of, or the prohibitive cost of, information inevitably leads to nonoptimal use of resources. But the obstacles to attaining efficient performance in the public sector are incentives. The managers of public enterprises operate within an incentive structure that extends little or no rewards for cost-saving efforts, or for more efficient operating procedures. Instead, the current reward system compensates the bureau conservation, or expansion, behavior demonstrated by state officials, by securing benefits in the form of prestige, tenure, and in-house comforts.

Government pursuit of macroeconomic and redistribution policies through nationalized corporations further impairs the efficient allocation of resources. Government intervention in the management of these enterprises encourages their employment for social and political objectives. The issue remains whether the taxpayer places a higher value on social returns rising from state ownership, or on the economic returns to shareholders rising from private management of these enterprises.

Only evidence accumulated after the transfer of denationalized enterprises to the private sector can substantiate whether the type of ownership determines efficiency. In the CONRAIL sale, we can openly speculate on the effects that a merger with NS would impose on the company's operation. The NS's management intentions were to eliminate duplicity of railroad services where parallel lines existed. As a consequence, several thousands of jobs would become obsolete. By the same token, those economies in services and manpower would mirror the antitrust problems facing Norfolk Southern. Had Norfolk taken over CONRAIL, only one railroad would remain for the state of Michigan. The NS was advised formally by the Justice Department to divest some of its lines to smaller competitors in the Northeast, to preempt antitrust claims brought by major competitors. Again, the lack of competitive conditions in the railroad industry complicated the validity of the efficiency argument. Moreover, it seems unfair to characterize CONRAIL's management as bureau conservationists or optimizers. The profit turnaround in 1983 underlines their market orientation.

In the case of British TELECOM, the issue becomes whether a private monopoly is more efficient than a public monopoly. In a private monopoly the forces of economic self-interest can translate into a fierce exploitation of the monopoly power. The hybrid status of British TELECOM further complicates the issue of efficiency. The coexistence of public-sector disincentives with economic motivations presents an ambiguous and ill-explored phenomenon, which potentially makes OFTEL's task more difficult.

The final argument in favor of denationalization concerns the reduction in public-sector subsidies or borrowing requirements (Heald and Steel 1982:342). In both the United States and the United Kingdom the considerable pu blic investment in the nationalized enterprises received great attention. Thus, the denationalization program was conceived to improve the current deficit picture, and to allow for allocation of funds for other, more productive and socially desirable purposes.

For years, CONRAIL remained a money-losing liability to the federal government. The administration regarded the future sale of CONRAIL to the public with dismay, for it feared an eventual return of the company to the public sector. The economic stagnation of the freight industry created serious doubts regarding the viability of an independent CONRAIL (U.S.R.A. 1980:13); thus, the administration preferred a future merger with a company with rich experience and with outstanding financial performance. To achieve such a deal, critics argue the administration planned to propose a sale with favorable terms for the NS. The initial agreed upon price of $1.2 billion was castigated as too low by both the members of Congress and the financial community. Furthermore, the issuance of favorable tax concessions to the NS, which permitted the carry-forward of losses and tax credits, raised public criticism. Although the price tag was later raised to $1.9 billion and the tax concessions retracted, the Congress still complained about the

small return compared to the government investment. Interestingly enough, CONRAIL was denationalized at a time when it was generating income and could potentially retire some of its debt to
the government.

Although the denationalization of TELECOM evolved in a different form, similar conclusions are reached. The emphasis assigned to public-sector borrowing requirements (PSBR) provided the major spur toward denationalization. To this date, the public sale of 50.2% of TELE-
COM's stock raised the largest direct contribution (£3.916 million) toward reducing the PSBR.
However, the issue of reliance on public funding by denationalized enterprises remains complicated. The Treasury decided that a public limited company would be excluded from the PSBR as
soon as, but not before, a majority shareholding has been sold to the private sector. Thus, conveniently, the borrowing of funds by hybrid corporations is excluded from the PSBR. But since the
government remains the single largest shareholder of British TELECOM, it is questionable
whether the effects of external financing now—payment of interest by the enterprise, and the
"crowinding out" of funds potentially used by the private sector—differ from the effects of PSBR
by the public ownership. In essence, the British government managed to reduce the amount of
PSBR artificially by utilizing accounting conventions; however, it did little to decrease public
expenditures that serve the interest of external financing, or to disseminate pressures on interest
rates caused by the "crowding out" effect.

Both examines of denationalization reveal the importance of sale procedures and conditions
to the implementation of these government programs. In the British case, the government showed
some reservation in magnifying the program's impact to further the competitive pressures in the
market. But in both nations the implementation of denationalization became problematic due to
the complexity of the program's hypothesis.

VI. COMPLEXITY OF JOINT ACTION

The implementation process of a government program requires that numerous actors behave in an
appropriate fashion. But the extent and significance of the actor involvement often determine
whether the program is implemented in a consistent and timely fashion. As Pressman and Wildavsky (1979:93) emphasize, the inclusion of numerous participants with diverse perspectives in
an impl.ementation process with mul.tiple decision points makes that process complex and convoluted. When more than one organizational unit of government is involved in the buyer selection
process, and in the administration and oversight of the denationalization program, the difficulties
and time involved in purchasing decisions multiply (DeHoog 1984:286).

The collective decision-making process installed in the implementation phase of the CON-
RAIL sale produced unusual delay and conflict. The DOT's plan for a merger with the NS demonstrated the administration's concerns regarding the future viability of CONRAIL, and led to the
negotiation with the single buyer of a series of Public Interest Covenants that would provide the
preservation of railroad services. But Congress, and particularly the House, instigated by CON-
RAIL's labor, management, customers, and other competitors, opposed NS's takeover bid, on the
basis of the low price tag attached to the sale, probable employment losses, and the antitrust sentiments that such a proposal created. The uncertainty inflicted on the economic future of the railroad industry by then relatively high interest rates and the reduction of the freight business elicited the reluctance by both parties to reach a quick agreement. The numerous access points
available to opponents of negotiated sale were conducive to the extensive bargaining among the
participants. However, these negotiations further delayed the implementation of the program. The
problematic features of the planned sale, the competition after the sale, and the amount of power
enjoyed by CONRAIL's future owner became more evident and exposed. Multilateral communication among all participants was permitted and even encouraged by the DOT to reduce the uncer-

tainty. But the lack of a definite time limit on the sale and the adversarial positions taken by CON-RAIL, NS, CSX, and other railroads prolonged the search for a resolution. The House was able to veto the DOT's plan by backlogging the program in the House Committee on Energy and Commerce and the House Subcommittee on Transportation. Moreover, the Administration lacked mechanisms at its disposal to induce the House to move on the proposed merger. In addition, the DOT remained almost inactive from mid 1985 to early 1986 because it preferred not to jeopardize its long-lasting valuable relationship with the House by lobbying extensively. Similarly, the House never rejected the denationalization concept, a top priority of the Reagan Administration, but it quietly objected to the proposed method. The House was concerned about the impact of that program on future legislation; thus, it desired to set a favorable precedent. In the CONRAIL sale a common theme emerged. The DOT, the House Committees, CONRAIL, and the NS wasted considerable energy in avoiding the responsibility of decision and defending themselves against maneuvers by the other participants. These activities eventually produced a sales plan based on consensus, but also considerable delay.

In the sale of British TELECOM, the ministry's plan was approved by both Houses with few alterations. The committee stage of the Telecommunications Bill in the House of Commons was concentrated on ensuring the adequate social provision of communication services. TELECOM's single but small competitor, Mercury, attempted to influence the decision-making process by requesting that OFTEL intervene in a dispute over the terms on which Mercury would interconnect with the TELECOM network (Curwen 1986:270). But the government refused to intervene in the dispute, in spite of its holdings in TELECOM, or to authorize OFTEL to intervene; thus, legal proceedings were instigated by both parties. The denationalization of TELECOM faced no opposition from the company's labor unions, or management, or from the other political praties, for reasons discussed in the following section.

It is apparent that the American political system has not yet developed an array of workable and legitimate inducements, sanctions, that public agencies and political institutions could deploy in the event of policy impases. This results in implementation delays, but also safeguards the pluralistic nature of American society. On the other hand, the British parliamentary system provides a more controlled setting for interactions among political organizations or actors who differ substantially about the government's objective, and who compete in attempting to affect both governmental decisions and actions. The centralized structure of policy authority, that is, the cabinet committee system and secretariats, appears to strengthen the implementation of government programs.

VII. ADVERSARIAL IMPLICATIONS OF DENATIONALIZATION

Compounding the implementation problem is how the denationalization programs affect various participants. These actors (unions, management, competitors, shippers, the Administration or Cabinet, and the Congress or Parliament) contemplate their reaction toward denationalization by identifying future program developments and implications potentially threatening to their existence. If indeed such threats are apparent, the actors will attempt to manipulate the implementation process to derive a more favorable result from denationalization. This section examines why adverse effects appeared with higher frequency and intensity in the CONRAIL sale than with the British TELECOM.

The Administration's plan to sell CONRAIL to the Norfolk Southern caused considerable resentment among the various participants in the implementation process. From the beginning, Elizabeth Dole, the Secretary of Transportation, saw her mandate as unequivocal: because the long-term prospects for CONRAIL were disheartening, the protection of a merger with a single, powerful company was sought. At the end of the bidding process, DOT made clear its intentions to sell CONRAIL to its largest competitor, the NS. The DOT argued that such a transaction would permit the government to require from the new owner the maximum level of economically justifiable service for 5 years after the sale. Also, provisions of the final sale agreement with the NS would ban the purchaser from liquidating all, or any part, of CONRAIL railroad assets for 5 years, preserve maintenance levels, and provide for a complex formula allocating CONRAIL's "excess cash" to the federal government. The NS's interests were to be promoted remarkably by this agreement. As the company claimed, NS could gain from traffic synergy and common threads between the two companies, and from the access to Detroit and to western railroads. These factors would enable the NS to compete from a better vantage point with other railroads and trucking firms in the Northeast. However, the other participants viewed the proposed sale with dismay, and employed their connections with the Congress to ameliorate the conditions of the denationalization program. CONRAIL's management voiced their opposition to the merger with the NS. Management was concerned that a merger would result in the abandonment of some of CONRAIL's facilities, the loss of thousands of jobs, and a move of headquarters. Unions similarly feared layoffs brought about either by the merger with the NS, or by the divestiture of CONRAIL or NS lines, as required by the Department of Justice. Unionized workers, paid wages 12% below industry norms since April 1981, were concerned about equity. Initially, the NS requested that wage concessions remained in place, even after the merger, in order to maintain the firm's profitability, but later withdrew that demand. CONRAIL's customers remain adamant in their opposition to purchase by any other railroad, or to a piecemeal sale. The shippers indicated that loss of rail services, and the increase of freight rates, might result from NS's acquisition. CONRAIL's other major competitors in the Northeast balked at the proposed merger, which would enable NS to have full control over several rail routes. They also claimed that the price attached on CONRAIL's sale, at three times its earnings of $449 million, was far below the standard for rail acquisitions, thus allowing the NS to obtain an unfair advantage. Finally, Congress, in response to intensive lobbying efforts by the opponents of the merger, contended the sale price was uncharacteristically low in view of the government's investment, and that the anticompetitive issues remained even after the Justice Department's affirmative report. These concerns and fears of future employment cuts and liquidiation of CONRAIL persuaded the House to opt for a public stock offering.

In the sale of British TELECOM, the amount of opposition to the program was decidedly less evident. During the Conservative Party's second term in office, in 1984, the Labour Party was embroiled in an internal crisis, regarding direction and leadership. Moreover, the creation of the SPD-Alliance party raised attritiaon fears among the Labour's leadership (King 1985:482). Thus, the criticism of the program in both Houses of Parliament lacked the intensity to alter the obujectives, or to cause implementation delays of the denationalization initiative. Moreover, considerable support was exhibited by the British public, which became disillusioned with the inadequate performance of nationalized enterprises. The management of British TELECOM was particularly supportive of the denationalization since they escaped the harsh financial control exercised by government auditors but still remained the dominanta force in the telecommunications industry and faced very few comnpetitive pressures. Further, the hybrid status guaranteed that in spite of the government's declared nonintervention policy, TELECOM's management could always accrue the benefits of government backing. Similarly, the trade union succumbed to TELECOM's denationalization, for no employment cuts were projected as a result of that transaction.

VIII. THE POLITICS REMAIN

In the American setting, the openness and accessibility of the policy process encouraged the frequent intervention of participants. These actors employed their power sources to devise several political means, in order to influence the program evolution. In one sense, the DOT and Secretary Dole failed to implement their plan, admittedly the toughest politically, because their position was viewed as inflexible and self-righteous. The DOT initiated the request for the Justice study and persuaded the NS to divest some lines, even reportedly completed a half a dozen "deals" with several Congressmen, but accomplished considerably less in mitigating Congressional concerns about substantial antitrust conflicts. Later, the DOT pressured the NS to raise its bid to $1.9 billion, and to forego tax benefits occurring from the merger, but still face the opposition of Congress. It seems the DOT, anxious to return CONRAIL to the public sector, committed itself to an agreement with the NS management. Further, the DOT refused to disengage from that commitment, and was unable to work out a compromise with Congress. For its part, the NS lobbied certain Congressmen and representatives of local governments to remind them of tax benefits for their region, had the transfer of ownership been completed. Also, it contacted officials from the unions and competing railroads to reduce anxiety about the merger, but with little success. The labor union especially utilized its close relationship with Congress to oppose the sale. Moreover, labor tabled its own proposal to buy CONRAIL from the federal government for the sum of $2.5 billion, which included only $500 million in cash. The government rejected that proposal. Further, labor attempted to stop the sale process, by filing a suit, contending the federal government had no right to negotiate a sales agreement that included the interest in CONRAIL owned by the carrier's employees. But the U.S. Supreme Court elected not to hear that case. Later, the union announced its support for the bid for CONRAIL by the Alleghany Corp., a nonrailroad company, to gain negotiating leverage against the Norfolk merger. For a similar purpose, Stanley Crane, CEO of CONRAIL, supported the purchasing proposal of Morgan Stanley, a Wall Street firm. Crane personally launched a lobbying effort, by urging CONRAIL's shippers to express their disapproval of the merger to Congress, to block the government's plan. That enraged the DOT and Secretary Dole, who resented that a public employee would publicly demonstrate opposition to the policy. Crane, however, was a powerful actor in the process, for he was viewed as responsible for CONRAIL's financial turnaround.

The secrecy that surrounds policy consultations in Britain, along with the cooptation of unions in the process, accounts for the lack of any effective attempts to rectify the implementation process in the British TELECOM sale. The Trades Union Congress, the central leadership of labor in Britain, rejected the denationalization program but was ineffective. In this case, the sale of British TELECOM set the record for employee participation. Ten percent of TELECOM's shares was reserved by the government on favorable terms for eligible company employees and pensioners. Indicative of the effectiveness of that approach is that 96% of eligible employees disregarded their union's opposition and applied for shares. Further, the Department of Industry initiated a plan to gain political approval of the sale. The crucial points of the sale, TELECOM's future form, regulatory authority, and financial structure, were agreed upon by TELECOM's representatives, politicians, and Treasury bureaucrats.

IX. CONCLUSION

In the problematic areas associated with implementation of denationalization, the British political system was more effective in maintaining the consistent and coherent delivery of governmental policies. As the sale of British TELECOM indicates, relatively few actors participate in the policy process, and do so in a way sympathetic to governmental objectives and instruments. On the other hand, multiple actors with adverse perspectives and interests dominate the American policy process. But with respect to the program theory, the extensive and open bargaining processes that prevail in the United States produced a program with nonincremental objectives. The Congress's plan for public stock offering cannot be characterized as a small adjustment, or change, from the previous base (nor for that matter can the DOT's plan for a merger).

What can we learn that explains these differences in implementation between the two countries? In Britain, the reduction of the size of the public sector consisted a major part of the Conservative government's policy. The opposition parties could not provide an alternative, viable solution to the problem of nationalized industries. The unions saw their power dwindle during that period. The civil service found no reason to oppose the government's policies on the denationalization issue. The hierarchical structure of Westminster reinforced the dominant position of the Treasury. The government showed great determination to proceed with its goals, despite opposition. But the strong rhetoric was not reflected in actions. If one word best characterizes government decisions, it is "pragmatism." The government never targeted for cuts or privatization the sacrosanct part of the British budget: the welfare services. Aware of the British moderate collectivist orientation, the government only modestly disengaged from market intervention (Britten 1984: 110).

Unlike Britain, where ideology ruled only in the government's rhetoric, in the United States ideology ruled in the administration's activities. The sale of CONRAIL was a small part of the administration's attempt to reduce the role of government. But the politics of American democracy corroded the administration's will. The administration faced a Democratic majority in the House, which had its own policy agenda. The interest groups reacted to decreases in government benefits, and willingly joined the battle to shape the postdenationalization environment according to their preferences. The conflict involved not the merit of privatization, but the appropriate strategy. It seems the administration's plan for a merger was perhaps a viable alternative considering the uncertainty in the industry, but it failed to address the important political consequences.

REFERENCES

Bardach, E. (1977). *Implementation Game: What Happens After A Bill Becomes A Law.* Cambridge, Mass: MIT Press.

Brittan, S. (1984). The politics and economics of privatization. *Political Quarterly 55*, 109–128.

Butler, M.S. (1985). *The Privatization Option: A Strategy to Shrink the Size of Government. The Heritage Lectures 42.* Washington: Heritage Foundation.

Butler, M.S., and Moore, S. (1988). *Privatization: A Strategy for Taming the Federal Budget Fiscal Year 1988.* Washington: Heritage Foundation.

Campbell, C. (1983). *Governments Under Stress.* Toronto: University of Toronto Press.

Curwen, J.P. (1986). *Public Enterprise: A Modern Approach.* New York: St. Martin's Press.

DeHoog, R.H. (1984). Theoretical Perspectives on Contracting Out for Services. In *Public Policy Implementation* (G.C. Edwards III, ed.). Greenwich, CT: JAI Press, pp. 227–259.

Fraser Institute. (1980). *Privatization Theory and Practice: Distributing Shares in Private and Public Enterprises: BCRIG, PETROCAN, ESOPS, GSOPS.* Vancouver, B.C., Canada: Fraser Institute.

Heald, D. (1985). Will the privatization of public enterprises solve the problem of control? *Public Administration 63*, 7–22.

Heald, D., and Steel, D. (1981). The privatization of UK public enterprises. *Annals of Public and Co-operative Economy 52*, 351–368.

Heald, D., and Steel, D. (1982). Privatizing public enterprise: an analysis of the government's case. *Political Quarterly 53*, 333–349.

Heidenheimer, J.A., Heclo, H., and Adams, C.T. (1983). *Comparative Public Policy: The Politics of Social Choice in Europe and America*, 2nd ed. New York: St. Martin's Press.

King, A. (1985). Governmental responses to budget scarcity: Great Britain. *Policy Studies Journal 13*, 476–493.

Newman, K. (1986). *The Selling of British Telcom.* New York: St. Martin's Press.

Peters, B.G. (1984). *The Politics of Bureaucracy*, 2nd ed. New York: Longman.

Pressman, L.J., and Wildavsky, A. (1979). *Implementation*, 2nd ed. Berkeley: University of California Press.

Rushefsky, E.M. (1984). Implementation and market reform. In *Public Policy Implementation* (G.C. Edwards III, ed.). Greenwich, CT: JAI Press, pp. 195–226.

Savas, E.S.M. (1982). *Privatizing the Public Sector: How to Shrink Government.* Chatham, NJ: Chatham House.

Selby, B. (1987). Inside the Conrail story. *Institutional Investor* April: 95–104.

United States Railway Association. (1980). *Federal Funding of Conrail: Rail Service. Objectives and Economic Realities.* Washington: U.S. Railway Association.

United States Railway Association. (1981). *Conrail at the Crossroads: The Future of Rail Service in the Northeast.* Washington: U.S. Railway Association.

12

A Shifting Center

Budgeting in the Thatcher, Reagan, and Clinton Administrations

Steven G. Koven   *Department of Urban and Public Affairs, University of Louisville,
Louisville, Kentucky*

I. INTRODUCTION

Budgets have long been recognized as reflecting more than lifeless prescriptions and techniques. Group conflict as well as conflict over ideas can be observed in the annual process of resource allocation. Some groups gain, others lose as they struggle over scarce monetary resources. Ideas, values, and philosophies also conflict as preferences struggle for acceptance. "Reaganism" and "Thatcherism" represented a set of values that gained ascendency in the 1980s in a conflict between dissimilar philosophical views of the world and disparate policy prescriptions. The administrations of Ronald Reagan and Margaret Thatcher were also marked by acceptance of conservative economic perspectives, a repudiation of liberal nostrums, and an alteration in accepted budgetary practices in the United States and Great Britain. The elections of Tony Blair in Great Britain and Bill Clinton in the United States suggest that the ideological pendulum shifted back toward the center in both countries, yet the central position itself has shifted to the right.

Early doubters of Reagan and Thatcher claimed that their electoral success merely reflected the personal popularity of these leaders and not a philosophical shift in mass sentiments. Policies in fact were not widely supported, yet paradoxically the leaders (Reagan and Thatcher) who advocated those policies continued to enjoy high levels of popularity, at least by recent historical standards. Margaret Thatcher's election in 1987 equaled the British record of winning three elections in a row. She exceeded the previous 20th-century record of occupying Downing Street for nine years without interruption. Ronald Reagan defeated Walter Mondale in 1984 by a margin of 525 electoral votes to 13. Reagan carried every state in the nation with the exception of Mondale's native Minnesota. His margin of victory in 1984 was even greater than in 1980, when former President Jimmy Carter secured 49 electoral votes in carrying four states (Koven 1991:53).

The popularity in the 1980s of both Thatcher and Reagan indicated that conservative ideals were not dead and that unabashed conservative politicians could capture the loyalties of a strong majority of British and American voters in the late 20th century. In 1980, Ronald Reagan carried on his broad coattails 33 new Republican members to the U.S. House of Representatives; in 1984, 16 new Republican members to the House of Representatives were elected. Twelve freshman

Republican senators were elected in 1980 when control of the Senate was taken from the Democratic party, only to be lost again in 1986. Senate and House of Representatives gains in 1980, however, established a base of Republican strength from which they would capture both chambers of Congress in 1994. To a great extent, contemporary conservative leaders such as Newt Gingrich, Trent Lott, Dick Armey, and John Kasich owe their success to Reagan's popularity.

Isabel Sawhill (1986:103–104) among others contended that economic policies of the Reagan administration differed fundamentally from his predecessor, Jimmy Carter. Policy focused upon fighting inflation and encouraging long-term growth rather than reducing unemployment and redistributing income. A primary goal of the Reagan administration was to shrink the size of government and curb taxation. Economic programs of Reagan included the 1981 cut in income taxes, cuts in social programs, and reducing tax rates. Monetary policy was featured as a method for holding the line against inflation. Reagan's basic message was quite straightforward. He attempted to tap into enduring ideals of the American consensus: individual freedom, distrust of centralized governmental power, free enterprise as the key to economic progress, and government as an assurer of equal opportunity, not as guarantor of particular results (Heclo 1986:39). These ideas were consistently employed in countering the status quo paradigm represented in the coalition built by Franklin D. Roosevelt.

The growing popularity of conservative ideas in the United States was also observed in the expanding influence of the so-called Christian right. In 1980 Jerry Falwell and the "moral majority" selected six liberal Democratic senators for defeat. From this "hit" list, five targeted senators failed in their reelection attempt: McGovern of South Dakota, Church of Idaho, Culver of Iowa, Bayh of Indiana, and Nelson of Wisconsin all were defeated. Only Cranstad of California was able to survive Falwell's targeting (Jorstad 1981:87). Pat Robertson's brief electoral successes and the successes of his followers at the state level validated the influence of conservative religious forces in the United States. The Republican capture of Congress in 1994 along with triumphs of conservatives in large states such as California, New York, and Texas suggests that an ideological shift to the right continued into the 1990s. In California, Pete Wilson discovered the electoral value of attacking immigration. In New York and Texas, George Pataki and George W. Bush (son of the former president) defeated liberal icons Mario Cuomo and Ann Richards.

The influence of shifts in political philosophy is observed and measured in public policy shifts and public sector budgets. Legislation of the 1990s was supportive of conservative ideas such as privatization, decentralization (as the case with welfare reform), free trade (fostered through the North American Free Trade Agreement), parental control in education (especially over sensitive topics such as sex education), and tax reforms that encouraged marriage. This chapter describes budgetary changes that occurred under the conservative leadership of Great Britain's Margaret Thatcher and America's Ronald Reagan. Budgetary outputs in these administrations are compared to revenue and expenditure patterns of the preceding time periods. Budgetary outputs and fiscal initiatives of the Clinton administration are also reviewed.

II. PHILOSOPHICAL FOUNDATIONS

A. Conservative Economic Perspectives

Economic policies of the Reagan and Thatcher administrations (and their philosophical underpinnings) represented a sharp break with policies of the post–World War II period and a return to theories that were discredited long ago. The resurrection of economist Jean-Baptiste Say (1767–1832) and the laurels heaped upon economists such as James Buchanan, Milton Friedman, and Arthur Laffer signaled an intellectual counterrevolution directed against the conventional wisdom grounded in Keynesian economics.

A number of fundamental assumptions were revived in the 1980s which provided the philo-sophical justification for conservative economic policies. Economic assumptions of both Thatch-er and Reagan maintained that state intervention in the economy would be counterproductive as a policy to reverse economic decline. Instead, these leaders advocated a macroeconomic, nonselec-tive approach to the economy. A revival of laissez-faire philosophies ensued as both those conser-vative leaders fundamentally rejected principles of state intervention (Freyman 1987:63). Macro-economic policy addressed issues such as national tax rates and money supply while leaving questions such as income distribution to the vagaries of free market competition.

The laissez-faire emphasis of Reagan and Thatcher can be traced back to the Scottish polit-ical economist Adam Smith and his classic work *An Inquiry Into the Nature and Causes of Wealth of Nations*, published in 1776. Smith maintained that the wealth of a nation and the wealth of indi-viduals within the nation would be maximized by leaving individuals alone to pursue their own objectives. Under this general perspective, values of individual freedom and liberty were priori-ties, and individuals should be free to pursue their own economic gains. Smith contended that a market system could combine the freedom for individuals to pursue their own objectives with the collaboration needed for the production of goods and services. In theory, as long as cooperation was strictly voluntary, exchanges would not take place unless all parties benefited. In Smith's par-adigm, an individual who "intends only his gain" was led by an "invisible hand." It was assumed that through pursuit of individual interests the "invisible hand" would promote the goals of socie-ty more effectually than if individuals deliberately set out to promote them (Friedman and Fried-man 1979:xvi).

Smith's insights are supported today by popular slogans such as "getting government off the back of the people" and "government is best that governs least." Friedman and Fried-man (1979:xx) stated that "an even bigger government would destroy both the prosperity that we owe to the free market and the human freedom proclaimed so eloquently in the Declaration of Independence." George Gilder, another modern-day advocate of free market capitalism, contend-ed that the problem of contemporary capitalism lay chiefly in the subversion of the morale and lack of inspiration of economic actors. The quality of capitalist societies, according to Gilder, depended on the creativity and leadership of investors. Gilder believed that creativity and leader-ship in turn could be fostered by lower taxes. As a result of lowering taxes, the scope and intru-siveness of government would decline, providing an environment for economic growth. In theory, economic growth would occur when investors and innovators were properly rewarded (Gilder 1981:46).

Economic policies of the 1980s followed monetarist and supply-side prescriptions. Mone-tarists stressed the importance of the supply of money to the overall stability of the economy. Lim-iting the supply of money was believed to be essential to control inflation. According to this per-spective, the only solution to inflation was to reduce the amount of monetary growth. Reductions in monetary growth would produce an uncomfortable but necessary period of unemployment (Robertson 1987a:21). The Friedmans stated that this cure for inflation was needed but politically hard to implement:

> A reduction in the rate of monetary growth is the one and only cure for inflation. Government
> must increase the quantity of money less rapidly. The only problem is to have the political will
> to take the necessary measures. Once the inflationary disease is in an advanced state, the cure
> takes a long time and has painful side effects (Friedman and Friedman 1979:258).

The monetary focus of Friedman, Thatcher, and Reagan shifted attention away from prob-lems of unemployment (the focus of Keynesian analysis) to problems of inflation. This represent-ed a sharp break with recent economic priorities and a triumph of conservative philosophies. Mon-etarism basically rejected policies of public intervention as well as income redistribution and reflected values of the Thatcher and Reagan administrations (Krieger 1986:26). Many of these ideas were condensed into a model that came to be known as "supply-side" economics.

B. Supply-Side Perspectives

The phrase "supply-side economics" was not devised by either Reagan or Thatcher. It was first coined in 1976 by Herbert Stein and referred to a set of propositions that explained how the macro-economy can enjoy increased tax revenue through a reduction in marginal tax rates (Alt and Chrystal 1983:71). According to this view, lower tax rates would stimulate aggregate growth, which would more than offset the tax reductions. This theory was also embraced by Arthur Laffer in his now famous Laffer curve. Laffer maintained that at higher levels of taxation people moved into the barter economy, worked less diligently, and substituted leisure for work. These actions in turn lowered the aggregate level of economic activity. It was believed that when tax levels were too high ("prohibitive range" of the Laffer curve), government revenues actually would increase if taxes were reduced. Since the curve is "backward bending," there are always two tax rates that will produce the same level of public funds: a low tax rate in a large, vibrant economy, and a high tax rate in a much smaller, constrained economy.

Advocates of the supply-side perspective explained that higher incentives to producers must be created. One method prescribed for increasing incentives to suppliers was to lower the rate of taxation. In the absence of such lower tax rates, the supply-side theory contended that investors would place their money in nonproductive tax shelters. Investors would also refuse to take risks if tax rates were high. According to supply-siders, investors would only take risks if they could retain for themselves the preponderance of earnings-in other words, if they could avoid high tax rates imposed by the government (Gilder 1981:43).

George Gilder (1981:39) is a leading advocate of the supply-side position. He claimed that taxes produced "sumps" of wealth that shifted money to nonproductive tax shelters. These monetary transfers (since they are less productive than other potential investments) reduce the level of growth in the aggregate economy. Government also has the ability to change the incentive structure:

> By altering the pattern of rewards to favor work over leisure, investment over consumption, the sources of production over the sumps of wealth, taxable over untaxable activity, government can directly and powerfully foster the expansion of real demand and income. This is the supply-side mandate (Gilder 1981:46).

The mandate of supply-side economics, however, was far from universally accepted. Critics maintained that it lacked convincing empirical evidence to support its propositions (Alt and Chrystal 1983:71–73; Stein 1984:245). Alfred Malabre (1987:78), news editor of the *Wall Street Journal*, stated that supply-side economics was a wonderful sounding notion that promised the proverbial free lunch, a perfectly painless, almost magical, way in which to strengthen the economy, cut the budget deficit, and take a large step toward economic utopia. According to Malabre, however, the supply-side idea was really hokum promoted by political activists who managed to gain President Reagan's ear. Early advocates of supply-side economics included economist Arthur Laffer, journalist Jude Wanniski, former Treasury Department official Paul Craig Roberts, and former Republican Congressman Jack Kemp.

The theory of supply-side economics was quickly converted into policy by the Reagan administration. The Economic Recovery Tax Act that was passed in 1981 reflected philosophies of the supply-siders. This act trimmed personal income tax rates by 23% over three years, reduced the tax on two-earner families, introduced indexing of income, and lowered taxes on investment income (Malabre 1987:78). With the passage of this act it was clear that conservative theories would play a major role in the development of policy in the coming years.

The ascension of Thatcher and Reagan to positions of power had other policy impacts. In regard to unemployment, each criticized strategies of public sector hiring and sought to transfer more responsibility to the private sector for solving problems such as unemployment (Robertson 1987b:89). In regard to industrial policy, Thatcher and Reagan espoused a macroeconomic non-selective approach to economic regeneration. Both believed that government intervention would distort market forces and therefore would be counterproductive in reversing industrial decline (Freyman 1987:62). Both leaders rejected Keynesian approaches advocating instead deregulation and privatization (Krieger 1986:15). Reagan and Thatcher therefore were at the forefront of a renewal of conservative thought in the 1980s.

When Reagan left office in 1988, however, there was little consensus concerning the accomplishments of supply-side strategies. Critics of the supply-side view claimed that these strategies favor the wealthy, represented nothing new, and were just a recycling of the same message that Andrew Mellon had conveyed to Calvin Coolidge in the 1920s (Koven et al. 1998:51; Schick 1990:70; Campagna 1987:486). Intellectual support for the revival of supply-side thinking had been provided by authors such as Milton Friedman (1962), George Gilder (1981), and Adam Smith (1904), as well as others such as Friedrich Hayek (1944) and Ludwig Mises (1944).

C. Clintonomics

While Bill Clinton could not be considered a supply-side advocate, neither did his policies replicate core beliefs of the Democratic party. Analysts asserted that as a "new Democrat" President Clinton attempted to break away from thinking that, according to some Democrats, had become an albatross around their necks. Policy initiatives that reformed the welfare system and balanced the budget did not exactly correspond to typical assumptions or policy prescriptions of the Democratic party. Other initiatives, however, such as Clinton's embrace of "enterprise economics," supported the liberal concept of stimulating economic growth through government activity. Initiatives such as "enterprise economics" represented an ideological pendulum swing away from the conservative policy prescriptions of the Reagan and Thatcher administrations back toward the center. The ideological center, however, appears to have moved to the right (more conservative) since the 1970s, as the Clinton administration supported some programs that were anathema to liberals. In addition, the 1997 budget agreement between congressional Republicans and the White House included many items that were favored by conservatives. These items included a tax credit of $500 per child to help families (a program long sought by the Christian Coalition and the "crown jewel" of the 1994 "Contract With America"), cuts in capital gains taxes, reductions in inheritance taxes, medical savings accounts, and changes in Medicare (Clymer 1997:A1).

"Clintonomics" is also associated with the liberal goal of increased government spending for specific areas. Recommendations of the Clinton administration included calls for "investment" in the areas of (1) "human capital," (2) technology, especially communications and transportation, and (3) infrastructure or roads, bridges, airports, and other capital investments (Dye 1995:230). Clinton is also associated with advocating government leadership in promoting the American economy as it competes internationally. In his inaugural address on January 20, 1993, President Clinton affirmed the three themes: of renewing America, investing in people and cutting the debt (Hunt 1995:501).

One should not be surprised if alterations in ideology were linked to budget priorities of the Thatcher, Reagan, and Clinton administrations. Analysis of the extent to which this linkage occurred is reviewed below. Growth of revenues and expenditures in the Thatcher, Reagan, and Clinton administrations are compared to outputs in a preceding, corollary time period.

III. BUDGETARY CHANGES OF THATCHER, REAGAN, AND CLINTON

A. Thatcher Administration

1. Revenues Under the Thatcher Administration

While Margaret Thatcher was not a professional economist, a great deal of evidence points to her strong commitment to cutting taxes as a means of stimulating economic growth. Thatcher's commitment to tax cuts was illustrated in the appointment of Sir Geoffrey Howe, a supply-side advocate, to the job of chancellor. Following Howe's shift to the foreign ministry, Nigel Lawson, another proponent of tax cutting, assumed the post of chancellor. In 1984, Lawson vowed to continue Howe's conservative policies (Waltman 1987:104). Analysis of revenue sources between 1979 and 1986 reveals that revenue strategies did indeed change under the leadership of Thatcher, Howe, and Lawson. Table 1 describes revenue collections in the first seven years of the Thatcher administration (1979–1986), revenue collections in the preceding seven-year period, and measures of revenue growth in both time periods. An "index of relative success" is calculated to describe relative growth of each source of revenue. This index simply compares the growth of individual sources of revenue with growth of total revenue. To compute the index, growth of individual revenue sources is simply divided by growth of total revenue. This index provides a handy method for seeing which individual categories have grown at a faster or slower pace than growth in aggregate totals (Koven 1988).

Two obvious changes in terms of revenue strategies of the Thatcher administration were discerned. First, growth in total revenue slowed considerably in the Thatcher period compared to the growth in the preceding seven-year period. Second, the composition of revenue sources changes as well. The Thatcher administration shifted taxes from the individual to the corporation. Growth of total revenue was higher (186% compared to 109%) in the pre-Thatcher era, suggesting a greater acceptance of taxation. An index of relative success of greater than 1 for corporate taxes, national insurance contributions, and National Health contributions indicates that the burden of taxation shifted from income taxes to these categories. These taxes are somewhat regressive, especially if corporate taxes can be successfully shifted to consumers in the form of higher prices.

The alterations observed in the growth and composition of taxes were consistent with the philosophical orientation of Thatcherism. Lower growth of public sector revenues is consistent with an antigovernment, pro-business philosophy. A shift from an income to a corporate tax structure also adheres to the conservative (in this case supply-side) doctrine of lower marginal tax rates assessed on individuals. Growth in corporate taxes should not be interpreted as a sign of tax progressivity or vertical tax equity because corporate taxes can often be passed on to consumers. If higher prices are assessed as a result of corporate taxes, burdens are borne by those less able to pay (Musgrave and Musgrave 1984). Lowering marginal tax rates to citizens ensures individual retention of a higher proportion of earnings, thus increasing the incentive for taking risks and earning profits. This lowering of the individual income tax rate is said to reflect the true "supply-side" mandate.

A greater emphasis on expenditure surtaxes (0.95 index of relative success compared to 0.83 index of relative success) was also noted in the Thatcher period, although the 104% growth rate trailed the rate of growth in total revenue. Taxes on expenditures included value-added taxes, taxes on hydrocarbon oils, tobacco taxes, a stamp tax, and others. Because upper-income individuals are likely to have higher savings rates, taxes on expenditures were generally considered to be

Table 1 Growth of Revenue Sources, Central Government, United Kingdom

Source of revenue	Amount in millions of pounds				Percent increase		Index of relative success	
	1971	1978	1979	1986	1971–78	1979–86	1971–78	1979–86
Income tax	6,184	18,707	20,343	37,618	203	85	1.09	0.78
Corporate tax	1,549	3,589	4,123	12,046	132	192	0.71	1.76
Total taxes on income	7,992	22,623	25,238	52,430	183	108	0.98	0.99
Total taxes on expenditures	6,722	17,094	23,107	47,166	154	104	0.83	0.95
National insurance contribution	2,547	9,157	10,432	23,104	260	121	1.40	1.11
National health contribution	230	761	882	2,256	231	156	1.24	1.43
Total revenue	19,022	54,359	65,225	136,037	186	109		

Source: Central Statistics Office, *National Income and Expenditures*, Majesty's Stationery Office, London (various years).

regressive. Consumption taxes of this nature, however, should encourage savings. This tax strategy is consistent with conservative economic priorities.

2.   Expenditures Under the Thatcher Administration

The spending priorities of the Thatcher administration were investigated through comparison of central government expenditures in the United Kingdom between 1971 and 1986. The extent to which spending grew between 1971 and 1978 as well as between 1979 and 1986 is displayed in Table 2. As with Table 1, patterns of the Thatcher period are compared with preceding patterns.

The Thatcher administration was able to moderate growth in total expenditures, total expenditures grew by 258% in the 1971 to 1978 time period, compared to 109% in the 1979 to 1986 period. When individual categories of spending were compared, growth of defense spending was found to be more robust under the Thatcher administration, almost keeping up with the growth rate of total expenditures. Some categories of social welfare spending, however, suffered from slower growth or actual cuts under Thatcher. Subsidies for housing actually declined in absolute terms. Other categories, such as grants to local authorities, and total subsidies, grew at a slower pace than growth in total expenditures. Within the social welfare function, categories such as social security and total grants to the personal sector did well.

Tables 1 and 2 illustrate the budgetary priorities of the Thatcher administration as well as change in those priorities. It appears from the data that ideological preferences of Thatcher did indeed influence budget outputs. Changes occurred in the growth of overall spending, growth of revenues, expenditure priorities, and strategies of taxation.

Whether similar patterns of influence can be detected for the Reagan administration can be assessed by use of the identical methodology. Differences in the structure of budgets are apparent when comparing Great Britain with the United States, which have largely contrasting systems of government. Power is more diffuse in the federal system of the United States than in the unitary system of Great Britain. Power is more centralized in the unitary system found in Great Britain. Taxes in 1982 as a percent of gross domestic product (GDP) were higher in Great Britain, 39.6%, compared to 30.5% in the United States. The United States was more dependent upon individual income taxes, while Britain relied upon consumption taxes to a greater extent (Whitman 1987:99–100). In Great Britain, the power to levy consumption and income taxes is reserved exclusively to the central government. In the United States, local and state jurisdictions also have the power to levy these taxes. It is clear that notable differences in regard to taxes exist between the United States and Great Britain, but these cross-national differences should not affect longitudinal analysis of changes between two periods of time within each nations.

B.   Reagan Administration

1.   Revenues Under the Reagan Administration

Ronald Reagan firmly embraced the supply-side doctrine, capturing the White House with the promise to cut taxes and reduce government involvement in people's lives. Table 3 compares the growth of revenue sources following Reagan's inauguration with growth of revenue in the preceding time period.

As was the case in the Thatcher administration, growth of total revenue was considerably slower in the administration of Ronald Reagan than in the preceding time period, 42% during the 1981 to 1987 Reagan years versus 96% in the comparable 1974 to 1980 time period. This can partially be explained by reductions in inflation. Like Thatcher, Reagan was successful in reducing reliance upon individual income taxes and in reducing marginal tax rates. Between 1974 and 1980 income taxes grew by 105%, a rate greater than the 95% increase in total receipts. In contrast,

Table 2 Growth in Expenditures, Central Government, United Kingdom

Category	Amount in millions of pounds				Percent increase		Index of relative success	
	1971	1978	1979	1986	1971–78	1979–86	1971–78	1979–86
Expend. on goods and services								
Defense	2,712	7,474	8,874	18,159	176	105	0.68	0.96
Health	1,949	7,246	8,310	18,238	287	119	1.11	1.09
Total expend. on goods and services								
Subsidies								
Housing	247	1,391	1,714	894	463	(48)	1.79	(0.44)
Agriculture, forestry, food	295	504	511	1,523	71	198	0.28	1.82
Assistance to coal industry	47	153	259	685	226	164	0.88	1.50
Total subsidies	841	3,129	3,670	5,389	272	47	1.05	0.43
Grants to personal sector								
University grants	255	740	800	1,574	190	97	0.74	0.89
Social Security	4,472	14,971	17,569	40,616	235	131	0.91	1.20
Total personal sector grants	4,612	17,049	20,069	46,314	270	131	1.05	1.20
Local authority grants	2,858	9,963	11,244	21,804	249	94	0.97	0.86
Total expenditures	16,037	57,415	67,119	140,476	258	109		

Source: Central Statistics Office, *National* Income and Expenditures, Majesty's Stationery Office, London (various years).

Table 3 Growth of Revenue Sources, Federal Government, United States

Source of revenue	Amount in billions of dollars				Percent increase		Index of relative success	
	1974	1980	1981	1987	1974–80	1981–87	1974–80	1981–87
Income tax	119.0	244.1	285.9	392.6	105	37	1.11	0.88
Corporate tax	38.6	64.6	61.1	83.9	67	37	0.71	0.88
Social insurance tax and contributions	65.9	157.8	182.7	303.3	139	66	1.46	1.57
Excise tax	16.8	24.3	40.8	32.5	45	(20)	0.46	(0.48)
Estate and gift tax	5.0	6.4	6.8	7.5	28	10	0.29	0.24
Customs tax	3.3	7.2	8.1	15.1	115	86	1.21	2.05
Total receipts	265.0	517.1	599.3	854.1	96	42		

Source: U.S. Census Bureau, *Statistical Abstract of the United States*, Government Printing Office, Washington D.C. (various years).

under the Reagan administration income tax revenues grew by 37%, a lower rate of growth than the 42% increase in total receipts that characterized the 1981 to 1987 time periods. The index of relative success for income taxes therefore is greater than 1 for the 1974 to 1980 period and less than one for the 1981 to 1987 period. Growing at a faster than average pace in the Reagan administration was the tax on social insurance and contributions. A shifting of the burden from the progressive income tax structure to the social insurance payroll tax is consistent with the supply-side philosophies, popularized in the Reagan administration.

In 1981, Congress significantly reduced individual income tax rates with the passage of the Economic Recovery Tax Act of 1981 (ERTA). This legislation had several implication. First, it represented a retreat from the principle of tax progressivity. Second, it led to high deficits. Tax reductions were most noticeable in the highest tax brackets, which fell from 73% to 50% over a three-year period. Aside from reducing marginal tax rates, another important feature of the 1981 tax reform was indexation. Indexing linked tax brackets to inflation, increasing the bracket in line with inflation and eliminating what was known as the problem of bracket creep (Cohen 1997:181).

The 1981 bill represented the first time in more than 50 years that Congress passed a tax bill that granted larger cuts to the better-off and to business. The tax cut was based upon the theory that tax cuts would stimulate savings, investment, and growth, and ultimately work to the benefit of all members of society (Cozzetto et al. 1995:42). In the Tax Reform Act of 1986, the tax rate structure was reduced from fourteen brackets, ranging from 11% to 50%, to two brackets of 15% and 28%. To compensate for the lower rates, many exemptions, deductions, and special treatments were reduced or eliminated (Dye 1995:257). The reduction in deductions were politically necessary to mobilize support for reducing rates and to maintain acceptable levels of income.

Unlike the experience in Great Britain, corporate taxes in the United States did not pick up any of the shortfall from the personal income tax reductions. In the United States, corporate taxes grew at a slower rate than the rate of growth in total receipts, producing an index of relative success of less than unity. The fastest-growing sources of revenue were found in the social insurance and customs tax categories. The social insurance tax grew at a pace that was more than 50% higher than the growth of total revenues (index of relative success of 1.57) while customs taxes grew at more than double the average rate for all receipts.

Income taxes, corporate taxes, and estate taxes grew at more moderate rates of growth than total revenues. Excise taxes actually fell in dollar terms between 1981 and 1987. This was attributed to the elimination of the windfall profits tax since taxes on alcohol and tobacco increased during the Reagan administration. The pattern of slower growth in total revenues, cuts in the rate of growth in both income taxes and corporate taxes, and higher growth in social insurance taxes is consistent with supply-side philosophies.

The Reagan administration outcomes even more closely approximated the supply-side doctrine than those of the Thatcher administration. This is attributed to the slower rate of growth in corporate taxes in the Reagan administration. A shifting of the burden to the social insurance tax is regressive since it is consistent with the philosophy of taxing lower-income groups more heavily. In theory, in this scenario, higher-income groups would benefit and invest more, take more risks, and work more diligently to stimulate economic growth. As of 1983, payroll taxes on wages only applied to the first $32,400 of wage and salary income (Musgrave and Musgrave 1984:724). The tax therefore led to a situation where higher-income levels (above $34,400) were free from the burden of the tax.

2. Expenditures Under the Reagan Administration

Expenditure levels and priorities were clearly altered in the Reagan administration. Total expenditures grew by 115% in the five-year period 1975 to 1980, compared to a 46% growth rate in the

1981 to 1986 time period. Some but not all of this difference can be accounted for by the lower rates of inflation after 1982. Alterations also occurred in the relative growth of individual categories of spending. Defense spending grew by 74% between 1981 and 1986, compared to an increase of 46% in total expenditures. This increase stands in sharp contrast to the 55% growth rate of 1975 to 1980, a period when total expenditures increased by 115%. Table 4 describes growth of expenditure categories in both the early years of the Reagan administration and the prior five-year time period.

Aside from the large increases in national defense spending, expenditures in the Reagan administration were characterized by high growth in spending for the category of agriculture and actual reductions or zero growth in the categories of (1) natural resources and environment, (2) community and regional development, and (3) education, training, employment, and social services. With the exception of agriculture, national defense, and housing, growth rates in discretionary programs lagged behind growth rates for total expenditures. Actual expenditures were lower in some categories of spending (i.e., community and regional development, and education, training, employment, and social services) in 1986 than they were in 1981. Spending on nondiscretionary, entitlement programs (such as health, Medicate, Social Security, and veteran's benefits) exceeded the average growth of expenditures during this time. This suggests that aggregate spending levels would have been lower if not for mandatory entitlements.

Expenditure patterns in the early years of the Reagan administration followed the conservative campaign rhetoric of reducing the size and scope of government. Reagan did not reduce aggregate spending levels; however, the rate of growth in spending was sharply curtailed. In addition, spending was targeted to functions that Reagan strongly supported, such as national defense. Functions that reflected more of a redistributive ethos (such as community development) did not fare as well in the spending decisions of the early 1980s.

C. Clinton Administration

1. Revenues Under the Clinton Administration

Prior to the election of 1992, Clinton outlined a plan that claimed to be "neither liberal nor conservative, neither Democratic nor Republican" but "new" and "different" (Clinton and Gore 1992:viii). The plan promised to restore economic growth by making the "wealthy" pay their "fair share," and reward people who worked hard to create jobs and start new businesses. Clinton moved quickly to reorient both revenue collections and expenditures. The Omnibus Budget Reconciliation Act of 1993 established a new top income tax bracket of 36%, a tax hike on some Social Security benefits, a gas tax increase, and an increase in corporate taxes. With the 1993 passage of this act, Clinton claimed that he had raised income taxes on only the top 1.2% of Americans and that he had effectively reversed the supply-side strategies of the Reagan administration (Koven et al. 1998:60).

Table 5 compares growth of revenue sources in the period prior to Clinton's taking office (1988–1992) with growth of revenue sources under the Clinton administration (1993–1997). As one might expect, based upon the Omnibus Budget Reconciliation Act of 1993, income taxes grew more robustly (32%) in the Clinton years. Also, consistent with the idea of tax progressivity, growth of corporate taxes was higher than average growth in total receipts and growth of regressive social insurance taxes lagged behind growth rates of total receipts. During the 1988 to 1992 time period social insurance taxes grew at a faster than average pace (index of relative success of 1.20), compared to the slower than average rate of 1993–1997 (index of relative success of 0.81).

Table 4 Growth of Expenditure Categories, Federal Government, United States

Category	Amount in billions of dollars				Percent increase		Index of relative success	
	1975	1980	1981	1986	1975–80	1981–86	1975–80	1981–86
National defense	86.5	134.0	157.5	273.4	55	74	0.48	1.60
Intl. affairs	7.1	12.7	13.1	14.2	79	8	0.69	0.17
General science, space and technology	4.1	5.8	6.5	9.0	45	38	0.39	0.83
Natural resource and environment	7.3	13.9	13.6	13.6	90	0	0.78	0
Agriculture	3.0	8.8	31.4	31.4	193	178	1.68	3.87
Transportation	10.9	21.3	23.4	28.1	95	20	0.83	0.43
Community and regional development	4.3	11.3	10.6	7.2	163	(32)	1.42	(0.69)
Education, training, employ.. social services	16.0	31.8	33.7	30.6	99	(9)	0.86	(0.20)
Health	12.9	23.2	26.9	35.9	80	33	0.70	0.72
Medicare	12.9	32.1	39.1	70.2	149	80	1.30	1.74
Social Security	64.7	118.5	139.6	198.8	83	42	0.72	0.91
Housing assistance	2.1	5.6	7.8	12.4	167	59	1.45	1.28
Veteran's benefits	6.6	21.2	23.0	26.4	28	15	0.24	0.33
Total expenditures	269.6	579.6	678.2	990.3	115	46		

Source: U.S. Census Bureau, *Statistical Abstract of the United States*, Government Printing Office, Washington D.C. (various years).

Table 5 Growth of Revenue Sources, Federal Government, United States

Source of revenue	Amount in billions of dollars				Percent increase		Index of relative success	
	1988	1992	1993	1997*	1988–92	1993–97	1988–92	1993–97
Income tax	401.2	476.0	509.7	672.7	18	32	0.90	1.03
Corporate tax	94.5	100.3	117.5	176.2	6	50	0.30	1.61
Social insurance tax and contributions	334.3	413.7	428.3	535.8	24	25	1.20	0.81
Excise tax	35.2	45.6	48.1	57.3	30	19	1.50	0.61
Estate and gift tax	7.6	11.1	12.6	17.6	46	40	2.30	1.29
Customs tax	16.2	17.4	18.8	17.3	7	(9)	0.35	(0.29)
Total receipts	909.0	1090.5	1153.5	1505.4	20	31		

*Estimate.

Source: U.S. Census Bureau, *Statistical Abstract of the United States*, Government Printing Office, Washington D.C. (various years).

2.   Expenditures Under the Clinton Administration

President Clinton endorsed a number of traditional Democratic programs such as housing, job training, environmental protection, and school programs. Other announced spending priorities of the Clinton administration included spending for community development, transportation, and crime prevention (Clinton and Gore 1992:11). Table 6 illustrates expenditure priorities of the Clinton administration and compares these preferences with spending patterns of the preceding time period.

The data indicate that, in many respects, President Clinton did not represent the stereotypical "tax and spend" Democrat. Growth of total expenditures was actually lower (16% during the 1993 to 1997 time period compared to 30% in the preceding period) during the Clinton period. Somewhat consistent with liberal priorities, the discretionary spending categories of national defense declined in both relative terms and in actual dollar terms between 1993 and 1997. Furthermore, the categories of housing assistance and community and regional development grew at a faster than average pace. Growth of the uncontrollable entitlement programs continued unabated. Medicare spending registered a particularly robust 49% growth rate of growth between 1993 and 1997, increasing from approximately $139.6 billion in 1993 to $194.3 billion in 1997. Ironically, President Clinton deserves credit for achieving the conservative goal of balancing the federal budget. Balance was achieved through restraining growth of total spending as well as shifting the burden of taxation to higher income groups.

IV.   CONCLUSIONS

It is logical to assume that strong leadership of any ideological orientation would have an impact on public policies. Just as Franklin D. Roosevelt influenced policy in 1932, Reagan and Thatcher had similar impacts in the 1980s. Palmer and Sawhill (1984:1) noted that Reagan presided over the largest redirection of public policies since Franklin Roosevelt. The Thatcher administration also had a significant impact on events. In 1988, strikes in Great Britain were at a 50-year low, union membership was 20% below its 1979 peak, inflation hovered around 3% (compared to 18% in 1979), top income tax rates were reduced, previously nationalized industries were returned to the private sector, the government budget was in surplus, the pound became one of the world's stronger currencies, and small firms opened up at rates unmatched since the 1920s (Knight 1988:33).

It appears that Margaret Thatcher was successful in reinvigorating a nation that was regarded in the past as the sick man of Europe. The "British disease" of continuous inflation led by wage increases, labor unrest, and slow growth in productivity appeared to be in remission if not totally eliminated (Shanks 1977:17). Thatcherism was not painless, but the malady diagnosed in the 1960s no longer seemed to be terminal.

In the United States, the rightward turn engineered by Ronald Reagan also appears to have produced some rewards. There was much less Carteresque talk about an American "malaise" permeating the nation. Discussing the virtues of entrepreneurialism, even greed, was in vogue as the capitalist system was exalted. All citizens did not agree that it was "morning in America," but the pessimism and desultory calls to sacrifice that marked the Carter administration dissipated with the Reagan era.

Liberals in both the United States and Great Britain were dejected by the electoral successes of Reagan and Thatcher. Both leaders were characterized as heartless—"reverse Robin Hoods" stealing from the poor to give to the rich. However, both leaders had a significant impact on reorienting budget outputs as well as polarizing debate. The coal miners strike of 1984–1985 in Great

Table 6 Growth of Expenditure Categories, Federal Government, United States

Category	Amount in billions of dollars				Percent increase		Index of relative success	
	1988	1992	1993	1997*	1988–92	1993–97	1988–92	1993–97
National defense	290.4	298.4	291.1	267.2	3	(9)	0.10	(0.56)
Intl. affairs	10.5	16.1	17.2	14.8	53	(14)	1.77	(0.88)
General science, space and technology	10.8	16.4	17.0	16.6	52	(2)	1.73	(0.13)
Natural resource and environment	14.6	20.0	20.2	22.8	37	13	1.23	0.81
Agriculture	17.2	15.2	20.5	10.2	(12)	(50)	(.40)	(3.13)
Transportation	27.3	33.3	35.0	39.3	22	12	0.73	0.75
Community and regional development	5.3	6.8	9.1	12.8	28	41	0.93	2.56
Education, training, employ., social services	31.9	45.2	50.0	51.3	42	3	1.40	0.19
Health	44.8	89.5	99.4	127.6	101	28	3.37	1.75
Medicare	78.9	119.0	130.6	194.3	51	49	1.70	3.06
Social security	219.3	287.6	304.6	367.7	31	21	1.03	1.31
Housing assistance	13.9	18.9	21.5	29.0	36	35	1.20	2.19
Veteran's benefits	29.4	34.1	35.7	39.7	16	11	0.53	0.69
Total expenditures	1064.0	1380.9	1408.7	1631.0	30	16		

*Estimate.

Source: U.S. Census Bureau, *Statistical Abstract of the United States*, Government Printing Office, Washington D.C. (various years).

Britain was viewed as a declaration of class warfare which produced class enmity (Krieger 1986:213). The PATCO air controller's strike in the early years of the Reagan administration set a similar tone in the United States. Both Reagan and Thatcher benefited from wide voter discontent with prior regimes. "Stagflation," or simultaneously rising levels of inflation and unemployment, undermined faith in the prevailing Keynesian economic thinking. This in turn produced a resurgence in the popularity of supply-side and classical economic thought.

The elections of Bill Clinton in the United States and Tony Blair in Great Britain signified a return to more centrist governance. It was apparent, however, that the ideological center did not return to its prior equilibrium point. President Clinton successfully reintroduced more progressive taxes in 1993, placing a heavier burden on those with greater abilities to pay. He also continued to reverse the buildup in national defense spending and increased funding for traditional Democratic programs such as housing and community development. While the Clinton administration adopted some traditional themes of liberal Democrats, other policy thrusts were more centrist and even conservative. These policies were warmly embraced by conservative Republicans.

Ironically, the legacy of the Clinton administration may be its success in shifting the Democratic party to the ideological center of the policy spectrum. Policies such as welfare reform, free trade, middle-class tax cuts, balanced budgets, and expenditure restraint all enjoyed wide support from conservative Republicans. Many of these policies were opposed by liberal Democrats in Congress. The budgets of the Clinton administration suggested that the era of old Democratic "tax and spend" may have been over, and that a "new Democratic" regime had emerged to guide policy. Budgets of the Clinton administration appear to have nudged the Democratic party back to the ideological center while at the same time moving away from ideological polarization that marked the early days of the Reagan and Thatcher regimes.

REFERENCES

Alt, J., and Chrystal, A. (1993). *Political Economics.* Berkeley: University of California Press.

Campagna, A. (1987). *U.S. National Economic Policy 1917–1985.* New York: Praeger Publishers.

Clinton, W. and Gore, A. (1992). *Putting People First: How We Can All Change America.* New York: Random House.

Clymer, D. (1997). Tax cuts, credit taken. *New York Times,* July 30:A1, A15.

Cohen, J. (1997). *Politics and Economic Policy in the United States.* Boston: Houghton Mifflin.

Cozzetto, D., Kweit, M., and Kweit, R. (1995). *Public Budgeting.* White Plains, NY: Longman.

Dye, T. (1995). *Understanding Public Policy,* 8th ed. Englewood Cliffs, NJ: Prentice-Hall.

Freyman, J. (1987). Industrial policy: Patterns of convergence and divergence. In J. Waltman and D. Studlar (eds.), *Political Economy Public Policies in the United States and Britain,* 44–68. Jackson: University Press of Mississippi.

Friedman, M. (1962). *Capitalism and Freedom.* Chicago: University of Chicago Press.

Friedman, M., and Friedman, R. (1979). *Free to Choose* New York:Avon Books.

Gilder, G. (1981). *Wealth and Poverty.* New York: Basic Books.

Hayek, R. (1944). *The Road to Serfdom.* Chicago: University of Chicago Press.

Heclo, H. (1975). *Modern Social Politics in Britain and Sweden.* New Haven, CT: Yale University Press.

Hunt, J., ed. (1995). *The Inaugural Addresses of the Presidents.* New York: Gramercy Books.

Jorstad, E. (1981). *The Politics of Moralism.* Minneapolis: Augsburg Publishing.

Knight, R. (1988). Thatcher's self-help Revolution. *U.S. News & World Report,* May 9, 38–39.

Koven, S. (1991). Turning right: budgeting in the Thatcher and Reagan eras. In A. Farazmand (ed.), *Handbook of Comparative and Development Administration,* 53–66. New York: Marcel Dekker.

Koven, S. (1988). *Ideological Budgeting: The Influence of Political Philosophy on Public Policy.* New York: Praeger Publishers.

Koven, S., Shelley, M., and Swanson B. (1998). *American Public Policy.* Boston: Houghton Mifflin.

Krieger, J. (1986). *Reagan, Thatcher and the Politics of Decline.* New York: Oxford University Press.

Malabre, A. (1987). *Beyond Our Means.* New York: Vintage Books.

Mises, L. (1944). *Bureaucracy.* New Haven, CT: Yale University Press.

Musgrave, R., and Musgrave, P. (1984). *Public Finance in Theory and Practice.* New York: McGraw-Hill.

Palmer, J., and Sawhill, P. (1984). Overview. In J. Palmer and I. Sawhill (eds.), *The Reagan Record.* New York: Ballinger.

Robertson, J. (1987a). Guiding and making policy: ideas and institutions. In *Political Economy Public Policies in the United States and Britain*, 16–46. Jackson: University Press of Mississippi.

Robertson, D. (1987b). Labor market surgery, labor market abandonment: the Thatcher and Reagan unemployment remedies. In *Political Economy Public Policies in the United States and Britain*, 69–97. Jackson: University Press of Mississippi.

Sawhill, I. (1986). Reaganomics in retrospect. In J. Palmer (ed.), *Perspectives on the Reagan Years*, 91–120. Washington: Brookings Institution.

Schick, A. (1990). *The Capacity to Budget.* Washington: Urban Institute Press.

Shanks, M. (1977). *Planning and Politics: The British Experience 1960–76.* London: Allen and Unwin.

Smith, A. (1904). *The Wealth of Nations.* (E. Cannan, ed.) New York: G.P. Putnam's Sons.

Stein, H. (1984). *Presidential Economics: The Making of Economic Policy from Roosevelt to Reagan and Beyond.* New York: Simon and Schuster.

Waltman, J. (1987). Changing the course of tax policy: convergence in intent, divergence in practice. In *Political Economy Public Policies in the United States and Britain*, 98–119. Jackson: University Press of Mississippi.

13

The Duality of Swedish Central Administration*

Ministries and Central Agencies

Olof K. Ruin   *Department of Political Science, University of Stockholm, Stockholm, Sweden*

I. INTRODUCTION

The central administration in Sweden is characterized by a number of relatively small ministries and a large number of central organs independent of the ministries. There are currently 12 ministries with a total staff of about 2500. The organs independent of the ministries number no fewer than about 300 and have a significantly greater number of employees than the ministries. Many of these authorities are very small. They have the character more of boards and secretariats, and their spheres of activity are limited. About 70 of them have a staff of considerable size, each responsible for essential parts or functions of society. These organs are referred to as central agencies (*centrala ämbetsverk*).

There are different kinds of central agencies. Some have responsibility for very important sectors in society, such as the National Board of Education for essentially all school education, and the National Board of Health and Welfare for all health care and social matters. Others have responsibility for more peripheral spheres. Some have produced goods or conducted outright business activity, such as the State Railways, which manage railway traffic in the country, and the National Telecommunications Administration, which supplies telecommunications. Some agencies have functioned more like staff organizations for the government. Agencies can also have tasks of paying out allowances, granting permits of various kinds, collecting taxes, issuing recommendations concerning special activities, etc. The tasks of agencies are thus very diverse. For this reason, the basis for classifying those units that are called agencies varies.

This special division into ministries and agencies has its origins in the Swedish Age of Greatness during the 1600s. During the first part of that century, five so-called administrative colleges were established. One of them, the chancery, received a special position in that in addition to managing matters of foreign affairs, it was also to forward matters of the other colleges. This chancery was the source of the ministries of today, while the four other colleges constituted precursors to the long line of agencies that were established, terminated, and merged with one another during the following centuries. Some of the agencies of today are in fact a direct continuation of those established during the 1600s (Herlitz 1967; Linde 1982; Söderling and Petersson 1986).

---

*Editor's Note: This chapter is a reprint, without revision, of the original chapter in *Handbook of Comparative and Development Public Administration*.

175

This division within the Swedish central administration, almost the result of historical accident, has since often been described and legitimized in terms of a classical dichotomy, that between policy and administration. It has been said that even though the two levels together form the Swedish central administration, they differ in that while the ministries deal primarily with policy, the agencies deal primarily with administration, in the sense of implementing various policies. The division of work between the two levels, like the interplay between them, has of course not always been so unambiguous in practice. There have been shifts in emphasis. There have also been continuous discussions concerning how reasonable or wise this characteristic division is. There have been waves of both praise and criticism.

This division between the ministries and independent agencies is also special in terms of the rules that are applied in communication between levels. Under each ministry there are several agencies; there are also close contacts between the individual ministries and the agencies under them. At the same time, it is the government as a whole that formally issues regulations and instructions of various kinds to agencies. Individual ministries do not formally have this power.

Toward the end of the 1900s, the situation changed to some extent with regard to the division of the Swedish central administration. Discussions concerned whether the division into ministries and independent agencies was itself of value or not. In addition, the actual division of work between the levels began to be directly and consciously changed, not least of all by changing the role of the agencies.

II. ADMINISTRATIVE MODEL AT THE ZENITH

At the end of the 1960s and beginning of the 1970s, the Swedish administrative model seemed to be working particularly well. The relationship between the ministries and the independent agencies was remarkably harmonious. This harmony coincided with a period in Swedish history during which the stability and ambitions of the Swedish welfare state had reached a peak.

One indication of the stability of Swedish politics is that the same political party, the Social Democratic party, had been in the government without interruption since the autumn of 1932 (with the exception of 100 days during the summer of 1936). Furthermore, since the autumn of 1957— at which time a six-year coalition government between the Social Democratic party and one of the three nonsocialist parties, the Agrarian party, was dissolved—the party had governed alone; in the general elections of 1962 and 1968 the party had even obtained more than 50% of the vote. The same person, Tage Erlander, had acted as prime minister continuously for no less than 23 years, from 1946 until 1969; he was succeeded in 1969 by one of his close collaborators, Olof Palme. Many of Tage Erlander's colleagues in the government—later on also colleagues to Olof Palme— had in turn acted as head of the same ministry during a long succession of years (Ruin 1990).

It is an indication of the great ambitions of the Swedish welfare state that reforms did not abate but, on the contrary, intensified along with the increase in the standard of living of the citizens. The work of establishing an advanced welfare state in Sweden—the term used in the beginning was "People's Home" (*folkhem*)—had been initiated during the interwar period. During the first decades of the postwar period, the basic philosophy for government action came to be that the citizens—when they became better off—would not have a lower demand but rather a higher demand for public service, such as better schools for their children, better health care for their sick, better roads for their cars, etc. The public sector, which includes both direct payments to private individuals and the services produced by public employees, was allowed to expand very rapidly in accordance with this philosophy. In no country in the world did the public sector increase as rapidly as in Sweden. In the beginning of the 1970s it was estimated to have comprised over 50% of the GNP.

The good relationship between the government and the agencies during these dynamic years was characterized by the fact that the ministers generally had great confidence in the agencies, and the agencies in turn were generally very responsive to the government. This relationship of mutual confidence and trust was promoted by the fact that many ministers had held their positions for a long time and many higher civil servants within the agencies had personal experience of work within the ministries. This was the case not least of all for those who were heads of the agencies, that is, the directors general (*generaldirektör*). Thus in the stable political situation that prevailed in Sweden during the 1960s and the beginning of the 1970s, many cabinet members inevitably came to know many agency heads very well, and vice versa.

A characteristic feature of the harmonious relationship between the government and the agencies was that the independent agencies were seen as having a central role in the process of political reform. It therefore also seemed natural that as the public sector accepted responsibility for new spheres of society, this responsibility should be reflected in the creation of new agencies. As examples, in 1965 the Swedish International Development Authority (SIDA) was established in order to increase the efficiency of Sweden's efforts for developing countries; in 1967 the National Environment Protection board (SNV) was established to deal with environmental problems and the National Board of Town and Country Planning for dealing with planning and construction matters in the country; in 1969 the National Immigration and Naturalization Board (SIV) was established to deal with matters that Sweden as a country of immigration faced; and in 1973 the National Industrial Board (SIND) began its work as an expression of the greater ambitions of the state in matters related to trade and industry. As a result of these newly established organs, the number of agencies increased. By the end of the war there had been about 50 agencies of importance; at the beginning of the 1970s there were more than 70 (Tarschys 1978). At the same time, mergers of agencies that had previously been separate from each other were undertaken. Efficiency was to be increased and coordination improved. An illustrative example of this tendency was the merger in 1967 of the Board of Medicine dating from the late 1600s with the Board of Social Welfare, which had been established in the beginning of the 1900s.

Many agencies also received more comprehensive tasks, as an expression of the confidence they enjoyed within the government and elsewhere in society. Their traditional role had—in line with the dichotomy of policy and administration—primarily been to put laws into practice and to implement goals formulated by the *Riksdag* and the government. As laws increasingly came to have the character of frame legislation, it was considered to be the responsibility of many agencies to fill the laws with substance in the form of regulations and guidelines of various kinds. Furthermore, it was also presumed that many agencies ought to devote themselves to planning within their respective spheres of responsibility and to undertaking independent initiatives. Rather substantial R&D resources were allotted to several of them so that they would be able to begin studies and inquiries and initiate research on matters within their spheres of responsibility (Premfors 1986). Finally, the agencies were in general to become more involved in providing service and information than previously. Thus, as has already been said, agencies, enjoying widespread confidence, had their spheres of activity significantly broadened.

III. MODEL QUESTIONED

A short time after the characteristic division in the Swedish administration seemed to have reached a peak—with the interplay between the levels functioning well—this division once again became the object of critical discussion. Criticism was directed less against the government than against the agencies. The criticism was rooted in several different factors.

One factor was to be found in the new and strengthened position of the agencies. The con-

ventional notion of what ministries and agencies should deal with—policy formulation and policy application, respectively—had not been strictly adhered to for a long time. The differences
between the levels had been further eroded. The work of the agencies had in significant respects
begun very simply to resemble that of the ministries. The former, as interpreters of frame legislation, had the task of working out detailed regulations of a type that the latter had primarily dealt
with. The former had furthermore started to become involved in conducting studies and inquiries
and in planning activity of a kind that resembled the traditional sphere of responsibility of the latter. All of this led many of the civil servants in the agencies to no longer see the application of laws
as their main task, as it had been for their predecessors. Instead, they perceived themselves as
activists characterized by an ambition to change society. With this, agency officials and ministry
officials also began to resemble each other more and more in their role as bureaucrats. This erosion of distinct roles among bureaucrats in Sweden was noted in an international survey that
included Sweden (Anton 1980; Mellbourn 1979).

At the same time as the two levels of the Swedish central administration seemed to have
converged more than before in terms of tasks, a more unstable political situation arose in the country, which further complicated matters. The long period of Social Democratic governance was
broken in 1976 when the three nonsocialist parties secured a majority in the general election and
formed a nonsocialist three-party government. Six years later in 1982, the nonsocialist two-party
government then in power was succeeded by a new Social Democratic one-party government.
These shifts were followed by a certain confidence gap between the government and the agencies.

There is no "spoils system" in Sweden in the sense of changes in governments being accompanied by changes in the leadership of agencies. Heads of agencies once appointed retain their
positions despite changes in government. As a result, many cabinet members and undersecretaries
in the nonsocialist government that assumed office in 1976 felt a certain estrangement from agencies having directors general who, according to them, had been too well entrenched in circles
around the outgoing Social Democratic government. In a corresponding fashion, cabinet members
in the Social Democratic government of 1982 felt a certain apprehension toward several of the
directors general who had been appointed by the nonsocialist governments; the new appointees
were considered to be either too well entrenched in the nonsocialist parties or not especially competent. Even if there is no "spoils system" in Sweden, a rather significant number of the heads of
agencies can be said to have clear political sympathies (DsC 1985:6).

The most important reason for the increasing criticism of the Swedish agencies during the
1970s and 1980s is, however, that many of them have to some extent been made the scapegoat for
the general criticism that was directed against advanced welfare states, like Sweden, at this time.
Thus it is not so much a matter of criticism based on economic problems that many welfare states,
including Sweden, were subjected to at the end of the 1970s and beginning of the 1980s: that continued financing of a persistently high level of public expenditure had become extraordinarily
problematic, that economic growth seemed to have decreased or completely ceased, that loans
from abroad had increased dramatically and the rate of inflation become high, that unemployment
had increased, etc. It was instead a matter of criticism related to the alleged difficulties of the modern welfare state in making decisions and directing developments in society.

One such difficulty, often expounded upon in international discussions of the welfare state,
was the overload that the state decision-making machinery was said to have been suffering from
as a result of all of the commitments that the central state had assumed. In Sweden this type of criticism was directed to some extent precisely against the agencies. It was the agencies in particular
that seemed to have been allowed to expand and proliferate. They were also criticized for not having the time to deal with everything they were supposed to deal with.

Another difficulty, to which attention is often drawn in international discussions, involved
trends toward sectorization and the negative consequences that could result from this. In the case

of Sweden, with the comprehensive welfare program of the country, there were certain agencies in particular that seemed to foster such tendencies. It had been a deliberate policy to create effective central agencies—sometimes through mergers of two or more previously independent authorities—with responsibility for large, clearly delimited spheres of state activity. These agencies, as agencies in general, had also received—in addition to the directors general—so-called boards of laypersons, which generally included politicians, representatives of interest organizations, bureaucrats, and experts of various kinds. These boards became breeding grounds for the growth of so-called iron triangles, coalitions between specialized politicians, representatives of interest organizations, and bureaucrats, in the defense of the interests of a specific sector. This became apparent, for example, in the situation in which Sweden, as other welfare states, found itself at the end of the 1970s and beginning of the 1980s, when the public sector was faced with the threat of reductions and reorientation.

Finally, there was a further aspect of the criticism of the welfare state that was particularly intense in Sweden and that indirectly also came to involve the agencies. It was claimed that trends toward corporativism, intimacy between the state apparatus and interest organizations, were especially evident in welfare states. In Sweden in particular there was a long tradition of powerful interest organizations. A large number of interests had been organized for a long time, the organizations had likewise incorporated a very large proportion of those who could potentially be organized, and the leadership of the organizations had held a strong position. During the 1970s the intimate contacts between organizations and the state apparatus intensified. The lay boards of the agencies were often presented as a typical example of this. Representatives of interest organizations occupied approximately 20% of all available positions on these boards (Hadenius 1978; DsC 1985:6). In addition, the practice of agency employees being represented on the board of their agency through their union organizations, though with limited voting rights, became more widespread during this decade. Through this practice, union organizations obtained double representation in the leadership of agencies in Sweden: they were considered both as representatives of a general interest by proxy and as representatives of the employees. This was seen as a flagrant example of precisely corporativist tendencies (Ruin 1974; Westerståhl and Persson 1975).

In summary, a rather rapid reversal in the assessment of agencies in Sweden had thus taken place and thereby also in the view of the relationship between the two levels of the central administration. At the end of the 1960s and beginning of the 1970s the agencies were still seen as important instruments in the continuing expansion of the Swedish welfare state. Rather soon thereafter criticism arose in many quarters. The agencies were felt to be both too unwieldy and too powerful and to have a tendency to pursue their own policies and defend their own territory. A political scientist and Liberal party politician, Daniel Tarschys, characterized the democratic process, in an often cited formulation, as running backward when agencies initiate and present plans that the government accepts and eventually also obtains approval for from the Riksdag (Tarschys and Eduards 1975).

IV. REFORM STRATEGY

At the same time that the Swedish administrative model was beginning to be questioned and the role of the agencies was being criticized in some quarters, two reform strategies were introduced which came to influence the structure and functioning of the central administration. They were influenced to some extent by the specific criticism of agencies that had been expounded, but they also arose independently of it, being characterized by general processes of change in society. In certain respects these reform strategies were the opposites of each other.

One of these involved transferring tasks from the central administration of the country to "lower" levels of decision making in society. While to some extent affecting the government level, it primarily involved transfer from the level of the agencies. This strategy was strongly associated with the spirit of the times, which emphasized decentralization, the importance of moving decisions closer to the people, of people having a greater opportunity for participating in the framing of decisions that concern them. But it was also a result of a feeling that many central agencies had become too large and thus had become unmanageable and even inefficient. In statements by the government and the Riksdag as well as in programs within specific sectors, traditional arguments in favor of decentralization were expounded with increasing intensity. Decentralization was argued to contribute to greater efficiency in decision making; it could provide greater possibilities for taking variations in local conditions into consideration in decision-making situations; it could raise the feeling of participation among the citizens, etc. (SOU 1978:52; Gustafsson 1987; Bladh 1987).

In Sweden the conditions for decentralization were particularly propitious since both the local and regional levels had been revitalized and strengthened through very deliberate reforms. On the local level were the municipalities, which had a long tradition of independent decision-making authority. The number of municipalities had been drastically reduced as a result of amalgamations during the 1950s, 1960s, and 1970s, primarily in order to promote efficiency; proper conditions were thereby foreseen for allowing the municipalities to take over responsibility for the day-to-day administration of various welfare programs from the central level. On the regional level there were both an expanded state regional administration in the form of regional administrative boards and a local government administration in the form of counties with responsibility primarily for health and medical care in the region. Elections to the approximately 280 municipalities and the 23 counties take place once every three years, at the same time as elections to the *Riksdag*.

The tasks on the central level that, in accordance with this decentralization drive, were successively transferred to the regional or local levels or terminated varied, of course, among different societal spheres. In general it can be said that there was a conscious attempt to decrease the role of the central level, particularly of the agencies, in supervision and detailed regulation and in issuing recommendations and providing instructions for lower levels and citizens to follow (Mellbourn 1986).

The other strategy of significance for the development of the Swedish administrative model was directly connected to the criticisms of the agencies. The supremacy of the government was emphasized more strongly than previously, and there were indications of a willingness to try to direct the independent agencies more forcefully than previously. The strategy was summarized for the Riksdag in a government proposition (Regeringens Proposition, 1986/87:90), which was in turn based on the work of two commissions of inquiry (SOU 1983:39, 1985:40). Arguments based on a particular conception of democracy were produced in support of increased control of this kind. It was argued that just as the government is responsible to the Riksdag, which is elected by the citizens in general elections, the agencies ought to comply with the wishes of the government. This type of relation of compliance was advanced as a final link in a democratic chain of decision making.

However, this emphasis on increased control on the part of the government involved a set of constitutional issues. There is a long-cherished notion in Sweden that the central agencies are not only organizationally independent from the government but also that the constitution guarantees them a large degree of independent vis-à-vis this higher level. This interpretation of the constitution, still sustained in various quarters in the country, has been essentially refuted though in connection with the current philosophy of increased control. On the other hand, there is general agreement over the fact that the current constitution in one specific respect guarantees the agencies independence from the government. Paragraph 11:7 of the Instrument of Government states: "No public authority, nor the Riksdag, nor the decision-making body of a municipality may determine how an administrative authority shall make its decision in a particular case concerning the exercise of public authority against a private subject or against a municipality, or concerning the application of law."

Thus, the government may not get involved in the decision of a central agency in a specific case if it is a matter of "exercise of public authority" and "application of law"; by "exercise of public authority" against a private subject is meant such matters as regard benefits, rights, obligations, disciplinary penalties, dismissals, etc. The rule of law in the determination of specific cases by administrative authorities is thereby supposed to be guaranteed.

The policy currently endorsed of attempting to direct the still independent agencies more forcefully than previously is not without problems. The means available are neither simple nor unambiguous.

One means that has not been considered is to issue detailed regulations to the central agencies. On the contrary, it has become a part of the public rhetoric to argue against centrally issued regulations, whether formulated on the level of the government or on the level of agencies. Instead, what has been discussed with renewed conviction in Sweden during the 1980s is directing through the specification of goals. This philosophy is said to be attuned to both an ambition to exercise less control—to decentralize—and to exercise more control in the sense of concentrating on what is essential. The philosophy has in turn aroused criticism of a traditional kind. It has been pointed out that goals formulated on the political level—by the *Riksdag* and the government—are of necessity very vague. The formulation of goals is often preceded by quite difficult negotiations between different interests, ideologies, parties, etc. Vague goal formulations, a precondition for being able to reach agreement at all, have only limited potential for serving a regulative function. Furthermore, if goals are made precise enough to be able to serve this kind of function, there would not be any great difference between these specific goals and out-and-out detailed regulation (SOU 1985:40, 227ff).

Another means of directing the work of the independent agencies that the government possesses is of course intensified informal contacts. Contacts of this kind have in fact existed for a long time, even though the formal principle in Swedish state administration is that it is the government as a whole—not individual ministers—who are to direct the work of the agencies. Thus many ministers have regular meetings with the directors general of the agencies falling under the ministry in question; many civil servants in the ministries maintain regular contact with agency officials, etc. (Jacobson 1984). It is now being suggested that these informal contacts be intensified in order to strengthen government control over agencies. However, there is obviously another side to contacts of this kind. The division of responsibility between what takes place on the level of the government and what takes place on the level of the agencies, respectively, is in danger of being completely eradicated. On the one hand, a cabinet member may increasingly be forced to accept responsibility for the actions of the organizationally independent agencies; on the other hand, the agencies may begin to lose their feeling of responsibility. The actual value of having an organizational division between the ministries and the agencies can be completely undermined in a situation in which the division of responsibility is unclear.

A further means is through the appointment of personnel. Demands have been made in public discussions in Sweden that the heads of the central agencies should resign when there is a change of government so as to increase the correspondence between the government level and the agency level and thereby facilitate government control. In recent decisions the *Riksdag* and the government have not wanted to go that far. There is still resistance to a direct spoils system. However, decisions have been made that make it possible to transfer heads of agencies in the middle of their terms of appointment, even against the will of the persons concerned, in an attempt to increase the possibility for the government of directing the work of the agencies. In this way a government would be able to relocate heads of agencies who are perceived as passive, obstinate, or inefficient.

In discussions during the past years on increased government control of agencies, the idea of using the layboards of the agencies as a means of directing the work of the agencies has come up. Something of that kind would, however, necessitate that the boards be populated solely by ministerial personnel or by politicians who share the political priorities of the government. However, the government and the *Riksdag* have not been prepared to propose this type of lay board. It has been felt that they should continue to include, as they have in the past, politicians both from the government and from the opposition, both representatives of interest organizations and experts of various kinds. All of these various categories of board members are expected to represent a general interest at the same time as boards composed in this pluralistic manner are assumed to provide the best opportunities for openness, for the input of public opinion, for the infusion of expertise, etc. At the same time, executive organs composed in this manner can make it more difficult for the government to direct the work of agencies, since they, precisely because of their comprehensive composition, can easily develop into a buffer around the agencies and the sectors of society that the agencies represent (Ruin 1983).

All of these means of directing agencies are associated with their own special limitations and problems. In the decisions taken by the *Riksdag* in the spring of 1987 concerning the relationship between the government and the independent agencies, other more or less vague means were mentioned that were all felt to be able to contribute to improved control of the work of the agencies. The cycle of the appropriation of funds that is the basis for the work of the agencies was modified; the importance of reviews of agencies by certain staff authorities as well as of evaluations by the agencies themselves of the work for which they are responsible was emphasized. A final impression is that it is nonetheless difficult for a government to attempt to direct the work of the agencies under it more forcefully without endangering their independent position, their own sense of responsibility, and their openness with respect to society.

Another solution for a government that does not have confidence in subordinate authorities is simply to assume responsibility for various matters. This has in fact happened. For example, the ministries have assumed responsibility for payment of subsidies and detailed planning of various kinds—matters that by tradition should reside on the agency level. It can thus be said that there have been recent trends toward centralization in the Swedish administrative system at the same time as there has been—in accordance with the previously mentioned reform strategy—a very clear ambition to decentralize, to transfer tasks from the agencies to lower levels, primarily to the local level. Thus tasks have been drained off from the agencies in two directions: both from above and from below.

V.   THE NEW SITUATION

The current division of roles between the two levels of the Swedish central administration has become somewhat different from what it was a few decades ago. In general, the ministries now have more to do and the agencies less. Some of the agencies, such as those that primarily produce goods, pay out subsidies, collect taxes, issue permits, etc., operate much as they did previously. Others have undergone distinct changes. The greatest changes seem to have involved agencies that have had responsibility for important sectors of the Swedish welfare society. Agneta Bladh (1987) has published a detailed account of changes in the work of three such agencies: the National Board of Education responsible for schools, the National Swedish Board of Universities and Colleges responsible for the system of higher education, and the National Board of Health and Welfare responsible for health and medical care as well as social policy.

The new focus of many agencies is often described by indicating what it is that the agencies do not do any longer. The level of ambition is said to be significantly lower than previously with regard to formulating regulations of a binding nature for lower levels in society. The agencies obviously also have less influence than before over how resources in detail are distributed within fields of activity which are being supervised.

The role of the agencies is also described by emphasizing what is new and different. Terms such as information, evaluation, followup, study and inquiry, service, etc. are used. Instead of attempting to direct their respective fields of activity by rules and subsidies as before, the agencies are said to aim at exerting influence both in a more indirect and in a more flexible manner. They are to disseminate information of importance. They are to undertake evaluations and followups of activities under their supervision. They are to have access to experts who can perform studies of various kinds and present proposals for plans concerning the work of the respective agencies. Finally, they are to be, in a more conscious manner than previously, service-minded, be prepared to support and assist in various ways those perceived as the "customers" of the agency. Presentations of what is new often tends to be rather vague. In accordance with the spirit of the times prevailing in the 1980s, models are borrowed both from the private sector, which has been in great favor, and from the local level, which has become increasingly important.

This new role that has been assumed by agencies, and that is constantly depicted in various semiofficial texts, has led to a degree of uncertainty. It is indicative that conferences of various kinds are often organized in Sweden nowadays concerning this role. The future of different agencies is studied, proposals for organizational changes are presented, and so forth. The source of this uncertainty is to be found both in the new modes of operation that are proposed and in the somewhat different position that the agencies occupy in the political system.

The training and experience of many agency officials has been primarily with purely administrative tasks, even though they may have worked on studies and inquiries of various kinds previously. With this kind of background, it may be difficult for many to adapt to a situation in which they are called upon to work almost exclusively with disseminating information and conducting studies. Since many agencies have had to decrease their personnel at the same time as they have assumed a new role, there has not been much in the way of new recruitment either.

The new position of many agencies in the political system can be expressed as a shift from being located along a vertical dimension to being located along a horizontal dimension. That is, the agencies were previously clearly subordinate to the government and superior to regional and local instances, having the job of interpreting the intentions of the government. The work was primarily directed toward lower levels of decision making and toward the citizens in general. Since the job of many agencies has become foremost that of furnishing the government with important background information, the work of agencies has come to be directed largely toward the government. Many agencies have begun to appear more as a resource for conducting studies than as a means by which the government can direct society.

It should be added that these transformed agencies are in no way the only source of studies and inquiries at the disposal of the government. On the contrary, the Swedish government system has a comprehensive system of commissions of inquiry (Meijer 1956, 1969). Every year a large number of state commissions of inquiry are appointed with the task of studying various problems and working out reform proposals. These commissions, which generally include politicians and representatives from organizations as well as experts of various kinds, have had a rather independent position vis-à-vis the government that has appointed them. This independence has been seen as facilitating the work of the commissions in reaching compromises and consensual solutions over policy (Premfors 1983).

There are a number of problems that arise as a result of a reorientation of the work of agencies from administrating to conducting studies. One concerns coordination with the traditionally strong Swedish system of commissions of inquiry. Who is to have charge over what? Another problem, and one of more general interest, concerns how meaningful it is at all to attempt to direct the work of agencies that assume this type of task. The question of directing the agencies more forcefully was brought to the fore precisely because they appeared to have become too powerful and unmanageable, but from the point of view of a government the situation would have to be quite another if the agencies are given the job of conducting studies. A certain degree of independence is usually advantageous for such tasks: it promotes impartiality and comprehensiveness. An attempt to reform the division of the Swedish central administration into two levels can clearly create contradictory situations.

VI. THE FUTURE

The future of the division of the Swedish central administration is naturally dependent both on general societal processes and on concrete experiences of the changes that have taken place in recent years.

Only one such process will be mentioned here. It involves the belief that politics on the national level in countries like Sweden is increasingly going to decline in importance. It is not only a matter of further municipalization of politics but also of Sweden's becoming increasingly dependent upon its international environment, not least of all on the accelerating integration in Europe. Many issues may in fact come to be decided in other capital cities or may be considered to be too large or too difficult to deal with on the national level. At the same time, it may turn out that other, less significant issues are best dealt with on the local level. With a development of this kind, the central administration of the country, regardless of how it is organized, would gradually be left with less to do.

At the same time that it is likely that Sweden's dependence on its environment is going to increase in the future, it is less likely that the local level is going to continue to increase-Parallel to the prevailing decentralization philosophy, there is at present a certain weariness with the lack of decisiveness that this philosophy encourages. Centrally issued instructions as to what is acceptable and not acceptable are often claimed to be lacking. It is perhaps indicative that the national organizations the municipalities and the countries have created—the Swedish Association of Local Authorities and the Federation of County Councils—have to some extent moved in and filled the vacuum that arose in certain areas when the central level, particularly the central agencies, failed to provide guidelines in accordance with the prevailing philosophy.

One concrete experience of the shifts that have occurred between the two levels in the Swedish central administration concerns the consequences for democracy. It has been claimed that both the concentration of tasks to the level of the government and decentralization of tasks to the local level would represent a gain in democracy, since these two levels have a more direct popular mandate than the independent agencies. The argument is formalistic. Consideration is not given to how decisions are in fact made.

A concentration of matters to the ministries in the name of democracy necessarily leads to an increase in ministerial personnel. There are already clear trends in this direction. Thus far, with rather small ministries and independent agencies, Swedish ministers have not needed to feel burdened by day-to-day administrative matters, as are their colleagues in other countries. A successive expansion of the ministries would change this. Ministers would find it more difficult to assert themselves against ministerial officials—to assume control over the work they head. One problem for democracy would thus be replaced by another. During the past decades this problem has been seen as a result of the agencies being unmanageable in relation to the ministries. Now this complex of problems can to an increasing extent come to be found within the ministries, in the relations between the politically appointed and the permanent ministerial officials.

At least three different scenarios for the future of the special division of the Swedish central administration can be imagined:

1.   The two levels are allowed to merge. The central agencies, several of which have

already assumed new tasks, are absorbed into the ministries under which they fall. They are simply transformed into divisions within the ministries. The idea of merging the two levels is in fact an old one in Sweden. At the beginning of this century, a state commission of inquiry that was very critical of this division proposed an amalgamation of this kind (SOU 1913). Duplication of work, waste of time, and increased administrative costs would thereby be avoided; preconditions would be created for uniform and systematic leadership of the administration, etc. However, no meaningful discussions of a total integration of the two levels are taking place today.

2.   The levels remain separate but the current trends in the division of labor between them are further intensified. A development of this kind is outlined, for example, by the political scientist Janerik Gidlund (1986:132) in a recently published study conducted for the Institute for Futures Studies concerning the public administration of the future. He anticipates, among other things, that the significance of the municipal level will continue to increase.

> The agencies will be tied more closely to the Ministries and local self-government will be given significantly greater independence and responsibilities. The Ministries will become larger at the same time as the agencies decrease significantly in size. A large portion of the increase in efficiency through increased municipal efforts will be extracted in the form of decreases in the state sector. The agencies will acquire an increasingly important role as service organs to the municipalities and as centers of knowledge. An important task will also be following up the work carried out in the municipalities and conducting long-term analyses.

Visions of the future like those depicted by Gidlund are often expounded in public discussions in Sweden today. The idea is that an administrative level should still remain between the ministries, on the one hand, and regional and local units on the other. But it is anticipated that the new focus of this middle level is going to continue and its independence and significance decline.

3.   The agencies generally regain to some extent the position they previously had. This means that in addition to everything that is part of the current philosophy—service, information, inquiry, followup, etc.—they are also given responsibility for tasks of a more regulatory and distributive nature. The assumption of a development of this kind is based on the idea of a greater need for central regulation for society, of a renewed appreciation of the fact that the ministries can be kept small by delegating tasks to the agency level, and also of an increased appreciation for the need for clearly demarcating the lines of responsibility between the ministries and the agencies.

My hope, rather than my prognosis, is that this third scenario is the one that will be closest to reality. The division of the Swedish central administration, which arose to some extent by historical accident, is today attracting increasing international attention. This could be seen, for example, at a conference that a subdivision of the OECD organized in May 1988 in Stockholm. The theme of the conference was "Policy Advice and Co-ordination at the Centre of Government," the participants being "senior officials from centres of government" (Statskontoret 1988). The flexibility that the division of the Swedish administration has helped in creating was emphasized. This arrangement had not previously met with any noteworthy recognition (Fulton 1968; Brown 1971). It would be paradoxical if Sweden itself were to be in the process of abandoning its special administrative model at the same time as the traditional advantages of the model are perhaps beginning to be recognized abroad.

REFERENCES

Andersson, S., Mellbourn, A., and Skogö, I. (1978). *Myndigheter i Samhället, Problem och utvecklingslinjer i statsförvaltningen.* Stockholm: Liber.

Anton, T.H. (1980). *Administrative Politics. Elite Political Culture in Sweden.* Boston: Martinus Nijhoff.

Bladh, A. (1987). *Decentraliserad förvaltning. Tre ämbetsverk i nya roller.* Lund: Studentlitteratur.

Brown, R.G.S. (1971). *Administrative Process in Britain.* University Paperbacks.

DsC. (1985). *Fakta om statliga myndigheters ledning. Civildepartementet* 16.

Fulton, Lord. (1968). *The Civil Service: Report of the Committee 1966–68.* Cmnd 8638. London: HMSO.

Gidlund, J. (1987). *Fria ämbetsverk eller självständiga kommuner. Strategier för morgondagens offentliga sektor.* Stockholm: Sekretariatet för framtidsstudier.

Gustafsson, G. (1987). *Decentralisering av politisk makt.* Stockholm: Carlsson.

Hadenius, A. (1978). Ämbetsverkens styrelser. *Statsvetenskaplig tidskrift 1.*

Herlitz, N. (1967). *Grunddragen av det svenska statsskickets historia.* Stockholm: Norstedts.

Jacobsson, B. (1984). *Hur styrs förvaltningen?—Myt och verklighet kring departmentens styrning av ämbetsverken.* Lund: Studentlitteratur.

Linde, C. (1982). *Department och verk. Om synen på den centrala statsförvaltningen och dess uppdelning—i en förändrad offentlig sektor.* Stockholm: Stockholm Studies in Politics.

Meijer, H. (1956). *Kommittépolitik och kommittéarbete.* Lund: Gleerup.

Meijer, H. (1969). Bureaucracy and policy formulation in Sweden. *Scandinavian Political Studies 4.*

Mellbourn, A. (1979). *Byråkratins ansikten. Rolluppfattningar hos svenska högre statstjänsteman.* Stockholm: Liber.

Mellbourn, A. (1986). *Bortom det starka samhället: socialdemokratisk förvaltningspolitik 1982–1985.* Stockholm: Carlsson.

Premfors, R. (1986). Governmental commissions in Sweden. *American Behavioral Scientist 26*(5).

Premfors, R. (1986). *Svensk forskningspolitik.* Lund: Studentlitteratur.

Regeringens Proposition (1986/87). *Ledningen av den statliga förvaltningen 1986/87:99.*

Ruin, O. (1974). Participatory democracy and corporativism: the case of Sweden. *Scandinavian Political Studies 9.*

Ruin, O. (1983). *Politik och förvaltning—Statsråd och generaldirektörer. Vägval, uppsatser om några demokratiproblem.* Stockholm: Brevskolan.

Ruin, O. (1990). *Tage Erlander. Serving the Welfare State, 1946–1969.* Pittsburgh: University of Pittsburgh Press.

Söderlind, D., and Petersson, O. (1986). *Svensk förvaltningspolitik.* Uppsala: Diskurs.

Statliga myndigheter, Verksamhet, organisation, ekonomi. (1986). Stockholm: Statskontoret.

SOU. (1986). *Departmentalkommitterades betänkande, Allmän del.* Stockholm.

SOU. (1978). *Lägg besluten närmare människorna. Huvudbetänkande från decentraliseringsutredningen 1978:52.*

SOU. (1983). *Politisk styrning—Administrativ självständighet. Slutbetänkande från förvaltningsutredningen 39.*

SOU. (1985). *Regeringen, myndigheterna och myndigheternas ledning, Huvudbetänkande från verksledningskommittén 40.*

Statskontoret. (1988). *Har centrala ämbetsverk en framtid. Statskontoret 6.*

Tarschys, D. (1978). *Den offentliga revolutionen.* Stockholm: Liber.

Tarschys, D., and Eduards, M. (1975). *Petita, Hur svenska myndigheter argumenterar för högre anslag.* Stockholm: Publica.

Westerståhl, J., and Persson, M. (1975). *Demokrati och intresserepresentation: en principdiskussion.* Stockholm: Liber.

14

Changing Values and Notions of Pay Equity in the Swedish Civil Service

Lois Recascino Wise   *School of Public and Environmental Affairs, Indiana University, Bloomington, Indiana*

Alf Sjöström   *Swedish Gallup, Stockholm, Sweden*

I. INTRODUCTION

The extent to which transitions in pay foster a balance among the competing norms and values in the pay administration process is critical to their long-term success. Wise and Jonzon (1991), among others, have described the way public sector employment in Sweden served as an instrument for putting into place the welfare state goals of income equality and equality between the sexes. But starting in the mid-1980s, Sweden began to implement decentralized and individually flexible pay after emphasizing solidaristic and collective wage setting and egalitarian earnings levels. Within 10 years, the central government pay system was transformed.

During the 1970s Sweden's already small wage differentials narrowed further as compensation policy in both government and industry was used as a mechanism to achieve the social goal of income equality (Jonsson and Siven 1986; Björklund 1987). Sweden's centralized pay negotiations were structured around solidaristic principles including the tenet that the profitability of individual firms should not drive wage formation (Meidner 1974). In principle, as in other Nordic countries, equity among sectors of employment and geographic regions was advanced and seniority was recognized as a legitimate factor for differentiation. But unlike Norway (Laegried 1996), for example, pay policy in Sweden did not reward educational attainment; rather, it sought to level earnings across educational groups. Many Swedes rejected the idea that work based on knowledge and mental skills was more valuable than manual work or that individuals' investments in their own human capital development should be rewarded with higher earnings. Moreover, the principle of comparability between sectors was undermined in Sweden by the tenet that the goods-producing sector should lead the wage negotiation process and make the process more responsive to international market forces (Edgren et al. 1973; Lundberg 1985).

This chapter analyzes attitudes and values toward pay setting among Swedish employees. Our main focus is to determine the extent to which the attitudes of work force members in Sweden appear supportive of or in tension with the reforms under way toward more flexible and contribution-based pay setting. The findings overall indicate that while a relatively small core group of employees remains faithful to the solidaristic pay-setting practices that characterized compensation policy in the Swedish public sector until the 1980s, a majority of Swedish employees are favorable toward a series of practices that shift the basis in pay setting from the positions people hold and the amount of time they have worked for a particular organization to the skills and abilities they bring to the workplace. These findings suggest that the reforms under way represent more than an economic adjustment or political intervention, but rather a fundamental shift in social values among both private and public sector employees (Wise and Sjöström 1997).

It seems apparent that the initial reforms were aimed at making central government more effective at recruiting and retaining valued and skilled workers and responding to the so-called imbalance in pay between the private and public sectors (Wise 1993). In the mid-1980s pay comparability between central government and the private sector was a policy recommended by the Ministry of Finance, and special "market" supplements were put into force which gave management some flexibility over centrally bargained wage rates for hiring and retaining. Government articulated the principle that pay setting in the public sector should be based on the activities of the agency and not on other social goals or objectives. Moreover, management gained flexibility in salary allocation during this period as the share of the wage pot available for local discretion was gradually increased.

The goal of income equality, which influenced pay setting in Sweden during the 1970s, was seen by some as a factor that had had dysfunctional consequences on skill development and educational attainment in the labor market and this was associated with a drive to increase wage differentials across occupational groups and between skill levels in the same occupational category (Jakobsson 1984; Lash 1985; Lundberg 1985; Jonsson and Siven 1986; Björklund 1987; Hibbs 1990; Verkstadsföreningen 1991). Within this context, larger differentials among individuals, occupational groups, regions, or firms were judged desirable by many and, in fact, were already apparent at the end of the 1980s (Gustafsson 1988; SCB 1991; Zetterberg 1994). Employers' associations promoted guidelines for managers taking up the task of differentiating among individuals in allocating pay during this period (Wennberg 1991; Bredbacka 1993), but no system of individual performance appraisal was promulgated by central government.

The reforms also emphasized efficiency and accountability in government administration. A public sector, large by any standard, was typically seen as limiting economic growth and viability, and demands to reduce the size of government and increase government efficiency were widespread and shared across political parties (Premfors 1991; Wise 1993). From 1985 to 1993, the Swedish central government reduced its work force by 25% through a variety of different techniques including reductions in force, privatization, reorganization, and mergers (Wise and Stengård, 1999). In this environment, agencies of government would normally focus on organizational survival and goal attainment but attention to mission and objectives was also promoted by a central government emphasis on measurable indicators of organizational performance (Premfors 1991; Ministry of Finance 1993; Wilkes 1996).

In response to these forces, the public sector wage-setting process was substantially decentralized and made much more flexible (Sjölund 1989; Gustafsson 1990; Wise 1993; Zetterberg 1994). Greater differentiation is apparent in the size of pay increases across occupational groups and among agencies. Differences are apparent between agencies of central government in the amount of funds made available for pay increases but we do not know whether these differences are ascribed to greater profitability or management efficiency.

The gap in average pay between the sexes in central government has also increased to the disadvantage of women, as others have noted (Gustafsson 1988; Zetterberg 1994), but gains are also noted for women. Women who were hired into the state sector from 1993 to 1995 were brought in with substantially higher salaries than the women who departed, while newly hired male employees received salaries that on average were lower than those of men leaving central government service (Arbetsgivarverket 1996).

But the key factor distinguishing pay reform in the Swedish central government was the abolishment of the formal, narrowly graded position classification system and with it the concept of holding a static civil service post. By eliminating the notion of "appointment," civil servants were sent the message that their work was being transformed and their jobs were becoming less secure (Wise and Stengård, 1999). A clear motive for pay reform in Sweden was to switch the emphasis in pay administration from personal status in the system to individual contribution to the organization (Göransson 1996). In discarding the old step-based pay system, central government employers signaled the work force that salaries were an instrument for achieving organizational results (Göransson 1996).

That such a sharp change in wage policy could be put into place in a relatively short time raises questions about the extent to which wage earners themselves have been supportive of pay reforms. Survey data show that both public and private employees in Sweden accepted public management reforms as necessary (Wise and Szücs 1996), but reforms such as these raise many questions about equity and perceived legitimacy in a public sector context (Lægreid 1996). The extent to which employees themselves accept the new compensation criteria as fair is a key question (Wise and Sjöström 1997). The pendulum of reform swings in a relatively restricted arc in Sweden, and the broad societal norm of egalitarianism is strong there (Sjöström 1992; Verba et al. 1988; Premfors 1998). Consequently, reforms designed to change the size of salary differentials between individuals or organizations or the criteria for allocating pay increases raise important questions about confidence in and acceptance of the new system (Levine and Kleeman 1992; Sjölund 1994; Lægreid 1996). The discussion now briefly reviews the underlying assumptions around flexible and individualized pay as well as the equity issues that impact individual perceptions of pay fairness.

II. EXISTING RESEARCH AND THEORY

The two key elements of pay reform in Sweden are greater differentiation among individuals in determining pay and decentralization of the responsibility for pay administration from central government to the agencies and from the agencies to line managers. An overall goal is to enhance flexibility in both employee behavior and organizational capacity to respond to new circumstances and demands for change.

The underlying assumption behind these reforms is that replacing individual neutral factors such as a defined position or length of time on the job with individually based criteria sends a signal to employees about the skills and behaviors that the labor market values while decentralization of decision making clarifies a manager's role in determining the amount of rewards and benefits an employee receives. Employees who acquire desirable skills and abilities and who make greater contributions to an organization should be recognized by their immediate supervisor and receive rewards and benefits commensurate to their level of contribution. For reforms like these to succeed, however, they must be perceived by a core group of employees as appropriate and legitimate and consistent with prevailing values about which behavior should be rewarded and how employers as paymasters should distinguish among different workers in distributing the goods and benefits derived from employment.

A. Prevailing Assumptions About Receptivity Toward Reform

It is often assumed that public employees are more resistant to reforms than people working in the private sector and that efforts to install progressive pay policies will meet with more hindrances in government than in the private sector, where competition and a profit motive make obvious the need for efficiency-based reforms.

This assumption has two weaknesses. The first is in assuming that all government employees assess the advantages and disadvantages of a given circumstance primarily from the perspective of their status as government employees. Research demonstrates that sector of employment is less important in accounting for employees' behavior than other interests people have in common, like their union affiliation (Blake 1991; Cousineau and Girad 1991; Wise and Szücs 1996), political ideology, or professional norms (Blake 1991; Lafferty and Knutsen 1984; Schwartz 1994; Wise and Szücs 1996). The second weakness in this assumption is that government employees do not act as a bloc with common interests based on their common characteristic of not working in the private sector. Central government and local government employees demonstrate significantly different belief structures and attitudes on many important issues (Dunleavy 1991; Wise and Szücs 1996).

B. Perceived Fairness of Pay Differentials

Pay equity is a complex construct. It has economic, social, psychological, and procedural components (Adams 1965; Aquino 1995; Goodman 1974; Greenberg 1990; Mammar 1990; Wise 1990). Perceptions of pay fairness vary from individual to individual and reflect existing salary conditions and prevailing value structures within a culture (Lowenberg et al. 1990). People appear to use multiple referents for assessing pay fairness, and the relative ratings of fairness on these criteria have different consequences for organizations. All methods for allocating monetary rewards in the employment relationship are subjective and reflect social values, beliefs, and assumptions about human behavior and labor market force, so no method of pay administration will be judged fair by all employees. A rational compensation policy will promote organizational success and survival and be judged fair and appropriate on equity dimensions that are critical to a core group of employees. Perceptions of pay inequity can be associated with reduced organizational attachment, lower performance output, and lower organizational compliance (Adams 1965; Aquino 1995; Goodman 1974; Taylor and Vest 1992).

C. Two Equity Constructs

Comparisons of pay fairness within an organization, corporation, or jurisdiction that functions as a single employer are sometimes referred to as assessments of internal equity. Some people think that a single employer should offer the same rate of pay for the same job in each organizational section or department in which the work is performed. Internal equity encompasses the idea of equal pay for equal work which can be at issue between women and men as well as among members of different divisions or departments of the same organization. Internal equity involves not only equal pay for equal work, but also the idea of increasingly more pay for increasingly more valued contribution or more difficult work. Issues of pay alignment among different occupational groups based on criteria such as work difficulty, educational standards, physical dexterity, or labor market demand, for example, are also an important aspect of internal pay equity in Sweden (Wise 1994).

A second equity construct pertains to issues of relative pay status between members of one organization and some external source. External comparisons may be based on the same work at the same level of difficulty in another organization, sector, or geographic region. This construct is sometimes referred to as external equity or pay comparability. The objectives of "harmonizing" pay and other conditions of employment between the public and private sectors is central to the reforms in Sweden (Zetterberg 1994; Wise and Stengård, 1999).

Many workers favor in principle the idea of structuring monetary rewards around an individual's contribution to the organization and consider this approach a fair and equitable way to distribute organizational rewards (Kanter 1987). Employees can contribute their training, skills, and knowledge as well as their energy and efforts. A concern for equity among some is whether opportunities for higher output are equally distributed among the work force or some workers have a better chance than others to have access to these rewards. To the extent that public sector pay lagged behind that offered by private sector employers, flexible and individualized pay can be positively viewed as an effort toward parity that attempts to improve the competitiveness of earnings between highly valued workers in government and their counterparts in the private sector.

The next section describes the methods used in the research. This is followed by a report of empirical findings based on an attitudinal survey. Finally, we draw some conclusions and point to a need for further research in this area.

III. METHODS

This section briefly describes the sampling procedures and the statistical methods. One survey instrument was used; the same questions with the same response categories in the same sequence were presented to all respondents. To assess the consistency between pay reform efforts and workers' attitudes in Sweden, data are presented from a survey of employees in the private sector, state sector, and local (county and municipal) government employment. Three samples of employees were drawn from work force registers. Telephone interviews were conducted by Swedish Gallup between March 29 and April 9, 1995. Respondents were screened on the basis of whether or not they were gainfully employed. The database includes 179 central, 91 local, and 157 private sector employees for a total of 427 respondents. Women made up 47% of the total sample, which is within one percentage point of their share of the 1994 Labor Force Survey conducted by Statistics Sweden (Statistics Sweden 1995).

Four different items provide information about how employees think pay differentials should be determined. The four questions try to capture the extent to which employees prefer traditional pay setting factors like time in service or assigned position in contrast with more flexible and individualized factors like competency, skill, and contribution.

These factors represent two distinct approaches to pay setting. One is called rank in position, which pertains to systems where it is the requirements of the position rather than the skills of the individual job occupant that determine the level of pay. These systems strive to be incumbent neutral. The second approach is referred to as rank in person; in this case pay is set according to the skills and abilities of a particular individual. Hybrid approaches consider both position-based and individual factors. The four constructs used are: support for position-based pay; support for pay based on individual skill and competence; support for skill-based over seniority-based pay; and support for profitability-based pay.

Since each sector represents a separate sample, a statistical analysis was used that controls for sector of employment. The computations were produced using a cross-tabulation procedure in SPSS for Windows. Sector was treated as a nominal variable. Statistical significance is reported at the .05 level or greater using the Likelihood Ratio.

The remainder of the paper is organized into two sections. The next section reports and summarizes the empirical findings regarding attitudes toward pay differentials and perceptions of pay equity. The last section attempts to draw some conclusions about the extent to which employees' attitudes are consistent with or distinct from flexible pay policies and explore the implications of these findings for managing the tension between pay flexibility and pay equity.

IV. FINDINGS

This section reports the extent to which employers in different sectors support different pay administration criteria, and gives some insight into the extent to which they adhere to the basic tenets of solidaristic wage policy. The data are presented in three tables.

A. Level of Support for Position-Based Pay

Employees were asked to indicate on a scale of 1 to 5 the extent to which they agree with the statement, "Employees shall be paid according to the position they occupy." Those choosing 4 or 5 indicated they agreed with the statement, while those choosing 1 indicated they did not at all agree. Agreement with the statement can be interpreted as indicating that an employee prefers traditional pay-setting practices based on job status rather than on individual factors. As the data reported in Table 1 show, about half of all employees in each sector indicate agreement with the statement. The differences among employees in different sectors of employment are not statistically significant.

B. Support for Pay Based on Individual Skill and Competence

Support for individualized pay was measured by the statement, "Employees shall be paid according to their skill and competence." The majority of employees in all three sectors of employment indicate that they agree with this statement. The share of private sector employees taking this position is largest, with about 7 in 10 concurring. For public sector employees, the rate is about 6 in 10. The differences between sectors, however, are not statistically significant. The two items indicate that there is a group of employees who support both pay philosophies. While almost two-thirds of central government employees polled supported competency-based pay, just under half affirmed that position should be a factor in pay setting.

C. Support for Skill-Based over Seniority-Based Pay

Respondents were also asked to choose between time in service within an organization and individual skill as a basis for determining salary levels. The share choosing time, skill, or a combination of the two is given in Table 2. Relatively few employees think that pay should be determined by time in service, or seniority, with less than 10% of private sector or central government employees supporting this traditional pay criterion. The share for local government employees is larger

Table 1 Support* for Different Pay-Setting Criteria by Sector[†]

	Private	Central	Local	N
Employees shall be paid according to the position they occupy.	54%	48%	52%	418
Employees shall be paid according to their skill and competence.	71%	63%	59%	411

Source: Swedish Gallup, 1995.
*Those choosing 4 and 5 on a five-point scale where 5 equals fully agree, 3 equals neither agree nor disagree, and 1 equals fully disagree.
[†]Differences between sectors are not statistically significant.

Table 2   Support for Time in Service and Skill as Pay-Setting Criteria by Sector
("Do you think that differences in pay should be decided according to time in service
in the organization or according to individual skill?")

	Private	Central	Local
Time in service	7%	8%	19%
Both	34%	38%	43%
Skill	59%	54%	38%

Statistics: Likelihood ratio = 14.518. Differences according to sector of employment are statistically significant at the .01 level. N = 417.
Source: Swedish Gallup, 1995.

(19%) but still weak. In comparison, more than half of all central government and private sector
employees say they think differences in salary should be determined by individual skill. While private sector (59%) and central government (54%) employees are quite similar in the share choosing skill, only about 38% of local government employees hold the same opinion.

About 34% of private sector and 38% of central government employees think a combination
of skill and time in service should determine pay levels. For local government workers about 4 in
10 hold this view. Overall, only a very small core of employees in any sector hold fast to the idea
that pay differentials should be based on seniority alone, and the majority of central government
and private sector employees choose skill over seniority as a pay setting criterion.

D.   Level of Support for Profitability-Based Pay

When employees were asked whether salary levels should be influenced by an organization's level
of profitability, the majority from each sector concurred, as shown in Table 3. About three-fourths
of private sector employees, 6 in 10 central government, and half of those in local government said
yes, pay levels should reflect firm profits. This represents relatively strong support for salary
reforms based on economic efficiency and a sharp departure from traditional norms regarding the
effect of profitability on workers' earnings. In contrast, note that about one-fifth of private sector,
one-fourth of central government, and one-third of local government employees reject this idea.
The number of respondents who were uncertain on this item is also noteworthy. While few private
sector employees (6%) did not express an opinion, about 1 in 10 local government and close to 2
in 10 central government employees were uncertain what they thought about the relationship
between firm profitability and salary levels. This uncertainty may reflect the fact that many
employees were reconsidering their values at the time of the survey.

V.   CONCLUSIONS

Overall, the responses demonstrate a definite transition toward flexible and differentiated pay and
away from solidaristic principles. Five in 10 local, 6 in 10 central, and three-fourths of all private
sector employees agree that an organization's profitability should have an influence on employees' pay levels. When asked to choose between skill and time in service as a standard for pay setting, 6 in 10 private sector and half of central government employees choose skill. About 4 in 10
local government employees make the same choice. When asked whether pay differentials should

Table 3 Support for Using an Organization's Financial Status as a Pay-Setting Criterion by Sector ("Do you think that an organization's profitability should influence pay levels for the employees in that organization?")

	Private	Central	Local
Yes	76%	58%	51%
No	18%	24%	37%
Don't Know	6%	18%	12%

Statistics: Likelihood ratio = 25.715 Differences between sectors are statistically significant at the .0001 level. N = 427.
Source: Swedish Gallup, 1995.

be based on skill and competence, half or more employees in all sectors indicate they strongly agree.

Consistent with other research, some important differences are apparent between state sector employees and their counterparts in local government. Local government employees were less supportive than other employees of the idea that an organization's profitability should impact individual pay, and were more likely than those in central government to think position and time in service more important than skill as a determinant of job worth.

These pay reforms are similar to those implemented in other countries (Chivers 1988; Elvander 1991). Gregg and Yates (1991), for example, report that the share of British managers thinking that wage setting was influenced by firm profitability, prevailing market wage rates, and local labor market rates increased substantially from 1985 to 1990, so that by 1990 more than three-fourths of managers surveyed thought these factors were important. But the trends toward flexible and individually differentiated pay in Sweden are in contrast with those in neighboring Nordic countries, where more centralized solidaristic practices remain (Engeset 1995; Pedersen et al. 1996). It might seem that because they share the notion that pay policy should be an instrument of managers rather than social engineers that the transformation in Sweden is simply another iteration of "new public management" (Sjölund 1996). Elements of new public management are apparent in Sweden (Wise and Stengård, 1999; Premfors 1991, 1998), but Sweden has pursued its own course to pay reform and it is unique. Unlike the United States, United Kingdom, Netherlands, and New Zealand, Sweden eliminated graded pay schedules for civil servants. Sweden did not go down the path of individually based pay for performance promulgated by OECD, but it has pursued the objectives of efficiency and cost saving (Gustafsson 1990; Premfors 1991). While practices vary from agency to agency, in Sweden pay policy is more likely to be linked to productivity through organizational or group-based measures of output and result than to individual ratings. This is consistent with overall government policy to hold agencies accountable for developing and applying organizational performance standards.

The transition toward a market orientation in Sweden impacts all employees, and people have to learn how to work in a new way (Häggroth 1993). As a consequence of different forces in Sweden, the boundaries between jobs became increasingly vague, the priorities in the public sector workplace were reorganized, and civil servants' traditional ways of working became dysfunctional in many cases. At the same time, dramatic reductions in force and reorganization were under way throughout the public sector and a new compensation system strengthened the position of line managers in the reward system. The compensation system has worked in concert with the organizational goal of transformation. A pay reform that appeared ad hoc in its early stages (Wise 1993) seems to be developing into an integrated and complementary component of human resource management. It advances organizational efficiency, human resource development, and governmental responsiveness, and at the same time it promotes a set of criteria for compensation that are perceived fair by the majority of employees. Most important, however, employees themselves were making a transition away from the pay policies introduced in the 1970s that minimized individual differences. New criteria for allocating pay including skill, ability, and cost efficiency have been accepted as fair and appropriate by a majority of employees. Sweden appears to be headed more toward pay based on contribution or value added to the organization, but that is not to say the country is rejecting the basic principles of social equality and small pay differentials.

As Lægreid (1990) observed, we should keep in mind that a consequence of human resource management reforms is that sometimes we merely change the way we perceive results. Nevertheless, in a period when many governments are exploring new systems of pay administration and new criteria for rewarding public employees, it may be useful to look more closely for the subtle but significant differences among these systems and in the paths taken to reform. All roads to flexible pay do not lead through pay for performance systems.

Differences in work cultures and prevailing norms can be reflected in unique interpretations and applications of global themes that provide insight into what is acceptable and legitimate in the eyes of the local work force. The Swedish case may offer an example of how a government can bypass a stage in the reform process and arrive at a result that is consistent with organizational needs and social values.

ACKNOWLEDGMENTS

The survey research was conducted by Swedish Gallup and funded by the Swedish Agency for Government Employers (*Arbetsgivarverket*). Any conclusions drawn or opinions expressed are those of the authors. The authors thank Per Stengård for his insightful comments and the Swedish Agnecy for Government Employers for the opportunity to use the data for research purposes.

REFERENCES

Adams, J.S. (1965). Inequity in social exchange. In L. Berkowitz (ed.), *Advances in Experimental Social Psychology*, Vol. 2. New York: Academic Press.

Ahlén, K. (1989). Swedish collective bargaining under pressure: inter-union rivalry and incomes policies. *British Journal of Industrial Relations 27*, 330–46.

Aquino, K. (1995). Relationships among pay inequity, perceptions of procedural justice, and organizational citizenship. *Employee Responsibilities and Rights Journal 8*, 21–33.

Arbetsgivarverket. (1996). *Personalförändringar och Löneutveckling: 1993–1995 (Personnel Transitions and Salary Development: 1993–1995)*. Stockholm: *Arbetsgivarverket*.

Björklund, A. (1987). Assessing the decline of wage dispersion in Sweden. In G. Eliasson (ed.), *IUI Yearbook 1986–1987*. Stockholm: Industrial Institute for Economic and Social Research.

Blake, D. (1991). Policy attitudes and political ideology in the public sector. In A. Blais and S. Dion (eds.), *The Budget-Maximizing Bureaucrat: Appraisals and Evidence* Pittsburgh: University of Pittsburgh Press.

Chivers, K. (1988). Flexible pay in the civil service. *Public Money and Management 8*, 51–54.

Cousineau, J.M., and Girard, A.M. (1991). Public sector unions, government expenditures, and the bureaucratic model. In A. Blais and S. Dion (eds.), *The Budget-Maximizing Bureaucrat: Appraisals and Evidence*. Pittsburgh: University of Pittsburgh Press.

Dunleavy, P. (1991). *Democracy, Bureaucracy, and Public Choice: Economic Explanations in Political Science*. Englewood Cliffs, NJ: Prentice-Hall.

Edgren, G., Faxen, K., and Odhner, C. (1973). *Wage Formation and the Economy*. London: Rushkin House.

Elvander, N. (1991). *Lokal Lönemarknad: Lönebildning i Sverige och Storbritannien (Local Wage Markets: Wage Developments in Sweden and Great Britain)*. Stockholm: FA-rådet.

Engeset, B.H. (1995). Lønnsreformer i ein skandinavisk kontekst (Pay reforms in a Scandinavian context). In P. Lægreid (ed.), *Lønnspolitik i Offentlig Sektor (Pay Policy in the Public Sector)*. Oslo: Tano.

Goodman, P.S. (1974). An examination of referents used in the evaluation of pay. *Organizational Behavior and Human Performance 12*, 170–195.

Göransson, U. (1996). Doing the unthinkable: from status to contribution. Paper presented at Civil Service Systems in Comparative Perspective. Bloomington: Indiana University, April 6.

Greenberg, J. (1990). Organizational justice: yesterday, today, and tomorrow. *Journal of Management 16*, 399–432.

Gregg, P., and Yates, A. (1991). Changes in wage-setting arrangements and trade union presence in the 1980s. *British Journal of Industrial Relations 20*, 369–376.

Gustafsson, S. (1988). *Löneskillnader Mellan Kvinnor och Män—Gapet Ökar Igen* (Wage differences between women and men—the gap increases again). *Ekonomist Debatt 3*, 209–215.

Häggroth, S. (1993). *From Corporation to Political Enterprise*. Stockholm: Ministry of Public Administration.

Hibbs, D.A. (1990). Wage compression under solidarity bargaining in Sweden. In *The Study of Power and Democracy in Sweden*. Uppsala: Maktutredningen.

Jakobsson, U. (1984). A note on incomes policy from a Swedish perspective. SAF document No. 1410 (June). Stockholm: Swedish Employers' Confederation.

Jonsson, L., and Siven, C. (1986). *Why Wage Differentials?* Stockholm: Swedish Employers Confederation.

Kanter, R.M. (1987). From status to contribution: some organizational implications of the changing basis for pay. *Personnel 64*, 12–36.

Lægreid, P. (1990). Changes in Norwegian public personnel policy. In OECD (ed.), *Flexible Personnel Management in the Public Service*. Paris: OECD.

Lægreid, P. (1995). *Perspektiv på Lønnspolitiken i Staten* (Perspectives on pay policy in the state). In P. Laegreid (ed.), *Lønnspolitiken i offentlig sektor (Pay Policy in the Public Sector)*. Oslo: Tano.

Lafferty, W.M., and Knutsen, O. (1984). Leftist and rightist ideology in social democratic states: an analysis of Norway in the midst of the conservative resurgence. *British Journal of Political Science 14*, 345–367.

Lash, S. (1985). The end of neo-corporatism? The breakdown of centralized bargaining in Sweden. *British Journal of Industrial Relations 23*, 215–239.

Levine, C., and Kleeman, R. (1992). The quiet crisis in the civil service. In P. Ingram and D. Kettl (eds.), *Agenda for Excellence*. New York: Chatham House.

Lowenberg, G., Lowenberg, G., and Dowhower, P. (1990). Individual differences in perceptions of appropriate pay differentials in the USA and Sweden. *Journal of Business and Psychology 4*, 343–356.

Lundberg, E. (1985). The rise and fall of the Swedish model. *Journal of Economic Literature 23*, 1–36.

Mammar, A. (1990). Employees' preferences for payment systems: theoretical approaches and an empirical test. *International Journal of Human Resource Management 1*, 329–340.

Meidner, R. (1974). *Coordination and Solidarity: An Approach to Wages Policy*. Stockholm: Landsorganisationen i Sverige.

Meidner, R. (1994). The rise and fall of the Swedish model. In W. Clement and R. Mahon (eds.), *Swedish Social Democracy: A Model in Transition, Studies in Political Economy*. Toronto: Canadian Scholars Press.

Pedersen, O.V., Lægreid, P., and Perdersen, D. (1996). *Forvaltning Spolitikkens Institutionelle Spor*. In P. Lægreid and O.K. Pedersen (eds.), *Integration og Decentralisering (Integration and Decentralization)*. Copenhagen: Jurist and Økonomforbundets Forlag.

Premfors, R. (1991). The "Swedish model" and public sector reform. *West European Politics 17*, 58–82.

Premfors, R. (1998). Reshaping the democratic state: Swedish experience in comparative perspective. *Public Administration 76*, 141–160.

Schwartz, H. (1994). Public choice theory and public choices: bureaucrats and state reorganization in Australia, Denmark, New Zealand, and Sweden in the 1980s. *Administration and Society 26*, 48–77.

Sjölund, M. (1989). *Statens Lönepolitik, 1977–1988 (The State's Pay Policy, 1977–1988)*. Stockholm: Almänna Förlaget.

Sjölund, M. (1994). Transitions in government pay policies: the problem of legitimacy. *International Journal of Public Administration 17*, 1907–1936.

Sjölund, M. (1996). *Lönepolitik och Institutionell Orden—Sverige* (Pay policy and institutional order—Sweden). In P. Laegreid and O.K. Pedersen (eds.), *Integration og Decentralisering (Integration and Decentralization)*. Copenhagen: Jurist and Økonomforbundets Forlag.

Sjöström, A. (1992). *SIFO Samhällsmonitor.* Stockholm: SIFO AB.

Sweden, Ministry of Finance. (1993). *Management of Government Administration and Financial Control for State Agencies.* Stockholm: Ministry of Finance.

Sweden, National Audit Board. (1992). *Human Resource Management in a Change Perspective.* Stockholm: Riksrevisionsverket.

Sweden, Statistics Sweden. (1991). *Löner i Sverige, 1982–1989 (Wages and Salaries in Sweden, 1982–1989).* Stockholm: Statistics Sweden.

Taylor, G.S., and Vest, M.J. (1992). Pay comparisons and pay satisfaction among public employees. *Public Personnel Management 21*, 445–454.

Verba, S. et al. (1988). *Elites and the Idea of Equality.* Cambridge, MA: Harvard University Press.

Verkstadsföreningen. (1991). *Lönebildning och Löneglidning 1989–1990 (Wage Development and Wage Drift).* Stockholm: VF.

Wilks, S. (1996). Sweden. In N. Flynn and F. Strehl (eds.), *Public Sector Management in Europe.* New York: Prentice-Hall.

Wise, L.R. (1988). Dimensions of public sector pay policies in the United States and Sweden. *Review of Public Personnel Administration 8*, 61–83.

Wise, L.R. (1990). Social equity in civil service systems. *Public Administration Review 50*, 567–575.

Wise, L.R. (1993). Whither solidarity? Transitions in Swedish public sector pay policy. *British Journal of Industrial Relations 31*, 75–95.

Wise, L.R. (1994). Implementing pay reform in the public sector: different approaches to flexible pay in Sweden and the United States. *International Journal of Public Administration 17*, 1937–1959.

Wise, L.R., and Jonzon, B. (1991). The Swedish civil service: an instrument for achieving social equality? In A. Farazmand (ed.), *Handbook of Comparative of Development Public Administration.* New York: Marcel Dekker.

Wise, L.R., and Sjöström, A. (1997). *Paradigmskifte inom Svensk Lönebildning.* In M. Sjölund, L.R. Wise, J. Perry, and A. Sjöström, *Lön för Mödan: Lönesättning i Offentlig Sektor.* Stockholm: Kommentus.

Wise, L.R., and Stengård, P. (1999). Assessing public management reform with internal labor market theory. In H.G. Frederickson and J. Johnson (eds.), *Public Management Reform and Innovation.* University, AL: University of Alabama Press.

Wise, L.R., and Szücs, S. (1996). The public/private cleavage in a welfare state: attitudes toward public management reform. *Governance 9*, 43–70.

Zetterberg, J. (1994). Effects of changed wage setting conditions on the male-female wage differentials in the Swedish public sector. *Public Administration Quarterly 18*, 342–358.

15

Public Administration in Germany

Continuity in Change*

Margaret F. Reid   *Department of Political Science, University of Arkansas,*
Fayetteville, Arkansas

I. INTRODUCTION

Germany has undergone one of its most important changes since the end of World War II. German unification has been largely couched in economic terms, both within Germany and abroad by its friends and allies. This interpretation is understandable, given the enormity and the speed with which this daunting task had to be accomplished. The political, constitutional, and administrative changes that have occurred at all levels of the federal system are no less deserving of attention, however. Within the context of Germany's own history, as well as that of European unification, these issues assume added significance.

The purpose of this chapter is to provide the reader with a general background of the often admired and sometimes maligned German administrative system on whose shoulders much of the future of the transformation after reunification of Germany will rest. The recent changes cannot be properly situated unless discussed within the context of Germany's administrative history. In the German case this look back is not only instructive, despite the many upheavals and massive societal changes to which the administrative apparatus had to adjust itself, but also essential lest we

*This chapter is dedicated to the memory of the great German political scientist and public administration scholar Thomas Ellwein whose writings mirror the transformation of German political thinking over the past three decades. His untimely death in early January 1998 at the age of 70 marks in many ways an end of an era that started a century ago with the works of Max Weber. Ellwein began his writings in the hope that politics could be designed in a rational, almost Hegelian, fashion. He concluded his scholarship on a far less optimistic note in the recently published second volume of his analysis of German public administration. His work is further evidence of the dynamic theoretical changes and developments in the field of public administration research as opposed to its sister discipline political science (in the U.S.) and law (in Germany). His careful blending of inductive research and vast theoretical knowledge of the field highlights the importance of postpositivist approaches to promoting knowledge creation in this important field of inquiry and practice when considering the topics discussed in this paper. His being a political scientist, and not a legally trained scholar, differentiates him from the majority of German administrative scholars and contributes to the richness of his writings, as did Weber's training.

miss the unique features of Germany's administrative development since the late 19th century. Public administration developed earlier than in many neighboring countries. The political realities, and the absence of a nation-state until late into the 19th century, gave rise to peculiarly German traits that continue to exercise their influences until today.

Thanks to efforts of the *grand seigneur* of German public administration, Thomas Ellwein, another thorough examination of German administrative developments and institutions is now available in German (Ellwein 1993, 1997). For the English-speaking reader few such comprehensive treatments can be found (see e.g. J Caplan 1988). For most political scientists and public administrationists the knowledge of German administration is limited to writings, however splendid, of Max Weber. The waning interest in comparative public administration, until recently, has further contributed to the perpetuation of certain stereotypical views of the German administrative system.

It is my hope that this chapter can present some of the lesser known features of German administrative developments, including the many challenges that have arisen in the wake of German reunification in 1990. In recent years, Germany has experienced its own version of "reinvention" in an effort to bring Germany in line with its western European neighbors. German administrative traditions of a strong State with a decentralized administrative apparatus makes this a less appealing option than in countries with either a unitary governmental system, such as France, or those with a civil-society tradition such as the United States, Britain, Australia, and New Zealand. Even so, despite Germany's cherished tradition of value consensus over which services should be delivered by state agencies, we now see some fraying of this consensus at its margins as will be explained below.

I will begin with a general exploration of the conceptual terrain explored in this chapter. In subsequent segments some central features of German administrative developments will be discussed in greater detail to support the theme of administrative continuity and stability in the face of political and societal discontinuities. I will conclude with a brief assessment of administrative modernization and transformation in the wake of reunification.

II. ADMINISTRATIVE MODERNIZATION AND INSTITUTIONAL CHANGE

Despite its often admired and sometimes maligned public service, systematic academic analyses, especially of the middle and lower tiers of the German bureaucracy, are still rare. Recent studies by Jeserich et al. (1983), Caplan (1988), Ellwein (1993, 1994), Ruck (1996), Kvistad (1999), and others (see notably Mommsen 1966; Huber 1968, 1978; Rebentisch and Teppe 1986 for the NS period; Heinrich et al. 1992; König 1995; Damskis 1997 for eastern Germany) fill important gaps. This is not to say that important work has not been done in examining some aspects of the German civil service from its infancy in 18th-century Prussia through a period of rapid industrialization and urbanization during the late 19th and early 20th centuries, the era most closely associated with Weber's conceptualization of the modern bureaucracy. Other studies are devoted to the pronounced differences between individual regions and territories such as Bavaria, southwest Germany, or Prussia; others have examined administrative subsystems (e.g., Ellwein 1993; Fenske 1993; Hess 1993; Ruck 1996). Likewise, a number of studies focus on specialized administrative functions such as financial, police, or social welfare administrations (e.g., Huber 1965; Weingarten 1993).

Notably absent are efforts to analyze reasons for the remarkable continuity of the German administrative state despite the political upheavals of the 19th and 20th centuries, the demographic and sociological changes, and the restructuring from an agrarian to modern industrial economy. The chapter asserts that in the German case several factors account for this continuity:

Administration perceived as the embodiment of the "state" and its constitutional authority (note the predominance of *Staatsverwaltung* as opposed to *Gemeindevwerwaltung*, the administration of the towns and cities)

The esprit de corps among civil servants, including powerful social associations that set the members of this social group apart from other professions and trades

The emphasis on rigorous academic training of the highest civil servants, predominantly by colleges of jurisprudence (especially administrative law and civil and constitutional law) in the belief that the central role of the administration was the execution of the laws, epitomized in Weber's rational bureaucracy theory at the beginning of the 20th century

The pronounced absence of any discussions of the relationship of democracy and bureaucracy (state and society were deemed separate institutional spheres) until after World War I

The varying interpretations of the relative influence of Napoleonic rule after 1806 and subsequently the role of the French Revolution in shaping concepts of state administration relationships in the 19th century (this last point while of interest remains unresolved in the academic literature and is beyond the scope of this chapter)

Suffice it to say, administrative developments in the German territories preceded the formation of the nation-state and the administration's crucial role in Germany's national formation and maintenance is certainly unrivaled in Western Europe. This is not to say, however, that the German civil service functioned as a homogenous body; more nearly, as society changed in the 20th century and democratic institutions began to assert their legitimate place, retaining its traditional aloofness from civil society became increasingly untenable.

In a broader context, the evolution of the modern German administrative state can serve as an object lesson of liberal institution building and problems with democratization, if one peels away some of the unique German features (see e.g. Kvistad 1999, for Germany's tortured relationship of state and society). On a positive note, it illustrates that a country can transform itself from an autocratic regime to a constitutional state, to a civil society. The German experiences make abundantly clear that a political system premised on a dualism of state and society cannot be sustained even with support of the best-trained and most loyal civil service, if other democratic institutions, civil and political, are not allowed to take their rightful place as important political transmission mechanisms.

Finally, it illustrates the importance of a viable federalist system with strong local communities to enhance state-building processes when the central state is politically weak or fractured.[1] Throughout history the strength of its regions, economically and administratively, has proved vital to much of Germany's development. Germany's cultural and economic diversity, the strength of regional centers outside the capital, compensated to some degree for the immature central political institutions and carried Germany at least through the industrial revolution. It was, however, the underdeveloped polity that contributed in large measure to disastrous miscalculations in foreign affairs, and the inability to incorporate an increasingly restless populace into public decision making and policy formation. A fully developed civil society had to wait until the middle of the 20th century.

By the beginning of the 20th century, it also became increasingly evident, that the German civil service was not the homogeneous loyal and neutral corps, as often portrayed, but an "increasingly diverse, expensive, and unwieldy bureaucratic apparatus" (Caplan 1988:13). It was by no means impervious to self-serving behavior of its members or immune to the effects of local or regional political cultures on individual bureaucrats. Germany's maturation as a civic body politic was paralleled by the steady erosion of its venerable system of social stratification (*Ständestaat*).

This process eventually undermined the carefully conserved social hierarchies within the German civil service as well. By the 1960s a total social and institutional transformation had been accomplished (Kvistad 1999; Ellwein 1994). The effect of the accession of eastern Germany with its more egalitarian social and economic system, but weak democratic institutions, on the rest of the system remains to be seen.

A. Role of the State

Central to the changes in the modern civil service system is the role of the state. Ellwein (1997) points to a simultaneous strengthening and weakening of the state. As society's demands on the state expands, its role as a central player is enhanced. In an effort to respond to respond by offering a greater variety of services, its control diffuses as it is forced to (inter)act within a more complex network of players. In the German case this system of cross-cutting interorganizational and inter-institutional relationships has evolved into what Scharpf called *cooperative federalism* (see e.g. Scharpf et al. 1976).

1.   Birth of the German Administrative State: 18th-Century Prussian Bureaucracy

Unfortunately, much of this voluminous literature is inaccessible to the non-German-speaking scholarly community. This has led to a somewhat undifferentiated and simplified view of administrative traditions and practices over the last 150 years: the role of the civil service in the evolution of the German administrative system, and its fundamental role in preserving the state as an institution throughout Germany's many political upheavals. Most notably, while often admired by 19th-century contemporaries, because of its perceived efficiency, German, or more precisely Prussian civil servants, were awkwardly positioned in a curious dualism of state and society alien to its west European neighbors (Ellwein 1993). Frederick William I and Frederick the Great, his son, laid the foundation for Europe's first modern bureaucracy. In absolutist Prussia a highly personalized and centralized apparatus was created to serve the military and economic needs of the kingdom. In order to compete militarily with more powerful neighbors, the creation of an efficient and noncorrupt revenue raising mechanism assumed utmost importance. Unlike other German territories, such as Saxony or Hanover and indeed most other European neighbors, where patronage was common practice, Prussian administrators were subject to rigorous training and testing before being appointed. Purchase or inheritance of a position, a common practice in France, also was prohibited (Dorn 1931:405). The Prussian civil service certainly outmanaged its commercial counterparts in its use of modern accounting practices, recruitment and training of its administrators, and in its active pursuit of economic development. It subsequently became a model of a rationalized administrative system that outlived the many political and societal changes over the last two centuries (Dorn 1931, 1932a,b; Spicer 1998).

Prussia had developed a complex five-tier hierarchical administrative structure by the end of the 18th century. The lowest level included the municipalities, from small villages to larger cities. With increases in size, administrative sophistication became a necessity. Public administration at the local level was self-administration, not self-governance. Participation of the citizenry, with the exception of the highest social strata, was nonexistent. Administration was viewed as a tool of central control, with allegiance to the monarch. Interestingly, it was this lowest tier that received a great deal of attention by reformers in the wake of Napoleon's success in 1806 and the demise of the Holy Roman Empire. Vom Stein's reforms sought a decentralized system with self-governing cities. He felt that only at the local level could one turn passive subjects into active citizens.

The next tier included the counties. The third tier were administrative districts to streamline revenue collection and monitor the implementation of rules and regulations from the center. The fourth tier were the provinces, to administer the far-flung Prussian territory and later its territorial acquisitions in eastern Europe. The fifth tier was composed of the central administration, thoroughly reformed in 1723 when line departments were introduced. Further reforms followed in the late 18th and early 19th centuries (e.g., von Hardenberg and vom Stein; *Städteordnung* of 1808; liberation of peasants). These subsequent reforms increasingly included calls for greater participation of male citizens in the political affairs of towns and cities (Heffter 1969). While the upper social strata were allowed greater involvement in local affairs, their political powers remained limited however (see especially Heinrich et al. 1992).

2.   German Civil Service—Guardian of a State-Society Dualism (19th to early 20th century)

After the German territories' transformation into a nation-state in 1871, a more decentralized state-centered administrative system was formed to serve as a bridge between the state and an increasingly complex civil society that emerged with the onset of the industrial revolution. These developments, in turn, required that the civil service be accorded a special role and special responsibilities toward the state. The industrial revolution and its social and economic changes caused major shifts in the political system as well. Reluctantly, an immature German political system undertook the tortured transformation from an autocratic monarchy with its loyalty to its supreme ruler, the monarch, to a modern body politic where loyalty was accorded to the law and a constitution. It required that civil servants were formally trained to take on the complex tasks of a modern administration but at an arm's-length relationship to society.[2] Furthermore, the introduction of a modern welfare system with its varied needs required a decentralized administrative system. Provinces and the newly emerging urban centers were the benefactors of these developments. Economic restructuring, population explosion and urbanization produced lasting, albeit incremental, changes in governance concepts as well. The absolutist monarchy was replaced by a constitutional monarchy. The welfare functions were now couched in legal terms rather than personalized ones.

In Germany a separate path was charted for the civil service that was unique in the western European context. The constitutional monarchy did not evolve as in Britain into a parliamentary system with the monarch serving essentiality in a representational role. Germany, late in becoming a nation-state, interpreted its constitutional notion of unity of its commonweal through retaining a strong center and its peculiar interpretation of "state." The monarch is the representative of national unity. The civil service is vital in maintaining this unity and thus becomes not merely a managerial tool, which it certainly was, but also an instrument, indeed an embodiment, of the state. In German constitutional interpretations, the state contained both a moral quality as well as a legal/administrative one. The creation of a civilian cadre of high-level administrators (the *Beamte*) with mostly legal training remains a uniquely German institution. The cadre was later expanded to include other academic specialties to include professionals in various economic areas, university professors, certain secondary school teachers, and physicians in state service. It was essential that the German administrative service remained removed from the day-to-day politics in order not to undermine its moral responsibilities as preservers of the unity of the state. These paraconstitutional functions of the civil service in virtually all areas of public decision-making made it difficult for the embryonic parliaments to carve out their rightful place in Germany's governmental system (Ellwein 1994).

Each tier in Germany's administrative system functioned as an extension of the central state. A strict hierarchy with small spans of control assured reasonable conformity with promulgated edicts and administrative orders, but also led to one of the largest civil service apparatuses in Europe.[3] With size came the need for greater control and thus even more rules and regulations. For example, each municipality until today has still an inordinate number of departments, many of them identical to their counterparts elsewhere.

Division of labor has been one of the central principles of German administration. It allowed the central state to maintain control of crucial decisions while delegating the implementation of policies to lower administrative levels with a fair amount of discretion given to those levels. The structural uniformity at each administrative level assured a rationalized system of bureaucratic decision making. Germany's civil service performed extensive welfare and regulatory functions: from an encompassing public health care system, unemployment insurance, an unparalleled educational system, the creation of public parks, recreational and cultural facilities, to maintaining law and order, constructing new roads and railroads, to monitoring compliance with regulations. The civil service thus constituted a modernizing *potential* that was largely negated by the fear of traditional elites of greater political participation of the citizenry (Ellwein 1993). It would take a major transformation of the German society itself to shake the normative foundations of the German civil service. This point will again be significant when we consider the most recent attempts at modernization in the 1990s.

Let us illustrate these issues with a brief example. Constitutionally, municipalities are assured a more independent position than in most other Western countries. Theoretically, it could be here, where removed from the immediate reach of the central state, that the greatest strides to self-government could be made. In addition, liberal trade and economic policies required a modernization of administrative rules and regulations, a modernization of agriculture and with it increasingly a rethinking of the complex relationship of the state and its administration. Yet, local political self-determination remained weakly developed as many of the social welfare functions were efficiently administered by numerous local bureaucracies with their cadres of administrators imbued with a strong *esprit de corps*. Thus, despite the increasing diversification and differentiation of administrative tasks in response to societal changes, the constancy of administrative behavior is one of the more notable features of the German civil service.

The Prussian model continued to influence the governance of many cities. Nineteenth century Prussian laws allowed cities to chose from a *magistrate* (collective executive body) or *Rhenish* (French-inspired) mayoral model. Many of the eastern and some central provinces adopted the Prussian system, while many western and southwestern regions favored the mayoral system.

After 1871, strong federalist elements shaped the national constitution to guarantee regional autonomy. This system allowed Germany to make rapid adjustments to the economic challenges of the industrial revolution while relieving the central government from both fiscal and administrative burdens.

B.   The *Berufsbeamtentum*

No analysis of the German administrative system would be complete without some comments on the German *Beamte*. The social transformation of Germany eventually contributed to a thorough restructuring of the civil service and its own perceptions of its conflicted societal role. A recapping of its history is instructive.

The composition of the German civil service ranks changed dramatically in the early decades of the 20th century. Civil servants (*Beamte*) were granted a separate employment status. Tenured for life, prohibited to participate in labor strikes, and their special legal employment conditions set them socially apart from other employee categories. The civil service of the 19th and early 20th centuries preserved the traditional class structures of the civil service corps. The lower civil service ranks (added as the societal demands for public services grew in the wake of the industrial revolution), e.g., postal carriers, did not differ much from non-*Beamte* of the same social strata. The middle and upper charges, however, enjoyed considerable social status. To advance to these positions applicants had to undergo extensive professional training and earn academic degrees, especially law degrees. The representatives of this group, typically teachers, and upper administrative officials were expected to show complete loyalty to the state and professional commitment to their administrative obligations. The highest ranks, mostly ministers and central administrative officials, were nearly always jurists. German public administrators, unlike their Anglo-American counterparts, are only now beginning to incorporate management training into their administrative education. The German public budgeting system (*Kameralistik*) remains antiquated and in need of major reform.

As the boundaries of the class structure within the traditional civil serve system began to blur, financial exigencies forced additional changes in hiring practices. Fewer employees were offered *Beamte* status, and more were hired on as regular blue or white color employees (*Arbeiter* or *Angestellte*), the latter often occupying the rapidly expanding staff positions in state (*Land*) and local administrations.

Sociologically, the blurring of status distances with the emergence of modern professions outside the civil service and the decreasing identification of the individual administrator with the state, undermined the ability of the central state to sustain the separation of state and society. Increased politicization of the general populace and demands for greater accountability of the administration to elected bodies, made necessary a reconceptualization of the role of the civil service in a modern polity. This development was interrupted with the accession of Hitler to power and the subsequent turmoil of World War II. It was only after the war that these developments could resume under a much stronger democratic auspices and increasingly mature political institutions.

III. CIVIL SERVICE IN A DEMOCRATIC POLITY: 1949–1990

After World War II, the most pressing questions were: What could be done to avoid the mistakes of the past (Sternberger 1949)? Could Germany muster the courage to deal with its own past and yet boldly write a new chapter in its history? What social and political order should be created that would build on the positive experiences of the Weimar Republic yet avoid its institutional weaknesses (Bracher 1975)? The founding generation of the new constitutional order (now referred to as the Bonn Republic) was very clear about the regime values that would have to be incorporated into the newly created democracy. At the core of its value system should be the centrality of the political parties as expressions of the popular. From the beginning there was an anticipation and acceptance of the possibility of conflict over the role of the state: would it be a protector of civil rights or a protector of the constitution (state) *against* its own citizens.[4] In this segment I will only consider administrative developments in the former West Germany (FRG).[5]

The redefinition of the role of the second pillar of the new republic—the professional civil service—has been a complex and contentious affair (Ellwein 1994). Staunch defenders of the German civil service pointed to its statist legacy and its independent role as protector of a legitimate political order. The Nazi period was viewed as an aberration in which public administrators were abused by an illegitimate regime. Western allies demanded a political neutralization of the civil service, creating in effect an administration—politics dichotomy, so familiar to students of the American public administration. This notion was roundly rejected. The founders viewed the civil service as a vital component in defense of the new constitutional order and it should thus be accorded a special status as protector of the state (Kruis 1979). The federal republic was however broadly based on a constitutional system in which the administrative actions were to be derived and legitimated by laws (*Rechtsstaat*). "Under the new constitution the rule of law was all-embracing. Hence the thick web of regulations: the elaborate legal prescriptions by which German local freedoms are realised and expressed" (Norton 1994:241). The preeminence of civil servants in policy making and implementation is a unique feature in both Germanys, even after the division.

Demands for more state action arose as Germany's economy and cities recovered from the devastation of the war. A flood of new laws was passed to provide detailed direction for state and local government administrations. Employment of new administrators and administrative judges increased manifold within a two-decade period. Other changes in the composition of the civil service are noteworthy as well. Technical specialties such as tax law, health administration, social services, economic development, urban and regional planning were introduced into traditional civil service ranks. Many advanced to middle management ranks without holding *Beamte* status. Some of these specialists were trained in technical universities rather than traditional comprehensive universities and law schools. These developments broadened opportunities for nontraditional social strata to join the civil service, and have led to increasing employment opportunities for women. Two decades after the formation of the FRG the social transformation of the German civil service had become apparent, if not complete.

The third pillar, a reconstituted federalist system, was intended to preserve historically grown territories. Institutionally, the parliamentary system with a popularly elected chamber (*Bundestag*) and an appointed federal chamber (*Bundesrat*) would suggest a tremendous conflict potential. Unlike in the United States, however, strong parties coupled with a parliamentary system minimized possible conflicts between federal and state (*Land*) interests (see e.g. Renzsch 1999). Consensus, albeit sometimes hard fought, has been the hallmark of the German federal system.

It is against this backdrop that the following discussions must be viewed. The administration of all federalist systems traditionally operates via a two-tiered civil service corps: a smaller for the federal level and an ever-expanding civil service system for state and local administrations.[6] Constitutionally, the two systems were given both separate and some joint responsibilities. The responsibilities of state and local levels were broadly designed. Unlike its western neighbors, the German federal constitution acknowledges (in Article 28) local government as a distinct sphere. The local communities are given an own resource base and the power to regulate their own affairs (under *Land* supervision) within the limits defined by law. As public law corporations they possess the right to self-government and self-administration, a measure thought to strengthen the democratic developments of the young republic. Their responsibilities include land use planning decisions; administering their own financial affairs; providing a broad range of social, recreational and cultural services to their citizens; preserving law and order; and hire, train and dismiss local administrative personnel. The *Land* government may ask its local governments to carry out additional tasks for which they receive additional funding.

Over the years, German federalism evolved a form of "cooperative federalism." The West German constitution, the Basic Law, envisioned a set of express powers accorded to the national legislature. The express responsibilities of the state and local levels were less clear. The states initially assumed tasks such as education, infrastructure projects, welfare, sponsoring of the arts, recreation, media, and enabling legislation pertaining to the local level (see Hesse and Ellwein 1997:89–90). What initially appeared as straightforward allocation of responsibilities across intergovernmental levels quickly became intertwined as the fiscal burdens exceeded the ability of the states and local governments to carry out those tasks on their own. Thus bureaucrats at all levels of government worked in close concert to design and implement public policies. Germany's cooperative federalism is further shaped by a strong equalizing tendency (the regime value of social market economy exemplifies this value, the *Sozialstaatsgebot* Article 72 of the Basic Law).

Fiscal equalization between the economically stronger states and their weaker neighbors has been a unique feature of Germany's value consensus.[7] From it, however, emanated the trend toward federalizing some tasks that were deemed to legitimately belong in the purview of the federal government arguing that only the federal government is uniquely positioned (and fiscally capable) to equalize access to vital services and educational opportunities, and to protect the health and welfare of its citizens. These centralizing tendencies (*Unitarisierung*) began in the 19th century and have continued since then (Kilper and Lhotta 1996:151ff). The recent reunification of Germany may provide further momentum.[8]

Finally, a brief discussion of the changes in the composition of the civil service is in order. Lecheler (1997:504) notes that one of the most significant changes that has occurred over the last 40 years is the social decoupling of the stratified educational system and the corresponding four tiers of the *Beamte* corps. The educational system offers more options for qualified degrees and credentialing than ever before. Knowledge, moreover, is constantly evolving. Contemporary public administration demands specializations that traditional education does not provide. It is not unusual to find that the normal hiring processes for *Beamte* are bypassed. The same is happening with regard to promotion of qualified candidates in order to retain highly motivated employees. In the absence of a comprehensive reform of the civil service system these must be seen as stop-gap measures to compensate for traditional personnel structures.[9]

IV. THE CHALLENGE OF REUNIFICATION: A CHANCE FOR REINVENTION?

German reunification in 1990 represents in many ways a significant political watershed and an event of great national significance. From an administrative perspective however this historic occurrence has been far less dramatic. For the western German civil servants reunification was almost an annoyance rather than an opportunity to fundamentally rethink entrenched administrative cultures that had experienced little change since the reforms of the 1970s. For eastern German civil bureaucracies the changes amounted to a metamorphosis of their bureaucratic cultures, structures, and processes. The change process itself, however, followed the traditional pattern of German administrative reforms: highly decentralized but with a strong emphasis on structural reforms to achieve the greatest amount of harmonization and uniformity possible. The outcome, intended or not, essentially amounted to the preservation of familiar western German administrative paradigms.

A brief recapitulation of the major German administrative reforms since the end of World War II will underscore this point more forcefully. Seibel (1997) identified four major administrative reform periods and two distinct reform-triggering impulses since the end of the war. The first two reform movements were triggered by *external* events. The latter by concerns over *internal* organizational efficiencies, at least in the FRG. The process of transformation in the East triggered by reunification resembled the externally induced changes of the early years of the Bonn Republic.

The first phase of German reforms lasted into the late 1950s and focused primarily on overcoming the effects of the war and to reinstitute a functioning civil service throughout the federal system. It was characterized by overwhelming support from all corners of society. The reforms could build upon the best of the old civil service traditions and civil service ethic. The successful re-establishment of an efficient administrative apparatus in a democratic polity laid the foundation for the survival of the young republic.

The reforms of the mid-1960s to the mid-'70s are probably the most interesting in German postwar history. Not only were they quite extensive, but they also occurred during a period of social upheaval that essentially tested the new democratic institutions of the Bonn republic and also provided a first indication of the emergence of mature democratic citizenry. The deference to the "state" that was so typical of the earlier eras was beginning to give way to streaks of rebelliousness, and calls for greater participation of the citizens in the affairs of state.

Interestingly, many of the administrative reforms targeted traditional state functions: finance, territorial reorganization, and bureaucratic reorganizations (the latter largely ineffective). However, a closer look will quickly show the influence of *external* reform stimuli: the recognition that only strong and efficient governing bodies (fiscal as well as territorial) would secure long-term economic prosperity. The financial reforms of the late 1960s produced the now maligned system of "fiscal equalization" among the states, the *Länder.* In tandem a territorial consolidation was needed as well. Within about a decade the number of *Regierungsbezirke* (an intermediate administrative unit lodged between the state and local levels) shrunk from 33 to 25; the number of counties and cities from 564 to 328, and general-purpose local governments from roughly 24,000 to 8500 (Seibel 1997:95). The effects on local self-government were twofold: the new larger units certainly were better equipped to serve the local citizenry. On the other hand, the reduction of local governments by nearly two-thirds, produced centralizing effects; e.g., new physical planning mechanisms required local governments to surrender local planning decisions to regional planning units. Arguments in support of these changes were that Germany occupied a small territory and careful regional planning was needed to preserve open spaces or to direct and coordinate economic development efforts.

Organizational reforms of the federal and state ministries and civil service systems were largely failures (building sufficient political support for such reforms is more difficult, and promised efficiency gains are not readily apparent or materialize over many years). A consensus to reform the civil service could not be established in the absence of support from the administrative elites.

By the mid-1970s the interest in reforms waned and was overshadowed by a severe recession. In the wake of the recession questions arose if Germany was able to afford the massive public sector growth that had occurred over the span of a decade.[10] "Debureaucratization," simplification of administrative processes and procedures through restricting the flood of new laws, became the new motto (administrative action in the German system is for the most part a direct result of laws passed in the national and state parliaments). By the late 1980s the call for greater citizen participation in public decision making and improved service delivery mirrored reform premises in other Western settings.

Finally, reunification produced a reform paradox. West German reformers were interested in continuing their modernization efforts of the antiquated financial and personnel systems and increasingly experimented with the infusion of private management practices. The process of reunification broadened these concerns beyond this narrow scope. Reunification imposed unforeseen fiscal stresses that raised serious questions if the carefully calibrated constitutional principle of roughly equal living conditions for all Germans was sustainable without a fundamental territorial restructuring. These concerns overshadowed the incipient debates about administrative modernization and *internal* efficiencies.

Reunification amounted to a wholesale transfer of western German institutions and administrative paradigms without much public debate in either part of Germany. On the surface this transfer was a complete success. Western administrators served as administrative midwives to establish a new civil service under democratic institutional auspices. The reality, however, turned out to be much more complex and varied than was originally anticipated by western experts. Eastern German administrators also began to impose their own brand of reforms. The transformation of socialist administrative cultures to democratic ones is in not comparable to that occurring in "developing" countries. We are dealing here with a systemic transformation not simply a "modernization," "reengineering," or "reinvention." Transformation, unlike modernization, involves changes in the entire societal value system, administrative cultures and organizational behaviors. The former East Germany can be characterized as a state-centered system with totalitarian features that encompassed all aspects of society. In the East German context some features of 19th-century Prussia remained intact for the lower administrative charges: professionalism, rational orientation, technical competence. The administrative elites, unlike their western counterparts, were a type of "political bureaucrats" or "administrative cadres" (*Kaderverwaltung*) (Balla 1972;

König 1992; Pitschas 1992; Damskis 1997), which presented a personnel policy dilemma: if and how to replace these leading administrators. The solution in almost all cases was to either recruit the new administrative elites from groups of administrators in the old regime that had minimal political ties or to import them from western Germany. Dasmkis' (1997) research showed that only about half of the new leadership was in equivalent positions before reunification. Many of the new elites claimed not to belong to a party. Naturally, there are differences between the various new states. Those closer to the capital were under more pressure to conform to regime values than those in the provinces. However, when examining the attitudes of western and eastern bureaucrats with respect to their task orientation differences are not significant. It is at the level of political and administrative values that most of the conflicts continue to occur.

Modernization and regime transformation are, ultimately, different but reconcilable goals. The opportunities afforded by examining regime and administrative values in a new national and international context represents a unique opportunity for administrative elites in both settings.

V. CONCLUSION

Criticisms of German bureaucrats for not effecting administrative changes abound. The highly touted reforms of the health care system, public financial and tax system, pension system, and most recently the hotly debated changes in spelling and grammar of the German language are seen by some as an inability of the German administrative system to reform itself. This conclusion, however, belies a long history of continuous improvements of the administrative processes that has insulated Germany from the management fads that many American readers are so familiar with. German reform efforts were often triggered in response to local or regional needs. Central reform programs such as *Next Steps* in Britain, the *New Public Management* experiments in New Zealand and elsewhere, and to some extent the reform discussions triggered by Gore's *National Performance Review* in the United States are rather unlikely occurrences in the German context. Klages and Löffler (1995:375) come to a similar conclusion: "Re-engineering as an 'everything or nothing option' management . . . has little chance of being realized in the German administration." There is a strong sense of administrative traditions that provides the undercurrent for the ongoing reform efforts, even one as massive as reunification. Moreover, the nature of the political and federal system renders radical reforms less likely.

However, Germany shares with other federal systems a penchant for experimentation at the lower levels of government that bode well for the continuous implementation of less visible reform efforts. Most federal systems have experienced strong centralizing tendencies in the post-war era due to internal economic or social pressures, and more recently due to the effects of economic internationalization. Countervailing trends at the local level and more significantly a growing discontent of citizens in all Western democracies may keep those developments in check. In continental and central Europe, with their strong social welfare state traditions, full-scale privatization is less likely. Fiscal exigencies may and do require a rethinking of management philosophies in both public and private sectors, but they are by no means synonymous with a radical withdrawal of the state. In the German case, administrative traditions are powerful retardants to radical changes as this chapter has attempted to show.

NOTES

1.   It is worth mentioning that even though the German federalist system was modeled after the American, it differs from the American in fundamental ways. The German constitution of 1848 never envisioned

independent territorial states alongside a national government. German states, unlike their American counterparts, possessed already well-developed administrative systems when they joined the union. To duplicate such efforts at the national level would have made little sense.

2. The many published case studies attest to the near impossibility of this demand. A large number of case studies from the various German regions illustrate the sociological and psychological problems of this transformation (see e.g. Caplan 1988; Runge 1965; Henning 1984).

3. Ellwein (1994:31) reports the following numbers: the civil service in 1950 had about 2.3 million members. This number had doubled by 1990. That means that about every sixth person is employed in some kind of civil service job. It largely reflects the increasing demand for more services, but also represents serious challenges for the reform minded who have called for a significant reduction of the public service sector (König and Beck 1997).

4. This interesting thesis has recently been explored in German and European constitutional discussions. Advocates of a "strong state" advance the argument that it is the legitimate role of the state to protect its citizens against those compatriots who not only violate constitutional rights of individuals but who are seen as a threat to the state (see, e.g., Leutheusser-Schnarrenberger 1999:316).

5. An extensive discussion of the administrative structures in the former East Germany can be found in König (1991); for the period after reunification, see especially Eisen and Wollmann (1996) for eastern German municipalities.

6. According to the national statistical office, in 1996, the public sector employed about 3.3 million individuals (2.6 million full time; 660 thousand part time) in the former western part and just under a million in the eastern part (290,000 full time and 178,000 part time). Women constitute 47% of all employees in the west and 65% in the East (1995 data). It is noteworthy, though, to look at the distribution between part- and full-time employees. Among full-time employees about 37% are women (former-West) and 60% (former East). Among part-time employees roughly 90% are women (with a slightly higher percentage for the West). Examining the percentage of women in public bureaucracy leadership positions reveals an even more unbalanced picture: Among *Beamte* only 13% occupied the two highest pay categories (up from 7% in 1960); among non-*Beamte* the women in the highest salary categories make up about 35% (up from about 29% in 1960). Women employed full time in research and teaching make up about 23% of that employee pool. Only 8% of all professors in 1996 were women (former West 5% in 1980) (Statistisches Bundesamt 1998:72–75).

7. A brief summary of the enormous sums of money involved in this system of intergovernmental redistribution can be found in an article by Döring that recently appeared in the conservative *Frankfurter Allgemeine Zeitung*. The author raises the question if these transfers are truly needed. He argues that there are differences in economic capacities between the states but that they are not severe enough to lead to a massive exodus from one state to another. Even the eastern states are beginning to catch up. He notes, however, that the fiscal equalization measures contribute as much as 25% in some states' tax coffers. If this is a trivial amount is open to debate. Over four decades those states that initially contributed more than they received are also not the same. As old style industries disappeared, the southern German states, notable Bavaria (Munich), Baden-Württemberg (Stuttgart), and Hesse (Frankfurt), emerged as the new economic engines. Similar regional discrepancies are becoming visible in the eastern part even after just 10 years.

8. Other manifestations of these centralizing trends are the harmonization of cultural, educational, and health policies through intergovernmental coordinating commissions. Most recently, the appointment of a fiduciary agency to privatize eastern German property, the *Treuhandanstalt*, may even be called illegal, as it bypassed traditional *Land* decision making powers/bodies, and was primarily accountable to ministries at the federal level (executive agencies).

9. A federal task force started a serious reform discussion in the early 1990s; it did not result, however, in any fundamental changes in established practices but concluded with the acknowledgement of a need for fundamental changes (see Lecheler 1997:507ff).

10. Seibel (1997:98) shows the following growth rates: total number of employees in the public sector increased from 1.8 million in the mid-1960s to 3.5 million in the mid-'70s. Of all gainfully employed, 13% worked for public agencies (compared to under 7% just a decade ago).

REFERENCES

Balla, B. (1972). *Kaderwaltung: Versuch der Idealtypisierung der "Bürokratie" sowjetischvolksdemokratischen Typs.* Stuttgart: F. Enke Verlag.

Bracher, K.-D. (1975). *The German Dilemma: The Relationship of State and Democracy.* New York: Praeger.

Bremers, M. (1997). Soziale Staatsziele und Verfassungsverständnis: Ein Rückblick auf die Verfassungsdebatte der deutschen Einheit. *Aus Politik und Zeitgeschichte B*(15–16), 21–32.

Caplan, J. (1988). *Government Without Administration: State and Civil Service in Weimar and Nazi Germany.* Oxford: Oxford University Press.

Damskis, H., and Möller, B. (1997). *Verwaltungskultur in den neuen Bundesländern.* Frankfurt: Peter Lang.

Damskis, H. (1997). *Politikstile und regionale Verwaltungskulturen in Ostdeutschland.* Wiesbaden: Deutscher Universitäts-verlag.

Döring, K. (1999). Milliarden für die "Einheitlichkeit der Lebensverhältnisse." *Frankfurter Allgemeine Zeitung* (218), Sept. 20:10.

Dorn, W. (1931). The Prussian bureaucracy in the 18th century. *Political Science Quarterly 46*(3), 403–423.

Dorn, W. (1932a). The Prussian bureaucracy in the 18th century II. *Political Science Quarterly 47*(1), 75–94.

Dorn, W. (1932b). The Prussian bureaucracy in the 18th century III. *Political Science Quarterly 47*(2), 259–273.

Eisen, A., and Wollmann, H. (eds.). (1996). *Institutionenbildung in Ostdeutschland: Zwischen externer Steuerung und Eigendynamik.* Opladen: Leske + Budrich.

Ellwein, T. (1994). *Das Dilemma der Verwaltung.* Mannheim: B.I.-Taschenbuchverlag.

Ellwein, T. (1993, 1997). *Der Staat als Zufall und Notwendigkeit. Die jüngere Verwaltungsentwicklung in Deutschland am Beispiel Ostwestfalen-Lippe* (2 vol.). Opladen: Westdeutscher Verlag.

Ellwein, T., and Hesse, J.J. (1997). *Staatsreform in Deutschland.* Baden-Baden: Nomos.

Heinrich, G., Henning, F.-W., and Jeserich, K.G.A. (eds.). (1992). *Verwaltungsgeschichte Ostdeutschlands 1815–1945.* Stuttgart: Kohlhammer.

Hess, U. (1993). *Geschichte der Behördenorganisation der thüringischenStaaten.* Jena/Thüringen: G. Fischer Verlag.

Hesse, J.J., and Ellwein, T. (1997). *Das Regierungssystem der Bundesrepublik Deutschland* (2 vol.), 8th ed. Opladen: Westdeutscher Verlag.

Jeserich, K.G.A., Pohl, H., and Unruh, G.C. (eds.). (1983). *Deutsche Verwaltungsgeschichte* (5 vol.). Stuttgart: Deutsche Verlagsanstalt.

Heffter, H. (1969). *Die deutsche Selbstverwaltung im 19. Jahrhundert.* Stuttgart: Deutsche Verlagsanstalt.

Henning, H.-J. (1984). *Die deutsche Beamtenschaft im 19. Jahrhundert.* Wiesbaden: Steiner Verlag.

Huber, E. (1968). *Deutsche Verfassungsgeschichte seit 1789, vol.* 2. Stuttgart: W. Kohlhammer.

Huber, E. (1965). Zur Geschichte der politischen Polizei im 19. Jahrhundert. In E. Huber (ed.), *Nationalstaat und Verfassungssstaat.* Stuttgart: Kohlhammer.

Kilper, H., and Lhotta, R. (1996). *Föderalismus in der BRD.* Opladen: Leske & Budrich.

Klages, H., and Löffler, E. (1995). Administrative modernization in Germany—a big qualitative jump in small steps. *International Review of Administrative Sciences 61*, 373–383.

König, K. (ed.). (1991). *Verwaltungsstrukturen der DDR.* Baden-Baden: Nomos.

König, K. (1992). Transformation einer Kaderverwaltung: Transfer und Integration von öffentlichen Bediensteten in Deutschland. *Öffentliche Verwaltung 45*(13), 545–556.

König, K. (1995). Personalpolitik bei der Transformation einer Kaderverwaltung in Deutschland. In W. Seibel and A. Benz (eds.), *Regierungssystem und Verwaltungspolitik.* Opladen: Westdeutscher Verlag.

König, K., and Beck, J. (1997). *Modernisierung von Staat und Verwaltung.* Baden-Baden: Nomos.

König, K., and Siedentopf, H. (eds.). (1997). *Öffentliche Verwaltung in Deutschland* (2nd ed.). Baden-Baden: Nomos Verlagsgesellschaft.

Kruis, K. (1979). Berufsbeamtentum—Ärgernis oder Forderung der freiheitlichen rechts- und sozialstaatlichen Demokratie? *Politische Studien 3*, 189–201.

Kvistad, G.O. (1999). *The Rise and Demise of German Statism: Loyalty and Political Membership.* New York: Berghahn.

Lecheler, H. (1997). Die Gliederung des öffentlichen Dienstes. In K. König, and H. Siedentopf (eds.), *Öffentliche Verwaltung in Deutschland.* Baden-Baden: Nomos Verlagsgesellschaft.

Leutheusser-Schnarrenberger, S. (1999). Neue Dimensionen des Politischen. *Zeitschrift für Rechtspolitik 32*(8), 313–316.

Misera, H.-U. (1992). *Organisationsveränderungen in der Verwaltung: Verwaltungswissenschaftlich untersucht am Beispiel der inneren Organisation der Finanzämter von 1919 bis 1992.* Frankfurt: Peter Lang.

Mommsen, H. (1966). *Beamtenpolitik im Dritten Reich.* Stuttgart: Deutsche Verlagsanstalt.

Pitschas, R. (ed.). (1992). *Verwaltungsintegration in den neuen Bundesländern.* Berlin: Duncker & Humblot.

Rebentisch, D., and Teppe, K. (eds.). (1986). *Verwaltung contra Menschenführung im Staat Hitlers.* Göttingen: Vandenhoek & Ruprecht.

Renzsch, W. (1999). Meist sinnvolle Ergänzung and nicht Konflikt: Zum Verhältnis von Parteiendemokratie und Föderalismus. *Frankfurter Allgemeine Zeitung 219*, Sept 21:12.

Ruck, M. (1996). *Korpsgeist und Staatsbewusstsein: Beamte im deutschen Südwesten 1928–1972.* München: Oldenbourg Verlag.

Runge, W. (1965). *Politik und Beamtentum im Parteienstaat: Die Demokratisierung der politischen Beamten in Preussen zwischen 1918 and 1933.* Stuttgart: Ernst Klett Verlag.

Scharpf, F.W., Reissert, B., and Schnabel, F. (1976). *Politikverflechtung: Theorie und Empirie des kooperativen Föderalismus in der Bundesrepublik.* Kronberg: Scriptor Verlag.

Seibel, W. (1997). Verwaltungsreformen. In K. König and H. Siedentopf, (eds.), *Öffentliche Verwaltung in Deutschland* (2nd ed.). Baden-Baden: Nomos Verlagsgesellschaft.

Spicer, M. (1998). Public administration under 'enlightened despotism' in Prussia: an examination of Frederick the Great's administrative practice. *Administrative Theory & Practice 20*(1), 23–31.

Statistisches Bundesamt (ed.). (1998). *Im Blickpunkt: Frauen in Deutschland.* Stuttgart: Metzler-Poeschel.

Sternberger, D. (1949). Demokratie der Furcht oder Demokratie der Courage? *Die Wandlung 4*(1), 3–18.

Wagener, F. (1969). *Neubau der Verwaltung: Gliederung der öffentlichen Aufgaben und ihrer Träger nach Effektivität und Integrationswert.* Berlin: Duncker & Humblot.

Weingarten, J. (1993). *Finanzverwaltung und Gesetzesvollzug: Anforderungen, Probleme und Vorgehen der Steuerverwaltung bei der Anwendung steuerrechtlicher Normen.* Opladen: Westdeutscher Verlag.

16

Institutionalizing Democracy

Governance in Post-1974 Portugal

Lawrence S. Graham   *Department of Government, University of Texas at Austin, Austin, Texas*

I. INTRODUCTION

Since 1974 enormous changes have occurred in Portuguese politics. Among them is the decentralization of political power, the consequences of which are a plurality of decision-making centers and constraints on executive-centered governmental action from Lisbon. Replacing a system in which the prime minister and the office supporting his work (the Presidencia do Conselho) were the center of politics and policy is a regime that has established a meaningful division of authority among the presidency, the prime minister, and the national assembly, coupled with guarantees of regional and local autonomy. An important outcome of this diffusion of power is a system in which there are numerous channels through which participation and public contestation of issues can take place. In such a context, the guarantee of meaningful subnational representation and governance has opened up a significant new arena in which local and regional issues can be expressed and attended to.

At the same time, within Portugal's new democracy, neither policy coherency nor impact in governmental programs at regional and local levels can easily be achieved. Severe deficiencies in the ability to coordinate and implement policy could already be noted in the state's administrative apparatus on the eve of the revolution, and these weaknesses have been compounded by the political changes that have ensued since 1974. Yet, while the problems presented by the lack of articulation between political and administrative structures are hardly new and have had far greater impact since 1974, what is of interest to development policy specialists is how despite these limitations Portugal has made notable advances both in institutionalizing a democratic regime and in attending to its development needs. This experience is instructive for other developing countries in that the solution to Portugal's administrative problems has centered on bypassing the national state in terms of development policy and taking maximum advantage of the supports and assistance provided by a regional association of states, the European Union. Freed from the need to engage simultaneously in state reform and economic and political restructuring, Portuguese leaders have been able to focus their attention first on consolidating a democratic regime. Then, once consensus was achieved among political elites to channel political conflict into competition at the ballot box and to resolve differences over legislation through the use of the majority principle in determining outcomes in the Assembly of the Republic, attention was directed at economic reform.

II. RESOLUTION OF GOVERNANCE ISSUES THROUGH NEGOTIATED SETTLEMENTS

What needs to be emphasized here are the contrasts between the very different political climate within which issues of governance are debated today and those that existed before 1974. Prior to the military coup of April 25 and two years of revolutionary upheavals (1974–76), the Portuguese state was a very different entity. Four decades of authoritarian rule and administrative change consonant with the concentration of power in the hands of the prime minister had produced a state with well-institutionalized procedures for centralized decision making on all important issues of public policy as well as effective mechanisms for excluding consideration of those issues most troubling to the dictatorship. A salient example is the regime's handling of its colonial question. Of central importance to all major groups in Portugal, the government of Marcelo Caetano (Salazar's successor, 1969–74) was able to exclude any open discussion of this issue until the eve of the revolution. When the government finally permitted General Spinola, an influential military officer, to publish his ideas for the creation of a Portuguese commonwealth in place of the colonial system, not only was his option no longer feasible in the context of an irreversible movement toward independence for Portuguese Africa, but also it was only a question of time before a captains' movement was to overthrow the regime itself, sideline the military hierarchy of which he was a part, and liberate the colonies.

If the Portuguese state of this era is examined from the standpoint of the centralized decision-making processes and issues dominating the government's agenda before 1974, it was for all effective purposes a centralized bureaucratic empire in which considerable effort and resources had been invested in linking two key regions in Africa—Angola and Mozambique—to decision-making centers in Lisbon. Once the regime was overthrown and independence of the overseas territories was guaranteed, huge adjustments had to be made. Not only was an extensive administrative apparatus radiating outward from the Ministry of the Overseas (Ministerio do Ultramar) dismantled overnight, but also overseas agents of the state, as public functionaries with legal guarantees of government employment, needed to be brought home and absorbed into the home service. While figures vary greatly on the number of Portuguese citizens returning to continental Portugal and the proportion of civil servants incorporated into the government, it is probably accurate to say that some 7% of the 600,000 returning were considered public employees and thereby entitled to continued public employment.[1]

III. REACTION AGAINST EXCESSIVE CENTRALIZATION OF POWER

Once the radical phase of the revolution had ended and commitment to the consolidation of a democratic regime took hold after 1976, the kind of unitary state that emerged was very different from what existed in the past. Following practices that have become common throughout southern Europe, rather than replace unitary forms of government with federal ones, regional autonomy statutes were provided for those regions where the pressures for independence were the greatest: the Azores and Madeira islands. But on the continent, despite much public debate concerning the desirability of regionalization, little was done initially nor has been done since to give new meaning to long-standing regional identities. Instead, attention has centered on revitalizing existing instruments for local government (concelhos municipais, juntas de freguesia, and local development authorities). Even when the Assembly of the Republic has made formal grants of authority to regional and local authorities, its control over public finance has placed real constraints on regional and local initiatives on the mainland. Only through the availability of funds from Brussels have regional and local authorities found it possible to bypass Lisbon.

The de facto system of governance that has emerged thus has reinforced disjunctures present in the new regime from the outset. Underwritten by the Constitution of 1976, this is a hybrid system of governance, with two tiers of elected of officials as well as two distinct sets of national and local institutions. Complementing these political institutions is a much older administrative system characterized by powerful central ministries housed in Lisbon with minimal representation in outlying areas. In such a setting, local authorities frequently find themselves without the capacity to respond effectively to the demands for improved public services in the areas under their jurisdiction, since many of these activities fall within the domain of ministerial action. At the outset it seemed that innovation in the form of mobile technical assistance teams—the *gabinetes de apoio tecnico* (GAT)—would serve to bridge this gap. But as the new system became institutionalized and as coordination and control of the *gabinetes* was vested in regional planning commissions, local authorities found the GATs far less likely to respond directly to local needs as articulated by leadership groups within the communities themselves. But, mitigating these constraints has been a continual infusion of regional and local development funds from the European Union, as Portugal thoroughly integrated itself into Europe after 1986.

Accompanying these developments at the local level has been a pulverization of responsibility in the central government as a consequence of the political events that dominated the public agenda from 1974 through 1976. During those years the reaction against centralized bureaucratic controls moved in two directions.

First, endeavors to dismantle institutions supporting the old order focused on the presidency of the council of ministers, the ministry of corporations, the internal security apparatus, and the overseas ministry. The first of these institutions was a supraministry. Created by Salazar, it was vested with all the control and coordination functions deemed to be important to the premier. The second institution was essentially an organ of social policy, which organized and regulated social groups (other than business) and administered social programs benefiting them, corporately. The third, internal security, was housed in an autonomous office, called the *Direcao Geral de Seguranca* (DGS: the directorate-general for security). Known originally as PIDE (*Policia Internacional de Defesa*) during the Salazar era, under Caetano it received a new name but little else changed; it continued to answer directly to the prime minister and retained an effective surveillance apparatus of its own, reaching throughout the mainland and the overseas territories. The last of the organizations of central coordination and control, the overseas ministry, consisted of directorates general matching each of the domestic ministries; these bureaus oversaw corresponding sets of activities overseas. At the provincial level—this was the basic colonial unit of governance—regional governments housed civil administration authorities with general oversight responsibilities as well as representatives of the directorates, under provisions of dual authority and supervision. Given the strictness of the controls exercised under the old regime, the strong sentiments expressed against them, especially the DGS, and the extensiveness of the changes after 1974, these organizations were dismantled uniformly and completely.

A second set of activities centered around removal of old-regime bureaucrats at the level of directors and directors general through a process known as *saneamento* (cleansing). Whereas Salazar had used the same process in the late 1920s and the early 1930s to remove senior bureaucrats identified with republican and liberal perspectives, the *goncalvistas*—military officers and civilians identified with the premiership of Captain (later General) Antonio dos Santos Vasco Goncalves—employed the same technique to remove those most closely identified with the authoritarian, corporatist, and repressive practices of the Estado Novo.

Under the impact of these actions from above and chaos from below, which accompanied mass mobilization and the occupation of places of work, vacant housing, and land, the administrative system ceased to function as a coherent body of institutions.[2] Once central controls disappeared, political movements outside the state wanting to restructure Portuguese public organizations converged with the actions of government employees from within, through worker commissions, to transform the conditions of work in the public sector. A twofold process ensued. At the senior management level there was a general exist of tenured civil servants (directors and directors general), while at the middle and lower levels new employees were taken on with each major cabinet change. Simultaneously, returning overseas civil servants were blanketed into the home civil service. Furthermore, as the local governments changed from administrative and regulatory bodies under the old regime, into separately constituted political entities, public employment at the local level expanded. The consequence of political clientelism—the blanketing into public jobs of one's own political following—was a rapid expansion in the number of the people working for the state. To these numbers must also be added those who worked in private-sector organizations nationalized by the government or transferred to the public domain as a consequence of bankruptcy or the exit of these firms' previous owners between 1974 and 1976.

Thus, whereas the central administration reported 155,200 in 1968 (the last public employee census before the revolution), by 1979 the total had increased to 313,800 and by 1983 to 442,000. At the local and regional level, the increase was from 41,542 in 1968 to 58,266 in 1979 and to 72,562 in 1983.[3]

This rapid increase in public sector employment coupled with expansion in the number of state-owned enterprises and the absence of central controls destroyed the coherency of the old administrative system without providing a substitute. In this context public administration drifted across 1975 and 1976 into 1977 and 1978. Although President Eanes attempted to bring about administrative reform during the era of technocratic cabinets (summer 1978 through fall 1979), none of the party-based governments gave anything other than lip service to the prospects of administrative reform. The more important issues concerned the constitution of new political institutions and questions of accountability and control between the presidency and the assembly, in which governments headed by a succession of prime ministers reflected continually shifting parliamentary majorities.

The hiatus between political and administrative structures has been the greatest at the local level. There specific programs and activities are carried out within a spatial context that superimposes civil governors overseeing political regions known as distritos, planning units staffed by regional authorities in key population centers, field offices with representatives of self-contained central ministries, and separately constituted local governments consisting of local assemblies and administrative institutions. The consequence has been a disjoined set of intergovernmental relations, characterized by three patterns.

First, field agencies of the central government remain constrained by the concentration of decision-making authority in Lisbon and, to a lesser extent, in such regional centers as Porto and Coimbra. Not only is funding for these agencies as limited today as in the past, but field representatives have even less capacity today to influence local affairs. Under the Estado Novo, central government agencies were charged with significant regulatory functions and few activities could be initiated at the local level without obtaining the necessary approval of governmental authorities.

Changes since 1974 have given great importance to local autonomy and local self-government. Responsible to local electorates, local authorities seek to maximize those activities that give credit to their claims to be exercising public office with responsiveness to public demands. The primary levers available to field agency officials are fiscal and technical. These are the external resources with which to enact many local programs, but both remain in short supply.

Second, municipal councils usually lack adequate professional staffs of their own to provide either new or expanded public services. While strong on representation, local councils and mayors have little or no influence over the local economy, and their capacity to extract new monetary resources is as limited today as in the past. The primary source of public funds for them domestically is the Assembly of the Republic and the provisions it makes for transfers to local governments in the annual budget. Third, prevailing intermediary structures, all of recent creation, are equally short of funds, technical staff, and influence to be able to respond to local needs. Because civil governors before the revolution were essentially representatives of the central government with strong powers to oversee and control local affairs, there has been little interest since in vesting them with much authority. Their powers today are largely symbolic, as representatives of the government in office, and the only real influence they can exert over local affairs is a function of their own individual personalities and whether or not they can convince others that they have a useful brokerage role to play.

In short, while the new political system remains strong in its ability to give representation to diverse interests, it is weak in its capacity to foment concrete programs and activities. Citizen perceptions still point to Lisbon as the source of change and as the place from which action, funds, and new personnel must come if anything is to be accomplished. The districts remain essentially political demarcations with little meaning except for the fact that the district capital continues to be the place to which one must travel when contacts with central government field services are required. Accordingly, even more so today than in the past, one must be willing to travel to recognized regional centers or the national capital to resolve local needs that fall outside the range of routine operations. When asked who were the most influential figures in public administration from the standpoint of programs in a survey this author conducted of local authorities in three representative districts during 1980, the answer was always the directors and the directors-general. Where were the decisions made that ultimately resolve anything? The answer uniformly was Porto, Coimbra, and Lisbon—especially the last.[4]

IV. CITIZEN PERCEPTIONS OF PUBLIC SERVICE

One way to evaluate the performance of governmental institutions is to examine the public services provided and citizen perceptions of their efficacy. Over the years, the Marketing and Public Opinion Division of NORMA in Lisbon has surveyed citizen attitudes periodically. While this work is more widely known in U.S. academic circles through the work Thomas Bruneau has published on voter preferences, in a survey conducted in April and May 1985, citizen attitudes regarding the state in terms of the services provided were also sampled.[5] Despite the fact that these data are now dated, they continue to have relevance to this discussion in that they were collected on the eve of Portugal's entrance into the then European Community (EC), now the European Union (EU), before deficiencies in the Portuguese administrative apparatus were mitigated by external factors. Portugal, along with Spain, joined the EC on Jan. 1, 1986, with provisions protecting it from full integration in the European common market until Jan. 1, 1992. After 1992 all barriers and protections for less competitive areas of the Portuguese economy ended.

In this particular survey, 995 individuals were interviewed randomly throughout Portugal. This information is recorded in Table 1. Eight questions, regarding different types of public service, were directed at this random sample of citizens. These questions asked whether the individual felt that the service in question had improved, worsened, or remained the same. These data are recorded in Table 2.

What is interesting about this survey is the insight it gives into citizen perceptions of public administration responsiveness once they are placed in an institutional context. Those public services in Table 2 that are provided by central government ministries through field offices are (1) public health services, (2) social security, and (3) tax collection. These are all instances where service delivery responds essentially to hierarchical norms. Public officials in these offices were aware of and in direct contact with the public, but the work environment was structured more by

Table 1   Distribution of Population Interviewed

	Sample size	Total population (in thousands)
Region		
Greater Lisbon	232	1584
Greater Porto	178	746
Atlantic Coast (Litoral)	212	2438
Interior of the North	178	1133
Interior of the South	195	978
Area		
Rural (under 2000 inhabitants)	250	3734
Intermediate (2000–10,000)	198	965
Urban (over 10,000 inhabitants)	547	2180
Sex		
Male	387	3301
Female	608	3578
Age		
18–34 years	296	2120
35–54 years	360	2611
55+ years	339	2148

Source: Divisao Publica, NORMA (Lisbon), unpublished survey results, May 1985.

the public organization of which he or she was an employee than by responsiveness to external groups receiving these services.

In these first three cases the perception revealed by the survey is that the services provided had worsened since 1974, especially outside the center. In some cases the contrast in the perception of the service performed before and after the revolution is dramatic; in others, the differences are less marked, and in still others—especially in Lisbon and Porto—services have either remained much the same or improved. For insight into these differences, consult Table 2 and the variations recorded there according to the area of the country.

Whereas the first three vertical entries in Table 2 are central government directed and controlled, the remaining five were all performed by public organizations outside the central administration. These were either public enterprises [e.g., TLP (Telefones de Lisboa e Porto) and CTT (Correios e Telecomunicacoes de Portugal)] or services operated by local governments (which were exercised directly by a municipal authority, a separately constituted local public organization, or a cooperative venture supported by a group of local governments).

Present here are two interrelated phenomena. Local government councils generally perceived successful performance of these services to be indicators of their responsiveness to local citizen demands.[6] Similarly, public-service-oriented state-owned enterprises at these points were apparently more sensitive to citizen demands and the representation of governmental authorities for expanded services than were central-government-operated services. In large part, this had come about as a consequence of more extensive field networks that brought these enterprises into closer contact with consumers (as, for example, in the expanded services provided by TLP and CTT in response to citizen demands and defense of these requests by local authorities).[7] Again, here as above, patterns varied considerably from one region to another. Still, what these data support is the interpretation that since the revolution the incorporation of meaningful local autonomy

Table 2 Citizen Attitudes by Percent on Public Services Since 1974 in Response to Question: Compared with before April 25, do you consider that:

	Total	Gtr. Lisbon	Gtr. Porto	Coast	Int. North	Int. South	Rural	Interme-diate	Urban	Porto	Lisbon
1. Public health services											
Improved	30.0	34.4	31.9	21.9	31.0	40.1	28.4	29.8	32.7	18.7	29.0
Worsened	41.0	37.1	38.3	46.2	45.4	31.0	43.4	38.7	37.8	46.5	38.8
Rem. same	16.7	40.5	21.6	16.8	7.0	18.2	13.4	23.7	19.4	11.0	18.5
No opinion	12.4	8.0	8.2	15.1	16.6	10.8	14.9	7.8	10.1	23.8	13.7
2. Social security											
Improved	31.5	45.3	24.9	22.1	31.6	37.3	27.0	25.5	41.8	32.4	31.8
Worsened	34.5	29.3	49.0	35.7	41.0	21.5	36.5	39.9	28.9	29.8	31.6
Rem. same	20.6	17.6	17.7	24.2	8.8	32.1	19.8	27.2	18.8	16.4	22.0
No opinion	13.4	7.7	8.3	18.0	18.6	9.1	16.7	7.4	10.5	21.4	14.6
3. Tax collection											
Improved	17.0	33.0	12.0	9.0	22.0	9.4	10.8	29.2	22.3	16.3	17.0
Worsened	48.1	47.9	54.8	47.9	52.3	39.2	50.4	37.9	48.7	40.6	51.8
Rem. same	21.1	12.0	22.7	26.7	8.3	35.6	21.5	26.8	17.9	14.3	18.0
No opinion	13.7	7.1	10.5	16.5	17.5	15.7	17.2	6.0	11.1	28.9	13.2
4. Water service											
Improved	41.2	44.6	24.7	41.1	51.6	33.0	44.0	45.2	34.6	22.2	26.5
Worsened	29.7	31.0	39.0	28.3	25.4	29.1	28.2	27.4	33.3	40.4	38.2
Rem. same	18.6	17.9	30.4	16.1	8.7	28.4	14.5	21.4	24.4	20.5	28.3
No opinion	10.5	4.5	5.8	14.5	14.4	9.6	13.3	6.0	7.8	16.8	7.0
5. Electrical service											
Improved	42.3	47.5	24.3	43.0	53.1	33.2	46.3	46.2	33.5	20.2	26.8
Worsened	31.2	30.9	41.7	28.9	27.4	33.6	30.0	24.0	36.4	46.2	39.7
Rem. same	17.9	17.0	29.3	16.4	8.1	26.0	13.5	24.6	22.6	20.0	28.0
No opinion	8.6	4.7	4.7	11.7	11.4	7.1	10.2	5.3	7.5	13.6	5.5
6. Public transportation											
Improved	37.5	48.8	34.6	27.7	50.3	30.8	36.6	43.7	36.3	33.6	28.1
Worsened	33.0	31.5	37.7	37.6	24.1	30.9	32.4	27.7	36.6	43.1	45.5
Rem. same	18.2	14.6	22.7	19.8	7.8	29.0	17.6	21.2	18.1	10.2	20.0
No opinion	11.3	5.1	5.1	14.9	17.8	9.2	13.5	7.4	9.1	13.2	6.5
7. Telephones											
Improved	36.1	40.9	32.2	30.4	52.0	26.9	37.1	41.4	31.9	23.4	19.6
Worsened	30.1	35.8	35.8	32.3	26.2	15.8	27.7	27.4	35.5	35.9	45.9
Rem. same	20.7	16.1	22.6	22.9	6.3	37.6	20.1	23.4	20.3	17.6	22.9
No opinion	13.2	7.3	9.5	14.4	15.5	19.8	15.1	7.9	12.3	23.1	11.6
8. Postal service											
Improved	37.4	42.5	31.3	31.1	55.3	28.3	37.6	38.7	36.3	29.1	24.8
Worsened	22.0	18.5	27.6	24.8	24.9	13.3	24.3	16.9	20.5	16.7	24.4
Rem. Same	25.6	24.5	27.7	25.7	7.5	47.8	23.7	30.4	27.2	23.8	33.7
No opinion	14.8	14.5	13.4	18.4	12.4	10.5	14.4	14.0	16.0	30.4	17.0

Source: Divisâo de Marketing e Opinião Pública, ɴᴏʀᴍᴀ (Lisboa), unpublished survey results, May 1985.

Note: In cases where percentages do not total 100%, the errors are in original data or due to rounding.

has had the effect of expanding basic public services to localities outside the center where such services were previously deficient or absent and where local authorities are now in a position to press for such services.

V. CHANGES IN PORTUGUESE PUBLIC POLICIES SINCE 1986

Between 1986 and 1992, major economic change took place in Portugal, as Portuguese political leaders consolidated their democratic regime and institutionalized democratic procedures. By 1986 a major breakthrough had occurred in removing the Portuguese military from participation in civilian affairs and in establishing an agreed-upon set of procedures for determining how its semipresidential parliamentary system would function. By 1989 revision of the Constitution of 1976 had been completed in the removal of the clauses which placed constraints on the development of a market economy compatible with Portugal's full integration in the European economic community by 1992.(8) By 1992 Portuguese political leaders had completed all the internal economic restructuring necessary to bring the country into a wider economic union.

As a consequence of these changes, the deficiencies noted above have in many respects been mitigated by two developments: the institutionalization of a successful market economy thoroughly integrated into the European common market and the impact of supranational policies and institutions developed in the course of the evolution of European integration. For a small, peripheral country like Portugal, the wider politics of regional accommodation in moving from a common market arrangement (the European Economic Community), to a more fully developed institutionalized regional association (the European Community), and from there into a political as well as economic regional authority with the capacity to act independently of individual member states (the European Union) gave it access to resources and innovations in development policy that were unavailable internally. The European form of supranational political association, through its use of the principle of subsidiarity, has been especially effective in breaking down the barriers to Portugal's economic modernization and the political and administrative constraints that earlier had the effect of making Portugal a peripheral European economic region. Under subsidiarity, development constraints that cannot be resolved at a lower level of governance (within the confines of individual national states as issue resolution moves from the local, to the regional, to the national level) can be forcefully dealt with at the Community level in accord with policies and programs developed in Brussels.

What this has meant in the Portuguese case is that the political costs of restructuring the public sector and engaging in major administrative reform have been bypassed. At the national level, where programs financed through the Community require working with national-level bureaucrats, parallel offices and delegates have established operations in cooperation with central government ministries and high-level governmental officials. At the regional and local level, both the availability of Community funds for development at the subnational level and the authority to set up again parallel offices and to deploy Community officials to work in cooperation with regional and local authorities have created a framework for cooperative initiatives that have accelerated the rate of economic as well as political and social change.

The significance of these changes should not be minimized. They are best reflected in World Bank rankings of Portugal since 1996. Before this date, Portugal fell in the category of an upper middle income country. Since 1996 Portugal has joined the league of the high income industrial countries.(9) While Portugal has received little if any attention in the U.S. setting, be it governmental or academic, the lessons of this transformation have not been lost on Eastern Europe. It should surprise no one that the East-Central European states are elated at the prospects of also joining Europe in the near future, for they too will likely be able to mitigate the tensions created by having to engage simultaneously in political and economic restructuring with limited domestic resources. In contrast, the Balkan states more than ever find their prospects for escaping from the legacies of the past increasingly difficult.

VI. CONCLUSIONS

Consideration of center-periphery relations and the interrelationships between political and administrative institutions, first under authoritarianism and later under more open, democratic arrangements, suggests the presence of an important dynamic in analyzing domestic change and the way in which governments function. Not only does such analysis serve as a corrective to some of the facile generalizations about the performance of authoritarian and democratic regimes, but it also calls attention to the utility of examining the wider context of intergovernmental relations and how activities in these areas give shape to such regimes. This is a dimension of politics integrating the bureaucratic component with political institutions and civil society warranting particular attention in newly constituted democratic regimes, especially during their consolidation, and how new forms of international cooperation, operating at a supranational regional level above individual national governments, can trigger breakthroughs in development policy.

In Portugal, the earlier pattern of disjoined intergovernmental relations suggested that there were a number of problems that lay ahead as expectations oriented to performance and results increased. Yet, with the shift of focus from resolving development problems within the constraints of a small, peripheral European state to the development of regional development strategies for southern Europe as a whole, the Portuguese leadership was able to respond effectively and access new financial and human resources from outside national borders that accelerated the rate of change and ultimately led to an economic breakthrough that accompanied the earlier political breakthrough. As a consequence, today Portugal is considered to be both a consolidated democracy and a consolidated market economy.

NOTES

1. Kenneth Maxwell uses the figure of 600,000 in reporting the number of Portuguese settlers who returned to mainland Portugal. See his article, "Regime Overthrow and the Prospects for Democratic Transition in Portugal," in Guillermo O'Donnell, Philippe C. Schmitter, and Laurence Whitehead (eds.), *Transitions from Authoritarian Rule: Southern Europe* (Baltimore: Johns Hopkins University Press, 1986), p. 134. Figures on the numbers of civil servants reincorporated into the home civil service vary between 35,000 and 45,000; for the purposes of this article, I would suggest using 40,000 as the approximate figure to match Maxwell's 600,000. See my article, "Bureaucratic Politics and the Problem of Reform in the State Apparatus," in Lawrence S. Graham and Douglas L. Wheeler (eds.), *In Search of Modern Portugal: The Revolution and Its Consequences* (Madison: University of Wisconsin Press, 1983), p. 238.
2. For an excellent discussion of the social movements outside the state that developed during the revolution, see John L. Hammond, *Building Popular Power: Workers' and Neighborhood Movements in the Portuguese Revolution* (New York: Monthly Review Press, 1988).
3. Public employment figures for Portugal are very difficult to pin down and one encounters large-scale discrepancies according to the sources used. The most reliable are probably those available from the Secretaria de Estado da Administracao Regional and these are the ones reported here, on the basis of the following source: Antonio Barreto, "Centralizacao e Decentralizacao em Portugal," *Analise Social* 20: 81–82 (1984), p. 207.
4. Lawrence S. Graham, "O Estado Portugues visto a partir de baixo," *Analise Social* 18 (1982), pp. 959–974.

5. See, for example, Thomas C. Bruneau, "Popular Support for Democracy in Post-Revolutionary Portugal: Results from a Survey," in Lawrence S. Graham and Douglas L. Wheeler (eds.), *In Search of Modern Portugal: The Revolution and Its Consequences* (Madison: University of Wisconsin Press, 1983), and *Politics and Nationhood: Post-Revolutionary Portugal* (New York: Praeger Publishers, 1984).

6. Graham, *op. cit.*, pp. 968–969.

7. See Telefones en 84: Oferta ultrapassou a procura em 50%, *Expresso* Feb. 9, 1985, p. 13.

8. For an in-depth discussion of these developments, consult Lawrence S. Graham, *The Portuguese Military and the State: Rethinking Transitions in Europe and Latin America* (Boulder: Westview Press, 1993).

9. For example, see the *1998 World Bank Development Report* (New York: Oxford University Press, 1998), passim.

17

Regionalization

A European Survey

Lon S. Felker and Paul C. Trogen   *Department of Economics, Finance, and Urban Studies, East Tennessee State University, Johnson City, Tennessee*

I. INTRODUCTION

Regionalism is "the practice of or belief in regional government" (McLean 1996:424). Regionalization, on the other hand, is a system of public administration put in place to achieve the goals and ends of regionalism. The two terms are frequently employed interchangeably. Regionalization is, in effect, the implementation of a regionalist plan.

In any event, the concept of regionalism is an old one, although it should not be confused with federalist or confederalist approaches to the organizational structure of governance. First, there is no claim of sovereignty on the part of regional governments within a centralized, unitary system. These are first and foremost administrative entities, created with the intent of serving as the regional implementers of the central government's public policy agenda, and not as units of policy making. Secondly, it follows that regionalization experiments are most frequently encountered within the context of unitary nation-states, such as France, Great Britain, and other nonfederal systems. This does not, however, entirely rule out the use of regionalization in federal systems. Canada, to cite one example, has embarked on a regionalized system of health care.

This raises another question: Do regional governments offer a full panoply of public services, or are they specialized in provision of only certain such services? The answer seems to be that both possibilities obtain. Certain governments use regionalism as foremost an economic development strategy, with the intent of generating balanced national growth through planned regional development. In such states, regionalism is focused on encouragement of economic growth, the decentralized realization of national policies, and the implementation of growth strategies slaved to a national master plan. The primary intent here is to move industrial and commercial development out of the metropolitan area, and to encourage the local economies in nonmetropole regions. Great Britain, France and Italy have all utilized such regionalist strategies in the past.

On the other hand, regionalized provision of services other than economic growth planning has occurred in a variety of settings. Such services include prison/police systems, health care, transportation, public housing, care of the elderly, education, waste disposal and broadcasting. Much depends in either case on the nature and scope of the regionalism/regionalization project—is it a piecemeal approach to service provision by a few or all national-level ministries, or is it a holistic approach to governance launched by the national political leadership with the intent of encouraging decentralization of the polity, economy, and society?

The arguments in favor of regionalization are many, but four stand out as significant: efficiency, economy, democracy, and balanced economic growth. First, the advocates of regionalism and regionalization contend that regional bodies would provide more expeditious and efficient services as well as provide a more flexible form of government than a centralized system (Irving 1975:28–29). This is so because of the shorter time and reduction in decision making that obtain when regional bodies make decisions that would otherwise have to be submitted to the centralized ministries for approval. Flexibility would be possible because regional governments would be capable of fitting central governmental legislation to local needs and conditions.

Secondly, economies would be forthcoming due to the high cost of operating a centralized administrative apparatus that functions only with considerable "red tape," duplication, and multiple decision-making centers. Third, democracy would result from locally focused bodies that would permit a higher degree of popular access and secure a greater degree of support. The remoteness of the central government in the metropole would be countered by the familiar and less impersonal nature of regional bodies.

Finally, regionalism would encourage balanced economic growth and development strategies that would be suitable for the region in which they have jurisdiction. Instead of the "one size fits all" approach of centralized planning, regional planning bodies would be capable of planning for development projects that serve the needs of the local economy, while simultaneously serving the overall goal of balanced national development.

The following sections will examine some regionalization schemes in several European nation-states. The main purpose of this survey is to provide a historical perspective on regionalization in Europe: a review of regionalism and regionalization efforts in several European settings. A secondary purpose is to draw certain conclusions based on this survey concerning the origins and gestation of regionalization.

II. EUROPE

Western Europe may be said to be embarked on one of the most ambitious centralization plans of all time—the European Union. The origins of this undertaking are traceable to the German-French coal and steel agreements in the post–World War II era. What seems to be evolving is a confederal system that is in transition to a federal form, and as such it offers a fascinating case of consolidation of nation-states into a supranational entity. The tariff union, the common currency, the Common Market, and a Eurobureaucracy headquartered in Brussels suggest that this is a maturing political form with the potential to subsume the sovereignty of the member states. One project within the EU is the regionalization of many government functions, with the intent of creating a "Europe of the regions," with regional development and growth along the lines required by the region as opposed to the nation-state.

It is within the nation-states of Europe, however, that regionalism has achieved something of a new lease on life. The various European nations have experimented with regionalism since World War II, and these efforts have taken a variety of forms.

A. France

In his *New French Revolution* (*1968*) John Ardagh remarks that De Gaulle, at the outset of the Fifth Republic, seemed "ready to sacrifice some Government sovereignty." In a speech in Lyons, in March 1968, De Gaulle had sketched some of his ideas for a series of regional assemblies, locally elected, with their own finances and some sovereign powers. This, as Ardagh remarks, was the "first blow in 150 years at the Napoleonic heritage of centralization" (1968:475; *Le Monde* 28 March 1968). But it is notable that neither the Constitution of 1946 nor that of 1958, the framing of both of which Gaullists had a major role in, contains any mention of the regions. The history of post–World War II regionalism and regionalization in France is somewhat more convoluted than it may appear.

In truth, this was by no means De Gaulle's first foray into regionalism, nor was it France's first experience with regionalist proposals. During the Vichy period (1940–44), Marshal Petain, De Gaulle's wartime rival, had implemented regional councils. Under the collaborationist Vichy regime, 18 regions were organized for police and economic administration, with a prefect in charge of each. Both De Gaulle and Petain seem to have gone to a common source for their regionalist projects—the right-wing, monarchical political philosophy of Charles Maurras. Part of Maurras' *Action francaise* platform had been the development of regional, decentralized government bodies to counter the overwhelming power of republican, centralized France (Muret 1972:298).

De Gaulle, with his aide Michel Debre, had drafted proposals for regionalization during the war. But these were never completed, and the decision was made to retain the Petainist system until this, too, was abandoned after De Gaulle's resignation (Andrews 1974:297).

Ironically, France's first postwar experience with regionalization, the retention of the Vichy regional prefects and councils created under German occupation (Andrews 1974:296–297), was only the first such effort in a long series. But this coincided with regionalization's popularity among provincial business interests in the immediate post-Liberation period, as the various provincial interests organized into lobbying groups in order to corner their share of aid and reconstruction funds. As part of this movement, regionalism was primarily popular with Alsatians and Bretons, who, in addition to worries about inequitable aid funding for regional recovery, also feared the submersion of their culture and language within the dominant culture of republican, centralized France. In fact, the establishment of the *Fonds National d'Amènagement du Territoire* (FNAT) within the Ministry of Reconstruction and Urban Development in 1950 had been inspired by the regional example in Brittany, the *Comité d'Etude et de Liaison des Intérets Bretons* (CELIB) (Irving 1975:19–20).

The initial proposal in the Fifth Republic for regional assemblies was defeated in the 1969 referendum. This was due first to De Gaulle's unpopularity following the May-June 1968 riots among students and workers in Paris, but also to the limited nature of local autonomy and heavy-handed central control that the Gaullist regionalization plan offered. In terms of a promised participatory revolution, voters found it too little, too late. But later Gaullist ministers, initially under Pompidou, had greater success in implementing this small "institutional revolution" (Ehrmann 1976:291). Enacted in 1972 and implemented in the fall of 1973, the new law offered a fresh conception of the counterweight of territory as a balance to overcentralization.

It was the need to find better areas for the administration of central services that had first led to the creation of standard regions, and throughout most of the 1960s France had embraced at best a "timid regionalism," which in many areas meant that the only regional development was the appointment of a regional prefect (Blondel 1974:225). With the establishment of the first semi-representative regional bodies in 1964, called *Comités de Développement Economiques Régionaux* (CODER), these committees served to express popular opinion in the region; they comprised a variety of local prominent representatives of the various political and social interests, and included local councilors as well (Blondel 1974:225).

The creation of 22 regions, it has been argued, exceeded one of the requirements of effective decentralization: to divide the nation into 10 to 12 regions that economists believed would be economically viable (Ehrmann 1976:292). Moreover, there was the choice between decentralization or deconcentration of decision making—the Gaullists opted for the latter. The rationale was that such regional bodies would provide regional initiative in launching development projects without the impetus from Paris, and without the heavy hand of the national bureaucracy overseeing every step. But even in the post-1972 incarnation of the CODER, these bodies possessed only "very limited" financial resources (Irving 1975:18). More to the point, these reforms had been directed at administrative deconcentration, not political devolution, which was what the committed regionalists, moderates, and some senior officials had been demanding. Without the devolution of decision making, many of these parties felt that regionalization was meaningless (Irving 1975:18).

The institutional arrangement was a classically French one. The chief executive of each region consisted of the *préfect* of the department in which the regional capital was sited (Ehrmann 1968:292; Hayward 1973:37–47). A special staff of civil servants comprised the *préfect*'s staff. The primary duties of the CODER were the oversight and coordination of economic development projects within the departments of the region. In short, the regional *préfect* became a *primus inter pares* among the *préfects* of those departments within the region. As for other services, these were coordinated with the field offices of the national ministries.

Mitterand's Socialist government, which took office in May 1981, inherited the regionalist system put in place by previous Gaullist regimes. Among its first legislative acts was the *lois de décentralisation* (*2 Mars 1982*), which attempted to modify and improve the relations between the central government and the provincial and local governments, as well as rationalize the administrative organization in terms of a division of labor (*Les locales collectivites*; http://www.fonction-publique.gouv.fr/les). As part of this reform package, the regions were upgraded to *collectivités territoriales*—much like the departments and the municipalities—which have democratically elected governing councils.

This represented a volte face for the French Left, having previously rejected regionalism as a plan rooted in monarchist and even fascist thinking. The Left had long feared that regionalism was a right-wing attempt to empower local notables and prominents—landowners and local conservative elites—at the expense of republican elements at the local levels. But Mitterand and a group of intellectuals within the newly constituted Socialist party had reconsidered regionalism during the 1960s, and the writing of Michel Rocard, especially his *Décoloniser la Province*, signaled a remarkable change in socialist though regarding regionalism and decentralization (Loughlin and Mazey 1995:1).

The regionalization effort in France has been modest. True decentralization has taken second place to deconcentration of decision making, and that only in limited spheres of activities, principally economic development projects at the regional level. This is not surprising given the long centrist and *dirigiste* traditions of the French state.

While the law of March 2 continued the economic planning functions under the regional prefects and their staffs, significant reforms occurred in the relationship between the regional governments and the ministerial field offices. The latter were, for the first time, brought under the direct control of the regional and departmental governments. Thus, local services were placed under local control, a formidable alteration of the pattern of centralized provision of services that had existed under all governments since the Fourth Republic.

Also, the fiscal capacity of the regions, while not being greatly enhanced in terms of state transfers of funds, were affected by the authorization of new taxes, principally the tax on automobile registrations (*taxe sur les cartes grises*). The abolition of a ceiling on regional fiscal resources was equally "progressive." However, these changes did not notably improve the position of the regions relative to those of the *départements* and municipalities. In 1983, new legislation transferred to the regions, among other educationally related functions, on-the-job professional training and apprenticeship administration, together with corresponding financial resources (Douence 1995:14–15).

Some advances in human resource capacitation for the regions was also forthcoming, but again, these were minimal when compared to those of the departments. The regions are bound to a system in which cooperation with other state and departmental bodies—advisory, assistance, and planning in nature—is necessary to implement programs. For example, in constructing a public school, the region must avail itself of the services of the rectorats (state regional-level educational offices) and the *Direction Départementale de l'Equipement* (DDE), and seek assistance from state employment agencies as well in setting up training plans and apprenticeship programs (Douence 1995:21). And yet it is worth noting that it is in educational planning—in the construction and improvement of *lycées*—that the regional councils have had their most widely recognized success (Douence 1995:19).

The offloading of the responsibility for building and maintaining schools to the regions, as well as being tasked with overall responsibility for secondary-school planning, suggests that the central administration is attempting to palm off this complex and expensive mission on the regions. Vincent Lemieux (1996:661ff.) has suggested that this pattern is common in regionalized systems, where the power relations dictate that the superior level of government will seek to preserve its power by maintaining its more important resources. A corollary to this might be that the superior level will transfer more expensive and/or less desirable functions and responsibilities to inferior levels.

The interest of the central government in controlling and even diminishing the political power of the regions is also demonstrated, in the opinion of Douence (1995:10–23), in the system of proportional representation elections mandated for the regional councillors. This has resulted in a fragmented and coalition-based governing group in nearly all of the regions. Douence (1995:16) notes that this is not the system found in the overseas regions, such as Corsica.

Some have argued that the Socialists have really not embraced regionalization as fully as they claim. Evidence of this is offered in terms of the Socialists' reluctance to arm the regions with a full panoply of planning and economic development powers. Yet few would argue that the regions have not, since 1982, become more powerful financially, politically, and economically (Loughlin and Mazey 1995:4). Moreover, the Socialists have encouraged movement of the regions into previously unknown policy areas, such as environmental planning and protection. Clearly, the Socialists changed their views on decentralization largely owing to their need to distinguish themselves from the Gaullists and the Right. Yet it is curious that when the Socialists suffered their first electoral defeat in 1986, the neoliberal Jacques Chirac government attempted revisions of many Socialist policies, but left regionalization alone (Loughlin and Mazey 1995:2).

The response of the national political elites to the new regionalism has been less than resounding acclaim. The national civil service, long trained in elite *grandes écoles* such as the Ecole National d'Administration (ENA), are socialized to become the arbiters and regulators of economic and political life. The bureaucrats view themselves as a *grand corps* imbued with a special mission and a sense of duty. This duty "involves the constant definition and defense of the general interest in the face of all who would assert particular or partisan interests contrary to the interests of the whole, or France" (Wilsford 1991:612).

And it is this limitation of the claims of the parochial and partisan that limits as well the influence of regionalization on French public policy processes. Probably a far more effective policy has been the privatization of many state-owned enterprises and the gradual reduction of state-directed business. The poor performance of the French economy in international competition has been a strong motivating factor in the privatization of enterprise, as well as the policy of ending subsidies to heavy industry that have long been a burden on the state (Wilsford 1991:616).

Yet another factor in regional economic development has been the European Union—most especially, the Common Market. Such cities are Strasbourg are evolving into major *European* cities due largely to their proximity to other nation-states and their centrality to international transportation networks. The European Union and the eventual preeminence of a supranational government are probably doing more to redirect French energies into new areas. While the policy of regionalism has been a first stepping stone to decentralization, more significant have been forces outside of France, within the European Union, as well as international economic trends which have forced reconsideration of the state's long-standing policies of interventionism. A Europe of the regions, *sans frontières intérieures*, is a long way from realization. And given the continued strength of French nationalism, it is doubtful that France will countenance a complete deconcentration of national institutions in the interest of a stronger European Union. In France, all roads still lead to Paris, although they sometimes have many provincial and regional byways.

B. Italy

The Italian Republic was born, much like Fourth Republic France, out of the turmoil at the end of World War II. What distinguishes the two nations, however, is the relative youth of Italy's political system compared to that of France. Italian unification had come rather late in the 19th century, while a unified France was centuries old. Italy's political history provided few instances of stable governance, and the rapid rise and fall of coalition governments in the new republic gave little indication that things were changing for the better. The major partisan division between the Left, which included no less than three militant political parties, and the Center-Right, of which the Christian Democrats were the anchor, was only one source of political and parliamentary divisiveness (Kopp 1966:92–93).

Unlike the French Vichy experience, Italy under Fascism did not embrace decentralization in the form of regionalism. On the contrary, the centralizing tendencies apparent since the *Risorgimiento* continued. A series of laws that ended with the Provincial and Communal Law of 1934 systematically eliminated all local and provincial authorities (for example, mayors were replaced with an appointed officer called a *podest'a*, who was advised by an appointed council—the *consulta*) and appointed state representatives were put in their place (Zariski 1987:97). Additionally, Mussolini attempted to suppress the ethnic minorities that had begun to find their voices after World War I. In areas such as Val d'Aosta and Bolzano (South Tyrol), the Fascists enforced Italianization, forbidding the use of the French and German languages. This would have adverse consequences for national unity when World War II ended and a reinvigorated sense of ethnic identity and regionalism emerged. As Zariski (1987:97–98) observes, "by carrying the centralizing tendencies of the pre-1922 liberal state to ridiculous extremes, fascism prepared the way for the regionalist resurgence that was to manifest itself after the Liberation."

The sense of region, the pull of place as a significant factor in Italian politics, has always been strong. So divided and lacking in consensus that Lijphart (1969:222–223) has classified the national political system as "fragmented and unstable," Italy lacked many of the attributes of the consociational democracies of the Low Countries and Scandinavia, and was rife with major cleavages of region, language, culture, class, party, and religion. But Italy's governments up to the end of World War II were unitary systems, with no significant autonomy for local levels of governance. It was therefore a dramatic departure when the 1948 Constitution included a provision for regional governments (Germino and Passigli 1968:56–60).

This proposal met with considerable opposition from a number of elements. Among these were many civil servants of the central state bureaucracy, numerous prefects and provincial officials, and the staffs of the central administration's field agency offices. In terms of the political party spectrum, there was a bloc of rightist parties opposed to regional autonomy. These included the moderate Liberals, the Monarchists, and the Any Man party (*Uomo Qualunque*), which together as a bloc constituted—fortunately for the forces favoring regionalism—the weakest coalition group in the Constituent Assembly in 1947 (Zariski 1987:100).

Some of the hostility to regionalism stemmed from the postwar situation, which at the close of the fighting in Italy found the Resistance groups in the North in firm control of many areas. These groups had formed regional councils or committees, called regional Committees of the National Liberation (CLN). These committees had developed a sense of autonomy and self-sufficiency by the end of the war, going so far as installing their own prefects over the career appointees from the state central administration (Zariski 1987:98).

Another factor in the opposition was the existence of centrifugal tendencies within various provinces, which were in several cases encouraged from without. At the close of the war, French troops had occupied French-speaking Val d'Aosta, and German-speakers in South Tyrol were interested in regional autonomy or merger with Austria. The Trieste border region in northeastern Italy had been the scene of fierce fighting at the end of the war, with Yugoslavs in both Trieste and Gorizia seeking union with Yugoslavia. In Sicily, an active secessionist movement led by Finocchio Aprile was demanding independence, while Sardinia saw the advent of the Sardinian Action Party (Zariski 1987:99).

While the Center (led by the Christian Democrats) and the Left-Center moderates (including the Republicans, the Action party, and a splinter faction of the Liberals) were the proponents of regionalism, they lacked an absolute majority within the Assembly. The balance of power was held by the Left—the Communists (CPI) and the Socialists. But the Left had every reason to believe (given their prominent role in the Resistance) that they were on the eve of taking power in Rome, and that any plan for regional autonomy would create a base of power for local elites opposing Communist central control. For this reason, the Left favored regionalism only for the islands of Sicily and Sardinia.

The 1948 Constitution's Article 5, under the heading of organization, encompasses the rules for autonomy and decentralization. The first of these rules imposes on the state the obligation to make accessible the administration to the general public, by "entrusting to the organs dependent on the central powers the direction of those interests that are not considered of national importance" (http://www.mi.cnr.it/WOW/deagosti/constitu/constitu4). The second rule, however, mandates administrative pluralism, providing as it does for the exercise of independent administrative power, different from that of the state but operating in tandem with the state's administrative entities.

It is the third rule that provides for the distribution of powers among the various administrative entities—state, region, province, and commune. The regions, described as "autonomous bodies with their own powers and functions," as established in Articles 114–133 of the Constitution, were conceived as a form of intermediary government between the national government and the provinces and communes (Adams and Barile 1972:54–55; Germino and Passigli 1968:56). Nineteen such regions exist: Piedmont, Valle d'Aosta, Lombardy, Trentino Alto Adige, Venezia, Friuli-Venezia Guili, Liguria, Emilia-Romagna, Tuscany, Umbria, Marche, Lazio, Abruzzi e Molise, Campania, Puglia, Bascilicata, Calabria, Sicily, and Sardinia. Five regions were singled out for special statutes providing "special forms and conditions of autonomy"—Sicily, Sardinia, Trentino Alto Adaige, Friuli-Venezia Guili, and Valle d'Aosta.

Article 121 sets forth the structure and offices of the regional governments. These consist of a regional council (termed an assembly—*assemblea*—in Sicily), an executive committee (*giunta*), and a president. Both of the latter two are elected out of the regional council from among the council's membership. It was not anticipated that the regional governments would develop an extensive bureaucracy but would rather serve as "coordinating bodies with reference to the local and provincial governments." (Germino and Passigli 1968:57; Adams and Barile 1972:131).

But these constitutional rules were moot, for it was to take another three decades for true regionalism to take hold as a force in Italian politics. The primary stumbling block was the highly partisan nature of postwar parliamentary politics, most particularly the split between the Left and Center-Right, which dominated the national political scene throughout the 30-year period.

A major problem up to the 1970s for regionalism in Italy was the refusal of the Christian

Democrat–dominated governments to approve the autonomy of regions in north-central Italy, especially in the so-called red belt—Umbria, Tuscany, and Emilia Romagna—around Bologna and Florence (Rousseau and Zariski 1987:11; Adams and Barile 1972:130). The Christian Democrats feared the emergence of a Communist stronghold in such regions, and the establishment of coalition governments inclusive of the CPI (Italian Communist Party) in these areas confirmed the Christian Democrats' fears. By a Fabian strategy of careful deliberation and consideration of the Communist-dominated regions' proposed constitutions, the parliamentary Christian Democrats managed to stave off recognition and formal empowerment of these regions up to the 1970s. While the special regions of Val d'Aosta, Trentino-Alto Adige, Sicily, and Sardinia were approved by the Constituent Assembly in February 1948, and the region of Friuli-Venezia was created in 1963 following the resolution of differences with Yugoslavia and the component provinces, it was only in 1970 that the ordinary regions were finally established.

The problem of linkage between the regional councils, their executives, and the national government was solved by creation of a Commissioner of the Government (Article 124), who would be headquartered in the regional capital and who assumed responsibility for coordinating the administrative functions of the state with those of the regional government, and for approving the legislation passed by the regional council within a month, unless there was opposition from the national government (Article 127; Germino and Passigli 1968:58). If the regional council exercises its legislative power in a manner the *commissario* deems inappropriate, unconstitutional, or not in the national interest or damaging to the interest of another region, then he informs Rome. The central government may then exercise a suspensive veto, which can be overridden by an absolute majority vote by the regional council in favor of the legislation. It is then up to the central government to appeal the case to the Constitutional Court (if it deems the legislation unconstitutional or illegal) or it may take the matter before the national parliament if the measure is deemed "inexpedient" (Adams and Barile 1972:131).

The *commissario*, whose office is essentially that of a state inspector, supervises the state's administrative regional functions and liaisons with the region and local services. At the provincial level the *prefecto* performs similar functions at the provincial level, coordinating local interprovincial state authorities. Among his most important responsibilities are public order and the administration of local elections (communal and provincial). In emergencies, the prefect assumes extraordinary powers over all public buildings, police and security services, and protection of the citizenry. Nevertheless, a number of the prefect's minor administrative functions have been assumed by the *commissario*, following the transfer of these to local administrations.

Finally, there is the *sindicato, or* mayor. This official functions at the municipal level, officially as a representative of the civil state and registry office. He, too, has police powers and, where they are lacking, may assume the functions of ordinary police jurisdiction. He assumes roughly the same functions of the prefect at the municipal level in the event of an emergency, controlling disaster relief and responsibility for the security of public buildings. The *sindicato* is also responsible for the administration of selective service for the military.

As in France, the Italian regional councils were to serve first and foremost as economic planning bodies. But as Clark (1975:66) notes, "regional economic planning in Italy has . . . been closely associated with—often coterminous with—attempts to solve the 'southern problem.' " A number of institutions have been set up since 1950 with the mission of developing the South, but the most important of these is the Fund for the South (*Cassa per il Mezzogiorno*), which spends at least 60% of its funds in that region (Clark 1975:66). The fund is administered by a Council of Administration made up of government-appointed experts, and is under the Minister of the South. Significant here is that there is no representative aspect to its composition; all members are central government appointees.

It is perhaps too easy to dismiss the regions as insignificant in to the ebb and flow of Italian politics, but this would be a mistake. In fact, the regions have developed political personae—not as strong as proponents might wish, but strong enough to evoke some attachment on the part of citizens. This is demonstrated in the increasing use of symbols, especially flags. The development of flags, or what might be termed banners or *gonfannons*, has been encouraged, indeed mandated, by President Scalfaro, who requested that all regions and autonomous provinces send their flags to be displayed at conferences (http://fotw.digibel.be/flags/it-reg.html#reg).

And yet, here too, there are differences and contradictions. First, many of the regional flags are based on the principal municipality's gonfalon, which is the town's coat of arms or official symbol. These gonfalons and gonfannons are hung vertically, and usually are displayed only on official buildings. Secondly, the flags of Sicily and Paglie that have been recently displayed are not the official ones adopted a number of years ago, giving rise to questions as to what constitutes the "official" regional or provincial flag. In at least one observer's opinion, this raises the question as to whether those who sent the flag were aware that an official flag already existed.

While Italian regions do not seem to have established themselves to the extent that the French regions have, they are nonetheless in a position to develop. Whether or not Italian regions will flourish depends on several factors: first, the degree to which separatism, decentralization, or even federalism becomes a force in parliamentary politics. To date, one party, the Northern League (*Legga Norte*), under Umberto Bossi, has seriously espoused separatism. In the 27 April 1997 local elections, this party fared badly. Previously, in the chamber of deputies elections of March 1994, Bossi and the League won 8% of the popular vote.

The Northern League has gone so far as to advocate the division of Italy into several nations—northern, central, and southern Italy—and to integrate at least northern Italy (to be called Padania) into the European Monetary Union (EMU). While this proposal strikes many Italians (as well as outsiders) as somewhat zany, there are many in Italy who see it as a serious proposition, one that has a certain merit. However, even in the League's "heartland" (northeastern Italy), few take the idea of secession seriously (*Economist* 1997:11). Some speculate that Bossi's real goals lie in the devolution of state power to regional governments. Still others see the Bossi and the Northern League as a tax reform movement, or as the espouser of an "erstaz federalism." For northerners, the tax question is an especially irksome one, for there is no doubt that the North pays most of the Italian tax bill, and that the tax burden has been a retardant on investment, profits and employment (*Economist* 1997:113).

Aside from partisan politics and popular sentiment, one other factor will affect the viability of the regions. This is the degree to which a regional public administrative presence can be established. Again, unlike in France, the heavily centralized Italian bureaucracy seems unlikely to cede its powers or open itself to regional or local competition. Article 118 of the constitution rigorously sets the regions' administrative responsibilities (under special statute), while reserving the remaining powers and responsibilities to the state. This seems to offer little leeway for regional administrative evolution. Despite its rhetoric of decentralization and autonomy, the reality is that the constitution does nothing to establish the regions as potentially significant policymaking and implementing institutions.

Because regions have few of their own resources, and have also failed to develop their own fiscal stances and expenditure patterns, this has resulted in the regions' spending large sums on specially assigned tasks, usually with earmarked funds from the state central treasury. But this has exposed the regions to periodic efforts by the central government to curtail spending, usually at the expense of the regions. As the public sector bargaining requirement has expanded in the course of the 1980s and 1990s, these efforts to check the regions' spending have increased (Hine 1996:114–115). With spending in a number of sectors increasing, especially with the regionalization of health care, and changes in the funding formulae in agriculture and transportation, the central government has issued regular calls for belt-tightening in the interest of reducing the national deficit, thus dimming hopes for future expansion of regional level projects. But this, according to Hine, has only increased the pressure from the regions to provide soft money in the form of additional grants and loans, leading to the passage of supplementary funding and other off-budget and end-run measures. The lesson here is that fiscal responsibility and self-sufficiency are not being developed at the regional level, nor will they be if this pattern continues.

Will Italy evolve into a truly federal system, or will the regions continue to be the last word in state decentralization? The Northern League offers one answer; perhaps another opinion is that the gradual integration of Europe into a "Europe of the regions" will answer the question very differently. Will the nation-state "wither away" in a Europe of no interior borders, leaving the regions as increasingly significant political units at the subunion level? If so, this development will certainly affect more than Italy.

Italy has had to overcome many obstacles in its regionalization experiments. These included the ebb and flow of partisan politics, the stultifying legacy of centralization under the Fascists, coupled with the equally centralizing goals of the postwar CPI, and the "deep distrust of centrifugal tendencies that autonomy was perceived to embody" (Zariski 1987:91).

If one is to judge Italy's regional experiment by the criterion of national unity, then there certainly are grounds for declaring it a success. Italy did not lose territory following World War II, and regionalism is one reason for that outcome. Sicily did not go off on its own, the French-speaking Val d'Aosta remained in the fold, as did as well the German and Slavic provinces.

There are grounds for viewing Italy's regionalism as a springboard to a more formal federalism. Certainly there is evidence that such a debate is under way, if the material on the Internet is any indication (see, for example, Franco Pizzetti, "Federalismo, Regionalismo E Riforma Dell Stato" at http://www.geslo.unitn..it/car-adm./Review/Constitutional/Pizzetti-1995/pizz2a.htm). If this happens, it will be only the second instance since World War II that a major West European state has adopted a federal system. Germany, which had a tradition of federalism prior to the Nazi period, was the first. Given the similarity in political history with Germany, this would not be surprising. Both nations were a patchwork of independent kingdoms, duchies, city-states, and other autonomous political entities prior to national unification in the 19th century.

While secessionist movements such as the Northern League seem to suggest a divisive future for Italy, they may be the harbinger of a more rationalist approach to national development, and an indication that a truly federalized nation-state is possible. They may well be an indication that a "Europe of the regions" is possible only with the withering away of the nation-state in the 19th-century sense.

C. Spain

The Spanish model of regionalization and regionalism has been one grounded in the historical experience of a nation that entered the modern era incompletely unified and institutionalized. Spain has a long tradition of minority ethnic and linguistic separatism that has yet to be fully absorbed into the national body politic. In fact, the Catalans and Basques have long asserted fordal rights that are even today held up as distinguishing certain "historical communities" from others. And there was, of course, that brief (1937–38) experiment known as the Autonomous Basque Republic that was one of the interesting offshoots of the Spanish Civil War.

Institutionally, Spain developed its political system largely through the incorporation of previously existing organs of state in the constituent kingdoms. Aragon, for examples, had a *cortes*, or legislative body, which began as the royal court in the 12th century, evolving into a sort of advisory body in which both the higher and lower nobility were represented (Kopp 1966:49). Castile's counterpart, on the other hand, was composed largely of a synod made up of clerical leaders. It is no wonder that Spain's long political history has frequently been marked by lapses in institution building. This lapse is equally evident in the modern era, when after a long hiatus in popular government, it was necessary to reinvent the institutional base of a constitutional monarchy in transition to democracy.

Emerging from the long midnight of Franco's rule in the 1970s, Spain was a veritable Rip van Winkle among European states. King Juan Carlos steered a cautious path to democracy and eventual elimination of the numerous manifestations of the recent Falangist past. Regionalism was one of the many reforms that were incorporated in the 1978 Constitution.

Unfortunately, the provisions for autonomous regions were more in the nature of vague proposals than carefully crafted legislation. Two different forms of regionalism were proposed, one requiring considerable popular approval and a lengthy probationary period, while the other, while conferring fewer powers, required far less in terms of popular approval. To further confuse the issue, there were later autonomous agreements emanating from the *cortes* that stipulated additional ways and means whereby regions could achieve autonomy.

All of this has to be seen against the backdrop of post-Franco Spanish politics, an atmosphere in which the old order stood ready to intervene, and on at least one occasion did so in a *golpe de estado* (coup d'état) that failed. The vastly improving economic conditions and the loosening of constraints on the press and popular expression did much to ensure a peaceful transition to democratic reform and regional self-rule. Despite the ambiguity, or perhaps owing in some small part to it, the regions have evolved into units of government that have developed a voice, an increasing visibility, and a sense of identity on the part of their inhabitants. The chief worry for the king and his ministers was that the loosening of state constraints for the non-Castillian areas might be viewed with alarm and spark a reaction in those less endowed Castillian-speaking sections (Zariski 1987)

One favorable development has been the growing unease with the violence and terrorism of the Basque underground group called ETA (*Euskati Ta Askatisuna*—Land and Freedom). This group has been active in assassination, bombings, and other violent acts, not only against Spanish officials but also against other Basques who are labeled collaborators. There have been various public demonstrations and rallies against terrorism in the Basque country, and this may be taken as a sign of increasing disenchantment with the methods, if not the aims, of ETA.

The Catalans, for their part, have always been more gradualist and less militant in their methods. This may reflect the larger Catalan population and the higher profile of Catalan culture and language relative to Basque. Catalan is a language related to Castillian Spanish and intelligible to speakers of both languages, whereas Basque is not even an Indo-European tongue. In January 1980, following an overwhelming vote of approval in home rule referenda, both the Basque country and Catalonia were granted autonomy. However, Basque extremists, most notably ETA, have continued a campaign for total independence.

Spain has sometimes been referred to as an "invertebrate" nation, in which the society resembles a multicelled organism without a central nervous system or core. In an article in *El Pais* (1996), "The Reinvention of Spain," Juan Antonio Ortega Bias-Ambrona remarks, "The idea we have today of Spain as a nation is . . . a recent invention." Indeed, the Spanish state seems to have evolved piecemeal, often through merger of kingdoms (Castile and Aragon) as well as conquest. The final expulsion of the Moors in 1492 marked only one milestone in the history of Iberian unification; others would follow over the centuries as Spain attempted to manage the problems of affluence and poverty, often with mixed results in both cases. That Spain is a patchwork quilt of nationalities, ethnicities, and languages has only added to the central issue of Spanish national identity.

To the linguistic and ethnic distinctiveness of the Basques, Catalans, and Gallegos (of Gallicia) must be added the ethnic communities among the Spanish (Andalusian, Valencian, Asturian, and Castillian) and the island communities of the Balearics and the Canaries. There were many missed opportunities for national unification throughout the period following the expulsion of the Moors, and the merger of the two kingdoms of Castile and Aragon to form the joint reign of Ferdinand and Isabella. However, the combination of fabulous wealth from the western hemisphere, dilatoriness at home, and the overzealous pursuit of empire abroad all conspired to postpone true national integration and the development of a centralized administration.

The reign of Phillip II (1556–1598) is illustrative of the difficulties facing Spanish rulers in the early modern period. Not only did Phillip have Spain to rule, he also had the Kingdom of the Two Sicilies, Portugal, as well as (as a result of Charles V's abdication in 1556), the Low Countries, and, of course, the Americas. As Argyle (1994:13) observed,

> Many of Phillip's—and Spain's—problems arose from the highly decentralized nature of the empire. Within Spain proper, Aragon, Catalonia, and Valencia had their own laws and tax systems; Portugal retained its separate system from its incorporation in 1580 to its independence in 1640; and Sicily had its own legislature and tax structure. . . . Yet the only stable source of revenue for Phillip II was Castile, and even there he had to deal with a strong Cortes, which was willing to vote taxes only on items from which the landed gentry were exempt. Spain continued to be plagued by problems of overextension and an inability of the center to control the empire.

The Napoleonic period of the early 1800s found Spain little prepared for what was about to beset her throughout that turbulent century, culminating as it did in the traumatic national experience of the Spanish-American War of 1898. Spain was not so much an actor as a reactor on the world stage, and seemed to be in a race with the Austro-Hungarian Empire, Russia, and Turkey for the title of Sick Man of Europe.

The Franco years saw Spain undergo a profound deadening of the spirit. The one saving grace was the fact that Spain's less than even-handed neutrality prevented it from being swept into the destructive maelstrom of World War II, providing a period in which much of the destruction of the its civil war could receive some attention. Toward the end of his rule, Franco opened Spain to foreign (initially mostly American) investment. This had unforeseen consequences. As Arango (1978:266) notes:

> But Franco, who had lived in such hermetic isolation for so long, failed to realize that by opening his society along one dimension he was setting in motion a process of modernization that could not be reversed—except, again, by total repression—and that would reverberate throughout the country transforming all those systems by which men organize their society: political, economic, intellectual, religious, psychological, moral, and ethical. Spain, as a result of Franco's decision, ceased to be a traditional, or closed, society and became a transitional society.

Still, it took many years for the effects of modernization to bleed into a new approach to political organization. And the basic problem of Spanish statehood, its incomplete emergence into a modern European nation-state, remained for the post-Franco reformers, mostly notably King Juan Carlos and his advisers, to address.

One residue of this incomplete centralization is the continuing existence of fordal rights in certain ethnic communities. These rights included that of collecting taxes through local or provincial means. It bespeaks a definite lack of administrative infrastructure that this "right" continued on into the 20th century. These fordal rights exemplify the often standoffish nature of regions toward the central administration. Indeed, the whole question of central-periphery relations is one that has proved most thorny for the post-Franco reformers.

The role of public administration in modern Spain has been a problematic one. The debate that centered around the new constitution tended to focus on questions of governmental-administrative dichotomy—the view that the civil service was an arm separate from the political forces of government. While the government has ruled under a number of statutes (Article 97, for example, enables the government to exercise legislative power through statutes), it has long been recognized that it would be impossible for the national government to provide all national public services through central administrative authorities (Subra de Bieusses 1983:80–81). Consequently, the country has been divided into areas which serve as the basis for local administrative authorities.

Traditionally termed the "peripheral" administration, this cadre of administrators is composed of civil governors who are considered "permanent representatives of the nation's government" at the provincial level. At the provincial level, too, there is a delegate from the different administrative state ministerial departments, each of whom oversees the work of the individual services provided at the provincial level by the ministry in question. By the onset of the new constitution, however, there was doubt that this system would survive the contemplated reforms (Subra de Bieusses 1983:81).

Article 2 of the new constitution deals with the matter of decentralization, national autonomy, and the redistribution of power to the regions. Recognizing that the juxtaposition of regional autonomy with a highly centralized, hierarchical state administrative apparatus would make little headway in achieving true autonomy, the constitutional framers instead took the view that certain public services, by their very nature, are local in character. Article 150 thus acknowledges that the state could "transfer or delegate powers within the domains which it heads." Or, it may choose to subdelegate a certain degree of autonomy on specific public services by conferring on them a legal personality, which would be essentially decentralization through services (Subra de Bieusses 1983:84).

The hope has been expressed by certain scholars that the decentralized civil service will lead eventually to "a system based on the notion of a closer link between the administration and the administered through the transfer of functions to subordinate territorial units which will act with full decision-making capacity" (Subra de Bieusses 1983:84–85). But while the Spanish regions seem to have more power than their Italian counterparts (see Zariski 1987:259), there is no overwhelming evidence to support the view that there is an upsurge in participatory democracy at the regional level. In fact, the historic regional communities sometimes seem ambivalent at best concerning the role of the local and provincial governments. Catalonia, for example, has restricted the role of local and provincial governments. But, according to Zariski (1987:259), most regional regimes have seen the logic of using local and provincial administrative resources in the implementation of public policy. This bodes well for the future of an integrative system of national, regional, provincial and local administration.

The Spanish regionalist experience appears to have taken root. The strong regionalist traditions of Spain certainly aided this development. As democratic government develops and flourishes in the context of a healthy economy, the regions may serve as a stimulus to grassroots political participation of a more moderate nature than has long been the case. Regionalism may even serve to ensure more efficient governance and more balanced economic growth.

III. CONCLUSIONS

The varying history and experiences with regionalization and regionalism in continental Europe suggest a pattern of sustained development. France, Italy, and Spain all demonstrate various levels of commitment to regional political and administrative arrangements. None of these nations, despite long histories of centrist traditions, seems bent on scrapping regions as administrative/political entities. This is all the more remarkable, given that regionalism as a political program in all of these states dates from the very earliest, the end of World War I.

A common thread in the adoption of regionalization as it has developed in western Europe has been the recognition that unified nation-states lack the flexibility to provide balanced economic growth in all areas. Regionalization provides some of this flexibility, as it serves as an ersatz federalism. As has been shown in France, local regional development councils have assumed many of the powers formally held by the Paris ministries. In Italy, too, the need for balanced and shared growth has accelerated the regional movement, to the point that it is now driving much of the national political debate. The Northern League would have an Italy comprised of three distinct nations, with the north separated from its less industrially endowed neighbors. It is doubtful that such a proposal will meet with widespread support outside of the north, and even there it is treated as less than serious by many political interests. The role of regionalism in economic development in Spain is a curious one. While Madrid and the Castile and Aragon regions have certainly had a disproportionate share of economic growth in recent years, it is in the North that industrialization has been significantly greater. Spain defies the model of metropole-dominated economic growth, and the role of regionalization as a balancer of economic growth is less obvious than in France and Italy. It is rather the second thread of regionalization—that of an incentive to popular political participation—that seems to dominate the Spanish political tapestry. The many linguistic and ethnic communities within Spain have long desired self government and self expression, and regionalism provides at least a modicum of this. Regionalism also seems to have diminished the credibility of radical separatist groups such as ETA, as now there are provincial and regional bodies which provide representation outside of the national cortes.

The future history of European regionalism and regionalization will be tied to the fortunes of European integration. As the European Union embraces a concept of a "Europe of the regions," it is very conceivable that strong nationalist traditions may be eclipsed as economic development and local political entities makes the regions significant players in the larger scheme of intra-European politics. Something akin to this is already occurring in border regions such as Strasbourg,

But what of the losers in the regional mosaic? What of those regions that will be net losers in the game of regional development? Will nationalist traditions continue to dominate these areas, while in more prosperous regions a sense of regional pride and loyalty effaces the past? Here the picture is far from clear. This underscores a point that needs making: regionalization does not constitute a panacea. It is not, and short of a change in constitution, can never be a total substitute for a federal system. The three nations whose experiences with regionalization have been considered here are all still very much unified nation-states.

REFERENCES

Adams, J.C., and Barile, P. (1972). *The Government of Republican Italy*, 3rd ed. Boston: Houghton Mifflin.

Andrews, W.G. (1974). The politics of regionalization in France. In M.O. Heisler (ed.), *Politics in Europe*, 293–322. New York: David McKay.

Arango, E.R. (1978). *The Spanish Political System: Franco's Legacy*. Boulder, CO: Westview.

Ardagh, J. (1968). *The New French Revolution: A Social and Economic Study of France, 1945–1967*. London: Secker & Warburg.

Argyle, N.J. (1994). Public administration, administrative thought and the emergence of the nation state. In A. Farazmand (ed.), *Handbook of Bureaucracy*, 1–16. New York: Marcel Dekker.

Aron, R., and Elgey, G. (1958). *The Vichy Regime: 1940–1944*. New York: Macmillan.

Bell, D.S. (ed.). (1983). *Democratic Politics in Spain: Spanish Politics after Franco*. New York: St. Martin's Press.

Blondel, J. (1974). *The Government of France*, 4th ed. New York: Thomas Y. Crowell.

Clark, M. (1975). Italy: regionalism and bureaucratic reform. In J. Conford (ed.), *The Future of the State*, 44–73. Totowa, NJ: Rowman & Littlefield.

Douence, J.-C. (1995). The evolution of the 1982 regional reform: an overview. In J. Loughlin and S. Mazey (eds.), *The End of the French State?* London: Frank Cass, pp. 10–23.

Economist, 8 November 1997.

Ehrmann, H.W. (1976). *Politics in France*, 3rd ed. Boston: Little, Brown.

El Pais, 26 September 1996.

Farazmand, A. (ed.). (1991). *Handbook of Comparative and Development Public Administration*. New York: Marcel Dekker.

Farazmand, A. (ed.). (1994). *Handbook of Bureaucracy*. New York: Marcel Dekker.

Germino, D.L., and Passigli, D. (1968). *The Government and Politics of Contemporary Italy*. New York: Harper & Row.

Hayward, J. (1973). *The One and Indivisible French Republic*. New York: Norton.

Hine, D. (1996). Federalism, Regionalism and the Unitary State: Contemporary Regional Pressures in Historical Perspective. In C. Levy (ed.), *Italian Regionalism: History, Identity, and Politics*, Oxford: Berg, pp. 109–130.

Irving, R.E.M. (1975). Regionalism in France. In J. Cornford (ed.), *Politics in Europe*, 14–43. Totowa, NJ: Rowman and Littlefield.

Kopp, H.W. (1966). *Parlamente: Geschichte, Groesse, Grenzen*. Frankfurt am Main: Fischer.

Lafont, R. (1971). *Décoloniser en France: Les Regions Face à l'Europe*. Paris: Gallimard.

Lemieux, V. (1996). L'analyse politique de la décentralisation. *Canadian Journal of Political Science 29* (4), 661–681.

Levy, C. (ed.), (1996). *Italian Regionalism: History, Identity, and Politics*. Oxford: Berg.

Lijphart, A. (1969). Consociational democracy. *World Politics 21*(29), 207–225.

Loughlin, J., and Mazey, S. (eds.). (1995). *The End of the French Unitary State: Ten Years of Regionalization in France (1982–1992)* London: Frank Cass.

Mazey, S. (1995). French regions and the European Union. In J. Loughlin and S. Mazey (eds.), *The End of the French Unitary State?* London: Frank Cass.

McLean, I. (1996). *The Concise Oxford Dictionary of Politics*. New York: Oxford University Press.

Le Monde, 28 March 1968.

Muret, C.T. (1972). *French Royalist Doctrines Since the Revolution*. New York: Octogon.

Newton, M. (1983). The peoples and regions of Spain. In D.S. Bell (ed.), *Democratic Politics in Spain*, 98–131. New York: St. Martin's.

Rousseau, M.O., and Zariski, R. (eds.). (1987). *Regionalism and Regional Devolution in Comparative Perspective*. New York: Praeger.

Rousseau, M.O. (1987). France: the bureaucratic state and political reforms. In M.O. Rousseau and R. Zariski (eds.), *Regionalism and Regional Devolution in Comparative Perspective*, 152–201. New York: Praeger.

Subra de Bieusses, P. (1983). Constitutional norms and central administration. In D.S. Bell (ed.), *Democratic Politics in Spain*, 78–97. New York: St. Martin's.

Wilsford, D. (1991). Running the bureaucratic state: the administration in France. In A. Farazmand (ed.), *Handbook of Comparative and Development Public Administration*, 611–624. New York: Marcel Dekker.

Zariski, R. (1987). Spain: The multinational state and the consequences of incomplete state building. In M.O. Rousseau and R. Zariski (eds.), *Regionalism and Regional Devolution in Comparative Perspective*, 202–267. New York: Praeger.

Zariski, R. (1987). Italy: the distributive state and the consequences of late unification. In M.O. Rousseau and R. Zariski (eds.), *Regionalism and Regional Devolution in Comparative Perspective*, 91–151. New York: Praeger.

18

A Framework for the Analysis of Changes in Australian Executive Branches

John A. Halligan and John Power *Centre for Research in Public Sector Management,*
University of Canberra, Canberra, Australia

I. INTRODUCTION

In the past two decades, the Australian public sectors have experienced an unprecedented period of change in which governments have sought to infuse new values into their bureaucracies and to reform structures and processes. Organizational change, however, is but the most visible manifestation of more profound, systemic changes that have been occurring within executive branches.

These fundamental shifts have been in part a response to the rapidly expanding demands on executive branches and in part a consequence of attempts by reformist governments to redistribute power within them. As a consequence, some traditional modes of operating have been supplanted. At one level, there has been a shift from administering to managing within the bureaucracy; at another, a shift from established structures to political managerialism. These shifts have meant not only a diminution of the influence of administration, but also, alongside the increasing importance of management, the resurgence of the political executive and its retinue of advisers vis-à-vis appointed officials.

These trends are of course international: the ascendancy of managerialism and politicization have been familiar processes in Western democratic countries. What makes the Australian situation of particular interest and potential theoretical significance is that there is a set of large and powerful units of government (the states are arguably the most significant of their type in the world) that have historically balanced not only administrative and political, but large managerial, components.[1] Despite the similarities in Australian constitutions, the mix of these three elements has varied sufficiently between the public sectors both historically and now—to offer the prospects of valuable insights into governmental reform. We have thus been in a position to undertake an examination of executive branch change through comparative analyses of several similar units of government at different development stages. It should be recognized at the outset, however, that the governments we analyze all belong to the Westminster family, which means that a single political body—the cabinet—controls both the executive and legislative branches.

We examined the existing literature on administrative reform in search of frameworks for exploring patterns of executive branch change. The limitations of the literature have led us to develop a new conceptual framework for the analysis of reform experience in Australia. Because this framework will be unfamiliar, we first provide a summary account of its overall structure.

There are two major components to the framework: policy systems and stratified interests.

Of central importance in any executive branch is a system of roles concerned with the maintenance of policy. This we term the administrative system. Alongside this system are two others also of great significance: the management system, which is composed of roles concerned with the implementation of policy; and the political system, which is composed of roles concerned with the steering of policies in ways that make them responsive to salient interests.

The relationships among these systems can differ substantially from one executive branch to another, and traditionally a critical influence on the nature of these relationships has been the character of the stratification of interests within the branch. For purposes of our analysis, we focus attention on only two sets of interests: those of superordinates (ministers, administrators, managers, other professionals in high office), and those of subordinates (especially those that are strongly organized through unions, churches, or labor parties, or various combinations of these).

In Australia for much of the 20th century, each of these interest sets tended to form close linkages with one of the two main political parties.[2] In a government that had undergone a long period of dominance by one party, its executive branch had tended to develop a distinctive regime character. Thus, in governments where non-Labor had enjoyed long periods in office, superordinate interests tended to predominate. We identify two types of regimes that developed in such circumstances: the *technicist*, where professionals such as engineers enjoyed great and autonomous power, and the *administrationist*, where aspirations toward the Whitehall model were partly realized. In governments where Labor traditionally had been preponderant, subordinate staff interests (especially those organized in unions) had succeeded in bureaucratizing much of the executive branch, to the point where a further type, the *bureaucratist* (but still strongly technicist), evolved.

In the 1980s, a new type—the *managerialist*—come into prominence, especially in Labor governments, which used managerial ideologies to reduce the powers of long-established professionals. The effects of this development on the interests of subordinate staff have been mixed, for they have depended on the variable capacities of union leaders to learn the new managerialist games.

The central section of this chapter is devoted to an elaboration of this framework and a fuller application of it to the interpretation of historical experience in Australia. In the concluding section, we test the framework still further by attempting to use it in some brief speculations about possible futures of executive branches. But first we briefly review the academic literature on administrative reform.

II. LITERATURE ON ADMINISTRATIVE REFORM REVIEWED

Divergent views exist about the state of the literature on reform. One view is that "administrative reform has emerged as an academic subject" (Ridley 1982:3), and indeed there is now an extensive literature on the field. But Ridley makes his remark in the sense of "broad patterns of administrative change and the often even broader factors that shape the process." A differing perspective saw "administrative reform as one of the underdeveloped in areas of study in public administration" (Chapman and Greenaway 1980:9). This was not necessarily inconsistent with the first observation because although there is quite a voluminous literature (in Ridley's sense) a large proportion of it was descriptive and without much relevance beyond a specific context. A good deal of it has not aspired to being more than informed commentary, although increasing sophistication has become apparent as the pace of an interest in reform has increased over the past decade.

The general reform literature can be broadly classified into four categories, roughly coinciding with causes, means, ends, and outcomes. Under the first head belong a number of theoretical perspectives, differing in foci and levels of analysis, which seek to explain why change has occurred (reviewed by Garnett 1980). Of the general processes associated with administrative change, environmental explanations are commonly used in seeking to identify major influences on reform (Johnson 1976; Caiden 1980, 1991).

The second type of study primarily focuses on strategies for reform: how to go about it and the problems associated with reforming. It seeks to account for the successes and failures of reform initiatives, to isolate the ingredients of reform, and to recommend means for improving the reform process. The titles of books convey the flavor: *Strategies for Administrative Reform* (Caiden and Siedentopf 1982), and *Changing Bureaucracies* (Medina 1982). Leemans seeks to derive a conceptual framework for studying reform, but as Ridley (1982:3) comments, it "is not so much concerned with the reform measures as with the factors that determine success or failure." Much of the more recent literature has been able to address the lessons from the rapidly accumulating experience of reform (Halligan 1996a; Weller 1993; Davis and Weller 1996).

A third theme in the literature has been essentially prescriptive. While we may all be "potential administrative reformers" (Caiden 1980:437), academics have been inclined to dabble rather than embrace a pronounced reform commitment. Moreover, much of the prescriptive literature has been, as Self (1978:312) remarks about "managerial reformism," "useless for analytic purposes because of its simplifications and dogmatism." A new wave of writing in the 1990s provided more sophisticated perspectives on how governments will need to function in the future (Barzelay 1992; Kettl et al. 1996).

The fourth theme, and broader activity, is the plotting of movement in systems and analyzing trends that result from general administrative change (e.g., Johnson 1976; Aucoin 1995; Halligan 1996b). There has been increasing Australian attention to trends central to this study: the growth of managerialism (Wettenhall 1986; Yeatman 1997; and several contributions in Considine and Painter 1997) and new modes of political-bureaucratic relations (Dunn 1997). This stream is in some respects closest to our interests, although some authors are more concerned with presenting a critique than an analysis of change, and the studies do not necessarily extend to the dynamic interaction between the several dimensions distinguished earlier.

This brief review of the principal streams in recent writings would seem to lend support to Self's early observation that "in seeking a framework for analysis, one looks in vain at much of the [then] limited literature on administrative reform" (1978:312). However, Self's response to this deficiency was to offer an "alternative and tentative approach" that differentiated "three arenas of behaviour and beliefs: the social, political and bureaucratic" and then refined them as social, political, and managerial agendas, the first two focusing on relations between bureaucracy and its environment, the last being intrabureaucratic (Self 1978:312–314). Wilenski differentiated types of reform—democratic, efficiency, and equity—that he saw as corresponding loosely with Self's categories. Like Self he has recognized the tensions that exist between different objectives and values in reform (Wilenski 1986).

Self's approach is relevant here not only because it represents the first serious attempt in Australia to provide a framework, albeit tentative, for the study of reform, but because it is concerned with deeper issues and alignments. His concept of "administrative change as the product of interaction between" the social, political, and bureaucratic arenas has been highly relevant to our explorations in this field.

Other writers have also sought to differentiate approaches to the interpretation of systems of public administration. Rosenbloom (1983), to cite one of the most stimulating essays, identified and elaborated three such approaches: the managerial, the political, and the legal. However, he stopped well short of indicating the ways in which these approaches typically are accommodated and reconciled in government. Rather, he has been content to present three more or less free-standing schools of thought, each firmly rooted in its own cultural tradition. Keeling (1972), in the context of British government, has identified a spectrum of systems with some resemblance to our distinctions: administrative, managerial, and diplomatic. It is our purpose to take up the challenge posed by Keeling and Rosenbloom of developing a theoretical framework adequate to encompass the principal approaches to the understanding of public administration and its reform.

III. CONCEPTUAL FRAMEWORK

The concept of policy is central to our understanding of the dynamics of the executive branch. Adapting somewhat the useful formulation of Schaffer (1977), we define policy as a politically contestable purposive construction placed on the existence of authoritatively committed structures of resources. It encompasses the relatively settled arrangements for the allocation of resources and the provision of services to the branch's clients. Thus conceived, policy embraces both the maintenance and the modification of the settled arrangements and the taking of decisions and launching of activities within the framework they provide.

We earlier distinguished three policy systems in the executive branch of government. In attending to the maintenance of policy, the administrative system within the executive branch is concerned with the maintenance of structures, rules, and principles that constrain the way resources and programs are disposed and committed. Within an administrative system the values of impartiality, continuity, and procedural correctness receive strong recognition. The second of the policy systems is management, which in attending to the implementation of policy is especially concerned with the application of formally rational techniques in the commitment of organizational resources. In contrast to the administrative system, management focuses on directing activities and processing resources. However, although actors in the administrative system are most characteristically constraining, they can also play proactive and enabling roles.

Johnson (1983:171) nicely expresses much of the distinction that we wish to make between management and administration:

> Management will simply be taken in its broad sense as the activity of organising for the efficient and effective performance of predetermined tasks . . . [O]ne feature distinguishing management in this broad sense from administration is the emphasis placed on using people . . . and on efficiency in the transformation of material resource . . . into outputs or results. Another feature is the stress on defining and, where possible, quantifying tasks or objectives themselves. In contrast, administration suggests looking after certain requirements and the effective performance of tasks according to whatever may be the operating conditions prescribed. There is less overt emphasis on the personnel factor and the explicit definition of objectives, as well as less emphasis on the efficient transformation of resources into outputs. Indeed, it is doubtful whether administration as traditionally conceived had much use for the notion of outputs at all, though it plainly embodied the achievements of effects and results.

As we have already indicated, the political system is concerned with the steering of policies in order to make the outputs of the branch as responsive as possible to politically salient interests (both inside and outside the formal boundaries of the branch). Although actors in the political system can have a keen interest in the quality and distribution of the outputs of the executive branch, such as the services and facilities it provides, they are usually at least at one remove from these outputs. They must rely on the administrative and management systems to mediate between the political system and the executive branch outputs, and they must develop and maintain appropriate patterns of authority to support and regulate the performance of this mediating function.

All executive branches experience periods when one or other of the management or administrative systems comes to enjoy a preponderant position. If Australian experience is any guide, however, there are strong pressures toward segmentation of any preponderant system, possibly because any newly ascendant set of interests has a tendency to divide the spoils of dominance. For example, the turn-of-the-century reforms, which were sustained in part by the emergent ideology of scientific management, led to a technicist segmentation of management between a range of autonomous, professionally dominated "guild authorities." An even more complex form of segmentation has characterized the bureaucratist type, for there the strong interests of subordinate staff have come to be superimposed on a continuing technicist structure. Between them, the technicist and bureaucratist types have been in the ascendancy in the Australian states for most of this century.

Table 1 displays these two segmented types, together with a corresponding pair of more centrally coordinated types. A regime characterized by a dominant but segmented management system is one that we designate technicist. At least in the Australian experience, the basis of this segmentation has been the emergence of distinctive types of technical expertise, each with its own "guild authority" bestowed on it by a sympathetic (usually non-Labor) government. The first and most durable example of this type in Australia was the state of Victoria, where the dominance of powerful public corporations was sustained by long periods of non-Labor rule (Sharkansky 1979). Another less pronounced example emerged alongside it in South Australia, which also experienced a lengthy non-Labor dominance. However, in that state, the segmentation of the technicist type was early modified by central managerial strength, albeit of an uneven and often informal kind.

The bureaucratist regime is one whose segmentation typically occurs on the basis of division between superordinates and subordinates (and their unions). The bureaucratist type emerges when some of the characteristics of a strong administrative system are superimposed on an executive branch that is otherwise in the technicist mode. The technicist origins remain significant, but are overshadowed by other interests that constrain rather than supplant it politically. This type is one which is likely to result from lengthy periods of governments that represent and maintain the interests of public service associations. It is also potentially the most resistant to change since it is segmented in two respects. Two examples of this type were Queensland and New South Wales, under traditionalist Labor governments of the 1930s through to the 1950s (in Queensland) and the 1940s through the 1960s (in New South Wales).

The administrationist regime occurs where a coherent and influential senior public service asserts a generalized influence within the executive branch. The type is characteristically associated with a central government with relatively minor responsibilities for direct service delivery, these being lodged in other spheres of government or authorities within the executive branch enjoying considerable operational autonomy. It typically functions with major financial resources at its disposal, light ministerial supervision, and few operational pragmatic responsibilities. The British administrative class represents an example of a highly developed generalist, senior civil service within a central government. This Whitehall model became especially influential in the Commonwealth government during the postwar period, although it was not well developed.

Table 1   Types of Executive Regimes

Character	Preponderant system	
	Administrative	Management
Segmented	Bureaucratist	Technicist
Centrally coordinated	Administrationist	Managerialist

The managerialist regime is one that introduces private sector ideologies and techniques into the executive branch and in an instrumental fashion seeks to "decompose" the organizations it influences into interchangeable roles and modules. Its appeal to the political system is widespread because it offers a range of mechanisms and techniques for reorganizing authority and structures within executive branches. The new pattern of political control that has been sought by contemporary Labor governments has received legitimation from the rational prescriptions that are inherent in the managerialist type.

Each type of executive branch originated in a period of innovation during which it was shaped by the political styles of dominant political forces. (This is an argument that is developed fully in our longer work: Halligan and Power, 1992.) Here we can only indicate that the evidence suggests the operation of cyclical processes in the longer term and identify the major periods of innovation as an indication of where the types can be located in time. The technicist and the bureaucratist types were products of developments in the nineteenth and early twentieth centuries, which produced distinctive regimes that flourished until recently. While administrative and management systems have long been present in public sectors, the administrationist and managerialist types are essentially phenomena of the second half of this century, the former a product of changes within the federal system in the period following World War II. As we have already suggested, the managerialist type is a product of the systematic attempts of new governments to regain control of their public sectors during the 1980s and 1990s.

IV. PATHWAYS TO MANAGERIALISM

To this point, we have developed and employed our framework in a somewhat static, classificatory fashion. We now wish to put it briefly to the test of interpreting the dynamics of recent executive branch changes.

In this section, we seek to trace three differing pathways to the common destination that currently seems to be awaiting all the executive branches we have studied—the managerialist type. In the succeeding and final section, we speculate about the ways in which this preponderant type may itself come to be transformed.

Table 1 suggests three main pathways: vertical (from the technicist), horizontal (from the administrationist), and diagonal (from the bureaucratist). These pathways have been listed in order of the speed with which governments have moved along them, and the table suggests some of the reasons why this order has been followed.

The technicist type has proven receptive to managerialism in significant part because of its reliance on technical expertise. Whenever specialist technical professionals come to believe (or at least can be brought to tolerate the proposition) that some validity can attach to the generalist planning and coordinating techniques of managerialism, the traditional autonomy of the guild authority will be breached. Similarly, the administrationist type is vulnerable to charges that obstructionist Sir Humphreys stand in the way of can-do managers.

To date, the bureaucratist type has been the most resistant to managerialism, because two interlocking structures of segmentation have together contributed a formidable "policy gridlock." However, a change of government can produce powerful pressures to propel even a bureaucratist regime down the pathway to managerialism. This seemed to have been happening in the largest Australian state, New South Wales, following the election in 1988 of a Liberal government, but the reform program was eventually stalled and the state remained only partly managerialized under the succeeding Labor government (Halligan and Power 1992; Laffin and Painter 1995).

This contemporary case of politically induced change prompts us to make a more general observation. In Australian governments, the emergence of each of the four types has been closely associated with one of the main political parties. Early in this century, the technicist type was fostered most strongly by governments of a non-Labor complexion, while the bureaucratist type emerged in governments undergoing long periods of Labor rule.

In more recent times non-Labor has most strongly promoted the administrationist type, and (to the surprise of many) Labor has progressed swiftly down the pathway to managerialism. The readiness of Labor to embrace managerialism may to a considerable extent be attributed to the fact that its stocks had been at a low level for much of the decades of the 1960s and (to a lesser extent) the 1970s. Coming to office after lengthy periods in opposition, Labor was then to grasp such tools for change as were available—the managerialist set lay ready to hand.

Many regimes have until recently been stable—if not ossified—because it appears that the party responsible for a type finds it extremely difficult to accomplish in office the paradigmatic changes necessary to shift its public sector to another type. The nexus between vested interests and a particular party government cannot be readily severed. It requires an incoming party, typically unencumbered by a compromising relationship with those entrenched interests, to accomplish the transformation. This proposition does not mean that a new government will necessarily be able to (or even wish to) reform the type previously cultivated by its opponents; it may either accept that type as an appropriate framework or simply succumb to its influence once it is comfortably settled into office. However, the current wave of activist governments, both Labor and non-Labor, seems unlikely so to succumb.

Just as the decade of the 1980s was one of Labor domination, that of the 1990s has proven to be that of conservative preeminence. In these two decades, the previously technicist states of Victoria and South Australia have exhibited markedly similar patterns of developments: Labor failure to implement successfully a managerialist reform agenda in the 1980s; followed by the most radical conservative governments (as evidenced by the reach of their privatization programs) in the 1990s. In contrast, the previously bureaucratist and administrationist regimes in NSW, Queensland, and the Commonwealth have moved much more cautiously down the road to managerialism.

V. CONCLUSIONS

All the pathways being followed by executive branches have been leading toward the managerialist type, but the extent to which they have so far travelled along it varies. Of these branches mentioned previously, Victoria has exhibited the most managerialist traits (Alford and O'Neill 1994), Queensland the least. The Commonwealth is well advanced down this path, but is unlikely to become as managerialist as the states (Campbell and Halligan 1992; Halligan and Power 1992). The reasons for these variations are complex. But they derive largely from the prior character of the executive branch.

Of the ubiquitous managerialism there is a strong argument that its principal function has been that of a mechanism for breaking down existing vested interests and enabling a new political executive to assume effective control. The appeal of managerialism to recent governments has lain in the leverage it has given them against the entrenched powers of the professionals-in-government, both the administrative brahmins (especially at the Commonwealth level) and the technical guilds (especially at the state level). Further, the reforms that have been introduced have benefited not only the political executive. The managerialist assaults on the established privileges of long-entrenched interests have done a good deal to open up employment opportunities for lateral entrants at all levels and have swept away many outmoded bureaucratic practices.

The very volatility of the managerialist type makes it extremely difficult to predict the forms it could assume if allowed a lengthy period of stability favorable to institutionalization. If we revert for a moment to our table, we may identify some of the pathways beyond managerialism that might well be opened up by a future phase of institutionalization. Such a phase would most likely favor the interests of some of the professions-in-government possessing a more substantive expertise about the outputs of government than that normally possessed by generalist managers. The strengthening of such interests could lead to a new vertical shift—not back to a technicist regime, for the dominance of engineers is unlikely ever to recur in Australian governments—but rather to one segmented into a number of loosely coordinated policy communities.

At the same time some administrative elements are reappearing in executive branches as a counterbalance to strident managerialism, even if there are located at a distance from the centre. The new segmentation resulting from privatization has produced the need for strong regulatory bodies as evidenced by new organizations such as the regulator-general in Victoria.

At the Commonwealth level, a lateral shift back to an administrationist regime is ultimately likely. There are, however, administrative features emerging under the current coalition govern-ment's reform agenda (Kemp 1998). A heavily downsized public service is focusing on core func-tions and contracting out most delivery of services, leaving policy and greater regulation as the primary roles (plus the responsibility of contract management, but minus corporate services, which is expected to be largely contracted out) (Halligan 1997). The administrative system may therefore be set to re-emerge in a regulatory (rather than a steering) form within a tempered man-agerialism appropriate for the national level.

A future government, more likely than not non-Labor in complexion, will find itself strong-ly attracted to an argument grounded in administrationist ideology that would advance the fol-lowing propositions: managerialist enthusiasms can achieve much that is valuable in the short term, but in the long run they can be no substitute for sound principles and structures of precedent, astutely administered. Properly handled, policy maintenance, which is the province of the admin-istrator, lies at the core of effective and efficient government.

NOTES

1. The principal components of the Australian federal system of government are the Commonwealth (national) government and six state governments (New South Wales, Victoria, Queensland, Western Australia, South Australia, and Tasmania). There are also two territories.
2. The Australian Labor Party, which is the nation's oldest, recently celebrated its centenary. Although it has held power nationally for less than a third of the century thus far, it has enjoyed long unbroken peri-ods in office—of two decades or more—in three of the six states. The main non-Labor party has pos-sessed a number of names this century although it has been "Liberal" since World War II. Under its sev-eral names, it has outperformed the Labor party throughout this century in terms of electoral successes at the national level and in the majority of the states.

REFERENCES

Alford, J., and O'Neill, D. (eds.). (1994). *The Contract State: Public Management and the Kennett Govern-ment.* Geelong, Australia: Centre for Applied Social Research, Deakin University Press.

Aucoin, P. (1995). *The New Public Management in Comparative Perspective.* Quebec: Institute for Research in Public Policy.

Barzelay, M. (1992). *Breaking Through Bureaucracy: A New Vision for Managing in Government.* Berkeley: University of California Press.

Caiden, G.E. (1980). Administrative reform. In G.R. Curnow and R.L. Wettenhal (eds.), *Understanding Public Administration*, 175–191. Sydney: George Allen & Unwin.

Caiden, G.E. (1991). *Administrative Reform Comes of Age*. Berlin: Walter de Gruyter.

Caiden, G.E., and Siedentopf, H. (eds.). (1982). *Strategies for Administrative Reform*. Lexington, MA: Lexington Books.

Campbell, C., and Halligan, J. (1992). *Political Leadership in an Age of Constraint: Bureaucratic Politics Under Hawke and Keating*. Pittsburgh: University of Pittsburgh Press.

Chapman, R.A., and Greenaway, J.R. (1980). *The Dynamics of Administrative Reform*. London: Croom Helm.

Considine, M., and Painter, M. (eds.). (1997). *Managerialism and its Critics: The Great Debate*. Melbourne: Melbourne University Press.

Davis, G., and Weller, P. (eds.). (1996). *New Ideas, Better Government*. Sydney: Allen and Unwin.

Dunn, D.D. (1997). *Politics and Administration at the Top: Lessons from Down Under*. Pittsburgh: University of Pittsburgh Press.

Garnett, J.L. (1980). *Reorganizing State Government: The Executive Branch*. Boulder, CO: Westview Press.

Halligan, J. (1996a). Learning from experience in Australian reform: balancing principle and pragmatism. In J.P. Olsen and B.G. Peters (eds.), *Learning from Reform*. 71–112. Oslo: Scandinavia University Press.

Halligan, J. (1996b). The diffusion of civil service reform. In H. Bekke, J.L. Perry, and T.A.J. Toonen, (eds.), *Civil Services in Comparative Perspective*. 288–317. Bloomington: Indiana University Press.

Halligan, J. (1997). New public sector models: reform in Australia and New Zealand. In J.-E. Lane (ed.), *Public Sector Reform: Rationale, Trends and Problems*, 17–46. London: Sage.

Halligan, J., and Power, J. (1992). *Political Management in the 1990s*. Melbourne: Oxford University Press.

Heatley, A. (1996). Political management in Australia: the case of the Northern Territory. *Australian Journal of Public Administration* 55(2), 54–64.

Johnson, N. (1976). Recent administrative reform in Britain. In A.F. Leemans (ed.), *The Management of Change in Government*, 272–296. The Hague: Martinus Nijhoff.

Johnson, N. (1983). Management in government. In M.J. Earl (ed.), *Perspectives on Management: A Multidisciplinary Analysis*. Oxford: Oxford University Press.

Keeling, D. (1972). *Management in Government*. London: George Allen and Unwin.

Kemp, D. (1998). *Reforming the Public Service to Meet the Global Challenge*. Ministerial Statement, Commonwealth of Australia, Canberra.

Kettl, D.F., Ingraham, P.W., Sanders, R.P., and Horner, C. (1996). *Civil Service Reform: Building a Government that Works*. Washington: Brookings Institution Press.

Laffin, M., and Painter, M. (eds.). (1995). *Reform and Reversal: Lessons from the Coalition Government in New South Wales 1988–1995*. Melbourne: Macmillan.

Leemans, A.F. (ed.). (1976). *The Management of Change in Government*. The Hague: Martinus Nijhoff.

March, J.G., and Olsen, J.P. (1983). Organizing political life: what administrative reorganization tells us about government. *American Political Science Review*, June:281–296.

Medina, W.A. (1982). *Changing Bureaucracies: Understanding the Organization Before Selecting the Approach*. New York: Marcel Dekker.

Ridley, F.F. (1982). Administrative theory and administrative reform. In G.E. Caiden and H. Siedentopf (eds.), *Strategies for Administrative Reform*, 3–15. Lexington, MA: Lexington Books.

Rosenbloom, D.H. (1983). Public administration theory and the separation of powers. *Public Administration Review*, May/June, 219–227.

Schaffer, B.B. (1977). On the politics of policy. *Australian Journal of Politics and History 23*(1), 146–155.

Self, P. (1978). The Coombs Commission: an overview. In R.F.I. Smith and P. Weller (eds.), *Public Service Inquiries in Australia*, 310–333. St. Lucia: University of Queensland Press.

Sharkansky, I. (1979). *Whither the State? Politics and Public Enterprise in Three Countries*. Chatham, NJ: Chatham Press.

Weller, P. (1993). Reforming the public service: what has been achieved and how can it be evaluated? In P. Weller, J. Foster, and G. Davis (eds.), *Reforming the Public Service: Lessons from Recent Experience*. South Melbourne: Macmillan.

Wettenhall, R. (1986). A missing link? Public administration and the managerialist tradition. *Canberra Bulletin of Public Administration XIII*(2), 120–129.

Wilenski, P. (1986). *Public Power and Public Administration*. Sydney: Hale and Irenmonger.

Yeatman, A. (1997). The concept of public management and the Australian state in the 1980s. In M. Considine and M. Painter (eds.), *Managerialism and Its Critics: The Great Debate*, 12–38. Melbourne: Melbourne University Press.

19

Public Administration in Japan

Past and Present in the Higher Civil Service

Masaru Sakamoto　　*Faculty of Law, Ryukoku University, Kyoto, Japan*

I. INTRODUCTION

In response to the enlargement of the scope of modern administration and changes in its function, many countries have had to grapple with the difficult problem of how to achieve a harmonious relationship between bureaucracy and democracy. Generally, the relationship of bureaucracy and democracy has depended on the bureaucratic status in the governmental structure of each country.

In Japan, the bureaucracy has traditionally exercised a strong political function. With the promulgation of the new Constitution in 1947, the old bureaucracy was replaced by a democratic civil service, and also the status of the bureaucrats transferred from one of servants of the emperor to one of servants of the people as a whole. However, despite its institutional reform, the traditional bureaucratic character still remains within the civil service.

This chapter will first trace the historical development of the Japanese civil service, and second describe the present conditions and problems of recruitment and promotion within the current higher civil service. Finally it will examine the discussions of the relationship of bureaucrats and politicians in policymaking, and also it will examine the recent development of restructuring and reforming of the civil service system.

II. PUBLIC ADMINISTRATION UNDER THE MEIJI CONSTITUTION

A. The Civil Service

Through the promulgation of the Meiji Constitution in 1889, a limited monarchy was adopted modeled on that of Bismarck's Germany. The personnel administration system was established two years earlier than the establishment of the Meiji Constitution (ILAS Tokyo 1982:7). In July 1887, the ordinances were issued establishing an examination commission and an examination system. Despite the regulations concerning examination procedures and requirements, it remained possible for applicants to substitute education or experience for taking an examination. The higher civil service examination, called *Kotoh Bunkan Shiken*, consisted of written tests in law, economics, finance, and in one or more fields of philosophy, ethics, logic, psychology, etc., and an oral test in law.

Since there was no separate central personnel agency, the direction of civil service was dispersed among other ministries and agencies, each maintaining its own personnel administration. Among ministries and agencies, the Ministry of Home Affairs was powerful enough to regulate or to set standards for government service. From 1910 to 1945, the ranks and grades of officials comprised the following: Persons of *Shinnin* rank (one grade) were appointed by the Emperor in person, and included the prime minister, cabinet members, privy council members, ambassadors, etc. Those of *Chokunin* rank (one to two grades) were appointed by the emperor based on the prime minister's recommendation, and included permanent secretaries, judges, procurators, bureau directors, and prefectural governors. The *Sohnin* rank (one to seven grades), including bureau secretaries and section chiefs, was appointed by ministers with the Emperor's approval. Appointments to *Sohnin* rank were, in principle, limited to persons who had passed the *Kohto Bunkan Shiken*. Persons of *Hannin* rank (one to four grades) were appointed by department heads on their own authority. The *Hannin* rank officials were required to pass an ordinary civil service examination or possess certain special qualifications, and were appointed to minor posts by department heads (Watanabe 1976:113).

Below these official ranks, there were the ordinary employees chosen by employing officials of each separate agency and governed by departmental regulations and ordinances. They were *Koin*, primarily clerical assistants to officials, and *Yohnin*, engaged principally as craftsmen or in custodial service. They enjoyed no civil service status and had no civil service protection. Of a recorded total of 858,543 employees in the government ministries, agencies, and monopolies, exclusive of the ministries of the army and navy, as of December 31, 1938, 2.2% were higher officials (77 of *Shinnin* rank, 1757 of *Chokunin* rank and 16,939 of *Sohnin* rank) and 17.3% (148,570 of *Hannin* rank) were lower officials, so that about 80% of all government employees had neither civil service status nor protection (GHQ/SCAP 1951:4).

B.   The Administrative Culture

In 1965, Dwight Waldo defined culture as "the totality of distinctive ideas, symbols, patterned behavior, and artifacts of a human group" (Waldo 1965:39). According to this definition, we can widely find this kind of culture within modern bureaucracy as the most typical human group. However, the nature of this bureaucratic culture is rather different from the historical development of the public administration in each country. Then what was the administrative culture like under the Meiji Constitution?

In Japan, the administrative culture traditionally evolved as a dominant culture covering the whole society, not as one of the subcultures in the larger social environment surrounding the civil service (Ide 1982:xvi). Since the formation of the nation-state as a result of the Meiji Restoration in 1868, the Japanese government wanted to modernize itself by absorbing the Western knowledge or skill, but, on the other hand, they intended to achieve it through inculcating the Japanese esprit de corps and eliminating the Western spirit in the modernization process. This intention had been largely achieved through a unified and centralized system of national education demanding loyalty to the Emperor as a divine being with comprehensive ruling power.

From 1887 until the end of World War II, the regulations governing Japanese civil service were often amended. However, the *Kanri Fukumu Kiritsu* (regulations concerning the discipline of officials) of 1887 remained in force with no revision for 60 years and contributed to the inculcation of a particular esprit de corps into Japanese civil service. According to Article I of *Kanri Fukumu Kiritsu*, "Officials shall regard loyalty and diligence to the Emperor and to His Majesty's Government as of primary duty, and shall discharge their duties in obedience to laws and ordinances." As this article suggests, the government officials were forced to serve as the "Emperor's servants" under very strict regulations demanding strong loyalty. However, on the other hand, they enjoyed privileged social status or honor such as court rank or decorations as a compensation for strong loyalty to the Emperor. In this context, Tadao Adachi defined the personnel administration in the prewar period as a spiritual or emotional administration based upon a sense of loyalty and honor (Adachi 1962:7, 1966:36). Besides, it followed, from the establishment of the personnel management system emphasizing special obligation and right that bureaucracy was permeated by a strong sense of *Kanson Minpi*, placing the government above the people.

C. Study and Education for Public Administration

In the prewar period, the study and education for public administration were exclusively represented by administrative law. Public administration has made comparatively little progress in Japan. In practice, a chair of administrative law was established at every law faculty in Japanese universities. It became a major compulsory subject necessary for the higher civil service examination in 1887, when the open entrance examination was introduced. The number of chairs of public administration was not only extremely limited, but the subject was not required in the entrance examination until 1959.

Generally, the development of public administration in Japan can be traced back to the early Meiji era (1868–1912). It is said that public administration during this period consisted of the translation of German cameralism and the theory of Lorenz von Stein. Lectures on public administration were offered at Tokyo Imperial University in 1883. However, when a system of administrative laws was established under the Meiji Constitution, public administration was replaced by administrative law and so on. After a long interval, a chair of public administration was established in the political science sections of the law faculties in Tokyo and Kyoto imperial universities in 1921. Masamichi Royama and Tokuji Tamura respectively offered lectures on the subject at these universities. This suggested that the development of the new methodology focused on the functional interpretation of public administration instead of the legal approach (Tsuji 1962:59). However, despite new development of the study and education for public administration, the total number of chairs of public administration was not more than five in the prewar period. Besides, many students in these imperial universities concentrated on lectures on administrative law and constitutional law for the reason that these lectures were offered by professors who were also examiners of the higher civil service examination. This contrast between administrative law and public administration suggests the nature of the study and education for public administration in prewar period.

In relation to the distinction between administrative law and public administration, Leonard D. White, the author of the first text in public administration in the United States, stated in 1926 that "the objective of Administrative Law is the protection of private rights," and "the objective of Public Administration is the effective conduct of the public business" (White 1926:5). According to this definition, it follows that in prewar Japan, the protection of private right against the abuses of the administrative power was achieved successfully as a result of the development of administrative law. However, Japan's administrative law exclusively contributed to the enforcement of the administrative power under the Japanese political environment.

This fact shows that the function of administrative law has two aspects (Adachi 1971:59) and also that each aspect depends on the nature of the constitutional system in each country. Indeed, the function of Japan's administrative law in the prewar period was exclusively limited to the one that Albert V. Dicey once criticized in relation to the meanings of the "rule of law" (Dicey 1904:198–199). In other words, the administration "by law" in this period did not mean the "rule of law" as a reflection of social will owing to the restriction of the parliamentary sovereignty (Tsuji 1952a:15). Rather, it resulted in a contribution to the establishment of the supremacy of the *Kan* (government or mandarin) to the *Min* (people). The existence of the administrative court gave impetus to this stream.

For this nature of Japan's administrative law or constitutional system in the prewar period, legal knowledge was considered to be essential to higher officials as the core of the emperor's government. In response to this request, *Kohto Bunkan Shiken* placed extreme emphasis on administrative law and related legal subjects such as constitutional law, civil law, criminal law, commercial law, and so on. Besides, the law faculties at imperial universities greatly contributed to legal education, since these lectures on the legal subjects were offered primarily at law faculties.

As a result of these institutional features, the higher civil service was dominated by men who had received legal training at law faculties. The law faculties at Tokyo Imperial University were especially noteworthy as the most important sources of higher officials, since these law faculties attracted the brightest students in Japan regardless of regional or social origin and also most of them desired to become higher government officials as a reflection of the founding process, since it was established for the purpose of training the government officials in 1877. In this sense, the objective of legal education at Japanese law faculties was quite different from that of the American law schools (Kubota 1969:77). The number of men having a desire to become private attorneys and judges was extremely limited due to the influence of a strong sense of *Kanson Minpi* guaranteeing high social status or privilege for the government officials.

In addition to this administrative culture, the political culture of restrained civil liberties made it difficult for scholars to criticize or do scientific research on the government administration, which was considered to be within the Emperor's prerogative. As a result, the objective of public administration that Leonard D. White defined in 1926 was not achieved. Red tape or maladministration continued to be practiced within the bureaucracy instead of the achievement of "the effective conduct of public business."

III.   PUBLIC ADMINISTRATION UNDER THE NEW CONSTITUTION

A.   Reform of the Bureaucracy

The new Constitution stated that "all public officials are to be servants of the whole people and not of any group thereof and that the people have the inalienable right to choose and dismiss their public officials" (Article 15). With the promulgation of the new Constitution, the reform of the bureaucracy that exercised political power over the people as "Emperor's servants" became an urgent need in order to substitute a body of democratically selected officials who would serve the people as "civil servants." The militarists and the *Zaibatsu* capitalists were dissolved through the powerful measures taken by the Allied powers. However, the bureaucracy, which functioned as an effective instrument for carrying out the policies of these groups, was permitted to survive, through the decision to utilize the existing Japanese government machinery to effect the Occupation policies. This decision inevitably involved the risk that ideologically hostile bureaucrats would nullify the effectiveness of policies for democratization by administrative sabotage. The risk was reduced to some extent by the removal of militarists and ultranationalists from public life. Table 1 shows the number of higher civil service officials who had been screened, passed, or removed or barred by January 4, 1947. Of the higher civil service officials of the ministries and agencies, 11.92% were removed or barred. In the ministry of home affairs slightly more than 60% were removed or barred, and in December this ministry was abolished (GHQ/SCAP 1951:26). Despite this purge and reorganization of the administrative system, the bureaucracy still survived with its machinery and traditional culture almost unchanged. For this reason, a drastic reform of the personnel system of the civil service was recognized as urgent necessary.

In response to the Japanese government's request, the U.S. Personnel Advisory Mission was sent to Japan in November 1946. On April 19, 1947, after five months of intensive study, the mission recommended the creation of a powerful central personnel agency to administer a civil ser-

Table 1   Screening of Higher Civil Service Officials Before January 4, 1947

Ministry/agency	Number screened	Number passed	Number removed or barred
Cabinet	144	138	6
Foreign Affairs	153	107	46
Home Affairs	564	224	340
Finance	223	218	5
Justice	252	215	37
Education	1,805	1,727	78
Welfare	120	97	23
Agriculture and Forestry	120	105	15
Commerce and Industry	69	59	10
Transportation	170	152	18
Communication	13	13	0
Other organizations	2,396	2,255	141
Total	6,029	5,310	719

Source: GHQ/SCAP, 1951:27.

vice system with standards based upon efficiency and equality of opportunity (GHQ/SCAP 1947). Another recommendation was to secure enactment of the proposed national public service law, providing service-wide standards of personnel administration under which a democratically oriented merit service could be established and the efficiency of the service promoted. In October 1947, the National Public Service Law based on these recommendations was passed by the Diet, laying down the legal basis for a fundamental reform of the Japanese civil service.[1]

Following the National Public Service Law amended in December 1948, the National Personnel Authority (NPA) was established, replacing the temporary National Personnel Commission created by the 1947 legislation. The NPA, composed of three commissioners, was empowered to issue rules of the authority concerning working conditions etc. of employees, to recommend rates and standards of compensation to the Diet, to conduct necessary research on personnel administration, to recommend changes in civil service laws, and to review appeals by employees. In addition, the NPA has been responsible for conducting various types of civil service entrance examinations.

In the prewar period, *Kohto Bunkan Shiken* operated to favor graduates of the law faculties of Tokyo Imperial University, which institution has come close to monopolizing the higher posts in the civil service. According to the special study by SCAP authorities in 1946, the eight permanent members of the Higher Civil Service Examination Committee (all higher career officials) were graduates of Tokyo Imperial University. In 1946, of 84 special members, 57 were graduates of Tokyo Imperial University and 17 of Kyoto Imperial University. Of the 32 of these examiners who were government officials, 25 had been graduated from Tokyo and two from Kyoto Imperial University (GHQ/SCAP 1951:67). Thus, the problem of a preference for the graduates of Tokyo Imperial University in the recruitment of the higher officials and the selection of the examiners seems to have been a very important issue for the reform of the old bureaucracy.

The National Public Service Law, amended in 1948, stipulated.

Officials holding positions from assistant section chiefs up to permanent secretaries, plus any other designated by the NPA, should be regarded as temporarily appointed to those positions for a period not to last beyond I July 1951. . . . The NPA might give appropriate examinations to any employees holding any government position whatsoever, and make transfers or removals (Article 9).

Based on this authority, the NPA announced in November 1949 that examinations would be held to fill designated positions up to permanent secretaries and that temporary appointments to these posts would lapse when appointments were made as a result of the examinations. A total of 12,200 applications were filed by 8076 persons, of whom 7815 were designated as qualified to take the examinations. About 25% of the higher officials lost their positions because of failure to perform adequately in the examinations. Incumbents were appointed to their original positions in 29 of 36 positions in grade 1, 108 of 139 in grade 2, 239 of 318 in grade 3, and 1473 of 1995 in grade 4—a total of 1849 incumbents retained for 2448 positions (GHQ/SCAP 1951:67).

The successful candidates of the qualification examination in 1950 were recognized as the efficient and democratic officials. However, the simple multiply choice examination angered the higher bureaucrats and especially unsuccessful candidates, because they considered the examination inappropriate for determining the qualification level as democratic officials. As a result, NPA had been involved intensely in these disputes of its abolition or reorganization for a long period, but through the creation of the personnel bureau within the prime minister's office in 1965 based on the recommendation of the First Provisional Commission for Administrative Reform in 1964, these disputes were put to an end (Sakamoto 1994:86–88).

B.   Study and Education for Public Administration

The promulgation of the new Constitution contributed not only to the transformation of the emperor's servants to the people's servants, but also to the removal of the political obstacle that impeded the progress of public administration. In an important event, the Japanese Society for Public Administration, an independent academic society, was established in 1950. In 1953, the society became a member of the International Institute of Administrative Sciences, and in 1982 it held the IIAS Round Table Conference in Tokyo. The society is composed of scholars and employees of central and local government, and its membership is 506 (individual members: 476; group members: 30 organizations) as of May 1999. It holds a general conference in May every year and also has issued publications as the result of its academic activity. For instance, the titles of recent annual studies from 1978 up to 1999 are as follows:

1.   Realm of Administrative Responsibility and Administrative Costs
2.   Thirty Years of Local Government
3.   Public Administration and Information
4.   Practice of the Field Organization of Central Government and Its Issues
5.   Present Conditions of Japanese Public Administration and Its Issues
6.   Administrative Discretion in Japan
7.   RINCHO and Administrative Reform
8.   Interdisciplinary Study of Administration
9.   Study of the Cabinet System
10.   Trend of the Civil Service
11.   Trend of Local Self-Government
12.   Administration in Times of Internationalization
13.   Comparative Study of Administration
14.   Education and Training for Public Administration
15.   Various Aspects of the Governmental System
16.   Administration Under Neoconservatism

17. Dialogue Between Public Administration and Administrative Law
18. Crossroads of Local Self-Government
19. Reform of Decentralization
20. Public Administration and Its Ideas in Comparative Perspective: Disaster and Administration
21. Public Administration and Its Accountability
22. Public Administration and Its Reform

Concerning the progress of public administration in university education, chairs of public administration, which had been limited only to Tokyo and Kyoto areas in the prewar period, were established at universities in other area on a nationwide scale. According to the preliminary survey by the Japanese Society for Public Administration in May 1988, the number of chairs of public administration amounted to 65 at the undergraduate level and 17 at the graduate level. Besides, the number of seminars of public administration was 25 at the undergraduate level and 8 at the graduate level. Including its related subjects such as local government, metropolitan studies, etc., the total number of chairs amounted to 96 at the undergraduate level and 31 at the graduate level, while the total number of seminars amounted to 41 at the undergraduate level and 9 at the graduate level. These figures are only tentative ones based on the voluntary response from the membership, but they show that the Japanese field of public administration has made big progress in the postwar period. In addition to the increase in the number of chairs of public administration and its related subjects in university education, public administration has grown in academic prestige, since it has been one of the elective subjects needed for the higher civil service examination since 1959. Also entering the 1990s, faculty and graduate school of public policy or public management have been established in Kanto, Kansai, and Kyusyu areas. This is another sign of academic growth of public administration.

Despite the new development of study and education for public administration in the postwar period, the traditional bureaucratic culture still remains within the civil service. This shows that the existing university public service education has not exerted an effective influence on the training of democratic administrators. In relation to this problem, Masamichi Royama, a founding father of Japanese public administration, criticized in 1958 that "the old Imperial university education system, said to have produced the old bureaucracy, has not improved substantially" (Royama 1958:31). This criticism still has merit even today. For instance, the curriculum of most of the law faculties in the postwar period has retained the same focus as it had at the imperial universities in the prewar period. Besides, many prospective students at law faculties tend to concentrate on the legal subjects needed for the higher civil service examination. As a result, the proportion of the law graduates in our higher civil service is still almost as high as in the prewar higher civil service, as shown in the following section. Given this, we need to establish a well-balanced higher civil service examination system effective for the resolution of modern public affairs.

C. The Civil Service

1. Size and Composition

According to the NPA Annual Report of July 1999, the total number of national civil servants of all administrative organizations (full-time and permanent positions) is 1,147,577. National civil servants are divided into two types of servants: regular services and special services. The number of regular service employees is 827,886. Of these, 501,498 are nonindustrial employees, including general administrative service (251,708), professional service (7819), taxation service (54,752), education service (70,257), research service (10,154), medical service (60,832), public security service (42,474), maritime service (1819), executive service (1683), and public prosecutor (2193). The remainder were industrial employees (313,436): postal service (297,105), national forest service (9004), printing (5938), and mint (1389). The number of special service employees is 319,691. Those engaged in special service include the prime minister, ministers of state, commissioners of the National Personnel Authority, judges and other personnel of courts of law, Diet personnel, and the self-defense forces. In addition, the number of local public employees is 3,272,207. Of these, 3,258,200 are regular service and 14,007 are special service.

2. Recruitment and Entrance Examination

(a) Recruitment

In the case of senior civil service entrance examination, initial appointment of employees is made, in principle, through a competitive examination conducted by the NPA that is open equally to all citizens. However, since the appointing power is vested in the head of each ministry and agency, the final appointment is decided by each ministry and agency through comprehensive evaluation of a specific written test, oral examination, and physical examination for the successful applicants selected from the entrance eligibility lists in which their names are entered in the order of their examination scores. Despite this appointment power in each ministry and agency, appointments to the positions of departmental section chief or higher in the central offices of a ministry and agency are subject to review and evaluation by the NPA, as provided by the NPA rule. The total number of these positions was 2323 as of March 1999. Thus, the number of the Japanese senior civil servants staffed at departmental section chief or higher posts amounted to 2323.

In relation to these senior posts, the typical career structure is as shown: permanent secretary or director general level posts (number: 59) ← departmental bureau chief level posts (number: 177) ← deputy bureau chief or councillor level posts (number: 529) ← departmental section chief level posts (number: 1562, as of October 1998 [information from the NPA]) ← associate section chief level posts (administrative service, pay grades 9) (number: 3326 including 1167 class I appointees) ← assistant section chief level posts (pay grades 7 and 8) (number: 31,131 including 2950 class I appointees) ← branch chief level posts (pay grades 4, 5, and 6) (number: 83,568 including 2747 class I appointees) ← Class I new entrants (number: 545 pay grades 3, 1999 NPA Annual Report, as of March 1998).

(b) Entrance Examination

In the national civil service, there are three categories of entrance examinations common to most ministries and agencies, in addition to 14 types of examination for candidates for specialist positions in specific ministries and agencies. They are class I, class II, and class III examinations. In addition to these examinations conducted by the NPA, the ministry of foreign affairs has conducted two types of entrance examination for candidates at the college graduate level, but its senior class examination was abolished through the integration into class I examination in 1999.

The class I examination (formerly known as senior A class examination, renamed in 1985) is the senior civil service examination open for candidates within the age group between 21 and 32. Annual gross wages is 3,363,600 yen for new college graduate recruits (as of April 1999). The class II examination (an integration of the formerly known senior B class examination and the intermediate examination in 1985) is an ordinary examination for the college graduate level within the age group between 21 and 28. Annual gross wages is 3,103,800 yen for new graduate recruits. The class III examination (formerly known as junior examination) is also an ordinary examination for the senior high school graduate level within the age group between 17 and 21. Annual gross wages is 2,525,400 yen for new graduate recruits. As seen from here, the age limit is imposed for all candidates in all class of the examinations. Apart from this, a person not holding Japanese nationality is deemed ineligible to take the entrance examination. The national regulation for becoming a civil servant limits the applicants to those of Japan except at the local government level.

3. Present Conditions of Appointment

According to the NPA Annual Report of 1999, the total number of candidates for class I examination is 35,754. Of these, the successful candidates are 1239, indicating a success rate is 3.5%. In the case of class II examination, the total number of candidates and successful candidates are 64,242 and 6542, respectively, indicating a success rate is 10.2%. Also in the case of the class III examination, the total number of candidates and successful candidates are 92,586 and 7928, respectively, indicating a success rate is 8.6%. It is especially worthy of note that the number of those passing the class I examination accounts for only 7.9% in the total number of successes among these three entrance examinations. It shows that our senior civil service examination is elite oriented, and this feature is especially prominent in both the law and public administration positions.

Despite this elite-oriented recruitment system, the number of applicants for the senior civil service examination as well as that of other type of examinations has been decreasing during the 1980s (see Figs. 1 and 2). This suggests that the circumstances surrounding the civil service are aggravating and also the senior civil service is losing its prestige. Especially worthy of note is the decline in the applicants for the technical positions. This tendency may be related to the lower prestige in the senior civil service and also the lower pay scales compared with the private sector.

However, entering the 1990s, while the private sectors cut down the new recruitments to battle the prolonged recession under their restructuring plans, the number of the candidates for the senior civil service examination and other type of examinations gradually increased towards the peak in 1994. However, the number of candidates for the senior civil service examination as well as that of other type of examinations has been decreasing again since 1996 (see Figs. 1 and 2). This suggests that the circumstances surrounding the civil service are becoming severe through the recent administrative reform and also that the prestige of the senior civil servant was tarnished as a result of a series of corruption scandals of bureaucrats. In addition, this decreasing tendency may have been caused by the end of the baby boom around 1996, although the decrease of the appli-

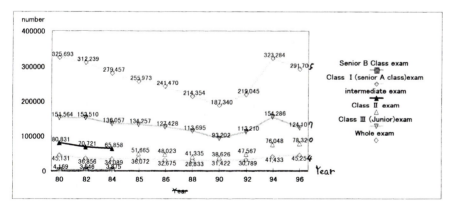

Figure 1   Changes in numbers of candidates in civil service entrance exams conducted by the National Personnel Authority (1980–1988). (From *NPA Annual Report,* July 1992:6, July 1999:73.)

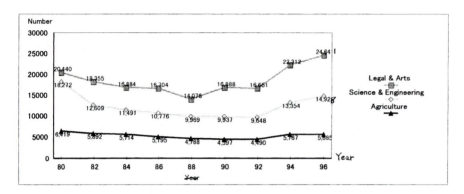

Figure 2   Changes in numbers of candidates in class I (senior A class) exam by academic specialty (1980–1998). (From *NPA Annual Report,* July 1992:36, July 1999:75.)

cants for the class III examination is apparently caused by an age limit that prevents applications from university graduates.

4.   Problems of Recruitment and Promotion

(a)   Problem of Recruitment

In relation to the recruitment to the higher civil service, it is important to pay attention to the existence of biases even in the presentation of statistical data. In particular, allegations of biases have focused on a preference for legal knowledge and a preference for Tokyo University graduates in the entry-level recruitment of the Class I Exam.

　　Preference for legal knowledge.   Table 2 shows the distribution of new appointees (class I exam) as of March 1998, divided by field of academic specialization and by ministry and agency. In the Japanese higher civil service, the fields of academic specialization such as public administration, law, economics, psychology, education, and sociology are regarded as clerical positions, while the other fields apart from these are regarded as technical positions. Traditionally the appointees of the clerical positions tended to aim for the top-level posts and also they tended to select prestigious ministries, such as finance, international trade and industry, posts and telecommunications, transportation, and construction. Generally, these economics-related ministries have close connection with business through the "administrative guidance system" and they also have jurisdiction for many public corporations staffed by their own personnel power. Thus, it is often said that their selection partly reflects their future prospects for entering business and public corporations after their retirement, since our civil service is, in principle, a career system of lifelong employment within a specific ministry and agency.

　　According to Table 2, the biggest group of appointees belonging to the clerical positions is in law, and its proportion among the total number of clerical positions is 53.4% (number: 121). Even if we consider the importance of legal knowledge in conducting administration based on the principle of the rule of law, its proportion seems to be too high. When we consider the characteristics of problems of modern public affairs, solutions solely dependent on legal knowledge have certain limitations. Besides, survey research made in 1977 by Michio Muramatsu shows that the top-level higher bureaucrats such as permanent secretary and bureau chief tend to point to the importance of economics as essential knowledge for their duties, although the higher bureaucrats at the level of section chief tend to emphasize the importance of legal knowledge (Muramatsu 1981:66). Therefore, to consider these respects, we need to maintain a well-balanced number of appointees in each subject area of the senior civil service examination through increasing the number of economics appointees and decreasing law appointees. To show the recent development, the number of law position appointees is actually decreasing (from 180 in 1986 to 121 in 1998), while the number of economics appointees is increasing (from 62 in 1986 to 67 in 1998).

A preference for legal knowledge in the Japanese higher civil service examination is in striking contrast to that of the British higher civil service. In the British higher civil service examination, critics have focused on the preference for arts graduates rather than social and natural science graduates. This means that the evaluation of the knowledge essential for the senior posts is greatly different in Japan and Britain. In both higher civil services, the problem of preference for legal graduates or art graduates has not been overcome. This shows the difficulty of deciding what area of knowledge is most important for the senior posts.

Preference for Tokyo University graduates.   The NPA has not published statistics to show the names of universities graduated by successful candidates and appointees of the class I examination. Media information indicated (*Asahi Shimbun*, Aug. 11, 1999) the proportion of successful candidates of Tokyo University in 1999 is 29.4% (number: 368). The next highest numbers were achieved by Kyoto (166), Waseda (76), Tohoku (62), Keio (58), Kyusyu (45), Hokkaido (40), Tokyokogyo (38), Osaka (33), and Nagoya (28). The total proportion of the successful candidates from the national university graduates represented by Tokyo University and Kyoto University was 81.2% in 1999, although the proportion is decreasing compared with 92.6% in 1975.

Especially, it is worthy of note that the appointee rate of Tokyo University graduates in the clerical positions (number: 207) amounts to 50.2% (104) in 1998, and also these new entrants of Tokyo university graduates occupy more than 70% in the clerical positions in such ministries as finance, MITI, welfare, transportation, and home affairs (*Yomiuri Shimbun*, May 25, 1998).

In addition to such bias, the rate of law graduates of Tokyo university amounts to 55.3% (71.1%, including other faculties; as of Aug. 1, 1996) at bureau chief level in five selected ministries—finance, international trade and industry, construction, health and welfare, labor—(total number: 38) and 70% (90%, including other faculties; as of October 1, 1996) at permanent secretary level (total number: 20) (Hayakawa, 1997:168–176). In this context, the dominant position of law graduates of Tokyo University has still been maintained in the postwar period. Certainly, in the recruitment procedure of class I examination, the initial appointment by the NPA has an objective rationality since it is based on the result of open and fair competitive examination. However, if we consider that the final appointment is decided by each ministry and agency, we need to examine closely the final appointment process, which is chiefly based on the oral examination conducted by examiners in each ministry and agency and dominated by Tokyo University graduates.

In relation to this problem, the Eleventh Report of the Expenditure Committee in Britain paid attention to the existence of biases (a preference for "Oxford and Cambridge" graduates, a preference for "Arts" graduates) in the recruitment of administration trainees. The committee recommended that "the Civil Service Commission should keep, assess and publish recruits, in terms of school and university attended, in order to ensure, and to be able to show, that equally able university graduates have equal chances of entering the service" (Eleventh Report, 1977a:xviii). With the commissioners' agreement to this recommendation, the Annual Report of Civil Service Commission has provided such statistics. Considering the dominance of Tokyo University graduates in our higher civil service, our NPA also needs to collect and publish statistics to show the type of degree and the name of university of applicants and recruits in the Class I examination (Sakamoto 1982b:29). It is also worthy of note that the Eleventh Report recommended the widening of the membership of the Final Selection Boards in relation to the problem of representativeness (Eleventh Report 1977a:xxi). Recalling the provision of our National Civil Service Law that "no two persons among the three Commissioners of NPA should be members of the same political part of graduates of the same ministry of the same university" (Article 4), we need to correct the bias of examiners in terms of university attended or type of degree in the final appointment process at

Table 2 Number of New Appointees (Women in Parentheses) in the Class I Examination by Topic of Examination and by Ministry and Agency (as of March 31, 1998)

Ministry/agency	Public administration	Law	Economics	Psychology	Education	Sociology	Mathematics	Physics	Geology	Information engineering	Electrical and electronics engineering	Mechanical engineering	Civil engineering	Architecture	Chemistry	Metallurgy	Mining engineering	Biology	Pharmacy	Agronomy	Agricultural economics	Agricultural chemistry	Agricultural engineering	Animal science	Forestry	Fishery science	Erosion control	Landscape architecture	Total
Board of Audit	1	2	1																										4
National Personnel Authority		1	2																										3
Prime Minister's Office		1											1																2
Fair Trade Commission	1		2																										3
National Police Agency		12(1)					1	1		1	3				1(1)														19(2)
Imperial Household Agency																													0
Management and Coordination		3(1)	3							1		1																	8(1)
Hokkaido Development Agency			1								1		6(1)										3						11(1)
Economic Planning Agency			6																										6
Science and Technology Agency	1	1(1)								1	1	5(1)			3(2)	2		1				1							16(4)
Environmental Agency		1(1)	2													1												2	6(1)
National Land Agency		1	1(1)																										2(1)
Justice	1	5(2)	5(1)	6(2)	2(1)																								20(6)
Public Safety Investigation	1	2																											3
Foreign Affairs																													0

Category	Entries (left → right)	Total
Finance	9(1) 8(1)	17(2)
Local Finance Bureaus	3 3(1)	6(1)
Custom Houses	3 1	4
Mint Bureaus	1	1
Printing Bureaus	1 1	2
Tax Administration Agency	5(1) 1 1	7(1)
Education	7 2(1) 2 1 2	19(2)
Health and Welfare	8(1) 2 2 2 3(1) 2 1	22(4)
Agriculture	11(1) 1 1 20(2) 9(1) 13(3) 18 7(2) 19(3) 6(2) 2 1(1)	111(5)
International Trade and Industry	12(1) 6 2 4 1(1) 3 2 2 2	34(2)
Industrial Science and Technology	1 2 2(1)	5(1)
Patent Office	5 7 12(1) 10 2 1(1) 7(2) 2 3 3(2) 2(2)	54(8)
Transportation	9(1) 1 5 3 10 1 4	32(1)
Maritime Safety Agency	5 1 1	2
Meteorological Agency	5	5
Post and Telecommunication	7 8(1) 2 1 4(1) 4 2	29(2)
Labor	21(1) 6(2) 2 1 1 1 2	18(5)
Construction	8 5(2) 4(2) 1 2 1 24(1) 10(1) 2 3 2(1)	58(5)
Home Affairs	10(1) 3 1 2 1	14(1)
Fire Defense Agency	1 1	2
Total	20(2) 121(14) 67(8) 10(4) 2(1) 5(1) 7 15 3 19(1) 30(1) 24(1) 51(3) 17(4) 21(6) 6 5 3 8(3) 20(2) 9(1) 18(5) 21 7(2) 19(3) 6(2) 6	545(66)

Source: NPA Annual Report, July 1999:332–333.

each ministry and agency in order to respond to the criticism of inbreeding and establish a fair and reasonable selection system.

In recent years in Japan, the Miyazawa cabinet paid attention to the above mentioned bias and decided at a meeting in April 1992 that Tokyo university graduates should make up less than half of high-level government workers hired over the next five years. Responding to the cabinet's decision, the National Personnel Authority instructed each ministry in May to use various criteria when hiring and to delete the question "university" on employment application forms. According to the information from the NPA, the appointee rates of Tokyo university graduates for clerical work are said to be 57.6% (1993), 54.8% (1994), 50.5% (1995), 49.1% (1996), 49.8% (1997), and 50.2% (1998) through whole ministries and agencies.[2]

(b)   Problem of Promotion to Senior Posts

Preference for the class I examination recruits.   Table 3 shows the number of staff by grade and type of entrance examination in the administration group. According to Table 3, the proportion of recruits staffed from class I examination (former senior A class examination) increases with approach to the higher grades, and this feature is especially prominent at the level of departmental section chief (grade 10 or higher), compared with the recruits staffed through the class II examination (former intermediate examination) and class III examination (former junior examination). This shows that the appointees of the senior A class examination have been recruited as the future executives and promoted rapidly in the bureaucratic hierarchy. So they are often called "career groups," meaning high fliers, while others are called "noncareer groups," whose prospect of promotion to the senior posts is low. However, this distinction between "career groups" and noncareer groups" in Japanese civil service is different from that between career executives (permanent civil servants) and noncareer executives (political appointees) in the U.S. federal higher civil service.

In the Japanese civil service, the former senior A class examination newly instituted in 1960 has played an effective role in recruiting able persons as future executives and compares well with the *Kotoh Bunkan Shiken* in the prewar period. However, such an elite-oriented examination has caused a decrease in morale on the side of "noncareer" civil servants, on the other hand. Therefore, it is important to establish the open promotion system in order to increase the morale of the noncareer civil servants under the present personnel system.

In Britain, the Fulton Report criticized the traditional class structure of the British civil service, dividing the service horizontally (between administrative class and other classes) and vertically (between generalists and specialists), and proposed the abolition of the class structure and its replacement by a unified grading structure covering the entire civil service. Following the Fulton Report, the previous three administrative, executive, and clerical classes were brought together in a single administration group under the unified grading system in 1971. As a result of this organizational reform, the previous executive and clerical officers had the chance to take the administration trainee examination, which is the gateway for senior offices. This AT examination is a promotion examination for the internal candidates, while it is an entrance examination for external candidates (Sakamoto 1982a).

In Japan, it is also necessary to establish this kind of promotion examination system for those recruited through the intermediate (class II) and junior (class III) examinations in order to give the chance to reach the senior posts regardless of the entry level of examinations. In response to this demand, in 1999, the NPA has introduced a special administrative training scheme designed to enhance knowledge and skills needed for the managerial posts for the able and experienced unit chief and section subchief level officers who have been recruited through class II and class III exams and to promote their promotion to the executive posts. This scheme is based on the NPA's guidance on their promotion to the executive posts shown to the ministries and agencies in March, 1999. The first administrative training course for the unit chief level officers was held in

Table 3 Number of Entrance Examination Appointees in Administrative Services, by Types of Examination and Pay Grades (as of March 1998)

Grade Type of exam	1 N (%)	2 N (%)	3 N (%)	4 N (%)	5 N (%)	6 N (%)	7 N (%)	8 N (%)	9 N (%)	10 N (%)	11 N (%)
Class I (senior A class) exam			1,872 (4.5)	691 (1.5)	1,072 (4.4)	984 (2.9)	756 (3.7)	2,194 (11.4)	1,167 (28.6)	1205 (55.2)	1,403 (85.9)
Class II exam		9,026 (35.8)	13349 (31.9)	4,607 (9.9)	548 (2.3)	39 (0.1)	—	—	—	—	—
Class III (junior) exam	12282 (96.6)	14825 (58.8)	22444 (53.7)	26878 (57.7)	13187 (54.2)	21267 (62.9)	11922 (59.0)	9018 (46.9)	1255 (30.8)	324 (14.9)	53 (3.2)
Senior B class exam		269 (1.1)	409 (1.0)	652 (1.4)	482 (2.0)	574 (1.7)	693 (3.4)	675 (3.5)	163 (4.0)	95 (4.4)	30 (1.8)
Intermediate exam		—	275 (0.7)	4926 (10.6)	3328 (13.7)	4333 (12.8)	2,540 (12.6)	3,333 (17.3)	741 (18.2)	301 (13.8)	43 (2.6)
Subtotal	12282 (96.6)	24120 (95.6)	38349 (91.8)	37754 (81.1)	18617 (76.5)	27197 (80.5)	15911 (78.7)	15220 (79.2)	3326 (81.5)	1925 (88.3)	1,529 (93.6)
Appointees by qualification and experience	434 (3.4)	1,096 (4.3)	3,446 (8.2)	8,799 (18.9)	5,709 (23.5)	6,589 (19.5)	4,299 (21.3)	4,000 (20.8)	754 (18.5)	256 (11.7)	104 (6.4)
Total	12716 (100.0)	25216 (100.0)	41795 (100.0)	46553 (100.0)	24326 (100.0)	33786 (100.0)	20210 (100.0)	19220 (100.0)	4080 (100.0)	2,181 (100.0)	1,633 (100.0)

Source: NPA Annual Report, July 1999:340–341.

October, and 46 officers including one woman selected from 23 ministries and agencies attended to the training course. The first administrative training course for section subchief officers will be held in fiscal 2000. This special administrative training scheme is expected to make it possible for these selected trainees to be promoted to the departmental section chief and above level posts (*Jinjiin Geppo*, January 2000:34–37).

Preference for the clerical officers at the top-level posts.   According to Table 2, the total number of new appointees who received academic training in natural science in college is larger than those who received academic training in social science and arts. Table 4 shows the composition of the senior posts by type of position in selected ministries and agencies generally considered to be agencies dominated by the technical field work. According to the tables, despite the larger proportion of technical officers (*Gikan*) at the entry level posts appointed through senior A class examination, the ratio of the section chief and higher posts occupied by clerical officers (*Jimukan*, especially those who received legal training) becomes very high especially at the top-level posts (permanent secretary and bureau chief) except for the science and technology agency, while the number of those staffed by technical career officers is extremely low. This bias is even more serious in other ministries and agencies apart from these administrative organizations. In relation to this problem, the development of the Senior Professional Administration Training Scheme (SPATS) in the British civil service is very suggestive. The main purpose of SPATS, instituted in 1972, is to provide specialist civil servants who have the potential to reach the more senior posts with an opportunity to broaden their experience in the wider fields of administration and management, and it is designed to make it possible for them to compete for the open structure posts (permanent secretary, deputy secretary, undersecretary) with the most able members of the administrative group (Eleventh Report 1977b:16).

In the Japanese civil service, we also need to provide those technical staff members showing the potential to reach the more senior posts with an opportunity to compete with the able generalist staffs through this kind of managerial training scheme. The open structure, enabling horizontal and vertical staffing in the higher civil service, will enhance the morale of the whole civil service and contribute to the establishment of the efficient civil service. Needless to say, the promotion process in the higher civil service should be open regardless of the entry level of examinations, type of position, educational background, and so on (Sakamoto 1982a:308).

(c)   Women's Representation in the Civil Service

Table 5 shows the number of applicants, passes, and appointees by general type of civil service examinations in 1975, 1984, and 1998. According to Table 5, the number of women applicants in the class I (former senior A class exam) examination and class II (former senior B class and intermediate exams) examination is greatly increasing, while the number of women applicants in the class III (former junior exam) examination is almost same. We can evaluate this change in accordance with the development of higher education of women. In practice, the ratio of women's entry into junior college and college has increased to more than 40% since 1992 and amounted to 49.4% in 1998, compared with 18% in 1970. With this major progress for women, the number of passes in both class I examination and class II examination is increasing.

Especially in the case of class I (senior A class) examination, it is worthy of note that the number of women who were successful increased from 34 (2.8%) in 1975 and 86 (5.6%) in 1984 to 176 (14.2%) in 1998. And the number of women appointees increased from 15 (2.2%) in 1975 and 47 (6.0%) in 1984 to 66 (12.1%) in 1998. Also, the number of women appointees in the class II examination increased from 93 (10.7%) in 1975 and 270 (11.9%) in 1984 to 683 (22.9%) in 1998. In addition, the proportion of the women passes in the class III examination in 1998 increased to more than 40%. Besides, women have progress in being recruited as air traffic con-

Table 4 Appointments to the Senior Posts by Types of Position in the Selection Ministry and Agency (as of April 1998)

Ministry/agency (central office)	Position	Total	Clerical officer (A)	Technical officer (B)	$\frac{B}{Total} \times 100(\%)$
Science and Technology	Permanent secretary	1	0	1	100
	Deputy secretary	1	0	1	100
	Bureau chief, director of the secretariat	6	3	3	50
	Deputy director general, Councillor	7	3	4	57
	Section chief etc.	76	17	59	78
Health and Welfare	Permanent secretary, director general	2	2	0	0
	Bureau chief, director of the secretariat	10	7	3	30
	Director, deputy director	13	9	4	31
	Section chief etc.	78	52	26	33
Agriculture, Forestry, and Fisheries	Permanent secretary, deputy secretary for international affairs	2	2	0	0
	Bureau chief, director of the secretariat, supervising councillor	9	7	2	22
	Deputy director-general, director, councilor	14	9	5	36
	Supervising section chief	16	14	2	13
	Section chief, counselor	164	57	107	65
Construction	Permanent secretary, deputy secretary for technics	2	1	1	50
	Bureau chief, director of the secretariat	6	4	2	33
	Director, deputy director	15	7	8	53
	Section chief	55	27	28	51
Posts and Telecommunications	Permanent secretary	1	1	0	0
	Bureau chief, director of the secretariat	10	9	1	10
	Director, deputy director	13	11	2	15
	Section chief	93	73	20	22
Transportation	Permanent secretary, director general	3	3	0	0
	Director of the secretariat, director of the bureau	14	11	3	21
	Councilor, director, Counselor	24	19	5	21
	Section chief, senior policy planner	163	97	66	40

Source: Report of the *Zen Gi Kon* in Science and Technology Agency, April 1998.

Table 5 Changes in the Number of Women Candidates, Passes, and Appointees in the General Types of Civil Service Entrance Examination (1975–1998)

Type of exam	Status	1975			1984			1998		
		Men	Women (%)	Total	Men	Women (%)	Total	Men	Women (%)	Total
Senior A class exam	Candidates	36,000	1,825 (4.8)	37,825	31,131	2,958 (8.7)	34,089	26,273	9,481 (25.8)	35,754
	Passes	1,172	34 (2.8)	1,206	1,476	86 (5.6)	1,562	1,063	176 (14.2)	1,239
	Appointees	663	15 (2.2)	678	742	47 (6.0)	789	478	66 (12.1)	544
Senior B class exam	Candidates	3,997	395 (9.0)	4,392	3,424	451 (11.6)	3,875			
	Passes	88	11 (11.1)	99	88	8 (8.3)	96			
	Appointees	54	3 (5.3)	57	37	5 (11.9)	42			
Intermediate exam	Candidates	37,538	9,478 (20.2)	47,016	51,190	14,668 (22.3)	65,858			
	Passes	1,410	212 (13.1)	1,622	3,946	627 (13.7)	4,573			
	Appointees	776	93 (10.7)	869	1,992	270 (11.9)	2,262			
Class II exam	Candidates							43,185	21,057 (32.8)	64,242
	Passes							4,793	1,749 (26.7)	6,549
	Appointees							2,299	683 (22.9)	2,982
Junior exam	Candidates	83,798	63,695 (43.2)	147,493	79,641	56,416 (41.5)	136,057	53,733	38,853 (42.0)	92,586
	Passes	12,310	5,562 (31.1)	17,872	14,095	6,489 (31.5)	20,584	4,716	3,212 (40.5)	7,928
	Appointees	5,064	1,749 (25.7)	6,813	8,776	3,121 (26.2)	11,897	1,159	583 (33.5)	1,742
Total	Candidates	161,333	75,393 (31.8)	236,726	165,386	74,493 (31.1)	239,879	123,191	69,391 (36.0)	192,582
	Passes	14,980	5,819 (28.0)	20,799	19,605	7,210 (26.9)	26,815	10,572	5,137 (32.7)	15,709
	Appointees	6,557	1,860 (22.1)	8,417	11,547	3,443 (21.2)	14,990	3,936	1,332 (25.3)	5,268

Source: *Jinjiin Geppo* (1985:10–11); 1998 data derived from NPA information.

trollers, maritime safety officers, and immigration guards, which are posts that have been occupied by men for a long time. This is another recent sign of progress for women.

According to the NPA Monthly Report (*Jinjiin Geppo*) of July 1985, in 1974, the proportion of the women employees retired at an age above 30 was 31.8% of the total number of women's retirees, while in 1983 it rose to 50.2%, and in 1996 it rose to 48.0%. Also, in 1974 the proportion of women employees retired at an age below 25 was 45.5%, while in 1983 it decreased to 28.2%, and in 1997 it decreased to 14.2%. These figures show us that the percent of younger retirees belonging to the below-25 age group is decreasing, while the percent of retirees in the age group above-30 is increasing (*Jinjiin Geppo* 1985:17 and information from the NPA).

Along with the tendency for women to remain longer in the civil service, they have made progress in being appointed to the senior posts. In fact, the total number of posts of departmental section chief or higher staffed by women was less than 10 in 1975, while its number rose to 27 including two bureau chiefs in April 1988. And in April 1997 its number rose to 30 including one permanent secretary and two bureau chiefs. Also, the total number of female professors at the national universities was 183 in 1974, while it amounted to 315 in 1986, and in 1998 it amounted to 821 (information from the Ministry of Education). The appointment of women to the senior posts is expected to increase in the near future as a result of the increase of women's appointees in the senior civil service examination and long-term career opportunities.

Despite these signs of progress for women, the NPA needs to take some positive steps based on the demands of the U.S. Equal Employment Opportunity Act of 1980. For instance, in the U.S. federal civil service, the Office of Personnel Management (and former Civil Service Commission) has published statistical data to show the number and percentage of minorities and women by grade and agency in order to respond to the demands of the Civil Rights Act of 1964 and the Equal Employment Opportunity Act (EEOA) of 1977.[3] In addition, in 1992 and 1996 the Merit System Protection Board published reports to answer the question of whether women and minorities face barriers—or what has come to be known as a "glass ceiling"—which constrain their career advancement, and found evidence that women continue to encounter barriers to advancement unrelated to their qualifications.[4]

To establish a fair and equitable personnel administration, the NPA should publish the statistics to show the number of women and percentage by grade in each ministry and agency, and also should seek to answer the question of whether a glass ceiling exists in each ministry and agency through the similar survey research of women career advancement in the national civil service. Needless to say, the promotion process in the higher civil service should be open regardless of the entry level, type of position, educational background, and sex.

5.   Mobility in the Civil Service

In the Japanese civil service, traditionally mobility has been developed within each ministry and agency. Principally, it means vertical mobility within the same ministry and agency. Certainly, this personnel policy was very effective in training a generalist administrator in the particular service in each ministry and agency. However, on the other hand, it caused the problem of ministerial sectionalism. Both reports of the First Provisional Commission for Administrative Reform (RINCHO) set up in 1961 and the Second Commission set up in 1981 emphasized the importance of interministerial mobility in order to overcome the problems of traditional sectionalism among ministries and agencies.

(a)   Interministerial Personnel Exchange

Following these recommendations, interministerial mobility at the departmental section chief level or higher posts has become more widely developed than has been expected. The number of interministerial moves at these posts in whole ministries has amounted to 737 and the total number of interministerial moves including nonmanagerial posts has amounted to 2320 (as of August 1999; see Table 6).

Here, let me elaborate the condition of interministerial mobility at section chief level posts in central office of ministry and agency. Among these officials who were promoted to section chief level posts since August 1998 (total number: 294), the number of section chiefs who have experience of interministerial transfer has amounted to 157 (53.4%) (information from the management and coordination). These show us the possibility that ministerial sectionalism of the higher bureaucrats based on strong identity to their employing ministries and agencies may be overcome. However, despite this improvement, interministerial mobility has a certain limitation in a sense that it often means one-way mobility based on a promotion plan weighed heavily in favor of prestigious ministries, not the equal two-way mobility between administrative organizations. This problem in interministerial personnel exchange has also occurred in personnel exchange between the national government and local governments.

Table 6 Number of Interministerial Transferees by Ministry and Agency (as of August 1999)

Ministry/agency	Section chief or higher officials[a]	Nonmanagerial officials[a]	Total
Cabinet/Prime Minister's Office	16	24	40
Ministry of Justice	40	60	100
Ministry of Foreign Affairs	35	26	61
Ministry of Finance	100	154	254
Ministry of Education	26	58	84
Ministry of Health and Welfare	54	103	157
Ministry of Agriculture, Forestry and Fisheries	57	226	283
Ministry of International Trade and Industry	96	125	221
Ministry of Transportation	44	144	188
Ministry of Posts and Telecommunications	20	84	104
Ministry of Labor	18	54	72
Ministry of Construction	79	192	271
Ministry of Home Affairs	40	44	84
Fair Trade Commission	5	13	18
National Police Agency	37	57	94
Imperial Household Agency	0	1	1
Management and Coordination Agency	7	13	20
Hokkaido Development Agency	0	46	46
Defense Agency	4	35	39
Economic Planning Agency	21	32	53
Science and Technology Agency	18	37	55
Environment Agency	8	25	33
National Land Agency	4	10	14
Board of Audit	1	8	9
National Personnel Authority	7	12	19
Total	737	1,583	2,320

[a]These officials are the persons and prosecutors employed by the class I (senior A) examination, national bar examination etc.

Source: Data from the Management and Coordination.

(b)   Personnel Exchange Between National and Local Governments

Personnel exchange between the national government and local governments is important in promoting the mutual understanding between national civil servants and local civil servants, fostering human resources and activating organizations. In Japan, however, this personnel exchange means one-way mobility to local governments, and it has been criticized as the main route of *amakudari* by national bureaucrats. What is the recent situation in intergovernmental personnel exchange?

According to Table 7 (as of August 1996), the total number of personnel transferred to the local governments amounts to 1197 persons including 951 class I recruits (managerial posts: 814, nonmanagerial posts: 137). By type of position, the number of clerical position is 416, and the number of technical position is 398. By ministry and agency, the construction (number: 246), home affairs (243), national police (210), agriculture (172), welfare (100), etc., are the big transferring ministries and agencies to the local governments. While the total number of accepting personnel of local governments to the national government amounts to 657 persons. By ministry and agency, the national police (number: 283), home affairs (122), education (60), agriculture (59), etc., are the main accepting ministries and agencies of personnel of local governments to the national government. Paying attention to this, the accepting personnel of local governments to the national government seems to be increasing more than has been expected. However, we can't exactly evaluate the advancement of transferees from local governments to the national government. As in these statistics, the total number of the accepting personnel of local governments to the national government includes the part-time transferees of less than one year term of office, we can't compare the actual condition of personnel exchange of full-time transferees of local governments with the one of full-time transferees of national government with more than one year term of office. Efforts should be made for the promotion of accepting personnel of local governments to the national government based on the principle of a two-way equal exchange system. In order to promote the two-way equal personnel exchange, it will be effective to enact the personnel exchange law like the U.S. Inter-Governmental Personnel Act enacted in 1970 (Sakamoto 1996:17–18).

(c)   Personnel Exchange Between the Public and the Private Sectors

Accepting personnel from private enterprises to ministry and agency is also important as it helps to activate the organization by the introduction of knowledge, skills, and working experience from the private sectors into the civil service. In the British civil service, this kind of personnel exchange started in 1977. Under the Thatcher government, the number of the outward secondments of public officials to the business and the number of inward secondments to the ministries such as defense, industry and trade, and environment from business have been increasing year by year (Sakamoto 1989:127–135).

In Japan, the Obuchi government decided to enact the Law of Personnel Exchange between the Public and the Private Sectors at the cabinet meeting on April 27, 1999, and the law was enacted on December 14, 1999. The law intends to foster the human resources and to activate the administrative operation through the personnel exchange between the public and the private sector. In relation to the institutionalization of personnel exchange between the public and the private sector, the law demands to give the following considerations: (1) necessity of acceptance from any private sectors, and (2) never having the person concerned assume any job related to the private sectors concerned. Also, the law requests the establishment of a mechanism under the review of the NPA that will enable to secure the fairness and reliability of civil service, and to prevent the public-private collusion. According to the law, the outward secondments of public officials at the section chief or branch chief level to the private enterprises are, in principle, within three years (maximum five years), maintaining the status of civil servants, and they are paid by the accepting

Table 7 Number of the Intergovernmental Transferees (as of August 1996)

Ministry/agency	Class I–III total	Class I Transferees total	Transfers to local governments from ministries and agencies						Transfers to ministries and agencies from local governments[a]
			Managerial posts			Nonmanagerial posts			
			Total	Clerical	Technical	Total	Clerical	Technical	
Cabinet/Prime Minister's Office	2	2	2	2	0	0	0	0	6
Ministry of Justice	0	0	0	0	0	0	0	0	0
Ministry of Foreign Affairs	5	4	4	4	0	0	0	0	33
Ministry of Finance	13	13	13	12	1	0	0	0	4
Ministry of Education	40	39	39	38	1	0	0	0	60
Ministry of Health and Welfare	100	91	82	29	53	9	3	6	28
Ministry of Agriculture, Forestry and Fisheries	172	151	101	24	77	50	6	44	59
Ministry of International Trade and Industry	35	33	33	25	8	0	0	0	20
Ministry of Transportation	73	54	54	18	36	0	0	0	3
Ministry of Posts and Telecommunications	17	7	5	3	2	2	1	1	2
Ministry of Labor	11	11	11	11	0	0	0	1	2
Ministry of Construction	246	238	226	36	190	12	1	11	8
Ministry of Home Affairs	243	189	154	153	1	35	33	2	122
Fair Trade Commission	0	0	0	0	0	0	0	0	0

National Police Agency	210	92	68	54	14	24	22	2	283
Environmental Disputes Coordination Commission	0	0	0	0	0	0	0	0	0
Imperial Household Agency	0	0	0	0	0	0	0	0	0
Management and Coordination Agency	0	0	0	0	0	0	0	0	0
Hokkaido Development Agency	2	2	2	0	2	0	0	0	1
Defense Agency	0	0	0	0	0	0	0	0	0
Economic Planning Agency	3	3	2	2	0	1	1	0	2
Science and Technology Agency	3	3	3	0	3	0	0	0	0
Environment Agency	15	15	11	3	8	4	0	4	17
Okinawa Development Agency	0	0	0	0	0	0	0	0	0
National Land Agency	3	3	3	1	2	0	0	0	2
Board of Audit	4	1	1	1	0	0	0	0	5
National Personnel Authority	0	0	0	0	0	0	0	0	0
Cabinet Legislation Bureau	0	0	0	0	0	0	0	0	0
Total	1,197	951	814	416	398	137	67	70	657

[a]The number of inward secondments to ministries and agencies includes full-time and part-time officials. Also, the inward secondments to ministries and agencies includes transferees to the foreign offices (embassies and consulates).

Source: Research on conditions of intergovernmental transferees by the Coordination and Management Agency.

private enterprises; the inward secondments to the ministries and agencies from business are proposed to be employed at the section chief level posts dealing with policy making, and their terms of office are also within three years (maximum five years), paid by the government.

As mentioned above, the recent mobility in the Japanese civil service has been developed in various ways. However, the evaluation of mobility tends to be a controversial issue. In the British civil service, traditionally personnel has been employed to train a generalist administrator through interministerial mobility. In the U.S. federal civil service, on the other hand, the value of professional specialists wed to single organizations or to narrow professional perspectives has been traditionally defended. The proposal to create a generalist administrator with mobility obligations between departments has been defeated through the strong opposition that mobility threatens the functional or organizational specialists. However, the creation of the Senior Executive Service (SES) in 1978 was based on the ideal of the mobile administrative generalist instead of functional specialist. Despite the greater flexibility of promotion based on interorganizational mobility, we need to pay attention to the view that SES needs to abandon the concept of the all-purpose generalist administrator. According to one observation as a practitioner, a government manager cannot move readily from defense to interior. He insists that personnel officers need to identify functional areas within government that are similar enough to require common training and to afford interagency mobility (Miles 1982:42–45; Smith 1982:5). The Japanese traditional vertical mobility in the same ministry may be effective in this respect, except for the drawback of sectionalism among ministries and agencies.

IV. RELATIONSHIP OF BUREAUCRATS AND POLITICIANS IN POLICY MAKING

The relationship of bureaucrats and politicians has chiefly depended on the status of bureaucracy within the governmental structure of each country. In Britain, the bureaucrats have been the servants of the monarch, then of the dominant political party under the patronage system, and finally of the people as a whole under the merit system. However, their institutional status remains that of servants of the Queen, as their duties and responsibilities are regulated by the civil service order in council, not by law. In the United States, the bureaucrats have been the servants of the dominant political party under the spoils system, and finally of the people as a whole under the merit system.

In Japan, the bureaucrats were the servants of the emperor until the end of the World War II, and the servants of the people as a whole with the promulgation of a new Constitution. In the prewar period, the concept of popular sovereignty or responsibility of government to the people did not exist. Along with the militarists and *Zaibatsu* capitalists, the bureaucrats tended to rule prewar Japan, but party politicians tried to weaken the strong bureaucracy through the political favors even if the practice emerged only for a limited period.

In 1919, Prime Minister Takashi Hara, the first one-party cabinet leader, drafted an ordinance opening more *Chokunin* posts without qualification restrictions and broadening the field of selection of *Sohnin* and *Hannin* rank officials. The proposal intended to open the bureaucracy through appointments granted as political favors (Masumi 1968:234). Removals were restricted under ordinances protecting officials against dismissals, but suspension that became permanent if not revoked within two years was permitted. A political party often ordered suspension because of "business rearrangements" within the agencies. This suspension order was used often as an excuse for flagrant abuse of the suspension provisions for the purpose of removing hostile officials, especially in the 1920s when the role played by partisan politics was most effective. As a result of the amendment of the ordinances in 1932, the suspensions and dismissals became subject to approval of disciplinary committees. Since then, party control over the appointment of the bureaucrats declined and the power and security of the bureaucrats increased.

From this historical development of Japanese bureaucracy, the first great problem in post-war period was that of making the bureaucracy responsible to the people. Thus, in March 1947, Tadao Adachi had to point out in his paper entitled "How to Reform the Japanese Bureaucracy" presented to the GHQ government section.

> We can find bureaucracy surviving at this turning point in our political history. It is true that some of the higher ranking officials were purged and that a few reforms were made to the administrative system of Japan. But were the defects of Bureaucracy ever abolished? Bureaucracy still remains with its unchanged machinery and tradition (Adachi 1947:1).

In 1952, Kiyoaki Tsuji pointed out in his famous study "A Study of Japanese Bureaucracy," which has influenced Japanese political science for many years, that "the causes of the bureaucratic supremacy lie in the Japanese historical development directly shifted from monarchy to the contemporary administrative state, skipping the stage of civil society" (Tsuji 1952b). These scholars who began to study politics and administration before and after the war as well as many other political scientists have focused their academic attention on the problem of democratization of the surviving old bureaucracy, and argued that the bureaucracy still has predominant influence in politics. In terms of the relationship of politicians and bureaucrats in policy making, the view represented by these scholars is called the bureaucratic-dominance model.

The second model also considers that the bureaucracy dominates policy making. This model's advocates are interested in the analysis of the political factors which influenced Japanese economic growth. For instance, the study entitled MITI and the Japanese Miracle by C. Johnson is a typical one. They insist that economy-related bureaucrats "actually increased their power under the Occupation's policies of economic recovery and post-occupation government's priorities for rapid economic growth" (Johnson 1982; Muramatsu and Krauss 1984:128). In addition, they consider that the personnel resources and the idea of the bureaucracy are almost the same as those of the bureaucracy in the prewar period. In this respect, both models have a common understanding on the bureaucratic role in policy making. However, the evaluation of the role of bureaucracy is different in these models. The former regards the bureaucracy negatively as an obstacle to the democratization of Japanese political system, whereas the latter positively evaluates the bureaucratic role played in policy making. The bureaucratic image in the first model is that of "emperor's servant," while the image of the second model is that of "sophisticated technocrat" (Yamaguchi 1987:7).

The third model of Japanese politics-administration relations is the party dominance model. This model is represented by Michio Muramatsu (Muramatsu 1981). The bureaucratic-dominance model has influenced the discussions of postwar politics. However, Muramatsu paid attention to the changing political environment surrounding the bureaucracy through the empirical study on the higher bureaucrats and politicians, and pointed out the following factors to show the party dominance:

> With the long duration of Liberal Democratic Party (LDP) governance and thus with many politicians gaining cabinet level and Diet committee experience, an increasing number of LDP members have developed the skills and knowledge necessary to understand and deal with complex policy issues. Further, LDP Diet members have increasingly formed policy study groups to share information and expertise and to discuss key questions. There has thus been a tendency toward the development of policy "tribes" (zoku) within the party who take a keen interest in, and have great knowledge of, specific policy area. The top party leadership has very substantial leverage and influence over the process of recruitment to top bureaucratic positions. And the fact that some top bureaucrats have long-range aspirations to run for the Diet as LDP candidates also gives additional leverage to the party leadership (Muramatsu and Krauss 1984:143).

Given these factors, he insists that the Japanese political system does not consist of the single bureaucratic-dominant structure, but pluralistic political process, and that party dominance is even more appropriate. In recent years, following this position, there also appeared the advocates who insist on extreme party dominance against the bureaucrats. They insist that the majority party politicians can control the bureaucrats through the rational choice theory based on the career expectation of bureaucrats (Ramseyer and Rosenbluth 1993). They emphasize the effectiveness of politicians' influence over the bureaucratic personnel issues including promotion and retirement management. However, the political autonomy in the bureaucratic personnel issues is not so strong as they insist. To consider the bureau's influence over promotion and *amakudari* personnel management in each ministry and agency, the bureaucratic autonomy in their personnel issues is still strong (Iio 1995:142–143).

In relation to the discussion of the relationship of bureaucrats and politicians in policy making, Masaru Nishio emphasizes the need for academic work integrating the above three models and argues as follows:

> First, it is important to analyze the relative status or role of bureaucrats in the governmental structure based on international comparative perspectives. Besides, it is necessary to examine the structure of the relationship between bureaucrats and politicians, not limiting the academic interest only to the issue of which role is more influential in policymaking process.
>
> Second, it is important to trace the development of the role and status of Japanese bureaucracy in historical perspective. In the postwar period, it is essential to classify it into three periods. The first decade is from the surrender of Japan to 1954, and the second is from the formation of the single, majority ruling party of 1955 to the middle of 1970s (end of the high economic growth), and finally from the end of 1970s to the present.
>
> Third, the relationship of bureaucrats and politicians seems to differ by the policy area, and also differ among ministries and agencies or even among bureaus. Thus, we should accumulate the various kinds of empirical case study, avoiding generalizations of particular tendency identified in a limited policy area (Nishio 1988:66).

According to his suggestion, let me here briefly examine the status or role of higher bureaucrats in the policy-making process from an international comparative perspective.[5] In the United States, for example, the Civil Service Reform Act (CSRA) of 1978 established the Senior Executive Service. The SES enabled the career civil servants to move and be promoted into policymaking positions without losing tenure in the process, and to play a policymaking role with political superiors. However, the politicization of the appointment of SES members and the role perception for the career executives limited to the administrative duties separate from policy role have caused serious conflict between political executives and career executives.[6]

CSRA intended to bring more efficiency into the civil service by reference to the economic concepts of business efficiency such as merit pay, performance appraisals, bonuses, and so on. Yet this intention did not succeed satisfactorily because of the financial problem. In recent years, this financial problem has been resolved, but the problem that the legitimacy or morale of the career executives declined as a result of the politicization has not been yet resolved. As Hugh Heclo suggests, the role and status of higher civil servants are not "something the apparitors of performance management can image," but "something that flows out of the evolving constitutional understanding" (Heclo 1984:105). In terms of the role of political appointees played in the executive management of the higher civil service, he considers that they are unfit managers and proposes to establish a higher civil service managed by career officials who are directly responsible to the President and Congress (Heclo 1984:108; Bingman 1984:4).

In the British higher civil service, the politicization into the appointment of top-level posts and reform of the career service based on the concepts of new public management since the 1980s have also brought the same kinds of conflicts between higher civil servants and politicians (Sakamoto 1989; Kimimura 1988, 1998a,b).

In the current Japanese higher civil service, such kinds of conflict will rarely happen, since the civil service is still permanent career service. However, in Japan, there is a powerful apparatus composed of Diet members within the LDP structure called *Seimu-chosakai* (Policy Affairs Research Council), which debates and ultimately decides legislation and legislative priorities. In particular, the Diet members called *Zoku* (policy tribes) tend to take a keen interest in the particular interests of their supporting business groups and promote them in the policy-making process of the council (Inoguchi and Iwai 1987).

The development of powerful influence of *Zoku* politicians under the LDP government, however, has involved the risk of sacrificing the public interest instead of representing vested interests of the particular business groups.[7] Thus, despite the Japanese traditional administrative culture, it was necessary for the higher bureaucrats to dispute the policy effectiveness with the related *Zoku* politicians and try to convince them from the perspective of the public interest. In this context, policy staffs of each ministry and agency may have a conflict with *Zoku* politicians on the issue of policy priorities or policy effectiveness. However, party dominance advocates will insist that it is difficult work for the higher bureaucrats who have aspirations to the top bureaucratic posts or Diet members as LDP candidates, although the influence of the top party leadership or each minister over the appointment to the top-level posts is not necessarily strong in a sense that it is only an option appointment power based on the arranged candidates lists.

To repeat again, the relationship of bureaucrats and politicians in the policy-making process depends on the characteristics of the constitutional framework in each country. In Japan, the Constitution stipulates that the Diet shall be the highest organ of state power, and shall be the sole law-making organ of the state (Article 41). Despite the stipulation, Diet members have depended heavily on bureaucrats even in the legislative process as well as in the policy-making process. The relationships between bureaucrats and politicians were so close that *Zoku* politicians came to represent the interests of ministries and agencies under the control of the LDP, which was in power continuously for nearly 40 years from 1955. However, in response to the changes of political culture under the coalition government since 1993, these relationship seems to be gradually changing.

In Japan, the relationship of bureaucrats and politicians in the policy-making process has been disputed as a zero sum game. The above-mentioned three-model advocates tended to limit their discussions only to the issue of which role is more influential in the policy-making process, but it is more important to discuss the problem of each accountability in the policy-making process. Especially, a series of cases including a number of banking bankrupts in 1990s, mistakes over the AIDS policy in 1996, and Tokaimura nuclear accident at a uranium processing plant in 1999 exposed the lacks of accountability and policy inabilities of the bureaucrats in prestigious ministries such as finance, welfare, and science and technology. Therefore, in order to secure the bureaucratic accountability, it is necessary to strengthen the political leadership over the bureaucrats. In this sense, a series of laws revised or enacted in 1999 are expected to promote the changes of relationship of bureaucrats and politicians in the policy-making process.

The law to revitalize Diet deliberations and establish a policy-making system led by politicians was enacted in August 1999. Based on the new law, a Standing Committee on National Basic Policy was set up in both chambers. At the meetings, to be held once a week, the leader of the ruling party and one from an opposition party hold discussions for about 40 minutes. The system modeled on the "question time" system employed in the Britain's House of Commons started from the ordinary Diet session in January 2000.

Under the system, the prime minister will not simply answer questions from the opposition leaders. Instead, the prime minister will conduct face to face debates with other party leaders. This format aims at testing the party leaders' abilities and also at invigorating the Diet deliberations.

Also, based on the new law, the "government committee member" system whereby top level bureaucrats (administrative vice minister and bureau chief) respond to questions in the place of cabinet ministers was abolished. The system was instituted in Meiji period under the Meiji Constitution (Article 54) and in the postwar period under the Diet Law (Article 69). Under the past Diet deliberations, it has been a stock phrase of ministers that "this is an important problem, so I will have a government committee member (bureaucrat) answer the question." However, through the abolition of the system, we can expect to transform "bureaucrat-centered" deliberations into a system centered on politicians. Under the new system, the mutually indulgent relationship between politicians and bureaucrats will disappear, and the Diet deliberations will be a sink-or-swim situation for cabinet ministers, vice ministers and deputy ministers, who are to be introduced in January 2001 with the restructuring of the government.

Furthermore, the revised Cabinet Law stipulates that the 20 state ministers with cabinet posts be cut to 14, and the revised National Government Organization Law stipulates that parliamentary vice minister posts be abolished. But, instead, the revised law stipulates to create 22 vice minister posts and 26 deputy minister posts dealing with policy making in each ministry and agency. And, the revised Cabinet Law stipulates to strengthen the prime minister's leadership in cabinet meeting and to beef up the functions of cabinet bureau through the increase of the number of political appointee posts.

The increase of the total number of cabinet level posts means the increase of political control over the bureaucrats. In the United States under the presidential system, its total number amounts to more than 200, and in Britain under the parliamentary system, its total number amounts to more than 100 (M. Nishio 1988:59). In Japan, the current total number of cabinet-level posts including cabinet ministers and parliamentary vice ministers has been limited to less than 50, but the total number will be increased to more than 60 under the revised law. The increase of cabinet-level posts will strengthen the political leadership over bureaucrats in the policy-making process. In addition, the committee system of the Diet was reorganized in January 1998. The House of Representatives set up a Standing Committee on Audit and Oversight of Administration in order to strengthen the Diet oversight function for the administration, and created a research bureau to boost the research ability, while the House of Councillors set up a Standing Committee on Oversight of Administration playing a role like ombudsman to make a research on the people's grievances for the administration. The reorganization of committees in the Diet will also beef up the political control over bureaucrats.

Although the situation seems to enable policy making by politicians, what is needed, above all, is the political leadership on the side of politicians which has been lacking. The politicians should strive to develop their policy abilities in response to the abolition of the "government committee member" system and the creation of vice minister and deputy minister posts. On the other hand, under the development of administrative reform, the bureaucratic status seems to be declining. In times of coalition government, it is essential for bureaucrats to maintain the neutrality of administration, and also develop their professional expertise in each policy area in order to dispute the policy effectiveness with the related politicians and try to convince them from perspective of the public interest.

However, the relationship of bureaucrats and politicians in the policy-making process mentioned above varies in the policy area in ministries and agencies. Therefore, we need to make various kinds of empirical research on their roles in policy making by each policy area and to examine their accountability and responsibility to the public.

V.   RESTRUCTURING AND REFORMING THE CIVIL SERVICE SYSTEM

The author once pointed out that "we need to remember the proverb that prevention is better than cure" for restructuring our civil service system (Sakamoto 1991:124). But now, our bureaucratic system is in the stage which needs an urgent "cure" for its institutional fatigue which has led to the inefficient coping with the fast-changing global society. Additionally, the great *Hanshin-Awaji* earthquake in January 1995 exposed the organizational problems of our bureaucratic system in crisis management (Sakamoto 2000). In order to examine the recent development of restructuring and reforming of the civil service system, it will be useful to elaborate the following Reports and Laws on the national civil service system.

A.   Report of Administrative Reform Council

The final report, issued by the Administrative Reform Council chaired by former prime minister Ryutaro Hashimoto, proposed in December 1997 that the existing bureaucratic structure of 22 ministries and agencies be replaced by one much strengthened cabinet office and 10 ministries and two agencies by 2001 (see Appendix 1). Toward streamlining the administrative organizations, the total number of secretariats and bureaus shall be drastically cut back, with the current total 128 to be reduced to around 90. The total number of "divisions" in the bureaus of ministries and agencies (currently about 1200) shall be reduced to around 1000 at the time of reorganizing ministries and agencies. Efforts shall be made to reduce this number ultimately to around 900. Also, in 2001, the initial year for the reorganization of ministries, the Law for the Total Number of Civil Servants shall be revised and a new plan for reduction of staff formulated.[8] And in the first 10 years of the plan, overall government staff shall be reduced by a minimum of 10%. Prime Minister Keizo Obuchi raised the target to 20% in 10 years, and then in talks between the LDP and Liberal party on forming the current coalition, the figure was raised to 25%. Furthermore, 131 of the government's 211 advisory committees shall be abolished.

   In relation to the restructuring of the civil service system, the report offers the following proposals. The first proposal recommends the construction of a two-tier personnel management system classified into policy-making and implementation functions. Based on the recommendation, the government is establishing the "independent administrative corporations" with independent legal status outside the state's normal organizational framework like the executive agencies in Britain. These corporations shall be designed to improve the efficiency and the quality of service of certain segments of the executive activities, and to ensure the transparency of such activities. In terms of employees' status, there shall be two types of corporations: those with employees given the status of national civil servants and those without. The government shall evaluate and determine the specific areas to be undertaken by these corporations. In April 1999, the Obuchi government decided to separate 88 organizations including four organizations without status of civil servants from ministries and agencies as the "independent administrative corporations." The organizations operating facilities, such as national universities, national hospitals, and sanatoriums, and national experimental and research institutes have been also targeted as future independent public corporations.

   The second proposal recommends a single entity management system for the section chief and higher level personnel through all government offices, regardless of the type of positions such as clerical positions and technical positions. The third proposal recommends the creation of a personnel system to recruit talented persons for the cabinet secretariat and the cabinet office from inside and outside of the civil service. The fourth proposal recommends the promotion of the active personnel exchange inside and outside of the civil service for securing various kinds of talented persons who are paid and promoted on the basis of merit or performance. The fifth proposal recommends the creation of the personnel management system for ensuring the availability of the aged ability through the review of the current retirement management system.

Regarding the reform of the current personnel system, the transfer of authority to appoint senior government officials from ministries to the prime minister or the cabinet was one of the key proposals in the report. Currently, each ministry hires its employees separately, but this personnel system has caused serious sectionalism among ministries and agencies which hire newcomers themselves. To prevent the traditional sectionalism, the reform council examined for a single entity to recruit entry-level personnel for all central government offices but faced strong objection. Some argued that depriving ministries of recruitment power will make it difficult to recruit talented people with special expertise. As a result, the council compromised with the third proposal for beefing up the prime minister's power along with the second proposal which promote the effectiveness of open personnel system.

In relation to the third and fourth proposals, the National Personnel Authority has decided to allow the hiring of specialists from research institutes and academic institutions as full-time government employees. The NPA revised the rules on hiring national government officials and started the midcareer employment plan from fiscal 1998. Under the current system, government officials are paid and promoted on the basis of their length of service. The new system, however, will allow professionals entering the civil service ranks from the private sector to be treated according to their abilities. These professionals will include veteran researchers at private think tanks, experts in the financial markets and analysts majoring in international affairs at graduate schools.

For the fifth proposal, it is important to examine the radical reforms of career management system in the civil service, including abolition of the practice of high-ranking bureaucrats of ministries and agencies taking early retirement and "parachuting" into executive posts in public corporations and private organizations. This early retirement practice is called *amakudari* (literally, descent from heaven). Up to the section chief level, so-called "career" bureaucrats who passed the class I exam and entered a ministry or agency at the same time are generally promoted simultaneously as "high fliers," but this practice ceases when bureaucrats are promoted to bureau directors or above. They are usually forced into early retirement in their early 50s, but they are promised second careers in the public corporations and private organizations under the jurisdiction of the ministries and agencies they have just left (Sakamoto 1994:109–111, 1996:134–136). This practice of *amakudari* is often blamed for contributing to corruption.

According to the NPA report published in August 1997, the NPA revised rules on reemployment to define that government officials who attain the rank of bureau chief and higher should be prohibited from working in any industry that their ministries and agencies supervise for at least two years after they retire. Although currently retired high-ranking bureaucrats are prohibited from taking positions directly related to their government posts, this revision is more far-reaching, covering all industries supervised by a bureaucrat's ministry. Under the new revision, all government employees should also be prohibited from assuming executive posts or other high-ranking positions that involve representing private companies. In addition, the NPA revised rules on retirement age to define that the retirement age for permanent secretaries and similar personnel should be extended to 62 years in July 1997.

B. Panel's Report on Civil Service System

The advisory panel reviewing the civil service system submitted a report to Prime Minister Keizo Obuchi on March 16, 1999. After a half-century without fundamental revision, the current civil service system has begun to show signs of institutional fatigue, such as the profusion of corruption cases and the widespread practice of *amakudari* in public corporations. Also, under the current personnel policy, with few exceptions, only so-called "career" civil servants who have passed the class I exam can be promoted to policy-setting posts in the government.

The report recommended that the seniority-based pay scale for civil servants be replaced by a merit-based remuneration system, and also recommended that the current seniority-based promotion system be changed to one based on civil servants' abilities and achievements. The panel recommended promoting the promising and ambitious "noncareer" civil servants to departmental chief or even higher posts, rather than limiting such posts to "career" civil servants.

Although the report acknowledges the public distrust of the civil service and proposes changes to increase openness and transparency and to place more emphasis on civil servants' abilities and achievements, its recommendations are not concrete and persuasive. If the panel wishes to implement the promotion system based on merit, "career" track should be abolished and the class I and class II exams should be combined. In the panel meeting, such drastic opinion was proposed by some members, but the panel concluded that the career track should be retained as an effective way to select and train senior officials (on the reform of the local public personnel administration, see Sakamoto 1999).

Furthermore, the report proposed to extend the retirement age until 65. Taking into consideration that people are living longer and remain healthy, the NPA has also prepared for the programs to allow reemployment of civil servants until they are 65 years old. Under the current system, the mandatory retirement age is 60. Since the age at which retirees can begin to receive public pension benefits has been raised, there is a need to increase employment opportunities beyond the age 60. However, given the practice of *amakudari*, it is hard to support the panel's plan. The panel should recommend the reform of the career patterns of the higher civil servants effective for the limit of practice of early retirement rather than extending their retirement age. If their career patterns will be changed, and reforms of the public corporations will be developed, it will be easy to support the panel's plan to extend the retirement age.

C. Freedom of Information Law

Recalling recent series of corruption scandals by elite bureaucrats, it is urgently necessary to establish an open administrative system enabling the public access to government documents. The only way to establish the public trust in our civil service system is to enact laws like the U.S. Freedom of Information Act. As a developed country, Japan has been too slow to enact such a law. After a long interval, the Freedom Information Law was enacted on May 7, 1999 (see Appendix 2). But it has already been more than 30 years since the U.S. Congress passed the Freedom of Information Act, in 1966. The major reason why Japan took so long to enact the law was that there was strong resistance from bureaucrats.

Although a series of information bills was proposed in the Diet in the 1980s by opposition parties, none of them was approved. On the other hand, many local governments were led by so-called *Kakushin* governors and mayors, reform-minded leaders supported by opposition parties. Therefore, the first legislation granting the public access to government documents came at the local government level.

In March 1982, Kaneyamacho, Yamagata prefecture, passed the nation's first ordinance to grant the public access to local government documents. In October of the same year, Kanagawa became the first prefecture to adopt a similar ordinance. Many local governments followed them. As of April 1999, 908 local governments have passed such ordinances. The ratio amounts to 27.5% of the whole (total number: 3299) (research by Ministry of Home Affairs).

The recent passage of the national Freedom of Information Law was made possible by the fact that the public has had over 10 years' experience of information disclosure at the local level. In addition, even bureaucrats had to give way to calm the mounting public uproar for the disclosure of government documents following the scandals stemming from cover-ups by officers in the following cases, which occurred in recent years.

In 1995, officials of the Power Reactor and Nuclear Fuel Development Corporation attempted to conceal the videotape footage and subsequently falsified reports related to the accident at *Monju* Reactor in Fukui prefecture. And in 1996, internal documents hinting at the health and welfare ministry mistakes over AIDS policy in connection with HIV-tainted blood being given to patients were discovered for the first time only after Naoto Kan, a member of the Democratic party of Japan, was appointed minister. The willful irresponsibility in handling of these incidents and the subsequent publicity spotlight thrown on it have apparently promoted the enactment of the law. The law shall go into effect by May 2001. Until then, we should get familiar with it, and the law needs to be revised to cover the documents of public corporations, which are currently exempted. This will encourage bureaucrats to become more accountable for their conduct and decision making. In order to change the attitude of bureaucrats significantly and to regain the public trust in them, it is also necessary to pass an ethics law for civil servants.

D.   Ethics Law for Civil Servants

A series of scandals involving the ministry of health and welfare and the ministry of finance prompted the political parties to submit ethics bills to the ordinary Diet session in 1998, but the bills were not deliberated. Taking advantage of growing calls for the passage of the bills, the ruling and opposition parties finally reached an agreement to pass the revised bills. On August 10, 1999, the Diet passed an Ethics Law to ban civil servants from accepting gifts or hospitality from companies in industries related to their duties.

   The law obliges bureaucrats holding the post of deputy section chief or higher at ministries and agencies to submit reports on gifts and hospitality received with a value of 5000 yen or more. The higher bureaucrats, at the level of bureau chief or above, are obliged to report their incomes and stock dealings. The law also stipulates that the NPA will set up an ethics committee consisting of five members to examine the reports submitted by bureaucrats. Also the Ethics Law for Self-Defense Forces was enacted, which regulates the value of gifts and hospitality that can be received by SDF personnel.

   There is an ethics code for civil servants stipulated by the National Civil Service Law. It states that the government can punish an official when he or she unlawfully commits an action deemed improper for a servant of the people (Article 82). In each ministry and agency, the voluntary ethics codes were created on this stipulation, but because these voluntary ethics codes were proven ineffective by a series of scandals, politicians decided to control bureaucrats' actions by enacting an ethics law. The bureaucrats must not do anything that might create public suspicion or distrust, such as receiving gifts from businesses that are under their authority. The law's existence is supposed to make bureaucrats feel guilty about receiving entertainment, but the best way for bureaucrats is to simply refuse any offer from business. The law goes into effect in April 2000, but the law must be strictly enforced. In addition, the law needs to be revised to regulate the politicians' behavior like the U.S. Ethics in Government Act in 1978, because the law can't regulate politicians as the civil servants of special services.

VI.   CONCLUSION

The transfer from the old bureaucracy under the Meiji Constitution to the democratic civil service under the new Constitution shows that the institutional relationship of bureaucrats and politicians has greatly changed in postwar period. Despite its institutional reform, the advocates of the bureaucratic-dominance model have paid attention to the fact that the old bureaucracy survived as the instrument of the indirect governance policy under the Occupation of Japan, and have argued that the bureaucracy still has a predominant influence in policy making (Adachi 1982). On the other hand, the advocates of the party dominance model have insisted that the Japanese political system is pluralistic and party dominance is even more appropriate. This model was productive in showing us the importance of the analysis of the changing political environment surrounding the bureaucracy. However, the bureaucratic-dominance model is still effective, since the Diet members have depended heavily on bureaucrats in the legislative and policy-making processes. In addition, the traditional administrative culture remains within the civil service,[9] and also the personnel system including recruitment, promotion, and retirement managements of the higher bureaucrats is almost the same as that of the old bureaucracy in the prewar period.

Further, the advocates of the model evaluating the bureaucratic role as the contributors to the rapid economic growth of Japan in postwar period helped to form a good bureaucratic image and promote bureaucratic prestige on an international scale. During the high-growth period, the bureaucracy has played a central role through the administrative guidance to catch up with and outpace other industrialized countries. However, the evaluation for such a bureaucratic role involved the risk that the personnel officers of each ministry and agency have overconfidence in the effectiveness of the current administrative and personnel systems and they act negatively for the reform of these systems. In fact, entering the 1980s and 1990s during the low-growth period, a number of serious problems have occurred which need the reform of bureaucratic functions. In addition, the recent eruption of corruption scandals caused by the higher bureaucrats in prestigious ministries such as those of health and welfare, finance, etc., have made bureaucratic prestige plummet.

In this context, the reform of the British civil service is very suggestive. Especially, the drastic reform of the British personnel system seems to have been closely related to the decline of the British economy, but regardless of the reason for the civil service reform, the development of the open personnel management system since the early 1970s suggests to us the importance of the establishment of an open personnel management system effective for enhancing the morale of all civil servants and regaining the public trust in the civil service. Therefore, as examined above, the recommendations in the panel's report of civil service system proposing to increase the openness and transparency in personnel management and to place more emphasis on civil servants' abilities and achievements should be promptly implemented.

Finally, it will be helpful to consider how to define the relationship of bureaucrats and politicians in the policy-making process. As mentioned above, in Japan, the bureaucracy has traditionally exercised a strong political function. As a result, the great task in the postwar period has been set to make the bureaucracy responsible to the people. Using the terms in Public Economy, the important problem is how the principals (politicians) elected by the people should control the activities of the agents (bureaucrats) (Tatebayashi 1999:85–86). In other words, it is the problem of how the Agents should be accountable for their policymaking roles to the principals.

In relation to the problem of administrative responsibility, there was once a famous dispute between Herman Finer and Carl Friedrich. Finer insisted on the importance of external formal check (accountability) by parliament and court, while Friedrich insisted on the importance of internal informal check (functional responsibility) within the administrative organizations. Despite the existence of traditional administrative culture that the bureaucratic-dominance model insists on, the evaluation for this dispute in the Japanese public administration tends to support the view of Friedrich rather than the view of Finer. As a result, they seem to have a tendency to neglect the external formal check that Finer proposed (T. Nishio 1998:68). As Takashi Nishio aptly points out, the following view of Masaru Nishio insisting on the importance of external check is very meaningful in these situations.

> I dare to support the Finer's view, and want to emphasize the need of the strengthening of external formal check in Japan. Paying attention to the present situations in the United States that

produced the internal informal check, we should never neglect the fact that the legislative and judicial administrative controls are much more stronger compared with those of Japan (M. Nishio 1974:107).

If the effectiveness of external formal check that he insisted on is accepted among the Japanese scholars, then it would have created the social impact to enact laws for securing bureaucratic accountability, and the series of corruption scandals by elite bureaucrats in the 1990s might have been prevented.

Although the Japanese Diet has been too slow to enact laws concerning the policy-making system led by politicians, the government information and ethics for bureaucrats, these laws were finally enacted. The new law to revitalize Diet deliberations and a policy-making system led by politicians will promote the transformation from bureaucrat-centered deliberations into politician-centered ones. The ethics law will be helpful to prevent the corrupt behavior and practice by government officials. And, the Freedom of Information Law enabling the public access to government documents will be expected to contribute not only to the establishment of the accountable and effective national civil service, but also to the further development of the study of public administration in Japan.

At any rate, a series of laws enacted in 1999 are expected to stimulate the changes of the traditional relationship between bureaucrats and politicians in policy making as well as changes in the traditional administrative culture in Japan. For 21st century, the Japanese civil service has taken a step forward to create a new civil service system.

ENDNOTES

1. The first National Public Service Law differed from the draft (Hoover report) recommended by the mission. In particular, it is interesting that the draft in its interim report (p. 13) and final report (p. 18) in April and June 1947 initially included the emperor in the top of the position lists of the special services of the civil servants, despite the status of the emperor as the symbol of the unity of the people in the new constitution in November 1946.
2. Despite the Cabinet's decision to pursue a "university-blind" policy when hiring college graduates, for instance, the Ministry of Education still recruited the bulk of its new career bureaucrats from prestigious universities. Although its 1996 questionnaire did not ask applicants to supply the name of universities, 90% of the 19 successful candidates for fiscal 1997 were graduates of Tokyo University (7), Waseda University (7), and Kyoto University (3). The ministry's Central Council for Education said in 1996 report that business and public agencies should come up with a system of hiring practices and promotion plans which are not influenced by employee's alma maters, but 67% of the ministry's section chief level or higher officials are graduates of Tokyo and Kyoto universities (*Daily Yomiuri* Aug. 5, 1997).
3. For the works of this issue, for instance, see David Rosenbloom, "Equal Employment Opportunity, Affirmative Action, and Public Personnel Management" (pp. 29–58) and Michael Cohen, "Problems of Women at Work" (pp. 59–72), in Michael Cohen and Robert Golembiewski, eds., *Public Personnel Update* (New York: Marcel Dekker, 1984); Masaru Sakamoto, "Renpo komuinsei no Daihyosei ni tsuite [Representativeness of the federal civil service] (1)(2)," in Kinki University, Kenlyu Kiyo 8(3) (March 1977, pp. 65–88) and 9(1) (July 1977, pp. 1–32).
4. On the problem of "glass ceiling" or "sticky floor" for women and minorities in the U.S. Federal civil service, see U.S. Merit System Protection Board, "A Question of Equity: Women and the Glass Ceiling in the Federal Government," Washington, D.C., October 1992; U.S. Merit System Protection Board, "Fair and Equitable Treatment: A Progress Report on Minority Employment in the Federal

Government," Washington, D.C., August 1996. These reports are introduced in Masaru Sakamoto, "Amerika Renpo komuinseido ni okeru Jinjigyosei no Doko [The trend of the Public Personnel Administration in the U.S. Federal Civil Service: Merit System vs Representation]," in Ryukoku University, Ryukoku Law Review 29(3) (Dec. 1996, pp. 1–112).

5. For instance, the study on the relationship between bureaucrats and politicians in the policy-making process in Western democracies by Aberbach/Putnam/Rockman is well known. They considered the four images of the relationship between bureaucrats and politicians: image I (policy/administration), image II (facts/interests), image III (energy/equilibrium), and image IV (pure hybrid). According to them, image I offers the differentiation as the Weberian distinction between professional bureaucrats and party politicians, whereas image II admits a certain policy-making role for bureaucrats. Image III concedes to bureaucrats a rather more political role, whereas image IV suggests that the last quarter of the 20th century is witnessing the virtual disappearance of the Weberian distinction between the roles of bureaucrats and politicians, producing what they call a "pure hybrid." The appearance of "pure hybrids" has been associated with an expansion of key central offices, such as the cabinet offices and White House staff which have absorbed increasing numbers of political administrators (Aberbach et al. 1981:4–23; Sakamoto 1986:18–21).

6. On the problem of politicization, for instance, see Bernard Rosen, "Effective Continuity of U.S. Government Operations in Jeopardy," *Public Administration Review 43* (1983, pp. 383–392); Statement of Bernard Rosen on the Senior Executive Service, before the Subcommittee on Post and Civil Service of the U.S. House of Representatives (Feb. 28, 1984); Masaru Sakamoto, "Amerika Renpo Komuinseido ni okeru Jinjigyosei Kaikaku [The reform of U.S, federal personnel administration]," *Kikan gyosei kanri kenkyu 33* (March 1986), pp. 3–33.

7. For recent activity of *Zoku* Diet members, for instance, those who represent vested interests and lobby for particular ministries and interest groups have been waging a counteroffensive, ever since the Administrative Reform Council's interim report in September 1997, chaired by former Prime Minister Hashimoto, proposed that the postal insurance service be privatized immediately and the postal savings be privatized eventually, with mail service remaining under state control. In the face of strong resistance from *Zoku* lawmakers (although many of them are from Hashimoto's LDP Diet members) and local postmasters, the council changed its position and proposed in the final report in December 1997 that a new type of public corporation be created in five years to take over the three postal service divisions. The prospects for the privatization of postal services have vanished through the resistance from *Zoku* politicians.

8. The Total Staff Number Law is the basic law concerned with the number of the national civil servants. The law sets the upper limit on the total number of "regular services" personnel to perform the duties of each ministry and agency. Before the law is enacted, the number of personnel in each ministry and agency was stipulated by each ministry or agency establishment law, but under the new law, the number of each ministry and agency have come to be specified by cabinet order within the maximum extent of the total number of personnel provided in the law. This made it possible to lay a prerequisite for implementing a dynamic and flexible placement of the number of personnel in response to the changing demands for administrative services.

9. For instance, the symbol of the traditional administrative culture showing the supremacy of the *Kan* (government) to the *Min* (people) is the decoration system. Although the system set up in 1873 was abolished during the Allied occupation of Japan, it was restored in 1963 under the Ikeda cabinet. Since then, the decoration system has been firmly administered, but in June 1999, the Japan Association of Corporate Executives, or *Keizai Doyukai*, criticized the present decoration system and compiled a report calling for the possible abolition of it because they regard it as a symbol of state supremacy and as a breeding ground for collusion between the government and the private sector. Under the decoration system administered by the decoration bureau of the prime minister's office based on the yardsticks of *Kan*, the decoration recipient is selected from the recommended list issued by the ministries and agencies. In order to establish the "citizenry" administrative culture and to promote a better relationship between the government and the private sector, the decoration system should be abolished (see Sakamoto 1994:112

REFERENCES

Aberbach, Putnam, Rockman (1981). *Bureaucrats and Politicians in Western Democracies*, Harvard University Press, Cambridge.

Adachi, T. (1947). How to reform the Japanese bureaucracy. In GHQ/SCAP, Government Section Records, March.

Adachi, T. (1962). The pattern of administration in the public service: an interpretation of the public service in Japan. Kwansei *Gakuin Law Review Annual Report 1.*

Adachi, T. (1966). *Gyosei kanriron [Public Management]*. Genbunsha, Kyoto.

Adachi, T. (1971). *Gyosei gaku [Public Administration]*. Nihon hyoronsha, Tokyo.

Adachi, T. (1982). *Shokugyo to shiteno Komuin [Civil Servant as a Profession]*. Komu shokuin kenshu kyokai, Tokyo.

Bingman, C. (1984). Statement on behalf of the Special Panel of the American Society for Public Administration on the Senior Executive Service, before the Subcommittee on Post Office and Civil Service of the U.S. House of Representatives, Feb. 28.

Dicey, A.V. (1904). *The Law of the Constitution*, 6th ed. Macmillan, London.

Eleventh Report from the Expenditure Committee: The Civil Service, Vol. I. (1977a). HMSO, London, July.

Eleventh Report: The Civil Service, Vol. II [Part 1] (1977b). HMSO, London, July.

GHQ/SCAP. (1951). Reorganization of civil service. In *History of the Non-military Activities of the Occupation of Japan 1945–1951*, Vol. V, part 6. Civil History Section Records.

GHQ/SCAP. (1947). *Report of the United States Advisory Mission to Japan*. (Records—RG331: Hoover Report, interim, April 24, 1947, and final, June 16, 1947.)

Hayakawa, S. (1997). *Kokka Komuin no Syoshin to Kyaria Keisei [Promotion and Career Formulation of the National Civil Servant.]* Nihon hyoron sha, Tokyo.

Heclo, H. (1984). A comment on the future of the U.S. civil service. In *The Higher Civil Service in Europe and Canada* (B.L. Smith, ed.). Brookings Institution, Washington.

Ide, Y. (1982). *Nihon kanryosei to gyosei bunka [The Japanese Bureaucracies and Administrative Culture]*. Todai shuppan kai, Tokyo.

IIAS Tokyo Round Table Organizing Committee, ed. (1982). *Public Administration in Japan, Tokyo, 1982.*

Iio, J. (1995). Seijiteki Kanryo to Gyoseiteki Seijika [Political bureaucrats and administrative politicians. In *Nihon Seiji Gakkai Nenpo [The Annals of the Japanese Political Science Association]*, Nihon Seiji Gakkai, ed. Iwanami Shoten, Tokyo.

Inoguchi, T., and Iwai, T. (1987). *Zokugiin no Kenkyu [A Study of LDP Policy-Tribes]*. Nihon keizai shin-bunsha, Tokyo.

Jinjiin Geppo [NPA Monthly Report] No. 414 (July 1985), No. 572 (September 1997), and No. 602 (January 2000).

Johnson, C. (1982). *MITI and the Japanese Miracle: The Growth of Industrial Policy, 1925–1975.* Stanford University Press, Stanford, CA.

Kimimura, A. (1988). Thatcher Seiken ka ni okeru Igirisu Komuin Seido no Henyo to Kadai [Transfiguration and problems of the British civil service under Mrs. Thatcher's Government]. *Doshisha Law Review*, No. 200.

Kimimura, A. (1998a). Gendai Igirisu no Gyosei Kaikau [Recent administrative reform in the U.K.]. *Doshisha Law Review*, No. 255.

Kimimura, A. (1998b). *Gendai no Gyosei Kaikaku to Agency [Recent Administrative Reform and Agency]*. Gyosei Kanri Kenkyu Center, Tokyo.

Kubota, A. (1969). *Higher Civil Service in Postwar Japan*. Princeton University Press, Princeton, NJ.

Masumi, J. (1968). *Nihon seito si ron [The History of Japanese Parties]*, Vol. 4. Todai Shuppan Kai, Tokyo.

Miles, R.E. Jr. (1982). Rethinking some premises of the senior executive service. In *Improving the Accountability and Performance of Government* (B. Smith and J. Caroll, eds.). Brookings Institution, Washington.

Muramatsu, M. (1981). *Sengonihon no Kanryosei [The Post-war Japanese Bureaucracies]*. Toyokeizaishin-posha, Tokyo.

Muramatsu, M., and Krauss, E. (1984). Bureaucrats and politicians in policymaking: the case of Japan. *American Political Science Review 78.*

National Personnel Authority. Komuin Haku Sho (*Annual Report*), Tokyo, 1992, 1997, and 1999.

Nishio, M. (1974). Gyosei kokka ni okeru Gyosei Sairyo [Administrative discretion in administrative state]. In *Gendai Gyosei to Kanryosei* [*Contemporary Administration and Bureaucracy*] (Ari et al., eds.). Todai Syuppan Kai, Tokyo.

Nishio, M. (1988). *Gyosei gaku* [*Public Administration*]. Nihon Hoso Shuppankai, Tokyo.

Nishio, T. (1998). Gyosei no Accountability to sono Naizaika [Administrative accountability and its immanency]. In *Nenpo Gyosei Kenkyu* [*Annual Study of Administration*] *33* (Nihon Gyosei Gakkai, ed.). Gyosei, Tokyo.

Ramseyer, M., and Rosenbluth, F. (1993). *Japan's Political Marketplace.* Harvard University Press, Cambridge, MA.

Report of the NPA Bureau of Recruitment, Tokyo, 1988.

Report of the Zen Gi Kon in Science and Technology Agency, Tokyo, 1998.

Royama, M. (1958). *Komuinseido no Honshitsu* [*The Issues of Public Personnel Administration*] (Nihon Gyosei Gakkai, ed.). Keiso Shobo, Tokyo.

Sakamoto, M. (1982a). Igirisu Komuinsei ni okeru opunka [The reform of the British civil service since Fulton]. In *Nenpo Gyosei Kenkyu* [*Annual Study of Administration*] *16* (Nihon Gyosei Gakkai, ed.). Gyosei, Tokyo.

Sakamoto, M. (1982b). Komuin no kyaria [Career pattern of the higher civil servant]. *Kihan Gyosei Kanri Kentyu 20.*

Sakamoto, M. (1986). Amerika Renpo Komuinseido ni okeru Jinjigyosei Kaikaku [The reform of U.S. federal personnel administration]. *Kikan gyosei kanri kenkyu 33.*

Sakamoto, M. (1989). Thatcher Seifu no Jinji Seisaku [Personnel policy under Mrs. Thatcher's government]. In Management and Coordination Agency (ed.), *Research Report on Improvement of the British Administrative Management.* Management and Coordination Agency, Tokyo.

Sakamoto, M. (1991). Public administration in Japan. In *Handbook of Comparative and Development Public Administrative*, edited by Ali Farazmand. Marcel Dekker, New York.

Sakamoto, M. (1994). Kokka Komuin Seido [The Japanese civil service system]. In *Seido to Kozo* [*The System and Structure*] (*Gyosei Gaku Koza*) (M. Nishio, M. Muramatsu, eds.), Vol. 2. Yuhikaku, Tokyo.

Sakamoto, M. (1996a). Amerika Renpo komuinseido ni okeru Jinjigyosei no Doko [The trend of the public personnel administration in the U.S. federal civil service: merit system vs representation]. *Ryukoku Law Review 29*(3).

Sakamoto, M. (1996b). Public corporations in Japan, with special emphasis on personnel management. In *Public Enterprise Management: International Case Studies*, edited by Ali Farazmand. Greenwood Press, London.

Sakamoto, M. (1999). Bunken Jidai no Jinji Gyosei [Public personnel administration in an era of decentralization]. *Toshi-Mondai Kenkyu 51*(9).

Sakamoto, M. (2000). Crisis management in Japan: lessons from the great Hanshin-Awaji earthquake of 1995. In *Handbook of Crisis and Emergency Management*, edited by Ali Farazmand, Marcel Dekker, New York.

Smith, B. (1982). Major trends in American public administration, 1940–1980. In *Improving the Accountability and Performance of Government* (B. Smith and J. Caroll, eds.). Brookings Institution, Washington.

Tatebayashi, M. (1999). Atarashii Seido Ron to Nihon Kanryosei Kenkyu [New institutionalism and the study of the Japanese bureaucracy]. In *Nihon Seiji Gakkai Nenpo* [*Annals of the Japanese Political Science Association*], Nihon Seiji Gakkai, ed. Iwanami Shoten, Tokyo.

Tsuji, K. (1952a). Hoochi gyosei to ho no shihai [Administration by law and rule of law]. *Shiso*, July.

Tsuji, K. (1952b). *Nihon kanryosei no kenkyu* [*A Study of Japanese Bureaucracies*]. Kobundo, Tokyo.

Tsuji, K. (1962). Public administration in Japan. In *Public Administration in South and South Asia* (S.S. Hsueh, ed.). International Institute of Administrative Science. Brussels.

Waldo, D. (1965). Public administration and culture. In *Public Administration and Democracy* (R.C. Martine, ed.). Syracuse University Press, Syracuse, NY.

Watanabe, Y. (1976). Nihon no Komuinsei [The Japanese civil service]. In *Gyosei no rekishi* [*The History of Administration*] [*Gyosei Gaku Koza*] (K. Tsuji, S. Yoshitomi, T. Adachi, B. Ari, K. Kato, M. Nishio, eds.), Vol. 2. Todai Shuppankai, Tokyo.

White, D. (1926). *Introduction to the Study of Public Administration.* Macmillan, New York.

Yamaguchi, J. (1987). *Okura Kanryo Shihai no Shuen* [*The End of the Treasury Control*]. Iwanami Shoten, Tokyo.

http://www.lasdec.nippon-net.ne.jp/

http://www.somucho.go.jp/jinji/chousa.htm

http://www.kantei.go.jp/jp/gyokaku/index.html

http://www.kantei.go.jp/foreign/diagram2.html

http://www.somucho.go.jp/gyoukan/kanri/kanri_f.htm

APPENDIX 1: PROPOSED JAPANESE NATIONAL GOVERNMENT IN 2001

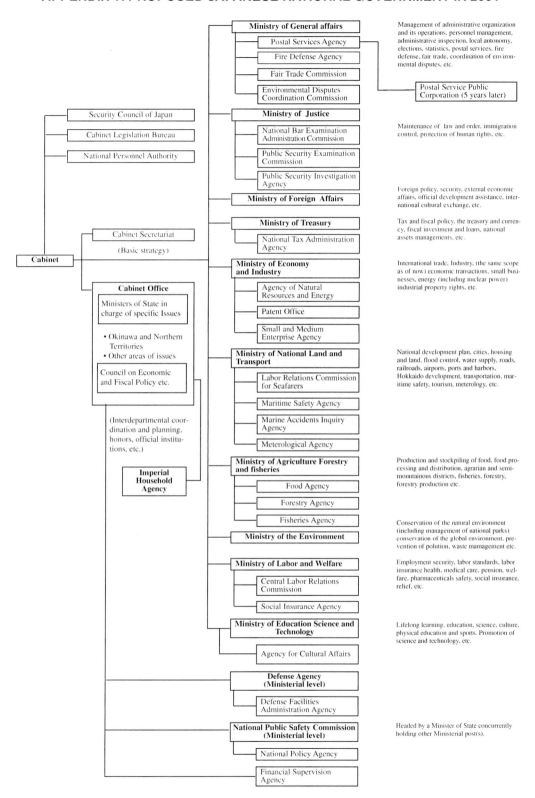

Source: http://www.kantei.go.jp/foreign/diagram2.html

APPENDIX 2

Law Concerning Access to Information Held by Administrative Organs

Chapter 1
General Provisions

Article 1
Purpose

In accordance with the principle that sovereignty resides in the people, and by providing for the right to request the disclosure of administrative documents, etc., the purpose of this law is to strive for greater disclosure of information held by administrative organs thereby ensuring that the government is accountable to the people for its various operations, and to contribute to the promotion of a fair and democratic administration that is subject to the people's accurate understanding and criticism.

Article 2
Definitions

1. For the purposes of this law "administrative organ" refers to the following organs.
(1) Organs within the Cabinet or organs under the jurisdiction of the Cabinet that were established pursuant to law.
(2) Organs established as administrative organs of the State as provided for in Article 3, paragraph 2 of the National Government Organization Law (Law No. 120 of 1948). (Provided that the organ is one in which an organ designated by the Cabinet Order referred to in the next subparagraph is established, the organ designated by the Cabinet Order is excluded.)
(3) Facilities and other organs under Article 8, paragraph 2 of the National Government Organization Law, and extraordinary organs under Article 8, paragraph 3 of the same law, that are designated by Cabinet Order.
(4) The Board of Audit
2. For the purposes of this law "administrative document" means a document, drawing, and electromagnetic record (Meaning a record created in a form that cannot be recognized through one's sense of perception such as in an electronic form or magnetic form. Hereinafter the same.), that, having been prepared or obtained by an employee of an administrative organ in the course of his or her duties, is held by the administrative organ concerned for organizational use by its employees. However, the following are excluded:
(1) Items published for the purpose of selling to many and unspecified persons, such as official gazettes, white papers, newspapers, magazines, and books.
(2) In the case of archives and other organs designated by Cabinet Order, as provided for by Cabinet Order, items that are specially managed as either historical or cultural materials, or as materials for academic research.

Chapter 2
Disclosure of Administrative Documents

Article 3
The Right to Request Disclosure

Any person, as provided for by this law, may request to the head of an administrative organ (Provided that the organ is designated by the Cabinet Order of the preceding Article, paragraph 1, subparagraph (3), that person designated for each organ by Cabinet Order. Hereinafter the same.) the disclosure of administrative documents held by the administrative organ concerned.

Article 4
The Procedure for Requesting Disclosure

1. A request for disclosure as provided for by the preceding Article (Hereinafter referred to as a "disclosure request.") shall be submitted to the head of an administrative organ as a document (Hereinafter referred to as a "disclosure application.") in which are entered the following items.
(1) The requester's full name or title, along with a permanent address or place of residence, as well as the full name of a representative in the case of a corporation or other group.
(2) The titles of administrative documents or other particulars that will suffice to specify the administrative documents relevant to the disclosure request.
2. When the head of an administrative organ concludes that there is a deficiency in the form of the disclosure application, he or she may, fixing a suitable period of time, ask the person making the disclosure request (Hereinafter referred to as "the requester.") to revise the request. In this case, the head of the administrative organ shall endeavor to put at the requester's disposal information that will be helpful in the revision.

Article 5
The Obligation to Disclose Administrative Documents

When there is a disclosure request, excluding cases in which any of the information mentioned in each of the following subparagraphs (Hereinafter referred to as "non-disclosure information") is recorded in the administrative documents concerned with the disclosure request, the head of an administrative organ shall disclose said administrative documents to the requester.
(1) Information concerning an individual (Excluding information concerning the business of an individual who carries on said business.), where it is possible to identify a specific individual from a name, birth date or other description, etc., contained in the information concerned (Including instances where through collation with other information it is possible to identify a specific individual.), or when it is not possible to identify a specific individual, but by making the information public there is a risk that an individual's rights and interests will be harmed. However, the following are excluded:

(a) Information that is made public, or information that is scheduled to be made public, as provided for by law or by custom.
(b) Information recognized as necessary to be made public in order to protect a person's life, health, livelihood, or property.
(c) In the case that the said individual is a public official (National public employees as described in Article 2, Section 1 of the National Public Service Law (Law No. 120 of 1947) or local public service personnel as described in Article 2 of the Local Public Service Personnel Law (Law No. 261 of 1950).), when said information is information that concerns the performance of his or her duties, from within said information that portion which concerns the said public official's office and the substance of the said performance of duties.
(2) Information concerning a corporation or other entity (Excluding the State and local public entities. Hereinafter referred to as a "corporation, etc."), or information concerning the business of an individual who carries on said business, as set forth below. Excluding, however, information recognized as necessary to be made public in order to protect a person's life, health, livelihood, or property.

(a) Where there is a risk that, by being made public, the rights, competitive standing, or other legitimate interests of the corporation, etc. or the said individual will be harmed.

(b) Where upon the request of an administrative organ it was offered voluntarily on the condition that it not be made public, and where in light of the nature of the information and the circumstances, etc. at the time, such as the corporation, etc. or the individual not ordinarily making the information public, the attachment of said condition is considered to be rational.

(3) Information that, if made public, the head of an administrative organ with adequate reason deems to pose a risk of harm to the security of the State, a risk of damage to trustful relations with another country or an international organization, or a risk of causing a disadvantage in negotiations with another country or an international organization.

(4) Information that, if made public, the head of an administrative organ with adequate reason deems to pose a risk of causing a hindrance to the prevention, suppression or investigation of crimes, the maintenance of public prosecutions, the execution of sentencing, and other public security and public order maintenance matters.

(5) Information concerning deliberations, examinations, or consultations internal to or between either organs of the State or local public entities that, if made public, would risk unjustly harming the frank exchange of opinions or the neutrality of decision making, risk unjustly causing confusion among the people, or risk unjustly bringing advantage or disadvantage to specific individuals.

(6) Information that concerns the affairs or business conducted by an organ of the State or a local public entity that, if made public, by the nature of said affairs or business, would risk, such as the following mentioned risks, causing a hindrance to the proper performance of said affairs or business.

(a) In relation to affairs concerned with audits, inspections, supervision, and testing, the risk of making difficult the grasping of accurate facts, along with the risk of facilitating illegal or unfair acts or making difficult the discovery of those acts.

(b) In relation to affairs concerned with contracts, negotiations, or administrative appeals and litigation, the risk of unfairly harming the State's or a local public entity's property interests or position as a party.

(c) In relation to affairs concerned with research studies, the risk that their impartial and efficient execution will be unjustly obstructed.

(d) In relation to affairs concerned with personnel management, the risk that the impartial and smooth maintenance of personnel matters will be hindered.

(e) In relation to the business of an enterprise managed by the State or a local public entity, the risk that legitimate interests arising from the management of the enterprise will be harmed.

Article 6
Partial Disclosure

1. In the case that non-disclosure information is recorded in a part of an administrative document concerned with a disclosure request, when it is possible to easily divide and exclude the portion in which the non-disclosure information is recorded, the head of the administrative organ shall disclose to the requester the portion other than the excluded portion. However, this shall not apply when it is deemed that meaningful information is not recorded in the portion other than the excluded portion.

2. In the case that the information of subparagraph (1) of the preceding Article (Limited to that which makes possible the identification of a specific individual.) is recorded in an administrative document concerned with a disclosure request, and if by excluding from said information the por-

tion of the description, etc., that makes possible the identification of a specific individual, such as a name or birth date, there is considered to be no risk of harm to an individual's rights and interests even though it is made public, then the portion other than the excluded portion shall be regarded as not being included in the information of the said subparagraph, and the preceding paragraph shall apply.

Article 7
Discretionary Disclosure for Public Interest Reasons

Even in the case that non-disclosure information is recorded in administrative documents concerned with a disclosure request, when it is deemed that there is a particular public interest necessity, the head of an administrative organ may disclose the administrative documents to the requester.

Article 8
Information Concerning the Existence of Administrative Documents

When non-disclosure information will be released by merely answering whether or not administrative documents concerned with a disclosure request exist or do not exist, the head of an administrative organ, without making clear the existence or non-existence of the documents, may refuse the disclosure request.

Article 9
Measures Concerning Disclosure Requests

1. When disclosing all or a part of the administrative documents concerned with a disclosure request, the head of the administrative organ shall make a decision to that effect, and notify the requester to that effect in writing as well as of matters determined by Cabinet Order relating to the implementation of disclosure.
2. When not disclosing any of the administrative documents concerned with a disclosure request (Including when refusing the disclosure request in accordance with the preceding Article, as well as when administrative documents concerned with the request are not held.) the head of the administrative organ shall make a decision to the effect of non-disclosure and notify the requester to that effect in writing.

Article 10
Time Limit for Disclosure Decisions, Etc.

1. The preceding Article's decisions (Hereinafter referred to as "disclosure decisions, etc.") shall be made within thirty days after the day of the disclosure request. However, in the case that a revision is requested as provided for in Article 4, paragraph 2, the number of days required for the revision shall not be included within this time limit.
2. Notwithstanding the preceding paragraph, when there are justifiable grounds such as difficulties arising from the conduct of business, the head of the administrative organ may extend the time limit provided for in the same paragraph for up to thirty days. In this case, the head of the administrative organ shall without delay notify the requester in writing of the extension period along with the reason for the extension.

Article 11
Exception to the Time Limit for Disclosure Decisions, Etc.

In the case that there is a considerably large amount of administrative documents concerned with the disclosure request, and there is a risk that by making disclosure decisions, etc. for all of them within sixty days of the disclosure request the performance of duties will be considerably hindered, notwithstanding the preceding Article, it shall be sufficient if the head of the administrative organ makes disclosure decisions, etc. for a reasonable portion of the administrative documents concerned with the disclosure request within the said period of time, and if disclosure decisions, etc. are made for the remaining administrative documents within a reasonable period of time. In this case, the head of the administrative organ shall within the period of time provided for in the first paragraph of the same Article notify the requester in writing of the following items:
(1) The application of this Article and the reason for its application.
(2) The time limit for making disclosure decisions, etc. for the remaining administrative documents.

Article 12
Transfer of a Case

1. When there is a justifiable reason for the head of another administrative organ to make the disclosure decisions, etc., such as when administrative documents concerned with a disclosure request were prepared by another administrative organ, the head of an administrative organ may upon consulting with the head of the other administrative organ transfer the case to the head of the other administrative organ. In this case, the head of the administrative organ who transfers the case shall notify in writing the requester to the effect that the case was transferred.
2. When a case has been transferred as provided for in the preceding paragraph the head of the administrative organ who has received the transfer shall make the disclosure decisions, etc. for the disclosure request. In this case, the acts prior to transfer by the head of the administrative organ who has transferred the case are considered to be those of the head of the administrative organ who has received the transfer.
3. In the case of the preceding paragraph, when the head of the administrative organ who has received the transfer makes an Article 9, paragraph 1, decision (Hereinafter referred to as a "decision to disclose."), that administrative organ head shall implement disclosure. In this case, the head of the administrative organ who has transferred the case shall cooperate as necessary in the implementation of disclosure.

Article 13
Granting Third Persons an Opportunity to Submit a Written Opinion, Etc.

1. When information regarding a person other than the State, a local public entity, or the requester (Hereinafter in this Article, Article 19, and Article 20 referred to as a "third person.") is recorded in the administrative documents concerned with a disclosure request, the head of the administrative organ, when undertaking disclosure decisions, etc., may communicate to the third person concerned with the information a representation of the administrative documents concerned with the disclosure request and other items determined by Cabinet Order, and may provide the opportunity to submit a written opinion.
2. In the event that either of the following subparagraphs apply, before making a decision to disclose, the head of the administrative organ shall communicate in writing to the third person con-

cerned with the information a representation of the documents concerned with the disclosure request and other items determined by Cabinet Order, and shall provide the opportunity to submit a written opinion. However, this shall not apply in the case that the third person's whereabouts are unknown.

(1) Where, in the case that the intention is to disclose administrative documents in which information relating to a third person is recorded, it is deemed that said information will fall within the information provided for in Article 5, subparagraph (1)(b), or within the proviso contained in subparagraph (2) of the same Article.

(2) When administrative documents within which information concerning a third person is recorded are to be disclosed under Article 7.

3. In the case that the third party who was provided an opportunity to submit a written opinion as provided for by the preceding two paragraphs submits a written opinion indicating opposition to disclosure of the administrative documents concerned, the head of the administrative organ, when making a decision to disclose, shall place at least two weeks between the day of the decision to disclose and the day that disclosure will be implemented. In this case, upon making the decision to disclose the head of the administrative organ shall immediately notify in writing the third person who submitted the written opinion (In Article 18 and Article 19 referred to as an "opposition written opinion.") to the effect that the decision to disclose was made, the reason, and the date of implementation of disclosure.

Article 14
Implementation of Disclosure

1. The disclosure of administrative documents shall take place by inspection or by the provision of copies for documents or drawings, and for electromagnetic records by methods determined by Cabinet Order that take into consideration their classification and the state of development, etc. of information technology. However, when disclosure of an administrative document is to take place by the inspection method, if the head of the administrative organ considers that there is a risk that difficulties in the preservation of the administrative document will arise, or for other justifiable reasons, a copy of the document may be provided for inspection.

2. The person who will obtain disclosure of administrative documents based upon a disclosure decision, as provided for by Cabinet Order, shall request the desired method of implementation of disclosure and other items determined by Cabinet Order to the head of the administrative organ who made the disclosure decision.

3. The request as provided for by the preceding paragraph shall be made within thirty days after the notification provided for in Article 9, paragraph 1. However, this shall not apply when there is a justifiable reason for being unable to make the request within this time limit.

4. The person who has obtained disclosure of administrative documents based upon a disclosure decision, within thirty days after first obtaining disclosure, may request to the head of the administrative organ to the effect of again obtaining disclosure. In this case the proviso in the preceding paragraph shall apply mutatis mutandis.

Article 15
Coordination with Disclosure Implementation by Other Laws

1. In the case that under the provisions of another law, administrative documents concerned with a disclosure request are to be disclosed to any person by a method the same as provided for in the text of the preceding Article, paragraph 1 (When the time limit for disclosure is provided for, lim-

ited to within that time limit.), irrespective of the text of said paragraph, the head of the administrative organ shall not disclose those administrative documents by that same method. However, this shall not apply when within the other law's provisions there is a provision to the effect that in specific circumstances disclosure shall not take place.

2. When the disclosure method designated by provisions of the other law is public inspection, said public inspection shall be regarded as inspection in the text of the preceding Article, paragraph 1, and the preceding paragraph shall apply.

Article 16
Fees

1. The person who makes a disclosure request, and the person who obtains the disclosure of administrative documents, as provided for by Cabinet Order, shall pay respectively a fee for the disclosure request and a fee for the implementation of disclosure of an amount determined by Cabinet Order and within the limits of actual expenses.

2. In determining the amount of the fee of the preceding paragraph consideration shall be given to see that it is as affordable an amount as possible.

3. When it is deemed that there is economic hardship or other special reasons, as provided for by Cabinet Order, the head of an administrative organ may reduce or exempt the fee of paragraph 1.

Article 17
Delegation of Authority and Functions

As provided for by Cabinet Order (In the case of organs under Cabinet jurisdiction and the Board of Audit, orders of said organ.), the head of an administrative organ may delegate to an employee of said administrative organ the authority and functions provided for in this Chapter.

Chapter 3
Appeals, Etc.

Section 1
References, Etc.

Article 18
References to the Review Board

When there is an appeal of a disclosure decision, etc. in accordance with the Administrative Complaint Investigation Law (Law No. 160 of 1962), the head of the administrative organ who is expected to make a ruling or decision on the appeal, excluding cases that fall within either of the following subparagraphs, shall make a reference to the Information Disclosure Review Board (When the head of the administrative organ who is expected to make a ruling or decision on the appeal is head of the Board of Audit, a review board separately provided for by law. In Section 3 generically referred to as the "Review Board.").

(1) When the appeal is unlawful and is rejected.

(2) When upon a ruling or decision the disclosure decision, etc. (Excluding decisions to the effect of disclosing all the administrative documents concerned with a disclosure request. Hereinafter in this subparagraph and in Article 20 the same.) concerned with the appeal is revoked or altered, and all the administrative documents concerned with the appeal are to be disclosed. However, this shall exclude cases in which an opposition written opinion regarding the disclosure decision, etc. has been submitted.

Article 19
Notification of Reference

The head of an administrative organ who makes a reference according to the provisions of the preceding Article (Hereinafter referred to as the "reference agency.") shall notify the following listed persons to the effect that the reference was made.
(1) The appellant and intervener.
(2) The requester (Excluding cases in which the requester is the appellant or intervener.).
(3) Third persons who have submitted an opposition written opinion about the disclosure decision, etc. that is concerned with the appeal (Excluding cases in which the third person is the appellant or an intervener.).

Article 20
Procedures in the Case that an Appeal from a Third Person is Dismissed, Etc.

The provisions of Article 13, paragraph 3, shall apply mutatis mutandis in a case in which the ruling or decision falls within either of the following subparagraphs.
(1) A ruling or decision to reject or dismiss an appeal from a third person regarding a decision to disclose.
(2) A ruling or decision altering the disclosure decision, etc. concerned with an appeal to the effect of disclosing administrative documents concerned with a disclosure decision, etc. (Limited to cases in which an intervener who is a third person has expressed an intention to oppose the disclosure of the administrative documents.).

Section 2
Information Disclosure Review Board

Article 21
Establishment

An Information Disclosure Review Board shall be established within the Prime Minister's Office in order to examine and deliberate appeals in response to references as provided for in Article 18.

Article 22
Organization

1. The Information Disclosure Review Board shall be composed of nine members.
2. Members shall serve part-time. However, not more than three members may serve full-time.

Article 23
Members

1. The Prime Minister shall appoint members from among those people of superior judgment who have been approved by both Houses.
2. In the case that a member's term expires or a vacancy occurs, and when the consent of both Houses cannot be obtained due to Diet adjournment or dissolution of the House of Representatives, the Prime Minister may, notwithstanding the preceding paragraph, appoint members from among those holding the qualifications as provided for in the same paragraph.

3. In the case of the preceding paragraph, ex post facto approval by both Houses shall be obtained during the first Diet session following the appointment. In this case, when the ex post facto approval of both Houses cannot be obtained the Prime Minister shall immediately dismiss the member.

4. Members' terms of office shall be three years. However, the term for a member filling a vacancy shall be the remaining portion of the former member's term.

5. Members may be re-appointed.

6. When a member's term expires that member shall continue to discharge his or her duties until a replacement is appointed.

7. When the Prime Minister concludes that a member is not able to carry out his or her duties due to a physical or mental difficulty, or concludes that a member has acted in contravention of official duties or that there has been some other misconduct unbecoming of a member, he or she, on receiving the approval of both Houses, may dismiss that member.

8. Members shall not disclose secrets they have come to know in the course of their official duties. The same shall apply after resigning from office.

9. While in office a member shall not be an officer of a political party or other political association, or actively take part in a political movement.

10. Full-time members, while in office, except where they have received the Prime Minister's permission, shall not engage in another job for remuneration, run a commercial enterprise, or conduct any other business the purpose of which is to profit financially.

11. Members' salaries are to be determined by a separate law.

Article 24
Chairperson

1. The position of Chairperson shall be established in the Information Disclosure Review Board, and the members shall elect that person from among themselves.

2. The Chairperson shall direct the affairs of and represent the Information Disclosure Review Board.

3. In the event that the Chairperson has an accident, the member who has been designated in advance by the Chairperson shall perform the duties of the Chairperson.

Article 25
Collegiate Body

1. The Information Disclosure Review Board shall examine and deliberate matters concerned with an appeal in collegiate bodies composed of three nominated members.

2. Notwithstanding the preceding paragraph, in cases designated by the Information Disclosure Review Board, matters concerned with an appeal shall be examined and deliberated in a collegiate body comprised of all members.

Article 26
Secretariat

1. A Secretariat shall be established within the Information Disclosure Review Board to manage the affairs of the Information Disclosure Review Board.

2. In addition to a secretary-general, the necessary staff shall be employed within the Secretariat.

3. The secretary-general shall direct the affairs of the Secretariat according to the Chairperson's orders.]

Section 3
The Review Board's Investigative and Deliberative Procedures

Article 27
The Review Board's Investigative Authority

1. When it is deemed necessary, the Review Board may request the reference agency to present the administrative documents concerned with the disclosure decision, etc.. In this case, no one may request to the Review Board the disclosure of those administrative documents presented to the Review Board.
2. The reference agency shall not turn down a request made in accordance with the preceding paragraph.
3. When it is deemed necessary, the Review Board may request to the reference agency that it produce and submit to the Review Board materials classifying or arranging in a manner specified by the Review Board the contents of the information recorded in the administrative documents concerned with the disclosure decision, etc.
4. In addition to the provisions of the first paragraph and the preceding paragraph of this Article, the Review Board may, in relation to the matter concerned with an appeal, request the appellant, intervener, or the reference agency (hereinafter referred to as "appellant, etc.") to submit written opinions or other materials, and may have persons deemed appropriate make statements about facts of which they have knowledge or request expert opinions or make any other necessary investigations.

Article 28
Statements of Opinion

1. When there is a petition from an appellant, etc., the Review Board shall provide an opportunity for that appellant, etc. to orally deliver his or her opinion. However, this shall not apply when the Review Board deems that it is not necessary.
2. As regards the text of the preceding paragraph, upon receiving the Review Board's permission, an appellant or an intervenor may appear together with assistants.

Article 29
Submission of Written Opinions, Etc.

Appellants, etc. may submit written opinions or other materials to the Review Board. However, when the Review Board fixes a suitable period of time within which written opinions or other materials should be submitted, the submission shall take place within that time period.

Article 30
Procedure for Investigations by Board Members

When it is deemed necessary the Review Board may have a designated member inspect the administrative documents that were submitted in accordance with Article 27, paragraph 1, investigate in accordance the same Article, paragraph 4, or hear statements of opinion by the appellant, etc. in accordance with the text of Article 28, paragraph 1.

Article 31
Inspection of Submitted Materials

1. The appellant, etc. may request to the Review Board to inspect written opinions or materials that were submitted to the Review Board. In this case, if it is not deemed that there is a risk that a third party's interests will be harmed, or if there is not another justifiable reason, the Review Board shall not refuse inspection.
2. The Review Board may fix the time, date and place for inspection as provided for in the preceding paragraph.

Article 32
Non-disclosure of Investigative and Deliberative Proceedings

The investigative and deliberative proceedings undertaken by the Review Board shall not be disclosed.

Article 33
Restriction on Appeals

It shall not be possible under the Administrative Complaint Investigation Law to appeal the dispositions made by the Review Board or its members according to the provisions of this section.

Article 34

Forwarding, Etc. of Report

When the Review Board submits its report regarding a reference it shall forward a copy of its report to the appellant and intervener, and also make public the substance of its report.

Article 35
Delegation to Cabinet Order

In addition to that which is provided for in this section, other necessary items related to the Review Board's investigative and deliberative procedures shall be determined by Cabinet Order (In the case of a Review Board that is separately provided for by law as referred to in Article 18, rules of the Board of Audit.).

Section 4
Exceptions, Etc. for the Jurisdiction of Lawsuits

Article 36
Exceptions, Etc. for the Jurisdiction of Lawsuits

1. In regard to lawsuits demanding the revocation of a disclosure decision, etc. or the revocation of a ruling or decision regarding the appeal of a disclosure decision, etc. (In the following paragraph and in paragraph 3 of the Additional Provisions referred to as an "information disclosure

lawsuit."), in addition to the court provided for by Article 12 of the Administrative Case Litigation Law (Law No. 139 of 1962), cases may also be brought before the district court (In the next paragraph referred to as a "specific jurisdiction court.") that has jurisdiction over the seat of the high court that has jurisdiction over the seat of the plaintiff's general forum.

2. When a suit is brought before a specific jurisdiction court as provided for by the preceding paragraph, and in the case that an information disclosure lawsuit involving the same or the same type or otherwise similar administrative documents is pendent in another court, the specific jurisdiction court, having given consideration to the addresses or whereabouts of the parties, the addresses of witnesses who should be examined, and characteristics common to the points in contention or the evidence along with other matters, when it deems it appropriate, may in response to a petition or on its own authority transfer the whole lawsuit or a part of it to the other court or a court provided for by Article 12 of the Administrative Case Litigation Law.

Chapter 4
Supplementary Provisions

Article 37
Management of Administrative Documents

1. To contribute to the proper as well as smooth application of this law, the heads of administrative organs shall properly manage administrative documents.

2. The heads of administrative organs shall both establish rules regarding the management of administrative documents as provided for by Cabinet Order, and make the rules available for inspection by the public.

3. The Cabinet Order referred to in the preceding paragraph shall determine standards for the classification, preparation, maintenance, and disposal of administrative documents along with other items necessary for the management of administrative documents.

Article 38
The Provision, Etc. of Information to Persons Who Intend to Request Disclosure

1. So that it is possible for persons who intend to request disclosure to request disclosure easily as well as accurately, the heads of administrative organs shall provide information helpful in specifying the administrative documents held by the administrative organ and take other appropriate steps that take into account the convenience of the person intending to request disclosure.

2. In order to secure the smooth application of this law, the Director-General of the Management and Coordination Agency shall provide for general inquiry offices.

Article 39
Publication of the State of Enforcement

1. The Director-General of the Management and Coordination Agency may request reports on the state of enforcement of this law from the heads of the administrative organs.

2. The Director-General of the Management and Coordination Agency shall annually collect, arrange, and publish a summary of the reports of the preceding paragraph.

Article 40
Enhancement of Measures for the Provision of Information Held by Administrative Organs

In order to comprehensively promote disclosure of the information it holds, the government shall strive to enhance measures concerned with the provision of information held by administrative organs, making clear to the people through timely as well as appropriate methods the information that administrative organs hold.

Article 41
Information Disclosure by Local Public Entities

In keeping with the spirit of this law, local public entities shall strive to formulate and implement measures necessary for the disclosure of the information that they hold.

Article 42
Information Disclosure by Public Corporations

Regarding corporations that were founded directly by law or founded through special establishing acts brought about by special laws (Excluding corporations not subject to Article 4, subparagraph 11 of the Management and Coordination Agency Establishment Law (Law No. 79 of 1973). Hereinafter referred to as "public corporations."), in accord with their character and type of business, the government shall take necessary measures such as legislative measures relating to the disclosure of information held by public corporations in order to promote the disclosure and provision of information held by public corporations.

Article 43
Delegation to Cabinet Order

Apart from the provisions of this law, items necessary for implementation of this law shall be determined by Cabinet Order.

Article 44
Punitive Provision

The person who in violation of Article 23, paragraph 8, discloses secrets shall be sentenced to a maximum of one year of imprisonment with hard labor, or a maximum fine of 300,000 yen.

Additional Provisions

1. This law shall come into effect on a date to be provided for by Cabinet Order, but not more than two years from the date of promulgation. However, the provisions of the part of Article 23, paragraph 1, concerning receiving of the consent of both Houses, Article 40 through Article 42, and the following paragraph, shall come into effect from the date of promulgation.

2. Approximately two years after promulgation, the government shall take the legislative measures referred to in Article 42 regarding information held by public corporations.

3. Approximately four years after this law comes into effect the government shall examine the state of enforcement of this law along with the manner of jurisdiction for information disclosure lawsuits, and shall take necessary measures based upon those results.

Source: http://www.somucho.go.jp/gyoukan/kanri/kanri_f.htm

20
Public Administration of Occupational Safety and Health

The Soviet Union and United States

Janice L. Thomas   *Department of Justice and Risk Administration, Virginia Commonwealth University, Richmond, Virginia*

I. INTRODUCTION

> Even if the incredible should happen (at Chernobyl), the automatic control and safety systems would shut down the reactor in a matter of seconds.
> —*Soviet Life*, February 1986

> As you all know, a misfortune has befallen us—the accident at Chernobyl Nuclear Power Plant.
> —Mikhail Gorbachev, May 14, 1986

The incredible happened on April 26, 1986, 1:25 a.m., at the Chernobyl Nuclear Power Station just outside of the Ukranian town of Pripyat. The Soviet Union's embarrassment over highlighting the safety of the U.S.S.R. power plant industry, and Chernobyl specifically, just less than two months before the accident, was eclipsed by the global tragedy of the nuclear disaster itself.

The "automatic control and safety systems" mentioned in the *Soviet Life* article did not work because they had been purposely turned off in order to run an unsanctioned and improperly supervised experiment. Although there are questions concerning the overall safety of Chernobyl-type nuclear reactors, it is now believed that design was not a primary factor in the accident. Instead, the Soviet investigation and subsequent legal action focused upon six men directly involved in the administration, operation, and government safety monitoring of the plant.

Chernobyl becomes only the most recent link in an international chain of technological safety and health disasters, many of which began in a workplace only to impinge upon the wider environment.

A. Questions for Consideration

What typically happens when a country perceives a risk to its citizens' safety and health? Do these national responses develop into structural and functional solutions that may be observed clearly from one country to the next?

In the United States, citizens expect their government to step in and regulate risk when it becomes "too dangerous," to "too close to home." For example, in December 1984, the world witnessed the death of thousands in Bhopal, India. During the next year the United States experienced a number of community chemical emergencies, including a "near miss" of the Bhopal type at Institute, WV. In direct response, the U.S. Environmental Protection Agency (EPA) began to work on national community right-to-know legislation that in ways closely paralleled workplace right-to-know legislation already implemented by the U.S. Occupational Safety and Health Administration (OSHA). These companion pieces of legislation now involve several federal regulatory agencies, all levels of state and local government, and the majority of workplaces in the private sector. Yet these two laws are only examples of a long list of regulatory actions being used by the United States to respond to perceived technological risks involving the workplace.

Are other countries doing the same? Should we be interested in their efforts? Would a comparison of administrative structures and specific functions be of use?

B. Scope of the Study

To date, no study has been published in English concerning the Soviet administration of occupational safety and health. In contrast, such studies of the U.S. system abound. Much concerning the Soviet administration of occupational safety and health can be gleaned from available literature on the social laws. In these pages we will simply begin to describe and contrast the two systems.

II. OCCUPATIONAL SAFETY AND HEALTH IN THE SOVIET UNION

It may be broadly stated that although there is evidence of individual and collective concerns over the many issues of occupational safety and health; these concerns have not produced a legislative reform movement within the Soviet Union.

The *Constitution of the Union of Soviet Socialist Republics* (1977) sets forth the basic laws of the nation, including two articles of interest to this study.

> ARTICLE 2. Industrial, office and professional workers . . . shall have . . . the right to healthy and safe working conditions. . . .
>
> ARTICLE 21. The state concerns itself with improving working conditions, safety and labor protection and the scientific organization of work, and with reducing and ultimately eliminating all arduous physical labor through comprehensive mechanization and automation of production processes in all branches of the economy.

These articles set clear mandates for protection in the areas of occupational safety and health. Yet what form does the administration of occupational safety and health, these "labor protections," take? Can we clearly follow the constitutional mandate of Article 21, through an administrative system, into the workplace?

Responsibility for occupational safety and health is shared by several diverse sectors of Soviet society:

1. Supreme Soviet of the Soviet Union and its pyramid counterparts at every other legislative level
2. Council of Ministers and its all-union and union-republic branches of the bureaucracy
3. Trade union organizations

4. Management at the individual worksites
5. Workers at the individual worksites
6. Procurator-General and the court system
7. Communist Party of the Soviet Union

Each of these groups, except the Communist Party, is legally enabled through two bodies of laws: (1) *The Fundamentals of Labor Legislation of the USSR and the Union Republics* ("The Fundamentals"); and (2) *The Labor Code*, enacted at the individual union-republic (state) levels of government.

The Fundamentals, adopted on July 15, 1970, are the national set of labor laws and serve as a model for similar legislation at the state level. (Throughout this study I have referred to an edition, edited by L. Smirnov, that includes amendments through March 1982.)

The Labor Code of the Russian Soviet Federative Socialist Republic (R.S.F.S.R.), adopted on December 9, 1971, will be used as our example of a set of state labor laws. In many places these are verbatim statements of the national legislation; in other areas, such as safety and health, they expand upon the national labor laws by adding more specific requirements. (An edition by L. Smirnov with amendments through 1985 was used.)

A. Legislated Responsibilities

The Supreme Soviet of the Soviet Union (U.S.S.R.) and the Soviet of the R.S.F.S.R. promulgate the federal and state labor laws placing overall executive and administrative control of labor legislation in the hands of the Soviets of People's Deputies. Here begins the pyramid government system that empowers the local legislative bodies, for example, the soviet of the city of Kiev. Neither the Fundamentals nor the Labor Code explain what form this control takes, but it appears this responsibility is actually passed on from the local soviet to the appropriate local office of the council of ministers.

The council of ministers, at both the federal and state levels, represents the actual bureaucracy of the government. This translates into specialized regional and local state bodies and inspectorates, for example, the State Committee of the U.S.S.R. on Supervision over Safe Working in Industry and Mines. All have responsibilities for approval of labor protection rules as well as socialized state inspection functions.

The trade unions appear to act as the primary regulators. The Fundamentals mandate that trade unions shall set up a system of "technical and legal labor inspectors" who shall supervise and control "the observance of labor legislation and labor protection regulations." The trade unions also approve "uniform regulation," inspect new enterprises, and give their authorization of safety prior to the commissioning (opening for operation) of the worksites (Smirnov 1982).

The managers of individual worksites or enterprises are reminded of their responsibility "to insure proper working conditions." At this point the manager begins to take on the functions of a Western private employer, becoming somewhat separate from the state.

The workers are also held responsible for their own safety and health by legislation that says they "shall be obliged to observe the labor protection instructions . . . to observe the established requirement for handling machinery . . . (for using) individual labor protection devices." The federal law also speaks to "compulsory preliminary medical examinations and regular periodic medical examinations" (Smirnov 1982).

The Procurator-General, the highest legal officer in the U.S.S.R., is "charged with supreme supervision of the strict and uniform observance" of the occupational safety and health laws (Smirnov 1982).

B. Safety and Health Inside a Workplace

Soviet literature refers to the worksite as the "level of endeavor." A key to labor protections at this level is the interaction between individual workers, the trade union officials, management, and others as they come together to write and implement a document called the collective agreement. This document, specific to each worksite, outlines management's commitment to safety and health.

The collective agreement is signed by members of the trade union committee who officially represent all the workers in that establishment. Management representatives also sign the agreement. After being signed, the collective agreement, and its supplements that outline the specific labor-protection and sanitary measures planned for the new year, are forwarded to the state government's regional economic council (council of ministers) and appropriate regional trade union councils. Funds are appropriated from these two sources for the new year's requested safety and health programs and improvements.

The Fundamentals remind us that the provisions of the collective agreement are to be considered "of a normative character," that is, an ideal set of standards that everyone has agreed to work toward. This is an important point: it becomes the primary responsibility of individual workers, and their trade union representatives, to do the work in fulfilment of these agreed upon goals. Two sets of worker representatives are identified for these purposes—the "labor protection activists" and the "volunteer labor protection inspectors." The labor protection activists are elected by their peers and are supposed to be the most experienced workers, who, under the guidance of the enterprise's trade union, will actively promote safety and health within their unit.

The second group of mandated safety and health representatives are the volunteer labor protection inspectors. These workers are elected to this office for a one-year term by their trade unions. They are "volunteers" only in that they are expected to serve as the official in-house safety inspectors, without additional compensation, while also performing their normal job assignments. These inspectors are responsible for safety and health surveys of the equipment, building, and worker operations. They also settle labor protection disputes between workers and foremen. They perform accident investigations and have the authority to issue reports to management describing discrepancies. The worksite inspectors are led by a "senior voluntary shop inspector" who has the authority to begin legal proceedings against the site's managers if breaches of the labor-protection laws are not corrected.

A hierarchical pyramid for safety begins to develop within the worker's environment. The workers are at the base with their most experienced representatives acting as labor-protection activists. At the next highest level are the trade-union-elected volunteer labor-protection inspectors, who are led by the senior volunteer inspector. This senior inspector also acts as the chairperson of the shop labor protection commission.

This commission is the locus for regular, formal discussions between the worker representatives (the activists and the inspectors) with their management counterparts. If the worksite is large, management will be represented at the level by medical staff, plant (safety) engineers, and other applicable technically oriented professions. If the workplace is small, it must be assumed that the actual supervisors will take a part in the commission's activities. The labor protection commission is just one of several specialized groups that report to and make up the work site's larger trade union committee. This describes the safety organization inside a shop; we may now turn to the shop door to identify those outside the level of endeavor who have an interest in the promotion of its safety and health.

C. Safety and Health Inspectors

Two types of "outside" inspectors may come through the shop door. One category of official will represent the Soviet bureaucracy in the guise of one or more state inspectors. The other type of inspector will arrive representing the appropriate trade union hierarchy and will be interested in technical or legal issues. Each inspector carries various responsibilities authorized through the Fundamentals and the Union Republic Labor Codes.

Trade unions, for the most part, carry out the role of the "outside" inspector. These officials operate from the local level and are divided into two types of oversight—technical and legal inspectorates. It is the technical inspector who visits the worksites and surveys the enterprise and its practices, equipment, materials, and workers for safety and health problems. The technical inspector also conducts accident investigations, monitors worker safety training and use of protective clothing, and has other specific responsibilities mandated by the labor codes.

The Soviet literature speaks of enforcement only when it outlines the responsibilities assigned to the trade union technical inspectors:

> The technical inspector has the right to give managements and individual executive and officials legally binding instructions to eliminate breaches of safety regulations and to control their execution. He can prohibit work . . . fine officials guilty of breaches of the safety rules, [and begin criminal investigation upon notification to the Procurator-General's office] (Livshitz and Nikitinsky 1977).

It seems relevant, in light of the power assigned to trade unions, to remember that they are not considered government agencies although they are enabled, by the labor codes, to exercise these controls over enterprises (Smirnov 1986).

All of this leaves us with many questions concerning the administration of the Soviet occupational safety and health system. How, in reality, is it actually administered? How often are inspections conducted at a worksite, by whom and with what results? How often are cases brought up for prosecution? What are the specific standards used to monitor worker safety and health? Is it true that these standards are not formally codified? These and other questions come to mind but must be put aside for further study.

IV. OCCUPATIONAL SAFETY AND HEALTH IN THE UNITED STATES

The U.S. plan for occupational safety and health protection is fairly well understood, in a general manner, by American workers. Citizens know that there is something called OSHA that is supposed to look out for their safety on the job. Workers in several specialized areas, such as mining and nuclear power, are aware of the federal programs mandated to protect their interests.

This national plan has slowly developed, from sporadic responses to social outcries at the turn of the century, to the sweeping regulatory reformation of the 1970s. For purposes of our study, we will focus upon the federal agency that is responsible for the safety and health of the majority of the U.S. work force—the Occupational Safety and Health Administration (OSHA). OSHA is able to affect almost every public and private sector workplace, within its mandated jurisdiction, either through its own organizational system or through agreements with counterpart agencies at the state level.

The Constitution of the United States does not speak specifically to the safety and health of the country's workers; instead, the preamble calls for promotion of "the general Welfare" of the "People of the United States." It is this "general Welfare" which Congress, at Section 8, is empowered to protect through various methods. One of these methods is "(t)o regulate Commerce with foreign Nations, and among the several States. . . ."

The ability of Congress to regulate interstate commerce becomes the constitutional key to the national legislation that was to wait 187 years before its enactment. The Occupational Safety and Health Act (Public Law 91-596) was signed into law on December 29, 1970, and became effective April 25, 1971. Its first two paragraphs clearly set forth the reason for the law, and the law's mandate.

> Sec. (2) The Congress finds that personal injuries and illnesses arising out of work situations impose a substantial burden upon, and are a hindrance to, interstate commerce in terms of lost production, wage loss, medical expenses, and disability compensation payments.
>
> (b) The Congress declares it to be its purpose and policy, through the exercise of its powers to regulate commerce among the several States and with foreign nations and to provide for the general welfare, to assure so far as possible every working man and woman in the Nation safe and healthful working conditions and to preserve our human resources—

The act outlines 13 ways it will fulfill its purpose and policy. These methods attempt to incorporate all levels of public and private, personal and organizational activity. Responsibility for occupational safety and health is shared by several groups:

1. U.S. Congress, and the legislative bodies of the states (and territories) of "state plan" states
2. The OSH administration, and the administration of a "state plan" state
3. The OSH review commission and federal court system, or the state judicial system in "state plan" states
4. Employers (both public and private sector)
5. Employees (both public and private sector)
6. Authorized representatives of employees (usually considered to mean a union representative)

Although under the OSH Act, each of these groups is recognized as having an interest or responsibility in occupational safety and health, only the first three have legal or enforcement powers under this law.

States that wish to participate in the national program must do so by applying for "state plan" status. For our broad purposes, a state program looks and acts like the federal program, thus allowing us to generalize about U.S. occupational safety and health without regard to the circumstances of any specific state. The federal OSHA program or a "state plan" is present in every state in the United States today.

A.   Legislated Responsibilities

Congress designed and wrote the Occupational Safety and Health Act in a way that places strongly worded duties upon the federal administrator of the law—the U.S. Secretary of Labor—and upon the employers covered by this law.

At Section 6 of the act, the Secretary is directed to promulgate occupational safety and health standards, allowing the public sufficient time for comment and input into the promulgation process. And "in order to carry out the purposes of this Act, the Secretary, upon presenting appropriate credentials to the owner, operator or agent in charge, is authorized," at Section 8, to enter workplaces, carry out inspections and investigations, talk to employees, and conduct all other business necessary to the support of the law.

The administration's regulatory process is also clearly outlined in the OSH act. The agency has supplemented the act by promulgating a supportive body of administrative law—the OSHA Regulations—which are used to guide their own, as well as employers', daily activities under the law. The OSHA Standards, several large volumes of specific and performance-oriented occupational safety and health requirements, complete the collection of OSHA regulatory paperwork.

The responsibility Congress placed upon the employer has become known as "the general duty clause" of the act.

> Sec.5.(a) Each employer—
>> (1) shall furnish to each of his employees employment and a place of employment which are free from recognized hazards that are causing or are likely to cause death or serious physical harm to his employees;
>> (2) shall comply with occupational safety and health standards promulgated under this Act.

The workers are also mentioned in the OSH act at Section 5 (b): "Each employee shall comply with occupational safety and health standards and all rules, regulations, and orders issued pursuant to the Act which are applicable to his own actions and conduct." Although these directions to employees are clear, they have never been used to legally hold employees responsible. Legal responsibility for the safety and health of the employee is placed singularly and firmly upon the employer's shoulders.

If an employer's worksite is inspected by OSHA and violations of the OSHA regulations and standards are observed, the employer will receive a citation stating the specific violation and giving the employer a certain amount of time to make corrections. In accordance with Section 10—Procedure for Enforcement—a penalty may or may not be attached to the citation, depending upon the seriousness of the hazard. The employer has the right to contest the citation, abatement dates, and penalty by taking the case to the Occupational Safety and Health Review Commission, or the appropriate first appeal level in a "state plan" state. Section 11 of the Act outlines this process of judicial review.

Labor unions are not officially recognized within the law and may only be interpreted as receiving mention by way of the phrase "representative of employees" used in the act and in the OSHA regulations.

B. Safety and Health Inside a Workplace

Normative agreements, such as the Soviet Union's collective agreement, are not a typical arrangement in America's workplaces. If a job site is unionized, a labor contract may stipulate broad safety and health benefits. It is generally acknowledged, by employers and their employees, that the codified OSHA regulations and the applicable safety and health standards are the minimum level of acceptable practice. This leaves individual industries and worksites to operate safety and health programs above and beyond this national baseline, as they see fit.

OSHA is currently considering a standard that would either advise or require that each workplace have an overall written safety and health program. This would represent a new level of standardization imposed by OSHA upon America's workplaces.

A microscopic view of the U.S. occupational safety and health policy may be accomplished by looking at a production company with a full-time employment of 500 or more workers. Usually a company of this size will have at least one person, in a staff or line position, who is in charge of the occupational safety and health program. The job title of this person or office varies too much to be of use to us here. This person may or may not have staff and dedicated budget, and may or may not have other duties outside of those of worksite safety.

Typically the state of the practice takes a number of forms, including a well-maintained written safety and health manual, site-specific programs for hazard recognition and loss control, and special programs for the education, training, and motivation of employees. Worker safety and health committees are a traditional unit within the safety and health organization of such a company.

In the United States, a prevailing philosophy says that occupational safety and health works best at the first line of supervision—between the individual workers and their immediate supervisor. Exactly how a private- or public-sector organization endorses and supports this concept depends upon the worksite. OSHA does not have a lot to say about it.

C.   Safety and Health Inspectors

OSHA's inspectors may enter a worksite for several reasons. Most visits are conducted as a result of (1) an employee complaint to OSHA, (2) an accident or fatality, (3) a special emphasis inspection program currently under operation, or due to (4) selection for a general inspection based upon the current scheduling regulations. There are also other reasons, stated in the law or regulations, that would lead to an inspector's first and subsequent visits.

An interesting and important characteristic of an OSHA inspection is that it is initiated without advanced notice to the employer. Congress realized that as "OSHA would not have resources to inspect all covered workplaces in the country, this authority (of inspection without notice), conscientiously implemented, would provide an incentive to all employers to abate workplace hazards, even before inspection" (Minz 1984).

Here lies a key to the philosophy of OSHA. If several different types of OSHA support systems (for example, education and training, consultation and research services) are paired with surprise enforcement visits, organizations would be able to, and in fact chose to, voluntarily comply with federal safety and health requirements. The philosophical, if not practical, concept of "voluntary compliance" emerges from this national scheme.

V.   COMPARATIVE ANALYSIS

One of the very helpful concepts in comparative analysis is that of functional equivalences. With this concept, we may compare the Soviet state bureaucracy, at the level of endeavor, to that of private sector management in a U.S. firm. Each is held responsible for the general welfare of their workers and the provision of a safe and healthful workplace.

Dogan and Pelassy (1984) note that functional equivalence is especially useful with two countries "when one is structured in an embryonic way and the other has reached a high level of structural differentiation." The U.S. federal occupational safety and health system can certainly be characterized as highly specialized, but I would not wish to use the word "embryonic" to describe the same functions in the U.S.S.R. Certainly a case could be made that states that the bureaucratic structure of the U.S.S.R. is currently under change. Gorbachev's pursuit of *perestroika* and the actions of the Nineteenth All Union Communist Party Conference (July 1988) may begin to produce new incentives in this area of occupational risk administration. Yet until these changes take place, it would be correct to characterize the bureaucratic administration of safety and health, within the U.S.S.R., as "power diffused," while the same type of administration in the United States is described as "power concentrated."

A.   Drawing Comparisons

We may begin to draw comparisons with a discussion of the enabling occupational safety and health legislation of each country. It is an important and symbolic first point that both countries have safety and health laws that emerged in 1970. The Soviet Union's Fundamentals were enacted in July 1970, while the Occupational Safety and Health Act was signed in December 1970.

Differences begin to take shape when we look at the administrative structures designed by each law. The national Fundamentals, brief in their enabling statements, simply give guidelines that are to be duplicated and supplemented at the Union Republic (state) level. The U.S. law, on the other hand, is detailed in its language and an important provision preempts all existing state safety and health programs. OSHA also requires those states that wish to operate their own programs to do so under a detailed federal model with federal monitoring. In the United States, administrative power is placed in concentrated form at the federal level while the same power is transferred to levels far below the Soviet Union's national structure.

The existence of a volume of national safety and health standards is another important point for comparison. The few obscure references to "maximum allowable concentrations" and "labor-protection standards" lead me to believe that the U.S.S.R. does not have a complete or codified body of specification and goal-oriented standards that may be used to evaluate the degree of safety and health within workplaces. And it is unclear as to how those standards that do exist are written and applied. In the U.S. system, government standards development and promulgation are performed with full public participation; procedures are clearly outlined in the OSH Act and further regulated by the U.S. Administrative Procedure Act. In addition, a robust body of consensus standards is developed by the private sector. Copies of all of these occupational safety and health standards are widely available and referenced.

While the point concerning standards is a significant contrast, the question of who has a general duty to protect workers is similar in the two countries. In several articles of Chapter VII of the Soviet Fundamentals, the managers of enterprises are told of their safety and health responsibilities. These statements can be seen to be the equivalent of the U.S. employers' OSHA "General Duty Clause." Similarly, each nation's laws instruct their workers to "observe the labor protection instructions" and "to comply with occupational safety and health standards. . . ."

Intuition tells me that the concept of "voluntary compliance"—the popular philosophy in OSHA activities—would also be valued in the Soviet workplace. Both sets of legislation seem to hint that there is a need for motivations that go beyond the negatives of enforcement. Within the Soviet workplace, we find that labor-protection activities are shared among many different organizational levels. Participation by the largest number of workers in daily safety and health activities is promoted. The position and duties of labor-protection activist, as described in the enabling legislation of the U.S.S.R., have a creative and positive tone. Here is an idea worthy of further consideration in the United States.

A significant difference in national or societal philosophy emerges when we continue to analyze the way enforcement of safety and health takes place within the workplace of the two countries. In the Soviet Union, the body of the trade union, although declared non-governmental, acts like a government entity. Through law it is asked to serve as the primary protector and enforcer of worker safety and health. For comparison's sake, we would want to say that the U.S. labor union movement looks and acts very similar to the Soviet trade union. Each generally represents the interests of the workers to management, while each may also serve as a support system for a specialized craft. Yet in the U.S.S.R., for purposes of enforcement, the trade union appears to be all-powerful while in the United States the same structure is virtually powerless.

A final point for comparison concerns the occupational safety and health administrators. We have said nothing about their organizational life in either country, nor anything concerning their profession's technical or educational backgrounds. Intuition nudges me to say that when these two groups are finally analyzed many similarities will be found. The risk administrators of the United States, even with their centralized power, are under challenge of identity and legitimization problems. In the Soviet Union, where administration of this state function is diffused, the problems of professional identity and legitimacy must certainly be compounded.

B. A New Era

The occupational safety and health systems of the U.S.S.R. and the United States are reaching maturity at a time when global conditions dictate a new model of communication and joint action. Critical events such as Chernobyl are obvious examples of this need. But other, just as pressing reasons may be found in the quieter events of everyday life.

The Soviet political environment appears to be growing more receptive to internal change including the introduction of new levels of foreign presence within the country. In response, American businesses are beginning to take advantage by seeking joint ventures, franchising, and other forms of interaction with the Soviet economy. The American scientific community is pursuing similar opportunities with its Soviet counterparts.

Technology will play a supreme role in all of these enterprises. But in partnership with technology are those risks—occupational, environmental, consumer, and so forth—that must be recognized, analyzed, and controlled. Therefore the risk administrator should and will become an important participant in this new era of cooperation.

Those risk administrators willing to work within the Soviet-American arena have inherited a bounty of material and a world full of motivations. An early comparativist, Alexis de Tocqueville, presented us with a lasting statement when he chose to analyze the emerging nations of America and Russia. "Their starting-point is different, and their courses are not the same; yet each of them seems to be marked out by the will of Heaven to sway the destinies of half the globe" (Heffner 1956).

With an understanding of each nation's administrative risk systems, and with joint efforts across the two cultures, we can begin to better control our shared technological risks in order that we each "sway" the destinies of the globe safely into the 21st century.

REFERENCES

Avanesov, P. (1986). Accident. *Soviet Life* September, 34–41.

Dogan, M., and Pelassy, D. (1984). *How to Compare Nations: Strategies in Comparative Politics.* Chatham, NJ: Chatham House Publishers, p. 34.

Goldsmith, F., and Kerr, L. (1982). *Occupational Safety and Health.* New York: Human Sciences Press, p. 245.

Heffner, R. (ed.) (1956). Alexis de Tocqueville's *Democracy in America.* New York: New American Library, p. 142.

Livshitz, R., and Nikitinsky, V. (1977). *An Outline of Soviet Labor Law.* Moscow: Progress Publishers, p. 104.

Minz, B. (1984). *OSHA: History, Law, and Policy.* Washington: BNA Books, p. 335.

Occupational Safety and Health Act, U.S. Code, vol. 29, sec. 2–34, 1970.

Smith, G. (1980). *Public Policy and Administration in the Soviet Union.* New York: Praeger, p. 9.

Smirnov, L. (1982). *Legislative Acts of the USSR, Book Two.* Moscow: Progress Publishers, pp. 61–99.

Smirnov, L. (1986). *Legislative Acts of the USSR. Book Five.* Moscow: Progress Publishers, pp. 13–99.

Vidmer, R. (1980). Administrative science in the USSR. *Administration & Society 12,* 69–87.

21
Regionalization in Russia

Paul C. Trogen and Lon S. Felker   *Department of Economics, Finance, and Urban Studies, East Tennessee State University, Johnson City, Tennessee*

> Leaders have never voluntarily parted with power in Russia.
>
> (Yeltsin 1994:291)

I. INTRODUCTION

A recent article suggests that offering limited autonomy to nationalist groups can prevent the breakup of multiethnic countries (*Economist* 1997b). The Russian experience offers an excellent opportunity to examine both the potential and the limitations of this strategy. Russia, the world's largest multiethnic state, has survived a tumultuous century and the collapse of two empires, yet remains essentially intact. Russia's ethnic diversity and its recurring cycle of decentralization and recentralization presents many opportunities to reflect upon how the strategy of offering limited autonomy contributes to national survival.

Imperial Russia, the Soviet Union, and the Russian Federation were each, in turn, the world's largest multiethnic state. The Russian Empire and the Soviet Union occupied more than 8.6 million square miles, or one-sixth of the Earth's land (Dunlop 1989:1; Bater 1996:22). The Russian Republic retained about 75% of the land of the former Soviet Union (FSU), or one-eighth of the world's land. This enormous size has lead to ethnic diversity. Only half the USSR's 290 million people were Russian; the other half was made up of 120 ethnolinguistic groups, making the county a tinderbox for nationalist movements (Clendenin 1992:22). Almost a fifth of the Russian Federation's population is non-Russian, and half the federation's territory belongs to ethnically designated subnational administrative units (Sharlet 1993:321).

Two factors contribute to the large number of changes in center-periphery relationships. Extensive Soviet centralization provided many potential opportunities for decentralization. While the country was formally a republic, in substance it was unitary with most decisions made in Moscow. Furthermore, the Soviet state had become a pervasive bureaucracy, embracing not only traditional government functions, but also economic and personal pursuits which are considered private in most societies (McCrea et al. 1984:74; Bater 1996:50). The center had many prerogatives it could offer the periphery.

The lack of sound institutions also caused frequent changes in center-periphery relationships. From the late 18th century onward, Russian political thinkers have rejected the Western idea that a well-organized society requires sound institutions (Lepingwell et al. 1995:2). Therefore, relations between the center and the periphery have been haphazard and fluid. In this uncertain environment, a decentralization/recentralization cycle emerged. Central leaders granted limited autonomy to the periphery to gain the periphery's support during power struggles. Weak institutions also allowed the center, once secure, to ignore local desires for autonomy, eliminate local privileges, and consolidate power back to the center. This chapter will trace the ebb and flow of power between the center and periphery and its role in holding a multiethnic empire together.

II. REGIONAL RELATIONS IN IMPERIAL RUSSIA

The twin drives to centralize authority whenever possible, and to grant concessions when necessary, were manifest in the tsarist period.

A. Political Centralization When Possible

Although the tsars were absolute monarchs, they initiated the pragmatic practice of allowing some degree of local autonomy when the center was weak, and centralizing control when the center was strong. In 16th century, there was a brief period of local self-government in the vulnerable young country (Walsh 1958:84). In the 17th century there was an attempt to strengthen central control and administrative governors were appointed to collect revenue and maintain order (Stoner-Weiss 1997:57). Peter the Great created eleven large regional governments, 50 provinces headed by governors (Stoner-Weiss 1997:58). Catherine the Great redrew administrative boundaries, abolished the 50 provinces, and attempted to separate executive, legislative and judicial powers (*ibid.*:58). Catherine also appointed prefects above the regional governors to be her official representative to each region (*ibid.*).

B. Decentralization When Necessary

The defeat of Russia in the Crimean War, however, exposed the shortcomings of the existing system, and the appearance of revolutionaries such as Herzen, Bakunin, and Chernishevsky prompted Tsar Alexander II to overhaul the system and devolve some authority (Walsh 1958:246; Medish 1985:44). In the 1860s, semiautonomous elected councils were established for local government, which were independent of the appointed governor's administration (Keep 1970:132; Stoner-Weiss 1997:59).

The assimilation of non-Russian peoples and the suppression of non-Russian nationalism was Russian policy (Hyams 1970:192; Shaw 1995:26). The Baltic peoples, Finns, and Poles, however, were accustomed to Western ideas, and to freedoms derived from feudal customs alien to Russian culture. Russia found it necessary to uphold traditional autonomies and freedoms in newly annexed areas: in Poland between 1813 and 1832, in the Baltic provinces down to the late 19th century, and in Finland from its annexation in 1809 until 1899. These concessions were still considered alien to Russian political theory and were later revoked (Shaw 1995:26). After Russia's defeat in the Russo-Japanese war and the revolutionary troubles in 1905, additional concessions had to be granted to these most recent annexations (Shaw 1995:26; Bater 1996:30).

III. REGIONAL RELATIONS UNDER LENIN

Lenin was a pragmatist who continued the policy of granting concessions to court the periphery when the center was weak, but taking them back when the center was strong.

A. Concessions to the Periphery

With the revolutions of March and November 1917 the Russian Empire ceased to function as a unitary state (Shaw 1995:27). Tsar Nicholas II dissolved the last Duma a few days before abdicating in March 1917, leaving no government (Bater 1996:41). Regional and local administration also ceased in March, 1917 when both provincial governors, who were agents of the Tsar, and those who worked under them were deposed or fled (Walsh 1958:386). The breakdown of authority encouraged many nationalities to seize the opportunity to escape Russian domination by declaring independence (Yeltsin 1994:112; Shaw 1995:27). By the end of 1918, 13 new states had come into being on the territory of the former Russian Empire (Shaw 1995:27). During the Revolution, the Bolsheviks recognized the declarations of independence of many non-Russian nations which had been absorbed into the Russian Empire. The policy of the Bolsheviks was purely pragmatic, as they realized arguing for their right of "self-determination" was the best way to ensure the support of the nationalities in the civil war (Hyams 1970:193; Nahaylo and Swoboda 1989:351; Shaw 1995:27).

B. Recentralize When Possible

Bolshevik declarations supporting national self-determination offered when Lenin needed support were quickly forgotten once the balance of power had shifted in favor of the Bolsheviks. Lenin was reluctant to give up even one bit of Great Russia's territory (Zwass 1995:8). The Red Army occupied as many countries of the former Russian Empire as possible, declared them Soviet Republics, and joined them to the Russian Soviet Federative Socialist Republic (RSFSR) by treaty (Medish 1980:189; McCrea 1984:144). Except for Finland, Poland, Latvia, Estonia, and Lithuania, all the Russian Empire was reconquered (Medish 1980:189; Nahaylo and Swoboda 1989:351). The Baltics, Finland, and Poland escaped reabsorption only because they offered stiff military resistance and Lenin feared a protracted war might destabilize his regime (Walsh 1958:408; Medish 1980:189).

C. Federation to Unitary State

Lenin was still reluctant to violate national sensitivities of the non-Russians, and therefore created a federation of nominally equal republics (Hyams 1970:193; Medish 1980:189; Shaw 1995:27–28; Nahaylo and Swoboda 1989:352). Actual power was concentrated in the unitary Communist Party, which was dominated by Russians (Nahaylo and Swoboda 1989; Allworth 1980:22). Undeveloped federal structures became rubber stamps for the party (Keep 1970:134). In the USSR, the autonomy allowed each of its members was limited to cultural areas, such as the preservation of languages and cultural identity (McCrea et al. 1984:143; Shaw 1995:27–28). Maintenance of ethnic languages and culture was governed by the principle "National in form, Socialist in content," meaning ethnic diversity was permitted as long as there was political uniformity (Desai 1985:38).

D. Economic Centralization

The Bolsheviks again granted concessions when they were weak, allowing the peasants to seize the land, and workers to take the factories in November 1917. When the Revolution was secure, both land and factories were nationalized (Walsh 1958:389). The economy floundered. By 1920, economic activity had fallen to one-fourth of its prewar level, and industrial output to one-sixth its 1913 level (Walsh 1958:417; Zwass 1995:6). In March 1921, with the regime in grave peril by shortages and popular uprisings, Lenin initiated the New Economic Policy (NEP) to placate the peasantry and consolidate Soviet rule (Keep 1970:129; Nahaylo and Swoboda 1989:59). Peasants were allowed to organize family production (Cox 1996:8). From 1921 to 1928 the NEP also allowed the resumption of private trade and small private industries (Walsh 1958:423; Dunlop 1983:5). The NEP was a successful devolution of economic control to preserve Lenin's revolution (Walsh 1958:425; Zwass 1995:4).

IV. REGIONAL RELATIONS UNDER STALIN

When Lenin died in 1924, Stalin became part of the collective leadership until 1934, when he emerged as the sole leader of the Soviet Union. Stalin revoked neither the concessions to the periphery in Lenin's national contract nor the NEP until his hold on power was secure. Once securely in power, Stalin no longer needed to court the periphery and took away what little linguistic, cultural and economic autonomy Lenin had granted to the periphery.

A. Breaking the National Contract

Like the tsars, Stalin would use assimilation of non-Russians to tighten his control over the periphery. Stalin abrogated the national contract created by Lenin (Nahaylo and Swoboda 1989:353). RSFSR party and administrative units were elevated and renamed Soviet Union-wide agencies (Medish 1980:190). Stalin declared all non-Russian nationalism a deviation of great danger (Hyams 1970:194), as it was often a factor supporting separatist movements which challenged the authority of the center. All suggestions of non-Russian nationalism in the USSR were ruthlessly suppressed (Shaw 1995:23; Bater 1996:311). Beginning in 1928, thousands of intellectuals, writers, scholars and artists from non-Russian lands were arrested in order to stamp out non-Russian cultural expression (Nahaylo and Swoboda 1989:65; Yeltsin 1994:112). Stalin's first purges targeted former members of non-Russian national communist parties and Bolsheviks who paid too much attention to their nation's interests (Nahaylo and Swoboda 1989:65). Forced russification, which was discontinued in 1917, reemerged in the mid-1930s, and the "melting pot became a pressure cooker" (Desai 1985:40). Russian-language instruction became compulsory in non-Russian schools in 1938 (Hyams 1970:194; Shaw 1995:31).

B. Centralize When Strong

At the end of World War I, Lenin was unable to regain the Baltics, Poland, and Finland, and signed treaties recognizing their independence. After Molotov signed a nonaggression pact with Hitler in 1939, the balance of power shifted, allowing Stalin to take back earlier concessions. In 1939, Stalin divided Poland with Hitler. In 1940, the three Baltic republics and Moldova were annexed (Shaw 1995:28; Desai 1989:32) and made Union Republics. Stalin also invaded Finland in the Winter War of 1940, which fought the Red Army to a standstill, and settled for an armistice granting Stalin some territorial concessions. Stalin had reclaimed almost all the territory granted independence during the Revolution. Stalin also grabbed the Tuvan's homeland on the border with China in 1944 (Kaiser 1995:427) and forcibly imposed a Soviet-style system on Eastern Europe in 1945 (Zwass 1995:12).

C. Centralization and the Party

Under Stalin all manifestations of dissent or initiative were dangerous (Shaw 1995:30). Stalin's use of terror created incentives for local party organizations to act as perfect prefects, carrying out directions from the center explicitly with little leakage of authority. Even when republics and local institutions had real responsibilities, they were supervised by USSR authorities and forced to operate under controlled budgets (Shaw 1995:30). Stalin established the practice of appointing Russians as second secretaries in all non-Russian Communist Party organizations (Hyams 1970:194). Until the end of the Soviet Union, Russians held key administrative, party and military positions in non-Russian republics (Rywkin 1980:182–183), and only Russians or "russified" members of subordinate groups assumed policy-making positions (Medish 1980:193; Rywkin 1980:185).

D. Economic Centralization

The economic centralization of the Stalin era caused an even greater loss of autonomy for the periphery (Smith 1995:39). As soon as Stalin consolidated power in 1928, he scrapped the NEP (Dunlop 1983:8; McCrea 1984:187).

1. Collectivization

During the NEP, the state bought grain at the market price. Stalin brought the peasantry under direct control through forced collectivization, to provide supplies of agricultural produce at minimum cost to the state (Dunlop 1983:10; Cox 1996:8). This internal colonization allowed Stalin to extract resources from agricultural areas at a fraction of their value, so the surplus could be redirected into rapid industrialization. There were more than 2000 uprisings, mostly in the Ukraine, the North Caucasus, the middle Volga area, Transcaucasia, and Central Asia (Nahaylo and Swoboda 1989:69). The Bolsheviks treated the peasants as conquered subjects. They were permitted no identification papers and were bound to their collective farms, as were serfs to their lord (McCrea et al. 1984:186; Zwass 1995:6; Cox 1996:8). Through collectivization, the economies of the Asian republics were turned into single crop economies, such as cotton in Uzbekistan (Zwass 1995:45), which made them dependent on other areas in the Soviet Union and ill prepared for independence.

2. Command Economy

The centralization of economic administration further limited republican autonomy. As soon as Stalin consolidated his power, he centralized the economy by introducing the command economy and five year plans. Stalin created a series of central economic ministries in Moscow, each to direct one sector of the economy (Shaw 1995:30). The center also practiced a policy of regional specialization, causing each region to depend on the rest of the country for all other goods (Smith 1995:36). The Soviet Union's centrally planned economy was designed to ensure that the republics and regions would find it difficult, if not impossible, to function on their own (Lepingwell et al. 1994:9). Economic colonialism exploited the resources of some regions in order to subsidize industry (Smith 1995:37). For example, oil and natural gas were sold internally at a fraction of the world market price, forcing energy producing regions to subsidize industrial areas in Russia (Aslund 1995:42).

E. Center-Periphery Structures Created by Lenin and Stalin

The federal system created by the Bolsheviks was asymmetrical, meaning ethnic areas had different political subdivisions from Russian areas (Poelzer 1995:205). The ethnic subdivisions initiated by Lenin and completed by Stalin would eventually include:

15 union republics (SSRs) including the RSFSR
20 autonomous republics (ASSR)
8 autonomous regions (AR) or autonomous provinces
10 autonomous areas (AA) or national okrugs (Medish 1985)

Nonethnic subdivisions were based on the territorial principle and included 120 oblasts, or provinces, and 6 krais, or territories (McCrea et al. 1984:171–174).

1.   Union Republics

Granting territories to ethnic groups was a radical departure from tsarist policy (Shaw 1995:31). Union republics were granted to peoples who had originally seized independence back in 1917–1918 and could claim equal status with Russia (Shaw 1995:28). The number of union republics continued to grow under Stalin. In 1936, Stalin divided the Transcaucasian SSR into three union republics: the Armenian SSR, Azerbaijanian SSR, and Georgian SSR. At that time Stalin also created two additional union republics out of territory which belonged to the Russian SFSR: the Kazakh SSR and the Kirghiz SSR. The union republics were enumerated in article 13 of the 1936 Soviet Constitution. The annexations of the Baltics and Moldavia, made possible after Stalin's 1939 nonaggression pact with Germany, resulted in the addition of the Moldavian, Lithuanian, Latvian, and Estonian SSRs to the Soviet Union. By 1940 there were 15 union republics.

2.   Autonomous Republics

Between 1918 and the mid-1930s, further federalization was taking place through the establishment of autonomous republics (ASSRs) within the Russian Federation to grant recognition of the national aspirations of ethnic minorities (Shaw 1995:28). Autonomous republics ranked just below union republics, and were granted to significant nontribal national groups which were still too small for union republic status (McCrea et al. 1984:170; Poelzer 1995:206). The so-called autonomous republics had less autonomy than the union republics (McCrea et al. 1984:171). Unlike the union republics, the status and borders of ASSRs were not guaranteed in the Soviet Constitutions of 1924 and 1936. Some territories annexed as a result of World War II became ASSRs rather than union republics. Territory annexed as a result of the Soviet victory in the winter war of 1940 against Finland temporarily became the Karelo-Finnish SSR, but this status was short-lived. As the least populated union republic, its name and union republic status intimated Stalin's intention to annex the rest of Finland. The annexation of Finland failed to materialize, and in 1956 the Karelo-Finnish SSR was downgraded to the Karelian ASSR. Tuva, which was annexed along the Soviet Union's border with China in 1944, also became an autonomous republic, the Tuva ASSR. Four ASSRs were eliminated due to accusations their populations collaborated with the Germans during the World War II. While two were later restored to their original territory, the Volga German ASSR and the Crimean Tatar ASSR ceased to exist.

3.   Autonomous Provinces

Autonomous provinces were granted to smaller nationalities which occupied remote areas of union republics and exercised administrative autonomy (McCrea et al. 1984:170). This status did not afford these nationalities any privileges.

4.   Okrugs

To recognize administrative and cultural autonomy of small tribal nationalities, small administrative units called okrugs were formed (Fig. 1) (McCrea et al. 1984; Poelzer 1995:206). In the

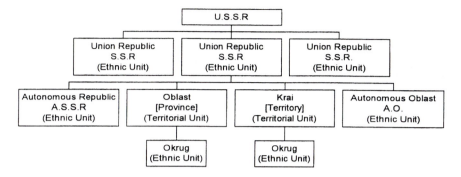

Figure 1 Regional structure of the former Soviet Union.

USSR, okrugs were always subordinate to an oblast or krai (Poelzer 1995:208) and exercised little autonomy (McCrea et al. 1984:171).

The boundaries of ethnic areas were drawn in such a way as to foil ethic attempts at independence. Territorial divisions do not match boundaries between ethnic groups, and many non-Russians often find themselves excluded from the polity in which the majority of their conationals reside (Smith 1995:34). For example, the borders of Tatarstan were drawn in so the majority of Tatars lived outside Tatarstan, and Tatars are not a majority within its borders (Lepingwell 1994:9). Nagorno-Karabakh was historically part of Christian Armenia, yet in 1923 Stalin included it with Muslim Azerbaijan (Smith 1995:40).

5. Oblasts and Krais

Where Russians were predominant, either oblasts or krais were established (Poelzer 1995:206). (Oblast can be translated "province.") There were 120 oblasts, and Moscow and Leningrad had the status of oblast. There are six krais, designed to provide some level of administrative decentralization to large, sparsely populated areas (McCrea et al. 1984:173). Oblasts and krais are purely administrative units whose present borders were drawn by Stalin beginning with the regional reform of 1929 until the mid-1930s (Stoner-Weiss 1997:61–62). The oblasts and krais belonging to each union republic were listed in Articles 22 through 29 of the 1936 Constitution, as were the okrugs and autonomous republics. Moscow and Leningrad also were given oblasts status. After World War II, the northern half of East Prussia was added to the RSFSR as the Kaliningrad Oblast.

The combination of territorial and ethnic subdivisions, initiated by Lenin as an accommodation to ethnic sentiments in a large multiethnic state, resulted in an asymmetrical administrative structure. This structure survived the former Soviet Union, and was inherited by the present Russian Federation.

V. REGIONAL RELATIONS UNDER KHRUSHCHEV

After Stalin's death, Khrushchev's hold on power was tenuous, so he courted the periphery.

A. Khrushchev's Restoration of the National Contract

Khrushchev proclaimed a restoration of Leninist principles in the nationalities question between 1956 and 1958 (Nahaylo and Swoboda 1989:353). Most ethnic groups deported by Stalin were allowed to return home and non-Russians were appointed to top bureaucratic positions in the ethnic territories (Medish 1980:192). In certain aspects of local planning and cultural issues, republics were granted some discretion, subject to higher authority (Shaw 1995:30). When controls were relaxed, people began airing grievances and calling on the Kremlin to honor the national contract (Nahaylo and Swoboda 1989:354). Khrushchev later backtracked on the national policy after threats to his leadership and unrest in Hungary and Poland emerged (Nahaylo and Swoboda 1989:353).

B. Khrushchev's Experiment in Economic Decentralization

In May 1957, Khrushchev limited the power of the state planning commission (*Gosplan*) and dissolved the branch ministries in which an entire industry was under the jurisdiction of a central ministry (Zwass 1995:14; Shaw 1995:30). Khrushchev moved from the branch principle to the territorial principle, in which, he delegated decision making powers to regional economic administrations (Zwass 1995:14; Shaw 1995:30). One hundred and five regional economic administrations were established (Zwass 1995:14). Regional economic authorities brought together larger industrial and construction firms under one roof (Zwass 1995:14). Because economic units were administrative units, some regions, like the Baltic republics, put regional interests ahead of those of the USSR (Bater 1996:69), which caused greater damage than the former segregation of industrial ministries (Zwass 1995:14; Shaw 1995:30). The number of regional economic administrations was reduced from 105 to 47 in 1963 (Zwass 1995; Bater 1996:69). The experiment ended in October 1964 with Khrushchev's fall from power (Zwass 1995:14).

VI. RECENTRALIZATION UNDER BREZHNEV

Under Brezhnev, de-Stalinization was halted, discussion of nationality questions was suppressed, and recentralization and russification were resumed (Nahaylo and Swoboda 1989:353).

A. Political Developments

Under Brezhnev, the political situation remained stable and no far-reaching reforms were introduced (Cox 1996:13). Although Brezhnev resumed russification, plans to do away with federalism in the new constitution of 1977 aroused so much opposition from non-Russian elements, that there was almost no change in the status of republics (Shaw 1995:32). Union republics, their theoretical right to succeed from the union, and protections against changing republican boundaries without the consent of the republics involved, were all retained.

B. Economic Recentralization

On the economic front, the Brezhnev era represented a return to centralized planning. Brezhnev abolished the decentralized economic administration introduced by Khrushchev (Zwass 1995:14). In September 1965, the Central Committee of the CPSU restored the state planning commissions (Gosplan) but central planning was only to be exercised on the most important areas of the economy (*ibid.*). Regional officials formally had administrative control over some industries and services (Aslund 1995:15; Cox 1996:16) but they were dependent on Moscow, both for resources and for funds (Cox 1996:16). On July 12, 1979, a resolution of the CPSU central committee and the council of ministers stressed central planning and vertical plans of the economic ministries were to be coordinated with horizontal development plans for large regions (Zwass 1995:15). This resulted in more centralized planning, not less.

The centralized hierarchical administration, like Khrushchev's decentralized administration, failed to sustain economic growth because planning mechanisms were incapable of handling the complexity as the economy became more sophisticated (Stoner-Weiss 1997:56). Under Brezhnev's leadership, economic growth rates fell from 7.5% per year in the five-year period from 1966 to 1970, to 2.5% in the last two years of the Brezhnev era (Zwass 1995:15). This weakness of the economy would grow into the undoing of the Soviet Union.

VII. GORBACHEV AND CENTER-PERIPHERY RELATIONSHIPS

Gorbachev inherited a floundering economy. The Soviet Union was matching U.S. expenditures in an arms race, but its economy was only a quarter the size of the U.S. economy. Gorbachev's reforms were driven by the fear that without reforms, the Soviet Union would degenerate into a third world country and cease to be a super power (Desai 1989:7; Aslund 1995:27). Perestroika and glasnost were intended to be limited devolutions of control which would revitalize the Soviet system and allow the USSR to maintain its superpower status. The processes, once begun, took on a life of their own and shifted the balance of power from the center to the periphery (Aslund 1995:27; Stoner-Weiss 1997:56).

A. Perestroika

Gorbachev's idea behind perestroika was to revitalize the Soviet system by technical adjustments such as those envisioned by Andropov, and deconcentrating more decision making to the local managers (Bater 1996:51), which was a very modest form of decentralization. The premise behind the reforms was that the overcentralization and lack of responsiveness of the Soviet system were not intrinsic to it, but the result of mistaken policies under Stalin and Brezhnev (Cox 1996:55). This later proved to be an overly simplistic analysis.

Gorbachev's early reforms combined several ministries to create superministries to make strategic decisions, and devolved operational decisions to regional bodies (Cox 1996:50). He also reduced the size of state administration, and subjected it to several reorganizations, leaving them overstrained and impaired in their ability to function (Aslund 1995:34; Stoner-Weiss 1997:39). Furthermore, the 1987 Law on State Enterprises shifted from mandatory central planning to a less comprehensive system of state orders (Cox 1996:53; Solnick 1996:223; Stoner-Weiss 1997:39) which only encouraged manipulation of the rules (Aslund 1995:29; Cox 1996:100). The reduced role of the State Planning Agency undermined state mechanisms for monitoring, coordinating, and controlling industry, without providing effective replacement mechanisms (Clarke and Graham 1995; Solnick 1996:223). Economic performance declined four years in a row (Zwass 1995:21).

Perestroika, instead of cleaning up the economy, deepened the crisis, as stagnation developed into a deep recession (Zwass 1995:70; Cox 1996:100). In the non-Russian republics, frustration levels were vested with ethnic meaning (Smith 1995:35), and many republics wanted independence (Zwass 1995:19). A rivalry developed between the conservative Soviet government, headed by Gorbachev, and the reformist Russian Republic government, headed by Boris Yeltsin, a popularly elected president (Cox 1996:53).

B. Glasnost

The plan behind glasnost was greater worker participation in the workplace and local affairs, a very modest and innocuous decentralization of authority. Gorbachev wanted to revitalize socialism by reversing the administrative capture of the soviets by the Party and restore them as actual governing institutions, as he believed was Lenin's original vision for soviets (Stoner-Weiss 1997:68). The soviets were originally spontaneous grass roots councils of workers and peasants. Gorbachev thought active discussion of local affairs and participation in the workplace would reinvigorate socialism.

Glasnost, or greater openness, removed much of the official censorship and the restrictions on organizing independent groups for discussion and community work (Cox 1996:52). When Gorbachev relaxed controls, non-Russians began airing grievances (Nahaylo and Swoboda 1989:354). Gorbachev's glasnost invited the union republics to pluralistic elections, giving nationalist movements a way to articulate decades of pent-up grievances against Moscow's rule (Smith 1995:35; Bater 1996:52). Glasnost also exposed the problems inherent in a command economy (Aslund 1995:32).

From December 1989 to March 1990, the union republics held parliamentary elections, which were more democratic than those of the Congress of People's Deputies of the USSR, so they enjoyed greater democratic legitimacy than the Soviet parliament. Local party organs, which acted as prefects for the center, were replaced by representative legislatures which owed their legitimacy to the electorate in the regions (Stoner-Weiss 1997:4). This provided legislators in the republics and those within Russia an independent power base from which to oppose the center and demand local control over local affairs (Stoner-Weiss 1997:57). Although Gorbachev initiated a "revolution from above," it soon became a revolution from below, with regions dictating its nature and tempo (Smith 1995:35; Bater 1996).

In 1989, with the party weakened, Gorbachev tried offering concessions to the periphery. Gorbachev proposed a restructuring of the Soviet Federation along the Leninist idea of equal states (Smith 1995:35). By this time, however, a number of republics, the Baltic republics, Georgia, and Azerbaijan began openly questioning the merits of remaining in the Soviet Union. By the end of 1990, five union republics (Estonia, Latvia, Lithuania, Georgia, and Armenia) had declared themselves independent, and 10 more had issued declarations of sovereignty, which implied autonomy. A war of laws over jurisdiction broke out that lasted until the Soviet Union was dissolved in December 1991 (Aslund 1995:35). The new Russian Congress of People's Deputies declared Russian sovereign in June 1990 (Aslund 1995:35; Cox 1996:123).

C.   Effect of the 1991 Coup on Center-Periphery Relations

Gorbachev attempted to revive the national contract as a way to keep the Soviet Union together. The catalyst of the coup event was the signing of the New Union Treaty scheduled for the day after the coup, August 20. Leading conservatives issued a manifesto calling for grass roots resistance to the New Union Treaty (Bater 1996:54). Yeltsin persuaded Gorbachev that the republics would join a new commonwealth only if Gorbachev replaced some of the hardliners, such as KGB chairman Gennedy Kryuchkov, who crushed the independence movement in Lithuania. This conversation may have precipitated the coup attempt, as transcripts later showed the conversation was electronically recorded (Yeltsin 1994:38).

After the failed coup, the government bodies of the Soviet Union were in suspension, leaving a vacuum in the political center. It became clear the real power was in the republics, especially Russia (Yeltsin 1994:105). The principle of ruling from the center had so compromised itself that the republics had little alternative but to opt for independence (Yeltsin 1994:105). Russian history had suggested that without strong institutions, there was no guarantee that the center would not someday be occupied by hard liners who, after they consolidate power, would withdraw Gorbachev's concessions to the periphery, erase new found republican autonomy, and reestablish central control. At this time, succession was possible, not because of changes in the constitution, but rather changes in the party that held it together. The mystery of the Bolshevik success, wrote

Jeane J. Kirkpatrick, was "violence and ideology" (Kirkpatrick 1992:7). The reason for their defeat, on the other hand, was the revision of the ideology that led the Soviet elite to hesitate over using force, not only in their sphere of influence in Eastern Europe but also later in their inner empire (Zwass 1995:43).

The Commonwealth of Independent States (CIS) was the only possible preservation of an integrated geographical region (Yeltsin 1994:114). All were ready to join the CIS except the Baltics and Georgia. The CIS decided not to have coordinating bodies, but the chiefs of state would meet once a month to resolve problems as they arose (Yeltsin 1994:121). This lack of central institutions prevents the creation of a new center which might someday attempt to recentralize power. Each former republic also formed their own army (Yeltsin 1994:153).

VIII. CENTER-PERIPHERY RELATIONS IN THE RUSSIAN REPUBLIC

This chapter began with the observation that from the late 18th century on, Russian political thinkers have rejected the Western idea that a well-organized society requires sound institutions, which caused relations between the center and the periphery to be asymmetrical, haphazard, and ever-changing (Lepingwell et al. 1995:2). This trend continues in the contemporary Russian Republic, where relations are asymmetrical between different types of regions (autonomous republics and oblasts and krais), across different republics, as a result of separate bilateral treaties between the periphery and the center, and across time, with more authority flowing outward to the periphery when power struggles weaken the center, and the recentralizing of authority when the center is strong.

A. Asymmetry Among Republics, Oblasts, and Krais

The Russian Federation retains the distinction of being the world's largest multiethnic republic and still has to manage a multi-ethnic polity in which nearly a fifth of its citizens is non-Russian (Smith 1995:36).

The new mission of Russia is not to regain the surrounding territory, but to retain territorial integrity within the present borders of Russia. The task of nation building is to convince its 21 ethnically designated republics, which contain half the land in the Russian Federation, that the federal arrangement gives them enough control over their political, economic, and cultural affairs (Smith 1995:36). At the same time, the center must not alienate the ethnically Russian oblasts, many of which pay much more into the central treasury than they get back. Federalism is a territorial strategy to avoid the breakup of Russia in which Yeltsin is trying to deflect support for succession (Smith 1995:38). So far, the strategy has worked.

Russia is formally a federation consisting of 89 subnational members. The type of federal arrangement in the Russian Republic, as in the FSU, depends on whether the population of the area was historically Russian or home to another ethnic group. Ethnically based subdivisions: 21 republics (former autonomous republics); 10 autonomous okrugs (national districts); and 1 Jewish autonomous oblast. Territorially based subdivisions: 49 oblasts (provinces); 6 krais (territories, sparsely populated); and 2 large cities (Moscow and St. Petersburg) (Hahn 1997:251–252). The majority of the regional boundaries, drawn in Stalin's time (Stoner-Weiss 1997:61) and in subsequent revisions, divide ethnic groups and reduce their cohesiveness (Clarke and Graham 1995).

Tensions between the republics and regions—the krais and oblasts—are fanned by the fact the federal system is not perceived as equitable by the majority of Russia's regions, the oblasts and krais (Lepingwell et al. 1994:8; Clark and Graham 1995). Special status granted to the republics on the basis of their ethnic identity is a constant source of irritation to the larger, richer, more populous, and more numerous regions (Lepingwell 1994:8). The oblasts and krais are responsible for paying most of the taxes to the federal government, yet the republics have greater powers (Lepingwell et al. 1994:7; Clark and Graham 1995). Ten regions, representing 25% of the population, are "donor" regions that pay 57% of the revenue to the federal budget (Hahn 1997:257; Slider 1997:456). Some prosperous parts of Russia have an incentive to opt out of the system to avoid the heavy tax burden. Regional leaders are agitating for more independence to stop paying Moscow and assume responsibility for services such as health care themselves (Lepingwell et al. 1994:7).

In addition to paying lower taxes, republics seem to get a disproportional share of federal revenue. As a republic, Sakha (Yakutia) receives asymmetrical budget transfers compared to its krai and oblast counterparts. In 1993, the Sakha Republic received 59,034 rubles per capita, compared to 5397 for the Novosibirsk oblast. The Sakha Republic received 955 billion rubles total, compared to 901 billion for the rest of the far east and Trans-Baikal areas (Poelzer 1995:211).

Taxes received by the center, in addition to paying for central expenditures, are supposed to be used by central authorities to equalize conditions across the regions. Often it appears political factors determine the size of financial flows (Slider 1997:456). A regression analysis suggested Yeltsin appeared to be bestowing the most benefits to satisfy regions that were generating problems, and it appears the tactic succeeds in demobilizing regional protests (Treisman 1996a:49). While the administrative structure inherited from Soviet times, with ethnic republics and nonethnic provinces, is not administratively logical, it has proved politically rational in the center's effort to give the ethnic republics political and economic incentives to remain in the Russian Federation.

B.   Asymmetry Due to Bilateral Agreements

First, instead of a fixed federal structure with well-defined powers, the Russian government pursued a policy of negotiating separate agreements with the regions. This is a continuation of the informal administrative bargaining which occurred under the Soviet system (Treisman 1996b:299). Most of these agreements have not been published, and there is no guarantee the agreements will not be overridden later by central authorities (Slider 1997:456). The way power is devolving is so haphazard and chaotic that it is impossible to discern any clearly established rules of the game (Lepingwell et al. 1994:8; Treisman 1996b:300). In 1992, Prime Minister Viktor Cheromyrdin was quoted as saying there was no regional policy in Russia (Treisman 1996b:300). Region-center relations have been in constant flux since Russian independence, with de facto arrangements emerging on a case-by-case basis (Slider 1997:448). At present, every territorial unit is out for itself, competing in a zero-sum game (Lepingwell et al. 1995:2).

Second, bilateral agreements are not uniform; rather than building a feeling of trust and fairness between regions, each region is pitted against the others to use whatever clout it has to negotiate the best deal for itself at the expense of the center (Lepingwell et al. 1994:8; Clarke and Graham 1995; Bater 1996:339). This competition poses some danger for the center. First, regional elites have an incentive to challenge the center, to prompt the center to grant it tax concessions, subsidies, and other benefits (Treisman 1996b:299). Both the constant challenges and mounting claims against limited central resources are likely to weaken the center in the long run. Rather than using Federal subsidies to reward supporters of the regime and regions which make progress on privatization, a statistical analysis suggests that federal funds were redistributed to appease regions which make trouble for the center, such as declaring sovereignty, having strikes against the government, and opposing the government in elections (Treisman 1996b:329). By giving money to regions that oppose his policies, Yeltsin may have kept the federation together until now, but the long-term consequence of this policy is that he has alienated his supporters without winning over his opponents (Treisman 1996b:330). This short term strategy may weaken his long-term ability to hold the nation together by creating incentives for regions to challenge the center and press separatist claims.

Regions that oppose the center have been rewarded with impressive concessions from the center. The republic of Sakha/Yakutia, which produces all of Russia's diamonds, negotiated a deal with Moscow by which it is allowed to keep all the taxes it collects (Lepingwell et al. 1994:8) and can dispose independently of 11.5% of its gold and 20% of its diamonds (Poelzer 1995:211) and a percentage of other minerals (*Economist* 1996).

Tatarstan signed a bilateral power sharing agreement with the Russian Federation in February 1994 (Lepingwell et al. 1994:9). The secret agreement between Tatarstan and Moscow allows it to transfer only 10% of the tax revenue to the central government compared to what Nizhy Novgorod had to pay each year (Economist 1995), and gives the Republic control over handsome oil revenues (Economist 1996) and the right to conduct its own "foreign economic policy" (*Economist* 1997), and grants both Tatarstan and Moscow sovereignty (Lepingwell et al. 1994:9; *Economist* 1996).

By May 1996, eight more republics signed such treaties (Hahn 1997:261). Ingushetia, next to war-ravaged Chechnya, negotiated a special tax status (*Economist* 1996).

Chechnya declared itself no longer part of the Russian Federation in November 1991, and has withheld taxes from Moscow since 1991. Chechnya has broken away almost completely, but at such cost few are likely to follow its example (*Economist* 1997).

Bilateral treaties have been negotiated with oblasts and krais (Hahn 1997:261) and government officials expect to conclude similar agreements with all subnational regions (Clarke and Graham 1995; Hahn 1997:261). The original intention was not to enter into treaties with oblasts (Stoner-Weiss 1997:85). Separatism in the oblasts and krais arose as a defense against the plunder of their natural resources by the center (*ibid.*). Fear that ethnic Russians at the oblast level would declare sovereignty against Moscow, supported by press articles finding parallels between these tensions and the dissolution of the Soviet Union led Moscow to negotiate with oblasts and let them retain some control over their economic resources (*ibid.*:86).

The center's practice of negotiating separate bi-lateral agreements with subnational units appears to preclude cooperation and solidarity between subnational governments. Divide and conquer, which has been a classical policy for empires, is now practiced by Russia. While the lack of cohesiveness among subnational units may preclude a united front against the center, bilateral agreements may have unintended consequences. Granting extra powers to some regions and not others, creates the potential for uneven economic and political development across the Russian Federation (Stoner-Weiss 1997:88), which may make holding the federation together more difficult in the long run. While bilateral agreements may buy time for the central government and temporarily diffuse opposition in the periphery, this strategy may weaken the long-term political and fiscal strength of the center (Treisman 1996b:329–330).

C. Asymmetry Over Time

The practice of the center to make concessions to the periphery to gain support when it is weak and to centralize when the center is strong has continued into the Yeltsin administration. The Yeltsin administration can be divided into two periods: a First Republic, which existed from the multi-candidate elections in March 1990 until Yeltsin dissolved the Russian Parliament in October 1993, and a Second Republic, which began after the dissolution of Parliament until the present (Sharlet 1993:316; Stoner-Weiss 1997:5). The First Republic was often characterized by weakness, as the government of the Russian Federation had to enlist the support of the periphery in order to establish autonomy from the Soviet Union and fend off attempts from hardliners to return to earlier arrangements. The Second Republic was more often characterized by greater strength in the center, after Yeltsin had weathered the challenges to his government and began institutionalizing more permanent center-periphery relationships.

1.   First Republic: Devolve When Weak

Yeltsin made concessions to the periphery when he was involved in a power struggle and needed support of the periphery. In his 1990 contest with Gorbachev for the support of local and regional elites, Yeltsin encouraged the regional elites to "take as much sovereignty as you can swallow" (Poelzer 1995:208; *Economist* 1995; Hahn 1997:252). Yeltsin supported the autonomist demands of Russia's ethnic regions, and encouraged them to declare themselves sovereign entities with greater political powers (Smith 1995:38). Yeltsin thus strengthened his own power base as President of Russia at the expense of Gorbachev's position as President of the Soviet Union. It would be a mistake to view devolution of power from Moscow simply as a collapse of central authority; various factions jockeyed for power and turned to regional and local elites for support (Poelzer 1995:208). The ethnic-regions boycotted Gorbachev's last-minute referendum in 1991 to keep the Soviet Union together, signaling their support for Yeltsin and the establishment of an independent Russia (Smith 1995:38).

The oblasts also gained from the devolution of power during the first Russian Republic. In 1990, the first session of the Russian Supreme Soviet elected a constitutional commission to draft a constitution revising the distribution of powers between the center and periphery. The resulting document recognized the autonomous republics as signatories to a federation treaty, but treated oblasts as branch representatives of the center (Stoner-Weiss 1997:83). The commission also proposed consolidating oblasts into a smaller number of "lands" for ease of administration, an idea which aroused strong opposition from the oblasts and was quietly abandoned (*ibid.*:84).

Three pieces of Russian Republic legislation symbolize devolution of power to the regions: the Law on Local Self-Government of 1991; the Federation Treaty of March 1992 (Poelzer 1995:208; Sharlet 1993:321); and the March 1992 Law on Oblast and Krai Soviets and Oblast and Krai Administrations (Stoner-Weiss 1997:79).

The Law on Local Self-Government provided for autonomously constituted local governments, which was a serious Soviet-era decentralization of power. Direct, contested elections for presidents in the 21 autonomous republics and governors of the 49 oblasts gave them independence they never had when they were appointed (*Economist* 1996, 1997). The center was no longer able to appoint republican presidents and provincial governors, and lost leverage over local officials and weakened the vertical hierarchy (Hahn 1997:259). In contrast to Russia, in China, for example, the center still appoints 4000 top officials, including all top posts in the regions and major cities, assuring that orders form the center are obeyed (Slider 1997:446). Reforms in the former Soviet Union radically weakened authority links within the hierarchies, while the reforms in China did not (Solnick 1995:210).

After the fall of the Soviet Union, the oblast soviets (or legislatures) elected in 1990 remained in power. The subnational governments became a natural refuge for former party officials, and a number of politicians opposed to Yeltsin's reforms were elected as provincial governors (Slider 1997:447) where they can use their democratic legitimacy and executive powers to resist Yeltsin's economic reforms (Slider 1997:448).

Therefore, while Russian government reformers have operated on the Soviet-era assumption that if a policy was adopted at the center, it would be implemented nationally, republic presidents and provincial governors have substantial ability to resist the policies of the center. Lack of central control over regional officials has left de facto authority to the regions (Slider 1997:449). While leaders in some areas, such as Nizhi-Novgorod, Novgorod, Samara, and St. Petersburg determined that market reforms were in their best interest and pursued them vigorously, other regional figures fear market reforms will undermine their authority and have resisted them (Bater 1996:87; Slider 1997:450).

The second piece of Russian legislation decentralizing power to the regions is the Federal Treaty of March 1992, which acknowledged the republics, krais, oblasts, and okrugs as constituent members of the Russian Federation and specified the powers each of them possessed (Poelzer 1995:208). Only two of the 21 republics—Tatarstan and Chechnya (Sharlet 1993:321; Smith 1995:38; Lepingwell et al. 1994:7–8)—refused to sign the treaty. As the Russian Constitution was being prepared, the balance of power seemed to shift further toward the periphery as Yeltsin and Parliament were locked in a power struggle (Sharlet 1993:322). While neither side wanted to offend the periphery (Sharlet 1993:322, 329), both feared the new federation was breaking up. Several republics drafted constitutions declared some sort of sovereignty (Clarke and Graham 1995). The federation treaty was an attempt to coopt centrifugal forces and define center-periphery relationships (Sharlet 1993:321).

A third piece of legislation, although not written to decentralize power, had a decentralizing effect. In March 1992, the Law on Oblast and Krai Soviets and Oblast and Krai Administrations further undermined the power of the center. Article 46 allowed oblast soviets to remove governors from office, and five oblasts removed the governors Yeltsin had appointed and scheduled new elections for 1993 (Stoner-Weiss 1997:79). When these 1993 elections were held, Yeltsin's candidates were beaten in a majority of oblasts. Yeltsin suspended further gubanatorial elections (Hahn 1997:253). Since many of the provincial soviets were so combative with the center, Yeltsin later suspended local soviets when he dissolved parliament.

2. Second Republic: Centralize When Strong

The First Russian Republic ended with the dissolution of parliament (Stoner-Weiss 1997:5). The regional soviets, a bastion of the conservatives, were also disbanded. Center-periphery relations began to change to reflect the new strength of the center. In December 1993, Yeltsin took advantage of his added power after storming the Russian Parliament to eliminate the Federation Treaty and the sovereignty clause from the Constitution (Clark and Graham 1995; Slider 1997:456). Representatives of the center had initially promised that the Federation Treaty would become part of the New Russian Constitution (Sharlet 1993:322; Clark and Graham 1995; Slider 1997:456). While the 1992 Federal Treaty granted ownership of natural resources to republics, the 1993 Constitution is mute on the question. The right to secede, which some claim was in the original Federation Treaty, was omitted from the Constitution (Smith 1995:38).

The 1993 Federal Constitution watered down some of the gains of the regions. The Constitution recognizes important differences between republics and regions. For example, only republics have the right to establish constitutions, and to establish an official language in addition to Russian (Poelzer 1995:209). The 1993 Constitution contains no article enumerating the responsibilities of the oblasts, nor are there mechanisms to enforce federal compliance (Stoner-Weiss 1997:87). While proclaiming Russia a federation, the constitution includes principles pertaining to a unitary state based on principles from the Constitution of the French Fifth Republic (Sharlet 1993:314; Stoner-Weiss 1997:299) to which constituent parts of the Russian Federation have already objected (Lepingwell et al. 1994:3). The December 1993 Constitution placed broad powers in the President and the executive, and weak powers to the legislature, which has led to a concern by many, both inside and outside Russia, about authoritarian rule (Lepingwell et al. 1994:3).

Some of the actions of the President also show a revitalized center taking authority back. In the wake of the 1991 coup, Yeltsin initially obtained the right to suspend elections of provincial governors for one year, and appoint them himself (Hahn 1997:252). In 1993, eight regions insisted on electing governors, with opposition candidates winning seven of those elections (Stoner-

Weiss 1997:78). Yeltsin did not permit additional gubernatorial elections until 1995. In a decree published in October 1994, Yeltsin reaffirmed his right to nominate and dismiss governors, and declared no elections of governors would take place without his permission (Hahn 1997:253). The appointment of governors is crucial as the evolution of regional government is toward virtually unlimited rule by regional governors. After the December 1993 Constitution, local legislative deputies stand for elections to relatively powerless local legislatures. Yeltsin allowed elections mostly, but not exclusively, in regions where the incumbents were likely to win. In the gubernatorial elections in 1995, Yeltsin's preferred candidates won in 10 of 13 races (Stoner-Weiss 1997:78). The rest of the governors were finally elected in regional elections in 1996 (Hahn 1997:253; Stoner-Weiss 1997:78). Republics also criticize Moscow for trying to 'dictate from the center' (Smith 1995:38). Center-building strategies to contain ethnocentrism are emerging, such as Yeltsin's December 1994 presidential decree to use force over the wayward autonomous republic of Chechnya (Smith 1995:40; Bater 1996:338) and arming local pro-federal organizations against secessionist movements in the North Caucasus (Smith 1995:40).

D. Overview of Regional Relations in Yeltsin's Russia

In the First Russian Republic, Yeltsin was locked in a series or power struggles, this required him to grant concessions to the periphery to gain support in the Second Russian Republic, Yeltsin used his political strength after he successfully dissolved parliament to bring power back to the center. Yet there have been some institution-building structural changes which may withstand attempts at recentralization. During the two Russian Republics, regional governments have been transformed from bodies that executed the center's will to representative bodies who implement their own policies, often to the consternation of the center. The popular election of regional governments, first initiated by Gorbachev, changed the political reference point from pleasing Moscow to pleasing local constituents (*ibid.*:192).

IX. CONCLUSION

Russia, which historically lacked strong institutions, has haphazard and fluid center-periphery relationships. In this uncertain environment, when the existence of the regime was threatened, the center has compensated, by granting concessions to the periphery to gain the support of the governed. Whenever the center is strong and has the opportunity, the center has attempted to reduce the difficulty of governing in an uncertain environment by centralizing as much power as possible in the center.

> Given the number of law-enforcement agencies, institutions of government and state employees . . . only one reason could explain the anarchy, the conveyor belt system of government was not working. . . . To put it bluntly, somebody had to be the boss in the country.
>
> (Yeltsin 1994:6)

To the degree Russia maintains weak institutions, the ebb and flow of power to and from the center will continue.

REFERENCES

Aslund, A. (1995). *How Russia Became a Market Economy.* Washington: Brookings Institution.
Bater, J.H. (1996). *Russia and the Post-Soviet Scene: A Geographical Perspective.* London: Arnold.

Clark, S.L., and Graham, D.R. (1995). The Russian Federation's fight for survival. *Orbis 39* (3), 329–352.

Clendenin, D.B. (1992). *From the Coup to the Commonwealth: An Inside Look at Life in Contemporary Russia.* Grand Rapids, MI: Baker Book House.

Cox, T. (1996). *From Perestroika to Privatization: Politics of Property Change in Russia.* Aldershot, England: Avebury.

Desai, P. (1989). *Perestroika in Perspective.* Princeton, NJ: Princeton University Press.

Dunlop, J.B. (1983). *The Faces of Contemporary Russian Nationalism.* Princeton, NJ: Princeton University Press.

Economist. (1995). Peripheral power: Russia's regions. *334* (7907), 54–56.

Economist. (1996). Russia's riddle of the regions. *338* (7958), 47–48.

Economist. (1997). The wounded bear. *344*(8025), 15–17; Devolution can be salvation. *344*(8035), 53–55.

Hahn, J.W. (1997). Regional elections and political stability in Russia. *Post Soviet Geography and Economics 38*(5), 251–263.

Hyams, N. (1970). Russian nationalism. In G. Schopflin (ed.), *The Soviet Union and Eastern Europe.* New York: Prager.

Kaiser, R.J. (1995). Prospects for the disintegration of the Russian Federation. *Post Soviet Geography 36*(7), 426–435.

Keep, J. (1970). Russia and the Soviet Union to 1956. In G. Schopflin (ed.), *The Soviet Union and Eastern Europe.* New York: Praeger.

Kirkpatrick, J.J. (1992). After Communism. *Problems of Communism*, January-April.

Lepingwell, J.W.R., Rahr, A., Teague, E., and Tolz., V. (1994). Russia: a troubled future. *Radio Free Europe/Radio Liberty Research Report 3*(24), 1–12.

McCrea, B.P., Plano, J.C., and Klein, G. (1984). *The Soviet and East European Political Dictionary.* Santa Barbara: Clio Press.

Medish, V. (1980). The special status of the RSFSR. In *Ethic Russia in the USSR: The Dilemma of Dominance.* New York: Pergamon Press.

Medish, V. (1985). *The Soviet Union.* Englewood Cliffs, NJ: Prentice Hall.

Nahaylo, B., and Swoboda, V. (1989). *Soviet Disunion: A History of the Nationalities Problem.* New York: Free Press.

Poelzer, G. (1995). Devolution, constitutional development and the Russian north. *Post Soviet Geography 36*(4), 204–214.

Rywkin, M. (1980). The Russia-wide Federated Socialist Republic (RSFSR): privileged or underprivileged? In E. Allworth (ed.), *Ethnic Russia in the USSR: The Dilemma of Dominance.* New York: Pergamon Press.

Sharlet, R. (1993). Russian constitutional crisis: law and politics under Yeltsin. *Post Soviet Affairs 9*(4), 314–336.

Shaw, D.J.B. (1995). Ethnic relations and federalism in the Soviet era. In D.J.B. Shaw (ed.), *The Post Soviet Republics: A Systematic Geography.* London: Longman.

Slider, D. (1997). Russia's market distorting federalism. *Post Soviet Geography and Economics 38*(8), 455–460.

Solnick, S.L. (1996). The breakdown of hierarchies in the Soviet Union and China: a neoinstitutional perspective. *World Politics 48*(2), 209–239.

Smith, G. (1995). Ethnic relations in the new states. In D.J.B. Shaw (ed.), *The Post Soviet Republics: A Systematic Geography*, London: Longman.

Stoner-Weiss, K. (1997). *Local Heros: The Political Economy of Russian Regional Governance.* Princeton, NJ: Princeton University Press.

Treisman, D. (1996a). Moscow's struggle to control regions through taxation. *Transition 2*(19), 145–149.

Treisman, D. (1996b). The politics of intergovernmental transfers in post Soviet Russia. *British Journal of Political Science 26*, 299–335.

Walsh, W.B. (1958). *Russia and the Soviet Union: A Modern History.* Ann Arbor: University of Michigan Press.

Yeltsin, B. (1994). *The Struggle for Russia.* New York: Random House.

Zwass, A. (1995). *From Failed Communism to Underdeveloped Capitalism: Transformation of Eastern Europe, the Post-Soviet Union and China.* Armonk, NY: M.E. Sharpe.

22

Devolution or Dissolution

Decentralization in the Former Soviet Union, Czechoslovakia, Yugoslavia, and the Russian Federation

Paul C. Trogen   *Department of Economics, Finance, and Urban Studies, East Tennessee State University, Johnson City, Tennessee*

I. INTRODUCTION

The federations of Eastern Europe—the Soviet Union, Czechoslovakia, and Yugoslavia—have dissolved into their constituent republics. The Russian Federation, which also retains a federal structure, is confronted by the same centrifugal forces which led to the demise of these federal systems. While a chapter cannot hope to explore all of the reasons for the dissolution of the East European federal systems, it can identify the reasons most often emphasized as influential. Those reasons are strikingly similar for all of the East European federal systems. Ethnic and religious differences evolved first into a sense of separate identity and then into nationalism. Economic hardship fueled resentment against other ethnic groups and against the central authorities. Economic differences generated resentment between regions: both among donor regions, which resented having to subsidize federal transfers to less developed regions, and among recipient regions, who blamed the central authorities for their relative deprivation. Stalemates at the federal level eventually prevented the center from effectively governing and precipitated the dissolution of all three previous federal systems.

II. HISTORICAL BACKGROUND

A. From Multiethnic Empires to Multiethnic States

The multinational federations of the Soviet Union, Czechoslovakia, and Yugoslavia were uneasy unions from their very beginnings. Each of them developed from the territory left by multinational empires, including the Romanov, Habsburg, and Ottoman empires. Within those multiethnic empires, settlement patterns included ethnic enclaves scattered throughout the empire, making it impossible to later divide these empires into separate nations along ethnic frontiers (Brubaker 1996:35). Although both Lenin and Woodrow Wilson proposed national self-determination as part of their programs for the postwar order, national self-determination would elude the people of the Soviet Union, Czechoslovakia, and Yugoslavia.

B. Broken Promises or Self-Determination

Both Lenin and Wilson promised national self-determination for national minorities. Lenin's call for national self-determination was more appealing to subordinate nationalities than the white slogan "One indivisible Russia" (Seton-Watson 1986:24) and helped secure the support of non-Russian nationalities during the Russian civil war (Hyams 1970:193; Brubaker 1996:32). Wilson included national self determination as one of his fourteen Points, and the Western powers promised Hapsburg minorities self-determination (Pearson 1983:135).

After the Revolution of March 1917, the Russian empire ceased to function as a unitary state and many nationalities seized the opportunity to declare independence (Yeltsin 1994:112). Thirteen states emerged in the former territory of the Russian empire (Shaw 1995:27). The Red Army occupied as many of these countries as possible and declared them Soviet republics and joined them to the Russian Soviet Federative Socialist Republic (RSFSR) by treaty (Medish 1980:189; McCrea 1984:144). Lenin was still reluctant to violate the national sensitivities of the non-Russians, and therefore created a federation of nominally equal republics (Hyams 1970:193; Medish 1980:189; Shaw 1995:27–28; Nahaylo and Swoboda 1989:352). The principle "national in form, socialist in content" allowed the preservation of ethnic languages and culture as long as political uniformity was maintained (McCrea et al. 1984:143; Desai 1985:38; Shaw 1995:27–28). The Soviet model of "national in form, socialist in content" came closer to realizing the promises of national self-determination than did the unitary states in interwar Czechoslovakia and Yugoslavia. This principle would later be applied in postwar Czechoslovakia and Yugoslavia.

The Pittsburgh Agreement of 1918 promised Slovakia a separate Diet and autonomy within a federal Czechoslovakia (Ulc 1996:332–333; Pearson 1983:153). The provisional Czechoslovakian government instead established a unitary system, which was codified into the constitution (Cox and Frankland 1995:75). Slovaks felt the Czechs were imposing colonial rule over them (Pearson 1983:153), and Sudetan Germans who protested the lack of self-determination were dispersed with bayonets and gunfire (Ryback 1996:166–167). For the majority of Czechoslovaks, the fall of the Hapsburg Empire merely replaced one foreign master with another.

National minorities also fared poorly in interwar Yugoslavia. Serbia, the largest nation of what would become Yugoslavia, became fully independent of the Ottoman Empire in 1879 (Brubaker 1996:73). Additional Serbs lived in the Hapsburg Empire and, after its demise, Serbia acquired parts of that empire. Although Croats and Slovenes believed they were entering a federation of equals (Staar 1988:221), the Serbs viewed the entire country as their own (Brubaker 1996:73) and extended Serbian administration over the newly acquired territories (Gotovska-Popova 1993:175). Serbian King Alexandar consolidated Serbian control by allowing Serbs to dominate the army, police, and courts (Emadi 1993:234–235), making interwar Yugoslavia a unitary state (Pearson 1983:156).

C. Postwar East European Federalism: Federal in Form, Unitary in Practice

The regimes established in Czechoslovakia and Yugoslavia after World War II were careful not to repeat the errors of their unitary interwar predecessors and followed the Soviet principle "national in form, socialist in content." The postwar federations thereby recognized the nationalities within their borders as nations, while maintaining unity through Communist Party discipline.

In Czechoslovakia, Communists were the leading party in postwar elections, aided by an anti-Western backlash after the betrayal of Czechoslovakia in Munich in 1938. The 1948 Constitution created a separate executive board called Slovak National Council and autonomy for Slovakia (Staar 1988:66). The asymmetrical federation, with a Communist Party of Slovakia within the Communist Party of Czechoslovakia and separate Slovak administrative structures within Czechoslovakia, recognized the status of Slovakia while centralizing power and pursuing an "integrationist strategy" (Cox and Frankland 1995:77). Czechs assumed leadership at the federal level.

In Yugoslavia, in the autumn of 1943, Tito announced the establishment of a de facto government, and decided the state should be built on a federalist system (Staar 1988:223). The 1946 Constitution recognized the six ethnic republics as separate nations, although they were subordinated in the most important matters to the federal government (Staar 1988:233). At the beginning, power was extremely centralized and expressions of national interests were restricted (Basom 1995:513–514). Later, republican party organizations were given more of the lead in policy making, subject to Tito's veto (Hodson et al. 1994:1539).

By 1948, all three East European federations had adopted similar structures which were federal in form but unitary in content. Later, each federation progressed through a functioning federalism and later to dissolution.

D. Attempts to Create Functioning Federalism

"National in form, socialist in content" recognized aspirations of national minorities without giving them real power. Nevertheless, the formal recognition of these national states within these Eastern European federations kept national identity alive and created national structures. These national governments became important after the Communist Party's hold on power began to weaken.

In the Soviet Union, Gorbachev introduced glasnost and perestroika in order to revitalize the Soviet system. The Soviet Union was locked in an arms race with the United States although GNP was about one-quarter the size of its adversary. Gorbachev's reforms were driven by a floundering economy and the fear that without reforms, the Soviet Union would degenerate into a third world country and cease to be a super power (Desai 1989:7; Aslund 1995:27). Gorbachev hoped to revitalize socialism by restoring the soviets, which were originally participatory grass roots organizations, as actual governing institutions, as he believed was Lenin's original vision for soviets (Stoner-Weiss 1997:68).

Glasnost invited the union republics to pluralistic elections, which unintentionally gave nationalist movements a way to articulate decades of pent-up grievances (Smith 1995:35; Bater 1996:52). From December 1989 to March 1990, the union republics held contested parliamentary elections, which replaced local party organs, which acted as prefects for the center, with representative legislatures which owed their legitimacy to the electorate in the regions (Stoner-Weiss 1997:4). Gorbachev proposed a restructuring of the Soviet Federation along the Leninist idea of equal states (Smith 1995:35).

A number of republics, however, began openly questioning the merits of remaining in the Soviet Union. By the end of 1990, five union republics (Estonia, Latvia, Lithuania, Georgia, and Armenia) had declared themselves independent, and 10 had issued declarations of sovereignty, which implied autonomy. A war of laws over jurisdiction broke out that lasted until the Soviet Union dissolved in December 1991 (Aslund 1995:35). Although Gorbachev initiated a "revolution from above," it soon became a revolution from below, with regions dictating its nature and tempo (Smith 1995:35; Bater 1996).

Czechoslovakia took a step backward before taking two steps forward to create a functioning federalism. The 1960 Czechoslovak Constitution removed Slovak autonomy, abolished the Slovak National Council, and aroused much resentment in Slovakia. This contributed to the overthrow of the Stalinist Antonin Navotny on January 5, 1968, and establishment of a federation on January 1, 1969 (Staar 1988:66; Cox and Frankland 1995:79). Navotny was replaced by Alexandar Dubcek, the first Slovak to lead the country (Staar 1988:66). A real federal system was introduced, with a symmetrical system with separate parliaments, government organs, and administration for both the Czech Socialist Republic and the Slovak Socialist Republic (McCrea 1984:145; Cox and Frankland 1995:80). Republic governments exercised control over education and culture, the Federal government retained control over foreign policy, defense and natural resources, and joint control was established for police and economic planning (Staar 1988:61). Alexandar Dubcek's efforts to create federalism continued despite the Warsaw Pact invasion in 1968, until he was replaced by another Slovak, Gustav Husak, on April 17, 1969. In 1970, when Husak consolidated his position, he took steps to recentralize authority, including creating federal veto power over laws passed by the republican governments, yet he retained the institutions of federalism as a "safety valve" (Cox and Frankland 1995:81).

In Yugoslavia, Tito was vigilant against nationalist movements outside the control of the party (Hodson et al. 1994:1538) but developed no alternative structures, outside of himself, for mediating national interests. After Tito's death in 1980, ethnic unrest reemerged. A 23-member collective leadership of the party was established, and the presidency of the central committee and the Republic rotated annually among the representatives of each republic (Emadi 1993:239).

III.   FACTORS LEADING TO DISSOLUTION

Similar causes are emphasized in the literature for the dissolution of all three of Eastern Europe's federal systems: the Soviet Union, Czechoslovakia, and Yugoslavia (Table 1). The first set of factors is related to nationality. Language often unites a nation, whereas these three federations were divided by multiple languages. Religion is also a common national unifier, but these federations were divided by multiple religious traditions. National populations often share common demographics, but these federations had growing and declining ethnic groups and related social instability. Nations usually have one national government; these federations each have multiple national governments for their multiple nationalities.

The second set of factors appear to have mobilized ethnic groups to pursue independence. In each case, economic adversity generated resentment against the center or other ethnic groups. Economic disparity led disadvantaged ethnic groups to blame the center for their relative deprivation and entertain the idea of pursuing independence. Economic disparity also led prosperous areas to resent transfers to less developed regions, and perceive that they too would be better off pursuing independence. And finally, political stalemates neutralized the central government and allowed the ethnic republics to declare independence.

A.   Ethnolinguistic Differences

The Soviet Union, Czechoslovakia, and Yugoslavia were multiethic states. At the time of dissolution, only half of the USSR's 290 million people were Russian. The other half comprised 120 ethnolinguistic groups (Clendenin 1992:22). Yugoslavia had five nationalities and four languages (Staar 1988:221). Czechoslovakia had Czechs, Slovaks, and Hungarians, each with their own language. Thus all three dissolving federal systems were divided by ethnicity and language.

B.   Religion

Religious distinctiveness between ethnic minorities and the dominant ethnic group can help prevent assimilation and preserve ethnic identity. When political manifestations of a nation are lost,

Table 1 Major Factors Contributing to Dissolution of East European Federal Systems

Contributing factors	Soviet Union	Czechoslovakia	Yugoslavia	Russian Federation
Ethnic subdivisions	15 ethnic union republics	2 ethnic republics	6 ethnic republics	21 ethnic republics
Higher birth rate of subordinate nationalities	Declining Russian and growing Islamic population	Slovak population grows faster than Czech population	Declining Serb and growing Albanian population	Declining Russian and growing Islamic population
Religious and cultural cleavages	Mostly Orthodox, with Islamic, Catholic, and Protestant Republics	Slovakia is Catholic; Czech Republic also has Hussites and is more secularized	Catholic, Orthodox, and Islamic republics and provinces	Mostly Orthodox, with Islamic and Buddhist republics
Economic frustration	Economic stagnation under Brezhnev and Gorbachev	Depressed Slovak arms industry after end of cold war	Declining living standards in late 1980s	Displaced and unpaid workers, falling living standards
Economic disparity	Russia and Ukraine subsidized central Asian republics	Czech Republic subsidized Slovakia	Slovenia and Croatia subsidized other republics	10 oblasts with 25% of people pay 57% of tax, subsidize others
Federal stalemate causes inability to govern	Coup suspends Communist Party and state organs	Slovaks block economic and Constitutional reform	Serbs and Allies block rotation of president, and economic reform	Regions usurp power, withhold taxes, and the Federation is bankrupt

the church often serves as the last bastion of national identity (Pearson 1983:22). Islam has been especially effective in preventing assimilation of Islamic minorities into the predominantly Orthodox populations of Russia and Yugoslavia.

In the Soviet Union, religious minorities helped preserve national identity. Islam created a "cultural bulwark" against assimilation (Wimbush 1986:219). making Muslims the least Russified community in the USSR (Bennigsen 1986:142). Islam is more than a religion, it is "a way of life, a culture, and . . . the basis for national consciousness" (Bennigsen 1986:141). Imperial Russia's initial attempts to convert Muslims to orthodoxy were a dismal failure, which only increased nationalism, and were abandoned (Seton-Watson 1986:22). The Romanovs decided to leave the existing social hierarchy intact when they expanded into Central Asia and did not interfere with Muslim cultural life (*ibid.*). The futility of trying to eliminate Islam resulted in a hands off policy which was continued into the Soviet era.

Yugoslavia's three religions played a major role in Yugoslavia's breakup (Mojzes 1994:116–117). Religion bitterly divides the Catholic Croats and Orthodox Serbs, even though they are of the same race and have the same language (Pearson 1983:22). The identity of Bosnia, a scene of much ethnic conflict, was based on Islam rather than race (*ibid.*). The Kosovo conflict between the Orthodox Serbs and Islam dates back to 1389, when Ottoman troops defeated the Serbian army in Kosovo and introduced Islam to the region.

The present-day Russian Federation is predominantly Orthodox, with Islamic areas in the South and Buddhist areas in the East. Islam is a contributing factor in the separatist tendencies in republics within the Russian Federation, including Chechnya, Dagestan, Northern Ossetia, and Ingushetia (Bryzko 1999:28–29). While the Islamic population in the Russian Federation is smaller compared to that in the former Soviet Union, the remaining Muslim areas have become more volatile than had been the Muslim union republics.

C.   Differential Birth Rates

Paul Johnson (1983:711), in his history of modern times, remarked, "One of the lessons of the twentieth century is that high birth rates in subject peoples is the mortal enemy of colonialism." This principle can also be applied to multinational states. Increasing population can increase the legitimacy of the claims of national minorities (Pearson 1983:16). At the same time, deteriorating demographic position of the dominant political group can make the it feel threatened and reawaken its own nationalism.

In the twilight of the Soviet Union, the Soviets were concerned about the projected depopulation of northern ethnic groups (Bernstam 1986:314). Russians no longer reproduced themselves, and the feeling of demographic decline has spurred a resurgence in Russian Nationalism (Harmstone 1986:249). At the end of the Soviet Union, Russians were less than half of the population and declining, while the population of Central Asia was growing rapidly. Only the break up of the Soviet Union prevented Russians, once the dominant ethnic group, from becoming a minority group.

Little attention has been focused on Czech and Slovak population growth rates. Evidence suggests interwar Czechoslovakia was 48% Czech, 23% German, 16% Slovak, and 5% Hungarian (Pearson 1983:151–152) for a 3-to-1 ratio between Czechs and Slovaks. The Germans were deported after World War II. By 1987, the population was 64.3% Czech, 30.5% Slovak, and 3.8% Hungarian, for about a 2-to-1 ratio between Czechs and Slovaks (Staar 1988:67).

The dominant ethnic group in Yugoslavia is also declining demographically, causing a resurgence of nationalism. Serbs, who were the dominant ethnic group in Yugoslavia, have a declining population and are not reproducing themselves (Mojzes 1994:7). In contrast, the Albanians in Kosovo had the highest birth rate in Europe (Pearson 1983:158; Mojzes 1994:7). In 1929, Kosovo was 61% Serbian: in 1998 that is down to 10%, in part due to the extraordinarily high

Albanian birth rate (Binder 1998:30). This demographic shift strengthens the pressure for some sort of Kosovar autonomy.

Russia faces the same demographic decline as Serbia. Russians are no longer reproducing themselves and its population is shrinking (Society 1998:5). The birth rate for Muslims, on the other hand, is rising (Kobishchenov 1995:1–3). The feeling of demographic and genetic decline is a factor in the reawakening of Russian nationalism (Harmstone 1986:249). At this rate, Russians will again decline from their current 80% of the Russian Federation population to only 50% by 2050 (Kobishchenov 1995:1–3).

D. Ethnic Subdivisions

Ethnic subdivisions, which were first conceived by Lenin, contributed to the dissolution of all three East European federal systems. Lenin and Stalin created the Soviet model for multinational federations when it created ethnically designated republics. The Soviet Union deliberately created 15 national republics and then limited the domain over which they were autonomous (Brubaker 1996:46) to language and culture. Ethnic republics eventually became an official recognition of ethnic identity and nationhood (Harmstone 1986:239). Yugoslavia and Czechoslovakia later borrowed this federal structure of ethnic republics, subordinated to the party. The significance of these republican governments increased dramatically by the end of the 1980s, when the Communist Party lost its hold on power.

Republic status is an important predictor of independence. Of the 15 union republics in the Soviet Union, all became independent. No subdivision that was not a union republic has gained independence.[1] Four of the six constituent republics of the former Yugoslavia have become independent, and no state that was not a republic has gained independence.[2] Both of the constituent republics of Czechoslovakia became independent, but its Hungarian minority, without a republic, has not gained independence.

The dissolution of the Soviet Union was primarily a result of a struggle between the center and the republics. The main players were Gorbachev, representing the center, and Boris Yeltsin, who championed the rights of the union republics against that center. The failed coup in 1991 may have been a reaction by communist hard-liners on the eve of a scheduled signing of a new Union Treaty, which would have given the ethnic republics more autonomy (Yeltsin 1994:38). After the failed coup, the government bodies of the Soviet Union were in suspension and the union republics became the de facto governments (Yeltsin 1994:105). The union republics, while lacking real autonomy during the Soviet era, had formally operated as nations within their respective borders. They became a ready alternative to the discredited center. After the coup, Gorbachev attempted to recreate a looser version of the Soviet Union. The union republics sided with Yeltsin in this center-periphery struggle, and withheld their support from Gorbachev's efforts to resurrect the Soviet Union. The Soviet Union dissolved.

The dissolution of Czechoslovakia was also due, in part, to a center-periphery struggle with one of its two republics. The creation of a true federation in 1969 created a platform for a center-periphery struggle, with not only a federal government, but also a president and national legislature for both the Czech and Slovak republics. This made conflict between the Slovak national government and the federal government likely. There are major differences between the Czechs and Slovaks. Slovaks distrusted the federation, which the Communists had used as a "facade" for centralized power (Innes 1997:393), where the Czechs identified with it. The Czechs were the economic powerhouse of the Austrian half of the Austro-Hungarian empire, whereas Slovakia was an agricultural hinterland of the Hungarian half of the same empire. Political conflict was reinforced by conflicting economic interests. Slovakia inherited large Soviet-style factories, and wanted to maintain state control over the economy (Svec 1992:379–380). The federal government, however, was intent upon market reforms, which were Czech reforms designed for the Czech economy

(Innes 1997:293). Furthermore, the International Monetary Fund (IMF) tends to impose conditions on aid which more closely resembles Hoover's response to the great depression than the New Deal (*Progressive* 1998:9–10). Slovak Prime Minister Vladimir Meciar blamed Prague's economic "shock therapy" for Slovakia's economic problems (Cox and Frankland 1995:84). On July 17, 1992, Slovakia declared autonomy and the federal government was dissolved on January 1, 1993 (Cox and Frankland 1995:86).

In Yugoslavia, Tito created a federal system with six national republics, four of which have become independent states. Tito's centralized control from Belgrade kept historic ethnic hatreds suppressed during his lifetime (Ornstein and Courson 1992:21). In Yugoslavia, part of the role of republic officials was to represent the interests of their national group to the center. This created many advocates for the republics, but Tito, as "President for life," developed no alternative institutions, outside of himself, to reconcile the competing interests of republics after he was gone. After Tito's death in 1980, the federal government was unable to mediate conflict among the republics. Republican governments, which had little real autonomy under Tito, assumed more importance after his death. When the Communist Party collapsed in 1990, the country fell apart (Ornstein and Courson 1992:22). Serbian President Slobodan Milosovic tried to renegotiate the federal arrangement and reassert Serbian pre-Tito dominance over the other republics (Talbott 1992:60). This hastened the drive for independence among the other republics. When the Serb dominated Yugoslav army was insufficient to prevent the succession of Slovenia, each of the republics, except for Serbia and Montenegro, declared independence.

Russia has replicated many of the mistakes of the Soviet federal structure. After the union republics succeeded from the Soviet Union, the 21 ethnically designated autonomous republics assumed the status of republics in the new federation. Yeltsin had to court the republics to get them to sign the Union Treaty, which was necessary to prevent a dissolution of the Russian Federation (Sharlet 1994:119). The autonomous republics, which had no autonomy or Constitutional guarantees under the Soviet system, negotiated a new favored status within the new federation. They now contribute less to the federal treasury than the oblasts (provinces), receive a disproportionate share of the revenue, and have control over their natural resources (Clarke and Graham 1995; Poelzer 1995:221).

E. Economic Frustration

Centrally planned economies suffered from low productivity and poor quality (Djilas 1986:376). Economic stagnation hit the Soviet Union during the Brezhnev era, Yugoslavia in the late 1980s, and Slovakia at the end of the cold war. Economic conditions are likely to worsen as newly independent nations find their former markets now beyond their borders.

In the Soviet Union, Gorbachev inherited a stagnant economy, and initiated glasnost and perestroika in the hopes they would stimulate productivity. Instead, economic performance declined four years in a row (Zwass 1995:21) into a deep recession (Zwass 1995:70; Cox 1996:100). In the non-Russian republics, frustration levels were vested with ethnic meaning (Smith 1995:35) and many republics wanted independence (Zwass 1995:19).

Slovakia also suffered under economic adversity. The end of the cold war was especially hard on Slovakia. In the 1980s, Czechoslovakia was had the highest per-capita arms exports of any nation in the world (Svec 1992:376). For strategic reasons, most of the armament industry was built in Slovakia (Ulc 1996:337–338). When the cold war ended, this asset became a liability (Svec 1992:376). Poor performance of Soviet-type tanks in the Gulf War reduced demand for Slovakian exports (Ulc 1996:337–338). Unemployment in Slovakia climbed to 12% (Svec 1992:379; Ulc 1996:339). Irreconcilable differences over economics later contributed to the divorce of the Czech and Slovak republics.

In Yugoslavia, growing inflation and unemployment also fueled nationalism (Nemeth 1991:32). In 1988, official figures suggest salaries dropped 24% in Yugoslavia, and living conditions dropped to 1960s levels. (Gotovska-Popova 1993:179). As economic results worsened, Croats blamed the Serb-dominated central government, and Serbs blamed Tito, a Croat, for setting up a federal system that left Serbia, the leading ethnic group, as only one nation among equals (Basom 1995:513). Serb efforts to redress this grievance later contributed to the breakup of Yugoslavia.

The Russian Federation suffers from a more severe economic crises than those that led to the collapse of the Eastern block federations. The Asian financial crisis frightened investors and slowed the flow of investment capital into Russia, and falling oil prices reduced Russia's export revenue (McFaul 1998:308). Enterprises have not paid their workers, suppliers, or taxes, and whenever payments are made, almost half the payments are made in barter (Gaddy and Ickes 1998:53–54; Goldman 1998:319). Most companies are bankrupt and unable to pay their taxes. Russian government revenues cover only 60% of its expenditures, the Russian Federation has defaulted on its loans, and the economy is beginning to resemble that leading to the collapse of the Soviet Union or the Germany's Weimar Republic (McFaul 1998:309–310). Losers in the transition to the flawed market economy by far outnumber winners (Rutland 1998:313–314). The economic shock is so traumatic that Russia is the first industrial country in history to have a declining population without war, famine, or disease (Powell 1998:335).

F. Economic Disparity

Economic disparity generates resentment, both on the part of less developed regions and also on the part of more developed areas. Underdeveloped areas feel relative deprivation (Dowley 1998:361). Prosperous areas can resent the subsidies which are extracted from them and distributed to other members of the federation in the form of transfer payments.

In the Soviet Union, regions whose production exceeded their income and investment became donor regions. For example, Ukraine consistently transferred 10% of its income to other republics (Schroeder 1986:307). This creates incentives to opt out of the union. Understandably, a little over three months after the unsuccessful coup, the people of Ukraine voted in a referendum for independence from the Soviet Union, killing Gorbachev's attempt to salvage the disintegrating multinational state (Yeltsin 1994:111). Central Asian republics, on the other hand, were constant recipients of interregional transfers (Schroeder 1986:307). Well-developed republics tended to succeed from the Soviet Union early in the breakup, while less developed tended to remain within the Soviet Union longer (Emizet and Hesli 1995:524).

Economic disparity also contributed to the demise of Czechoslovakia. Czech lands were the industrial heart of the Habsburg Empire (Ulc 1996:332–333). Every year from the beginning of Czechoslovakia in 1918 to its demise in 1992, with the exception of the years during World War II, when Slovakia was independent, the Czechs subsidized Slovakia (Ulc 1996:333–4). The breakup of Czechoslovakia saved the Czechs almost $1 billion a year in subsidy to Slovakia, or about 7% of the national budget (Ulc 1996:337–338). The subsidization of Slovakia was a drain on the Czechs. A survey a couple years after the breakup showed 57% of Czechs are happy with the breakup of Czechoslovakia, compared to only 36% of Slovaks (Ulc 1996:348–349).

Even though Slovakia was the beneficiary of transfer payments, their relative deprivation also caused resentment. Like most Soviet-era industry, Slovak productivity is low and energy consumption is high (Ulc 1996:337–338). Both the end of the cold war and economic reforms hit Slovakia harder than the Czech Republic. Prague's economic reforms were also unkind to Slovakia's inefficient Soviet-era plants. The growing disparity between the Czech and Slovak economies became a source of tension. Unemployment in Slovakia climbed to 12%, compared to 4% in the

Czech Republic (Svec 1992:379; Ulc 1996:339). Slovak politicians blamed Prague for the economic suffering (Cox and Frankland 1995:83) and eventually declared independence.

In Yugoslavia, economic disparity also contributed to dissolution. Yugoslavia had a north-south split, with the northern republics of Slovenia and Croatia being much more prosperous than the other republics of Yugoslavia (Lawday 1991:33). Slovenia and Croatia were the main contributors to Yugoslavia's GNP (Gotovska-Popova 1993:179). Croatia generated about half of the foreign trade and was the main foreign-currency earner for the federal budget (*ibid.*). The underdeveloped regions of Yugoslavia included Macedonia, Montenegro, Bosnia-Herzegovina, and Kosovo (Staar 1988:230; Graff 1991:44). The social plan for 1981–85 concentrated on "faster development of economically underdeveloped republics," and between 20% and 30% of the Slovene GDP is diverted to the southern republics (Staar 1998:230). Despite the transfers, economic output in Slovenia and Croatia grew twice as fast as those areas with generous investment (Staar 1998:230). Slovenia and Croatia resented taxation to support the less-developed regions of the federation (Gotovska-Popova 1993:179; Basom 1995:113) and acted in their own best interest to resist all centralizing measures (Staar 1998:230). As was the case with the Soviet Union, the most prosperous republics, Slovenia and Croatia, declared independence first; the less-developed republics stayed in the federation longer.

Economic disparity also plagues the current Russian Federation. Ten of the 89 republics, provinces, and territories, representing 25% of the population, are net donors to the federal budget, and pay 57% of federal revenue (Hahn 1997:257; Slider 1997:456); the other 79 units receive more back from Moscow than they contribute in taxes (Rutland 1998:376). The federal system is not perceived as fair by the majority of the regions—the oblasts (provinces) (Lepingwell et al. 1994:8; Clark and Graham 1995). This creates an incentive on the part of the donor regions to try to opt out of the federal system (Smith and Graham 1995; Lepingwell et al. 1994:7).

G.   Catalyst for Collapse: The Inability to Govern

Institutional failure at the center allows nationalities on the periphery to achieve independence (Dowley 1998:359). The Soviet Union, Czechoslovakia, and Yugoslavia continued to function as federal systems for many years, despite having multiple nationalities and languages, religious differences, rising population among subdominant groups and ethnic subdivisions, poor economic performance, economic disparity, and ethnic tension. The catalyst that triggered the dissolution of each multinational federation was a crisis in which one of the players incapacitated the federal system so it was no longer able to govern.

Factors contributing to the disintegration of the Soviet Union were divided political elites at the center, and jurisdictional disputes between the center and the republics (Brubaker 1996:41). The first division was between political elites in the central government—Gorbachev and the reformers on one side, and the hardliners who staged a coup on the other. A new Union Treaty to replace the Soviet Union was scheduled to be signed on August 20, 1991. Hardliners detained Gorbachev and staged their unsuccessful coup on August 19. When the coup eventually failed, it left the institutions of the center in suspension. Then the second division came into play, pitting the center against the union republics, who wanted to wrest control away from the center. Gorbachev's reforms had revitalized the union republics. With the governing bodies of the Soviet Union in suspension, the union republics filled the vacuum as the de facto governments in the former Soviet Union (Yeltsin 1994:105). An orderly transition was possible only because the republics had already existed as quasi-nation-states (Brubaker 1996:41). After the coup, the union republic elites were unwilling to sign a treaty to resurrect the Soviet Union. The failed coup created a window of opportunity for the union republics to leave the Soviet Union.

The problem that brought the Czechoslovak Federation to a standstill was a challenge from Slovakia. The federal system created in 1969 created Constitutional safeguards for both Czechs and Slovaks. These protections enabled either partner to hamstring the federal government (Innes 1997:393) to protect their interests. One of the houses of parliament, the House of Nations, had parity, or equal representation, of the two republics (Ulc 1996:340–342). In 1990 and 1991, constant disputes with the Slovak deputies tied up the federal parliament and slowed economic reforms (Gotovska-Popova 1993:180). Slovak nationalists in parliament also blocked the reelection of Vaclav Havel as President of Czechoslovakia (*Economist* 1992:52). The stalemate also prevented a resolution of the relationship of Slovakia within a federal Constitution. Since passage of Constitutional amendments required a three-fifths vote in both chambers, 31 members could paralyze the process. While this was not a problem in the Soviet era, when the body easily ratified any measures approved by the Communist Party, Slovak nationalists now held sufficient seats to block drafts of a new federal Constitution (Ulc 1996:340–342). Slovak President Vladimir Meciar was bargaining for a confederation where Slovakia would be internationally recognized but still receive subsidies from Prague (Ulc 1996:341–343). Federation President Vaclav Klaus was unwilling to be drawn into protracted negotiations. On July 17, 1992, the Slovak parliament declared independence (Cox and Frankland 1995:86). On November 11, 1992, the federal parliament approved the final dissolution of Czechoslovakia (*ibid.*).

Regional leaders also caused a stalemate in the federal government of Yugoslavia. In 1990, Yugoslavia had multiparty elections. The prime minister, Ante Markovic, attempted to carry out economic reforms, but contentious ethnic and regional groups prevented the implementation of these programs (Cohen 1992:371). The major republics, Croatia, Slovenia, and Serbia, had drastically different visions of Constitutional reforms, preventing any progress on a negotiated reorganization. Serbian leader Slobodan Milosovic charged that the federal government was anti-Serb, and on March 15, Milosovic announced Serbia would no longer obey the authority of Yugoslavia's collective presidency (*Economist* 1991:54). In May 1991, Serbia, its two provinces, and Montenegro blocked the annual rotation of the federal presidency to the Croatian representative (Cohen 1992:373). The ability of the Serbs to prevent the proper functioning of federal institutions intensified Croatia and Slovenia's desire for independence and foreclosed the possibility of maintaining the federal system.

Russia still faces a stalemate between the parliament and president. The 1993 standoff between the Russian president and parliament is an example of a stalemate. During that power struggle, between Yeltsin and the Supreme Soviet, the balance of power shifted to the republics (Clarke and Graham 1993). Conflict at the center allowed the periphery to usurp authority from the center. Although both Yeltsin and the Supreme Soviet feared the federation was falling apart, neither could afford to alienate the periphery, so neither challenged the leakage of authority. While Yeltsin survived this dangerous stalemate, the deeply divided government which led to the stalemate has not changed. While Yeltsin has been able to hold the country together, his departure may leave a vacuum similar to that resulting from the death of Tito in Yugoslavia.

Another ominous development is the economic crisis. In the past, Yeltsin has held wayward republics and provinces in the federation by giving troubled areas tax concessions and federal subsidies (Treisman 1996:329). Now, there are no more funds to use to win cooperation. A number of regions have withheld tax revenue from the national treasury (Sharlet 1994:121). The federal government is collecting only enough revenue to meet half its budget, and is in default on its loans (McFaul 1998:308). The economic crisis may incapacitate the center, which would allow the republics and oblasts to declare independence.

IV. CONCLUSION

The problems that unraveled the multinational federations of the Soviet Union, Czechoslovakia, and Yugoslavia are very similar, and these same problems still face the Russian Republic. The

Russian Federation still includes 21 ethnic republics within its borders, including Chechnya. The country still has a growing Islamic population, which is resistant to assimilation and is now being influenced by separatist movements. Economic frustration is mounting, and economic disparity encourages republics and oblasts to each look after their own interests, to the detriment of the federation. The federation is bankrupt, which has impaired its ability to govern. Moscow has little carrot or stick to offer its constituent republics and oblasts. Russia is practically ungovernable.

Dissolution is a real possibility. The critical factor which is missing for dissolution is a political stalemate which would neutralize the center long enough for the independence-minded republics and oblasts to establish their independence.

Devolution is a second possibility. The current asymmetrical system based on bilateral treaties has led to a slow, piecemeal erosion of central authority and capacity to govern the periphery. There is more devolution in practice than is permitted in the Constitution. Taxes are being withheld by republics and oblasts, contributing to the bankruptcy of the Russian Federation. Policies are being implemented at the periphery which contradict the policies of the center. If contenders for power avoid forcing a stalemate at the center, devolution is likely as the periphery usurps more power from the center.

Two structural changes make the reconcentration of power in Moscow less likely than in the past. Contested elections in republics and oblasts gives local officials an independent power base from which to challenge center, making a pre-Gorbachev level of centralization extremely difficult. To dominate functioning federal structures, greater party discipline would be required than the Communist Party of the Soviet Union was able to muster at any time since Stalin. It is unlikely that a party or coalition of parties could be both broad based enough to win at all levels of government across the Russian Federation and also disciplined enough to enforce a consistent policy across all levels of government. The second change making recentralization of authority difficult is the decentralization of the revenue structure. The periphery has withheld revenue from the center as a form of protest since Gorbachev. The center does not have the resources to subdue the periphery without the periphery's cooperation. As long as contested republic and oblast elections are held and revenue is collected by the periphery, power will remain decentralized.

ENDNOTES

1. Chechnya was an autonomous republic within Russian Republic, which was one of the 15 union republics. This designation was one level lower than union republic in the Soviet hierarchy, and did not provide any real autonomy. This status has not been sufficient to lead to independence for Chechnya.
2. Kosovo was an autonomous region inside one of the Yugoslav republics, Serbia, until 1989, when that status was revoked. While external forces have intervened on its behalf, its status as an autonomous region was insufficient to obtain independence by political means. Vojvodina, the other autonomous region, is ethnically diverse and has also remained part of Serbia.

REFERENCES

Aslund, A. (1995). *How Russia Became a Market Economy.* Washington: Brookings Institution.

Basom, K.E. (1995). Prospects for democracy in Serbia and Croatia. *East European Quarterly* 29(4), 509–529.

Bater, J.H. (1996). *Russia and the Post-Soviet Scene: A Geographical Perspective.* London: Arnold.

Bennigsen, A. (1986). Soviet minority nationalism. In R. Conquest (ed.), *The Last Empire: Nationality and the Soviet Future.* Stanford, CA: Hoover Press.

Bernstam, M.S. (1986). Demography of Soviet ethnic groups in world perspective. In R. Conquest (ed.), *The Last Empire: Nationality and the Soviet Future*, 314–368. Stanford, CA: Hoover Press.

Binder, D. (1998). Ignorant "Albright doctrine" entangles U.S. in ancient disputes. *Insight on the News 14*(6), 30.

Brubaker, R. (1996). *Nationalism Reframed: Nationhood and the National Question in the New Europe.* Boston: Harvard University Press.

Bryzko, N. (1999). Separatism: is greater Russia falling apart? *World Press Review 46*(2), 28–29.

Clark, S.L., and Graham, D.R. (1995). The Russian Federation's fight for survival. *Orbis 39*(3), 329–352.

Clendenin, D.B. (1992). *From Coup to Commonwealth: An Inside Look at Life in Contemporary Russia.* Grand Rapids, MI: Baker Book House.

Cohen, L.J. (1992). The disintegration of Yugoslavia. *Current History 91*(568), 369–375.

Cox, R.H., and Frankland, E.G. (1995). The federal state and the breakup of Czechoslovakia: an institutional analysis. *Publius 25*(1), 71.

Cox, T. (1996). *From Perestroika to Privatization: Politics of Property Change in Russia.* Aldershot, England: Avebury.

Desai, P. (1989). *Perestroika in Perspective.* Princeton, NJ: Princeton University Press.

Djilas, M. (1986). Eastern Europe within the Soviet empire. In R. Conquest (ed.), *The Last Empire: Nationality and the Soviet Future*, 369–380. Stanford, CA: Hoover Press.

Dowley, K.M. (1998). Striking the federal balance in Russia: comparative regional government strategies. *Communist and Post Communist Studies 31*(4), 359–380.

Economist. (1991). Body and soul. *318*(7699), 54–55.

Economist. (1992). Ripping velvet. *324*(7769), 52.

Emadi, H. (1993). The last years of Yugoslavia. *Contemporary Review 263*(1534), 233–242.

Emizmet, K.N., and Hesli, V.L. (1995). The disposition to secede: an analysis of the Soviet case. *Comparative Political Studies 24*(4), 493–536.

Gaddy, C.G., and Ickes, B.W. (1998). Russia's virtual economy. *Foreign Affairs 77*(5), 53–68.

Goldman, M. (1998). The cashless society. *Current History 97*(621), 319–324.

Gotovska-Popova, T. (1993). Nationalism in post Communist Eastern Europe. *East European Quarterly 27*(2).

Graff, J.L. (1991). Serbia's land grab in Yugoslavia. *Time 138*(11), Sept 40–41.

Hahn, J.W. (1997). Regional elections and political stability in Russia. *Post Soviet Geography and Economics 38*(5), 251–163.

Harmstone, T.R. (1986). Minority nationalism today, an overview. In R. Conquest (ed.), *The Last Empire: Nationality and the Soviet Future.* Stanford, CA: Hoover Press.

Hodson, R., Sekulic, D., and Massey, G. (1994). National tolerance in the former Yugoslavia. *American Journal of Sociology*(6), 1534–1559.

Hyams, N. (1970). Russian nationalism. In G. Schopflin, (ed.), *The Soviet Union and Eastern Europe*, New York: Praeger.

Innes, A. (1997). The breakup of Czechoslovakia: the impact of party development of the separation of the state. *East European Politics and Societies 11*(3), 393–435.

Johnson, P. (1983). *A History of the Modern World: From 1917 to the 1980s.* London: Weidenfeld and Nicolson.

Kobishchenov, Y. (1995). Can Russia deal with major influx from the South: who will be living in the 21st century. *Current Digest of the Post Soviet Press 47*(6), 1–3.

Lawday, D., Green, P.S., and Trifkovic, S. (xxxx). The fire this time, why Yugoslavia is a candidate for creative destruction. *U.S. News and World Report 111*(3), 33–36.

Lepingwell, J.W.R., Rahr, Al., Teague, E., and Tolz, V. (1994). Russia: a troubled future. *Radio Free Europe/Radio Liberty Research Report 3*(24), 1–12.

McCrea, B.P., Plano, J.C., and Klein, G. (1984). *The Soviet and East European Political Dictionary.* Santa Barbara: Clio Press.

McFaul M. (1998). Russia's summer of discontent. *Current History 97*(621), 307–312.

Medish, V. (1980). The special status of the RSFSR. In *Ethic Russia in the USSR: The Dilemma of Dominance.* New York: Pergamon Press.

Mojzes, P. (1994). Balkan travels: the case of Solvenia. *Christian Century 111*(8), 254–258.

Nahaylo, B., and Swoboda, V. (1989). *Soviet Disunion: A History of the Nationalities Problem.* New York: Free Press.

Nemeth, M. (1991). Balkan breakdown. *Macleans 104*(11), 32.

Ornstein, N., and Courson, K. (1992). As the world turns democratic, federalism finds favor. *American Enterprise 3*(1), 20–25.

Pearson, R. (1983). *National Minorities in Eastern Europe, 1848–1945.* New York: St. Martins Press.

Poelzer, G. (1995). Devolution, Constitutional development and the Russian North. *Post Soviet Geography 36*(4), 204–214.

Powell, D.E. (1998). The dismal state of health care in Russia. *Current History 97*(621), 335–341.

Progressive. (1998). Russia's agony. *62*(10), 9–10.

Rutland, P. (1998). A flawed democracy. *Current History 97*(1998), 313–318.

Ryback, T.W. (1996). Dateline Sudetenland: hostages to history. *Foreign Policy 105*, 162–178.

Schroeder, G.E. (1986). Social and economic aspects of the nationality problem. In R. Conquest (ed.), *The Last Empire: Nationality and the Soviet Future.* Stanford, CA: Hoover Press.

Sharlet, R. (1994). Federalism in Russian Constitutional politics. *Publius: The Journal of Federalism 24*(1994), 113–127.

Shaw, D.J.B. (1995). Ethnic relations and federalism in the Soviet era. In D.J.B. Shaw (ed.), *The Post Soviet Republics: A Systematic Geography.* London: Longman.

Seton-Watson, H. (1986). Russian nationalism in historical perspective. In R. Conquest (ed.), *The Last Empire: Nationality and the Soviet Future.* Stanford, CA: Hoover Press.

Slider, D. (1997). Russia's market distorting federalism. *Post Soviet Geography and Economics 38*(8), 455–460.

Smith, G. (1995). Ethnic relations in the new states. In D.J.B. Shaw (ed.), *The Post Soviet Republics: A Systematic Geography.* London: Longman.

Society. (1998). Russia's population shrinks. *35*(5), 5–6.

Staar, R.F. (1988). *Communist Regimes in Eastern Europe*, 5th ed. Stanford, CA: Hoover Press.

Stoner-Weiss, K. (1997). *Local Heros: The Political Economy of Russian Regional Governance*, Princeton, NJ: Princeton University Press.

Svec, M. (1992). Czechoslovakia's velvet divorce. *Current History 91*(568), 376–380.

Talbot, S. (1992). End of an empire. *Time 139*(26), 60.

Treisman, D. (1996). The politics of intergovernmental transfers in post Soviet Russia. *British Journal of Political Science 26*, 299–335.

Ulc, O. (1996). Czechoslovakia's velvet divorce: formal dissolution into Czech and Slovak states 1992. *East European Quarterly 30*(3), 331–350.

Wimbush, S.E. (1986). The Soviet borderlands. In R. Conquest (ed.), *The Last Empire: Nationality and the Soviet Future.* Stanford, CA: Hoover Press.

Yeltsin, B. (1994). *The Struggle for Russia.* New York: Random House.

Zwass, A. (1995). *From Failed Communism to Underdeveloped Capitalism: Transformation of Eastern Europe, the Post-Soviet Union and China.* Armonk, NY: M.E. Sharpe.

23
Process of Democratization and Local Governance in Poland

Renata Wanda Siemieska   *Institute of Sociology, Warsaw University, Warsaw, Poland*

I. INTRODUCTION

Poland regained independence in 1918 and became a republic after nearly 150 years of partitioned existence under foreign rule by Russia, Austria, and Prussia. In 1939, Poland was an economically underdeveloped agricultural country with a low level of urbanization. In 1931, only 25% of the total population were urbanites (*Small Statistical Yearbook* 1939). Twenty-three percent were illiterate, with illiteracy higher among women (28%) than men (18%) (Siemienska 1989).

Poland was a mosaic of diverse ethnic cultures and religions, including Roman Catholics, Greek-Catholics, Greek Orthodox, Protestants, and Jews. Roman Catholicism, however, was hegemonic and held a special place in the cultural and psychological makeup of the Poles. Poland's geopolitical location lent special importance to her ties to the Roman Catholic church. The situation changed after World War II. The Polish borders were changed; the eastern part of Poland was included into the Soviet Union and, as compensation, some eastern German territories became part of Poland. The ethnic and national structure of the population was dramatically changed. As a consequence of the Holocaust the Jewish population was almost totally exterminated. Some Ukrainians, Belorussians, Lituanians, etc. became citizens of the Soviet Union when the eastern territories were incorporated to the state. As a result Poland became an almost ethnically homogeneous country.

After World War II the Communist system was established in Poland, as it was in other Eastern European countries. In Poland the system broke down in 1989 after semifree parliamentary elections. The Polish events opened the way for similar political changes in 1989–1990 in other states in this part of Europe.

II. POLITICAL STRUCTURE IN POSTWAR POLAND

The political system was highly centralized, with the center located at the confluence of the highest organs of the Communist party—the Polish United Workers Party (PUWP) and state structures. It had final authority, derived from the supremacy of state power and the hegemonic position of the Communist Party. The United Peasant Party (UPP), made up of farmers, and the Democratic Party (DP), composed primarily of craftspeople and small producers, were urged to cooperate with the PUWP as the hegemonic party in a spirit of understanding and accord. The

PUWP was defined in the Constitution as playing a leading role in the life of the country. According to a reform carried out in 1972–75, the commune became the basic administrative unit. Under the new People's Councils Act of 1975, the presidium was changed from an executive body to a policy-making and supervisory one.

The people's councils and the commune head and his staff were organs of state power acting within the commune. Local party units provided ideological and political guidance and roles of leadership and control vis-à-vis elective self-government organs and their staff. Commune committees of the United Peasant Party were expected to cooperate with the PUWP committees. Local organs of power had only some prerogatives because, in the highly centralized Polish system, they were subordinated to higher-level party authorities that had considerable powers of their own. The leading role of the PUWP was reflected in institutional structures and personnel policy. Most ranking officials in the economy, administration, education, judiciary, etc., were PUWP members.

Three periods can be distinguished in Poland's postwar history until the 1980s, similar to that of other Communist countries: a struggle for power, an intensive industrialization phase, and a period of economic modernization. During the first period, there was a fierce power struggle between the PUWP and other groupings and parties. Loyalty to the new authorities was the chief recruitment criterion. Little or no attention was paid to the candidate's education, skills, job experience, etc. What counted above all was prior active membership in the wartime Communist party, in the Resistance movement, or in an army unit that had fought alongside the Soviet Army during World War II. It also helped to have a working-class or peasant background.

These same criteria were strongly emphasized in the second period, also. Since the mid-1950s, because of priority given to socioeconomic development, leaders were pressed to adapt to the new situation by seeking more education. At the same time, a new generation of recruits was also brought into the party system who could not meet all of the immediate postwar criteria. A limited number of cadres, who rotated among positions, filled leadership posts at the local level. People already holding leadership positions were on the roster of the "reserve cadre" (members of the so-called nomenclature) and were among the first to be considered for vacant leadership positions. In Poland, this was called the "job merry-go-round." When the crisis of August 1980 occurred, many protested that people who failed in one job were simply moved to another (Siemieńska 1983).

This recruitment system hindered the active participation of women in politics. Fewer women than men had been members of the Communist party before World War II, fewer had fought during the war in underground military forces that were connected with the reestablishment of the Communist party in 1943, and fewer had joined the Communist party or other parties cooperating with it following World War II (Siemienska 1990). Women's promotion to leadership positions in most cases was centrally decided and was generally determined by a quota system that provided for representation of women, as it did for representation of young people and other recognized social and political groups. Described above criteria for appointing managerial personnel, combined with certain cyclical crises serving to integrate society around problems important for both rather than just one gender, created conditions that, since 1945, favored men over women in the world of politics, even at the local level, as will be explained below.

III. TRANSITION TO DEMOCRACY

A. Change of the Political System

The crisis at the beginning of the 1980s in Poland had economic, political, and moral dimensions. The independent trade union Solidarity, created at the time, had a membership of about 10 million (the Polish population was at the time 36 million). In public opinion surveys, Poles demonstrated a lack of confidence in existing institutions. The introduction of martial law in 1981, with its restrictions on personal freedoms, whetted popular demand for the democratization of government, greater citizens' influence in decision making, and economic reforms. Poland's economic system totally broke down at the end of the 1980s. In the winter of 1989, negotiations were held between representatives of the ruling Communist party (PUWP) with their allies and the opposition led by Lech Wałęsa's Solidarity, with the Catholic church in the role of observer. The talks resulted in the legalization of Solidarity, thus creating conditions for political pluralism and for conducting partially free elections for parliament in June 1989. The result was an overwhelming electoral success for the citizens' committees (at the time, the advisory political body created by their leader, Wałęsa). The political changes opened the way for major political and economic reforms, designed to transform the Polish political system from totalitarianism to democracy and the Polish economy from centrally planned and controlled to market oriented.

The new government replaced a number of people in managerial positions, most of whom had been Communist party members, with those who had been politically in opposition during the Communist regime. The change in the political system did not improve the political status of women. In the partially free elections in June 1989, when the Communist party was defeated, women constituted 13% of members of the lower chamber (Seym) of parliament and only 6% of the higher chamber (the Senate). In the parliament elected in 1991, the respective figures were 9% and 8%. In the parliament elected in 1993, it was 13% and 13% and the same percent in the parliament elected in 1997. (The highest number of women in the parliament under the Communist regime was 23%, in 1980–85.) In the first free elections to the local self-government held in May 1990, women constituted only 11% among those elected. In the next elections, in 1994, more women were elected (13.2% in total: in districts up to 40,000 inhabitants, 12.8%; in larger districts, 16.7%). In comparison with the elections in 1990 to the local governments, the elected deputies were slightly older, particularly the men. The most numerous group among women consisted of councillors aged 41 to 50 (42%), and among the men, also 41 to 50 (36%). The councillors elected in 1994 were better educated: in 1990 44% of the women and 28% of the men had university-level education; in 1994, 54% of the women and 35% of the men in the elections to the local self-government in 1998 the number of elected women increased to 15.7%.

In the first government dominated by non-Communists created in September 1989, there was only one woman minister. In the second and third governments formed in the 1990s, there were none. In the fourth government, created in 1992, a woman was made prime minister—the first in Polish history. Women constitute 10 of the 229 members of the government and 2% of the 98 heads and deputy heads of provinces. The largest proportion of women managers work in the ministries of health and social protection, work and social policy, and culture and arts, where they constitute 58%, 47% and 41%, respectively, of the managerial labor force. The smallest proportions of women managers work in the ministry of transportation (none), foreign affairs (6%), and foreign economic cooperation (9%). Women have greatest access to managerial positions in the professions in which a large proportion of those employed are women.

B. Legal Basis of Local Government and Its Functioning in the 1990s

The basic reform of territorial (local) governments was carried out before the elections to local councils in 1990, and local governments were granted a larger degree of autonomy than they had before the change of political system. The main idea behind the reform launched by the first government led by the non-Communist prime minister was to move from a centralized political and economic system to one in which local units were empowered. During the next few years the reform did not progress, leaving the problem as a subject of political controversy. The decision was finally made in fall 1998.

One of the main aims of the reform is the reintroduction of the intermediate or second tier of local government—county (*powiat*), and the enhancement of the legal basis for the organization and functioning of the commune (*gmina*). The reform is part of the global reform of the structure and functions of public administration and division of the country to new provinces. Sixteen provinces were created instead of existing 49 provinces to make stronger economic units. (Piekara and Niewiadomski 1998).

According to the Constitutional provisions made at the beginning of the 1990s, local government was the basic form of organization of public life. It was assumed that the *gmina* jurisdiction is not "delegated" by the state but is provided by law, particularly by the Constitution. *Gmina* constitutes a democratic community authorized by the people to perform its legislative functions. The inhabitants of the *gmina* make decisions concerning the election of *gmina* authorities by a universal ballot or through referenda. *Gmina* authorities are authorized by both the people who have the legislative power and the inhabitants as the electorate. The responsibility ascribed to *gmina*, an execution of a "vital part of public tasks" by local government authorities, imposes an obligation to satisfy the collective needs of the community. According to the Constitution, *gminas* have the right to "establish their internal structure freely within the limits of law" (statute-dependent autonomy). The provisions of the statute cannot grant the *gmina*'s statutory authorities responsibilities over matters that fall within the exclusive jurisdiction of the *gmina* council. The abolition of *gminas* requires a Constitutional amendment. The establishment or windening up of other units of local government requires an act of parliamentary. The scope of activity of *gminas* embraces local or delegated tasks which fall within the terms of reference of the civil service. The nature of the Local Government Act delegating a task and the provision of financing from the state budget obliges a *gmina* by law to carry out delegated reponsibilities. The autonomy of a *gmina* is substantially reduced, since a *gmina* cannot question the validity of the task but can only decide on the best method of its realization.

The *gmina* council is elected by a universal and secret ballot. The *gmina* council as the decision-making authority passes resolutions in such matters as the establishment of the *gmina*'s internal organization, the election and recalling of the council executive, the decisions on the directions of its activities, the passing of financial plans, local land development plans, economic programs, and cooperation with other *gminas*.

The council executive is made up of the *gmina* executive officer (*wojt*) or mayor (town president in towns with over 100,000 inhabitants) as the chairman of the council executive, his deputy, and the remaining council executive members (four to seven persons), all elected by secret ballot. The council executive "shall implement the resolutions of the *gmina* council and the responsibilities of the *gmina* defined by the provisions of the law" (Article 30 of the LGA).

The two bodies of authority appear to be complementary in some matters, for example, the budget: the *gmina* council passes the gmina budget while the council executive implements it (Kidyba and Wrobel 1994; Piekara and Niewiadomski 1998).

IV. SOCIODEMOGRAPHIC CHARACTERISTICS OF LOCAL AUTHORITIES

A. Local Authorities in the 1980s

In 1983 and 1984, studies were conducted on the functioning of the local authorities in the Kalisz and Siedlce *voivodeships* (provinces) (Wiatr 1987). Among the 564 top members of the local authorities (282 from each *voivodeship*), only 13% were women (Siemienska 1990; 1994). The research combined elected heads of local councils, local party committees, and appointed heads of local offices into a single category because the system was such that those allegedly elected were in fact appointed. The studies found that since twice as many women (36%) as men were born in the place where they currently worked, fewer women than men were employed in provinces to which they were officially transferred (43% of men vs. 21% of women). This suggests that either women were less mobile than men, which is a career constraint, or, alternatively, that women were offered job transfers less frequently than men, perhaps because women are assigned to lower-level positions in organizations.

The social backgrounds of women and men leaders were similar, even though their professional careers differed. One-third of the women began as office workers, with a significant, but decidedly smaller, number beginning as teachers and technicians. By contrast, more men began as manual workers, teachers, and instructors of cultural activities. The latter was usually associated with the activities of a political party.

The proportion of women employed as top civil servants in local administration was higher than that of men. Although many women officially occupied relatively high positions, in fact they had much less responsibility for influencing local matters (see Table 1). Women tended to work in institutions that had little influence on the allocation and distribution of resources. For example, in the PUWP, women were much more likely than men to occupy the less influential positions of deputies. Women were virtually never the heads of divisions of provincial offices. Moreover, women stayed longer in the same position than men. This fact is not surprising since the PUWP authorities changed people (usually men) more often in the higher positions. When new politicians took office at the top, they usually preferred to have their "own" people, whom they could trust, as subordinates. As a result of this pattern, women, who generally occupied less influential positions than men, were more convinced than their male counterparts that after five years they would remain in the same position. Men, almost twice as frequently as women, stated that they did not know what they would be doing in five years' time (Bartkowski 1990; Siemienska 1990).

Table 1 Jobs of Local Leaders in Kalisz and Siedlce *Voivodeships* (1983–84)

Sector	Men % (n = 493)	Women % (n = 70)
Administration	35.3	47.1
PUWP party	26.8	14.3
Youth organizations	2.4	2.9
United Peasant party	1.6	1.4
Democratic party	1.8	—
Production/directors of industrial enterprises, farming collectives	6.7	1.4
Municipalities, housing cooperatives	7.1	11.4
Trade	1.8	1.4
Courts of justice, public prosecutor's office	2.2	—
Militia, army	2.4	—
Local authorities, PMNR*	1.4	1.4
Education	2.2	1.4
Other	6.9	14.4
No data	1.4	2.9

*PMNR, or Patriotic Movement of National Rebirth, was created after the introduction of martial law on Dec. 13, 1981. The main goal of this organization was to gather citizens, irrespective of their organizational affiliation, around the program of overcoming the crisis proposed by the Communist party.
Source: Siemienska (1990).

One of the most common reasons given to explain why women advanced at a slower pace than men is the limited amount of time and energy that women can devote to professional work, primarily because they must combine professional duties with family duties. A related impediment to women's advancement was their more limited access to higher education once on the job. Men, more often than women, continued to raise their educational level during their careers. At the beginning of their professional careers, women were, on average, slightly better educated than men (Siemienska 1990:215). By 1984, however, almost 70% of men had acquired university level education, compared to only 52% of women. It is impossible to conclude whether this gender difference in human capital accumulation was caused by women's more burdensome social roles, by women's lower incentive to get more education due to their lower likelihood of promotion, or by superiors less frequently encouraging women than men to further their education.

The discovered similarity in women and men managers' attitudes may have resulted from the selection process. Since women were elected or appointed based on similar criteria to men, perhaps they were in fact selected because they shared the views of their male colleagues (Siemienska 1990, 1994).

B. Local Authorities in the Early 1990s

The situation at the local political level was similar to that at the national level. Solidarity, as a trade union, and the citizens' committees, as its political branches, were the most powerful political forces at the time of the elections in 1990.

In spring 1991, a national study was conducted of members of the local authorities in randomly selected medium-size cities by the Institute of Sociology, University of Warsaw, and was repeated in 1995. Its purpose was to create a profile of the new leaders in local governments. The study included 686 persons—162 (24%) women and 524 (76%) men. Leaders were identified on the basis of positions held and public reputation. The groups compared were administrators (people holding managerial positions in mayors' offices), politicians (chairpersons of the local committees of political parties, citizen's committees, and Solidarity), and people elected to the local councils.

The distribution of women and men among the three major positions differed significantly (see Table 2). Over half the women were administrators, and about one-quarter were elected members and politicians. Among the men, the distribution was more even, with the largest group being elected officials. Administrators have far less political clout than either elected officials or politicians; women's underrepresentation in the categories, therefore, means that their potential impact on the system and their ability to influence the future promotion of women is more limited. As in the past, women are more likely to occupy deputy positions and positions of directors of departments in mayors' offices. Over 70% of the local leaders were new in their positions and were appointed or elected since the beginning of 1990, compared with 19% first appointed between 1982 and 1989; only about 10% had been appointed earlier than 1982. More men than women were new to their positions—about 10% more in each of the analyzed groups (administrators, politicians, councillors).

The political changes in the 1990s, as expected, brought more local people into local leadership than previously. The majority were born in the community where they now live, or at least in the same province. This, however, is less the case for local politicians and councillors, who more often than the local administrators were born in other parts of the country. The pattern is even stronger among women than men. The tendency became even stronger in a middle of 1990s when only 21% of members of local authorities were people born in other parts of the country than the town, province or neighboring province where they actually work (Jasinska-Kania 1997). According to the same study conducted in 1995, only 7% of local authorities are people who live in their

Table 2 Positions of Local Leaders in Poland in 1991 by Gender (Percent)

Positions	Women (N = 162)	Men (N = 524)
Administrators (n = 84 women, 141 men)	51	27
Mayor	2.4	6.3
Deputy mayor	6.1	5.6
Secretary in mayor's office	14.6	3.3
Treasury officer in mayor's office	11.6	1.3
Department director in mayor's office	16.5	6.8
Councillors (n = 40 women, 201 men)	25	38
Local council chairperson	3.0	6.3
Local council deputy chairperson	3.7	7.4
Local council chairperson of committee	11.0	10.6
Chairpersons of local committees (n = 38 women, 182 men)	24	35
Solidarity	0.6	5.5
Citizen's committee	4.3	4.8
Political parties	11.6	15.5
Deputy, senator of the parliament	6.7	4.3

Source: Siemienska (1994a).

respective communities less than 10 years. The findings show that the local origin became one of the most important determinants of fast promotion to local authorities in the 1990s (Bartkowski 1996). From the early 1990s a mean of age of local elites is higher (43.6 years) and in 1995 even higher (45.2 years) than it was in the early 1980s. The change is caused by change of "political generations." The Communist government at the time wanted to increase its legitimacy by bring young people (activists of youth organisations) to the power positions. After the change of political system, people who replaced them were former activists of Solidarity in the early 1980s and in general opposition, and to some extent they stayed in power after the changes caused by next elections to local councils in 1994. In 1995, 53% of members of local authorities, compared to 41% in 1991, were over 45 years old.

In all the categories of local leaders, women are more than 20% more likely to be unmarried or divorced. However, the majority of female local leaders are married, with single women constituting a rather small fraction of the leader population. The local leaders of the 1990s are, on average, less educated than their predecessors in the early 1980s: 67% of the local leaders have a university education, compared with about 80% in the 1980s. Politicians of both genders are less well educated, with only half having a university education. The level of education is higher among local administrators and local councillors. Among administrators, men more often than women have completed university education (82% vs. 64%). Among the councillors, the reverse is true: 80% of women and 61% of men are university educated. Differences in the educational pattern can be explained as follows: women administrators hold lower positions than men, positions that rarely demand a university education. By contrast, women competing in elections to become councillors have to have more "educational capital" than men to make them competitive in the eyes of voters.

Women and men university graduates who become managers specialize in different fields. For example, the largest group of men administrators has a diploma in a technical field (57%), followed by law and administration (16%) and economics (12%). Among women administrators, the largest group gained their diploma in economics (34%), followed by law and administration (27%) and technical fields (27%) (Table 3). Professional expertise is becoming an increasingly important route for women to enter politics. Women are usually appointed to positions in the lower levels of the political structure on the basis of their professional qualifications. Given the strong prejudice against women as leaders and decision makers, women succeed far less frequently in achieving positions when they compete against men in public elections (Vianello et al. 1990).

The new policy encourages selecting administrators on a basis other than political affiliation, especially for lower-level positions. This policy appears to work in favor of women. Membership in political organizations played a less significant role in 1991 than it did under Communist rule: 33% of the local leaders were not currently members of any political organization, nor had they ever been. The majority of the local leaders (56%) had never been members of a political party or political association prior to their election. Sixty-seven percent were currently connected with some political party or trade union such as Solidarity or Individual Farmers' Solidarity.

Among administrators, there were no differences between women's and men's former political party membership. However, among politicians and councillors, a greater proportion of women than men had not been organizationally active in the past. Among former Communist party members, men indicated a stronger orientation to the left, and women were more aligned to the right and center—a finding that requires further study (Table 4). The comparison of answers of the members of local authorities in 1991 and 1995 shows decreasing number of the people who consider themselves as independent (from 27% to 9%). The finding might be interpreted as a prove of crystallization of multiparty system and its growing role in selection of members of local elected bodies as well as local administration (Jasinska-Kania 1998).

Women at the local level appear to be more stable in their jobs than men, probably because they hold less politically sensitive positions and consequently also have less political clout. The

Table 3 Education of Local Leaders by Gender in 1991 (%)

| | Administrators | | Politicians | | Councillors | | |
Educational level	F	M	F	M	F	M	Total
Primary	1	—	5	3	5	—	2
Basic, vocational	—	—	2	7	—	5	4
Uncompleted secondary	—	—	2	4	—	1	1
Secondary, vocational	21	8	13	15	2	20	15
General secondary	8	2	18	5	2	3	5
Post-high school courses	7	5	8	11	10	9	8
University	63	82	52	55	80	61	64
No data	—	3	—	—	1	1	1
University field							
Teaching	2	2	33	13	24	9	9
Law/administration	27	15	—	12	6	7	12
Other humanities	3	5	22	15	13	6	8
Economy	34	12	11	8	15	10	13
Engineering	26	57	16	32	18	41	39
Math/computers	—	—	—	—	—	—	—
Medicine	—	—	—	5	21	7	5
Agriculture	7	7	5	11	—	10	8
Other	1	2	13	4	3	10	6

Source: Siemienska (1994a).

Table 4   Relationship Between Past Political Membership and Left-Right Orientation of Local Leaders by Gender (1991) (%)

Current political orientation*	Membership of political parties under Communist regime											
	Administrators				Politicians				Councillors			
	Women		Men		Women		Men		Women		Men	
	Yes	No	Yes	No	Yes	No	Yes	No	Yes	No	Yes	No
Left	8	7	18	3	40	5	26	10	22	3	22	8
Center	64	64	56	60	54	60	42	42	66	70	50	50
Right	21	29	26	37	6	26	32	46	11	18	27	38
No data	7	—	—	—	—	7	—	2	1	9	1	4

*Left: 1 to 4 on 10-point scale; center: 5 and 6; right: 7 to 10.
Source: Siemienska (1994a).

growing women's lobby in Poland is expected to create pressure on politicians to pay more attention to women's appointments to managerial positions in the future.

V. ETHICAL REASONING OF LOCAL OFFICIALS IN THE EARLY 1990S

The change of political system caused among others by moral dissatisfaction with the Communist system, replacement of "old" officials by newly elected and appointed ones raised a question what system of moral reasoning is characteristic for them. From December 1993 through January 1994 289 public administrators and 196 elected officials in 12 towns in two contrasting provinces (Lodz and Lublin) were interviewed (Stewart et al. 1997). The provinces differ in respect of level of urbanization, industrialization, and density of population. To assess the level of ethical reasoning in government settings, an instrument based on theory and research in cognitive development was used. The Stewart-Sprinthall Management Survey (SSMS) has been created over the past decade and employed in a wide variety of public administration settings in the United States (Stewart and Sprinthall 1994). The instrument contains three scenarios depicting issues that a public offical might face on the job: friendship in promotion; accepting favors in return for favorable treatment of a contract proposal; and manipulating a dataset to cover up an error.

The three stories were adapted slightly for the Polish situation. The levels of alternative considerations offered to respondents were devised from extensive theory and research based on Kolber's work on moral/ethical development. The levels were following:

1. Concern for obiedence and punishment
2. Concern for cooperation and reciprocity in a single instance
3. Concern for enduring personal relationships
4. Concern for law and duty
5. Concern for abstract principles (P score) of societal cooperation

The most striking finding was that local officials in newly democratic Poland paralleled almost precisely their counterparts in the United States, with their distinct preference for law and duty as the basis for decision making. Overall, the average score for the Polish officials across the board was 47% for law and duty, while the average law and duty scores for public administrators in the United States were 48% in one sample and 47% in a second sample. For principled reasoning in Poland a P score was 34.6%; in the United States samples were 38% and 39%. In Poland the results are strikingly similar for the elected and the appointed officials. For example, the total score for principled reasoning are 34.7 for elected officials and 34.5 for appointed officials. Similarly the total scores for law and duty reasoning (stage 4) are 45.8 and 47.4, respectively. This finding is consistent with a recent literature review that reported similar value structures for elected and appointed officials in the United States (deLeon 1994).

We found no differences in P scores in the Polish sample related to the functional role respondents held. There were also no significant differences in P scores related to the rural or urban settings of officials, their religiousness and, surprisingly, between those reporting past membership of Communist party and those denying such history. As far as education was considered the significant difference occured only between those trained in law and administration (P score 32.4) and those trained in economics (P score 38.7). But we found that gender makes a difference in modes of ethical reasoning and that the difference is stronger among public administrators than among elected officials. When the two groups are combined, the female mean P score of 36.9 is higher than the male score of 33.9. It was also the significant relationship between the overall decommunization measure and capacity to reason at a principled level. The respondents with significantly different and lower P scores were not decisive on the issue of decommunization. Higher P scores were associated with decisiveness.

Five aspects of "decommunization," being a subject of political discussion in the early 1990s, were addressed in the interviews. The officials reported strong support for decommunization when asked if justice requires punishment of collaborators or if the public could trust a government that employed collaborators, but shunned decommunization as a practical matter by agreeing that the secret police records were simply not accurate enough to permit a fair and just screening process. In all cases elected officials were clearly more supportive for active decommunization than their public administration colleagues, with statistically significant differences on four of the five questions. Somewhat lower pro-decommunization response was on the part of respondents with a Communist party background, none of these was significant at the .05 level.

The above-described way of ethical reasoning does not say how local officials behave in reality. But it is significant that, asked to solve hypothetical ethical dilemmas in their work settings, they are turning to principles as do U.S. administrators, public servants of one of the oldest democracies.

VI. VALUE ORIENTATION

One of the aims of the study conducted by Siemienska, Stewart, and Sprinthall in 1993–94 was to find out to what extent the local officials in the early 1990s were in favor of democratic changes and transformation of economic mechanisms from a command economy to a market oriented (Siemienska 1995a). The basic hypotheses were based on an ideal model of profile of values of politicians and administrators in a democratic society:

1.   Members of the new local governments are more sensitive (in the subjective sense) to local needs and therefore their perception of the needs is close to the perception of inhabitants of their communties and also are ready to consider inhabitants' expectations as the most important as "vox populi."

2.   Councillors being elected in free elections means having support of the voters, and administrators, appointed by a new government which has a high support of the Poles, give a feeling of political competence to average people.

    3.   The new people in local governments are tolerant toward minorities, and also in general (when the F scale is used to measure the level of tolerance) (Lane 1972).

    4.   The new government has a high level of trust among the people.

    5.   They are postmaterialist oriented (using Inglehart's terminology) (Inglehart 1977, 1990).

    6.   They are in favor of changes leading to a free-market economy and a limited role of state as a provider of benefits.

    7.   They are in favor of a government which is elected according to democratic rules and that consists of people who are honest and ready to act in congruence with principles of justice and recognition of human dignity.

A. Authoritarianism and Tolerance

The analysis of distribution of answers to the statements of F scale showed that local leaders are rather authoritarian oriented toward what can be perceived as persistent feature of the leaders and society over time (Siemienska 1988, 1991). The leaders demonstrated some inconsistency in this respect; only some items of the scale were correlated. The statement "Young people need a strong discipline from parents" was only the item which was correlated with at least two others. It was correlated with the last quoted statement "Strong leader can do more for the country than discussion etc." ($r = .24$, $P < .001$) and also with the statement "People who do not achieve anything do not have enough strong will" ($r = .14$, $P < .01$). The fourth item of the scale, "personal harm should not be forgotten," was not significantly correlated with others. But still it was rather highly correlated ($r = .12$) with the statement that in so complicated a world it is the only way to know what to do, to rely on leaders and specialists. There were no other significant correlations among the items of the scale.

B. Trust

The councillors and administrators have been divided to two groups, almost equal in size, to what extent people can be trusted; 45.6% of the respondents believed that you can never be too careful in relations with people and 39.4% were convinced that people can be trusted (14.8% had no opinion). The distribution of the answers is significant taking into consideration that the majority of the respondents were people connected with Solidarity movement and it could be assumed that earlier experience of common fight against the Communist regime could bring the people together: those who were elected and those who elected them. But it was not the case.

C. Materialist-Postmaterialist Orientation

Cross-national studies consistently show that an intergenerational shift from materialist toward postmaterialist priorities already is taking place in majority of countries, not only highly developed (Inglehart 1977, 1990). Materialist values are characterized by the fact that they give top priority to economic and physical security, while postmaterialists emphasize self-expression and the quality of life over economic and physical security. The original four-item index constructed by Inglehart and used in the majority of the studies consists of two items that tap materialist orientation and two that tap postmaterialist orientation. Those people whose top priorities in politics during the next 10 years are given to "maintain order" and "fight rising prices" are classified as materialists. Those whose top two priorities are given to "freedom of speech" and "more say in government" are classified as postmaterialists. Those who select any combination of the two types of goals are classified as mixed types.

The studies conducted in Poland on national random samples in 1980 and 1984 (Inglehart and Siemienska 1988; Siemienska 1988) showed that Poles at the time were more postmaterialist oriented than populations of many developed countries. After overthrowing the Communist regime and entering the path of political and economic reforms, Poles expressed much greater interest in material issues (maintaining order in the nation, fighting rising prices), because in social perception the freedom of speech was accomplished as a result of political change in 1989. The study conducted after the change of political system, in December 1989 (Siemienska 1994) and in 1992–95 (Cichomski and Morawski 1996), demonstrated that the new political situation has caused significant changes in the materialist-postmaterialist priorities which tend to be a "stabilized pattern" during the last few years. The number of people with postmaterialist orientation was twice lower than earlier.

The comparison of distribution of answers of the local councillors and administrators with the distribution of answers of (1) Polish random national sample interviewed in 1989, 1992, 1993, 1994, and 1995; (2) national sample of teachers of private and public primary schools interviewed in 1992; and (3) parliamentarians interviewed in 1992 showed that the local councillors and administrators were most postmaterialist oriented, more than any other group of respondents. Next to them (and very similar to them) were parliamentarians. Teachers were more materialist oriented than the two groups. But the most materialist oriented was national sample studied over time. For example, postmaterialists constituted 21.9% of local leaders, but only 5.4% of teachers of nonpublic schools and 2.2% of teachers of public schools. The respective numbers of materialists were 13.9%, 41.9%, and 40.7%. Respondents of mixed orientation were 64.2%, 52.7%, and 57.1%, respectively (Siemienska 1994b). As in the West, the younger and more educated tended to be more often postmaterialist oriented.

D.   Acceptance of Free-Market Mechanisms (Liberal-Nonliberal Orientation)

The elites, who came to power in 1989 in Poland, as in many Central and Eastern European countries, have seen a way out of the actual economic situation in far-reaching economic reforms. They envisage a departure from a centrally controlled economy, with the state concentrating the ownership of the means of production in its own hands, to an economy in which the market mechanisms will be the basic regulators of economics processes and to a certain extent social ones as well. Resignation from the welfare role of the state, developed by the Communist system, is one of the elements of the reforms undertaken. The state is passing on the responsibility of the fate of individuals to the members of society and discarding the principle of economic equality and substituting it by the principle of creating possibilities for individual accumulation of wealth as a path leading to the creation of the capital necessary for privatization processes. The introduction of such a "package" of reforms has met with an incoherent reaction of the society, on the one hand wishing for changes in the economic order, and on the other being stripped of a series of privileges in the process. Therefore the attitudes of local elites are important in to what extent they share the attitudes of national political elite and to what extent they differ from it.

The attitudes of the councillors and administrators to a given concept of economic and social order was measured here in three dimensions:

1.   Attitudes toward economic equality ("Incomes should be made more equal" or "There should be greater incentives for individual effort"; scale: 0–10)

2.   Concept of ownership of the means of production ("Private ownership of business and industry should be increased" or "Government ownership of business and industry should be increased"; scale: 0–10)

3.   Individual or state responsibility for the situation of individuals ("Individuals should take more responsibility for providing for themselves" or "The state should take more responsibility to ensure that everyone is provided for"; scale: 0–10)

The attitudes of the local councillors and administrators were congruent with the direction of reforms launched by the national political elite after 1989, and in general they demonstrated highly pro-reform attitudes. Although, the degree of acceptance of the reform on particular dimensions varied. Differentiation of income was the most accepted (mean = 7.9). Two other dimensions of the reform were a little bit less; the increase of private ownership (mean = 4.1), the individual responsibility (mean = 4.4). Those who accepted differentiation of income have been in favor of the increase of private ownership ($r = -.16$, $P < .001$), their attitudes toward the individual responsibility less pronounced ($r = -.09$, nonsign). But there was strong correlation between the last two attitudes ($r = .40$, $P < .001$); those who have opted for the increase of private ownership have been strongly for the individual responsibility of people. The answers to the three questions were used to built an index which classified the respondents to four groups unequally represented in the population: (1) "liberals" (opted for the differentiation of income, for the increase of private ownership of means of production, for responsibility of individuals for themselves), who constituted 36.5% of the respondents; (2) "egalitarians" (have opposite opinions), 4%; (3) "centrists" (systematically placed themselves in a center of all scales), 3.2%; and (4) others (who had mixed attitudes toward introduced reforms placing themselves in different points of the scale depends on an issue), 59.9% of respondents. Distribution among the four groups shows that a large group of the local elites had mixed feelings toward the reform, how far they would like to go. From another side it is reasonable to stress that almost 40% of the local leaders were strongly committed to the launched reforms.

Their priorities demonstrated above were highly congruent with their choice of which is more important—freedom or equality—when respondents were asked to choose. Those who emphasized differentiation of income, emphasized also an importance of freedom ($r = .16$, $P < .001$). Those in favor of state ownership of means of production and state responsibility to provide people with protection were strongly for equality when choosing between equality and freedom as two important values. The respective correlations were .26 and .24, in both cases $P < .001$.

E. Left-Right Orientation

In democratic systems it is believed that placing one's opinions on a left-right continuum is one of the basic methods for defining one's position in the world of politics. Studies show that in different societies the concepts of "left orientation" and "right orientation" are different (Fuchs and Klingemann 1990), especially when countries differ in their political histories. In the Communist countries, several months after the overthrow of the governing Communist party (e.g., Siemienska 1994, 1995), it was not just choice in ideological categories. In the first place, it was a chance to be for or against the Communist regime, to be for something which was or an attempt to return to the past or the vision of constructing a democratic society with the economy based on free-market mechanisms. The subsequent development of the political situation showed how internally differentiated was the opposition, formerly integrated by opposition to the existing political system. Taking into consideration the mass character of the political opposition to the Communist system in Poland, it was clear that the number of people identifying themselves as left-oriented was small at the beginning of the 1990s, smaller than in many other post-Communist countries (Siemienska 1997). Also, a significant number of people pointed to difficulties in describing themselves on the left-right axis, perceiving society in categories also used by the political opposition of "us" (the average people) and "them" (people associated with the Communist authorities) (Siemienska 1997).

The majority of the councillors and administrators identified themselves (according to their self-placement on 10-point scale) as center (46%) or right-oriented (39.3%). Only 14.6% of respondents considered themselves as left-oriented.

F.   Concept of Authority in the Context of Kohlberg's Theory

There is an assumption that it is a relationship between a level of moral development (as it is characterized by Kohlberg 1981) and a concept of desired authority. The councillors and the administrators were asked the three most desired characteristics of authorities. The respondents replied: (1) "The authorities should act according to the principles of justice and to respect human dignity" (postconventional orientation) (80% of respondents); (2) "People who govern should be honest" (conventional orientation) (67.4%); (3) "The authorities should be elected in a democratic elections" (postconventional orientation) (55.5%). Less than half of them pointed out (1) "The authorities should establish order in a society" (conventional orientation) (44.7%); (2) "The authorities should improve economic situation of people" (preconventional orientation) (39.8%); or (3) least popular feature of the authorities, "The authorities should be strong and be able to execute order" (preconventional orientation) (10.1%). The distribution of answers demonstrates that the councillors and administrators are mostly postconventional oriented as expected, according to Kohlberg, in a democratic society. He considers the postconventional stage as the highest stage of the moral development. Comparison of the findings with data collected in 1992 in the sample of teachers shows high similarities between the two populations. The teachers as often as the local leaders pointed out the importance of "The authorities should act according to the principles of justice and to respect human dignity" (postconventional orientation) (91.9% of teachers of nonpublic schools and 80.2% of public schools), "People who govern should be honest" (conventional orientation) (70.3% of teachers of nonpublic schools and 72.5% of teachers of public schools). However, there are differences as far as the third characteristic among the most important is mentioned. The teachers of nonpublic schools pointed out "The authorities should establish order in a society" (54.1% of respondents), while teachers of public schools "The authorities should improve economic situation of people" (71.4% of respondents) (Siemienska 1994b). The findings demonstrate that the local leaders represent a higher stage of moral development but that in all the compared groups postconventional orientation is highly recognized. We can also assume that low income, particularly of teachers of public schools, might influence their responses to the question.

In conclusion, values and attitudes of the councillors and administrators were similar to the values and attitudes of the political elite on the national level, and to some extent different from those shared by society. Councillors and administrators differ in their evaluation of accomplishments of actual authorities at the time the study has been carried out, while their concept of authorities as they should be, are very much the same in both groups. The administrators more often than councillors believed that "the authorities improve economic situation of people" (preconventional orientation) ($r = .14$, $P < .01$), "People who govern are honest" (conventional orientation) ($r = .19$, $P < .001$), "The authorities are elected in a democratic elections" (postconventional orientation) ($r = .13$, $P < .01$), and "The authorities act according to the principles of justice and to respect human dignity" (postconventional orientation) ($r = .25$, $P < .001$).

The evaluation of accomplishments of actual authorities showed that the councillors were significantly more critical than the administrators. The councillors considered freedom as more important than equality, which can be considered as more congruent with their more strongly pronounced postconventional orientation, but astonishingly, they more often opted than the administrators for less-differentiated incomes of members of society.

The multiregression analyses (MCA—Multiple Classification Analysis) performed for materialist-postmaterialist orientation, right-left orientation, and liberal-nonliberal orientation of the local leaders showed that province and the role played in local elites (councillor or administrator) proved to differentiate the values and orientations much less than many other factors. Age occurred to be insignificant, which might appear to be inconsistent with the results of many studies. However, it is necessary to remember that there were small age differences among respondents from the point of view of some theories (like Inglehart's theory) which emphasize an importance of generational differences. In this case all respondents belong more or less to the same generation, with generally similar life experiences. Respondents' income (its subjective evaluation) also occurred to be not so important a factor as differentiat values system and political orientations. However, the differences in the claimed income were small.

Mothers' and fathers' occupations of the respondents were found as important differentiating factors; in some cases mother's occupation even more than father's. The findings confirm once more the importance of social milieu of individuals in process of their socialization for shaping their value systems, and also deficiency of many studies which did not include mother's occupation and education as important factors determining values and attitudes of their children when they become adults. Contrary to many studies focused on values and attitudes of elites, gender proved to be one of fairly important differentiating factors at least in a case of some values. Its role varies, depending on analyzed political values and orientations. The same it might be said about the role of religiosity.

The materialist-postmaterialist orientation of the local elites is explained ($R2 = .062$) first of all by father's and mother's occupations, gender, and such political orientations as liberal-nonliberal and left-right (mentioned according to their importance based on beta coefficients) among 10 predictors included in the analysis. In the case of the right-left orientation ($R2 = .232$), the most important predictors turned to be liberal-nonliberal orientation, membership of organizations under Communism system, religiosity, mother's occupation, and gender (mentioned according to beta coefficients). The liberal-nonliberal orientation is explained ($R2 = .209$) by the same variables as the materialist-postmaterialist orientation, but they explained much larger variance in the case. The most important were left-right orientation, respondent's education, mother's occupation, gender, and father's occupation.

The left-right orientation played a minor role in explaining materialist-postmaterialist orientation. Inglehart believes that the axis reflecting differences in the system of values of individuals is becoming increasingly important, that the previous basic conflicts in society, expressed on the left-right axis, are now substituted by conflicts regarding the realization of given values (Inglehart 1990, 1997).

The importance of the left-right orientation as an explaining factor of liberal-nonliberal orientation and vice versa indicates a crystallization of the political orientation in a congruent way with that found in countries without the Communist past. At least, it is possible to say this about the politicians and administrators serving on local level, elected shortly after the change of the political system.

VII. LOCAL LEADERS AND THE POPULATION

After three years of being in office the councillors and administrators had strong feeling that their perception of local needs was different from people living in the communities: only 13.2% considered that their perception was the same as the local populations, 66.4% partially different, 19.7% different. Majority of them also believed that members of local governments have only a limited obligation to follow wishes of inhabitants; 64.1% rather or totally disagree that local leaders should follow wishes of inhabitants even if they think that the people are not right ($r = .15$, $P < .01$). An overhelming majority (70.8%) believed that in so complicated a world, the only way to know what to do is to rely on trusted leaders and specialists. Therefore also, a correlation between the last statement and one of the items of the F scale "Strong leader can do more for the country than discussion, debates, etc." was very high ($r = .20$, $P = .001$). But also was significant with other item of the scale "Young people need a strong discipline from a side of parents" ($r = .12$, $P < .01$).

Another study conducted more than a half year earlier (April 1993) on the national random sample of 1452 respondents (Local Authorities, Councillors, and Officers before the Reform of the Local administration, 1993) showed that the general opinion about functioning of local governments improved in a comparison with 1989. However, the respondents believed that the majority of councillors in their work first of all take into account their own interests (19%), the interests of their friends and relatives (10%), and their political party (15%). Less often they think that the councillors represent interests of inhabitants of towns/*gminas* (24%) and their voters (7%). Perception of local administrators' work was highly correlated with perception of councillors' work. Maybe the quality of administrators' performance is considered by respondents as a measure of efficiency of elected local authorities. In 1993, 49% of respondents stressed that the administrators of the closest office of public administration to them were "patient and benevolent," 40% that they work "fast and efficiently." Criticizing administrators' work, the respondents underlined most often "their unpleasant behavior" (25%), "lack of competence" (19%), and "expectation of receiving bribes" (12%). However, a large number of respondents had no opinion about different aspects of public administrators' work. For example, in the case of "expected bribes," 43% considered that the administrators do not expect them, and 45% had no opinion.

Inhabitants of smaller administrative units, less educated, had more favorable opinions about activities of councillors and public administrators than more educated people living in big cities.

VIII. CONCLUSIONS

The political change at the beginning of the 1990s was connected with a basic administrative reforms giving more say inhabitants about issues of their local communities. At the time, large numbers of elected and appointed local officials were replaced by new ones. Women did not benefit in the transitional process, being again clearly underrepresented among councillors and public administrators. After the first free elections to local councils and new appointments to administrative positions, many of the new people had experience of earlier activity in the political opposition under the Communist system. The officials, despite our expectations, felt fairly alienated (like their predecessors), seeing a divergence between their own perception of local needs and the perception of inhabitants. In their value orientation they were more pro-reform oriented than other social groups and the random national sample. In their ethical reasoning they were, surpringly, very similar to the American public administrators, which probably might be explained by the deep moral dissatisfaction with the functioning of Communist system in the past which produced higher (at least on a verbal level) sensitivity to principles of ethical behavior. In other words, our hypotheses concerning characteristics of new people in local authorities received very moderate support in findings of cited studies. One of the main conditions of the creation of an efficient modern democratic state and implementation of administrative reform, enlarging autonomy of administrative units, is having professional civil service personnel not engaged politically and also not subject to changes as a consequence of changing political situation after following elections on national and local levels.

REFERENCES

Bartkowski, J. (1990). *Kariery działaczy lokalnych* (*Careers of Local Leaders*). Warsaw: Institute of Sociology, University of Warsaw.

Bartkowski, J. (1996). *Lokalne elity władzy w Polsce w latach 1966–1995* (*Local Elites of Authority in Poland 1966–1995*). Warsaw: Institute of Sociology, University of Warsaw.

Cichomski, B., and Morawski, P. (1996). Polish General Social Surveys 1992–1996. Warsaw: Institute for Social Studies, University of Warsaw.

deLeon, L. (1994). The professional values of public managers, policy analysts and politicians. *Public Personnel Management 23*(1), 135–152.

Fuchs, D., and Klingemann H.-D. (1990). The left-right schema. In. *Continuities in Political Action* (M. Jennings, J. W. K. van Deth, et al., eds.). New York: de Gruyter.

Inglehart, R. (1990). *Culture Shift in Advanced Society.* Princeton: Princeton University Press.

Inglehart, R. (1997). *Modernization and Postmodernization.* Princeton: Princeton University Press.

Inglehart, R., and Siemienska R. (1988). Changing values and political satisfaction in Poland and the West. *Government and Opposition 23*, 440–457.

Jasińska-Kania, A. (1998). Kim sąlprzedstawiciele lokalnych elit władzy? (Who Are Representatives of Local Political Elites?). In J. Wiatr (ed.), *Władza lokalna w warunkach demokracji (Local Government in the Conditions of Democracy)*. Warsaw: Scholar, 35–46.

Kidyba, A., and Wróbel, A. (1994). *Public Administration in Poland. Its Structure and Powers.* Warsaw: Friedrich Ebert Foundation.

Kohlberg, L. (1981). *Essays in Moral Development.* San Francisco: Harper and Row.

Lane, R. E. (1972). *Political Man.* New York: Free Press.

Local Authorities Councillors, and officers before the Reform of the Local Administration (1993). Warsaw: Center for Studies of Social Opinion.

Piekara, A., and Niewiadomski, Z. (eds.). (1998). *Samorząd terytorialny. Zagadnienia prawne i administracyjne. (Territorial Self-Government. Legal and Administrative Issues)*. Warsaw: Wydawnictwo Prawnicze.

Siemieńska, R. (1983). Local party leaders in Poland. *International Political Science Review 4*(1), 127–136.

Siemieńska, R. (1988). Political materialist-postmaterialist values and their determinants in Poland in cross-national perspective. *International Review of Sociology 3*, 173–212.

Siemieńska, R. (1990). *Plec, zawod, polityka. Kobiety w zyciu publicznym w Polsce (Gender, Occupation, Politics. Women's Participation in Public Life in Poland)*. Warsaw: Institute of Sociology, University of Warsaw Press.

Siemieńska, R. (1991). Popular demands and local leadership responses in periods of economic retreat in Poland. In A. Farazmand (ed), *Handbook of Comparative and Development Public Administration*, 155–167. New York: Marcel Dekker.

Siemieńska R. (1994). Viejos y nuevos elementos de los valores democraticos en polonia, desde una perspectiva international w: *Tendencias mundiales de cambio en los valores sociales y politicos* (J. D. Nicolas, R. Inglehart, eds.). Madrid: Fundesco, 375–404.

Siemieńska, R. (1994a) Women managers in Poland: in transition from Communism to democracy. In N. J. Adler, and D. N. Izraeli (eds.), *Competitive Frontiers. Women Managers in a Global Economy.* Cambridge: Blackwell, 243–262.

Siemieńska, R. (1994b) Szkoła panstwowa i niepaństwowa a wartości demokratyczne (Public and Non-public Schools and Democratic Values). *Kwartalnik Pedagogiczny* (special volume) Szkoły niepaństwowe w polskim systemie edukacyjnym (R. Siemieńska, (ed.) *1–2*(151–152), 55–78.

Siemieńska, R. (1995). Dylematy transformacji w Europie Środkowej i Wschodniej. Analiza systemu w perspektywie porównawczej (Dilemma of Transformation in Central and Eastern Europe. Analysis of System in Comparative Perpective). In E. Tarkowska (ed.), *Powroty i kontynuacje. Warsaw*: IFiS PAN, 117–135.

Siemieńska, R. (1995a) *Value Orientation of Councillors and Local Administrators in Transition to Democracy,* unpublished paper delivered at the conference organized by North Carolina State University, Raleigh.

Siemieńska, R. (1997). The changing world of ideological conceptions in Central and Eastern Europe. *International Review of Sociology 7*(3), 461–484.

Small Statistical Yearbook. (1939). Warsaw: Main Statistical Office.

Stewart, Sprinthall, Siemieńska. (1997). Ethical reasoning in a time of revolution: a study of local officials in Poland. *Public Administration Review 57*(5), 445–453.

Vianello, M., Siemieńska, R., et al. (1990). *Gender Inequality. A Comparative Study in Discrimination and Participation.* London: Sage.

Wiatr, J. (ed.), (1987). *Władza lokalna w warunkach kryzysu (Local Government in the Crisis Conditions)*. Warsaw: University of Warsaw Press.

24

Building Community Organizations and Local Governments in Former Soviet Republics

Earl Frank Mathers   *International Institute, USDA Graduate School, Washington, D.C.*

I. INTRODUCTION

The object of this chapter is to underscore salient aspects of civil society development in transitional democracies with particular attention to local level initiatives that may be promoted through government collaboration with civil society organizations (CSOs) and nongovernmental organizations (NGOs). In this context, much of the information presented is drawn from international development experience in post-Soviet societies including the author's observations and implementation efforts in Lithuania as well as brief illustrations from other countries that are at different points on the democratic transition continuum. Although emphasis will be on transitional democracies, the noteworthy legacy of civil society and community activism in the United States will not be ignored. In fact, observations of U.S. experience and the current redefining of practical approaches to citizen involvement in this country will serve as a reference points, despite the laments from various sources regarding the decline of community action in America and related debates.

The U.S. Agency for International Development (USAID) and other donors in Central and Eastern Europe and the New Independent States (CEE/NIS) have placed considerable emphasis on the need to build civil society as a means of promoting and consolidating democratic reform, improving the potential for the decentralization of government authority, increasing access to government, and enhancing service delivery. Civil society is, from the USAID perspective, one of the four critical building blocks of democracy.[1] Recognition is growing that working through community-based organizations can have salubrious effects on peace building for postconflict societies and in grappling with community conflict (Silver 1999). In many situations, however, severe resource constraints, ineffective leadership, and interrupted or nonexistent histories of civil society activity are factors that discourage the development of a vibrant CSO/NGO community and inhibit the implementation of viable solutions to these vexing problems. Public apathy, the lack of an adequate legal environment, suspicion, limited public understanding of the sector, and the documented excesses of a small segment of profiteering NGO officials are additional factors that continue to delay the emergence of more viable civil society in many CEE/NIS countries. USAID has created an NGO "sustainability index" that measures the overall strength of the NGO community in the CEE/NIS and operates on a 7-point scale. The criteria used to evaluate the viability of the NGO sector in a given country are listed in Table 1.

Although USAID developed the *sustainability index* to evaluate the strength of NGOs in the

CEE/NIS region, it is clear that measuring organizational or nonprofit sector capacity and efficacy in the United States along some of the same parameters would be an equally viable methodological approach. From a comparative perspective, it is not that NGOs in advanced democracies are confronted with different developmental obstacles than those that challenge their CEE/NIS counterparts; the differences are more in terms of order of magnitude. How often, for instance, have we heard U.S. nonprofit executives grumble about the difficulty of achieving tax-exempt status or express concern that viable prospects for staff development are too costly for austere organizational budgets?

My personal experience managing nonprofit and quasi-governmental entities in the United States, undoubtedly replicated by thousands of others around the country, suggests that the fight to maintain financial viability requires sustained effort. The seasoned executive will, in fact, maintain some degree of continuous focus on the revenue generation capacity of his or her organization by documenting achievements, devising creative fund-raising strategies and adding value to products. The difference for many organizations in the CEE/NIS region is that attributes such as a well defined and relevant organizational mission, creative approaches to fund raising, persistence in negotiating the bureaucratic labyrinth, and strident calls for volunteer support may not be enough to overcome systemic problems and the paucity of financial resources available in severely stressed economies.

Informed observers agree that the legacy of Communism in the CEE/NIS, while generally negative, is not uniform in terms of infrastructure condition, severity of social problems, economic vitality, or latent capacity of the various countries in question to address these concerns. As the development of civil society—vibrant in some cases and virtually nonexistent in others—attests, some countries are better equipped to manage than others. Adroit management and leadership are more likely to produce the desired results when other conditions are favorable as well.

II. REFORM AGENDA

Program implementation in transitional democracies for USAID involves deliberate effort to advance established components of the reform agenda as identified in the form of strategic objec-

Table 1   NGO Sustainability Index[2]

Aspects of NGO sector for analysis	Representative evaluation criteria
Legal environment	Ease of registration
	Taxation and procurement
	Legal status of NGOs
	Legal knowledge of sector
Organizational capacity	Critical mass of mature organizations
	Support infrastructure for development
Financial viability	Revenue generation capacity
	Philanthropy and volunteerism
	Financial management capacity
Advocacy	Record of influencing policy
	Extent of active monitoring
Public image	Public awareness and perception
	Media coverage
	Government's willingness to collaborate

tives and intermediate results. Most other donors also provide some parameters for program design, implementation, and performance measurement. For example, "Increased development of a politically active civil society" and "More transparent and accountable government institutions" are strategic objectives that are directly relevant to the current discussion in terms of their potential for civil society programming.[3] Consultants working with recipient institutions and governments must be committed to designing and implementing activities that fulfill the intermediate results that are in turn subordinate to the strategic objectives that comprise the reform agenda. More specifically, consultants are concerned about improving government accountability and transparency, increasing levels of voter registration, enhancing access to the legal system and establishing any of a host of other acknowledged attributes of a well functioning democracy.

Particularly at the local level, however, these same consultants may be confronted with another set of issues that focus on the practical economic, social, and quality-of-life needs of the community. Local government officials and other community leaders, regardless of their awareness of, or commitment to, the democratic reform agenda, are usually under pressure to address and ameliorate these very real community problems, often with inadequate resources. For the adviser-consultant assigned to work in the areas of democratic reform and/or civil society development, one key issue may be how to devise a strategy that integrates the fulfillment of two sets of objectives; one from the mission and one from the local community or institution that is the designated recipient of his or her services.

Programs of technical assistance for good governance often promote decentralization, and this typically involves facilitating the creation of an enabling environment in which local governments can meet the needs of constituents efficiently and in a way that reflects the genuine interests of citizens. It is widely accepted that the proximity of local government to citizens makes it more representative and more responsive to local issues. Decentralization, under the right conditions, can also produce governments that are increasingly self-sufficient and innovative in their approaches to service delivery. Johnson and Minis suggest that *legitimacy*, *accountability*, *management effectiveness*, and the *availability of information* (transparency) are accepted by most observers as the attributes of good governance.[4] Axiomatically then, programs that build the relationships between citizens, the organizations that represent them and local governments will focus on legitimacy, accountability, transparency, and, in some cases, management effectiveness. The case study from Lithuania toward the end of this chapter discusses an approach that successfully integrated local program objectives with those of USAID in a program of training and project planning involving local governments and NGOs.

III. SPECIAL PROBLEMS

As stated above, similarities exist between problems confronting civil society organizations in nascent and in advanced democracies. The order of magnitude of the problems, however, may be quite different. Several examples may help to illustrate this point. A recent public opinion poll in Russia reveals that only 4% of Russians have ever participated in nonprofit work and, as recently as 1997, only 32% of the population could name one NGO.[5] Actually, these numbers have improved incrementally in recent years and, throughout the region, NGOs are becoming increasingly cognizant of the need to increase public awareness of the positive aspects of civil society activity. In the recent past, however, the primary exposure the public has had to the nonprofit sector has been negative media coverage of organizations engaged in activities such as money laundering and tax avoidance schemes. Although similar problems and others such as the misappropriation of charitable donations for excessive personal enrichment and influence peddling have occurred in the United States, the maturity and diversity of the nonprofit sector in this country prevents these anomalies from destabilizing the sector. Indeed, the nonprofit sector in the United States is a tightly woven component in the fabric of American life that, if not fully understood by the public, is comparatively well known and accepted.

Early in my experience as a long-term government consultant to Lithuania, I was enlightened by several revealing expressions that Lithuanians would use to help explain their former relationship with the Soviets. One adage that seems especially applicable in this context is: "They pretended to give us jobs and we pretended to work."

This homily helps to explain an interesting point. While civil society was generally restricted during the Soviet period, those innocuous organizations that were permitted and those that directly supported the system were blessed with comparatively high levels of participation because primary employment was in organizations that were often dramatically overstaffed. Consequently, workers often had the flexibility to donate their time to community activities because the value of an individual's time was of no consequence and the serious concerns about competition were confined to moving through the party ranks or the sports field. Today, the struggle to compete in emerging market economies requires that people work diligently, sometimes in more than one job, so that little time or discretionary income is available to support civil society programs. Another vestige of the Soviet era that predisposes people to reject the idea of volunteerism are negative stereotypes regarding the "voluntary" labor they were compelled to give the state during that period.[6] This situation is exacerbated in Lithuania by the fact that volunteerism is a legal non sequitur and organizations may experience tax liability if they rely on volunteer labor due to ill-conceived statutes governing civil society. Gradually, these statutory anomalies are being addressed in Lithuania as the country develops a more enabling climate for civil society.

Another illuminating Lithuanian expression is "Because nobody owned it, nobody cared about it." People rarely felt a sense of pride or ownership in their communities during the Soviet period. In fact, many people refer to that period as one of "occupation" and reliance on the remote Soviet state to manage and finance all physical and program development created a host of pervasive and lingering problems. The legacy of communism, though somewhat uneven, is one of varying degrees of infrastructure decline; limited preventive maintenance; inefficient, uncomfortable, and wasteful design; and, in most cases, marginal service quality. Recognizing that people in the West did not live like this, expectations of dramatic improvement ran high during the early years of the transition. Unfortunately, these expectations were inflated. Overcoming problems of the immensity found in post-Soviet societies will require considerable time. Effective collaboration between citizens and their governments in resolving these problems, especially at the local level, can lead to community capacity building and more vigorous resource development.

At present, NGO survival in the CEE/NIS frequently demands reliance on donor or foundation assistance which may be tenuous if donors lack confidence in an organization or the potential for reform in a particular country. This limits the number of viable NGOs and PVOs and is a locational factor as well leading to higher concentrations of civil society programs in capital cities where the donors typically have offices. In Moldova, for instance, we found that most NGOs were based in the capital city despite the fact that 72% of the population is classified as rural.[7] Infrastructure decline and poor or nonexistent public services, exacerbated by severe economic stress, have combined to create a situation in which quality of life for most Moldovans is low, wages are frequently well below poverty levels, and a persistent crisis of confidence in government exists. World Bank data indicate that 45% of Moldovans lived below the absolute poverty threshold of $18.30 per month at the end of 1998. Local governments, particularly in smaller communities, lack the capacity to respond effectively to public needs, and in many instances basic services such as water and heating are intermittent and/or threatened. Political instability and unmanageable levels of external debt create additional stress and limit the ability of government at all levels to respond to citizen needs. Not surprisingly, in this context, the overall number of registered NGOs has declined in recent years.[8]

Despite the severity of the crisis in Moldova, certain NGOs, including the Viitorul Foundation, continue to fulfill important roles in areas such as policy analysis and representation for local governments. The general climate for NGO development in Moldova is unfavorable, however, and falls short on many of the criteria established by USAID's sustainability index. In particular, neither NGOs nor the local governments that might choose to work with them to build community capacity has the financial viability or organizational capacity to move forward in this vein aggressively. The training resources that exist in Moldova are underdeveloped and unlikely to become self-sustaining for some time since few institutions would be able to pay for much needed human and/or organizational development services. Donor assistance has helped in some instances, but Moldova's instability and tenuous hold on the ladder of democratic transition will inevitably slow program development on the part of donors and result in additional conditionality. The severe disruption of the Russian and NIS economies in 1998–99 has created a ripple effect in Moldova with its heavy dependence on impoverished and unstable trading partners in the region and weak local economy. This adversely impacts the potential for the development of local government and community organizations by stanching the flow of capital into the country and diminishing the financial viability of those institutions while exacerbating the service delivery needs of residents. As the BASA Press reported on Aug. 4, 1999, Moldovan export trade for the first seven months of 1999 declined by 45% from the already low levels of the same period in 1998. The irony is that the donor community may be justifiably reluctant to invest program or capital funds in certain countries due to unstable conditions. While these countries may not be fertile ground for development programming, their need for assistance is great.

IV. POTENTIAL FOR COLLABORATION AND PARTNERSHIP

In response to resource constraints and the desirability of involving citizens and the organizations that represent them in the governing process, many local governments in the United States and other Western democracies are increasing their reliance on planning techniques and implementation strategies that actively engage community-based organizations. Adherents believe that such strategies will result in improved decision making, increased support for program implementation efforts, and better local-government accountability to constituents. It is also clear that practitioners and elected officials are often responding to external pressure to engage and empower citizens. This pressure may be exerted by citizens themselves, through the mandates of higher levels of government or from conditions attached to donor funding. In addition, some practitioners have discovered that actively engaging and empowering citizen groups has the potential to significantly augment local resources although others complain that devoting time to working with citizen groups and facilitating the resulting initiatives demands inordinate amounts of time. My belief is that increasing levels of representation in government goes to the essence of democracy and produces more relevant programs.

During the early assessment phase of the Strengthening Local Government Project in Lithuania for which I was Chief of Party, I began to recognize that some of the same strategies that are effective in the United States had the potential for successful adaptation in that Eastern European country. I was aware that this potential to build the capacity of the community could have positive ramifications for many different areas of public administration practice including social services programming, public utilities and housing, infrastructure development, recreation, education, and economic development. American cities like Des Moines, Iowa, have made remarkable strides in their approaches to citizen involvement while effectively prioritizing infrastructure improvements and building community decision-making capacity.[9] Officials in Des Moines and other American cities would undoubtedly concede, however, that achieving success with their approaches to citizen involvement required sustained effort, significant resource deployment and a well-conceived planning process. If the incomplete fulfillment of these requirements sometimes inhibits civil society program development in the United States, to what extent would these and other factors limit similar initiatives in Lithuania? There have been many donor-sponsored programs of NGO assistance taking a variety of forms and utilizing an array of strategies. The same can be said of programs designed to assist local government. Significantly, there has been growing recognition within the development community that it makes sense to work concurrently with the two sectors in order to achieve objectives of common interest.

One area of established interest to local governments and community organizations in CEE/NIS cities that recently has been acknowledged by donors is economic development. For many Lithuanian cities in the mid-1990s, issues like job creation, business development, and privatization overshadowed other community needs. The resident city to which I was first assigned was no exception and economic development became a priority focus for collaborative program development involving city officials, community organizations representing the business community and the local university.[10] Donor interest has solidified in recent years and, in November 1998, a regional conference was held in Bucharest to consider the opportunities and challenges associated with local economic development in the CEE/NIS. The primary theme of the conference, *Mobilizing Community Resources for Local Economic Development*, is suggestive of the importance the donor community is now placing on building partnerships between community organizations and local government. In the CEE/NIS, economic development seems to be particularly fertile ground for the formation of such partnerships although collaboration in a variety of service delivery areas is possible if certain conditions are met. At the Bucharest conference, which was sponsored by USAID, the World Bank, the Open Society Institute of the Soros Foundation, and the Council of Europe, participants identified the key characteristics of successful economic development partnerships, namely:

Common goals and objectives
Involvement of stakeholders from different sectors
Clearly defined roles and responsibilities
Collaborative approaches to problem solving
Mobilization and pooling of resources to achieve shared objectives
An understanding that working together makes sense
Agreement on the roles, responsibilities and resources of the partners[11]

The following examples may help to illustrate the importance of the characteristics identified at the Bucharest conference in practical terms. Despite the challenges of retrofitting antiquated facilities and overcoming sometimes irksome attitudinal problems, it is possible at times to take advantage of the infrastructure that remains after the demise of the Soviet Union. In Russia, the *Technopolis* concept involves the coordination of local resources to engage underutilized scientific and technical capacity formerly attached to the military-industrial complex in the Urals region.[12] With leadership and training by the Urals branch of the Russian Academy of Science and active community involvement, the program was designed to build human and reorient local resources to the market economy. Combining resources and identifying common goals were important characteristics of the formation of partnerships in several formerly closed communities in the region.

An especially dramatic example of collaboration to build community capacity involved a group of Lithuanian public administrators I worked with in 1997–98. In this case, Donatas Jankauskas, mayor of the Kaunas regional municipality, and his colleagues successfully converted the former Soviet electronic spying facility known as Linksmakalnis to a small community with housing, schools, and economic opportunities for residents.[13] Working in concert with citizens, prospective investors and the central government, the officials of the Kaunas region were able to develop incentives, attract public and private investment in Linksmakalnis and to lure residents back to the community while improvements were in progress. In this case, the most innovative feature of the program at Linksmakalnis was the creation of incentives such as below-market rent and lease rates, under certain conditions, for prospective residents and investors. Although these examples may be exceptions, there is potential for the application of locally originated strategies of community development to succeed under the right conditions in former Soviet republics and in Russia. Clearly, people become committed to such community development initiatives when the prospects for success are reasonably strong and the potential benefits to collaboration and hard work are significant.

Community mobilization efforts have been successfully nurtured in other established and emerging democracies. In fact, many local governments are contemplating more aggressive programs of citizen and NGO involvement. It is also reasonable to assert that the characteristics of successful economic development partnerships identified above also characterize other fruitful collaborative efforts. The remainder of this chapter describes one successful model of promoting collaboration that engendered the development of these characteristics.

V. CASE STUDY: LITHUANIA

Although conditions for community development in Lithuania, as assessed by the NGO sustainability index or less rigorous observation, were not completely favorable in 1997, there was potential and a clear desire in many cities to build capacity. Despite the fact that public understanding of jurisdictional authority for various types of services was cloudy at times, there was increasing reliance on local governments to meet a broad array of community needs, usually with comparatively scarce resources. The following sections discuss an innovative program of local government/NGO training and collaborative project planning that was conducted in eight Lithuanian cities during the winter of 1997–98. This program was developed and conducted by Development Associates, an Arlington, Virginia-based consulting firm and the Municipal Training Center (MTC) at Kaunas Technological University in Lithuania. Funding for the project was provided by USAID. The design of the program coincided with strategic objectives established by the USAID mission in Vilnius, Lithuania, and responded to the specific needs of the communities selected for the program.

The fundamental premise of this paper has been that efforts to involve citizens and mobilize community organizations are consistent with a broader, paradigmatic shift toward more participative approaches to public management. Contemporary public administration, in advanced and emerging democracies, requires flexibility, responsiveness and a willingness to consider a diverse array of values and issues in the context of planning and decision-making. Therefore, citizen involvement is practical and desirable in terms of operational efficiency and political expediency as well as governmental accountability and responsiveness. I believe that emphasis on broad-based participation will continue in the future although new models of collaboration and involvement may emerge. Involving citizens and various external organizations in planning, decision making, and resource deployment processes is beneficial in terms of framing issues, enhancing the exchange of vital information and promoting understanding between competing interests and local government.

A. Context

Lithuania and the United States are very different democratic countries. While the United States is a mature democracy with well-established institutions, Lithuania continues to move through the transition from Soviet-era central planning to a system that relies fully on democratic institutions and a market economy. The transition is an arduous process, and both structural and psychological vestiges of the communist system linger, sometimes hampering democratic reform efforts. In addition, severe resource constraints exacerbate the myriad problems confronting local governments in Lithuania.

Fifty years of Soviet dominance in Lithuania bridled public management and altered the quality of interest group activity, citizen involvement, and acknowledgement of the interdependence of local government and constituents. As a result, widespread cynicism and public apathy eroded confidence in government at all levels. Economic conditions continue to negatively impact citizens as well as local government revenue generating capacity, creating a downward spiral of personal financial stress and ever-increasing demands on public institutions. In addition, the residual effects of Communism in Lithuania and throughout the region, including shoddy construction practices, delayed maintenance and a failure to upgrade technology present, a particularly vexing set of challenges for governments that are faced with many demands and insufficient means.

The structure of the system in Lithuania favors political adroitness over administrative efficacy. Local governing bodies vary in size from 21 to 51 members depending upon the size of the city. Members are elevated to their positions on city boards or councils on the basis of their standing in their political party and the degree of success that party has had with the electorate. In other words, the composition of the city board reflects the percentage of the popular vote garnered by the various political parties. Local political leaders, therefore, are not directly elected and are often highly partisan in their allegiance. The problem of indirect representation is compounded by the fact that high attrition among administrative officials also limits the continuity of relationships between local government and citizens. Abysmally low salaries in local government are a primary cause of this high attrition.

According to the NGO support center in Vilnius, Lithuania, as many as 4000 to 5000 non-governmental organizations (NGOs) exist in Lithuania. Many of these are hunting, gardening, fishing, and sporting societies, however, and the NGO support center maintains an active mailing list of only 1500.[14] A much smaller percentage is actively involved with local government. Fortunately, the body of statutes governing NGO affairs is undergoing revision because existing laws are both restrictive and cumbersome.

While many of the factors mentioned above impose restrictions on the effectiveness of NGO/local government collaboration, close observers of the Lithuanian democracy transition process strongly believe that stimulating this process will lead to greater transparency, responsiveness, and accountability in government. For this reason, our program was developed and implemented in Lithuania during the fall and winter of 1997–98.

B.   Training and Collaborative Project Facilitation Program

Based on the collective experience of the trainers and considerable substantive contact with local government and NGO representatives from around the country, program organizers possessed insight regarding training needs in the context of collaborative program development. The organizers had presented a series of local government training events the preceding year and were able to draw upon training needs assessment information as well. It was expected that the program would be presented in eight cities that are geographically distributed across Lithuania. City selection criteria included size, level of NGO activity, and expressed willingness to engage in collaborative project planning and implementation.

A training manual covering eight topics was developed for the project. In practice, there were some variations in the actual program presented from city to city as the trainers developed greater receptivity to the needs of the local government and NGO officials present. The following topics were included in the training manual: strategic planning, consensus building, conflict management, citizen participation, project management, cost/benefit analysis, sustainable community development, and proposal writing and fund raising. In addition, considerable amounts of time during the course of the three-day events was reserved for facilitating project planning activities with the active involvement of participants. Table 2 summarizes program participant information.

In general, the local government officials attending the events were department directors, assistant directors, and several city administrators. A comparatively small number of elected officials attended as well. Virtually all of the NGO representatives in attendance had management responsibility as executive level staff or board members for their organizations.

Participants were surveyed before and after each of the training and project facilitation events. Of particular interest to the program organizers were the factors which inhibit the development of cooperative problem solving between NGOs and local government. Table 3 lists several of the more common responses to survey questions that touched on this issue. Although it is clear that the participants were able to identify specific factors which inhibit collaborative effort, the relations between the two groups in the interactive environment of the training and project facilitation activities were generally amicable and supportive. Although Table 3 relates information specific to the community level, two of the most common constraints identified (legal environment and financial capacity) are also found in USAID's NGO sustainability index, and several others are consistent with information emanating from the Bucharest conference.

In most cases, the participant groups were reasonably well balanced in terms of the number of representatives from local government and those from the NGO community. Leadership in group activities emerged from both sides, although key city department heads most frequently assumed leadership roles. In general, the participants were either uninitiated to the topics presented in training or had only a limited degree of familiarity with them. It is likely that none of the participants had previously engaged in the types of facilitated project planning activities that were utilized by the trainers in that phase of the program. The program was, in fact, a ground-breaking

Table 2   NGO/Local Government Participant Summary Information

Number of program cities	8
Overall number of participants	154
Average attendance per city	19.25
Percent NGO representatives	56%
Percent local government officials	44%

Table 3   Factors Inhibiting NGO/Local Government Cooperation

1. Lack of funding for cooperative programming
2. Poor communication between NGOs and local government
3. Limited experience in working together on projects
4. A lack of understanding between NGOs and local government
5. Problems associated with the legal/statutory environment that restrict activities
6. Knowledge and technical expertise limitations on the part of government officials
7. Time restrictions due to excessive workloads

effort and the techniques used, including environmental scanning and consensus building were virtually unknown in Lithuania.

C. Program Methodology

As mentioned above, the cities in which the program was conducted were selected with some care in recognition of the fact that the level of NGO activity and degree of local government responsiveness to community needs varies considerably from place to place. While program objectives were primarily focused on improving NGO/local government collaboration at the community level in eight cities, it was also anticipated that program success might result in replication in additional cities. In addition, the methods of collaboration that were demonstrated could be readily applied to future project planning efforts in the eight program cities and thus produce significant and sustainable benefits.

The three-day events were organized in such a way as to intersperse training segments with project-planning activities in a logical progression. Two presenters conducted the events and delivered the various training modules while facilitating the progressively more detailed planning activities. In essence, the program moved from loosely structured brainstorming and environmental scanning activities, to more regimented strategic planning efforts and on to the development of detailed and actionable operational project plans. At the appropriate points, one- to two-hour training components were presented in accordance with the informational needs of the participants at that particular stage in the process. This structure stimulated consistent and active participant involvement throughout the entire three-day event. Exit surveys indicate that the participants were highly satisfied with the process and the results of the program. Table 4 summarizes the cities and issues that became the focal areas of the eight program events.

The cities in which the events were conducted are listed in chronological order in Table 4. They range in size from approximately 30,000 to 420,000 and are geographically distributed in every quadrant of Lithuania. Although participant groups were almost exclusively from the communities in which the event was conducted, the broad geographic distribution may enhance replication because neighboring communities tend to communicate frequently and exchange information regarding important issues.

Fifty percent of the program communities selected as their primary area of focus issues related to public utilities and housing. Given present circumstances in Lithuania, this common concern is not surprising. Much of the public housing stock and utilities infrastructure is in poor condition and in need of either replacement or major renovation. The level of deterioration has

Table 4 Cities and Issues Covered by the NGO/Local Government Program

City	Primary issue area
Marijampole	Services for the handicapped
Klaipeda	Handicapped/disadvantaged
Panevezys	Cultural center development
Siauliai	Public utilities
Kedainiai	Public housing
Kaunas	Tourism development
Mazeikiai	Public housing and utilities
Taurage	Public housing and utilities

been exacerbated by deferred maintenance, and local governments have neither the cash reserves nor revenue generation capacity to effectively address problems of this magnitude in most cases. In addition, energy prices have been rising to market levels in recent years. This aspect of the transition to a market economy has outstripped the capacity of many citizens to absorb increases in the price of heating and other utilities. For those residents of public housing and in rural areas with minimal income potential, the problem is especially severe. Consequently, large numbers of people are in arrears with respect to utility payments. There are also cases in which local governments have been unable to make energy payments to the higher levels of government that control supplies. The participants of our program also attributed a variety of social problems including high rates of alcoholism and family violence to the financial distress of citizens.

Evidence of physical deterioration abounds in most Lithuanian communities. It is also clear that many types of social programming including services to the aged, people with disabilities, the poor, and those with substance abuse problems are not well developed by the standards of local service providers and fall far short of Western standards. Additional concern exists regarding the need to develop youth programs. While only two cities designated projects that would serve social programming needs specifically as their top priorities, most of the other participant groups acknowledged many of the same problems. The participants also recognized the interrelationship of many social and economic problems and believed that ameliorating one type of problem may produce positive spillover effects in other sectors. The interrelationship among social variables is, in fact, well known. Putnam, for example, states that "informal social control can be more effective than law enforcement in reducing criminality and violence."[15]

Program participants were strongly encouraged to prioritize projects on the basis of both importance and feasibility. As program managers in their communities, they are in the best position to judge the importance of the community development projects under consideration and able to realistically assess implementation potential. The completed plans moved from the strategic to the operational level, following a model the author developed several years ago.[16] Beginning with a mission statement that synthesizes related community visions, the plans present goals, objectives, and action steps at increasing levels of specificity. At the action step level, participants were required to assign specific responsibilities (preferably to individuals) and designate time frames for activity completion.

D. Program Impact

At this juncture, at least seven of the eight cities have implemented some components of the project plans developed during the program. One other participant group has obtained a commitment from the city board to fund their major capital improvement projects over the next several fiscal years. Many of the projects entail capital investments of several hundred thousand U.S. dollars. The participant groups have thus far been able to maintain sufficient enthusiasm and momentum to convince governing bodies and other groups to financially and logistically support project plans. In several cases, external financing will be required to fully implement plans and for obtaining external support were developed during the project facilitation events.

To a remarkable extent, the participants at the eight training and project facilitation events were eager to participate and committed to following through with plans. Although this may be partly attributed to effective program design, the fact that prospective participant groups were informed in advance regarding the process and the anticipated results of the program helped produce a high level of preparedness on the part of the participants. More specifically, they approached the event with the conviction that they would be able to make substantive progress in dealing with an issue of major significance to their communities. It is possible to generalize regarding factors that influence project success based on the experience gained from this program which is augmented by additional experience in the provision of technical assistance to Lithuanian municipalities. Table 5 presents several key factors.

E. Analysis and Comparison

During the course of the training events, I was somewhat surprised to learn that participants believed there were actually higher levels of community participation during the Soviet era. Conventional wisdom has it that the Soviet system effectively quashed all forms of social-political activity that was not linked to the Communist party. Indeed, community organizations were generally required to register with party officials and often fell under the malodorous scrutiny of the KGB as well.[17] Despite these constraints, community organizations did operate in Lithuania during the Soviet era and citizens were probably more active in them than they are today. As described above, this may be partly attributed to economic reality. During Soviet times few incentives were associated with hard work, with the exception of notorious black-market activities. Today, many Lithuanians work two or more jobs in order to survive. Others are engaged in lucrative business activities that place a premium on their time. While it is generally true that there is a very limited history of volunteerism in Lithuania, there may be some collective memory of community organizational activity that can be effectively revived in a new context, particularly as the transition advances and social-political-economic stability increases.

Kretzman and McKnight advocate what they refer to as "asset-based community development" and suggest that this type of internally focused approach can produce significant rewards in terms of identifying and mobilizing existing resources.[18] Valuable resources exist in our communities, and efforts to effectively harness those resources in a way that contributes to community capacity building may have potential in Lithuania as well as the United States. Mobilizing those resources is often problematic, however. In America, public administration has been concerned about a "crisis of confidence" in public institutions. There is little doubt that distrust of government is highly pervasive in Lithuania as well. Apathy and suspicion may bring about withdrawal. Commenting about the situation in America, Boyte and Kari say that "our real crisis is the disengagement of ordinary people from productive involvement in public affairs."[19] Economic conditions have been mentioned as a factor that has contributed to public disengagement from community activities in Lithuania. Putnam mentioned several other causal factors in his discussion of the decline of civic associations in the United States. While mobility and other factors may contribute, Putnam cites the desocializing influence of television as the most significant reason for this decline.[20] In the developed world, other forms of technological innovation and adaptation also reduce our contact with both neighbors and institutions in a way that is heralded for increasing productivity but may have deleterious effects in terms of public involvement.

It has been argued that citizenship no longer carries the same set of responsibilities that it did a few decades ago. Indeed, there is much discussion of "global citizenship" today in our world

Table 5 Factors Strongly Influencing Successful Project Development

---

Degree of consensus and intragroup cohesion achieved at the end of the training and project planning process.

Involvement of key city officials such as the mayor, administrator, and department heads.

Perception among event participants that the municipal governing body would support the cause financially and otherwise.

Extent to which participants were able to focus on manageable issues.

---

of instant communication and multinational business and financial dealings. People continue to live in communities, however, and public administration at the local level is responsible for solving problems in those communities with inevitable resource limitations and ever-changing demands. Community-based planning, decision making, and program development make sense because the individuals involved may have superior understanding of community resources, culture, and needs as well as the ability to devise the specific kinds of strategies that will work in their cities. The model that we used in Lithuania worked, and there may be a number of other approaches that will work equally well. The concepts presented by Richard Box in *Citizen Governance*, for example, will inspire considerable discussion and, hopefully, practical application leading to empirical growth in the field.[21] Given the evidence, however, it would be misleading to suggest that building collaborative relationships and promoting citizen involvement will yield the benefits described in this chapter uniformly. Clearly, there are preconditions at both the national and local levels that influence the likelihood of achieving success. The program that works well in America or Lithuania may be ineffective in Russia and Moldova for a variety of reasons. Discussing the application of best practices in new venues is, in Blair's words, "both promising and fraught with potential" and "heightens the chances that the seeds of democratic governance will grow only in fertile spots, offering little to less promising and marginal areas."[22]

Community development can mean many things. Generally, the focus is on improvements in services for residents, enhancing quality of life, or meeting an unmet demand at the community level. The author has been involved in an eclectic mix of projects in the United States that involved local government cooperation with NGOs. In general, the factors that contribute to successful project development and implementation in Lithuania also enhance collaboration between community organizations and local government in the United States. Although interest group conflict is inevitable in both countries, there is considerable potential for coalition building and conflict management through the process of planning community development projects. If interdependent relationships between interest groups with common goals can be established and these groups are able to engage in further collaboration with local government, community capacity for various types of development can be expanded.

Collectively, the projects which were planned during the events described in Lithuania involved a relatively large number of NGOs. Although paid staff formed a portion of the participant group, the NGO board members present were often local businesspeople, including joint stock company executives and entrepreneurs, who were willing to apply their expertise and leadership skills to community interests. In some cases, these volunteers had a vested interest in the success of the program. Parents of developmentally disabled children were active participants in two cities, for example. Whether or not these effective volunteers have a strong personal interest in the program, their contribution can be valuable if their commitment is strong. In addition, such volunteer groups are sufficiently close to community problems to have a very clear impression of what real solutions will be. Some years ago, Buss and Vaughn presented convincing evidence that the program solutions to important community problems devised by local governments are sometimes at odds with the actual needs of recipients because their input was not sought.[23] More active involvement of the people close to the problems can, therefore, promote the efficient and effective use of public resources.

Volunteerism and charitable giving are less developed in Lithuania than in the United States at present. The participants in our training program suggested that wealthy business owners were reluctant to contribute financially for fear of incurring the unwanted scrutiny of the tax authorities. Several of the factors that limit the amount of time Lithuanians are willing to devote to community development have been cited above as well. However, it is clear that in the Lithuanian cities that appear to be most successful in applying the concepts presented in the NGO/local government program, the degree of commitment and leadership qualities of both local officials and NGO participants are very important factors. These leadership skills can be applied to nurturing the development and investment of social and financial capital in the community.

VI. CONCLUSIONS

That citizen involvement in democratic government strengthens and improves the quality of governance is axiomatic. Assuming that many NGOs and PVOs are established to perform a variety of functions in the community interest can also be accepted as fact. Further, it can be acknowledged that NGOs have resources, expertise, knowledge, and capacities that may, for one reason or another, elude local government. Community associations in the broadest sense might include service clubs, churches, business organizations, and a host of other affiliations in addition to human services providers and other entities that are commonly thought of as NGOs. In Lithuania, Catholic charitable organizations were very active in a number of community service activities and maintain a more refined image than many other groups. These organizations, as well as less formally organized groups, are closer to certain elements within a community than is city government. This closeness and personal familiarity produces a sense of belonging that local government will not be able to duplicate. It may be possible, however, to tap the creative energies and resources of those close associations in a way that enhances the more general sense of community that people feel. Compelling evidence exists that local government, working in tandem with NGOs and other community organizations, can solve community problems more efficiently and effectively, both in the United States and in Lithuania. Working with community organizations benefits public officials in many ways such as framing debate over important issues, improving decisions by increasing the level of information available and building rapport with a larger segment of the community. In this context, Reich has suggested that "higher-level public managers have an obligation to stimulate debate about what they do."[24]

From an American perspective, acting upon this obligation to nurture and refine participative democracy is generally considered an exemplary characteristic of public sector managers. By contrast, observations in Lithuania suggest that a significant portion of public leaders in that country continue to demonstrate a reluctance to involve either citizens or subordinates in the decision-making process. During the Soviet period, coordination with community organizations was used as a means of control and orientation to the Communist party, a fact that may continue to compromise efforts to develop citizen trust in collaborative programs today.[25] It is encouraging to note, however, that the NGO/local government program of training and project facilitation in Lithuania did achieve promising results that have the potential be replicated elsewhere and appeared to overcome some initial cynicism. The following statements summarize several of the more prominent benefits derived from this approach to NGO/local government collaboration in Lithuania:

1.   In the Lithuanian cities that were concerned with services to the handicapped and disadvantaged, underutilized city-owned buildings will be used as the locus of expanded program services and newly created citizen committees will work together to obtain external funding for improvements. Multilateral learning and improved communication occurred in all the program cities.

2.   In some cases, areas of duplicative effort, poorly designed services or other types of programmatic inefficiency were identified and addressed.

3.   Specific mechanisms for communication, problem identification, and conflict management were developed in several cities in the form of standing committees. This should help to reinforce newly established levels of cooperation.

4.   Participants acquired expertise in a variety of areas that will enable them to solve community problems more effectively in the future by deploying available resources more efficiently.

For example, participants in two cities identified new approaches to public housing problems such as a system of cooperative solid waste collection that produces better economies of scale.

5. In most of the program cities, there was favorable media coverage of the events, sometimes involving television interviews with organizers and participants.

6. The program participants in one city recast their group as an advocacy body and confronted the central government over jurisdictional issues involving local service needs.

Though not a primary objective, the NGO/local government program did enhance the process of institutional capacity building for implementing partner, the Municipal Training Center (MTC). The cofacilitator (now a member of the Lithuanian parliament) and center director were both very actively involved in the project, as were other staff members and graduate students. Implementing this and other projects funded by USAID has augmented the capacity of the MTC. The organization is now self-sustaining and the demand for the services provided by MTC extends beyond the borders of Lithuania.

While there are distinct differences between Lithuania and the United States in terms of the structure of local government, resource availability, and the attitudes of the people involved, many of the problems confronting local government, NGOs, and the communities they serve are similar, although generally of greater magnitude in the Baltic country. The experiences described in Lithuania suggests that utilizing training and project facilitation events can be effective in stimulating NGO/local government collaboration under the right conditions in transitional democracies. Similar techniques have also been used in the United States to clarify decisions, mobilize resources, and build support for community development activities. In order to improve the likelihood of developing strong commitments, facilitators should encourage participants to focus on strategies and specific plans for programs that address significant community problems to which practical solutions are possible. Because the approach used was a radical departure from traditional methods of managing community problems in Lithuania, creativity and innovation seemed natural and acceptable to the participants, and coalition building was a stated purpose of the events. In this context, it was comparatively easy for those involved to subordinate possible differences in the interest of mutually beneficial outcomes.

ENDNOTES

1. *Report on Assistance for Democracy Development* (Washington: USAID 1998), p. 5.
2. *NGO Sustainability Index for Central & Eastern Europe and the New Independent States* (Washington: USAID 1998), 3–4.
3. *Handbook of Democracy and Governance Program Indicators* (Washington: USAID, 1998).
4. Johnson, R., and Minis, H. *Toward Democratic Decentralization: Approaches to Promoting Good Governance.* RTI Center for International Development, staff working paper, p. 2.
5. Topoleva, Elena. Russian public warms to nonprofits. *Give and Take: A Journal on Civil Society in Eurasia* 2(2), 1999, p. 5.
6. Forster, Amy. *Kazakhstan's NGOs Intensify Outreach,* 1999, p. 7.
7. Beals, Mathers, and Sommers. 1998. *Moldova Local Government Assessment Report* for USAID/Kiev, p. 24.
8. *Non-Governmental Organizations in the Republic of Moldova; Their Evolution and Future.* (1998). World Bank and NGO Contact Center.
9. Mathers, E. Organizing public participation at the neighborhood level. *Public Administration Times,* October 1998.
10. Mathers, E. *Strengthening local government in lithuania. Public Administration Times,* May 1997.
11. *Mobilizing Community Resources for Economic Development.* Conference Report: USAID and the International City/County Management Association, 1998, p. 3.

12. Mathers, E. *Assisting in the transformation of the Russian economy. Economic Development Review*, fall 1995, pp. 78–79.

13. Mathers, E. *Linksmakalnis: the remarkable transition of a Lithuanian town. Public Administration Times*, April 1998.

14. Conversation with NGO support center staff on March 24, 1998.

15. Putnam, Robert. Bowling alone, revisited. *The Responsive Community*, spring 1995, p. 19.

16. Mathers, Earl. Economic development gauge and exchange, winter 1994, and in Mathers et al. *A Guide for Local Officials*. Kaunas, Lithuania: Kaunas Technological University, 1997, p. 19.

17. Based on conversations with training program participants and Alvydas Andrenas, Director of the Department of Economic Development and Investment, Kaunas, Lithuania.

18. Kretzman and McKnight. *Building Communities From the Inside Out* Center for Urban Affairs and Policy Research, Northwestern University, 1993.

19. Boyte and Kari. *Building America: The Democratic Promise of Public Work*. Philadelphia: Temple University Press, 1996, p. 14.

20. Putnam, 1995, *op. cit.*, p. 29.

21. Box, Richard. *Citizen Governance: Leading Communities into the 21st Century*. Sage Publications, Thousand Oaks, CA, 1998.

22. Blair, Harry. *Spreading Power to the Periphery: An Assessment of Democratic Local Governance*. USAID–Center for Development Information and Evaluation, 1998, p. 47.

23. Buss and Vaughn. *On the Rebound*. Washington: Council of State Policy and Planning Agencies, 1988.

24. Reich, Robert. *Policy Making in a Democracy*. In Robert Reich, editor, *Public Ideas*. Harvard University Press, Cambridge, 1988.

25. Andrenaite, Zivile. Unpublished brief entitled *Non-Governmental Organizations in Soviet Totalitarian Society*, 1998.

25
Prospects for Modernization of Public Administration in Postdictatorial Greece

Platon N. Rigos *Department of Government and International Affairs, University of South Florida, Tampa, Florida*

I. INTRODUCTION

In his exhaustive study of flaws and shortcomings in the study of comparative administration, Heady (1996:3–34) assigns much of the explanation for slow administrative reform in transitional societies to the results of a social condition labeled "clientelism" (Eisenstadt and Roniger 1984; Roniger 1994). Clientelism is a system of client-patron relationships and decision rules that are ascriptive and particularistic, as opposed to merit-based and universalistic which characterize societies that are in transition from a traditional system to a modern legal-rational. Even in democratization studies there is a tendency inherited from comparative government to look upon transitional societies with clientelism and corrupt bureaucracies as hopeless cases of political decay[1] (Huntington 1965, 1968:3). Moreover, in studies of democratic consolidation (Diamond 1996; O'Donnell 1994), the role and growth of a merit-recruited, neutrally competent, and responsive bureaucracy (the working definition of modernization here) has been ignored. Much of the emphasis is placed justifiably on the emergence of a civil society.

This pessimistic view on the chances that transitional nations may adopt Western administrative practices prevailed through the 1980s. It was partly buttressed by a concept of clientelism that attributed immutable features to what Riggs (1964) called the prismatic society. This view is not only culturally biased—only those with a Western culture can achieve civil society and merit-based bureaucracies—but historically flawed as well, since it does acknowledge that Western nations were once replete with clientelistic features and patronage bureaucracies. If it was possible for them to move out of that status, why could it not happen elsewhere? Few social scientists noticed that the end of the Soviet empire might remove major obstacles to administrative modernization such as one-party rule models and command economies. Few of them predicted the spread of democratization and pluralistic ideals.

This paper seeks to show that administrative modernization can take place just as much through top-down administrative reforms as by changes in the society within which a bureaucratic structure operates. External inputs such as imported conceptions of merit recruitment and neutrality of the civil service and the demand of foreign entities (large firms and international organizations) have greater impact in a setting where the state is no more able to ignore global currents. Internal inputs such as the growth of independent associations, a freer television system and more independent local governments can also contribute to the total effort. The role of long periods of prosperity in decentralized settings has also been ignored.[2]

Until 1996 studies of the Greek administrative structure in English have been rare,[3] short, and vague (Danopoulos 1991; Legg and Roberts 1997:167–71). All studies, including the most exhaustive (Sotiropoulos 1996), have documented the shortcomings in most "reform" efforts and the persistence of political criteria for recruitment. Entry into the Greek civil service is generally regulated by competitive examinations supervised by a board of civil servants. Public personnel is organized into categories which distinguish between university graduates and other levels of educational attainment (Shinn 1995:215). As such, it has some basic attributes of a modern bureaucracy, but political favoritism is rampant and despite the recent (1985) construction of a school for public administration staffing remains highly political.

Yet the political and economic climate has changed radically since the death of Andreas Papandreou, the charismatic leader of the party in power, PASOK (Pan Hellenic Socialist Movement) throughout most of the last 18 years (1980–89 and 1993–98). It is then appropriate to ask if the more hopeful signs in the economy and polity can also warrant a more hopeful prospect for the Greek civil service.

Although PASOK's elites of intellectuals and idealists genuinely believed and sought to produce major reforms (Shinn 1985:238, as cited in Danopoulos[4] 1991:605), most of the party leadership and cadres practiced a semi-Leninist model of a strong party takeover of the state (Sotiropulos 1996:7). The results of the first eight years of PASOK (1980–89) in power were the expansion of an already large bureaucracy into a huge and even more partisan make-work machinery.[5]

By 1989, Greece had made the jump from a classic clientelism of personality-based spoils system, to a party-based mass clientelism. Lyrintzis (1984) has labeled this pattern "bureaucratic clientelism," where state posts are offered to large classes of people simply because they are part of the party's constituency. The differences between party and state jobs, party allegiance, and ideological coherence were blurred. Fueled with European Community funds and excessive deficit spending, this model was a threat to the survival of democracy itself. The tight grip of a charismatic leader undermined basic democratic features, from party affairs to labor union elections[6] (Lyrintzis 1993:125). PASOK came close, even if in the end it failed to achieve total control of the state and other aspects of Greek society.

Surprisingly, upon the death of its leader, PASOK emerged intact and proceeded to undo some of the damage done to the economy over the years. This has recently been given an added impetus by the national consensus to enter the European Monetary Union and the European Community's strict rules for admission to what is called the "Euro Eleven." PASOK changed its strategy of total control to one that would allow civil society to flourish. Its biggest task remains the restructuring of the giant government machinery. Any reduction in size requires that large sectors be privatized.

This paper begins with a theoretical framework that emphasizes the role of bureaucratic professionalism and independence in the building of democratic systems. A short historical overview of Greek political developments sets the stage for tracing the tortuous evolution of Greece's administrative practice, then turns to a number of social, political and economic changes that augur well for administrative modernization. Among these, is the growth of local government activism in a nation once smothered by an all-powerful, yet bumbling central state. This represents a change in the conception of democratic and bureaucratic development in a group of nations labeled as "semiperipheral"[7] They are located in Southern Europe, Latin America and parts of Asia. Their attributes are that they have achieved some level of economic development, but have had long periods of problematic parliamentarism (Mouzelis 1987; O'Donnel 1994) in a climate of clientelism. Some new democracies of Eastern Europe could probably be added to that group.

II. THEORETICAL FRAMEWORK

While the availability of "free-floating" resources is crucial to the initial emergence of a powerful secular bureaucracy (Weber 1958), the development of several centers of power that compete for such resources is also viewed as necessary in order to limit a powerful bureaucracy's excesses (Eisenstadt 1959). In cases where the bureaucracy developed meritocratic standards, its total domination of a society (as existed in ancient China) was eventually the cause of its own downfall.

With democratization and industrialization, these power centers change into civic organizations and create a civil society (Diamond 1995). A new equilibrium between the bureaucracy and independent interest groups (unions and business groups) can reduce some clientelistic practices. Ideally an independent civil service will command respect from various groups for its standards of efficiency and impartiality. Respect will also increase as the best of university graduates are inducted into a system increasingly in need of technical expertise. Technical expertise can impose merit standards in some segments of the bureaucracy, even if the rest of it remains influenced by politics.

The equilibrium of political forces may often be unstable (as in France throughout the 19th and 20th centuries), if other parts of the political system (army, political parties) are still not fully modernized or have not shed antidemocratic ideologies. Brief revolutionary or dictatorial episodes and government instability will not impede the march toward democratic development as long as the bureaucracy maintains its independence (Timsit 1986) and professionalism. Italy, Germany, and Japan provide similar examples.[8] On the other hand, if these episodes take place before the bureaucracy has acquired widespread acceptance and trust, the organization will be subject to systematic purges, every time a new government or a new leader comes to power.[9]

When the equilibrium of a civil society is not yet achieved, political parties take over the bureaucracy and destroy any meritocratic tendencies that may have been budding. As in Russia, when a political party takes over the state for 70 years, it eliminates independent centers for decision making. The introduction of a free market and democratic structures leads to the collapse of the civilian and the military bureaucracies and induces massive corruption and inefficiency. The political party domination takeover completes the destruction of civil society and in the ensuing chaos, the only organizations that prevail are those that carry out criminal activities (Fukuyama 1995).

Independent, professional media presence is useful to bureaucratic modernization, because newspapers and television stations thrive in exposing corruption and scandals. Particularly critical is the emergence of large audience television stations occupying mostly the middle of the political spectrum.[10] The middle-of-the-road channels allow their reporters and commentators greater freedom to exercise an independent sense of journalistic professionalism.

External inputs such as successful colonial efforts (Britain's in India[11]), or the modernization of the American South, which began, with the Social Security amendments of 1940 (U.S. Civil Service Commission 1978:70), also help the spread of administrative professionalism.[12] Other external inputs can include the demands of international organizations like the United Nations or the European Union. As external inputs, schools of public administration and the training of civil servants overseas can help, but the postwar era is replete with failures. Nigeria has been blessed with a number of schools of public administration organized by the best American universities, and yet it is rife with the worst corruption seen anywhere.

The role of a strong ethic of professionalism in the business community has often been overlooked. Again the development of the American administrative system (U.S. Civil Service Commission 1978) shows that when business organizations acquire meritocratic standards and reject nepotism,[13] they will eventually demand that the same standards can be found in governmental affairs. Increased emphasis on the creation of business schools is indicated. Owners of enterprises have to abandon views that the corporation is their personal property, and leave the day to day decisions to professional managers. This change rarely develops spontaneously, in clientelistic or low trust societies (Fukuyama 1995), but foreign corporations can implant that seed in the local business climate. More recently, the partial or full privatization of public enterprises creates a new class of managers who have to respond to market conditions (including a demanding stock market) and not as much to politically inspired directives.

Finally, in studying bureaucracies in transitional societies, there is an important consideration to make. Most political systems undergo a process of "political incorporation" (Browning et al. 1983, 1997; Lyrintizis 1990; Collier and Collier 1991) of previously oppressed, underrepresented classes, workers, or ethnic groups, so as to democratize successfully. Political incorporations unfortunately, can be disruptive, chaotic and unsuccessful (Collier and Collier 1991: 161–95). The bureaucracy is affected because whether a populist or left party carries out the process, it often nationalizes or controls major industries to create jobs. This has often meant a substantial increase in the size of the public sector and the inclusion of employees on bases other than merit. In assessing the progress accomplished in a transitional bureaucracy that has just been subjected to the impacts of political incorporation, we must expect some amount of overstaffing and the lingering of political consideration in recruitment. These characteristics recede as the healing of political wounds proceeds and citizens begin demanding greater efficiency and effectiveness.

III. OVERVIEW OF THE GREEK POLITICAL SETTING

An overview of the political setting is needed because administrative reform is closely linked to changes in government that have constantly disrupted and weakened the foundations of the Greek civil service. The Greek State resembled the classic legal-rational bureaucratic model when it was founded in 1823. It borrowed heavily from French and German models. Yet four major impediments to modernization and democratization stood in the way. The first was that Greece was still basically an agrarian society with a heavy tradition of clientelism and patrimonial local bureaucracies, left over from Ottoman dominant rule.[14] Part of that past included the reinforcement of Greek individualism and localism.

The second impediment was the task of nation-building efforts which distract many new nations. In the Greek setting this effort often called the "*megali idea*" (the Grand Idea) was the search for a larger Greece that would encompass all large Greek communities living in the Ottoman Empire. Greece's effort was more ambitious for such a small nation and met with success throughout the late 19th Century and in the early 1900s (the Balkan wars of 1912–14) as it doubled Greek territory. Unfortunately, the pursuit of that goal distracted Greek economic modernization efforts for 100 years and strengthened a central state that weakened local government and much of civil society (Legg and Roberts 1997).

The third impediment was the emergence of a royalist/anti-royalist cleavage that made mass purges of the bureaucracy a well-accepted phenomenon. Moreover, this cleavage was not even expressing the more meaningful cleavage of upper classes opposing lower classes in the middle of a world-wide economic crisis.[15]

A fourth impediment was the constant, foreign intervention in Greek affairs on the side of royalist and right wing factions. Great Britain was first and the United States continued the practice from 1948 until 1974, when the military dictatorship came to an end. Finally, the political incorporation of Greek workers and lower classes was a traumatic process that had to be repeated more than once and involved a violent civil war. Throughout the interwar era (1918–1940) mass purges in the bureaucracy were normal. Even Elevtherios Venizelos, the first great modernizer of Greece who sought to build a Westernized, liberal state resorted to such tactics. Venizelos is still revered for his doubling of Greek land mass. For reasons that have been discussed elsewhere,[16] he chose to express the drive toward modernity more as a zero-sum, take-no-prisoners clash between the monarchy and his supporters. This made incorporation of workers and modernization of bureaucratic traditions a case of fits and starts that left both processes incomplete.

Finally, Greece had the misfortune of facing World War II, the Nazi occupation, and an intense Civil War between right and left for almost a decade (1940–49). The Civil War itself was quite bloody and destructive and left the country even poorer. The Civil War left a heavy legacy of deep divisions between left and right. The left having come close to gaining power during the last part of the Nazi occupation felt cheated. There are few examples of democratic regimes emerging after a civil war as Spain's experience shows. Such regimes encounter the problem of the political incorporation of the defeated (Rigos 1999), the left in the Greek case. The conservative parties ruling Greece after the Civil War, were incapable of bringing that about, not in a climate of a worldwide clash between Soviet Communism and American power that distorted the politics of many large and small nations. The armed forces remained fiercely pro-monarchy and anticommunist, the secret police and paramilitary elements fought and jailed a number of leftist leaders very much in the style of Latin American nations at that time. Similarly, the American CIA intervened to support these elements (Rigos 1998a).

In the middle of this climate of conspiracy and repression, Greece nonetheless thrived economically, rebuilt its infrastructure and parts of its welfare state (social security, unemployment compensation, a minimal public health care system). Under a conservative like Caramanlis (1955–63), the state established a prominent role in the economy, owning banks, phone companies, and major industries (Clogg 1990). In politics, however, the antagonisms did not abate. The center and left accused Caramanlis of rigging the general elections of 1961 and of keeping extensive files on voters of the opposition parties. The bureaucracy was viewed as the ideal job placement for members of the middle class (Vergopoulos 1981:298–308).

The colonels' regime in 1967 was the last gasp of military intervention that had harmed democratic and administrative development so often. The military clique took aim at the bureaucracy one more time, changing recruitment patterns and pressing for efficiency. The debacle that brought about the occupation of Cyprus in 1974 was so bad that Caramanlis was summoned from exile. His New Democracy Party held sway until 1981, seeking to occupy the center and discredit the more extreme elements of the old right, but in 1981 it lost the elections to PASOK, a new party with a populist agenda and a formidable organization. PASOK was the first mass party ever seen in Greece. Its organization reached into every village, hamlet, or island.

PASOK proceeded to radically change Greek society and complete full political incorporation of previously deprived or excluded strata. By 1988, the project was complete (Lyrintzis 1990) and the state agencies were filled with its supporters. Part of the incorporation process was an effort at total state control. A series of financial scandals reported by a press and media that had come very close to being controlled by the party, proved to be the nation's salvation, and PASOK was momentarily defeated. In the hiatus of 1989–90, even the Communist party joined an interim government aimed at adjudicating the scandals. Unnoticed by most observers, the increased independence of various local governments (controlled by opposition parties) and the growth of independent television and radio stations[17] became the bulwark against one-party domination.

After Papandreou's death, the new prime minister, Constantine Simitis, proceeded hesitantly, and with great opposition from within his own party, to reverse the pathologies created by 16 years of chaos. He will be embroiled in battles over privatization, the taming of inflation and a huge budget deficit at least until the next elections in 2000.

IV. GREEK BUREAUCRATIC DEVELOPMENT

In covering the complex path of Greek reform effort, I have sought to maintain a historical perspective and an organizational concern, that groups issues of personnel administration. The sheer volume and changes in direction reflected in PASOK's administrative initiatives in the 1980s have necessitated a separate section of its own with its own thematic subsections. This first section on Greek administrative developments will begin with the development of some basic concepts of administrative modernization like tenure and job security and their shaky status in the post–World War I era. The post–World War II era until 1974 is also an ideal setting for discussing the issue of political pressures and abrogation of basic employee rights brought to bear on a dispirited civil service. A fourth segment will analyze some basic features of the Greek administrative system under conservative rule in the late 1970s. To some extent some topics may overlap with the conservative era of the 1950's and have relevance for Greek administrative practices in general. In the section dedicated to PASOK initiatives, separate segments will consider the effort at wrenching control from the conservative order, the meritocratic and egalitarian tendencies displayed by each various reform effort.

A. Early Reform Attempts (1883–1917)

The highly centralized state administration (built on French and German models) was nonetheless completely dependent on alternating governing parties during that era. Civil servants, the police force, judges, tax collectors, local financiers, and local prefects looked to members of parliament for protection. Parliamentary politics reflected more a clash of personalities than any partisan or ideological conflict. This was traditional clientelism in its purest form. Prime Minister Charilaos Trikoupis in the 1880s tried to build an independent civil service by establishing strict codes on the firing, transfers and promotions of government workers, but these changes were quickly ignored. Sotiropoulos (1996) calculates that during the 1870s, there were seven times more civil servants per 10,000 inhabitants in Greece than in Great Britain.

    Legally speaking, the concept of tenure for civil servants became an integral part of the "modern" Constitution of 1911, but even that development did not root out old practices. Constitutional guarantees have rarely meant much in Greece, since they were often flouted by decrees of subsequent regimes. The blatant flouting of statutory or Constitutional guarantees with laws or implementations that contradict them is common in a country that at the same time reeks of excessive legalism and formalism (Mouzelis 1987). All such regimes have been able to count on a subservient judiciary.

B. Civil Service Under Political Assault (1917–1974)

As early as 1917, Venizelos, the great modernizer, began purges of his political enemies in the bureaucracies. Four other similar purges would occur from 1911 until 1950 (Sotiropoulos 1996:24). The Metaxas dictatorship (1936–1940) continued the purging tactics against Venizelos supporters and Communists, too. The Greek Civil War marked the beginning of more severe blows to the standards of an independent civil service. The governments of that era (1945–61) purged the civil service of Communists, socialists, and other members of the left. In a single year (1947), 12% of civil servants were dismissed (Sotiropoulos 1996).

    With the arrival of virulent anti-Communism, a registry of "disloyal" civil servants became the first tool of political control. Some personnel legislation was inspired by anti-Communist American legislation (Alivizatos 1979). Many of these practices continued under the seven-year dictatorial regime.

The Civil Service Code of 1951[18] introduced the first uniform grade structure and centralized personnel management. A central council managed the comprehensive competitive examinations for entering public service while personnel councils within each ministry decided on promotions. Yet the code also included all sorts of intrusions into the private and political life of state workers. For example, before appointment could become final, civil servants had to fill out a questionnaire on their "social opinions." Special "councils of loyalty" could also be used (Sotiropoulos 1996:28). Political neutrality was expected, yet this feature was more often used to control the ideology of civil servants. In one clause of the code, a civil servant was not obliged to follow an illegal order, but another clause created two loopholes wide enough to negate its meaning.[19]

C. Civil Service and Regional Organization Under the New Right (1974–81)

The New Democracy (ND) party came to power pursuing a centrist social policy and denouncing elements of the extreme right associated with the royalty and the colonels. Yet very little changed in the bureaucracy from the patterns set in the 1950s. ND as a party is still replete with elements that have learned to feed off the state and Caramanlis belonged to that wing of the party. It is only recently that it has developed a true free market wing within its ranks and that wing does not dominate.

Ministers were given the right to have their own little cabinets to which they appointed their close personal and political associates. The secretaries-general in each ministry controlled promotions and transfers. The prime minister selected officials called "directors-general" who were career bureaucrats with tenure. They were superior to all civil servants except for the secretary-general. In 1975, the ND government created the new position of "alternate director-general," to provide jobs for the large numbers of qualified civil servants pressing for promotion in ministries. Directors general and alternate directors general were allowed to stay on in the service more than 35 years. Even more durable were those who occupied the post of director. On the other hand, technical and consultative committees and councils kept expanding, because of a need to circumvent the more inefficient mechanisms of individual ministries.

A reliance on temporary employees, while still conducting examinations for permanent civil servants, was and still is a common recruitment policy. Since the ministry intervened to affect the final list of finalists, the formal recruitment procedures were undermined. Only fractions of the successful applicants were finally hired by the state, while the rest of the finalists had to wait to be hired until the next round of recruitment.

The central administration maintained its superiority over the local government by controlling the decisions of local authorities (e.g., municipal councils). They also minimized the limited funds to selected regions on the basis of their electoral significance for the ND government in general and for the reelection of individual ministers in particular. In every prefecture, there was a prefect, a political appointee, selected by the government among retired civil servants, former military officers, and unsuccessful parliamentary candidates of the governing party. As in France, the prefect not only supervised local elected governments of towns and villages but was the arm of the ministry of the interior in his region.[20]

Despite a number of pathologies such as bribery and bending exam rules to favor one's relatives, the ND era included some attempts at meritocratic standards. The 1951 code established a classification system based on the degree of education achieved and the results of competitive exams.

Civil servants were not passive observers of the situation. From the late 19th century, government workers intervened to help rig elections (Dertilis 1977). They took care of their own interests through unionization. As in other aspects of Greek economic and public life, labor unions accumulated a large amount of power, first under ND, and even more under PASOK.[21] Since labor unions in different sectors often support each other's strikes, work stoppages are frequent and disruptive. In the 1998 struggle to privatize one of the largest public banks, the public employees received a great amount of support from other unions. The endurance and continued political radicalism of the Communist party unions also complicate the role of unions in the privatization issue.

The power of the public sector is also reflected in its sheer numbers. Sotiropoulos (1996) calculates that as early as the 1900s, 11% to 12.5% of the total population of Greece worked for the civil service. His figures for 1976 put the size of the service at about 8.5% of the population. Although figures are shown to rise under PASOK to 10.1% in 1988, other estimates (Legg and Roberts 1997:168) put this percentage to 16% of the labor force in 1992. Legg and Roberts (1997) also cite Reed (1990) who in including all state enterprises arrives at a figure of 40% of that same labor force.

V. CIVIL SERVICE REFORM UNDER PASOK

During its two terms in government PASOK was intent on radically changing the civil service both at the central level and at the local level, but it had contradictory impulses. On one hand, it sought total control of the state bureaucracy all the way to the smallest village, and through it, its perpetuation in power. Part of this overall goal was to institutionalize a new party by creating and nurturing constituencies through government jobs. On the other hand, various cadres in the party wanted professionalization at all levels and decentralization to help revive local governments. These two sets of goals would clash and the first would most often prevail. Still, some professionalization initiatives were useful in setting the stage for future efforts. Included within the first goal of achieving total party control, were the initiatives to reverse the conservative regime's structures of control and replace them with its own. Within this first goal, was a continued centralization trend. Part of this effort was also a short-lived attempt to control the national media through the prime minister's office.

The second goal sought to experiment with a meritocracy through the creation of a school of public administration and other efforts to recruit engineers and experts. Yet this goal, too, was contradicted by egalitarian and social welfare tendencies within PASOK. The result was a series of recruitment practices that overlapped or contradicted with each other.

Policies aimed at changing local government in the 1980s were also poorly thought out. PASOK introduced a number of decentralization reforms yet treated the recruitment and promotion of municipal officials in the same centralized way (Christophilopoulou 1994). Still, central policy between 1982 and 1984 improved the human resources available to local government. Although the added resources amounted to yet another layer of patronage, the indirect effects of more personnel on financially starved local governments helped some units emerge out of a total archaic state. The additional resources and the expansion of demands for local action transformed local governments into unlikely sites of experimentation and innovations.

A. Destroying the Conservative Tools of Control

In December 1982, the government abolished the two highest ranks of the public administrative hierarchy. The posts of director-general and alternate director-general were abolished. Newly created "advisers" were brought in to bypass the directors. But the directors (who worked under the directors-general) remained influential, because while the advisers came and went with each cabinet reshuffle (Papandreou reshuffled his cabinet sixteen times in the eight-year period 1981–89), they stayed. In 1982, loyalists of the new government replaced all incumbent local prefects that had been appointed by ND.

B. Centralization of Power

In 1982, it was explained that the prime minister's technical support needs warranted the appointment of new top administrators. Yet the office of prime minister as in other European countries, already had ample technical staff available. This initiative added a number of "mini" central government offices called "bureaus of the prime minister" and included the law bureau, the diplomatic bureau, the economic bureau, the security bureau (in charge of the personal safety of the prime minister), and the political bureau.

The size of PASOK cabinets kept expanding. By November 1988, it reached the unheard of number of 57 ministers, deputy ministers, and junior ministers. In this period, the inclusion or exclusion of a high-ranking PASOK member in the cabinet was always decided at the last minute by Papandreou himself. Other measures of centralization can be found in the powers granted to the "minister of the presidency of government," a direct appointee of Papandreou's. The minister was given complete control over transfers, the power to determine how many new employees were needed, and how to increase the remuneration of the newly created advisers to ministers. Finally, Papandreou's personality and leadership style made the whole governmental structure top-heavy, confusing and unproductive. During that period, protesting groups and dissenting ministers would head for the prime minister's private residence in Ekali, a northern suburb of Athens.

Part of the centralization effort was a dangerous effort to eliminate some Greek institutions that might have had an ounce of independence or autonomy. As all scholars know, such a development can destroy civil society and makes a political system vulnerable to total control. As early as 1982, a 100-year-old public institution, the Law Council of the State, was abolished. The law council was staffed by lawyers hired through competitive examinations who enjoyed a status as prestigious as that of members of the judiciary. The law council could issue opinions on the legality of some administrative actions.

Part of the same effort was placing the audit office that had been under the ministry of finance, directly under the supervision of the prime minister himself. Now that we know the accusations of shifting public funds brought on the prime minister in the late 1980s, it is not surprising that Andreas Papandreou wanted control of the institution that could uncover criminal financial practices.

C. Creating Dependent Constituencies and Building the Party

PASOK needed to give additional salaries to PASOK cadres working full time for the government. Soon PASOK replicated its organizational structure and grafted it on the state bureaucracy to feed off the public trough. The cabinet was greatly expanded and through frequent reshuffling the cabinet gave more than 100 parliamentarians and PASOK cadres a chance to become ministers, alternate ministers, or junior ministers from 1981 to 1989. As a result, they also became quite wealthy.

In what was presented as an attempt to undo ND's multiple salary system, PASOK included exceptions that actually increased multiple remuneration. Multiple compensation could be allowed if the goal was to provide public jobs to the unemployed, to distribute the "social income" in a more just way. In this new conception of the state as a dispenser of income to political clienteles, PASOK was ushering in the new bureaucratic clientelism, which would not replace but supplement old-fashioned clientelism.

In what was explained as an effort to reform recruitment criteria, PASOK abolished entrance examinations altogether in 1983. Instead it instituted a system of points which sought to favor applicants from the middle classes that had not had a chance to enter government service before. The point system emphasized demographic characteristics describing the candidate and his or her family. The system did not last long because it was complicated and hurt the effort to recruit technically competent employees. However, it was successful in appealing to a new constituency.

From 1984 to 1987, the personnel needs of the state were met by ad hoc ministerial ordinances. According to Sotiropoulos (1997) positions were "created by fiat," without resorting to either the traditional competitive entrance examinations or the "point system." In the 1987–89 period as election time neared, the party proceeded to expand the public payroll (as ND had done), to improve its electoral chances. But the effort this time was massive. In a time span of only six months in 1989, 96,000 new public employees were hired. This is the equivalent of 2.6 million new employees in a country the size of the United States.

Similarly the problem of temporary employees resulted in overstaffing. These employees may have been hired for legitimate needs to speed up the completion of a project or for purely political reasons but it did not matter. Most of them would be granted tenure in the next recruitment waves regardless of merit. In 1984, for example, 80,000 temporary employees received permanent status.

D. Meritocratic Tendency

PASOK did not altogether abandon the concept of a meritocracy, at least not for the higher levels of the bureaucracy. In 1983, a law on recruitment founded an elite school of public administration, following the prototype of the French Ecole nationale d'administration (ENA). The new law established a center for professional training of civil servants. The center consisted of two branches, a national school of public administration, offering preentry training to prospective top administrators, and an institute for the in-service training of current civil servants. Admission to the school was based on competitive entrance examinations among university graduates. Graduates of the school were promised at least a job in some ministry. The school's program reflected a preference for legal studies, reproducing a well-known trait of the Greek civil service. Once placed however, graduates were not exactly embraced by the other civil servants. Given the egalitarian tendencies introduced by other PASOK initiatives (see upcoming section), it will take a long time for these graduates to develop the sense of mission and pride instilled in the graduates of the French ENA.

E. Egalitarian Tendency

Concurrent with the meritocratic concerns was a much stronger tendency toward egalitarianism. In 1986 each ministry was given the right to create its own committee of five employees to decide on promotions. Political forces within each ministry (the labor unions and PASOK supporters) were aligned so as to enhance the chances of high school and vocational school graduates. A less educated civil servant could supervise higher educated ones. This could happen if, for instance, a high school graduate, known for his support of PASOK, was selected by the committee to head a unit where university graduates worked. Finally, heads of administrative units were frequently rotated to weaken the role of seniority. In reforming pay scales, pay level became even less related to position. Under the 1984 pay scale system, public workers with a high school diploma or better, could move from one salary level to the next every two years, even when there were no positions available at that higher salary. The impact of these egalitarian initiatives had its cost in dampening the ambition and motivation of more motivated workers.

VI. PASOK'S COMEBACK

The fall of PASOK from power in 1989 was associated with allegations of scandals in which a few of its ministers and its main leader were implicated. Papandreou was sued by the Greek parliament, and a special court later acquitted him. Two of his ministers of finance were found guilty on various charges of financial mismanagement.

In its brief stay in power (1990–93) New Democracy reverted back to its own brand of clientelism. ND was eager to replace as much of the personnel appointed by PASOK as soon as possible. It was helped by multiple line and staff posts open to political appointments, which had been created by PASOK in 1981–89. It preserved the new top-heavy organizational charts created earlier and recreated the abolished post of director-general.

Claiming correctly that ND had forced some PASOK sympathizers to resign by frequent transfers, PASOK made sure that these employees could return if their resignation any time in 1990–93 was due to political reasons. Despite a looming financial crisis and a promise of fiscal restraint, the government decided in the spring of 1994 to increased recruitment in the civil aviation authority, the ministry of culture, and the state-run postal service.

PASOK resumed its contradictory modernization strategy. Once again it created an independent public authority in charge of all personnel recruitment to the civil service while allowing the minister of the presidency of the government to determine its composition. In addition, every general manager of state-run companies was given the right to recruit three new political appointees. On the other hand, the new personnel authority continued to conduct entrance examinations. PASOK did not immediately attack the directors-general put in place by ND. It sought to replace them gradually by changing the composition of promotion councils mentioned above.

Another set of contradictions emerged when some new regulations favored candidates with high professional credentials while other rules favored socially disadvantaged candidates, such as unemployed older persons or unemployed candidates with children. Why women or young unemployed youth did not merit similar treatment was never explained.

VII. POLITICAL MODERNIZATION

Another new sweeping reform effort that is the result of a two-year study is pending enactment in late 1998. It is too early to tell how it will be implemented. Given the long track of reform failures detailed above, it is hard to be too hopeful. Developments in other segments of Greek life give any observer more hope.

The first reason for hope is that Greece's economic situation and its dedication to enter the European Monetary Union (through limiting inflation and budget deficits) dictate very restrictive goals. The dedication to enter the European monetary system is so strong (any government would pursue it at almost any cost), because most Greeks understand that full integration with Europe constitutes the best defense against a bellicose neighbor with territorial demands. When the bureaucracy is already very large, old policies that cater to the needs of party constituencies must change.

The government's resolve has been severely tested. In the spring and summer of 1998 the first efforts at privatization of major public institutions took place. Privatizing the national airline proved to be too difficult, but one of the largest publicly held banks[22] was sold. The government faced huge demonstrations and strikes. Another test of the government's dedication to these goals has come from electoral losses as the austerity measures created dissension within PASOK's left. In October 1998, the government and parties of the left were not able to avert large losses in local and regional elections.

Part of the more realistic approach of the new PASOK leadership has been a willingness to grant major contracts for urgent projects (the new Athens airport and the Athens rapid transit system) to large foreign firms. The new regime has also been forced by threats of losing Euro funds to loosen competition rules for contracts on infrastructure projects. PASOK is no longer insisting that all projects must go to its supporters. In general, E.U. regulations are reaching deep even in the operations of small businesses.

The second major reason why prospects for modernization in all areas of Greek society seem imminent has to do with nothing less than the construction of a civil society. Legg and Roberts (1996) emphatically denied that such a project was underway. The growth of civil society is documented in great detail by Kostas A. Lavdas (1997) in his work on interest group associations in Greece and how they have been effectively "Europeanized." Lavdas contends that the impact on Greek associations began as early as the late 1950's as the entry into the Common Market was being considered.

Just as important to the creation of civil society is the growth of independent media institutions and the growth of local government independence. As mentioned earlier, radio and television media became independent through a challenge issued by the mayor of Athens. The new networks provide serious debate of public issues in a more intensive context than even in the United States. They add a civility to the public debate process that has been lacking from the tabloid journalism still thriving in the main press.

The growth of the role of local governments has taken place through a "de facto" decentralization and small undetected changes (Christofilopoulou 1994). Some of the changes are attributed to central government initiatives, whereby new functions were shifted to local government and units of supervision (the prefects) were reorganized. PASOK's belief in decentralization was genuine, but was still part of a policy of extending control to areas that might be bases for the opposition. Still, it must be given credit for putting more emphasis on political organization at the local level. This in turn provoked the ND party to follow its example as it found itself in the role of the loser trying to come back from defeat.

It must be remembered that local governments under ND had been severely underfunded and restricted through heavy central control. PASOK did not change the degree of centralization, but poured a lot of resources in the form of political appointees and special advisors to mayors of larger units. Even though these new employees were centrally appointed and functioned more as the eyes and ears of the central administration, they nonetheless expanded the size of mayoral staffs that had been skeletal up to then. Large number of professionals and engineers were hired on limited contracts and eventually became more useful to mayors that wanted to pursue a more independent policy. They clashed with generalists appointed by the ministry of Interior. While this clash was to affect local government decisiveness, their sheer presence helped local governments and new ad hoc units (see below), build an economic development infrastructure (Christophilopoulou 1994).

Local government has traditionally been the place where opposition parties lick their wounds, while hoping to come back to power in the next national elections. At a time when the central government seemed more preoccupied with redistributing rather than producing income, local government was recognized as the institution whose main task was to promote local economic and social development. ND mayors and local councils were ideally placed to benefit from this new emphasis. Intermunicipal cooperation increased and a new system of finances was adopted (Christophilopoulou 1994). A new top tier of local government was created at the level of the prefectures and the new concept of regions was introduced as new administrative divisions of the central state.

What truly increased local effectiveness was the inclusion of new semiprivate institutions similar to the American special district. These new authorities emerged as in the United States because municipalities were not up to the task of running highly technical functions like water treatment and supply.[23] In 1980, the financial situation was so difficult that the ND government had to borrow from international financial institutions (the European Investment Bank) which demanded strict accountability for the loaned funds. This could only be guaranteed by the creation of separate specialized administrative units solely responsible for water supply. Gradually, similar units called "municipal enterprises" spread throughout Greece. Although some of the latter were totally controlled by the nearby municipality, they proved to be more flexible in the provision of services.

PASOK introduced the concept of "popularly based firms" which were units jointly owned by the municipality and cooperatives of private citizens. These were encouraged by development incentives 15 times larger than for private firms (Christofilopoulou 1992:11) and given greater flexibility in management practices. Soon these municipal enterprises proliferated in all functions of local government from tourism to housing. They also entered new fields such as manufacturing, mining, and construction. Even elsewhere (in the United States and Europe), municipal representatives on the boards of these enterprises have confessed to their own inability to exercise political control over the units. Despite the concern for fragmentation that has also been heard elsewhere, there is little doubt that in Greece, the emergence of these new units has increased the capacity for local service delivery.

Even more ambitious "development companies" emerged at the regional level to assist in the absorption of E.U. funds for infrastructure development. These new units have helped in intermunicipal cooperation. In yet another bold step, PASOK forced the merger of minuscule and nonviable municipal units into fewer slightly larger units. The "Kapodystrias Project Law," as this local reorganization was called, was adopted in 1997.

Electoral successes at the local level in October 1998, by the opposition ND party give it an opportunity to continue the effort at local self governance started by PASOK. There are indications that ND politicians have understood that the local level can be an even greater site for showcasing effective government to the nation than it has been before. Very much like in the United States, where successful governors make excellent candidates for the presidency, successful mayors (particularly those who serve in Athens) catapult them into the spotlight by great local accomplishments and stunning electoral victories. Finally, the topic of local self-governance has become a rallying cry for serious reformers of all political stripes at all levels and in academia. This would have been unheard of just 15 years ago.

VIII. CONCLUSIONS

This paper has shown that Greece still suffers from leftovers of the two forms of clientelism (traditional and bureaucratic) and political overstaffing. PASOK's impulse to totally control the nation in the 1980s thwarted most of its reformist agenda. Unfortunately for Greece, the other major party (ND) did not inspire hope that it could do that much better in the 1974–1980 period and in its briefer stint in 1990–93. Despite the admittedly meager signs of administrative reform, Greece has come closer and closer to European economic standards. The best indicators come from the economy, where an inflation rate of 22% has been brought down to about 4.5%. The annual national deficit is down to 4% of GDP, yet unemployment is better than in Spain. This contradiction between fast economic accomplishments and lagging political and administrative improvements (the "Greek paradox") show that the country's economic potential is so large that it can accommodate even inefficient institutions if the nation's consensus and its government are focused on an urgent goal—full integration in the European Community.

Other transitional societies suffering from various forms of clientelism and difficult incorporation periods, like Spain and Portugal, have shown that they can modernize even more rapidly because they do not have to spend a huge portion of their national budget on defense. The outlook should be similarly good in countries like Brazil, Argentina, and Chile. The key in all such nations is the control and reversal of government bloating.

The future of administrative reforms in Greece will depend first of all in a continued prosperity that lifts all classes to the best standard of living they can remember. The prosperity and sincere appreciation of the mistakes of the past (those of Caramanlis and those of Papandreou) has brought about a new moderation in the policy debate that is ideal for the solution of administrative issues in a less threatening setting. Still, a lot of difficult choices await Greeks and their leaders. Having achieved national healing, completed the political incorporation of forgotten masses, and acquired a modern mass media, they must now accept that the cost of mistakes of the past must be paid. The political leadership available is promising. Prime Minister Simitis has proved to be a technocrat with a politician's savvy and some opposition figures also inspire hope.

ENDNOTES

1. The concept of decay is basically flawed when applied to newly created political systems. How can a living entity something that has not begun to grow can be already decaying.
2. There is a downside to unfettered growth in underdeveloped markets and economies, as the East Asian and Russian debacle show.
3. One of the first works in English to include meaningful coverage of the Greek administrative state is Tsoucalas, C. (1969), *The Greek Tragedy* (Baltimore: Penguin). For early parts of Greek administrative patterns see also Mouzelis, Nicos P. (1980), "The Greek State and Capitalism," in Richard Scase, ed., *The State in Western Europe* (New York: St. Martin's):241–273, and Vergopoulos, C. (1981), "The Emergence of the New Bourgeoisie, 1944–1952," in Iatrides, J.O. ed., *Greece in the 1940s: A Nation in Crisis* (Hanover, NH: University of New England Press), pp. 298–318. For the only Greek-language comprehensive treatment of Greek bureaucracy, see Poules P.E., *History of the Greek Public Administration, 1821–1975* (Athens: Sakkoulas, 1987).
4. In a more recent edition of the study called *Greece: A Country Study* (1995), this time edited by E. Glenn Curtis, the segment on "Government and Politics" authored by Eleni Mahaira-Odoni does not display enthusiasm about reform efforts under early PASOK rule. Referring to efforts by the two major parties in the 1980s, Mahaira-Odoni concludes, "the impact of this legislation seemed meager apart from broadening the immediate political influence of the governing party."
5. As in Peron's Argentina, the party in power sought to reduce unemployment by creating jobs that the economy did not need.
6. Only one party congress was convened during Papandreou's hold on power.
7. Greek sociologist Mouzelis (1987) and others (Arrighi 1985; Larrabee 1990; Seers, 1979) have developed the concept.
8. This emphasis on the role of bureaucracy in democratic development is purely mine although some scholars of political development (La Palombarara 1967), and development administration experts (Riggs 1967) have toiled in that area for years. Still, the bulk of democratization literature ignores this important role of bureaucracies.
9. There is a great contrast between the record of bureaucratic stability and independence in France throughout its long rotations of government and that found in Argentina, Chile, Greece, and to a lesser extent, Spain.
10. From personal observation throughout Europe (France, Italy, Greece, and Great Britain), it seems that large audience television stations must aim for the political center of the political spectrum, where most of the shoppers are.
11. India's unusual case involved a native culture that had its own long bureaucratic tradition and unusual leadership in the formative years of the democratic system.
12. This is where we find evidence of how bureaucratic professionalism can be imported gradually into political subsystems that have large doses of clientelism and ascriptive criteria for personnel recruit-

ment. The entire American South was still very much in the grips of clientelism until the 1960s, even though the social security amendments mandating that all programs funded directly by the federal government be administered by merit-based civil service, had been complying since the 1940s.

13. Clientelistic societies usually have a heavy system of nepotism within their businesses, which as Fukuyama (1995) has shown, makes them fail faster.

14. Danopoulos (1994) and Legg and Roberts (1996) emphasize that under Ottoman rule, the only contact between subject people and the Muslim authorities came when the officials needed tax collection or forced labor.

15. Many countries (e.g., France and Italy) have suffered from the distortion created by a royalist/antiroyalist cleavage, but for both countries it had become irrelevant by the mid-1930s.

16. This was a period of intense foreign intrigue often on behalf of the monarchy and these considerations may have played a role in Venizelos's reliance on the army to fight "fire with fire."

17. A story that has assumed the dimension of a legend is the one about how the then mayor of Athens, Miltiadis Evert, in 1988 challenged state monopoly of the air by establishing the first municipal radio station. Private radio and TV stations sprouted overnight. Six TV stations now outdistance the government networks in audience ratings.

18. According to Sotiropoulos (1996) some of the influences on the Greek code of 1951 were the French (1946) and German (1937) civil service codes. Italian laws on the status of public administration employees and some British institutions inspired the writers of the code. Some general guidelines formed by decisions of the Greek Council of the State were also included.

19. In one instance, the subordinate may not refuse to obey an order if the text of the order justifies its illegality by stating "reasons of general interest." An illegal order can be reissued. One small deterrent to abuse is that after having obeyed an illegal order, the subordinate can and should inform the immediate supervisor of his or her supervisor.

20. See Paraskevi D. Kaler-Christofilopoulou, *Decentralization in Post-Dictatorial Greece.* London: London School of Economics and Political Science, 1989:60, 67, 217.

21. Under ND and PASOK, the labor unions had power by their sheer ability to disrupt everyday life through frequent strikes. Lyrintzis (1991) argues that labor union's autonomy was reduced under PASOK.

22. The National Bank and the National Telephone Company are partly privatized and traded on the stock exchange.

23. In the United States, it was the construction of airports and large highways that began the explosion of special districts after World War II.

REFERENCES

Argyriades, D.C. (1965). Some aspects of civil service reorganization in Greece. *International Review of Administrative Service 31*(4), 297–309.

Alivizatos, N. (1979). *Les Institutions Politiques de la Grece a Travers les Crises 1922–1974.* Paris: Pinchon,

Arrighi, G. (1985). *Semi-Peripheral Development: The Politics of Southern Europe.* Beverly Hills, CA: Sage.

Browning, R.P., Marshall, D.R., and Tabb, D.H. (1985). *Protest Is not Enough: The Struggle of Blacks and Hispanics in Urban Politics.* Berkeley, CA: University of California Press.

Browning, R.P., Marshall, D.R., and Tabb, D.H. (1997). *Racial Politics in American Cities*, 2nd ed. New York: Longman.

Christofilopoulou, P. (1992). Professionalism and public policy-making in Greece: the influence of engineers in the local government reforms. *Public Administration 70*, 99–118.

Christofilopoulou, P. (1994). Organizational fragmentation in Greek local government: municipal bureaucracies and municipal enterprises. *Research in Urban Policy 5*, 1–19.

Collier, D., and Collier, R.B. (1991). *Shaping the Political Arena.* Princeton, NJ: Princeton University Press.

Danopoulos, C. (1994). Greek bureaucracy and public administration: a persistent failure of reform. In A. Farazmand (ed.), *Handbook of Comparative and Development Public Administration.* New York: Dekker.

Dertiles, G. (1977). *Social Change and Military Intervention, 1880–1909* (in Greek), 2nd ed. Athens: Exantas.

Diamond, L. (1996). Toward democratic consolidation. In L. Diamond and M. Plattner (eds.), *The Global Resurgence of Democracy, 2nd ed.* Baltimore. Johns Hopkins University Press, 227–240.

Einsenstadt, S.N. (1959). Bureaucracy, bureaucratization, and debureaucratization. *Administrative Science Quarterly 4*(3), 302–320.

Eisenstadt, S.N., and Roniger, L. (1984). *Patrons, Clients and Friends: Interpersonal Relations and the Structure of trust in Society.* London: Cambridge University Press.

Fukuyama, F. (1995). *Trust.* N.Y.: Free Press.

Heady, F. (1996). *Public Administration: A Comparative Perspective, 5th ed.* New York: Marcel Dekker.

Huntington, S.P. (1965). Political development and political decay. *World Politics 17*, 386–430.

Huntington, S.P. (1968). *Political Order in Changing Societies in Changing Societies.* New Haven, CT: Yale University Press.

La Palombara J. (1963). An overview of bureaucracy and political development. In J. La Palombara (ed.), *Bureaucracy and Political Development.* Princeton, NJ: Princeton University Press, 3–61.

Kaler-Christofilopoulou, P.D. Decentralization in post-dictatorial Greece. Ph.D. dissertation. London: London School of Economics and Political Science, 1989.

Larrabee, S. (1990). The southern periphery: Greece and Turkey. In P.F. Shoup (ed.), *Problems of Balkan Security: Southeastern Europe the 1980's.* Washington: Wilson Center Press, 176.

Lavdas, K. (1997). *The Europeanization of Greece: Interest Politics in Greece.* New York: St. Martin's Press.

Lenin, V.I., (1932). *State and Revolution.* New York: International Publishers.

Legg, K., and Roberts, J.M. (1997). *Modern Greece: A Civilization on the Periphery.* Boulder, CO: Westview.

Lyrintzis, C. (1993). PASOK in power: from "change" to disenchantment. In R. Clogg (ed.), *Greece, 1981–89: The Populist Decade.* New York: St. Martin's Press, 120–130.

Lyrintzis, C. (1984). Political parties in post junta Greece: a case of "Bureaucratic clientelism"? *West European Politics 7*(3).

Mahaira-Odoni, E. (1995). Government and politics. In G. Curtis (ed.), *Greece: A Country Study.* Washington: Federal Research Division, Library of Congress.

Mouzelis, N.P. (1980). The Greek state and capitalism. In R. Scase (ed.), *The State in Western Europe.* New York: St. Martin's, 241–273.

Mouzelis, N. (1986). *Politics in the Semi-Periphery: Early Parliamentanism and Late Industrialization in the Balkans and Latin America.* London: Macmillan.

O'Donnell, G. (1994). Delegative democracy. *Journal of Democracy 5*, 55–69.

Poules, P.E. (1987). *History of the Greek Public Administration, 1821–1975* (in Greek). Athens: Sakkoulas.

Reed, C. (1990). Greece at the precipice. *International Management 45*(May), 70–77.

Riggs, F.W. (1964). *Administration in Developing Countries: The Theory of Prismatic Society.* Boston: Houghton Mifflin.

Rigos, P.N. (1998a). Political healing in democratizing systems: the case of post-dictatorial Greece. *Florida Political Review* (Spring).

Rigos, P.N. (1999). Greece: the perils of political incorporation. In F. Rimanelli (ed.), *Comparative Democratization and Peaceful Change in Single Party Dominant Polities.* New York: St. Martin's Press.

Roniger, L. (1994). The comparative study of clientelism and the changing nature of civil society in the contemporary world. In L. Roniger and A. Gunes-Ayata (eds.), *Democracy, Clientelism and Civil Society.* Boulder, CO: Lynne Rienner.

Shinn, R.S. (1986). *Greece: A Country Study.* Foreign Area Studies, Washington: American University, 223–286.

Seers, D. (1979). The periphery of Europe. In D. Seers, B. Schaffer, and M.-L. Kiljunen (eds.), *Underdeveloped Europe: Studies in Core-Periphery Relations.* Atlantic Highlands, NJ: Humanities Press. pp. 3–34.

Sotiropoulos, D. (1996). *Populism and Bureaucracy: The Case of Greece Under PASOK, 1981–1989.* London: University of Notre Dame Press.

Timsit, G. (1987). *Administrations et Etats: Etudes Compares.* Paris: Presses Universitaires de France.

Tsoucalas, C. (1969). *The Greek Tragedy.* Baltimore: Penguin.

U.S. Civil Service Commission, Office of Public Affairs (1978). *Biography of an Ideal, A History of the Federal Civil Service.* Washington: USGPO.

Vergopoulos, C. (1981). The emergence of the new bourgeoisie, 1944–1952. In J.O. Iatrides (ed.), *Greece in the 1940s: A Nation in Crisis.* Hanover, NH: University of New England Press, pp. 298–318.

Weber, M. (1958). Politics as a vocation: In H. Gerth and W. C. Mills (eds.), *From Max Weber: Essays in Sociology.*

26

The Public Administration of the Republic of China on Taiwan

Lee-Jinn Hwa   *College of Law, National Chengchi University, Taipei, Taiwan, Republic of China*

I. INTRODUCTION

In the past 40 years, the economy of the Republic of China on Taiwan (ROC)[1] has developed so rapidly as to be praised as a miracle. Moreover, ROC's social, cultural, and political modernization has kept step with economic developments.[2] No doubt its public administration has played an important role in all these developments. Therefore, the public administration of ROC should not be ignored.

Unlike many developing countries whose administrative systems are imitative rather than indigenous, and usually patterned after a particular national administrative model (Heady 1984:281), ROC's administrative system has evolved through long history; though much influenced by Western countries, it certainly is not after any Western country's pattern. It is a very unique system that is mixed with elements of Chinese traditions and those of Great Britain, the United States, Germany, and others.

Though Taiwan was ruled by Japan as a colony for 50 years, the present administrative system was very little influenced by Japan, because Taiwan was returned to China after World War II, not severed from Japan as a new nation—something like Alsace-Lorraine returned to France after nearly 50 years of German rule. And the influence of Japan on ROC might be even less than that of Germany on Alsace-Lorraine, as the Taiwanese used the Chinese language under Japanese rule, while Alsace-Lorraine had a large German-speaking population.

II. EXTRAORDINARY POLITICAL ENVIRONMENT

The political environment of ROC is really without parallel in the world in many aspects, and the most significant one is the fact that at present China is one of the split countries, but, unlike Korea and Germany, the separation was caused not by international agreements but by actual forces of both sides. The one with the title of Republic of China controls the area of Taiwan and some nearby islands, the other with the title of People's Republic of China (PRC) controls the mainland, and in between the two is the Taiwan Strait. Both governments claim the jurisdiction of whole China and the reunification of China.

The PRC's forces attacked ROC's nearby islands in 1949 and 1958 unsuccessfully. Communist leaders have announced several times that when Taiwan declares independence or violent conflicts happen in Taiwan, they will use military forces to subdue rebellion or seek peace for the people.

From the viewpoint of international law, there is only one sovereign China, rather than two sovereign Chinas. The war between ROC and PRC is not an international war, but a civil war. The conspicuous thing is that, unlike Germany and Korea, the split two parts are far from equilibrium. PRC is so large, with more than one hundred million people and the China mainland, while ROC is so small, with 19 million people and the island of Taiwan, the smallest of the 35 provinces of China. Hence, most countries in the world, including major powers, recognize PRC, but only around 20 countries recognize ROC, and it causes much difficulty for ROC's government of conduct foreign relations.

In reality, the ROC has been, is, and will be under the constant threat of Chinese Communist military attack and subversive activities.

Naturally, the ROC's government has to take measures to cope with the threats, and this is why the ROC's politics is a kind of crisis politics. The most serious measure taken was the enforcement of martial law in 1950, which was not lifted until 1987. But the martial law was used in a limited way: it was not equal to military government, so political development toward democracy could proceed steadily.

Sooner or later, the two sides of the strait will be reunited under one government rule. Administrative system is the subsystem of political system. Obviously, the future of ROC's administrative system depends on the future of China's political system.

III.   HISTORICAL DEVELOPMENT OF THE CHINESE ADMINISTRATIVE SYSTEM

No doubt the ROC's administrative system is one of the systems with the longest history of gradual evolution in the world. According to credible historical data, a rudimentary form of administrative system was established in Yin Dynasty (or Shang), which reigned old China from about 1766 to 1122 B.C. In this era, the feudal system was erected.

In the Ch'un Ch'iu ("Spring and Autumn") period (722–481 B.C.) and the Chan Kuo ("Waring States") period (481–221 B.C.), the old feudal structure declined and new monarchies rose. Ch'in unified China in 221 B.C. and the king claimed the title of *Shih Huang Ti* (the First Sovereign Emperor). Shih Huang Ti abolished the feudal system completely and extended the local system of prefectures and counties into whole China. Shih Huang Ti also established the structure of central government under the emperor. The basic principles of the emperor system were not changed until the establishment of the Republic of China in 1912. Ch'in was short-lived. The Han dynasty was founded in 202 B.C. and developed a civil system that was followed by later dynasties. The main features were as follows:

1. Recruitment was open to all who possessed suitable qualities.
2. A rank-and-salary system was established.
3. Promotion could be from the lowest grade to the highest.
4. There was no demarcation of civil service between central governments and local governments.

All these four features were found in subsequent dynasties. It was under Yang Ti (reigned 605–618) of Sui dynasty that the regular competitive examination system was established. The significance of the open examination system cannot be overestimated for traditional Chinese society, politics, and administration. It was by this system that the traditional Chinese vertical social mobility became rather high. Beginning with the Southern Sung dynasty (1126–1279), over 50% of chancellors came from commoners whose family had no officials in three generations before them. It was in this sense that traditional China after Southern Sung dynasty could be considered as an open society. And thus, we can say that there was no ruling class in traditional China. It goes without saying that this system helped the government get competent people to serve in governments.[3]

In the late Ch'ing dynasty, beginning with the Opium War (1839–1842) between China and Great Britain and its resulting Nanking Treaty, Imperial China suffered defeat in a series of wars against imperialistic countries and signed unequal treaties. To cope with the successive defeats, the Ch'ing authorities did make a lot of domestic political reforms but with little success on the whole.

The Republic of China was established in 1912, but the new central government was unable to govern the country. China was in reality disunified and was controlled by different political forces in different parts of China. Therefore, the old civil service system collapsed but no new system was established. Different political forces used their own system to suit their own convenience. It was not until 1927 when the new central government was established in Nanking that the civil service system was reestablished step by step. But owing to civil war and World War II, the Chinese political situation was not very stable, and the new system could not be institutionalized firmly in all governmental agencies and all levels of governments. Since the central government moved to Taipei in 1949, ROC has had political stability for 40 years. Now it cannot be denied that the ROC has made a new institutionalized civil system after the collapse of the traditional system in 1911 revolution.

IV. DEVELOPMENT ADMINISTRATION AND ADMINISTRATIVE DEVELOPMENT

In the past 40 years, there has been an economic, cultural, and political development syndrome in ROC. Various development programs have been planned and implemented one after another. No doubt administrative system did play an important role to achieve developmental goals. It is in this sense that ROC's public administration can be called development administration (Heady 1984:12). At the same time, public administration must not lag behind; in other words, administrative development must be one aspect of the development syndrome. Otherwise, various development programs could not be carried out. There is no common indicator of the development, but we can see the change from the following factors.

A. Increase in Number of Government Workers

Table 1 shows the increase in the number of government workers.

B. Creation of New Governmental Agencies

New agencies that have been created since 1954 are:

> Vocational Assistance Commission for Retired Servicemen (1954)
> Atomic Energy Council (1955)
> National Youth Commission (1966)
> Central Personnel Administration (1967)
> National Science Council (1968)
> Research, Development, and Evaluation Commission (1969)

Table 1   Total Numbers of ROC Government Workers, 1957–1980

Year end	Grand total	Administrative offices	Public enterprises	Public schools
1957	157,656	75,529	33,079	49,048
1962	217,162	89,626	51,104	76,396
1967	254,931	97,361	63,308	94,262
1972	312,467	114,388	74,501	123,578
1977	382,729	136,155	136,155	143,781
1982	453,842	157,513	157,513	157,954
1986	498,909	176,395	176,395	165,919

Source: Statistical Book of Examination Yuan of ROC (1987).

> Department of Health (1971)
> Council of Economic Planning and Development (1977)
> Central Election Commission (1980)
> Council of Cultural Planning and Development (1981)
> Council of Labor (1987)
> Department of Environment Protection (1987)

C.   Developing Public Human Resources

It seems that human resources development is getting more and more important in personnel administration all over the world. In-service training has been an important part of ROC's public personnel administration. Over the years, the personnel administration departments of various agencies have augmented its use. Nowadays the agencies not only do a lot of training to improve employees' performance on the present job, but also provide learning to improve employees' performance on a future job, and learning not job related to improve employees' overall capabilities. The following are the most important training methods:

   1.   Training and education at various agencies' own training institutes. There are more than 50 training institutes belonging to various ministries, departments, local governments, public corporations that train and educate their own employees.
   2.   The Center for Civil Service Education was created in 1983. It provides various educational programs for middle and upper-middle civil officials to improve their overall capabilities.
   3.   Administrative officials and public school teachers are permitted, encouraged, and sponsored to study at universities for different programs, credit courses, or even degrees. The junior college of Public Administration on the Air was created in 1978 and it offers government workers (including military servicemen) the chance to study on television and radio for a diploma program of college credits.
   4.   Sending government workers (including military servicemen) to study abroad.

D.   Administrative Reforms

1.   Reform of Personnel System

Personnel rank system is a traditional system having lasted for more than 2000 years in Chinese bureaucracy. Surely it has some merits, but it seems too loose to be used in the present, postindustrial society. In early 1960's, some U.S. AID (Agency for International Development) advisers proposed that the personnel system be reformed into an American-style position classification system. This was adopted in 1968. Due to traditional norms, behavioral habits, and impracticality of the design, the new system was far from perfect (Hwa 1982). Then there was a new reform in 1986. It was a mixture of traditional rank system and the position classification system. Having been implemented for 2 years, though some drawbacks did show, the new system is going fairly well. It is safe to say the new system has laid the foundation for the ROC's personnel administration in the conceivable future.

2.   Emphasis on Research and Development

Facing the rapid change of knowledge and techniques in the postindustrial society, the ROC's government has long been aware of the importance of research and development in public administration. In 1969, the Research, Development, and Evaluation Commission was created in the Executive Yuan under the direction of the Premier. Moreover, there is a unit in charge of R&D in all the governmental agencies except the lowest local governments. All of the R&D programs have practical purposes but are based on academic theories. A great many of the R&D programs, especially important ones, were conducted by college professors or under the direction or help of professors.

3.   Increasing Use of Advisory Committees and Public Hearings

In order to get more information and achieve better decision making, various administrative agencies have created many permanent and temporary advisory committees whose members are mostly scholars and specialists of different academic disciplines. On the other hand, public hearings have been held more and more times by representative bodies and administrative agencies with the view of making public policies more responsive to the people's demands so as to facilitate the democratization movement in ROC's politics.

Beyond all these governmental transactions, it is worth noting that in the past 40 years, the ROC's education has made such impressive progress that government agencies are able to recruit more capable people. Also notable is the fact that Chinese scholars in general are willing to help the government, so it is not difficult for various governmental agencies to get professors and specialists to conduct research, to serve in advisory committees, and to instruct in governmental training and education institutes. Such favorable environments are very helpful for administrative development.

V.   STRUCTURE AND MANAGEMENT

A.   Government Organization

According to the Constitution, all government agencies are as shown in Figure 1. Such a structure of government is really unique in the world. It is a mixture of traditional Chinese system, modern Western democratic system, the innovation of Sun Yet-sen (founder of the Republic of China), and the compromise of the different political forces in the Constituent Assembly in 1946.

Some unusual features of the governmental system are as follows:

1.   The National Assembly, with its functions of electing and recalling the president and amending the Constitution, and with the powers of initiative and referendum on condition, is a unique body. All delegates of the assembly are elected by the people, but they only convene once in six years for said purposes.

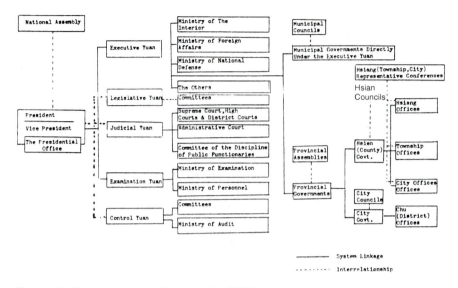

Figure 1   Government organization of the ROC.

2.   In addition to the legislative yuan, the executive yuan, and the judicial yuan, there are the control yuan and the examination yuan, and they make the five-power government, a new form of separation of powers and of checks and balances.

3.   As regards the powers of the president and the premier and their relationship with the legislative yuan, the French system bears some resemblance—a semipresidential and semiparliamentary system, a dual executive system. The president, elected by the National Assembly for a six-year term, is more than a titular head and is given power to command the army, the navy, and the air force of the whole country and to take measure to cope with emergencies. On the other hand, the Premier should be responsible to the legislative yuan and countersigns on laws and mandates promulgated and issued by the president. The members of the legislative yuan are elected to serve a term of three years and they do not have the power to overthrow the premier by vote of nonconfidence, while the president and the premier do not have the power to dissolve the legislative yuan, but they in cooperation can veto bills passed by the legislative yuan. So far, this executive dualism has not led to serious conflicts because all presidents and premiers have come from the same party—the Nationalist Party (KMT, Kuomingtang). What will happen if the two come from opposition parties? A cohabitation like that of France in 1986 to 1988? No one can tell now.

B.   Administrative System

Strictly speaking, from the legal point of view, there is only one system of public administration. Except for commanding the military forces and managing the office of the president, the president has no administrative functions. No doubt the highest manager of ROC's administrative system is the premier, who has under his direction all ministries, committees, and other agencies of the executive yuan and all three-tier local governments. There is no such thing as the U.S. independent regulatory commissions that are out of control of the highest executive.

Local governments are subordinate organs of the central government. The central government can delegate powers to local governments, but it keeps full scrutiny and control power. The local governments bear responsibility of implementing national legislation. Therefore, except for the taxation offices, there are few field services of the central government.

There are three tiers of local units:

1. Provinces and special municipalities: Provinces are something like U.S. states, and a special municipality is like the city of Washington, D.C.
2. Hsiens and shihs: Hsiens are rural areas, like U.S. counties.
3. Hsiangs and chens.

National laws provide the organizations and functions of all local governments. Hence, the organizations and functions are similar in same level units. At the present, there are only one province and two special municipalities under the jurisdiction of the ROC's central government. Such a system was used for all of China, which is divided into 35 provinces and 14 special municipalities. It is criticized as cumbersome and inefficient for such a four-tier (including the central) governmental system of ROC, but in consideration of the final reunification of China it is understandable.

Another thing worth special note is that the local governments are under double direction, from their own chief manager and from their upper authority of similar functions. For instance, the department of education of the provincial government is under the direction of the governor and the ministry of education of the central government, and in the same way, the bureau of education of the Hsien government is under the direction of its own magistrate and the department of the education of the provincial government. Conceivably, such a system causes conflicts and inconveniences, but they are usually solved by usages, compromises, and political arrangements.

C. Public Corporations

Public corporations are sponsored and controlled by different ministries, agencies, and local governments. The political and economic reasons for the establishment of public corporations are:

1.   According to the political principle of livelihood of the Constitution, private capital should be limited and national capital should be enlarged. Public corporations are of national capital.

2.   In order to protect the public interests and avoid private monopoly of some industries, public corporations are necessary.

3.   Only the government, especially the national government, has the capability to provide huge capital and recruit high-level specialists to establish corporations like the Chinese Petroleum Corporation and China Steel.

4.   Public corporations can be used as an adjustable means for economic development. When the private sector is booming, public corporations can be restricted in order to avoid inflation. When the private economy sector is in stagnation, public corporations can be used to stimulate economic growth by public investment.

Public enterprises have been playing an important role in the country's economy, but in the past 40 years their importance has diminished greatly. The ratio between private sector and public of distribution of industrial production by ownership in 1952 was 43.4 private to 56.6 public and in 1986 was 85.2 private to 14.8 public (*Taiwan Statistical Data Book* 1987:89). Since privatization of public enterprises is the present economic policy of the government, their role will continue to shrink, but, in consideration of their political meaning, they will survive.

D. Public Schools

Public schools constitute a very important of ROC's public administration. In terms of personnel, public school teachers and administrators make up around one-third of all government workers. Education is administered at three levels. At the national level, the ministry of education is in charge of policymaking and administering higher education, and the presidents of national universities are appointed by the ministry. At the provincial level, there is a department of education that is mainly in charge of administering senior high schools. All county governments have their bureau of education, which is mainly in charge of administering the primary school education.

VI. PUBLIC SERVICE PERSONNEL

Excluding the armed forces, approximately half a million people work in the public sector. These may be divided into three categories, namely, civil servants, public school teachers, and public enterprises employees. Each category makes up roughly one-third of them, as Table 1 shows. Obviously, these three categories of public workers are different in kind. Naturally, their personnel systems are different. The systems of public schools and public enterprises need not be explored here. The system worth noting is that of the civil servants.

Unlike the system of the civil servants in the United States, which has more than 1000 political appointments but has no clear delineation between the political and nonpolitical positions (Heady 1988:410), there are in ROC's system, legally, many fewer political positions but there is a clear delineation between these two types. In every ministry, only the minister and one or two vice-ministers are of the political positions, and all other civil servants under the permanent secretary are nonpolitical. It has long been criticized that the political positions are so few as to make it difficult for the minister to conduct a ministry.

Under the new rank position combined system, all career civil servants are divided into 14 grades vertically and 53 groups horizontally. Civil servants are recruited through open competitive examinations that are held several times for different purpose every year. They are really open to all, unlike those of the United Kingdom, whose higher civil servants are to be drawn from a narrow social and education stratum (Smith 1988:74).

There is a very free transfer and promotion system. One can be promoted from the bottom to the top grade, and some really make it. Theoretically, political officials and career officials are different in kind. In practice, highest level career officials, usually permanent secretaries of ministries, can be moved to political offices, and this is considered an honorable promotion and a reward for their excellent performance. The division of groups is not absolutely definite; one can transfer from one group to another group conditionally. Moreover, civil servants can transfer among different agencies, even between central agencies and local agencies. There are many cases when a high-level, central, non-head official has been appointed to be the head of a provincial agency.

Laws and regulations promulgated by the central government concerning examinations, appointments, salaries, performance, job evaluation, insurance, and retirement are used for all civil servants. Consequently, civil servants of the same grade in different agencies, no matter whether central or local, get the same treatment of all things.

As regards the personnel administration, it is so extraordinary that it is difficult to understand without explanations. As mentioned above, ROC's central government is a five-power system; one of the powers is examination power. The Examination Yuan is in fact the personnel yuan and it comprises (1) the ministry of examination, which conducts all types of examinations of civil service, professions, and technicians, and (2) the ministry of personnel, which is in charge of screening of the appointment, removal, promotion, demotion, transfer, rank, pay, and performance records of officials.

On the other hand, the Central Personnel Administration (CPA) under the executive yuan, subject to the direction of the examination yuan, is responsible for the personnel administration of all government agencies, public schools, and public enterprises, including local governments under the executive yuan. There is a personnel unit in every agency, public school, and public enterprise under the executive yuan, and all the units are under the supervision of the CPA. The personnel unit is a part of the body in which it is placed, and personnel officers are the staffs of the head of the body. The personnel officers are under the direction of the agency head to conduct personnel administration according to laws and regulations, but the chief of the personnel unit is responsible to his upper personnel unit, and the assignment, removal, and transfer of the personnel chief is up to his upper unit, not up to the agency head. As a rule, the personnel chief serving at a post is limited to a rotating three-year term. The purpose of such an institutional arrangement is to avoid nepotism and to ensure exact implementation of the personnel policies. But it often causes conflicts between the agency head and the personnel chief, and therefore it is criticized as being both functional and dysfunctional in terms of administrative effectiveness and efficiency.

As a matter of fact, there is no clear-cut demarcation of functions and duties between the examination yuan and the central personnel administration, and their conflicts seem unavoidable.

VII.   THE BUREAUCRACY AND POLICYMAKING

No matter how the controversy is going about the role of top civil officials of policymaking, the actualities are that bureaucrats are bound to be a part, an important part, of policymaking (Heady 1988:409–410). Especially in the case of ROC, in whose governmental structure there are only two of the three political leaders in a ministry, it is just impossible for them to formulate policies without the involvement of their top civil officials. As knowledge relevant to public problems and programs grows and deepens, political leaders, usually generalists, must rely heavily upon the information, analysis, judgment, and suggestions of the career officials (Mosher 1978:523). In general, high-level career officials participate in policymaking in the following ways:

1.   The budget is on annual basis. Every unit of an agency is responsible for the preparation of a budget of its own. When preparing the budget, the responsible officials can initiate new programs and enlarge or shrink ongoing programs.

2.   According to the regulations, every agency must make annual administrative guidelines and annual administrative programs. In reviewing and compiling the guidelines and programs, career officials are making policies.

3.   When political leaders initiate policies, they must ask career officials for information and suggestions. What these respond positively or negatively, they make the substantial policy contents.

4.   Since the political leaders are so few, as mentioned, the policy initiative role of career officials of ROC should be more important than their counterparts of other countries.

In all important economic programs, the high-ranking civil officials played the key roles. Generally speaking, the highest executives—the premier and the ministers—set the policy principles, and then the civil officials prepare the various programs and draft the related bills and budgets for the consideration of the legislative yuan. Sometimes the civil officials initiate policies based on their expert knowledge.

Considering that the successful development syndrome in the past 40 years is the result of so many programs that were designed by career officials under the directions of political leaders, we may safely conclude that the role of ROC's high-level civil officials in policymaking is obvious, significant, and successful.

VIII.   ADMINISTRATIVE ACCOUNTABILITY

There are multiple controls over public administration of ROC as follows.

A. Legislative Yuan, Provincial Assemblies, and Local Councils

All the representative bodies have the right of questioning. In recent years, the questioning has turned to being very critical, or even, we may say, very harsh. The answers are usually oral and instant.

B. Control Yuan

As the title demonstrates, this body's sole function is to control governmental agencies. The Constitution invested in it the following powers of control:

1. Power of impeachment: It may institute impeachment proceeding against a public servant of the central or local governments, including the President of the Republic and judges.
2. Power of censure: It may file a written censure against a functionary whose offense requires immediate remedy.
3. Corrective measures: It may propose corrective measures for the inappropriate operations of the agencies of the executive yuan.
4. Power of audit: It exercises its power of audit through the ministry of audit, which establishes audit bureaus in various area.

C. Judicial Yuan

1. Administrative Court

Any person who deems that his rights are violated by reason of any administrative action rendered by a governmental agency may institute administrative proceedings before the court.

2. Committee on the Discipline of Public Functionaries

This committee may make disciplinary measures against a public servant for malfeasance, dereliction, or any other neglect of duty.

D. Examination Yuan

As mentioned before, this body conducts all civil service examinations and regulates personnel administration.

E. Executive Yuan

Finally, it goes without saying that there are hierarchical channels of supervision over all administrative agencies. Though there is such a multiple control, the effectiveness of the executive yuan is in dispute. Obviously, corruption in government, though not rampant, is not uncommon at least in ROC.

IX. CONCLUDING REMARKS

As a developing country, ROC has made many development programs and most of them have been carried out successfully. In comparison with other developing countries, ROC's achievements are marvelous. These facts have proved that ROC's development administration is rather good. At present, ROC's government is planning to turn ROC into one of the developed countries before the end of the 20th century, and there are development programs to be designed and carried out. If the new administrative development can be advanced, then all these programs can be carried out successfully as before, I believe. Therefore, based on the case of ROC, it is safe to say that a developing country must make its administrative development and development administration go synchronously; otherwise, there can be no development at all. This is why many U.S. AID programs to some developing countries had no results.

Though the ROC's administrative system has changed much in the past 40 years and is bound to change much in the future, it is already an institutionalized system of public administration. It is a system far different from that of Western countries and those of all other developing countries, which are probably imitative of Western patterns, especially their colonial governments. Though it can be deemed a good administrative pattern for developing countries, it is not, in consideration of its uniqueness, one suitable for export to other developing countries.

Though the administrative system has played an important role in the development syndrome, it is still being criticized as corruptive, inefficient, and ineffective. In reality, there are problems, such as the cumbersome four-tier structure of government, the conflicts of personnel administration between the examination yuan and the central personnel administration, etc. These are apparent but difficult to solve. Over the years, they have been tolerated or ignored by the public. In recent years, the public is getting more and more aware of public affairs and less and less tolerant of administrative weaknesses. Under public pressure, new reforms are unavoidable.

The political future of ROC is still unclear, as is the future of its public administrative system. If the Chinese Communists control Taiwan in the near future, this system will disappear totally; if the final reunification of China takes place in another way, such that the ROC government has a say, then this system, or some features of this system, will spread to all of China and will be imitated as a model by other countries in the future.

ENDNOTES

1. In order to avoid misunderstanding, it is helpful to define a few related but easy to confuse and often misused terms as follows: (a) China—Refers to the great country China generally, including ancient and modern China. (b) The Republic of China—The new title of China from 1912. Sun Yat-sen and his followers overthrew the Ching dynasty in 1911 and established officially the Republic of China in 1912. Nowadays, people in the Republic of China on Taiwan and anti-Communist overseas Chinese all over the world still use this term to refer to the whole China. It is also used by many to denote Republic of China on Taiwan. (c) The People's Republic of China—The new title of China by the Chinese Communists since 1950. (d) Taiwan—Legally speaking, this is one of the provinces of China, the Republic of China, and the People's Republic of China. It is widely used to denote the Republic of China on Taiwan to avoid getting confused with PRC. But it is obviously an incorrect use, because there is no country called Taiwan in the world. (e) The Republic of China on Taiwan—Refers to the political entity under the official title of the Republic of China, but its real jurisdiction includes only Taiwan Province, Taipei Municipality, Kaohshiung Municipality, Penghu Island (Pescadores), Kinmen, Matsu, and Nansha Chuntao of the Republic of China. This is not an official title, and it is used by this writer and many others to denote this political entity without getting confused with the other terms above. Incidentally, one thing deserves special mention: In ROC's official view, the PRC is a rebellious regime according to the Constitution of the Republic of China. On the other hand, in PRC's official use, the Republic of China is one of the dynasties in Chinese history such as Ming and Ching; the dates Dynasty of the Republic of China were 1912 to 1949.
2. Pye (1884) says, "Political developments in Taiwan do not lag far behind economic and social modernization." And Gold (1986:vii) points out, "I have not put quotation marks around the word 'miracle'

in the title of this book for the simple reason that I think the people of that island non-nation have made miraculous progress at rapid growth, structural change, improved livelihood, and political democratization."

3.   For the evolution of traditional Chinese administrative system, see Yang (1976).

REFERENCES

Gold, T.B. (1986). *State and Society in the Taiwan Miracle.* Armonk, NY: M.E. Sharpe.

Heady, F. (1984). *Public Administration—A Comparative Perspective*, 3rd ed. New York: Marcel Dekker.

Heady, F. (1988). The United States. In *Public Administration in Developed Democracies* (D.C. Rowat ed.). New York: Marcel Dekker, pp. 395–417.

Hwa, L.-J. (1982). Position classification plan: the experience of the Republic of China. Paper presented at the 1982 Conference of the American Society for Public Administration. *Chinese Journal of Administration 33*, 56–76.

Mosher, F.C. (1978). The public service in the temporary society. In *Current Issues in Public Administration* (F.S. Lane, ed.). New York: St. Martin's Press, pp. 521–537.

Pye, L.W. (1984). Taiwan developments and their implications for US-PRC relations.

Smith, B. (1988). The United Kingdom. In *Public Administration in Developed Democracies* (D.C. Rowat, ed.). New York: Marcel Dekker, pp. 67–86.

Taiwan Statistical Data Book. (1987). Council for Economic Planning and Development, Republic of China.

Yang, S.V. (1976). *A History of Chinese Traditional Civil Service* (in Chinese). Taipei: Sung Min Press.

27

Public Administration as a Discipline in the People's Republic of China

Development, Issues, and Prospects

King W. Chow   *Department of Political Science, The University of Hong Kong, Hong Kong, China*

I. INTRODUCTION

In 1982, only a few scholars in the People's Republic of China considered public administration (PA) an academic discipline. Now, more than 1000 academicians claim PA as their specialty or major research interest; more than 200,000 state employees have received or are receiving formal training in administrative management.

The development of the discipline has been impressively rapid; its impacts upon China could be substantial; more importantly, its development issues are relevant to probing the field of PA in Western democracies. In view of these points, this chapter, based on a review of current Chinese PA literature and interviews with Chinese PA scholars and government officials conducted between August 1983 and April 1988,[1] examines the development, issues, and prospects of Chinese PA in order to shed light on PA as an academic discipline.

A. China as a Developing Country

After the Nationalists retreated to Taiwan in 1949, the Communist Party of China (CPC), under the leadership of Mao Zedong, proclaimed the formation of the People's Republic of China on October 1, 1949. The CPC under Mao succeeded in consolidating its power in the early 1950s and began to launch various political campaigns to develop the country. While the Chinese Communists have accomplished much in the past decades, they have also experienced many setbacks.[2] The Great Leap Forward movement (1958–1960), which resulted in economic disaster, and the Cultural Revolution (1966–1976), which literally shattered the economic, social, and political systems, were two incidents proving that revolutionary romanticism and class struggle could not be the basis for modernization. Even one prominent leader, Chen Yen, who served as a member of the standing committee of the Politburo of the CPC between 1978 and 1987, was pessimistic about the development of the country. In view of the critical problems confronting the leadership, Chen prophesied that China would soon suffer from one of three disasters—"the economy would collapse, the army would stage a coup, or there would be a popular rebellion" (Butterfield 1982: 231–232).

Whereas Marxism-Leninism in China under Mao was in trouble, Marxism-Leninism in China under Deng Xiaoping is in revision. After the fall of the "Gang of Four" in 1976 and the subsequent purges of the "radical leftists" from the leadership circle, Deng and his followers have pushed for fundamental reforms.[3] Recently, the "pragmatic" leadership has even called for the adoption of a theory of "the primary stage of socialism,"[4] which, as the public philosophy, will legitimize and effectuate capitalist practices in socialist China. Drastic changes have occurred in the past few years, all geared toward the attainment of rapid modernization. China under Deng in the 1980s is in essence what Kallgren (1979) described as a society caught up in the streams of development and modernization, striving to raise the standard of living of its population, and trying to preserve its cultural heritage.

B. Bureaucracy and Development

While the "pragmatic" leaders recognize that economic development and societal changes demand an efficient and effective operation of the administrative system, they are utterly disappointed with the performance of the state bureaucracy. The most vivid criticism of the performance deficiencies of the state bureaucracy was presented by Deng in an enlarged working meeting of the CPC Politburo convened on August 18, 1980. According to Deng, bureaucratism was typical of a phenomenon that had reached a state that could no longer be accepted. He described many of its features, including authoritarianism, routinism, elitism, corruption, shirking responsibility, deceit, laziness, talentlessness, formalism, red tape, nepotism, and the seeking of special privilege (Deng 1983:287).

Reform of the bureaucracy is an immensely difficult mission because administrative problems in modern China are interrelated and their causes are interlocking (Chow 1985; Harding 1981). Nevertheless, Deng and his followers are determined, and they are taking unbelievably forceful reform actions to transform the bureaucracy into an efficient and effective instrument. These include the latest efforts to establish a merit-based civil service, to separate the Party from the state, and to redefine the scope and nature of functions of state organs.[5]

Upgrading the knowledge, skills, and abilities of the 27 million state cadres[6] is vital to the leadership's pursuit. Training and retraining of cadres are thus emerging as a critical task. Naturally, public administration becomes a glamourous subject matter in China in this age of reform.

II. DEVELOPMENT OF PUBLIC ADMINISTRATION IN CHINA

Before the CPC came into power, American influence was pervasive in China's academic life. Naturally, American PA was a legitimate field of study. American-trained scholars, such as Xia Shu Zhang of the Zhong Shan University (who received his Ph.D. from Harvard University) and others, offered such PA courses as Introductory Public Administration and Organization Theory in major Chinese universities. Those courses, reflecting the concurrent American theories concerning the nature of PA, were politics-oriented and focused primarily on the society and bureaucracy interface.

After 1949, major universities continued to offer PA courses. In 1952, however, Mao Zedong and his followers considered administrative theories based on capitalist values to be irrelevant to their socialist pursuits; they thus instructed universities to eliminate PA courses. Subsequently, the leadership also rejected political science, and all political science departments were abolished in 1955.[7] PA as a field of study vanished between 1952 and 1981, and scholars shifted their teaching and research focus from public administrative theories to other areas, such as political economy, Marxist-Leninism, and history.

Since the late 1970s, the shift of policy focus from class struggle to economic development has highlighted the severity of problems of the state bureaucracy. Reformers began to look for remedies, and PA scholars were eager to salvage their discipline. Professor Xia Shu Zhang took the lead by publishing a journalistic article on January 29, 1982, in *Remin Ribao* (*People's Daily*)—the official newspaper of the CPC—in which he called for a systematic study of administration. In December 1983 and January 1984, Professor Xia offered a two-month program on public administration for university teachers interested in the subject matter. Close to 40 scholars attended the training program held in Shanghai. Subsequent developments indicated the significance and success of Xia's program: program participants openly advocated the establishment of PA as an academic discipline; various cadre training colleges[8] and major universities began to offer PA courses; some cadre training colleges offered PA as a major; and many provinces established PA associations.

Scholars' efforts to establish PA were formally endorsed by the "pragmatic" leadership in an official meeting on the development of PA held in the city of Jilin in August 1985. The meeting was cosponsored by the State Council and the Ministry of Labor and Personnel; attendants included high-level officials from the state council, the three largest major cities, and provinces.[9] Major resolutions adopted in the meeting included (1) the endorsement on the establishment of PA as an academic discipline, which shall be characterized by scientism, modernity, and legalism; (2) the building up of a massive team of PA scholars in China; (3) the setting up of an organizing committee for the establishment of a national association of public administration;[10] and (4) the promotion of a cooperative relationship between the government and the PA scholars in areas of joint research, inservice training, and management consultancy.

The rapid development of PA in China is impressive. By the end of 1982, only one journalist article on public administration (Xia 1982) had been published, and few scholars considered it their specialty. By mid 1987, however, there were more than 100 institutes offering PA courses; 20-plus PA books were in print,[11] with more than 30 books nearly ready for marketing; close to 10 academic journals devoted to the advancement of the art and science of public administration were in circulation; more than 1000 scholars had claimed to have an expertise or a genuine interest in PA; there were six associations of public administration at the provincial level; more than 100 students were enrolled in graduate programs with PA as a concentration; and two universities— Zhengzhou and Wuhan—had formally established a department of public administration, which together enrolled approximately 100 undergraduate students, and a few more universities were developing such programs.

Chinese scholars are generally pleased with the rapid development of PA in the past few years. However, they considered that the efforts expended were merely for the promotion of the discipline in China. As one scholar commented, "Public administration has never had a root in China, and a massive campaign is needed to promote and legitimize the study; now, as more people, particularly government officials and academicians, are aware of the significance of the discipline, PA is likely to be a well established field of study in the coming decade."[12]

III.   DEVELOPMENT OF CHINESE PUBLIC ADMINISTRATION: ISSUES

A.   The Scope of PA

In the course of development of the discipline, a few critical issues arise. The first one concerns the scope and nature of PA. Regarding the scope of PA, there is a consensus among Chinese PA scholars: they consider PA a distinct field of study, differing from business administration and other functional administration, such as judicial administration or management of tertiary institutions. Such a consensus is based on three basic assumptions: first, public administration is a practice that involves the exercise of state (public) authority and implementation of Party and state policies; second, it is a value-free process through which state objectives are accomplished in the most efficient and effective manner; and third, it is a unique activity with its efficiency and effectiveness not readily measurable in terms of dollars and cents.

In this light, Chinese PA scholars generally treat the state bureaucracy as the unit of analysis. Moreover, their teaching and research interests primarily center around causes and effects of administrative actions taken by state organs. In Western democracies, the above conception of the scope of PA is acceptable, even though some PA scholars would argue that scholarly research attention should also be extended to the management of nonprofit organizations and (private) actions taken by large corporations. In socialist China, however, the above conception is problematic. Administrative actions in China affect every aspect of social, economic, and political activity. More importantly, many administrative actions, having the effect of law, are being undertaken by "nongovernmental organs." In this light, the currently conceived scope of PA is obviously too narrow: other administrative units and their actions must be accounted for if Chinese PA scholars are to develop a comprehensive understanding of the complex administrative reality in China.

B. The Nature of PA

Regarding the nature of PA, Chinese scholars also share a common understanding. Heavily influenced by professor Xia, they perceive that PA is a practice-biased and problemsolving-oriented activity. Such a conception of the nature of PA influences the general Chinese definition of PA: public administration as an activity is the management of public affairs, and thus public administration as a field of study is an applied science for coping with the problems of administration. Thus, unlike other social scientists, who are primarily concerned with basic research and have a genuine interest in the pursuit of systematic knowledge for the sake of knowledge, most PA scholars in China consider PA a science that is interdisciplinary and applied.

The above popular definition of PA, however, does not prescribe the core of PA study. A review of the current PA curricula in major universities, cadre training colleges, and research institutes[13] reveals a high degree of similarity among institutions: Introductory Public Administration, Political Economy, Political Theory, Public Personnel Administration, Decision-Making Theories, Leadership Science, Public Budgeting and Financial Administration, and Computer Applications are all listed as core courses, while other courses, such as Administrative Law, Management in State Organs, Municipal Management, Social Psychology, Microeconomics, Policy Studies, Public Relations, and Office Management are listed as electives. Nonetheless, in-depth interviews with PA scholars from the three types of tertiary institutions indicate that the curriculum design is grossly misleading. In reality, according to respondents, most schools, due to the lack of textbooks and competent teachers, could offer very few PA courses. Moreover, materials covered in courses under different labels are often similar or even repetitive. Furthermore, the contents of the PA courses being actually offered lack uniformity: with Public Personnel Administration, as an example, a politics-oriented teacher would primarily discuss political issues of personnel administration, while a management-oriented teacher would teach only personnel administration "theories." Such a lack of uniformity reflects the absence of a consensus on the nature of PA.

Indeed, at the current stage, five schools of thought prescribe the nature of PA from different perspectives: public management, administrative law, political economy, decision making, and political science. The public management scholars, similar to their American counterparts, believing in the significance of management training for public executives, consider management the basis of PA. They argue that the nature of PA is interdisciplinary, and thus they call for the introduction of established theories from various disciplines to cope with administrative problems. These scholars are actively advocating the rapid development of PA by increasing the number of training programs, both long and short term, formal and informal, regular and irregular. Moreover, they call for more field research to be conducted by PA scholars so as to develop a better understanding, which will result in the establishment of "theories" for practitioners to cope with their problems in the workplace. As one public management scholar noted, "Administrative problems confronting cadres are theoretical problems confronting scholars; we (PA scholars) are responsible for introducing theories, either developed locally or imported from other countries, to cadres so that they may effectively resolve their administrative problems."[14] At present, public management scholars are very influential: most PA curricula in universities and cadre training institutes reflect that PA courses are primarily practice-oriented.

Four other groups of scholars are also competing for influence with public management scholars. The first group, composed of legal scholars from such universities as Zheng Fa University, considers the core of PA study to be administrative law. These scholars, arguing that the underdevelopment of administrative law is the fundamental cause of bureaucratic problems in China, call for systematic study of statutes, ordinances, decrees, and executive orders, which (1) determine the scope and nature of functions of state organs, (2) define the powers and privileges of state organs, and (3) govern and regulate the behavior of state cadres. These legal scholars have been active in pursuing research on law and reform; many also teach at cadre training institutes as adjunct faculty members, offering short courses in administrative law. As the current popular sentiment in China, both among the masses and within the leadership, is in favor of revitalizing the legal system, administrative law scholars have received much recognition. Due to the limited number of legal scholars engaged in the teaching and research of PA, however, they are the least influential in defining the field of PA.

Another group of scholars who are trained in economics generally define PA as a study of political economy. Perceiving that the state administrative apparatus functions to facilitate and promote economic development, these scholars, who are mainly faculty members of cadre training institutes and Party schools, call for (1) delineation of interactional relationships among the political, economic, and administrative systems, (2) establishment of "theories" of economic development in the "primary stage of socialism," and (3) application of microeconomic theories in the management of state organs. The curriculum designs of PA programs in cadre training institutes reflect the extent of influence of this group of scholars: almost all programs list Political Economy or Economic Theory as a required course. Political economy scholars are well established in both the academic community and the polity: most of these scholars received their university education in the 1950s and 1960s and have been actively involved in teaching and research in the past two decades; the "pragmatic" leadership is further pushing for more rapid economic reforms, and thus scholars with expertise in economic development are commanding much respect. Therefore, they are emerging as one of the major forces in shaping the course of development of PA.

Another major school of thought stresses decision making and considers it the core of PA study. Scholars subscribing to this school of thought are mainly those who have had received training in economics and quantitative analysis. They advocate systematic study of prescriptive theories of decision making and models and techniques for decision making. Their concerns for improvement of decision making are reflected in *all* current PA curriculum: students are required to take at least one course, usually labeled as Administrative Decision Making. One important point about the current wisdom of this school of thought is that while scholars have not employed the concept of policy analysis, they have set the distinction between the so-called "administrative decision making at the state level" and "administrative decision making in state organs": the former carrying the characteristics of policy analysis as described in American PA literature, and the latter referring to the daily problem-solving activities. Since the "pragmatic" leadership has repeatedly called for improvement of efficiency and effectiveness in state organs, and thus has placed a premium on rational decision making, these scholars are well received in both the academic community and government offices, and are heavily influencing the perception of PA students toward the dynamic nature and characteristics of the discipline.

The last major group of scholars competing for influence in the course of development of PA in China is political scientists. These scholars are primarily faculty members of major universities or researchers in academies of social science at the Central or provincial levels. Almost all of these scholars taught and conducted research on Marxist-Leninism, international communism, and related political theories before developing their interest in PA. Now these scholars stress political analysis of bureaucracy and society interface, and call for political reform as *the* solution to administrative problems. Currently, these politics-oriented scholars have been extremely effective in developing rapport with the "pragmatic" leadership. As a result, some have been appointed to serve on important committees concerning political reform; others have received formal authorization from the State Council to train PA teachers or write textbooks; and still others conduct comprehensive analysis for submission of administrative reform proposals to the State Council.

While political scientists are getting increasingly influential at the current stage of PA development, they resemble American PA scholars who receive their PA training in political science departments in their stress on political aspects of administrative management; moreover, the overwhelming majority of these Chinese PA scholars are trained in qualitative analysis and prescriptive political theories. Naturally, their research and publications have received much criticism from both inservice students and scholars subscribing to other schools of thought: their "theories" of PA are either irrelevant to resolving critical problems confronted by practitioners or too abstract to be operationally applicable in the real world.

The above review of the five major groups of scholars indicates that while most Chinese PA scholars consider PA interdisciplinary and applied, there is still a lack of consensus among PA scholars about the core of PA study.

C. Theory Building

Whereas Chinese PA scholars generally believe in the uniqueness of PA as a field of study, Chinese PA still lacks a unique identity as an academic discipline for the resolution of another critical issue—theory building—is awaiting. As of 1987, in print are approximately 20 Chinese PA textbooks, which primarily focus on (1) introduction of PA "theories" imported from western democracies, particularly the United States; (2) prescriptions of institutional and administrative arrangements from the official perspective; and (3) description of officially prescribed practices of management in state organs. Scholars and practitioners, however, are utterly dissatisfied with the quality of these publications. As one scholar noted:

> The primary problem of the development of PA at this point of time is theory-building. More people are now accepting PA as a field of study. Nevertheless, if PA is to become a legitimate discipline, it must have a set of theories applicable to explaining and predicting administrative phenomena in socialist China. Current publications, however, lack these elements.[15]

Another scholar commented,

> It will be mistaken to consider the study of problems in the workplace an academic discipline; without a preconceived mission—generating systematic knowledge about administrative process—we (PA scholars) are nothing but practitioners or journalists interested in public administrative issues.[16]

A review of major PA books and articles indeed indicates that most contemporary Chinese PA scholars are, from the perspective of behavioralists, "unconscious thinkers." Their works are merely descriptive studies, critical analysis of administrative issues, or "how-to-do-it" prescriptions of management processes; they are, at best, interpretive research aimed at the development of a better understanding of administrative phenomena in China. Interpretative research has its place in theory building (White 1986a): description and interpretation are essential to developing a somewhat complete understanding of certain relationships in this world characterized by complexity and uncertainty. But it must be kept in its place: interpretative research should result in a basis for empirical research leading to establishment of theoretical propositions; otherwise, scholars will remain in the state of "getting ready to get ready" (Sigelman 1976:623), and theories will never be constructed.

Seemingly, the causes of underdevelopment of theories are three. First, Chinese scholars have always had difficulties in gaining access to information from government officials. Although the state council has recently instructed state organs to release unclassified information to researchers when requested, administrative secrecy remains the norm. Thus, PA scholars still find empirical research to be either unfeasible or frustrating.

Second, complete research methodology has yet to be developed: Chinese scholars have been employing mainly qualitative methods, such as historical analysis, case study, content analysis, and interviewing, which are less rigorous as compared with quantitative methods in terms of their utility to building "elegant" theories. Chinese PA scholars have to take remedial actions if they are to be able to systematically account for administrative events: first, importation of such empirical research techniques as experiments and surveys; and second, strict application of normative methodology or logical procedures, including formulating research problems, constructing theories, deriving hypotheses, and operationalizing concepts.

Third, resolution of the problem of trained incapacity is waiting: few Chinese PA scholars are capable of conducting rigorous empirical research or committed to theory building because they have received very little or no training in positive research. Related to the issue of underdevelopment of methodology as aforementioned, this problem is likely to remain serious. While there are approximately 100 graduate students taking PA courses or claiming PA as their major, they are still receiving training in philosophical study and qualitative analysis, with a primary focus on either the political aspect of administrative management or management principles imported from Western democracies. Moreover, Chinese PA teachers, concerned mainly with dissemination of information, employ lecturing technique in the classroom, and rarely use discussion and seminars to promote brainstorming, critical analysis, and independent thinking. Thus, both the graduate and undergraduate students of PA are still receiving training in "know-how" instead of "know-what." Furthermore, income inequality has become an increasingly severe problem as China progresses, and academic jobs are becoming less attractive as compensation is relatively inequitable, thus resulting in unsuccessful recruitment of talented scholars.[17] In short, unfavorable conditions exist and the building of a team of rigorously trained PA teachers is very difficult.

The supply of teachers, however, will improve somewhat in the coming few years. By mid 1989, the first batch of PA graduate students will complete their master's program and reinforce the teaching team at the university level; a year later, 100-plus undergraduates will be qualified to teach at cadre training institutes. Nonetheless, while the sheer number of teachers may increase, methodological rigor and teachers' commitment to quality research cannot be guaranteed. One prominent Chinese PA scholar commented: "One may claim to be a PA teacher, but without going through rigorous, comprehensive training, one has a long way to go in the searching for scholarship."[18]

Obviously, promotion of commitment among PA students to advance systematic knowledge of PA, revitalization of compensation system for academicians, and requirement of training in both empirical and normative methodology are essential to the enterprise of theory building in China.

IV. PROSPECTS

To most socialist Chinese, PA is a young field of study. Its dramatic development in the past few years is impressive, and many of the aforementioned issues about the discipline are challenging. Given the facts that the "pragmatic" leadership is pushing for rapid economic development, PA, being generally considered as an applied science, is likely to become an increasingly important field of study.

Nonetheless, whether or not Chinese PA can become a comprehensive field and acquire a unique identity depends on how PA scholars, both within China and without, attempt to shape its course of development. Two points are important. First, a consensus among Chinese scholars about the scope and nature of PA is essential to guiding research, and thus to theory building and practical problem solving. At the moment, five major groups of scholars attempt to define the field from unique perspectives. The recent proliferation of PA programs with different curriculum designs tailored to the needs of various segments of the population has increased the popularity of PA as a field of study, but this development further confuses the unique identity of the discipline. The Chinese may eventually find themselves in the same situation experienced by American scholars in the early 1970s when the "identity crisis" occurred; the Chinese, like their American counterparts, may simply choose to treat PA as an "enterprise," a term broad enough to comprehend every public administrative element (Brown and Stillman 1985:462). Regardless of their preferences, core issues concerning faculty development, curriculum design, and promotion of professionalism must be dealt with.

Second, in order to establish PA as a legitimate discipline, Chinese PA scholars must attempt to advance systematic knowledge of PA and continue to highlight the significance of public administration as a practice. The latter will hardly be a problem: the "pragmatic" leadership has recently endorsed the policy to establish a "civil service," which is to be based on "merit" principles—appointment by credentials and reward/punishment for performance—and, in this light, further systematic training for civil servants will be arranged, thus generating a greater demand for rapid development of a PA enterprise.

The advancement of systematic knowledge, however, is likely to remain problematic. The organizing committee of the national association of public administration has already set up a research agenda, identifying specific research areas as follows: functions of state organs, organization theory, reforms of state organs and cadre system, application of general management theories, management in functional departments (for example, police and health), management in local governments, management in different socioeconomic regions, and administrative law. According to one respondent, the organizing committee is determined to see to it that the eventual formation of the association will influence all Chinese PA scholars both to promote the development of PA as a discipline and to direct their research attention to items on the agenda. In view of the problems aforementioned, however, the coming of age of PA as an academic discipline may be observable only in the twenty-first century. International cooperation may result in a more speedy development of the discipline.

V. DISCUSSION

In terms of probing the field of PA in Western democracies, the development of the discipline in China represents more than another ongoing activity of the regime undertaken to revitalize its administrative system or another continual effort in a developing country to attain modernization. It is relevant to gaining a better understanding of the issues of the discipline: this report indeed indicates that the critical issues confronted by Chinese PA scholars and those confronted by American PA scholars differ in degree and not in kind. Two points about the development of PA in China are particularly noteworthy. First, the Chinese experience indicates that there is a striking regularity among the courses of development of the discipline in different countries: socioeconomic development has always resulted in political and administrative reforms, and thus the emergence of PA as a field of study; such a relationship exists due to the perceived instrumentality nature of PA as an applied discipline. In view of the applied nature of PA, scholars must not be obsessed with abstract theorizing: indeed, the Chinese practitioners, just as their American counterparts have expressed their frustration with irrelevant or impractical "theories." Nonetheless, basic research is equally important if the PA "enterprise" is to flourish; thus, scholars should not be merely concerned with critical problems of practitioners.[19] Seemingly, PA scholars shall appreciate this challenge and aim to conduct research that is both theoretically and practically significant.

Second, the "identity crisis" that occurred in the early 1970s in the United States endures. A review of the current graduate PA programs (Ellwood 1985) suggests the absence of a consensus among American PA scholars on the scope and nature of the discipline. Moreover, any random interviews with public executives in Western democracies may indicate that they identify more with their specialty or program than with the "profession of public administration." Seemingly, the only thing shared among PA scholars in their teaching and research is the word "public;" the only thing shared by public executives and policy analysts is that they are government employees. Given that academicians do not share much in common, and that practitioners lack an identification with the "profession," PA may merely be something that encompasses everything, in turn, making itself "nothing."

In this regard, the Chinese experience is valuable to the effort to resolving the "identity crisis." Chinese PA teaching adopts a prescriptive tone. Pervasive in Chinese PA publications and curricula is the element of ethics. In the past, "serve the people" was advocated; now, "efficient consumption of scarce resources" is stressed. Together, these ethical principles serve to compel Chinese cadres to perform efficiently and effectively. More importantly, they compel cadres to have a sense of mission and a sense of identity: a one high-level cadre, an economist, echoed, "I specialize in economics, but as far as I am concerned, I am more a civil servant than an economist because I am responsible for proper exercise of state powers to make this a better country."[20]

American PA scholars in general have been cautious about injecting values in their research and teaching. The "new Public Administration" scholars have attempted to incorporate such values as social equity into the PA "enterprise." Their efforts to develop a normative theory of PA are admirable, but the applicability of such a theory has been problematic due to the political arrangement of the United States. After all, a PA theory is inevitably a political theory (Sayre 1958:105), and the "new Public Administration" prescription is in effect calling for a redistribution of policy-making powers within the political system. In this light, students of PA and practitioners are still searching for guidance, and the potentials of values as a bond pulling PA academicians and practitioners together go unrealized. PA remains an "enterprise" rather than a unique discipline and a profession.

If the PA "enterprise" is to learn from the Chinese experience, it should be the recognition of the significance of commitment to administrative values—be it commitment to excellence, to efficient consumption of scarce resources, to advancement of humanity and civilization, or to all of the above. Promotion of PA, both as a discipline and a profession, is more than expression of appreciation of quality services delivered by civil servants, as expressed by Naomi Lynn (1985:455), the former president of the American Society for Public Administration (ASPA). It should be done by dedicated efforts to produce more "committed PA professionals" and to advance the art and science of public administration, which are based on a set of cosmic public administration values.

All in all, Chinese PA is still at its early stage of development. While it is likely that PA will become a very popular field of study in China, a Marxist-Leninist state with more than one billion population, Chinese PA scholars must resolve a few critical issues, which are endemic in even developed countries.

ACKNOWLEDGMENTS

An earlier draft of this paper was presented at the 1988 National Conference of the American Society for Public Administration, Portland, Oregon. The author wishes to thank Michael Davis, Jean Hung, and J. Oliver Williams for their helpful comments on the earlier version of this paper.

ENDNOTES

1. This researcher made 11 visits in China between 1983 and 1988. The lengths of the visitations ranged from two days to one month; 162 cadres, scholars, and residents were interviewed. Nevertheless, information about the development of PA was primarily collected from 46 academicians.
2. For a review of the setbacks and political crises, see Dittmer (1981). For analyses of issues of modernization in China, see Baum (1980), Kallgren (1979), and Mabbett (1985). See also Harding (1981) for an excellent treatment on Chinese bureaucratic problems.
3. For discussions of various reform measures, see Israel and Lee (1983); for reviews of the current political and administrative reforms, see Lee (1983, 1984), Tung (1987), and Wu (1987).
4. For details of the theory, see Zhao Ziyang's Work Report to CCP Congress reprinted in *Beijing Review 30* (November 9–15, 1987):III–VI. See Chang (1987) and Rosen (1988:42) for a brief review of the theory.
5. For details of the reform proposals, see *Beijing Review 30* (November 9–15, 1987):XV–XIX.
6. The term cadre can be used to mean anyone with a formal position of leadership or state employees above a certain rank. For discussion of this term, see Whyte (1974:58), and Burns (1988:224). It has become typical in China today that all state employees are being referred to as cadres, regardless of their ranking. Thus, the term cadre is used in this chapter as a state employee, while leading cadre is someone at the executive level.
7. Nevertheless, the leadership eventually recognized the significance of the study of international politics and thus authorized the establishment of a department of international politics in the Peking University in 1957 and in the Fu Dan University in 1959.
8. In China, each one of the State Council ministries and provinces has its own cadre training college to provide cadres with inservice training. In theory, these colleges were to offer short courses for the upgrading of cadres knowledge, skills and abilities; in practice, these colleges, like Party schools, primarily offered courses on the study of Marxist-Leninism and Mao Zedong's political theories. Since the early 1980s, these colleges have begun to offer a variety of job-related training courses. Now, a few of them even offer a two-year program leading to a "diploma of tertiary studies," a qualification similar to a junior college degree in the United States.
9. According to one respondent, Premier Zhao Ziyang personally endorsed the meeting and appointed vice-premier Tian Qiyun to chair the meeting. Although Tian was then on special assignment to Tibet and thus unable to attend the meeting, such an arrangement indeed reflected that the leadership was placing a premium on the development of PA in China.
10. According to one respondent, the national association will be a semiofficial organization with institutional memberships. The officer-in-charge will be a high-level cadre, and staff of the association will be on government payroll. One PA professor wrote in July 1988 to inform the author that the association would be formally established in October 1988, and a cadre at the vice-minister grade will serve as the president of the association.
11. The best sellers include Chen (1984), Guo (1984), He (1985), Jiang (1986), Li (1984), Song (1987), Wang (1984), Xia (1985), Ying and Zhu (1985), Zhang (1986), and Zhu (1987).

12. Interview with a PA professor in Tianjin on August 9, 1987.

13. In China, some researchers in research institutes serve also as professors. They adopt the British graduate training approach and supervise graduate students pursuing either a master's degree or a Ph.D. Thus, research institutes, such as the Academy of Social Science of China, do have informal curricula for graduate students pursuing PA studies. (At present, only students at the master's level are receiving training in PA.)

14. Interview with a PA faculty member of a cadre training institute in Beijing on July 7, 1987.

15. Interview with one PA researcher at the Academy of Social Sciences of China in Beijing on August 11, 1987.

16. Interview with PA professor in Beijing on August 15, 1987.

17. For a discussion of the inequity issue, see Chow (1987, 1990).

18. Interview with one PA researcher at the Academy of Social Science of China in Beijing on August 11, 1987.

19. For critics of research biases among American PA scholars, see Perry and Kraemer (1986), White (1986b), and Stallings (1986).

20. Interview with a bureau-grade cadre in Beijing on August 6, 1987.

REFERENCES

Baum, R. (ed.). (1980). *China's Four Modernization.* Boulder, CO: Westview Press.

Brown, B., and Stillman, R.J. (1985). A conversation with Dwight Waldo: an agenda for future reflections. *PAR 4*, 459–467.

Burns, J.P. (1988). The Chinese civil service. In *The Hong Kong Civil Service and its Future* (I. Scott and J.P. Burns, eds.). Hong Kong: Oxford University Press.

Butterfield, F. (1982). *China: Alive in the Bitter Sea.* New York: Times Books.

Chang, C.P. (1987). On the theory of the initial stage of socialism. *Issues and Studies 12*, 12–21.

Chen, T.S., ed., (1984). *Ling Dao Ke Xue Jiao Cheng* [The Syllabus of the Science of Leadership]. Beijing: Qi xiang chu ban she.

Chow, K.W. (1985). The diagnosis of Chinese bureaucratic maladies. Proceedings of the Seventh International Symposium on Asian Studies, Hong Kong, pp. 77–84.

Chow, K.W. (1987). Equity and cadre job performance: causation and implications. *Issues and Studies 9*, 58–71.

Chow, K.W. (1989). The management of Chinese cadre resources: reforms, problems, and implications of pay administration, 1949–1984. *Public Budgeting and Financial Management*, *1*, 67–98.

Chow, K.W. (1990). Super-optimum solutions in developmental policy. *Public Budgeting and Financial Management.*

Deng, X.P. (1983). *Selected Writings of Deng Xiaoping.* Beijing: People's Publishers.

Dittmer, L., (1981). China in 1980: modernization and its discontents. *Asian Survey 1*, 31–50.

Ellwood, J.W., (1985). A morphology of graduate education for public service in the United States. Draft report of the NASPAA's Mellon Project, National Association of Schools of Public Affairs and Administration.

Guo wu yuan ban gong Xing diao zha yan jiu shi [The Research Section of the Office of the State Council], ed. (1984). *Zhong guo xing zhheng guan li xue chu tan* [Preliminary Enquiry About Chinese Public Administration]. Beijing: Jing ji ke xue chu ban she.

Harding, H. (1981). *Organizing China: The Problem of Bureaucracy 1949–1976.* Stanford, CA: Stanford University Press.

He, Z.X. (1985). *Xian Dai Guan Li Xue Gai Lun* [Introduction to Modern Management]. Zhe jiang: Zhe jiang jiao yyu chu ban she.

Israel, J., and Lee, H.Y., eds. (1986). *The Limits of Reform in China.* Boulder, CO: Westview Press.

Jiang, H.T., ed. (1986). *Xing Zheng Guan Li Xue* [Public Administration]. Chang Sha: Hu nan ke xue ji shu chu ban she.

Kallgren, J. (1979). China 1978: the new long march. *Asian Survey 1*, 1–19.

Lee, H.Y. (1983). Deng Xiaoping's reform of the Chinese bureaucracy. In *The Limits of Reform in China* (J. Israel and Y.Y. Lee, eds.). Boulder CO: Westview Press.

Lee, H.Y. (1984). Evaluation of China's bureaucratic reforms. *Annals* AAPSS *476*, 34–47.

Li, F. (1984). *Xing zheng guan li xue gang yao* [Essence of Public Administration]. Beijing: Lao dong ren shi chu ban she.

Lynn, N. (1985). Commemoration, celebration, and challenge. *PAR 4*, 453–458.

Mabbett, I. (1985). *Modern China: The Mirage of Modernity.* New York: St. Martin's Press.

Perry, J.L., and Kraemer, K.L. (1986). Research methodology in the *Public Administration Review*, 1975–1984. *PAR 3*, 215–226.

Rosen, S. (1988). China in 1987: the year of the thirteenth party congress. *Asian Survey 1*, 35–51.

Sayre, W.S. (1985). Premises of public administration: past, and emerging. *PAR 2*, 102–105.

Sigelman, L. (1976). In search of comparative administration. *PAR 6*, 621–625.

Song, S.Q., ed. (1987). *Wen shu xue* [The Study of Secretarial Work]. Beijing: Shi fan xue yuan chu ban she.

Stallings, R.A. (1986). Doctoral programs in public administration: an outsider's perspective. *PAR 3*, 235–240.

Tung, R. (1987). Communist China's economic reforms in the wake of the CCP's thirteenth national congress. *Issues and Studies 12*, 40–65.

Wang, F.X. (1984). *Ren shi dang an guan li gai lun* [Introduction to Management of Personnel Dossier]. Hubei: Hu bei ren min chu ban she.

White, J.D. (1986a). On the growth of knowledge in public administration. *PAR 1*, 15–24.

White, J.D. (1986b). Dissertations and publications in public administration. *PAR 3*, 227–234.

Whyte, M.K. (1974). *Small Groups and Political Rituals in China.* Berkeley: University of California Press.

Wu, A.C. (1987). The possible impact of the political reform on mainland China's politics. *Issues and Studies 12*, 22–39.

Xia, S.Z. (1982). Ba xingzheng xue de yanjiu ti shang richeng shi shihou le [It is Time to Place the Study of Public Administration on the Agenda], *Remin Ribao* January 29:5.

Xia, S.Z., ed. (1985). *Xing Zheng Guan Li Xue* [Public Administration]. Tai yuan: Shan xi ren min chu ban she.

Ying, S.N., and Zhu, W.J., eds. (1985). *Xing zheng fa xue zong lun* [Introduction to Public Administration Law]. Beijing: Gong ren chu ban she.

Zhang, Y.F., ed. (1986). *Ren shi guan li xue* [Personnel Administration]. Chang sha: Hu nan ke xue ji shu chu ban she.

Zhu, J.L. (1987). *Guan Li Mi Shu Xue* [The Study of Managerial Secretaryship]. Beijing: Jing ji ke xue chu ban she.

28
Politics of Governance Reform in Thailand

Bidhya Bowornwathana   *Department of Political Science, Chulalongkorn University, Bangkok, Thailand*

I. INTRODUCTION

As we stand on the edge of the 21st century, several countries around the world are transforming their public sectors with new reform paradigms under names such as the new public management (Hood 1991), entrepreneurial government (Osborne and Gaebler 1992), and governance (World Bank 1992; OECD 1995; Frederickson 1997). These new reform paradigms have many common characteristics. Scholars are debating whether there is a global governance paradigm or not.[1] I proposed elsewhere to use the term "democratic governance" paradigm (DGP) to refer to the new administrative reform approach (Bowornwathana 1997a). I shall here refer to the DGP as "governance."

Scholars have recently paid attention to the study of the consequences of reform diffusion of governance in particular countries. For example, in the United Kingdom, some scholars have observed the "hallowing of the state" or the "governance without government" phenomenon (Rhodes 1997; Peters and Pierre 1998). Another scholar, Moshe Maor, has argued that experiences of Australia, Canada, the United Kingdom, Austria, and Malta on governance result in the paradox of managerialism: the loss of control of political executives over the implementation of their policy bureaucracy, make them hunger for more control over the bureaucracy (Maor 1999).

Using public sector reform in Thailand as a case study, I shall argue that the diffusion of governance is not weakening the strong central government of Thailand. Moreover, governance has provided politicians with greater power vis-a-vis the senior bureaucrats. Thus, the politician-bureaucrat relationship is changing to the advantage of the first group.

An important methodology used here is the classification of public sector reform into dimensions: power, organization, accountability, and fairness. The four public sector reform dimensions are derived from my previous argument that there is a new democratic governance paradigm (DGP) which serves as a model for the transformation of bureaucracies into the twenty-first century. In short, the DGP calls for a government that is smaller and does less, global vision and flexible organizations, accountability, and fairness (Bowornwathana 1997a). These four principles of the DGP represent the four public sector reform dimensions proposed in this paper.

The paper is divided into five parts. First, I shall explain the nature of public sector transformation process from government to governance along the four public sector reform dimensions: power, organization, accountability, and fairness. Second, I shall provide a brief political background of the Thai public sector. Third, I shall describe recent governance reform initiatives to transform the Thai public sector by explaining the changes made along the four public sector reform dimensions. Fourth, I shall discuss the politics of governance in each public sector reform dimension. Finally, I shall make some concluding remarks.

II. TRANSFORMING FROM GOVERNMENT TO GOVERNANCE

Nowadays, public sector transformation for many countries is a process of change from government to governance. For conceptual purposes, one can distinguish between two opposite ideal-type models of public sector systems: the *governance model* and the *government model*. Four public sector reform dimensions are depicted to make comparison between the two public sector systems: power, organization, accountability, and fairness.

A. Power

How should power be distributed in the public sector? According to the government model, the power to govern the public sector rests solely in the hands of ministers and senior bureaucrats in a single hierarchical bureaucratic system with the prime minister on top. The government model postulates a strong central government approach. Under a highly centralized government, central government officials are in complete control of the public sector. They make policy decisions and are also in charge of the implementation of policies in the public sector. Citizens are recipients of public services delivered by the powerful central government bureaucrats.

On the other hand, the central thrust of the governance model is the desire to alter the power structure in society by curtailing the power of the central government and the bureaucracy, while increasing citizen control over the government apparatus. It is a process of change from a society controlled by the state to a society controlled by the citizen. The principle of a smaller government that does less in the governance model calls for the central government to disperse power to control the public sector to other actors outside the central government. The governance model is predicated on the belief that power should not reside in the hands of a small group of cabinet ministers and senior bureaucrats of the central government. On the contrary, power must be decentralized or distributed widely to other power centers outside the central government machine.

In the final stage, the governance model envisages a shrunken central government with much reduced powers. The dispersion of power from the central government to other power centers will enable citizens to gain more control over the public sector. The new public sector will consist of a plurality of actors from central government, local governments, civil society organizations, communities, business companies, international actors. Each actor is in charge of the production and management of specific public goods. The central government becomes much smaller, relinquishing control over most parts of the public sector to the newly emerging public units. Scholars have called this phenomenon "the hallowing of the state," (Rhodes 1996) and "governance without government" (Rhodes 1997; Peters and Pierre 1998). Eventually, "power" in the new public sector becomes highly pluralistic creating a new kind of polity.

Key measures used to create a smaller central government that does less are: downsizing, privatization, decentralization, and nongovernmental organizations. These measures shift the power, and also the burden (Hall and Reed 1998), of central government over certain public activities into the hands of new non-central government actors. Downsizing of the central government through drastic reduction in the number of bureaucrats will significantly cut personnel costs. Privatization of state enterprises will disperse the power to run state enterprises from the monopolies of central government officials (such as in the case of Thailand) to outside actors. Decentralization of power from the central government to various local government units further disperses the concentration of power in the hands of central bureaucrats. A strong civil society will enable non-government actors to take over many areas of responsibility previously assumed by the central government.

B. Organization

How should the new public sector be organized structurally? The government model advocates a structure of government based on one single hierarchical pyramid consisting of ministries, departments, and divisions. Ministers and senior bureaucrats are in charge of every public activity in the public sector. Meanwhile, The Governance Model represents an escape from the old practice of government to organize the public bureaucracy under a single hierarchical structure to the new multiple organizational structures which helps avoid the necessity for all public agencies to be under the command of ministers, permanent secretaries, and director-generals. The new multiple organizational structures also open ways for alternatives in organization design for better service delivery to the citizens.

Furthermore, the argument for the establishment of many new power centers is a solution to the overloaded central government, or Toeffler's "too many eggs in one basket" analogy (Toeffler 1994). A major purpose is to separate policy organizations from implementing organizations: to allow the later more freedom and flexibility to perform their public functions. The traditional model of government with ministries, departments, and divisions is to be transformed into a more complex networks of numerous kinds of implementing organizations such as contract organizations, executive agencies, civil society organizations, and business companies. The new envisaged public sector or "governance", in R.A.W Rhodes's opinion, can be conceptualized as "self-organizing interorganizational networks" (Rhodes 1997). Policy success depends on the ability of these networks of actors to collaborate and form "partnerships" (Bogason and Toonen 1998).

C. Accountability

What kind of accountability should be practiced in the new public sector? Though the government model supports en efficient system of internal accountability such as internal auditing, the model does not advocate strong external accountability. Under the government model, there is no outside accountability mechanism which could effectively monitor and check the use of authority by central government officials. Few top bureaucrats and political executives monopolize government power. Against the state, the citizen is powerless.

On the other hand, the governance model supports the idea that the citizen should exercise control and monitor the work of the central government. In other words, the governance model calls for an open and transparent government. Government agencies must be closely scrutinized by non-government actors: civic watchdogs, news media, interest groups, professional associations, communities, non-governmental organizations, and the individual citizen. The emphasis is on external rather than on internal accountability mechanisms within the bureaucracy such as the typical auditor-general office and the counter corruption agency. As the public sector transforms itself to incorporate multiple organizational structures, the nature of accountability changes from exclusively internal to incorporate external accountability mechanisms. More outside actors move in to check and monitor the performance of the old central government. At the same time, the new actors that assume control over many parts of the public sector are themselves subjected to external accountability. At the end, actors in the new public sector monitor one another, forming complex networks of accountability within the public sector.

To facilitate the institutionalization of external accountability mechanisms, a legal reform is launched to introduce new public laws such as the freedom of information act, the ombudsman act, the administrative procedure act, and the administrative court act, into the society. Non-legal methods to guarantee accountability must also be developed simultaneously. For example, citizens should form watchdog groups to monitor the work of specific government agencies.

D. Fairness

What kind of fairness should be the rule in the new public sector? In the government model, "fairness" is at the will of government bureaucrats. As government officials, they make their own judgements about what is right and what is wrong. Though bureaucratic discretion in the government model are generally based on the rule of law that bureaucrats were instrumental in issuing, in practice, patronage and nepotism take precedence. In contrast, the governance model argues that "fairness" of government action in a public sector is determined by the citizen. The use of discretionary power by public officials as to who should get what when, how, and why must be based on the principles of democratic governance. Both Thai citizen, international actors, including the United Nations and the United States, have campaigned for new governance values. Governance values must overrule traditional values such as patronage and nepotism. Examples of the new governance values are human rights, sustainable development, children and women's rights, social justice, equal treatment under the law, reduction of the gap between rich and poor, education and health for all. To transform from government to governance, public officials and also citizens must go through a value change process so that new governance values can be integrated into Thai society.

In its ideal form, the governance model creates a new public sector in which the power to govern is completely decentralized; better services are provided by multiple organizational structures; external accountability of the public sector is extensively practiced; and the new fairness becomes the criteria for making government decisions. We move from a system ruled by a small group of ministers and senior central government officials to a new system ruled by a complex network of government and non-government actors who are under the close scrutiny from the citizen. In short, the central government becomes very small and its power over the public sector, though not necessarily weak, becomes very limited. In contrast, under the government model, the central government remains big and extremely powerful in the public sector.

III. POLITICAL BACKGROUND

For centuries, the Thai public sector has a long tradition of being ruled by the few. Under absolute monarchy, kings exercised authoritarian rule over the public sector. The establishment of constitutional monarchy in 1932 paved the way for the powerful bureaucratic elite, especially the military, to assume control over the public sector (Riggs 1966; Bowornwathana 1988). From the 1980s onward, the business elite have joined hands with the old bureaucratic elite to form a new alliance dictating the direction of the Thai public sector.

At present, the Thai public sector system very much resembles the government model. In Thailand, a small group of political executives and senior bureaucrats who sit on top of the central government machine possess the sole authority to run the public sector. They exercise control over the national budget and two million public servants, and they have authoritative decision-making power over the state machine. The central government has a single hierarchical structure consisting of ministries, departments and state enterprises. Citizens have little say in the manner that the public sector is being governed by the old political order of traditional elite: the cabinet, the military and senior civil servants. The Thai central government practices internal accountability; but external accountability is almost nonexistent. Government discretion is based on patron-client relationships (Neher and Bowornwathana 1986) rather than on the principle of fairness.

To reshape the Thai public sector with governance is therefore a radical departure from the present realities of the Thai public sector. Not surprisingly, strong resistance to administrative reform under governance comes from the power-holders: political executives and senior bureaucrats (Bowornwathana 1999, 1997, 1996a,b,c, 1994). For example, the difficulty of a local government such as the Bangkok Metropolitan Administration (BMA) to foster governance has to do with the overwhelming authority the central government has over Bangkok Metropolitan affairs (Bowornwathana 1998a,b,c).

The transformation of the public sector from government to governance is a widespread phenomenon in the Asia-Pacific Region (Maidment 1998, Chapter 11). Two recent developments contributed to the governance movement in Thailand: the promulgation of the October 1997 Constitution, and the economic crisis in July 1997. For Thailand, it was not until after the 1992 May bloodshed that democratic political reform gained momentum resulting in the promulgation of the 1997 constitution. Though Thai democracy history is marked by the promulgation and the abolishment of many constitutions, the new 1997 constitution is a very special one because it contains clauses which are very supportive of governance principles.

As constitutional reform gained momentum in 1997, Thailand was hit by an economic crisis on July 29, 1997 (the day Thailand requested emergency assistance from the IMF), triggering the collapse of many financial institutions, banks, and private companies (Bello 1998; Dixon 1999; Mallett 1999; Unger 1998; Warr 1996; Gough 1998, Delhaise 1998; Gill 1998; Siamwalla and Sopchokchai 1998). Previous sound economic progress can not be sustained without an effective public administration system (Bowornwathana 1995:388–397). As Ranjit Gill observed, "A potent of mix greed, bad governance and unchecked globalization sent the Asian miracle off tangent" (Gill 1998). Social problems such as rising unemployment, poverty, and education dropouts followed. Economic reform became the central theme of the central government. And in the eyes of the Thai government and international funding agencies such as the World Bank, the IMF, and the Asian Development Bank (ADB), "governance" has become the buzz word for successful economic and social recovery (Royal Thai Government, 1997, 1998a,b,c,d; TDRI 1998; Root 1996; World Bank 1994, 1991; Nunberg and Nellis 1995; Nunberg 1995) Under the economic recovery plans of these international funding agencies, governance has become a must, not a choice, for public sector reform in Thailand.

IV. GOVERNANCE REFORM INITIATIVES

I shall describe recent governance reform initiatives in Thailand by examining the four dimensions of public sector reform: power, organization, accountability, and fairness.

A. Power

The major governance reform initiatives under the power dimension are: downsizing, privatization, decentralization, and non-governmental organizations.

1. Downsizing

The policy to downsize the Thai bureaucracy has been around for two decades. Unfortunately, the experience to downsize the Thai bureaucracy is marked by a cycle of thundering policy statements by the new government, cabinet resolutions consisting of complicated standardized bureaucratic downsizing measures, and ironically, ending up with upsizing of the bureaucracy. For example, on December 23, 1980 the cabinet approved a resolution proposed by the administrative reform commission to limit the growth of the numbers of government officials and employees by no more than 2% annually. However, from 1981 to 1995, only five annual growths are under the two percent ceiling. Six annual growths are above 3%. Part of the problem is that there are too many exceptions to the rule. National manpower committees, central agencies such as the secretariat of the civil service commission could not block the personnel increases sought by some ministers and government bureaucrats. In 1981 the civil servant and permanent employee workforce nationwide stood at 1,032,802. In 1995 it rose to 1,464,557.

Under the 1997 economic crisis, the problem of the bloated Thai bureaucracy becomes more serious because the government has less money, while the expanding bureaucracy is taking away a larger sum of the national budget. During 1986–98, personnel expenses, that is, salaries and welfare benefits of government officials and employees, were about 34% to 39% of the national budget. In fiscal year 1999, however, personnel expenses swallowed up to 42.5 per cent of the 800 billion baht national budget: partly due to the massive shortfall in revenue of one-fifth of the estimated revenue. At the same time, the IMF loan to Thailand requires that the size of the public sector be drastically reduced. The World Bank and Thai authorities have drawn up a blueprint for a $400 million public sector reform loan in order to overhaul the cumbersome bureaucracy (Nation, August 10, 1998:1).

In April 28, 1998, the Chuan government adopted a cabinet resolution approving the proposal of the administrative reform commission to prohibit the creation of new positions from the fiscal year 1998 onwards, and to abolish 80 per cent of retired officials' posts. The remaining 20% of the vacancies will be allocated by a government committee. In 1998, 9085 government officials retired. The government will abolish 7585 (83%) of their positions, leaving only 1500 positions to be filled. The committee would consider the requests of government agencies in line with three priorities: first priority are judges, public prosecutors, university lecturers and scientists, and lab technicians for universities; second priority are teachers and police; third priority are specialists like doctors, nurses, engineering and legal experts for the office of the council of state (Nation, January 25, 1999:A2).

2.   Privatization

Though efforts to privatize state enterprises in Thailand started two decades ago during the Prem administrations in the 1980s, not much has been achieved. Before the 1997 economic crisis, only 13 state enterprises with less than 2% of all state enterprises' assets had been fully privatized (Changsorn 1999). Like downsizing, privatization of state enterprises has been a dismal failure. The share price of Thai Airways International was a disappointment to the public. Northeast Jute Products Co collapsed after privatization because it wandered off into the real estate business. PTT Exploration and Production Co. was too much of a domain for foreign institutional investors to benefit small Thai investors. A subsidiary of the Electricity Generating Authority of Thailand did well in the stock market because of good management. Nevertheless, privatization did not create confidence among the Thai people on the benefits of listing state enterprises in the stock market (Nation, February 17, 1998).

The economic crisis of 1997 has forced the Chuan II government to take privatization seriously. Privatization of good state enterprises will bring in much-needed cash. Under the economic bailout program of the IMF and the World Bank in mid-1997, privatization of state enterprises has become a condition for obtaining loans. For example, a condition of the IMF is for Thailand to privatize all state enterprises by 2001. The IMF had proposed that the establishment of a regulatory framework consisting of a national committee in charge of reviewing privatization proposals under a master plan. From the sells of blue-chip state enterprises, the government expected to raise between 80 billion to 100 billion baht in 1998. These blue-chip state enterprises are Thai Airways International Plc, Bangkchak Petroleum Plc, Electricity Generating Plc, PTT Exploration and Production Plc, Esso (Thailand) Plc, and the Electricity Generating Authority of Thailand's Rachaburi power plant (Nation, February 5, 1998, Sect. B).

In the second letter of intent to the IMF, the Thai government agreed to reduce its 93% stake in the national airline to 51% in two years, sell off its entire 72.2% stake (including that of the Petroleum Authority of Thailand) in Bangchak Petroleum. Officials said the privatization of these two state-controlled agencies would involve foreign partnerships. The government also plans to reduce its stake in PTT Exploration & Production to 51%, in Ecco to 20%, in ESSO (Thailand) to 0%, in EGAT's Rachaburi power plant, which is yet to be commissioned for production, to 0% (Nation, February 5, 1998, Sect. B).

For the Thai government, privatization reduces the government's investment burden and raises much needed funds. The following steps are being taken by the Chuan II government to facilitate the privatization process. First, the government will establish an Office of State Enterprises and Government Portfolio (OSEGP) supervised by the Finance Ministry, The OSEGP office will support and coordinate the privatization of state enterprises, develop private participation in infrastructure, monitor state enterprises, and manage government portfolio.

Second, the government will draft a master plan for long-term state enterprise reform. A national committee on state enterprise reform chaired by the Deputy Prime Minister Suphachai Panitchpakdi received funding and technical assistance from the World Bank to draw the blueprint. The priority of the Thai government is to privatize state enterprises in the energy, transport, communications and public utilities sectors. An independent regulatory framework for each sector will be finalized (Nation, May 21, 1998:B3). Regulatory bodies to oversee services' standards, secure competition among operators, and prevent monopolies will be set up. Half of the proceeds from the privatization will be used to offset losses incurred by the Financial Institutions Development Fund from its attempt to prop up troubled banks and finance companies over the past two years. The other half will be used to fund social and education programs (Bangkok Post, August 30, 1998:3).

Third, the introduction of a new corporatization bill (or the state enterprise capital bill) will transfer state enterprises into legal corporate entities. The new legal status of Thai state enterprises will allow the private sector, including foreign investors, to hold shares in public utilities sectors. The corporatization bill will enable the government to create shares in state enterprises based on their assets, and then sell the shares to the private sector. Under the new corporatization bill, a national privatization committee, chaired by the prime minister, will decide what assets of which state enterprise will be transformed into corporate shares. Then, a working committee chaired by the permanent secretary of the ministry or bureau that the privatized state enterprise is attached to will work out the details for the formation of the corporate.

3. Decentralization

Before the 1997 constitution, local government in Thailand has been under the interior ministry for a century. Previous attempts to reform the Thai local government system which would challenge the traditional authority of the interior ministry had met with stiff resistance from the interior minister and officials. Past efforts to grant more autonomy to the local governments have failed. However, the new 1997 constitution is a major step toward decentralization of power to local governments in Thailand because the constitution recognizes the rights of local communities to self-government. The central government must strictly limit its regulatory role on local government (Article 283). The 1998 constitution provides a general guideline for the decentralization process

(Article 284). First, the authority and responsibility of local governments vis-à-vis central government must be clearly spelled out by a new law which will specify the new inter-organizational relations. Second, a law must be issued to set proportions of taxes collected to be shared between the state and local administrative bodies under the principle of greater local autonomy. Third, a committee must be set up to oversee the decentralization process.

Under the new 1997 constitution, members of local councils come from elections. Executive of local administrative bodies come from direct elections or are approved by local councils. The interior minister officials in the provinces can no longer become directly involved in local government. The provincial governor can not be chair of the provincial administrative organization. The district officer can not be chair of sukhapiban organization. Local communities have the right to manage and utilize their natural resources and environment, a power formerly vested in the central government.

Since decentralization laws have not yet been passed by parliament, we still do not know what the final new structure will look like. The Chuan II government has set up a national committee to facilitate the decentralization process as stipulated by the 1997 constitution. On 24 February 1998, the cabinet approved five decentralization bills: *sukhapiban* abolishment bill, *tambon* council and administrative organization bill, provincial administrative organization bill, municipal bill, and *Pattaya* bill. In late June 1998, the Chuan II government announced plans to create a central state mechanism to supervise and accelerate the decentralization process. A national committee chaired by the prime minister consisting of permanent secretaries from interior and finance ministries; the director of budget bureau; the secretaries-general of the civil service commission, the national social and economic development board, and the council of state; and the director-general of the department of local administration (DOLA) of the interior ministry, 10 representatives from the Bangkok metropolitan administration, municipalities, provincial administration organizations, and *tambon* and special local administrations; and 10 experts in political science, law, economics, and public administration. The national committee will be responsible for drawing up decentralization plans, specify the ratio of revenue sharing among the central and local governments (Nation, June 29, 1998:A3).

4.   Nongovernmental Organizations

Nongovernmental organizations (NGOs) are basically organizations set up by private individuals, instead of governments. NGOs do not make profits but try to help people at local, community, and global levels. These nonprofit organizations are in all fields: from church groups to people's assemblies, environment and human rights watchdogs, government oversight bodies, and relief organizations (Kulawat 1998:8). In the governance model, nongovernmental actors are very important because they are supposed to become strong and more active so that they can monitor government action and assume control of several functions originally performed by the central government.

It is understandable that with a strong central government tradition, NGO-government relationship in Thailand has been rather confrontational. Generally speaking, the central government treats NGOs with suspicion. According to Kamol Sukin (1998), Thai NGOs are moving toward a network-style management. Thai NGO networks can be divided into four groups: First, the hot-issue group works on selected cases such as pollution, nuclear power, industry and dams. They protest to demand a solution from the government. Second, the cold-issue group deals with general issues such as women, children, consumers, green product, health, community-based savings, and environmental awareness. The cold-issue group normally avoids confrontation. Third, the Assembly of the Poor, established in 1995, works on six problems affecting 121 groups of poor people from 35 provinces concerning land rights, the negative impact of dam construction, slums, occupational health, the results of government development projects, and farming issues. The aim of the Assembly of the Poor is to get government compensation for errors in past development policies and to suggest changes. Protests are applied to pressure the government to resolve all 121 issues. This usually ends up with negotiation or scrutiny by ad hoc committees. The last is the pro-civil-society group. It was formed after the drafting of the Eighth National Economic and Social Development Plan. The pro-civil-society group believes that national administration at all levels should draw on a partnership of five sectors (the "penta party"): government, business, communities, academia and nongovernmental organizations (Sukin 1998). The recent economic crisis of 1997 is causing financial problems to NGOs. Only the pro-civil-society group has accepted loans from the World Bank and the ADB designed to ease social problems stemming from the economic crisis. The central government has been very slow in providing financial support to Thai NGOs (Nguak 1998).

B. Organization

I shall discuss three reform initiatives: the Public Organization Act, independent public organizations, and size reduction of the public sector.

1. Public Organization Act

Under the Chuan II government (1997 to the present), a major reform innovation is the creation of a third type organization, the "public organization." (The first type includes the ministry and the department; the second type is the state enterprise.) According to the Public Organization Act of February 13, 1999, a public organization is a nonprofit, autonomous, executive (created by the executive) state agency. Since the Public Organization Act of 1999 is new, there has been no public organization created yet under the new act. According to Minister Abhisit Vejjajiva, who is also deputy chairman of the administrative reform commission, the government has made a commitment with the Asian Development Bank (ADB) that all state universities be made "autonomous" by 2002 (Memorandum of Understanding 1998). Becoming a public organization is one way to fulfill that promise. Another possibility is to transform state hospitals into public organization hospitals (Bangkok Post, February 25, 1999:2). On July 28, 1988, the cabinet approved in principle to turn the following state agencies into public organizations: certain hospitals, education evaluation units of the ministry of education, TV Channel 11, and the department of science service of the ministry of science, technology, and environment (Nation, August 13:A2).

2. Independent Public Organizations

Are there any types of organizations besides the public organization? In the near future, the birth of new types of organizations is expected. The classification possibilities are: profit or nonprofit; autonomous or nonautonomous; permanent or ad hoc; and executive, parliamentary, or judicial. Thus, many types of state organizations are possible. For example, "public organizations" in accordance with the Public Organization Act of 1999, are nonprofit, autonomous, executive state agencies. The governance model also opens the door for private sector organizations to participate in the provision of public goods in the new public sector.

The creation of new "independent" agencies in the public sector is coming soon. The 1997 constitution contains clauses for the creation of new types of organization. According to the 1997 constitution, several new state, institutions are required to be established; national human rights commission; ombudsman; constitutional court; administrative court; national countercorruption commission; and auditor-general commission. These new constitutional institutions will need "independent" bodies to help administer their work.

New independent agencies may also be established to fulfill a policy obligation specified in the 1997 constitution. For example, Article 40, which regards radio, TV, and telecommunications frequencies as national resources, requires establishment of an independent agency to allocate the frequencies (Nation, February 15, 1999:A3). The 1997 constitution's call for local decentralization (Chapter 9 on local government) of administrative power will require that an independent office be created to manage the decentralization process. The policies of environmental protection (Article 56) and consumers protection (Article 57) have also led to the felt need to set up independent agencies. The setting up of the constitutional court, the administrative court, and the court of justice under the 1997 constitution has led to discussions about establishing independent offices for the courts. The new proposed economic and social advisory board under the 1997 constitution (Chapter 5) to give advise to the cabinet on economic and social issues and recommendations before the national economic and social development plan is launched, has led to proposal of setting an independent office.

Otherwise, proposals to create new independent agencies may come from individual actor. For example, the finance ministry's proposal to the cabinet to form an independent budget audit unit that will work full time in all ministries and provide the government with effective tool to check abuses and corruption in state agencies. The new independent audit unit will also work on the highly controversial project-bidding systems of each ministry, where corruption through collusion between state officials, politicians and private firms is widespread (Nation, November 8, 1998:1).

3.   Size Reduction of Public Sector

Besides creating new types of state agencies outside the old bureaucratic system of ministries and departments, there are other ways to reform the organizational arrangements in a public sector. One drastic way is to reduce the role of the state and enhance the participation of the private sector in the provision of public sector services. A well-known example in Thailand is the Bangchak gas station project. Communities are encouraged by the Bangchak Petroleum Company to use their existing agricultural cooperative organizations to run gas stations selling gasoline supplied by the Bangchak Company. Private-public partnerships should be developed in the new public sector. Another way to change the nature of the public sector is to downsize the public sector by reducing the dependency of the citizen on the state. His Majesty the King of Thailand's suggestion to the people to go back to the simplest forms of living by practicing what he called "self-sufficient economy," known as the "new theory," in order to survive the economic crisis is a case in point (Nation, December 5, 1998:1; Bangkok Post, December 5, 1998; 1).

C.   Accountability

Reform initiatives with regard to accountability are quite recent in Thailand. There are two major developments. First, several public laws are promulgated, while several others are on the pipeline. Second, there is an increasing awareness of the importance of accountability among the Thai people, including government officials of the central government.

1.   New Public Laws

The accountability movement takes the form of the passing of a package of public law bills. In 1996, the Administrative Procedure Act and the Public Officials' Violations Act were both promulgated on September 27. Next, the Official Information Act (Freedom of Information Act) was passed on September 2, 1997. In accordance with Article 6 of the Official Information Act, a new office of the official information commission was created in the office of the permanent secretary of the prime minister.

According to the 1997 constitution, the following mechanisms related to the accountability of the government officials are required to be established: three parliamentary ombudsmen, the national human rights commission, the national countercorruption commission, and the auditor-general commission. (Another commission, the elections commission, is concerned with the election process of politicians.)

The three ombudsmen, who are selected by the senate, are empowered to examine complaints concerning failure of abide by the law, or negligence of duties or violations of human rights by civil servants, state enterprise officials, and local administrators. The national human rights commission comprises 11 members nominated by the senate. It is duty-bound to monitor violations of human rights or ignorance to violations of human rights approved by Thailand for reporting to parliament. The national countercorruption commission, whose chairman and eight members will be nominated by a 13-man panel made up of presidents of the supreme court, the constitution court, and the administrative court; six rectors of state universities; and four representatives of political parties, will no longer be an agency under the supervision of the prime minister. It has the power to investigate corruption allegations against the state authorities and politicians and to submit reports to the senate, the political tribunal, and the national countercorruption commission. The auditor-general commission will become an independent body instead of being under the supervision of the prime minister.

2.   Public Awareness

The second important event is the increasing awareness among the Thai people about accountability. I shall explain civic awareness, bureaucrat awareness, government awareness and business awareness.

a.   Civic Awareness

The idea that government officials can be monitored and questioned by the citizen is new. The promulgation of the 1997 constitution and new laws supporting a more open and transparent government mark the beginning of a new democratic reform of the Thai bureaucracy. The reform process will take a long time because it involves changing the values and culture of the old bureaucratic system. For example, the Official Information Act of 1997 calls for the right to know runs counter the culture of secrecy in the Thai bureaucracy (Chongkittavorn 1999a). In the transformation process, the mass media play a key role in socializing the public about the right to know. Daily newspapers have columns presenting news and discussions about the benefits of an open, transparent, and accessible government. Television and radio programs regularly broadcast lectures by respected members of the society such as Anand Punyarachun and Prawese Wasi on the importance of cultivating a culture of external accountability. Civic watchdogs must be stronger to be able to call for more openness and transparency of the government. To improve the quality of the press, journalists have signed a declaration to set up a national press council, an independent and self-regulating body that will enforce a code of conduct for journalists (Bangkok Post, July 5, 1997:1).

b.   Bureaucrat Awareness

Under the government model, a lingering problem has been corruption in the public sector. Under the governance model, corruption within the bureaucracy will be minimized because the activities of the government officials will be closely monitored by a stronger anticorruption mechanism and public watchdogs. Not all government officials are corrupt, of course. In fact, former and present government officials can form watchdogs to monitor corruption and malfeasance. For example, a watchdog network has been set up by former and contemporary senior public health officials and experts following the medical supply scandal which has tarnished the image of the public health ministry (Bangkok Post, November 23, 1998:4).

c.   *Government Awareness*

The increasing public concern for government transparency is illustrated by another recent case: the so-called Miyakawa Fund of 53 billion baht provided by the Japanese government as short-term stimulus on the Thai economy. The mounting fear expressed by the public and mass media that the funds will be spent by recipient ministries hastily and purely for politically reasons, has prompted the government to impose measures to ensure transparency in the disbursement of funds and to battle possible corruption in the use of the fund. The Thai finance minister, Tarrin Nim-manahaeminda, named the five antigraft measures: full details of the projects must be posted at state agencies for public scrutiny; each village or area will carry complete information on projects being carried out so that the local people can participate and check on the implementation; complete details of the projects will be posted on the Internet; a team from the national economic and social development board, the budget bureau, and the comptroller-general will file progress reports on the projects to the cabinet every two weeks; and the cabinet secretary was instructed to coordinate the implementation of an internal auditing mechanism (Nation, March 25, 1999:A3).

Another example of concern shown for accountability is the effort to revise the 1992 prime minister's office procurement regulations so that government contracts awarded can become more transparent, political interference can be removed, and more specific bidding requirements and harsher penalties can be added (Nation, February, 27, 1998:A5).

d.   *Business Awareness*

The emphasis on good corporate governance as a panacea for economic recovery also helps people to see the importance of the accountability movement in the public sector. The believe is that the Thai economy crunched because the business sector did not practice good corporate governance. There was no transparency in the decisions of banks and financial companies in approving loans. The result is that the nonperforming loans (NPL) are so large that the central government has to move in. Therefore, a package of economic bills must be passed in parliament to restructure the business sector. These bills include: social security act amendment bill, bankruptcy court bill, bankruptcy amendment bill, civil code amendment bill on miscellaneous cases, foreclosure bill, bill on court appointments, state enterprises corporatization bill, alien business law amendment bill, bill on property lease and rights, land code amendment bill, and condominium ownership bill (Nation, March 16:A3).

D.   Fairness

The promulgation of the 1997 constitution and the 1997 economic crisis reinforced the significance of the new principles of fairness. The 1997 constitution has provided the government with a general framework of fairness practices to follow. The important principles are: human rights, environmental protection, and better justice.

1.   Human Rights

According to the 1997 constitution, a national human rights commission (NHRC), for the first time, will be established. The NHRC will comprise 11 members nominated by the senate with a term of six years. The NHRC members must be experts on the protection of the rights and freedoms of the people and must accept participation by representatives of private human-rights organizations. In Chapter 1 on "general provisions," the 1997 constitution stipulates that human dignity and the rights and freedoms of individuals must be protected. The rights and freedoms guaranteed by the constitution must be respected and protected by parliament, the cabinet, the court, and state agencies and their officials. Discrimination based on sex, race, language, religious beliefs, age, education, physical condition, financial status, and political opinions is prohibited in Chapter 3.

2. Environmental Protection

In the new 1997 constitution (Chapter 5 on basic state policy guidelines), the state must encourage the people to participate in maintaining and using natural resources and the environment. Local communities are encouraged to take part in managing, maintaining and using natural resources and the environment. In this regard, an independent body represented by environmental-related private organizations and educational institutions will give opinions on public projects affecting the environment (see Chapter 3 on the rights and freedoms of the people). Concern for environmental protection is in line with the United Nations' objective for nations to follow the principle of sustainable development.

3. Better Justice

The 1997 constitution (Chapter 8) has reformed the justice system of Thailand. First, new general provisions are stipulated to solve previous injustice problems due to the shortcomings of the Thai judicial process. For example, the case of arrest warrants. Previously, arrest warrants can be issued with the approval of provincial governors or the interior ministry inspectors-general. Under the 1997 constitution, the issue of arrest warrants must be ordered by a court. Arrest warrants can be issued only when there is sufficient evidence and when there are grounds to believe that suspects may escape, threaten witnesses, or pose other dangers. The second example is the rights of suspected criminals to lawyers. Under the 1997 constitution, suspects in criminal offences have the right to have their lawyers present during interrogations. Previously, the state helps provide lawyers for criminal cases during trials only. The third example is the detention power of authorities. The 1997 constitution stipulates that authorities have power to detain suspects for 48 hours. Court approval must be sought for further detention. Before, police can arrest and detain suspects of not more than 72 hours and are required to file the case in court as soon as possible. The fourth example concerns the quorum of judges. Under the 1997 constitution, the number of members of a panel of judges is fixed. Court executives who do not sit on the panel from the beginning cannot conduct trials or give rulings. Previously, no regulations concerning a quorum of judges existed. Therefore, a senior judge or court executive may sign on the court verdict on behalf of judges who handled the case from the beginning without having to take part in the case. The last example is about witnesses' protection. The 1997 constitution stated that witnesses in criminal suits have the right to protection and compensation from the state. The former constitution did not state such a right.

Thailand's court system consists of four courts: the constitution court, the court of justice, the administrative court, and the military court. The constitution court and the administrative court are new. The constitution court has the power to consider bills which one-tenth of MPs, one-tenth of senators, one-tenth of members of both houses, or the prime minister see as unconstitutional. The constitution court comprises a president and 14 judges selected as follows. The supreme court votes secretly to select five supreme court judges to become constitution court judges. The administrative court selects two of its judges. The supreme court president and four deans of law schools and four deans of political science schools of state universities jointly nominate 10 law experts and six political science experts. The senate then selects five of the law experts and three of the political experts. The administrative court has the power to settle disputes among government agencies, state enterprises or authorities, and the people, or among state agencies themselves. The administrative court will be established under the dual court system, with its general-affairs section independent from controls by both the executive and judicial branches, but attached to the supreme administrative court president. An important new clause included for the court of justice is the composition of the judicial commission with two members appointed by the senate, who must not have been judicial officials before. Another is the stipulation that the court and its general-affairs section are independent bodies attached to the supreme court president. Also, the political tribunal is set up under the court of justice with nine supreme court judges empowered to consider corruption complaints against politicians. Their rulings are also considered final.

Two major implications of the new fairness are public socialization about fairness in governance, and new institution building to support the principles of fairness. First, the adoption of fairness as guidelines for government action requires that the values and culture of Thai government officials and citizens be changed. The value change process takes a long time. One indication of the fairness movement in Thailand is the increasing commitment shown by the Thai citizen to call for standardized codes of conduct or ethics for every professions: civil servants, politicians, judges, businessmen, etc. Second is the process of institution building to accommodate new ideas of fairness is underway in Thailand. In the near future, new laws, government institutions, and independent bodies will be formed both in the public and private sectors to take charge of human rights, environmental protection, consumer protection, and social justice. The reform process should create a stronger central government at the expense of the citizen. More power must be given to the Thai people.

V. POLITICS OF GOVERNANCE

I shall explain the political consequences of governance reform initiatives on the nature of the strong central government and the politician-bureaucrat relationship by considering each public sector reform dimensions. Before doing so, two general observations are made about governance reform in Thailand. First, since under the present government structure the central government exercising full control of the Thai public sector, major decisions on the transformation process are in the hands of central government elite: the cabinet and senior bureaucrats. Second, even though the new constitution of 1997 which laid down a foundation for governance was drafted by a group of people selected by parliament, the implementation details such as future organic laws are left in the hands of the ruling central government.

A. Power

Transforming from government to governance should result in the reduction of central government's authority over the public sector, and increase in citizen's power to govern the public sector. Questions asked are: Has the central government become a smaller unit that does less? Have the new power centers emerged to take over former power domains of the central government?

Previous attempts to create a smaller government that does less were not successful because of failures to downsize, privatize, and decentralize the central government. To downsize the bureaucracy is not a wise move on the part of the political executives. If you are a minister, your popularity among your subordinates in the ministry will be enhanced if you can fight for more positions and expand the ministry's domains (Bowornwathana 1997b). Your clout does not expand by downsizing your ministry. This explain why there is a lack of political will to downsize the bureaucracy. Drastic measures to reduce the size of the bureaucracy such as massive layoffs have not been introduced by the political executives. Politicians have been very lenient toward the bureaucrats because they need the support of bureaucrats to implement their policies successfully. Despite the economic crisis of 1997 and the shrinking national budget, the political executive have not yet drastically cut the salary of bureaucrats. Only minor measures are introduced, such as no two-step salary increases for senior officials, no meeting allowance, and temporary suspension of foreign trips by government officials. Since bureaucrats are paid at a very low rate in Thailand, being in government is like being on welfare.

The urgency to downsize the bureaucracy due to the economic crisis has make politicians who are cabinet members more powerful vis-à-vis bureaucrats. The situation has also increased the power of central agencies such as the civil service commission and the budget bureau because they function as staffs of the political executives in making downsizing decisions. The line ministries are in a disadvantage position to bargain for new positions.

Failure to downsize the Thai bureaucracy meant that the central government is still very large and strong. So far, the Thai experience indicates that there has been no progress in downsizing the central government. The announcement of the Chuan II government to stop filling new positions and, at the same time, abolish 80% of the retired positions and fill only 20% (about 1500 positions) must not be taken lightly if the government really meets the target in the near future. Though a minor move, it will be the first time that the Thai government is able to halt increases in the number of government officials.

If Thailand's privatization policies under the IMF conditions are successfully implemented, all state enterprises will become private corporations. It will be the end of state enterprises in Thailand. The central government will lose control of state enterprises. Ministers will lose control of state enterprises attached to the ministry. Thus, the central government will become smaller and will loss control of several key functional domains in the public sector such as electricity generation and telecommunications services.

However, during the privatization process, it is the political executives who have gained power substantially. All of the sudden, political executives have the power to sell state enterprises. This is a victory of the political executives over the government employees working in state enterprises. For Thailand, it is a rather unusual situation because state enterprises are known to be closed systems, and the state employees wield considerable political power. In fact, employees in profitable state enterprises are known to have enjoyed a generous sum of annual bonuses and salaries that very much surpasses those of ordinary civil servants. Their protests and strikes had shaken and can still shake the stability of the government. Judging from previous experiences, one can not rule out the possibility that politicians may find ways to benefit from the privatization process. What if a minister is bribed by a private company which intends to buy the shares of the privatized state enterprise? How can we be sure that the funds obtained from the sell of state enterprises will not be misused by the political executives?

Opposition to privatization from the state employees is expected because they stand the risk of losing the most. First, they may lose their jobs. Second, those that remain in the new corporate will find themselves that their jobs are no longer secure for life and that they have to perform under a new business culture. They cease to be a part of the traditionally well protected and prestigious central government. Instead, they become private employees who would lose their privileges and welfare benefits they used to gain from their state enterprise status.

Government officials from central agencies such as the Fiscal Office Policy of the Ministry of Finance, which is responsible for overseeing more than 70 state enterprises nationwide, will gain more power during the privatization process. They will set out a general framework and implementation details for privatization. However, in the long run, government officials may stand to lose power and privilege. For example, the practice of senior government officials to be appointed as board members of state enterprises will be terminated. This is a major blow for senior bureaucrats in ministries with state enterprises. For example, several senior officials from the Finance Ministry who used to supervise all state enterprises would no longer be members of state enterprise boards.

Under economic crisis, privatization of state enterprises will bring in foreign investors. Public utilities and the telecommunications, energy, and transport sectors may be under the ownership of foreign companies. Fear of foreign control of former state enterprises is also a reason why privatization in Thailand will not be easy.

Decentralization process in accordance with the 1997 constitution has been progressing slowly. Once completed, the strong central government will lose its firm grips on the administration of provinces. A stronger system of local governments will emerge as new centers of power in local affairs. National politicians and bureaucrats will become less powerful in local affairs. But since the decentralization process has not been finalized yet, the ongoing process is a struggle for power between national and local actors. The proposal by the government to set up a national committee will strengthen the positions of national political executives and senior bureaucrats. At the same time, the struggle at the national level for control of local governments will go on. Representatives from the Interior Ministry will try to maintain some control over local governments. That is why the Interior Ministry wants the new decentralization office to be under the ministry. Recently they even suggested the creation of a department of local government in the interior ministry to oversee decentralization. Central agencies such as the civil service commission, the budget bureau, and the ministry of finance will want to have more say in the new decentralization system by proposing relevant standardization procedures. Local leaders, of course, call for more autonomy.

Though NGOs in Thailand are not strong enough to seriously undermine the traditional power of the central government, the existence of NGOs is a nuisance to the power holders, both bureaucrats and political executives. There is a continuing distrust among political executives and government bureaucrats about the activities and organization of NGOs. For example, some ministers have showed concern over the efficiency of NGOs with respect to participation in a 21.6 billion baht loan scheme to create employment opportunities for low-income groups (Nation, May 13, 1998:1). In short, the NGO movement in Thailand seem to have strengthened the politician-bureaucrat alliance.

B. Organization

Moving from government to governance is a process of changing the structure of the public sector from a single hierarchical structure to multiple structures. The new multiple structure consists of various types of organizations especially those that function independently from the old hierarchy of ministries and departments, and are managed under the principles of flexibility and autonomy. Escape from the former bureaucratic system to new flexible organization systems is expected to enable the state to provide citizens with better quality services. How far have we moved ahead?

In my opinion, the new Public Organization Act of 1999 reinforces the strength of the central government by giving power to the cabinet to establish public organizations through executive orders without the need to seek approval from the parliament. Cabinet members or the political executives gain control over the new public organizations through their power to decide on the creation and abolishment of public organizations; their power to appoint board chairman and members; their power to specify the management arrangements of a particular public organization so that more management autonomy and flexibility in budgetary and human resources will result in better performance of the public services delivered; and, their power to monitor and control the new public organizations. All these new powers are bestowed on the political executives, not to the permanent secretaries and directors-general. However, the possibility of government officials from ministries, departments and state enterprises of leaving their government jobs and become employees of the new public organizations is not only opened, but policywise encouraged because the transformation of departments into public organizations symbolizes the escape from the old inefficient bureaucratic system, and will therefore eventually produce a more effectively-run public sector.

How has the structure of the public sector changed with the introduction of the new public organization? My argument is that the new public organization initiative has created a new structure within the central government which parallels the old hierarchical bureaucratic system of ministries and departments. As more and more new public organizations are established, the nature of the public sector will change. Political executives will retain control of the old system, and gain control of the new system of public organizations. Central bureaucrats in the old system will have no control of the new world of public organizations, and may lose control of the old bureaucratic system as departments and state enterprises are transformed into public organizations. In short, the political executives, that is, the central government, become more powerful. They will not loss control over the implementation of their policy because the Thai public organization model incorporates a strong board, not a strong chief executive, model. The citizen, on the other hand, is rather removed from the new public organization structure because they do not directly exercise authority over public organizations.

C. Accountability

The transition from the government to the governance involves the strengthening of external accountability mechanisms to ensure openness and transparency in government so that the citizen will have more power to monitor and control state agencies in the public sector. How far has the accountability movement gone in Thailand?

It would be accurate to say that governance reform on accountability has just started and it looks strong. As the accountability movement is taking shape, resistance to change from the old bureaucratic system is also very strong. Though the Official Information Act was passed in 1997, most central government agencies pay little attention to the new law. Many government ministries have not set up their own mechanism and assigned officials to respond to public enquires for information. Public awareness over the right of access to public information has not significantly increased. The first test of the Official Information Act is the petition filed by Ms. Sumalee Limpa-owart, a mother of a daughter who failed the entrance examinations for primary students of the demonstration school at Kasetsart University, to the official information commission (OIC) to seek disclosure of results of the entrance examinations. Though the OIC ruled that Kasetsart University, a state university, must reveal the exam record, the Kasetsart authorities refused to comply. And when they did later on comply after a ruling from the civil court, the exam result was shown without identifying the names of students. That the new office of the official information commission is under the office of the permanent secretary to the prime minister meant that the prime minister and other political executives have a new political instrument to exercise control over the state bureaucracy and bureaucrats.

The accountability movement is changing the nature of the central government. By putting new accountability agencies under the political executives and parliament, politicians are equipped with a new set of instruments to contain and balance the strong power of the traditional bureaucracy. Since the accountability movement at the initial stage is a legal reform process, the new forces are legal experts specializing in the field of public law who work in the council of the state and in university's law faculties. As in the case of the establishment of the administrative court, the process can be characterized as a struggle within the legal community involving judges on one side, and the council of the state and public law university lecturers on the other side. A major concern of the judges is the possibility of the administrative court to intervene in the affairs of the judicial commission (Bangkok Post, January 2, 1999). Thus, citizen may have more say in the future about government affairs, but the legal institutions are again displaying their powerful position in the Thai society.

The commissions required by the 1997 constitution to be established are the national human rights commission, the ombudsman, the national countercorruption commission, and the auditor-general commission. These new commissions will strengthen the power of parliament to check and monitor the work of the executive. But since political executives of the coalition government are from the same group of political parties that control the majority in parliament, the reigning coalition government can easily overcome the monitoring from parliament. Under the 1997 Constitution, the political executives are losing control of two former executive agencies under the prime minister, namely the counter corruption agency and the auditor-general, which will eventually move out of the executive branch to become independent agencies under parliament. But since the prime minister also heads the major coalition party, he can indirectly monitor the two agencies which are supposed to check him.

Another development which reaffirms the importance of being a senior government official is the fact that in practice, commission members are chosen from persons with a background in central government services. For example, all members of the national countercorruption commission recently selected by the senate on March 26, 1999, are or were former high-level central government officials. The question is: can they remain impartial on corruption cases involving their former friends and enemies in the bureaucracy? The distrust some people have on leaving corruption abatement solely in the hands of politicians and bureaucrats has pushed citizens to form their own corruption watchdogs. For example, Prawese Wasi proposed that a "social countercorruption commission" be formed as an informal independent body to monitor graft in government agencies and pass the information to the media for further investigation (Nation, September 30, 1999:A8).

D. Fairness

Public sector transformation from government to governance also entails a process of adopting of new democratic egalitarian value system and standards of behavior on the part of government officials and the citizen. In the governance model, bureaucratic discretion is based on the principle of fairness rather than on conventional bureaucratic practices and regulations. What has happened in Thailand?

Governance reform on fairness has just started in Thailand. Therefore it is premature to make any conclusive statements about the politics of governance. Two preliminary observations are made. First, the enforcement of the new fairness principles such as human rights, better justice, environmental protection, and consumer protection should give more power to the citizen, and end the monopoly of the central government to make judgements about the policies without taking into consideration the wishes of the people. Once stronger civic groups and institutions emerge, the public should be better-off. In the meantime, reform proposals of the central government should be carefully scrutinized as they may contain conditions which perpetuate the monopoly of power by the state.

An example of the struggle between the state and the citizen is the human rights bill. According to the 1997 constitution, Article 334, the human rights bill must be passed by October 1999. Recently, 14 private human rights organizations challenged the changes made on the bill by the Council of the State, the legal advisory body of the executive. They argued that the provisions authorizing the ministry of justice to direct the National Human Rights Committee (NHRC) went against articles 199 and 200 of the 1997 constitution, which require that the committee be an independent body. The human rights groups also oppose the fact that only civil service lawyers and politicians are allowed to sit on a panel to select the 11 NHRC members. They also object to the idea of permitting government officials to work part time as NHRC commission members (Bangkok Post, March 2, 1999:1). For the NHRC to be under the justice ministry means that the central government will become stronger, and central government officials will become more powerful. As proposed by the council of the state, the NHRC will be under the prime minister, not parliament, as many human rights groups have wished (Chongkittavorn 1999b; Pratoomraj and Bhattacharjee 1999).

Moreover, recent developments in the fairness dimension indicate that political executives are reluctant to make decisions that run counter to central bureaucrats. Reform initiatives on the judicial process approved by the prime minister and the cabinet favor government bureaucrats. Sometimes, reform decision have nothing to do with granting of more power to the citizen over the public sector. For example, the recent restructuring of the police department of the ministry of interior into a national police office under the prime minister has nothing to do with improving the quality of police services delivered to the public. However, the creation of the national police office gave the police greater autonomy and power.

VI. CONCLUSION

The transformation of the Thai public sector from government to governance is still at an early stage. The promulgation of the 1997 Constitution and the 1997 economic crisis are critical factors which have helped boost the governance reform movement in Thailand. It is still premature to make final judgments about the impact of governance on the Thai public sector. Nevertheless, governance reform can be conceptualized as a struggle among the political executives, bureaucrats, and citizens.

The four public sector reform dimensions in Thailand are changing at different paces. In the power dimension, measures to disperse power from the central government such as downsizing, privatization, decentralization, and nongovernmental organizations are not making much progress because of strong resistance from central government officials. The citizen is still too weak to challenge the traditional state. As for the organization dimension, political executives seem to have gained from the new Public Organization Act of 1999. After several public organizations are established, we will then have an empirical base to make judgment. Accountability has made the most progress among the four public sector reform dimensions. However, one needs to wait and see whether in future the new accountability laws will function well under the governance framework. The last dimension, fairness, is also progressing very slowly because conflicting perspectives of central government officials and citizens.

The difficulty in determining whether reform choices of the central government do indeed foster the goal of governance to empower citizens to control the public sector is obvious. One suspects that reform decisions claimed by political executives to be based on governance have hidden motives such as establishment of supremacy over permanent bureaucrats. Clearly, the recent introduction of governance principles in Thailand has not resulted in a weaker central government. The balance of power in Thai government, however, is shifting in favor of politicians and political executives who are gaining a firmer grip over the public sector. That is, the power of the prime minister, ministers, and members of parliament is increasing at the expense of the traditional bureaucratic elite: military generals, permanent secretaries, and directors-general.

ENDNOTES

1. Recent observation by scholars center on the question whether there is a global governance paradigm or not. International organizations such as the World Bank (1992) and the OECD (1995) support the globalization of the governance or the new public management (NPM) paradigm. Though scholars accept that there are similar public sector reforms under the NPM umbrella taking place in various countries, they also pointed out that country-specific variations are widespread (Masser 1998). Therefore, a uniform "one-track" picture is not at all accurate (Pollitt and Summa 1997), and the NPM's overall suitability for different regimes remain uncertain (Galnoor et al. 1998). Public sector reforms must be understood as interacting rather than overruling a country's government traditions. National political structures, cultures, and power relations interact with reform programs to create many governance arrangements (Jensen 1998). A satisfactory explanation of the differences must include an analysis of governmental traditions that make public sector reform distinctive everywhere (Rhodes 1998). Leading British scholars such as Rhodes (1998) and Hood (1995, 1998) went even further to argue recently that there is no such thing as the NPM: the case for NPM as a global paradigm was overstated. In this paper, the author argues that though it is true that country-specific variations are important, it is also equally true that the similarities exist. Model construction of the governance has its comparative utility.

REFERENCES

Bangkok Post, July 5, 1997, p. 1.
Bangkok Post, Aug. 30, 1998, p. 3.
Bangkok Post, Nov. 23, 1998, p. 4.
Bangkok Post, Dec. 5, 1998, p. 1.
Bangkok Post, Feb. 25, 1999, p. 2.
Bangkok Post, March 4, 1999, p. 1.
Bello, Walden, Shea Cunningham, and Li Kheng Poh (1998). *A Siamese Tragedy*: *Development and Disintegration in Modern Thailand*. London: Zed Books Ltd.
Bogason, Peter, and Theo A. Toonen, eds. (1998). Comparing networks. *Public Administration*: *An International Quarterly 76*(2).
Bowornwathana, Bidhya. (1999). Administrative reform and the politician-bureaucrat perspective: visions, processes, and support for reform. In Hon S. Chan and H. K. Wong, eds., *Handbook of Comparative Public Administration in the Asia-Pacific*. New York: Marcel Dekker, 69–77.
Bowornwathana, Bidhya (1998a). Fiscal reform of Bangkok metropolitan administration: from bureaucracy to governance. Paper presented at the International Workshop on Issues and Innovations in Metropolitan Development Financing organized by the United Nations Centre for Regional Development and the Korea Research Institute for Human Settlements, 7–9 September 1998, Seoul, Republic of Korea.
Bowornwathana, Bidhya (1998b). Bangkok metropolitan administration into the twenty-First century: the practice of good local governance. In Josefa S. Edralin, ed., *Metropolitan Governance and Planning in Transition*: *Asia-Pacific Cases*. Nagoya, Japan: United Nations Centre for Regional Development, 147–164.
Bowornwathana, Bidhya (1997a). Transforming bureaucracies for the 21st century: the new democratic governance paradigm. *Public Administration Quarterly 21*, 294–308.
Bowornwathana, Bidhya (1997b). Thailand: bureaucracy under coalition governments. Paper presented at the International Conference on Civil Service Systems in Comparative Perspective, Indiana University, Bloomington, April 5–9.
Bowornwathana, Bidhya (1997c). The governance of the Bangkok metropolis: the old system, the new city, and future governance. In Josefa S. Edralin, ed., *Local Governance and Local Economic Development*: *A New Role for Asia Cities*, Nagoya, Japan: United Nations Centre for Regional Development, 87–114.

Bowornwathana, Bidhya (1996a). The politics of reform of the secretariat to the prime minister. *Australian Journal of Public Administration 55*(4), 55–63.

Bowornwathana, Bidhya (1996b). The phenomenon of new ministries and the politician-bureaucrat perspective. *Asian Review of Public Administration 8*(2), 23–32.

Bowornwathana, Bidhya (1996c). Political realities of local government reform in Thailand. In Susumu Kurosawa, Toshihiro Fujiwara, and Mila Reforma (ed.), *New Trends in Public Administration for the Asia-Pacific Region: Decentralization.* Tokyo: Local Autonomy College, Ministry of Home Affairs, 79–88.

Bowornwathana, Bidhya (1995). Response of public administration system of Thailand to global challenges. In Sirajuddin H. Salleh and Ledevina V. Carino, eds., *Globalisation and the Asean Public Sector.* Kuala Lumpur: Asian and Pacific Development Centre, 365–430.

Bowornwathana, Bidhya (1994). Administrative reform and regime shifts: reflections on the Thai polity. *Asian Journal of Public Administration 16*(2), 152–164.

Bowornwathana, Bidhya (1989). Transfers of bureaucratic elites by political bosses: the question of political versus bureaucratic accountability. *Asian Review of Public Administration 1*(1), 18–37.

Bowornwathana, Bidhya (1988). Public policies in a bureaucratic polity. Paper presented at International Political Science Association meeting, Washington, D.C.

Changsorn, Pichaya (1999). Privatization lingers in the slow lane. *Nation*, Feb. 16, 1999, p. A4.

Chongkittavorn, Kavi (1999a). Information act challenges culture of secrecy. *Nation*, Jan. 23, p. A4.

Chongkittavorn, Kavi (1999b). Chuan betrays trust with revised rights bill. *Nation*, March 22, 1999, p. A4.

Dixon, Chris (1999). *The Thai Economy: Uneven Development and Internationalisation.* London: Routledge.

Frederickson, H. George (1997). *The Spirit of Public Administration.* San Francisco: Jossey-Bass.

Galnoor, Itzhak, David H. Rosenbloom, and Allon Yaroni (1998). Creating new public management reforms: lessons from Israel. *Administration and Society 30*(4) 393–420.

Gough, Leo (1998). *Asia Meltdown: The End of the Miracle?* Oxford: Capstone.

Hall, M. H., and P. B. Reed (1998). Shifting the burden: how much can government download to the nonprofit sector? *Canadian Public Administration 41*(1), 1–20.

Heady, Ferrel (1996). *Public Administration: A Comparative Perspective.* New York: Marcel Dekker.

Hood, Christopher (1998). *The Art of the State: Culture, Rhetoric, and Public Management.* Oxford: Oxford University Press.

Hood, Christopher (1991). A public management for all seasons? *Public Administration 69*(1), 3–19.

Hood, Christopher (1995). Contemporary public management: a new global paradigm? *Public Policy and Administration 10*(2) 104–117.

Jensen, Lotte (1998). Interpreting new public management: the case of Denmark. *Australian Journal of Public Administration 57*(4), 54–65.

Kiel, L. Douglas and Euel Elliot (1999). Long-wave economic cycles, techno-economic paradigms, and the pattern of reform in American public administration. *Administration And Society 30*(6), 611–615.

Kulawat, Suchada (1998). NGOs: a star is born: *Bangkok Post*, Jan. 6, 1998, p. 8.

Maidment, Richard, David Goldblatt, and Jeremy Mitchell, eds. (1998). *Governance in The Asia-Pacific.* London: Routledge.

Masser, K. (1998). Public sector administrative reforms. In J. Shafritz (ed.), *The International Encyclopedia of Public Policy and Administration.* Boulder, Westview, 1851–1862.

Mallet, Victor (1999). *The Trouble with Tigers: The Rise and Fall of South-East Asia.* London: Harper Collins.

Memorandum of Understanding (1998). *Proposed Social Sector Program Loan.* Memorandum of Understanding Between the Fiscal Policy Office of the Ministry of Finance of the Kingdom of Thailand and an Appraisal Mission of the Asian Development Bank, Jan. 16.

Moar, Moshe (1999). The paradox of managerialism. *Public Administration Review 59*(1), 5–18.

Nation, Feb. 5, 1998, Sect. B.

Nation, Feb. 17, 1998, p. A4.

Nation, Feb. 27, 1998, p. A5.

Nation, May 13, 1998, p. 1.

Nation, May 21, 1998, p. B3.

Nation, Aug. 10, 1998, p. 1.

Nation, Aug. 13, 1998, p. A2.

Nation, Sept. 30, 1998, p. A8.

Nation, Nov. 8, 1998, p. 1.

Nation, Dec. 5, 1998, p. 1.

Nation, Jan. 25, 1999, p. A2.

Nation, Feb. 15, 1999, p. A3.

Nation, March 16, 1999, p. A3.

Nation, March 25, 1999, p. A3.

Neher, Clark D., and Bidhya Bowornwathana (1986). Thai and Western studies of politics in Thailand. *Asian Thought and Society 11*(31), 16–27.

Nguak, Nok (1998). Are NGOs equal to the task? *Bangkok Post*, Sept. 8, 1998, p. 8.

Nunberg, Barbara (1995). *Managing the Civil Service: Reform Lessons from Advanced Industrialized Countries*. Washington: World Bank.

Nunberg, Barbara, and John Nellis (1995). *Civil Service Reform and the World Bank*. Washington: World Bank.

Osborne, David, and Ted Gaebler (1992). *Reinventing Government: How the Entrepreneurial Spirit is Transforming the Public Sector*. Reading, MA: Addison-Wesley.

Organisation for Economic Co-operation and Development (OECD) (1995). *Governance in Transition: Public Management Reforms in OECD Countries*. Paris: OECD.

Peters, B. Guy, and John Pierre (1998). Governance without government? Rethinking public administration. *Journal of Public Administration Research and Theory 8*(2), 223–245.

Pollitt, Christopher and Hilkka Summa (1997). Trajectories of reform: public management change in four countries. *Public Money and Management. 17*(1), 7–18.

Pratomraj, Sarawut and Ken Bhattacharjee (1999). Stop playing politics with right commission bill. *Nation*, April 3, p. A5.

Rhodes, R.A.W. (1996). The new governance: governing without government. *Political Studies XLIV*(4), 652–668.

Rhodes, R.A.W. (1997). *Understanding Governance: Policy Networks, Governance, Reflexivity and Accountability*. Buckingham: Open University Press.

Rhodes, R.A.W. (1998). Different roads to unfamiliar places: UK experience in comparative perspective. *Australian Journal of Public Administration 57*(4), 19–32.

Root, Hilton L. (1996). *Small Countries, Big Lessons: Governance and the Rise of East Asia*. New York: Oxford University Press.

Riggs, Fred W. (1966). *Thailand: The Modernization of a Bureaucratic Polity*. Honolulu: East-West Center.

Royal Thai Government (1997). *The Cabinet's Policy Address by the Prime Minister to the House of Representatives*. Bangkok: Office of the Secretariat to the Cabinet.

Royal Thai Government (1998). *Sixth Letter of Intent to the IMF*, Dec. 1.

Royal Thai Government (1998). *Fifth Letter of Intent to the IMF*, Aug. 25.

Royal Thai Government (1998). *Fourth Letter of Intent to the IMF*, May 26.

Royal Thai Government (1998). *Third Letter of Intent to the IMF*, Feb. 24.

Royal Thai Government Gazette (1999). *Public Organizations Act 116*(9).

Royal Thai Government Gazette (1996). *Constitution of the Kingdom of Thailand 114*(55).

Siamwalla, Ammar, and Orapin Sopchokchai (1998). Responding to the Thai economic crisis. Thailand Development Research Institute, August.

Sukin, Kamol (1998). The various challenges to the NGOs. *Nation*, Oct. 28, 1998, p. A5.

Thailand Development Research Institute (1998). A draft proposal to build good governance. Working Group on Good Governance, Thailand Development Research Institute. (In Thai.)

Thailand Development Research Institute (1997). *Thailand's Boom and Bust: Collected Papers*. Bangkok: Thailand Development Research Institute.

Toeffler, Alvin, and Heidi Toeffler (1994). *Creating a New Civilization: The Politics of the Third Wave*. Atlanta: Turner Publishing.

Unger, Danny (1998). *Building Social Capital in Thailand: Fibers, Finance, and Infrastructure.* Cambridge: Cambridge University Press.

Warr, Peter G., and Bhanupong Nidhiprabha (1996). *Thailand's Macroeconomic Miracle: Stable Adjustment and Sustained Growth.* Washington: World Bank.

World Bank (1998). *Thailand Economic Monitor.* Bangkok: Thailand Office, World Bank.

World Bank (1994). *Governance: The World Bank's Experience.* Washington: World Bank.

World Bank (1991). *The Reform of Public Sector Management: Lessons from Experience.* Washington: World Bank.

29

Innovations for Administrative Reforms in Korea

A Case of Local Autonomy System

Jong-Hae Yoo   *Department of Public Administration, Myongji University, Seoul, South Korea*

I. INTRODUCTION

The South Korean local autonomy system was begun in 1952 and was implemented for nine years until it was suspended by the military regime in 1961. But it was reinstated before the staging of the Seoul Olympics in the fall of this year. This democratic self-governing system will be able to contribute, not only to achieving national balanced development toward the year 2000, but also to maximizing citizen participation. Also, government's responsiveness and accountability to citizens will be enhanced, even though it is not necessarily expected to be successful in the light of past experiences.

This chapter provides an academic basis for reinstating local autonomy by making a systemic review of local self-governing experiences and by analyzing needs and potentials for the local autonomy system in South Korea. In the light of some critical factors, an attempt is also made in this study to propose a desirable and feasible system that will be appropriate for Korea.

Korea has experienced two decades of rapid economic development and industrialization, during which its per-capita GNP increased from $80 in 1960 to $8850 in 1997. The stages of this growth in Korea can be broken down into three periods: (1) the period beginning with the establishment of the South Korean government in 1948 and up through the 1950s, that is, the stage of nation building; (2) the period of the 1960s and 1970s, which is called the stage of economic take-off and construction of the national economy; and (3) the period of the 1980s and 1990s which may be regarded as the stage of the welfare state for equitable distribution of income and greater participation by the people.

During the stages of nation building and economic takeoff, a powerful centralized government and its bureaucratic administration functioned as the most appropriate apparatus in guiding economic planning and implementation of developmental policies. In these stages, a significant number of local developmental projects were planned and managed by central officials and planners within the context of national development plans. Critical resources were also mobilized and allocated primarily by the central government through the guidance of its formalized administration.

Since the 1980s, however, significant changes have taken place in South Korean society, especially a wave of major social changes, such as the higher education level of the general public, the increase of income levels, and the greater demand for a higher quality of life. This has had a greater impact on people's political expectations. Moreover, there is a new distrust of and resistance to the excessive centralization of government power.

These factors tend to enable the people to ask for greater opportunities to participate in decision-making processes, and thus for decentralization of power at the local level. These demands for decentralization must be interpreted in connection with the strong and sincere desire of the people at all levels of society for both "democratization" of the political process and active participation in their own government. People at the local level are beginning to want local solutions to local problems and are increasingly advocating broader discretionary power. Local officials also express feelings of inconvenience with stringent national government control over local affairs. Finally, in response the government has advocated that local autonomy would be reinstated gradually in the early part of 1987. This was later postponed until after the 1988 National Assembly elections.

The reason that people want to participate in policymaking processes, especially in the regional development policy, is due to the failure of the centralized metropolitan policy to address practical needs. Thus, there has been a serious disparity between metropolitan and provincial areas. In South Korea, the overconcentration of the population in metropolitan areas such as Seoul, Pusan, Taegu, Inchon, and Kwangju has accelerated since the rapid industrialization of the country. The physical size of Seoul is only 0.63% of the land mass, but more than 10 million people, one-quarter of the population live in Seoul. Furthermore, as of 1985 not only important facilities and resources—such as 51.0% of banks, 62.2% of deposits and 61.4% of loans, 51.6% of the composite income tax, 72.6% of the corporation tax, 57.2% of the wholesale business, 22.3% of electric power consumption, 40.0% of motor vehicles, 30.1% of hotels, 38.8% of hospitals, and 46.7% of universities—but also substantial opportunities for socialization of people were concentrated in Seoul (Christian Institute for the Study of Justice and Development 1987). It is in this respect that Seoul is sometimes cynically called "the Republic of Seoul." Under these circumstances, one of Korea's national policy goals is to redisperse the population and capital of the metropolitan areas back to the rural areas, and to develop middle-sized and small cities by encouraging so-called "U-turn" migration (Cho and Kim 1983). In order to accomplish these policy objectives, it seems essential that a desirable system and strategy for local autonomy should be one that encourages people to live in localities.

Based on a review of the contextuality of South Korean local autonomy since 1949, the presupposition of this chapter is that local autonomy is the best avenue for local participatory democracy and one of the best solutions for overpopulation in metropolitan areas.

II. HISTORY OF SOUTH KOREAN LOCAL AUTONOMY

A. Changing Process of the Local Autonomy Act

Established on August 15, 1948, the Republic of Korea was introduced to the local self-government system by the promulgation of the Local Autonomy Act on July 4, 1949 (see Table 1). By this Act, local assemblies were constituted in such localities as province (do), city, town (eup), and township (myon), even though the chiefs of local government were not elected directly be residents. This local autonomy system was very new to South Korea, which had a long tradition of centralized power. But it has been radically changed since the first amendment to the Local Autonomy Act on December 15, 1949.

The first popular elections for local assemblies in the cities, towns, and townships were held in April 1952, during the Korean War. With the exception of Seoul, Kyunggi, and Kangwon

Table 1 Changing Process of Local Autonomy Act, by Amendment

Key items	Local Autonomy Act (July 4, 1949)	First amendment (Dec. 15, 1949)	Second amendment (Feb. 13, 1956)	Third amendment (July 8, 1956)	Fourth amendment (Dec. 26, 1958)	Fifth amendment (Nov. 11, 1960)	Sixth amendment the provisional (Sept. 1, 1961)
Units of local autonomy	Province, Seoul city, town (eup), township (myon)	Province, Seoul city, town (eup), township (myon)	Province, Seoul city, town (eup), township (myon)	Province, Seoul city, town (eup), township (myon)	Province, Seoul city, town (eup), township (myon)	Province, Seoul city, town (eup), township (myon)	Province, Seoul, Pusan, city, county
Term of local assemblymen and chiefs	4 years (assemblymen) 4 years (chiefs)	4 years 4 years	3 years 3 years	3 years 4 years	4 years 4 years	4 years 4 years	Stopped Stopped
Selection of the mayor of Seoul and of governors of provinces	Appointment	Appointment	Appointment	Appointment	Appointment	Direct election by residents	Appointment
Selection of local chiefs of basic unit (such as city, town, township)	Election by local assembly	Appointment until the organization of the local assembly	Direct election by residents	Direct election by residents	Appointment	Appointment	Appointment
Power of "no-confidence" vote against local chiefs	Established	Established	Abolished	Abolished	Established	Established	Stopped
Power of disbanding local assembly by chiefs	Established	Established	Abolished	Abolished	Established	Established	Stopped
Set limit of meeting days	None	None	Limited	Limited	Regulated	Limited	Stopped

provinces, which were in war zones, elections for provincial assemblies were held in May of the same year. The fact that local elections were held despite the nation's involvement in war does not necessarily mean a strong desire for decentralization and grass roots democracy, but may imply the hidden political intentions of the central government. At that time, because the opposition party had more seats than the ruling party in the National Assembly, which elected the president, the government tried to weaken the power of the National Assembly through local autonomy. For this reason, it might be said that the purpose of local autonomy of Korea differed from Western countries from the very beginning.

The Local Autonomy Act was amended twice in 1956. Since four years of local autonomy experience had revealed many irrationalities, such as an excessive number of assemblymen, no set number on meeting days, and frequent uncomfortable relations between the local assembly and the chiefs of local government, a second amendment was passed. Through this amendment, the chiefs of local government were to be directly elected by popular vote. Both the power of the "no-confidence" vote of assemblymen against the chiefs and the power of disbanding the local assembly of chiefs were abolished. In contrast to the substantial change in the second amendment, the third produced little change. For example, it preserved the 4-year term of the incumbent local chiefs and assemblymen elected in 1956. Many considered it an instrument to postpone elections of local assemblymen until the presidential election in 1960.

Two years after the amendments of 1956, the Local Autonomy Act was substantially amended again. As local chiefs, a number of opposition party members was engaged in local government. The government made an amendment that replaced direct election with an appointment system for local chiefs. The purpose of this amendment was to allow the national government under President Syngman Rhee to control local government easily and effectively.

The Local Autonomy Act, revised four times during the First Republic period, was dramatically changed by the Second Republic, established by the student revolution on April 19, 1960. The Democratic party government that replaced President Rhee's Liberal party strengthened local autonomy. For example, it reestablished the direct election system of local chiefs, including the mayor of Seoul, the governors of Provinces, and even chiefs of neighborhood associations such as Dong and Ri. It reintroduced the power of the no-confidence vote of the local assemblies against their chiefs. Throughout the whole nation the third election of all chiefs and assemblymen was held in December 1960.

But local government under the Second Republic was abruptly ended by the military coup of May 1961. The new military government, led by the late President Chung Hee Park, enacted the Provisional Act on Local Autonomy, which held the Local Autonomy Act in abeyance. According to this law, only provinces, cities, and counties (gun), including towns and townships, were eligible for self-governing units. Actually, the law empowered the national government to dissolve local assemblies and to appoint the chiefs of local governments. The functions of the provincial and Seoul assemblies were delegated to the ministry of home affairs. Other city and county governments were placed under the provincial governors appointed by minister of home affairs. Thus, since 1961, local self-government has not existed due to a philosophy that placed efficiency, based on centralization, over people's direct political participation through decentralization.

These frequent amendments to the Local Autonomy Act were not made due to the needs of the local residents, but rather they were made to suit the various political purposes of the parties in power in the central government. Thus, local autonomy was distorted as a policy instrument to strengthen the centralization of the government rather than to decentralize the power.

Along with the Local Autonomy Act, the Provisional Act has also been amended six times, and even today it is still in the forefront of discussion. Nevertheless, the Provisional Act has come under fire since the ruling and opposition parties agreed in 1985 that local assemblies in some form would be constituted by the first half of 1987. However, due to other political issues such as the election of the National Assembly, the amendment to the Local Autonomy Act was not taken into deliberation by the last National Assembly. At this time, it seems possible that a local self-governing system will be established soon after the election of the 13th National Assembly on April 26, 1988.

B.   Present Situation of Local Autonomy

1.   Hierarchical Structure of Local Governments

Local governments in South Korea are created and charged with the administration of the policies and programs initiated by the central government. Within the city administration, there is a three-level hierarchical structure. The city of Seoul, a "special city, " is under the direct supervision of the Prime Minister, while the direct-jurisdiction cities (Pusan, Taege, Inchon, and Kwangju) are under the direct control of the minister of home affairs. They have a population over one million. The other 56 common cities have populations of more than 50,000, and are controlled by the provincial governors, who in turn are subject to the supervision of the ministry of home affairs (Fig. 1).

The ministry of home affairs (Fig. 2) is one of the most powerful bureaucratic organizations in the national government. Of course, each ministry in the central government has the power to supervise and direct special subdivisions of the local governments within that ministry's jurisdiction.

There are three bureaus—local administration, local finance, and local development—in the ministry of home affairs. Each bureau administers all local affairs under the guidance of the minister. Furthermore, the power of appointment of provincial governors, mayors, county chiefs, and many other important local officials belongs to the ministry of home affairs. In reality, the local governments are hardly self-governing at all. They are operated more like branch offices of the national government. In the light of this present hierarchical structure, the South Korean local

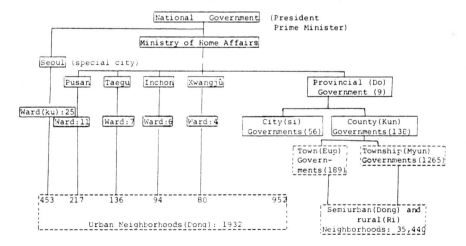

Figure 1   Hierarchical structure of local governments in Korea (as of 1988).   ☐ = autonomous administrative units; ⌐⌐⌐ = subordinate administrative units. (From Ministry of Home Affairs.)

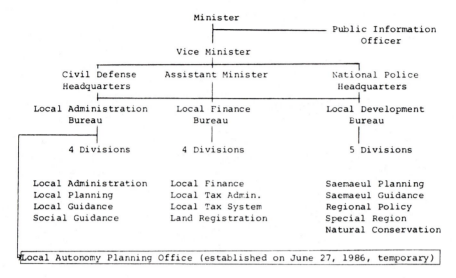

Figure 2   Organization of the Ministry of Home Affairs. (From Ministry of Home Affairs, 1988.)

government system may be called a self-governing system in name only. However, it could be said that the present local government system will be changed be reinstating local autonomy.

2.   Financial Self-Sufficiency of Local Governments

In 1986, the average level of financial self-sufficiency of local government was only 57.7% and the average rate of local revenue was only 13% of the national total (Table 2). In comparison to Seoul and the other four direct jurisdiction cities, the self-sufficiency rate of counties was only 25.9%, with the common cities rate at 57.8%.

Among the 138 counties, the highest in terms of financial self-sufficiency was Sihung-kun (49.1%) and the lowest was Jangsoo-kun (11.7%). Of the 56 cities, the highest was Woolsan (96%), and the lowest was Dongduchun (61.1%). During the past 10 years, from 1976 to 1985, the financial self-sufficiency of the provinces, cities, and counties, did not improve very much. The average degree of financial self-sufficiency only changed from 42.5% to 57.7% during the period 1976–1986. The real situation has been that city governments and other local governments have depended financially on general and categorical assistance grants from the central government (see Table 3). It should be noted that nearly all local governments are financially weak and politically vulnerable to the influence of the national government. Only Seoul and three of the four direct jurisdiction cities (Pusan, Taegu, and Inchon) are not dependent on the national government.

For that reason, by changing the cigarette sales tax rate, which is a part of local revenue, the central government is distributing about $266 million to local governments, with the exception of Seoul and the other four major cities. According to this amendment, starting at February 1, 1988, every city and county government, will be entitled to receive 22% (previously 2%) and 55% (previously 22%) of the profits from the cigarettes sold in its own area. But, it should be said that this amount of financial resource is still insufficient for making local governments financially independent. Therefore, the national government is considering an increase of tax revenues by providing local government with the power to autonomously appropriate the items and rate of taxation for local assemblies. For this reason it seems that local financial self-sufficiency can be improved through reformation of structure and exploration of new sources for local taxation.

Table 2 Financial Self-Sufficiency of Local Governments as of 1986

Name of region	Rate (%)
Metropolitan city	
Seoul	(97.5)
Pusan	(85.5)
Taegu	(87.5)
Inchon	(89.7)
Kwangju	(63.1)
Province	
Kyungki	(63.7)
Kangwon	(28.4)
Chungbuk	(33.3)
Chungnam	(42.0)
Chunbuk	(27.9)
Chunnam	(28.8)
Kyungbuk	(31.3)
Kyungnam	(45.1)
Cheju	(35.0)
Average of cities and provinces	(64.1)
Average of cities	(57.8)
Average of counties	(25.9)
Average of national total	(57.7)

Source: *Hankook, Kyungje Shinmoon*, Dec. 29, 1987, p. 13.

3. Increase in Number of Local Public Officials

The local government organizations have been extended as a result of increasing trends in public service needs. This increase raised the need for local public employees. In addition, the workload of the local governments has been increased by the mandate system, which delegates additional matters to local agencies by the central government. As shown in Table 4, between 1965 and 1986, the number of local public service employees increased amazingly by 425.5%. This also reflects that people wanted to receive more services through their local government because of accessibility. Accordingly, it can be said that local autonomy in Korea is needed to check extended local government functions and to respond to local residents' demands by establishing a local self-governing system.

III. AFFIRMATIVE INFLUENCES ON LOCAL AUTONOMY

In general, the failure of local autonomy in the 1950s was due to certain socioeconomic factors such as a low educator level, insufficient fiscal-self support capacity,[1] narrow scope of governing of local affairs,[2] excessive control of national government, and government intervention by top political leaders (*Cho-Sun Ilbo*, May 30, 1986, p. 5). But these factors have been changing for the

Table 3   Revenue Sources of Local Governments (in Millions of Won)

Revenue source	Seoul	4 Direct jurisdiction cities	9 Provinces	56 Cities	138 Counties
Total revenue	1,149,906	852,567	1,895,609	1,066,479	2,009,318
Local tax	879,943	459,768	357,192	337,201	322,196
Nontax revenue	239,355	238,723	332,810	235,640	215,984
Local share tax	0	35,084	446,625	223,584	750,000
Subsidy	30,608	118,792	758,982	270,054	721,138

Source: Ministry of Home Affairs, 1987.

past 28 years. The education level of the general public is rapidly increasing. Low financial self-sufficiency will be improved by reclassifying national tax revenue with local tax revenue. This shows that national government is affirmatively changing its attitude toward local autonomy in response to the strong demand of the people. The following three factors constitute affirmative influences on the reinstatement of local autonomy in South Korea.

A.   Education Level of the General Public

The education level in South Korea has developed so rapidly that it cannot be compared with any other example in the world. The percentage of school-age children attending school in 1950 was 69.8%, but in 1987 the percentage of elementary school children in school reached 93.9%. The number of secondary education students in the middle and high schools increased almost 56 times during the 40 years from 1954 to 1986. During the same 40 years, the number of students receiving higher education, including university education, increased 38 times (Ministry of Education 1986). This rapid increase of the numbers being educated demonstrates the growth of the citizens' capability for and understanding of local self-government. Of course, high education level is not a necessary condition for operating a local self-governing system successfully. But it means that people will not experience the same failure of local autonomy caused by the 30% illiteracy rate in the 1950s.

Table 4   Increase in Number of Public Officials

Level	1965	1970	1975	1980	1986	% Increase 1965 to 1986
National public service*	253,973	344,171	365,390	471,438	467,306	184.0%
Local public service†	47,760	68,681	107,385	185,729	203,329	425.5%

*Numbers of public employees belonging to the national government.
†The officials of the ministry of education and Seoul are included in the numbers of local public servants.
Sources: *Statistical Year Book of Korea of 1982*, and Ministry of Government Administration, *Public Personnel System*, 1976.

B.   Government Attitudes Toward Local Autonomy

It is no longer valid to say that due to the low fiscal self-capacity of local government, local autonomy cannot succeed in South Korea. In preparation for local autonomy, the national government changed the Local Tax Revenue Act in 1986. According to this amendment, as mentioned before, the cigarette sales tax was allocated to local tax revenue. The national government is still considering various methods to enhance local financial capacity. For example, the government is trying to amend the Local Tax Share Act toward improving serious regional disparities. Within the national government, the ministry of finance and the economic planning board are considering coordinating the rate of tax revenue shares and transferring fares and taxes such as power, telephone, and transit from central to local governments. Also, the government is giving consideration to levying a tax on tourist resorts and on environment pollution as new financial resources for the local autonomy system.

However, it should be said that the most important factor for the operation of local autonomy is the attitude of national government, which gives discretionary power and autonomy to local governments without any intervention.

C.   Maturity of People's Political Consciousness

In 1960 when the third and last election period for local assemblies of self-governing communities was held, the per capita income was only 80%. Many people say that local elections were fraught with corruption and injustices, including selling votes in order to earn money. But, as of 1987, per capita GNP has reached $2850. With a rapid increase in income and material stability the citizens have begun to express their desire for democracy and direct participation in government affairs.

Furthermore, a recent study, which was based on a public opinion survey, indicates that 87% of the interviewees agreed to reinstating local autonomy. Especially among that 87%, about 50% of them responded that local autonomy has to be carried out throughout the whole nation. Only 8.9% disagreed with the concept of local autonomy; this was because of its inefficiency and financial burdens.[3] In this respect, it could be said that many people expect to organize local assemblies, as well as to operate local governments.

Moreover, South Korean people have experienced the importance of participation through nationwide movements, such as the democratization movement in June 1987, which resulted in the peaceful replacement of a regime. We can say that the local autonomy system provides people with an opportunity to participate in democracy.

IV.   DESIRABLE FORMS OF THE LOCAL AUTONOMY SYSTEM

Local autonomy entails decentralization, meaning the distribution of concentrated power of the national government to local government. Therefore, in operating the local autonomy, one of the most important points is to set up an ideal relationship between central and local governments.

Compared with other countries, such as Japan, China, and some in Western Europe, South Korea has a far different tradition of local government. Those countries that have a long history of local government have to concentrate and coordinate the dispersed power of local governments in the process of modern state building (Chung 1985). South Korea, on the other hand, is experiencing a reversal of this process. From this perspective, it is very difficult for Korea to make a feasible and desirable local autonomy system.

Numerous methods for structuring the local governments in line with power decentraliza-tion have been suggested by both scholars and politicians. A feasible system in this present sociopolitical context will be proposed in this chapter by considering the local self-governing units and types, the method for selecting local chiefs, the relationships between central and local governments, and the local governments' financial situations.

A.   Units of Local Self-Government

It is very important that people experience direct democracy through local autonomy systems. A local self-governing system provides residents with an opportunity to make government respon-sive to their own needs, and it enables people to enhance public responsibility.

Such local self-governments will be most productive if they are reorganized into a two-tier local self-government system consisting of a small local government unit and a large government unit. For effective administration, the large units should include Seoul (a special city), the direct jurisdiction cities, and the provinces, while the small units, as the basic units, should include wards of Seoul and four other major cities, and common cities as well as counties. The current multihierarchical system of local government with three or four local levels has posed adminis-trative problems.[4] It has overlapping functions in local governments.

For example, county government has operated as an intermediary between town and town-ship governments when they needed to refer to the provincial government. This practice reduced the township governments to secondary roles in that preparation of necessary reports for higher levels became a major portion of their duties, rather than functioning as self-governing units.

Such unnecessary problems could be lessened, though not eliminated, by organizing the system into a two-tier local government unit with the province as the large local government unit as well as the ward, city, and county as the small local government unit (Fig. 3). Furthermore, the problems that could arise from distance as a result of the rearrangement can be prevented by estab-lishing county branch offices where necessary.

The traditional grass-roots governments, the towns (eups) and townships (myons), would no longer be recognized as local self-government units in this new system. In place of town and town-ship governments, county government branch offices would be instituted so that they could deal locally with the policy and administrative affairs within the boundary of the county. The county branch offices would not be hierarchical subdivisions of the county government. Rather, they would carry out the same functional duties as the county government. The services provided by the county branch offices would get rid of any inconveniences that the county residents might have in getting services from the remotely located county government office. The administrative affairs of the towns and townships would be properly executed by the county branch offices without referring matters to the county government offices. They would function only on a broader juris-dictional basis.

There are still several reasons behind selecting the county as the basic local government unit instead of the town and township governments. In 1952, with the establishment of local assem-blies, the national government practiced local self-government at the town and township levels for the first time. From the outset there were many functional problems, which resulted mainly from the paucity of professionally trained personnel and the lack of financial resources, which was par-ticularly severe. Accordingly, the township governments had difficulty in providing adequate facilities and services for their local residents.

There are also several reasons for considering the ward of major cities the basic unit of the local self-governing system. In major cities, residents would hardly be able to participate in a pol-icymaking process beyond casting a vote in local elections such as assembly and mayors, if ward assembly could not be organized.

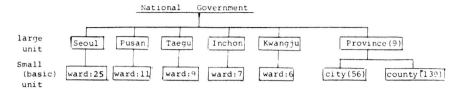

Figure 3   Proposed units and types of the local self-governing system. ☐ = autonomous unit.

B.   Election Method of Local Chiefs

How to elect local chiefs is a determinant factor in operating local autonomy. Currently, the chief executives of local government in South Korea are not popularly elected by the citizens but rather are appointed by the president. It follows that those who are appointed by the president tend to pay attention to the president's interests rather than to the local residents' interests in their administrative work. In the Local Autonomy Act Amendment presented to the last National Assembly, direct election of local chiefs was recommended. But, as an additional rule, an appointment system will be selected instead of direct election for the time being, because the national government and the ruling party think that it would be too easy to cause inefficiency and instability in local government.

However, since the appointment system does not work effectively for the betterment of the local residents, the direct election system is desirable for local autonomy; directly elected local chiefs can exercise strong political leadership in policymaking without consideration of the national government, and they will take a serious view of residents demands. In these respects, the mayor council and professional administrator system would be one alternative for both facilitating citizen participation in local politics and improving administrative specialization and efficiency. As the chief executives of the local governments, the county chiefs and mayors would have the power to appoint and remove managers, who can direct and supervise administrative and policy affairs.

In addition, the locally elected legislative body such as the local assembly will be able to check and supervise the executive body. Without the participation of political parties, democratic local autonomy cannot function. For this reason, the election of political party members as local chiefs, mayors, and assemblymen should be allowed.

C.   Functional Relationships Between National and Local Governments

The New Local Autonomy Act provides that local autonomous bodies shall deal with local public matters and matters delegated to the entity by laws and ordinances. However, there are no detailed criteria to delegate functions specified. In the self-governing system, the proper share of administrative affairs has not yet been assured. Accordingly, it is necessary to distribute as many functions as possible to the basic unit of local government such as ward, city, and county by making clear criteria. For example, such public affairs as conservation of environment, military, labor, and agriculture have to be considered as functions, of basic local autonomous bodies. Not only these functions but also welfare administration such as health insurance and the national pension have to be distributed as local public affairs.

Of course, the local governments should operate in partnership with the national government in such functions as integrated regional development planning and programs. But for establishing the tradition of grass-roots democracy the national government has to limit intervention in local governments in the process of reinstating the local autonomy system.

Thus, initiatives or referendums (Naisbitt 1984:164) should also be popularly practiced at the local level in the future of South Korea, because they are methods of direct legislation by which voters may enact laws or constitutional amendments without action by the legislature. The referendum is a type of direct legislation similar to the initiative.[5]

D. Proposal for Improving the Local Financial System

The financial capacity of local governments is weak. In 1982, 42% of the total revenues for local governments came from outside sources in the form of subsidies of local share taxes provided by the central government (Ahn and Kim 1987). Local governments still depend heavily on the subsidies from the national government to supplement their financial shortages (Table 3). The reason is that the present tax system puts more priority on national tax than on local tax. The total tax revenue of South Korea was comprised of 87% national tax and 13% local tax in 1986. Therefore, it is necessary that some of the national tax items, such as transfer income tax, telephone tax, and the amusement, eating, and drinking tax, provide for the sufficiency of local self-governments.

But the most important thing is not to levy any new local tax on local people in order to reinstate local autonomy. Rather than new local taxes, a strategy for developing the local economy should be considered by inviting manufacturing companies to set up plants. Each local government should also establish a long-term financial planning system. In addition, scientific management tools such as computer analysis, organization and methods, and management information systems should be introduced to local self-governments to enhance efficiency and economy.

V. CONCLUSIONS

The structure and governance of local governments was frequently changed throughout the nine-year period 1952 to 1961. It was even suspended. But local autonomy is about to be reinstated in Korea. To revitalize and innovate local self-government, national government will have to take proper actions on the following three points.

1.   Without any intervention and control, the national government and other concerned authorities should distribute their power to local self-governments in order to maintain autonomy.

2.   The national government should relocate industrial complexes to the provincial areas in order to activate local economies and to result in balanced growth among the regions.

3.   The national government should encourage people to participate in local politics and give related information to them through public relations activities.

It is more important to keep in mind that the operation of local autonomy does not depend on the system, but on the people who operate the system. Accordingly, those who are influential in the operation of local autonomy have to show their will toward democratic local government. For example, President Roh, directly elected by the people, should develop his endeavors for reinstating real local autonomy by holding elections for local assembly and chiefs in the near future. Also, "ordinary people" should show their active participation in elections and local politics with a democratically oriented attitude.

ENDNOTES

1.   Average rate of financial self-sufficiency was 28% in 1960.
2.   The rate control of local affairs was only 32%, 43%, and 33% in provincial, city, and county governments, respectively, in 1960 (Kim 1988).

3. *Chung Ang Ilbo*, April 2, 1985. This survey was originally made by the Institute for Development of the National Assembly, Seoul, South Korea.
4. The system of national, provincial, city, county, town, and township governments are hierarchically structured in terms of supervisory and regulatory responsibilities. Therefore, lower units of local governments are controlled by and reported in much red tape to upper governments.
5. The initiative and referendum as instruments of direct legislation are commonly found together. However, they are separate instruments and one may be used independently of the other.

REFERENCES

Ahn, C.-S. ed. *The Local Political System in Asia*: *A Comparative Perspective.* Seoul National University Press, Seoul, 1987.

Ahn, C.-S., and Kim, K.-D. Korea. In *The Local Political System in Asia*: *A Comparative Perspective* (C.-S. Ahn, ed.). Seoul National University Press, Seoul, 1987, p. 51, Table 4.

Chung-Ang Ilbo, March 7, 1985.

Chung-Ang Ilbo, April 2, 1985.

Cho-Sun Ilbo, May 30, 1986.

Cho, Y.H., and Kim, Y.S. The challenge of urban overpopulation and public policy: the case of metropolitan Seoul. *Journal of East and West Studies XII*(2), 1983.

Cho, Y.H., and Kim, Y.S. The national fiscal assistance system and the local government of Korea: its effects on city finance and environment correlates. *Journal of East and West Studies XIV*(2), 1985.

Christian Institute for the Study of Justice and Development. *Social Justice Indicators in Korea.* CISJD, Seoul, 1987, pp. 24–29.

Chung, S.-W. Relations between national and local autonomous entities toward the year 2000 (in Korean). Presented to seminar *On Local Administration Toward the Year 2000*, Seoul, South Korea, Sept. 18–10, 1985.

Chung, S.-W. Local self-governance in Korea: retrospect and prospect. *Korea Local Administration Review* 2(2), 89–105 (1987).

Hill D.M. *Democratic Theory and Local Government.* George Allen and Unwin, London, 1974.

Institute of Seoul Municipal Research (Cizung Young Koo Dan). *Reports on the Research of Basic Needs of Seoul Citizens* (in Korean), 1983.

Jun, J.S. Decentralization and local administration: a step toward democratic governance in Korea. *Political Studies Review 1*:57 (1985).

Kim, A.-J. Brief History of Local Autonomy in Korea, *Comparative Local Administration 17*:44–57, 1988.

Kim, S.-J. Public officials' expecting desirable local autonomy. *Comparative Local Administration 17*:17–23, 1988.

McCandleness, C. *Urban Government and Politics.* McGraw-Hill, New York, 1970.

Ministry of Education. *Statistical Book of Education.* Ministry of Education, Seoul, 1986.

Ministry of Government Administration. *Public Personnel System.* Ministry of Government Administration, Seoul, 1986.

Naisbitt, J. *Megatrends: Ten New Directions Transforming Our Lives.* Warner Communications, New York, 1984.

Park, E.-K. Assessment of the importance of local government in Korea. Prepared for the Joint International Seminar on *Local Self-Government*, Dec. 9–13, Seoul, 1987.

Quigley, J. *Perspectives on Local Public Finance and Public Policy*, Vol. 2. JAI Press, London, 1985.

Yoo, J.-H. Administrative reforms in Korea: local autonomy system in the future. Presented at the 12th General Assembly of EROPA Conference at Manila, Nov. 23–28, 1987.

Yoo, J.-H. Local autonomy and citizenship. *Local Administration Review 36*(409), 1987.

Yoo, J.H. Tasks for democratization of local autonomy system. *Local Administration Review 37*(412), 1988.

30

Public Enterprise Reforms and Privatization in India

Anil Kumar Monga   *Department of Evening Studies, Panjab University, Chandigarh, India*

I. INTRODUCTION

Public enterprises in India are passing through a process of crucial change. For the last four decades, India has been pursuing a path in which the public sector was expected to be the engine of growth. It was to hold the commanding heights of the economy. As a result of this policy, public enterprises grew in terms of number, area of operation, investment, turnover and exports. Today, these enterprises operate at three levels of government, central, state, and local, and have been organized mostly in three forms: departmental public enterprise, public corporation, and government companies. The total number of public enterprises is about 1200 in the country. There are 236 public enterprises at the central level with an investment of $2020 billion (*Economic Survey* 1998–99). There are 900 state-level public enterprises with an investment of $20 billion. The municipal public enterprises are around 50 in number and have an investment of about $1 billion (Mishra 1998).

The public enterprises operate in a wide-ranging area of economic activities. They deal with manufacturing and service activities. The manufacturing activities range from production of steel to the generation of power. The enterprises engaged in services are involved in private consultancy services, financial services, development finance, dairy development activities, etc. The state-level public enterprises are engaged in manufacturing, trading and service, development finance, and promotional and welfare activities. In the field of manufacturing, they mostly operate in consumer durables, electrical, electronics, and light engineering goods industries. The trading and service enterprises at the state level mainly deal with state trading, warehousing, and civil supplies activities. The financial enterprises at the state level are extended arms of the All-India Development Bank engaged in extending financial assistance by way of risk and debt capital to the entrepreneurs in the various states of the country. The promotional enterprises include small-industries development corporations, fisheries corporations, leather industries development corporations, etc. The welfare enterprises are enterprises dealing with the elevation of the weaker sections of society, although on a commercial basis. The municipal enterprises are local-level enterprises handling activities such as water supply, drainage, milk supply, etc.

A cursory look at the postindependence era reveals that the period from 1950 to 1980 saw the very rapid growth of public enterprises, under both the central and the state government. It was during this period that a large number of public enterprises were set up and huge funds were invested in them. However, by the early 1980s, disenchantment with the public enterprises started due to its failure in meeting one of their major objective—generation of surpluses. The situation became alarming in the beginning of 1990s. For example, the ratio of net profit to capital employed was only 2.23 in 1990–91 and declined marginally to 2.00 in 1991–92 (*Economic Survey* 1992–93). The poor financial performance of PSUs made them a constant drag on the government exchequer. Domestic resource crunch coupled with pressures from the IMF–World Bank combine forced the government of India to withdraw budgetary support and announce drastic measures in its "new industrial policy" (NIP), 1991, to restructure PSUs. (Table 1) The 1991 NIP, influenced by market forces, reduced the monopoly of the public sector and assigned increasing role to the private sector. The major components of 1991 NIP are as follows:

> Portfolio of public sector investments will be reviewed with a view to focus the public sector on strategic, high-tech and essential infrastructure. Whereas some reservation for the public sector is being retained, there would be no bar for area of exclusivity to be opened up to the private sector selectively. Similarly, the public sector will also be allowed entry in areas not reserved for it. Public enterprises which are chronically sick, and which are unlikely to be turned around will, for the formulation of revival/rehabilitation schemes, be referred to the Board for Industrial and Financial Reconstruction (BIFR), or other similar high-level institutions created for the purpose. A social security mechanism will be created to protect the interests of workers likely to be affected by such rehabilitation packages. In order to raise resources and encourage wider public participation, a part of the government's shareholding in the public sector would be offered to mutual funds, financial institutions, general public and workers. There would be greater thrust on performance improvement through the Memorandum of Understanding (MOU) system through which management would be granted greater autonomy and will be held accountable. Technical expertise on the part of government would be upgraded to make the MOU negotiation and implementation more effective. Boards of public

Table 1 Disinvestment in PSUs Since 1991

Year	Month	No. of PSUs disinvested	Amount realized (Rs. in crores)	Total amount (Rs. in crores)	Amount targeted (realized crores)	Average price Per share (*Rs.*)
1992–92	December 1991	30	1,427.00	—	—	27.65
	February 1992	16	1,611.00	3,038.00	2,500	45.25
	October 1992	8	681.95	—	—	52.99
1993–93	December 1992	14	1,183.83	—	—	58.10
	March 1993	9	46.13	1,911.91	3,500	57.83
1993–94	March 1994	6	2,290.90	2,290.90	2,500	202.00
	October 1994	6	2,230.62	—	—	531.44
1994–95	February 1995	5	330.568	2,619.92	4,000	77.6
1995–96	October 1995	4	168.62	168.62	7,000	110.21
1996–97	March 1997	1	390.00	390.00	5,000	10,000.00
1997–98	—	—	—	—	—	—
1998–99	November 1998	6	6,619.74	6,619.74	9,000	—

Sources: Economic Surveys, Department of Public Enterprises, Finance Division, Government of India, and the *Economic Times*.

sector companies would be made more professional and given greater powers (Government of India 1996–97).

The successive governments between 1991 and 1998 have sworn to introduce these reforms in PSUs. The aim of this paper is to review the various initiatives made by the Government of India.

II. DERESERVATION

The government of India, by announcing NIP 1991, has initiated the process of opening up the areas to the private sector which were hitherto reserved for the public sector. The industrial policy of 1956 had made provision for reservation of 17 industries for the public sector. The NIP 1991 brought this number down to only eight and further on March 26, 1993, it was reduced to six: defense products, atomic energy, coal and lignite, mineral oils, railway transport, and specified minerals. Last year, coal and lignite and mineral oils were also dropped from this list (*Economic Survey* 1998–99:96–97). Thus, since 1991, a deliberate attempt has been made to bring down the role of the public sector and focus on only strategic, high-tech, and essential infrastructure and envisaging a greater role for the private sector in the economy. However, it is observed that areas which are being opened to the private sector require huge investments, sophisticated technology, and a long gestation period. The private sector in India still does not have either the capacity or the technical know how to venture into these areas. The NIP 1991 recognizes this fact and goes all out to woo foreign capital. It has been decided to provide approval for direct foreign investment up to 51% foreign equity in high-priority industries. This is being done with the understanding that it will provide much-needed foreign exchange and would lead to injecting a heavy doze of investment in the high-priority industries. However, it is feared that in our enthusiasm to welcome foreign capital, we are endangering our economic sovereignty. Once foreign capital is permitted free entry, the distinction between high-priority and low-priority industries is likely to disappear, and under pressure from the multinationals, the government would be forced to open up lines of production to facilitate foreign investment. The excessive freedom to foreign capital will ultimately affect our economic sovereignty as push the country further into debt. Thus, the need of the hour is to be selective in permitting foreign investment flows, and the government should reconsider its open-door policy.

III. DISINVESTMENT

One significant policy component of the Government of India announced in 1991 was disinvestment in PSUs. The major objectives of this policy on public sector were to promote ownership of public enterprises by the general public, exposing PSUs to the discipline of market, involving workers as PSU shareholders, and mitigating the fiscal deficits in the government's budget.

In the national union budget 1991–92, it was announced to raise Rs. 2500 crores through disinvestment. During that year, equity of 31 PSUs was disinvested in December 1991 and February 1992. The PSU shares were grouped on a random basis into bundles. The government realized Rs. 3038 crores against the targeted amount of Rs. 2500 crores. However, the comptroller and auditor-general (C&AG) of India has indicated the government for underselling the PSU shares: "The Government did not conduct adequate preparatory study before launching the disinvestment exercise. Efforts were not made to generate necessary enthusiasm among potential buyers" (C&AG Report 1993:9–10).

The C&AG even criticized the method of sale of shares in bundles. According to C&AG the process of bundling of shares had adversely affected the value realization of PSU shares. In 1992–93 three rounds of disinvestment were completed, and the government discontinued the practice of clubbing shares of PSUs into bundles. The total amount to be mobilized through disinvestment during this year was Rs. 3500 crores. However, the total realization worked out to be just half of this (Rs. 1911.91 crores). The average realization per share (with a face value of Rs. 10) was to the tune of Rs. 56.30. In the year 1993–94, the equity of six PSUs was disinvested in the month of March 1994. The government realized Rs. 2290.90 crores against the targeted amount of Rs. 2500 crores during that year. Analysis of 1994–95, 1995–96, and 1996–97 reveals the similar picture. In the year 1994–95, the government was able to mobilize Rs. 2619.92 crores and the targeted amount was Rs. 4000 crores. The average realization per share was Rs. 77.6. During the year 1995–96, the government was able to raise just Rs. 168.62 crores against the targeted amount of Rs. 7000 crores with are average price per share of Rs. 110.21. In the year 1996–97, the targeted amount was as high as Rs. 5000 crores, and government could mobilize only Rs. 390.0 crores.

The government's disinvestment program for 1997–98 began with the then union finance minister P. Chidambaram announcing a selloff target of Rs. 4500 crores. In a sudden move, the then united front government planned a series of strategic sales and revised the target to Rs. 7200 crores. But in the end, 1997–98 turned out to be a very dismal year. Except for the disinvestment of 47 million shares of Mahanagar Telephone Nigam Limited (MTNL) through the global depository receipts (GDR) route, no other blue-chip disinvestment took place. The Indian Oil Corporation's (IOC) international public offering was first stalled because there was no policy on dismantling the administered pricing mechanism (APM); and when the policy statement did come, the Southeast Asian crisis knocked the sails off the global capital markets. Gas Authority of India (GAIL), too, became a victim of this crisis.

The government agreed to divest 210 million shares—around 10% of its capital—appointed lead managers, and even initiated road shows at Asian and European financial centers. But, due to depressed market conditions, the core group on disinvestment decided to postpone the issue. Ditto for the Container Corporation of India (CONCOR) float, where the government agreed to divest 6 million shares. The issue nearly made, but for the whims of the minister in charge of the administrative ministry, another one bit the dust. In case of strategic sale, bids for appointment of global advisers for Bharat Aluminum Co. (Balco) and Kudremukh Iron Ore Co. Ltd. (KIOCL) were received. The bids were required to be opened by an interministerial group comprising officials from the union ministries of mines, industry, and finance, in the presence of bankers from SBI-Caps and IDBI, who were consultants to the strategic sale. January 15, 1998, was set as deadline, but the entire process got derailed because of the elections and the demise of the United Front government. A similar exercise was planned for Modern Foods and India Tourism Development Corporation (ITDC) also, but bureaucratic delays and pressure groups within the administrative ministries stalled the selloff plans in these two companies.

In the year 1998–99, government announced in budget to raise Rs. 5000 crores by disinvesting specified portions of equity from IOC, GAIL, VSNL, and CONCOR (*Economic Times* June 2, 1998). The government started well by selling CONCOR's 9 million shares, The issue first to be launched during 1998–99 fiscal year was able to generate interest among all the categories of investors. The government was successful in generating amount to the tune of Rs. 225 crores by selling shares on discount of 30% to the market price. This was followed by the GAIL issue which raised Rs. 180 crores by selling 30.58 million shares through the book-building process at a price of Rs. 60.00. The next issue was of VSNL, which was a composite book-building issue, where a book for a Global Depository Receipts (GDR) issue and a domestic issue simultaneously collected Rs. 786.25 crores. The domestic issue flopped while the GDR issue went through.

The government was able to raise Rs. 561.49 crores by restructuring NALCO. The government converted 50% of its equity into debt. The debt was placed to banks and financial institutions by way of private placement of six-year, 14.5% (semiannual) bonds. The government, due to the depressed economic conditions and poor market for Asian stocks in the global capital markets, decided not to initiate disinvestment in any other PSUs. However, they came up with two schemes—cross-holdings and buyback of PSU shares—to pick up cash from the listed government companies. It also revised the disinvestment target to Rs. 9000 crores in the wake of these policy decisions. Government decided that oil companies, flush with funds, would buy part of the government's stake in these companies and thereby create cross-holdings in each other. The oil companies, including IOC, ONGC, and GAIL, would swap equities, whereas MTNL would buy back part of the government's stake in it. This was preferred as there was no transaction cost involved and also it would be done quickly unlike disinvestment in domestic or international markets.

The government has been successful in raising Rs. 6619.74 crores through disinvestment of its holding in PSUs in 1998–99. Out of the Rs. 6619.74 crores, Rs. 4867 crores was raised through the crores-holding in various oil companies. While the 2.5% stake in ONGC by GAIL saw Rs. 600 crores go into the government kitty, a 10% stake in ONGC and a 5% stake in GAIL by IOC saw the government richer by Rs. 2567 crores. The 10% stake in IOC and 5% in GAIL by ONGC saw Rs. 1700 crores come into the exchanger (Table 2).

Thus, the government has been successful in transferring PSU surplus funds to the central exchequer. This is nothing but a bizarre new version of the government looting the publicly listed, government-controlled companies. Government's initiatives on buy-back and cross-holding have weakened the PSUs considerably. These have massively destroyed shareholders wealth, including the government.

The total market capitalization of the *navratna* PSUs units on the Bombay Stock Exchange (BSE) has been winedof by around Rs. 20,000 crores or 23% in a month following the governments decision to promote crossholdings between PSUs to achieve its disinvestment target (Table 3). Most of the leading PSUs—BPCL, GAIL, HPCL, IOC, MTNL, ONGC, and VSNL—have seen a sharp erosion in the values of their shares in the recent weeks. However, in the case of IPCL, the market capitalization recorded a gain of 48% mainly on account of expectations of a high price

Table 2

Public enterprise	Amount raised (Rs. crores)
Domestic/GDR issue	
CONCOR	225.00
GAIL	180.00
VSNL	786.25
Cross holdings	
GAIL in ONGC	600.00
(2.5% stake)	
IOC in ONGC and GAIL	2567.00
(10% stake in ONGC and 5% in GAIL)	
ONGC in IOC and GAIL	1700.00
(Stake of 10% in IOC and 5% in GAIL)	
NALCO recast plan	561.49
Total	6619.74

Source: *Indian Express*, March 28, 1999.

Table 3   Market Capitalization in Rs. Crores of Nine Navratra PSUs

Public enterprises	Market capitalization		Percent change
	Jan. 11, 1999	Feb. 17, 1999	
BPCL	3,825	3,000	−22
GAIL	7,087	5,243	−26
HPCL	5,954	4,264	−28
IOC	16,557	11,863	−28
MTNL	12,789	10,836	−15
ONGC	28,233	19,321	−32
VSNL	7,600	6,764	−11
IPCL	1,750	2,586	48
SAIL	3,180	3,242	2
Total	86,975	67,119	−23

Source: *Economic Times*, Feb. 19, 1999.

at which the government is likely to sell its holding very soon. The SAIL is another PSU which gained moderately 2%. Thus, it can be inferred from the above that the government ended up collecting far less than what had been targeted for the year and has harmed long-term interests of the PSUs in the country which is a matter of serious concern.

Another significant objective behind the disinvestment exercise, as mentioned earlier, was wider public share ownership and workers participation by selling the equity shares of PSUs to general public and workers. However, so far, government has failed miserably on this front also. During the initial rounds of disinvestment, the government allowed participation of only selected financial institutions for bidding of the shares. Consequently, the Unit Trust of India purchased 69.4% of the total shares sold during 1991–92 followed by General Insurance Corporation (7%) and Life Insurance Corporation (6.1%). In the year 1992–93, the government offered shares to the general public also but the government fixed very high limit of minimum bid (Rs. 2.5 crores in October 1992, Rs. 10 lacs in December 1992, and 1 lac in March 1993). However, in a country like India, where one-third of the population is living below the poverty line, the achievement of the objective of wider share ownership with minimum bid involving lakhs of rupees has no meaning. Therefore, the government should offer equity shares to workers free of cost up to a number, on matching basis and in the form of open sale, as has been done very successfully in the United Kingdom, to achieve the objective of wider share ownership.

Government projected marketization of PSUs as one of the basic objective of public enterprises reforms. However, it restricted the level of disinvestment in most of the cases less than 20% and that too to only a financial institutions and mutual funds. There has not been significant change in the internal working of the PSUs. Their procedures with regard to recruitment, promotion, fixation of salaries, internal audit, and management information system remain unchanged. The government nominees continue to dominate their boards. The disinvestment has made no impact on the performance of disinvested PSUs (Mishra 1998).

IV.   DISINVESTMENT MACHINERY

In response to the problems faced during the initial rounds of disinvestment, the government of India set up a committee under the chairmanship of V. Krishnamurthy on February 26, 1992, to look into issues concerning disinvestment. The committee was reconstituted in November 1992 with C. Rangarajan as its chairman. The committee submitted its report in April 1993 and recommended, among other things, setting up a statutory committee on public enterprise disinvestment. The then congress government at the center did not set up a committee for disinvestment. However, the United Front Government, immediately after resuming office, constituted a Public Sector Disinvestment Commission by a resolution on August 23, 1996, initially for a period of three years. It was a five-member commission under the chairmanship of G.V. RamaKrishana. The major objectives of setting up of this commission were to prepare an overall, long-term disinvestment programme for public sector undertakings referred to the commission; determine the extent of disinvestment; select financial advisers to facilitate the disinvestment process; supervise the overall sale process and take action on instruments, pricing, timing, etc.; monitor the progress of the disinvestment process; and advise government on possible capital restructuring to ensure maximum realization through disinvestment. Initially, the government referred 40 public sector undertakings to the commission, and added 10 more later on. Subsequently, Government withdrew seven public sector undertakings from the commission. Of the remaining 43, the commission has examined and made its recommendations in respect of 41 public sector undertakings.

The commission has not taken an ideological approach to disinvestment. It has examined each PSU and classified it as strategic, core, and noncore. The commission has suggested no disinvestment in PSU classified as strategic. However, in the case of core and noncore PSUs, the commission recommended disinvestment upto 49% and 74% respectively. So far, the commission has submitted nine reports and has made specific and general recommendations. After detailed examination of each PSU referred to it, the commission recommended trade sale in case of six PSUs; strategic sale in 18 cases; partial sale of equity in five cases; no disinvestment in one case; disinvestment to be deferred in seven cases; and closure/sale of assets in four cases. The major general recommendations include establishment of disinvestment fund; delinking the disinvestment process from the budgetary exercise of the government; creation of standing empowered group to ensure smooth implementation of its recommendations; granting graded autonomy to all PSUs; establishing a preinvestigation board; strengthening the investor's interface; and voluntary retirement schemes (VRS) with stable and attractive terms with long-term perspective for workers.

Although the commission has gone into the working of PSUs very seriously and made valuable recommendations, it has been facing rough weather since its inception. There has been a lot of resistance from the bureaucracy due to its lack of control over it. The commission was constituted in the industry ministry, and gradually a rift developed between the commission and its parent ministry. Bureaucrats in industry ministry irked by the functioning and utterances of the commission chairman wanted the commission to be shifted to finance ministry (*Tribune* May 26, 1997). In the absence of any action on this suggestion, the industry ministry announced policy decisions such as granting of autonomy to eleven leading enterprises under the title of *Navratna* and later extending it to additional ninety one enterprises without consulting the commission. The tussle between industry ministry and the commission got intensified and finally on January 12, 1998, the powers of the commission were trimmed by a resolution of the ministry of industry making it an advisory body. The paragraphs relating to monitoring and supervision of disinvestment process were deleted from the original terms of reference announced on August 23, 1996, thus diluting its role and making it an ineffective body. The Bhartiya Janta Party (BJP) coalition government since coming to power has made many noises about prioritising the disinvestment process, but has done precious little in practice. Despite the occasional soothing noise made by industry minister, finance and industry ministry bureaucrats continue to share an uneasy relationship with the disinvestment commission chairman G.V. Ramakrishna.

Thus, in nutshell, the response of the governments toward the disinvestment commission has not been favorable. It seems that the government is not interested in the disinvestment commission's recommendations nor wants it to play a role in the implementation. If the government is serious about the disinvestment, it should restore all the powers of the disinvestment commission at the earliest. Further, the commission should be made a statutory body as has been done in various countries which has carried out disinvestment program like France, Malaysia, Singapore, and the Philippines and as originally proposed in India in order to take it out of the octopus grip of the bureaucracy. This would not only enhance the status of the disinvestment commission but also smoothen the disinvestment process in the country.

V. MEMORANDUM OF UNDERSTANDING

The government of India has adopted performance contract system approach for improving public enterprises performance. The practice of improving performance through this approach is in progress in many countries. The generic name for this policy is "performance contract"; it is also referred to as "performance Agreement," "contract plan," "contract de programme," and "letter of agreement." However, in spite of the diversity in the names used, the general essence of the policy has remained intact in all the countries overtime. The concept of performance contract is very simple.

It is supposed to be a freely negotiated performance agreement between government, acting as the owner of a public enterprise, and the public enterprise. It is expected to clearly specify the "intentions," "obligations," and "responsibilities" of the two parties. Once it is signed, the government is expected not to interfere in the day-to-day operations of the enterprise and to judge the enterprise performance at the end of the year only on the basis of the mutually agreed performance parameters laid down in the performance agreement. The philosophy behind this policy is to simultaneously increase autonomy and accountability. The approach has been widely used in many countries—viz., France, Korea, Pakistan, Bangladesh, Senegal, etc.

The review of country experiences reveals that broadly there are two varieties of performance contracts: the "French contracting system" and the "signaling system." There is much more that is common than what is different between these two approaches. Both approaches have emerged as an attempt to find a solution to the basic problem of public enterprises, i.e., they face multiple principals who have multiple goals, which are often conflicting. Both approaches try to define the rules of the game. Further, these two approaches also have a similar structure. Each contains the obligations of the enterprises and the obligations of the Government. Although, the spirit and the philosophy of these two approaches may be similar, yet there are very important differences which make them two very distant approaches. In the contracts belonging to the French system, one could only point out whether a particular target was met or not. Here, no effort in made to assign weights to targets. This creates a great difficulty in making an overall judgment regarding enterprise performance. This difficulty with the French system was overcome by the signaling system. It proposed a simple way to arrive at a "composite score" which measures the ability of an enterprise to meet its commitments. If an enterprise signing MOU does exceedingly well with regard to all its commitments, the value of composite score at the end of the year is 1. If it is dismal failure on all fronts, it gets a value of 5. A combination of good performance on some fronts and poor performance on other fronts gets it a score between 1 to 5.

India is perhaps the only country that has the distinction of having experimented with both French system and the signaling system. The MOUs signed for the first time in the year 1987–88 were patterned on French model. Later on, the contracts based on signaling system were signed in 1989. Since the inception of this system, the number of PSUs signing the contract has increased manifold. In the year 1987–88, only four PSUs signed MOU, and their number has increased to 110 in the year 1996–97. In the year 1997–98, MOU signing PSUs were 108 (Table 4). The majority of the MOUs signing PSUs have been ranked as grade A (excellent) followed by grade B (very good). More than three-fourths of the undertakings fall in these two performance evaluation categories. Except 1990–91, throughout the period under review, none of the PSU has been categorized as poor. It has been pointed out that the performance criteria has been made more fair to the manager and less fair to the country. The PSUs are showing good results in terms of profits only by sacrificing the long-term interests of the PSUs. "Long-term gains have been scarified at the cost of short-term gains. For instance, a number of PEs have scaled down the tempo of incurring expenditure on R&D, and thereby inflating their profits" (Mishra 1998).

The MOU system has failed to improve the enterprise government interface and grant operational autonomy to the PSUs. In order to be successful, the MOU should have been a truly bilateral negotiated documents between two equal parties (Iyer 1990). However, lack of equality between the secretary of the administrative ministry and the managing directors of the various public enterprises has put the public enterprises to great disadvantage (Mishra 1998). The practice of holding management responsible for results has not been introduced. If the performance is good, management claims the credit; however, in case of poor or average performance, the responsibility is shifted to the violations of the assumptions upon which MOU targets were based. The whole process of signing of MOU between the government and the public enterprise has been a mere eyewash. The process is delayed for months and gets completed in the month of January/February instead of September/October, leaving hardly any time for the management to understand the obligations and the government to fulfill their commitments toward the PSUs.

The government has not made any effort to spread the MOU culture throughout the organization by signing MOU between management and workers. Thus, the culture of accountability has not percolated down to the lower levels of the enterprise. However, inspite of these limitations, the MOU system can help in mitigating many problems of PSUs in India. There is need to create conditions for the successful implementation of the MOU system in India. First, there is need to unshackle the PSUs from the grip of the bureaucracy and grant autonomy to them in real sense. Second, the performance criteria should be laid down very carefully after free and frank negotiations at the beginning of the year. It should be fair to the manager; i.e., it should encompass only areas within the control of public enterprise management. Also, it should be fair to the country; i.e., public enterprise management should not be rewarded for actions which, though may indicate improved performance according to the criterion chosen, infact does so at the cost of the nation's

Table 4 MOU System in India

Year	No. of MOUs signed	Grades				
		A	B	C	D	E
1987–88	4	Grading not done				
1988–89	11	Grading not done				
1989–90	17	8	4	5	NIL	NIL
1990–91	23	14	8	NIL	NIL	1
1991–92	71	31	25	11	4	NIL
1992–93	102	28	22	10	7	NIL
1993–94	101	46	29	12	10	–
1994–95	99	39	26	–	–	2
1995–96	104	51	31	–	–	2
1996–97	110	46	27	19	11	7
1997–98	108	45	25	13	22	3

Sources: 1. Economic Surveys, Government of India, Ministry of Finance, Economic Division, New Delhi. 2. Department of Public Enterprises, Government of India, Annual Reports, New Delhi.

overall welfare. Third, there is need to spread the MOU culture throughout the organization which can be achieved by signing MOUs between management and workers. Fourth, efforts should be made to link the performance with a system of incentives or disincentives.

VI. BOARD OF INDUSTRIAL AND FINANCIAL RECONSTRUCTION (BIFR):

The government of India announced in 1991 to remove the dichotomy in the government policy toward sick units in the public and private sector. In December 1991, the government amended the Sick Industrial (Special Provision) Act of 1985 to enable the chronically sick public enterprises to be referred to BIFR for revival/rehabilitation. According to this amended act, any public enterprise with seven years of incorporation whose net worth has been completely eroded and has made losses for two continuous years can be referred to the BIFR (*Economic Survey* 1992–93:151).

As of November 31, 1998, out of 225 references received from central and state public sector undertakings, 157 cases have been registered (Table 5) BIFR so far has provided revival package in respect of 50 cases. Winding up has been recommended in the case of 29 public enterprises. Winding-up notices have been issued in case of six public enterprises. The employees of one public enterprise have obtained stay orders from the High Court on the proceedings of BIFR. The cases of 23 public enterprises are under enquiry with BIFR. As many as 30 cases have been declared nonmaintainable. The close examination of the working of BIFR reveals that although the board was created seven years ago, so far nothing concrete has been done. The decision making process of the BIFR is very slow. The resources at its disposal are inadequate. In addition, lack of political will to implement the turnaround package suggested in some cases have compounded its problems. Government has no clue how to deal with surplus workers and its approach toward their redeployment and retraining is muddle headed.

In order to protect the interests of workers and provide a social safety net for workers, a National Renewal Fund (NRF) was set up in February 1992. Various schemes have been proposed to assist the employees in retraining, redeployment, and counseling. Provision of funds through NRF also exists for cases where workers retire voluntarily (VRS) or are declared surplus. To implement the NRF schemes, an empowered authority has been created. Between 1992–93 and

Table 5   Status of PSU Cases Referred to BIFR as of November 30, 1998

	Central PSUs	State PSUs	Total
References received	82	143	225
Registrations delivered	15	51	66
Under scrutiny	—	2	2
References registered	67	90	157
Dismissed as nonmaintainable	5	25	30
Rehabilitation schemes approved/sanctioned	21	29	50
Winding up recommended to High Court	10	19	29
Draft schemes issued	9	3	12
Winding-up notice issued	4	2	6
Under inquiry	12	11	23
Schemes failed	2	1	3
Stay ordered by courts	1	—	1
Declared no longer sick	2	4	6

Source: *Economic Survey*, 1998–99, Government of India, p. 111.

1997–98, Rs. 3407 crore was provided as budgetary allocation under NRF, of which Rs. 2227 crore was transferred to public account and the actual spending was Rs. 2083 crore. The majority of the funds under this scheme is being spent for VRS activities, and the allocations for non-VRS activities have been declining. The non-VRS allocation component declined from 20% in the first year to 11% in the second year and came down to 4% or at times even to zero in the later years (*Economic Times* 1998). Thus, the main thrust of the NRF has largely been confined to VRS, making little headway in terms of identification and survey of workers, counseling, vocational training, and entrepreneurship development.

Even in VRS, no preliminary study was done in each PSU to identify the areas and departments that were planned with redundancy of workers. The scheme was generalized and was made open to all, resulting in the flight of young and talented engineers and managers from PSUs to the private sector. The thoughtless introduction of this scheme has siphoned off the cream of PSUs to the private sector, leaving the public sector with employees whose opportunity cost in the market has been lower than their present wage levels. In case selective VRS had been offered to redundant workers, the NRF could have been used in more effective and economical manner. Thus, it is observed that the NRF was used mainly to finance VRS only and even that by having negative effect on productivity and efficiency.

A. Restructuring of Board of Directors

The government of India has expressed its resolve to reform the institution of board of directors of PSUs. It has been noticed that there has been excessive representation of government nominees on their boards. Also, these members of the board have very short tenures. Due to slow decision making in the government, a number of position on the boards remain vacant and sometimes PSUs remain headless for months. The administrative ministries do not clear the names on one pretext or the other. It takes an inordinately long time to get vigilance clearance for the nominated persons.

In order to overcome these limitations, the government announced *Navratna* and *Mini-Ratna* policy, which envisaged two key changes: professionalization of governing boards so that the company functions as a board-run rather than ministry-led organization, and (2) allowing the companies the freedom to choose joint venture partners and make fresh investments without government permission but subject to certain conditions. But more than two years after the launch of the policy of giving autonomy, not much has been achieved.

The government of India constituted a search committee comprising the chairman of the Public Enterprise Selection Board; secretary, Department of Public Enterprise, Ministry of Industry; chairman, Standing Conference of Public Enterprises (SCOPE); secretary, concerned ministry and heads of PSUs, to select professionals for the PSU boards. The committee went through the entire exercise of selecting professionals for the boards twice. The first round of selection was completed under the United From government. The panel of names was sent to the respective ministries. But the ministers delayed clearing these names. In the meanwhile the United Front government fell and the Bhartiya Janata party (BJP) came to power. The search committee had to repeat the entire exercise again. Of 11 Navratna PSUs, only three PSUS—BHEL, NTPC, and SAIL—have seen changes in their boards. In rest of the cases, the names of the professionals await clearance from the administrative ministries. Now the government has quietly disbanded the search committee (*Indian Express* July 3, 1998).

The policy of granting autonomy to the PSUs has failed to take off because there is lack of coordination between the industry ministry and other ministries. While the industry ministry announced the policy, other ministries did not put their weight behind it. They have not found it important enough to push through the changes quickly. In addition, while the policy on PSUs is formulated and announced by the Department of Public Enterprise of the industry ministry, it does not have powers to ensure quick implementation. There is a need to bring all types of PSUs reforms under one umbrella and create a single authority to implement PSU reforms effectively in the country.

B.   Government Control

The central government has been controlling its PSUs by issuing guidelines from time to time. These guidelines gave hardly any elbow room for PSUs to take independent decisions. So long the management of the PSUs are in good books of the powers that be, these guidelines do not affect them. Once they fall out with powers, these are invoked readily to harass them. Recently, a committee headed by N. Vital was constituted by the government to review these guidelines. The committee recommended that of 892 guidelines, 762 needed deletion, 25 required modifications, and only 105 should be retained. It would be worthwhile to scrap all the guidelines; instead, a model code of conduct of ethics for PSUs as well as administrative ministries should be adopted as suggested by guidelines committee (Guidelines Committee Report 1997:12). Further, the PSUs in the country are in complete grip of comptroller and auditor-general of India (C&AG), the Central Vigilance Commission (CVC), the Central Bureau of Investigation (CBI), and the Committee of Public Undertakings (CPU). The PSUs represent the investment of the tax payers money and we have the parliamentary system.

   The role of these agencies in keeping a watch on the management of the PSUs, and monitoring them cannot be avoided. However, over the years, the attitudes and the activities of these agencies and their penchant to look into and magnify small procedural lapses has, in effect, destroyed the entrepreneurial attitudes that were taking roots in the PSUs. Another issue which needs immediate attention is amendment of Article 12 of the Indian Constitution. Under this article, the PSUs in which the government holds more than 51% equity are treated as "state" for all purposes. As a result, the employees of the public sector have more rights than the employees in the private sector. In view of this, the PSUs are more run under the government culture rather than business culture. This has become a problem especially in the context of liberalization where PSUs which were monopolies earlier are now facing competition. In the current liberalized environment, the PSUs have to be very quick on their feet. The issue of corporate governance is vital for ensuring the survival and prosperity of the PSUs. Thus, Article 12 needs to be amended to overcome this obstacle.

VII.   CONCLUSIONS

Public Enterprises in India is ushering in a new era. The new policy of the government of India is based on the philosophy of the free-market economy which has assigned limited role to the public sector. A series of measures have been announced, including the opening up of areas to the private sector by merit; disinvesting a part of government's share holding in public sector units to raise resources; introduction of performance contract system; reference of terminally sick public sector units to Board for Industrial and Financial Reconstruction; and granting autonomy to the public enterprises. The review of the various initiatives made by the government of India reveals that government by adopting open-door policy to attract foreign capital may endanger economic sovereignty and push the country into debt further. Government has announced to disinvest in some selected blue-chip public sector companies. However, instead of concentrating on the process and key areas of disinvestment, various administrations have showed their concern only about fixing the disinvestment targets. They have failed miserably in their objectives, namely, promoting share ownership of public enterprises among the general public and exposing public enterprises to market discipline, because of their lackluster approach toward disinvestment. The MOU system introduced by the government has also not been successful in improving government-enterprise interface. The whole process of signing MOU between government and public enterprise has been a mere eyewash. Government has done well by removing dichotomy in the government policy toward sick units in the public and private sector. However, the Board for Industrial and Financial Reconstruction, created for the purpose, has not been able to do much due to inadequate resources, slow decision making, and lack of political will. The National Renewal Fund is being used to finance the voluntary retirement scheme, and even that is having a negative effect on productivity and efficiency. There has been a lot of governmental control over the PSUs through its various agencies, and there are a large number of guidelines issued by the government from time to time. The PSUs are more run under the government culture rather than business culture due to Article 12 of the Constitution. If the government is serious about granting real autonomy to the PSUs, it must address these issues urgently.

REFERENCES

Abdul Hazfeez Shaikh (1987). Performance evaluation of public enterprises: lessons from the Pakistan experience. Prajapati Trivedi (ed.) (1990). *Memorandum of Understanding: An Approach to Improving Public Enterprises Performance.* International Management Publishers, New Delhi, p. 460.

Basu Prahlad Kumar (1991). *Performance Evaluation for Performance Improvement.* Allied Publishers, New Delhi, p. 100.

Comptroller and Auditor General of India (1993). Report on Disinvestment of Government Shareholdings in Selected Public Enterprises, New Delhi.

Department of Public Enterprises, Ministry of Industries, Government of India, New Delhi. *Public Enterprises Survey,* 1996–97, Vol. 1, pp. 1–3, 41–43.

Disinvestment Commission Report I–IV (February 1997–August 1997).

Disinvestment Commission Report V (November 1997).

Disinvestment Commission Report VI (December 1997).

Disinvestment Commission Report VII (March 1998).

Ghuman, B.S. (1994). Public sector policy and economic reforms. The Indian case. *Social Sciences Research Journal.*

Ghuman B.S. (1998). Disinvestment of government shareholding in public enterprises—the Indian experience. Paper presented in IASIA Conference, Paris, 14–17 September.

Gopalakrishan, M. (1997). Dis-investment and restructuring of public enterprises in India—some reflections. *Journal of Institute of Public Enterprise 20*(3,4).

Jones, Leroy P. (1981). Towards a performance evaluation methodology for public enterprises: with special reference to Pakistan. Paper presented at International Symposium on Economic Performance of Public Enterprise, Islamabad.

Mishra, R.K. (1998). Public enterprises in India under economic liberalization. Paper presented in IASIA Conference, Paris, 14–17 September.

Park, Young C. (1986). *A System for Evaluating the Performance of Government-Invested Enterprises in Korea.* Public Sector Management Division, World Bank.

Rajeshwari Kurup (1991). MOU—no panacea for all the ills. *Economic Times* Jan. 3:12.

Ramaswamy R. Iyer (1990). Past experiences with public enterprises performance evaluation systems in India. In Prajapati Trivedi (ed.), *op. Cit.*, p. 768.

Shaikh, Abdul Hafeez (1986). Performance evaluation of public enterprises: lessons from the Pakistan experience. Mimeo, Howard University.

Sucheta Dalal (1998) PSU disinvestment bungling all the way. *Indian Express* Dec. 27.

Suresh Kumar (1990). Memorandum of understanding and performance improvement. *Economic Times* Aug. 11:6.

Trivedi, Prajapati (ed.) (1990). *Memorandum of Understanding: An Approach to Improving Public Enterprises Performance.* International Management Publishers, New Delhi.

Economic Times, Aug. 9, 1996; Feb. 1997; Nov. 17, Aug. 3, and Dec. 25, 1998; Jan. 7, Feb. 12, Feb. 16, and Feb. 19, 1999.

Tribune May 26, 1997.

Indian Express, March 28, 1999.

United Nations (1992). United Nations Conference on Trade and Development Report, New York, p. 137.

World Bank (West African Division) (1985). *Project Completion Report for the First Technical Assistance Project to the Parapublic Sector in Senegal.*

World Bank (1993). Managing state-owned enterprises. World Development Report, Washington, p. 79.

31

A Decade of Public Administration and Political Flux in India: 1987–1998

Krishna K. Tummala   *Department of Political Science, Kansas State University, Manhattan, Kansas*

I. INTRODUCTION

India has successfully weathered two major political traumas—one in 1975, with the declaration of Emergency by Prime Minister Indira Gandhi, and the other in 1979, when the coalition Janata government fell, resulting in Gandhi's return to power (Tummala 1979). The aftermath of Indira Gandhi's assassination in 1984 once again tested the national mettle. The summer of 1987 saw the country on the brink of disaster. The 1996 general elections wreaked political havoc as India entered into a new political phase of coalition governments at the Center (as the federal government is commonly known). The elections of 1998 only confirmed this phenomenon. While the stability of the nation itself is under no serious threat, the state of political flux and its impact on administration deserve serious study. The following pages are devoted to a capsule analysis of some important issues in government, and of governance stemming from a decade of uncertainty.

II. ISSUES IN GOVERNMENT

A. Prime Minister Versus President

India did not discard the British constitutional tradition on becoming independent. It retained the parliamentary form of government while accepting an elected constitutional head of state—the president, not altogether different from the crown. And right from the beginning of the Republic, the relationship between the prime minister, the head of government, and the President, the head of state, came under stress. However, an all-time low was reached with the election of Zail Singh as the President of India in 1982, who appointed Rajiv Gandhi prime minister in 1984.[1] Three questions muddled the relationship between the two august offices: (1) Can the president return a bill duly passed by parliament led by the prime minister for reconsideration? (2) What type of information is the president entitled to from the head of the government? (3) Can the president dismiss the prime minister who commands a majority in parliament? If so, under what circumstances?

President Zail Singh returned for reconsideration the Indian Post Office (Amendment) Bill of 1986—a bill that would have empowered the government to censor personal mail. Under Article 111 of the Indian Constitution, the president can send back a bill (presented for his signature) to the parliament, and not to the cabinet. But once it is reconsidered by the parliament with or without the amendments he may have suggested, the president has to assent. Also, Article 143 allows the president to refer a bill to the Supreme Court on a question of "law or fact," and in the public interest.

Article 74 provides for a council of ministers "to aid and advise the president." The 42nd Amendment passed during the Emergency in 1976 amended this article to make it obligatory for the president to act in accordance with the advice given by the council of ministers. But after the defeat of Indira Gandhi, the new opposition Janata government in 1978 passed the 44th Amendment providing the president with some leeway in that he could refer the advice already given, back to the council of ministers for reconsideration one more time.

Article 78(a) laid down that it is the duty of the prime minister to communicate to the president all decisions of the council of ministers "relating to the administration of the affairs of the Union and proposals for legislation." Section (b) of the same article also permits the president to seek similar information. And Article 86(2) allows the president to send messages to parliament which shall be considered at convenient dispatch. While the president can seek information, it was decided in the *Shamsher Singh* case in 1975 that he is not a rival source of power, and must act on the advice given by the council of ministers. Yet, the president is not necessarily an "expensive inconsequence."

To clarify the relationship between the president and the prime minister, one might turn to the intent of the Constitution. Contrary to the suggestion of the Constitutional adviser, the Constituent Assembly on July 28, 1947, decided not to confer any "special powers" on the president. Similarly, during the debate in the Constituent Assembly in December 1948, the amendments proposed by K.T. Shah to give greater powers to the president were also denied. Introducing the draft Constitution, the chairman of the drafting committee, B.R. Ambedkar, commented thus:

> (T)he President occupies the same position as the king under the English Constitution. He is the head of the State but not of the executive. He represents the nation but does not rule the nation. . . . The President of the Indian Union will be generally bound by the advice of his Ministers. He can do nothing contrary to their advice nor can he do anything without their advice . . . (s)o long as his Ministers command a majority in Parliament (Shiva Rao 1968:341).

It is important here to see how Zail Singh and Rajiv Gandhi came to occupy their respective positions. Consequent to the drubbing they received in the May 1982 elections, the opposition parties talked of a consensus candidate to be the president. Instead, the then prime minister Indira Gandhi set up Zail Singh, former chief minister of the Punjab and home minister of the Government of India. This was a calculated move on her part, as always, in that she could placate the Punjabis in the face of the continuing political crisis in that state by making a Punjabi the president. Moreover, Singh came from a "backward" caste, which also meant good politics to garner support from the minorities. But, not only did several question his credentials, Zail Singh himself raised many an eyebrow by saying almost servilely that if the leader asked him to sweep the floors, he would gladly take up a broom.

After the assassination of Indira Gandhi in November 1984, her son, Rajiv Gandhi, was called upon by President Singh to head the government with the least regard to the basic canons of parliamentary democracy in that Rajiv Gandhi was not even elected as the leader of the parliamentary Congress (I) party. The appointment, some thought was a payback from the president for Indira Gandhi's generosity of making him the president by making her son the prime minister. Surely the appointment was an arbitrary one, though vindicated later, when in 1985 Rajiv Gandhi went to polls and returned with the largest majority the Congress (I) ever had winning 80% of all seats contested (415 of 542 contested). Given such a background, perhaps the expectations on the part of the president and the prime minister as to who is to be obliged to whom may have been altogether different.

However, soon the two began drifting apart. As already mentioned, the returning of the post office bill, which was much sought by Prime Minister Rajiv Gandhi, aggravated the situation. While the president pressed for all the information on the defense contract scandals (see below), the prime minister in his turn did not even brief the president on the several foreign trips he made (despite the fact that it is required by protocol), had not cleared several foreign visits of the president (at one time nearly 40 such invitations for the president were said to be pending), refused sending normal government information, and finally stopped even calling on the president in person. In a society where respect for elders is a cherished value, this kind of treatment by a prime minister who was in his early 40s toward a president who was almost twice his age was not taken lightly. In response to a statement by the prime minister in the parliament that he was informing the president regularly, the president in his turn retorted that "the factual position is somewhat at variance with what had been stated" (*Hindustan Times*, March 14, 1987).

In the meantime, the President opened up his official residence to any one who wished to see him, and began meeting with several opposition leaders from the various states, thus leaving the impression that he was cultivating the opposition. He sent letters to some governors of states admonishing them for taking active political stances, mostly against opposition parties in power. In fact, he even reminded some union cabinet ministers that they served at his "pleasure," and encouraged "alternative leaders."

The prime minister himself had not helped the situation much insofar as he did not control his party members calling the president names both in parliament and outside. Finally, as the clamor of the opposition parties and the press became vociferous, the prime minister called upon the president on March 28, 1987, for over 130 minutes. Thus was the formal communication channel reopened between the head of state and the head of government. Several other scenarios were rumored to have been played out during the summer of 1987. For one, Zail Singh for a while toyed with the idea of running for a second term as president as an opposition candidate when Congress (I) had already decided to have R. Venkataraman, then vice president, as the official candidate. If indeed Singh ran and won the election, it would have created a nightmarish confrontation between the president and prime minister. If he lost, which was more likely, it would have been a humiliating defeat at the hands of his own former vice president. In either case, he finally decided not to run. For, to win, Singh not only would have needed all the opposition support but also some crossover votes from the Congress (I), which he could not have counted upon.

Another was the possible dismissal of the Prime Minister Rajiv Gandhi by President Zail Singh. The jurists he consulted did advise the president that he has special powers under Article 74 of the Constitution, which, as seen above, actually provides for a council of ministers to aid and advise the president in the exercise of his functions. And Article 75 states that they shall hold office at the pleasure of the president, as noted above. Indeed, the president did meet in private with V.P. Singh, who was the former finance, and later defense, minister in Rajiv Gandhi's cabinet, and was considered a rival to the prime minister, a point proved to be quite correct not too long after. Rumor had it that if he accepted the mantle of power as the leader of the Congress (I), he would be sworn in as the prime minister after dismissing Rajiv Gandhi. If some such thing ever happened, it would indeed have been absurdly unconstitutional to dismiss a prime minister who commanded more than three-fourths majority. Moreover, to succeed in such a venture, the announcement of dismissal and the appointment of the new prime minister would have to be gazetted under the signature of the seniormost civil servant, the cabinet secretary, who might or might not have obliged. If he did not cooperate, he might have to be dismissed as well and a new and compliant secretary found. And in this equation what the army, which has been known for its apolitical stand all along, would do must have been an imponderable. In either case, any such dismissal would have meant a serious blow to parliamentary democracy in India, and certainly made a martyr of Rajiv Gandhi. The danger, however, passed with the president backing off by an open announcement that he does not contemplate a dismissal. The fear of possible dismissal must have been felt by the prime minister, after all. Otherwise, there was no reason for his decision to only adjourn the *Lok Sabha*—lower House of Parliament—sine die, and not prorogue it as is customary, after the completion of legislative business. By adjourning, he could quickly recall the parliament to prove his strength, if necessary (Katyal 1987:9).

The 1996 and 1998 general elections resulted in a hung parliament in that no party got the majority to form a government with the result coalition governments became the norm. And the relationship between the president and the prime minister became crucial for two reasons: one, the appointment of the Prime Minister, and the other the strength of the advice given by the prime minister to the president.

The 1996 general elections proved to be a turning point on the Indian political scene (Tummala 1998a). While no party got the majority to form a government, the Bharatiya Janata party (BJP), with only 160 seats, but supported by an assortment of other parties, claimed that it had a strength of 195 seats which was around a third of the total *Lok Sabha*. But true to parliamentary traditions, the president invited the BJP leader Atal Behari Vajpayee to form the government, and stipulated that he prove his strength in the parliament within a fortnight. Vajpayee's first political test came in the form of the election of the Speaker of the House. The opposition United Front (UF) put up a Congress (I) candidate who handily won the position. The BJP thus lost the war before the battle was even begun, and the prime minister resigned from office which lasted the shortest span in Indian history—a total of 13 days.

Then it was the turn of the United Front, a conglomeration of nearly 15 different parties, including Congress (I), with a total strength of 179. This coalition put up Deve Gowda as their leader. As irony would have it, he came from the Janata party, which had only 43 seats. He himself was not a prominent person, but was least objectionable to the coalition partners. Given his minority status, Gowda much depended upon the support of the senior coalition partner, Congress (I). And its new president, Sitaram Kesri, who fancied himself as of prime ministerial stature, pulled the rug under the feet of Gowda after 10 months, and the United Front government fell consequently.

When approached by Kesri with the request that he be allowed to form the government, the president this time demanded to know his strength, and when Kesri failed to show proof, he was denied the opportunity. But once Gowda was removed, Kesri was willing to support any other UF leader, and the mantle fell on Inder Kumar Gujral. But the president this time insisted that the coalition partners show some evidence of their continued commitment to support the UF choice of candidate, and only then did he appoint Gujral as prime minister. But Kesri did not live up to his assurances, and led to the downfall of Gujral government too. And the President was advised to call for a general election.

Thus, within two years new elections were forced upon the nation. The 1998 general elections led to the same scenario with no party getting the majority, and the BJP entered into a coalition of 13 different regional parties. Its leader, Atal Behari Vajpayee, who previously had been prime minister for 13 days, was appointed again with the proviso that he prove his strength in the *Lok Sabha*, which he did. And that government has been tottering in power since. This experience shows that the president although does not have the prerogative to pick any one as his choice of the prime minister can, and did, insist on some guarantees of political stability while making the appointment.

The second issue was that of the strength of the advice given by the head of the government to the head of the state. The constitutional dynamic of the relationship between these two offices is already seen above. But then, under a coalition government, could the president, knowing full well that the prime minister is on a shaky ground, act independent of the advice of the prime minister (and his cabinet)? There have been two occasions when the advice rendered by the prime minister was not accepted by the president outright. In both cases, it was to dismiss a state government belonging to a party opposed to that of the prime minister at the Center. United Front Prime Minister Gujral recommended in November 1997 that the BJP government of Kalyan Singh in Uttar Pradesh be dismissed. But the president did not see that there was a breakdown of Constitutional machinery, and referred the matter back to the prime minister and his cabinet for reconsideration, as he is empowered to do. The Gujral government backed down, and Kalyan Singh was saved.

Similarly, in September 1998, the BJP government at the Center recommended the dissolution of the Rashtriya Janata Dal (RJD) government of Rabri Devi in Bihar. Again, the president did not see that the dismissal was warranted, and sent back the recommendation for reconsideration with the result the BJP government backed off, and Rabri Devi's government was saved. However, these two experiences need not be interpreted as the president snubbing a coalition prime minister whose strength is not much to talk about in the first place. It is perhaps so because that the incumbent president, K.R. Narayanan, is a Constitutional stickler. But the point is that the president did not like the attempts at the partisan use of the constitution to dismiss a state government of a party opposed to the Center. More importantly, it also appears that for this president a bad government is not synonymous with a failing government, and certainly a breakdown of Constitutional machinery there could not be inferred. In any case, it is obvious that the president has started to flex his Constitutional muscles to muzzle the partisan manipulation of the Constitution by a minority government (Tummala 1998b).[2]

B. Prime Minister Versus Parliament

There are two cardinal features of a parliamentary system that are of interest here. One is collective responsibility of the cabinet, which implies that for all decisions made by either individual cabinet ministers or the cabinet as a group, the cabinet as a whole takes responsibility. This means not only collegiality among the members of the cabinet but also the expectation in particular that individual ministers do not dissent from, and much less oppose, the prime minister once a decision is made, although in the discussions of the cabinet they may enjoy full freedom to express their opinions. The second important attribute is the presence of a "loyal opposition" which is ready and waiting to take over the reins of government should the government of the day fall. The role of the opposition parties thus is normally a constructive one in that they do not simply criticize the government but do that to keep them in check while offering differing opinions and alternate public policies. In other words, the opposition should not necessarily play the role of simple obstructionists.

Turning to collegiality, Rajiv Gandhi had at least 24 cabinet reshuffles in 42 months—the last one in July 1988. Two trends are discerned in this context. One, several prominent ministers left the cabinet in protest against the prime minister, and were later dismissed from the Congress (I) altogether. The most controversial of all was V.P. Singh. His anticorruption effort, as finance minister, along with the collection of delinquent taxes from several of the big and influential industrial houses who regularly contributed munificently to the Congress (I) party coffers, not only resulted in a furor but also caused serious embarrassment to the prime minister. As a result, he was moved from finance to defense. And in April, within four months of the transfer, consequent to the institution of inquiries into several defense contract corruption deals, he had to resign altogether from the cabinet. On July 19, 1987, he was expelled from the Congress (I) for alleged antiparty activities. (Ironically, only three days prior to the dismissal, his offer of resignation was turned down.)

With each reshuffle, several state-level Congress (I) leaders have been rehabilitated as cabinet ministers. For example, the last cabinet of Rajiv Gandhi had eight former chief ministers of states, provoking one opposition party leader to comment that the central cabinet "was fast becoming the dust bin for rejected state leaders" (*Hindu International Edition*, July 2, 1988:2). Simultaneously, some of the former cabinet members were posted as governors who turned out to be highly controversial partisan characters, particularly in those states where the opposition parties were in power. Events such as these cast a long shadow not only on the collegiality in the cabinet but also on the good faith of the prime ministers.

In times of coalition governments, the clout that the prime minister exercises will of necessity diminishes. The reason for this is simple enough. Just to be in office, the prime minister needs the support of the various constituent parties which in the first place in all probability would have bargained for cabinet berths of their choice, and whenever the prime minister tended to be less accommodating, they might in turn threaten to walk out and thus could bring the government down. They could turn around and put together yet another coalition. Thus, the instability of coalition governments is well known. The worst part of this scenario is that governments busy in being in power can do little constructive for the country as such, and are always on the look out for partisan gain. It is no secret that the Samatha party leader, Mulayam Singh Yadav, in return for his party's support of the United Front government very much wanted the home portfolio; instead he ended up with the defense portfolio. Once the United Front government fell, he went out and even entertained thoughts of being the prime minister, and later started what came to be known as the Third Front as an alternative. Furthermore, take the example of Jayalaltiha from Tamil Nadu, who has not even two dozen members supporting her but kept threatening perennially the Vajpayee government that unless they obliged her in various ways (including scrapping some corruption cases going on against her), she would pull out and thus lead to the fall of the government. In other words, having been a partner in the government, she has been taking the government almost for ransom.

A responsible opposition ready to assume the reins of government is the sine qua non of a parliamentary form, just as a constructive opposition is to good government. In the presence of a monolithic Congress (I) party, historically the opposition had not much of a chance in India, except for the brief Janata rule in 1977–79. However, consequent to the success of several regional parties many of the state governments have come under the power of parties other than the one in power at the Center. Given the rival ambitions of the regional leaders for the national spot, and the fact that they are spread over the right-left spectrum, it was well nigh impossible to get even a minimum understanding among the coalition governments at the Center, and between the Center and state governments as such. Thus, it tended to be a constant tussle between levels of government in a federal form, and within the central government itself.

The relationship between a disunited opposition and the monolithic ruling Congress (I) normally took either of two forms. One, the Congress (I) tried to logroll its writ. For example, when the opposition parties demanded a probe into financial irregularities in defense purchases, the prime minister characterized it as a "Constitutional coup" and an attempt at "destabilization." The point lost is that the opposition has the right to know about the governance of the country and the obligation to keep the government in check. Two, knowing full well their incapacity to influence the policies of the party in power, the opposition indulged in "oppositional mentality," taking umbrage in simple dilatory, even obstructive, often destructive, tactics of noncooperation. Moreover, until the passage of the 52nd Amendment in March 1985 outlawing defections, legislators switched parties at will and as opportunity arose for either office or profit, leading to what came to be known as "market politics."

The best illustration of noncooperation to the point of confrontation on the part of the opposition may be seen from their intransigent attitude on the issue of the appointment of a joint parliamentary committee (JPC) to conduct inquires into the corruption issue that consumed the entire monsoon session of the parliament in July–August 1987. Lung power to shout was substituted for reasoned argument, and parliamentary give and take gave way to legislative stalemate. Gone are the depth of policy statements and wit and wisdom in political speeches; invective and rancor have come to reign supreme. Parliamentary debate as an educated spectacular now degenerates often into a sorry spectacle with the government and opposition benches vying with each other, and at times even coming to fisticuffs and the use of microphones and furniture as missiles.

Along with the deterioration in parliamentary standards, a fall in personal standards of behavior is also apparent. To illustrate the point, K.K. Tewary from the treasury bench accused President Zail Singh (offering no proof) of having harbored Sikh extremists in his abode—the *Rashtrapati Bhavan*. Even after becoming minister for state enterprises, unchecked by the prime minister, he took pride in irresponsible behavior, leading the president to finally insist that he be dropped from the cabinet. (He was dropped, but restored to a cabinet position in a later reshuffle.) In a later session, he stomped in and out of the *Lok Sabha* after having been asked to leave the chamber for unparliamentary behavior. Similarly, Ajoy Biswas (CPI-M) snatched papers out of the hands of Defense Minister K.C. Pant only to be followed by another Congress (I) member who retrieved and returned the papers to the minister, leading to the expulsion of the former from the house. Even the hospitalization of legislators (at least at the state level) stemming out of fracas in state legislatures is not uncommon. Prime Minister Rajiv Gandhi himself had been accused of "irritability, petulance, smart-aleckness in serious situations" (*India Abroad*, Feb. 15, 1987:2). Under Vajpayee's coalition government, one female member of parliament (MP) assaulted a male colleague right in front of the table of the Speaker of the House.

C. Center Versus States

During the last decade or more, not only was the parliamentary form put to test in India but also the federal principle itself came under severe stress. Among the several constitutional provisions, three are of particular importance in this context: (1) the governor of a state is appointed by the Center (2) under Article 356, using the Emergency powers, the Center, on receipt of a report from the governor, can dismiss a duly elected government of a state and take over its administration directly; and (3) federal grants to states are not based on any formula but are purely discretionary. On top of these, there is the administrative arrangement of the All-India Services (IAS, IPS), whose personnel management is under the control of the Center but whose members occupy crucial administrative positions at the state level. When the same political party was in power at the Center and in the states, as was the case for a long time while the Congress (I) party held hegemony, these provisions had not caused any serious tension. But of late, almost all of India at the periphery came under the rule of several opposition parties, with the Center controlling only what is commonly known as the "Hindi belt" in the heart of India with the result the Center-state relations tended to be much more threatened.

The governors of states are appointed by the president on the advice of the government of the day and serve during his pleasure, as already seen. Initially, this office served well, but soon all sorts of characters were appointed to the position. These included defeated state politicians otherwise needing rehabilitation, at times personal minions of the prime minister (as was the case during Indira Gandhi's days), retired senior army officers, and even some bureaucrats—almost all on the basis of their political affiliation, not necessarily for any other accomplishment. Once appointed, they began acting as the agents of the Center, and even worse as the subordinates of individual cabinet ministers. The most telling example of this was the appointment of Romesh Bhandari as the governor of Uttar Pradesh who played a prominent role in the dismissal of the Kalyan Singh government at the behest of the defense minister Mulayam Singh Yadav (Tummala 1998b).

Perhaps crucial for a federal form of government is that the governor's report to the president is the basis on which the state governments are dismissed. Since the beginning of the Republic, nearly 100 state governments were dismissed invoking the Emergency provisions of Article 356. In 1984, the dismissal of the popular government of N.T. Rama Rao in Andhra Pradesh was considered to be the most blatant use of this power to get rid of an opposition government (Tummala 1986). A similar fate befell on the governments of Tamil Nadu and the Punjab later. In March

1988, the 59th Amendment to the Constitution was passed empowering the Center to dismiss the government of the Punjab for "internal disturbance" alone. Several governors, appointed as they were for partisan reasons as mentioned above, tended to serve, contrary to constitutional intent, as agents of the Center and began meddling in their respective state administrations, much to the discomfiture of the ruling opposition governments. Thus the federal form is assaulted continuously and remains under the threat of degenerating a unitary government. And the tension between the Center and states abounds, particularly when it comes to grant monies necessary for development administration.

With the rise to power of the several regional parties, leading not only to the loss of hegemony of the Congress (I) but also to the later inauguration of the new phenomenon of coalition governments, one would have thought that the federal form of government would be strengthened. But in fact, the experience turned out to be contrary. The major partners of the coalition government who had scores to settle with state chief ministers, particularly when they belonged to an opposition party, often tried to use the Emergency powers to dismiss such governments. Two telling examples were the attempt to dismiss the BJP government in Uttar Pradesh during the United Front regime in October 1997, and a later attempt of the BJP government to dismiss the RJD government in Bihar in September 1998. In both cases, as mentioned above, the president stepped in and advised the government of the day to reconsider the suggestion of dismissal. And in both cases, the respective government backed off. The president prevailed and showed that he was not going to sit back and carry on at all times the partisan dictates of the government.

The Sarkaria Commission, which was appointed to study Center-state relations, argued in its 1978 report in favor of a strong central government. Yet it recommended that the Emergency powers to dismiss state governments be used sparingly, and that too after serious consultations with the concerned state government, and only after exhausting all other sources of preventing the breakdown of administration. While several opposition leaders argued for the abolition of the position of the governor, the commission recommended its retention, but suggested that active politicians should not be appointed as governors, and that in the case of a state ruled by an opposition party, the governor ought not to belong to the ruling party at the Center. But then, these were recommendations only, and the Center has not acted favorably since. Consequently, the state governments continue to complain bitterly that they are often at the mercy of the Center for their very survival.

III. ISSUES OF GOVERNANCE

Outside of the governmental institutions, there are other serious issues pertaining to the governance of the country, each interacting with the other. The foremost of these is the organization of the parties themselves. For example, the democratic intentions of Congress (I) Prime Minister Rajiv Gandhi and the later presidents of the party are often judged by the way the party is run. Astonishing as it may sound, there were no organizational elections of this party from 1972 until 1998. Even its parliamentary board met only rarely, and only when it had to select candidates for election. Elections to the 25 Pradesh Congress Committee (PCC—state level) officeholders are also held very infrequently, and often most of the District Congress Committees (DCC—local level) are exclusively selected by the All-India Congress Committee (AICC). Added to this, the operations of the Youth Wing of the party headed by a riotous young president caused a serious commotion when its members harassed, threatened, and even assaulted some of the dissidents within the party. All this led to the criticism that the party under Rajiv Gandhi became highly centralized and authoritarian. Since his assassination, and the loss of power of the Congress (I) after the elections in 1996, the party has been in disarray. Its leaders, unable as they were to come together and work for party unity had to turn to Rajiv Gandhi's widow, Sonia, an Italian born, to head the party and rebuild it. That a nation of nearly a billion people with established political institutions and democratic rule spanning over half a century had to turn repeatedly to one family—commonly and often derisively called as the Nehru-Gandhi dynasty—speaks of the state of the party, and perhaps the nation as well.

The authoritarian behavior of the party was further criticized, particularly when it tried to control the voting behavior of its members. For example, the party issued a three-lined whip directing its members to vote for the official presidential candidate, R. Venkataraman. Some claimed that this was a violation of Article 55(3), which prescribes that the election shall be by secret ballot, Article 19 permitting freedom of expression, and also the Representation of People Act as well as the Vice Presidential Election Act of 1952, which prohibit use of "undue influence" (Antony 1987). A similar whip was issued while setting up a joint parliamentary committee to inquire into the Bofors deal. These actions came to be understood not as mere party discipline but as actual suppression of internal party dissent.

The experience of the current ruling BJP is in a way listless as it is torn as under with its three fundamentalist constituents—the Vishwa Hindu Parishad (VHP), Rashtriya Swayamsevak Sangh (RSS), and the Bajrang Dal—who want a sort of Hindu theocracy in India. Present Prime Minister Vajpayee, as a moderate, is consistently under pressure of these right-wing partners within the party, not to mention the demands of other coalition partners. To illustrate the misery, these groups within the party, joined by yet another prominent right-wing group in Maharashtra called Shiv Sena, are trying to prevent a Pakistani cricket team from playing in India in early 1999. The BJP government is in a quandary as to how to stop these groups, and allow the cricket matches continue without disruption and certainly without any serious break down of law and order.

Perhaps the worst issue of governance of late is rampant corruption—a subject big enough for a separate book. Corruption was not invented by the Indians; it is a universal phenomenon. Only the scale and frequency differ. But in India it is ubiquitous. Even the opposition leaders who preach against corruption are not immune from these charges! Prime Minister Rajiv Gandhi himself, who was originally called "Mr. Clean," came under a terrible cloud concerning foreign defense contracts, with names such as HDW (Howladt Deutsche Werke), Fairfax, Bofors, and Sam Progatti becoming common in this context.

Several top-level politicians and a few bureaucrats have been charged with corruption. These include former Prime Minister P.V. Narasimha Rao, former Chief Minister of Bihar Laloo Prasad Yadav, and several cabinet ministers from both the Center and several states. Perhaps the most egregious case is that of the former chief minister of Tamil Nadu, Jayalalitha, against whom as many as 18 different cases are being heard in three different special courts set up for this singular purpose. Despite the several cases, it is to be noted that so far not a single politician has spent any time worth mentioning in jail. Not only are they let loose on bail, but the proceedings of the courts often drag on for years. And the same politicians continue to use their political clout, whether they are in or out of government, all for personal gain, and some for partisan well-being.

Certainly as the Congress (I) came back to power and started its New Economic Policy in 1990, several economic liberalization policies were inaugurated, and the country came out of a severe financial crisis. The Nehruvian socialist policies have been slowly shown the door, and free enterprise is steadily taking over. And then came the coalition governments who, preoccupied as they are in just staying in office, are unable to do much for the development of the country. The BJP has to come begging the several nonresident Indians for capital with favorable conditions. And the current BJP finance minister keeps stressing that the economic reform proposals would continue despite the pressure for indigenous economic growth coming from the BJP constituents. The only thing that caught the eye of the world was the explosion of nuclear devices in 1998.

There were three major problems that confronted Rajiv Gandhi during the last part of his life and career, which a decade later are only exacerbated: regionalism, communalism, and terrorism.

A. Regionalism

The whole of India was never under the same ruler, historically. Even the British had to leave some parts of India untouched. And students of the Constitution know pretty well that it is "union," not federation, of India which is contemplated to counter the several centrifugal forces in the country. Reorganization of Indian states on a linguistic basis in the 1950s only helped emphasize the fact of regionalism. On one hand, there is the north-south schism which came into full force when attempts were made to "impose" Hindi as a national language. (It is only an "official" language now.) On the other, what with the emergence of several regional parties, Rajiv Gandhi lost state after state for the opposition—Andhra Pradesh, Assam, Haryana, Karanataka, Kerala, the Punjab, West Bengal, and so on. This enhanced regionalism, at times bordering on chauvinism, only aggravates the already existing problems with federalism, as seen above, and threatens national unity. With the loss of hegemony of the Congress (I), and in the absence of a national party (despite the claims of the BJP for that status) that can command the respect of a majority of Indians, this regional fervor is only exaggerated by self-serving regional political satraps.

B. Communalism

Ever since the partition of India following its independence, Hindu and Muslim communal frictions and riots have been common. Yet, in the past they did not disrupt the social fabric as they do currently. Consequent to the storming of the Amritsar Golden temple (the most sacred religious place of the Sikhs), a new element entered into this fracas—the Sikhs. Having become more militant, they went as far as to demand a separate nation of theirs called Khalistan. This was only further strengthened by the perception that the same government that balks at interfering in other religions does it regularly and with impunity with the majority Hindu religion. For example, the government reacted to the Supreme Court decision on the Shah Bano case (under the belief that the court stepped over the Muslim religion) by passing the controversial Muslim Women (Protection of Rights on Divorce) Act in May 1986, virtually reiterating the Islamic religious tenets when it came to personal married life (Mody 1987). Contrarily, the government goes to the extent of managing the properties of the Hindu temples under the Hindu Religious Endowment Act. In response to these and the continuous efforts of the government to make good some of the promises made, constitutionally and otherwise, for the uplifting of minorities, a Hindu backlash is seen (Tummala 1989). Consequently, even a simple religious procession is often turned into a show of strength, occasionally violent. The government itself acknowledged that as many as 167 were killed and 358 injured in communal riots during the first half of 1987.

With the demolition of the Babri mosque in Uttar Pradesh in December 1992, and with the *Hindutwa* slogan of the BJP pressing India for Hindus, not only the secular nature of India came under a cloud, but also the Muslims, in particular, came under threat (Tummala 1993). Abetted by Shiva Sena in Maharashtra in particular, the communal divide has only widened. Currently, the Christians are also at the receiving end from some of the misguided Hindu nationalists, particularly in the state of Gujarat.

C. Terrorism

With the 1984 attack on their sacred temple in Amritsar, not only have a few Sikhs become militant, but some of their actions also turned out to be brazen. In early July 1987, on two consecutive nights, in the two contiguous states Punjab and Haryana, two buses were stopped and 76 innocent passengers, mostly women and children, were massacred. Not to be outdone, the Hindus retaliated whenever and wherever they could. Even in the capital, New Delhi, several assassinations took place, notable among them being members of the BJP. Following the demolition of Babri mosque, several Hindus and many Muslims were also killed. One could not have missed the barricades raised in and around the capital with several armed police patrolling the streets and checking all vehicles. Prime Minister Rajiv Gandhi himself lived in a fortresslike home and moved around under the constant threat of assassination, which in fact was successfully carried out in 1989.

Perhaps the most pernicious development is the unholy, but convenient, marriage between politicians and criminals. Lacking a philosophical fervor as to how to shape society, or for that matter govern, politics and crime came to be fused together in the only pursuits available—occupy public office and make money, in whichever way possible. For example, it is reported that in the state of Uttar Pradesh alone there are at least 96 armies of gangsters operating with nearly 57 of them being patronized by one political party or the other. As many as 209 candidates contesting in the 1996 elections had criminal records, 10 of them being convicts. Thirty-two of those elected to the legislature have criminal records (*India Today*, April 15, 1997:15). Prime Minister Gujral himself openly stated that as many as 70 members of parliament had criminal records.

Of particular concern in this context is the relationship between the government and the bureaucracy. Rarely, if ever, has a political executive paid compliments to the bureaucracy in public. But many a politician scored electoral points often enough by indulging in bureaucratic bashing. While it can be readily admitted that the bureaucracy is no Caesar's wife, it serves no public interest if the political executive uses it either as a shield to hide behind or, worse, as a sacrificial lamb. Bureaucrats need political support as well as confidence. Much has been written exhorting the two to work as a team: the political amateur seeking the permanent expert experience and advice, and the administrator being admonished about "what the people won't stand."

The case of a former foreign secretary, for example, has not served this cause at all. A.P. Venkateswaran was a distinguished foreign service officer with 36 years of experience. But only 10 months after his appointment as secretary, he was kicked out of office most unceremoniously. Without any prior notification, and certainly to the surprise of everyone present including the secretary, the prime minister at a televised press conference in February 1987 simply announced that he was being replaced without mentioning any reasons. Humiliated, the secretary resigned from service altogether.

Particularly at the district level, where the administration is closer to the client and where the politician would like to have a say in terms of delivery of services and distribution of grant largess, the pressures on the bureaucracy are phenomenal. And those who do not toe the political line find themselves moved out in search of a pliant civil servant. Such transfers have become so frequent and far-reaching that the average tenure of district officers had dropped to nine months. Prime Minister Rajiv Gandhi himself, deploring it, suggested that the term should be at least three years (*Hindu International Edition*, June 4, 1988:6). Similarly, at the secretariat level, transfers, sometimes en masse, have become quite common as may be seen from the extreme experience of Uttar Pradesh when higher-level civil servants have been transferred by succeeding governments (with the ostensible belief that the previous government picked its own henchpersons to occupy top civil service positions who work closer to the politicians).

Besides transfers, blatant supersession of seniority, either in search of a compliant secretary or to accommodate the pressures of a politician or civil servant with political connections, had demoralized the administrative class to the point they are now either striking back in exasperation, or worse, becoming fully compliant to the point of becoming collaborators in the several political shenanigans and corrupt practices.

In addition to these serious pressures, the capacity of the administration seems to be coming under severe test, particularly just before election time. Governments in power, in an effort to win reelection, make promises, however outlandish they might be. The most serious one is what has been called the "loan mela"—the loan festival, where the government shows its generosity by bestowing loans. Not to be outdone, some of the opposition parties outpromise to write off past loans worth hundreds of millions of rupees, as was the case in Haryana when the Lok Dal leader, Devi Lal, did that and won the election which was considered to be a test for Rajiv Gandhi. Several projects get started only to be forgotten following the election. Many an inaugural stone pock-marking the length and breadth of the country stands in mute testimony to the election year ploy. These hastily made political decisions, with little regard either to the impact on the economy or to the administrative capacity, have only added an additional dimension to the problems of development administration.

The growing influence of groups that had found new sources of power, either by way of access to decision makers or simply by being vociferous, places further demands on administration. While participation in the political process is salutary in itself, "demand politics" become destructive when emergent groups turn intolerant of each other, obstructing even the publication of books and release of films under the pretext that they hurt the religious or cultural sentiments of one group or the other, either true, perceived, or, worse, even trumped up. The net result is a monumental tieup of administration, not to mention the serious law-and-order problems. One would perhaps like to believe that all these are manifestations of growing pains inherent in a pluralist political process. But there is no escaping the fact that the bureaucrats are under severe strain. How do they cope?

As a classic expression of Victor Thompson's "bureau pathology" (Thompson 1961), the Indian officialdom at lower levels developed a stratagem of major profundity. They never answer a client's request either affirmatively or negatively. It is almost always, "Let us see," or "No problem," or "Don't worry." The case is then put off for the time being, leaving the subliminal message that things can be "managed" if only the proper influences are brought to bear upon or, worse, the required bribe is rendered. This modus operandi also enhances the personal ego of the officer concerned while putting the client in the "proper place." Thus, administratively there is nothing that cannot be done if only one has proper connections, or enough monetary resources. Very little moves on its own merits at the first try, all of which paves the way for corruption.

At the higher levels, some civil servants become sycophants; others are either cowed down, or hide behind the rules of procedure. One way out is to be a strict Weberian bureaucrat who would act in the "spirit of formalistic impersonality," and "without hatred or passion, and hence without affection and/or enthusiasm" (Weber 1947:329–341). Past efforts at making civil servants "committed" had proved to be controversial and failed, and the civil servants have shown that they are largely "establishment" oriented (Tummala 1981). Perverse though this might sound within the context of development administration where the bureaucrat is to act as a "change agent" and the administration is expected to penetrate the far corners of the country, there is some virtue in being a Weberian bureaucrat. It certainly would take the pressure off the bureaucrat, and would also insulate the administration from political meddling. And it might help even continuity, at least preventing discontinuity as governments change from party to party. This kind of behavior has been extolled within the French bureaucracy (Diamant 1957). But it has also been criticized as the hallmark of a "stalemate society" (Crozier 1964). Surely, this dampens developmental efforts.

IV. CONCLUSION

India has survived intact for many millennia despite the fact that it was conquered by myriad rulers from many parts of the world. In fact, it has historically shown a great resiliency and absorbed many of the foreign cultures that thus arrived. The best of parliamentary institutions that came as a legacy of the British have taken root since independence. And India now is a nuclear power, the 10th-largest industrial nation with the fifth-largest economy. But not all is well, as seen above. So, what to be done?

There has been no dearth of discussion and moralizing at the state of affairs. Several suggestions have been made as a remedy to the present ills. These include the establishment of a presidential form of government, better enforcement of anticorruption measures, and what not. The current BJP government went as far as to suggest a review of the Constitution in an effort to rewrite it to suit the present conditions. One can easily see that the problem is not with the Constitution. To paraphrase Woodrow Wilson, it is easy to write a Constitution, but not that easy to make it work.

The crucial problem, it appears, is the prevailing political culture which in fact turned all canons of political behavior on their heads. It is the triumph of one of the seven sins identified by Mahatma Gandhi—politics without principle. And the Constitution is reduced to a piece of parchment which can be tossed around at will for partisan and political gain. For this, the blame must be placed squarely on the shoulders of political parties and their leaders. So, any reform must start there. If the political parties clean up their act, much of the current curse would be lifted, and India could look forward to much greatness.

ENDNOTES

1. It should be noted that true to the tradition of parliamentary government, the appointment of the prime minister is a foregone conclusion, and the role of the president in this regard is only formal. The leader of the majority party is automatically recognized as the prime minister, and the president has no choice but to make such an appointment. In case of a coalition government, the president may have a more onerous responsibility, though not much discretion.

2. It should be noted that the use of Emergency powers, particularly under Article 356 of the Constitution, is nothing new in India. Nearly 100 times such a thing occurred in the past. See Tummala, "The Indian Union and Emergency Powers," *International Political Science Review 17*(4), 373–382. Except the difference now is that the president played an active role in defense of a state government much against the recommendation by the prime minister at the Center.

REFERENCES

Antony, M.J. (1987). Is the whip a Hukumnama? *Indian Express*, July 15, pp. 1 and 6.
Crozier, M. (1964). *The Bureaucratic Phenomenon.* Chicago: University of Chicago Press.
Diamant, A. (1957). The French administrative system: the republic passes and the administration remains. In *Toward the Comparative Study of Public Administration* (W.J. Siffin, ed.). Bloomington: Indiana University Press, pp. 182–218.
Hindu International Edition, June 4; and July 2, 1988; and Aug. 15, 1987.
Hindustan Times, March 14, 1987.
India Abroad, Feb. 15, 1987.
Katyal, K.K. (1987). Alert still on PM's side. *Hindu International Weekly*, May 30.
Mody, N.B. (1987). The press in India: the Shah Bano judgement and its aftermath. *Asian Survey XXVII*(8).
Shiva Rao, B., ed. (1968). *The Framing of India's's Constitution: A Study*, Vol. V. New Delhi: Indian Institute of Public Administration.
Thompson, V.A. (1961). *Modern Organizations.* New York: Knopf.
Tummala, K.K. (1979). *The Ambiguity of Ideology and Administrative Reform.* Allied Publishers, New Delhi, 1979.

Tummala, K.K. (1981). Higher civil service in India: 'Commitment' or 'Establishment'? *Politics, Administration, Change VI*(2), 17–40.

Tummala, K.K. (1986). Democracy triumphant in India: the case of Andhra Pradesh. *Asian Survey XXVI*(3), 378–395.

Tummala, K.K. (1989). 'Reservations' in the Indian public service. In *Equity in Public Employment Across Nations* (K.K. Tummala, ed.). Lanham: University Press of America, Chap. 3.

Tummala, K.K. (1990). India at crossroads in 1989. *Asian Profile XVII*(4), 353–364.

Tummala, K.K. (1993). Religion and politics in India. *Asian Journal of Political Science I*(2), 57–76.

Tummala, K.K. (1996). The Indian union and the emergency powers. *International Political Science Review XVII*(4), 373–384.

Tummala, K.K. (1998a). India's experiment with coalitions: the 1996 general elections and since. *Asian Profile XXVI*(6), 497–510.

Tummala, K.K. (1998b). Constitutional government and politics in India: the case of Uttar Pradesh. *Asian Journal of Political Science VI*(2).

Weber, M. (1947). *The Theory of Social and Economic Organization* (trans. A.M. Henderson). New York: Oxford University Press.

32

Capacity Building for Municipal Governance in Kenya

A Profile of Technical Cooperation

Itoko Suzuki   *Ritsumeikan Asia Pacific University, Beppu, Japan*

I. INTRODUCTION

Governance, especially, good governance, has become a major worldwide concern. Many conferences these days focus on and emphasize governance approach which entails decentralization to the capacity building of local government. Contrary to the frequent reference to these themes, the progress of decentralization and intended outcome of governance approach is extremely slow. Both the Brettton Woods institutions and the UN and UNDP have encouraged all the recipients of their technical cooperation to promote decentralization and governance approach. The term governance is used to mean participatory public management that would include nongovernmental organizations and private sectors in order to democratize a nation and mobilize all people in public affairs.

Many African countries have complied with the donors' ideas, as national leaders need to get funds for their governments on one hand, and must show the electorate that they are in favor of democratization (people empowerment) on the other. Even with their good intentions, decentralization and democratization are not easy undertakings in these countries, as both decentralization and democratization may slow down the very development of their economies. Also, why give up one's own power to someone else? When a central government has no resource to give to local municipalities; local municipalities have no adequate competence to manage resources; why can central government decentralize or deconcentrate their resources to local government to manage? Similarly, why privatize, when there is very little private sector business in a country? There is no way to consider for a central government, under these circumstances, to deconcentrate or decentralize their resources or vested powers and authorities to local governments or private businesses.

Theoretically, decentralized governments can certainly serve better to the local communities as they are more knowledgeable about the local issues. And participatory policy making and implementation are much better for the morale of the local communities. Private sector can do more efficient jobs in delivery of many services than public sector by using competitive mechanism and profit and outcome oriented principles.

Despite the dilemmas and difficulties, many African countries repeatedly took pains of initiatives, particularly the elected officials of larger municipalities and ministry of local government (as differed from substantive ministries). In general, local government ministry needs to play a leadership role to decentralize the government machinery and hence is destined to be isolated from other ministries in charge of substantive sectors, and ministry of finance. In any way, it is usually the ministry of local government that has to show to the donors and citizens that the government will carry out the decentralization policy (often pushed by donors). This is the situation that Kenya has been put in place.

Municipal governance in Kenya provides a stark example of dichotomy between stated intentions of governance approach and decentralization, and the realities on the ground. This short essay will review the most current efforts taken by the Ministry of Local Government (officially Ministry of Local Authorities) and four major Municipal Councils of Kenya. It will particularly focus on a profile of the efforts taken together with the United Nations and UNDP and will draw some lessons of experience for the donors, technical cooperation agencies, and the recipient governments.

II. OVERVIEW OF THE UN PROJECT

The central government of Kenya decided in early 1990s to promote the role of municipal authorities as an integral part of national decision-making structures (instead of using the notion of decentralization). Five-year plans of economic and social development as well as the most recent Presidential Commission of Local Authorities (*Omamo Report* 1995) considered the municipal councils as the key institutions for democratization, and nation building. Particularly, the Omamo report recommended the elevation of four larger municipalities, i.e., Mombasa, Kisumu, Nakuru, and Eldoret, to city status (at this point, Nairobi is the only municipality that has city status in Kenya).

While the United Nations was during that period implementing a project of Capacity Building of Municipal Council of Nairobi, mayors of these four municipalities in question approached both the Ministry of Local Authorities and the United Nations. It happened at the time of joint workshop with the UN and the Kenyan government held in February 1997 when the sector review of the administration and management of the municipality of Nairobi was being discussed. The mayors of these municipalities requested the United Nations to undertake a similar sector review of their municipal management. Both UNDP and the government of Kenya approved the requests and hence the UN was designated to backstop sector review and the capacity building project of these four towns with the project funding from the UNDP.

This new project for the four municipalities took a similar form and the course of the previous one for Nairobi. A sector review of management of four municipalities was organized by the United Nations. Based on the questionnaire established by the United Nations, Winnie V. Mitullah undertook the review of Kisumu and Eldoret as a national consultant to this project; likewise, John M. Nderi prepared the review of Nakuru and Mombasa. Both authors conducted a few field trips to these municipalities and a few surveys were undertaken in each municipality during their research. The United Nations, the Ministry of Local Government of Kenya, and the UNDP studied their draft reports of the sector review. In order to review the draft reports of the sector review and formulate remedial measures to tackle the problems raised in the reports, a Conference of Capacity Building for Municipal Governance was organized during 12–13 October 1999 in Mombasa (hereinafter cited as the Conference).

The sector review and hence the Conference concentrated on the following governance issues[1] of municipalities raised in the draft reports of the national consultants:

Reforming structure and management of policy development of the municipal councils
Improving the personnel management
Strengthen the financial management
Improving the municipal service delivery
Exploring building partnership between government and NGO/Private sector (particularly for urban environmental management)

The October 1999 Conference was attended by about 120 central government and municipal officials as well as scholars. Notably, J.J. Kamotho of the Ministry of Local Government, senior officials of the central government including Edwin Osundwa, permanent secretary; Francis Ndooli, deputy secretary; F.G. Mathenge, undersecretary; M. Thairu, SPSC, who performed as UNDP coordinator for this project; and others took part. From municipalities, Mayor of Mombassa Municipal Council, Mwalimu Masudi Mwahima, Josiah Magut of Eldoret Municipal Council, F.H. Ogendo Ponge of Kisumu Municipal Council, Marine Nderi of Nakuru Municipal Council as well as town clerks and other councilors and senior officers of all the four municipalities in question attended. The mayor of Nairobi, town clerks, and other senior officers were invited in order to compare this current exercise with the previous one in Nairobi. Also present as guests from other countries were O Mlbaba of Durban Metropolitan Council (equivalent of mayor), John S. Kibitz, mayor of Kampala City, E. Canker, Commissioner of Harare, C. Keenja, Dar-as-Salaam City Commissioner, and D. Alusandika, Chief Executive of Blantyre City (Malawi). From UNDP, the deputy resident representative, program officers, and consultants attended. From the United Nations, Chief of the Governance and Public Administration Branch (myself) and two other staff in charge of the project participated. This two-day Conference included both plenary meetings and working groups sessions. It should be noted that the town clerks and the heads of the Department of Environmental/Health Affairs of the participating municipalities also participated in the two-day Conference due to the arrangement of the programme, which included a small special session on ecopartnership building.

III.   LEGAL PARAMETERS OF THE KENYAN MUNICIPALITIES

Specifically, this two-day Conference included, after the formal greetings and statements, the following events:

1.   Presentation of major issues in the plenary by the sector review authors of the four municipalities in question, as well as the presentation of the UN team addressing to focus on the issues set above during the Conference (i.e., policy development, personnel management, financial management, service delivery, and partnership building).

2.   Working-group sessions to discuss each municipality's pragmatic problems based on the issues presented in the plenary (four working groups on municipalities in question and one guest city group).

3.   Presentation of the results of the working-group discussions in the plenary.

4.   Second-day morning plenary on ecopartnership building as an example of partnership building within a municipality and across the municipality (even across the region such as Asia-African municipal cooperation).

5.   Individual consultative meetings with each municipality (which was attended by also officials from the UN, UNDP, and ministry of local government) for practical consultation to determine how to solve the problems/issues identified by each municipality.

Municipal councils are units of the local government system in urban areas of Kenya, which comprises the Ministry of Local Authorities (formerly the Ministry of Local Government), provincial and district local government offices, and the city, county and town councils. Councils are corporate bodies and established under the Local Government Act. They are not, however the autonomous bodies and subject to being dismantled by the Ministry of Local Authorities. The current councils in question were constituted in 1998 after the December 1997 general elections. It was the first multi-party elections held in Kenya since the early 1960s. Different political parties are in control of different local authorities. Each council (there are at present 47 local councils in Kenya) is headed by a mayor, who is selected among the councilors.

The Local Government Act stipulates that the Minister for Local Authorities performs supervisory functions over the local authorities which include to establish local authorities; to create or alter local authorities including ward boundaries which each individual local councilor represents; approval of annual local authority budgets, level of local taxes, fees and charges; approval of local authority by-laws; upgrading the status of local authorities; dissolution of local authorities.

The United Nations Sector Review and the Mombasa Conference paid considerable attention to the impact of the existing Local Government Act on municipal operations. The Local Government Act of 1973 went through a number of amendments including provision of inspectors of local government, transferring of services of education, health and roads to central ministries (at some points, but later the functions returned to local authorities), auditing of accounts by the controller and auditor-generals, removal of taxation powers from local authorities, etc. The abolition of personal tax clearly weakened the local councils, as it served as the principle source of major revenues for all local authorities.

In his opening statement of this conference[2], Minister Kamotho cited two basic tenets of public policy on local authorities that are outlined in sessional paper No. 1 of 1986 and 1994. The first is the rural-urban balance strategy for national development, which entails the improved urban management. The second is fiscal decentralization, which entails the enhanced autonomy in determining expenditure priorities by local authorities, as well as the enhanced taxation and revenue raising authority. (On the second point, however, the Conference participants from the four municipalities in general did not appear to enjoy such authority, as expenditure priorities set by the local authorities must be in fact approved by the Ministry of Local Authorities.) Sessional Paper No. 1 of 1994 on recovery and sustainable development to the year 2000 emphasizes that development must involve the participation of all the citizens in policy development and implementation. Minister urged the four participating towns to work closely with the community groups and private sector in municipal governance. He also cited the Kenya Local Government Reform Program, which demanded accountability mechanisms at central and local government level.

The draft reports of the sector review[3], however, claimed that the Local Government Act gives too many supervisory authorities to the Minister of Local Government and that it denies the local authorities the necessary autonomy and evolution in creating a responsible system in the councils. The act is rather ambiguous and is subject to various interpretations by the ministry officials. Centralization of power and the overwhelming influence of the ministry over the councils and small administrative details of municipal administration significantly reduce the decentralization codes. In the Conference all the council officials including mayors expressed that the councils could hardly do anything without approval of the minister. The Conference noted that the length of time to approve proposals from the municipalities and the procedural requirements did impair the functions of councils and municipalities.

The Minister of Local Government is empowered, mainly, to nominate one-third of councilors, in proportion to the distribution of elected councilors to political parties. The minister has also the power to transfer municipal officers to other municipalities. The Conference noted that this practice resulted in a feeling among municipal officers that they are accountable to the central government and not to the municipalities. This legal context also attributed immensely to the mistrust between the councilors and the municipal officials.

A most far-reaching change in the legal status of local authorities occurred in 1984 when the power of appointments of the town clerk, the treasurer, and senior officers in the council was vested in the Public Service Commission, causing a weakening effect on the authority of elected members over these officials. On the other hand, the continuing political interference of the elected council members particularly in relation to tenders, transfer and employment of lower level officials (which the municipalities have the power to recruit) has resulted in excessive use of patronage instead of following established procedures of personnel management. These basic legal parameters alone indicated the participants of the Conference that the proposed change of the status of four municipalities to city level would require certain major adjustments in the Local Government Act.

IV. CONTEXTUAL ISSUES

It is evident that these local councils have become unable to cope with increasing demand for services due to rapid population expansion, shift towards urbanization, lack of resources, poor infrastructure or environmental concerns, etc. Above all, the management capacity continued to suffer due to basically the above-cited legal parameters set for the municipalities.

Among the four municipalities in question, in Kisumu, rapid population growth of about 5% is attributed to migrants from the provinces, natural increase and decrease of infant mortality rate. Current population is estimated as 400,000. Informal settlements are extended in the municipality. Main economic activities of Kisumu are agricultural farming-tea, coffee, pyrethrum, sugarcane and cotton, and fishing and fish processing for foreign exchange earning.

Eldoret is one of the fastest growing urban sectors in Kenya having an inter-census population growth rate of almost 8%, one of the highest in Kenya's urban areas. At present its population is about 248,000. Like Kisumu, the urban growth is attributed to natural population increase, migration and industrial expansion. Eldoret is the fifth largest town in Kenya and is one of the seventeen districts in the Rift Valley province. It is an industrial and commercial center for western Kenya.

Mombasa is the second largest town in Kenya and the main seaport for eastern and central African countries. Annual population growth rate is 4.5%, and its current population is 646,000. It is the administrative center for Coast Province and Mombasa Island. Its major economic activities include tourism, agriculture, and agroindustry.

The town of Nakuru is the center of provincial administration in the Rift Valley province. Its population growth is estimated to be 7% per annum. At present, population is estimated as 410,000. The main sources of employment are provided by agricultural industries and tourism. It is the fourth-largest town in Kenya and was once regarded in the 1970s the cleanest town in East Africa.

According to the draft sector review[4], as well as the presentation of the Mombasa Conference, common problems of all these municipalities include water shortage, unemployment and uncollected garbage as well as uncollected dues and rates. Rapid growth of urban areas has put a severe strain on municipal service provision. Most of those living in these municipalities do not pay for the services, although they use the services provided by the councils. Most businesses in the areas are not properly regulated and do not pay any fees. All these practices created a vicious circle, and convinced the Conference participants that unless concrete regulatory and financial management were put in motion, capacity building could not be effectively started. Social impact of these problems in terms of crime, school dropouts, vandalism, and malpractices are becoming prevalent and the situation has been deteriorating. Poor infrastructure, including road, telephone facilities, and lack of capital investment, is making the rate of unemployment extremely high.

Despite all these economic and social situations in the four municipalities, as noted ealier, the central government decided to promote the role of the local authorities and to elevate the status of the four towns, Mombasa, Nakuru, Kisumu, and Eldoret to city status, the status the capital city Nairobi has been enjoying. But the actual reforms along proclaimed lines have not been initiated[5].

The central government considered it a luxury at the moment to do much more beyond its current resources and possibilities. According to the draft sector review[6], the central ministries are impatient with limited managerial capacities of municipal councils. The result was almost direct administration from the central government. In the past, on a few occasions, the government had superseded municipal councils and appointed commissions for short periods, for example in Mombasa. There are also interagency overlaps in the roles of officers of the council, district-level of central government. Municipal staff was considered to be inferior and ineffective.

In the above context, technical cooperation agencies and donors considered that the thrust of municipal governance in most developing countries is being focused on decentralization with appropriate measure of delegation in administrative and financial operations for improving service delivery and making the local authorities self reliant. This entails deliberate initiatives for modernization of administrative structure, management practices, and procedures and decision making to bring municipal councils close to the public they serve in collaboration with the private sector and the civil society. A strategic requirement, therefore, is to assess the existing level of administrative and management with a view to adopt an integral capacity building measures.

With the foregoing legal parameters and context, the United Nations undertook the sector review of the four municipalities of Kenya and the above-cited Conference was organized.

V. MAIN PROBLEMS PRESENTED

The problems presented in the Conference can be summarized in the context of the five following sections[7].

A. Policy Development

Kenya's local authorities (local councils) do not have either autonomy or power to implement the decisions made by the committees and sub-committees of the council without the approval of the Ministry of Local Government. This is stated in the Local Government Act. The Conference heard a number of complaints on this lack of autonomy. All the working groups of four municipalities repeatedly underlined following related issues.

1.   Lack of independent decision-making authorities in the municipal councils and mayors in running their own municipal affairs including minor matters.

2.   Need to involve citizens in policy formulation and executions. However, a question was raised about how to empower the community to induce their participation. It was also mentioned that the elite in the community do not come out or participate during elections and yet they complain later on incompetent leadership.

3.   Ambiguities regarding the role of mayors and chief officers which tended to create internal conflict and animosity between councilors and the chief officers (who were from the central government).

4.   Need to train senior officials of the four municipalities in question to acquire policy analysis skills and the legal personnel in the Ministry of Local Government.

5.   Local authorities expressed the desire to negotiate directly with the donors, rather than all aides from international and intergovernmental bodies through Ministry of Local Government.

B. Financial Management

The Conference revealed that the financial management was the weakest among other problems in all the municipalities in question. The basic problem was that the municipalities were not given the right to tax. However, part of the revenue collection is decentralized to the local level, such as land rates, water charges, licensing, market fees, etc. In general, the four councils do not have the proper administrative infrastructure in place to collect the revenue.

On the other hand, it was very interesting to learn, at the Conference, from the Minister of Local Authorities, Kamotho (he proclaimed in his opening statement) that the government had launched the Local Authority Transfer Fund (LATF) to improve the local financial management and revenue mobilization. Initially 2% of the national income tax collections would be disbursed to local authorities during the fiscal year 1999/2000. While 60% of LATF is to be allocated for service delivery on a population basis, LATF will also be allocating 40% of the monies to provide incentive to local authorities to improve financial management, revenue mobilization and debt resolution. This performance-based component of LATF will be given to local authorities in exchange for financial management information and revenue mobilization and debt resolution plans. The minister indicated that through establishment of a LATF advisory committee, which includes both public and private sector professionals, the publication of LATF allocating criteria, and amounts by local authorities, the LATF mechanism would improve accountability between central and local governments. However, the participants from the municipalities did not argue much about this scheme, which again would provide wide discretion and power to the Ministry of Local Authorities. The actual impact of this scheme on decentralization would need to be assessed when the scheme was fully operational.

1. Budgeting

The central government is at present planning to develop a comprehensive budgeting and accounting system for local authorities. Six municipal councils are participating in this pilot project. The German Government Development Corporation (GTZ) is funding this project and a general guideline on budgeting was prepared in 1995. The major issue was the fact that the budget process was too long and approval took long time from the central government.

As a positive sign, the Municipal Council of Eldoret has been able to improve its collection of water revenue and computerized its operations. To improve its liquidity, the Council has established a debt collection section with a sole function of collecting outstanding debt. The Conference recognized that the local citizens were so reluctant to pay the fees; and local officials must collect the fees more efficiently by establishing mechanisms such as computerized collection systems.

2. Accounting

A major issue identified was the absence of local authorities' accounting standards, which could be used as a reference in the preparation of books of accounts. Due to shortage of qualified and motivated staff, accounting systems have been left for a long time as they were and training and installation of modern accounting system have been long called for.

The level of liquidity of the councils are so low that they are not able to pay the debts to the creditors such as Kenya Power and Lighting company, water, national housing corporations, etc. The councils are faced additionally with over drafts on their accounts. As a consequence, they are not trusted in the eyes of the private business community. The end result was a very unstable supply of electricity and water to the citizens.

3.   Auditing

A major problem was that there was no separation between accounting and auditing. The audit function is part of the treasury department. The Conference revealed that the councils were not pleased with this arrangement. As stated numerous times in the draft reports of the sector review, many of the departments and offices in the municipalities were understaffed; such as treasury department where some positions had been vacant for a number of years. Cashbooks of some councils had not been audited since 1991. In the case of Nakuru, final accounts have not been audited for the last three years.

C.   Human Resource Management

1.   Staffing

One serious problem recorded in the Conference was the common practice of the central government (Ministry of Local Government) that transferred officers who have been trained by a particular council to other councils at its discretion. The Conference participants called for formation of a Local Government Service Commission to handle local authorities transfers instead of the Public Service Commission. That proposed commission should include recruitment authorities for local municipal councils. At present, the Public Service Commission carries out the recruitment of staff currently at scales of 1 to 9, whereas recruitment of staff on a scale of 10 to 20 is the responsibility of the councils. Therefore, each municipal council needs to work closely with the Ministry of Local Government and the Public Service Commission in order to get efficient staffing arrangement. Recruitment of these lower officials was often arranged by the power politics within the council. There is a clear-cut necessity to establish a guideline for recruitment at the lower level (scale 10 to 20).

Another, related issue was rotation. Many staff on acting positions and those who are on the same positions have been left out for several years in the same positions. For avoiding any corruptions, or improving the morale, it is essential to get the positions in place by facilitating appointment of officials rather than stabilizing them as acting. Rotation and promotion should be logically arranged with a solid guideline.

There was a serious concern expressed among many participants, that the roles were not very clear or not understood clearly about the senior positions of the municipality and the council. There was a suggestion that an internationally organized workshop, such as this could be used to train senior officials including chief officers and councillors of joint municipalities, in order to have understanding and appreciation as to the functions they are performing and to have a clear understanding the respective roles and establish a cooperative atmosphere for management.

2.   Recruitment

The Conference suggested to have a mechanism of incentives in kind to attract qualified staff. Also suggested was the streamlining of the procedures for recruitment of lower-level staff and preparation of a guideline for recruitment to avoid nepotism. It was suggested to carry out a job analysis exercise to match the number of employees needed with actual posts in order to avoid overstaffing at the lower level. It was also suggested to find a way to match remuneration package with qualification.

3.   Training

The Conference acknowledged the need for training of officers across the board, although the type of training should vary depending on the level and extent of training. Group training is cost effective and beneficial to councils rather than individualized training. Such concept would apply to joint training of both councilors and senior officials of the municipal administration as stated earlier. Many participants agreed that facilities within Kenya could be used to train staff at all levels to save costs. Training programme introduced under the aforementioned GTZ could be beneficial in setting up performance targets and annual staff appraisal system. Ideally, training needs assessment should be carried out to prioritize specific training. Some officers however expressed reluctance to be trained. Municipalities should create an atmosphere that training is valued at the council.

D. Service Delivery

At the opening of the Conference, Minister J.J. Kamotho underlined the need for cooperation among the four municipalities and policy dialogue among these municipalities to improve municipal governance. He also underlined the importance of ecopartnership as was initiated by the United Nations. He emphasized that capacity building was really needed to improve the service of the municipalities in order to crystallize the efforts of the government in cooperation with municipalities. Sustainable development should be initiated by the improved service of the municipalities and he requested the UN and UNDP to strengthen their efforts to this end. At the same time, he appealed the residents to cooperate to improve their own local environment.

After all, the ultimate role of a governmental body is to deliver services in exchange for taxes paid by citizens. Despite the limited mandate given to the municipal councils, they provide their communities with a wide range of services, including, primary school education, health services, transportation, garbage collection, water, electricity, etc. The results of the assessment of residents experience with service delivery reported[8] were to be far from satisfaction in all the municipalities in question. The sector review reports indicated that residents complained bitterly about the inefficiency or lack of service provision, including the length of time it takes to get access to water supply, overflowing sewerage, garbage collection, and sanitation.

Evidently the major reason for the lack of service delivery was directly correlated with the lack of revenue collection of the councils. For instance, most of the councils collect less than half of the water bills. Additionally, the councils were not able to account for loss of over 47% of water produced during a year.

Some municipalities have contracted out some of the municipal responsibilities to the NGOs, and the private sector. For instance, the Nyeri Water and Sewerage Company is now fully operational. Kenya Breweries sought partnership in the area of water provision. As a large consumer of water, the breweries have offered to either provide material support or take over the operation of the water plants. Councils are aware of the potential that lies in this type of partnership. Partnership or contracting out does not however mean that the councils are not responsible for the public service. Privatization (sector review used the term *commercialization*) requires the councils to monitor and supervise if the particular contracted out service is properly provided equally to the public. Councils are not sufficiently effective in monitoring or supervising and the provisions of service of water or electricity are not constant. Dialogues with citizens or communities including private sector are not sufficient and citizens are often left out. Partnership concept, which is essential for municipal governance, is still not a reality in Kenya's municipalities.

E. Building Partnership for Service Delivery (Ecopartnership)

The Minister of Local Government also underlined the necessity for cooperation among municipalities to promote sustainable development and improved municipal governance. The importance of policy dialogue between developed and developing municipalities and cities can be addressed particularly in urban environmental management, which has been neglected in many African countries.

In this context, it should be explained here that the idea for human resource development for ecopartnership building in local governance has been originally emanated from two previous United Nations undertakings. The first one is the Eco-Partnership Tokyo Conference, which was held in May 1998 by the United Nations and Tokyo Metropolitan Government. This world conference affirmed that establishing environmentally sustainable society needs cooperation and partnership of all people, particularly participation of nongovernmental sectors including NGOs and private sector in formulating and implementing environmental policies. Another initiative of the United Nations was the Second Tokyo International Conference on African Development (TICADII), which was held in Tokyo in October 1998.

After these two world conferences, a project was organized by the United Nations to promote Asia and African municipal partnership in developing human resources to manage urban environment. The primary objective of this eco-partnership post conference project is to build the human resource capacity in municipalities for implementation of initiatives through north-south cooperation. After all, the partnership among all stakeholders—citizens, NGOs, the private sector, various specialists, research institutions, and local and central government—can be the foundation for creating a sustainable municipal governance which would guarantee the service delivery for all. During the Mombasa Conference, a half-day workshop was organized to promote the idea of partnership building among municipalities and within a municipality and to exchange ideas, views, and best practices with the aim of transferring and cross-fertilizing new ideas in the management of environmental issue in municipalities.

Theoretically, the basic tenet of municipal governance means, particularly in today's world, to value grass root actions and participative management involving nongovernment sectors and communities. Civic action can be superior to that of public administration in terms of promptness, flexibility, and originality. Local residents are likely to become aware of such problems as street cleaning, garbage collection, river water pollution of their own municipalities, before the government does. Such civil action is more effective when undertaken within a cooperative framework with other parities, particularly with a municipality, as the municipal authority has legitimacy, if not financial or expert knowledge. Cooperation between local authorities and citizens who are highly sensitive to social needs enhances the efficacy of policy making. Experience of such cooperation can further help local authorities to act more productively. When such cooperation becomes partnership, local authorities could enhance their service delivery.

This theory is in general practice in developed countries. However, in Kenya, the draft sector review reports indicated only sporadic endeavors in environmental management or partnership building. The draft reports indicated that all these four councils lagged behind any sound standards of municipal functioning, particularly in garbage disposal, solid waste management, sanitation, public health, road repairs and fire fighting. When the citizens are evading even paying the dues, and municipalities are providing poor services, it would be extremely difficult to create such consciousness for partnership building. How can the municipal administration solicit the participation of civil society to tackle local environmental issues or any service delivery? There was no solid answer to this primary question in a situation given in Kenyan municipalities.

VI. METHODOLOGY FOR IMPROVEMENTS

As mentioned earlier, the Conference included four consultative sessions, which took place after presentation of four municipal working group presentations in the second-day afternoon plenary. The consultative session was held with an objective to sort out the action plans to redress the issues prepared by each municipality during the Conference. Each session was attended by the mayor, town clerk, senior officers present in the Conference from each municipality, permanent secretary, and the senior officers of the Ministry of Local Government, UNDP Deputy Resident Representative (later Program Officer), and United Nations project officers including myself. The consultative session for each municipality took about one hour and half each, and four sessions were held. This event took altogether about seven hours.

Rather than enumerating the content of the problems and actions sorted out which was the original objective of the consultative sessions, I found it very interesting (and rewarding) that the sessions served a forum of a dialogue between the local authority and the central government. Sometimes, it served as a mediating session by UN and UNDP, although UN officers tried to serve mainly as advisors to the dialogue between the local and central government. A most striking thing was that sometimes, the consultative session turned to a quick decision-making forum by the permanent secretary of the Ministry of Local Government on matters which have been outstanding for long. For instance, short-term measures proposed by Nakuru municipality on the pending issues of recruitment of town planner and establishment of full-fledged physical planning department (town engineers department) both of which require the approval of the Ministry of Local Government, were approved on the spot by the permanent secretary. The senior officials took the notes of the decisions. The sessions were characterized as a civilized argumentative consultation and negotiation and deepened the understandings of the different interpretations between the central and local authorities. Probably that is the reason why a workshop like this organized by the technical cooperation agency attended by both parties in question would be useful. This matter can be argued separately as an important methodological point for capacity building for local governance (after all stakeholders and neutral body were present in the sessions).

The content of the actions sorted out into the three following ways:

1.   Some illustrations of short-term measures that can be accomplished mainly by municipalities with or without approval of the Ministry of Local Government:

> Recruitment of senior officers such as town planners
> Formalization of pending establishment of departments
> Implementation of by-laws by the council (such as air pollution by-laws)
> Council to require bond for officers to be trained in order to prevent brain drain

2.   Some illustrations of long-term measures that need approval of the ministry and may require donors' cooperation:

> To conduct joint training of senior officers and councilors in professional and technical training
> To conduct training needs assessment and establish a training calendar
> To improve the data collection and processing by computerization, particularly collection of rates and charges to improve revenues
> To commercialize the water supply services and other services such as garbage collection, street cleaning, etc.
> To install incinerators and drainage facilities
> To organize sensitization session for citizens, officers, etc.
> To enact by-laws such as environmental bills

3.   Some illustrations of long-term measures that require changes in the Local Government Act (as bulk of the municipal activities are delegated but require approval of the Ministry of Local Government, a number of proposed measures require amendments of Local Government Act):

> To establish a Local Government Service Commission to replace the overburdened Public Service Commission

Abolish transfer from one council to another and to guarantee cross transfer and suitable replacement

To delegate the authority of employment, and budget approval to provincial public service commissions for the scales of 10 to 20 for approval

Establishment of municipal courts by the Municipal Council to deal with cases of tax evasion

Approval of by-laws for the local authorities to publish the abstracts of accounts in the media

To legislate the separation of internal auditing function and account from the Treasury Department

VII. FROM GOVERNANCE TO GOVERNMENT

The Mombasa Conference indicated there was little partnership created between government and nongovernment sectors in the municipalities. Despite the appeal and the stated objective of the senior officials of central government including the Minister of Local Government, the Conference revealed the nonexistence of the practice of participatory governance.

Another way of looking this situation is the efficacy of governance approach to municipal management. Unless government is established and able to deliver services to the citizens, citizens may not feel inclined to cooperate with the government. Likewise, it may be quite a Western idea to rely on NGOs or community organizations for local service delivery when the government does not function properly.

During the Conference, it was questioned about how to raise consciousness of municipal officials in order to solicit participation of private sector. Before municipal officials approach stakeholders in municipal governance, government officials must first realize the efficacy of governance approach. When the municipal officials are not even alleged to their own municipalities due to political situation and public administration framework, how can one expect them to do additional thing such as involving citizens. The Conference revealed that they were not well paid and sometimes they had to worry when and or whether their salaries would be ever paid. Municipalities must first establish a viable organization before partnership be sought with outside.

Another, related question was raised during the Conference if the private sector was strong enough to invest for the environmental businesses, such as recycling or garbage collection. A related issue was whether the government or municipalities are willing to privatize some services. While few cases of partnership have been experienced recently in water supply, garbage collection, sanitation, they have not been replicated in other wards and the original initiatives have not continued long. Proposals for privatization and commercialization have not been explored fully.

Having reviewed a profile of the four local authorities in Kenya, it is evident that the governance approach which emphasize the participatory management is not on the way yet. Both central and local authorities in Kenya agree, however, that the capacity of local authorities must be upgraded and for that end, the Local Government Act must be amended to redress the major issues that have stagnated the changes in the management of local authorities.[9] Two things must happen to improve the capacity of the municipalities: first, amend the Local Government Act, and then strengthen the local authority to become a decentralized local autonomy. Perhaps in countries like Kenya, for the improved local governance, local government must be first established by changing the Local Government Act. Local authorities must be created as autonomous bodies given appropriate level of authorities from the central government. Unless a decentralized system is created, municipalities cannot properly function as a viable institution to serve the local communities. Donor community should therefore aim at the creation of local government, rather than local governance that would emphasize the relationship of municipalities with non-governmental sectors. To that end, both donor community and the central government need to refocus their priority, for the sake of truly building sound local governance for the long run.

ENDNOTES

1. In fact the discussion paper on the sector review for the Mmobasa Conference was prepared by the UN secretariat based on the draft reports of the national consultants for the sector review of the four municipalities in question. See References 1–3.
2. Minister J.J. Komotho participated in the entire Mombasa Conference. His 10-page written statement was made available during the Conference, entitled Opening Speech for the Partnership Building Conference on Municipal Governance for the Four Towns. National consultants for the four municipalities were critical of current arrangements made by the Ministry of Local Authorities.
3. All the participating mayors and town clerks of the four municipalities made presentation on the current practice and the proposed remedial measures.
4. The opening statements of both the Minister of Local Authorities and the UNDP resident representative, McLeod Nyirongo, clarified this point as the background for holding this capacity-building project for these four municipalities.
5. See the draft reports for the sector review listed in References in 2 and 3.
6. UN Secretariat had singled out these five issues summarizing the draft reports prepared by the national consultants for the purpose of facilitating discussions on the challenges facing the municipalities and for formulating during the conference remedial measures by the participating municipal officials. See the Discussion Paper listed in the Reference 1.
7. The national consultants undertook surveys and field trips during their sector review preparation.
8. See the opening statement of Minister Komotho for the Mombasa Conference.
9. At least the Mombasa Conference confirmed on this point.

BIBLIOGRAPHY

1. United Nations. Discussion Paper on the Sector Review for Mombasa, Nakuru, Kisumu and Eldoret for the Conference on Capacity Building for Municipal Governance (prepared by U. Andersen, A. Almaz, and I. Suzuki of Governance and Public Administration Branch, DESA, United Nations Secretariat for the Conference, 12–13 October 1999, Mombasa, Kenya).
2. United Nations. Draft Report of Sector Review on Capacity Building for Municipal Governance in Nakuru and Mombasa (prepared by John M. Nderi, national consultant for the Conference on Capacity-Building for Municipal Governance, Mombasa, Kenya, 12–13 October 1999).
3. United Nations. Draft Report of Sector Review on Capacity Building for Municipal Governance in Eldoret and Kisumu (prepared by Winnie V. Mitulla, national consultant for the Conference on Capacity-Building for Municipal Governance in Kenya, 12–13 October 1999).
4. Itoko Suzuki. (1998). Reforming local governance: Kenya; with special focus on Nairobi. EROPA Local Government Center: *Reforming Government: New Concepts and Practices in Local Public Administration* (Tokyo, Japan), pp. 149–170.
5. UNDP. (1998). *Country Cooperation Framework for Kenya, 1999–2003*, Nairobi, 22 June 1998 (UNDP, Nairobi, Kenya).
6. Government of Kenya. (1986). *Local Government Act (Chap. 265)*, Republic of Kenya.
7. Tokyo Metropolitan Government and United Nations. (1999). *Eco-Partnership Tokyo Conference Report (CD-ROM)*, Tokyo, Japan.

8. United Nations. Tokyo Metropolitan Government, *Eco-Partnership Tokyo*, (Executive Summary Report of the World Conference on International Cooperation of Cities and Citizens for Cultivating an Eco-Society, May 26–29, 1998, Tokyo), New York, 1998.
9. United Nations, UNDP. (1997). *Local Governance*, (Report of the United Nations Global Forum on Innovative Policies and Practices in Local Governance.) New York, United Nations.

33

Decentralization and Development Administration in Nigeria

Olatunde J.B. Ojo   *Department of Political and Administrative Studies, University of Port Harcourt, Nigeria*

Peter H. Koehn   *Department of Political Science, University of Montana, Missoula, Montana*

I. INTRODUCTION

Since independence, African states have engaged in periodic public-sector reforms seeking to rationalize institutional structures, clarify goals and objectives, and introduce improved management systems and procedures into their civil services, public profit- and non-profit-making enterprises or parastatals, and local governments (for a review see Adamolekun 1995:34–43; Balogun 1995:13–33). Although the results have not met expectations (because all but improved pay measures fail of implementation), public sector reforms still command a great deal of attention today. Culpability of the public sector in the economic crisis and decline since the 1980s have raised compelling questions about the proper role of the sector in the task of local and national development, specifically about the scope and responsibilities of the central government vis-à-vis state-owned business enterprises and local government. Academics and practitioners have argued against the expanded role of the state; some suggest a move away from the paradigm of development administration to that of development management (Rasheed and Luke 1995:1–11).[1] However, there is no getting around the fact that the state in Africa has to be the primary and fundamental agent of economic transformation. The reason is clear: "When the public sector is weak, so is the private sector" (Balogun 1995:20).

It is within this context that decentralization has reemerged as a priority policy objective in the search for African development. Long prescribed as a political-administrative cure for Africa's sociopolitical ills, decentralization measures, like those of the larger public sector reforms, achieved unimpressive results in the 1960s and 1970s. Today, in line with the worldwide trend toward democratization and popular participation, decentralization is being demanded by local pro-democracy movements and, as a conditionality, by many donor agencies (Ayee 1996:32 *New York Times* 7 April 1996).

This chapter presents an assessment of recent initiatives in decentralization and development administration in Nigeria. It explores the nature and extent of decentralization at the grass roots where, in the light of NGO successes, it is now believed that the public sector can equally make a similar impact. Our focus is on policy measures that enhance local capacity and autonomy that are deemed to be the essential foundation of national development and democracy. We are concerned with the extent of decentralization, looking specifically at the powers and functional jurisdiction of local governments or councils, their revenue resources and size in relation to functions and needs, and, more importantly, the impact of these on rural and urban service provision, development planning, and community empowerment. We analyze the role of development administrators associated with the impact of decentralization and conclude the chapter by suggesting changes that could overcome some of the observed weaknesses and lead to a more efficacious decentralization and development administration.

II. WORKING DEFINITIONS

Among the available approaches to decentralization, the one adopted here is devolution described by Rondinelli (1981:37–39) as "the most extreme form." The reason is that decentralization of the devolution variety is the one political-administrative approach which holds out the best prospect of (1) advancing democratic governance through expanded popular participation in the decision-making process, and (2) promoting socioeconomic development. It is the approach that requires the transfer of power and authority from central institutions and actors to constitutionally distinct, community-based institutions and actors (Koehn 1995:72). It thus can take advantage of institutions and actors that are well-informed regarding local conditions and are therefore flexible, innovative, highly motivated, and productive (Osborne and Gaebler 1992:252–253). Moreover, by facilitating the development of respected governmental structures at the grass roots that energize and channel the efforts of civil society in the delivery of essential public services, devolution also can attenuate practices that undermine governmental capacity and weaken the legitimacy of the state (also see Koehn 1995:79).

Development administration is used here to refer to the complex of agencies, management systems, processes, and methods used by governments at all levels to implement policies and plans designed to meet development objectives (Riggs 1970:6–7; Gant 1979:20). Its value, as Swerdlow (1975:345) puts it, is in calling attention to the special importance of public administration in the [development and] modernization process." Development administrators, then, are those public servants (political and bureaucratic) whose activities bring about change to enhance local and national autonomy and self-reliance, satisfy basic needs, and promote economic growth along with greater social equity—all important development objectives (Koehn 1991a:240).

III. RECENT DECENTRALIZATION INITIATIVES

For years after Nigeria's independence, the prevailing political impact of the center on the locality was antidemocratic. Overconcentration of power and lack of accountability resulted in the dissociation of public policy from social needs, the transformation of politics into warfare, and the widespread abuse of political and bureaucratic authority. Indeed, the ordinary people came to perceive the state as a hostile force to be resisted and thwarted (Ake 1992:42). Military rule, spanning 29 of the 38 years of independence, facilitated overconcentration of power. However, the military also made conscious attempts at decentralization aimed to help nurture development and democracy. The implications of the contradictory policies are the subject of our analysis.

The 1976 reforms provided the initial entry point for the Federal Military Government's (FMG) definition of the boundaries, functions, and finances of local government. (For an overview and critical analyses, see Adamolekun and Rowland 1979; Gboyega 1987:134–157; Gboyega and Oyediran 1978:266; Aliyu 1978.) The exercise enhanced the potential capacity and authority of the new 301 local governments in the country to execute key local development functions and to deliver services to a degree hitherto not feasible. However, local councils remained effectively under the jurisdiction, constraints, and encroachments of the states (Aliyu and Koehn 1982:53–75). States still had the constitutional mandate to provide by law for the establishment, composition, structure, function, and finance of local governments, and state-centered elites grossly abused this mandate, especially during the Second Republic. Indeed by the time of the Buhari coup in January 1984, the Nigerian local government system was generally believed to be in complete disarray (see Graf 1988:180–200; also Suberu 1994).

The short-lived Buhari regime sought to insulate local governments from state and even federal machinations. But it was the successor Babangida administration that undertook the more profound and extensive structural reorganization. First, it increased the number of local government areas from 301 to 449 in 1989, and then to 591 in 1991. It also inaugurated the system of executive chairpersons in order to bring local government into conformity with the presidential government that operated at the state and federal level. The extent of authority devolution is examined at two levels: political and functional autonomy, and financial resources and autonomy.

A. Functional Jurisdiction and Political Autonomy

In theory, local government councils have exclusive legislative authority over a wide range of issues, including the establishment and maintenance of cemeteries, homes for the destitute or infirm, motor parks, and public conveniences; the establishment, maintenance, and regulation of markets; construction, equipping, and maintenance of primary schools; and registration of births and deaths. They also are charged with the responsibility of bringing socioeconomic development to their area of jurisdiction. This gives them authority to consider and make recommendations to the state governments on the economic development of the state as it affects their respective council areas. And, they can prepare development programs for submission to state governors in accordance with the state governments' guidelines. Local governments also share Constitutional and statutory authority with state governments on a wide range of issues, including for example primary and secondary education, health services, and certain categories of roads and urban markets. Indeed there is evidence of some collaborative efforts. One example is the provision of 200 boreholes in Adamawa state in which the local councils contributed 30% of the cost, the benefiting communities 10%, and the state government the balance of 60% (*Guardian*, 6 February 1997:4).

In an apparent effort to attenuate the past tendency of state governments to control and erode the functions of local governments, the Babangida administration in 1989 abrogated state ministries of local government that previously performed regulative and supervisory roles over local authorities. It permitted only an inspectorate division within the state governor's office to offer guidance and ensure the attainment of targets set by local councils (see text of independence anniversary broadcast, *National Concord*, 1 October 1988; Osaghae 1989:359). It also granted local governments autonomy to recruit, train, promote, and discipline their junior staff. However, the State Local Government Service Commission remained in charge of the recruitment, training, transfer, promotion and discipline of middle-level and senior local government officers. To enhance the prestige of that bureaucracy and help it attract highly qualified personnel and strengthen its professional autonomy, the federal military government (FMG) harmonized the positions and conditions of service in the local governments with those in the state and federal services.

The practical reality is rather different from the theory, however, and decentralization and autonomy measures have not fulfilled the ostensible intentions of their protagonists and creators. One major problem appears to be contradictions among the professed goals, the policies to bring them about, and the implementation of those policies. For instance, the contradiction between the policy of a national salary structure and identical conditions of service among all three tiers of government and the goal of federalism, decentralization, and autonomy, did not sink in until the worsening economic crisis and structural adjustment programs made implementation of the policy problematic. Subsequent directives by both Babangida and Abacha allowing each state to determine its own wage structure failed to be carried out. The states that tried implementation quickly found that trade unions, which by law belong to one national umbrella union, would accept nothing but the federal wage structure and conditions of service. The states have come to see, and argue, that until there is resource federalism which restores state resources to the states and allows independent revenues, there can be no wage federalism (*Guardian* 24 Feb. 1996:28; *Guardian on Sunday* 26 Jan. 1997:A7).

B.   Financial Resources and Autonomy

What has been said of political and functional autonomy applies with even greater force to the related issue of financial autonomy. The professed goal is vitiated by policies that essentially substitute local government dependence on the federal government for dependence on state governments.

1.   Tax Base

In line with the notion of federalism and of decentralization of the devolution genre, each tier of government is accorded tax jurisdiction over certain activities. In the most recent listing of these, the federal government is given exclusive jurisdiction to determine and collect education, value-added, petroleum profit, and companies' income taxes; stamp duties from corporate entities; capital gains tax on Abuja residents and corporate bodies; and personal income tax on armed forces personnel, the police, external affairs officers, and residents of the federal capital territory, Abuja. The states collect federally determined income and capital gains taxes on all other individuals; stamp duties by individuals; motor vehicle and road taxes; taxes on pool betting, lotteries, and gaming; state-determined levy on business premises and registration up to a maximum of N10,000 per annum in urban areas and N5000 in rural. States also determine and collect development levy on individuals, but only to a maximum of N100 a year; also, fees on naming of streets in the state capital, on right of occupancy of land in the state capital, and on markets in which state finances are involved (*Guardian* 2 April 1997:1–2).

In the light of the often heard complaints by local government officials about lack of tax bases, especially in the poverty-stricken rural areas, the tax jurisdiction of this layer of government is instructive. According to the 1997 approved list, local governments had authority to levy and collect rates on shops, kiosks, and tenements; taxes on cattle; licenses to sell beer and wine; fees on slaughter slabs; registration of marriages, births, and deaths; fees on naming of streets outside the state capital; fees on bicycles, hand trucks, wheelbarrows, canoes, radio, and televisions; fees for permits to put up signboards and advertisement, to bury the dead in customary and religious burial grounds, to block roads for ceremonies and parties; and fees for public convenience, sewage and refuse disposal, and for wrong parking.

In the rural towns and villages most of these items are few and far between: public convenience, sewage or refuse disposal do not exist; there are only a handful or no cars and lorries to charge for wrong parking; few or no streets to name; few lock-up shops or kiosks; hardly any cattle other than those brought in for slaughter; few radios and bicycles; hardly any television sets; and few beer parlors. Indeed, many local government areas have no electricity at all (except where the rare well-to-do citizens who have not migrated to the urban centers possess personal generators).

As for the other sources of revenue, most are hardly enforceable for reasons of either inadequate manpower, or fear of resistance and violence, or both. Collective memory of the 1969–70 peasant revolt (*agbekoya*) cautions against provoking rural dwellers about taxes on their cherished cultural norms, especially where they are not involved in the decision making on why and how the monies are collected or spent. Marriages and land ownership, despite the land use decree vesting the latter in the state governments, are still largely transacted under customary law which traditionally required no registration. The same is true of deaths and burials. Only enlightened self-interest, because of the increasing importance of birth certificates for various benefits, may increase the number of registrations of births. Even this is doubtful as long as sworn declaration of age is permissible and officials exist willing to issue back-dated certificates for a fee. In sum, most local governments find that they have limited resources to tap and often times expend substantial funds and manpower to collect little.

2. Federal and State Government Sources

Over the years, the federal government, in the name of making local governments autonomous, has progressively institutionalized its direct financial relationships with local governments and has expanded the latter's share of federally allocated statutory funds. The current revenue-sharing arrangement allocates 48.5% of federally collected revenues to the federal government, 24% to the states, and 20% to the local authorities. The balance is distributed to special allocations such as that for the rehabilitation and development of mineral-producing areas or special grants for peculiar problems in the states. In addition each state is statutorily required to set aside 10% (previously 5%) of the internally generated revenue in its annual budget for disbursement to the local governments in that state.

The local government portion of state and centrally allocated revenues currently is distributed on the basis of equality (40%); population (30%); social development factors (10%); internal revenue generation effort (10%); and land mass and terrain (10%). Suberu (1994:6) points out that allocation of only a 10% weight to the criterion of internal revenue generation effort reflects the intense political opposition that has developed everywhere in Nigeria (except in the oil-producing areas) to derivation as a principle of revenue allocation. That opposition has been so intense (and attempts to cheat by inflating internal revenue generation effort so widespread) that this index has now been replaced by the relatively more reliable index of primary school enrollment. The apparent exception to the opposition to derivation is in respect of the federally collected value-added tax (VAT). Currently VAT amounts to about N40 billion a year. For 1998 the federal share is 25% (as against 35% in 1997), the states' share 45% (up from 40% the previous year) and local governments' share 30% (up from 25% in 1997) (*Guardian on Sunday*, 11 January 1998:11). But even here there is controversy arising from Lagos' share which is alleged to be inflated by the fact that company head offices in Lagos usually ascribe to that state alone production and consumption figures collated from their branches throughout the country. In the near future education tax on companies, already being collected by the federal government, also will be divided among the three tiers of government.

For now and the foreseeable future, Nigerian local governments, like the component states of the federation, depend heavily on centralized distribution of revenue for their activities. The extent of dependence is illustrated by the following typical examples: Out of the N33.35 million budgeted for fiscal 1992/93, in Gummi local government, in rural northern Nigeria, the federal government was expected to contribute N31.4 million (94.2%), the state government N250,000 (0.7%), and only N1.7 million (5.1%) from its own internal sources (*National Concord*, 31 March 1992:14). And in Ikeja, an urban local government in the South, N185.1 million of its 1998/99 budget of N304 (i.e., 60.9%) was expected to come from the FMG, comprising N99.4 million from the federation account and N85.7 million from VAT. The state government was expected to contribute N49.5 million or (16.3%) while the balance, N69.4 million (22.8%), was to be generated from internal sources (*Daily Times*, 18 March 1998:4). When one recalls that the previous year this local government realized only N4.7 million (only 6.7%) out of the projected internal revenue of N70 million, the internal goal for 1998/99 appears grossly overambitious. In effect, *both* urban and rural local governments have problems of limited internal resources to tap, hence their dependence on federal subventions.

3.   Stoppage of State Interference

To buttress the initiatives ostensibly mounted to ensure fiscal autonomy for local government, President Babangida reacted positively to complaints that state governments did not always fully or promptly forward to local councils the funds allocated to them from the Federation Account. First he issued a directive that the monies accruing to local governments from the Federation Account be paid *directly* to them (see Tordoff 1994:572–573). He also gave the order that where the mandatory 10% of state revenue to local governments was not disbursed to the respective local authorities, the amount was to be deducted from the offending state's share of the Federation Account (*National Concord* 1 October 1988; Osaghae 1989:359). Periodically the Finance Minister reminded states of these directives by issuing warnings over illegal deduction of local council funds (see, e.g., *Guardian*, 15 August 1996:40).

These directives appeared to have emboldened some local governments to assert their autonomy. For instance, all the local government councils in Kwara state refused in 1988 to pass to the state government that portion of their statutory grant from the federal government that, hitherto, paid for their share in the joint responsibility of funding secondary schools and health services. They would rather directly finance that part of their responsibility themselves. For another instance, the Calabar municipal government came into conflict with the Cross River state government when it decided to operate free primary education contrary to state policy. It also dragged the State to court when the state environmental sanitation task force forbade it to dispose refuse within the Calabar municipality (Osaghae 1989:357–358). More recently the 30 local councils in Osun state, accusing the state government of failure to remit the councils 10% of its internally generated revenue as required by law, retaliated by withholding the personal income tax they statutorily collect for and on behalf of the state (*Guardian*, 10 January 1998:3).

It will be fair to conclude that while federal policies ostensibly aim to nurture and strengthen the fiscal autonomy of local governments vis-à-vis the states, they also underscore the reality of the centralization of intergovernmental financial relations and a shift from local government dependence on states to dependence on the center. Rotimi Suberu (1994:8) puts it succinctly: "current revenue-sharing practices in Nigeria have encouraged the financial hegemony of the center, the chronic dependence of constituent states and localities on the centralized redistribution of resources, the massive transfer of revenues from the oil-producing areas to the other parts of the federation and in general the development of a highly integrated and unified public financial system."

This dependence on centralized redistribution rather than on subunit financial autonomy can be said to encourage demands for further fragmentation. With little cost to themselves and much to gain, every town or village yearns to become a local government. A case can be made, however, that there is merit in having every town or village become a self-governing local government unit (see later). It suffices to say here that regardless of whether funds continue to be centrally disbursed, or some of the lucrative revenue sources currently controlled by the center come under local control, grassroots people in Nigeria feel that they would be better off if they controlled their own destiny through political and economic empowerment of their traditional communities than under the present arrangements. This is their message to the Committee on State Creation, Local Government, and Boundary Adjustment (the Mbanefo Committee), which, halfway through its work, was already inundated with requests for over 3000 local government areas (*Guardian*, 28 March 1996:40). In the end the Abacha regime created only 183 new local governments in December 1996, bringing the total to 774 in the country.

However, the struggle for political and economic empowerment of local communities continues and manifests itself in many other ways. One way is in the intensive pressures for fairer treatment by the petroleum-producing states and local communities. This is symbolized by Ken Saro-Wiwa and the autonomist agitation in the Ogoni local government areas and by the increasingly more violent demonstrations ostensibly against oil companies in Warri and the delta areas for not conferring direct benefits, (see, e.g., *Guardian*, 13 March 1998:6). Most of the states in the southern part of the country support these agitations which strengthen their own demands for a more equitable revenue allocation system (see Oyelegbin 1998:6). Another way is direct protests and confrontation by state workers, like the one at Ibadan in 1996 when the Accountant-General of the Federation, instead of deducting the total emolument of all teachers in a state from VAT allocations before sharing the balance among the state's local governments, changed to making allocations to the local councils first before deducting the emoluments of their respective teachers. This had an adverse effect on the urban councils such as the five in the city of Ibadan which tended to have disproportionately large number of teachers while it favored rural councils where teachers usually do not want to serve (Fabowale 1996:3). Given this confrontational trend, the impact that FMG directives will have on revenue generation drives will be interesting. On the one hand most people will applaud the FMG's abolition of the practice of sealing off the business premises of tax defaulters, and of using armed forces or police personnel or the mounting of road blocks to collect taxes and levies (*Guardian*, 2 April 1997:1–2). On the other hand, by adversely affecting internal revenue receipts, the directives may further fuel what is called the "national question"— a crystallization of opposition to the integration by centralization that characterizes Nigeria's federal system.

IV. IMPACT ON DEVELOPMENT

What has been the impact on the grassroots of the decentralization efforts that began in earnest over 20 years ago? In analyzing the impact we concentrate on three major components of development and the role of local government in each: rural and urban service provision, development planning, and community participation and empowerment.

A. Rural and Urban Service Provision

Despite heavy statutory subventions by the federal, and to a lesser extent, state governments, local governments remain plagued by inadequate funds. What is more, the bulk of these goes into escalating recurrent budgetary commitment to staff salaries and emoluments, and to office operations and purchases of equipment. For example, Ikeja, Eti-Osa, Kosofe, and Mainland, four urban councils in Lagos with relatively broader effective internal tax bases, budgeted N304 million, N342.3 million, N207.3 million, and N327.8 million respectively for the 1998/99 financial year. At the exchange rate of N84 = $1, these budgets translate to $3.62 million, $4.08 million, $2.47 million, and $3.90 million—minuscule indeed relative their needs. Typically, recurrent commitments comprise well over half the budgets, leaving little for the development of the local government area. For example, the recurrent commitment at Ikeja comprised 66.88% of the budget, 58.02% of Eti-Osa's, and 67.75% of Kosofe's (*Guardian*, 19 March 1998:12; *Daily Times*, 18 March 1998:4).

It is not surprising then that, as in the past (see Koehn, 1991a), many essential urban services remain inadequate (e.g., potable water, electricity, health services, motorable roads, etc.). Inadequate as government services generally are, their grossly uneven distribution remains an equally common characteristic of urban centers. Cities have highly serviced, poorly serviced, and nonserviced areas that generally correspond to the class backgrounds of neighborhood inhabitants. Moreover, as Green observed awhile ago (1977:15, 18), lack of coordination among state, local, and parastatal agencies hampers service provision throughout the urban area.

People in the countryside struggle with even less of the benefit of vital services. In the entire Surulere local government of Oyo state, for example, not one town or village enjoyed electricity as of July 1997, when one of the authors visited. It had no hospital and most towns and villages did not even have dispensaries or maternity centers. Until the local council began sinking and ringing 21 deep wells (evenly distributed among its 10 wards), streams, pools, privately owned shallow wells, and rainwater were the main sources of drinking water. Feeder and access roads were ungraded, making it virtually impossible for communities to be linked with their neighbors or to move farm produce to the market except by human portage. The only interstate road linking the area with Ogbomoso, the urban state capital to the West, and Osogbo, the capital of the neighboring state to the East, was rough, untarred, and unmotorable during the long rainy season (see also *Sunday Tribune*, 16 March 1997:11).

Performance results with respect to education are even more alarming. Although the largest proportion of local government revenue continues to be spent on education, the bulk of it on teachers' salaries which are now deducted at source from VAT and statutory allocations, there continues to be irregularity in the payment of salaries. Many school buildings are dilapidated; new classroom blocks are uncompleted and abandoned; books, equipment, and facilities are in short supply; and standards have drastically fallen (*Daily Sunray*, 5 March 1993:3; *Guardian*, 19 March 1998:3; Koehn 1990:259–260, 1991a:243–244).

In effect, Stren's (1988:21) and Stock's (1985:472–477) observations of Makurdi and Ida (Benue state) and Kano state, respectively, remain applicable to many other areas of Nigeria today. Richard Stren had found that residents identified "poor water supply as their single most serious neighborhood problem," while Robert Stock documented both inadequate and uneven distribution of public health service, finding for instance that less than 15% of the rural population lived within 8 km of a health facility that offered inpatient services. Currently, many state governments berate their local governments not only for not providing essential services but also for financial recklessness and failure to maintain or rehabilitate vital infrastructures the state had provided them (*Daily Times*, 15 October 1996:4; *Guardian*, 13 March 1997:7; *Sunray*, 12 March 1997:5). Ordinary citizens also accuse local government officials of being preoccupied with lining their own pockets, of forgetting about the actual business of governance, and of being accountable literally to no one. One Lagos state resident expressed the feelings of many when he opined that the only thing that shows that local governments exist is the intimidating presence of their security outfits who go about harassing motorists and other citizens in the course of revenue drive (*Guardian*, 3 April 1996:11, 13 March 1997:7, 11 March 1998:4). The military governor of Ondo state was less charitable. The local government executives in the state, he said, were a "bunch of empty brains who lack vision to transform their rural communities." They could not even furnish him with "the details on three kilometers of road to be rehabilitated in their areas." Worse, most deceived constituents by pointing to state projects as their own accomplishments (*Guardian*, 13 March 1997:7).

While inadequacy of resources partly accounts for this deplorable performance, self-aggrandizement, mismanagement, lack of commitment, and lack of effective accountability are also part of the equation as we shall presently see. Local council officials, however, claim that too much political and administrative interference adversely affects their performance. They point to restrictive federal guidelines, to dictates by state governors, to bureaucratic controls by state and federal institutions and functionaries, and to erosion of their functions by state encroachment. Many see the role of State Local Government Commissions, on balance, to have been detrimental to the effectiveness of local government administration (*Guardian*, 15 August 1996; 13 March 1997:7, 11 March 1998:4). All of this has some validity. However, most of the control measures, like the FMG's Financial Memorandum (FM) which they find particularly irksome, are intended to help stem administrative and financial irregularities and recklessness. The FM spells out the precise duties and responsibilities of executives and other officials in respect of local government financial administration—funds, stores, revenue generation, records, etc. It is one way to ensure some accountability in the absence of effective political structures, forums, and community empowerment to make local government operators directly accountable to the people.

Overall we can safely conclude that what the Political Bureau observed more than 10 years ago (Nigeria Political Bureau, 1987:116) still remains true today: that "despite the strategic importance of local government to the national development process, its contribution has been minimal." This situation has led to increased demand for more of the partial privatization of certain services, which Stren (1988) first observed in some cities. It has also fueled increasing reliance upon self-help everywhere, notably in the ubiquitous launching of development funds by the various town's and village's Progressive Unions and Annual Day Celebrations.

B. Development Planning

The uninspiring performance record compiled by LGs in Nigeria underscores the need for, and importance of, effective local-level development planning. Unfortunately, the unstable political situation in the country and in the local governments, particularly from 1993 to 1998, has made serious long-term development planning almost impossible. Nevertheless, earlier experience with development planning and with activities pertaining to capital investments and annual budgets offer insights on the impact of local governments on contemporary development planning activities and outcome at the grassroots. We already noted that the bulk of the limited financial resources not spent on education goes to recurrent expenditures, mostly on salaries and emoluments of professional staff, leaving little for significant development projects (see also Otobo 1986:118, 121–126). Even here, however, local officials, like their counterparts at the higher tiers of government, consistently select projects, set priorities, and advance and execute policies and programs which principally benefit themselves.

To begin with, officials have exhibited gross self-aggrandizement in land acquisition and allocation, a particularly important subject since land is a major resource or service of capital in development. Frequently using their strategic position and broadly defined powers under the 1978 Land Use Decree (which was originally intended to protect the poor against greedy speculators), local, state, and federal officials have manipulated state land allocation policies and procedure to acquire the land of the poor and powerless occupants who rely on land for their survival. Usually, inadequate or no compensation is paid. The weapon the officials often use to intimidate or apply pressure on their victims is the Certificate of Occupancy (CO) issued by the governor or local government chairman in whom the decree respectively vests urban and rural lands as trustees. They use personal favoritism, inside information, and connections to procure COs on choice residential, rental, and business properties and then use government housing loans and/or loans obtained from commercial banks where they are preferred customers to satisfy the requirement that allocated land be "developed" (i.e., built upon) within a short period of time (see Nigeria, Political Bureau, 1987:54; Koehn 1984:59–75, 1987:163–186, 1990:143–172).

The courts have begun to curtail this abuse of office, ruling that the Land Use Decree does not (and was not intended to) "abolish existing instruments of title to land, nor, *a fortiori*, replace them with another 'indefeasible' title document in the name of a C of O." Neither the grant of a piece of land by the governor or chairman, nor the CO issued in support of the grant could defeat the prior interest of the original title holder under customary law or other valid instruments (see Ogunniran 1996:29, 1989:162). As one state attorney general recently asked rhetorically: "How can you be a trustee over a land you don't have?" (see *Thisday*, 13 March 1998:3; *Post Express*, 26 May 1997:28).

No laws or courts have yet come to the aid of the poor with regard to officials' unfairness in decisions regarding local government or state capital investments in annual or longer-term planned expenditures. Ideally, the most important goals and factors that should guide decisions regarding which proposals to incorporate into such plans include: projects which are development oriented, require labor-intensive methods of execution, and have wide distribution of benefits, particularly among rural residents and the poor (Koehn 1991a:244). In Nigeria, as Koehn's study of the 1981–85 development plan in Bauchi and Kaduna local governments shows, this is far from the case. While the bulk of their capital investments (41.2% and 54.8%, respectively) went into social services, including education, roads, and other infrastructures, neither of the local governments did much about economic goods production. Here they invested a mere 1% and 1.7%, respectively. Yet Bauchi, a more rural area, could profitably invest heavily in agricultural goods production, for example. It chose instead to invest 39.1% of its capital outlay on revenue-generating projects of dubious economic or social value—motor parks, markets, slaughter slabs (Koehn 1990:198–202) and, more recently, on mass transit programs, tractor-hiring services, and a revolving loan program for drug purchases (*Post Express*, 26 May 1997:5). Studies of Bendel state also show the proclivity to construct too many markets, motor parks, civic centers, and similar projects which are generally underused, a product of the need to engage in revenue-yielding projects rather than on socially relevant and development-enhancing programs (Okafor 1984:253, 256; King-Akesode, 1988).

A related problem is the basic misconception of development that equates it with skyscrapers, flyovers, and neon lights, a belief that social or economic development is best indicated by the number and size of physical structures. This accounts for the heavy emphasis on building projects and other capital-intensive construction works in the capital expenditure estimates of local and higher tier governments (Aliyu 1980:12–13). It is also one of the reasons for demands for more local governments and the associated deadly riots over the siting of their headquarters which have plagued Nigeria in recent years. In the prevailing view, headquarters means fancy office buildings; beautiful houses—even if only for officials; and amenities like pipeborne water and electricity.

A compelling argument can be made that the most important factor in assessing a development proposal is the likely beneficiary. The reduction of inequality lies at the heart of development. In development planning, this goal is realized by rectifying socioeconomic and gender disparities and locational (urban/rural, area A vs. area B) imbalances. Thus, the first step in a development planning strategy directed toward ameliorating poverty and inequality is for those involved in the project selection process to raise "who benefits" questions.

Nigerian local governments can play a vital role in identifying pressing needs, addressing existing disparities of means and opportunity, incorporating local priorities into the national development planning framework, and promoting and defending citizen interests at higher levels of policy review and budgetary allocation. The effective performance of these roles requires a conducive process and the application of feasible and relevant planning methodologies. The planning choices that have predominated to date at the local level in Nigeria reflect the top-down and technocratic nature of the prevailing plan formulation process. Entirely different orientations and results are likely to be forthcoming when planners and policy makers develop and apply appropriate criteria in the submission, analysis, and selection of project proposals (see Hyden et al. 1996:44–45).

C.   Community Participation and Empowerment

In light of its central connection to sustainable development, a compelling case can be made that community participation and empowerment is (or should be) the fundamental aim or objective of decentralization. Community empowerment involves building people's capacity to formulate and implement local development initiatives, to analyze and choose among alternative approaches, to realize benefits from projects that produce improved living conditions, and to share in the evaluation of outcomes. Community empowerment is realized through self-reliant organization and political mobilization; education, training, and awareness-building for all members; the capacity to assess and articulate collective needs; and the ability to generate and utilize vital material and human resources. Thus, heightened community participation is viewed as a critical element in the development process (see Cheema and Rondinelli 1983:3–11)

In Nigeria, although the decentralization and local government reforms make rhetorical references to empowering local communities, little or nothing in practice has been done to advance this goal. The record of citizen empowerment is poor. A major limitation of local governments, indeed of governments at all levels, is the inability to mobilize local communities for participation in socioeconomic development. There also is little grassroots participation in the assessment of community needs, planning, and decision making (see Adedayo 1985). One reason is the attitude toward community development and participation that local government administrators hold. Local government officials and councils simply assume that local needs are obvious (dispensaries, potable water, electricity, markets, roads, etc.) and see little in the provision of these that the community and people can do beside faithfully paying their taxes. Only occasionally do they involve local communities in the implementation of projects. At such times, villages or beneficiary communities may be requested to contribute a certain proportion of the cost, provide some materials, or contribute labor. Grassroots governing bodies seldom emerge to give a sense of proprietorship, to monitor performance, and/or to assure sustainability. As in the past, there is little or no civic interest group participation in project identification, priority setting, design, or selection.

This attitude and the failure to involve communities stem from a number of factors. First is the belief that development planning is too complex for the illiterate masses to comprehend while the scope of skills and costs associated with programs and projects are too intricate to appreciate. To attempt to explain these to the people is viewed as a slow, time-wasting, and fruitless endeavor. Nigerians have yet to heed Fanon's admonition that the whole people must plan and decide even if it takes twice or three times as long. Nor do they yet appreciate that "the time taken up by explaining, the time lost in treating the worker as a human being, will be caught up in the execution of the plan" (Fanon 1963:118, 193, 197–198; Koehn 1991b:748). Thus, for example, most of the 399 GL 03-13 local administrators studied by Hay et al. (1990:156–160) held the view that the public should not participate in the planning of community development programs, that officials should determine goals and the framework for collective action at the local level, and that certain information that is crucial for effective involvement in project formulation and evaluation should be withheld from the local populace.

Related to the fear of slowing down "progress" is the concern that informed and empowered masses could challenge elite and urban-oriented programs and privileges. As long as the elite can get away with skewed benefits and privileges because there are no effective forums of the type associated with local communities to engage and challenge them, the attitude described here can continue indefinitely. It would be a different matter when there is avenue for community involvement. A case in Oba, Olorunda, local government is instructive. The initial position of the elite on the choice of development projects had been to give priority to electricity while the grassroots preferred a pipeborne water project. However, under the aegis of the Oba Progressive Union and Annual Day celebrations, the grassroots prevailed after a series of debates complete with a cost-effective strategy of actualization.[2] Clearly, community participation can have salutary effect on awareness, mobilization, democracy, and self-reliant development. It is one of the main reasons, apart from fairness, why Nigerian communities have made demands for large numbers of local governments.

The demands for more local governments are also a product of the fact that extant structures lack firm roots in the respective communities. Olufemi Vaughan (1995:501–518) explains this rootlessness in terms of the top-down formulation and implementation of reform and local government policies. The celebrated Ife-Modakeke case (see *Guardian*, 23 May 1977:40) epitomizes a problem that looms in the background in many parts of the country.[3] (For other cases see, e.g., *Guardian*, 2 April 1997:11, 8 January 1997:26). In the Ife-Modakeke case, the newly created Ife East local government merged the town of Modakeke and surrounding villages with parts of the city of Ife. The headquarters of the new local government was sited at the Enuwa ward in Ife. Following bitter protests against what Modakeke saw as government insensitivity to its long history of struggle against claims of Ife suzerainty, the federal government changed the headquarters to Modakeke. Ife, however, would not accept what it saw not only as a "treacherous plot for illegal autonomy [of Modakekes] as settlers on Ife land" (*Guardian*, 23 May 1997:40) but also as subordinating Ife to the indignity of bowing, its own land, to those it considers its former vassals (*Guardian*, 24 March 1997:5). For a while the new council operated two secretariats—one in Modakeke, the other at Ife—as the indigenes of Modakeke and Ife reported for work in their respective home headquarters. A seven-day ultimatum by the State Local Government Service Commission threatening to dismiss those who continued to absent themselves from work at the Enuwa headquarters precipitated a civil war between the two communities in which 200 people were killed and more than 400 houses razed within the first three months (*Guardian*, 11 January 1998:3, 12 April 1997:28). Structures congruent with social forces and community traditions and forms of governance will clearly need to be created if the collective energy of the community people is to be harnessed and applied rather than turned off or dissipated.

V. ROLE OF DEVELOPMENT ADMINISTRATORS

The evidence is overwhelming that little has been accomplished in Nigeria by way of genuine development administration. To understand this situation, we must consider prevailing bureaucratic inclinations. Two levels of analysis are useful here. First, one often encounters an absence of commitment to public service. In addition, we need to examine the presence of attitudes that are conducive not to development but to underdevelopment administration.

A. Commitment to Public Service

One expects public officers to translate their knowledge, power, and strategic advantage into opportunity to serve the people. Instead they tend to be self-serving, constituting themselves into a parasitic institution that consumes a huge amount of resources but provides little in return by way of goods and services (Balogun 1995:23–24; Joseph 1987). Balogun has argued that as the sole operators of an alien (mostly Western) institution, bureaucratic public officials turn even the simplest procedure into a "ritual object" that their clients must worship. Many actually "see themselves as rulers" rather than as public servants (Takaya 1980:67–68). For their part, political public officials "come into politics without any clear conception of what it is a politician does, other than wield power" and "stay in power." Hence, whether in civilian or military garb they show aggression in order "to make up for lack of role perception," and, because office alone is their reason for existence as a political class, their "main concern is to offer rewards and bribes to anyone who can contribute to keeping them in power." It is this "heavy weight of political and bureaucratic power," to adapt Fred Riggs' well-known phrase, that opens the door to "egocentric norm-lessness and [political and] administrative prodigality." In Nigeria this has taken several forms.

First, federal and state leaders have turned local governments into instruments of local dom-ination and political control, not units of a truly independent third tier of government. Civilian governments often dissolved local councils at will, replacing them with sole administrators or caretaker committees. Many failed to remit to their local governments the federal statutory allo-cations paid through state accounts. Most also minutely scrutinized and altered local-government budgets, and often seconded, as local-government secretaries, state administrative officers loyal to the state government rather than to their local-government superiors. Military politicians invoked nebulous security reasons for preserving the smoothness of the transition to civilian rule to sus-pend difficult local council chairmen (e.g., Sam Orji of the Enugu council), or forbid them from holding meetings or traveling outside their local-government area without the governor's permis-sion. Some suspended chairmen on the ground of alleged fraud, as in the case of all 18 council chairmen in Kaduna state.

At the highest level of government, both Babangida and Abacha manipulated local govern-ments to enable them to succeed in their attempts at personalist transformation from junta leader-ship to civilian president. Their complicated maneuvers—from designating local-government areas as constituencies for federal elections to requiring elections to the councils on a no-party basis only to demand repeat elections within a year, this time on partisan basis; from nonrecogni-tion of parties in which opposition elements predominated to behind-the-scenes activities and financial support for preferred candidates; and from disqualifications of candidates before elec-tions to disqualifications of poll winners even after their assumption of office—left no doubt that the junta's purpose was to "ease [its] control over the democratization process" and attain person-al objectives rather than to "build strong and independent units of government at the grassroots" (Egwurube 1989:38). In the Abacha regime, specifically, elections were seen as a tool for select-ing people "the government will be able to control" for the formation of "a government party to support [the junta leaders'] 5-year hidden term" (*Guardian*, 3 April 1996:11). In what proved to be a prophetic insight, Ayodele Akinkuotu (1996:8–13) suggested that "somewhere along the line, [Abacha would] get the chairpersons to vote that in view of the political situation in the country, the General should stay on to save the country from dismemberment or serious social and politi-cal chaos" (see also Useh 1996:10–14). As it turned out two years later, Abacha did exactly that, manipulating each of the five parties he had recognized to put him forward as the sole presidential candidate for the scheduled election of August 1998 which was aborted only by the event of his sudden death in June (*Tempo*, 8 January 1998; *Thisday*, 10 March 1997:3).

Secondly, at the local government level, as at the state and federal level, high officials usual-ly used the power of office to settle personal scores, intimidate opponents or, as we have noted above, to become overzealous in respect of tax and levy collection, resulting in tax raids, road blocks, and abuses of human rights. Thirdly, as a number of other scholars have observed, there is a relative lack of devotion to public service that one finds at all levels of government in Nigeria. The problem manifests itself in different forms. At the middle and lower ranks of the technical and pro-fessional cadre, for instance, Chris Ukaegbu (1985:505–580) reports that the "culture of unex-plained absence" is widespread. Ebong Ikoiwak's research (1979:247) uncovered an "absence of commitment to the public interest" among federal civil servants at all levels of employment (also see Nigeria, Political Bureau 1987:111). Fully 91% of the respondents in Ikoiwak's study (1979:227) indicated that a "wrong attitude toward work" constituted a performance obstacle among their fellow civil servants. Similarly, Bala Takaya (1980:64) contended that while postre-form local government "is now physically nearer to the people, it is not people oriented." He con-cluded that the 1976 reforms brought about "no noticeable change in terms of attitudes toward the people."

Little has changed since these studies. In fact, under the strains of structural adjustment, especially the devaluation of the naira in the 1990s and the concomitant runaway inflation, most public officials in the junior and middle cadre find that their monthly salaries can pay for either two weeks of rent and food or transportation to and from work. Few show up for work three or more times a week unless their units provide free or subsidized transportation. Most look for alternative ways of survival, mainly farming and trading, and pay less attention to their formal employments (Bangura and Beckman 1993:84).

B. Underdevelopment Inclinations

Even more insidious than the absence of devotion to the welfare of the masses is the presence among public administrators of attitudes that actively support exploitation and underdevelopment. Fraud appears to be the preferred means: councillors and chairmen divert resources (e.g., fertilizers) meant for their constituents to private use, or, in collaboration with state officials overseeing local government affairs, they connive with officials in Federal Pay Office to defraud their councils of millions of naira (*Thisday*, 16 October 1996:3; *Guardian*, 16 October 1996:1). The ubiquitous kickbacks that have made Nigeria a veritable "*contractocrazy*" often pitch councillors against their chairmen for alleged mismanagement of funds on the part of the latter. Sometimes the allegation ostensibly is about "sidelining the councillors in the administration of the council" but really about excluding them from contract awards or about appointments to cash disbursement committees. For their part, the bureaucratic officials often disregard payments approved by political officials to "certain contractors, but only pay those contractors *known to them*" (*Guardian*, 13 March 1997; *Punch*, 10 January 1998:27).

Many councils have "ghost workers" on their pay roll while financial recklessness has resulted in unnecessary debts for many others (*Daily Times*, 15 October 1996:4; *Guardian*, 11 March 1998). Nearly all the caretaker committees passed on huge debts and staff claims to the newly inaugurated councils in 1996, ranging from N13 million and N15 million in Aboh/Mbaise and Ihitte/Obama councils, to N98 million in the Calabar council (see *Guardian*, 11 April 1996:25, 3 April 1996:5). The same has been true of the 1997 councils (*Sunray*, 12 March 1997:5). This situation compromises the ability of local governments to engage in vital dimensions of the development process, in particular capital projects.

The prevailing inclination to pursue self enrichment leads public administrators to focus their attention on the protection of privilege rather than on development activity. This requires keeping the grassroots in the dark rather than informed; suppressing popular interests rather than promoting change. In this fundamental way, bureaucratic officials become agents of underdevelopment.

VI. CONCLUSIONS

An emerging consensus among those who study public administration in Africa holds that structural performance is deteriorating and that public policy makers frequently act in ways that are inimical to the needs of the rural and urban poor (Stren 1988:243; Hyden 1983:xii, 106, 120; Koehn 1984:72–73, 1990). The basic will and capacity of state functionaries to serve as agents of development is seriously questioned. The failings of the public service account in large measure for the state of perpetual crisis in which African states find themselves.

The most important issue with respect to the future of decentralization for development administration in Nigeria concerns the role commitments adopted by political and administrative personnel at all levels of government. Will public servants, both political and bureaucratic, utilize their elite social status and powerful policy-shaping position in the political system primarily to engage in further self-aggrandizement, to pursue class interests, or to promote the design and execution of effective local governments that can engage in public projects that enhance sustained, self-reliant economic development and bring about substantial improvements in the living conditions encountered by the vast majority of the country's rural and urban populations?

A.   Past Performance

On its face, devolution has progressed further at times in Nigeria than it has in most other African contexts. Nevertheless, these efforts typically have not resulted in pronounced socioeconomic development. Nor have they contributed to democracy. Leaders have not had sustained commitment to the design and implementation of local government reforms that simultaneously seek to promote local democracy and socioeconomic development. They have not had sustained willingness to provide the kind of structure, authority, and resources needed to ensure success in the mobilization of the energies and resources of local people for their own development; nor have they employed effective implementation strategies that address and remove principal constraints.

We suggest that this is in part because decentralization has been used and/or captured by political forces bent on pursuing a personal *cum* national agenda that rules out community empowerment. This is most evident in the top-down, one-size-fits-all manner in which local governments have been created, financed, and given identical functional jurisdiction and authority, identical administrative structures and procedures, even identical political modus operandi. There are, in addition, underdevelopment inclinations and attitudes on the part of officials. The lesson from the Nigerian experience is that for sustainable socioeconomic gains to be realized, community empowerment must be the goal of devolution.

B.   Structural Reform and Accountability Proposals

Goran Hyden (1983:132) has suggested that one way the reorientation of local government councils can be realized is "by allowing groups in society, through intermediary non-governmental organizations, to exercise pressures in such a direction." This will not be enough, however. To be efficacious decentralization must be of the devolution kind and designed to maximize the advantages associated with small size, local knowledge and concerns, and community involvement (Oyovbaire 1985:273; Wilks 1985:271; Koehn 1990:290–291). It is empowerment of the rural and urban masses that generates a powerful countervailing force against bureaucratic privilege and exploitation (see Yahaya 1982). The evidence examined here suggests that the basic challenge of decentralization in Nigeria involves transferring material and human resources, along with decision-making power, from the center to local governments in a manner that satisfies indigenous aspirations expressed through community empowerment.

The primary unit of organization and service in such a system would be the rural village, the town, or the city (or townships comprising the city). In Nigeria each of these constitutes a natural community at the center of which is a traditional ruler or king, the embodiment of the political norms as well as the sociocultural traditions of the community. The paramount-chieftaincy institution provides the rallying point for communal spirit, energy, aspirations, and loyalty. This is so even among the Igbo, whose claim to be acephalous rests only in the fact that, unlike, say, the Yoruba or the Hausa-Fulani, "the office is an acquired one open to any male agnate in either a royal clan . . . or a royal maximal lineage . . . who is of good character and who can afford to join particular title societies and to pay the required fees and expenses of the installation ceremonies" (Nzimiro 1972:21).

In most parts of the country what Saburi Biobaku says of the Yoruba holds true as well; that is, the meaningful form of leadership resides in traditional or paramount chieftaincy and not in the is modern form of government. Vaughan (1991:313, 319–322), citing this eminent historian as well as Takaya (1984) and other influential champions of formal roles for paramount chiefs, has argued that while the political and administrative elites in the modern structures of government possess ultimate political authority, they often lack legitimacy and must seek the support of the incumbents of a well-tested and respected institution in order to mobilize support. Vaughan sees in the ubiquitous longing for chieftaincy titles (which only paramount chiefs can confer), and the high level of enthusiasm that often accompanies their conferral, attestation by the Nigerian political class to the fact that the paramount-chieftaincy institution retains some normative attributes that could enhance their standing in society by bestowing status and recognition. It is thus an instrument of legitimatization. Those who eschew the institution and have sought to undermine it have failed, often with tragic results.[3] Indeed, it is to this institution that modern political leaders often turn for help in times of serious crisis and disturbances. For instance, peace came to Ife-Modakeke only after the Yoruba paramount chiefs stepped in.

Given this reality, the paradox of contemporary situations, as Biobaku puts it, lies in the universal grassroots support and overwhelming elite recognition of the paramount-chieftaincy institution and its lack of formal political functions. To compound the paradox paramount chiefs are paid from the 5% of state revenue statutorily allocated for that purpose. It is this anomaly that must be redressed by integrating the village, town, or city townships into the governmental system as the third tier of Nigeria's local-government structure.

In the proposed structure every village, town, or city township with a paramount chief would become a self-governing unit. The central and state funds which currently go to local governments would be shared among them, using appropriate formulas and a similar process and method as are now used to pay the paramount chiefs. This way the dynamic interaction among chiefly authority, the masses and elite sons and daughters, which enables self-help organizations to become the vaunted engines of growth at the grassroots, becomes an integral part of governance in the new local-government unit. It is the complex interaction of these societal forces and institution that enables chiefs and elite sons and daughters to employ "formal and informal networks that penetrate the policy arena [to] serve as important conduits between the center and the periphery" for the funds needed for their town's development (see Woods 1994:465–483; Vaughan 1995: 516). It is the dynamic interaction that generates enthusiasm and mass participation, the dedication and loyalty of the elite, and, thus, the ability to convert physical capital and human skills into concrete development products. By making the town or village a unit of local government, it becomes possible to integrate the self-help activities of hometown associations or development/improvement unions into the formal structure of local development administration. As such local governments become imbued with the same level of mobilization, participation, responsiveness, and accountability we have come to associate with hometown self-help groups, the role of local administration in development, hitherto elusive, becomes achievable.

For purposes of service provision, a town or village which cannot go it alone could have joint programs or projects with similar villages or towns by free choice and negotiations, with one set of like-minded communities on one issue, with another set on a different issue, and so on. This helps eliminate deadly forced unions of the Ife/Modakeke kind, while at the same time promoting democratic governance. It enables democracy to be built from the ground up in contrast to the top-down efforts that have been a source of much grief in African political history.

C. Bureaucratic Reorientation

Nigerians at all levels of government are capable of engaging in effective development administration. Moreover, the building blocks necessary for fundamental reorientation of the bureaucracy and improved public sector performance are known and within grasp. They are changes in policy-making processes, diminished dependency, distributive policies, the adoption of uncomplicated and participative approaches to development, and the assumption of a new set of inclinations by public officials. The primary challenge comes down to how the role of public administrators can be transformed from an essentially "parasitic class" that is primarily inclined toward preserving and enhancing self-aggrandizement into a committed, effective force for social change and independent economic development. Although leadership by example and devotion to ethical behavior are crucial in the long run, the historical record offers no indication that further education and retraining, or approaches that rely on bureaucratic initiative and voluntary compliance, will provide the impetus for reorientation of the public services. Increasing democratization of structures at all levels of government offers a more promising avenue for effectuating such a transformation.

The overwhelming influence that administrative officers exercise over public policy making in Nigeria results in part from the intellectual and technical dependency of political actors. Therefore, moving the bureaucracy in a more responsive direction awaits the arrival of informed, aware, forceful, and effective representatives of the rural and urban poor. An indispensable first step in this direction is local government at village, town, or city township level accompanied by the political mobilization and education of the peasantry and poor city dwellers. Meanwhile the importance of removing restrictions on citizen access to governmental information cannot be overemphasized (Adamolekun 1983:213). As Sheth (1987:163–165) points out, "the consumers of development cannot be kept out of the process of formulation of norms of alternative development—however inconvenient this might prove . . ."

Empowerment of the rural and urban masses would generate a persistent and powerful countervailing force against bureaucratic privilege and exploitation (Yahaya 1982). In the absence of this kind of check at the base of the political system, public servants will continue to be inclined to act primarily as self-serving agents of underdevelopment.

ENDNOTES

1. Unlike the former, which sees development as solely a state or public sector responsibility, development management focuses on the "involvement of all sectors and institutions of society: state and civil society, public and private enterprises and NGOs and cooperatives." As such it is "concerned with all types of organisational settings—micro-, small-, or large-scale; informal and formal; and public, private or voluntary" (Rasheed and Luke 1995:4, 5).

2. The strategy was simple. A neighboring town was providing itself with pipeborne water by constructing a damn on the Otin River on their common border. Since a large part of the resulting lake would cover Oba people's farmlands, they would insist on the extension of the piped water to Oba as a quid pro quo. Oba would finance the cost of pipes, tanks, etc., for its own side. One of the authors, a citizen of Oba, was a participant observer in this matter.

3. Vaughan recalls the most notable, relatively recent case: Abubakar Rimi, who had won an electoral landslide to become the governor of Kano state, overestimated his popularity and legitimacy by consistently undermining the influence of the Emir of Kano, a supporter of the opposition party. The hostilities came to a head in July 1981 when the governor queried the emir, charging him of disrespect to the state government and giving him 48 hours to show cause why he should not be disciplined. This insult to the emir led to instigate violence and arson in which the state government Secretariat was burnt down and several lives were lost, including one of the governor's aides, Bala Mohammed. Chief Moshood Abiola's warning with a Yoruba proverb is indeed apropos: "a wild horse cannot be ridden by force; if it throws you, you'd be lucky to escape with your life"—the lesson being that attacking the formidable, traditional paramount-chieftaincy institution in the absence of a revolution of French or Bolshevik proportions is tantamount to individual and collective suicide.

REFERENCES

Adamolekun, L. (1983). *Public Administration: A Nigerian and Comparative Perspective.* London: Longman.

Adamolekun, L. (1991). Promoting African decentralization. *Public Administration and Development 11*(3), 285–291.

Adamolekun, L. (1995). Reassessing thirty years of public administrative reform efforts. In S. Rasheed and D.F. Luke (eds.), *Development Management in Africa*, 34–43. Boulder: Westview Press.

Adamolekun, L., and Rowland, L. (1979). Epilogue. In L. Adamolekun and L. Rowland (eds.), *The New Local Government System in Nigeria: Problems and Prospects for Implementation,* 293–301. Ibadan: Heinemann Educational Books.

Adedayo, A. (1985). The implications of community leadership for rural development planning in Nigeria. *Community Development Journal 20*(1), 24–31.

Ake, C. (1992). *The New World Order: A View from the South.* Lagos: Malthouse Press.

Akinkuotu, A. (1996). On the march again? Booby-traps against handover. *Tell* 11 March, 8–13.

Aliyu, A.Y. (1978). As seen in Kaduna. In S.K. Panter-Brick (ed.), *Soldiers and Oil: The Political Transformation of Nigeria,* 270–287. London: Frank Cass.

Aliyu, A.Y. (1980). Local government and the administration of social services in Nigeria—the impact of the local government reform. Paper presented at the National Conference on Local Government and Social Services Administration in Nigeria, held at the University of Ife, February 1980.

Aliyu, A.Y., and Koehn, P.H. (1982). *Local Autonomy and Inter-Governmental Relations in Nigeria.* Zaria: Institute of Administration, Ahmadu Bello University.

Ayee, J.R.A. (1996). The measurement of decentralization: the Ghanaian experience, 1988–92. *African Affairs 95*(1), 31–50.

Balogun, M.J. (1995). A critical review of the changing role of the public sector. In S. Rasheed and D.F. Luke (eds.), *Development Management in Africa*, 13–33. Boulder: Westview Press.

Bangura, Y., and B. Beckman, B. (1993). African workers and structural adjustment: a Nigerian case-study. In A. Olukoshi (ed.), *The Politics of Structural Adjustment in Nigeria.* London: James Currey & Ibadan: Heinemann Educational Books.

Cheema, D.S., and Rondinelli. (1983). "Introduction." In G. S. Cheema and S. Rondinelli (eds.), *Decentralization and Development: Policy Implementation in Developing Countries.* Beverly Hills: Sage.

Gboyega, A. (1987). *Political Values and Local Government in Nigeria.* Lagos: Malthouse Press.

Gboyega, A., and Oyedirah, O. (1978). "A view from Ibadan." In S.K. Panter-Brick (ed.), *Soldiers and Oil. The Political Transformation of Nigeria,* 257–269. London: Frank Cass.

Graf, W.D. (1988). *The Nigerian State: Political Economy, State Class and Political System in the Post-Colonial Era.* London: James Currey.

Green, H.A. (1977). Urban management and federalism: an overview of the Nigerian situation. *Nigerian Journal of Public Affairs 7,* 7–24.

Hay, R., Koehn, P., and Koehn, E. (1990). Community development in Nigeria: prevailing orientations among local government officials. *Community Development Journal 25*(2), 147–160.

Hyden, G. (1983). *No Shortcuts to Progress: African Development Management in Perspective.* Berkeley: University of California Press.

Hyden, G., Koehn, P., Saleh, T. (1996). The Challenges of Decentralization in Eritrea. *Journal of African Policy Studies 2*(1):31–51.

Ikoiwak, E.A. (1979). *Bureaucracy in Development: The Case of the Nigerian Federal Civil Service.* Unpublished Ph.D. dissertation, Atlanta University, Atlanta, GA.

Joseph, R. (1987). *Democracy and Prebendal Politics in Nigeria: The Rise and Fall of the Second Republic.* Cambridge: Cambridge University Press.

King-Akesode, M.C. (1988). *Localism and Nation Building.* Ibadan: Spectrum Books.

Koehn, P. (1984). Development administration and land allocation in Nigeria. *Rural Africana 18,* 59–75.

Koehn, P. (1987). Political access and capital accumulation: an analysis of state land allocation process and beneficiaries in Nigeria. *Afrique et Developpement 12,* 163–186.

Koehn, P. (1990). *Public Policy and Administration in Africa: Lessons from Nigeria.* Boulder: Westview Press.

Koehn, P.H. (1991a). Development Administration in Nigeria Inclinations and results. In A. Farazmand (ed.), *Handbook of Comparative and Development Public Administration,* 239–254. New York: Marcel Dekker.

Koehn, P.H. (1991b). Revolution and public service in the third world. In A. Farazmand (ed.), *Handbook of Comparative and Development Public Administration,* 745–754. New York: Marcel Dekker.

Koehn, P.H. (1995). Decentralization for sustainable development. In R. Sadiq and D. Luke (eds.), *Development Management in Africa. Toward Dynamism, Empowerment, and Entrepreneurship,* 71–81. Boulder: Westview Press.

Nigeria. Political Bureau. (1987). *Report of the Political Bureau.* Lagos: Federal Government Printer.

Nwosu, H.N. (1977). *Political Authority and the Nigerian Civil Service.* Enugu: Fourth Dimension Press.

Nzimiro, I. (1972). *Studies in Ibo Political Systems: Chieftaicy and Politics in Four Nigerian States.* Berkeley and Los Angeles: University of California Press.

Ogunniran, H.D. (1989). The certificate of occupancy as a muniment of title. *Nigerian Journal of Contemporary Law 162.*

Ogunniran, H. (1996). The real worth of a certificate of occupancy. *Guardian,* 14 May 1996:29.

Okafor, F.C. (1984). Dimensions of community development projects in Bendel state, Nigeria. *Public Administration and Development 4,* 249–258.

Osaghae, E. (1989). The strengthening of local governments and the operation of federalism in Nigeria. *Journal of Commonwealth and Comparative Politics 27*(3), 347–364.

Osborne, D., and Gaebler, T. (1992). *Reinventing Government: How the Entrepreneurial Spirit Is Transforming the Public Sector.* Reading, MA: Addison-Wesley.

Otobo, D. (1980). Bureaucratic elites and public sector wage bargaining in Nigeria. *Journal of Modern African Studies 24,* 101–126.

Oyelegbin, R. (1998). Oyo, Ekiti protest revenue allocation formula. *Guardian,* 3 March:6.

Oyovbaire, S.E. (1985). *Federalism in Nigeria: A Study in the Development of the Nigerian State.* New York: St. Martin's Press.

Rasheed, S., and Luke, D. (1995). "Introduction: Toward a New Development Management Paradigm." In S. Rasheed and D. Luke (eds.), *Development Management in Africa: Toward Dynamism, Empowerment, and Entrepreneurship,* 1–11 Boulder: Westview.

Riggs, F. (ed.). (1970). *Frontiers of Development Administration.* Durham, NC: Duke University Press.

Rondinelli, D.A. (1981). Government decentralization in comparative perspective: theory and practice in developing countries. *International Review of Administrative Sciences 47*(2), 133–145.

Sanni, L. (1996). Okuku, Oyinlola's hometown, celebrates self-help spirit. *Guardian* (Lagos), 9 April:12.

Sheth, D.L. (1987). Alternative development as political practice. *Alternatives 12,* 155–171.

Stock, R. (1985). Health care for some: a Nigerian study of who gets what, where, and why. *International Journal of Health Services 15,* 469–484.

Stren, R.E. (1988). Urban services in Africa: public management or privatisation? In P. Cook and C. Kirkpatrick (eds.), *Privatisation in Less Developed Countries,* 217–247. New York: St. Martin's Press.

Suberu, R.T. (1994). Integration and disintegration in the Nigerian federation. Paper presented at the Integration et Regionalisme Colloque Internationale, Talence, France, 27–30 April.

Swerdlow, I. (1975). *The Public Administration of Economic Development.* New York: Praeger.

Takaya, B.J. (1980). Failures of local government reforms in Nigeria: in search of causal factors. In S. Kumo and A.Y. Aliyu, (eds.), *Local Government Reforms in Nigeria,* 61–71. Zaria: Institute of Administration, Ahmadu Bello University.

Takaya, B.J. (1984). Politics of hegemony and survival. Paper presented at the National Conference on the Role of Traditional Rulers in the Governance of Nigeria, Institute of African Studies, University of Ibadan, 11–14 September.

Tordoff, W. (1994). Decentralisation: comparative experience in Commonwealth Africa. *Journal of Modern African Studies 32*(4), 555–580.

Ukaegbu, C.C. (1985). Are Nigerian scientists and engineers effectively utilized? Issues on the deployment of scientific and technological labor for national development. *World Development 13,* 499–512.

Useh, A. (1996). Abacha strategies: fit of desperation. *Tell* 26 February:10–14.

Vaughan, O. (1991). Chieftaincy politics and social relations in Nigeria. *Journal of Commonwealth and Comparative Politics 29*(3), 308–326.

Vaughan, O. (1995). Assessing grassroots politics and community development in Nigeria. *African Affairs 94*(377), 501–518.

Wilks, S. (1985). Nigerian administration—in search of a vision. *Public Administration and Development 5*, 265–276.

Woods, D. (1994). Elites, ethnicity, and 'hometown' associations in the Côte d'Ivoire: an historical analysis of state-society links. *Africa 64*(4), 465–83.

Yahaya, A.D. (1982). The idea of local government in Nigeria: the need for a redefinition. In A.Y. Aliyu (ed.) *The Role of Local Government in Social, Political and Economic Development in Nigeria 1976–1979,* 55–66. Zaria: Ahmadu Bello University, Institute of Administration.

34
Conduct of Managerialism and Its Performance in Southern African Countries

Ogwo J. Umeh *Department of Public Administration, California State University, Hayward, California*

Greg Andranovich *Department of Political Science, California State University, Los Angeles, California*

I. INTRODUCTION

The recent literature on public management in Africa has become more complex as deficiencies in earlier approaches and studies have been addressed. The nature of the African state in development; the relationship among institutions of the state, the economy, and society; and the integration of African countries into the international political economy have become topics of research (Hyden 1983; Balogun and Mutahaba 1989; Mehretu 1989; Blomstrom and Lundahl 1993; Siddiqui 1993). Much of this research has adopted dynamic frameworks for analyzing change, particularly in how the state, economy, and society are changing and how these changes affect the role and function of the state in modern African societies. The global context of this change has been recognized as occurring within the international political economy, mediated by both public and private sector organizations. At the center is the fragile African state—its political and governmental institutions and administrative capacity severely strained.

In this paper we undertake an exploratory examination of the use of administrative management skills in the conduct and performance of managerial work within the context of administrative management, specifically in nine SADC countries in southern Africa (the Southern African Development Coordinating Conference is now SADC and includes South Africa, Mauritius, Namibia)—Angola, Botswana, Lesotho, Malawi, Mozambique, Swaziland, Tanzania, Zambia, and Zimbabwe. Although the term "relationship" suggests a two-way process—a political system influences the conduct and performance of public management; the prevailing management capacity implicitly shapes the regime's policies—our analysis focuses on the former aspect.

In the following section, background information on the political economy of the nine SADC countries is provided as context for the exploration of administrative characteristics in different political regimes. Next, the methodology for data collection is described. The novel use of "critical incidents" provides an interesting view of the use of managerial skills and their effectiveness, in the SADC countries during the 1980s. In the final section of the paper, the implications of the SADC data for the ongoing discussion of building public management capacity for implementing intensive growth in southern African countries are explored.

II. POLITICAL ECONOMY OF SOUTHERN AFRICA

The political economy of contemporary southern Africa is rapidly changing terrain. Many have lamented the absence of political leadership skills that has plagued the African countries that became independent after World War II. One result has been the public bureaucracies, although constrained by policy decisions made by political leaders, have played a central role in the performance of leadership functions (e.g., Esman 1974; Vengroff et al. 1991).

After an in-depth survey of many African developing countries, Heady (1991) noted five commonalities about the nature of political leadership which, in effect, suggest that knowledge of political processes in the developing countries is understandably still fragmentary and tentative. According to Heady, the absence of strong political leadership in these countries has resulted in political regimes that can be characterized by: (1) widely shared developmental ideologies as the source of basic political goals; (2) high reliance on the political sector for achieving results in society; (3) widespread incipient or actual political stability; (4) "modernizing" elitist leadership accompanied by a wide political gap between the rulers and the ruled; and (5) imbalances in political institutions, with the public bureaucracy often playing a more dominant role than other institutions.

The politics of development in southern Africa has been colored by the Republic of South Africa's regional economic and military strength, and the economic and political linkages of the neighboring countries to South Africa (most, like Mozambique, derive from colonial times). In recent years preceding the end of apartheid, the Republic of South Africa's neighbors developed several regional associations (e.g., Preferential Trade Area of Eastern and Southern Africa; SADC) to pool economic resources and develop their political strength and regional infrastructure and to combat the continued domination of the region by South Africa (see Thompson 1986; Msabaha and Shaw 1987). As Thompson has noted (1986:264), the colonial wars in this region were among the last, and the countries neighboring South Africa have been somewhat slower to start down the road to independence than the rest of the continent.

All of the southern African countries except Angola and Mozambique (formerly Portuguese colonies) were British colonies or were within the sphere of influence of the Republic of South Africa; by the mid-1980s all except Zimbabwe had more than a decade of independence; and population growth rates across the nations are similar. The economies of these countries appear considerably different, with Zimbabwe, Tanzania, and Zambia having the largest GNPs and Botswana and Malawi the smallest. The microeconomies of Lesotho and Swaziland should be viewed as somewhat separate cases (Young 1982:191).

The average GNP per capita (again, excluding Lesotho and Swaziland for the moment) provides another perspective on the national political economy, with Botswana and Zimbabwe showing relatively higher income levels and Mozambique, Malawi, and Tanzania showing relatively lower levels. However, it is important to bracket this information because all of these nations are relatively poor (World Bank 1986) and the estimates for per capita GNP reflected a downward trend in the late 1980s in most of the SADC nations (see Nyang'oro 1989; Blomstrom and Lundahl 1993).

This political economy has profound effects on the management of the public bureaucracy. Kiggundu, among others, has alluded to the organizational face of the "soft state": society pervades public organizations which are not "mature" enough, in the Weberian sense, to prevent this occurrence (1989:44). Nti (1989) has suggested that the political economic crisis has resulted in the further penetration of society into the state, with societal conditions replicated within the states administrative organizations. Nti (1989:124) identified some of these conditions: "shortages in pencils, duplicating papers, functioning typewriters, and photocopiers are rampant in many ministries and departments in a number of African countries." Together, these factors account for the description of the African state as a commons susceptible to tragedy (see Leonard 1991:279–281).

A. Design

The public management literature suggests that administrative characteristics may be represented by the set of skills used by public officials in accomplishing organizational missions (e.g., Mintzberg 1973). The identification of public management skills in studies of bureaucracies in developing countries has followed similar lines (see McCurdy 1977; White 1987; Vengroff et al. 1991). In addition, much emphasis has been placed on the degree of importance of these skills to accomplishing developmental programs, thus effectively linking conduct to performance (see NASPAA 1985; White 1987; Ronan 1993). For example, McCurdy compiled a list of the most frequently exported management strategies needed to help developing nations. Among these strategies were the implementation of modern management techniques, including organizational management techniques, technical skills, development planning, and financial and budgetary strategies (McCurdy 1977:305).

After extensive research on development management in Africa, Morgan came up with similar skills to those identified above. According to Morgan, "management qualities crucial to effective implementation of centrally inspired policy include skills in negotiation, representation, coordination, motivation, advocacy, work planning and allocation, monitoring, reporting, and so on" (Morgan 1984:4). Montgomery (1986a) suggested that there are certain issues over which bureaucratic politics were waged, including finances, turf, and people (staff, clients, and other bureaucrats). In an in-depth examination of managerial work in the Central African Republic and the SADC countries, Vengroff et al. (1991:107) found several common roles in public management. These were the roles of: spokesperson (disseminator), technical expert, executive, and "operating rules and procedures" (a non-Western managerial role characterized by "knowledge and adherence to juridical rules and regulations"). Kiggundu clarified the conceptualization of managerial work by delineating managerial work into critical operating tasks (those tasks that are necessary to keep the organization functioning) and strategic management tasks (those tasks that help position the organization in its environment). He cites evidence showing that strategic management tasks are paid "little or no attention" and that the conduct and performance of critical operating tasks (which tend to focus on intraorganizational needs) is "equally problematic" (Kiggundu 1989:150).

Sorenson (1990:15) has noted the shift from *extensive* to *intensive* growth; that is, a political economic reframing away from an emphasis on the global economy toward the domestic and regional economies. This shift will require new capacities to formulate and implement growth policies, including greater flexibility, communication, adaptability and innovation in all sectors of society. At the same time, White (1990:36) notes that even recent reports by international development organizations (e.g., World Bank) have recognized the need for "joint diagnostic exercise[s] . . . with a mix of technical, organizational and political analysis, and with due attention to organizational processes." Vengroff et al. (1991) suggest that although certain roles and characteristics are common to public managers in different African countries, contextual differences occurring on a country-by-country basis undermine generic management education and development efforts. These important observations are in stark contrast to earlier models of development which suggested that tropical Africa has been modernized from "without" rather than from "within" (e.g., Kautsky 1972:162–163). The attendant need for greater flexibility, communication, adaptability and innovation in governmental, as well as private and not-for-profit sector institutions has placed additional burdens on African political regimes (Esman 1991:153; Picard et al. 1994:124–126).

After reviewing the transferability of management education and development from the

West to Africa, however, Jones suggested that African managers require somewhat different skills than do Western managers. Jones (1989:84–85) suggests that more highly developed political and diplomatic skills are needed by Malawian managers in monitoring events that may affect them in relation to their bosses, other superiors, colleagues, subordinates, as well as demands from outside the agency, such as family or kinship groups (see also Hyden 1992). To this we can add Rondinelli's (1983) caveat: the imposition of modern management techniques (e.g., participatory management) cannot be implemented successfully without first preparing the participants, those in government and out, who will be assuming new or different responsibilities. All of this suggest that greater flexibility, communication, adaptability and innovation in public management may not be enough; institution building may be needed as well to illuminate the path of intensive growth (see Balogun 1989; Picard and Garrity 1994b). The implications of this have been nicely captured by Ronan (1993), who has advocated shifting away from competency-based approaches toward seeking the greatest return on management education investment because this would link internal organizational efficiency to external effectiveness.

B. Methodology

We examined management events gathered from public officials or their deputies in the nine nations that took part in a cooperative effort in alliance with the National Association of Schools of Public Affairs and Administration (NASPAA). In 1984, with funding from the U.S. Agency for International Development (USAID), NASPAA launched a major study of management training needs in these countries.[1] Rather than using traditional survey research techniques, a critical incidents methodology was employed (for various descriptions of this study see NASPAA 1985; Montgomery 1986a–c, 1987, 1991). The methodology was based on a collection of management events in the public, private and parastatal sectors, with the event representing the unit of analysis (we are only using the public sector data subset in this paper).

Unlike survey methods, which rely on statistical sampling techniques to prevent distortion, the critical incidents method focuses on the most recent experience of the respondent. It is the incident and not the respondent that constitutes the data point. This method is random in the sense that the selection of events requires each respondent to cite the most recent incident in his/her experience. In the SADC study, the respondents were asked by the training authorities of their own government to participate in the survey.

The management events collected from officials or their deputies were aimed at identifying skills needed in the region. Using a "highly inductive" approach each of the collected events was coded or classified into nearly 50 identifiable management skills derived from the incidents (Montgomery 1987:357). This process identified administrative skills used in the conduct of managerial work in the SADC nations, as well as whether the skill contributed to the resolution of a particular event. If the skill used in the event contributed to effective public management it was coded positive; otherwise, it was classified as negative. This procedure provided some evidence of managerial performance.

Although the SADC events provided some valuable data and insights, the database does suffer from methodological and conceptual weaknesses (see Vengroff 1990). Two methodological weaknesses involve the timing of the data collection and the make-up of the respondents. A third, more general problem arises in the coding of events, particularly with intercoder reliability.[2]

In a previous paper comparing the managerial work conducted at different administrative levels, we found that the most frequently reported skills were in intraorganizational management (Umeh and Andranovich 1992). The next category for managerial work was in the interoganizational arena. Community relations was the least reported, yet skills in this area tended to yield positive performance outcomes. In light of these findings as well as those of White (1990) and Vengroff et al. (1991), we have reexamined the sadc management events to ascertain the extent of their use in the conduct and performance of managerial work.

Categorization of events into six skill clusters was based on two criteria. First, these are the most frequently mentioned skills in studies of bureaucracies in developing countries (e.g. McCurdy 1977; Jones 1989). Second, the conduct of managerial work tends to be focused on three levels—internal organizational processes, interorganizational relations between public agencies, and between the public sector and the larger society. In addition, much emphasis has been placed on the degree of importance of skills clustered at these three levels in accomplishing developmental program goals (see naspaa 1985; Kiggundu 1989; Vengroff et al. 1991). Further, the performance dimension of managerial work requires both efficiency and effectiveness (Ronan 1993);—that is, flexibility, adaptability, and willingness to experiment and learn from failure (Rondinelli 1983). For example, both Kiggundu (1989) and Vengroff et al. (1991) note that more attention to the context or environment of specific countries and the empowerment/responsibility of stakeholder groups is necessary for successful capacity building to occur.

These levels of managerial competencies consist of several related skill groups. At the level of intraorganizational management are three skill clusters. Clerical skills consist of secretarial, technical, and mathematics and computational events. General management consists of personnel and organizational management, and planning and coordinating events. Policy analysis consists of policy, program and project analysis, financial management and evaluation, and monitoring events. Given the overwhelming focus on the conduct of intraorganizational relations (Umeh and Andranovich 1992), the strict adherence to juridical rules and regulations (Vengroff et al. 1991), and the importance of critical operating tasks to public management (Kiggundu 1989), skills in the general management and policy analysis clusters are those that would be most likely to foster and enhance intensive growth through the conduct of intraorganizational relations.

The arena of interorganizational management consisted of two clusters. Adaptability clustered organizational management, skills at organizing, ability to change the environment, and leadership and initiative. The political maneuvering cluster included political environment, negotiation, bureaucratic politics, and interorganizational relations. Both clusters identify strategic management skills necessary in managing the political and administrative environments that are important to intensive growth (Kiggundu 1989; Montgomery 1991).

Finally, community relations included events coded as public relations, community relations, and communication. This cluster might be the key to successfully embarking on the path of intensive growth because of the importance of community loyalties and community values in African governance (Hyden 1992). In addition, the recent emphasis in implementing sustainability suggests a reliance on decentralized implementation structures and processes (Picard and Garrity 1994a). As Esman (1991:143) has noted, this process can be effective only if it is possible to learn from local practices that have shown their effectiveness.

Table 1 provides an overview of the distribution of respondents and management events in the nine nations. As can be seen, not only did the respondents vary by nation, but so did the distribution of management events. Zimbabwe, Lesotho, and Botswana had the most respondents overall (with 60, 55, and 34, respectively). Similarly, Zimbabwe and Lesotho account for about half of the events. This is not surprising given the data collection strategy of the original study (e.g., Montgomery 1986b:212), but does provide a cautionary note to interpreting these data.

III.   RESULTS

As noted above, there are a variety of political paths to development in Africa. We utilized the public sector subset of the sadc management training needs database to undertake an exploratory

Table 1 Distribution of Respondents and Management Events

	Number of respondents (n = 239)	Number of events (n = 1709)
Angola	5	17
Botswana	34	194
Lesotho	55	360
Malawi	9	41
Mozambique	21	126
Swaziland	9	96
Tanzania	24	179
Zambia	22	149
Zimbabwe	60	547

examination of the use of administrative management skills in the conduct and performance of managerial work within the context of the different countries.

The inward, departmental focus of public managers across the nine southern African countries is shown in Table 2. Public officials in these countries seemed to exhibit tendencies that illustrate that managing intraorganizational relations is the core activity of managerial work. In all of these countries, general management was the most noted skill cluster. The application of general management skills does include planning and coordinating, two skills that have the potential to lead to greater flexibility in public management. The mixed outcomes obtained from using these skills (Table 3), however, preclude us from drawing such a conclusion. Policy analysis skills, although used less often, potentially are more useful in fostering intensive growth by linking the various channels through which regime policies are implemented. Although the outcomes are mixed (see Table 3), using policy analysis skills did contribute to effective management practice more frequently than not. This difference is particularly noticeable in Angola, Lesotho, Mozambique, and Tanzania. Public officials did, however, elicit management events that suggest a preoccupation with the more routine clerical tasks, again with mixed outcomes.

Interorganizational management, or managing and steering the department through the maze

Table 2 Conduct of Managerial Work by Skill Categories

	Number	Percent
Intraorganizational relations		
Clerical (n = 332)	332	19
General management (n = 523)	523	31
Policy analysis (290)	290	17
Interorganizational relations		
Adaptation (n = 62)	62	4
Political maneuvering(n = 320)	320	19
Community relations (n = 182)	182	10
Totals	1709	100

Table 3   Performance (outcomes) of Managerial Work by Skill Categories (N = 1709)

	Positive performance		Negative performance	
	No.	%	No.	%
Intraorganizational relations				
Clerical	166	19	166	20
General management	251	28	272	33
Policy analysis	169	19	121	15
Interorganizational relations				
Adaptation	43	5	19	2
Political maneuvering	151	17	169	21
Community relations	106	12	76	9
Totals	886	100	823	100

that makes up the public sector in most of these countries, and an important component of intensive development strategies, was a distant second to the conduct of intraorganizational relations. In part, this may reflect how the data were coded, nonetheless, it does point up a major gap in skills needed for intensive growth. Regardless of country, the SADC public managers' responses demonstrate a stronger preference for political maneuvering than adaptation (Table 2); this trend was particularly pronounced in Swaziland and Lesotho, respectively. In both areas (i.e., political maneuvering and adaptation skills), the performance outcomes across these countries were mixed to negative (i.e., the skills used did not contribute to effective management; Table 3).

One exception was in Botswana and Zimbabwe, in which the use of adaptation skills (i.e., leadership and initiative, skills at organizing, ability to change the organization's environment) more generally resulted in effective managerial performance. Unfortunately, adaptation skills were one of the lesser used skills overall; a more in-depth analysis of the use of these skills in Botswana and Zimbabwe might prove useful. If the data could be generalized to the concept of risk taking, the absence of events in leadership and initiative and the ability to change the environment categories would suggest that innovation and adaptability are indeed rare occurrences in the public sector (Leonard 1991).

Community relations, an integral component of intensive growth, was woefully lacking in all these countries (Table 2) (Rondinelli 1983; Caiden 1991). Like adaptation skills, however, the use of community relations skills (community relations, communication, and public relations) generally resulted in effective management practices (Table 3).

IV.   DISCUSSION

Rapid political and economic changes are converging in much of the world and are resulting in a recasting of global power and politics (see Attali 1990). In southern Africa, a peripheralized region at best in the *fin de siecle*, the need to confront the effects of these changes from a different perspective is necessary. Sorenson's (1990) observation that flexibility, communication, adaptability and innovation are skills in great demand should not be lost in translation when assessing the strengths and weaknesses of public managers in southern African nations. The SADC data do suggest that these skills are currently used, with varying degrees of effectiveness, in intraorganizational management, interorganizational management, and community relations. Yet overall, these skills tend not to have a reference point in sadc bureaucracies. Blunt and Jones (1992:69–70) note that little attention has been paid to these skills, and to develop them would require linking capacity building to institutional environments that support such behavior.

Although this exploratory examination of the sadc data regarding the conduct of managerial work and its performance on administration tends to support several existing negative observations regarding public management in southern Africa, the data also point to fruitful paths for rethinking management capacity building strategies in the region. In large part, African bureaucracies tend to operate in a similar, familiar fashion, regardless of regime type. The caveat that all but two of the nations represented have a British colonial heritage may not be meaningful here; Vengroff (1990) compared the sadc data with a former French colony, the Central African Republic, and found no variation attributable to colonial regime heritage. Hence, other factors such as level of political (institutional) and administrative (organizational) development may be key to explaining the lack of any noticeable variation (Leonard 1987).

The sadc data showed that most public managers in these southern African countries seemed to focus much of their effort on the internal workings of their agency or department, often around routine tasks and not achieving effective results. These data support Kiggundu's (1989:41–42) observation that critical operating tasks are delegated upward in the administrative hierarchy, due to several possible factors: the politicization of administrative work; management style; previous experience; or internal weakness in the performance of these tasks.

When African managers do engage in other activities in the interorganizational or community arenas, the effectiveness picture changes slightly. Although generalization from the sadc data may not be warranted, it does appear that organizing skills, communication skills, and negotiation skills did pay dividends in the effective performance of managerial work. Kiggundu (1989) has described these skills as necessary for completing strategic management tasks. The sadc data confirmed Kiggundu's assertion that these skills are generally lacking in developing countries. Kiggundu (1989:61) suggests several reasons for this, including: the highly volatile political, social, and economic environments don't give public managers time to plan; weaknesses exist in carrying out the basic operating tasks; the lack of strategic management skills; and structural institutional weaknesses. Several of these factors seem to have been at issue in the sadc countries. For example, volatile economic and political environments, the weaknesses in carrying out basic operations, and structural institutional weaknesses may account for the lack of use of these skills (also see Montgomery 1991).

Adapting these skills, and permitting them to evolve locally, would seem to be the next order of business in shoring up the administrative and political institutions in the SADC countries (Gulhati 1991; Ademolekun 1991; Esman 1991). For example, many researchers and practitioners are calling for the linking of administrative skills to institution building (e.g., Balogun 1989; Picard and Garrity 1994a). This is important because as the sadc data illustrate, public management practices show a similar pattern across these countries. In addition, institution building needs to link management education and development in public, private, and not-for-profit organizations and institutions, as each supports the other and self-reliant private and not-for-profit sectors would be a tremendous aid to intensive, long-term growth efforts (Balogun 1989; Esman 1991).

V. IMPLICATIONS FOR MANAGEMENT DEVELOPMENT

As is currently the leading edge of practice, management education and development needs to be learner-centered, and based in theories of adult education and experiential learning (Blunt and Jones 1992:317–318). We would highlight the need for management education and training to be interactive and involve managers in its design, conduct, and evaluation (Youker 1989). As Esman

(1991:130–143) has noted, such a reorientation of management development can emphasize a bottom-up strategy of management reform, even when focusing on the familiar terrain of intraorganizational management skills. But lessons must be learned in the context of local political conditions, especially for interorganizational and community relations skills, because politics will influence success and failure in policy making and implementation. Esman (1991:159) describes these new skills as going beyond the emphasis on efficiency and effectiveness, the typical organizational standards for successful management practice. Capacity building for intensive growth would profit from the use of other barometers, including outreach (i.e., local participation and resource contributions), responsiveness (meeting actual demand), and sustainability (continuity through innovation and adaptation) (see also Ronan 1993).

To this, we would add the need for two generic process skills—communication and nonadverserial conflict resolution—that help mediate and lubricate organization/environment interaction. The sadc data show that communication and negotiation skills, although not frequently used, did pay dividends in the effective performance of managerial work. In the United States, these process skills are becoming an increasingly important component of capacity building but face the problem of being consensus-based; in U.S. politics—unlike in many African countries—individualism, conflict, and competition establish an institutional environment that favors majority rule (winner takes all) over consensus (Kelman 1991). Achieving consensus means that all stakeholders—public, private, not-for-profit—in a given problem domain continue to work to achieve each stakeholder's interests or until agreement becomes impossible (e.g., Fisher and Ury 1981). Achieving consensus can be a difficult and time-consuming process; furthermore, it may threaten the balance of power in a particular problem domain because it is inclusive of all stakeholders or participants. Interest-based collaborative processes are premised on identifying common ground based on mutual recognition of a shared future, whether economic, cultural, political, or geographic, *and* recognizing the legitimacy of other stakeholders' perceptions and claims. Together, these skills present an opportunity to strengthen the state, to provide a buffer against the tragedy of the state commons.

Our analysis shows both the problems and the promise of African managers. As Leonard (1991:300) observed, the necessary conditions of excellence appear to be political demand for particular services and a professional group sustaining its values. SADC, as a regional organization, may be in a position to provide greater leadership in refocusing the regional political economy toward the national and regional shared interests of intensive growth, particularly since the apartheid regime has finally been dismantled in the Republic of South Africa (see sadc, 1992). A variety of management skills are being used in public organizations, and perhaps it is in this area that technical assistance programs can be of greatest value: replicating successes and identifying, correcting, adapting, and learning from errors (i.e., local experience) may be the best tonic for southern African managers in the decade ahead.

VI.   THE FUTURE OF SKILL DEVELOPMENT IN THE SADC REGION

With regard to skill development in the southern African region, there is evidence that efforts are ongoing in all fronts by the individual member countries of the Community, the SADC organization itself, and several bilateral and multilateral aid organizations worldwide. According to an FY 1997 usaid Congressional Presentation, "perhaps the most striking change in Africa over the last few years has been the emergence of a strong cadre of sophisticated, well-trained, self-confident professionals." The report goes further to suggest that "these men and women are taking charge of the development process and are looking at donors as partners rather than as managers and financiers of development (usaid, Africa Regional, 1997). These views by the usaid underscore the degree of importance attached to the problem of skill development by the southern African countries.

In Namibia, for instance, a recent focus of the USAID has expanded into a comprehensive human resources development strategy which provides for degree-level training in U.S. colleges and universities, and short-term management training. According to the USAID FY 1997 program, "management training and skills development will create more opportunities for the majority population to increase incomes and participate fully in the country's development." (USAID Congressional Presentation FY 1997, Namibia).

Within the context of the USAID efforts, other programs had been launched. The USAID launched the Improved Training Performance and Education/Training Opportunities for Historically Disadvantaged Namibians. The objective of this intervention was to develop various modules for short-term management training programs (up to one year's duration) which will, over the life of the activity, produce some 400 well-trained, highly competent managers in both the public and private sectors, many of whom will, after learning advanced business skills on the job, elect to use this expertise to form their own companies (USAID Congressional Presentation FY 1997).

Finally, the following is a partial listing of areas where skill development efforts are ongoing: training on agricultural research; strengthening policy-analytic capacity for development; linking U.S. expertise and African expertise in a mentoring role; development of improved African analytic capacities for conducting strategic assessments; development of capacity to analyze, accelerate, and rationalize the process of decentralization and devolution of authority; improvement of students' mastery of basic literacy and math skills; strengthening of management at the district and schools level, and ability to decentralize resources; basic education training; skills in environmental education and community-based natural resources management; human resource development, performance appraisal, and organizational structures; training and consultancy; motivation, organization culture, team building, communication, management style, and conflict management; tax planning, finance planning and structuring; project review and supervision. For additional sources of information related to skill development and training in the SADC countries, we offer the following Internet websites:

Country	Internet Address
Angola	www.sadc-usa.net/members/angola/default.html
	www.angola.org/relief/index.htm
Botswana	www.sadc-usa.net/members/botswana/default.html
	www.worldbank.org/html/extdr/offrep/afr/btswbck.htm
Lesotho	www.sadc-usa.net/members/lesotho/default.html
Malawi	www.sadc-usa.net/members/malawai/default.html
Mozambique	www.sadc-usa.net/members/mozambique/default.html
Namibia	www.sadc-usa.net/members/namibia/default.html
SADC Organization	www.nsrc.org
Swaziland	www.sadc-usa.net/members/swaziland/default.html
	www.realnet.co.sz/real/sbyb/tran&com.html
Tanzania	www.sadc-usa.net/members/tanzania/default.html
Zambia	www.sadc-usa.net/members/zambia/default.html
Zimbabwe	www.sadc-usa.net/members/zimbabwe/default.html

ENDNOTES

1. The SADC dataset was obtained from J.D. Montgomery for Umeh's doctoral dissertation. The importance of the dataset—it is one of the most comprehensive collections of the managerial experience in Africa (Montgomery 1991)—and the many questions raised in the course of completing the dissertation have led to the preparation of this paper. The events methodology, the heart of the SADC data,

derived from the "critical incident" procedure which was developed during World War II to determine whether and how training and organizational changes could improve the performance of combat pilots. It has since been employed many times for the purpose of studying human performance in different contexts in the private, professional, military, and civilian sectors. The seminal work in this area is by Flanagan (1949:419–425); for a recent bibliography on the subject, see Fivars (1980).

Data collection proceeded as follows. First, members of the study team interviewed public and private officials during a scheduled site visit. At the time of the interview, 10 permanent secretaries or managing directors or their equivalents, or deputies, were invited to complete a short Management Events Diary listing five or six events that occurred over a period of five to 10 days. The public officials were in large civilian ministries that conducted training (e.g., Health, Personnel, Economic Affairs, Finance, Education, Minerals and Water, Local Government and Lands, Agriculture, Labor and Public Service, Communication and Works, and Trade and Industry; see Montgomery 1986b:212). This procedure called for the description of activities that took an hour or more of the respondent's time, or that seemed important for other reasons.

Next and separately, a questionnaire was administered to groups of officials at different levels; the questionnaire was scheduled in conjunction with a training exercise or official meeting devoted to the discussion of organizational problems, usually held in the capital city. The questionnaire asked for a brief, 20- to 50-word reports describing as specific experience or event associated with either the exercise or absence of a managerial skill or administrative knowledge. The events were to have occurred recently and involve the respondents themselves as well as colleagues, subordinates, and superiors. Montgomery is careful to note that the data collected do not rely on the opinions of the respondents, but rather ask for a narrative of specific events. The data were then coded by 20 students at the Kennedy School of Government. Elsewhere, Montgomery notes that the coding of the data took into account "their impact or outcome as well as their intent or objective" (Montgomery 1986c:17).

2. Regarding timing, there is the assumption that events identified are in fact random because they represent the most recent management activities on the part of the respondents. This fails to take into account of the fact that certain management activities are not randomly distributed throughout the year. Budgeting, planning, and inventory management are examples of managerial events which may be associated with distinct periods of time during the year (see Vengroff 1990). The timing of data collection may have a major influence on the relative frequency with which these types of events appear in the data.

Second, the size of the sample of events and the number of actual respondents may be crucial factor for analytical purposes. Where a relatively small number of individuals are interviewed, the peculiarities of a particular position or individual can become magnified and appear quite important (Leonard 1991). In the case of several of the countries in the SADC study (Malawi, Swaziland, Angola, and Mozambique), a few individuals drawn from a particular service or with a particular interest can grossly distort the findings for that country. This can occur if the individual is either very active in citing cases or somewhat reticent (the average number of instances cited in the SADC study was eight, but the range was from one to 15). Thus, rather than viewing management events in general we may be attaching undue weight to the experiences of relatively few individuals. Finally, there is the issue of intercoder reliability given the nature of the data (i.e., written events) and the number of skill categories (50) and coders (20).

Conceptually, the skill categories, although linking process with performance (positive or negative outcomes indicating the relative effectiveness of management), tend to adopt a tool-oriented, Weberian focus (i.e., the classical bureaucracy). As others have pointed out, using a Western code of administration and a Western skills orientation masks important differences between how we in the West tend to think of administrative management and how African managers administer public affairs (see Rondinelli 1983:116–120; Jones 1989; Caiden 1991; Ronan 1993).

REFERENCES

Ademolekun, L. (1991). Public sector management improvement in sub-Saharan Africa. *Public Administration and Development 11*, 223–227.

Atali, J. (1990). *Millennium.* New York: Random House.

Balogun, M.J. (1989). The role of management training institutions in developing the capacity for economic recovery and long-term growth in Africa. In M.J. Balogun and G. Mutahaba (eds.), *Economic Restructuring and African Public Administration,* (225–238). West Hartford, CT.: Kumarian Press.

Balogun, M.J., and Mutahaba, G. (eds.). (1989). *Economic Restructuring and African Public Administration.* West Hartford, CT.: Kumarian Press.

Blomstrom, M., and Lundhalh, M. (eds.). (1993). *Economic Crisis in Africa: Perspectives on Policy Responses.* New York: Routledge.

Blunt, P., and Jones, M.L. (1992). *Managing Organizations in Africa.* New York: Walter de Gruyter.

Caiden, N.J. (1991). Unanswered questions: planning and budgeting in poor countries revisited. In A. Farazmand (ed.), *Handbook of Comparative and Development Public Administration,* 421–434. New York: Marcel Dekker.

Esman, M. (1974). Administrative doctrine and developmental needs. In E.P. Morgan (ed.), *The Administration of Change in Africa,* 3–26. New York: Dunellen.

Esman, M. (1991). *Management Dimensions in Development.* West Hartford, CT.: Kumarian Press.

Fisher, R., and Ury, W. (1981). *Getting to Yes.* New York: Penguin.

Fivars, G. (1980). *The Critical Incidents Technique: A Bibliography* (2nd ed.). Palo Alto, CA: American Institute for Research.

Flanagan, J. (1949). Critical requirements: a new approach to employee evaluation. *Personnel Psychology 2,* 419–425.

Gulhati, R. (1991). Impasse in Zambia. *Public Administration and Development 11,* 239–244.

Heady, F. (1991). *Public Administration: A Comparative Perspective* (4th ed.). New York: Marcel Dekker.

Hyden, G. (1983). *No Shortcuts to Progress.* London: Heinmann.

Hyden, G. (1992). Governance and the study of politics. In G. Hyden and M. Bratton (eds.), *Governance and Politics in Africa,* 1–26. Boulder, CO: Lynne Rienner.

Jones, M.L. (1989). Management development: an African focus. *International Studies of Management and Organization 19,* 74–90.

Kautsky, J.W. (1972). *The Political Consequences of Modernization.* New York: Basic Books.

Kelman, S. (1992). Advesary and cooperationist institutions for conflict resolution in policymaking. *Journal of Policy Analysis and Management 11*(2), 178–206.

Kiggundu, M. (1989). *Managing Organizations in Developing Countries.* West Hartford, CT: Kumarian Press.

Leonard, D.K. (1987). *The political realities of African management. World Development 15,* 899–910.

Leonard, D.K. (1991). *African Successes.* Berkeley: University of California Press.

McCurdy, H.E. (1977). *Public Administration: A Synthesis.* Menlo Park, CA: Cummings.

Mehretu, A. (1989). *Regional Disparity in Sub-Saharan Africa.* Boulder: Westview.

Mintzberg, H. (1973). *The Nature of Managerial Work.* New York: Harper and Row.

Montgomery, J.D. (1986a). Bureaucratic politics in southern Africa. *Public Administration Review 46*(5), 407–413.

Montgomery, J.D. (1986b). Life at the apex: the function of permanent secretaries in nine southern African countries. *Public Administration and Development 6,* 211–221.

Montgomery, J.D. (1986c). Probing managerial behavior: image and reality. Paper prepared for Annual Meeting of the African Studies Association, Madison, WI, Oct. 29–Nov. 1.

Montgomery, J.D. (1987). How African managers serve developmental goals. *Comparative Politics 20,* 347–360.

Montgomery, J.D. (1991). The strategic environment of public managers in development countries. In A. Farazmand (ed.), *Handbook of Comparative and Development Public Administration,* 511–526. New York: Marcel Dekker.

Morgan, E.P. (1984). Development management and management development. *Rural Africana 18,* 3–15.

Msabaha, I.S.R., and T.M. (eds.). (1987). *Confrontation and Liberation in Southern Africa: Regional Directions after the Nkomati Accord.* Boulder, CO: Westview.

NASPAA. (1985). *Improving Management in Southern Africa: Final Report to the Regional Training Council of the Southern African Development Coordinating Conference.* Washington, DC: National Association of Schools of Public Affairs and Administration.

Nti, J. (1989). The impact of economic crisis on the effectiveness of public service personnel. In M.J. Balogun and G. Mutahaba (eds.), *Economic Restructuring and African Public Administration*, 121–129. West Hartford, CT: Kumarian Press.

Nyang'oro, J. (1989). *The State and Capitalist Development in Africa: Declining Political Economies.* Westport, CT: Praeger.

Picard, L.A., and Garrity, M. (1994a). Improving managerial performance in Africa. In L.A. Picard and M. Garrity (eds.), *Policy Reform for Sustainable Development in Africa: The Institutional Imperative*, 127–149. Boulder, CO: Lynne Reinner.

Picard, L.A., and Garrity, M. (eds.). (1994b). *Policy Reform for Sustainable Development in Africa: The Institutional Imperative.* Boulder, CO: Lynne Reinner.

Picard, L.A., Liviga, A.J., and Garrity, M. (1994). Sustainable policies, management capacity, and institutional development. In L.A. Picard and M. Garrity (eds.), *Policy Reform for Sustainable Development in Africa: The Institutional Imperative*, 113–126. Boulder, CO: Lynne Reinner.

Ronan, N. (1993). Developing the African manager: the good, the bad and the competent. *Management Education and Development 24*(winter), 388–394.

Rondinelli, D.A. (1983). *Development Projects as Policy Experiments.* New York: Methuen.sadc. (1992). *Human Resources: Primary Factor in Development.* Windhoek: Republic of Namibia.

Siddiqui, R.A. (ed.). (1993). *Sub-Saharan Africa: A Subcontinent in Transition.* Brookfield, VT: Ashgate.

Sorenson, G. (1990). *Democracy, Dictatorship and Development.* London: Macmillan.

Thompson, C.B. (1986). *Challenge to Imperialism: The Frontline States in the Liberation of Zimbabwe.* Boulder, CO: Westview.

Umeh, O.J., and Andranovich, G. (1992). Capacity building and development administration in southern Africa. *International Review of Administrative Sciences 58*, 57–70.

usaid Congressional Presentations FY 1997: http://www.info.usaid.gov/pubs/cp97/afr/afrreg.htm

usaid Briefing for the President: Overview. http://www.info.usaid.gov/regions/afr/new_day/overview.htm

usaid Congressional Presentation FY 1997: Namibia:http://www.info.usaid.gov/pubs/cp97/countries/na.htm

Vengroff, R. (1990). Rural development, policy reform, and the assessment of management training needs in Africa: a comparative perspective. *Public Administration Quarterly 14*, 353–375.

Vengroff, R., Belhaj, M., and Ndiaye, M. (1991). The nature of managerial work in the public sector: an African perspective. *Public Administration and Development 11*, 95–110.

White, L.G. (1987). *Ceating Opportunities for Change.* Boulder, CO: Westview.

White, L.G. (1990). Policy reforms in sub-Saharan Africa. *Studies in Comparative International Development 25*, 24–42.

World Bank. (1986). *World Bank Atlas, 1986.* Washington, DC: World Bank.

Youker, R. (1989). Lessons from evaluation in Africa for external funding bodies. In J. Davies, M. Easterby-Smith, S. Mann, and M. Tanton (eds.), *The Challenge to Western Management Development: International Alternatives*, 75–84. New York: Routledge.

Young, C. (1982). *Ideology and Development in Africa.* New Haven, CT: Yale University Press.

35
State Tradition and Public Administration in Iran: Ancient and Contemporary Perspectives

Ali Farazmand   *School of Public Administration, Florida Atlantic University, Fort Lauderdale, Florida*

I. INTRODUCTION

State tradition and public administration have existed ever since the beginning of human civilization. As a bridge land between the Eastern and Western civilizations of the ancient world, Iran has been one of the oldest centers of world civilization and a pioneer in the development of state building, bureaucracy, and public administration. This chapter attempts to present a brief historical discussion of Iranian state and public administration from the earliest time to the present. This essay is mainly drawn from the author's forthcoming book on Iranian civilization, state, and public administration from 6000 B.C. to the present. It is also based on numerous primary and secondary sources, of which some of the better known are cited here—hence a lack of detailed references. The following discussion is organized into three major historical periods of Iranian public administration: the prehistory Susa and the Federal Elamite state (6000–650 B.C.); the ancient Median State and the World-State of the Persian Empire (720 B.C.–651 A.D.); and the Medieval and the Islamic periods under Saljughs, Safavids, and Qajars (651 to the 19th century), and the 20-century modern Iran.

II. ADMINISTRATION OF THE FEDERAL STATE OF ELAM

The earliest experience of state tradition and administrative functions on a massive scale began around 6000 B.C. in Susa. As one of the oldest sites of ancient civilization, Susa began political and administrative life first as a city-state contemporary and rival to Sumer in the Mesopotamia, then as the capital of one of the oldest empires of antiquity, Elam. Established in the late fourth millennium B.C., the Elamite Empire was the first Iranian experience in empire building and state tradition. As a major rival to Sumer, Babylonia, and Assyria, the federated state of Elam practiced public administration in Iran long before the arrival of the Aryans on the Plateau around 1000 B.C. The federal system of Elam was composed of several major kingdoms (the Kassite, the Guti, the Lullubi, Susiana, and Elamite), all being of the same racial group of the pre-Aryan people. The Elamite over-lordship in Susa was the main power of the federated states, the heads of which frequently assembled for political and military purposes. Decision making was based on equality, and cooperation was key to the coordinated system of government in a federal structure. The "golden age" of the united federal Elam was toward the end of the second millennium B.C., when, after a period of decline, the empire enjoyed a renaissance of power and achievement in arts and architectures; one of the federated states, Kassite, conquered and ruled Babylonia for 567 years, and Elam expanded to almost all of Mesopotamia and Asia Minor (*Cambridge Ancient History* CAH-I-1, 1970; CAH-I-2, 1971; Cameron 1968; Farazmand, in press; Ghirshman 1954; Mallowan 1965, Willis 1982).

While internal independence of the member states was respected, intergovernmental relations on civil administration were regulated by various administrative rules and ordinances. Public administration flourished under the 2500 years of the strong federated state of Elam, which made significant contributions to Iranian and world civilizations. The organization of the federated state of Elam was based on two pillars, the military and civil administrations, and there was a generally respected separation of these two functions. The civil administration was headed by a coordinating body of appointed functionaries who discharged the administrative responsibilities of the "federal state" at Susa. This administrative body handled the financial, regulatory, and other civil affairs, and coordinated the intergovernmental relations with the member states in the system. Thus its experience in federalism and intergovernmental relations administration was perhaps the oldest in recorded history (CAH-I-1, 1970; CAH-I-2, 1971; Ghirschman 1954).

Among the major administrative achievements of the Elamite Iran were the development and management of a gigantic system of underground irrigation, *qanats*, an earlier Iranian invention turning an unworked country into an agricultural land; the invention and development of the written language of Elamite and its extensive use in the administration of the federated state; and the construction and maintenance of numerous public enterprises like roads, bridges, cities and towns, communication centers, and economic trade centers with the neighboring states. Elamite Iran was relatively prosperous because of its rich minerals and precious metals, as well as other industries and arts. After all, agriculture, bronze, painted pottery, and perhaps iron were invented and/or discovered in Iran, barley and wheat were also discovered by Iranians, and metallurgical industries were much more advanced on the Plateau than in Mesopotamia or elsewhere. Economic management of Elam had improved along with Babylonia, and the long tradition of state in the federated Elam provided the foundation for the later development of public administration and the establishment of a bureaucracy that became the main institution of governance in the united "World-State" Achaemenid Empire of Persia (*Ibid.*; Farazmand, in press).

III.   THE STATE AND ADMINISTRATION OF THE MEDES

The arrival of the Aryans, a people of Indo-European origin, on the Plateau during the second migration wave at the turn of the first millennium B.C. gradually changed the composition of the native population and of the political power in Iran. This group of young pastoral-agriculturist people slowly assimilated the native Iranians and was destined to change the history of the Near East and the mankind by conquering the known world in a single generation. They established an administrative state that was politically effective and managerially efficient, a system that surpassed any that had existed in antiquity. The first of the two settled branches of this powerful nomadic-pastoral people, the Medes, formed a strong kingdom on the highland of central Iran, and established itself at the capital city of Ecbatana, meaning "place of assembly" (modern Hamadan). The median state soon evolved into a major power, which was destined to capture Nineveh, the capital of the Assyrian empire, and to finish that world power forever in 612 B.C. (Dhalla 1977; Frye 1963, 1975; Olmstead 1948).

And after absorbing completely the federated state of Elam in 600 B.C., it became one of the three major empires of the time, the other two being the Chinese and the Egyptian empires. Thus, in the words of Ghirshman (1954:75), the first half of the first millennium B.C. was "a turning point in human history," for the "center of the 'world politics' of the age shifted," from the watered valleys of the Nile and the Mesopotamia to the less climatically favored region of the north and Iran. The three main players of the drama were the Semitic Assyrians, the Asiatic kingdom of Urartu, and the Iranians, who emerged the most victorious of all and who were destined to dominate the world politics for the next millennium (Ghirshman 1954).

Borrowing from the federal Elam and from the bureaucratic state of Assyira, but making their own original contributions, the Medes also established an empire state, which was superior to Elam and did not have the colonially destructive and bureaucratically oppressive features of the Assyrian empire. Like the federated Elamites, the Iranian Medes also governed Iran by collective system of decision making, though the king's orders were considered final. The magian priests also had a major role in the administration of the state, but it was the established and respected institution of the "collective body" of Aryan warriors in the "place of assembly," *Ecbatana*, that determined the significant political and military decisions of the state. In addition to their remarkable military successes, the Medes are known to have reached a high degree of achievement in state building, in organization and structure of governance, and in administration of state functions (CAH-1-1, 1970; CAH-1-2, 1971; Cameron 1968; Dhalla 1977; Farazmand, in press; Frye 1963, 1975; Ghirshman 1954).

The Medean state was organized on the basis of "kingship" and "administrative efficiency." Economy and efficiency in the administrative processes, record keeping and strict observation of laws and procedural rules, taxation and financial management, departmentation of state functions, and organizational hierarchy and unity of command were among the stressed features of the Medean state and public administration. The bureaucracy grew under the Medean state, and public administration assumed an increasingly large domain in the economy and society, though market economy prospered. The concept of "state" was for the first time in history adopted officially by the Aryans, who later turned that concept into reality. This was especially true under the Achaemenid Empire of Persia. When Cyrus the Great subdued the Medean state, he found an established administrative system that was already developed and experienced, but the state Cyrus had founded required a different organization (Ghirshman 1954).

IV. THE WORLD-STATE OF THE PERSIAN EMPIRE

While the Medean empire was at the zenith of its power and was preparing for conquest of the rest of Mesopotamia, Babylonia, the other branch of the Aryans (Iranians), the Persians, were developing their own kingdom in Parsa (modern Fars) on the plain land of south Iran. Eventually, the Persian forces led by Cyrus II, the Persian King, defeated the Median army in a battle waged and commanded by the Median overlord, Astyages, who had aimed at punishing Cyrus for refusing to denounce an alliance with the last Babylonian prince, Nabunaid. Thus emerged one of the most brilliant leaders of antiquity, Cyrus the Great, who led the young and vigorous Persians in their "turn on the conquest of the world" (Ghirshman 1954:113). The Achaemenid Persian Empire founded by Cyrus the Great and expanded by Darius was the largest and greatest empire the world had ever known. It governed for more than two centuries (559–329 B.C.) 47 different nations and states, which stretched from India in the east to Europe and north Africa in the west, a vast territory covering virtually the entire known world, except the isolated China—hence a "World Empire." Included in the Empire were Mesopotamia, Babylonia, Asia Minor, Greek cities and islands, Egypt and North Africa, India, and Europe. How was such a huge, world empire governed and what was its administrative system like?

Cyrus was very much conscious of the settled civilizations of some of the conquered peoples, and sought to create a "synthesis of ancient civilizations" aimed at uniting all the human world. He adopted a liberal policy of tolerance and of universal treatment of different nationalities on the basis of laws, and of granting the right to local self-government to conquered peoples. The administrative achievement of the Achaemenid Empire bears no resemblance to that of the earlier Assyrians who destroyed the conquered nations and their peoples' costumes, or the later Romans who forced conquered peoples to "adapt themselves to the common culture and to participate in the collective economy" (Ghirshman 1954:126).

Unlike the Romans, the Achaemenid Persians governed the Empire by a well-organized administrative state and based on a number of liberal principles that were original and innovative. Cyrus used the Medean expertise of state building and administrative practice, and adopted in principle the organization of the Assyrian empire, but made significant innovations in the administrative system of the Empire. He created a system of *satrapy*, an enormous territory including several nations and peoples, at the head which governed a satrap appointed by the Great King, or King of Kings, from the capital Susa. He divided the entire Empire into 23 satrapies, a territory that was maintained under Darius and his successors. Also, one of the most significant innovations of the Achaemenid Persians was that, like the Medes, they conceived of Iran as a "state" and "turned that concept into a reality" (Ghirshman 1954:127). The adopted concept of "state" replaced the concepts of nation, kingdom, and the like, and reference to the "state of the united world" was the key to the administration of the diverse peoples of the Empire: hence the concept of the one "world-state" of the Achaemenids. The Persian tradition of collective decision making continued under Cyrus and the "college of seven princes" may date from this period, a "collective" body of decision making that functioned as a "royal council" for selection of the right successor to the king and in the strategic governance of the united state of Persia. While Cyrus was a great conqueror and organizer, Darius was an outstanding administrator and financier who had great interest in administrative details and in managerial efficiency (Ghirshman 1954:128; Frye 1963, 1975; Olmstead 1948).

A.   The Satrapy and the Bureaucracy

The administrative system of the Achaemenid World State was politically effective and managerially efficient. This was especially true under the great reformer Darius onward. This was achieved through the satrapal system of governance and the centralized bureaucracy of the state. The satrapal system of administration in the united state was based on several principles and institutions of political control. These principles included religious and cultural tolerance, centralization combined with a sufficient degree of decentralization, multiplicity of institutional control, equality of peoples before the law, divine status of the Great King as also the head of the united state, and the standardization of the state functions and administrative processes. The satrapal system was based on five major institutions of government. At the center of the system was the satrap—meaning the protector of the realm—appointed by the Great King from the central government in Susa. The satrap was granted a broad range of authorities, powers, and responsibilities. He ruled a vast territory covering different nations and peoples, even monarchies, and was surrounded by a miniature court of his own. He was the highest judicial authority and the head of the state administration in the satrapy. However, he had to refer decisions on policy issues to Susa. His responsibilities included maintenance of law and order, oversight of general administration, collection of taxes, mobilization and supply of military forces for wars and defense, maintenance of the universal postal and communication routes, building and maintenance of public works, managing intergovernmental affairs with both the central government and other satrapies, and dealing with the neighboring satrapies on political and military matters. Toward the end of the Empire, the satraps also assumed military powers of the state, but their widest functions remained in civil administration, and periodic reorganization of the state resulted in subdivision or consolidation of certain satrapies, an administrative practice that was mainly based on the consideration of personality and influence of certain satraps as well as on financial and geographical criteria.

To forestall any possible disaffection and revolt, Darius added four other institutions of checks and balances to the system of satrapy. These included an independent commander-in-chief of the armed forces, an "eyes of the king" who performed as a "state attorney" in legal matters, and an "ears of the king" performing as an "inspector general of the state," all being independent from each other and appointed by the central government; they also reported to the central government. The latter institution was highly admired by monarchs of the ancient world, and was adopted by Charlemagne, the first Holy Emperor of Rome to secure "cohesion between the various parts of his empire" more than 1000 years later (Ghirshman 1954:144). To this multiple system of administration was added the fifth institution, the periodical examiners of the state or representatives of the Great King who gave unexpected visits to administrators and reported any corruptions and mismanagement in the satrapies to the central government. The central government was obviously administered by a huge bureaucracy that was centrally organized and extended throughout the entire empire. It maintained an effective system of coordination and control over the administrative institutions and processes of the satrapies.

The administrative capital of the state was Susa and the religious, ceremonial, or dynastic center was Persepolis, while Ecbatana (modern Hamadan), Babylon, and other major cities served as commercial, strategic, or provincial capitals. Elamite, Akkadian or Aramaic, and the Old Persian language of cuneiform script written on clay tablets were the main languages, but Elamite and Aramaic continued to dominate the bureaucracy while the cuneiform script (Old Persian) served mainly royal purposes. The bureaucracy grew rapidly in terms of number of personnel and various functions and processes. This resulted in the development of a highly educated castelike group of scribes or strata of bureaucrats who promoted "closed-union" features of their organization to the outside world. "Everywhere the armies of the great king went, there the Achaemenid bureaucracy was planted with all of the combatants of administration—military, financial, and judicial—and communication with other provinces and [satrapies] was insured by the official language" (Frye 1963:97). This bureaucracy and administrative state performed several major administrative functions of the united state. But the legal and administrative reforms of Darius made fundamental changes in the economy and society of the Empire, as well as in the administrative state that was assigned to govern it. The following is a highlighted account of Darius's reforms.

B. The Administrative Reforms of Darius

Darius's reforms were comprehensive, with far-reaching consequences. These reforms in the governance system of the Achaemenid world state covered the main areas of postal service and communication, taxation, economic management and financial administration, legal affairs and justice administration, and local government. The communication system was developed to keep the central administration in constant touch with the satrapies, and to disseminate information necessary for the administration of the state. A system of roads was founded and expanded that linked all parts of the Empire to Susa, and it was "excellently maintained and secured," as Herodotus describes it. The roads were measured in *parasángs* (=3³/₄ miles). The most famous of these roads was the royal highroad connecting Susa to Sardis in Europe, which, like other roads, had posting stations at regular intervals with well-maintained inns and caravansarais, and with garrisons at various stations. These roads also served the innovative system of riding postal services, though it was used mainly for royal and administrative purposes. The riding messengers were ready on all stations, where by day and night and under all weather conditions they rode swift horses and delivered messages. While the normal travellers took about 90 days to travel the Sardis—Susa road, the riding messengers passed it in less than a week. The couriers were all state employees and were paid by the state. Although the postal network was used primarily for government communication, private and commercial ends were also served. In addition to the developed network of road communication, sea transportation was extensively used since Darius's time, when the world's first and largest oceanic navigation was carried out from the Hindus to the African shores and the Mediterranean via the Red Sea and the Suez Canal, which was built under Darius (Ghirshman 1954; Frye 1963; Olmstead 1948).

Rarely among ancient monarchs do we find rulers like Darius "who so thoroughly understood that the successful state must rest on a sound economic foundation" (Olmstead 1948:185). Darius's economic and tax reforms included fiscal and monetary reforms affecting the tax structure, public finance, price system, and the banking and financial institutions throughout the united State of Persia. For the first time in the Near East a fixed taxation system was administered and stabilized, and the weights and measures were standardized with great details. Lands were carefully surveyed and individual and collective income taxes were collected, as well as a wide range of other taxes and tributes. These included municipal and public enterprise taxes, tolls on major roads and waterways, taxes on harbors and market places, animal taxes, property taxes, and the like. Tributes were also fixed on conquered satrapies. Also, the economy was stabilized and flourished under the Achaemenids, whose monetary reforms affected the price and interest rate systems guided by the state (Olmstead 1948:185–194; Frye 1963; Ghirshman 1954).

In this connection, a universal coinage system was established and, through an emphasized policy of rapid urbanization, a monetary economy developed and replaced the barter system to a great extent. Gold and silver coins were used mainly for military, political, and administrative purposes, while copper coins were used for various economic activities. While gold was rare and gold coins, *darics*, could be coined only by the Great King, silver and copper coins were minted by major satraps for payment to soldiers and for commercial and public administration purposes. The general term for tax was the Old Persian *baji*, the tax collector was *bajikárá*, and the central treasury was at Susa and Ecbatana. Accountants, *hamarakárá*, and treasurers, *ganzabárá*, were carefully selected and well paid. While an individualized market system was promoted and free enterprise flourished in banking and commercial activities, state regulations stabilized and monitored the whole economy. As a result, economy and society prospered during the two centuries of peaceful government of the Empire. Banking activities expanded on a large scale for the first time in the ancient world, and the number of bankers proliferated. The two most famous banking houses of Marashu and Sons and of Egibi operating in Babylon only were but two examples. However, over-taxation often caused hardship and misery for the peasantry, who carried the largest financial burden in the Empire, and this contributed to the eventual fall of the Empire (*ibid.*).

Darius's legal and judicial reform was probably one of the most famous and recognized elements of the administrative reform package. Like the universal coinage and standardization of weights and measures and the comparative values of prices in the economy, Darius introduced a "Universal Ordinance of Laws" and codes that applied equally throughout the Empire. The Universal Law of Darius recognized no status or favoritism, and was applied by the Persian judges who, according to Herodotus and other Greek sources, never failed to serve universal justice. And as stated in the Bible, "the laws of the Medes and Persians do not change" (Frye 1963:98–103). Although borrowed from the previous Babylonian law of Hamurabi, the Law of Darius was distinctive. Unlike any previous laws, Darius's laws were both comprehensive and universal; they covered almost every aspect of economic, social, political, military, and administrative systems, and were universally applied throughout the entire empire. The Old Persian terms of *dátá* and *dátá-bárá* were used for law and judges respectively, and local judges, *dayyán*, were also used in local court trials. Thus administration of justice constituted an essential component of Darius's administrative reforms, for he believed that justice and fairness were foundations of state stability, and to him only a universal system of law and justice administration could serve that objective. But injustice and repression were not uncommon to observe from time to time after Darius (Frye 1963). The central government was composed of the royal court, the military establishment, and the civil administration headed by the prime minister, *hazárapáti* (meaning "a thousand-leader"). The institution of the Prime Minister became more elaborate and its organizational structure and functions rapidly developed as the Empire became older. He was the closest confident of the royal court and, as the head of the bureaucracy, his authorities and functions were widest in civil administration, though he was also a military advisor to the Great King (*ibid.*; Farazmand, in press).

Local government in the satrapies was modeled on the central government and its administrative structure. Similar administrative functions were performed by the local governments within the satrapies, though variations were found in certain local governments in which local traditions and costumes were preserved. As mentioned above, flexibility was allowed in the local government structures and in their leadership selections. Nevertheless, stress was placed on coordinated uniformity and standardization of administrative processes, and the centralized bureaucracy maintained a professionalized system of control and coordination over the satrapal and local bureaucracies. This was a major achievement of the administrative state of the empire, which was almost entirely adopted by the following Selucid, Parthian, and Sasanian empires. Thus, despite the temporary interruption caused by the Macedonian invasion, the "Golden Age of Persia" continued to dominate the world politics and society, only to be followed by the more glorious fame of the Sasanian state (*ibid.*).

The Achaemenid bureaucracy or administrative state was a centralized system of administration that had major political, socioeconomic, and administrative orientations. It was by far the most organized and best administrated system of institutionalized governance in a huge scale of the ancient time. This system of administration remained intact after the fall of the Empire to Alexander the Great, who invaded Persia and destroyed Persepolis, but married the natives, was conquered by the Persians' rich culture, and became Persianized himself. The Persian system of administration was adopted with few modifications and remained in operation throughout the 467 years of the following Parthian Empire (240 B.C.–227 A.D.). The Parthian Iran was a decentralized state characterized by administrative fragmentation, bureaucratic dispersion, numerous official titles, poor central coordination, and decreased efficiency in financial system of administration. However, the decentralized and powerful state of Parthia also provided great flexibility to its satrapal and local systems of government, which functioned with major administrative autonomy and with speed inspired by the Great Seven Noble Families who inflicted several military defeats on the Roman empire and who actually chose the kings of the Parthian Empire. The powerful state of Parthia was a world power and a major rival to Rome militarily and economically. This status was achieved especially after the major defeat of the Romans under the command of counsul Crassus by the forces of a Persian noble, Suren, who "put Parthia on an equal if not superior plane with Rome in the minds of men from the Mediterranean to the Indus" (Debevoise 1983:93). Unlike many Roman governors who "had mistreated the subject peoples," the "Parthian administration" was generally popular, especially under Pacarus (Debevoise 1938:116–117), making the Parthian state a powerful rival to Rome only to be followed by a more formidable state, the Sasanian Empire (Debevoise 1938; Frye 1963, 1975; Ghirshman 1954; Olmstead 1948).

V. THE SASANIAN STATE AND ADMINISTRATION

The Sasanian Empire was a highly centralized state with a highly advanced system of administration and with a developed organization of economy and society. It was indeed a bureaucratic empire with an efficient administrative state, which, after its fall in 651 A.D., became the model state for the following Islamic Empire (Eisenstadt 1963; Frye 1963). It is impossible to even summarize adequately the main features of the Sasanian administrative state here. Suffice it to say that virtually the entire world was divided between the world's two greatest empires of Sasanian Iran and Rome. Despite their military and political rivalries, the two superpowers entered from time to time into treaties and pacts for common defense against invading barbarians and for economic cooperation. The economy and society were regulated, and the state had maintained monopoly over a number of developed industries and commercial enterprises, while agricultural and other economic activities were privately operated. During the 428 years of the Sasanian "golden age" the economy and society prospered, science and technology advanced, medical training and university education system (the medical school attached to the Gondi Shapur University) were established and promoted, military science advanced, and religion and public administration gained major strength and extended their domains. The Persians made significant contributions to the theory and practice of state and government, a legacy that has benefited not only Iran and the Islamic empire, but also the modern nation-states of the West as well as the Middle East (CAH-I-1, 1970; CAH-I-2, 1971; Farazmand, in press; Frye 1963, 1975; Ghirshman 1954; Olmstead 1948; Dhalla 1977).

The Sasanian state adopted the Achaemenid system of administration and bureaucracy and advanced it through its own original contributions in the theory and practice of state and government, and in administration and management. This was done through several government reorganizations and administrative reforms. The most famous reforming kings of the Sasanian House were Shapur and Anushirvan, who showed great interest in administrative efficiency of the state. The following is a short listing of some of the highly advanced characteristics of the Sasanian administrative system:

1.   The formal stratification of society resulted in the division of the population into four estates: religious classes, warriors, the bureaucracy, and peasants. Zoroastrianism of the Achaemenid Iran became an official state religion, and the bureaucracy and professionals gained high status in society. The administrative class grew larger and along with the religious leaders played a powerful role in the Empire. While the *mobad mobadán* was the "highest priest," the *vazurg farmandár* was the "Grand Vizier," or prime minister who was recruited from the same professional "administrative class" (Dhalla 1977; Frye 1963, 1975; Ghirshman 1954; Lambton 1980:VII-3; Olmstead 1948).

2.   The royal court was highly organized and staffed with various professional people, and "the splendour and pomp exhibited by the Sasanian court was not equaled by any royal court of the time" (Dhalla 1977:312–313). In this court several new administrative and legislative structures developed, which were then adopted throughout the empire (Frye 1963, 1975; Ghirshman 1954; Olmstead 1948).

3.   A council of state (cabinet) was created as part of the reorganization of the bureaucracy, as well as the laws of tax reform, which added new additions to Darius's fiscal administration. The council had a consultative role and consisted of governors, high-ranking military generals, the strategic administrative elite, and the royal princes who included a number, but not all, of the nobility. This was because most of the Sasanian kings tried to weaken the power of the independent nobility and to centralize the political and administrative control of the state throughout the empire (Olmstead 1948).

4.   The reorganized bureaucracy extended its domain as the Empire expanded and public administration functions increased in scope, size, and complexity. The number of functional departments or ministries was increased and included the Office of the Prime Minister or chief executive, *vazurg farmandár*; the Ministry of State, headed by the Secretary of State, *dapiran mahist* or *Iran dapirát*; the joint Commander-in-Chief of armed forces, *arteshtárán sálár* or *Iran*

sipahát; and the Ministry of Agriculture, headed by the *vastryosán salár*, who also controlled commerce, labor, and similar departments. He was also called the *huokhshapát*. These departments or ministries were well organized on the bases of functional specialization and of increased professionalization of the state, and several central agencies coordinated the functions and activities of the respective departments of the bureaucracy at satrapal and local levels. This system of public bureaucracy and administration became the "prototype of the *Diváns* or ministries" under the Abbasid empire, which, like its predecessors, had completely adopted the Sasanian state structure and administrative system centuries after the fall of the Persian Empire in 651 (Olmstead 1948).

5.   The well-institutionalized office of the prime minister and the council of ministers (cabinet) were developed, and assumed major legislative and policy functions for the state and bureaucracy. The prime minister also headed the cabinet and was a key adviser to the Great King in domestic and foreign affairs.

6.   The satrapies remained as the main organizational division of the empire until the seventh century, when some changes were introduced in the system. The earlier names of satrapy and satrap were replaced by *ostán* and *ostandár* (the modern Iranian provincial governor-general bearing the same title *ostandár*) and *marzpán* (mainly for the border satrapies or ostáns), and subdivision within ostáns or satrapies became more common with county governors and district/local governors at their heads. These governors were called *shahrikáns* or *dehkháns*, and had tremendous amount of power in local affairs. In still other cases, consolidation resulted in the creation of a Grand Marzpán supervising several *marzpáns* in, for example, Khurasán, while present-day Iraq, or the Lakhmid province, was headed by one *marzpán*. This reorganized system of administrative distribution of the empire and its names and titles have remained mainly unchanged throughout the history of Iran, and is still the basis of political and administrative organization of the modern Iranian state. The later reorganization of the state under Khosrow Anushirvan divided the expanded empire into four major administrative districts created at four corners of the state. Several large satrapies or ostáns were consolidated together and were then headed by a vice-king who supervised the *marzpáns* and *ostandárs* or satraps, and reported directly to the Great King. While this new administrative reorganization was intended primarily for military consolidation of the empire, the arrangement centralized further the administrative system of the state and its gigantic bureaucracy which had established itself throughout the four corners of the realm (Olmstead 1948; Farazmand, in press).

7.   The name *Iranshahr* was adopted the official name for Sasanaian Iran, which included Iran and non-Iran satrapies. The capital was in Ctesiphon (Middle Persian: *Tyspwn*) in southwest Iran, and was called the "heart of Iranshahr." The official language of the bureaucracy was the Middle Persian *Pahlavi* or *Dari*, which continued to be in use in the bureaucracy of the Islamic caliphate for centuries (Olmstead 1948; Eisenstadt 1963).

8.   The bureaucracy became the most powerful institution of government after the army, and later in the empire it sought and exercised autonomy and ruled the state. Its system of personnel recruitment, promotion, and compensation was professionalized, and the bureaucracy extended its domain far from the capital, expanding to huge public enterprises. These large public projects and enterprises were established mainly for managerial efficiency and organizational improvement, and operated in the areas of irrigation and energy, postal services, communication and roads, municipal management, tax collection, and the like. In essence, they covered a wide range of economic sectors in urban and rural areas, for the state was the largest employer and had monopolized most of the industrial, agrarian, commercial, and social activities in society. They also took charge of certain military-related functions across the borders of the empire—for example, the many defensive walls, *khandaghs*, built in the frontiers against the nomadic raids in the north and the west, and between the Caucasus mountains and the Caspean Sea, where the most

famous of these walls were built and maintained against the invading barbarians. As part of a pact with Iran, the Byzantine Empire frequently "paid large sums of money to Iran as part of the cost of maintaining the forts and fortifications in the Caucasus against inroads of Huns" (Frye 1963:14, 225; Eisenstadt 1963).

9. The financial administration was also reformed under Anushirvan, who also changed the tax system and had the lands surveyed and registered under the farmers' names. Fixed taxation on individuals and collective entities were levied, and crops and industrial products were taxed, but priests and bureaucrats were exempt. Other taxes included the ones collected under the Achaemenid state. Coinage was used, gold and silver coins were circulated widely, and the money economy was highly advanced as rapid urbanization and economic growth continued. This contributed to a further development of the bureaucracy and its political power in society. And as the political authority weakened and or became repressive by overtaxation toward the end of the Empire, the bureaucratic abuse of power increased. The urban workers as well as the peasantry carried the burden of hardship (Frye 1963; Ghirshman 1954; Olmstead 1948).

10. The Sasanian legislative system was developed and the judicial administration became more complex. The collective system of policymaking at the top of the government and by the council of ministers functioning under the general supervision of the kings of Sasan was the major institution of legislation, along with the Zoroastrian religious institutions, which exercised a great deal of judicial power in society. The earlier Persian "collective body of warriors" or "royal council" also continued to play an important legislative role in the Sasanian state, but its power diminished at times when increased centralization of state power was pursued in full force. This resulted in increased power for the bureaucracy. In the area of the judiciary, the role of the religious leaders, *mobadán*, and their law book, *Avesta*, was pervasive after the judicial powers of the King and his appointed judges. Judicial administration and court trials became more elaborate, and major improvements were achieved over the Achaemenid system. But religious heresies were not tolerated and were dealt with cruelly. The best example of this was the brutal massacre of 500,000 adherents of the popular Mazdakite (Communist) movement in 528 A.D. (Dhalla 1977:321–331; Frye 1963; Ghirshman 1954).

11. The use of a merit system in personnel administration was common for a long time and was emphasized during Kavadh I and Khosrou I. "Strong emphasis on universal values" of administration was prevalent as the power of the aristocracy in imposing patronage demands on the bureaucracy was weakened. The merit system in turn contributed further to the professionalization of the administrative state and stimulated various innovations in the theory and practice of state governance. And as the society achieved a higher degree of structural differentiation, so did the bureaucracy, which attained a high degree of recognition in the stratified social structure and sought autonomy and political power. This also resulted in an increased tendency in the bureaucracy to manifest several orientations, which included self-interest and aggrandizement orientation, servant of the state or community orientation, public service orientation, aristocratic or strong interest orientation, regime/ruler orientation as an oppressive instrument, and professional independent orientation. The latter orientation gave the bureaucracy an image of neutral public servant functioning for judicial-like tasks in society, roles that challenged some autocratic rulers as well as patronage-demanding princes. In this role the bureaucracy served society and upheld ethical and professional codes of behavior, legitimizing its status in society. In short, the administrative state enjoyed several bases of legitimacy, which included (1) its legal and political position in society as the main institution of the state, (2) the rational and professional status gained from its expertise and organizational capacity, (3) the aristocratic support it received from the nobility and other special strata, and (4) the ideology of public service orientation it developed in society (Eisenstadt 1963:153–260; Frye 1963, 1975; Ghirshman 1954).

The increased structural differentiation and functional specialization of the bureaucracy continued at full speed as the society and the governmental responsibilities of the empire became more diffused, expanded, and differentiated. As a result, theoretical contributions to organization and structure of government and to public administration increased and were promoted—hence Persian intellectual contributions to the knowledge of organization theory and public administration (Ghirshman 1954). Cases of this literature are too many to cite here, but some of the major works include the special works of the men of pen, *Dapirán*, the numerous councils to rulers and administrators, *Andarz* books, the numerous "administrative handbooks," and advice to rulers and governors or "Mirrors of Princes." Moreover, the Sasanian law book, *Datastán Namak* (also called the Book of a Thousand Laws), was periodically updated and heavily used in administration of the state. Finally, the prime minister, the *Vazurg farmandár*, who as chief executive of the state heading the bureaucracy, had to be highly educated and knowledgeable in the specialized fields of finance, organization, and administration. His appointment and tenure of office were also contingent upon continuous intellectual contributions of significance to the theory of state and government from within the administrative class. A particular example is the late prime minister Rozbeh, who wrote several treatises on government and, after the fall of the empire in 651 A.D., translated them into Arabic (Ghirshman 1954; Olmstead 1948; CAH-IV 1960).

VI. ADMINISTRATION OF MEDIEVAL ISLAMIC IRAN

Despite the Islamic/Arab conquest of Persia, the Persian administrators, bureaucrats, and scholars continued to make significant contributions to the theory of state and public administration. Since the entire system of Sasanian government and administration was adopted as the "model state" by the Islamic caliphate under the Umay'yeds and Abbasids, the Persian bureaucracy and the Pahlavi language served as the main institutions of administration in the Islamic Empire for centuries. But the Persian bureaucracy and administrators took over virtually the entire Abbasid caliphate, making it more a Persian than Arab system of government. The rise of the Abbasids was followed by a "transformation of the administration and society under the influence of Sasanian tradition" (Lambton 1980:I-407). The "pre-Islamic Persian forms of court etiquette and features of the old Sasanian bureaucracy increased in importance under the Abbasids," to the extent that the question at stake "was not Islam or Iran, but rather a Persianized bureaucratic empire" (Frye 1953:53, 1963, 1975).

Meanwhile, intellectual contributions of Persians to the theory and practice of government and administration continued to grow under Islam, though through the innovated sect of Shia Islam. Some of the most notable Iranian scholars who contributed to political and administrative theories during this period include Ibn-al-Moghaffa (the former Sasanian prime minister Rozbeh), who translated into Arabic his books on politics and administration (*Adab-e-Kabir, Adabe-e-Saghir*, and *Sahabiyeh*); Key Kaous and his *Qabous Nameh*; Mavardi's *Principles of Government*; Ghazzali and his *Theory of Government* and *Counsel of Kings*; Farabi, who is known in history as the second teacher after Aristotle and the first Islamic teacher, and his *The Good City*; the great scientist and philosopher Ibn-e-Sina (Avicenna) and his numerous books and treatises on government and science; Fakhradding-e-Razi and his works; Nasir-al-Din Tusi and his *Nassirian Ethics* (in which he stratified the society into four ordered estates, men of pen, men of the sword, men of affairs, and husbandmen); Najmaddin-e-Razi and his books on government; Hosein Vaez Kashefi and his *Good Ethics of Mohseni*; Al-Tur Tushi and his *Siraj al-Muluk*, emphasizing rule of law; Ibn-al-Balkhi and his *Fars Nama*; and the prime minister under Saljughs (1063–1091 A.D.), Nizam-al-Mulk Tusi, whose *Seyasat Nameh* (Book of Government) and other contributions made him known in Iranian and Islamic history as an "excellent administrator" (Frye 1953:53). Nizam-al-Mulk continued the Sasanian state tradition and initiated "the formation of an administrative class." Some of these works were mirrors of princes inspired from the Sasanian period, while others were on administration and government (for details see Farazmand, in press; Lambton 1980:II-131, VII-3).

Persian bureaucracy continued to control the governments of Iran and Islam for centuries, though it was not as centralized and powerful as it was in the Sasanian and Abbasid times. Changes in rulers usually meant only change in the recipient of taxes, and the bureaucracy was content to continue working for new masters. The Persian renaissance under the Samanids, who revived the sasanian tradition of state and civilization, also contributed to the growth of Iranian administrative theory and practice. But while the devastating Mongolian invasions destroyed much of Iranian civilization in the north, perhaps the most powerful Iranian state since Islam has been the Safavid Empire, which once again revived the glory of the Sasanian state. Established in 1501 and lasting until 1737, the Safavid state made Shia Islam a state religion of Iran, and reorganized the administrative system in which merit principles were introduced to the personnel administration. Once again, public finance, personnel administration, communication systems, and gigantic public works and enterprises received special attention on the agenda of administration in the state.

Like the Achaemenids and Sasanians, the Safavids turned the concept of state into reality. The functions and legacies of public administration under the Safavids are too many to name; the number of public roads, buildings, mosques, transportation and communication systems, ports, educational centers, etc. are too many to name and are still in operation in present day Iran. In addition to the practice of "meritocracy" in the centralized bureaucracy, the local administration under the Safavids was also reformed with a new institution to appear more extensively in Iranian administrative history, though it was founded by the Sasanians. That institution is the *kadkhodá*, the village headman, who had performed as the political and administrative representative of the state in village until the 1960s. The reorganized system of administration and the theory of government under the Safavids also received a number of concepts and terms such as *Arkan-e-Dawlat* (pillars of the state), *Dawlat* (state), *Iitamad-al-Dawla* (the trustee of support or prop of the state, given to the *vazir* who headed the bureaucracy and civil administration), and a well-defined system of cabinet, a council of ministers, composed of up to 11 ministers. The religious institution was incorporated into the bureaucracy, but "there was a movement away from the theocratic state" as the administration of the empire became more elaborate. Again, the increasingly formalized stratification of the society and structural differentiation of the administrative system also resembled that of the Sasanian state (Lambton 1980:III-132; Savory 1980; Farazmand, in press).

After the fall of the Safavids, the bureaucracy continued again to operate and even ruled in times of turmoil and political instability, which governed Iran for several decades until the revival of a powerful Iran under the "Napoleon of Asia," Nader Shah, followed by a period of stagnation under the Qajar dynasty. The highly decentralized state of the Qajars during the 19th century made no improvement in the administrative system of Iran. Indeed, the often destabilized state of the Qajars was highly dependent on a feudal system of economy and society and became the battleground for foreign influence of the West and the East. It lost several major provinces to Russia during the two wars in the nineteenth century. The historical reputation of the Iranian administrative system lost its fame to corruption, patronage, and selling of office, and the ancient principles of efficient administration were pushed to the back seats of the political machine driven by feudal tendencies, royal corruption, and exploitative interferences of imperialist Britain and Russia. Reforms of the two most famous *Sadr-e-Aazams* (prime ministers), Amir Kabir and Mirza Hosein Khan Sepahsalar, to modernize the administrative system, including the religiously controlled judicial administration, failed. These two ingenious and great statesmen lost even their lives to the reform opponents, who had much to gain from the status quo. Thus, while Western Europe was coming out of the age of Feudalism and despotism and was in the process of rapid industrialization, Iran lagged behind politically, economically, and administratively (Farazmand, in press; also see Nashat 1982).

VII. BUREAUCRACY AND ADMINISTRATION IN MODERN IRAN

The Constitutional Revolution of 1905–1911 abolished the absolutist monarchy in Iran and established for the first time a constitutional system of government with a parliamentary legislature and independent judiciary. It gave hopes for democracy and administrative development in twentieth century Iran, but the movement failed badly as Britain and Russia continued their interference in Iranian domestic affairs during World War I, and the rise of the Pahlavi autocracy under Reza Shah killed any possibility of democratic reforms in Iran. Several anti-imperialist and national democratic movements in Gilan, Azerbaijan, and Khurasan were suppressed, all political parties were abolished, and state monopoly of economic and social affairs of the society continued until World War II, when the Nazi sympathizer Reza Shah was forced to abdicate the throne. Under Reza Shah several economic and administrative reforms were introduced, which created in the Western tradition a centralized bureaucracy aimed at controlling the population and at changing the feudal system of economy into a *comprador* capitalist economy linked with the international capital. The centralized bureaucracy attempted to penetrate rural areas through a rural police (*gendarmerie*), not to destroy the feudal power, but rather to reinforce its changed character (Bill 1972; Farazmand 1989; Zonis 1971).

The national democratic movement under premier Mosaddegh, like Amir Kabir of the nineteenth century, was an attempt to revitalize Iranian political and economic independence from foreign influence, but the successful military coup d'état by the American CIA killed that opportunity and installed in Iran the notorious dictatorship of the Shah, who lacked any major legitimacy. Several antiregime and popular movements, including the religious movement of the 1960s led by Ayatollah Khomeini, were suppressed and the Pahlavi autocracy established a highly centralized "bureaucratic state" that was administratively corrupt, managerially inefficient, and politically repressive. But its centralized bureaucracy penetrated all of rural Iran and established for the first time firm control of the state over all the population. The U.S.-consulted agrarian and administrative reforms of the regime in the 1960s and 1970s actually transformed the Iranian economy and society from a relatively independent society into a *comprador* capitalist system of society almost totally dependent on international powers, especially the United States. The administrative reforms created institutional channels for this economic system, and the bureaucracy became the main instrument of "system maintenance and regime enhancement" (Farazmand 1989) and kept "people busy" (Sherwood 1980). Public administration assumed tremendous number of functions, as the state extended its monopoly power in every sectors of economy and society in the thoroughly bureaucratized Iran. The Iranian administrative system was control-oriented and autocratic, and its bureaucracy was a highly developed repressive instrument in the service of the regime and its inner circle elite. While subservient to the Shah, the bureaucracy played a formidable role in the bureaucratic state. It was a powerful institution of dependency through which the economic, social, technological, and cultural dependence on the West was promoted and maintained. The major beneficiaries of this system were the Shah's regime and the military, economic, political, and bureaucratic elites, as well as their Western partners (Cottam 1979; Farazmand 1989; Halliday 1979; Zonis 1971).

The revolution of 1978–79 abolished the system of monarchy in Iran and established an Islamic Republic system of government, which is based on separation of powers and is a combination of parliamentary, presidential, and Islamic systems of government. The revolution also caused several changes in the bureaucracy and administrative system of Iran. In short, public administration in postrevolutionary Iran has also been expanded and strengthened as the theocratic state under the Islamic Republic, which recognizes no separation of religion and politics, has taken over many sectors of the economy and society through nationalization policies, and has paid much attention to political, economic, and administrative independence. But the recent trend of privatization under former President Hashemi Rafsanjani is claimed to solve some of the gigantic problems of economic inefficiency and the growing bureaucratism in administration. Whether or not this controversial policy will succeed to produce positive economic results remain to be seen, for critics argue that it would lead to increased inequality and economic exploitation of the lower classes. Organizational and administrative reforms have received considerable attention, but they have a long way to go. And unless a genuine and fundamental reform is introduced and implemented in the organizational structure and administrative processes, the past and current characteristics of the self-serving bureaucracy will persist and cause major disenchantments and frustrations among the citizenry (for details on the Pahlavi and the Islamic Republic states see Farazmand 1989).

VIII. SUMMARY AND CONCLUSION

As a bridge land between the East and the West, Iranian civilization begins from the earliest time of human civilization. While the tradition of state and public administration has existed since at least 6000 B.C., the real practice of public administration on a state scale began with the federated Empire of Elam around the beginning of the fourth millennium B.C. The arrival of the Aryans on the Plateau in the beginning of the first millennium B.C. changed the history of the entire Near East and the world, and resulted in the establishment of the first "World-State" Empire of the Achaemenid Persia founded by Cyrus the Great. The centralized administrative system of the Persian Empire turned the concept of state into reality and left major legacies and made significant contributions to public administration and political theory. The Parthian and Sasanian states of Iran also continued that tradition, but the Sasanian bureaucratic state made innumerable contributions to the theory of state, government, and public administration. As the two superpowers, the Sasanians and Romans ruled virtually the entire world and developed an administrative state that has left a great many legacies to the following empires and nation-states, including the modern societies. The fall of the Persian Empire to the Islamic caliphate did not stop Persian intellectual and practical contributions in politics and administration; rather they continued that tradition, and indeed captured the new system and Persianized the administration of the Islamic empire. However, this historical original tradition began to decline with the eighteenth century, as foreign influence and domestic despotism gained strength in Iran. Economic dependence and political repression of nineteenth and twentieth century Iran under the Qajars and Pahlavis transformed this country of numerous originalities in politics, administration, and culture into a wasteland of domestic self-interested elites and their Western legitimizing powers. The revolution of 1978–79 was aimed at changing the administrative system of Iran as much as it was against the Pahlavi regime. Despite some major changes that have taken place in the structure and organization of the new state under the Islamic Republic government, fundamental reforms are still needed to improve the Iranian administrative system if socioeconomic development and national independence are ever to be achieved.

   Public administration as it is practiced in Iran today is primarily an ancient Sasanian structure, reformed by the modern Western managerial and organizational principles introduced by the Pahlavi regime, and influenced by Islamic concepts and traditions. The Iranian traditions of state and public administration have thus been transformed from a powerful world-state Empire to a nation-state system of politics and administration. However, Iranians have always been conscious of their past culture, civilization, and glorious past, and the proud feeling of their past is a powerful foundation for their outlook of the future, no matter how unfavorable and undesirable the temporal conditions may be. This is an integral part of the Iranian culture and tradition that has never died for centuries, in spite of the foreign invasions and temporal declines. What was Persia in the ancient time is probably America today, and only history can tell about the distant future. This is how the human civilization has been changed and shaped.

IX. UPDATE ON THE 1990S

A new movement of reform in politics and administration was ushered since the election of the President Mohammad Khatami. Khatami's agenda has been to implement a number of political, administrative, and economic liberalization policies, including massive privatization well beyond most governments have in the world. His proposed Third Five-Year Development Plan (2000–2005) included a comprehensive program of privatization, which, surprisingly, the conservative-controlled National Assembly approved, but the Guardian Council, a higher body of governance, vetoed it for being unconstitutional. It is unlikely that such an extreme measure of policy option would be ratified. But with the return of the legislation to the parliament for revisions, or with the possible intervention of the High Expediency Council in charge of determination of the final fate of legislation as well as other issues cardinal to the political system, a compromise may be reached. However, very few legislation has ever reached the High Council, and the Supreme Leader of the Islamic Republic does not intervene in such administrative, legislative, or judicial policy issues.

The president's administrative reform measures have been totally unclear, except for downsizing and surgical operations often advocated by public choice theorists, and those recommended by the World Bank and International Monetary Fund. His administration has been trying to please the World Bank and IMF for international aid and investment concessions, but the price the country will have to pay would be further increasing dependence on these supragovernmental organizations that take their instructions from the U.S. departments of treasury and state. Yet, contradictions appear in his policies. Indications point to the fact that the president is aware of the social and political consequences of creating massive inequality, labor displacement, and the underprivileged people whose dependence on a gentle public policy is unavoidable in a country that has gone through a dramatic revolution and millions of people have high expectations.

President Khatami came to power on a populist platform backed mostly by intellectuals, university students, landowners in town and country, and liberal or semiliberal forces, but these people all together constitute less than twenty percent of the population. Ignoring the preferences of the majority of the population with labor, peasantry, and lower-class backgrounds would be a fatal mistake, undemocratic, and unfair, and would have serious political consequences for the president as well as for the Republic. This is one reason why many of his reform policies and approaches to administration and economic management are opposed by the traditional forces—both conservative secular and religious authorities, including the Supreme Leader, Ayatullah Khameneii, and many of others in society. Broadening political freedom is very important, but most important—and imperative—is the economic performance and improvements in productivity, employment, production, and general economic welfare for the majority of Iranian citizens.

REFERENCES

Bill, J. *The Politics of Iran: Groups, Classes, and Modernization.* Columbus, OH: Charles Merrill Press, 1972.
Binder, L. *Iran: Political Development in a Changing Society.* Los Angles, CA: University of California

Press, 1962.

The Cambridge Ancient History, IV. The Persian Empire and the West. Cambridge: Cambridge University Press, 1960.

The Cambridge Ancient History, I, Part 1, 3rd ed. Cambridge: Cambridge University Press, 1970.

The Cambridge Ancient History, I, Part 2, 3rd ed. Cambridge: Cambridge University Press, 1971.

Cameron, G.G. *History of Early Iran.* New York: Greenwood Press, 1968.

Cottam, R. *Nationalism in Iran.* Pittsburgh: University of Pittsburgh Press, 1979.

Debevoise, N.C. *A Political History of Parthia.* Chicago: University of Chicago Press, 1938.

Dhalla, M.N. *Zoroastrian Civilization.* New York: AMS Press, 1977.

Eisenstadt, S.N. *The Political Systems of Empires.* New York: Free Press, 1963.

Farazmand, A. *The State, Bureaucracy, and Revolution in Modern Iran*: *Agrarian Reforms and Regime Politics.* New York: Praeger, 1989.

Farazamand, A. *State and Bureaucracy in Persia (Iran)*: *5,000 Years of Public Administration.* New York: Praeger, in press.

Frye, R. *The Golden Age of Persia.* New York: Harper and Row, 1975.

Frye, R. *The Heritage of Persia.* New York: World Publishing Company, 1963.

Frye, R. *Iran.* New York: Henry Holt, 1953.

Ghirshman, R. *Iran: From the Earliest Times to the Islamic Conquest.* New York: Penguin Books, 1954.

Halliday, F. *Dictatorship and Development.* New York: Penguin Books, 1979.

Lambton, A.K.S. (ed.). *Theory and Practice in Medieval Persian Government.* London: Variorum Reprints, 1980.

Mallowan, M.E.L. *Early Mesopotamia and Iran.* London: Thames and Hudson, 1965.

Nashat, G. *The Origins of Modern Reforms in Iran, 1876–80.* Chicago: University of Illinois Press, 1982.

Olmstead, A.T. *History of the Persian Empire*: *The Achaemenid Period.* Chicago: University of Chicago Press, 1948.

Savory, R. *Iran under the Safavids.* Cambridge: Cambridge University Press, 1980.

Sherwood, F. Learning from the Iranian experience. *Public Administration Review 40*:413–421, 1980.

Willis, G. *World Civilization.* Lexington, MA: D.C. Heath, 1982.

Zonis, M. *The Political Elite of Iran.* Princeton, NJ: Princeton University Press, 1971.

36

Reform Managers in Iran

Heros of Civil Society?

Abbas Monavvarian   *Department of Public Administration, State Management Training Centre, Tehran, Iran*

I. INTRODUCTION

Anechiarico (1998) renumerates five elements of civil society: issue nonclosure, coalitional decision, associative emphasis, professional trusteeship, and civil models of reform. He argues that all of the elements are related to public administration. These elements are indicative of civil society in the United States and may not be applicable in other places. However, it seems that at least some of them are necessary to achieve civil society in every country. Among them, reform of public administration is, in this study, under consideration, and is considered necessary to reinforce the civil society.

The connection between administrative (reform) and civil society was an issue on the agenda of the New Public Management (NPM) in the 1960s and 1970s, when social equity and popular empowerment were raised by critics of government management (Fredrickson 1996). More recently, the reinventing government movement has stimulated both interest in and criticism of the impact on civil society of public sector entrepreneurship. Most of the reform rethoric at the end of the century, including privatization and public-private competition, indeed the whole entrepreneurial approach to public administration, is a product of the development of civil society described by Sandel (1996). Therefore in some scenes, it can be argued that reformers, as far as the connection between civil society and administration is considered, can be the heroes of the civil society. Now the question is whether the reformers in Iran were heroes.

II. REVIEW OF THE LITERATURE

Planning, implementation, and coping with change has been, and seems likely to remain, one of the main challenges facing managers in both private and public sectors today (Carnall 1990:2). The management of change is viewed as a complex and difficult area, worthy of special attention and study.

A number of writers have promoted their views of the characteristics of excellent organizations: *Change Masters* by Rosabeth Moss-Kanter (1983) (mostly business enterprises); *In Search of Excellence*, by Peters and Waterman (1982); *A Passion for Excellence* by Peters and Austin (1985); and *Organizational Culture and Leadership* (1992) are a few examples. The authors argue that effectiveness is likely to emerge from organizational cultures which encourage accountability, synergy, cross-cultural skills, managing interfaces, and financial realism (Carnall 1990). The focus of these books is mostly on change in companies and individual organizations. Due to the magnitude of reform at national level, consisting of a network of complicated organizations, the role of reform managers is much more challenging and can be expected to require more effective and different expertise. In addition, since, "the good of public organizations and their programs tend to be multiple, vague, shifting and at times conflicting" (Thomas 1996:13), the public sector reform managers, and in general, the change agents typically face a range of paradoxes, and of apparently conflicting tasks, responsibilities, and priorities.

A.   Different Perspectives on Change Agents

Review of the literature reveals at least three broad perspectives (project management, participative management, and sociological approach) concerning the main agendas of the change agents. The project management literature emphasizes content and control agendas (see for example, Darnell and Dale 1985; Dinsmore 1990; Harrison 1985; Gunton 1990; Birchall 1975; Leech and Turner 1990). Based on the logical-rational approach of this perspective, it has been labelled as 'rational-linear' model of change (such as the logic of rational problem solving).

The participative management approach considers the social process as a central factor to effective change (see for example, Pettigrew 1985; Coch and French 1948; Buchanan 1979; Lawler 1986; Peters 1987). This approach was described by Pettigrew (1985) as the "*truth, trust, love and collaboration approach*" to change. The underlying assumption of the approach is that if people get involved in the process of change, they will feel ownership and more commitment to implement the desired change at its best.

The third approach, that is, the sociological approach, emphasizes the political and cultural nature of the change process (Quinn 1980; Pettigrew 1985, 1987) and seeks to demonstrate how the rational and political dimensions are intertwined (Buchanan and Boddy 1992). The model of the effective change agent emerges from this approach, and "concerns sensitivity to the power and influence of key individuals and groups in the organization, including the change agent(s), and to how patterns of power and influence will be altered by a particular program of change" (Buchanan and Boddy 1992:26).

Whatever approach or perspective is adopted, given the complexity of working as a reform manager, the competence and expertise of people involved in the design and implementation of the reform program is imperative.

Studies of the managerial skills, behaviors, roles, attributes, and competencies linked to effective management practice are extensive (Hunt 1995; Bigelow 1994; Sandwith 1993; Hearn et al. 1996; Hunt and Wallace 1997). However, in regard to "how competences are generated, how they can be identified and how the association between competences and performance can be measured and established" (Kamoche 1997:273), there is not consensus. Hunt and Wallace (1997) identified three perspectives that have thus far influenced the debate surrounding the competence movement:

1.   Competence consists of attributes possessed by individuals, including knowledge, skills, and attributes, all of which are directly measurable and quantifiable based on predetermined categories and criteria (Boyatzis 1982; Klemp and McClelland 1986; Gonczi et al. 1990).

2.   Competence is best viewed as being oriented to tasks in specific situations (National Training Board 1991; Dall'alba and Sandberg 1993). Based on this perspective the attributes of an individual are identified and evaluated precisely as they relate to the demands of specific organizational or job-related tasks.

3.   Competence is best understood in terms of the manner in which the activities and work-related tasks are conceived by the individual (Sandberg 1991).

Defining areas of competence and expertise depends on the given situation (Buchanan and Boddy 1992; Hunt and Wallace 1997). Underpinning this view is the belief that to achieve successful performance entails identifying the organization's core business and strategic activities and resource implications, and then nurturing the required skills and necessary competences. Due to the fact that "public organizations are not always able to articulate their strategic objectives, or to define their productive activities unambiguously" (Kamoche 1997:276), identification of the areas of competence and expertise necessary to reform public bureaucracy is more challenging.

The review of the literature indicates that, despite efforts of managers and academicians to achieve consensus in definition and understanding of the term competence, they do not yet share a common language when talking about skills, attributes, and qualities of effective management performance (Mangham 1986; Slater 1992). There are several definitions of competence (e.g., Boyatzis 1982; Training Commission 1988; Hunt and Wallace 1977; Sandberg 1991; Gonczi et al. 1990). One of the definitions, however, which considered more appropriate to the context of this study, is the one offered by the Training Commission (1988). Based on this definition competence is defined as ability to perform the activities within an occupation which "encompasses organization and planning of work, innovation and coping with nonroutine activities. It includes those qualities of personal effectiveness that are required in the workplace to deal with co-workers, managers and customers" (Training Commission 1988:14).

In the following, by considering the overall context of Iranian public sector and cultural attributes, the expertise of Iranian reform managers is analyzed. The analysis is based on attributes or competences considered more important for the reform managers.

III.   METHOD

A.   Subjects of the Study

The respondents included 174 persons (32 female and 142 male), who all were reform agents in different Iranian public organizations. For the total group of 174 persons, 8 were top managers, 58 were middle managers, 8 were low-level managers, and 96 were nonmanagers (for the rest, position was not recorded). Accumulated experience of managers in any position was 21 to 25 years, 16 to 20 years, and 16 to 20 years respectively for top managers, middle managers, and low-level managers. Also, their experience as reform managers was 11 to 15 years for all managers at different levels.

B.   Measurement

The questions of the self-administered questionnaire are derived from a study by Buchanan and Boddy (1992) which sought to establish the competence of effective change agents, particularly change managers operating with a change program in an environment characterized by "high hassle, high vulnerability."

In summary, the original study revealed five clusters—goal setting, role specification, communications, negotiating skills, and managing up—and 15 attributes as follows:

Goal setting
   1. Sensitivity
   2. Clarity
   3. Flexibility

Roles

    4. Team building
    5. Networking
    6. Tolerance of ambiguity

Communication

    7. Communication
    8. Interpersonal skills
    9. Personal enthusiasm
    10. Stimulating motivation

Negotiation

    11. Selling
    12. Negotiating

Managing up

    13. Political awareness
    14. Influencing
    15. Helicopter perspective

The five clusters and 15 attributes were described as core competences—the "tool kit" of the change/reform managers. It was argued that:

> The core competences are necessary . . . [but] they are not sufficient, in the creation of change agency expertise. The effective change agent is able to deploy these core competences appropriately in context, and is not merely able to display those individual competences separately (Buchanan and Boddy 1992:115).

In the current study, a modified version of the survey was used to analyze the competences of the reform managers in different departments of Iranian government. The survey questions were based on the above-mentioned clusters. However, the questions (or attributes) under each cluster were chosen based on those competences considered more important for the reform managers, in the context of Iranian bureaucracy. Hence, the number of questions (or attributes) was reduced from 30 (in the original study) to 17. The adopted scale was also different from the original one to be able to assess the degree of competences and skills of reform managers: a five-point Likert scale, ranging from 1 (not at all) to 5 (a very great extent), while 3 represents the medium level.[1] Respondents were asked to rate the skills and competences of their immediate supervisors (the person in charge of a reform committee) in terms of the given attributes. The results are summarized in Tables 1 to 5.

IV. ANALYSIS OF FINDINGS

A. Goals

Those involved in a reform program or affected by it, will more probably accept changes if they have a clear, well-communicated picture of the future. If, with any degree of certainty, forecasting of the direction of changes and the probable results would not be possible, those involved in the reform processes will show less commitment and motivation toward the program. It is argued by Buchanan and Boddy (1992:96) that, in setting the reform goals, "clarity is inadequate on its own. The goals and objectives have to be realistic, and have to be seen to be realistic."

Fundamental reform programs inevitably never run as they were planned. Especially for reform of public sector organizations, flexibility of plans is needed even more. Reform managers should expect a series of intractable issues and problems to resolve. Therefore, the reform managers' ability to predict different situations, and have variety of scenarios to revise the prespecified objectives as conditions change, seems necessary.

In addition, every change and reform in any sector can affect other sectors and groups of people. To understand the internal and external effects of any change, it is vital to reduce the resistance to change by insiders, and attract the cooperation of outsiders. This calls for a system perspective to see the effects of changes in a broad scale to gain the advantages of synergy, or cooperation and collaboration.

Table 1 includes the summary of the responses of the survey subjects about the level of expertise of reform managers in regard to the goal setting cluster: clarity of goals, revision of strategies as conditions change, and recognition of implications of changes elsewhere. The mean scores for the items are 3, 2.7, and 3, respectively. The mean score for this cluster (goals) is close to midpoint (M = 2.96, SD = .981). The analysis indicates that 58.6% of the respondents assessed the skills and capabilities of their immediate supervisors at midpoint or below that.

B. Roles

Large-scale reform programs, such as that adopted in the first plan of Iran, typically involve a large number of players, which needed to be formed into organized groups or teams. Hence, team-building abilities of reform managers is necessary if the reform is to be succeed. Together with the clarity of objectives discussed above, a clear idea of what is expected of each person involved in reform projects is among the signs of an organization with "strong culture." Carnall (1990:163) defined a strong organizational culture as "one in which people may have a clearer idea of what is required of them, a clear sense of the objectives being pursued."

In addition, increased commitment to change depends on how well managers succeed in establishing cooperation and collaboration among the team members. Nobody has all necessary skills and competences to change a situation properly; so it is the power of the team that is important, not the separate skills or competences of individuals.

Despite the potential benefits of teamwork, the teams initially established to achieve coordination and cooperation, may often result in greater conflict and frustration rather than cooperation (Sims 1986). To prevent such a conflict, reform managers are required to posses a high competency in management of team(s) and to establish effective working groups.

The aforementioned skills and competences are classified under the "roles" cluster. Table 2 includes the items related to this cluster. The respondents were asked to rate the skills and competences of their immediate supervisors regarding clarification of responsibilities inside and outside of the organization, and cooperation of various groups working on the given reform program. The summary of the responses are shown in Table 2. The mean scores for the three competences listed

Table 1 Goals: Assessment of Skills and Competences of Reform Managers (% and mean)

Skills and competences	1[a]	2	3	4	5	Mean
Ability to get agreement on clear and accepted goals	6.9%	27.6%	25.3%	25.3%	12.6%	3
Revision of strategies as conditions change	13.8%	33.3%	24.1%	23%	5.7%	2.7
Recognizing the implication of changes elsewhere	4.6%	26.4%	36.8%	23%	9.2%	3

[a]1, *not at all*; 5, *to a great extent*; 3, *a moderate extent*.

Table 2   Roles: Assessment of Skills and Competences of Reform Managers (% and mean)

Skills and competences	1[a]	2	3	4	5	Mean
Early clarification of who was responsible for each part of the job	16.1%	27.6%	26.4%	21.8%	8%	2.8
Ensuring other staff understand their own roles adequately	10.3%	24.1%	37.9%	23%	3.4%	2.8
Ensuring that various groups working on the change worked well together	12.6%	26.4%	40.2%	18.4%	2.3%	2.7

[a]1, *not at all*; 5, *to a great extent*; 3, *a moderate extent.*

under the roles cluster are 2.8, 2.8, and 2.7, respectively, leading to the aggregate mean of 2.8 for the cluster.

C.   Communication

Effective communication and consideration of interests of all affected groups are preconditions for commitment of interest groups. Such involvement helps people understand the change, and gives the participants confidence that management is trying its best to make use of different ideas. Also, the communication skills of the reform managers to transmit effectively to all stakeholders the need for changes in project goals, and in every individual tasks and responsibilities are very important. Motivated stakeholders can have a multiplier effect on the change initiatives. Their optimism and assurance, communicated to the rest of the members and stakeholders will encourage them to persevere during chaotic or painful periods in the reform efforts.

Lippitt et al. (1985:111) believe that "the most important element contributing to success is the art and act of communicating." The entry from the diary of the Logic Manager Electronics depicted in Buchanan and Boddy (1992:101) also illustrates the importance of communication and some problems of ineffective communication:

> Good communication and the involvement of representatives from all affected groups are mandatory for commitment. Also, politics is more likely to be a factor if communication is not handled efficiently. If strategy is left to filter through, problems will result. Individuals with perceived positions of power can impose their own strategies to achieve their own political desires. Communication is vital. More information should be made available to more people at all levels. Especially important is the ability to be able to listen to ideas from lower levels in the organization.

However, based on Table 3, the mean score for the communication cluster is 2.6 ($SD = .848$), indicating that Iranian reform managers during the period of first development plan did not possess an effective communication ability to exchange the ideas, inform all affected groups and staff, understand the reasons for change, and so on.

One possible explanation for low rates of competency of reform managers in communication (as well as team building) attributed by their subordinates, is the individualistic culture dominant In Iranian society, and in public organizations as well. According to Grint (1995:170): "Individualistic cultures . . . have a leadership style that is authoritative, if not necessarily authoritarian. It takes the gap that exists between subordinate and superordinate as crucial to the maintenance of the entire system and rejects participatory developments by the subordinates."

Table 3 Communication: Assessment of Skills and Competences of Reform Managers (% and mean)

Skills and competences	1[a]	2	3	4	5	Mean
Activity seeking information about changes affecting the concerned reform	11.5%	39.1%	26.4%	18.4%	4.6%	2.4
Ensuring all departments involved know what is expected of them	8.1%	34.9%	40.7%	14%	2.3%	2.6
Ensuring staff understand the reasons for the change	12.9%	34.1%	38.8%	12.9%	1.2%	2.6
Improving communication between different people involved in the change	17.2%	25.3%	33.3%	23%	1.1%	2.8

[a]1, *not at all*; 5, *to a great extent*; 3, *a moderate extent.*

D. Negotiation

Development and communication of a clear image of the future, according to Beckhard and Harris (1977), is one of the first and most critical step for managing the reform programs. During the period of fundamental reforms, which normally takes a long time, resistance and confusion frequently develop, because people are unclear about what the future state will be like. Thus the goals and purposes of the reform become blurred, and individual and group expectancies get formed on the basis of information that is frequently erroneous. In the absence of a clear picture of the future, rumors develop, people design their own fantasies, and they act on them. So, together with development of a clear picture and image of the future, it is important to communicate information to those involved in the change or affected by it. The information could include about what the future state will be like, how the reform will come about, why the change is being implemented, and how the people affected see benefits of value to them.

Negotiation skill includes the competency of selling ideas to get the agreement of interested parties about targets and objectives. Peter Kean (1981) argues that the change agent should rely on face-to-face interaction to sell, influence, and otherwise persuade other members of the organization to accept change. This skill and communication, motivation, and conflict resolution are called by Buchanan and Boddy (1992) "soft" skills or competences which are intangible, invisible, and unquantifiable abilities that in many organizational settings undervalued but that are critical nevertheless.

The results of survey analysis, concerning the negotiation skills of reform managers summarized in Table 4, indicates that the subjects assessed the negotiation skills and competence of

Table 4 Negotiation: Assessment of Skills and Competences of Reform Managers (% and mean)

Skills and competences	1[a]	2	3	4	5	Mean
Ensuring people affected see benefits of value to them	12.6%	33.3%	35.6%	11.5%	6.9%	3
Ensuring other staff understand their own roles adequately	8%	27.9%	24.4%	27.9%	11.6%	2.8
Ensuring that various groups working on the change worked well together	6.9%	33.3%	25.3%	28.7%	5.7%	2.9

[a]1, *not at all*; 5, *to a great extent*; 3, *a moderate extent.*

their immediate supervisors, below the midpoint (mean = 2.9, *SD* = .849). It might mean, the reform managers developed their negotiation skills at slightly below moderate level, which was not enough to sell the reform ideas properly.

E. Managing Up

Managing up, according to Buchanan and Boddy (1992:108), "incorporates aspects of the other four clusters, but represents the exercise of those competences in a different and significant contex, but merits allocating to a distinct category." It is argued that one of the most important tasks of reform managers is managing people with widely different and changing values and expectations (Devine 1988). In the absence of this integrative role, "the divergent style groups . . . form cohesive norms and set up strong resistance to integration" (Schroder 1994:112). To build such an integrative competency calls for awareness that agreement among different interests is necessary if the reform program is to be succeed.

Working as a reform manager, when fundamental changes of the system under consideration are necessary, calls for competence in marshalling support for reform. In addition, in fundamental reforms, challenging existing political and cultural considerations is inevitable. The goals of the reformists may not always be seen as consistent with the goals of other stakeholders or players in the system and may in some circumstances be regarded as suspect. As Pettigrew (1985:443) explains:

> The content of strategic change is thus ultimately a product of a legitimization process shaped by political, cultural considerations, though often expressed in rational/analytical term. This recognition that intervening in an organization to create strategic change is likely to be a challenge to the dominant ideology, culture, and systems of meaning and interpretation, as well as the structures, priorities, and power relationships of the organization, makes it clear why and how the processes of sensing, justifying, creating, and stabilizing strategic change can be so tortuous and long.

Therefore, the reform manager, *inter alia*, is expected to (1) consider the impacts of any change of the attitudes on all stakeholders, (2) reinforce establishing consensus and agreement among different interests to enjoy the benefits of collective support of key players, and (3) posses a wide, broad, and long-term vision, and a "helicopter"[2] perspective to visualize how all the dimensions of the reform program fit together.

The results of survey analysis, in regard to the "managing-up" skills of reform managers summarized in Table 5 indicate that the subjects assessed the skills and competences of their

Table 5 Managing up: Assessment of Skills and Competences of Reform Managers (% and mean)

Skills and competences	1[a]	2	3	4	5	Mean
Anticipating how one decision or change can affect people's attitudes to the whole change	6.9	36.8	28.7	23	3.4	3
Awareness that agreement among different interests is necessary	8	28.7	33.3	25.3	4.6	3.1
Ability to visualize how all the dimensions of the project fit together	9.2	29.9	21.8	35.6	2.3	3

[a]1, *not at all*; 5, *to a great extent*; 3, *a moderate extent.*

immediate supervisors, at midpoint (mean = 3, *SD* = .881). It means that the reform managers, based on the perceptions of their staff developed their negotiation skills at moderate level.

The summary of findings regarding the overall skills and competences of reform managers, based on five specified clusters, is shown in Table 6.

F.   Correlation Between Expertise Factors and Reform Program Dimensions

The correlation analysis between the overall expertise of the reform managers and success/failure of reform program indicates that there is a statistical relationship between these two (multi)variables (χ^2 = 11.15525; *df* = 2, *p* = .00378). The phi coefficient of 0.25320 (*p* = .00378) indicates that the correlation is statistically significant. By considering the huge number of factors affecting the results of a reform program at national level, it could be said that the correlation is moderate.[3]

It could be said that, the more the competencies of reform managers, other things equal, the more the probability of success of reform programs. This is consistent with the results of the study of Schroder (1994:110) on managerial competence and style that "the organizational effectiveness will be highest . . . when managers possess the competencies to perform the tasks demanded by their jobs and the climate of their organization. . . ." To find the details and direction of relationships between expertise of reform managers and (success of) the reform program, to provide the reform managers and decision makers a useful guide, factor analysis of the items would be necessary.

The 17 items of the questionnaire related to the level of skills and competences of reform managers were factor-analyzed. The data reduction led to only two factors, which explained 67.7% percent of the total variance (Table 7). Examination of the items of factors suggested the following descriptive titles:

1.   Factor 1: Coordination

This factor (alpha .93) with eigen value of 10.47, which is representative of 61.6 variance, is considered as the most important factor. The factor, as its title indicates, is related to items in relation to coordination between and among different groups, and ensuring that all the involved people, groups, and departments understand their roles, know what is expected of them, understand the reasons of change, and see benefits of value of them.

2.   Factor 2: Prediction-Based Management

This factor (alpha .92) is composed of items related to the prediction capability of managers in different areas. Items such as anticipating the effect of one decision or change on the attitudes of people, visualizing how all the dimensions of the project fit together, and recognizing the implications of change elsewhere, are categorized under the second factor. Also the factor includes items relating to revision of strategies whenever conditions change, negotiating new arrangements to cope with temporary difficulties and early clarification of who is responsible for each part of the job.

Table 6   Summary of Results of Analysis of Competencies of Reform Managers

Goals		Roles		Communication		Negotiation		Managing up		Overall	
Mean	SD	Mean	SD	Mean	SD	Mean	SD	Mean	SD	Mean	SD
2.96	.981	2.8	.92	2.6	.85	2.9	.85	3	.88	2.8	.88

Table 7 Results of Factor Analysis (Varimax) for Competence of
Reform Managers

Items	Factor 1	Factor 2	h[a]
6	.87		.60
7	.80		.64
8	.76		.67
5	.74		.73
9	.73		.68
15	.68		.74
12	.60		.61
10	.59		.70
11	.59		.59
17		.78	.72
3		.76	.77
2		.72	.67
14		.70	.58
13		.66	.76
4		.65	.62
1		.62	.73
16		.57	72
Eigenvalues	10.5	1.03	
percentage of variance	61.6	6.1	

[a]h = communalities.

Table 8 Correlation Between Expertise and Reform Program Scales

	Expertise dimensions	
Reform program dimensions	Coordination	Prediction-based management
Training and Research	.16 (.032)*	.14 (.014)
Simplicity and Capacity Building	.23 (.002)**	.28 (.001)*
Participation and Delegation	.27 (.001)*	.24 (.002)*
Pay System-Performance Dependency	.09 (.225)	.06 (.42)
Procedures and Coordination	−.10 (.18)	−.08 (.31)

*p < .05; **p < .01.

Table 8 represents the relationship between expertise factors and reform program dimensions. The results (Table 8) reveal that relationships between "Training and Research" and both factors of expertise are statistically significant ($r = .16$, $p < .05$; and $r = 0.14$, $p < .05$, respectively). It may mean that accomplishment of the items (or goals) included in the training-and-research factor is associated with (and is in need of) both coordination and prediction-based management of reform managers.

The "Simplicity and Capacity Building" dimension of the reform program is significantly related to "Coordination" ($r = 0.23$, $p < .01$) and "Prediction-Based Management" ($r = 0.28$, $p < .01$) factors. The correlation coefficient at the case of Prediction-Based Management is the highest, and indicative of its importance. The results indicate that accomplishment of goals related to simple procedures and rules and regulations, and also goals related to capacity building in the Iranian public sector are significantly related to both types of expertise of reform managers.

Based on the results presented in Table 8, the relationships between the Participation and Delegation dimension of reform programs and two factors of reform managers' expertise are also significant and positive ($r = .27$, $p < .01$; and $r = .24$, $p < .01$, respectively). The relationships between the other two factors of reform program and two dimensions of reform managers expertise are not statistically significant. The analysis of correlation between the whole reform program and the factors of expertise indicates that the program has significant correlations with both factors of the expertise (see Fig. 1).

VI. LIMITATIONS

The analysis presented in this chapter may have some limitations. The first limitation may arise from the difference between intended and actual point of reference. The study intended to receive the perceptions of the respondents about the expertise of their immediate managers. However, since most of the respondents, together with working as agent of reform, had other positions, too, they might have been described the skills and competences of supervisors other than reform managers. This limitation can cause disparity in the unit of analysis on which an individual is asked to focus.

The next limitation may arise from the adopted measurement. As explained, the questions for measurement of expertise of reform managers derived from the study of Buchanan and Boddy (1992), which sought to establish the competence of effective change agents at organizational level. Nevertheless, the intention of the current study is to measure the expertise of reform managers working at the national level. So, although the selected questions include those attributes, probably, the most appropriate ones for subjects of the study, it seems the limitation still exists.

VII. SUMMARY AND DISCUSSION

The questions in section 3 of the questionnaire were designed to assess the skills and competences of reform managers, in regard to five clusters—goals, roles, communication, negotiation, and managing up. Possession of core skills and competencies analyzed here is "equivalent to possession of the right tool kit—which does not necessarily mean that one is able to use the tools effectively to do the job" (Buchanan and Boddy 1992:7). Also it is argued that the expertise of the change agent includes not only the tool kit, but also the diagnostic, evaluative, and judgmental capabilities required to use the tool kit effectively.

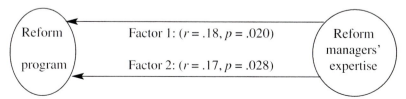

Figure 1 Correlation between expertise factors and reform program.

It is presumed that the effective change agent is the one who is able to deploy those core competencies appropriately in context—the process of change varies from context to context—and is not just able to deploy those individual competencies separately. Therefore, it is the ability of change/reform managers to use the tool kit appropriately that counts, not so much the possession of the foregoing or any other collection of attributes.

Based on the definition adopted, competence is ability to perform the activities within an occupation which encompasses organization and planning of work, innovation, and coping with nonroutine activities. It includes those qualities of personal effectiveness that are required in the workplace to deal with coworkers, managers and customers (Training Commission 1988:14). With this definition, it is expected of the reform managers to be able to use the tool kit appropriately to: deal properly with their coworkers (other reform managers and reform agents); establish a team work and improve their commitments; deal in an appropriate manner with their own managers to receive political support; and deal in a well-ordered manner with the clients and customers (the general public or other organizations) to satisfy their needs and requirements.

The findings of the study, however, indicate that the reform managers, according to the perceptions of their subordinates, did not have enough expertise or core competences to shape, manage, or socially construct the reform process through which the public organizations were moved. In other words, during the period under consideration, their staff thought they did not acquire enough interpersonal, social, organizational, and political skills to implement changes according to the original expectations. The findings reveal that the reform managers had, on average, considerable years of experience as follows: accumulated experience of managers in any position was 21 to 25 years, 16 to 20 years, and 16 to 20 years respectively for top managers (N = 8), middle managers (N = 58), and low-level managers (N = 8). Also, their experience as reform managers was also considerable: 11 to 15 years for all managers at different levels. It means that almost all managers had more than one decade of experience working as "reform agent." Theoretically this could have been a bountiful time for them to acquire the core competencies discussed above, through training or experience (even through trial and error method).

The overall result of analysis of the responses of reform agents about the competencies and skills of reform managers, however, reveals that, the reform manager's capability to implement the objectives of reform programs was regarded slightly below the middle point (average score for all studied skills and competence was 2.8). Theoretically it could be possible to assess the skills of reform managers slightly below acceptable level (midpoint as criterion). The reform program in Iran was expected to bring about fundamental changes in all aspects of the administrative system and in the values of the bureaucrats to cope with the new expectation of the general public. Therefore, setting a minimum yardstick for evaluation of expertise of reform managers is contradictory with the expectations and specified goals. But, even at this minimum level, too, the acquired level of competence was not satisfactory.

The overall result of analysis of success rate of reform program and the expertise of reform managers indicates that the reform managers not only did not acquire enough skills and capabilities, they were also apparently unable to use the tool kit effectively. It may mean that if the reform managers want to be the heroes in the civil society of Iran, they should improve their competencies or leave their positions and let other people with more skills and expertise substitute them.

ENDNOTES

1. In the survey conducted by Buchanan and Boddy (1992), respondents were asked to rate the contribution to project success of thirty different skills and competences. The scales used were rated as *very helpful*, *somewhat helpful*, and *not at all helpful*.

2. The term is borrowed from Buchanan and Boddy (1992:107). It is explained that "from a helicopter one obtains, first a good overview of the ground directly beneath and, second, a good forward view of the horizon."

3. Some statistics texts provide arbitrary rules for evaluating the magnitude of a correlation coefficient, such as: "a correlation that is less than 0.30 is small, a correlation that is between 0.30 and 0.70 is moderate, a correlation that is between 0.70 and 0.90 is large, and a correlation that is greater than 0.90 is very large." Although such rules provide general guidelines to interpretation, they can be misleading in many specific situations. To tell whether a correlation coefficient is large or small, you have to know what is typical (Jaeger 1983).

REFERENCES

Anechiarico, F. (1998). Administrative culture and civil society: a comparative perspective. *Administration and Society 30*(1), 13–35.

Beckhard, R., and Harris, R. (1977). Organizational transitions: managing complex change. In D. Buchanan and D. Boddy (eds.), *The Expertise of the Change Agent: Public Performance and Backstage Activity.* New York: Prentice-Hall.

Bigelow, J. (1994). International skills for managers. *Asia Pacific Journal of Human Resources 32*(1), 1–10.

Birchall, D. (1975). *Job Design.* Gower: Aldershot.

Boyatzis, R. (1982). *The Competent Manager.* New York: Wiley and Sons.

Boyatzis, R. (1982). The role of management training institutes in developing capacity for economic recovery and long-term growth in Africa. In M.J. Balogun and G. Mutahaba (eds.), *Economic Restructuring and African Public Administration.* Hartford, CT: Kumarian Press.

Buchanan, A.D. (1979). The development of job design theories and techniques. In D. Buchanan and D. Boddy (eds.), *The Expertise of the Change Agent: Public Performance and Backstage Activity.* New York: Prentice-Hall.

D. Buchanan and D. Boddy (eds.), *The Expertise of the Change Agent: Public Performance and Backstage Activity.* New York: Prentice-Hall.

Carnall, C.A. (1990). *Managing Change in Organizations.* London: Prentice Hall International.

Coch, I., and French, J.R.P. (1948). Overcoming resistance to change. *Human Relations 1*, 512–532.

Dall'alba, G., and Sandberg, J. (1993). A competency-based approach to education and training. *Herdsa News 15*(1), 57–71.

Darnell, H., and Dale, M.W. (1985). Total project management: an integrated approach to the management of capital investment projects in industry. In D. Buchanan and D. Boddy (eds.), *The Expertise of the Change Agent: Public Performance and Backstage Activity.* New York: Prentice-Hall.

Devine, M. (1988). Flexibility's the aim for the global manager. In D. Buchanan and D. Boddy (eds.), *The Expertise of the Change Agent: Public Performance and Backstage Activity.* New York: Prentice-Hall.

Dinsmore, P.C. (1990). *Human Factors in Project Management*, 2nd ed. New York: American Management Association.

Gonczi, A., Hager, P., and Oliver, I. (1990). *Establishing Competency-Based Standards in the Professions.* National Office of Overseas Skill Recognition, Research Paper No. 1. Canberra: AGPS.

Grint, K. (1995). *Management: A Sociological Introduction.* Polity Press.

Gunton, T. (1990). Inside information technology: a practical guide to management issues. In D. Buchanan and D. Boddy (eds.), *The Expertise of the Change Agent: Public Performance and Backstage Activity.* New York: Prentice-Hall.

Harrison, F.L. (1985). *Advanced Project Management*, 2nd ed. Gower: Aldershot.

Hearn, G. Close, A., Smith, B., and Southey, G. (1996). Defining generic professional competencies in Australia: towards a framework for professional development. *Asian Pacific Journal of Human Resources 34*(1), 44–62.

Hunt, J. (1995). *Key Components in the Development of Senior Executives in Australia.* Executive Development and Leadership Report: 1995. Sydney: Excelsior Pacific Management Consultants.

Hunt, J.B., and Wallace, J. (1997). A competency-based approach to assessing managerial performance in the Australian context. *Asian Pacific Journal of Human Resources 35*(2), 52–66.

Itami, H. (1987). *Mobilizing Invisible Assets.* Cambridge, MA: Harvard University Press.

Jaeger, R.M. (1983). *Statistics: A Spectator Sport.* Sage Publications.

Kamoche, K. (1997). Competence-creation in the African public sector. *International Journal of Public Sector Management 10*(4), 268–278.

Kanter, R. (1983). *The Change Masters.* London: George Allen and Unwin.

Kean, P. (1981). Information systems and organizational change. In D. Buchanan and D. Boddy (eds.), *The Expertise of the Change Agent: Public Performance and Backstage Activity.* New York: Prentice-Hall.

Klemp, G., and McClelland, D. (1986). What characterizes intelligent functioning among senior managers? In R. Stemberg and K. Wagner (eds.), *Practical Intelligence: Nature and Origins of Competence in the Everyday Wordls.* Boston: Cambridge University Press.

Lawler, E.E. (1986). *High Involvement Manager: Participate Strategies for Improving Organizational Performance.* San Fransisco: Jossey-Bass.

Leech, D.J., and Turner, B.T. (1990). *Project Management for Profit.* Ellis Horwood.

Lippitt, G.L., Langseth, P., and Mossop, J. (1985). *Implementing Organizational Change.* Jossey-Bass.

Mangham, I. (1986). In search of competence. *Journal of General Management 12*(2), 5–10.

National Training Board (1991). *National Competency Standards: Policy and Guidelines.* Canberra: AGPS. Occasional Paper 91.4. Melbourne: ERADU.

Peters, T. (1987). *Thriving on Chaos: Handbook for a Managerial Revolution.* London: Macmillan.

Peters, T., and Austin, N. (1985). *A Passion for Excellence.* New York: Random House.

Peters, T., and Waterman, R.H. (1982). *In Search of Excellence.* New York: Harper and Row.

Pettigrew, A.M. (1985). *The Awakening Giant: Continuity and Change in ICI.* Oxford: Basil Blackwell.

Pettigrew, A.M. (1987). Context and action in the transformation of the firm. In D. Buchanan and D. Boddy (eds.), *The Expertise of the Change Agent: Public Performance and Backstage Activity.* New York: Prentice-Hall.

Quinn, J.B. (1980). *Strategies for Change: Logical Incrementalism.* Homewood, IL: Richard D. Irwin.

Sandberg, J. (1991). Competence as intentional achievement: a phenomenographic study.

Sandwith, P. (1993). A hierarchy of management training requirements: the competency domain model. *Public Personnel Management 22*(1), 43–62.

Schein, E.H. (1992). *Organizational Culture and Leadership*, 2nd ed. Jossey-Bass Management Series and the Jossey-Bass Social and Behavioral Science Series.

Schroder, H.M. (1994). Managerial competence and style. In K. Michael (ed.), *Adaptors and Innovators: Styles of Creativity and Problem Solving.* Routledge.

Sims, D. (1986). Interorganization: some problems of multiorganizational teams. *Personnel Review 15*, 27–31.

Slater, W. (1992). The preparation of a generic list of supervisory management skills and the feasibility of defining and assessing these skills as competencies. Australian Institute of Management, SA.

Training Commission (1988). Classifying the components of management competences. In D. Buchanan and D. Boddy (eds.), *The Expertise of the Change Agent: Public Performance and Backstage Activity.* New York: Prentice-Hall, p. 14.

37

Bureaucrats as Agents of Development in the Middle East

John G. Merriam   *Department of Political Science, Bowling Green State University, Bowling Green, Ohio*

I. INTRODUCTION

The state in the Middle East is the principal means by which the society is guided toward development (Heady 1984:257). Bureaucracies are called upon to provide regulatory and service functions to plan and implement essential, far-reaching socioeconomic programs. Mobilist regimes have generated unmet demands on an unprecedented scale. If the bureaucracy does not provide adequate services the populace will be resentful and the political system possibly destabilized by alienation rooted in economic shortages and dislocation, thus undermining ambitious long-range plans for modernization.

The term "modernization" as used here is interchangeable with "development," with the stipulation that true modernization comprises meaningful, beneficial, in-phase, integrated socioeconomic and political change. The term is not merely synonymous with economic growth, which cannot take place over the long term without appropriate evolution in the administrative structures and genuine pluralism for the growing number of "moderns."

With typically authoritarian, centralist traditions, the bureaucracy rather than the underdeveloped private sector is crucial to development; yet a private sector role may emerge in the countries under study here. Most but by no means all of these states, fueled by inflows from oil revenues, high aid flows, or long-term loans, look to their bureaucracies to implement far-reaching plans. (For a survey of the civil service in Middle Eastern countries, consult Appendix 1).

II. ROLE OF THE STATE

Bureaucracies are agents of the state, which by definition is the political structure that has supreme civil authority and political power, and serves as the basis of government of a people permanently occupying a defined territory and possessing an organization politically subordinate to a sovereign government.

A distinction should be made between the state and state elites, those chosen or self-designated definers of development goals. The state, while shaping and directing the society, cannot help but be shaped in turn by societal, economic, political, and historical processes. Bureaucratic tradition may better explain public behavior when there is an established civil service tradition as in Turkey (Heper 1987:12).

The state according to Anderson (1987) is "an analytically distinct actor," but to what extent it succeeds in achieving and maintaining "autonomous capability" may depend on exogenous challenges. To achieve order within its territory and to implement its development goals, a state requires an ongoing administrative capability, a military to maintain security and protect against foreign threats, and the institutionalized means for collecting and disbursing monies to achieve these ends.

Middle Eastern states here range from those beneficiaries of the historical legacy bequeathed by the quintessential Ottoman Empire to countries today that are barely states in name. In the modern context the nation-state, not empire, is the norm, but the Ottoman legacy remains relevant if in vestigial form (Anderson 1987:1–3). The Middle East is broadly defined here as stretching from Morocco in the west to Pakistan in the east and extending north to Turkey and as far south as the Sudan. Excluded in this essay are Iran, Israel, and Libya. Future studies may wish to include these countries and, as research opportunities and the public dissemination of information become available, the newly independent Caspian region states. Although most Middle Eastern countries are covered here, an emphasis has been placed on Egypt.

The energy-rich Caspian states, for example, vary in "stateness," as do other states in the Middle East. This term looks to the quality of statehood. "Strong" states may be conceptually distinguished from "weak" states (Rosenau 1988:15). Following the Ottoman legacy of centralized administration, of which modern Turkey and Egypt are examples, strong states are "statist" or "parastatal" and can extract resources from, and provide services to, the population. Revenue-surplus states, whether from petroleum or other sources (functionally the distinction is not significant), form exceptions. Citizens now look to the state for services well beyond the basic maintenance of physical security, thus increasing opportunities for administrative penetration (downward flow) but also the generation of popular demands (upward flow).

The bureaucracy is necessarily subordinate to the political leadership in matters considered crucial to regime enhancement, legitimacy, and survival. Bureaucracy, however, will play some role, whether positively or negatively, in rule making or determining policy outcomes. Strong states will preempt the rule-making function; strong bureaucracies will affect policy making.

III. PUBLIC BUREAUCRACY DEFINED

The administrative civil service comprises part of the public bureaucracy in which may be included the public sector and even the state companies. The military, a bureaucracy unto itself, is normally quite distinct; yet it may assume administrative tasks, particularly if there is a large peacetime standing army as in Egypt.

Aid from the United States and some other Western industrial states often requires as an implicit precondition an enthusiastic endorsement of privatization with its marketplace panacea (Esman 1988:127). The very antitheses of state dominance, privatization may be viewed by some Middle Eastern elites as an alien concept to which more lip service than genuine commitment is displayed.

The role of the private sector in Egypt, for example, continues to be substantial, although one should distinguish between large-scale and small-scale, stall-type enterprises. The public sector continues to be of major importance in the post-Nasser era, if difficult to define. It may include the joint public sector *infitah*, private *infitah*, and joint foreign-private ventures, among others (Moench 1988:181). The *infitah* was Sadat's economic "opening" to foreign trade and investment. Egypt's labor force in 1983 is shown in Table 1.

Table 1 Labor Force, Egypt, 1983 (in hundreds)

	Government	Public sector	Private	Informal, private	Total
Urban					
Male	11,058	8,525	21,975	3,997	45,555
Female	4,674	1,211	2,918	1,957	10,760
Total	15,732	9,736	24,893	5,954	56,315
Rural					
Male	7,626	3,317	41,930	3,170	56,083
Female	764	128	9,142	955	10,989
Total	8,390	3,445	51,112	4,125	67,072
Total					
Male	18,684	11,842	63,945	7,167	101,638
Female	5,438	1,339	12,060	2,912	21,749
Total	24,122	13,181	76,005	10,079	123,387

Source: CAPMAS [Center for Public Mobilisation and Statistics], *Bath al-amalat bil'einat* (Study of the Labor Force in the Arab Republic of Egypt according to the results of the May, 1983 Survey). In Arabic. Cairo: CAPMAS, 1985, p. 50.

While it is agreed that the Egyptian economy is dominated by a somewhat inefficient public sector, the private sector must also be faulted as it has made "minimal commitment to the long-term development of the state" (Leila et al. 1986:325). If the public sector is to continue to regulate and dominate, restructuring is essential.

The public sector is an extension of the administrative structure. By definition it pursues pubic policy objectives by means of majority ownership and/or control of nonfinancial public enterprises involved in the production and sale of market goods and services, and also by means of majority ownership and/or control to public financial institutions. In sum, the governmental institutions, the nonfinancial public enterprises, and the public financial institutions constitute the public sector and are the means to achievement of public policy objectives (International Monetary Fund 1987:iii). (For comparative purposes, central government expenditures as a percentage of GNP for the countries of the Middle East are provided in Table 2.

IV. BUREAUCRATIC PROLIFERATION

Accompanying the phenomenon of the preponderance of the state is the proliferation of bureaucratic structures. The vast increases in the number of administrative personnel have often exceeded the rate of population increase.

The Ottoman and, in its own right, the Egyptian models amended by colonial experiences of the recent past have provided a base for the increases. Egyptians, Pakistanis, and Palestinians, for example, often provide expatriate expertise to the newer states with less-developed structures. As exporters of their bureaucratic systems, these itinerant resource persons provide a transfer of knowledge and the justification for expansion. Indigenous bureaucrats themselves may have studied abroad, coming back with foreign models convinced that more bureaucratic proliferation is better. Increasingly, these aspiring civil servants are receiving training at home country institutions, however.

Are enlarged bureaucracies the means to and the guarantor of development? Most Middle East countries go beyond controlling the population to the provision of services and the longer

Table 2 Central Government Expenditure, 1985*

Middle East countries	Defense	Education	Health	Housing, amenities, soc. sec., welfare	Economic services	Other	Total expenditure (percentage of GNP)
Bahrain	n/a	n/a	n/a	n/a	n/a	n/a	n/a
Egypt, Arab Republic	17.5	10.6	2.4	14.4	7.9	47.1	48.1
Iran, Islamic Republic	10.2	16.2	7.4	13.3	25.0	28.0	30.8[†]
Iraq	n/a	n/a	n/a	n/a	n/a	n/a	n/a
Israel	27.8	7.1	3.5	3.5	5.4	36.0	97.6
Jordan	27.7	11.3	4.2	14.5	24.8	17.5	42.9
Kuwait	14.6	11.6	6.5	17.9	26.6	22.8	43.1
Lebanon	n/a	n/a	n/a	n/a	n/a	n/a	n/a
Libya	n/a	n/a	n/a	n/a	n/a	n/a	n/a
Morocco	14.9	19.2	3.1	7.0	25.8	30.1	33.5
Oman	43.0	7.7	4.2	1.5	23.3	20.3	62.1
Pakistan	n/a	n/a	n/a	n/a	n/a	n/a	n/a
Qatar	n/a	n/a	n/a	n/a	n/a	n/a	n/a
Saudi Arabia	n/a	n/a	n/a	n/a	n/a	n/a	n/a
Sudan	24.1[†]	9.3[†]	5.4[†]	15.8[†]	15.8[†]	44.1[†]	19.2[†]
Syrian Arab Republic	37.2[†]	11.3[†]	1.4[†]	3.6[†]	39.9[†]	6.7[†]	28.8[†]
Tunisia	7.9	14.3	6.5	12.4	33.1	25.7	40.4
Turkey	10.9	10.0	1.8	3.6	19.6	54.1	25.7
United Arab Emirates	45.3	9.7	6.2	5.0	5.1	28.7	16.3
Yemen, Arab Republic	30.1	20.6	4.4	n/a	8.7	36.1	33.3
Yemen, PDR	n/a	n/a	n/a	n/a	n/a	n/a	n/a

*Figures in italics are for years other than those specified. Data may not reflect current realities but are nevertheless provided for comparative purposes.

[†]1972 figures.

Source: World Bank (1987:246–247).

term state-held development goals. Some argue (Ayubi 1986:201) that excessive bureaucratization may be the barrier, not the means, to true development (as opposed to mere growth). Nevertheless, the widespread enthusiasm for development administration seems boundless, justified or not. Appropriately, Egypt has a minister for development administration.

Excessive numbers are on the face of it irrational, and much has been written about the example of the Egyptian government being the "employer of last resort." But Ayubi, citing Saudi Arabia as well as Egypt, notes that public employment is a "political safety valve" (Ayubi 1988:22). The underlying, unexpressed hiring rationale may be politically motivated cooptation and control of would-be dissidents. Yet economic reality does impinge, for the Egyptian government has implemented a delayed-entry program. Some will find employment elsewhere, but all too many will continue to look to the central government.

Notwithstanding the tradition of a major government role, perceptions are mixed. Despite the almost omnipresent examples, big government has not always been regarded in Esman's words as the "beneficent instrument" by the targeted population. The state's agenda was to be carried out by a dedicated elite who understood with almost Rousseauian self-assuredness the true will of the people. Certainly, this "transforming minority" (Esman 1988:125) has penetrated traditional insularity to affect individuals in new and unprecedented ways.

Or at least that has been the design exemplified by Egypt's Gamal Abdul Nasser, though less so by his successors Anwar Sadat and Hosni Mubarak. Modern elites under the guidance of the state and such strong-willed leaders of the past as Mustafa Kemal Ataturk may force the pace of modernization by increasing public spending levels and the numbers of administrative personnel to do their will, but with little attention paid to the stressed institutions and the radicalized political environment.

Larger numbers do not always translate into greater societal impact, however. The sporadic harshness and arbitrariness of "forced draft modernization" may be tempered by less than thorough bureaucratic implementation, a lack explainable as much by administrative inertia as by the self-serving bureaucratic desire to preserve their corporate interests. A retreat from big government purportedly characterizes the recent decades. The call by well-intentioned foreign intervenors is for decentralization, presumably in the name of efficiency and in keeping with the global economic liberalization trend, and for a democratic antidote for Middle Eastern authoritarianism.

Disillusionment and mistrust of central bureaucracies have not resulted in widespread displacement by local problem solvers. Nevertheless, even as the number of upper-level state bureaucrats has grown, some increase and genuine development have taken place at the provincial or village council level. There the "elders" can often be quite rational in mobilizing local resources, bypassing the provincial governor if need be, to interact with the national level authorities. Conversely, local elites may resist disruptive reforms mandated from above.

V. BUREAUCRATS AS AGENTS OF DEVELOPMENT

Bureaucrats, however narrowly or broadly defined, are increasingly viewed as agents of development by modernizing mobilist regimes. Indeed, their expansion may in large part be justified in terms of their redefined roles. Bureaucrats not only administer laws but in the absence of parliamentary institutions usually do much to create them (Halpern 1963:340 et seq.). In fact, while legislative bodies are by no means uncommon, they may be periodically suspended as in the case of Kuwait or not play an assertive role as in Egypt.

Well-established bureaucracies like Egypt's but also states such as Saudi Arabia forced the pace of modernization. Development can be aid driven or oil revenue driven. For Halpern

(1963:340), bureaucracies play a multifunctional role: "They not only license, supervise and tax, but also often organize and manage agriculture enterprises." Permanently in place they certainly seem to be, but whether they possess the expert and effective cadre requires individual country assessment. It is generally agreed that development goals necessitate new kinds of orientation and, above all, training in the fields of economics and politics—to which should be added sociology. New directions can have unmitigated societal consequences.

Saudi Arabia is illustrative, for it does not have the long bureaucratic tradition of Turkey or Egypt. As an oil revenue surplus rentier state, it has not evolved with well-developed procedures for collecting tax monies, unlike more normal bureaucracies. Nevertheless, the Saudi bureaucracy needs to develop structures and procedures adequate for massive disbursements. A survey of bureaucrats found them quite aware of shortcomings in performance in a less than fully supportive "motivational climate," particularly in the intermediate and lower echelons. Chackerian and Shadukhi (1983:319) noted "an overconcentration of authority at the top of administrative hierarchies and a passionate avoidance of responsibility at the bottom, mismatches between position requirements and training, a lack of trust between administrators and the public. . . ."

Studies find fault with many bureaucracies, and the Saudi bureaucracy is no exception, but Max Weber, against whom all bureaucratic performance, Western and non-Western, seems to be judged, recognized that his model was an ideal seldom if ever reached. Bureaucracies in such countries as Saudi Arabia do for the most part manage to function despite well-founded criticism. The same survey more positively recognizes that "While workers are not highly motivated, they do seem to be responsive to demands from their superiors. Hierarchical information flows are quite effective" (Chackerian and Shadukhi 1983:319, 221).

In sum, bureaucrats whose justification depends in part on an expanded role as agents of modernization may prove to be inadequate, or even obstacles to development, if internal contradictions compounded by external pressures are not resolved.

VI.   THE MILITARY AND THE BUREAUCRACY

Some Middle Eastern states have turned to a sector with its own bureaucratic base, one relatively free of traditions inhabiting development. Nevertheless, modernizing military juntas in order to effect their goals may establish a symbiotic relationship with the civilian bureaucracy (La Palombara 1963:31).

When Egypt's Nasser came to power after the 1952 revolution he recognized that the military would have to work with, and in the process control, the bureaucracy by staffing key positions with army officers. To make up for deficiencies in training, officers went back to school for management degrees.

Egypt's military went much further under the direction of Field Marshall Abu Ghazala, the minister of defense, branching out in nonmilitary areas as well as in joint private business-military-industrial ventures. In a more conventional mode, Egypt's military manufactures arms and has joint overseas ventures (Springborg 1987:11). The military's administrative structures and powerful leadership overshadow (and preempt) the president and the state's civilian administrative apparatus; they, too, are agents of development.

VII.   DEVELOPMENT-ORIENTED REGIMES COMPARED

Looking at Turkey, Tunisia, Egypt, Algeria, and Syria in earlier years, Tahtinen (1973) examined the role of the single party in the modernization process. His observations together with appropriate updates are instructive. Nasser seemed to be on the path of party-induced modernization. The regime did build a party, named after the 1962 Arab Socialist Union, but it "never achieved much autonomy or assumed many real functions" (Hinnebusch 1985:19), unlike some other Middle Eastern polities. Tahtinen affirmed that a military regime cannot achieve large-scale modernization without a dominant single-party system, but appeared to contradict himself by noting in the Egyptian case the alliance with the bureaucracy and the placing of officers in key administrative posts, as much for control purposes as to guide modernization. In Egypt, with its well-established bureaucracy, the party, whether yesterday's ASU or today's ruling National Democratic party, is not the catalyst.

Administrative development in Turkey underwent rationalization under Ataturk with emphasis on achievement versus ascription. As one of the early development-oriented regimes, Turkey required competent economic managers, sound planning, and qualified expertise. The RPP (Republican Peoples Party) at one time played a strong, pragmatic, as opposed to ideological, oversight role (Tahtinen 1973:44–47).

But commitment to rational economic planning has not always been the norm in the intervening years. Nevertheless, we saw a return to this commitment under the then incumbent prime minister. Coming to power in the 1983 elections, Turgut Ozal, an economist by training, sought, with his team of technocrats, to lead Turkey out of the economic and social chaos.

The late Prime Minister Ozal, like many other truly modern leaders worldwide, recognized that the key to legitimacy is economic performance; yet much remains in Turkey of the former state-controlled "etatist" structure established in the 1920s and 1930s by Ataturk (*Middle East Review* 1988:173–179). Ozal's ruling Motherland party won an overwhelming victory in the general elections held (under the military rule) November 29, 1987, an endorsement for the new breed of politicians and further economic rationalization.

Administrative activity under Tunisia's pragmatic Destourian Socialist Party, or PSD, has been significant. The single party's leadership role was facilitated by minimal administrative disruption following independence. The relatively smooth transition was aided by trained Tunisians and retained French personnel. The National School of Administration in Tunisia encouraged development of a basically achievement-oriented bureaucracy, but political controls largely preempted the rule-making process. Significantly, agricultural development was accorded priority, although hampered by lack of management expertise. For the most part, however, the bureaucrats have been experienced and efficient and have shown honesty and industriousness in the distribution of goods and services (Tahtinen 1973:75–79).

Tunisia is now pressing ahead with a major effort to reform its flagging economy. The memory lingers of the January 1984 riots when the government had to reverse a decree doubling the price of bread. Economic reform advocates confronted unacceptable political costs. The government began a gradual adjustment of the dinar exchange rate and of commodity subsidies, but reforms were not comprehensive. The structural reforms implemented during 1987–1991 called for significant planning efforts (*Middle East Review* 1988:168–171). On November 7, 1987, Tunisia's ailing president-for-life, Habib Bourguiba, who led his country to independence in 1956, was replaced by General Zine al-Abidine Ben Ali—a premier example of economic as well as political rationalization.

In stark contrast, independent Algeria was left with virtually no administrators. Even as the numbers grew with indigenous rather than French personnel, a paucity of qualified bureaucrats remained for many years. And then there was, Tahtinen found, the problem of an apathetic, conservative, clan-ridden, even antisocialist bureaucracy at a time when Ben Bella sought to build a socialist state. The FLN (National Liberation Front) had not been successful in controlling the bureaucracy. Troubled by internecine conflict and parochial loyalties, it had lacked the unified will to organize the countryside effectively.

Ben Bella's successor, Houari Boumedienne, sought technological competence. His crackdowns on bureaucratic corruption, racketeering, and recruitment on the basis of achievement compared favorably with Tunisia. The industrial sector, accorded higher priority, proved a greater success than the agricultural, and more successful than Turkey's RPP stressing heavy industrial development or Tunisia's pragmatic PSD with its strong grass roots emphasizing agricultural development (Tahtinen 1973:104–111).

Algeria, 98% dependent on hydrocarbon exports, was hard hit by the 1986 price collapse. A depressed market continued in 1988. Solutions included dismantling the state economic structure initiated in the 1970s by Boumedienne, the predecessor of Bendjedid Chadli. New reliance was placed on private investments and market forces, in contrast to the *dirigiste* centrist governmental approach to management of the economy. Resistance nevertheless continued from FLN hardliners (*Middle East Review* 1988:35–39).

Egypt's revolutionary regime inherited a highly experienced if not always effective bureaucracy. While distinctive in its own right, the administrative structure in 1952 resembled Ottoman Turkey. Recruitment often took place not on achievement criteria but less commendably on the basis of ascriptive norms. Political or family connections, not ability, were stressed. Inefficiency and overstaffing caused problems.

The regime sought to control and steer the bureaucracy to achieve its development goals. The introduction of "new blood," including army officers over the ensuing years, some with freshly minted management degrees in hand, expanded the military junta's capacity for penetration and control. The net result was a proliferation of bureaucrats in an already overstaffed bureaucracy, but the rationale was a development base on which to build; specialists at the time of independence were not lacking. Indeed, their expertise placed them at an advantage initially over the young officers (Tahtinen 1973:141).

Then and now, expertise often quite impressive at the top has seldom translated into middle- and lower-level competence or the assumption of responsibility. Urban-based bureaucrats are reluctant to make extended field visits. Nevertheless, despite these administrative shortcomings, local-level and rural deficiencies are being remedied in more recent years, thanks to the sheer number of educated personnel and the amenities increasingly available in the countryside. Rural electrification has provided an incentive for nonurban development, in contrast to the preoccupation with urban and industrial development exhibited by so many regimes. "Urban bias" and the consequent neglect of the critical rural base work against true, national development. Muhammad generalizes: "If development is to take place evenly and where it is most desirable, real authority must be placed in the hands of the local population." Yet he acknowledges the political obstacles (Muhammad 1988:20–21).

Acceptance of government-induced rural modernization programs has grown as government employees become more adept at field visits. Men are more likely than women to leave city-bound desks for the field, but female extension agents need to communicate with the farm women. Urban investment has all too often come at the expense of rural needs.

Shortcomings continue in many cases on the part of administrative personnel supposedly addressing the rural target populations. Farmers are more likely now to have some schooling and urban impressions through personal or family-member travels to the major cities or other foreign, usually Arab oil-producing, countries. However, remittances from overseas workers have often contributed little to agricultural activity directly. Interestingly, small-farmer loans, which, it should be noted, often have a commendably high repayment rate, produce two effects: to channel unbanked funds into government hands through the loan repayment medium, and to foster rural bureaucratic structuring.

Problems abound, but the government is determined to press on with development. Complaints about the bureaucracy recall President Nasser's assessment on the second anniversary of the revolution: "We have inherited a heavy legacy: a ruined treasury, an unbalanced budget, and corrupt government." Indeed graft, party conflict, personal interest, and the abuse of influence by government officials were rife. Nevertheless, for Berger, "further professionalization and rationalization can be expected" (Berger 1957:123, 177).

Syria's Ba'thist party, Tahtinen maintained, inherited a mostly secularized civil service. However, since 1963, loyalty to the party rather than professional competence is the litmus test at a time of heavy demands on the bureaucracy. Foreigners, including Palestinians and other exogenous Arabs, are to be found in technical/managerial positions. The sole party remains the principal arbitrator, guide, and rule maker. But Tahtinen found the Ba'th party less effective than the other one-party systems in effecting administrative modernization (Tahtinen 1973:166). The economy of Syria, for its part, is troubled by foreign exchange shortages and a costly peace-keeping role in Lebanon. The bureaucratic environment compounds the difficulties in doing business, thus contributing to capital flight—a form of disinvestment.

In a move toward economic rationalization, the 1986–1990 plan, indicated Syrian Minister of State for Planning Sabah Baqjaji, called for only a slight increase in investment. Reductions in defense spending were being considered, while investment in agriculture and industry was scheduled to increase (*Middle East Review* 1988:161–167). General Hafez al-Assad, who continues as president of the Syrian Arab Republic, faces a substantial number of political challenges and pressing economic and social problems.

Tahtinen concluded by awarding highest praise in his earlier assessments of Turkey, Tunisia, Algeria, and Egypt (Tahtinen 1973:179). Tunisia, more than the others, under the PSD was fortunate to enter the postindependence era with a substantial number of effective, indigenous administrative personnel to fulfill the development agenda. Furthermore, the Tunisians reduced potential administrative disruption by pragmatically retaining essential French administrators while moving toward an all-Tunisian bureaucracy. Admittedly, Tunisia's relative homogeneity and lack of disruptive ethnic cleavages have contributed favorably.

Tahtinen and others frequently speak in Weberian terms of the importance of merit over ascriptively based criteria for recruitment of the effective, modern bureaucracy needed to implement the development agenda. While this is undeniably true, the first task in countries of divided political loyalties, of localistic rather than national-level orientation, is to build that loyalty. Then, too, modernizing regimes can pragmatically recruit on a merit basis from among the ranks of the faithful and therefore meet in part some of the achievement-based criteria. Loyalty and competence need not be mutually exclusive terms in bureaucratic structures where political criteria take priority.

Ben Aissa questions the appropriateness of Weberian-dominated foreign models. Speaking to the subject of administrative neutrality in the Arab countries, he perceptively argues that politicization of the bureaucracies is undeniably the ascriptive norm. In fact, "In the eyes of political leaders, administrative neutrality is tantamount to a lack of civic responsibility." He makes the case for a strong intermediary role, which works against a disinterested bureaucracy. The public in turn demands "access" to the bureaucracy, if only to make the system work to personal advantage (Ben Aissa 1986:50).

VIII. RECENT STUDIES

Egypt's historically rooted bureaucracy continues to be subject to critical scrutiny. Lauri Neff, while agreeing that it is "the place to be" for foreign investors because of its geographic location and that many acknowledge President Hosni Mubarak has provided a "real push" for reform and the creation of a more investment-friendly environment, nevertheless finds that the biggest problem remains the bureaucracy (Neff 1996:76–77).

Jreisat concludes that "excessive rules inhibit investors, delay business transactions, and frustrate citizens, compounded by overstaffing, low salaries and low motivation" (Jreisat 1995). It may be added that the Egyptian government's commitment to the social policy of being "employer of last resort" has created even more problems. The government has tried to reduce the number of new recruits with a longer waiting period. The net result, however, is that some do indeed find jobs elsewhere, but they are usually the "best and the brightest," leaving the less qualified for eventual civil service jobs.

Subramanian points to a "formidable reform agenda" including privatization of utilities and infrastructure sectors, invigorating the financial system and further integrating Egypt into the world economy with a trade liberalization program (IMFWP/97/105).

Kuwaitis in their almost unique entity comprise (1996 est.) only 41.1% of the population of Kuwait. The remaining 58.9% include other Arabs, South Asians, Palestinians (though in reduced numbers following the trauma of the 1990–91 Gulf War), and *Badoun* (stateless migrants). Yet, Kuwaiti citizens constitute nearly 92.7% of the government sector. Non-Kuwaitis in 1995 had declined to 11.8% in the public sector thanks in part to the policy of "Kuwaitization" (*Arab Times* 1996).

Saudi Arabia, a classic rentier state with its massive though now stressed oil revenues, has, now that it no longer relies for the most part on tax gathering, seen "a decline of the information-gathering capacity associated with the regulatory and tax bureaucracy" (Chaudhry 1997:143).

The record on Syria's economy is mixed. While a 1991 investment law initially attracted foreigners and Syrian expatriates, and the proportion of the private sector rose from 35% to 70%, the legal system discourages private investment as it is almost impenetrable. State planning continues to be important, although President Hafez al-Assad is "not hostile" to private investment, says *The Economist* (1998).

Tunisia is another one of the Arab countries that has been opening up its economy since 1986, moving from import substitution and state intervention to a more market-based and export-oriented approach. Nevertheless, the banking system remains under state control and may be influenced by the government's larger agenda (IMF No. 97/57:8, 45).

In Turkey, the economy is highly diverse, led by a new generation of private sector companies.

What are some of the Arab world trends? "Large public sectors . . . have tended to crowd out private initiative, and resulted in lack of investment opportunities for foreign and domestic capital" (IMFWP/97/125:33). Nevertheless, a state may act positively by helping to "nurture and strengthen a private sector," but all too often the state (e.g., Libya since 1975) is "strangling" the private sector. In fact, precisely because of the challenges of the global market to which many Middle Eastern states have been slow to respond, unlike the Asian economies, bureaucrats may rationalize the need for a continued key role in structural transformation (Richards and Waterbury 1996:174). State-owned enterprises (SOEs), a World Bank study generalizes, are often part of the problem, remaining "stubbornly large" despite increasing investiture (World Bank 1995).

IX. CONCLUSION

Are bureaucrats of the Middle East effective agents of development or are they part of the problem? Jreisat, looking at Iraq, Jordan, Morocco, Saudi Arabia, Sudan, Syria, and what was then

North Yemen, pessimistically observes that "these structures have proved unequal to the demands of development plans and expanded needs for regular public services," the most crucial shortcoming being "inadequate public sector capacity" (Jreisat 1988:89). In sum, "bureaucratic torpor" remains a problem.

The public sector strongly persists, even when government leaders talk about its deemphasis, perhaps in keeping with Middle East history, cultural values, and geography. Little evidence exists of macro-level private sector capacity for modernization. Rationalization of administrative and public sector structures is necessary if the state is to realize development goals. These reform efforts should include better training and adequate funding for middle and local-level bureaucrats, plus more attention to rural initiatives.

So many new demands have come so quickly that building the requisite cadre has not come fast enough. Generalizations are unwise in the diverse Middle East, but growing sophistication and better training do seem to raise the prospect of bureaucrats becoming the effective agents of development.

APPENDIX 1: CIVIL SERVICE IN MIDDLE EAST COUNTRIES

Algeria

Locked in an ongoing insurgency since the cancellation of the January 1992 elections, oil and gas revenues nevertheless continue to flow. Algeria seeks to further structural adjustment despite problems of persistent unemployment and domestic markets unintegrated with the global economy.

Bahrain

No information currently available on the Bahraini civil service. Excessive dependence on declining oil revenues has been partially offset by Bahrain's entrepôt role.

Egypt

The civil service constitutes the largest employment sector in Egypt, already employing in the early 1970s more than 1 million persons in 12 grades terminating at the assistant under secretary of state level. Two supergrades are for higher officials. Provisions exist for automatic salary increases and promotions on a seniority basis. Parity in pay exists between male and female employees, but disparities exist with regard to career development and training opportunities. The civil service is administered by the Civil Service Commission, which handles recruitment and enforces discipline. Of a formal labor force of 13 million (1985), the government (national and local) comprises 36%. Despite some privatization measures, the public sector continues to play a major role.

Iraq

The civil service is governed by the Civil Service Law and Cadre Law (1962). Civil servants fall into two categories, with officials holding one of nine grades in government departments and as employees of semigovernment bodies. The Ministry of Interior has the largest number of officials. The civil service is administered by the General Service Board, regulating recruitment, promotion, and discipline. The Ministry of Finance is responsible for establishing the quota of civil servants in each ministry, transferring officials and investigating misconduct. Open to all Iraqi citizens over 18 years of age, recruitment is based on competitive examinations. The 1980–88 war with Iran followed by the 1990–91 Gulf War resulted in many more female employees. Administrative divisions consist of 18 provinces under centrally appointed officials.

Jordan

The Jordanian civil service was originally based on the British model. Selection is by competitive examination, with training provided by the School of Public Administration in Amman. Administrative responsibilities comprise eight governorates under centrally appointed officials. (West Bank and Gaza Strip are not included.)

Lebanon

The Civil Service Board and the State Inspection Department supervise the civil service. The National Public Administration School provides training. Civil servants receive such benefits as travel, disability, and travel allowances. Out of a total labor force of 650,000 (1985) the government constitutes 10%. The country has been torn by the 1975–90 civil war and continued foreign intervention. The administrative divisions comprise four provinces.

Morocco

Patterned after the civil service established under the French protectorate, the civil service was completely Moroccanized by 1970. The *chefs de service* head each department. The Moroccan School of Administration is the most prestigious of the seven institutes of administrative training. The administrative divisions are the 36 provinces (does not include Western Sahara) and two provinces (Rabat-Salé and Casablanca). Approximately 400,000 people (15%) are employed by the government. Structural adjustment remains a challenge.

Oman

One province (Dhofar), two governorates (Musandam and Muscat), and numerous other *wilayats* (districts) form the administrative divisions.

Pakistan

The All-Pakistan Unified Civil Service was established (1973) with 22 pay grades. Recruitment is done by the Central Public Service Commission, 20% on the basis of merit, and 80% on the basis of regional parity. Lateral entry is permitted for specialists, professionals, and scientists. The administrative divisions comprise four provinces (Baluchistan, Northwest Frontier, Punjab, Sind) and one territory (the Federally Administered Tribal Areas).

Palestinian Authority

The Authority comprises the legislative and executive body exercising powers devolved by Israel to autonomous Palestinian areas pursuant to the September 1993 Oslo Accord.

Qatar

No information is currently available on the Qatari civil service. Sheikh Hamad bin Khalifah ath-Thani, who deposed his father in 1995, continues to possess major control of Qatar's reserves.

Saudi Arabia

The unified civil service is open to all Saudis. Below the rank of minister are nine grades. Appointments to grades 1 to 3 are made by ministers, and through qualifying examinations for grades 4 to 9. Out of a labor force constituting one-third of the population, 45% are in commerce, government, and related fields.

Sudan

Out of a labor force of 6 million (1982), 6% are in government service. Nine regions form the administrative divisions.

Syrian Arab Republic

Below the ministry level all government positions are filled from the ranks of the civil service. A system of examinations form the basis for entry and promotion. Administrative divisions consist of 13 provisions and the city of Damascus.

Tunisia

The General Civil Servants Law (1968) regulates employment. Seventy percent of civil service vacancies are filled by competitive examinations, another 20% by specialized examinations, and 10% by internal promotions. At the highest level political appointments are the rule. Lateral entry is provided for mid- and lower-level teachers and technicians. In 1962 the *Ecole nationale d'administration* was established to provide specialized training for the bureaucracy. Twenty-three governorates form the administrative divisions.

Turkey

Each ministry provides for its own recruiting and training programs. Above the level of district administrators, the Institute of Public Administration in Ankara provides additional training. Political participation by civil servants is forbidden. Sixty-seven administrative divisions constitute the administrative divisions. The government has not moved quickly enough on essential budget cuts or privatization, and a rigorous remedy for inflation now running at nearly 100% annually.

United Arab Emirates

Out of a labor force of 580,000 (1985 est.), 5% are in government. The UAE comprises the member states of Abu Dhabi, Ajman, al-Fujayrah, Dubai (Dubayy), ash-Shariqah, Ra's al-Khaymah, and Umm al-Qaywayn. The UAE leads the gulf states in that almost 90% of the work force comes from overseas.

Yemen Arab Republic

Eleven administrative provinces form the administrative divisions.

Yemen PDR

Six governorates form the administrative divisions. The two countries were united May 21, 1990, to form the Republic of Yemen with San'a as the capital.

REFERENCES

Abbott, K. (1996). Palestine: the shape of government. *The Middle East* 13–15 (October), 1994.

Arab Times. Expats 83.4pc of labour force. Kuwait City, October.

Anderson, L. (1987). The state in the Middle East and North Africa. *Comparative Politics 20*(1), 1–18.

Ayubi, N. (1968). Bureaucratization as development: administrative development and development administration in the Arab world. *International Review of Administrative Sciences 52*(2), 201–222.

Ayubi, N. (1988). Arab bureaucracies: expanding size, changing roles. In *Beyond Coercion: The Durability of the Arab State* (A. Dawisha and I.W. Zartman, eds.). London: Croom Helm, pp. 14–34.

Ben Aissa, M.S. (1986). Report on the Arab countries. *International Review of Administrative Sciences 52*(1), 45–54.

Berger, M. (1957). *Bureaucracy and Society in Modern Egypt.* London: Oxford University Press.

Chackerian, R., and Shadukhi, S.M. (1983). Public bureaucracy in Saudi Arabia: an empirical assessment of work group behavior. *International review of Administrative Sciences 49*, 319–322.

Chaudry, K.A. (1997). *The Price of Wealth: Economies and Institutions in the Middle East.* Ithaca, NY: Cornell University Press.

Encyclopedia of the Third World (G.T. Kurian, ed.), rev. ed., 3 vols. (1978). New York: Facts on File.

Esman, M.J. (1988). The maturing of development administration. *Public Administration and Development 8*, 125–134.

Halpern, M. (1963). *The Politics of Social Change in the Middle East and North Africa.* Princeton, NJ: Princeton University Press.

Heady, F. (1984, 1996). *Public Administration: A Comparative Perspective*, 3rd ed. rev. and 5th ed. New York: Marcel Dekker.

Heper, M. (1987). The state and public bureaucracies: a comparative and historical perspective. In *The State and Public Bureaucracies: A Comparative Perspective* (Metin, ed.). Westport, CT: Greenwood Press, pp. 9–26.

Hinnebusch, R.A. Jr. (1985). *Egyptian Politics Under Sadat.* New York: Cambridge University Press.

Hiro, D. (1996). *Dictionary of the Middle East.* New York: St. Martin's Press.

International Monetary Fund. (1997a). *Globalization and Growth Prospects in Arab Countries.* Prepared by P. Alonso-Gamo et al.

International Monetary Fund. (1997b). *The Egyptian Stabilization Experience: An Analytical Perspective.* Prepared by Arvind Subramanian.

International Monetary Fund. (1997c). *Tunisia-Selected Issues.* Prepared by H. Ghesquiere.

International Monetary Fund. (1987). *International Financial Statistics: Supplement on Public Sector Institutions.* No. 13.

Jreisat, J.E. (1988). Administrative reform in developing countries: a comparative perspective. *Public Administration and Development 8*, 85–97.

Jreisat, J.E. (1995). Faltering bureaucratic reforms: the case of Egypt. *Journal of Developing Societies II*, 221–232.

La Palombara, J. (1963). An overview of bureaucracy and political development. In *Bureaucracy and Political Development* (J. La Palombara, ed.). Princeton, NJ: Princeton University Press, pp. 3–33.

Leila, A., Yassin, E.S., and Palmer, M. (1986). Assessing attitudes of Egyptian bureaucrats toward public service and the Egyptian public. *International Review of Administration Sciences 52*(3), 325–338.

Sources: *Encyclopedia of the Third World* (1978), *World Factbook* (1987), and Richard and Waterbury (1996).

Merriam, J.G., and Fluellen, A.J. (1992). Arab world privatization: key to development? *Arab Studies Quarterly 14*(2 & 3), 57–67.

Middle East Review, 14th ed. (1988). Essex, U.K.: World of Information.

Ministry of Planning, Central Statistics Office. (1996). *Annual Statistical Abstract, 1996, Edition 33.* State of Kuwait.

Ministry of Population. (1996). *Morocco in Figures.*

Moench, R.U. (1988). Oil, ideology, and state autonomy in Egypt. *Arab Studies Quarterly 10*(2), 176–192.

Muhammad, F. (1988). Public administration: prevailing perceptions and priorities. *International Review of Administrative Sciences 54*(1), 3–36.

Neff, L. (1996). Parting the red tape: in Egypt. *Middle East Insight 12*, 76–79.

Richards, A., and Waterbury, J. (1996). *A Political Economy of the Middle East*, 2nd ed. Boulder, CO: Westview Press.

Rosenau, J.N. (1988). The state in an era of cascading politics. *Comparative Political Studies 21*(1), 13–44.

Springborg, R. (1987). The president and the field marshall: civil-military relations in Egypt today. *Middle East Report 147*, 5–16.

Tahtinen, D.R. (1973). The role of the single party in the modernization process of five Middle Eastern states. Ph.D dissertation, University of Maryland.

The Economist. (1998). Syria's economy: the party's over. *346*(8051), 42.

World Bank. (1995). *Bureaucrats in Business: The Economics and Politics of Government Ownership.* Washington: World Bank.

World Bank. (1987). *World Development Report, 1987.* Washington: International Bank for Reconstruction and Development/World Bank.

The World Factbook. (1987). *CPAS WF 87-001.* Washington: Public Affairs.

38

The Regionalization Experience in Latin America

Lon S. Felker   *Department of Economics, Finance, and Urban Studies, East Tennessee State University, Johnson City, Tennessee*

I. INTRODUCTION

Regionalization is a theme that has appeared in the public administrative literature of Latin America since the 1960s. This concept, regionalization, refers to the move to decentralize the administrative apparatuses of centralized governments, such as exist in most Latin American nations. Decentralization along regional lines is a variation on a persistent trend in Latin America, that of the transfer of power out of the hands of the national bureaucracy and into the hands of regional or at least subnational levels of government. Another aspect of the decentralization movement, as it has historically developed in Latin America, is the creation of independent agencies and government corporations, which has its roots in the tradition of state corporatism as well as the widespread acknowledgement of the patronage nature of much of the regular civil service and the lack of professional and neutral competence in many areas of the national bureaucracy.

But regionalization is more than a variant of the decentralization movement. It is a movement with social, political, economic, and even cultural overtones and dimensions. In the Andean nations, for example, the long-standing neglect and retarded development of the sierra regions of many of the countries can be traced to the overly central lines of government and administration. Some writers (Stavenhagen, for example), speak of an internal colonialism with respect to the models of economic growth in many areas of Latin America. In this view, the metropolitan areas enjoy higher levels of growth, development, and industrialization at the expense of the hinterland regions.

While regionalization and decentralization in general are not sufficient cures in themselves to the problems alluded to, they do offer the beginnings of a palliative to the problems. As a fairly recent contribution to the developmental administration literature, it is worth noting how seldom the terms "regionalism" or "decentralization" are to be encountered in the administrative writings of two decades ago. Even so, the problems that regionalization addresses were widely acknowledged by knowledgeable observers. Roberto de Oliveira Campos (1967) notes that the administrative problems of the region could be summarized as:

1.   The prevalence of paternalistic attitudes, or state paternalism, which affects every aspect, personnel as well as budgetary, of the operation of the administrative apparatus.

2.   The overcentralization of decision making, which contributes to the weakness of provincial and local governments, leading to overconcentration at the center.

3.   The lack of an adequate and realistic theory on the role and limits of governmental

intervention, which expresses itself in the popular mind as complete disbelief in government as a regulator while marked at the same time by overconfidence in the managerial abilities of government.

Most of the points that De Oliveira Campos remarks on have been noted by others. The reform movement in public administration in many Latin American countries has targeted these criticisms for attention. The major obstacle has been the long-standing traditions of bureaucratic centrism and statist paternalism coupled with the absence of set limits on state action. Still, a change in the literature was evident with the late 1960s. As Linn A. Hammergren (1983:5) observes:

> In the earlier literature (roughly 1950 to 1970) reform was the *only* change policy and was also a principal theme. An abrupt shift, beginning in the late 1960s radically altered this situation. Following a few years in which what little was written on reform programs aimed at questioning and criticizing them, the emphasis is now on outlining alternatives to reforming and devising new approaches to improving administrative performance.

In view of the major role that regionalization was to play in the reform planning of a number of Latin American governments after 1970, it is noteworthy that in a work devoted to strategies for public administrative development (Honey 1968), the words regionalization, decentralization, and debureaucratization do not appear. Perhaps these were already established as concerns in Latin American reformers' lists of priorities prior to their emergence in the North American administrative reform literature. In the following section, some of the Latin American sources for regionalization and decentralization will be considered.

A.   Origins of Latin American Regionalization

There are a number of sources citable for the origins of Latin American regionalization, decentralization, and bureaucratic reform in general. The following discussion is not a comprehensive one, focusing as it does on the highlights and major trends and influences within the region.

1.   Early Latin American *Pensadores* and Regionalization

It is customary to trace the centralizing tradition in Latin American public administration to the Spanish imperial period and the consequent influence of this (and a similar Portuguese tradition) on the evolution of administration in the New World. Omar Guerrero Orozco (1985) has noted the continuity of the centralist administrative tradition after the French Revolution, and the influence of the "new" centralized administrative theory on the nations of Spanish America. One can note, however, the federalist nations that were frequently linked to the liberal political tradition in a number of Central and South American nations: Argentina and Colombia, for example. Here the linkage can be largely explained by the rejection of the centralizing Iberian tradition and the influence of federalist ideas emanating from the United States. Whether the victory of the liberals necessarily led to the endorsement of federalism and regional autonomy is a quite different question.

2.   Twentieth Century Writings

A number of writers in various countries developed a critique of the prevailing centralist tradition in the early part of this century.

In Peru, both Raúl Victor Haya de la Torre (1986) and Jose Carlos Mariategui were vocal critics of the lack of attention to the problems of the interior. Mariategui (1968) especially, in his now classic *Seven Interpretative Essays on the Peruvian Reality*, wrote of the legacy of neglect and the forces that worked to keep the inhabitants of the interior, principally the Indian, in a state of low development. He linked the regional imbalance in development with the nature of land tenure (*gamonalismo*) and the low status of the Indian in Peruvian society. Mariategui (1968:161) further realized that true administrative decentralization required more than municipal autonomy; it required as well the development of the region as a governmental entity in its own right.

Haya de la Torre, the founder and leader of the American Popular Revolutionary Alliance (APRA), today the oldest and largest political movement in Peru, gave evidence of his concern over the course of rural development in the Plan of Action of the Apista party in 1931. The agrarian program of this plan had five parts: (1) the national agrarian policy; (2) the farming production; (3) zoning and colonization; (4) agricultural education; and (5) agrarian public administration. APRA was the first political party to see the rural labor force as a mobilizable political force. The role of the public sector in assisting rural development was a key element of APRA's strategy (Rojas Samanez 1986:183–184).

Despite such early evidence of support for regionalization among the intellectual community, the fact is that very little in the way of concrete effort was forthcoming in bringing about regionalization until the 1960s. In Peru, Raúl Lizárraga Bobbio (1985:28) cautions that movements for regionalization/decentralization had a long history of not always laudable ends, and were, likely as not, dominated by some local political or military chief (*Caudillo*), or what might be termed the "traditional bourgeoisie" (local landowners and *hacendados*). In either case, true regionalization and decentralization were absent, and regional development was not on the agenda. Only in the present context does the legal and policymaking system support the participation of popular local groups in a movement directed at regionalization.

B. Beginning of Regionalization

By the end of the 1950s, a number of influences and trends were shaping the regionalization movement. For one, the writings of such keen social observers as Mariategui and others were receiving attention. A second set of factors was the external pressures of international bodies, such as the United Nations and its many constituent units, the international financial community, and the U.S. aid and assistance missions. Other forces were at work to open Latin America to a rich variety of new influences, not the least of which were the opportunities for education abroad that many younger Latin Americans enjoyed. The expansion of secondary and higher educational systems in the region resulted in more opportunities for representatives of some remote and isolated communities to receive a higher education. New leadership and a more popular base of support for regionalization and administrative decentralization and reform were only some of the political consequences of these developments.

In a few states, regionalization efforts got an early start due to the recognition that certain areas of the nation had failed to develop at the same pace as others. The attempts to rectify this situation present the first real efforts at regionalization.

1. The Brazilian SUDENE

The example of Brazil's Superintendency for Development of the Northeast (SUDENE) was one such effort. Established in 1959 under a legal formula in which the Superintendency was set up as an autonomous federal organ under the direction of the President of the Republic, the model that SUDENE provided served for the establishment of other such development agencies in other parts of Brazil (Alves Da Silva 1976:60).

Under the legal formula adopted, the agency had administrative as well as financial autonomy. SUDENE was tasked with planning, coordinating, executing, and evaluating the development of the Brazilian Northeast, a region noted for its low level of development relative to the rest of the nation. SUDENE's significance lies in its creation prior to the advent of national planning. This provided SUDENE with a period of relative independence from national planning priorities, thus permitting it to develop ties to its political base and its natural constituency. SUDENE evolved as a policymaking and initiating body prior to the imposition of the first national plan.

Dr. Celso Furtado and his associates were particularly instrumental in the creation and success of SUDENE (Pichardo Pagaza 1976:99–103). It was Furtado and his group that first approached the developmental problems of the Northeast in a comprehensive analysis. They suggested alternative paths to development for the region. The fact that SUDENE's creation predated that of the ministry of Planning meant that SUDENE had the opportunity to develop its own decision-making patterns and to establish goals for the region outside the context of a global plan for the nation.

As a consequence of its success, other such superintendencies were set up to develop other regions: the Amazon (SUDAM), the Central East (SUDECO), and the South (SUDESUL). The initial success of SUDENE can be said to have spurred interest and positive action toward federally initiated regional development programs in Brazil (Alves Da Silva 1976:63–64). In time, of course, the work of the superintendencies was brought under the coordination of the Ministry of Planning (formally created in 1967). But by then, a medium in the form of the superintendencies had been set up in which the states could participate in decision making relative to the distribution of federal funds to the regions. This had a decisive impact on future state participation in the allocation of such funds (Stöhr 1976:237).

2.   Mexican Regional Development

By the early 1960s another pattern of regionalization was emerging in a number of states. This was what Walter B. Stöhr refers to as centralized systems for the development of regions. A prime example was Mexico's Commission for the Development of River Basins, which were placed under the control of the Secretariat of National Hydraulic Resources (Stöhr, 1976, p. 236). In the Mexican case, economic bases of regional development seem to predominate. River basins were targeted under the Chontalpa Plan for development, while arid regions were placed under the National Commission for the Arid Zones. In both cases, the primary external influence seems to have been the example of the U.S. Tennessee Valley Authority. It is significant that this was an effort directed by the U.S. federal government to develop the resources of a specific region. The most critical issue in such efforts has been the highly centralized nature of Mexican political life; local efforts at regional planning and development must have the blessing of the Mexico City authorities. As Pichardo Pagaza (1976:84) remarks, "In Mexico, until the very recent epoch, the tendency has been to strengthen all the factors of central direction in regional programs."

The Mexican case demonstrates the problems in attempting regional development through a policy of deliberately created national subunits without fiscal or administrative autonomy. Although the TVA served as the model, it is difficult to perceive in the present Mexican context any viable regional organizations that have developed the same strong ties to the region as the model. Mexico is not alone in this particular problem; the legacy of administrative centralization from above is very much a factor in federalized political systems such as Mexico and Brazil, as well as in the unified systems of government more common in the region.

3.   Aldo Piras and the XVI International Congress of Administrative Sciences

Yet another influence on the shaping and growth of regionalization as a movement in Latin American public administration was the work of Aldo Piras at the XVI International Congress of Administrative Sciences, held in Mexico City in July 1974 (Pichardo Pagaza 1976:67).

By nationality an Italian, Aldo Piras served as coordinator of the sessions on regionalization at the Congress. Piras presented a typology of structures for purposes of determining the stages of development of various efforts at regionalization in industrialized countries, although a number of Latin American participants saw the relevance of Piras's analysis to Latin American regions. In particular, Piras identified the major problems as a pattern of deterioration in the public sector due to the inability of highly centralized governments, such as France and other unified political systems, to perceive, manage, and solve the problems of subnational units. This tendency was compounded by the state's administrative apparatus, which paralled in most respects the centralized pattern of the rest of the political system.

In response to this, Piras advocated a decentralized regional administration in which the regional organs coincide with logical geographic, economic, and ethnocultural areas. Such a system would require the national government to cease attempting to administer the entire national territory through field offices. Instead, a number of different organs and regional institutions would be set up to resolve short-term as well as long-term developmental problems. Aside from the typology, Piras suggested that there are two essential components of regionalization:

1.   Concentration of administrative powers in a single agency that replaces certain functions of the minor local authorities.

2.   Existence of a "grand region" in order to capitalize on economies of scale and economies in the provision of public services (Pichardo Pagaza 1976:71).

Piras's typology and concepts had a definite if difficult-to-delineate influence on Latin American regional administration. Certainly the 1974 Congress served as a useful stimulant to many reform-minded individuals, who recognized in Piras's typology many of the problems of their national administrative systems. In Mexico, for example, the following year (1975) saw the creation of the National Commission for Regional Development, which was tasked with (among other duties) the promotion of socioeconomic development. The national commission established state-level committees for this purpose. In the setting of the priorities of these committees, the role of the state governors proved crucial. There may have been other cases where Piras's influence is notable, although the evidence is lacking.

II.   REGIONALIZATION IN SPECIFIC COUNTRIES

The pattern of regionalization from nation to nation has been markedly different. No single path to regionalization is apparent from an examination of the various national plans and efforts. Even regionally, there seems to be a distinct amount of variation. Peru, Columbia, and Venezuela, all Andean states, have had significantly different experiences. Colombia's experience with regionalization was marked by a frustrating inability of regionalized programs to incorporate themselves in the national bureaucracy, by widespread complaints of lack of funding, and by a fairly universal recognition toward the end of the 1970s of the inefficiency and lack of coordination of local and departmental services. Peru and Venezuela were more distinguishable from Columbia and more similar in certain respects. This was probably due to the more centralized nature of these nations' two political systems.

More to the point, Linn A. Hammergren's (1983) analysis of these three nations suggests that the nature of the political system played a lesser role than the level of institutionalization of the political system. In the case of Peru, the military regime in power from 1968 to 1980 suffered from a problem of legitimacy, and this contributed to the authority of the planners and managers brought in to plan and administer the regionalization programs (Hammergren 1983:164–166). In the case of Venezuela, frequent changes in political party control of the government may have contributed to the varying fortunes of the regionalization program under the COPEI (Social Christian Party) and AD (Accion Democratica Party) governments. The rise and decline of oil revenues during the 1970s also had consequences on the fiscal side of regionalization. Indeed, the entire reform movement in Venezuela, of which regionalization was only one aspect, suffered from the vicissitudes of the oil market.

A. Chile

In the case of Chile, the initial effort under the Frei government (1964–1970) underwent significant changes, first under the Socialist Allende regime (1970–1973) and later, after the right-wing military coup-d'état, under the military regime of Pinochet (1973–1990). Under the Frei government, the basic thrust was on popular participation in decision making, including decision making at the local levels of government. By the mid 1960s, there were some stirrings about concern with the spatial dimension of development and the inequities and disequilbria of national development (Raczynski 1986:8).

Some attention was being paid to regional planning by the advent of the Allende government. This regime further encouraged the participation of all relevant groups in the decision-making process, including groups outside the greater Santiago de Chile area. A number of regional bodies were created, most of them with some discernible developmental focus (the Board for the Development of Arica, the Corporation of Magallanes, the Corfo-Aysen Institute, and the Programming Committee of Iquique and Pisagua, for examples). Under the Christian Democratic Frei government, the term "growth poles" had been used to indicate the essentially developmental focus of regionalization. While the Allende government spoke instead of "integrated spaces," the developmental aspect was still present (Boisier 1984; Raczynski 1986).

In understanding the regionalization movement in Chile, it is important to comprehend the nature of the Chilean bureaucracy at the time of the inception of regionalization. As in many Latin American governments, Chile had two basic types of state agencies, those that were centralized and nonautonomous, and those that were decentralized. The latter were regarded as "semi-fiscal, autonomous corporations, or state industries," which

> profited from direct authority links to the president . . . ; they usually had a large percentage of guaranteed revenue; they were liberated from sending their regulatory decrees to the General Comptroller's office for prior approval; they could change their organizational chart and number of personnel without going through Congress, and they could set their salary scales above the levels of the centralized portion of government. (Cleaves 1974:10–11).

In effect, a status difference existed in Chilean bureaucracy, between the centralized and less prestigious agencies and the more prestigious, decentralized ones. Here the term "decentralized" should not be construed as indicating a regionalized form of organization. Rather, it indicates a greater degree of organizational "flexibility" and "agility" in response to problems, and a much higher degree of freedom from political forces, especially those in the legislature.

What is significant about the dual nature of Chilean (and by extension Latin American) bureaucracy is the ability of the decentralized agencies to engage in regionalization strategies with greater ease and facility than the decentralized elements of the state bureaucracy. But a problem in achieving meaningful regionalization of decentralized agencies is the composition of their personnel, which tend to be drawn from elite metropolitan social classes, many of whom would regard an assignment in the provinces as a form of exile. This is not simply a Chilean dilemma, but one far more common to Latin American state bureaucracies at large.

Throughout the 1960s, the lack of sufficient scope in regional autonomy within Chile was largely justified by the lack of trained personnel to send to regional offices (where they existed), and the absence of adequate structures for effective administration (Stöhr 1976:238). One pattern that continued without significant change was the concentration of investment in education, health, and housing in the metropolitan areas. This may reflect the absence of effective representation of various rural and nonmetropolitan elements in Chilean political life, as well as the absence of effective regional organs of representation and administration.

Since 1973 and the advent of military rule, the pattern of regionalization has been largely one of top-down orientation. The Pinochet regime's interest was directed toward enhancing the central government's capacity to affect change at all levels, rather than the creation of autonomous organs of local and regional government. Raczynski (1986) reports that since 1973, there has been a significant and rather permanent drop in social expenditures by the state in health, education, and social security. She notes that for the period 1974–1981, the level of social expenditure did not rise to the level of 1970.

It is a curious series of starts and shifts in emphasis through which regionalization policy has traveled in Chile: first under Frei, as a government-directed effort to establish developmental councils and committees at the local and regional level, and later under Allende, as a policy of popular participation and economic development, and last of all, as a measure by the military government since 1973 to strengthen the administrative and control functions of the central government. None of these efforts has resulted in a viable set of local organs capable of operating with a reasonable degree of autonomy in the setting of regional priorities and the administration of regional-level programs.

B. Colombia

The early influences on regionalization in Colombia were French. At least four French missions visited Colombia in the course of the 1950s. This source of influence is markedly different from that of Mexico and Peru, for example, where the Tennessee Valley Authority model seems to have had a definite impact.

Another difference from other Latin American neighbors can be found in Colombia's unique political system. Colombia had a strong tradition of federalism throughout most of the last century, largely emanating from the Liberal Party. The high polarity of the political party system coupled with a dominant elite system and a fairly conservative social structure make Colombia, while not exactly unique, certainly a special case. The extreme degree of civil violence (*La Violencia*) that characterized the nation from the late 1940s until the end of the 1950s placed severe strains on the social fabric and the policymaking capacities of the political system.

Exhausted by the level of violence, the strong elite-dominated political system was weakened to the extent of permitting the first military regime, that of Rojas-Pinilla (1953–1957), to take power. Following this not entirely successful experiment, the two major political factions worked out a power-sharing compromise, the National Front, that lasted for a period of 16 years (1958–1974), with regular alterations in the presidency every 4 years. This political background is necessary to understand the course of regionalization in Colombia.

Regionalization and decentralization as administrative reform issues were considerably affected by violence and the elite-dominated nature of Colombian political life. Indeed, Hammergren (1983:158–159) refers to these issues as "orphans of the administrative reform movement." The high degree of fragmentation among power centers, coupled with the delicate power balance crafted by the two major political parties in the form of the National Front, made regionalization and decentralization too potentially controversial and volatile an issue to confront in the 1970s.

Colombia lacked both leadership and coherence in taking on the problem of overcentralization of the national administration. Although some agreement existed on the nature of the problem, consensus on a solution was sadly lacking. Authority was divided among at least four different units and agencies: the National Department of Planning (DNP), the Administrative

Department of the Civil Service (DASC), the Higher School of Public Administration (ESAP), and the Secretariat of Administrative Organization (SIAP). All of these agencies competed to one degree or another for jurisdiction over these issues. The result was a welter of plans that were often contradictory.

This pattern is extremely unfortunate in view of the trend toward rural depopulation in much of the nation, coupled with the increasing demand on urban social services as the result of internal migration and urban population growth. Griffin and Williams (1980:21) observe that

> Even today, much of the rural area lacks the most basic social services. Gains are being made in electrification, but most of the countryside still lacks electricity. Rural schools are increasing in numbers, but their quality remains low, and there are not sufficient spaces for all school-aged children or teachers to teach them. Despite government efforts to improve health care in the countryside, few doctors are available to rural peasants, and rural clinics and hospitals are few. Government programs such as minimum-wage laws go unenforced, thus not only creating economic hardships for peasants and their families, but also exaggerating the existing perception of great economic distinctions between urban places and the countryside.

Unfortunately, the above could serve as a description of the state of public services in the rural areas of many nations in the region. In Colombia and other nations, this situation has long-term consequences on the rural-urban migration patterns, contributing to further imbalance in the rates of regional economic development.

Development and its linkage to decentralization have been cited by one former President of Colombia, Julio Cesar Turboy Ayala, as the key to the social welfare issue (Amaro Guzmán 1986:265–266). Turboy Ayala, a Liberal who occupied the presidency from 1978 to 1982, noted that

> Development is closely linked to decentralization and we cannot attempt—although we have a typically centralized administration—to succeed until the vigilant presence of the state and the testimony of progress reach all parts of the country. In simultaneously conducting administrative decentralization and development, the day will not be far off when Colombia sees all its energies channeled towards the high goals of social well-being.

The problem in Colombian regionalization and reform has been that each president, since the initiation of the National Front, has introduced new reform plans without much effort to coordinate with past efforts and build on previous work in the area. The result has been a kind of anticipatory minimalization of the impacts of such reform programs, with the bureaucracies and the opposition political groups working together to devise strategies to limit the thrust of the new reforms. Furthermore, there was a distinct lack of political reality in some of the planners' conceptions of regionalization, at least in the early phases. A relentlessly theoretical view, with poles of development, regional boundaries having no basis in historical precedent, and a less than firm grasp on the need to coordinate planning with the existing ministerial offices all were characteristic of Colombian regional planning in the 1970s.

The results were less than encouraging. Programs set up under one presidential administration tended to be deemphasized under the next. The Pastrana administration (1970–1974) encouraged the establishment and management of urban development enterprises, which were deemphasized under Lopez Michelson (1974–1978), to site one example (Hammergren 1983:163). At times the National Department of Planning's support of the departmental development corporations wavered, as there was little evidence that those corporations, formed mostly at the subdepartmental level, were in any sense superior to the departments in which most of them existed (Hammergren 1983:163). In short, the whole decade saw little consistent progress and many aborted efforts.

C. Peru

Following the takeover by progressive military leaders in 1968, Peru embarked on an ambitious series of reforms, regionalization being only one of these. The military's goal of centralizing institutional development and channeling it to desired ends encouraged professional planners to think in terms of global regionalization strategies.

As the more progressive elements of the military gave way to more conservatively inclined ones, the enthusiasm for this holistic approach gave way to more pragmatic approaches. The influence of the U.S. Agency for International Development (USAID) was quite pronounced in Peruvian regional planning. Some pilot projects were launched with AID support, such as the Integrated Regional Development Project (IRD). USAID/Peru also worked in conjunction with the Disaster Reconstruction, Relief, and Rehabilitation (DRRR) project, and also financed a number of studies, reports, evaluations, workshops, seminars, and publications.

By the 1980s, the major thrust of the drive toward decentralization and regionalization took several forms: (1) the National Micro-Regional Program with its emphasis on creating and building microregional planning and implementation capacity; (2) the formation of regional governments, consisting of popularly elected regional assemblies that would manage all internal regional affairs (a deadline for this goal was set for 1988); (3) the reestablishment of the CORDES, or Regional Development Organisms, to act as transitional regional governments during an interim period (1978–1988); (4) the extension of technical assistance and training capacity to the municipalities, in part through the Municipal Development Fund; and (5) efforts by the government to decentralize the nation's development banking system (Hess 1986:27).

While all major political parties in Peru (with the exception of the right of center Popular Christian Party; PPC) paid rhetorical lip service to decentralization, it is difficult to see how any political party, including APRA and the United Left, could be persuaded to surrender control of the highly centralized process through which the CORDES receive their funding. It would be a serious loss of direct influence at the regional and local level, something that any political party is loath to lose.

Still, substantial progress has been made toward decentralization in Peru, and the foundations that were laid in the 1970s and early to mid 1980s should provide the necessary support for the next phase of development, always presuming that the political will to continue the process of regionalization and decentralization maintains itself.

III. CONCLUSIONS

The pattern of regionalization policy from nation to nation demonstrates few consistent similarities. While each nation shares a common legacy, the centralistic Iberian tradition of governmental administration, it is equally true that each country in the region has had a largely independent political development since at least the 1820s.

And while it would be simple to explain the lack of progress in some nations toward regionalization and decentralization in terms of the common Iberian legacy, the preceding examination of three nations' experiences suggests otherwise. Even in a nation such as Colombia, which has had a rather stronger tradition of regional autonomy than many other states in the region, the obstacles to achieving regional reform were daunting. In Colombia the main problems were to be found in the elite nature of the society and the unique political solution in the form of the National Front to the long-standing problem of partisan violence.

Throughout Latin America, the rise of mass-based political parties has complicated the attainment of true regionalization and decentralized administration. Such political organizations require large amounts of campaign financing and patronage in order to maintain themselves and remain electorally viable. These needs are in fundamental conflict with the goals of regional fiscal autonomy and professional public administration in a decentralized context.

Where the military has taken power and pursued regionalization, as in Chile (1973–1990) and in Peru from 1968 to 1980, the centralizing trend has been little different. The military has tended to perceive the need for regionalization, but rather as a means of achieving more effective administrative control at the local and regional levels. While this is perhaps in harmony with military notions of organizational design, it denies the regional units any true autonomy.

The immediate prospects for achieving regional-based, decentralized administration are at best mixed. The growing realization of the long-standing inequities of national development, the increasing demands of the masses for political participation, and the successful examples of other nations, most notably in Europe, are all long-term sources of encouragement for the Latin American regionalization movement.

REFERENCES

Alderfer, H.F. *Local Government in Developing Countries*. McGraw-Hill, New York, 1964.

Alves Da Silva, L. Planificación administrativa, regionalización del desarrollo y regionalización administrativa como predondiciones para el desarrollo regional. In *Administración regional en Améerica Latina* (A.B. Rofman, ed.). Ediciones SLIP, Buenos Aires, 1976, pp. 47–65.

Amaro Guzmán, R. *Introducción a la Administración Pública*. McGraw-Hill, Mexico City, 1986.

Barrenecha, C. *Regionalización y Lucha Descentralista: Analisis Global y Propuesta para Puno*. Tarea, Tecira and C.I.E.D., Lima, Peru, 1984.

Bedrack, M. *La Estrateqia de Desarrollo Espacial en Chile, 1970–73*. Ediciones SIAP, Buenos Aires, 1974.

Boisier, S. Pobres, desarrollo regional y decentralizacón. *Estudios Sociales 40* (trimester 2), CPU, 1983.

Boisier, S. Un dificil equilibria: centralización y decentralización en planificación regional. *Estudios de Economia V*(1), (1984).

Busey, J.L. *Latin American Political Guide*, 18th ed. Robert Schalkenbach Foundation, New York, 1985.

Carpio Muñoz, J.G., Chaves Belaunde, F., Lozada Stanbury, J., and Simons Camino, S. *Como Hacer Gobierno Regionalo*. Intercampus, Lima, Peru, 1984.

Centro Peruano de Estudios Para el Desarrollo Regional. *Dictamen de Mayoría y Minoría del Proyecto de Ley de Bases de Regionalización*. C.E.R., Lima, Peru, 1986.

Chetwynd, E., Hatch, J., Hammergren, L., Johnson, R., Rondinelli, D., and Salinas, P.W. *Integrated Regional Development: Final Evaluation*. USAID, Lima, Peru, June 1985.

Cleaves, P. *Bureaucratic Politics and Administration in Chile*. University of California, Berkeley, 1974.

De Althaus, J., Delgado, C., Guerrero, E., and Lopez, C. *Communidad, Gobierno Local y Desarrollo Provincial: El Caso de Chancay*. Centro Peruano des Estudios Para el Desarrollo Regional (C.E.R.), Lima, Peru, 1985.

De Oliveira Campos, R. Public administration in Latin America. In *Readings in Comparative Public Administration* (N. Raphaeli, ed.). Allyn and Bacon, Boston, 1967, pp. 283–294.

Franco Temple, I. Algunos problemas cuyas soluciones estan fuera del alcance de las corporaciones departamentales de desarrollo y que han obstaculizado su gestion. Mimeograph, Lima, August 1986.

Funes, J.C. Aspectos Financieros del Desarrollo Regional. In *Administración Regional en América Latina* (A. Rofman, ed.). Ediciones SIAP, Buenos Aires, 1976.

Furtado, C. *Obstacles to Development in Latin America*. Anchor, New York, 1970.

Gilbert, A. *Latin American Development: A Geographical Perspective*. Penguin, Baltimore, 1974.

Gordillo, A. *Problemas del Control de la Administración Pública en América Latina*. Editorial Civitas, Madrid, 1981.

Gonzales Roberto, E., and Durand, E. *Descentralismo y Planificación: Balance y Propuesta*. Centro Peruano de Estudios Para El Desarrollo Regional, Lima, 1985.

Griffin, E.C., and Williams, L.S. Social implications of changing population patterns: the case of rural depopulation in Colombia. In *Internal Migration Systems in the Developing World* (R.N. Thomas and J.M. Hunter, eds.). G.K. Hall and Schenkman, Boston, 1980, pp. 17–25.

Guerrero Orozco, O. *Introducción a la Administración Pública.* Harper & Row Latinoamericana, Mexico City, 1985.

Hammergren, L. *Development and the Politics of Administrative Reform,* Westview Press, Boulder, CO, 1983.

Hartlyn, J., and Morley, S.A., eds. *Latin American Political Economy.* Westview Press, Boulder, CO, 1986.

Haya de la Torre, V.R. *El Antiimperialismo y el APRA.* Ediciones Lyder, Lima, 1986.

Heady, F. *Public Administration: A Comparative Perspective.* Marcel Dekker, New York, 1984.

Hess, D. Decentralization in Peru: USAID/Peru Contributions to the National Policy Dialogue, 1984–1986. Mimeograph, USAID/Peru, Lima, May 1986.

Honey, J.C., ed., *Toward Strategies for Public Administration Development in Latin America.* Syracuse University Press, Syracuse, NY, 1968.

Hopkins, R. *Desarrollo Designual y Crisis en la Agricultura Peruana: 1944–1969.* Instituto de Estudios Peruanos, Lima, 1981.

INFOM-AID. *Diagnostico de Goviernos Locales a Nivel National 1985.* Program de Assistencia Technica y Capacitacion a Municipalidades, Lima, 1985.

Jiménez Nieto, J. *Teoria Administrativa del Gobierno,* Vol. 1. Universidad del Pacifico, Lima, 1977.

LaFont, R. *Decoloniser en France.* Editions Gallimard, Paris, 1971.

Lizárraga Bobbio, R. *Estrategias para la Decentralizacion y el Desarrollo Regional.* Centro Peruano de Estudios para el Desarrollo Regional, Lima, 1985.

Lizárraga Bobbio, R., and Izquierdo Larrea, H. *Sistemas Financiero y Propuestario Descentralizados.* C.E.R., Lima, 1986.

Makón, M. El presupuesto del sector público regional. In *Administración Regional en América Latina* (A. Rofman, ed.). Ediciones SIAP, Buenos Aires, 1976, pp. 167–191.

Mariategui, J.C. *Siete Ensayos de Interpretacion de la Realidid Peruana.* Biblioteca Amauta, Lima, 1968.

Monroy, D. La experiencia de Venezuela en cuanto a regionalizacion de los ingresos y gastos publicos. In *Administración Regional en América Latina* (A. Rofman, ed.). Ediciones SIAP, Buenos Aires, 1976, pp. 191–227.

Montgomery, J.D., and Siffen, W.H.J. *Approaches to Development: Politics, Administration and Change.* McGraw-Hill, New York, 1966.

Negron, M. La planificación urbana como complemento de la planificación regional. In *Administración Regional en América Latina.* Ediciones SIAP, Buenos Aires, 1976, pp. 125–145.

Niera Alva, E. Desarrolio regional en América Latina; Utopia o estrategia de desarrollo nacional. In *Administración Regional en América Latina* (A. Rofman, ed.). Ediciones SIAP, Buenos Aires, 1976, pp. 247–289.

Pichardo Pagaza, I. El análisis instrucional de la administración regional. In *Administración regional en América Latina* (A. Rofman, ed.). Ediciones SIAP, Buenos Aires, 1976, pp. 67–111.

Raczynski, D. *La Regionalización y la Politica Economicosocial del Regimen Militar: El Impacto Regional.* Notas Tecnicas No. 84. Corporación de Investigaciones Economicas para Latino-américa, Santiago, Chile, July 1986.

Raphaeli, N., ed. *Readings in Comparative Public Administration.* Allyn and Bacon, Boston, 1967.

Rebaza del Pino, J.J., Garcia de Romana, A., and Monge, F. *Estructura y Gestion del Estado Descentralizado.* C.E.R., Lima, 1986.

Rodwin, L., and Associates. *Planning Urban Growth and Regional Development: The Experience of the Guayana Program of Venezuela.* M.I.T. Press, Cambridge, MA, 1969.

Rofman, A., ed. *Administración Regional en América Latina.* Sociedad Interamericana de Planificación, Buenos Aires, 1976.

Rojas Samanez, A. *Partidos Politicos en el Peru,* 5th ed. Centro Documentacion Andina (CDI), Lima, 1986.

Stavenhagen, R. Seven erroneous theses about Latin America. In *Latin American Radicalism* (I.L. Horowitz, J. de Castro, and J. Gerassi, eds.). Vintage, New York, 1969, pp. 102–117.

Stecher, A., Gonzáles, J., and Bernex de Falen, N. *Descentralización-Regionalización-Microregionalización.* C.E.R., Lima, 1986.

Stöhr, W.B. La regionalización como instrumento de la política de desarrollo. Algunos enfoques comparativos de la experiencia latinoaméricana. In *Administración Regional en América Latina* (A. Rofman, ed.). Ediciones SIAP, 1976, pp. 229–246.

Stone, R. *Dreams of Amazonia.* Penguin, New York, 1986.

Travieso, F. Planificación del desarrollo regional. La planificación regional como instrumento. In *Administración Regional en América Latina* (A. Rofman, ed.). Ediciones SIAP, 1976, pp. 113–124.

Wiarda, H., and Kline, H. *Latin American Politics and Development*, 2nd ed. Westview Press, Boulder, CO, 1985.

Wilson, P. *Problematica Regional y Política Central en el Peru.* Universidad del Pacifico, Lima, November 1983.

39
Merit Reform in Latin America

A Comparative Perspective

Karen Ruffing-Hilliard   *U.S. Agency for International Development, Cairo, Egypt*

> Between the splendor of the word and the sadness of the reality falls a shadow.
> —Jaime Vidal Perdomo

I. INTRODUCTION

The history of merit reform in Latin America spans more than three decades. While in the first half of the twentieth century isolated attempts were made to legislate civil service systems and to create central personnel offices to administer them, the bulk of merit reform activity occurred during the cold war period. A baseline study commissioned by the Organization of American States in 1954 concluded that among the 20 Latin American republics one encountered 20 different varieties of public personnel systems. These ranged from complete civil service systems, which included civil service legislation, a central personnel office charged with recruitment, selection and promotion on the basis of merit, and an established retirement plan, to systems that functioned entirely on the basis of spoils (Fonseca Pimentel 1966:198).

Consequently, the 1950s and 1960s witnessed a massive infusion of technical assistance provided by institutions like the International Cooperation Administration, the United Nations Division for Public Administration, and later the Agency for International Development (AID). These donor agencies focused on assisting the developing nations in drafting career civil service legislation and establishing a central personnel agency to oversee its implementation.

Nevertheless, in spite of technical assistance projects in several Latin American countries including Colombia, Venezuela, Ecuador, and Brazil, Fonseca Pimentel (1966:200) could find only seven that had civil service legislation and a central personnel agency in place. Only Brazil, Peru, Costa Rica, Panama, Argentina, Colombia, and Ecuador could be said to evince even these elementary features of a merit-based personnel system. Even so, more in-depth studies by Gilbert Siegel and Kleber Nascimento (1965), Jaime Vidal Perdomo (1982), and Karen Mangelsdorf and Zane Reeves (1988) revealed that the early optimism surrounding merit reforms in Brazil, Colombia, and Ecuador may have been unfounded.

Yet if merit reform programs in Latin America have failed or had only mixed success, it has not been for lack of trying. In fact, many countries succeeded in passing or decreeing civil service laws. Recent studies suggest that it is in the implementation phase of the policy process that these systems appear to break down. Nevertheless, donor agencies forge ahead with reform programs in countries as diverse as Somalia and Zaire without stopping to assess the results of previous efforts (Jumelle 1974).

It is the purpose of this chapter to examine and evaluate the success or failure of merit reform policies in Latin America using the framework for implementation analysis advanced by Daniel Mazmanian and Paul Sabatier (1983:1–30). The discussion will focus on reform attempts in Ecuador, Venezuela, and Costa Rica. Examples from the Dominican Republic, Colombia, and Brazil will also be incorporated into the analysis. The information will be derived from a review of the extant literature regarding civil service systems in developing nations as well as field research conducted in Ecuador between 1984 and 1986.

II. CONCEPTUAL MODEL

The conceptual framework posited by Mazmanian and Sabatier grew out of the author's observations regarding the implementation of regulatory policies in the United States. The discussion that follows is drawn from their ground-breaking work, *Implementation and Public Policy* (1983:1–43). Despite the domestic roots of the model, the relationships hypothesized therein are sufficiently universal to make the framework applicable to policy environments in less developed nations as well. The framework identifies several independent variables that are believed to influence the outcome of policy reform programs. The authors divide the independent variables into three broad categories: (1) those indicative of the tractability of the problem, (2) those concerned with the nature of the statute itself and the extent to which it structures implementation, and (3) the nonstatutory variables affecting implementation.

The term "tractability" refers to the amount of difficulty encountered when solving a problem. Factors such as the availability of appropriate technology, knowledge of the causal linkages underlying a problem and the ability to develop inexpensive performance indicators determine to a great extent the facility of solution.

Furthermore, several factors related to the target group itself are relevant to the analysis. The extent and diversity of the behavior change desired and the size of the target group relative to the total population affect problem solving. According to Mazmanian and Sabatier (1983), fewer behaviors, a smaller target group, and less behavior change are positively associated with successful policy implementation.

The second set of independent variables measures the extent to which the statute defines the parameters for implementation. If a policy is to be successful, the statute or executive order must define precisely the objectives of the policy and rank them in order of priority. This conveys clearly to the implementing agency not only the nature of the policy directive, but the priority it is to receive among other programs that compete for staff time and attention. The statute should explicate the causal theory underlying the reform. It is imperative that the policy directive stipulate the agency responsible for implementation as well as its place in the overall administrative hierarchy. This approach assumes great importance when coordinated action among semiautonomous agencies is desired or when the policies of a central bureau are to be carried out by agencies at lower levels in the hierarchy.

The degree of commitment of agency officials to the policy is crucial when assigning responsibility for implementation to an existing agency. Because the choice of implementing officials is often severely constrained in practice, policymakers will often create a new agency to carry out their mandate.

The extent to which participation by outsiders can be biased in favor of the achievement of legal objectives may also determine the success or failure of the policy. Target groups (or interest groups) are often well organized and possess the financial resources to influence policy, yet the beneficiaries (often the general public) may lack the resources to participate in support of the statute. By providing for equal access by beneficiaries in the statute itself, implementation may be enhanced. Provisions for judicial, legislative, or executive participation in implementation may help or hinder the process, depending on the degree of support for the policy on the part of these entities. Nevertheless, allowances for judicial review, legislative veto, independent evaluation, etc. should be clearly spelled out in the statute. Finally, an initial allocation of resources in sufficient quantity to ensure implementation is clearly required.

The third and final category of variables encompasses those that are outside the scope of control of the statute. This category includes factors such as the emergence of other social problems that take precedence over the original statute, the need for periodic infusions of political support from executives, legislators, and the general public, changing attitudes and resources of constituency groups, and the commitment and leadership skills of the officials responsible for implementation.

The stages in the implementation process comprise the dependent variables in the model. The initial policy outputs of implementing agencies must be followed by compliance with the outputs on the part of target groups. Compliance alone, however, does not ensure the success of the policy. The statute must also achieve the desired impact. This is contingent in large part on the validity of the underlying causal theory. The final phase of the implementation process is the perception of the policy's impact by the public and possible revision of the policy.

The aforementioned framework assumes a democratic form of government where interest groups and the general public have an explicit role in policymaking and where executive, legislative, and judicial functions are separate and relatively well defined. It is not difficult, however, to adapt such a model to a military, corporatist, or even a totalitarian system. While the political institutions may vary, conflicting interests still surface and are mediated to some extent by all governments. Nevertheless, the strength of the original model is its ability to explain how conflicting forces in a democratic environment mold the process of policy implementation. Consequently, the framework provides a useful tool for assessing how the implementation process has fared in the changing political environment of Latin America.

III. MERIT REFORM: THE PROBLEM

The sense of urgency regarding merit reform in Latin America during the late 1950s, 1960s, and 1970s is inextricably tied to the attitude toward development that prevailed during the cold war period. The perceived Soviet threat, the Korean War, and the subsequent revolution in Cuba led to a widely shared perception that it was "five minutes to midnight" in Latin America. If development did not occur, and occur quickly, Latin American countries were at risk of falling prey to leftist-inspired revolutions.

Development, it was thought, required not only increased economic growth but a measure of reform and redistribution. For example, assistance provided under the Alliance for Progress was often contingent upon agrarian reform. While equity considerations did not initially constitute the driving force behind donor efforts, they gained importance in the 1970s with the advent of the New Directions programs in donor agencies like AID. Due to the broad range of activities to be undertaken, host countries were required to submit national development plans. The need for central planning and coordination among sectors and the expanded role of the state in the direct provision of services led to increased public employment and public spending. These trends logically prompted concern regarding the skill levels of public servants.

The inevitable comparison between the need for skilled civil servants and the quality of existing government employees led to complaints about low performance levels among bureaucrats, the dearth of trained professionals, and the problems associated with the recruitment and retention of qualified personnel (Graham 1976:43).

At the same time that these nations were engaged in developing their economies, they were also concerned with developing their polities. In Latin America the populist movement reached its apex. This grassroots movement eschewed political parties in favor of charismatic leadership by the strong man (or *caudillo*). Both the populists and the more organized political parties that vied for power with them were more interested in the political loyalties of public servants than their competence.

Hence, the dilemma of the civil service in Latin America came to be viewed as a dichotomy that pitted neutral competence against political responsiveness, merit against spoils. The spoils system soon became the culprit when the Latin American public sector failed to live up to its promises regarding national development. This conceptualization of the underlying tension in the public sector has persisted into the 1980s. Richard Kearney summarized the problem thus:

> . . . one must recognize that the almost unfettered worship of political responsiveness has not been conducive to social and economic development. Patronage and spoils may be useful for promoting political loyalty but they do nothing to staff a civil service with competent, technically proficient employees who are responsive to the public interest and capable of carrying out development programs (Kearney 1988:70).

The diagnosis was that progress in an era of increased public sector involvement in developing country economies could not occur without a politically neutral, competent civil service in the Weberian sense. The cure that followed logically from this conclusion was to install a merit-based civil service system similar to those possessed by developed nations. These assumptions formed the underlying causal theory for the policy reforms that would follow.

Once the problem had been identified, its tractability revolved around the availability of technology to solve the problem, the diffusion of that technology, and the means to measure its impact. In this case, the timing could not have been better. Public administration in the United States was enamored with the management science approach. Problem solving was merely a matter of matching the dilemma with the appropriate technological solution.

The United States had over half a century of experience with merit systems that could be brought to bear on the problems of the Latin American civil service. Western technical know-how regarding civil service legislation, civil service commissions, centralized personnel agencies, and classification plans was believed to be directly relevant to not only the Latin American but the Asian and African situations as well (Sharma 1981:60–66). The technology was therefore available, and it fell to donor agencies like the United Nations and AID to identify the most appropriate means of disseminating it.

The model chosen by the donors for diffusion of innovation is what Barbara Nelson terms point-source diffusion (1984:1–30). Point-source diffusion, as opposed to horizontal diffusion, occurs when a technical or policy innovation is discovered at some central level of government. Normally, model legislation is written and attempts are made to coax lower-level governments or administrative bodies to adopt the recommended policies. This model is most commonly used to describe the diffusion of innovation in a federal system within one country. However, the process that occurs when international donors, bilateral or multilateral, attempt to encourage the adoption of new technologies in the developing world appears quite similar.

The case of merit reform in Latin America appears to follow such a pattern of diffusion. For example, the U.N. Division of Public Administration was actively involved in reform attempts in several Latin American countries. Where bilateral donors such as AID were concerned, frequently the same consulting firms were used to write legislation and structure reforms in more than one country. The Chicago-based firm of J.L. Jacobs and Company provided technical assistance to both the Ecuadorean and Venezuelan governments. The civil service system that took root in Costa Rica closely resembled the ideal system outlined in the U.S. Intergovernmental Personnel Act (Hayes and Reeves 1984:34–35; Kearney 1988:74). The Costa Rican Constitution of 1949 provided for merit appointment of civil servants, removal only with just cause, and paved the way for the drafting of a career service statute. This statute was approved in 1953 and implemented in 1955. The law provides for a chief administrator, or director general, who is appointed by a board but is accountable directly to the president. His office oversees recruitment and selection, position classification, compensation schedules, promotions, performance appraisal, training, discipline, and dismissal. Coverage of the executive branch reached 78% in 1986, although parastatals still remain outside the merit system. A civil service tribunal (which mirrors the old U.S. Civil Service Commission) hears appeals on dismissals and disciplinary actions (Kearney 1988:74). Job security is high, although it is reportedly lower than that enjoyed by Brazilian civil servants (Fonseca Pimentel 1966:204). Fringe benefits include health care, vacations, and pensions. Advances in merit system coverage have been constant and measurable. In short, Costa Rican reform has led to a merit system not unlike that of the United States.

The early success stories of Costa Rica and Brazil led U.S. experts to believe that diffusion of the innovation to the remaining Latin American nations was only a matter of time. Measurement of progress was viewed as simple. It was based on the presence of structures such as a career civil service law, a classification plan and salary schedule, a central personnel agency to implement them, and fringe benefits and retirement. The functioning of the system could be measured using indicators such as the number of employees recruited through competitive or assembled exams, number of employees with tenure, and number and type of institutions covered by the career law.

With these criteria in mind, donor agencies set out to reform the civil service of the remaining Latin American countries including Ecuador, Venezuela, Panama, Colombia, and, later, the Dominican Republic. The reform programs contemplated nothing less than a total overhaul of the host country personnel systems, the drafting of legislation, the creation of implementing agencies, and the coverage of all existing ministries and agencies within the target countries (Groves 1967:439).

As Roderick Groves (1967:439) and Richard Kearney (1988:72) have observed, the new systems being advocated amounted to nothing less than a total break with past practice. Whereas heretofore appointments were made on the basis of particularistic criteria such as friendship, kinship ties, and political loyalty, the new system was to be based on objective criteria of merit. The Venezuelan case is illustrative of the extent of the behavior change required.

Venezuelan politics revolved on the concept of personalist rule derived in part from its Iberian culture heritage and in part from its own political history of successive dictatorships. Prior to the discovery of oil, all other resources, especially land, had been controlled by a tiny elite interrelated by ties of kinship and regional association. Consequently, political rule in Venezuela depended more on personal than partisan loyalty.

The traditional bureaucratic system accorded the president the right to appoint and remove top ministerial executives, who in turn exercised great discretion in the appointment and removal of their subordinates. There was no pressure to relate work and compensation, least of all from the employees who were acutely aware of their vulnerability. The reformers intended to transform this system with the package previously outlined: (1) a merit system law, (2) a classification plan, and (3) a compensation plan. Furthermore, the prerogative of hiring and firing was to be removed from line executives and centralized in the hands of a director general along the lines of the Costa Rican model. The target group was to include all 13 ministries and the autonomous institutes.

The basic provisions of the reform attempt in Ecuador were nearly identical. They included a basic career law, a classification plan, a compensation schedule, and a central national personnel directorate with agency-level equivalents in 15 ministries. Coverage of all white collar employees was to be achieved by 1969 (Thrash 1966:124). The magnitude of the proposed change from a traditional to a "modern" personnel system was equally great in Ecuador. Ecuadorean politics, characterized by strong populist tendencies, had a history of strong-man civilian presidents who were repeatedly overthrown by military juntas. In fact, the major political figure of the 20th century, Velasco Ibarra, was elected president six times between 1933 and 1972. He was overthrown or prevented from taking office all six times. Nevertheless, his personalist style dominated Ecudorean politics until his death in 1979. Hence, Ecuador, like Venezuela, had a strong tradition of political patronage based on personal rather than partisan loyalties, which extended to the very lowest levels in the public bureaucracy.

Finally, the case of the Dominican Republic is similar in that totalitarian rule by the dictator Rafael Trujillo persisted from 1930 to 1961. Western-style partisan political activity developed during the three administrations of Joaquin Balaguer (1966–1978). Nevertheless, the concept of centralized, personalistic decision making through presidential appointments to all public-sector positions persisted even though it adopted a veneer of partisan loyalty. The relatives and friends of the president are the first to reap the benefits of the spoils system (Kearney 1986:pp. 145–147).[1]

In sum, an analysis of the tractability of the problem reveals mixed results. The causal linkage, the technology, the model for diffusion, and the means of measuring change were all considered to be self evident at the time. The overwhelming optimism that characterized development efforts well into the 1970s seemed to reduce, if not obscure entirely, the magnitude of the policy change that was contemplated. This optimism sprang from the conviction that Western technology was the answer to the problems of the developing world. This optimistic outlook was confident that an accurately and comprehensively designed project would succeed in spite of cultural and political obstacles. Therefore, a closer look at the mechanics of reform is warranted.

IV. THE REFORMS

Detailed examination of the civil service legislation of all of the Latin American nations that purport to possess merit systems is clearly beyond the scope of this study. A brief examination of the Ecuadorean case should suffice to point out the difficulties inherent in structuring implementation by means of statute or executive decree.

The Ecuadorean case illustrates nicely the second set of variables proposed by Mazmanian and Sabatier and bears out the difficulties inherent in structuring implementation by means of statute or executive decree. The Ecuadorean Civil Service and Administrative Career Law of 1964, rewritten in 1978, shows clear evidence of the underlying causal theory explicated. The legislation links a merit system and stable career civil service with efficient delivery of government services and the social and economic transformation of the nation. A trained and diligent bureaucracy is regarded as a positive force in the nation's progress (Comision de Legislacion 1983:4).

The law establishes eligibility requirements for the civil service. Nepotism is outlawed. All nominations for the public service must be registered with a central national personnel directorate (NPD).

The NPD is headed by a presidentially appointed director, who reports directly to the chief executive. The director has the authority to appoint the personnel with the NPD. Responsibility for expanding the merit system to all dependencies of the state and for elaborating administrative regulations corresponding to the law rests with the NPD. It oversees position classification, remuneration, testing, and training. The NPD is charged with all recruitment, selection, and promotion decisions except those it may delegate to the corresponding offices in each ministry. The ministerial offices are primarily concerned with implementing training programs, maintaining statistical records, evaluating and disciplining employees, and fulfilling whatever technical functions may be delegated to them by the NPD (Comision de Legislacion 1983:22–23).

The law provides for a Board of Appeals that hears grievances. Dismissal must be based on just cause and can be appealed to the Board. Certificates of tenure are awarded to those who serve the initial probation period of six months. Provisions for fringe benefits and retirement are clearly outlined in the law.

The coverage of the career service is presented as being universal with several exceptions including the armed forces, diplomatic corps, blue collar workers, legislative and judicial personnel, political appointments at the apex of central government agencies, teachers, and those subject to other laws. This effectively excludes employees of the numerous autonomous agencies and parastatals that operate in the country. In addition, the director of the NPD may recommend the exclusion from the merit system of certain categories of civil servants whose functions are essentially political (Comision de Legislacion 1983:22–23).

Though the law appears comprehensive on the surface, the effect of these provisions is the exclude 81% of all public employees from the career civil service. In fact, in 1982, the proportion of the total number of bureaucrats employed by autonomous institutions not covered by the law was 17.4%, nearly equal to the proportion covered by the merit system (19%) (Mangelsdorf and Reeves 1988:11).

There are several other "transitory dispositions" that serve to limit the coverage of the law. These include provisions for grandfathering incumbents of positions that now fall under the administrative career law as long as they meet the basic requirements for the position. If they do not, they may present their credentials for a noncompetitive examination. If found to be otherwise qualified, they need not meet the established job requirements. Finally, those offices within the ministries that have traditionally selected employees for positions may continue to do so until advised by the NPD that personnel selected through the merit system are available for a particular type of position. These ministerial appointments must be registered with the NPD and are considered provisional (Comision de Legislacion 1983:22–23).

These exceptions to the law are not uncommon elsewhere in Latin America. They are present to a greater or lesser extent in all Latin American civil service systems. Exceptions for parastatals and decentralized (autonomous) agencies are present in Costa Rica, Colombia, and Venezuela (Groves 1967:444; Vidal Perdomo 1982:81). The result is that merit reform legislation often lacks the "teeth" to enforce compliance on the part of even the executive branch agencies. Yet insofar as the legislation has the potential to effectively structure implementation, its success is contingent upon continued political and social support for the principles upon which it is based. In essence, success or failure of administrative reform depends largely upon social, economic, and political variables that are outside the scope of the legislation per se.

V. THE ENVIRONMENT

Returning to our conceptual framework, it becomes clear that a variety of factors that can alter the course of policy reform are beyond the reach of the policy itself. Policy reforms are experiments and, unlike those that occur in the laboratory, subject to changing environmental conditions. A problem that one day captures the attention of the lawmakers and the public is supplanted the next by a new, more pressing dilemma.

Merit reform, considered a burning issue in the Latin America of the 1960s, was replaced by a heightened concern for the expansion of programs to serve the disadvantaged in society. The urban and rural poor continued to exert pressure on democratic and military governments alike to address social concerns like education, public health, and social welfare. The traditional government ministries in both Ecuador and Costa Rica were viewed as too large and inefficient to address the specific concerns of constituent groups, hence the proliferation of smaller, more flexible autonomous institutions that fell outside the established civil service system. Their exclusion, as seen in the Ecuadorean case, was deliberate. Traditional classification and compensation plans were viewed as obstacles to recruitment of the most qualified applicants. Systems used by autonomous agencies permitted the payment of higher salaries and better benefits.

Even in the core ministries, pressures related to the administration of enlarged social programs necessitated rapid hiring of new employees. In Ecuador, the number of public servants increased from 150,000 in 1976 to 240,000 in postelection 1981. The hiring of new employees had not yet peaked. In 1983 alone, over 12,000 new employees joined the government service. The pressure to respond to the staffing needs of the ministries took precedence over the observance of strict merit principles. In 1983, competitive examinations were given to less than 300 of the new employees. Fewer than 1500 were hired by means of assembled examinations (Mangelsdorf and Reeves 1988:4–14).

The periodic infusion of support so crucial to the implementation of policy reforms was often absent in Latin American polities. Successive administrations tended to view reforms passed by a predecessor as limitations on the freedom of the new chief executive to appoint and remove employees. Moveover, since reforms were often initiated by military dictatorships immediately prior to new elections, they failed to consider the need of candidates to consolidate political support and reward backers once elected. Not surprisingly, reforms begun by military regimes in Brazil in 1930, Venezuela in 1958, and Ecuador in 1978 all suffered setbacks under the democratic regimes that followed (Garcia-Zamor 1969:315).

Regardless of whether candidates favored the merit system in principle, they also had to take action to ensure political stability by consolidating the support of elements opposed to dictatorship. For example, in postelection Venezuela, the Betancourt government was confronted with two choices: (1) purge the incompetent and unreliable in the existing bureaucracy and replace them with employees selected on the basis of merit, or (2) incorporate the old bureaucracy into civil permanence. The first alternative was viewed as dangerous to political stability in that the opposition would surely side with the now unemployed civil servants. In fact, public employee unions, fearing just such a purge, had voiced their opposition to the new merit system in Congress. Clearly a purge would threaten to destabilize the regime. The second alternative, the wholesale incorporation of the existing bureaucrats into the permanent civil service, would have subordinated competence completely to the need for political stability. It also meant the even opponents of the regime would be given tenure. This was not an attractive option either. Hence, the logical response of the government was to support merit reform in principle and apply it in practice only selectively, if at all. Political appointments were used to strengthen bureaucratic competence at strategic levels in ministries, but where political stability might suffer, the incumbents were left alone. The commission that spearheaded the reform was allowed to function and make recommendations, yet most appointments were made in the traditional manner. The president had the best of both worlds. He could appear "modern" by supporting the reform outwardly without having to implement it (Groves 1966:443).

In the case of Ecuador, because a few competitive exams were administered and the national personnel directorate continued to set standards for the system as a whole, the illusion of progress toward a merit system was maintained while in reality little occurred. For example, during the Roldos-Hurtado administration only 26,000 civil servants had been tenured by 1982, a mere 10% of the total (Mangelsdorf and Reeves 1988:6).

Implementation of policy reform also relies on the support of constituencies and/or beneficiaries in addition to that provided by the executive branch. Again merit reform has tended to suffer from a lack of support from both groups. On the one hand, the groups most likely to be affected by the reform (the civil servants, government employee unions, and employees of the autonomous institutions) have little to gain from reform and often much to lose. While the concepts of job security and due process are attractive to some, they are only attractive if the employee is the lucky one who retains his job once a merit system is instituted. The employees of the autonomous institutions strongly oppose the incorporation of their agencies into the system because they stand to lose their increased salaries and benefits.

On the other hand, the general public, which stands to gain from a more efficient and effective bureaucracy, is poorly organized, has a diverse set of concerns, and has little access to the policy process. Moreover, as is the case in the Dominican Republic, the public may simply resign itself to the corruption and inefficiency of the spoils system. Government jobs are viewed as the path to riches and power and everyone simply waits his turn. Hence, the desire to change the system may be absent among the general public, as everyone believes that one day he may benefit from spoils (Kearney 1988:72). All of these factors combine to hinder the implementation of reforms like a merit-based personnel system.

VI. DISCUSSION AND CONCLUSION

Returning to our theoretical framework, the foregoing sections illustrate that the problem of merit reform was not as amenable to an infusion of Western technology as was previously believed. Reform programs relied heavily on superficial technical solutions that ignored the cultural and political dimensions of change. The scope of the reforms and the degree of behavioral change attempted in retrospect seem monumental, yet during the optimistic decade of the 1960s they appeared attainable.

Though the technology needed to reform the system existed, as did the means to disseminate it, even by the standards of measurement set at the time, the reforms have failed in most countries. Even Costa Rica, which possessed the most advanced merit system in Latin America, had classified only 78% of its executive branch employees as of 1986. Parastatals and other autonomous agencies, which are excluded from the civil service system, employ 55% of all government employees. Their personnel systems continue to operate on the basis of particularistic criteria rather than merit (Kearney 1988:74). In Ecuador, which was also considered by Fonseca Pimentel (1966:209–210) and Thrash (1966:124) to be a success story, only 19% of government employees are covered by the Administrative Career Law. Patronage appointments that occur under the guise of a "review of credentials" by the NPD are rampant (Mangelsdorf and Reeves 1988:13).

The ability of statutes to structure implementation is limited because interest groups that oppose civil service legislation usually manage to dilute their content. Exceptions for autonomous institutions and loopholes regarding merit versus patronage appointments result in laws that lack "teeth." Adherence to laws and administrative rules is formalistic. Agencies give lip service to merit system provisions while they are busy devising ways to circumvent them. Systems such as position classification plans are widely adapted to particularistic criteria: people rather than positions are classified (Siegal and Nascimento 1965:175–176).

Perhaps more importantly, the periodic infusions of political support have not been forthcoming. Floundering democratic regimes have been too concerned with trying to stay afloat to risk jeopardizing political support for the sake of merit principles. With neither the bureaucrats not the general public pressing for reform, politicians have been content to exercise the wide discretion allowed by a spoils system.

The notable lack of enthusiasm on the part of Latin American polities where merit reform is concerned must then force us to reexamine the fundamental assumptions that drove this bustling reform activity of the past three decades. Perhaps the fault lies not with the regimes but with the reforms themselves. In the first place, these imported reforms failed to take into account the unique political environment of Latin America. Perhaps the fact that Costa Rica has been the most successful nation in Latin America in implementing merit reform is no coincidence. It is also the most stable democracy. It could be argued that to expect fledgling democracies on the rest of the continent to put political development on the back burner while they pursue a merit-based civil service is akin to "putting the cart before the horse." It seems only natural in a region where democratic regimes are sandwiched in between military dictatorships, and where populism has retarded political development, for politicians to use patronage to edify political parties. This concept should hardly be foreign to a country that was home to the Jacksonians. Furthermore, the Latin American nations did not have the benefit of a triggering mechanism as dramatic as the assassination of a president to galvanize them to action.

Finally, perhaps we should examine the causal linkage that served as the basis for technical assistance in merit reform. The assumption went something like this: If development is to occur, the government must expand its role in the process. This will required technically competent professional civil servants. A spoils system is antithetical to a qualified, competent public service. Therefore, the solution is a reform program to establish a merit-based civil service system.

While this causal theory appeared sound to Western public administrators, their Latin American counterparts did not necessarily view the dichotomy between neutral competence and political responsiveness as quite so absolute. As the Venezuelan case illustrates, chief executives found a middle-of-the-road solution that involved using traditional patronage appointments to achieve technical competence in strategic programs while opting for political stability elsewhere in the bureaucracy.

Lawrence Graham (1976:45) has suggested that the emphasis placed on "how-to" merit reforms was disproportionate to their actual performance. No assurance could be given to political or administrative leaders that the day-to-day activities of a ministry would necessarily become more economic or rational or that target populations would be better served merely because bureaucrats were selected on the basis of merit.

Even if one accepts that a merit system is a necessary condition for efficiency and effectiveness, it is not sufficient. The poor performance of merit reforms in practice casts further doubt on their utility. In retrospect, these results suggest that scarce resources might have been better spent on training the Latin American bureaucrat to become a policy entrepreneur in the context of the administrative environment in which he must operate.

ENDNOTE

1. The remarkable feature of the Dominican reform attempt is that, by virtue of the fact that it came as late as 1986, the law was derived from the Ecuadorean, Colombian, and Puerto Rican experiences, thereby constituting an example of horizontal diffusion of innovation.

REFERENCES

Comision de Legislacion. *Ley de Servicio Civil y Carrera Administrativa.* Gobierno del Ecuador, Corporacion de Estudios y Publicaciones, Quito, Ecuador, 1983.

Fonseca Pimentel, A. La administracion de personal en America Latina. *International Review of Administrative Sciences 32*(3):197–210 (1966).

Garcia-Zamor, J. An ecological approach to administrative reform: the Brazilian case. *IRAS 35*(4):315–320 (1969).

Graham, L.S. *Public Personnel Dilemma in Developing Countries: The Latin American Experience.* Institute of Latin American Studies, Offprint Series No. 182. University of Texas, Austin, 1976.

Groves, R.T. Administrative reform and the politics of reform: the case of Venezuela. *Public Administration Review 27*(5):436–445 (1967).

Hayes, S.W., and Reeves, T.Z. *Personnel Management in the Public Sector.* Allyn and Bacon, Boston, 1984.

Jumelle, L., La reforme administrative au Zaire, *IRAS 40*(2):171–181 (1974).

Kearney, R.C. Political responsiveness and neutral competence in the developing countries. *Review of Public Personnel Administration 8*(2):66–80 (1988).

Kearney, R.C. Spoils in the Caribbean: the struggle for merit-based civil service in the Dominican Republic. *PAR 46*(2):144–151 (1986).

Mangelsdorf, K.R., and Reeves, T.Z. *Implementing the Merit System in Ecuador.* Mimeo, Florida State University, Tallahassee, 1988.

Mazmanian, D.A., and Sabatier, P.S. *Implementation and Public Policy.* Scott Foresman, Glenview, IL, 1983.

Nelson, B. *Making an Issue of Child Abuse: Agenda-Setting and Social Policy.* University of Chicago Press, Chicago, 1984.

Sharma, S.K. Centralization of personnel functions: an Asian perspective. *IRAS 47*(1):60–66 (1981).

Siegal, G., and Nascimento, K. Formalism in Brazilian administrative reform: the example of position classification. *IRAS 31*(3):175–184 (1965).

Thrash, R.M. Establishing a merit system in Ecuador. *Public Personnel Review 27*(2):122–124 (1966).

Vidal Perdomo, J. La reforma administrativa de 1968 en Colombia. *IRAS 48*(1):77–84 (1982).

40

Local Government in Authoritarian Chile*

Alfredo J. Rehren   *Instituto Ciencia Política, Universidad Catolica de Chile, Santiago, Chile*

I. INTRODUCTION

In September 1973, Chile moved from being a competitive multiparty system to an authoritarian regime.[1] Previous to the dissolution of congress and political parties and almost immediately after the coup, the military junta ordered all elected mayors and local councillors to cease in their functions and transferred all their powers to newly junta-appointed mayors. The regime promoted the creation of new channels of controlled participation to replace outlawed political parties in the context of what has been described as an "authoritarian-corporate infrastructure" (Kaufman 1976 :36). Municipalities and local interest groups were viewed as important institutions and social actors.[2] The first were seen as having a "transcendental role as a vehicle of social organization" (Junta de Gobierno 1974:9–10) and were called upon to be the most important organic channel of citizens' expression . . . incompatible with politicization" (Pinochet 1980). As far as local interest groups were concerned, they were called to "defend their corporate interests" and to be a "technical channel" of participation, but "it cannot be accepted that their objectives are distorted by a partisan instrumentalization of them" (Junta de Gobierno 1974:29–32).

The municipality was envisaged as a key institution; located at the base of the system, it would offer the best opportunity for the "organized participation" of the community (Pinochet 1974:14). A municipal reform was designed to disarticulate the brokerage network that characterized Chilean local politics by making the municipality a public service integrated within a hierarchically organized system of national administration, impervious to the influence of political parties.[3] The creation of communal development councils in each commune, integrated by representatives belonging to neighborhood associations, community organizations, local interest groups, and municipal bureaucrats, was intended to replace local elected officials and congressmen both as local interest mediators and brokers.[4]

Communal development councils were first established in July 1974. They were to be presided over by the mayor, and their function would be to participate in the approval of local policies, plans, and programs (Decree Law No. 573, Articles 17 and 18). The Municipal Law of 1976 (Articles 15–18) was more specific and stated that the communal development council would set priorities in the formulation and implementation of specific programs and projects and would

*The research for this article was realized in Chile during 1984–1985, thanks to a doctoral fellowship granted by the Inter-American Foundation. The points of view hereinafter expressed are exclusively those of the author and do not represent those of the foundation.

make observations on the municipal budget. On the basis of instructions emanating from the Ministry of the Interior, councils started to function sporadically, with great variations in terms of the number of councillors and composition across localities.

The military has thus introduced a basic reconceptualization of Chilean local politics, providing the regime with a potential space for manipulation and cooptation at the local level. Cooptation responds to the needs of the regime to gain legitimacy or consent of the governed and the need to impose central direction and bureaucratic controls.[5] Bureaucratic petitioning assumes particular salience. In the absence of political parties, the deconcentration of functions and strengthening of local government, helps to replace grass-roots, independent involvement, and makes bureaucratically directed demand-making a controlled, predictable, and manipulative process (Dietz 1980:136, 189). This chapter sheds some light upon the nature of the authoritarian program by drawing a picture of its functioning from below.[6]

II.   AN AUTHORITARIAN ADMINISTRATIVE REFORM

The government established a hierarchical system of territorial units and authorities with similar functions, equivalent decision-making capacities, and tight integration under the single line of command of the executive power. The process, called regionalization, was conceived as an administrative deconcentration strategy guided by the principle that the center cannot realize actions that could be performed more efficiently in the regions or communes (Canessa 1979:17–18).

But if the regionalization process was to create a deconcentrated administrative structure to enhance the state's effectiveness in rendering better services, it is no less true that it integrated all localities into a pyramidal organization throughout the nation. In the words of Pinochet (1974:14), the process of regionalization did not "imply a weakening of the central government power, but on the contrary, the exercise of a delegated, duly supervised power, strengthen[ed] it." Regionalization thus "does not constitute a form of political decentralization," but responds to the need to "maximize the efficiency of the political system," through the installation of a rigid chain of command running from the president down to the mayor and the local community (González 1979:262).[7]

The nature of the municipality has changed in a fundamental way compared to what it was in the past. Its limited powers have been enlarged with the addition of new important functions such as the elaboration and implementation of a communal development plan and a municipal budget in which purportedly the communal development council has participation.[8] However, the new legislation established the concept of local administration in place of local government. Incorporated into the state's administrative apparatus, the municipality lost its political autonomy, which was incompatible with the regime's technocratic ideology that emphasizes local government efficiency. Municipalities became a public service despite initial remarks made by Pinochet (1975) that assured the government's respect for their attributes as "direct representatives of the local community." The National Commission of Administrative Reform, comparing the old municipal legislation with the new municipal code, stated that under the old conception, the municipality was a "political organization of a passive character" and has become now a "public service, active in the state's administrative apparatus" (CONARA 1976:57).

The precarious state of pre-1973 municipal finances did not improve much during the first years of the military government, and thus deep changes were needed for the municipalities to comply with their new role. To change this situation, the government enacted a new law of municipal revenues in December 1979, which increased municipal income considerably. According to the new legislation, municipalities were allowed to keep 100% of property taxes, the most important source of revenue, which in the former system was collected by the central government, leaving only a share of 25% for municipalities. Other sources of municipal income came from central government transfers and payments for the implementation of social programs and for the management of public services such as education and health. Municipal revenues increased over four times from 1975 to 1983 (Odeplan 1984:396).

However, the most significant impact was the implementation of the Municipal Common Fund, which redistributed a substantial amount of resources to the small communes of the country and achieved a quantitatively and qualitatively different composition of municipal expenditures as compared with the pre-1973 situation. The percentage of municipal budgets spent on development projects rose from 4% in 1975 to 30% in 1983 (Odeplan 1984). In the region where the field research was conducted, the three poorest and smallest communes had a 1984 municipal investment per capita ratio two or three times that of the three richest and highly populated communes. Also, the proportion of total revenues they allocated to investment projects was twice that of the richest communes.

The inflow of more resources into the municipalities does not, however, necessarily mean financial autonomy. The controls to which the municipalities are subjected in the allocation of resources by provincial and regional authorities and the scarce participation of communal development councils in the planning and budgeting processes offsets this positive trend. However, the reforms of the authoritarian government in this area constitute, according to some observers, a redeemable aspect. It gives the municipalities a "significant margin of potential autonomy," which together with increased powers provides structural opportunities for further participation in the future (Tomic 1984:22–24).

III. DECISION MAKING IN DEVELOPMENT COUNCILS

Local participation has been defined by the regime as a "process of direct information to the citizen of the country's political course" and the citizen's "communication to the government of his desires, and belief that his opinion will be heard through intermediate organizations" (Benavides 1978:31). Accordingly, the municipality's role is to regulate and direct the action of these organizations to make them cooperate with municipal tasks. Within this scheme, the function of the communal council is to integrate local interest groups and organizations into municipal plans and the mayor's actions. As an alternative way to political and electoral participation, the regime offered the administrative process as an instance of community integration: "It is vital for the councilor to integrate himself into the formulation, approval and evaluation of the commune's development plan and municipal budget because they are true sources of creative community integration" (Zamora and Blanche 1983:179).

However, the data collected show that participation of councils in the formulation of the local plan, assigning priorities to projects, allocating resources to the municipal budget, and selecting municipal personnel was extremely low. In those stages such as planning and the allocation of priorities to projects, where according to the government's goals they should be most influential, only 40 and 36% of the councillors considered that councils did participate. In the last two stages the influence of councils was practically nil; 14% of the councillors agreed that the council participated in allocating resources to the municipal budget, and only 5% considered that the council had any participation in personnel selection.

Before being presented to formal council meetings, all projects and the budget were usually approved within a technical committee composed only of municipal technicians and presided over by the mayor. The manipulation of this process by the mayor and municipal bureaucrats was corroborated by data obtained on the source of project initiative. Forty-seven percent of the councillors mentioned the mayor as the source generating projects, and 26% mentioned both the mayor and municipal technicians as sharing such initiative; only 11% agreed that they had the initiative or shared it with the mayor. Compared with the 1960s, when only 26% of the councillors saw the mayor as taking the initiative, and 46% thought the initiative came from all of the councillors and the mayor as well, the present scheme has concentrated all initiative in presenting new development projects in the person of the mayor. This lack of collective action has left councillors as mere spectators of a process controlled by the mayor and municipal technicians.

As a consequence, a sense of frustration and skepticism could be observed among councillors, who looked at local planning and the municipal budget as a fait accompli, a situation that led to a low level of individual participation. Only half of them had ever indicated or suggested development projects, and only 14% had participated in the elaboration of the budget. Only 5% of the councillors stated that they participated in both activities. The data suggest a general level of inactivity and apathy, which contradicts the government's goal of incorporating the councillors into basic municipal tasks.

Communal development councils had a passive and receptive role indeed. Although they met monthly, an examination of meeting minutes in all municipalities revealed they were superficial, routine, and informative of the mayor's activities. The agenda was always set by the mayor, and there had never been any extraordinary meetings called by the councillors themselves to debate matters they deemed important. Councillors avoided presenting their own viewpoints in council meetings. There was apprehension of being misinterpreted by the mayor or by the provincial governor or regional intendant, to whom copies of monthly meeting minutes were sent. While the conflict and rivalry of the past between the mayor and councillors to gain political credit for local initiatives or to accommodate local problems to central party designs have been suppressed, nowadays councillors appear as very passive elements and ineffective articulators of local demands in the locality.

The nature of the demands reaching the municipality has not changed since the 1960s.[9] The most important problems today, as conceived by councillors, were more or less the same: unemployment, housing, education, roads, transportation, poverty, and health care. But while in the 1960s the overwhelming majority of petitions were cleared in advance outside of the municipal building with one of the elected councillors, nowadays the appointed local councillor is not a channel to address petitions. Only 5% of the councillors considered that people approached them when they had a problem, 21% said people would address either a councillor or a municipal officer, and 64% maintained people would go straight to a municipal officer, if not directly to the mayor, to have their problems solved. On the whole, this situation defeats the government's objective of making the councillor a link between local government and the community and of transforming local functional organizations into articulating bodies, by supposedly putting the population into direct contact with municipal bureaucrats.

Few councillors were also an effective link of the municipality with higher administrative levels. At the most they traveled to the provincial capital, the next hierarchical center, and ventured very little beyond to centers that were regularly visited either by the mayor or the provincial governor. Fifty-five percent of the councillors traveled to the provincial capital, and only 36% and 26% went to the regional capital and Santiago, respectively. Compared to 1968 when 30 out of 70 regidores had made at least one trip to Santiago and 24 more than three trips (Valenzuela 1977:121), in 1984 only 14 councillors had made one trip to Santiago, and only three of them had traveled more than three times a year. It was also found that only nine councillors (out of 66) had traveled to the three capitals provincial, regional, and national—to deal with municipal problems. Of these, seven were employed by the municipality, either as technicians or teachers. This is a significant finding because it stresses the bureaucratic context of center–regional–local relations, making it an administrative process dominated by those councillors who were members of the local bureaucracy, and not by those who purportedly represented local interest groups and community organizations. The latter engaged in largely protocol and ceremonial activities. The reason for this plight lay in the poor organization of interest groups at the local level and the lack of leaders who could be influential at higher administrative levels. Continuity in municipal affairs was usually obtained by the direct intervention of the mayor.

IV. PREDOMINANT ROLE OF THE MAYOR

To become mayor, it was indispensable to count on the government's political sanction. This came first from the provincial governor and then from the regional intendant, who finally remitted the names for presidential approval. While the democratic mayor exercised authority because of his elective position, the authoritarian mayor is "the representative of the President of the Republic" and concentrates all power at the local level (Pinochet 1978:20). Further, he enjoys a good salary and the perquisites of a position well above the socioeconomic level of the local population (especially in rural areas). He is required to give absolute loyalty to the government and cannot belong to any party organization or movement. Not surprisingly, the government has relied upon a dwindling number of former politicians to occupy mayoralties (see Table 1).

Officially, the mayor provides the channel of communication between the ruler and the ruled, and he is required in addition to integrate the community into municipal activities. He must "guide the local population" and avert "political deviations . . . guarding constantly against political infiltration" (Soto 1980:86). He must identify and select persons within the community, able to assume leadership positions in community organizations and to capture public opinion to avoid its falling into the hands of the opposition (Montero 1983:39–40). Local projects and programs are not worthwhile if the "people do not identify themselves with the ideals and goals of those who made them possible" (Benavides 1978:35). Thus the mayor is expected not only to function within a hierarchical chain of command, but also to reach out and integrate the community under his leadership.

Usually, mayors looked for persons who were well-known and linked to the community to integrate them in local councils. Local chambers of commerce, farmers, and neighborhood asso-

Table 1   Distribution of Mayoralty Posts by Party: 1973–1983

Political party	September 1973	December 1974	April 1978	April 1983
Christian Democratic	91	70	16	2
National	48	79	59	39
Padena and Dem. Radical	15	20	3	2
Socialist	60	—	—	—
Communist	36	—	—	—
Radical	20	—	6	3
Christian Left	4	—	—	—
Military	—	29	28	14
Catholic Church	—	—	1	1
Other and Independent	12	81	172	255
Total	286	279	285	316

Source: For 1973 and 1974 see Valenzuela (1977:222); for 1978 and 1983, the lists of mayors attending annual meetings were cross-checked with the lists of elected councillors from 1960 to 1971, published by the Dirección del Registro Electoral.

ciations were the preferred institutions, in addition to the municipality itself, to recruit local councillors. Facing a dilemma between the need to incorporate the organized community and the necessity of being efficient to the request of superior authorities, mayors decided to surround themselves by municipal bureaucrats and loyal friends in order to avert dissension in the council, a situation that could jeopardize their position. For instance, almost one-third of the councils studied were composed of municipal bureaucrats and teachers who were also hired directly by the mayor. Besides, mayors had a clear preference not to have councillors elected by their own organizations. A survey of 239 mayors carried out in 1980 showed that 68% of the mayors of the country preferred to appoint directly all neighborhood representatives to the council, while only 4% preferred to have them elected in general neighborhood assemblies. In relation to the generation of representatives from local groups, mayors also preferred to appoint them freely from members of the community in 86% of the cases (Peña 1981:10). Councillors assigned to themselves a low level of prestige compared to other local positions (ranking 4.8 in a prestige scale going from 1 to 9), with the exception of rural communes where they saw themselves with more prestige among the population. Given the lack of participation of local interest groups and community organizations in their appointment, councillors considered themselves not representative within their communes.

Mayors faced a difficult task in achieving integration and were exposed to multiple role strains. They were imposed on the local community with very little local input and sometimes against local opposition. Moreover, mayors did not belong in most cases to the commune where they had been appointed. The latter provoked a feeling of resentment among local councillors. Half of them would have liked to have a native as mayor, elected within the commune, rather than an outsider or a native appointed by the central government. Although the form of election was not specified, the finding is significant because it represents a partial rejection of the present system as implemented by the regime. The demand was for the election of the mayor by the local council together with more participation in municipal decision making. But it was recognized that any *apertura* would be conducive to party politics, even if the mayor was elected by the same council. In an authoritarian regime, whose objective is to eliminate party politics from the local level, a locally elected mayor, even one elected by local councils, would undermine the control imposed by central authorities. This situation has created obstacles for the new type of bureaucratic mayor to reach out into the community and integrate it into municipal activities.

Despite its military character, the regime has not relied upon a cadre of active military officers to control municipalities, as Table 1 shows. During the initial 5 years of the regime, military mayors made up no more than 10% of all mayors and have since then been increasingly replaced by civilians. The regime recruited its local authorities initially from former elected local councillors, especially from parties to the right of the political spectrum, whose members increased considerably after the coup. Together with the elimination of all mayors belonging to Marxist parties, the regime maintained a significant number of Christian Democrats until 1977, especially in urban communes with leftist political leanings. After that year, all democratic parties were outlawed and a major qualitative change took place. By 1983 former elected councillors from democratic parties had been virtually excluded from all mayoralty positions and constituted only 15% of the mayors. The latter demonstrates the regime's will to exclude party politics from the local level.

V. LOCAL PARTY POLITICS

There has been much speculation upon the effects of the authoritarian regime policies at the local level, but empirical analysis is scarce. Some scholars have suggested that after a decade of military authoritarian rule, nondemocratic structures have penetrated and now dominate life in small communities (Grupo de Estudios Constitucionales 1984:3). Others have argued that political parties are "likely to gain a significant foothold in the new organizational space provided paradoxically, by the military regime to destroy partisan politics" (Gil 1983:2). Finally it has also been argued that the removal of local elected councillors and political parties did away with democracy and "severely undermined the ability of local communities to obtain the necessary services for basic survival" (Valenzuela 1977:xii).

Given the highly competitive nature of Chilean local party politics before 1973, the question remained whether traditional political parties still represented strong local institutions or whether they had withered away. It was found that parties showed a great power of resilience. Eighty percent of the councillors estimated that political parties were active in their localities. Party activity was usually associated with parties opposed to the regime, and was carried out under covert conditions, especially in rural areas. Party activists usually gathered in the provincial capitals, which were relatively isolated from politically active centers, especially Santiago. Among the parties mentioned by councillors, the Christian Democrats, the Communist, and the Socialists headed the list. Only 6% of the councillors mentioned progovernment parties (e.g., National, Radical Democracy), despite the fact that 30% of the councillors had belonged to them in the past. This would suggest that the demobilizing policies of the regime have also been detrimental to proregime parties.

Despite evidence of certain party realignments taking place at the national level, the traditional party spectrum seemed not to have subsided at the local level. In fact, the historic tripolar arrangement of political forces—left, center, and right—that has dominated Chilean politics since the 1960s continues to be alive. The disorganized parties of the right found political space in local councils, especially through some of their local notables who had pledged loyalty to the regime, and the parties of the center and the left competed with each other in creating structures parallel to government-controlled organizations, to which they had little access.

The elimination of elected councillors has not left communities abandoned, but has changed the nature of center-local relations. In democratic Chile, the brokerage network operated by centralized political parties led from every locality to the center, and allowed the manipulation of the central bureaucracy by political parties. Nowadays, appointed mayors and councillors need to not be political entrepreneurs but rather to be administrative activists in order to extract resources from the center.[10] And with the introduction of a new administrative structure that deconcentrated power both at the regional and local levels, they do not need to contact the center as much as they did in the past. If contacting is necessary to solve local problems, it is limited to the provincial and regional levels following the hierarchical line of command established by the regime.

By eliminating party politics from municipal affairs, the regime disarticulated brokerage politics and isolated centralized political parties from their basic source of local political power: the access to the resources of the local bureaucracy to deliver electoral favors.

VI. CONCLUSIONS

The relevant problems are to what degree councillors can really articulate local demands that represent the problems of the community, what problems they transmit to the municipality for solution or take directly to superior hierarchical levels, and the extent to which they are an effective link for the local community with outside power centers. From this perspective, the communal development council is not an effective interest representation mechanism, and makes impracticable the authoritarian goal of replacing clientelistic brokerage politics by a style of local corporatist representation. Administrative deconcentration has centralized power in the hands of the mayor and the municipal bureaucracy, leaving the local development council to play a symbolic role. The regime has only reproduced at the local level a system of authoritarianism, where the real allocation of power to the local development council as a counterweight to the mayor—the representative of the president in the commune—has been avoided, because of the fear of politicization.

It would seem that the root of the problem for the regime lies in the tension between the need to institutionalize mechanisms of controlled local participation and the need to maintain discretionary power through the appointment of mayors. The fear both of losing centralized control and of politicization of the local level have played an important role in blocking the regime's own plans. The Minister of Interior asserted in 1978 when addressing the First Congress of Mayors: "The politics of participation is planned . . . but several risks are involved, among them the resilience of the bad habits of party politics." This standstill situation was defined at the same time as dangerous because the community's ideals "could deviate toward negative courses of action or simply disappear in an improductive negativism" (Benavides 1978:32–34). Seven years later, speaking to the Socioeconomic Council on the problem of participation, the Undersecretary for Regional Development stated that after a decade of the implementation of the regionalization process, "the majority of the citizens considers it as a process exclusively inherent to the state administration and do not identify with it" (*El Mercurio*, June 13, 1985).

The relationship between municipality and local community in the present conditions, in which the communal development council appears as a ceremonial instrument to solve local problems, will be unlikely to generate a true participatory scheme. After all, the same political parties that the regime has sought to eliminate have been forced to search for new ways to control a rejuvenated municipality. By deconcentrating certain functions at the local level, the regime has opened up new spaces for party penetration, and by increasing the financial resources of local governments, it has provided with the means to satisfy future electoral clienteles.

ENDNOTES

1. The Chilean regime that emerged in September 1973 has been characterized by most scholars as "authoritarian-corporate" or "bureaucratic-authoritarian" and most of its analysis has been performed within the framework of an already vast literature on the theme. See Collier (1979), Hammergren (1977), Kaufman (1976), Malloy (1977), O'Donnell (1973, 1978), Philip (1980), Pike and Strich (1974), Remmer (1979, 1980), Stepan (1978), and Wiarda (1981).

2. For the role of "regional-provincial councils of functional groups" which have since the 1930s striven for regional decentralization, corporatist regionalism, and administrative decentralization, see Drake (1978:95–97). For the coexistence of Chile's traditional multiparty system with a functional style of interest representation, see Bicheno (1972), Carriere (1975), Cea (1976), Cleaves (1974), and Menges (1966).

3. According to a report of the Commission on Municipal Constitutional Norms sent to the Ministry of Interior in March 1973 "politics [should] be removed from the new municipality," replacing former elected municipal councils by nonelected communal development councils (Fernández 1981:55). In 1974 the National Commission of Administrative Reform, evaluating the municipal situation, stated that municipalities lacked powers, had scarce resources, delivered poor services, lacked integration with other levels of the administration, did not apply modern budgeting and programming techniques, and were extremely politicized (CONARA 1976).

4. Regular and highly contested municipal elections took place in Chile every four years, but none of the parties was able to get more than 30% of the vote from 1935 to 1971, except for the Christian Democratic party in 1967, which obtained 36% (Valenzuela 1977:11). Yet community participation in municipal decision making was absent. In the words of a prominent advocate of municipal reform during Frei's government, the municipal system did not "effect citizen participation in the municipal structure by a simple election every four years" (Cleaves 1969:46). In fact, after voting, the citizen had no power to intervene in community problem solving. The municipality was an isolated decision-making

body with no important organized constituencies that could deliver support for a given project (Valenzuela 1977:85). A study in the 1960s demonstrated that about half of the demands on the municipality were originated within the same municipal bureaucracy and that the other half were external demands of a particularistic kind, asking mostly for individual benefits (Martinez 1969). Chile's major policy dilemma was to make municipal action more responsive to local needs and to stimulate local innovations through a wider participation of local interest groups in decision making and program implementation (Friedmann 1970:229). For a recent critical review on the functioning of local government from 1925 to 1973, see Chaparro (1985) and Pike (1974).

5. Cooptation does not envision the transfer of power but shares the responsibility for power with those groups whose organized forces would be able to threaten formal authority. They are included in the decision making process as a recognition and concession to the resources they can independently command, a feature that becomes an essential component of styles of interest intermediation characterized as corporatist. For the definition of cooptation see Selznick (1949), and on the relationship between cooptation and corporatism as a style of interest intermediation see Schmitter (1979).

6. See Rehren (1986). The research was realized in six communes of the Región del Biobio, in southern Chile, five of which had been studied by Valenzuela (1977). The five communes were selected from Valenzuela's random sample on the basis of their diverse political settings before 1973 and their socioeconomic characteristics; a metropolitan commune was added to provide a contrast with these five small rural communes. A questionnaire containing some questions asked in 1969 was applied to 66 local councillors and 6 mayors. Interviews were also held with municipal officers, members of the community, and provincial governors. Finally, minutes from previous local council meetings were examined in each municipality and the author also attended several council meetings. The study intended to increase within-country comparison at the local level, not only across time but also in the context of contrasting political regimes.

7. For a discussion on the administrative reform implemented by the military regime see Blumenwitz (1984), Boisier (1981), Borel and Mergudick (1976), and Cumplido (1983).

8. See Decree Law No. 1289, Article 3 in Fernández (1981:234), and the 1980 Chilean Constitution, Article 110.

9. See Wayland-Smith (1969:23–24), Cleaves (1969:24), and Valenzuela (1977:74–76).

10. For the difference between political entrepreneurs and administrative activists, see Tarrow (1977).

REFERENCES

Benavides, R. Discurso en el acto inaugural del Primer Congreso Nacional de Alcaldes, Primer Congreso Nacional de Alcaldes, Santiago de Chile, 1978.

Bicheno, H.E. Anti-parliamentary themes in Chilean history: 1920–1970. *Government and Opposition* 7:351–388 (1972).

Blumenwitz, D. La autonomia administratativa en el sistema democrático: considerando especialmente el desarrollo constitucional de Chile y de la Rebública Federal de Alemania. *Estudios Públicos 15:* 255–272 (1984).

Boisier, S. Chile: continuity and change, variations of centre-down strategies under different political regimes. In *Development from Above or Below?* (W.B. Sthohr and D.R. Fraser Taylor, eds.). John Wiley, New York, 1981.

Borel, E., and Mergudick, C. *Algunos Aspectos Administrativos del Gobierno Regional y Perspectivas de Desarrollo del Nuevo Municipio Chileno.* Universidad de Chile, Santiago, 1976.

Canessa, J. *La Regionalización: Sus Proyecciones y la Nueva Institucionalidad.* CONARA, Santiago de Chile, 1979.

Carriere, J. Conflict and cooperation among Chilean sectoral elites. *Boletin de Estudios Latinoamericanos y del Caribe 19*:16–75 (1975).

Cea, J.L. La representación functional en la historia constitucional de Chile. *Cuadernos de Ciencia Politica* 9 (1976).

Chaparro, P. *Organización y Funcionamiento del Gobierno Local en Chile, 1925–1973: Una Apreciacion*

Critica. Centro de Estudios para el Desarrollo, Materiales para discusión No. 69, Santiago de Chile, 1985.

Cleaves, P.S. *Developmental Processes in Chilean Local Government.* Institute of International Studies, University of California, Berkeley, 1969.

Cleaves, P.S. *Bureaucratic Politics and Administration in Chile.* University of California Press, Berkeley, 1974.

Collier, D., ed. *The New Authoritarianism in Latin America.* Princeton University Press, Princeton, NJ, 1979.

CONARA. *Chile Hacia un Nuevo Destino: Reforma Administrativa.* Comisión Nacional de la Reforma Administrativa, Santiago de Chile, 1976.

Constitución Politica de la Republica de Chile. Editorial Juridica, Santiago de Chile, 1980.

Cumplido, F. *La Estructura Institucional del Modeio de Descentralización.* Documento de trabajo No. 3, Centro de Estudios del Desarrollo, Santiago de Chile, 1983.

Dietz, H.A. *Poverty and Problem Solving Under Military Rule: The Urban Poor in Lima, Peru.* University of Texas Press, Austin, 1980.

Drake, P. Corporatism and functionalism in modern Chilean politics. *Journal of Latin American Studies 10*:95–97 (1978).

El Mercurio, Santiago, Chile.

Fernández, J. *Régimen Juridico de la Administración Municipal.* Editorial Juridica, Santiago de Chile, 1981.

Friedman, J. Urban-regional policies for national development in Chile. In *Latin American Urban Research,* vol. 1 (F.F. Rabinovitz and F.M. Trueblood, eds.). Sage Publications, Beverly Hills, CA, 1970.

Gil, F. *Chile: The Background to Authoritarianism.* Occassional Paper Series, Institute of Latin American Studies, University of North Carolina, Chapell Hill, 1983.

González, A. Las corporaciones provadas de desarrollo como instrumentos de participación y de desarrollo regional en Chile. In *Informe Final: I Seminario Internacional Sobre Participación del Sector Privado en el Desarrollo Regional* (CONARA, comp.). CONARA, Santiago de Chile, 1979.

Groupo de Estudios Constitucionales, Sub-Comisión Organizatión del Poder Politico Local. Bases programáticas para la formulación de una normativa constitucional acerca de la organizacion democrática del poder politico local. Santiago de Chile, 1984.

Hammergren, L. Corporatism in Latin American politics: a reexamination of the unique tradition. *Comparative Politics 9–10*:443–461 (1977).

Junta de Gobierno. *Declaración de Principios del Gobierno de Chile.* Editora Gabriela Mistral, Santiago de Chile, 1974.

Kaufman, R.R. *Transitions to Stable Authoritarian-Corporate Regimes: The Chilean Case?* Sage Professional Papers, Comparative Politics Series 1, No. 01-060, Sage Publications, Beverly Hills, CA, 1976.

Malloy, J.M. *Authoritarianism and Corporatism in Latin America.* University of Pittsburgh Press, Pittsburgh, 1977.

Martinez, G. El municipio como sistema politico. *Cuadernos de Desarrollo Urbano-Regional 12*:5–91 (1969).

Menges, C. Public policy and organized business in Chile. *Journal of International Affairs 20*:343–365 (1966).

Montero, E. *Intervención del Señor Ministro del Interior.* Quinto Congreso Nacional de Alcaldes, Santiago de Chile, 1983.

Odeplan. *Informe Social 1983.* Oficina de Planificación Nacional, Santiago de Chile, 1984.

O'Donnell, G. *Modernization and Bureaucratic-Authoritarianism: Studies in Southern Politics.* Institute of International Studies, University of California, Berkeley, 1973.

O'Donnell, G. Reflections on the patterns of change in the bureaucratic-authoritarian state. *Latin American Research Review 12*:3–38 (1978).

Peña, J. *Integración y Atribuciones de los Consejos Comunales de Desarrollo.* Ministerio del Interior, Santiago de Chile, 1981.

Philip, G. The military institution revisited: some notes on corporatism and military rule in Latin America. *Journal of Latin American Studies 12*:421–436 (1980).

Pike, F. Chilean local government and some reflections on dependence. *Inter-American Economic Affair 31*:63–71 (1974).

Pike, F.B., and Stritch, T.T., eds. *The New Corporatism.* Notre Dame University Press, Notre Dame, IN, 1974.

Pinochet, A. Manifiesto del Presidente de la Junta de Gobierno y Jefe Supremo de la Nación, Don Augusto Pinochet Ugarte, con motivo de la iniciación del proceso de regionalización del pais. In *Estatuto Juridico de la Regionalización* (D. Hernández, ed.). Ediciones Juridicas de América, Santiago de Chile, 1974.

Pinochet, A. Speech at the 15th Inter-American Congress of Municipalities, Primer Congreso Nacional de Municipalidades, Santiago de Chile, 1975.

Pinochet, A. Discurso de Su Excelencia en el Acto Inaugural del Primer Congreso Nacional de Alcaldes, Santiago de Chile, 1978.

Pinochet, A. Discurso de S.E. el Presidente de la República al Inaugurar el Segundo Congreso Nacional de Alcaldes, Santiago de Chile, 1980.

Remmer, K. Public policy and regime consolidation: the first five years of the Chilean junta. *Journal of Development Areas 13*:441–461 (1979).

Remmer, K. Political demobilization in Chile, 1973–1978. *Comparative Politics 12*:275–301 (1980).

Schmitter, P. Still the century of corporatism? In *Trends Toward Corporatist Intermediation* (P. Schmitter and G. Lehmbruch, eds.). Sage Publications, Beverly Hills, CA, 1979.

Selznick, P. *TVA and the Grass Roots: A Study in the Sociology of Formal Organizations.* University of California Press, Berkeley, 1949.

Soto, R. Fortalecimiento del rol del alcalde y mejoramiento de las municipalidades como organismos de participación de la comunidad y prestación de servicios. Segundo Congreso Nacional de Alcaldes, Santiago de Chile, 1980.

Stepan, A. *The State and Society: Peru in Comparative Perspective.* Princeton University Press, Princeton, NJ, 1978.

Tarrow, S.G. *Between Center and Periphery: Grassroots Politicians in Italy and France.* Yale University Press, New Haven, CT, 1977.

Tomic, B. *Examen Critico de Tres Intentos Oficiales de Planificación Descentralizada y Participativa.* Oficina Internacional del Trabajo, PREALC, Documento de Trabajo 37, Santiago de Chile, 1984.

Valenzuela, A. *Political Brokers in Chile: Local Government in a Centralized Polity.* Duke University Press, Durham, NC, 1977.

Wayland-Smith, G. *The Christian Democratic Party in Chile: A Study of Political Organization and Activity with Primary Emphasis on the Local Level.* Sondeos No. 39, Centro Intercultural de Documentación, Cuernavaca, Mexico, 1969.

Wiarda, H.J. *Corporatism and National Development in Latin America.* Westview Press, Boulder, CO, 1981.

Zamora, G., and Blanche, E. Las organizaciones comunitarias territoriales en la integración de los codecos. Quinto Congreso Nacional de Alcaldes, Santiago de Chile, 1983.

41

State Administration in Socialist Cuba

Power and Performance

Sheryl L. Lutjens   *Political Science Department, Northern Arizona University,*
Flagstaff, Arizona

I. INTRODUCTION

The study of public administration in a socialist state raises critical questions about the foundations of comparative research. If, as Ferrell Heady argues, some common framework or "organizing concept" is necessary for comparative public administration and to "avoid burial under an avalanche of data," the choice of framework and concepts matters greatly. For Heady, that choice is "bureaucracy," an organizing concept "at the core of modern administration even though public administration and public bureaucracy are not synonymous, and which has impinging upon it all the other forms that have in the past interested students of public administration" (1984:60). The concept of bureaucracy can indeed serve to orient comparative studies of administration. When socialism, not capitalism, is the political-economic context of the public organizations under study, however, it is especially important to recall the contested theoretical terrain within which beliefs about bureaucracy exist.

The concept of bureaucracy must be unpacked if it is to guide comparative research. An overview of administration in socialist Cuba provides the opportunity to explore the concept in two ways. First, the dominant Weberian perspective on bureaucracy is outlined briefly, focusing on efficiency as the ideal of administrative performance *and* the presumed basis of organizational power. Second, a review of Cuban administrative development contrasts state administration in capitalism and socialism, introducing a Marxist alternative to the Weberian perspective on bureaucracy. The purpose here is thus twofold: (1) to use the Cuban case to demonstrate where the theory and practice of socialist administration challenge prevailing ideas about the efficiency and power of bureaucratic organization; and (2) to argue that historical analysis of the source and nature of organizational power must precede the evaluation of administrative performance in Cuba and any other setting, be it socialist or capitalist. Ultimately, comparative research must pursue analysis, rather than description or categorization according to an unexplored model of bureaucracy.

II. THE POWER OF EFFICIENCY

Max Weber, though not the first student of bureaucracy or public administration, conceived an ideal type of bureaucracy that has since been at the heart of theorizing about modern organizations. Weber's inventory of characteristics and conclusions about the efficiency, power, and inevitability of bureaucracy have contributed to an enduring, though problematic, Weberian tradition. Marked by internal debates and fitful recognition that Weber's ideal type was an analytical tool for sociological investigation, the Weberian tradition has created a theoretical dilemma that affects comparative research: its central concern with organizational efficiency is confounded by the acceptance of an ahistorical "logic of bureaucratization."

Weber defined bureaucracy with a description of the structural characteristics of the efficient modern administrative organization. While normative definitions have proliferated,[1] Weber's remains as the model. According to Weber, modern bureaucracy has a hierarchical organization of offices, salaried officials appointed on the basis of technical qualification, and strict and systematic discipline according to impersonal official obligations (Weber 1978:220). The superiority of bureaucracy derives from its "indispensable" technical knowledge and its machinelike performance. Pure bureaucratic administrative organization—monocratic bureaucracy—is "from a purely technical point of view, capable of obtaining the highest degree of efficiency and is in this sense formally the most rational known means of carrying out imperative control over human beings. It is superior to any other form in precision, in stability, in the stringency of its discipline, and in its reliability" (1978:223). The rationality of bureaucratic techniques—"the achievement of an optimum *in the relation* between the results and the means to be expended on it" (1978:65–66)—makes efficiency a property of hierarchical organization.

The perception of efficiency as the *goal* of modern organization, rather than simply a structural property, abetted the acceptance of the Weberian model as a normative one. Weber's celebration of bureaucratic efficiency bolstered an existing "machine" theory of public and private organization already characterized by a concern with efficiency through hierarchical control.[2] As Gulick wrote in 1937, before Weber was translated, "In the science of administration, whether public or private, the basic 'good' is efficiency. The fundamental objective of the science of administration is the accomplishment of the work in hand with the least expenditure of man-power and materials. Efficiency is thus axiom number one in the value scale of administration" (1970:100). By positing the superiority of modern bureaucracy, Weber's work reinforced scientific principles of hierarchy, sanctified the elevation of efficiency as a "good" above others, and became part of the formal school of organization theory.

Skeptics before and after Weber challenged the correlation of hierarchy with efficiency, though criticism of hierarchy scarcely altered the appeal of efficiency or the momentum of a Weberian perspective. Human relations theorists focused on informal groups and relationships, denying the presumed efficiency of formal structure and rules of control. Hierarchy, moreover, was attacked for being authoritarian and for conducing "inefficiency." *Achieving* efficiency, however, became more important as the nature and failings of formal hierarchy were identified.[3] Critics in the "informal" school created a deep conflict within the emergent Weberian tradition.

A tension exists in thinking about efficiency and bureaucracy. The search for efficient organization no longer automatically equates efficiency with bureaucratic hierarchy. Yet that search is a reactive one, theoretically and practically, since bureaucracy *is* the dominant organizational form in the modern context. The source of the calculability, speed, discipline, *and* efficiency that the Weberian model posited—and that are still desirable—remain unclear. The Weberian tradition limits its potential for resolving the theoretical and practical problems of efficiency. How?

Prevailing assumptions about organizational power transform the debates about hierarchy and efficiency into a true dilemma. This dilemma of efficiency inheres in accepting the *logic* of Weber's model without acknowledging the analysis that underpinned the concept of bureaucracy. Weber wrote about the power, origins, and effects of bureaucratic organization within modern capitalist society. Bureaucracy, moreover, was seen as a form of domination, not simply as a specific structure. In accepting Weber's conclusions, but not his methodology, efficiency and power have both been treated—and debated—as ahistorical properties of formal organizational structures. Power *inside*, not *of*, the organization has been the focus.

In Weber's sociological and historical explanation, modern bureaucracy emerged via the rise of rational-legal authority from within Western capitalist society. The rationalization that propelled obedience to impersonal and "specifically analyzable rules," in contrast to more personal traditional or charismatic authority, was integral in the development of capitalism and the development of bureaucratic administration in all large organizations. Bureaucracy, wrote Weber, "offers the attitudes demanded by the external apparatus of modern culture in the most favorable combination" (1978:975). Capitalism welcomed bureaucratic organization, capitalist businesses were organized as "unequalled models of strict bureaucracy" (1978:974) and a capitalist market economy required state administration to perform with equivalent speed and precision, with calculable rules, and "without regard for persons" (1978:975). The power of bureaucracy as "the most rational means of carrying out imperative control over human beings" thus issued from societal development.

An incomplete appreciation of Weber's methodology renders power *inside* the organization the predominant concern. The formal school easily located administrative power with formal hierarchy, finding authority in the position.[4] Critics of the formal school located power in informal groups, behaviors, and dynamics—in other words, as it diverged from formal structures but still within the organization.[5] More recently, an important though partial destruction of the theoretical insulation of organizations is achieved by systems approaches and by empirical studies of the penetration of public bureaucracies by private power.[6] Simple assumptions about the power of bureaucracy have thus been partially impeached, although thinking about power generally relies on exchange theory, not a theory of domination.[7] Attention to the larger context within which power creates organizations, rules of control, and the impulse to efficiency is preempted by deeply held assumptions about the universal logic of bureaucratization.

An acceptance of Weber's argument that bureaucracy is inevitable, in capitalism and in socialism, sustains the Weberian tradition with an ahistorical approach to both efficiency and power. Weber predicted and in many ways lauded an inexorable rise of bureaucratic organization: "it would be sheer illusion to think for a moment that continuous administrative work can be carried out in any field except by means of officials working in offices" (1978:223). If capitalism needed and nurtured bureaucracy, socialist economic planning would require even more formal bureaucratization to replace the contribution that private business made to technical efficiency in a capitalist system (1978:223–224). Though he proclaimed that the "future belongs to bureaucratization," Weber also found the "iron cage" of bureaucratic rationality disturbing. He feared bureaucracy's effects on individual freedom, its resistance to political control in capitalism, and the loss of the countervailing power of private bureaucracy in socialism.[8]

Weber's ideal type, however, was conceived as an analytical tool. The power that specific bureaucracies possessed was not to be explained by *a priori* conclusions about the indispensability of bureaucratic organization in capitalism or socialism. According to Weber, real bureaucracies confront remnants of older institutions, encounter tendencies toward substantive rationality that might contradict the "spirit" of bureaucracy, and use "official" knowledge to pursue power beyond that granted on the basis of technical knowledge (1978:225). Though Weber announced the relentless spread of "escape-proof" bureaucracy—a "chilling foresight" that may actually stem from rigid "historical hindsight"[9]—he called for conclusions about real bureaucracies based on the use of the ideal type for the purposes of analysis.

It is the ahistorical treatment of power, not simply the debates about the efficiency of hierarchy, that create the theoretical conundrum of the Weberian tradition. The source, extent, and effects of organizational power, as well as the standards of administrative performance, remain critical empirical issues. Investigation cannot proceed from a reification of the concept of bureaucracy, the reduction of power to efficiency, or the acceptance of an ahistorical logic of bureaucratization. As an examination of administration in Cuba reveals, there are indeed structural alternatives to the pursuit of efficiency through Weber's bureaucracy and theoretical alternatives to the Weberian tradition. There is, however, no useful alternative to historical analysis of the societal context of organizational power that conditions real administrative performance.

III. CUBA: EFFICIENCY AND SOCIALISM

Cuba has adopted a Marxist perspective on state administration that contrasts with the approach of Weber *and* the Weberian tradition. Central to this perspective is the assumption that capitalist bureaucracy serves the purpose of class domination.[10] Lenin, for example, argued that the administrative system of the capitalist state served ruling-class interests; state bureaucracy was merely disguised by claims of neutrality, expertise, and efficiency. Lenin predicted that socialism would destroy the "old bureaucratic machine" by separating the control functions of bureaucracy from the technical ones and permitting democratic participation in administration (Lenin 1976). The demise of the Soviets and the use of Western Taylorism to improve centrally planned production suggest that bureaucracy was not diminished in Lenin's time. Indeed, efficiency is a vital concern in socialist administration, though Marxist theory maintains its antibureaucratic assumptions.

Cuba's antibureaucratic attitudes are a product of Cuban history, Cuban socialism, and Marxist theory. Efficiency is an official standard of administrative performance. How is efficiency defined and pursued? What are the source and extent of administrative power? A review of pre- and postrevolutionary administrative structures, standards, and dynamics begins the analysis that answers these questions.

A. Prerevolutionary Administration

Prior to the 1959 revolution, a dependent capitalist society was the context in which Cuban public administration developed. After four centuries of Spanish rule through a bureaucratic imperial system,[11] and the Spanish-Cuban-American war for independence at the end of the 1800s, the United States occupied Cuba and ushered in the modern era of public administration. Centralization characterized administrative organization, though political manipulation of administration precluded efficiency. The social development of capitalism in Cuba produced what has been called a "cleptocracy."

Military rule from 1899 until 1902 established a centralized republican system fashioned after the U.S. government and standards of efficiency derived from North American theory.[12] Seeking to recover Cuba from the devastation of the independence struggle and corruption of colonial rule, the military government preached frugality, fiscal accountability, accurate record keeping, and discipline of employees. The military governor practiced a moncratic rule based on personal control and military methods. By formal independence in 1902, elected national officials and 97% of public employees were Cuban.[13] The centralization characteristic of Cuban administration until 1959 precluded efficiency, however, for several reasons.

Patronage became a mainstay of Cuban politics and the defining feature of public administration. Beginning with the occupation practice of appointing "friendly" Cubans, a Cuban spoils system operated until 1958. Its characteristics included purges of elected and appointed officials at all levels upon electoral victory; the *botella* or sinecure; kickbacks, bribes, and other profit-making activity; and theft. State expenditures rose 600% by 1922; by 1923 annual defrauding of the public treasury amounted to $15 million. By 1950, 80% of the central budget was spent for salaries and a third of all employees were suspected of doing no work.[14]

The patronage dynamics of Cuban politics enmeshed the public bureaucracy in a costly game of domestic and international alliance. Party competition engendered political violence and, under the aegis of the Platt Amendment to the 1901 Cuban constitution, repeated U.S. military interventions. The U.S.-guided reform efforts did little to alter centralization or its dynamics. In the 1906–1909 occupation, for example, an attempt was made to legalize a civil service. Apparently seeking a professional bureaucracy, the occupation addressed Cuban unrest by administering "Cuba as a Tammany problem in patronage," creating more unnecessary jobs to satisfy competing groups (Beals 1933:208). The U.S. oversight was direct until the 1930s. By the 1930s, the failure of the state to represent the interests of all Cubans had provoked unrelenting demands for sovereignty and for political and administrative reforms. The United States let Cuban president Gerardo Machado fall in Cuba's 1933 revolution.

The dynamics of state administration before and after the 1933 revolution are more fully explained by considering the domestic conditions of what is called neocolonialism. Overt U.S. control was replaced by the Good Neighbor policy, strategic allies such as Sgt. Fulgencio Batista, and coups by the latter in 1933 and 1952. Continuing centralization may have served North American interests, but it had deep domestic roots. The U.S. investment in the sugar-centered Cuban economy amounted to $1.15 billion by 1928. Nationalist reforms after the 1933 revolution sought to reclaim the profits of the economy through state regulation. Though the character of U.S. interests shifted thereafter, planned investment for the 1955–1965 period amounted to $205 billion and in 1955, 73.4% of Cuban imports originated in the United States.[15] A dependent capitalist society thus conditioned the practices and possibilities of state administration.

In this context, the spoils system was symptomatic of the nature of administrative power. With limited access to property and profits, elected and appointed offices became a political "industry." Poverty, unemployment, and illiteracy expressed the social inequality among Cubans and between rural and urban Cuba. More specifically, the maldistribution of education had significant effects on the potential of administration. The 1952 census counted only 86,000 technical and professional persons, the majority attorneys or in the arts; in a work force of 2 million, there were but 2500 engineers (Jolly 1964). If personnel practices demonstrated the nexus of political and administrative power, distorted economic development nourished the former and constrained any change in the nature of the latter.

The dynamics of administration in prerevolutionary Cuba proved impossible to reform, though efforts were made. The nationalist constitution of 1940 resurrected the civil service career and created a Tribunal de Cuentas to ensure fiscal probity. A school of public administration was created in the University of Havana in 1940. The merit system, technical improvement, and regularization of procedures desired by Cuban critics were not realized, however. *Botellas* reached their zenith in 1944–1946, when 10,000 employment changes were made in the Ministry of Education alone.[16] The Cuban people mounted their last revolution in the 1950s with the reform of patronage politics among their demands.

B. Postrevolutionary Administration: The 1960s

Centralization continued after the 1959 revolution, though political, economic, and social change altered the scope of state administration and the conditions of administrative power. Capitalism gave way to an unique Cuban model of socialist development as the revolution pursued sovereignty, economic development, and a redistribution of property, wealth, and opportunities. The first decade of organizational change shows how new standards of performance emerged in the process of administering in a revolutionary context.

State organization remained provisional during the 1960s, though old structures and practices gave way to new ones as nationalist policy unfolded. Existing administrative arrangements were not immediately dismantled, though by March 1959 approximately 50,000 of 160,000 public employees were replaced when *botellas* were withdrawn and *batistianos* fled (Domínguez 1978:234). Agrarian reform and the extension of education, health care, social security, welfare, and employment opportunities required some new organizations *and* effective performance. Several new ministries and the National Institute of Agrarian Reform (INRA) were created in 1959. Staffed by the Rebel Army, INRA had responsibility for implementing land redistribution, for road building, health, housing, and, by the late 1960s, for more than half the industrial activity in Cuba. By 1961, 85% of industry was nationalized and people's stores were created; after the 1963 agrarian reform, 70% of agriculture was under state control. A central planning board and further ministerial change accompanied the restructuring of the Cuban economy.

The first few years of revolutionary administration were characterized by "guerrilla administrators" and a *por la libre* (free-wheeling) approach to policy implementation. The voluntary exodus of public and private administrators opposed to the revolution drained Cuba of some 15,000 to 20,000 professionals by 1961, exacerbating the scarcity of trained administrators at a time when the state had more to administer. "Guerrilla administration" was the term used by Che Guevara to identify mistakes made in this situation, even by the Rebel Army. It meant administration by untrained but revolutionary administrators who were unconstrained by information and personified guerrilla warfare in the realm of management. It produced a *por la libre* approach to policy implementation, or chaotic, uncoordinated administration, according to Cuban and foreign critics.[17]

Attempts to improve performance became part of a distinct Cuban model of socialist development. Between 1961 and 1963, an imported Czech centralized planning system was tried. In 1961, the JUCEIS (Juntas de Coordinación, Ejecución e Implementación) were created for coordinating central policy at the provincial and local levels. Both confronted a shortage of economic information and skilled personnel. By the mid 1960s the Cuban model of centralization without the discipline of formal hierarchy linking the bottom to the top emerged.

The Cuban model expressed a political idealism that affected administrative standards. Its characteristics included "ad hoc" economic planning in which sectoral plans were made with little central coordination; a vanguard party created in 1965 (Partido Comunista de Cuba, PCC); a stress on collective participation in mass organizations, moral incentives and the creation of a "New Man" with discipline, generosity, and socialist consciousness; and antibureaucratic attitudes. The idealism of the 1960s led to an attempt to overcome the objective constraints of an underdeveloped economy by harvesting 10 million tons of sugar in 1970. It also envisioned an administrative "new man" who could eradicate old and new administrative problems.

Cuban standards of administrative performance increasingly emphasized political criteria as *burocratismo* (bureaucratism) became the new label for administrative problems. Such problems included a surplus of personnel, insulation from the people, and rigid work methods, all stemming from but not identical with guerrilla administration. A lack of experience, organization, and skills was seen as producing poor information flows, a desire for more personnel, and endless meetings to get things done. The political critique produced the 1965–1967 Campaign against Bureaucracy, which attacked bureaucracy and bureaucratic attitudes. The first stage of the campaign implemented a reduction (rationalization) of administrative personnel. Some 21,066 positions were eliminated in Havana by 1966. The second stage began at the end of 1966, eliminating 31,000 jobs and focusing on high-level administrators. Administrative personnel from central state offices were sent for agricultural labor one week each month; more than 1000 party officials began three years of work in the countryside.[18]

In 1967, a series of editorials explained the Cuban position on bureaucracy that engendered the campaign. The problems with bureaucracy were described in terms of political power. As early as 1962, Che Guevara had called for administrative *cuadros* (cadres) with administrative abilities *and* political consciousness. By 1967, however, it was a bureaucratic concept of administration, not trial-and-error, that was seen as the cause of *burocratismo*. An "ideological battle" was necessary to combat the "belief that the world is created from an office" and the danger that it might "prevail among a special stratum of men whose relation to the means of production and political decisions places them in a position of leadership."[19]

Cuban administration in the 1960s was not oriented by the standard of efficiency. The party and state hierarchies considered typical of socialist organization were neither desired nor produced in the centralization of the 1960s. The PCC remained small and weak in its supervisory role. The discipline of the Rebel Army proved instrumental in organizing the efforts for the 10-million-ton harvest. The Cuban people were increasingly mobilized to implement policy. And Castro remained the source of many decisions and the prime example of an "ambulating bureaucrat" who used unbureaucratic work methods and resolved problems spontaneously (Petras 1973:290). Administrative dynamics reflected an underdeveloped administrative capacity, a conscious preference for revolutionaries rather than experts, and escalating criticism of undeserved bureaucratic power.

C.   Postrevolutionary Administration: The 1970s and Beyond

The shortfall of the 1970 harvest propelled major adjustments in the Cuban model and a "state-building" period in the 1970s. Despite a record 8.5-million-ton harvest, serious self-criticism ensued. For Cuban administration, state building entailed a reorganization of administrative structures, technical training for administrators, and a stress on efficiency unseen in the previous decade. Cuban standards for administrative performance suggest the addition of efficiency, rather than the loss of the idealism of the 1960s, however. The more mature revolution of the 1970s and 1980s has adopted a participatory approach to efficiency.

State building involved strengthening central capabilities and decentralizing reforms, both geared to improving the efficiency of an administrative system with extensive responsibilities. A more pragmatic approach to economic management included stronger central coordination, enterprise budgeting based on prices, income, costs, and profits, long-term planning, and a return to material incentives and work quotas. The renovation of planning culminated in the implementation of the Economic Management System in 1977, a system that invited worker participation in planning. The Communist Party was strengthened so that it could better fulfill its vanguard role. The PCC had its first Congress in 1975, expanded its numbers from 55,000 in 1969 to 202,807 by 1975, and adopted statutes and a program. Internal reorganization of the PCC included a bottom-up system for reviewing performance and electing leadership.[20] As party and planning institutions assumed stronger organizational capacities, the military formally returned to the barracks.

The political institutions of a socialist state were inaugurated in 1976, accompanied by decentralizing administrative change. Called Poder Popular (People's Power) and tested from 1974 to 1976 in the province of Matanzas, it is a three-tiered representative system that has administrative functions. At the national, provincial, and local levels, assemblies of elected delegates are to represent the population and to oversee the administration of specific activities withinin their jurisdiction. Local assemblies manage local enterprises and service units. Thus, management of 75% of commercial and public facilities, 86% of educational units, and 50% of health care units passed to the municipal level in 1976 (Alonso 1980:109). Activities that have a national or provincial scope or involve normative or technical standards remained in the jurisdiction of the center—the sugar industry, labor norms, and salaries are examples. Administrative decentralization is at the core of the new political arrangements.

The decentralization required by Poder Popular and apparent in other organizational changes in the 1970s was part of the pursuit of improved efficiency. The better performance of administrators was to be achieved in two ways. Technical training of administrators became a priority. Between 1971 and 1977, 120 technical and professional schools were created. A National School of Economic Management for higher-level management was created in 1976, and by 1980 10,100 managers had graduated. Between 1975 and 1980 there was a 65% increase in educated technicians in the agricultural sector, and in 1985 Cuba had 11,700 economists.[21] On the other hand, efforts to rationalize personnel continued. Though administrative personnel were reduced by 23.4% in the Matanzas dry run, a 178% nationwide increase occurred between 1973 and 1984. While this may be the sign of successful policy, as with the 18,000 new *cuadros* needed between 1975 and 1980 because of the expansion of secondary schooling, both rationalization and technical improvement are ongoing efforts.[22]

The technical capacity of administration is now considered integral to Cuba's development strategy, though political criteria were not entirely displaced. Automated management systems are used in economic planning; attention is given to computerized information banks, systems techniques, and especially to socialist principles of scientific management.[23] Yet Cuba's first cadre policy, adopted by the PCC in 1976, weighed political, managerial, and technical qualities equally. The idealism and antibureaucratic attitudes characteristic of the 1960s, moreover, remained apparent in the state-building period.

Cuba's pursuit of efficiency joined idealism and antibureaucratic attitudes in a participatory approach to efficiency. Antipathy to bureaucracy did not disappear in 1970. Paper shuffling, making decisions in ignorance of the people's needs, usurping privileges, and corruption are still viewed as symptoms of *burocratismo*; officially, bureaucracy is considered "one of the permanent risks of socialism."[24] The design of the state system anticipated decentralization through Poder Popular as a means for promoting efficiency in an antibureaucratic fashion: "By its immediate proximity to the masses, by its most direct and daily contact with them, deficiencies can be discovered earlier, the manifestations of *burocratismo*, inefficiency or carelessness can be countered more effectively" (Roca 1978:8).

The participatory approach to efficiency combines the pragmatism of the 1970s with the idealism of the 1960s. State administration now functions according to a principle of double subordination that structures two types of control: hierarchical control from the central ministries, and popular control through elected representatives at each level. The means for local control of both types are several: local assemblies name and remove heads of departments; local planning requires review of expenditures and performance; permanent and temporary standing commissions composed of specialists and citizens conduct investigations, evaluate performance, and attempt to resolve specific problems. Elected delegates have a crucial role: their representative activities are to provide information about the performance of local administration; and they are to take *direct* action to resolve all problems identified by the community (see García Cárdenas 1986).

In the mid-1980s official criticism of the performance of Cuban socialism introduced a process of Rectification of Errors and Negative Tendencies. Acknowledging successes and external constraints, Castro's February 1986 report to the Third Party Congress stressed domestic problems and Cuban mistakes, among them shortcomings in the planning system, the preparation of state cadres, and the use of material incentives (Castro 1986). The rectification process launched in April 1986 to correct errors and eliminate symptoms and perceived sources of poor performance—including corruption, *burocratismo*, and technocratic or economistic attitudes, promotes revolutionary consciousness reminiscent of the 1960s *within* the organizational framework created in the 1970s (see Martínez Heredia 1988). Pragmatic still about the need for efficiency and committed to centralization, administrative development, and the better functioning of existing institutional arrangements, Cuba's rectification process reasserts politics, ideology, and the importance of participation.

In the process of reforming administration after 1959, Cuba's thinking about efficiency and bureaucracy changed. Republican politics bequeathed the revolution a corrupt and inefficient state administration. Once the economic and political arrangements sustaining the "cleptocracy" were eliminated, including a break with the United States, the old state administration was replaced by administrative arrangements and standards reflecting Cuba's Marxist theory and the opportunities and constraints of socialist development. How has the administrative system performed? What is the source and nature of administrative power? These questions call for some conclusions about Cuba and about comparative analysis that can account for the theoretical contest over bureaucracy.

IV. CONCLUSIONS: ANALYZING POWER AND PERFORMANCE

An evaluation of administrative performance in contemporary Cuba confronts the deep theoretical differences between two contending perspectives on bureaucracy. The historical analysis of organizational power necessary for understanding administrative arrangements, standards, and performance must therefore entertain critical choices about the concept of bureaucracy. Though such an analysis of Cuban administration will not be finished here, its direction and utility are suggested. Socialist efficiency, the societal context that empowers administration and conditions performance, and the Cuban alternative to Weberian bureaucracy are briefly considered in turn.

Efficiency, generally considered in terms of a ratio of inputs to outputs, is a standard of performance shared by capitalism and socialism. Though problems persist in its pursuit of efficiency, Cuban state administration has improved its performance since 1959. Given Cuba's socialist goals, the "material welfare" of the Cuban people has been served by successful implementation of health care, education, food, and employment (see Brundenius 1984). Economic growth and labor productivity, so central to judgment about the efficiency of socialist administration, reveal accomplishments. Productivity, for example, increased at an average annual rate of 5.2% in the 1981–85 period.[25] Figures, however, explain little about the problems and possibilities of performance in a system where the obligations and the scope of state administration have expanded exponentially. Though the desire for efficiency may appear similar in capitalism and socialism, the organizational and societal contexts within which it is pursued differ.

Cuba's participatory approach to efficiency clearly differs from the Weberian ideal in terms of administrative arrangements, yet it is the socialist context of organizational power that explains Cuban standards and actual performance. Weber supposed that the power of knowledge-based hierarchical control would be extended from capitalism to socialism. Cuban capitalism did not generate the technical development that propels a Weberian process of bureaucratization, and the pace of postrevolutionary improvement in technical efficiency has been constrained by underdevelopment, bipolar international hostility, and deliberate Cuban choices. Yet the power of real bureaucracies, as Weber suspected, is never that of a pure technical efficiency. Historical analysis of the context of organizational power, not an abstract process of bureaucratization, provides the basis for conclusions about the performance of state administration in Cuba.

An analysis of the socialist context of administration, about which Weber had little to say,[26] requires analytical choices and a forray into contested theoretical terrain. First, acknowledging that organizations are products of society, Cuba's socialist context must be described and explained. It is a context profoundly different from capitalism. Given the facts of state management of production and collective property, centralized decision making and a Communist party, a complex relationship with the Soviet Union,[27] and an official vision of a future free of bureaucracy and all other forms of domination, the nature of authority must be determined, not assumed. Second, by taking Cuban standards of performance seriously, the specific sources of organizational power can be explored empirically. The antibureaucratic standards of Cuban socialism, as well as the use of technical expertise, have social and historical roots. By distinguishing problems of inadequate knowledge or experience from the use of knowledge or position to gain or maintain privileges and power, performance can be analyzed with reference to competing theories of the origin, nature, and effects of bureaucratic organization. Finally, all conclusions that presume the performance of socialist administration on the basis of its pursuit of efficiency, the structures of administration, or an ahistorical logic of bureaucratization must be set aside.

Cuba's participatory approach to efficiency provides an alternative to Weber's pure bureaucratic organization and challenges us to rethink our understanding of the power *and* the inevitability of bureaucratic domination, in capitalism and in socialism. While evaluation of the results of Poder Popular and the antibureaucratic pursuit of efficiency is part of the further investigation of the relationship of organizational power and administrative performance advocated here,[28] practical alternatives to traditional hierarchies keep the critical debates about bureaucratic organization alive. It may indeed be possible to resolve an apparent dilemma of efficiency. Comparative analysis organized around the concept of bureaucracy has an immanent role in that project.

ENDNOTES

1. Heady (1984:61–64) sorts definitions according to three tendencies: to define around structure, around behavior (both functional and dysfunctional), and around purpose. Lane (1987) identifies at least 11 definitions.
2. Other names associated with the formal school include F.W. Taylor and H. Fayol (scientific industrial management), and L. White, L. Gulick, and L. Urwich (generic or public management science). See Morgan (1986) and Denhardt (1984) for an overview of the development of organization theory.
3. Human relations theorists include F. Roethlisberger and W. Dickson (1939), E. Mayo (1933), A. Maslow (1943), D. MacGregor (1960), and C. Argyris (1964). Two of the most important contributors to management theory critiqued the emphasis of formal theory without redefining the purposes of the organization. Barnard explained management functions according to the variable human element in organizations (1948); Simon explained the limits of rationality in organizations while defending decisionmaking with efficiency as its end (1976). Humanistic approaches have proliferated, producing critiques of organizational values and, in the 1970s, a call for a new public administration. See Thayer (1973), Hummell (1987), and Marini (1971). That efficiency remains a critical concern is seen in the rise of the public choice paradigm (see Lane 1987).
4. As Morgan explains: "By giving detailed attention to patterns of authority and to the general process of direction, discipline, and subordination of individual to general interests, the classical theorists sought to ensure that when commands were issued at the top of the organization they would travel throughout the organization in a predetermined way, to create a precisely determined effect" (1987:27).
5. Seminal works by Follet (*Dynamic Administration*), Barnard (*The Functions of the Executive*), and Crozier (*The Bureaucratic Phenomenon*) looked at organization in light of new perspectives on the location of power, though in different ways. The trend has been to locate power lower in the organization than the formal school did.
6. J.D. Thompson (1967) identified two strategies for studying organizations. The closed system approach tends to ignore the external environment, treating the organization as a rational system. The open systems approach focuses on uncertainty and interdependence with external environments. Classic empirical work on the permeable boundaries of public organizations includes Selznick's study of the TVA (1949) and Kaufman's study of the U.S. Forest Service (1960).
7. Clegg and Dunkerley describe the treatment of power in terms of resource exchange: "The topic becomes *exercise* of power from within an equilibrium position, where that exercise is premised on the possession of some resource(s) by the power-holder" (1980:432). The structure itself is then taken for granted, as is the distribution of power resources. See Clegg and Dunkerley (1980, Chap. 4) for a discussion of specific theorists.

8. See Mommsen (1987) for Weber's view of the predicament of liberal democracy, and Krieger (1979) and Kilker (1987) for Weber's views of socialism.

9. Kilker (1987:35) suggests that Weber's analysis of socialism relied too heavily on historical experiences, ignoring the "uniqueness of modern technological innovation and cultural values."

10. The development of the Marxist perspective is not treated here; Lenin is used since he restated the work of Marx and attempted to carry theory into the practices of the Soviet Union. See Marx (1974), Lenin (1976), and for subsequent Marxist positions, Heydebrand (1977), Goldman and Van Houten (1977), and Fischer and Sirianni (1984).

11. On the Spanish imperial bureaucracy, see Haring (1947); on colonial rule in Cuba, see Pino Santos (1984).

12. See Hitchman (1971) and Lockmiller (1969) on the occupations.

13. In 1868, Cubans held only 135 of 532 positions in the colonial bureaucracy, mainly in poorly paid posts in education (Portuondo 1965:392).

14. Figures in Trelles (1923:20) and International Bank for Reconstruction and Development (1951:453, 683).

15. Figures in Pino Santos (1984:255, 464), and Smith (1960:166). On economic relationships see Benjamin (1984) and Pino Santos (1984).

16. See Diez del Valle (1953) for Cuban criticisms. Figure for *botellas* in Stokes (1949:356).

17. See Guevara (1970:176–183) and Dumont's (1970) criticism of INRA. Tortolani (1979) calls this early period "muddling through."

18. *Granma Weekly Review*, March 5, 1967, p. 4; March 26, 1967, p. 3; and LeoGrande (1979).

19. *Granma Weekly Review*, Feb. 10, 1967, p. 2, and March 5, 1967, p. 3.

20. On the development of Cuban planning after 1959 see Valdés (1979).

21. Figures from Kolésnikov (1983), Morales (1982), Messmer (1984), and *Granma Weekly Review*, Dec. 29, 1985, p. 2. A Cuban study of the development of *cuadro* policy is found in Machado Bermúdez (1983).

22. Zimbalist (1987:14) (an increase from 90,000 to 250,000). The growth in educational *cuadros* was reported in Ministerio de Educación. *Informe . . . a la Asamblea Nacional del Poder Popular Sobre Logros, Dificultades, Deficiencias y Perspectivas Inmediatas*, Havana: Asamblea Nacional del Poder Popular, pp. 274, 279 (1981).

23. The principles of socialist management are explained in Carnota Lauzan (1981). Space prohibits discussion of Cuban management theory or its treatment of Western theory.

24. Statement by Carlos Rafael Rodríguez, Political Bureau member, in a 1980 interview (1983).

25. Codina Jiménez (1987:139). The following are average annual rates of economic growth: 1962–1965, 3.7%; 1966–1970, 0.4%; 1971–1975, 7.5%; 1976–1980, 4%; and 1981–1985, 7.3% (Zimbalist and Eckstein 1987:10).

26. A more detailed exploration of what Weber did and did not write about socialism is not possible here, though most agree that he devoted scant attention to it; see Krieger (1979) and Kilker (1987).

27. Cuba's relationship with the Soviet Union does not duplicate its prerevolutionary relationship with the United States. The argument bears a fuller explanation than can be provided here, given the complexities of aid and alliance and the effects of both on economic, political, and administrative development.

28. See Harnecker (1979) and Lutjens (1987, Part II), where an effort is made to assess decentralization, participation, and the extent of local control.

REFERENCES

Alonso, J. *Cuba; el poder del pueblo.* Editorial Nuestro Tiempo, Mexico City, 1980.

Barnard, C. *The Functions of the Executive.* Harvard University Press, Cambridge, MA, 1948.

Beals, C. *The Crime of Cuba.* J.B. Lippincott, Philadelphia, 1933.

Benjamin, J.R. *The United States and Cuba: Hegemony and Dependent Development, 1880–1934.* University of Pittsburgh Press, Pittsburgh, 1974.

Brundenius, C. *Revolutionary Cuba: The Challenge of Economic Growth with Equity.* Westview Press, Boulder, CO, 1984.

Carrión, M. El desenvolvimiento social de Cuba en los últimos veinte años. *Cuba Contemporanea* 27(Sep. 1921):6–7, 19–20.

Carnota Lauzan, O. *Curso de administración para dirigentes*, 3rd ed. Editorial de Ciencias Sociales, Havana, 1981.

Castro, F. *Main Report: Third Congress of the Communist Party of Cuba.* Editora Política, Havana: 1986.

Clegg, S., and Dunkerley, D. *Organization, Class and Control.* Routledge & Kegan Paul, London, 1980.

Codina Jiménez, A. Worker incentives in Cuba. In *Cuba's Socialist Economy: Toward the 1990s* (A. Zimbalist, ed.). Lynne Rienner, Boulder, CO, 1987.

Denhardt, R.B. *Theories of Public Organization.* Brooks-Cole, Monterrey, CA, 1984.

Diez del Valle, M. *La Administración Pública en Cuba. Principales Problemas y Possibles Soluciones.* Editorial Lex, Havana, 1953.

Domínguez, J. *Cuba, Order and Revolution.* Harvard University Press, Cambridge, MA, 1978.

Dumont, R. *Cuba: Socialism and Development.* Grove Press, New York, 1970.

Fischer, F., and Sirianni, C., eds. *Critical Studies in Organization and Bureaucracy.* Temple University Press, Philadelphia, PA, 1984.

García Cárdenas, D. *State Organization in Cuba.* José Martí Publishing House, Havana: 1986.

Goldman, P., and Van Houten, D. Managerial strategies and the worker: a Marxist analysis of bureaucracy. *Sociological Quarterly*, Winter: 108–125 (1977).

Guevara, E. Contra el burocratismo. In *Obras 1957–1967*, Vol. I. François Maspero, Paris, 1970:176–183.

Gulick, L. Science, values, and public administration. In *The Administrative Process and Democratic Theory* (L.C. Gawthrop, ed.). Houghton Mifflin, Boston, 1970.

Haring, C.H. *The Spanish Empire in America.* Harcourt, Brace & World, New York, 1947.

Harnecker, M. *Cuba: Dictatorship or Democracy?* Lawrence Hill & Company, Westport, CN, 1979.

Heady, F. *Public Administration: A Comparative Perspective.* Marcel Dekker, New York, 1984.

Heydebrand, W.V. Organizational contradictions in public bureaucracies: toward a Marxian theory of organizations. *Sociological Quarterly 18*:83–107 (1977).

Hitchman, J.H. *Leonard Wood and Cuban Independence 1898–1902.* Martinus Nijhoff, The Hague, 1976.

Hummel, R. *The Bureaucratic Experience*, 3rd ed. St. Martin's Press, New York, 1987.

International Bank for Reconstruction and Development. *Report on Cuba.* Washington, D.C., 1951.

Jolly, R. Education. In *Cuba, The Economic and Social Revolution* (D. Seers, ed.). University of North Carolina Press, Chapel Hill, 1964.

Kaufman, H. *The Forest Ranger: A Study in Administrative Behavior.*, Johns Hopkins University Press, Baltimore, MD, 1960.

Kilker, E. Max Weber and the possibilities for socialism. In *Bureaucracy Against Democracy and Socialism* (R. Glassman, W. Satos Jr., and P. Rosen, eds.). Greenwood Press, New York, 1987.

Kolésnikov, N. *Cuba: Educación Popular y Preparación de los Cuadros Nacionales 1949–1982.* Editorial Progreso, Moscow, 1983.

Krigier, M. Weber, Lenin and the reality of socialism. In *Bureaucracy: The Career of a Concept* (E. Kamenka and M. Krygier, eds.). St. Martin's Press, New York, 1979.

Lane, J. Introduction: the concept of bureaucracy. In *Bureaucracy and Public Choice* (J. Lane, ed.). Sage Publications, London, 1987.

Lenin, V.I. The state and revolution. In *On the Dictatorship of the Proletariat.* Progress Publishers, Moscow, 1976.

LeoGrande, W.M. Party development in revolutionary Cuba. *Journal of Interamerican Studies and World Affairs* November: 475–480 (1979).

Lockmiller, D. *Magoon in Cuba: A History of the Second Intervention, 1906–1909.* Greenwood Press, New York, 1969.

Lutjens, S.L. The state, bureaucracy and politics: administrative reform in Cuba. Ph.D. dissertation, University of California, Berkeley, 1987.

Machado Bermúdez, R. *La Formación de Cuadros y Dirección Científica Desde el Subdesarrollo.* Editorial de Ciencias Sociales, Havana, 1983.

Marini, F., ed. *Toward a New Public Administration: The Minnowbrook Perspective.* Chandler, San Francisco, 1971.

Martínez Heredia, F. *Desafíos al Socialismo Cubano.* Centro de Estudios sobre América, Havana: 1988.

Marx, K. The civil war in France: address to the General Council. In *The First International & After* (D. Fernbach, ed.). Vintage Books, New York, 1974.

Messmer, W. Cuban agriculture and personnel recruitment policy. *Studies in Comparative International Development* Spring: 3–28 (1984).

Mommsen, W.J. Max Weber and the crisis of liberal democracy. In *Bureaucracy Against Democracy and Socialism* (R.M. Glassman, W.J. Swatos, Jr., and P. Rosen, eds.). Greenwood Press, New York, 1987.

Morales, R. La preparación de los cuadros dirigentes de la economía del país. *Cuba Socialista* September–November: 108–133 (1982).

Morgan, G. *Images of Organization.* Sage Publications, Beverly Hills, CA, 1986.

Petras, J. Cuba: fourteen years of revolutionary government. In *Development Administration in the Third World* (C.E. Thurber and L. Graham, eds.). Duke University Press, Durham, NC, 1973.

Portuondo, F. *Historia de Cuba Hasta 1898.* Editorial Nacional de Cuba, Havana, 1965.

Pino Santos, O. *Cuba, Historia y Economía: Ensayos.* Editorial de Ciencias Sociales, Havana, 1984.

Roca, B. *Discurso Pronunciado por el Compañero Blas Roca Durante el Acto de Constitución de la Asamblea Provincial del Poder Popular en Matanzas Celebrado el 21 de Julio de 1974.* Asamblea Nacional de Poder Popular, Havana, 1978.

Rodríguez, C.R. An interview with Carlos Rafael Rodríguez, December 1980. In *Fidel Castro Speeches,* Vol. III. Pathfinder Press, New York, 1983:316–321.

Selznick, P.A. *TVA and the Grassroots: A Study in the Sociology of Formal Organization.* University of California Press, Berkeley: 1949.

Simon, H.A. *Administrative Behavior: A Study of Decision-Making Processes in Administrative Organization,* 3rd ed. Free Press, New York, 1976.

Smith, R.F. *The United States and Cuba: Business and Diplomacy, 1971–1960.* College and University Press, New Haven, CT, 1960.

Stokes, W.S. The Cuban parliamentary system in action, 1940–1947. *Journal of Politics* May: 335–364 (1949).

Thayer, F. *An End to Hierarchy! An End to Competition!* New Viewpoints, New York, 1973.

Thompson, J.D. *Organizations in Action.* McGraw-Hill, New York, 1967.

Tortolani, P. Cuba 1959–1970: the evolution of an administrative system in a revolutionary context. Ph.D. dissertation, New York University, New York, 1979.

Trelles, C.M. *El Progreso (1902 a 1905) y el Retroceso (1906–1922) de la República de Cuba.* Havana: Imprenta El Score, 1923.

Valdés, N.P. The Cuban revolution: economic organization and bureaucracy. *Latin American Perspectives* Winter: 13–37 (1979).

Weber, M. *Economy and Society* (G. Roth and C. Wittich, eds.). University of California Press, Berkeley, 1978.

Zimbalist, A. Introduction: Cuba's socialist economy toward the 1990s. In *Cuba's Socialist Economy: Toward the 1990s,* (A. Zimbalist, ed.). Lynne Rienner, Boulder, CO, 1987.

Zimbalist, A., and Eckstein, S. Patterns of Cuban development: the first twenty-five years. In *Cuba's Socialist Economy: Toward the 1990s* (A. Zimbalist, ed.). Lynne Rienner, Boulder, CO, 1987.

42

Internationalization or Indigenization

Alternatives on the Path from Dependency to Independence

Keith M. Henderson   *Department of Political Science, State University College of New York at Buffalo, Buffalo, New York*

I. INTRODUCTION

In this chapter, I will examine the alternatives of internationalization and indigenization as options on the road to administrative independence. The former is dominant in contemporary thinking and argues for independence within the framework of Northern-dominated institutions; the latter usually argues either for the impossibility of independence on the periphery of the world economy or, more positively, for the possibility and desirability of political, economic, and/or administrative detachment from other systems.

Internationalization is well understood and widely discussed; indigenization less so. Various bottom-up indigenization strategies suggest the feasibility of replacing the existing multinational corporate structures with grassroots economic units (e.g., Ekins and von-Uexkull 1992; Korten 1997); others seem mere ideal administrative worlds with little likelihood of realization. Existing power relationships would have to be overturned—in either instance—to establish independence based solely on indigenization.

In the discussion to follow, both internationalization and indigenization will be characterized, and then consideration will be given to the prospects for merging the two approaches. A realizable "unity in diversity" is posited, replacing the "one size fits all" Northern model.

II. INTERNATIONALIZATION

In its administrative dimension, internationalization involves a continued reliance on and a further empowering of Western-style (Northern-style) public administration in the developing world. Systems originally established by colonial rulers or copied from the West/North would be further integrated—in their present male-dominated, elite-oriented mode—into a global system without appreciable local (indigenous) content. This would occur along with debureaucratization and privatization, making remaining administrators even more dependent for their continued livelihood on outside forces. As Dwivedi indicates:

Development administration in the past has been concerned mainly with transplanting and replicating ideas and institutions of the North. It continues to practice statecraft in a hierarchical, bureaucratic, and centrally planned manner. But as the events of 1989 [*sic*] (fall of the Berlin Wall, separation of Eastern European countries from Russia) have demonstrated, that strategy was one of the causes of stagnation in the former communist regimes of Eastern Europe. Developing nations must now employ alternative institutional designs to escape from further damage to their system (Dwivedi 1994:147).

Under the current trend toward further internationalization, linkages to the North would be solidified with conditional financial assistance, policy advice and insistence on democratic governance into a seamless web of administrative interaction. Internationalization—thought of this way—suggests "development with aid" and a necessary administrative relationship between North and South. Unequal power is obvious in the current arrangements and implied in projections of "structural adjustment" and other lending patterns. The overwhelming problems associated with nation building and socioeconomic development along with the lack of resources and skills in developing countries argues for the importance of loan or grant programs at the same time that it restricts self-reliant human needs centered/sustainable administration (Dwivedi and Henderson 1999).

As the 21st century gets underway, there is every indication that the Washington/London/Bonn/Paris/Tokyo consensus will prevail. More than in the past there is today a remarkable degree of consensus among Northern lenders as to the way in which administrative systems—along with economies and polities—would be drawn into the international system (OECD 1996). Differences among the important Northern powers (the G7) remain over the appropriate proportion of the national budget for development assistance (with the United States near the bottom of the list), over appropriate roles for private enterprise and voluntary organizations, over tying of aid to advantages for domestic business, over bilateral-multilateral linkages, and other matters.

At the same time, there is both more coordination of programs and more support for the World Bank/IMF approach than previously existed. Reinforcing the centripetal tendencies are the end of the cold war, limited availability of funds, "graduation" of some countries which had been aid recipients, strategic considerations, agreement on the importance of proper governance, the telecommunications revolution, the influence of the United Nations, and other factors. The dominant reasoning remains economic and the ideal administrative world envisioned is one of honest, competent, but limited government administration which promotes a facilitating environment for business unfettered by red tape or overregulation and secure in property rights and judicial redress mechanisms. The single barrier-free worldwide marketplace would be complemented by the existence of regional trading arrangements overseen by the World Trade Organization, successor to the General Agreement on Trade and Tariffs (GATT).

An internationalizing of public administration in accordance with the above would require the promotion of Northern values and practices with administrators in all world areas performing in essentially the same fashion. Conferences, Internet interaction (overwhelmingly in the English language), publications, and standards of performance would be Northern dominated; OECD countries (particularly the G7) and some newly industrialized countries (NICs) would be looked to for guidance.

A.   World Bank Role

The predominant economic emphasis underlying administrative reform places the World Bank (and its sister organization, the International Monetary Fund) in a more crucial role than, for example, the United Nations, which does not have the same leverage for inducing change. In its own words and stated policies, the World Bank is a benevolent institution concerned not only with economic development but with human needs and a sustainable environment.

In its widely discussed analyses of performance by individual countries and the correlation between development (as the Bank defines it) and policy, several themes stand out. *The East Asian Miracle* (1993) advanced the debate by suggesting—for the first time in an official Bank release—that no single model could capture the success of East Asian economies; government interventions to promote industrial advance were varied, widespread, and prolonged among the NICs and Japan. Targeted industries, in the Bank's view, generally did less well than those left to the marketplace. The basic notion that markets are efficient and governments inefficient remains; the neoliberal position is vindicated in the Bank's judgment. Some revisions in its position, however, were necessitated by the unanticipated collapse of the East Asian miracle in 1997 and 1998 (World Bank 1998).

In its analyses of African economies, not surprisingly the Bank concluded that those regimes which had consistently followed Bank requirements did better than those that did not. In one important study, 29 sub-Saharan countries which had undertaken structural adjustment policies in the 1980s were reviewed. Although no country was found to have an ideal macroeconomic strategy, those that made the most improvement in policy also did best economically. Ghana headed the list, followed, in order, by Tanzania, Gambia, Burkino Faso, Nigeria, and Zimbabwe (World Bank 1994).

In academic circles and in the world of practice, the Bank's conclusions were strongly criticized. Reforms in Ghana, for example, were found in one study to benefit the elite and some rural dwellers but not the urban middle class, students, or civil servants (Jeong 1995).

Imbalances and human suffering have resulted from many of the conditionalities imposed by multilateral and bilateral lending organizations and apparent successes—even in strictly economic terms—are sometimes short-lived or of benefit only to certain groups. It is interesting to note that indigenous administrators are often one of the disadvantaged groups.

Self-correcting mechanisms within the Bank and IMF—as well as within bilateral agencies—have yielded a rhetoric which has encouraged many influential leaders in both the developing and developed worlds to regard the Bank somewhat more positively. These mechanisms are reinforced by both the direct impact of the "reverse agenda" of civil society movements such as nongovernmental organizations (NGOs) and the indirect influence of United Nations organs, themselves influenced by the "reverse agenda." Heightened gender, environmental, and human rights concerns have been particularly important outcomes of United Nations conferences such as the Fourth International Conference on Women held in Beijing in 1995 and the Earth Summit held in Rio in 1992. Additional Bank/IMF responsiveness may be expected, along with redirection to respond to crises such as in East Asia.

Significantly for students of Development Administration, the Bank's *World Development Report 1997, The State in a Changing World*—the 20th annual edition of the Report—acknowledges that the emphasis upon market-friendly policies and state downsizing may have gone too far, neglecting the role of the state in insuring a prosperous economy. The critical factor, the Bank suggests, is not the *size* of the state but its *capabilities*; roles must be matched to capabilities. This is not a return to standard development administration prescriptions from an earlier era but a renewed stress on the importance of secure property rights and a reliable legal system—largely for the direct benefit of business—with the recognition that these are obtained only through governmental institutions and actions. In support of the argument is the Bank's survey of 3600 entrepreneurs in 69 countries who were asked about such basic governmental functions as securing property rights. The Bank converted the responses into an index of credibility. Countries with the higher credibility bring in greater investment and have faster economic growth (World Bank

1997). Again, the irony was that the model often used by the Bank and others—the NICs of East and Southeast Asia—was not able to guide uninterrupted, sustained development.

In spite of indications concerning their flexibility and constructive shifts in thinking along with competitive pressures from private lending, the argument can be made that deeply rooted organizational characteristics of the World Bank and IMF will outlast the best intentions of reformers. Using the Bank's own memoranda and interviews with staff, Paul Nelson has documented this convincingly. Staff is under pressure to make loans, usually large ones; a rigid project cycle exists along with an insular information management system; and the Bank suffers from an organizational myth of apolitical development (Nelson 1995). He is pessimistic about the prospects for Bank–private sector–third sector cooperation (a sine qua non for the future) even though the assumption of the Bank presidency by a reform-minded Australian interested in environmental and social development issues (James D. Wolfensohn) holds out promise, in his view. "But he takes over a large and conservative bureaucracy whose entrenched interests, myths and organizational dynamics have resisted and reshaped changes promulgated by previous leaders" (Nelson 1995:28).

For the early part of the 21st century, it is likely that the Bank (and IMF) will continue to dominate administrative reform efforts—for better or worse—in an increasingly interdependent world. Increased private sector lending and lack of credibility of the Bank/IMF—as well as reluctance to provide funds by the U.S. Congress—will compromise but probably not displace that leadership.

III. INDIGENIZATION

The concept "indigenization" is somewhat less familiar than internationalization (or the broader idea, globalization) and has been used in a variety of technical ways to refer to native populations. It is used here as the reciprocal of internationalization to indicate all those activities, processes, organizational structures, and target groups that are native to a geographical area and are *relatively* immune to outside forces—i.e., not driven by Northern imperatives. Every administrative system is to some extent a mix of exogenous and indigenous elements; the distinguishing factor is the proportion and importance of the exogenous. Nearly all administrators, of course, are indigenous but few of their *formal* administrative activities, processes, or structures in the third world (and former "second world") were originated locally. The Northern argument is that where there is internal origin, then localized customs and traditions distort proper administration. Thus, nearly all informal patterns and administrative particularities are considered undesirable in Northern views, and often as seen by the ill-served client populations in the countries themselves.

In its perverse mode, indigenous administration is corrupt and self-serving following time-honored practices. Bribery is the tolerated norm; favoritism and nepotism are taken for granted; close patrimonial ties exist between administrative personnel and political leadership; and overstaffing is widespread. State-owned enterprises are allowed to proliferate, providing favors and employment opportunities for the privileged. Officials are arrogant, even abusive, and do little to readjust a status quo which favors existing power holders. Often, business or land-owning interests control the direction of government administration through intricate—and often invisible—tradeoffs. An ironic formalism—in which precise and detailed procedures are specified—is accompanied by locally developed mechanisms for circumventing the rules and regulations. Officials themselves or immediate family members may own and/or operate business and agricultural enterprises. At the top hierarchical level they are part of the elite; at middle and lower levels, they are linked to the elite. Geographic, clan or tribal, political, religious, and/or other commonalities characterize the entire administrative system or important parts of it.

Over many years, administration in the public sphere has accommodated more and more growth through formalized regulations (stamps and signatures required in large number for simple transactions conducted by small armies of underpaid, low-level clerks), extension of government activities (parastatals, marketing boards, etc.), and "employer of last resort" policies.

Northern advisers recommended overall restructuring; new planning, and organization and methods units; civil service modernization; campaigns against corruption; extensive training and education for the public service and other "improvements." Organizational and procedural changes were superimposed on the inefficient and ineffective bureaucracies resulting in a hodge-podge of updated colonial and neocolonial practices. The comparative public administration/development administration literature is replete with studies of indigenous practice, Western/Northern technology transfer, and documented failures in earlier reforms. It is not surprising that continual reform has been called for over many decades by nearly all elements except those immediately benefiting from the status quo.

The response to the widely understood inadequacy of government administration, however, has seldom been to seek precolonial patterns or other culturally relevant reforms for unique circumstances but, rather, to continue to require logical, rational—recently, neoliberal—change strategies. There is no spiritual element in these strategies nor participatory, bottom-up correction of perceived deficiencies.

In its less perverse dimension, indigenization may be a culturally desirable alternative to Northern impositions and may lead to preferred political, economic, and social results in the 21st century. It might have lead to better results in the postwar period, particularly when judged in terms of human-needs-centered/sustainable development and from the vantage point of self-reliance. In referencing "the events of 1989" (fall of the Berlin Wall, retreat from Communism, etc.), Dwivedi has called attention to the administrative inadequacies of Central and Eastern European governments while under Russian hegemony. The Communist brand of administration—with its rigid central planning and enforced ideology—ill served the post–World War II countries under its influence and did little better for the mother country. Transitions occurring since 1989–1990 provided opportunities for indigenous administration which were largely eclipsed by neoliberal conditions for economic aid. Preservation of culture and tradition without submergence in Northern patterns remains a popular theme, stimulated both by the perceived inadequacies of outside influences and by increasing pride in indigenous capacities. However, little movement is evident toward truly indigenous administration in most areas of the world; China and Iran at the national level stand out as exceptions, and a few other examples on a small scale may be found.

IV. TWO VIABLE EXAMPLES OF INDIGENIZATION

It is sometimes forgotten that China consciously rejected the Russian Communist model of administration many years before the collapse of Communism and turned to indigenous patterns. After Russian advisers were summarily dismissed and their Russian ideas rejected, attempts were made to develop characteristically Chinese solutions. Tragically unsuccessful at first under Mao, in more recent times the Jeng and post-Jeng reforms show the possibilities for indigenous administration. The situation, of course, was quite different than in Central and Eastern Europe but nevertheless may be broadly instructive. In fact, a great deal of attention has been given to the Chinese reforms and their long-range implications, and only a brief review is warranted here.

The first target of policy change under Deng was the agricultural sector, for which a new rural management system was introduced. The industrial sector was then addressed, with attempts to modify the large state-owned enterprises originally designed and operated with Russian assistance. Generally, the command economy was decentralized and designated areas of the country were used for pilot projects which, if workable, were extended to other regions.

The gradualist reform policies of Chinese political leadership gave prominence to administration throughout the 1980s and 1990s. Problems relating to corruption, nepotism, and procedural obstacles—along with issues of continued Party control—were the objects of reform. The *Gengshen* reforms attempted broad shifts in the roles of the Party, army, and government itself. In a case study of the Ministry of the Machine Building Industry, Oliver Williams showed how the mandate to modernize administrative management was carried out. He pointed out that even though advanced management techniques from other countries were studied—including computerized information processing—the Party maintained its cells and committees to "ensure that party and state policies were effectively implemented" (Williams 1993).

State enterprises have been granted considerable autonomy even though they are still subject to constraints imposed by government departments. Enterprise managers were subject to a revived "manager responsibility" system which gave managers clear authority and separated them from party secretaries.

In 1987, the National People's Congress passed a law reforming village committees through formal elections by villagers of their leaders. This was a belated response to the decollectivization of rural agricultural communes which had been replaced by township governments and village committees unpopular with the peasants. The new system has been more successful, ironically, in seeking implementation of central government directives (Manion 1996).

Health care in China has always had indigenous characteristics and its evident successes have been a model for other countries. The "barefoot doctors" brigade managed health stations, cooperative medical care insurance schemes, and other aspects. Changes in the early 1980s replaced a three-tiered system under each county in which communes controlled brigades and brigades controlled teams. Dismantling of the communes in 1983 introduced a less uniform pattern emphasizing financial rather than strictly ideological incentives with consequent regional disparity (Yin-bun 1995).

Among numerous other reforms in China since Mao's time is the introduction of a unique civil service system. In 1987, at the Thirteenth Party Congress, a new system was announced and was moving toward full implementation until the Tiananmen Square catastrophe in June 1989. In 1993, the "Provisional Regulations of State Civil Servants" were finally promulgated with the same intention of replacing a monolithic cadre system. The debate over the development of this system in China reveals why and how it differs from formal Western systems: "It would be misleading to call the attempt to create a civil service system in China just an administrative reform" (Lam and Chan 1995:1303).

More recently, Prime Minister Zhu has undertaken widespread reorganization of administration, announcing merging or elimination of 15 ministries and massive downsizing in the numbers of civil servants (*Economist* 1998:45). The role of the Communist party and its previous tight control over management of cadres was reformed in both instances, in a uniquely Chinese manner. Party-state relations and state-society relations were both affected.

The example of China's incremental approach within a Communist framework to public administration reform suggests an important alternative to Northern patterns. Prolonged economic success and accommodation with the North have been accomplished without rejecting Asian Communist principles. The vast English-language literature on modern China—some of it incorporating administration—attests to the recognition of its growing importance.

Arguably, the one other Southern country which has undertaken large-scale administrative reform at the end of the 20th century on its own terms is Iran. Its approach, while considerably different from China's, is also "non-Northern" and—in the 1990s—equally viable.

Islamic revivalism or "Islamism" in its Iranian form as well as its other radical manifestations throughout the Muslim world (usually called Islamic fundamentalism) presents an unappealing prospect to the North. Administratively, a distinctly non-Western concept of carrying out services and providing goods for a population on a religious basis is found. Religion and government are intertwined and attempts are made to address the whole individual; "state" and "society" are inseparable. In the Islamic concept of governance, officials are not regarded as detached, objective implementors; their religious identity is crucial and their skills are judged first and foremost on religious grounds. Shia Islam is the official religion of Iran and Islamic law is the basis of authority. Islamic ideals and beliefs provide the foundation of customs, laws, and practices including public administration.

As Ali Farazmand has explained, the ancient roots of administration—dating to many hundreds of years B.C.—have not been interrupted by colonial impositions and can form the basis of a distinctly Iranian pattern (Farazmand, 1999).

Administrative behavior in Iran should conform to the Sharia—the religious law—as interpreted by the Muslim clergy. Farazmand notes that the bureaucracy in Iran—while growing—is far less powerful than its counterpart under the Shah (Farazmand 1994).

In Iran more than in other countries the revolution brought a concerted effort to eradicate Western influences, considered the bane of Islam and the source of much of the world's difficulties. In the bureaucracy, as Farazmand and other observers have explained, this meant a purging of outside influences and the substitution of Islamic correctness. Translated into terms of administrative structure, procedure, and new or rehabilitated personnel, this resulted in a unique combination of revolutionary groupings (such as the Komiteh committees) and organizations such as the Islamic Revolutionary Guards Corps ministry.

Indigenous aspects of the new Iranian bureaucracy include the Martyrs Foundation, which was designed to assist the families of those who die for Islam. Ayatollah Khomeini initiated it in February 1980 for those killed in the 1977–79 period and its task expanded enormously—along with its resources—during and after the conflict with Iraq when hundreds of thousands of young men died in the eight-year war (Hiro 1985:252). While similar in many ways to the Islamic welfare organizations found in other parts of the Islamic world, the Martyrs Foundation and other foundations (*bonyads*) appear to enjoy—by their scope and importance in relation to other organizations—an integral place in Iranian administration. They have billions of dollars in assets and engage in numerous business enterprises (Kazemi 1997:43).

Observers have arrived at mixed reactions to the innovative "administrative reforms" of the Mullahs and their contributions to economic and social development. Farazmand is one of the most important public administration sources and he is somewhat optimistic. Omid argues that the failure to truly rationalize administrative structures has yielded bureaucratic confusion resulting in an increase in poverty (Omid 1994). Schirazi agrees and argues that administrative reforms have brought forth more problems than solutions. Chaos and confusion, he believes, have followed land reform and "production management" reform carried out in the name of Islam (Shirazi 1993).

V. OTHER CASES: SARVODAYA AND LIBERATION THEOLOGY

In addition to Asian Communist administration as evidenced in China and Islamic Revivalism as found in Iran, there are other indigenous administrative examples worthy of note which have not attained systemwide success. Sarvodaya and Liberation Theology represent the attempt to organize civil society at the grass roots and provide social services through nongovernmental organizations or unorganized grass roots movements. They are based on cultural factors with a religious/spiritual core and provide assistance—in the absence of adequate government programs—as an adjunct to their mobilization of disadvantaged populations. As development models, they would be implemented by indigenous administrators or volunteer workers within their regions (i.e., the subcontinent and Latin America, respectively) without appreciable outside direction. Financial aid would be accepted, if at all, without compromising the integrity of the model.

Again, the historical experience for Sarvodaya and Liberation Theology is instructive, although not entirely sanguine, and provides insights into alternatives for bureaucracy as usually construed. Both Sarvodaya and Liberation Theology represent spiritual models of development not unlike many other such efforts throughout history but with extensive, contemporary "real-world" records.

As an ancient Indian philosophy emphasizing truth, love and nonviolence Sarvodaya was included in Mahatma Gandhi's programs for social development (Macy 1985; Sharma 1982). Gandhi, regarded as the father of independent India, was a proponent of *satyagraha*—passive resistance to British rule. His rejection of Western culture was based on Hinduism but he believed in the unity of humanity under one god and preached Muslim and Christian ethics as well as Hindu. Gandhi's stress on self-sufficiency and rejection of mechanical technology and material "benefits" of a money economy suggests the superiority of a people-based spiritualism for administration and administrators. In its Sri Lanka application, Sarvodaya dates to the mid-1950s, when a group of idealistic high school teachers in Colombo organized Shramadana work camps in which students from the city volunteered to share their time and effort in the poorest villages, whether Sinhala, Muslim, or Tamil. By the mid-1970s some 1000 villages were involved and 20 years later some 8000 to 10,000 out of a total of 23,000. However, political violence has impeded the movement and it has not been able to prevent the terrorism and bloodshed in Sri Lanka (Ekins and von-Uexkull 1992:111).

Liberation Theology—more politically active than Sarvodaya—has been attacked for its Marxist leanings and militaristic mobilization of the poor and oppressed to combat capitalist domination. Since the collapse of Communism, it seems to have turned more towards spirituality than social activism but still is an important presence in thousands of base communities throughout Latin America. Like Sarvodaya, its influence has been felt in other regions (Black Liberation Theology was an important element of the antiapartheid movement in South Africa; a feminist variant also exists) although it remains identified primarily with the liberal wing of the Catholic Church in Latin America. It is now facing competition from a growing Pentecostal movement in Latin America which also provides services on a limited basis to the poor, and it has never had enthusiastic support from the Vatican.

In the opinion of one observer, the Christian base communities in Brazil and other Latin American communities may still represent "the most revolutionary Catholic movement since the Reformation" (Burdick 1992:171).

Movements such as Sarvodaya and Liberation Theology which espouse a religious/spiritual ideology are inevitably involved in political controversy. Other movements ranging from the Zapatistas in southern Mexico to Kurdish nationalists in the Middle East have clear political agendas and provide basic services beyond the available governmental and Northern voluntary ones as an adjunct to their priority concern with seeking justice. Both the Hizballah in southern Lebanon—which provides a wide range of educational and social services and operates modern hospitals (Norton 1998:148)—and the Tamil Tigers in Sri Lanka are commonly identified as "terrorist organizations" with little attention to their administrative role. Regardless of their relationship to established political units, the administrative uniqueness of such organizations is frequently marked by dedicated volunteers in place of career officials, disdain for administrative detail including accounting and budgetary matters, and ambivalent status vis-à-vis other service-delivery agencies.

Other small-scale indigenous development efforts, often with unusual but effective administration, have existed within established governmental structures for many years. Indigenous water organizations, for example, are not uncommon. One well-studied instance is the water temples of Bali which illustrate the inseparability of social organization from production relationships. As an elaborate irrigation system involving rituals and beliefs, the water temples are an integral part of Balinese society:

> My argument is that the ritual system of water temples defines the symbolic meaning of productive relationships. A weir is just a weir, but the concept of holy water from a weir shrine transforms the weir into the symbol of a specific social unit (Lansing 1991:129).

Dutch colonials installed bureaucratic management systems in Bali which persisted after independence but ultimately were readjusted for traditional practice.

These examples suggest that indigenous administration is, indeed, workable in a variety of situations and often—but not always—preferable to Northern impositions or conventional, central-government programs. Decentralized arrangements, contracting out, and, of course, privatization are additional options. However, all raise the specter of the state turning over power to politicized groups concerned only with their own well-being.

The possibilities of precolonial revivals are also real and, in much of Africa for example, the custom of village councils and self-administered services through local initiatives has remained. In fact, rural development programs which were indigenous creations and later received external funding are fairly numerous in Asia, Africa, the Middle East, and Latin America as are small-scale financial initiatives such as credit facilities modeled after Bangladesh's well-known Grameen Bank (Mead and Liedholm 1998).

VI. MERGING INTERNATIONALIZATION AND INDIGENIZATION

Thought of as directions or choices on the path to independence in administration, internationalization and indigenization appear on the surface to be contradictory. The first leads to interdependence (if not dependence) and uniformity; the second to separateness and diversity. There is evident conflict between the two approaches with the former having the advantage of controlling resources, dominating international systems, and setting standards.

A more hopeful perspective is suggested here which leads to partial *reconciliation* ("unity in diversity") at the same time as it reduces administrative homogenization and Northern dominance. Possibilities of merging internationalization and indigenization should be explored in order to avoid further conflictual interaction, resentment of the North, and dependence. Desirable instances of such merging are discussed at length in an edited volume just completed (Henderson and Dwivedi 1999) and in Dwivedi's *Development Administration, From Underdevelopment to Sustainable Development* (1994).

In addition to the examples of China and Iran—where any merging is on their own terms—and the spiritually based approaches such as Sarvodaya and Liberation Theology—no longer at the peak of their effectiveness—are instances of success of a different character.

Sharing of power with NGOs through partnership and coordinated service delivery is among the most promising "new wave" of diverse administrative styles attuned to indigenous concerns. NGOs are proliferating around the globe and have been proven able to share in service delivery—particularly for very poor populations—without overturning established institutions. An important "reverse agenda" has arisen as increasingly influential Northern and Southern NGOs and grassroots movements demand policy changes from existing governments. This is true not only for the spiritual/religious NGOs and grass roots movements such as Sarvodaya and Liberation Theology but also for those organizations which individually and collectively (in networks, consortia, public forums, etc.) advocate human rights, gender inclusiveness, child welfare, sustainable development, environmental action, or other concerns (Henderson 1999:Chap. 3). More study needs to be done concerning the ways in which Northern sponsors can support NGO–host government collaborative efforts without coopting them or encouraging their absorption by host governments.

Creating new "people-centered" organizations such as the National Irrigation Administration (NRI) in the Philippines is another approach. NRI involves a radical participative approach following a "learning process" ala David Korten (1988) which eschews top-down blueprints and embraces the concept of learning from errors (Turner and Halligan 1999:Chap. 6). Bolivia's Popular Participation Law is an additional example of "people-centered" administration based on enhancement of citizen participation and decentralization through strengthening of local government. Most of the underserved rural population in Bolivia are indigenous people living in very small communities and historically marginalized (Rosenbaum 1998:133).

Additionally, there are revitalized central administrative agencies in some countries staffed by the people affected, such as Indian groups in Latin America (Meacham 1999). Beyond symbolic efforts, such agencies could truly serve the needs of neglected populations and encourage additional self-reliance through culturally based administrative patterns.

Recognition of diverse cultural elements in administration as neither an obstacle to merging of indigenization and internationalization nor an aberration in need of correction is found in the acceptance of "Asian values" in administration, most widely appreciated in the case of Japan:

> Typical values are identified as group rather than individual reference; conflict avoidance; the importance of face; respect for authority and seniority; paternalism; respect for academic credentials; undervaluation of the professional role of women; belief in cosmology and superstition; and the importance of family support (Turner and Halligan 1999).

The "undervaluation of the professional role of women"—also found in other than Asian applications—is one aspect of the listing which is problematic. Gendered—as well as ecological—thinking is a key element of meaningful merging of internationalization and indigenization (see Tremblay 1999).

In short, diversity can be accepted, alternative forms of administration encouraged, and gendered/ecological thinking incorporated in existing bureaucracies. Administrative independence can be attained as an adjunct of political development without merely copying the Northern/Western style of administration.

Undergirding the new thinking is the report of the World Commission on Culture and Development which recommended a broad-based rethinking of the development process. Its international agenda includes the rights of women and children, the recognition of indigenous peoples, and a "coalition of cultures" approach to development recognizing the authenticity of other cultural voices. (UNESCO 1995). As a UNESCO project (the United States is not a member of UNESCO, having withdrawn in 1984) there is widespread representation including the United Kingdom and Scandinavia as well as developing countries. Along with numerous other reports of United Nations organs, this represents a consensus beyond the "Washington consensus."

There is reason to hope that trends under way at the moment will lead to an administrative world in the 21st century in which gender and ecological awareness are prominent in all elements of the polycentric state and in which North/South divisions have been bridged by administrative understandings, networks, and partnerships that succeed in reducing poverty and distress through provision of needed services. Neither the demanded dependence of the North nor the idiosyncratic and maladaptive behavior of the South would prevail.

REFERENCES

Burdick, J. (1992). Rethinking the study of social movements: the case of Christian base communities in urban Brazil. In A. Escobar and S. Alvarez (eds.), *The Making of Social Movements in Latin America.* Boulder, CO: Westview.

Dwivedi, O.P. (1994). *Development Administration, From Underdevelopment to Sustainable Development.* London: Macmillan.

Dwivedi, O.P., and Henderson, K.M. (1999). Alternative administration: human needs centered and sustainable. In K.M. Henderson and O.P. Dwivedi (eds.), *Bureaucracy and Its Alternatives in World Perspective.* London: Macmillan.

Economist, March 14, 1998.

Ekins, P., and von-Uexkull, J. (1992). *A New World Order: Grassroots Movements for Global Change.* London: Routledge.

Farazmand, A. (1999). Bureaucracy and its alternatives in the Middle East. In K.M. Henderson and O.P. Dwivedi (eds.), *Bureaucracy and Its Alternatives in World Perspective.* London: Macmillan.

Farazmand, A. (1994). Bureaucracy, bureaucratization, and debureaucratization in ancient and modern Iran. In A. Farazmand (ed.), *Handbook of Bureaucracy.* New York: Marcel Dekker.

Henderson, K.M., and Dwivedi, O.P. (eds.). (1999). *Bureaucracy and Its Alternatives in World Perspective.* London: Macmillan.

Hiro, D. (1985): *Iran Under the Ayatollahs.* London: Routledge and Kegan Paul.

Jeong, H. (1995). Liberal economic reform in Ghana: a contested political agenda. *Africa Today 4,* 82–103.

Kazemi, F. (1997). The Iranian enigma. *Current Affairs 96*(606), 40–46.

Korten, D. (1990). *When Corporations Rule the World.* West Hartford, CT: Kumarian.

Korten, D. (1980). Community organization and rural development: a learning process approach. *Public Administration Review 40*(5), 480–511.

Lam, T.C., and Chan, H.S. (1995). Designing China's civil service system: general principles and realities. *International Journal of Public Administration 18*(8), 1298–1315.

Lansing, J.S. (1991). *Priests and Programmers: Technologies of Power in the Engineered Landscape of Bali.* Princeton, NJ: Princeton University Press.

Macy, J. (1985). *Dharma and Development: Religion as a Resource in the Sarvodaya Self-Help Movement.* West Hartford, CT: Kumarian.

Manion, M. (1996). The electoral connection in the Chinese countryside. *American Political Science Review 90*(4), 736–748.

Meacham, C. (1999). Development administration and its alternatives in Latin America and the Caribbean: reforms and redirection. In Henderson and Dwivedi, *op. cit.*

Mead, D.C., and Liedholm, C. (1998). Dynamics of Micro and Samm Enterprises in developing countries. *World Development 26*(1), 61–74.

Nelson, P.J. (1995). *The World Bank and Non-Governmental Organizations, The Limits of Apolitical Development.* London: Macmillan.

Norton, A.R. (1988). Hizballah: from radicalism to pragmatism? *Middle East Policy 5*(4), 147–155.

OECD Development Assistance Committee. (1996). *Shaping the 21st Century: The Contribution of Development Assistance.* Paris: OECD.

Omid, H. (1994). *Islam and the Post-Revolutionary State in Iran.* New York: St. Martins.

Rosenbaum, A. (1998). Strengthening civil society and local democracy through national initiatives: the case of Bolivia's "Popular Participation Law." *International Review of Administrative Sciences 64,* 133–136.

Sharma, S. (1982). An alternative strategy of social development. *Social Development Issues 6*(2), 45–57.

Schirari, A. (1993). *Islamic Development Policy in Iran.* Boulder, CO: Lynne Rienner.

Tremblay, R.C. (1999). Inclusive administration and development: feminist critiques of bureaucracy. In Henderson and Dwivedi, *op. cit.*

Turner, M., and Halligan, J. (1999). Bureaucracy and its alternatives in East and Southeast Asia. In Henderson and Dwivedi, *op. cit.*

UNESCO. (1995). *Our Creative Diversity: Report of the World Commission on Culture and Development.* Paris: UNESCO.

Williams, O. (1993). An outsider's perspective. In M. Mills and S. Nagle (eds.), *Public Administration in China.* Westport, CT: Greenwood.

World Bank. (1993). *The East Asian Miracle.* New York: Oxford.

World Bank. (1994). *Adjustment in Africa: Reforms, Results, and the Road Ahead.* New York: Oxford.

World Bank. (1997). *World Development Report 1997, The State in a Changing World.* New York: Oxford.

World Bank. (1998). *Poverty Reduction and the World Bank: Progress in Fiscal 1996 and 1997.* Washington: World Bank.

Yin-bun, C. (1995). Community mobilization and health care in rural China. *Community Development Journal 30*(4), 317–326.

43

Understanding Small-State Governance

An Emerging Field

Ian Thynne   *Department of Politics and Public Adminstration, University of Hong Kong, Hong Kong*

Roger Wettenhall   *Centre for Research in Public Sector Management, University of Canberra, Canberra, Australia*

I. INTRODUCTION

This chapter focuses on the concerns and problems of a group of states which may be developed, developing, or underdeveloped, and whose distinguishing characteristic is smallness, sometimes compounded by remoteness. Of particular interest are the various institutional arrangements which have been adopted as innovative responses to smallness and the need to achieve appropriate degrees of political and administrative integration.

The study of the governmental problems of small and island states has been emerging as a subfield of public administration as the number of such states has grown dramatically over the past generation. The subject communities have mostly, of course, long existed: what is new is that many of them have acquired the institutions of statehood as the result of the breakup of empires in the recent period of decolonization and, as small statehood has thus become better understood, other oddities such as the proverbial "little countries of Europe" (Luxembourg, Monaco, Andorra, San Marino, Liechtenstein: AGS 1969) have also been recognized fully as states in their own right, often moving on to United Nations membership.

Two explanations are immediately required. First, in this body of scholarship the word *state* is used in a generic sense and is broader than the international law sense which requires recognition of full formal sovereignty. It refers to any territory that has a degree of governmental autonomy or separateness, and so covers not only fully sovereign countries but also "associate" states such as the Cook Islands, self-governing colonies and territories, and constituent states or provinces within federations. It is likely that the new category of "special administrative region" (Palestine in its present relation to Israel, and Hong Kong from 1997 and Macao from 1999 under Chinese sovereignty) will also qualify. It is convenient to regard states of this sort as "quasi-states." Within the Australian federation the Australian Capital Territory (ACT), the Northern Territory and Norfolk Island are, since the granting to them of self-governing institutions, states in this sense as well as the six founding (or constitutional) "states," but not some other tereritories, notably the Cocos Islands, Christmas Island, and the Australian Antarctic Territory, which have no distinct governments of their own. Overseas French possessions which are treated governmentally as though they are *départements* of metropolitan France (Réunion in the Indian Ocean, Martinique and Guadeloupe in the Caribbean, Guyane in South America) would also not be regarded as states (on France's overseas possessions: Aldrich and Connell 1992).

Second, there is no universally accepted definition of *smallness*. The word is often used in a somewhat emotional sense, which can work in opposite directions: either reminiscent of Schumacher's dictum that "small is beautiful" (1973), or of the view of a senior Beijing student in the Australian Capital Territory in the late 1980s (when self-government was conferred on that territory) that it was ridiculous for a community of just 300,000 people to enjoy its own governing institutions. It is all relative: thus, relating to the larger states in which he served, a Singaporean diplomat described his own country as "tiny" (Lee Koon Choy 1993), but with around 3 million people Singapore is a giant compared with many others; thus again, an administrative historian described Malta as a "microstate" (Pirotta 1996), but with around 350,000 people it is 35 times larger than the largest of the microstates discussed as case studies later in this chapter.

In an endeavour to be more rigorous, several studies have adopted the rule of thumb of population less than 1 million; a few have preferred 500,000 or less (see Raadschelders 1992 for discussion). Small population often goes with small size, but not always: Australia's Northern Territory is small in population but large in area. Sometimes, of course, the reverse applies: very small in area but comparatively large in population (Singapore again, Hong Kong or Mauritius). Many small states are islands, some remote and some not so remote. Some are landlocked, and they can be parts of tightly linked economic communities (like Luxembourg, Monaco, or Vatican City) or virtually as isolated as remote islands (Lesotho and Swaziland when apartheid prevailed in surrounding South Africa).

It is not surprising that a special branch of public administration scholarship has developed to study the characteristics and needs of these states and quasi-states, for they are numerous and often face major problems of limited resources and inadequate government machinery. For a while, through the 1950s and '60s as the former imperial powers were seeking ways of disposing of what were often referred to as "fragments of empire," the United Nations played with the notion of establishing a new category of "associate member" to accommodate them (Boyce 1977). But that idea fell through, and in the event many joined the UN as full members. Today almost 40 UN members (out of a total current membership of 189) have populations of under 1 million, with another dozen or so not much bigger; around 25 do not have more than 300,000 people (UN 1996). Moreover these statistics ignore the fact that a few small sovereign states (such as Kiribati, Nauru, Tonga and Tuvalu until 1999–2000) have found the cost of UN membership too high and so have not joined. Small-state membership of the Commonwealth of Nations is also high: some two-thirds of the heads of government attending the 1997 Commonwealth Heads of Government Meeting (CHOGM) in Edinburgh came from small independent states. And these counts, of course, ignore all the quasi-states. Some international bodies do, however, provide for them, the Commonwealth Parliamentary Association being a conspicuous example. It grants full membership to the legislatures of states within federations and of self-governing territories, and it was thus that Norfolk Island's legislators were able to establish some international connections and particularly to discover the important role of Jersey—a small and comparatively affluent quasi-state with its own overseas aid program—in facilitating meaningful collaboration between all the small states of the Commonwealth (Potter 1986). The institutions of the European Union are now also making special arrangements for the autonomous regions and dependencies of some member countries, such as Catalonia, the Åland Islands, the Azores, and Madeira.

II. AN IASIA INITIATIVE

The Small and Island States Working Group of the International Association of Schools and Institutes of Administration (IASIA) has been actively engaged in studying administrative problems and developments in such states for a decade and a half. In a chapter written partly in the ACT, it is appropriate to point out that the group was actually launched in Canberra, at the 1981 IASIA Annual Conference held at the Canberra College of Advanced Education (now University of Canberra): the original sponsors of the group were the Commonwealth Secretariat and the Australian International Development Assistance Bureau (now AusAID).

That first meeting of the group noted three major areas of concern for small and island states in ensuring effective administration:

1. Development of adequate, appropriate experience and a more versatile manpower base.
2. Establishment of regular communication between the centre of government and the outer islands and rural areas.
3. The need to explore ways of reconciling the differences between indigenous traditions and imported or imposed administrative systems (Hoyle 1981:183).

The meeting in West Berlin in 1983 identified eleven specific problems that had to be faced:

1. The small scale and limited scope for expansion of economic activities are serious difficulties.
2. There is a limited range of natural resources available.
3. Diseconomies of scale and the lack of a critical mass are characteristic of public administration and economic and social overhead capital. Such diseconomies of scale lead to a high per capita cost of both public administration and economic and social infrastructure.
4. There are inadequate levels and a narrow range of trained human resource skills.
5. Small and island states are particularly susceptible to natural disasters (mainly hurricanes, floods, and volcanic eruptions) that may devastate an entire country because of its small size.
6. Small and microstates that have to deal with a wide range of developmental activities often do not have the volume of work to justify the establishment of differentiated structures. Multipurpose ministries and departments, however, create problems for public administrators who have to deal with a wide variety of subject areas and a larger number of middle and lower level staff than can be effectively managed.
7. In small states the separation of functions between generalist administrators and specialist implementers greatly reduces the capacity of the total system to make an impact on the development process.
8. The public service in small states is usually the single largest employer of labour. Consequently, the system does not possess the capacity to pay competitive salaries and is therefore unable to attract or retain the best qualified staff. In some technical areas it may not be able to locate anyone with adequate training.
9. Inherited rational models of public administration are often inappropriate to the social milieu of the small states.
10. There is a continuous widening of the gap between public expectations and demands and the capacity of public administrative systems to meet these demands.
11. Small and island states suffer from an inadequate supply of appropriate educational and training institutions and programmes, as well as from a scarcity of relevant resource material for training (Barrett 1983).

This identification of areas of concern and problems has served fairly adequately to guide the group in its subsequent work. There were further group meetings in Bloomington, Indiana (1984), Tunis (1985), Amman (1986), Milan (1987), Brisbane (1988),[1] Marrakech (1989), Bath (1990), Kota

Kinabalu (1991), Vienna (1992), Toluca (1993), Hong Kong (1994), Dubai (1995), Durban (1996), and Quebec (1997). Then a special workshop was held in the Seychelles, also in 1997, in association with the Commonwealth Association for Public Administration and Management (CAPAM), and the group joined with the Islands and Small States Institute established by the University of Malta to host a conference on the Governance of Small Jurisdictions in late 1999 (mostly adapted from earlier report in Wettenhall 1992a; on the Seychelles meeting see Warrington 1997).[2]

Three general collections of papers presented at Group meetings have been published (Baker 1992; Warrington 1994; Warrington 1998). In its more recent work the Group has tended to focus on particular areas of concern for small states, one being the external relations environment and another machinery of government innovation.

In terms of "their place in the world," many of these small states have sought, sometimes controversially, to exploit special situational and historical factors. Thus Kiribati has seen some advantage in its isolation in negotiating with China, Japan, and the United States for the establishment of rocket-launching or satellite-tracking stations; the large-scale sale of fishing licenses has brought it more revenue. Ironically for a strongly Christian society, Tuvalu made itself somewhat notorious by leasing its telephone code to a foreign country to provide a communications network for the sex-by-phone industry. Far out in the Pacific, both these nations have focused their domestic higher education effort on maritime training colleges (*EWYB* 1997:1900–1901, 3298–3299). The Marshall Islands, site of early U.S. nuclear bomb testing, has captured large funds by way of compensation for the victims of that testing, and now offers itself as a repository for nuclear waste. Its Micronesian neighbor, Palau, has oppositely determined to be nuclear free, and this has been a dominant factor in its negotiations for a form of "free association" with the United States. Like small St. Vincent in the Carribean, the Marshall Islands has also exploited its maritime position to provide an international shipping registry and take business from Panama and Liberia, and it competes with other small states like Liechtenstein, Bermuda, the Isle of Man, and the Cayman Islands in providing offshore banking facilities with the tax advantages which often come with them. Where possible the Micronesian states have also exploited their proximity to U.S. military installations on Guam to attract business; as one Micronesian scholar has reported, the factor of "strategic locale" has operated to prevent the realization of hopes for the governmental unity of all Micronesia (Alkire 1977:97; and generally Wettenhall 1997).

The list of such situational adaptations goes on: Monaco has found a niche with its top-class casino; Liechstenstein has found more prosperity through a focus on boutique industries such as the production of dental prosthetics; oil-rich Brunei and Kuwait have become great international investors, and to a degree they have been joined by Nauru as it has tried to secure a future from the sound placement of royalties from its dwindling phosphate deposits (unfortunately the placements have sometimes been far from sound). Brunei, Monaco, and Tonga make much of their royal dynasties. In the Maltese case the strategic factor was for long the country's fortress position in the central Mediterranean; but Britain's retreat from the East and the declining importance of shipping produced a major crisis almost simultaneously with Malta's emergence as a modern independent state—failure to retain the naval dockyard required major economic adaptation. And Baker has shown how small Caribbean states like Dominica and St. Lucia, with almost total economic dependence on their ability to get good prices from exporting their banana crops, have sought to exploit their geographic situation across the drug routes from South America as a bargaining card to play against importing countries (Baker 1996).

III. MACHINERY OF GOVERNMENT INNOVATION

Most importantly for present purposes, this innovative capacity sometimes runs to structures and processes of government. At the beginning, many of these small states unreflectingly retained most of the governmental structures inherited from departing colonial regimes, which mostly reflected structures of the metropolitan power itself. Of course new domestic governments replaced colonial governors. But under them the old departmental apparatus carried on, and the legislatures, which had mostly passed through a long evolutionary process with effective authority moving gradually to elected representatives and apprentice ministers, also reflected metropolitan structures and behaviors. However, some perceptive practitioners and observers—such as New Zealander Sir Colin Allan, who joined the British Colonial Service and as governor saw the Solomons and the Seychelles through to independence; Sir Albert Henry, who was first Cook Islands premier after self-government (later discredited, but for other reasons); and Englishman Professor David Murray, who spent time at the University of the South Pacific in Fiji—argued that these inherited systems were entirely inappropriate for new states and sought to design more streamlined systems. This quest has produced considerable innovation, with sometimes impressive outcomes.

Murray advocated that, in the design or redesign of their administrative systems, small states ought to adopt a strategy of "scaling down the prescriptions and enlarging up the actual administrative situation." Thus, for example, the number of departments, agencies, or branches could be "scaled down" to a very small number, leading to the work of each being correspondingly "enlarged up," so that there is both an aggregated administrative superstructure and a relatively undifferentiated allocation of responsibilities (Murray 1977:572). Such an arrangement has considerable integrative potential at all levels of organizational authority and can be bolstered by the effective use of flexible, organic structures of one form or another.

Allan variously headed administrations in the New Hebrides (now Vanuatu), the Seychelles, and the Solomons. Early in his career he noted the unhappy consequences of fragmented administration in the New Hebrides condominium, and he developed the firm view that small states should not seek to replicate the bureaucratic apparatus of the larger metropolitan countries with which they had been associated. In the Seychelles, as it moved to independence, he found allies among local politicians who had already experimented adventurously with the committee system in lieu of a ministerial system at the central government level. The agreed agenda was to decide what functions the new state should fulfil at home and abroad, then to get cost-benefit (or organization and methods) experts to show what administrative apparatus was needed to serve those ends—so avoiding the fate of other small states which were "threatened with engulfment by their own bureaucracies." Accordingly, after a thorough investigation by an English consultant, all the bits and pieces of the old administration were consolidated in the mid-1970s in a structure of seven or eight coordinated ministries (Allan 1982; Wettenhall 1986:215–217).

In the Cook Islands, a small Pacific state in free association with New Zealand, Premier Albert Henry reasoned fairly similarly. Formerly a Cook Islands public servant, he began questioning why he and his ministers found it so hard to implement government policies, and soon concluded that thoroughgoing structural reform was necessary. Around a score of departments inherited from the former New Zealand administration—and more or less matching New Zealand's own arrangements—were consolidated in 1973 into seven ministries on a one-minister/one-ministry basis that was then fairly novel in decolonizing regimes, and strenuous efforts were made to ensure "finger tip" policy control by ministers and effective management under them by competent permanent secretaries. That this bold reform did not "hold" simply indicates that there were very deep behavioral patterns in the island society which militated against acceptance of such a streamlined system of government (Henry 1971; Wettenhall 1986:205–210).

The Seychelles experiment with executive committees in lieu of ministers points to another significant reform possibility. This way of arranging for political direction of administrative departments is familiar enough in local government systems in larger states, but it is not generally known at central government level. Perhaps it lends itself better to small-scale operation, although we are not aware that this proposition has been tested. What is clear is that the arrangement does not sit easily with tightly disciplined political parties competing for the spoils of government and that, whatever their disadvantages, small states often seem better able to escape the stranglehold these parties so often have on governmental processes. There have been several such experiments in smaller states. Today Jersey stands as the great exemplar: the advantage claimed is that government by multimember executive committees promotes consensual rather than conflictual parliamentary behavior and spreads responsibility widely among members. So government becomes shared (or collegial), and, in the words of former Jersey Senator Ralph Vibert, *all* the talents of a legislature are applied positively to governing, in lieu of the more familiar pattern in which virtually one-half are committed to opposition and thus to pulling down the contributions of the other half (Vibert 1981, 1990, 1994; also Grey 1980; Wettenhall 1983:25–30; Le Hérrissier 1996).

One other area of difference, actual or potential, may be mentioned. In many small states, there is sensibly also little or no division between "state-type" and "municipal-type" structures. Such a distinction arises almost inevitably in larger states, where issues of decentralisation and devolution have high importance. But the condition of small states is different, and here also they should not slavishly follow large state models. It is here that the German city-states assume great relevance: while their populations are not tiny, they show how it is possible to fuse the two levels of government effectively. This is already done in many of today's small states, including the Australian Capital Territory (see Grundy et al 1996; Wettenhall 1998; Halligan and Wettenhall 2000).

IV. THREE MICROSTATES CONSIDERED

For illustrative purposes, we looked at three of the world's tiniest states: Nauru, Niue, and Norfolk Island.[3] All three are situated in the South-Central Pacific and are appropriately classified as "microstates" in terms of geographic area, population, and economy. Each has a land mass of less than 300 square kilometers, a population of less than 10,000, and a gross national product of less than US$90m. They are each among the world's 12 smallest countries on the basis of either two or all three of these factors.

We were especially interested in the ways in which the administrative structures in these states have been integrated into the wider constitutional and political arrangements. Earlier research into such arrangements in other states—including Australia's small island state, Tasmania—had identified numerous examples of rather odd linkages and relationships which suggested that, as independent or self-governing states emerged from colonial rule, little or no thought was given to the possible redesign and restructuring of administrative systems to meet the demands of responsible government (Wettenhall 1986a,b). This led us to consider why this might have been so, and to advance four broad propositions. The first is that the processes of change have been so dominated by moves to alter the balance of political power and authority within a system that the appropriateness of administrative arrangements has simply been overlooked or ignored. The second, in contrast to the first, is that the lack of administrative change has actually been the result of a firm belief that the structures already in place were quite adequate to the tasks at hand and that it was sufficient just to subject them to effective political leadership. The third builds on the second by arguing that established structures have been retained not only because of their assumed adequacy but more importantly because of the equilibrium effect of providing an unbroken link between the past and the future. The fourth, like the first, is concerned directly with questions of power and authority, but this time the focus is on the extent to which key officials have been successful in keeping administrative change off the political agenda and thereby in ensuring the survival of existing structures largely intact.

We were conscious that one or more of these propositions could well serve to explain many of the mismatches found in various systems. But, at the same time, we recognized the need to account for those changes in other systems that were clearly, or presumably, the product of some conscious and quite innovatory thinking. In this regard, we were generally convinced that, in some contexts, one of the explanations has to do with the small scale of the systems and societies involved: that the condition of smallness has sensibly prompted institutional designers and reformers to look beyond the experiences of larger states and to propose arrangements appropriately attuned to local circumstances and needs. This has certainly been the case in Nauru, Niue, and Norfolk Island.

Nauru gained independence in 1968, having immediately before then been administered by Australia as a trust territory under the United Nations; Niue became internally self-governing in free association with New Zealand in 1974 after more than 50 years of direct rule by New Zealand; and Norfolk Island became a self-governing territory in 1979 almost a century after having become the home of descendants of the *Bounty* mutineers and their Tahitian associates and more recently having been constituted as a territory under the Australian Commonwealth. All three states adhere to the Westminster model of government in one way or another and thus have political executives which are part of the legislature rather than outside of it, as in the U.S. congressional-presidential model.

Each of these states has responded in interesting and, in some cases, contrasting ways to the recognized need to streamline its administrative system and subject it to effective political leadership and control. In all three cases, the structural arrangements have sought to facilitate a high degree of administrative and political integration that is not usually found, or so clearly prescribed, in larger governmental systems. The degree of coordination attempted is even tighter than that attempted in the ministry systems of Seychelles and the Cook Islands, both of which are (though small) considerably larger than Nauru, Niue, and Norfolk Island.

A. Nauru

In Nauru, integration has been provided for in or through the office of president, the collectivity of cabinet, the roles of the chief secretary, and the relationship between ministers and their ministries. The president is both the chief executive and head of state but, unlike the U.S. President, he must be and remain a member of parliament, is elected by parliament, and is not directly vested with executive authority. As part of the established system of checks and balances, the executive authority is formally vested in the cabinet which is headed by the president and comprises four or five other members—ministers—who are appointed by the president from parliament and who are each individually responsible for a single ministry. The cabinet is "collectively responsible to parliament" for the "general direction and control of the government." The collective responsibility is complemented by the chief secretary who is both the chief adviser to the government and the commissioner of the public service and who, as such, provides a unified form of subministerial control. Thus, at one and the same time, the head of state, the parliament, the executive and its administrative arm(s) become cemented together sufficiently to achieve a considerable degree of coordination both laterally and vertically, but not so firmly as to remove all limits to the exercise of power within the system (*EWYB* 1993:2041; for background to Nauru, see Weeramantry 1992).

B. Niue

The need for some form of subministerial leadership and control has also been recognized, indeed to an even greater extent, in Niue. There, the premier and his three ministerial colleagues are each responsible for two or more departments, so the integrating effect of the Nauru-type one-to-one relationship between ministers and their ministries is not provided for. But, in practice, this is not that significant, for the total number of departmental employees has never been more than 600 and therefore the number of departments under each minister has had few implications for the efficacy of ministerial control and accountability. Also, more importantly, there is a secretary to the government who, operating under the direct control of cabinet, is administratively responsible for the activities of all departments. In this capacity, and given that he has a unique right under the Constitution to attend and speak but not vote at all meetings of cabinet, he is clearly the managerial centerpiece of the governmental system. The effective facilitation of a close and workable partnership between politicians and officials rests very much in his hands (Chapman 1976:76–77; also Thynne 1981).

C.   Norfolk Island

On Norfolk Island, the integrative arrangements have involved the bringing together of the legislative assembly, executive, and administration in a way that is clearly uncommon in Westminster-based systems. Most notably, the offices of the chief minister and the president of the assembly have often been occupied by the same person who in turn could be (as in mid-1990) supported in the executive not only by the deputy president and four ministers drawn from the assembly, but also by all other members of the assembly serving as assistant ministers. In addition, the public service, which comprises less than 200 staff, is organized into "branches" rather than departments or ministries and is subject to the direct managerial control of a chief administrative officer, not unlike the situation in both Niue and Nauru (for background see Grundy and Wettenhall 1977; Wettenhall and Grundy 1992).

V.   SUGGESTIONS FOR FURTHER RESEARCH

It is beyond serious question that the more successful of the small states have sought deliberately to design new systems appropriate to their own circumstances. We suggest here that it would be useful to undertake further comparative research on small state governance, and we think that this research should move out from what we have reported about the situation in three microstates to consider how political and administrative leadership functions in three interrelated arenas as influenced, at least in part, by the managerialist trends of recent years. The first arena comprises those arrangements which are internal to government and which serve to complement the integrating effect of a centralised system of subministerial control as manifest in the roles, for instance, of Niue's secretary to the government. The second arena encompasses the first but also includes the market and the community and, as such, could likewise have an important integrating effect within a state. The third arena extends beyond the state into the wider international sphere to the extent that governments have recognized, or simply have been forced to concede, the need increasingly to respond to external pressures and demands in the administration of public affairs.

The analysis of the first arena concerning internal arrangements could usefully build on the ideas expressed by Murray, Allan, and Henry. The integrative potential of the innovations addressed by them could be further realized, and no doubt is in many cases, through the use of a set of matrix-type structures that are designed to overlay departments at various levels within the hierarchy of authority and to be readily adaptable to changing circumstances and needs (see Flynn 1993:ch. 8; Thynne 1994:207–208). The efficacy of such structures is very dependent on the competence, personal commitment, and dispositions of all concerned, as well as on the chairing, agenda setting, resourcing, and other procedural arrangements that are made. All of these factors could well have particular significance in small-scale administrative systems and, accordingly, where structures of this kind exist, it will be important to investigate any special, smallness-related aspects of their forms and modes of operation.

The second arena worth exploring has to do with the notion of subsidiarity, which envisages the movement of state activity "outwards" to the market and "downwards" to the community. Certainly, in large(r) states, the last 10 to 15 years have witnessed a host of market-oriented developments involving various forms of privatization, as well as initiatives resulting in more and more authority being devolved to community associations, trusts, and the like. In all cases, there has been a reshaping and realignment of state activity and power, such that the state-market and state-community nexi and divides have been altered, often quite significantly (Thynne 1998a; Wettenhall and Thynne 1999). But, in small states, we would assume that, where similar developments have occurred, the structural and functional boundaries among the state, market, and community have remained as fluid and fuzzy as ever in keeping with the highly personalized nature of the societies. Accordingly, we would expect to find that, for the leaders of these states, the processes of change and of accommodation to emerging realities have raised issues and posed problems of a different order from those raised and encountered in large(r) states. We hope that, in addressing these and related matters, the nature and significance of small-state experiences can be discerned and appreciated.

An increasingly important element of that experience involves administrative decentralization which, as an issue of governance, gains wide attention today in larger states, as demonstrated (for example) by the central theme of a recent conference of the Eastern Regional Organization for Public Administration in Tokyo (Kurosawa et al. 1996). Our three microstates are, as single, compact islands, marked by a lack of provincial-type concerns. But in still small archipelagic or scattered-island states the position may be different: thus, in the Cook Islands, a Ministry of Outer Islands was established in 1995 in an effort to overcome the perceived problem of "nonequity of benefits" as between Rarotonga, the central island, and the others (Puna 1996:6).

Another important issue of special relevance to the second (and also the third) arena concerns the nature and implications of political and administrative relationships with institutions of civil society. There is a growing literature on the idea of "social capital" and the extent, for example, to which it is, or ought to be, an expected outcome of public-private cooperative activity in the context of community affairs (see e.g., Putnam 1993; Evans 1997a). Questions are raised about whether such "capital" can be "constructed" or is largely an "endowment" which needs naturally to be buit up over a long period of time (Evans 1997a,b). These and related questions are quite closely aligned to Hau'ofa's reflections on a "sea of islands" and the idea of "a New Oceania" (Hau'ofa 1993; see Thynne 1996). They deserve serious attention and could yield some significant findings on the processes and consequences of various forms of governance in small (as well as larger) states.

The third arena, which is clearly the most complex and uncertain of the three, is that which extends well beyond the geographical boundaries of the state into the wider international sphere of political, social and economic activity. This is the world of global communications, markets and manoeuvring, in respect of which it would be important to identify the network of structures and relationships that seek to enable the leaders of small states to maintain some kind of balance between the competing demands and pressures of international integration and state autonomy.

With reference to the future of another geographically small state (small in area if not in population) whose status has recently undergone dramatic change, namely Hong Kong, it has been argued that integration and autonomy each need to be seen as comprising both positive and negative possibilities in terms of their institutional manifestations and likely consequences for state activity. The two broad sets of possibilities are captured and contrasted in Figure 1(Thynne 1998b).

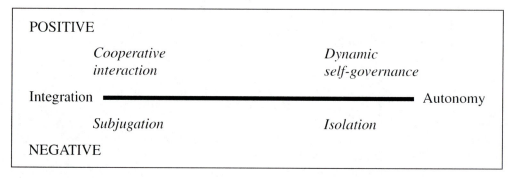

Figure 1   Integration and autonomy in perspective.

We suggest that valuable comparative analysis of governance structures in small states could be pursued in relation to all the arenas which we have identified. The various elements of these arenas are interrelated but can be isolated and adapted for separate and detailed treatment. For example, while the integration/autonomy schema was obviously developed for the special case of Hong Kong, we believe that it can be usefully applied in the analysis of other small state experiences. It highlights broad possibilities and, in so doing, it indicates the challenges facing the political and administrative leadership, particularly in those small states which are in some kind of prolonged transition.

ENDNOTES

1. In this Australian bicentennial year a number of the participants also took part in the *Islands '88* conference held at the University of Tasmania in Australia's small island state (for the proceedings, see Chapman et al. 1988).
2. A selection of papers from the Malta meeting will appear as a symposium in an early issue of the new *Public Organization: An International Journal.*
3. For our fuller expolration see Wettenhall and Thynne (1994). What follows is a digest of what we discovered in preparing the earlier paper. We have not tried to update this material. Thus, although we know that the title of the Norfolk Island Legislative Assembly President was changed to Speaker in 1995, we do not know how that has affected the arrangements here described.

REFERENCES

AGS (American Geographical Society). (1969). *Five Little Countries of Europe.* Volume in Around the World Program, Nelson Doubleday, New York.

Aldrich, R., and Connell, J. (1992). *France's Overseas Frontier: Départements et Territoires d'Outre-Mer.* Cambridge University Press, Cambridge. (Reviewed in Wettenhall 1993.)

Alkire, W.H. (1977). *An Introduction to the Peoples and Cultures of Micronesia,* 2nd ed., Cummings Publishing Co., Menlo Park, CA.

Allan, C.H. (1982). *Constitution Making in New Island States.* Legal Research Foundation Inc., Auckland.

Baker, R. (ed.). (1992). *Public Administration in Small and Island States.* Kumarian Press, West Hartford, CT.

Baker, R. (1996). The Effect of a Micro-State's External Relations on Domestic Policies and Institutions: A

Concept Paper. Paper for Small and Islands States Working Group, International Association of Schools and Institutes of Administration (IASIA) Annual Conference, Durban, July (revised as "Small, Isolated States in a Rapidly Reconfiguring World: Challenge, Threat or Incentive?" in Warrington 1998).

Barrett, I.R. (1983). Working group V: administration of small and island states. In W.G. Schaeffer (ed.), *IASIA Working Group Reports 1983.* IASIA and Canberra College of Advanced Education (now University of Canberra), Canberra.

Boyce, P. (1977). Microstate diplomacy. In *Forieign Affairs of New States: Some Questions of Credentials.* University of Queensland Press, St Lucia.

Chapman, R.J.K., Herr, R.A., Murfett, P., & Clark, C. (1988). *Islands '88—Proceedings.* University of Tasmania, Hobart.

Chapman, T.M. (1976). *The Decolonisation of Niue.* Victoria University Press and New Zealand Institute of International Affairs, Wellington.

Evans, P. (ed.) (1997a). *State-Society Synergy: Government and Social Capital in Development.* University of California at Berkeley (International and Area Studies), Berkeley.

Evans, P. (1997b). Introduction: development studies across the public-private divide. In Evans 1997a.

Evans, P. (1997c). Government action, social capital, and development: reviewing the evidence of synergy. In Evans 1997a.

EWYB (*Europa World Year Book*). (1993). Vol. II, Europa Publications, London.

EWYB. (1997). Vol. II, Europa Publications, London.

Flynn, N. (1993). *Public Sector Management*, 2nd ed. Harvester Wheatsheaf, Hemel Hempstead.

Grey, I. (1980). Editorial note. *Parliamentarian*, *61*(3).

Grundy, P. and Wettenhall, R. (1977). Norfolk Island versus the Nimmo Report. *Current Affairs Bulletin*, *54*(5).

Grundy, P., Oakes, B., Reeder, L. and Wettenhall, R. (1996). *Reluctant Democrats: The Transition to Self-Government in the Australian Capital Territory.* Federal Capital Press, Canberra.

Halligan, J. and Wettenhall, R. (eds.) (2000). *A Decade of Self-Government in the Australian Capital Territory.* Centre for Research in Public Sector Management, University at Canberra, Canberra.

Hau'ofa, E. (1993). Our sea of islands. In E. Waddell, V. Naidu, and E. Hau'ofa (eds.), *A New Oceania: Rediscovering Our Sea of Islands.* University of the South Pacific in association with Bleak House, Suva.

Henry, A.R. (1971). The government of the Cook Islands today. Part II of *Rambling Thoughts of the Premier*, Rarotonga.

Hoyle, A.R. (1981). Working group 8: administrative problems of small and island states. In E.N. Scott (ed.), *International Perspectives in Public Administration: Proceedings of the IASIA Round Table, Canberra, July 1981.* Canberra College of Advanced Education in association with IASIA, Canberra.

Kurosawa, S., Fujiwara, T., and Reforma, M.A. (eds.). (1996). *New Trends in Public Administration for the Asia-Pacific Region: Decentralization.* Local Autonomy College, Ministry of Home Affairs, Tokyo.

Le Hérrissier, R. (1996). A small state at the crossroads: the development of a policy-making capacity on the island of Jersey. Paper for Small and Island States Working Group, IASIA Annual Conference, Durban.

Murray, D.J. (1977). A problem in the administrative development of small island states. In S.K. Sharma (ed.), *Dynamics of Development: An International Perspective*, vol. 1. Concept Publishing Co., Delhi.

Pirotta, G. (1996). *The Maltese Public Service 1800–1940: The Administrative Politics of a Microstate.* Mireva Publications, Msida, Malta.

Potter, E. (1986). Jersey: host to the small countries. *The Parliamentarian*, *67*(3).

Puna, P. (1996). *Cook Islands Country Paper.* Commonwealth Association of Public Administration and Management Conference, Malta, April.

Putnam, R. (1993). *Making Democracy Work: Civic Traditions in Modern Italy.* Princeton University Press, Princeton, NJ.

Raadschelders, J.B. (1992). Definitions of smallness: a comparative study. In Baker 1992.

Schumacher, E.F. (1973). *Small Is Beautiful: Economics as if People Mattered.* Harper and Row, New York.

Thynne, I. (1981). The ministerial system in Niue. *Public Administration and Development*, *1*(1).

Thynne, I. (1994). The need to take stock: a question of values, work and organisational design. In I. Scott and I. Thynne (eds.), *Public Sector Reform: Critical Issues and Perspectives.* AJPA, Hong Kong.

Thynne, I. (1996). Public administration in troubled waters: organisations, management and "a new Oceania." *Australian Journal of Public Administration, 55*(2).

Thynne, I. (1998a). Integrative governance: challenges for the senior public service. *International Review of Administrative Sciences, 64*(3).

Thynne, I. (1998b). 'One country' or 'two systems'?: integration and autonomy in perspective. In I. Scott (ed.), *Institutional Change and the Political Transition in Hong Kong.* Macmillan, London.

Thynne, I. and Wettenhall, R. (1996). Innovation in leadership structures in small and island states. Paper for Fifth Pacific Islands Political Studies Association Conference, Airai, Republic of Palau, December.

UN. (1996). *Statistical Yearbook: Forty-First Issue.* United Nations, New York.

Vibert, R. (1981). Parliament without parties: the states of the island of Jersey. *Parliamentarian, 62*(1).

Vibert, R. (1990). *Parliament Without Parties: The Committee System in the States of the Island of Jersey.* States of Jersey, St Helier.

Vibert, R. (1994). Using *all* the talents of a legislature in governing. *Australian Journal of Public Administration, 53*(1).

Warrington, E. (ed.). (1994). Symposium on the governance of small and island states. *Asian Journal of Public Administration, 16*(1).

Warrington, E. (1997). Professional developments: the Seychelles CAPAM/IASIA small and island states conference. *Public Administration and Development, 17*(3).

Warrington, E. (1998). The impact of external relations on the domestic policies and governing institutions of micro-states (Symposium). *Public Administration and Development, 18*(2).

Weeramantry, C. (1992). *Nauru: Environmental Damage Under International Trusteeship.* Oxford University Press, Melbourne. (Reviewed in Wettenhall 1992b.)

Wettenhall, R. (1983). Governmental structures: models and options. In A. Hodgkinson (ed.), *Towards Territorial Government.* Canberra College of Advanced Education in association with Australian Institute of Urban Studies (ACT Div.), Canberra.

Wettenhall, R. (1986a). Questions about departments, with special reference to the Australian states. In *Organising Government: The Uses of Ministries and Departments.* Croom Helm, Sydney.

Wettenhall, R. (1986b). Modes of ministerialisation. In *Organising Government* (as above).

Wettenhall, R. (1992a). Small states: some machinery of government considerations. In Baker 1992.

Wettenhall, R. (1992b). Review of Weeramantry 1992. *Australian Journal of Public Administration, 51*(4).

Wettenhall, R. (1993). Review of Aldrich and Connell 1992. *Australian Journal of Public Administration, 52*(1).

Wettenhall, R. (1997). Notes on the microstates of Micronesia. Paper for Small and Island States Working Group, IASIA Annual Conference, Quebec, July.

Wettenhall, R. (1998). The external relations of a small quasi-state within a federal system: the case of the Australian Capital Territory. In Warrington 1998.

Wettenhall, R. and Grundy, P. (1992). *Norfolk Island and the Electorate of Canberra: "Community of Interest?" Report to the Norfolk Island Government*, Canberra.

Wettenhall, R. and Thynne, I. (1994). Machinery of government innovation in micro-states: the cases of Nauru, Niue and Norfolk Island. In Warrington 1994.

Wettenhall, R. and Thynne, I. (1999). Emerging patterns of governance: synergy, partnerships and the public-private mix." *Asian Journal of Public Administration 21*(2)

44
Administrative Reform

Gerald E. Caiden   *School of Policy, Planning and Development, The University of Southern California, Los Angeles, California*

I. INTRODUCTION

Over the past two decades, the United Nations Programme in Public Administration and Finance has given administrative reform top priority (United Nations, 1983). Indeed, since its interregional seminar in 1971 in Brighton, there has hardly been a year in which somewhere in the world there has not been an international meeting of administrative reform experts to exchange information and review experiences (Caiden and Siedentopf 1982). Such meetings have emphasized again and again that countries that already possess high administrative capacity are capable of implementing elaborate reforms but those deficient in administrative capability still cannot (Adedeji 1975; CARICAD 1981; Chaturvedi 1985; Hammergren 1983; Kliksberg 1983; Mathur 1986; Rowat 1980).

The latest rush to overhaul administrative systems and to rejuvenate public organizations around the globe has been prompted largely by a worldwide decline in public finances and the need to get more for less. Governments have had to cut back, to reduce expenditures, staff, investments, and services, and to demand higher productivity and better performance from their sluggish public sectors. In trying to position their countries better in the emerging world economy, governments have been forced to redefine their role and reconceptualize strategies. In this, almost all have faulted the dead hand of bureaucracy—more particularly, the poor performance of public bureaucracies and the daily annoyances of irksome restrictions, cumbrous redtape, unpleasant officials, poor service, and corrupt practices. Government itself had become too big, had taken too much upon itself as insurer and guarantor of economy and society, manager of natural and human resources, and sponsor of intellectual and cultural talent, all well-intentioned activities but beyond its administrative, political, and technical capacity to realize.

This questioning of Big Government has lifted administrative reform well beyond traditional managerial concerns to a critical review of the role and functions of the administrative state. Similar questioning has been undertaken in the post-Mao China (where Mao's "Twenty Manifestations of Bureaucracy" had long raised serious doubts about excessive statism there) (Cabestan 1986; Falkenheim 1980; Lee 1982), in the post-Stalin Soviet Union culminating in the current reconstruction (*perestroika*) of the Soviet economy, in Prime Minister Thatcher's revamping of the British administrative state (Greenaway 1984), and in Brazil's debureaucratization program (Belmiro et al. 1986; Joao 1984). The primary concern has been the remapping of the state itself, the redefinition of its boundaries, before turning to the administrative, bureaucratic, managerial, and professional features that might need redesigning. The dead hand of bureaucracy has to be replaced by a new, invigorating concept of public management and clear proof that public organizations are value for money. What follows is a survey of major thrusts of this new administrative reform agenda as devised by the most frequently cited reform proposals (see Table 1).

II. PRIVATIZATION AND COPRODUCTION

Failures of capitalism before World War II induced governments thereafter to manage their economies and run major industries. For a time, collectivization and nationalization appeared to succeed or meet public objectives better than superseded private organizations. But in time their performance fell below expectations, productivity declined, and often public enterprise was not any improvement on private enterprise. The social costs of forced collectivization proved prohibitive. Public enterprises exploited their monopoly position. Detailed public management of the economy failed to safe guard public investments or provide sufficient incentives to raise performance. The less dogmatic Marxist states acknowledged the fact and allowed a greater degree of liberalization, until television revealed to all that the collectivized economies were still being outperformed by some liberal economies. Without the abandonment of cumbersome, inflexible, and coercive economic direction, the gap would widen. It was left to more pragmatic leaders in China and the Soviet Union to justify in ideological terms economic reforms and the attendant administrative reforms that would promote private initiatives, self-regulation, and consumer choice.

The term "privatization" took on a more precise meaning when British Prime Minister Thatcher assumed office in 1979 on a populist platform centered on "rolling back the state." The financially strapped government decided to denationalize several state industries where ready private purchasers could be found. This gave it a beneficial injection of sorely needed finance and relieved it of the burden of managing marketable public goods and services. Its success enticed other governments around the world similarly to divest themselves of public enterprises, particularly in telecommunications, airlines, public housing, hotels, and bus service. As a result, governments everywhere began reexamining what businesses they could divest and devising various ways of transferring public enterprises into private hands under public supervision.

Privatization shifts government-owned industries into the private sector, automatically reducing the size of government, state controls, and the public budget. It relieves governments of detailed management and possibly contentious subsidies. It enables the new owners to offer their wares at market rates, to streamline operations, and to rid themselves of publicly protected featherbedding. Their example of economic efficiency, client satisfaction, and investment returns pressurizes the whole public sector to reconceptualize operations. Privatization has appeared to reverse the prospects of several unprofitable government ventures, to improve performance, and to reduce industrial disputes. On the other hand, it has involved the sale of undervalued public assets to private parties that have not proved capable of operating them at previous performance levels, and it has not relieved governments of determining what criteria other than economic efficiency should be applied to economic enterprise. In poor countries, privatization has been more of a mixed blessing, with several scandals associated with the sale of public enterprises and their failure under private management.

As a middle ground between direct delivery and privatization, governments have preferred to contract with other public bodies or private parties. Governments have increasingly resorted to contracting with other public bodies or devising joint delivery arrangements or transferring operations to special public authorities. Such intergovernmental arrangements have largely been responsible for the multiplication of government organizations. General-purpose governments have contracted specific services to another government organization that can concentrate on delivering them more efficiently on a user cost basis, more as a private business yet still publicly

Table 1   Most Frequently Cited Administrative Reform Proposals

Australia	Royal Commission on Australian Government Administration (Coombs), 1976 Administrative Decisions Judicial Review Act, 1977 Review of New South Wales Government Administration (Wilenski), 1982
Brazil	Under Secretariat for Modernization and Administrative Reform, 1964 National debureaucratization Program, 1979
Canada	Royal Commission on Government Organization (Glassco), 1962 Operational Performance Measurement Systems (OPMS), 1975 Royal Commission on Financial Management and Accountability (Lambert), 1979 Committee on Personnel Management (D'Avignon), 1979
China	Third Plenum of C.C.P. Central Committee, 1979 Zhao's administrative reform program, 1982
France	Ministry of Civil Service and Administration Reform
Japan	Provisional Commission on Administrative Reform (RINCHO), 1983
Netherlands	Committee on the General Structure of Government Services, 1979
Soviet Union	Gorbachev's reconstruction (*perestroika*) policy, 1986
United Kingdom	Committee on the Civil Service (Fulton), 1968 Committee on Personnel Social Services (Seebohm), 1968 Central Policy Review Staff, 1970 Local Government Act, 1972 Privatization program, 1979 Management Information for Ministers (MINIS) Management and Personnel Office, 1981
United States	Congressional Budget and Impoundment Control Act of 1974 Civil Service Reform Act of 1978 Cutback management programs, 1978 Paperwork Reduction Act of 1980 President's Council on Integrity and Efficiency (PCIE), 1981 President's Private Sector Survey on Cost Controls (Grace), 1983 President's Council on Management Improvement (PCMI), 1984 Reform '88 program, 1984

accountable. Consequently, complex government has become even more complex, government even more fragmented, and the delivery of public goods and services even more dominated by professional managers.

Closer to privatization has been contracting out to private enterprise. While governments have always contracted for readily available "on the shelf" items, it is now more common practice to contract out for services and one-of-a-kind items unavailable in the marketplace for which the government is the sole purchaser (Gilbert 1983). Often governments have only the vaguest idea what they want; nobody knows whether it can be supplied at all or to detailed specifications. Such forms of contracting out create nonmarket delivery systems solely dependent on public funds with a strong contractor interest in sole source supply (monopoly), higher returns (waste), loose supervision (low accountability), and follow-on contracts (political lobbying). In the United States, some local governments contract out all key services—police, fire protection, social welfare, public works—while others make their own municipal agencies bid against private contractors. The federal government has even been encouraging public employees to form their own private companies to contract for newly privatized activities.

In all these experiments, the public have been passive onlookers. But as public resources have diminished, so governments have sought to cut costs by relying more on the voluntary participation of people in public organizations to takeover some of the work load and by encouraging people to do more things for themselves instead of looking to government to do things for them. Despite bureaucratic and professional opposition, governments have also attempted fitfully to devolve some activities to communal organizations and various public-private partnerships. Here, the public are encouraged to share in the delivery of public services though privately financed participation, hopefully reducing public alienation and making citizenship more meaningful (Levine 1984). Unfortunately, such coproduction works only on a small, local scale and relies heavily on private funding, local self-interest, and community organization. Its potential for generating private inputs into government is likely to lead to novel partnerships in the future.

III. DEBUREAUCRATIZATION

Privatization and coproduction are part of a larger effort to reduce government intervention and bureaucratic controls. Such streamlining and simplification of public bureaucracy—termed debureaucratization—also seeks to end the ways people have devised to evade government controls and cut through the bureaucratic maze. Eventually, debureaucratization should improve public trust and confidence in government, which has dropped sharply over the past decade, and should minimize the need to use intermediaries employed by people to deal with the public bureaucracy for them. Debureaucratization views government from the public's standpoint with the overarching objective to eliminate bureaucratic dysfunctions or bureaupathologies, not the bureaucracy itself, and to transform the mindless bureaucrats of the imperious state into caring public servants of the community.

Debureaucratization incorporates the whole gamut of administrative reform:

Improving public policy making and government decisions
Streamlining the machinery of government
Deconcentrating power and authority
Increasing public-sector productivity
Devising measures of performance and insisting on better performance
Tackling bureaupathologies, such as fraud, waste, and corruption
Adopting up-to-date information and administrative technology
Simplifying and rationalizing administrative processes
Reducing unnecessary red tape, featherbedding, and paperwork
Devising organizational innovations
Diversifying public service delivery systems
Providing and ensuring greater responsibility
Allocating scarce resources more rationally

Providing incentives for cost consciousness and public savings
Reducing public debts
Improving forecasting and simulation
Deregulating marketable services
Consolidating fragmented units
Emphasizing effective consultation and coordination
Enforcing financial management controls
Attracting and retaining better qualified public employees
Transferring and retraining surplus employees
Educating public managers to manage
Retuning public employee skills
Improving public-sector working conditions
Demanding higher professional standards and stricter discipline
Speeding up operations
Stressing public ethics and norms
Restoring public confidence in public institutions
Investigating and ameliorating public complaints
Allowing greater direct public participation in public administration
Educating public officials and public on how to behave with one another

All these elements are contained in the National Debureaucratization Program in Brazil, a model for other countries in Latin America, first launched in 1967 by Helio Beltrao, who explained its major purpose as being "to deliberately reduce excessive government interference in economic activities" (Carneiro 1986:6). Every area of federal government administration in Brazil has since been reviewed, several hundred legal documents have been revised, and millions of documents have been eliminated. Regulations have been modified or discontinued and new information technology has reduced red tape. Some activities have been decentralized to quicken decision making, and attempts have been made to humanize public administration. The task has been overwhelming and has failed to change the disposition of both officials and public to each other (Belmiro et al. 1986; Joao 1984). Public administration is still seen as management of the public with decisions imposed from above and afar while the public still believe their overcentralized government to be out of touch, too exploitive, and self-serving.

The main thrusts of the Brazilian program—deregulation, decentralization, modernization, personalization, and greater public accountability—have been repeated elsewhere around the globe. Deregulation has gone beyond the lifting of government restriction on business activity to the revision of all statutes and official instructions to reduce unnecessary restrictions on individual liberty and to eliminate needless bureaucracy that people have been forced to endure to obtain required documents. Improvements in face-to-face contact could not have been achieved without a willingness on the part of central authorities to delegate authority, inevitable as the multiplication of detailed paperwork threatened to paralyze government altogether (Bayley 1979; Graham 1980). The aim has been to relieve the center of detailed minutiae and to reduce the amount of routine matter being passed along instead of being decided locally. Local officials have been encouraged to decide more for themselves and to consult more locally in reaching their decisions.

Almost universally, the revised education and training of public officials have encouraged them to be more proactive, enterprising, creative, sensitive, responsive, human, and humane. New cadres are being taught to challenge tradition and devise improvements, to modernize and personalize public administration. They are increasingly identifiable individually; anonymity is considered passé. More attention is paid to civility in conducting public business and to the provision of proper facilities for people who have business to conduct. But the personalization of public bureaucracy has not touched the deeper malaise of bureaupathologies and institutionalized wrongdoing. In response to mounting public concern, traditional watchdog agencies (audit offices, inspectorates, ombudsmen) have been reinforced and some novel safeguard devices such as "hot lines" installed.

IV. REORGANIZATION

Reorganization of the machinery of government used to be considered the primary need in administrative reform. And governments did indeed reorganize only to be disillusioned when their expectations of economy, efficiency, productivity, effectiveness, and responsiveness did not materialize. Often the managerial prescriptions in regrouping administrative units, redistributing functions among them and other structural transformations, did not pay off at all and they were not worth the cost of the political upheavals involved or the time and effort (Boyle 1979; Kaufman 1977; Stanton 1981). In short, reorganization has been recognized as "a domain of rhetoric trading, problematic attention, and symbolic action" (March and Olsen 1983:291). Consequently, it has been administratively if not politically relegated as a strategy of administrative reform. Nonetheless, governments continue to reorganize and rearrange in the belief that bureaucratic performance will be improved thereby.

Where once the focus of reorganization was on consolidation of small units and the integration of similar activities, it is now recognized that the consolidation of units created massive impersonal organizations that lost touch with the publics they were supposed to serve and that the integration of similar activities is endless given the multiplicity, diversity, and complexity of contemporary government activities. Instead, there has tended to be a search for decentralizing activities that could and should be better performed at a more local level closer to their intended publics and for restructuring regional and local governments to allow greater direct public participation. Overcentralization has produced much needless bureaucracy and paperwork, with too much public business being funneled to the center where channels tend to get clogged, decisions delayed, and details just lost altogether.

Several countries have began serious review of relocating the central government away from a choked capital city or at least relocating major administrative units out of the capital city to less crowded towns, thereby deconcentrating public employees and geographically spreading public investments. But few schemes have been implemented, partly because of the costs but mainly because few senior officials have been willing to leave the capital. Similarly, schemes to devolve central government on special regional governments have not gone far, this time because the regions had insufficient access to public resources to support their activities and the central government did not want to create political rivals (Rowat 1980). Decentralization has not been just a reaction to over-centralization but a genuine attempt to facilitate effective popular participation in national development and to improve local delivery of government services, particularly in rural areas of poor countries.

More concern has been expressed in decentralizing national administrations and the incorporation of local representative institutions than, as formerly, creating several layers of autonomous regional and local governments, although multilayered governmental systems have been established where they did not previously exist. Nonetheless, "the majority of decentralization programs are seen as attempts to *decentralize the national government*, rather than to establish a second tier of government" (Conyers 1983:105), although the actual degree of decentralization has been quite limited and has rarely contributed to rural development, and local popular participation has been low (Saxena 1980).

Many countries, rich and poor, are still experimenting with local government reorganizations and their fit into decentralized national government organization, the redistribution of governmental activities among the different tiers, the size and number of local government authorities, and various forms of community organization and public participation. They echoed the sentiments of French president Mitterrand to give the state back to the people with a "new citizenship" for the individual, a new division of economic power, and new influences for submerged ethnic and cultural minorities.

In reality the reforms have been much less radical, although they have increased the influence of local government in national policymaking. It has proved difficult for centralized governments to relinquish any power, and supposedly autonomous tiers have been highly dependent on central governments to subsidize them. Reorganization for decentralization has been largely cosmetic. Local government has been reorganized, not reformed, with central government authority usually prevailing over local proposals, with emphasis on rationality, economy and efficiency, and improved service delivery, rather than increased public participation and identification, and local autonomy with relatively minor activities being reallocated (Rondinelli et al. 1983).

V. MORE EFFECTIVE PUBLIC MANAGEMENT

Rather than dramatic reorganizations, governments have been trying to achieve the same results by shaking up the top management of public organizations, the senior officials who set the style and tone of conducting public business, and who almost universally have been much criticized for being unduly privileged, unworldly, arrogant, unenterprising, and "badly trained, lacking in expertise and devoid of the managerial skills necessary in an era of complex interventionist government" (Greenway 1984:67). Required is a new philosophy that emphasizes mission over control, a new emphasis on managerial qualities and skills, a new freedom for public managers to manage, a new leadership "more concerned with broad management policy and experimentation with innovative management approaches, linked to evaluation and reporting of agency managerial performance than detailed operational controls" and with "greater emphasis on pressing for innovation, research, the redesign of outdated systems, and the attainment of managerial excellence" (National Academy of Public Administration 1983:viii).

The model for this new style of effective public management has been the Senior Executive Service (SES) established by the U.S. federal government following the passage of the Civil service Reform Act of 1978 (Bowman 1982; Dillman 1986; Godwin 1981; Ingraham and Ban 1984). The SES was to be

> a general civilian officer corps, staffed by highly trained and broadly experienced men and women who could be shifted from assignment to assignment as the needs of government required. In return for higher pay, performance bonuses, and enhanced career opportunities, SES members were to forego many of the protections of the traditional civil service system and be held to higher standards of performance. The SES would, in brief, create the vigorous, competent, and spirited bureaucracy that democratic government requires (Twentieth Century Fund 1987:29).

Other countries have adopted similar principles, namely, opening up closed career systems, banding senior officials together to overcome departmentalization, remuneration based on annual performance ratings, bonuses (incentives) for superior performance, and possible demotion and removal. In practice, the hopes of civil service reformers have been thwarted because the initial base salaries were kept too low and turnover has been high as identifiable good performers have been seduced to leave public service. Mobility within has been low in the face of department opposition, while the executive training that was supposed to accompany appointment has rarely materialized. The performance appraisal and bonus systems have proved difficult to apply to technical specialists. But the real block has turned out to be accusations of politicization of senior positions as governments have relished their new freedom to pick and choose bureaucratic chiefs at will.

VI. VALUE FOR MONEY

The central theme behind most recent reform campaigns has been that government does not give enough value for money. Privatization will reintroduce market principles and economic efficiency. Debureaucratization will eliminate unnecessary, parasitic, and unproductive government activities. Reorganization will improve government performance and improve service delivery. More effective public management will increase productivity and reduce incompetence. But none of these deals adequately with overspending and waste, due primarily to the lack of incentives in public budgeting to save public money. Bureaucratic performance, so mythology would have it, has tended to be measured by outlays and staff size, not effectiveness and opportunity costs. There has to be something seriously wrong when governments that cannot cover expenses pile debt upon debt. Budget reforms, such as PPBS and zero-based budgeting ZBB), which had promised to stop the rot, had done no such thing. Nor had sunset legislation. Far from there being too much slack, the opposite was true: public organizations were strapped for funds to do better, and they continued to put in their claims.

The economic crisis of the 1970s forced governments to insist on cuts all around. Some way had to be found to control runaway government expenditures, rising inflation, and mounting debts. Cutback management became the order of the day—cut budgets or at least cut estimates and claims, cut staff or at least freeze establishments, cut services or at least postpone things that did not have to be done right away (Levine 1980). The opportunity was taken to do some things that had been politically unpopular or had been resisted by public employee unions, now much weakened by the economic situation. Programs were terminated and organizations reduced, sometimes cosmetically by transferring the activities to nongovernmental organizations, but largely with the least harmful effects by putting off long-term public works, reducing maintenance, inducing early retirements, diminishing reserves, lowering real conditions of employment, leaving vacancies unfilled, and generally enforcing austerity.

Governments sought to reduce, not eliminate, their debts and deficits. They added another step in the budget process, that of preparation, rather than reforming the budget process itself. Prepreparation set overall spending and borrowing limitations beforehand, later to be translated into broad budgetary ceilings and (reduced) program targets. This new step was a centralized top-down integrated rationing process, involving

> The use of tight fiscal norms and targets to constrain spending demands, strict enforcement of budget ceilings and the use of baselines to set cutback targets, the conversion of multiyear budgets from program plans into spending controls, and greater attention to the preparation phase of budgeting (Schick 1986:216).

This way the objectives of budget reforms—multiyear cycles, programic content, prioritizing requests, performance appraisal, and baseline auditing—were achieved in substance but not form, although the deeper intractable problems of public budgeting directed thinking toward more radical reforms in process.

The budget imperative of more for less did accelerate the adoption of other administration reforms. Wherever possible, government organizations were made individually more financially self-contained and reliant through self-financing by way of user fees and other charges more in line with the actual costs of delivery. In this way, government organizations became more aware of their expenses and the public more aware of the real costs of public services. Attempts were made to reduce entitlements and other universal legal rights to public services for people who did not need them or could afford to pay for them on a commercial basis, but proposals were dropped where such cuts were interpreted as a rolling back of the welfare state or a failure to maintain the level of private-sector employment. Another target for reform was overspending and seepage of public funds through fraud, waste, and corruption. Significant savings could be made if such loopholes were blocked. Similarly, public funds could be boosted if the government's collection of monies were improved, not just loans never collected but taxes that had been avoided and evaded. Finally, not only was prepreparation added to the budget process but preauditing was also boosted. Even before money was allocated, claims and requests were to be audited as to their public worth and value, not just legality and appropriateness. Altogether, government auditing was tightened, with previously exempt public organizations now included.

The "value for money" approach in administrative reform has been greatly assisted by the upsurge over the past decade of policy analysis and public productivity research (Dillman 1986; Miller 1984), dispelling doubts that much government performance could not be measured and evaluated. Their impact has been to switch attention from process to substance, from general government arrangements to specific improvements in individual public organizations (Brown 1979; Hawker 1981; Tierney 1981). At all levels of public education, for instance, it is recognized that better value can be obtained by raising education standards rather than by further bureaucratization of the administration of education. Social security insurance schemes are being transformed by new information technology, and the quality of care in public institutions is being improved. Technology and competition have prompted reforms in such public businesses as mail delivery, telecommunications, and airlines.

VII. LIMITATIONS OF REFORM

While these administrative reforms proceeded with reasonable success, the more ambitious comprehensive reforms faltered and proved a great disappointment in poor countries that had pinned such high hopes on them. While the National Debureaucratization Program (NDP) in Brazil dwindled in impact, its imitators in other Latin American countries could not match the NDP's initial successes. In Africa, administrative reform initiatives collapsed in one country after another, victim to political corruption, bureaucratic inertia, and social disharmony (Abudin 1986; Chikulo 1981; Williams 1987). In Asia, bureaucratic resistance defeated reform campaigns in the Indian subcontinent (Khan 1980a; Maheshwari 1981; Tummala 1979), while political corruption took its toll in the Philippines, Indonesia, South Korea, and Taiwan, political turmoil upset reform programs in the Indochinese peninsula and China, and in Thailand reforms hardly affected bureaucratic attitudes (De Guzman et al. 1982; Khan 1980b; Krannich 1980). As in the past, the administrative systems most in need of reform could not muster the political support, administrative capacity, and public participation to implement reforms, while those possibly least in need among the more wealthy countries in the world could (Al-Saigh 1986; Mayo-Smith and Rutter 1986).

The reform of public bureaucracy had in practice to "be implemented by and within that same bureaucracy" (Smith and Weller 1978:310–311). The public bureaucracy was consulted and involved throughout the reform process, as governments sought to tap inside ideas on how to make the system work better. Also, governments realized that provided they minimized any personal damage that might befall victims of reforms, public officials had the good sense to go with the times to meet the challenges presented. The fact that governments were able to function so well given general belt-tightening was testimony to bureaucratic resilience. While outside critics might use this as evidence of previous slack, more knowledgeable insiders realized that the public bureaucracy had responded despite an appreciable degree of demoralization that boded ill for the longer term. In the meantime, the public bureaucracy had been faced in a different and more desirable direction.

In this realistic reappraisal of public-sector performance, a number of myths were exposed. Government could not be run like a business, though it could be more businesslike. What it had to do was quite different from business, and how it went about doing what it did also had to be different. The public sector had a logic of its own. Furthermore, given its context and limitations, the public sector performed much better than often realized. Indeed, its productivity may have been rising at a higher rate than private-sector productivity, and it was often managerially more enterprising and creative. Outside criticism had been overdone and if persisted in might prove to be self-fulfilling prophecy. Panaceas for government ills could not be found in political abstractions or business practices or in purely managerial prescriptions or constant harassment of public officials. They could not be conjured up from foreign administrative cultures or from general manuals of management or even from neighboring public organizations.

Realistic reform required a pragmatic experimental approach, perhaps confined to one specific public activity or one set of public organizations or one class of public employees. While outside experts, public inquiries, new laws, new organizations, new people, and new coordinating mechanisms could make a difference, reform success depended on the everyday operations of government and the hundreds of thousands of permanent officials who daily handled public business to devise for themselves better ways of doing their jobs. By using the system in place, the reforms had guarantees of system supports, adequate resources, and opportune timing. But this strategy could only work where the existing system was already performing reasonably well and the people who directed it were politically sensitive, professionally sophisticated, and identified with the reforms. Unfortunately, in many countries, it was the system itself that was grievously faulty and no amount of tinkering around with it would overcome built-in deficiencies.

Recent experience confirms that a crusading spirit is still essential in administrative reform. A burning spirit of righteous indignation is crucial to overcome bureaucratic inertia, political indifference, and public apathy. And as many countries and reformers have found, idealism is all too easily crushed in the daily frustrations of reform programs. All the bureaucratic opposition has to do is wait until the initial reform momentum declines and personally ambitious reformers move to more promising opportunities. Public memory is short; scandals quickly fade away. Since most people do not know any different, the reformers and their reforms are often seen as meddlesome interferers, whose motives are suspect, trying to draw attention to themselves so they can take the system over and do exactly the same as those they criticize. Imperfections will remain even if their reforms are adopted (Feldman 1981). Reform can only control, not cure, the ills of public administration. It exposes maladministration and proposes alternatives that promise to reduce maladministration, but it cannot guarantee good administration nor can it prevent the reappearance of maladministration.

REFERENCES

Adedeji, A. Strategy and tactics for administrative reform in Africa. In *A Decade of Public Administration in Africa* (A. Adedeji, ed.). East African Literature Review, Nairobi, 1975, pp. 223–230.

Al-Saigh, N.M., ed. *Administrative Reform in the Arab World: Readings.* AOAS, Amman, 1986.

Bayley, L. *Local Government: Is It Manageable?* Pergamon Press, New York, 1979.

Belmiro, V., Castor, J., and Franca, C. Administracao public no Brasil: exausto e revigorameto do modelo. *Revista de Administracao Publica* 20(3):3–26 (1986).

Bowman, J., ed. Civil service reform. *Review of Public Personnel Administration 2*(2) (1982).

Boyle, J.M. Reorganization reconsidered: an empirical approach to the decentralization problem. *Public Administration Review 39*(5):458–465 (1979).

Brown, R.G. *Reorganizing the National Health Service: A Case Study in Administrative Change.* Blackwell/Robertson, Oxford, 1979.

Burns, J.P. Reforming China's bureaucracy, 1979–82. *Asian Survey 23*(6):692–722 (1983).

Cabestan, J.-P. Commentary on the article by You Chunmei on current administrative reform in China. *International Review of Administrative Sciences 52*(1):145–150 (1986).

Caiden, G.E., ed. Symposium on public policy and administrative reform. *Policy Studies Journal 4*(8) (1980–1981).

Caiden, G.E., and Siedentopf, H., eds. *Strategies for Administrative Reform.* Lexington Books, Lexington, MA., 1982.

Calilsta, D.S. *Bureaucratic and Governmental Reform.* TAI Press, New York, 1986.

CARICAD. *Final Report of the Round Table on Administrative Reform.* Caribbean Centre for Development Administration, Barbados, April, 1981.

Carneiro, J.P. *National Debureaucratization Program: Three Years of Debureaucratization.* National Debureaucratization Program, Brasilia, 1982.

Chang, K.Y. Whither mainland China: reforms and problems. *Issues and Studies 20*(7):13–20 (1984).

Chapman, R.A. The rise and fall of the CDS. *Policy and Politics 11*(1):41–61 (1983).

Chapman, R.A., and Greenaway, J.R. *Dynamics of Administrative Reform.* Croom Helm, London, 1980.

Chaturvedi, T.N., ed. Administrative reform—revisited. *Indian Journal of Public Administration 31*(3) (1985).

Cheema, G., and Rondinelli, D.A. *Decentralization and Development: Policy Implementation in Developing Countries.* Sage, Beverly Hills, CA, 1983.

Chikulo, B.C. The Zambian administrative reforms: an alternative view. *Public Administration and Development 1*(1–4):55–65 (1981).

Chunmei, Y. Current administrative reform in China. *International Review of Administrative Sciences 52*(1):123–144 (1986).

Conyers, D. Decentralization for regional development: a comparative study on Tanzania, Zambia, and Papua New Guinea. *Public Administration and Development 1*(1):107–120 (1981).

Conyers, D. Decentralization: the latest fashion in development administration. *Public Administration and Development 3*(2):97–109 (1983).

Conyers, D. Decentralization and development: a review of the literature. *Public Administration and Development 4*:187–197 (1984).

Curnow, G.R., and Wettenhall, R.L., eds. *Understanding Public Administration.* Allen and Unwin, Sydney, 1981.

De Guzman, R., Pacho, R., and Legada, R.T. *Institutional Organizational Arrangements for Planning and Implementation of Administrative Reform.* College of Public Administration, University of the Philippines/EROPA, Manila, 1982.

Dillman, D.L. Personnel management and productivity reform: taming the civil service in Great Britain and the United States. *International Journal of Public Administration 8*(4):345–367 (1986).

Eltayeb, H. Administrative reform theory: approaches and tentative strategies. *Sudan Journal of Economic and Social Studies 2*(2):19–36 (1978).

Falkenheim, V.C. Administrative reform and modernization in post-Mao China. *Pacific Affairs 53*(1):5–28 (1980).

Feldman, D.L. *Reforming Government.* Morrow, New York, 1981.

Garnett, J.L. *Reorganizing State Government: The Executive Branch.* Westview Press, Boulder, CO, 1980.

Gilbert, C.E., ed. Implementing governmental change. *Annals of the American Academy of Political and Social Science 466*(March) (1983).

Godwin, P., and Needham, J. Reforming reform—challenging the assumptions for improving public employees' performance. *Public Personnel Management 10*(2):233–243 (1981).

Graham, L.S. Centralization versus decentralization in the administration of public service. *International Review of Administrative Sciences 46*(3):219–232 (1980).

Greenaway, J.R. Bureaucrats under pressure: the Thatcher government and the Mandarin elite. *Teaching Politics 13*(1):66–84 (1984).

Gunlicks, A.B. *Local Government Reform and Reorganization: An International Perspective.* Kennikat Press, Port Washington, NY, 1981.

Hammergren, L.A. *Development and Politics of Administrative Reform: Lessons from Latin America.* Westview Press, Boulder, CO, 1983.

Hawker, G. *Who's Master, Who's Servant? Reforming Bureaucracy.* Allen and Unwin, Sydney, 1981.

Ingraham, P.W., and Ban, C. *Legislative Bureaucratic Change: The Civil Service Reform Act of 1978.* State University of New York Press, Albany, NY, 1984.

Joao, B.O. *Desburocratizacao e Democracia.* Papirus, Sao Paulo, 1984.

Kaufman, H. Reflections on administrative reorganization. In *Setting National Priorities: The 1978 Budget* (J.A. Pechman, ed.). Brookings, Washington, DC, 1977.

Keating, M., and Hainsworth, P. *Decentralization and Change in Contemporary France.* Gower, Aldershot, 1986.

Khan, M.M. Administrative Reform. *Indian Journal of Public Administration 24*(2):170–180 (1980a).

Khan, M.M. Ruling elites and major administrative reforms: the case of the Pakistan civil service. *Indian Journal of Political Science 41*(4):729–760 (1980b).

Khan, M.M., ed. *Administrative Reform: Theoretical Perspectives.* Center for Administrative Studies, University of Dacca, Dacca, India, 1981.

Kliksberg, B. Administrative reform in Latin America: a review of the conceptual framework. *Venezuelan Review of Administrative Development 3* (1983).

Konig, H. *Implementation of Administrative Reforms Related to Economic Changes: The Federal Republic of Germany.* Institute of Administrative Sciences, Military University, Hamburg, 1986.

Krannich, R.L. Administrative reform and role responses in Thailand. *International Journal of Public Administration 2*(3):263–296 (1980).

Larmour, P., and Qalo, R., eds. *Decentralization in the South Pacific.* University of South Pacific, Suva, 1985.

Lee, H.-Y. Deng Xiaoping's reform of the Chinese bureaucracy. *Journal of Northeast Asian Studies 1*(2):21–36 (1982).

Levine, C.H. *Managing Fiscal Stress: The Crisis in the Public Sector.* Chatham House, Chatham, NJ, 1980.

Levine, C. Citizenship and service delivery: the promise of coproduction. *Public Administration Review 44*:178–187 (1984).

Maheshwari, S. *Administrative Reform in India.* Macmillan, Delhi, 1981.

March, J.G., and Olson, J.P. Organizing political life: what administrative reorganization tells us about governing. *American Political Science Review 77*(2):281–296 (1983).

Mathur, H.M. *Administering Development in the Third World: Constraints and Changes.* Sage, Beverly Hills, CA, 1986.

Mayo-Smith, I., and Ruther, N.L. *Achieving Improved Performance in Public Organizations: A Guide for Managers.* Kumarian Press, West Hartford, CT, 1986.

Miewald, R., and Steinman, M., eds. *Problems in Administrative Reform.* Nelson-Hall, Chicago, 1984.

Miller, T.C., ed. *Public Sector Performance: A Conceptual Turning Point.* Johns Hopkins University Press, Baltimore, 1984.

Muttalib, M.A. *Trends in Administrative Reform.* Indian Council of Social Science Research, New Delhi, 1983.

National Academy of Public Administration. *Revitalizing Federal Management: Managers and Their Overburdened Systems.* Washington, DC, 1983.

Owojaiye, G.S., and Smith, B.C. Reforming local government: lessons from Britain. *International Review of Administrative Sciences 4*:404–412 (1983).

Pierce, W.S. *Bureaucratic Failure and Public Expenditure.* Academic Press, New York, 1981.

Plowden, W., et al. New directions in administrative reform. *International Review of Administrative Sciences 49*(1):96–109 (1983).

Prasser, S. Public inquiries in Australia: an overview. *Australian Journal of Public Administration 44*(1):1–16 (1985).

Preston, M.B. *The Politics of Bureaucratic Reform: The Case of the California State Employment Service.* University of Illinois Press, Urbana, 1984.

Rhodes, G. *Committees of Inquiry.* Allen and Unwin, London, 1975.

Ro, C.-H., ed. *Social Change and Administrative Reform: Towards the Year 2000.* Development Management Centre, EROPA, Seoul, 1985.

Rondinelli, D.A., Nellis, J.R., and Cheema, G.S. *Decentralization in Developing Countries: A Review of Recent Experience.* World Bank, Washington, DC, 1983.

Rowat, D.C., ed. *International Handbook on Local Government Reorganization.* Greenwood Press, Westport, CT, 1980.

Saxena, A.P., ed. *Administrative Reforms for Decentralized Development.* Asian and Pacific Development Administration Centre, Kuala Lumpur, 1980.

Schick, A., ed. *Perspectives on Budgeting.* ASPA, Washington, DC, 1986.

Scott, E.N., ed. *International Perspective in Public Administration.* A.C.T. CCAE/IASIA, Canberra, 1981.

Smith, R.F.I., and Weller, P., eds. *Public Service Inquiries in Australia.* University of Queensland Press, Brisbane, 1978.

Stahl, O.G., ed. *Improving Public Services.* USAID/ICIPMP, Washington, DC, 1979.

Szanton, P., ed. *Federal Reorganization: What Have We Learned?* Chatham House, Chatham, NJ, 1981.

Tierney, J.T. *Postal Reorganization: Managing the Public's Business.* Auburn House, Boston, 1981.

Tummala, K.K. *The Ambiguity of Ideology and Administrative Reform.* Allied Publishers, Bombay, 1979.

Twentieth Century Fund. *The Government's Managers.* Priority Press, New York, 1987.

United Nations. *Enhancing Capabilities for Administrative Reform in Developing Countries.* Department of Technical Cooperation, New York, 1983.

United States Government. *Strengthening Management Through Partnership.* President's Council on Management Improvement, Washington, DC, 1987.

Wilenski, P. Administrative reform—general principles and the Australian experience. *Public Administration 64*:257–276 (1986).

Williams, R. *Political Corruption in Africa.* Gower, Aldershot, 1987.

Wright, D.S., and Sakurai, Y. Administrative reform in Japan: politics, policy and public administration in a deliberative society. *Public Administration Review 47*(2):121–133 (1987).

Yates, D. *Bureaucratic Democracy: The Search for Democracy and Efficiency in American Government.* Harvard University Press, Cambridge, MA, 1982.

45

Government Reform and Reorganization in an Era of Retrenchment and Conviction Politics

B. Guy Peters   *Department of Political Science, University of Pittsburgh, Pittsburgh, Pennsylvania*

> I was to learn later in life that we tend to meet any new situation by reorganizing . . . and a wonderful method it can be for creating the illusion of progress while producing inefficiency and demoralization.
>
> —Petronious, AD 66

I. INTRODUCTION

Reorganization and reform are, as Petronious said, a wonderful way to create a sense of activity in government. Governments spend a good deal of their time attempting to reorganize and reform their own structures and procedures. Since at least the time of the Romans almost every government that has come into existence and remained viable for any period of time has sought at one time or another to reorganize and reform itself. The efforts at change have usually had the same disappointing results as those reported by the Romans. It is perhaps a tribute to the resilience and optimism of the human species (or at least that nonrandom sample of it involved in government) that governments continue down the same well-worn paths of reorganization and reform. The perpetuation of interest in reorganization is, however, also a testament to the continuing difficulties in developing structures and procedures that will enable governments to perform as citizens and political leaders would like them.

This general predilection of decision makers toward reforming government has been spurred on to greater heights by two elements of political life in the 1970s and 1980s. One is the continuing fiscal problems faced by almost all democratic governments, with deficits and debts increasing and with no apparent mechanism to reduce public expenditures without a major political confrontation. The second element, not unrelated, is the emergence of "conviction politics," especially on the political right. In a number of countries—the United States, the United Kingdom, and Canada as three prime examples—conservative politicians have come into office with definite agendas to reduce the size of government, and to restore (or create) the dominance of the free market over economic allocations. The combined pressures of real fiscal strains and the convictions of politicians have challenged the reform capacity of governments to the point that some—even Sweden with a long history of successful adaptation and change—have not been able to produce the types

669

of change desired or expected (Mellbourn 1986). Many of the reforms that have been produced are rather simplistic answers to complex questions, and address the needs of conviction politicians more than the needs of managers or taxpaying (or service-consuming) citizens.

This chapter will be a discussion of those two dominant pressures for change faced by contemporary governments, especially for change by the permanent civil service and the institutions usually associated with the civil service. These pressures will be discussed in the context of specific recommendations for change that have been put forward and in some cases implemented in western European and North American democracies. These examples of reform have been drawn from a variety of settings and require some effort to classify them, along with the strategies for achieving better government that they imply. Finally, we will examine alternative explanations for the choice of reform strategies, and begin to explore some ideas about a possible analytical approach for explaining reform and reorganization (Olsen 1988; March and Olsen 1989).

II. FISCAL STRESS AND COMMITTED POLITICIANS

As noted above, governments have had to face both real fiscal stress and politicians who believed that they understood the causes and solutions of those financial problems. In fact, in many instances, the one followed the other closely, as the comfortable period of certain economic growth and agreement on social and economic policy that characterized postwar politics came to an end with the first OPEC oil embargo in the early 1970s (Kavanagh 1985). Referred to as "Butskellism" in Great Britain, and widely accepted even where there was no specific title, the Welfare State and Keynesian economic management were the cornerstones of domestic policy in a postwar period with widespread agreement about public policy. Politics in that era was primarily about minor variations on those themes, and certainly not about the whole new approaches to solving the policy problems of industrialized societies—those were assumed to have been solved. The assumption of having solved the problems of governance, and the consensus on the means, should be understandable, given that the period following the Korean War was one of almost continuous economic growth and increasing prosperity. In the eyes of most citizens, whatever government was doing appeared to be successful, and they saw no reasons for change in those basic directions. But that comfortable period was not to last, and real problems for government were soon introduced.

A. Fiscal Stress

The first difficulty to arise was the real economic problem of scarcity. The economic successes in Western democracies after 1952 had made many citizens and politicians forget about scarcity, but it remained a very real constraint and governments were soon forced to learn about it again. The 1970s and 1980s have been an era of real or perceived fiscal difficulty for governments in most industrialized societies. Talk of cutting budgets, cutting public employment, and perhaps above all cutting taxes has dominated political life. These financial difficulties for the public sector have been in part a function of the uncertainty of future economic growth, following several decades of sustained and rapid economic growth (Rose and Peters 1978). Although economic growth in the mid and late 1980s has been more sustained and somewhat greater than in the decade immediately after the oil crisis of 1973, a nagging uncertainty remains in the minds of many policymakers. That practical uncertainty is accentuated by the absence of an accepted economic dogma to guide decision making after the collapse of Keynesianism. The discussions of "fine-tuning" the economy after the collapse of Keynesian methods that were common in the 1960s now appear dated, and optimistic if not actually naive. Subsequent attempts by monetarists and supply-siders to formulate a new paradigm never gained the widespread acceptance enjoyed by Keynesianism.

The fiscal difficulties of government also have been a function of the continuing commitments of governments to fund social programs begun in the 1950s and 1960s (or even 1930s). Demographic changes, inflation, and political pressures for enhanced benefits have made these entitlement programs more expensive year by year. Those increasing program costs have become even more uncontrollable by the legislated indexation of benefits to meet increases in prices and/or wages (Weaver 1988). The costs of these social programs have led some to question the advisability of their being continued. The desire to reduce program spending may actually be more deep-seated and ideological, but financial problems have provided a useful justification for the public. In the language of the time, governments were "overloaded," with too much to do and inadequate resources to meet all their commitments (King 1975).

Finally, after the initial financial shocks around the times of the oil crises, the apparent fiscal distress of governments has been generated as much by ideological changes and citizens' backlash against taxation as by real economic conditions. As noted above, economic growth is currently more problematic than in the late 1950s and 1960s, but continues to occur and for European countries appears likely to get stronger. The unpredictability of growth that plagued the 1970s now appears to have been reduced, and growth is predictable if not always large. However, whether in California, Denmark, Wellington or wherever, groups have mobilized to lower or at least stabilize taxes, and thereby have been able to place, wittingly or unwittingly, fiscal pressures on government (Hadenius 1986; Taylor-Gooby 1985).

B. Commitment

The above discussion of the ideological dimension associated with fiscal stress leads us to a second source of pressure for change in government—the growth of conviction politics. Politicians in the late 1970s and early 1980s came into office with real commitments to alter the manner in which the public sector has been operating. They came to office riding on a wave of popular discontent about the way in which government had been managed, as well as with some particular programs. The "Era of Retrenchment" has been more than just simple demands for government to spend less money or employ fewer people. In many countries it has been associated with a more sweeping indictment of government as usual, and an attempt to impose an alternative ideological vision on government. While most political leaders of this era do not have ideologies in the sense of an integrated and coherent vision of state and society, they do have a set of beliefs about government. Further, they have had the capacity to communicate those ideas to their fellow citizens, and the tenacity to place their ideas into practice to an almost unprecedented degree (Jones 1988; Kavanagh 1987; Netherlands Scientific Council 1983). This set of beliefs at the elite level has successfully permeated mass thinking about government in many countries; the notion of an "enterprise culture" in Britain is the most obvious example. It appears that citizens no longer first look to government to solve societal problems, but rather seek those solutions in the private sector or simply no longer consider that "problems" exist. The era of retrenchment and the leaders it has spawned have produced a major cultural change concerning government, and governing has come to mean coping with this cultural change as much as coping with more tangible factors such as inadequate money and personnel. In the words of two authors, the public sector has now moved "from hubris to helplessness" (Downs and Larkey 1986).

Although retrenchment is usually discussed as a fiscal concept, it has numerous managerial and leadership ramifications as well. In the first place, some of the reasons behind the perceived need for budgetary retrenchment are managerial. Governments are usually discussed as "bureaucratic," bumbling, inefficient, and poorly managed (and those are the most polite terms used). Many critics of government see its fiscal problems arising as much from the inefficiency of its own internal management practices as from external fiscal pressures (see, for example, Savas 1982; for a contrary view see Goodsell 1985). These critics then propose the private sector as the proper exemplar of good management for government (Downs and Larkey 1986:23–58). Evidence of corruption—whether in defense procurement in the United States or the management of the Property Services Agency in Britain or wherever—only adds to the appearance of poor public-sector management (Rose-Ackerman 1978; Doig 1984). The phrase "fraud, waste, and abuse" in the United States has come to encapsulate a general feeling that many of the financial problems of government can be laid at its own doorstep, and that something must be done to make government work better.

Complaints about government and its apparent inability to accomplish its tasks in an efficient and effective manner (leaving aside for the time being just what those two terms mean in the public sector) are not new. What is different is that a cadre of politicians has come to office believing that government is almost inherently inefficient as it is currently organized and managed, and that this cadre has a commitment to do something dramatic about those perceived weaknesses. In some instances, this has meant attempting to dismantle a large portion of the apparatus of government, but in almost all cases it has meant undertaking major changes. In addition, unlike many previous change programs concerning the apparatus of government, these changes did not assume that what government did was inherently valuable. On the contrary, most of these politicians came into office with an assumption that a good deal of what the public sector did, if it should be done at all, could be done better by the private sector. Hence, words like "privatization" and "deregulation" became powerful slogans for a new generation of political leaders who appeared quite willing, and even anxious, to dismantle a great deal of public-sector activity.

These demands for improved (or simply less) management in the public sector have provoked a number of responses. In some instances the responses have been merely budgetary changes and gimmicks (Tarschys 1985); some change little more than the style of presentation without any real impact on levels of public expenditure. Other responses fall under the general rubric of "cutback management" (Levine 1978, 1980; Tarschys 1981) and involve the effective micromanagement of organizations as they respond to declining resources and probably also declining personnel figures. Other responses involve large-scale changes in the manner in which government is organized and managed. At one time or another, almost all governments of industrialized democracies have attempted all three types of reform, very often one after the other in a predictable sequence (Ingraham and Peters 1988), albeit with varying degrees of success.

The new ideologues in government, and their demands for managerial skills, in turn require some rethinking of the role of political executives and the role of the career civil service. It may require even more careful rethinking for political leaders who succeed the current crop of leaders in office. The rules of the governing game have been changed, and in some cases changed very fundamentally. Those rules have been changed primarily to tilt the playing surface in the direction of the politicians' end of the field, and to enhance their capacity to score goals. It may be that subsequent leaders can learn and build an even greater capacity to get things done with their own resources, or they may want to return to a governing system vesting greater responsibility for policy in the career service. If indeed times are tough, it may pay politically to minimize responsibility for what happens and attempt to place the blame elsewhere (Weaver 1986; Hood and Schuppert 1988). Whatever their desires, those future leaders will have to understand and react to the managerial and policy developments of the past decade.

III. ATTEMPTING TO COPE WITH CHANGING DEMANDS

Governments have adopted a number of strategies to deal with their problems in the era of retrenchment and commitment. This section will catalog and briefly describe those coping strategies, ranging from very mundane tinkering to very fundamental reorientations of the public sector. These reforms will, however, serve only as a backdrop for subsequent attempts to address the more crucial point about reform: the question of choice. There is an entire cafeteria of choice available for decision makers, and if we assume that those leaders do indeed want to produce change, how can they choose among the alternatives in a way that will maximize the probability of desired changes? There is as yet very little in the way of positive theory to guide the eager reformer in the selection of an alternative that will produce the most results in a particular setting. The question then becomes whether such a positive theory, perhaps in the form of a contingency approach (Pfeffer 1978), would be possible and further whether it would be desirable. It may be that most reforms arise from a "garbage can" (Cohen et al. 1972), or that they are only experiments (Campbell 1969), or arguments (Dunn 1982), and lack any real possibility of certainty and predictability. Further, as with Simon's (1947) proverbs of administration, it may be that improving performance on one dimension may require sacrifices on another. There is still a great deal that is not understood adequately about the difficult and complex task of reforming government.

In addition, with the committed leadership that now exists in many governments, it may be difficult to distinguish a belief about the appropriateness of a particular remedy from the reality of its efficacy for changing government. Most of the committed leaders coming into office in the 1980s have brought with them beliefs that the means of management and intervention used in the private sector are superior to those of the public sector, and that whenever possible the public sector should either emulate the private sector or simply privatize the function. In addition, centralized control over policy has generally been seen as undesirable by those leaders, so that quasi-markets have been created to perform what had been managed centrally. A great deal of the revealed wisdom of the reformers has little basis in organizational theory or policy analysis, but this has not stopped attempts at implementing the reforms. Thus, if we are concerned about the role of any theories of policy choice, we should begin with those that posit simple, objective rationality on the part of decision makers. This may be possible here because this crop of politicians appears to have a simpler and more uniform set of preferences than do most. Further, they will not bow, it appears, to popular political forces, because the unpopularity of many reforms that have been proposed has deterred their advocates very little if at all. As with almost any group of ideologues, there is the belief among this group that the reforms are "right."[1]

A. Targets of Reform

With some understanding of the political setting in which reforms have been undertaken, we can begin to categorize them as an aid to further discussion and analysis (see Table 1). One dimension of classification for the attempts of government to cope with demands for change is the content of those reforms. Where were the problems in government identified as needing "fixing" that generated a particular intervention? What is the apparent diagnosis for the ills of government? While far from ambiguous, it appears that we can think usefully of these targets of reform in four basic content categories: the budget, structures, procedures, and relations between the permanent civil service and political leaders (see also Ingraham and Peters 1988).

1. The Budget

The simplest of these categories of reforms contains attempts on the part of public decision makers to change the manner in which their budgets are made, or the type of analysis or thinking that goes into their construction. As can be seen by reference to the second dimension of Table 1, there are a number of strategies and devices through which this manipulation of the budgetary process has been undertaken (see Tarschys 1985; Schick 1988; Midwinter 1988). Furthermore, to a greater

Table 1 Types of Reorganization and Reform

	Targets			
	Budgetary	Structural	Procedural	Relational
Load shedding	Privatization	Privatization	Deregulation	Politicization
Snakes and ladders	Subnational responsibility	Decentralization	—	Task forces
Automaticity	Gramm-Rudman Hollings	Japanese personnel	Paperwork reduction	—
Priority setting	(PPBS)	—	(Planning)	Priorities and planning
Squeezing	Main alternative	Grace Commission	Grace Commission	—
Management	FMI/Next Steps	Quangoization	(MBO)	FMI/Next Steps

or lesser extent, all the methods developed to cope with retrenchment appear to have had some success, although almost always less success than promised by their advocates. The successes in producing retrenchment actually have been greater than most previous attempts at budgetary reform (e.g., Planning-Programming Budgetary Systems, Rationalisation des Choix Budgetaires, Public Expenditure Survey Committee, and the like), in part because the goals of the recent reforms have been more modest. While many strategies for budgetary reform in the 1960s and early 1970s had something approaching comprehensive rationality as a goal, most contemporary budgetary reforms have had simpler intentions, such as merely reducing the budget (Peters 1989: Chap. 7; Hood 1988). Hence, strategies such as the "main alternative" for the Swedish budget (Ericksson 1983), which is simply a 2% reduction of the previous appropriations, have very clear and attainable goals. Even contemporary budgetary reforms with greater analytic content, such as the reconsideration initiatives in the Netherlands, have as their fundamental goal reduction of public expenditures rather than the more grandiose goals of achieving some Pigovian optimum of allocations among competing purposes. In the case of budgetary reform at least, the hubris may be gone but there is no sense of helplessness.

2. Structures

As the name implies, structural changes involve transformations of the organizational framework that provides government services. These changes range from the simple jiggling and poking of government structure that is common in any era, faced with retrenchment or not (Peters and Hogwood, in press), to very fundamental changes in the institutional fabric that provides public services. It is by no means uncommon to think that if the organization of government is correct, then those institutions will actually function smoothly. Organization is important but, despite their frequent occurrence, structural reorganizations of government are really not very well understood either by those that implement them or by students of government (Leemans 1976; Pollitt 1984; Campbell and Peters 1988; Hult 1987; Ståhlberg 1987). As a consequence, reorganizations frequently do not meet the goals—especially those of enhanced efficiency (Salamon 1981b)—that have been posited for them and often produce more disillusionment and disappointment than significant change in the way government works.

Among the most fundamental structural changes tried has been the shedding of burdens through privatization and deregulation (Young 1987). Even when programs have been retained in the public sector, there has been a tendency to hive them off into smaller, presumably more accountable and mission-oriented, organizations and to reduce the relative power and authority of the mainline departments. This has been seen in, among other examples, the formation of *administrations de mission* in France and Belgium (Rigaud and Delcros 1984; Timsit 1987), *Projektgruppen* in West Germany (Lepper 1983), and in the proposed creation of mission-oriented agencies by the reform called "Next Steps" in the United Kingdom (Jenkins et al. 1988). Also, there have been a number of efforts at decentralizing (or even centralizing) government to attempt to promote efficiency, accountability, and a host of other political values by involving other levels of government. It would appear that one common reaction to the perceived inability of existing government structures to deliver the goods in a manner that most people would desire is to attempt to alter the existing structures for service delivery. This is hardly a new response to the problem, but it remains interesting the extent to which old reforms continue to become new problems.

Again, we should not be terribly sanguine about the capacity of structural reforms to produce any tangible improvements in the performance of the public sector. The reforms do have two advantages, however. The first is that they give the appearance of action in dealing with problems for which there may be no real solution, and political leaders may need that image created. This need to demonstrate activity may be especially important for committed political leaders who came into office with a pledge to do something about the "mess in X" (fill in the name of the capital city). Further, as with some of the budgetary "reforms," structural reforms may give the illusion that expenditures have been reduced when in fact they are only being made at another level of government, or by a quasi-public organization that does not show up in the budget (Peters and Heisler 1983; Hood and Schuppert 1988).

3. Procedures

Along with changing the structures, governments have sought to alter the procedures by which they conduct their business and make their decisions. Again, unlike many of even the nonbudgetary procedural remedies adopted during the 1960s and early 1970s (e.g., management by objectives, MBO), many of the procedural reforms emerging in the later 1970s and into the 1980s have been very little concerned with substantive rationality. Rather, they have been more concerned with the simple task of trying to produce some improvements in output per unit of input, or at a minimum making those managing programs in government conceptualize their tasks in those terms. Other reforms have been concerned with procedural rationality and providing the appearance that government does in fact perform its role properly.

One focus for the procedural reforms has been increased managerial accountability and enhanced scrutiny of administrative performance. Many components of this category could be considered either procedural reforms or structural reforms. Procedures rarely can be introduced on their own but require an organization to develop and implement them. So, for example, were the Rayner scrutinies in Britain a procedural reform or were they a structural change, that is, the creation of the Efficiency Unit? In this analysis we will be considering reforms of this type as procedural because it was the change in procedure, or the addition of new procedures, that was designed to produce the result. Reorganization or the creation of a new organization was coincidental with the procedural change. Further, some procedural reforms may come very close to being budgetary in nature. The Financial Management Initiative in Britain, for example, had a good deal to do with the spending of money, although the primary purpose appeared to be altering how government did its business rather than saving candle ends through changes in the formal budgetary process.

Similar to budgetary, and especially to organizational, reforms, however, some of the most important and effective of the procedural reforms have involved reducing the number of procedures. This is seen externally through deregulation and governments' decisions to impose fewer rules on the conduct of economic and social life in their countries. Internally, in government itself, this type of reform has manifested itself in several ways. One has been through Paperwork Reduction Acts and their equivalents. Another has been the abrogation of some procedures that may have protected civil servants, such as the Priestley system of pay research in the United Kingdom, or the principle of pay comparability between the public and private sectors in the United States. One meaning of "reform" has been simply to eliminate what were perceived as slow and costly procedures (for France, see Fournier 1987) in favor of quick decisions by elected political leaders or their appointees.

4. Relational Reforms

Finally, governments have sought to address political demands for retrenchment and greater commitment to political goals through altering the working relationships between the career civil service and temporary political executives. A dominant theme of most of the "ideological" governments in the 1970s and 1980s (especially those of the Right) has been that policymaking has been dominated by the career civil service. The alleged poor management skills of the civil service, and their thinly disguised policy agendas, have been argued to be the fundamental cause of all that is wrong with government in Washington, Whitehall, or wherever. Further, civil service systems are argued to protect and disguise a cadre of organizational politicians who have their own views about policy and who have been successful in implementing those views (see, for example, Butler et al. 1984; Hoskyns 1983). The view that politics and administration could not be separated has long been the conventional wisdom in academe (Aberbach et al. 1981), but it has now permeated the "real world." With the popularity of this view, and the determination of a new breed of politicians to implement their programs, the public bureaucracy has become a scapegoat for the very need for retrenchment, and political leaders have been effective in deflecting attention from their own managerial shortcomings onto the civil service (Milward and Rainey 1983).

Given the diagnosis of the illness of government that has been offered, the remedies prescribed should not surprise. In the 1980s, a number of attempts have been made to interject more political control, and more political appointees, into the career services. This has progressed to the point that politicization of the civil service has become a significant concern in a number of countries (Meyers 1985). Even in countries such as the United Kingdom with a long tradition of an apolitical and largely respected and influential civil service, attempts have been made to impose greater political control and involvement of outsiders (Ridley 1985; Drewry and Butcher 1988:165–168). In countries such as France and West Germany, where civil servants have been more identified with political parties, the importance of that identification appears to have intensified (Derlien 1988; *Pouvoirs* 1987; Ståhlberg 1987). It now appears to be widely believed among elected political leaders that if they can only get more committed people into managerial and leadership positions in government, then the commonly identified problems of government will have been solved, or at worst ameliorated.

5. Summary

This has been a catalog of the types of targets that reformers in the public sector have to shoot at. This is to some degree the totality of government, but the selection of targets will reflect something of the diagnosis of the pathologies that the reformers perceive in government. It will, everything else being equal, be easier to make minor adjustments in the budget or in a few agencies, and hope that everything will then work well. If, however, the diagnosis is that governmental structures and operations are more fundamentally flawed, then the reforms will have to be more extensive and more basic. Some of the strategies, ranging from the simple to the very profound, are detailed in the following section.

B. Strategies of Reform

In addition to dealing with specific contents of problems in government, the reforms that have been adopted can also be classified according to the strategies of reform they attempt to impose. Although some styles appear especially closely tied to specific contents (e.g., automaticity with budgetary reforms), there is a rather wide distribution of almost all styles in the several content categories. Faced with the very daunting problem of attempting to change the manner in which government conducts its business, political (and administrative) leaders have cast their net very widely and have tried a number of "solutions." What does appear general, however, is the denigration of "rationality" in favor of more political, ideological, and nonanalytic responses to managerial problems. There are some counterexamples, as MBO is reborn in several Scandinavian countries and program budgeting is revived in Australia, but the general approach has been that commitment and political will are more important than analysis. This does not mean that the tools taught in schools of public administration and policy around the world are being allowed to rust. Rather, the tools appear now to be used more overtly to justify preconceived notions rather than to "discover" new solutions and new information about policy issues.

1. Load Shedding

One of the simplest strategies governments can adopt for dealing with the perceived need to retrench is to shed some of the policy load it has been carrying, and require the private sector to do more. We have already noted that this is infeasible for many large-expenditure, entitlement programs, but is has proved to be very possible for a number of programs (Veljanovski 1987; Savas 1987). Even for the big-ticket items, however, some governments have undertaken serious evaluations of the possibilities of privatization. In addition, international organizations such as the World Bank and the International Monetary Fund have been instrumental in carrying the gospel of privatization to many nonindustrialized countries, so that this strategy has become a worldwide response to perceived governmental and economic failures.

Load shedding need not, however, just be privatization. Deregulation is another important form of load shedding that has been adopted in varying degrees in different countries. Not only have governments reduced their ownership of productive enterprises, but they have sought to allow private industries greater autonomy in making their own decisions. This strategy presumably both lessens the decision-making burden within government and permits greater economic development through the operation of the free market. It should be noted, however, that it may not be possible to employ these two load-shedding strategies simultaneously. Privatizing industries that meet the usual criteria for regulation (Wolf 1987) may require that those new private industries be regulated (Pelkmans and van Nie 1985). For example, very soon after British Telecom was privatized, the Office of Telecommunications was established in Whitehall to protect the public from a potential monopolist and to encourage competition.

It is also important to remember that load shedding, especially in the form of privatization, is not universally regarded as an acceptable strategy to cope with all the problems that afflict government. This is especially true in Northern European countries with a well-developed statist tradition in the provision of basic public services and the benefits of the welfare state. When a conservative Danish government, for example sought to introduce widespread privatization, the attempt was rebuffed (Kristensen 1984). The term "privatization" was then dropped, and some of the same changes were introduced successfully under the more acceptable rubric of "modernization" (Olsen 1988). Other types of governmental reforms have been implemented in the Scandinavian countries using that same rubric of modernization. In these cases, at least, the ideologues did not triumph completely, and some of the underlying commitment of the societies to public programs was preserved.

2. Snakes and Ladders

Not all movement of power and decision making is between the public and private sectors. Another reform style is to redistribute the tasks of government among different actors within government itself, even if all the activities do remain governmental responsibilities. Some functions may be centralized and others decentralized, but if there is a problem then shifting the level of government may be proposed as the answer. Of course, all this shifting of responsibilities may only be a facade to hide the intractibility of the problems. Or it may be a means of one level of government trying to gain some apparent fiscal responsibility at the expense of others. This strategy may be especially powerful for a goal of fiscal restraint if the function can be forced onto a level of government that is not permitted to run a deficit, such as the states in the United States (Nathan and Doolittle 1987; Beam 1984). As with privatization, the same function performed elsewhere still costs somebody something, but the political appearance is often as important as the reality of the reform.

Interestingly, different governments when faced with somewhat similar demands for retrenchment or at least improvement of governmental performance have approached the problem of who does what somewhat differently. This to some degree may be a function of their respective starting points; highly centralized regimes could centralize further only with great difficulty, so that there may be a tendency to move toward more centrist strategies. This is not entirely the case, however, as the United States, which began with a decentralized regime, decentralized even more during the Reagan administration. Of the two types of response, decentralization has appeared to be the more popular choice. France, Spain, and Italy have undertaken major decentralization efforts in what had been centralized regimes (Keating 1988; Putnam 1988). Local government reforms in a number of European countries appear to have made giving more power to the localities a real possibility (Gustafsson 1981). Only the United Kingdom (Jones 1988) has seen a major effort at centralization of control over local government, albeit combined with a broad effort at load shedding to the private sector. Other countries have, however, centralized some functions (especially in budgeting and finance) in an attempt to enhance political control.

Also, as mentioned earlier, a certain amount of decentralization has been occurring with the central government itself (Salamon 1981a). This has occurred through the creation of small, mission-oriented organizations with limited lifetimes and very specific purposes (Rigaud and Delcros 1984). These organizations are created outside the usual ministerial structures of government, with the hope that they can be made more accountable to political control, to the market, or to their "customers." One of the most extensive attempt to create organizations of this sort is "Next Steps" in the United Kingdom, which would radically decentralize most of central government (Taylor 1988). New Zealand is undertaking a perhaps even more radical reorganization of the functions of central government into autonomous or quasi-autonomous agencies or corporations. There are, however, some contrary changes that would centralize control, as for examples attempts made to reduce the autonomy enjoyed by the boards and agencies in Swedish central government (Ruin 1988).

3. Automaticity

As noted above, this strategy is closely associated with problems in public expenditure and the budget. It has been argued frequently that it is difficult for political organizations, or any public organization with close links to clients, to make difficult decisions about reducing public expenditure. Therefore, if those actors can agree in advance on automatic mechanisms for imposing reductions, then some of the political onus will be removed from those decisions. American readers will recognize the logic of the Gramm-Rudman-Hollings plan to eliminate the budget deficit in this statement, and similar mechanisms have been imposed in other political systems. In some, such as Japan, similar mechanisms have been applied to cutting the size of the civil service (Muramatsu 1988). The fundamental approach to reform here is to remove as much discretion as possible from those whose political careers might be damaged by making decisions on cuts. Such a strategy enables politicians committed to fiscal restraint to place a mortmain on any growth in the public sector, and possibly to reduce the size of government.

Automaticity has also been introduced as a means of preventing governments from enhancing their revenues through inflation. With a progressive income tax, as their incomes increase, taxpayers move into higher brackets and have to pay a larger portion of their income in tax. If increases in income are due to inflation rather than real economic growth, the individual taxpayers will be able to retain only a smaller real income. To prevent this "fiscal dividend" from being received by the public sector, a number of governments have introduced automatic adjustments of bracket thresholds for inflation (Rose 1985). With this arrangement, if governments want more tax revenues they must go through the difficult political battle needed to change the law, rather than receiving an automatic fiscal dividend through increases in price levels.

4. Priority Setting

One of the standard complaints about "big government" is that it has been allowed to grow without much rhyme or reason. This has meant that it has often grown in very incoherent, and therefore excessively costly, directions (Rothstein 1986). One standard example is the Surgeon General of the United States spending a substantial amount of money to discourage smoking at the same time that the U.S. Department of Agriculture supports tobacco farmers. Thus, if clear policy priorities could be established then the "burdens" of government could be reduced and better government produced for all. The need for priority setting is argued to exist especially in the budget (see Natchez and Bupp 1973), but it also exists in a range of governmental activities. Further, while some of the rational reforms of the 1960s and 1970s also sought to impose priority setting (Klein et al. 1988), governments in the 1980s have sought to determine and implement those priorities by more politicized means.

Attempting to establish and implement clear priorities in government may not take sufficient account of the multiplicity of worthwhile goals that exist within government. In addition, placing a greater emphasis on priority setting in government will tend to drive decisions upward, away from the career civil service and toward the political executives. This is much the same idea as Campbell's (1984:24) "planning and priorities" style of executive behavior, and to some extent similar to Dror's (1985) concept of the "central mind of government." These approaches to governing assume that there should be a single set of priorities in government, and that policy should be controlled from the center. This style may be difficult to execute, but it would place politicians firmly in control.

In moving decisions upward, this style of governing will very obviously affect the relationships between civil servants and politicians—in ways apparently desired by most contemporary politicians. Thus, initiatives such as the Financial Management Initiative and its sequel Next Steps in the United Kingdom are intended to have as one of their several impacts making civil servants as the managers of frameworks (expressions of priorities) established elsewhere rather than advisors on policy. This will, in turn, reduce their importance in governing.

5. Squeezing

One assumption of conservative critics of government is that government budgets and staffs are almost inevitably too large for the demands of the tasks that are to be performed (Niskanen 1971; but see Lane 1987). If that assumption is accepted, then an important strategy to improve efficiency would be to squeeze the fat out of those budgets. While this may be done through the automatic methods discussed above, it can also be done more selectively. That selection may be done on the grounds of efficiency, such as selecting targets regardless of their political popularity because they appear to have a great deal of available slack. Reviews of defense procurement (even prior to the bribery scandals) would be an example of this approach. Lane's (1988) ideas about systematic comparison of the costs of organizations and subnational governments would be another. A more common strategy appears to be selecting as targets of opportunity programs that have minimal political support, and then scrutinizing their budgets very carefully. Finally, often the most politically popular, even if logically undesirable, method of approaching the problem of "squeezing the fat" out of budgets is across-the-board cuts, or "equal misery."

One way to produce the desired squeeze on government is to involve people who have little or nothing to protect in the current programs and arrangements for administration. This is typified by the Grace Commission (Kelman 1985; Goodsell 1984; Baber 1987) in the United States, with a very similar mechanism being employed subsequently in Canada (Wilson 1988) in the form of the Nielsen Task Force. Other countries that do not permit outsiders to come roaming through their governments cannot enjoy all the benefits of these exercises,[2] but exercises such as the Rayner scrutinies in the United Kingdom serve much the same purpose by using civil servants, albeit somewhat atypical civil servants (Metcalfe and Richards 1984). Whether it is a one-time exercise (Grace) or an ongoing exercise (Rayner), this search-and-destroy tactic provides a great deal of ammunition for those who want to reduce the size of government. This strategy does, however, run the risk of cutting the good along with the bad. This danger is especially evident because, as we point out immediately below, the analogies between the public and private sectors may well be false.

6. Managerialism

Finally, there has been a major movement in government circles to attempt to make government itself more like private enterprise, and to make managing government organizations more like private-sector management. This approach to governing sometimes parades under the banner of "managerialism," as if there had been no management in government prior to the time it was advocated (Duffy 1988). This "managerial" approach tends to ignore all the warnings about the fundamental differences between managing government organizations and those in the private sector (Allison 1986; Rainey et al. 1976) and proceeds to attempt to transplant private-sector ideas to government. As might be imagined, this approach has been championed by the political right, although it has not been without its more moderate and even liberal advocates. Managerialism has been characterized, however, by some scholars as almost hopelessly muddled and as a "reign of error" (Metcalfe 1988).

The managerial approach to improving government's performance in the face of retrenchment has been widely accepted; it is very comforting to politicians to think that all that is really wrong with government can be cured without addressing any fundamental program choices. Examples of managerialism are numerous. The Reagan administration, through its general approach to government, characterized by projects such as the Grace Commission and "Reform '88," has sought to make government function more like a business (Newland 1983; Benda and Levine 1988). Similar themes have emerged in Canadian and Australian government (Aucoin 1988; Wilenski 1986; Yeatman 1987). Major efforts at understanding and improving government management are under way in the Scandinavian countries.

Nowhere, however, has managerialism been a more visible and important strategy for addressing the perceived ills of government than it has been in Mrs. Thatcher's Britain. Beginning with the MINIS information system (Likierman 1982), going through the Financial Management Initiative (Lee 1984; Gray and Jenkins 1986), and now pushing even further along the managerial trail with the Next Steps program (Jenkins et al. 1988), the Conservative governments since 1979 have been attempting to produce a basic change in the culture of the British civil service. The fundamental idea is that career civil servants should serve as managers, and policy ideas should be the province of the political executives. This thinking pervades several of the substantive areas of reform, but is especially evident in thinking about relational issues in governance.

7.   Summary

Governments have not been remiss in trying to cope with the problems presented to them by retrenchment and conviction politics. On the contrary, they have been extremely creative in producing reforms that address, if in no more than symbolic terms at times, the many challenges they face. The classification and enumeration of reforms contained here in many ways only scratch the surface of the complexity of change in the public sector. They do, however, serve as the background and prologue for an attempt to understand something of the dynamics of choice in reform and reorganization. These reforms have not appeared by magic but are the products of some process of choice within government. That process is, however, still understood very poorly. The concluding section of the chapter will attempt to at least provide some tentative ideas about those processes for choosing reform.

IV.   PROBLEM OF CHOICE

After detailing one classification of the many changes that have been tried by governments in Western democracies in attempting to cope with change, we are faced with the difficult task of attempting to explain why those choices would have been made. There are some similarities among the "solutions" adopted, but there are also some important differences. There are even greater differences in the levels of apparent success of the same remedies in different settings. This then leaves us with two questions of choice rather than just one: Where do the ideas for change come from, and what explains differential levels of success?

A.   Agenda for Reform

To have an impact on the performance of the public sector, a reorganization or reform proposal must be able to gain a place on the public agenda. This is perhaps the least understood stage in the policy process, despite some important advances in conceptualization (Kingdom 1984; Walker 1977). For many of the reforms we have been discussing, however, getting on the agenda was not that difficult; they were (in principle if not in detail) a part of the commitment that politicians made when campaigning for office. Given the greater dedication of conviction politicians in many countries to their stated programs, the fact that proposals have been forthcoming is not surprising.

In addition, Grafton's (1984) analysis of the impact of "novelties" on reorganization argues that social, economic, and technical changes are principal driving forces behind change in government. He demonstrates this with an extensive analysis of change in the federal government of the United States. If this analysis is correct, then the economic showdown in the late 1970s can be seen as an anomaly sufficient to produce major reorganization and reform efforts by government. Although we can well understand how general pressures for change may have originated, the specific proposals appear to have come from a variety of sources.

One of the most obvious sources has been borrowing from the private sector. Having the public sector borrow administrative ideas from the private sector is an old story, and a number of the more rationalist reform ideas in the 1960s and 1970s were borrowed directly from industry—most notably PPBS. What may be different in the 1980s, however, is that as well as borrowing the techniques, governments have also been encouraged to borrow the ethos of "market forces" that accompanies the techniques. It remains unclear, however, just how market forces are able to provide managerial guidance for many of the programs in government. One might argue, in fact, that many are in government for the simple reason that they could not be managed effectively using those market forces.

Another set of reforms has been borrowed from other governments, either from different levels of government within a single country, or from governments of other countries. Take, for example, the idea embodied in the Grace Commission of having private-sector executives loaned to government to scrutinize management and make recommendations for cost savings. This was used in well over half the states in the United States and some cities before being adopted at the national level (Peters 1986). The idea was later exported to Canada (Wilson 1988). In most of the cases of reform we have been discussing the borrowing has been by the free will of the government involved, but countries in the Third World have not been as fortunate, having reforms such as program budgeting and later privatization thrust upon them as a condition of receiving aid (Premchand 1983).

In both the cases of borrowing from the private sector and borrowing from other governments, there is a strong possibility of "false learning." That is, the borrowing may be guided by false analogies and a failure to match carefully the conditions undergirding the reform, whether those be social, cultural, economic, political, or whatever (see Hall 1980). This is most clearly the case when ideas from the private sector are imported willy-nilly into the public sector, without the clear definition of output or success that would be available in the world of business. It may well also be the case for public-sector programs that do not conform to the cultural milieu into which they are being introduced, such as the example of privatization in Denmark given above. Thus, borrowing is easy but the clothes that are borrowed often do not fit the borrower as well as they did the lender.

Another source or reform might be termed "regression toward the mean." A number of the reforms discussed here and elsewhere involve moving along a continuum on which all political systems must be located. This is most obvious in the use of centralization or decentralization as reforms; all governments must have some sort of division of powers with subnational governments, and with the components of their own administrative apparatus. Often, then, reforms involve merely moving along that continuum, usually moving from a more extreme position to a less extreme position. What appears especially interesting, however, is that some proposed reforms in the 1980s involve moving from one extreme position to another. So, for example, if the British scheme contained in the Next Steps document is actually implemented, it will involve moving from a very centralized administrative structure in the ministries to a very decentralized structure of agencies.

Another important factor for promoting reforms and for getting them placed on the public agenda is having organizations in government with their primary responsibility to investigate management and produce proposals for improvement. This may be successful to some degree with specific task forces, such as Brownlow and Hoover in the United States, established for that purpose, but is more likely to be successful if there is a standing organization concerned with the structure of government and improvements in management. There is, of course, some danger here as an organization dedicated to change will find a large number of things that need changing, and we have few objective criteria (as in the private sector) of when a change is really required. There will need to be some balancing of the pressures for change, although the simple inertia of organizations may prove to be an effective counterweight for any pressures toward unwise reform.

Finally, we cannot dismiss the role of ideology in generating proposals for reform in government. Although for many politicians coming into office in the 1980s learning management from the private sector is something of an ideology in itself, other reforms have been generated from ideological commitments. Decentralization is a good example. It appears that in the political climate of the 1980s centralization or any other hierarchical control mechanism is readily dismissed in favor of decentralized systems more responsive to the environment. The relevant feature in that environment may be the market or it may be "the people." Interestingly, the decentralization strategy appears to be adopted as readily by the political left (Mitterrand) as by the political right.

In summary, although reform is a frequent topic of discussion around governmental circles, it is still rarely easy to move from that discussion stage to the stage of formal consideration. As with any exercise in agenda setting, the social condition in question (inefficiency? the budget deficit?) must be defined as a sufficient problem to require action. There appear to be more ideas for reform around than there is legislative time to adopt them. This may be fortunate in some ways, because too much change is disruptive and counterproductive. This is an often-used defense in organizational circles but it still contains a substantial element of truth (Hogwood and Peters 1983). What has been discussed here is a set of factors that can provide the system of government with some "sail" to counter the many anchors that existing organizations are all too willing to throw out to slow or stop the implementation of reforms.

B. From Agenda to Implementation

If we can provide some explanations for why proposals to reform government do reach institutional agendas for resolution and even adoption, we are still faced with the task of attempting to explain why some proposals might be implemented more successfully than others. The majority of research on implementation has been focused on implementing programs intended to affect the external environment of government—purposive goals in Mohr's (1973) analysis. Many of the same principles, however, that influence the implementation of service programs should also influence the implementation of reforms within government itself—reflexive goals. Even if that is the case, the problem is far from solved because, as Sabatier (1986) and O'Toole (1987) and many others have argued, the guidance supplied by implementation research for the design of public programs is disappointingly sparse. That literature provides a much better catalog of why things do not work than of how they can be made to work.

We might approach the problem of implementing reforms in government from the "bottom up," and consider that this is a problem of gaining adequate information and compliance from the lowest echelons of the organization, and from clients, prior to designing or attempting to design any organizational changes. We have already argued that there are several empirical and normative weaknesses in this approach (Linder and Peters 1987), in reference to purposive programs, and the difficulties encountered concerning governmental reforms would be more pronounced. If the intention of reforms in the public sector is to alter the manner in which government has been conducting its business—often in very fundamental ways—then depending upon existing patterns of organization and procedure for guidance would appear to be exactly the wrong thing to do. This should not be taken to mean that politically motivated reformers of the public sector are correct and that the status quo is fundamentally flawed. What it does mean is that if the premise of the reformer is that the status quo is indeed flawed, then understanding that status quo is only a preliminary step to implementing any desired reforms.

We could therefore rely more heavily on the alternative, "top-down" approach to implementation. This approach attempts to produce implementation of policies through the application of law and other authoritative instruments of government. While the usual caveats advanced by the "bottom up" school concerning the necessity of generating compliance beyond mere authority must be taken into account (Hjern 1982), still for reforms within the public sector itself this approach does appear to have greater promise. Public sector organizations have shown substantial capacity to resist reform and change, but they also at times have demonstrated extraordinary capacities to change in positive directions (Mazmanaian and Nienaber 1979). Thus, we might expect somewhat greater probabilities of implementing reforms in the public sector from the top down than we might expect outside of government. This would be especially true when the civil service is predominantly trained in law and has a legalistic conception of their role, as in Germany and Scandinavia. This does not, however, answer the question of which laws, when, and how. That may require an even more complex answer.

The simplest answer to the question of successful implementation is that we cannot know in advance, and that the research for effective reform in government is yet another "garbage can" (Cohen et al. 1972) in which problems and solutions find each other (or not) to some degree by serendipity. If, however, we want to enhance the probability of success of a particular reform, there are still some design steps that can be taken. Building on the relative successes and failures of reforms over the past several decades, some factors do emerge as central elements in successful reforms. Time is important in thinking about this question, and strategies that might have been effective in having reforms adopted when resources were more plentiful and the culture was more supportive of government are less likely to be effective in the 1980s.

Perhaps the most obvious idea of improving the probability of implementation is that the simplest ideas are often the most successful. Much has been written, for example, on the failures of PPBS in almost every public-sector setting into which it was introduced (Schick 1973; Wildavsky 1979). While this budgeting system was extremely appealing to an academic audience because of its reliance on rationality and the systems concept, once faded with the realities of government decision making, where rationality is expensive or just impossible because of competing goals, PPBS was capable of doing relatively little to alter the manner in which money was being allocated. Simpler reforms of the budgetary process, such as cash limits in the United Kingdom, have been more successful in actually producing change.

Following from the above point concerning simplicity, it appears that the appeal of a reform proposal is enhanced if it can be encapsulated in a relatively simple slogan or can be summarized with a simple concept. This would be true even if the reform itself involves a number of more complex implications for governance. Thus, some of the success of recent reforms in many governments attempting to make the public sector function more like the private sector (success being defined here as the successful implementation of procedures borrowed from industry rather than necessarily a successful "bottom line") is that there is a very readily explained rationale behind the changes. The reality may be much more complex, and scholars can point to any number of ways in which the public sector is *not* like the private sector, but the idea could still be marketed easily. A more complex rationale for change, which might in the end produce more real results, will have a more difficult time being adopted.

Another point, derived from the literature on reforming purposive policies rather than reflexive policies, is that *catalytic* controls are more likely to be effective than are *coercive* controls (Gormley 1987). That is, everything else being equal, it will be more effective to employ mechanisms that manipulate incentives than to employ techniques that attempt to use hierarchy and authority to generate change. Although appearing very similar, this advice is actually somewhat different from that offered by the "bottom up" school of implementation studies. The point here is not to allow the lower echelons of the organization, or the clients, to determine what the organization should do or what the policy should be. Rather, this is a choice to implement the changes decided upon in a less coercive manner. This may be especially important as governments have both developed more negotiating and bargaining styles in managing their own personnel, and attracted more professionally trained civil servants into government. These individuals would generally expect to have greater autonomy in their work than traditional civil servants, and would therefore resent attempts at the hierarchical imposition of reforms. It may well be that coercive or authoritative methods for implementing reforms simply will not produce the managerial results intended, while a carefully constructed set of incentives could. This may be even more the case because incentives can be altered and adjusted without the reform appearing to have "lost," while altering more coercive controls might be taken as a sign of weakness or capitulation to the organizational forces that almost inevitably will oppose change.

The intentions of the reform will also influence its likelihood of success. Salamon (1981b) and others have argued that efficiency as a goal for reorganization is unlikely to be achieved. Their argument is that the systemic factors constraining administration in the public sector are so influential that any great improvements in efficiency are unlikely. On the other hand, reorganization and other reforms can affect policy choices. The policy changes may come about for very mundane reasons, such as changing who interacts with whom, but they are achievable. Therefore, it would appear to make more sense to concentrate attention of achieving policy change through reorganization rather than chasing efficiency—the "will o' the wisp" (Miles 1978).

Finally, we would argue that comprehensive reforms, everything else being equal, would not be as successful as more piecemeal reforms. This would be true for two reasons. The first is that comprehensive reforms tend to be premised upon some sort of rationalist or theoretical basis, and if the underlying theory is shown to be wrong, then the entire reform program will also be flawed. Second, and perhaps more importantly, comprehensive reforms may be more threatening to organizations, employees, and clients than are piecemeal or increment reforms. Any change can be threatening to established interests in an organization (Hogwood and Peters 1983), but the greater and more fundamental the change, the more threatening it will be. Therefore, to the extent that reforms can be undertaken in pieces, or that large-scale reform programs can be made to appear smaller (through reasoning by analogy, phased implementation, etc.), they will be more likely to meet with success.

This brief catalog of possible explanations for the relative success of reorganization and reform proposals getting onto the public agenda, and then their relative success in implementation, has been far from definitive. However, there is as yet very little definitive information on the topic (Leemans 1976; Hult 1987). In particular, with respect to this chapter, we did not investigate the effects of the characteristics of individual organizations on either proposals for reorganization or success in reorganization and reform. There are any number of possible factors, including the nature of the work force, the clientele of the organization, and the age and status of the organization, that could influence the likelihood of attempted changes and their success.

What this catalog does point to more than anything else is the need for more detailed explication of the logic of reforming government, and the correlates of success in these efforts. We do believe that an initial step in that direction has been the development of this classificatory scheme for the proposals, although that may well require refinement and expansion. What does appear most certain in all is that the political leaders of most modern democracies will be cooperating in this scientific endeavor through their continuing efforts to make the public sector function "properly," or at least to make it function to suit themselves. This continuing activity will provide an ongoing laboratory for the investigation of reform and reorganization in the public sector.

ENDNOTES

1. This is true even when reforms are nominally guided by an academic theory (see Bobrow and Dryzek, 1987). Very often the theories are trivialized or stereotyped simply to do what the politician in question wants to do rather than providing the real guidance for the reform. This can be seen to some degree in contemporary reforms in New Zealand based on the public choice approach.
2. I can say this with more reason than most, having served as an outside "expert" in the review of a state government in the United States.

REFERENCES

Aberbach, J.D., Putnam, R.D., and Rockman, B.A. *Bureaucrats and Politicians in Western Democracies.* Harvard University Press, Cambridge, MA, 1981.

Allison, G.T. Public and private management: are they fundamentally alike in all unimportant respects. In *Current Issues in Public Administration* (F.S. Lane, ed.). St. Martin's Press, New York, 1986.

Aucoin, P. Contraction, managerialism and decentralization in Canadian government. *Governance 1*:144–161 (1988).

Baber, W.F. Privatizing public management: the Grace Commission and its critics. In *Prospects for Privatization* (S.H. Hanke, ed.). Academy of Political Science, New York, 1987.

Beam, D. New federalism, old realities: the Reagan administration and intergovernmental reform. In *The Reagan Presidency and the Governing of America* (L. Salamon and M. Lund, eds.). Urban Institute, Washington, DC, 1984.

Bekke, A.J.G.M. Private organizations and the state: mutual prisoners blocking de-bureaucratization. In *Limits to Government: Dutch Experiences* (I.T.M. Snellen, ed.). Kobra, Amsterdam, 1985.

Benda, P.M., and Levine, C.H. Reagan and the bureaucracy: the bequest, the promise, and the legacy. In *The Reagan Legacy: Promise and Performance* (C.O. Jones, ed.). Chatham House, Chatham, NJ, 1988.

Bobrow, D.B., and Dryzek, J.S. *Policy Analysis by Design.* University of Pittsburgh Press, Pittsburgh, 1987.

Butler, S., Sanera, M., and Weinrod, W.B. *Mandate for Leadership II: Continuing the Conservative Revolution.* Heritage Foundation, Washington, DC, 1984.

Caiden, G.E. The vitality of administrative reform. *International Review of Administrative Sciences 54*:331–357 (1988).

Campbell, C. *Governments Under Stress: Political Executives and Key Bureaucrats in Washington, London and Ottawa.* University of Toronto Press, Toronto, 1983.

Campbell, C., and Peters, B.G. *Organizing Governance: Governing Organizations.* University of Pittsburgh Press, Pittsburgh, 1988.

Campbell, D.T. Reforms as experiments. *American Psychologist 24*:409–429 (1969).

Cohen, M.D., March, J.G., and Olsen, J.P. A garbage can model of organizational choice. *Administrative Science Quarterly 17*:1–25 (1972).

Derlien, H.-U. Repercussions of government change on the career civil service in West Germany: the case of 1969 and 1982. *Governance 1*:50–78 (1988).

Doig, A *Corruption and Misconduct in Contemporary British Politics.* Penguin, Harmondsworth, 1984.

Downs, G.W., and Larkey, P.D. *The Search for Government Efficiency: From Hubris to Helplessness.* Random House, New York, 1986.

Drewry, G., and Butcher, T. *The Civil Service Today.* Blackwell, Oxford, 1988.

Dror, Y. *Policymaking Under Adversity.* Transaction, New Brunswick, NJ, 1985.

Duffy, H. Are civil servants 'all managers now'? *Financial Times* November 23 (1988).

Dunn, W.N. Reforms as arguments. *Knowledge: Creation, Diffusion, Utilization 3*:293–326 (1982).

Ericksson, B. Sweden's budget system in a changing world. *Public Budgeting and Finance 3*:64–80 (1983).

Fournier, J. *Le Travail Gouvernmental.* Dalloz, Paris, 1987.

Goodsell, C.T. The Grace Commission: seeking efficiency for the whole people? *Public Administration Review 44*:196–204 (1984).

Goodsell, C.T. *The Case for Bureaucracy*, 2nd ed. Chatham House, Chatham, NJ, 1985.

Gormley, W.T. Institutional policy analysis: a critical review. *Journal of Policy Analysis and Management 6*:153–169 (1987).

Grafton, C. Response to change: the creation and reorganization of federal agencies. In *Problems in Administrative Reform* (R. Miewald and M. Steinman, eds.). Nelson-Hall, Chicago, 1984.

Gray, A., and Jenkins, W.I. Accountable management in British central government: some reflections on the financial management initiative. *Financial Accountability and Management 2*:171–185 (1986).

Gustafsson, G. Local government reform in Sweden. In *Local Government Reform and Reorganization* (A.B. Gunlicks, ed.). Kennikat, Port Washington, NY, 1981.

Hadenius, A. *A Crisis of the Welfare State.* Almqvist and Wiksell, Stockholm, 1986.

Hall, P. *Great Planning Disasters.* Weidenfeld and Nicolson, London, 1980.

Hogwood, B.W., and Peters, B.G. *Policy Dynamics.* Wheatsheaf, Brighton, 1983.

Hood, C., and Schuppert, G.F. *Delivering Public Services in Western Europe.* Sage, London, 1988.

Hood, C., with Dunsire, A., and Thomson, L. Rolling back the state: Thatcherism, Fraserism and bureaucracy. *Governance 1*:243–270 (1988).

Hoskyns, J. Whitehall and Westminster: An outsider's view. *Parliamentary Affairs 36*:137–147 (1983).

Hult, K.M. *Agency Merger and Bureaucratic Redesign.* University of Pittsburgh Press, Pittsburgh, 1987.

Ingraham, P.W., and Peters, B.G. The conundrum of reform. *Review of Public Personnel Administration 8*:3–16 (1988).

Jenkins, K., Caines, K., and Jackson, A. *Improving Management in Government: The Next Steps* (Ibbs Report). HMSO, London, 1988.

Jones, G.W. The crisis in central-local government relations in Britain. *Governance 1*:162–183. (1988).

Kavanagh, D. Whatever happened to consensus politics? *Political Studies 33*:529–546 (1985).

Kavanagh, D. *Thatcherism and British Politics: The End of Consensus?* Oxford University Press, Oxford, 1987.

Keating, M. Does regional government work? The experience of Italy, France and Spain. *Governance 1*:184–209 (1988).

Kelman, S. The Grace Commission: how much waste in government? *Public Interest 78*:65–77 (1985).

King, A. Overload: problems of governing in the 1970s. *Political Studies 23*:284–296 (1975).

Kingdon, J.W. *Agendas, Alternatives and Public Policies.* Little, Brown, Boston, 1984.

Klein, R., et al. *Joint Approaches to Social Policy.* Cambridge University Press, Cambridge, 1988.

Kristensen, O.P. Privatisering: modernisering af den offentlige sektor eller ideologisk korstog. *Nordisk Administrativt Tidsskrift 65*:96–117 (1984).

Lane, J.-E. *Bureaucracy and Public Choice.* Sage, London, 1987.

Lane, J.-E. Evaluating service delivery. Paper presented at Finnish Academy of Management, Vaasa, Finland, 1988.

Lee, J.M. Financial management and the career service. *Public Administration 62*:2 (1984).

Leemans, A. *Managing Change in Government*, Martinus Nijhoff, The Hague, 1976.

Lepper, M. Internal structure of public offices. In *Public Administration in the Federal Republic of Germany* (K. König, H.J. von Oertzen and F. Wagener, eds.). Kluwer, Boston, 1983.

Levine, C.H. Organizational decline and cutback management. *Public Administration Review 38*:316–325 (1978).

Levine, C.H. *Managing Fiscal Stress: The Crisis in the Public Sector.* Chatham House, Chatham, NJ, 1980.

Likierman, A. Management information for ministers: the MINIS system in the Department of the Environment. *Public Administration 60*:127–142 (1982).

Linder, S.H., and Peters, B.G. Relativism, contingency and the definition of success in implementation research. *Policy Studies Review 7*:116–127 (1987).

March, J.G., and Olsen, J.P. *Political Institutions.* Free Press, New York, 1989.

Mazmanian, D.A., and Nienaber, J. *Can Organizations Change?* Brookings Institution, Washington, DC, 1979.

Mellbourn, A. *Bortom det Starka Samhellet.* Carlssons, Stockholm, 1986.

Metcalfe, L. The logic of public management. Paper presented at International Political Science Association World Congress, Washington, DC, August 29-September 1, 1988.

Metcalfe, L., and Richards, S. Raynerism and efficiency in government. In *Issues in Public Sector Accounting* (A. Hopwood and C. Tompkins, eds.). Oxford, Philip Allen, 1984.

Meyers, F. *La Politisation de l'Administration.* Institut International des Sciences Administratives, Brussels, 1985.

Midwinter, A. Local budget strategies in a decade of retrenchment. *Public Money and Management* 8:21–28 (1988).

Miles, R. Advice for a president bent on reorganization. *Public Administration Review 38*:155–162 (1978).

Milward, H.B., and Rainey, H.G. Don't blame the bureaucracy. *Journal of Public Policy 3*:149–168 (1983).

Mohr, L. The concept of organizational goal. *American Political Science Review 67*:470–481 (1973).

Muramatsu, M. Recent administrative developments in Japan. *Governance 1*:468–478 (1988).

Natchez, P.B., and Bupp, I.C. Policy and priority in the budgetary process. *American Political Science Review 67*:951–963 (1973).

Nathan, R.P., and Doolittle, F.C. *Reagan and the States.* Princeton University Press, Princeton, NJ, 1987.

Nelson, R.R. *The Moon and the Ghetto.* Norton, New York, 1977.

Netherlands Scientific Council for Government Policy. *A Reappraisal of Welfare Policy.* Netherlands Council, The Hague, 1983.

Niskanen, W. *Bureaucracy and Representative Government.* Aldine/Atherton, Chicago, 1971.

Nobelen, P. Kwijend Corporatisme en Stagnerende Verzorgingsstaat. In *Coproratisme en Verzoringsstaat* (T. Akkermans and P. Nobelen, eds.). University of Leiden, Leiden, 1983.

Olsen, J.P. The modernization of public administration in the nordic countries: some research questions. *Hallilnnon Tutkimus 7*:2–17 (1988).

O'Toole, L.J. Policy recommendations for multi-actor implementation: an assessment of the field. *Journal of Public Policy 6*:181–210 (1987).

Pelkmans, J., and van Nie, M. *Privatization and Deregulation: The European Debate.* European Institute of Public Administration, Maastricht, 1985.

Peters, B.G. State cost control commissions. Paper presented at Annual Meeting of the Midwest Political Science Association, Chicago, 1986.

Peters, B.G. *The Politics of Bureaucracy*, 3rd ed. Longman, New York, 1989.

Peters, B.G., and Heisler, M.O. Thinking about public sector growth. In *Why Governments Grow: Measuring Public Sector Size* (C.L. Taylor, ed.). Sage, Beverly Hills, CA, 1983.

Peters, B.G., and Hogwood, B.W. The application of population ecology models to the public sector. *Research in Public Administration 1* (in press).

Pfeffer, J. *Organizational Design.* AHM Publishers, Arlington Heights, IL, 1978.

Pollitt, C. *Manipulating the Machine.* George Allen and Unwin, London, 1984.

Pouvoirs. Special issue. Des fonctionnaires politises? (1987).

Premchand, A. *Government Budgeting and Expenditure Controls.* International Monetary Fund, Washington, DC, 1983.

Putnam, R.D. Institutional performance and political culture: some puzzles about the power of the past. *Governance 1*:221–242 (1988).

Rainey, H.G., Backoff, R.W., and Levine, C.H. Comparing public and private organizations. *Public Administration Review 36*:223–244 (1976).

Ridley, F.F. Politics and the selection of higher civil servants in Britain. In *La Poliltisation de l'Administration* (F. Meyers, ed.). Institut International des Sciences Administratives, Brussels, 1985.

Rigaud, J., and Delcros, X. *Les Institutions Administratives Françaises, les Structures.* Presses de la Fondation Nationale de Sciences Poliltiques, Paris, 1984.

Rose, R. *The Problem of Party Government.* Macmillan, London, 1974.

Rose, R. Maximizing tax revenue while minimizing political costs. *Journal of Public Policy 5*:289–320 (1985).

Rose, R., and Peters, B.G. *Can Government Go Bankrupt?* Basic Books, New York, 1978.

Rose-Ackerman, S. *Corruption: A Study of Political Economy.* Academic Press, New York, 1978.

Rothstein, B. *Den Socialdemokratiska Staten.* Studentlitteratur, Lund, 1986.

Sabatier, P. Top-down and bottom-up approaches to implementation research. *Journal of Public Policy* 6:21–48 (1986).

Salamon, L. Rethinking public management: third-party government and the changing forms of government actions. *Public Policy* 29:255–275 (1981a).

Salamon, L. Reorganization—the question of goals. In *Federal Reorganization: What Have We Learned?* (P. Szanton, ed.). Chatham House, Chatham, NJ, 1981b.

Savas, E.S. *Privatizing the Public Sector.* Chatham House, Chatham, NJ, 1982.

Savas, E.S. *Privatization: The Key to Better Government.* Chatham House, Chatham, NJ, 1987.

Schick, A. A death in the bureaucracy: the demise of federal PPB. *Public Administration Review* 33:175–180 (1973).

Schick, A. Micro-budgetary adaptations to fiscal stress in industrialized countries. *Public Administration Review* 48:523–533 (1988).

Schulman, P.R. *Large-Scale Policymaking.* Elsevier, New York, 1980.

Sears, D.O., and Citrin, J. *Tax Revolt—Something for Nothing in California.* University of California Press, Berkeley, 1982.

Seidman, H., and Gilmour, R. *Politics, Position and Power*, 4th ed. Oxford University Press, New York, 1986.

Simon, H.A. *Administrative Behavior.* Free Press, New York, 1947.

Ståhlberg, K. *Utvardering av en forvaltingsreform.* Åbo Akademy Press, Åbo, 1987.

Tarschys, D. Public policy innovation in a zero-growth economy: a Scandinavian perspective. In *Policy Analysis and Policy Innovation* (P.R. Baehr and B. Wittrock, eds.). Sage, London, 1981.

Tarschys, D. Curbing public expenditure: current trends. *Journal of Public Policy* 5:23–67 (1985).

Taylor, R. Thatcher takes Swedish lesson in bureaucracy. *Financial Times* November 23 (1988).

Taylor-Gooby, P. *Public Opinion, Ideology and State Welfare.* Routledge and Kegan Paul, London, 1985.

Timsit, G. *Administrations et Etats: Etude Comparée.* Presses Universitaires de France, Paris, 1987.

Toonen, T.A.J. Implementation research and institutional design. In *Policy Implementation in Federal and Unitary Systems* (K. Hanf and T.A.J. Toonen, eds.). Martinus Nijhoff, Boston, 1985.

Veljanovski, C. *Selling the State: Privatisation in Britain.* Weidenfeld and Nicolson, London, 1987.

Walker, J.L. Setting the agenda in the U.S. Senate. *British Journal of Political Science* 7:423–445 (1977).

Weaver, R.K. The politics of blame avoidance. *Journal of Public Policy* 6:371–398 (1986).

Weaver, R.K. *Automatic Government: The Politics of Indexation.* Brookings Institution, Washington, DC, 1988.

Wildavsky, A. A budget for all seasons: why the traditional budget lasts. *Public Administration Review* 38:501–509 (1979).

Wilenski, P. Administrative reform—general principles and the Australian experience. *Public Administration* 64:257–276 (1986).

Wilson, V.S. What legacy? The Nielsen Task Force program review. In *How Ottawa Spends, 1988/89: The Conservative Heading into the Stretch* (K.A. Graham, ed.). Carleton University Press, Ottawa, 1988.

Wolf, C. Jr. Market and non-market failures: comparison and assessment. *Journal of Public Policy* 7:43–70 (1987).

Yeatman, A. The concept of public management and the Australian state in the 1980s. *Australian Journal of Public Administration* 46:340–353 (1987).

Young, P. Privatization around the world. In *Prospects for Privatization* (S.H. Hanke, ed.). Academy of Political Science, New York, 1987.

46

Is Democracy a Substitute for Ethics?

Administrative Reform and Accountability

B. Guy Peters   *Department of Political Science, University of Pittsburgh, Pittsburgh, Pennsylvania*

I. INTRODUCTION

A central problem of the public bureaucracy is the problem of bureaucratic discretion. Even in the most clearly defined and legalistic administrative systems the individual administrator is granted a great deal of latitude for making decisions on his or her own (Lewis and Birkinshaw 1993; Hoff 1993). In most instances this discretion creates no real problem for the public; the public servant merely follows the law and/or has a reasonable ethical sense so the citizen is treated fairly. Indeed, there is some evidence (Lipsky 1980; Nilsson and Westerstahl 1997) that citizens, in their role as program clients, may be treated more than fairly, and that public servants can become advocates for their clients. In these cases it is citizens as in their role as taxpayers who may not fare so well when bureaucratic discretion is being applied. Of course, there are other cases in which actions by the police, tax authorities, immigration officials, and even doctors and teachers demonstrate very clearly the possibilities for the abuse of administrative discretion.

There are several well-established ways for political systems to cope with the problem of administrative discretion (see Hood 1998a). Some systems have attempted to develop a highly professionalized administrative corps which functions as a closed career system, with the assumption that the professional values will ensure appropriate behavior. Another strategy is to employ primarily lawyers, and to utilize legal training as a means of inculcating the desired norms into the public servants. Still other administrative traditions make use of a number of internal control devices that enforce accountability and attempt to prevent the exercise of much autonomy by public servants, even those at the very top of the administrative pyramids. Day and Klein (1986) point to a number of alternative ways to conceptualize accountability, as well as to the increasing complexity of the accountability relationships within modern government.

These methods for coping with the problem of administrative discretion rapidly resolve themselves into the familiar Friedrich vs. Finer debate (see Brehm and Gates 1999). Does any amount of formalized, external control defend the public against the public servant who has individual goals, or perhaps even wants to abuse his or her discretion? Or does it really cause damage to the professionalism of public servants to supplement the positive values of most bureaucrats with a goodly amount of oversight and external control? The obvious resolution of this debate is that it is premised on a false dichotomy and that administrative systems need both types of control, internal and external, if they are to function as most citizens would like. Even if the external controls are not really necessary, their existence helps to legitimize the system, assure the more skeptical citizen, and to "encourage" the few public servants who have not internalized a code of conduct.

Christopher Hood (1998b) provides another approach to understanding the problem of control in bureaucracy. Building on cultural theory, he argues that a "hierarchicalist" conception of public administration tends to focus attention on failures of administration that result from inadequate control from above, and excessive free-lance decision-making on the part of individual public servants. In this model the control appears to come from within the organization, but it could also be external. "Egalitarian" conceptions of public administration, on the other hand, are more concerned with the inherent *dysfunctions* of hierarchy, and the perceived need for greater individual initiative to prevent and correct those dysfunctions (see also Peters 1996:Ch. 3).

These positions concerning controlling discretion are well known, but are none the less important because of their familiarity. Indeed, it helps to be reminded of these on-going debates as governments are proceeding down roads of reform that appear to ignore questions of discretion and its control. The issues to be raised in this paper revolve around the effects of numerous recent reforms of the public sector that have tended to reduce both the hierarchical and the internalized controls over the bureaucracy (but see Hood et al. 1999). While these reforms may be motivated by desires to make administration both more efficient and more "user friendly," the outcomes may be less positive. In the process of producing change, some important questions of administrative control may have been ignored, or at least have been assigned a subsidiary position.

The need for imposing some form of control over the bureaucracy has not been forgotten entirely in the process of reform. Although some market-oriented reforms do appear to ignore accountability,[1] substituting the value of efficiency for equity and fairness (Self 1993), other strands of administrative reform have been concerned explicitly with creating new forms of accountability. One manifestation of that concern has been the explicit introduction of mechanisms of popular, democratic control over bureaucracy, these controls being conceptualized as substitutes for the internalized values of a professionalized civil service or for the internal controls of hierarchy (see Brehm and Gates 1994). The idea is that if representative democracy is not capable of exerting control, then more direct mechanisms can and should be substituted.

The alternative reaction has been to substitute partisan political controls for the ethical and hierarchical controls, assuming that those instruments also have some democratic legitimacy, and that they may be the only effective controls remaining in a less hierarchical public service (see Rouban 1997). The development of the "appointed state" in the United Kingdom, for example, has been a means by which political parties have sought to exercise control over organizations by the appointment of loyalist in key staff positions (Skelcher 1998). Even appointive positions that have been available to prime ministers or ministers for some time now appear to have become even more politicized, with the clear intention of using placement of people as means of controlling discretion.[2]

II. THINKING ABOUT CONTROL

The criterion of *responsiveness* is, to a great extent, replacing ideas of *responsibility* and *accountability* in the control of the public bureaucracy. These terms are often used interchangeably, but should be seen as implying rather different things about the control over bureaucracy. Accountability means simply having to render an account for one's actions, usually to parliament. Thus, in Westminster systems accountability is conceptualized in parliamentary terms, with the minister being (at least in principle) accountable for all the actions of his or her department (Aucoin, forthcoming). While emphasizing the importance of representative democratic controls over the bureaucracy, this form of accountability also tends to emphasize exposing failure and exceptions (often for political reasons rather than administrative reasons) rather than assessing the performance of the bureaucracy on a more regular basis. Further, this form of accountability tends to be very much ex post facto, with the deed to be exposed publicly already having been done.

The concept of responsibility, on the other hand, implies commitment on the part of officials to a set of ethical and legal standards. Responsible civil servants are expected to make most of their own decisions without close supervision, but to do so within a clearly defined legal and/or ethical principles. The control here is largely ex ante, with the internalized values of the public servant preventing malfeasance. Both responsibility and accountability imply that the focus of control over public administration resides largely at the elite level. In one instance the source of control is externalized, while in the other it is internalized, but in both citizens are left with their agents (elected or permanent public servants themselves) performing the important democratic task of exercising control over the public bureaucracy.

Responsiveness is a more manifestly democratic term, implying that the bureaucracy will respond to the demands of the public, perhaps as mediated through political elites of some sort. Responsiveness of administration here is conceptualized as being both to political leaders as well as more directly to the public at large. That is, the response of the administrator in a responsive mode may be to a member of parliament functioning as an advocate of a constituent's interest. When the response to parliament is in an accountability mode it tends to be to the institution as a whole, or perhaps to a committee, rather than to an individual member. Likewise, the purpose of that response to the politician tends to be different. One should note here that a responsive bureaucracy may not be responsible, and may encounter difficulties when held to account for its actions, given that those actions may serve more particular than general interests.

After describing the nature of the public sector reforms that have engendered the greater use of both democratic and political means of control, we will proceed to discuss the likely effects of these forms of control versus others. The basic argument is that political leaders are searching for some means of controlling the organizations within the public sector. These leaders have been elected to provide direction to government, but may find that they are being thwarted by the nature of the administrative system within which they are working. This does not imply venality on the part of the public service, or even the quasi-public organizations, so much as it implies an absence of levers that can be pulled to produce desired actions.

The administrative reforms in question have created a number of avenues for citizens to express their concerns about government, but fewer ways for them to exert effective control. In Christopher Hood's (1986) terms for describing policy instruments these democratic forms of control are useful "detectors" but tend to be less well suited as "effectors." Further the public themselves possess few effective mechanisms for producing appropriate actions by their governments. These mechanisms almost always depend upon the involvement of other, political actors in order to produce the required types of changes in behavior by public employees.

The second part of the argument is that these more overtly participatory mechanisms for control of bureaucracy may, to the extent that they are effective, actually generate somewhat perverse incentives for organizations in the public sector. Further, these forms of accountability may mis-specify the values that should be implemented by public sector organizations, and often may do so in a manner that is potentially destructive of important public sector values. This concern with the effects of reform certainly should not be taken as an argument against democracy, nor one against more open government. It should, however, be taken as an argument in favor of the use of internalized means of control where possible, or at least the coordinated use of both populist and professional forms of accountability. It should also be taken as some skepticism about the apparent efficacy of substituting seemingly participatory means for well-established professional means for policing and controlling administration.

III.   FORMS OF PARTICIPATORY CONTROL

To this point I have been going on at some length about mechanisms of participatory control over bureaucracies without specifying what empirical referents were intended by that statement. Another word that has been applied to some of the changes I have been describing as the "democratization" of control over the bureaucracy is the "consumerization" of policies. As we argued earlier (Hood et al. 1996), this phrase is itself extremely ambiguous. In both conceptualizations of change, however, there is an attempt to facilitate the public affected by government action in having greater influence over the policies that impact them.[3]

Participation as a means of bureaucratic control can be effective because there are relatively direct ways for the public to monitor poorly performing organizations and individuals within the public sector (see Klein and Schmalz-Bruns 1997). One of the more pervasive of these concepts has been that of the "citizens' charter" or, perhaps more appropriately, the "consumers' charter" (Bellamy and Greenaway 1995). In the United Kingdom that initial "populist" element in the accountability regimen has been followed by the Complaints Task Force, and elsewhere by even more populist conceptions of accountability. The assumption guiding these programs is that citizens (largely functioning in their role as consumers of public services) are capable of assessing the performance of many public organizations. It is further assumed that they are also capable of transforming those assessments into enforceable decisions about what government should do, and how it should do it.

An associated version of the democratization of control over the public bureaucracy is the creation of various user groups that function as virtual boards of directors for public sector organizations (see Jensen 1998; Adley et al. 1990). This form of control over service provision has been most apparent for policies such as education, social housing, and health care where there are numerous clients who want to, and indeed often now demand, to exert some greater control over the activities of service providers. The groups that function as the mechanisms of accountability may be elected from the clients, therefore having some direct democratic mandate for enforcing accountability over the providers, albeit at the same time excluding other citizens from some means of influence over the program.

There is another way in which democracy now comes into play in the control of administration, and this is through the use of political appointments to an increasing number of positions in government. As noted, number of components of contemporary administrative reforms have tended to "deinstitutionalize" bureaucracy, i.e., to reduce its conformity to rules and to change the meaning of public employment. For example, the internal deregulation of bureaucracies has shifted the focus from formalized rules for the system as a whole to more particularistic rules and procedures (see Peters 1996:Ch. 5). This change has meant, for example, that traditional civil service systems are devalued, and a variety of alternative forms of managing personnel are being implemented, permitting greater discretion on the part of the individuals making the appointments.

Another major aspect of this deinstitutionalization has been to move a good deal of implementation activity out of formal government organizations and to move it into either deconcentrated organizations or into quasi-private or private organizations. The former locus refers to organizations such as the "agencies" now a dominant (in personnel terms) and familiar part of British government. The latter refers to any number of options such as quangos, or increasingly entirely private organizations operating with contracts from government (Salamon 2000; Kettl 1988; Hogwood 1993). Both of these structural changes tend to reduce the capability of conventional means of accountability to function adequately, and create more patronage opportunities.

When using either less formal personnel systems or the decentralized organizations government may lose a good deal of its direct control over policy, and over the implementors of its policies. This loss of control is obviously evident when there is an increasing use of nongovernmental, or quasi-governmental, organizations as major implementors of policy. Indeed, much of the purpose of these reorganizations of the public sector has been to reduce the level of governmental control over organizations delivering public services to enable them to be more efficient and effective, following the dictates of the new public management (Hood 1991). The consequence of this change in organizational formats may be a loss of conventional accountability, or at least the need to rethink how accountability can be enforced.

The other format for deinstitutionalizing the public bureaucracy has been deregulation, or the loosening regulation of personnel systems and the elimination of many formal civil service requirements (Horner 1994). This strategy is also in part a mechanism for enabling government to emphasize managerialism, and presumably to enhance its efficiency. The argument implicit, or explicit, in these reforms is that traditional civil service laws have been straight jackets for managers, limiting whom they can hire and how they can motivate, and if necessary punish, their employees (DiIulio 1994). Likewise, an exclusive career civil service system closes government to the best possible talent, while the ability to move in and out make government a more attractive employer for some of the best talent.

The final means for deinstitutionalizing the bureaucracy is by the use of what the Canadians refer to as "citizen engagement," perhaps the most overtly democratic component of the changes mentioned here (see also Klein and Schmalz-Burns 1997). The purpose of citizen engagement is much like the consumerization of policy—to permit the public to have a direct impact over policy and administration. In terms of controlling the bureaucracy these mechanisms depend upon the public being able to identify malfeasance and nonfeasance on the part of the bureaucracy and then perhaps also having at its disposal the mechanisms for, at a minimum, beginning a process of rectification of problems.

The deinstitutionalization of public bureaucracies opens these reformed systems to greater patronage and to more over tampering with the administration of personnel. Positions that at one time might have been covered by merit appointments are now subject to direct political appointment. The assumption is that managerial values will be used to make these personnel decisions, and indeed in many cases that may be the case. There is, however, little to prevent other less desirable criteria from being applied in the selection of personnel. For example, Paul Light (1996) has described the "thickening" of the federal government in the United States, with more and more manifestly political appointees being placed in control positions over the permanent federal bureaucracy. Further, these appointments have tended not to be made at random, but rather have gone differentially to more politically sensitive departments and agencies (Ingraham, Thompson and Eisenberg 1995). This pattern indicates the clear interest of politicians to use these appointments as instruments of control over potential sources of embarrassment.

The United States has a long history of political appointments in the federal bureaucracy but there also appears to be increasing levels of political selection of personnel in other countries. For example, in European countries with a reputation for highly institutionalized public services and meritocratic values there are increasing uses of political appointees as means of exercising control over the public sector. Rouban (1998, 1997), for example, points to the increasing use of political appointments in France, and the desire to ensure that some form of accountability and control is thereby assured. In Scandinavia there is also an apparent increase in the number and influence of political appointments (Pierre 1998; Virtanen 1998). The list of cases of politicization could be extended rather easily, but the basic point remains that merit is being replaced, or at least supplemented, by political appointment. The principal purpose of this change in recruitment is exercising control and creating a form of accountability.[4]

It may be that the spoils system is, however, the only effective means of control available when some of the conventional forms of control have been eliminated or devalued. Although citizens in industrialized democracies have become accustomed to a more professionalized form of personnel management, the spoils system has been reintroduced as a means of selecting personnel. In some ways this may be a more democratic means of selecting personnel, given the well-known problems of ensuring that the civil service complies with the wishes of the elected government (Rose 1976).

IV. IMPACTS OF POLITICIZED ACCOUNTABILITY

For individuals raised and trained in the tradition of the merit system in industrialized democracies, there is an almost visceral reaction against the increased use of patronage appointments—the spoils system (see Hoogenboom 1968). In addition to this negative reaction, there may be more rational reasons for concern about the institutional changes described above. The use of the political mechanisms, whether direct or through partisan institutions, may introduce rather perverse incentives for participants in government, and produce a form of accountability that was not thought of when these changes in the public service were introduced.

In most institutionalized democratic regimes, the status of political controls—other than through parliament or ministers—over the bureaucracy is suspect. Most governments have invested a good deal of time and energy in ridding themselves of patronage and other forms of political involvement in administrative life, only to see them reemerge as a mechanism for control over public organizations when the traditional mechanisms have been weakened. Although we are reasonably sure we understand the implications of such a change in accountability systems, it may still be worth a brief discussion.

The use of these political controls is often seen by political leaders as a necessary step once some of the other mechanisms for enforcing accountability and control have been weakened, or even terminated through the reform process. This political need arises because although a public service may be delivered by a private organization, or perhaps by a quasi-public organization, to the average member of the public it remains a public service. Therefore, the minister who heads the ministry in question may be seen as the ultimate locus of responsibility. Thus, the minister may be perceived a being responsible over programs over which he or she has little real influence, an untenable political position.

V. CAN WE ESCAPE LAW AND FORMALIZED ACCOUNTABILITY?

To this point I have been engaged in something of a polemic concerning the populist, and democratic elements of contemporary administrative reforms, and the effects of those reforms on accountability regimes in contemporary political systems. There do appear to be some genuine problems if these democratic mechanisms are taken to the extreme, and if they are assumed to be the panacea for problems of accountability in democracies. This is especially true if the patronage mechanisms play a major role in defining accountability. We should, however, also recognize the resilience of ethical, and especially legal, mechanisms for imposing accountability in public administration in these same countries. While the populism is based on democratic and deinstitutionalizing premises about administration,[5] it also appears that the democratic elements often become translated into rights, and therefore easily can become justifiable. This movement towards creating rights is found despite numerous political attempts to enhance the discretionary character of many policies, especially social policies, and thereby to deny the entitlement basis of many benefits.

This transformation to rights can be seen in the experience of the Citizens' Charter in the United Kingdom, and to some extent in analogous charters in other political systems (see Fortin and Van Hassel, forthcoming). While charters may have begun simply by establishing appropriate standards of service for various public organizations, and by assuming a populist method of implementation, those standards are generally transformed from "appropriate" in a normative sense to "right" in a legal sense (Page 1999), and become in some instances justiciable. Further, control over bureaucracies appears to be becoming increasingly legal and judicialized. This is true even in the United Kingdom (Harlow 1997; but see Sainsbury 1994) which has had a relatively low level of judicial involvement in policy and administrative issues.[6]

Depending upon one's perspectives, this resilience on the part of more formalized modes of control over the bureaucracy is either the good news or the bad news. If one is a believer in the efficacy of populist forms of control, and the need to consumerize the public sector, then this is indeed bad news; well-intentioned populist methods are seemingly being captured and then converted to their own purposes by the more traditional political institutions. On the other hand, if one is more skeptical about the utility of the populist and politicized mechanisms for accountability then these evolving instruments for legal intervention are an important way of addressing the problems perceived in those nominally democratic mechanisms. Like so much else of importance in politics, the important issues here become those of perceptions.

VI. SUMMARY

This paper has attempted to demonstrate that despite the many virtues arising from administrative reforms, and especially from those reforms that have a participatory character, there are also some important negative consequences. The principal problem identified here is that of the potential loss of accountability, or the shift of the central focus of accountability from a broadly defined public interest to a more narrowly defined set of personal or group interests. Somewhat paradoxically reforms that have as at least one goal to open public administration to the public may in the end actually reduce the level of democratic accountability.

Of course, a large part of the reason that these very reforms have been undertaken is the perceived failings of the career bureaucracy to always supply the type of accountability that many citizens would like to see. We may laud professional ethics and norms in the abstract, but they may not have been so laudable in practice. What may be required, therefore, is some mixing of norms of professional conduct with political mechanisms that place some pressure on the enforcement of those norms. Finding the golden mean is usually a means of solving problems, especially problems arising from dichotomous choices. This appears yet another example.

ENDNOTES

1. In fairness, some of the market-based concerns with performance and quality do have elements of accountability, but not the procedural accountability with which the political system typically has been accustomed.
2. The politicization of the appointment of the director of the BBC in June 1999 is a clear case in point.
3. The obvious difference is that in one version the emphasis is on shaping general policy, while in the other the focus is on detecting and redressing maladministration at the implementation stage.
4. Elsewhere we distinguish between "traditional clientelism" and "managerial clientelism" (Dudek and Peters 1999) to make the point that although this may appear simply to be old fashioned "jobs for the boys and girls," the root causes may be importantly different.
5. Deakin (1994) refers to this as the "state and the citizen agenda" that had been fostered by the New Right.
6. The increased use of legalistic controls in the U.K. is in part a function of Europeanization, with the ECJ and the ECHR beginning to have real impacts.

REFERENCES

Adley, M., Patch, A., and Tweedie, J. (1990). *Parental Choice and Educational Policy.* Edinburgh: University of Edinburgh Press.

Aucoin, P. (Forthcoming:) Accountability and performance. In B.G. Peters and D.J. Savoie (eds.), *Revitalizing Governance.* Montreal: McGill/Queens University Press.

Brehm, J., and Gates, S. (1994). When supervision fails to induce compliance. *Journal of Theoretical Politics 6,* 323–344.

Brehm, J., and Gates, S. (1999). *Working, Shirking and Sabotage: Bureaucratic Response to a Democratic Public.* Ann Arbor: University of Michigan Press.

Budge, I. (1997). *The New Challenge of Direct Democracy.* Oxford: Polity.

Chapman, R.A. (1994). *Ethics in the Public Service.* Edinburgh: University of Edinburgh Press.

Day, P., and Klein, R. (1986). *Accountabilities.* London: Tavistock Press.

Deakin, N. (1994). Accentuating the apostrophe: the citizen's charter. *Policy Studies 15,* 46–58.

DiIulio, J.J. (1994). *Deregulating Government.* Washington, DC: Brookings Institution.

Dudek, C.M., and Peters, B.G. (1999). Clientelism in cold climates: the changing forms of political involvement in the bureaucracy. Unpublished paper, Department of Political Science, University of Pittsburgh.

Hoff, J. (1993). Medborgskap. brugerrolle og makt. In J. Andersen et al. (eds.), *Medborgskap, demokrati og politisk deltagelse.* Herning: Systime.

Hogwood, B.W. (1993). Restructuring central government: the 'next steps' initiative. In K.A. Eliassen and J. Kooiman (eds.), *Managing Public Organizations,* 2nd. ed. London: Sage.

Hondeghem, A. (1998). *Ethics and Accountability in a Context of Governance and New Public Management.* Amsterdam: IOS Press.

Hood, C. (1986). *The Tools of Government.* Chatham, NJ Chatham House.

Hood, C. (1991). A public management for all seasons? *Public Administration.*

Hood, C. (1998a). Remedies for misgovernment: changing the remedies but not the ingredients. In A. Hondeghem (ed.), *Ethics and Accountability in a Context of Governance and New Public Management.* Amsterdam: IOS Press.

Hood, C. (1998b). *The Art of the State: Culture, Rhetoric and Public Management.* Oxford: Oxford University Press.

Hood, C., James, O., and Jones, G. (1999). *Regulation Inside Government: Waste Watchers, Quality Police and Sleaze Busters.* Oxford: Oxford University Press.

Hood, C., Peters, B.G., and Wollmann, H. (1996). Sixteen ways to consumerize the public sector. Public Money and Management 25.

Hoogenboom, A. (1968) *Outlawing the Spoils: A History of the Civil Service Reform Movement, 1865–1883.* Urbana: University of Illinois Press.

Ingraham, P.W., Thompson, J.R., and Eisenberg, E.F. (1995). Political management strategies and political/career relationships. *Public Administration Review 55,* 263–272.

Jensen, L. (1998). Cultural theory and democratizing functional domains: the case of Danish housing. *Public Administration 76,* 117–139.

Kettl, D.F. (1988). *Government by Proxy: (Mis)managing Federal Programs.* Washington, DC: CQ Press.

Klein, A., and Schmalz-Burns, R. (1997). *Politische Beteilung und Buergerengagement in Deutschland.* Bonn: Bundeszentrale fuer politische Bildung.

Lewis, N., and Birkinshaw, P. (1993). *When Citizens Complain.* Buckingham: Open University Press.

Light, P.C. (1996). *Thickening Government: The Federal Government and the Diffusion of Responsibility.* Washington, DC: Brookings Institution.

Lipsky, M. (1979). *Street-Level Bureaucracy.* New York: Russell Sage.

Nilsson, L., and Westerstahl, J. (1997). Representiv demorati. In S. Jonsson et al. (eds.), *Decentraliserad valfardsstad.* Stockholm: SNS.

Page, A. (1999). The new administrative law, the citizen's charter and administrative justice. In M. Harris and M. Partington (eds.), *Administrative Justice in the 21st. Century.* London: Hart.

Peters, B.G. (1996). *The Future of Governing.* Lawrence: University Press of Kansas.

Pierre, J. (1998). Depolitisee, repolitisee ou simplement politique? La bureaucratie suedoise. *Revue francaise d'administration publique 86*(avril-juin), 301–310.

Rose, R. (1976). *The Problem of Party Government.* London: Macmillan.

Rouban, L. (1997). *La Fin de Technocratie.* Paris: PFNSP.

Rouban, L. (1998). La politisation des fonctionnaires en France: obstacle ou necessite? *Revue francaise d'administration publique 86*(avril-juin), 167–182.

Sainsbury, R. (1994). Internal reviews and the weakening of Social Security claimants' rights of appeal. in G. Richardson and H. Genn (eds.), *Administrative Law and Government Action.* Oxford: Clarendon Press.

Salamon, L.M. (2000). The analysis of policy tools. In L.M. Salamon (ed.), *Handbook of the Tools Approach to Public Policy.* New York: Oxford University Press.

Skelcher, C. (1998). *The Appointed State: Quasi-Governmental Organizations and Democracy.* Buckingham: Open University Press.

Self, P. (1993). *Government by the Market?* Boulder, CO: Westview.

47

Environmental Policy in the Balkans

The Albanian Experience

Constantine P. Danopoulos   *Department of Political Science, San Jose State University, San Jose, California*

Andrew C. Danopoulos   *College of Social Sciences, University of California at Davis, Davis, California*

Filip Kovacevic   *Department of Political Science, University of Missouri–Columbia, Columbia, Missouri*

I. INTRODUCTION

The violent disintegration of Yugoslavia and the carnage in Bosnia that followed helped focus public and scholarly attention on a vital but largely neglected area of the world: the Balkan peninsula. An ever-proliferating number of academic as well as more narrative-oriented works appeared seeking to fill the void and shed light on the causes, effects, and implications of the crises in the area. A concerted effort has been made to analyze and understand the political, economic, and social transition unleashed by the collapse of Communist regimes in the Balkans as well as other countries of the former Eastern bloc.

Preoccupation with more immediate concerns has left little time to the new and ever-swelling ranks of Baklanologists to examine other important aspects of life on the peninsula. One of the most neglected areas is the environment. This is an effort to fill a small part of the void by examining the specifics of the Albanian case. The Land of Eagles, as Albania is known in folklore tradition, shares many social, political, and economic characteristics, as well as environmental problems, with its Balkan neighbors. Albania is also unique in that until the fall of the Communist regime in 1991, it was considered one of the most isolated and xenophobic countries in the world.

The following pages will summarize Albania's environmental record and will discuss, analyze, and evaluate the efforts of the Albanian state to deal with the nation's environmental problems. There is a scarcity of scholarly work on Albania. This paper is based on whatever little data can be gleaned from such sources as well the lead author's on-site observations and interviews when he visited the country a few years ago. Those interviewed included then President Sali Berisha, his national security adviser Adem Chopani, Professor Gramoz Pashko, and other government officials and academics.

II. FROM INDEPENDENCE TO WORLD WAR II

Myriad geographic, historical, geopolitical, religious, and other factors contributed to render the Balkan peninsula one of Europe's most ethnically heterogeneous, politically unstable, isolated, and undeveloped regions. As a result, independence arrived late, state formation and consolidation faced enormous difficulties, and industrialization and economic development lagged behind the rest of the continent. In turn, these factors delayed awareness and efforts to arrest environmental degradation, even though signs of human damage to the area's ecological system appeared as early as other parts of Europe, if not earlier. For example, deforestation of the once forest-covered mountains surrounding Athens, Tirana, Skopje, Sarajevo, and other parts of the peninsula could be considered as the first and most noticeable sign of environmental damage. Ironically, the very word "Balkans" derives from the Turkish term for wooded mountains. Today the visitor would have to stretch his vision to catch a glimpse of green around Athens, Istanbul, Tirana, or other once-lush areas.

Albania's experience matches closely the situation just outlined. Nationalism coupled with parochialism and strong clan attachments characterize the Land of Eagles. As descendants of the Illyrians, the Albanians have one of Europe's oldest traditions. Nevertheless, they were among Europe's last groups to achieve national independence and statehood. These did not come until 1913.

Owing to its strategic location and mineral resources, Albania was occupied by a number of great empires prior to 1913. The kingdom of Illyria was subdued by the Romans in 167 B.C., but when the Roman Empire was divided in A.D. 395, Albania fell under the jurisdiction of the Eastern Empire. It remained a Byzantine province until the 1450s, when the Ottoman Turks overran Constantinople and dissolved the already weakened empire.

Albania's largely Christian population converted to Islam to take advantage of lower taxes levied against Muslims in the multireligious Ottoman Empire. As the economic fortunes of the Ottoman Empire declined, the Porte increased taxes and imposed compulsory military service, all of which alienated the local population and gave rise to an Albanian national movement. Although the 1878 Prizren (a city in contemporary Kosovo) uprising failed, it had the effect of making the great powers aware of the "Albanian question."

Taking advantage of the 1912 Young Turk Revolution and the turmoil that followed, the Albanians rose up again, and with great power encouragement and diplomatic support forced the Ottoman authorities to allow the creation of an autonomous Albanian state in 1912. While Italy, Austria-Hungary, and Russia were debating the new entity's frontiers and future, neighboring Balkan states, which had long-held claims on Albanian territory, overran it. President Woodrow Wilson's decisive intervention saved the new state from dismemberment, and the Conference of Ambassadors (1921) finally settled the Albanian question.

The new state faced enormous economic, social, and political difficulties. Half of its arable land belonged to great estates; infrastructure, industry, and modern communications facilities were virtually nonexistent. The country's overwhelmingly rural population was largely illiterate and in revolt. Parochialism ran supreme, and clannishness and clan activities thwarted efforts to end anarchy and establish a semblance of political stability.

Before independence, much of Albania was an environmentally pristine, bucolic, but very poor land. Derel Hall states.

> Game-shooting [there] was much easier than in the other areas of the Balkans. . . . Mixed shooting along the whole coast was reported to being available—partridges, pheasant, snipe, quail, hare—with the best of woodcock, boar and roe deer being available between October

and December. . . . The whole seaboard and river mouths offered "splendid chances." Trout was abundant in the streams running into the Shkoder and Ohrid lakes.[1]

Environmental hazards were not totally absent, though. Severe shortage of employment opportunities coupled with population expansion led to increased sheep and goat herding, which resulted in overgrazing, deforestation, and soil erosion. In addition, lack of fuel for cooking and other household purposes also contributed to tree cutting and deforestation which, in turn, caused soil erosion and river and lake pollution. The country's most environmentally degraded area was the Myzeqe Plain which is located in the southwestern part of Albania. As early as 1920, Austrian geographer G. Veith described Myzeqe as "a desolate wasteland covered with spreading water areas and impassable swamp forests . . . inundated in winter and dried up in summer."[2]

Dean S. Rugg blames the deterioration of the plain in the exploitive Turkish land tenure system, which forced peasants to leave the fields uncultivated and to move into mountain areas, as well as land misuse which had begun in antiquity. Rugg had this to say about Myzeqe's condition before World War I:

> The cycle of deterioration included overcutting and overgrazing followed by loss of soil from the steep, bare slopes during winter rains; this transported sediment then filled the beds of the main streams as their gradients were radically reduced on reaching the plain; and the result was flooding, swamp conditions, and malaria. The deposits of the Shkumbin, Seman, and Vijose rivers eventually expanded the plain outward into the sea.[3]

Although cancer and cardiovascular diseases were rare, the country's population, especially in rural areas, suffered from a multitude of other disease. Tuberculosis was widespread among Muslim women, syphilis and intestinal parasites were common, undernourishment was everywhere, and mortality was high in many parts of the country. Malaria, anthrax, and other epizootic diseases were also endemic in river valleys and coastal plains, especially around Myzeqe.

Ahmet Zogu, a wealthy Muslim bey who represented the interests of the country's landlords and clan leaders, assumed power in 1924 and managed to impose a semblance of authority. Three years later Zog proclaimed himself Zog I, King of the Albanians. Facing monumental foreign and domestic problems, Zog was forced to give in to Italian pressure. Albania became an Italian satellite. Zog's rule came to an end in April 1939, when Mussolini's armies invaded and annexed the Land of Eagles.

Zog's years brought some political stability, but the country's economic conditions saw little improvement. With Italian help, the Hotel Dajti, a few other buildings, and some roads were built. Trees were also planted along the main boulevards of Albania's capital, Tirana, a dusty town of about 30,000 inhabitants. A Rockefeller Institute–organized effort was made an attempt to drain some marshlands. These projects did little to improve public health and land conditions, or alter the exploitive mode of land ownership. In 1933, for example, Albania's underfunded and understaffed Directorate of General Health reported that one-fourth of the population suffered from malaria. Even though the Rockefeller-funded marshland project appeared to have reduced malaria somewhat, it resulted in the destruction of a number of wetland habitats.[4]

The interwar period saw much deforestation and wood cutting. Derek Hall documents that "many forest areas, containing all of the best European hardwoods as well as conifers, had been devastated by reckless cutting for fuel or charcoal burning. Walnut had almost disappeared. . . . Preservation and planting had not been considered."[5] An Austrian botanist visiting the area in the mid-1930s wrote: "One notices how hard this pitiless deforestation makes the outlines of the hills, as if they had been cut out of cardboard." The visitor also observed that the newly built roads were used by the highlanders "chiefly to aid in their deforestation [activities]."[6]

III. ENVIRONMENT UNDER COMMUNISM: 1945–1991

The Italian occupation of Albania lasted until their surrender in September 1943; they were succeeded by the Nazis. Three separate liberation groups emerged, united in their opposition to occupation but with widely different political views. The liberation forces spent more time fighting one another than the occupiers. The better-organized and disciplined left, led by the Albanian Communist Party, which later became known as the Albanian Party of Labor (APL), favored a Soviet-style people's republic. They collaborated with Josip Broz Tito's Partisan movement in neighboring Yugoslavia. When liberation arrived, the Communists, headed by Enver Hoxha, reached power through the sword and did so without Soviet assistance. Hoxha and his colleagues swiftly liquidated their opponents and established a Marxist-Leninist regime along the line of the Soviet prototype which lasted until the early 1990s.

Though Communist, the Hoxha APL was inspired by strong nationalist sentiments. They regarded their conservative opponents at home as reactionaries and puppets of foreign powers. Albania's troubled history lent credibility to their position. Under the circumstances, it did not take long for Hoxha and his group to break with their close wartime ally, Tito, whom the Tirana regime perceived as seeking to expand Belgrade's influence on Albania. Hoxha purged the pro-Yugoslav elements within the APL, and Tirana quickly joined the Soviet-dominated Council of Mutual Economic Assistance and later the Warsaw Pact. In a very short time, Albania became a full-fledged Soviet satellite.

The Tirana-Moscow honeymoon lasted 12 years (1948–1960). But the nationalistic and ideologically rigid Hoxha regime ultimately found itself in disagreement with the Soviet Union and broke with Moscow. At this point, Albania's xenophobic leaders turned their eyes toward Mao's China. The Albanian-Chinese love affair lasted longer (1961–1978) than previous engagements the Hoxha regime had entered into. During this period, Beijing provided some financial and technical assistance, and a number of mutual visits involving civilian and military personnel took place. In actuality, the relationship this partnership never had the depth that previous ones had. Few Albanians learned Chinese—in sharp contrast with respect to Russian, which Albanians were taught even after the Soviets were long gone.

Growing disagreements as well as the Albanian leadership's xenophobia brought this strange relationship to an end. After 1967, self-reliance "became one of the most dominant themes of Albanian propaganda."[7] This fortress mentality outlived Hoxha's death in 1985, despite the modest efforts of his hand-picked successor, Ramiz Alia, to end the country's isolation. Together, Albania, North Korea, and perhaps Mongolia earned the dubious distinction of being the most hermetically isolated and closed societies in the world. Its economy was and remains the poorest in all of Europe.

Despite the break with the Soviet Union and later with China, Albania's economy retained its Stalinist centralized characteristics to the very end. Like other Marxist-Leninist regimes, the APL regime collectivized agriculture, emphasized the development of heavy industry, and forbade private initiative. There were some notable achievements. The Myzeqe and other swamps were drained and some of the country's rivers were dammed. As a result, cultivable acreage increased and Albania became self-sufficient in electrical power. The policy of self-reliance, coupled with Draconian restrictions on telephone or other forms of contact with the outside world (including watching foreign television or reading foreign literature) and prohibition against any form of foreign borrowing, all but eliminated commercial activity in or out of Albania.

More so than in other Eastern bloc counties, consumerism and individual liberties received very low priority. Ownership of private automobiles was illegal, foreign travel in and out of the country was severely restricted, and expression of religious beliefs was forbidden. Albania became the world's first officially atheist state. In this "Mediterranean gulag" of fewer than 2 million people, enforcement was stringent, justice was swift, and the much-feared and ever-present secret police, the Sigurimi, brooked no dissent. Violators or would-be violators and their families were treated harshly; internal exile, forced labor, and executions were common. For example, it is estimated that between 1955 and 1966, over 80,000 people were arrested; 16,000 of them died in prison. Things got ever harsher in the late 1960s and 1970s.[8]

Despite the fact that Albania's constitution stipulated that each citizen had a responsibility to protect the country's environment, Albania, like other Marxist-Leninist countries, suffered considerable environmental damage during the period of Communist rule. Concentration on heavy industry, along with isolation, self-reliance, minimal pollution control, antiquated equipment and technology, poor quality of solid fuels, and lack of government and managerial interest in environmental protection were among the many culprits. Owing to severe restrictions on private automobile ownership—coupled with the country's agrarian, poor, and consumer-weak society—Albania's environmental degradation was more latent and did not reach the near catastrophic levels associated with other Communist countries, like Poland, Romania, or Czechoslovakia. Nevertheless, the country's air, soil, drinking water, rivers, lakes, and work environment experienced considerable deterioration.

The major source of atmospheric pollution included the many antiquated, poorly constructed, and inefficient chemical, metallurgical, and thermal power plants. Constructed in or near major population centers, these industrial enterprises emit large quantities of carbon dioxide, sulfur, soot, nitrogen oxide, and other harmful gasses, solid particles, and other polluters. The situation is aggravated by the fact that most major Albanian towns are built in valleys and river basins surrounded by high mountains which trap pollutants. Using a variety of sources, including his own observations, Hall lists 16 types of industrial pollutants, the type of activity they perform, and the amount and type of pollution they emit.[9] Located in over 25 cities and scattered around the country, these plants were built with inferior and outdated domestic, Soviet, or Chinese technology. The overwhelming majority of them operate on poor-quality oil, low-grade coal, or other solid fuels; their belching chimneys did not and do not have even the most elementary flue filters.

The Elbasan metallurgical combine, Albania's largest industrial plant, was a case in point. Construction was begun by the Chinese but was delayed by the breakup of relations between the two countries. The complex was completed during the height of self-reliance. Using "obsolete technology [and] machinery and other equipment produced in the plant's own engineering works," the Elbasan combine is totally bereft of environmental provisions. As such,

> Atmospheric pollution is poured into the surrounding Bradshesh valley, encompassing forests with huge quantities of carbon monoxide, sulphur ashydrite, sulphur dioxide, cyanic acid, ammonia, phenol, cyanuric acid, dusts and soot ashes produced. Thirty-five million cubic meters of effluent have been discharged into the Shkumbin river annually, including 180t of ammonia, 1.2t phenols, 450t sulphates, 6t cobalt, 3t copper, 1.2t magnesium, 1.6t cyanide, and 1.5t zink. Most of the river's water is used for irrigation in the Elbasan and Durres districts, causing contamination of land and of the food produced.[10]

In addition to environmental degradation, these plants are characterized by poor working environments. Airborne pollution (especially in chemical and textile mills), exposed machinery, wet floors, excessively high noise levels, poorly constructed scaffolding, and other work-related hazards prevailed in Albanian industrial plants. Protective devices—such as helmets, ear plugs, and masks—are almost totally absent in all sectors of Albanian industry. The Chinese-built Berat textile mill is a case in point. Its faulty design, old equipment, and ineffective extractor facilities have created severe health hazards. Isolation and lack of foreign exchange also caused severe shortages in agricultural machinery and replacement parts. This forced workers to cannibalize parts, and frequently to operate faulty, dangerous, and polluting equipment.

The destruction of vegetation by acid rain is another byproduct of industrial pollution. In the Rubik, Kukes, and Ballsh areas, for example, acid rain spewed by petrochemical, copper-smelting, and cement plants has caused considerable damage to vegetation and olive trees. Wood-burning stoves, especially in rural areas, and the use of charcoal and coal for house heating and other domestic needs, coupled with clouds of dust from unpaved streets and debris of nonbiodegradable polythene used for hothouses, vehicle covering, and other purposes, add to the problem.

Seawater and freshwater contamination is another major environmental and public health problem. The sources of water contamination are multiple. Windborne polythene pieces end up in rivers, lakes, and irrigation canals, causing water and beach pollution; they also clog canals. The use of ammonium and highly toxic pesticides for agricultural purposes poses considerable water contamination as do leaky sewer pipes and lack of water and waste treatment facilities. In addition to ammonia, arsenic, and nitrates from the nearby Fier fertilizer plant, the Seman river "receives . . . an estimated 14 barrels per day of petroleum seepage from the poorly maintained oil wells scattered across arable cultivation." Hall further observes, "The lower reaches of many streams and rivers in the central part of the country already appear to be organically dead."[11] Overpumping increased the level of salinity in the nation's lakes and rivers. All these, in turn, wreaked havoc on Albania's flora, vegetation, and aquatic and fauna life.

Soil also suffered considerable damage due to salination and erosion. Scientists have observed soil salination on the Myzeqe Plain and other drained marshes. The few data that have been collected have not given scientists enough information to determine the exact level of salinity; nevertheless, soil salination appears to be increasing rather rapidly. During the height of isolation and self-reliance, the Hoxha regime opened for cultivation large portions of virgin land. Under the slogan "Let us take to the hills and mountains to make them as beautiful and as fertile as plains," the regime urged terracing and cultivation of hillsides. But the topsoil on these hillsides was "too shallow and the scrub too fragile for working."[12] This, along with rapidly increasing deforestation in the late 1980s and early 1990s, led to significant soil erosion.

Finally, the more than 300,000 bunkers built by the paranoid Communist regime to protect Albania from American and/or Soviet invasion added to the problem of soil contamination. Built in the middle of wheat fields, by the beach, on hillsides, and everywhere else, these costly and strategically useless concrete pillboxes occupy valuable space and interfere with land cultivation and harvest.

Despite some efforts aimed at protecting rare animals, birds, and plants, and provisions in the Constitution to protect the environment, the Albanian Communist regime's environmental record was very weak. A few additional and largely token efforts were made in the late 1980s, including the establishment of the Central Commission for the Protection of the Environment. But these efforts received little backing from the authority that counted, the APL.

However, in December 1987, a little over two years after Hoxha's death, Albania participated in a conference on Balkan ecology in Sofia, Bulgaria. The conference accomplished little. A weak joint was issued in which Balkan states agreed to exchange information on the environment. Nevertheless, Tirana's participation signified that Albania was coming out of its self-imposed isolation and showed willingness to rejoin the world.

IV.   THE POST-COMMUNIST RECORD

The winds of democratization that swept the Communist regimes in Eastern Europe and the Soviet Union eventually reached distant Albania. Political opposition surfaced in early 1990, which set in motion a process that culminated with the victory of the Democratic Party in the March–April 1992 elections. The APL was soundly defeated and Albania acquired a democratically elected government for the first time in its history. Headed by President Sali Berisha, the new government took over a country in profound crisis. The economy was in a state of near collapse. Industrial production was down by almost 80% and agriculture was not far behind; people by the thousands were leaving the country in search of employment. If this were not enough, the disintegration of neighboring Yugoslavia and the ensuing crisis on the peninsula added to the new Albanian government's long list of domestic and foreign policy problems.

The new regime moved to privatize agriculture and other sectors of Albania's economy, create a legal framework, introduce new modes of social relationships, and establish new—and one hopes democratic and legitimate—political institutions. To keep the country afloat and to start up its economy, Berisha and his ministers traveled the world in search of financial and other forms of aid. Although the record is mixed, the government's efforts met partial success. Remittances from Albanians working in Greece, Italy, Germany, and other European countries as well as Canada and the United States have brought a slight improvement in living standards. Land privatization increased food production, but Albania's obsolete industrial sector remains largely idle. Unemployment or underemployment is estimated as high as 60% of the work force while per-capita income remains well below $1000 per year. For example, the August 1, 1997, issue of *The Chronicle of Higher Education* reports that university faculty salaries range from $45 to $125 per month.[13]

As far as the environment is concerned, the Berisha government submitted and parliament enacted legislation aimed at addressing the country's air, water, soil, and work environment-related pollution. However, very little if any of it has been implemented owing to the country's severe and ongoing economic crisis. Since the 1990s, some aspects of Albania's environment have improved while others have deteriorated, although the government per se played only a small role on behalf of the nation's ecology.

Ironically, the virtual shutdown of the country's industrial sector has reduced water pollution. Hall quotes a conversation with an Albanian environmental expert who stated in 1993:

> With industrial closures . . . rivers and coasts were revealing . . . a noticeable improvement in water quality. To the north of Durres, for example, identification of the first hermit crab was a significant indicator of improving biodiversity.[14]

The same factors account for air quality improvement in other parts of the country with heavy industrial concentration. Industrial closures are also responsible for similar improvements in neighboring Yugoslavia and Macedonia. For example, water in the Sava and Vardar rivers is noticeably cleaner than five or six years ago and some aquatic life has reappeared.

These improvements, however, have been offset by deteriorating conditions in other sources of pollution or the appearance of new polluters. Worsening conditions in the countryside prompted thousands of rural Albanians to migrate to large cities, especially Tirana, aggravating the chronic housing shortage and putting additional strain on already weak water and sewage facilities. As a result, the supply of water has become more erratic and leaky water and sewer pipes have created serious contamination. Archaic and badly maintained oil facilities continue to damage Albania's soil and underground water supplies. Very little has been done to address salination and soil erosion problems which have been aggravated by the widespread deforestation and tree cutting that took place during the chaotic 1990–92 transition period.

Housing shortages have prompted many poor Albanians to convert many of the concrete bunkers into living quarters. Without running water and sanitation facilities the areas around these bunkers have become cesspools of contamination and disease. The financially strapped Berisha administration was unable or unwilling to have these monstrosities removed.

In addition, with the legalization of private ownership of automobiles, smog-related pollution has entered the picture. Many Albanians who fled abroad in search of employment return home from Western European countries behind the wheel of recently acquired vehicles. These mostly aged cars are poorly serviced due to lack of replacement parts and money, and burn low-grade gasoline. Narrow and inadequately maintained roads add to the problem. As a result, Albanian cities are choked in automobile emission and clouds of dust, and the countryside is littered with broken motor vehicles abandoned by their owners.

Finally, like other East European and third world countries, Albania became a dumping ground of toxic waste emanating from Western European countries, mainly Germany. Hall reports that during the height of political upheaval (1991 into early 1992), more than 600 tons of East German-produced highly toxic pesticides were shipped to Albania by Schmidt-Cretan, a joint venture between a Hanover-based waste contractor and an Albanian toy company. The shipment was billed as "humanitarian aid for use in agriculture," but contained pesticides banned from the German market. Hall further reports that Albanians emptied out the content and used the barrels for food and water storage. Additional shipments containing organoclorides and herbicides arrived often in damaged and leaky barrels. Although the German and Albanian governments announced steps to control future shipments, widespread corruption and the desperate state of the country's economy made control enforcement very difficult, indeed.[15] The situation worsened with the recent, and in some respects ongoing, state of anarchy and chaos which resulted from the failed money pyramid schemes.[16] While hard evidence is difficult to come by, there are indications that the dumping of toxic waste substances on Albanian soil may have intensified.

V. ENVIRONMENTAL ROADBLOCKS

Like its East European, Soviet, and Chinese counterparts, and despite occasional official rhetoric to the contrary, Albania's Communist rulers paid little attention to the environment. Emphasis on quick industrialization, isolation from the outside world, political repression, and the Marxist-Leninist belief that "man" can triumph over nature account for the general state of environmental neglect.

The Albanian case displays these and other more idiosyncratic characteristics. While considerable, environmental damage in the Land of Eagles did not reach the near-catastrophic levels of other East European countries and parts of the former Soviet Union, and was less visible. Even though urbanization increased during the APL regime, Albania retained its bucolic character and remained Europe's most rural society. These factors partly explain the almost complete absence of an environmental movement in Albania. While environmental movements in East European countries, and to a lesser extent in the former Soviet Union, were at the forefront of the struggle that eventually spelled the demise of Communist regimes, the first Albanian Green party was the creation of the Alia regime and never got off the ground. The Greens, who later joined forces with the Ecologists, received less than half of a percent in all electoral contests since 1992; they did not even field candidates in the July 1997 elections.

The clan-dominated nature of the Albanian society also contributed, and continues to impede environmental awareness. For Albanians, attachment and allegiance to local clans outweigh allegiance to the nation. The ancient, unwritten law, known as the Kanun (Canon), and not state laws, ultimately set the parameters of individual behavior. Words or actions that shame one's own or one's family's honor must be avenged. The shooting of an opposition legislator by a political rival a couple of years ago, as the former was entering parliament, exemplifies deep-rooted laws of revenge and blood feud. As a result, localism is very strong and government actions and intentions are highly suspect and distrusted. The chaos, rampage, and destruction of government property (including schools, brigdes, and communications facilities) that occurred a few years ago, which eventually brought down Berisha and his Democratic party, can be seen in that context.

Under the circumstances the development of environmental awareness and enforcement of relevant policies face powerful roadblocks, no matter who is in power.

In addition to these more subjective elements, other, more objective factors continue to impede environmental awareness and policy making and implementation in Albania, especially in the post-Communist period. The poor state of the nation's economy forced the Berisha government to concentrate on more pressing needs; the environment was seen as a luxury that could wait. Aside from a loose association of academics, scientists, and a small number of nature lovers, there was (and still is) no organized effort in support of the environment. There are no signs of an environmental movement in Albania similar to the one that emerged in the Black Sea whose aim is to protect the "region's damaged environment, . . . including the Danube delta."[17] Nongovernmental organizations "play an essential role in [the] political process in assuring the social accountability of both public and private institutions [and] in serving as watchdogs for the regulators and regulatees."[18] With no environmental lobby hot on their heels, government leaders could afford to sidestep environmental issues.

Colin Kirkpatrick and Norman Lee argue that in their effort to privatize their economy and attract foreign capital, post-Communist regimes are often tempted to go along with "a firm's incentive to maximise profits on existing activity levels, by avoiding the costs of reducing pollution or by overextraction of resources." Similar considerations may also lead to "less rigorous environmental standards, whether locally or foreign owned."[19] The environmental policy adopted by the Berisha government was a case in point. Though well-intended, the government's policy was rich in rhetoric but short on specifics, particularly in terms of implementation. Michael R. Reich and B. Bowonder argue that "lack of . . . a well formulated set of priorities is a major obstacle to effective implementation."[20] Inability or unwillingness to establish priorities and set specific targets allowed for manipulation by corrupt and often incompetent governments officials, police officers, and bureaucrats.

Moreover, environmental policy suffered from multiple and often competing responsibilities and turf battles. Even though the Ministry of Economics has primary responsibility, a host of other government agencies were also involved in environmental matters. Lack of funding impeded the collection of relevant data and rendered enforcement and compliance nearly impossible.

Finally, the Albanian parliament, which is vested with some oversight responsibility on environmental and other areas of public policy, is poorly equipped and lacked a competent staff and access to information to exercise its oversight responsibilities effectively. The legislature's rubber stamp status during the long Communist era provided little historical precedent in oversight or other responsibilities. There is virtually no independent authority to oversee policy implementation. These shortcomings continue to undermine parliament's effectiveness.

No change has taken place since Berisha's defeat and the return to power of the reformed Communists, and none is expected. Albania's severe economic woes and the ongoing Kosovo crisis offer little ground to be optimistic that the return to power of the socialists and their allies will make the country's environment an important priority.

ENDNOTES

1. Derek Hall, *Albania and the Albanians* (London: Pinter, 1994), 142.
2. Cited in Dean S. Rugg, "Communist Legacies in the Albanian Landscape," *The Geographic Review*, vol. 84:1 (January 1994), p. 60.
3. *Ibid.*, 60.
4. Hall, *Albania*, 142.
5. *Ibid.*, 42.
6. Cited in *Ibid.*, 43.

7. Peter R. Prifti, *Socialist Albania Since 1944: Domestic and Foreign Developments* (Cambridge, Mass.: MIT University Press, 1978), 212.
8. Hall, *Albania*, 57.
9. *Ibid.*, 144.
10. *Ibid.*, 146.
11. *Ibid.*, 151.
12. *Ibid.*, 150.
13. Theresa Agovino, "Exodus from Albanian Universities," *The Chronicle of Higher Education*, Aug. 1, 1997, A37.
14. Cited in Hall, *Albania*, 153.
15. *Ibid.*, 167.
16. For more details see Elez Biberaj, *Albania in Transition: From Comminism to Democracy* (Boulder: Westview Press, 1998).
17. *The New York Times*, Oct. 19, 1997, pp. 1 & 6.
18. Michael R. Reich and B. Bowonder, "Environmental Policy in India: Strategies for Better Implementation," *Journal of Policy Studies*, vol. 20:4 (1992), p. 657.
19. Colin Kirkpatrick and Norman Lee, "Market Liberalization and Environmental Assessment in Developing and Transition Economies," *Journal of Environmental Management*, vol. 50 (1997), 240.
20. Michael R. Reich and B. Bowonder, "Environmental Policy in India," p. 650.

48

Problems of Public Policy Implementation in Developing Countries*

Jean-Claude Garcia-Zamor *School of Policy and Management, Florida International University, North Miami, Florida*

I. INTRODUCTION

Successful public policy implementation in developing countries has been hampered by three major problems: (1) the constraints on policy implementation that may be part and parcel of foreign aid, (2) the overly centralized structure of their administrations, and (3) a blind adherence to Max Weber's bureaucratic model.[1] These three features of the public policy environment have great influence on how implementation is to proceed.[2]

The ultimate goals of public policy are to improve the quality of future governmental decisions and to work toward improving the quality of some aspect of human life (Portney 1986:216). In view of this, public policy implementation is an important element in the developing countries' efforts to move forward. A crucial factor for implementation is the ability of public bureaucrats to identify all the variables that affect the achievements of their objectives (Mazmanian and Sabatier 1983:21; Pressman and Wildavsky 1984: xxiii). Implementation forges a causal goal between vague and sometimes conflicting policy objectives. Koenig (1986:156) states, "Because policy goals are usually multiple, conflicting, and vague, and because of policy-makers' cognitive limitations and the unpredictable dynamics of the environment, it is impossible to anticipate all the relevant constraints applicable to a policy when it is adopted. Instead, they are discovered as implementation proceeds."

II. CONSTRAINTS OF FOREIGN AID

The first major problem for policy implementation in developing countries is a byproduct of the limits and possibilities of international cooperation and the role of foreign aid. One of the obstacles to the achievement of developmental goals in the third world is the inability of the public

*An earlier version of this essay was originally prepared for presentation at the XVth World Congress of the International Political Science Association in Washington, D.C., August 1988. I am indebted to Professor Joseph P. McCormick, II, my former colleague at Howard University, and to Professor Harold Fuhr of the University of Konstanz, West Germany, for their insightful comments and criticism.

bureaucrats to formulate plans and to implement them properly. Even when innovative policies, inspired by foreign donors, are formulated, the ineffectiveness of the public servants in implementing them is an obstacle to the success of development assistance. As Bryant and White (1982:22) point out, administrative incapacity is often characterized by swollen bureaucracies encumbered with formalistic procedures that delay rather than expedite service delivery and program implementation. Contrary to the industrialized societies where public policy implementation involves countless routine tasks by the public servants, in developing countries the ultimate goal of public policy implementation is the attainment of developmental objectives expressed in the national development plans. These plans are usually inspired by foreign donors and are based primarily on expected technical assistance from abroad. In addition, most developing countries do not have the administrative framework to handle the requirements imposed by donors of foreign aid.

Many developing countries are now realizing that international development assistance is not going to solve their long-range problems. Some have reached the point where they have to pay more interest on past aid than they take in new aid. These countries incurred large debts in the 1970s because of the sharp increase in oil prices and now find it difficult to repay their loans because of depressed exports and the low prices of their commodities. Most of them are asking the international banks to renegotiate their debts on easier terms. Figures published by the World Bank reveal that for the period from 1970 to 1985 the outstanding debt of oil-importing developing countries rose from $50.9 billion to $484.7 billion. During that same period the increase for the oil-exporting developing countries was from $17.7 billion to $226.5 billion (World Bank 1986:44). Most developing countries were unable to obtain new net lending from private sources, except under rescheduling agreements. Negotiations for the rescheduling of existing debt in 1985 covered 19 World Bank members, including 10 from sub-Saharan Africa and seven from Latin America. In addition, many aid programs involve economic conditions that for a variety of reasons recipients would prefer to avoid. Furthermore, there is an increasing awareness that there is not a strong relationship between the amount of development assistance a country receives and its rate of development. Indeed, some studies show that aid correlates negatively with growth: those countries that have received the most aid also have had subsequently unimpressive growth rates (Mende 1973:Ch. 7).

The 1980 report of the Independent Commission on International Development Issues, under the chairmanship of Willy Brandt, called for at least $4 billion in aid over the next decade for the world's poorest countries. In addition, it called for an international system of universal revenue mobilization based on a sliding scale related to national income.

The developed nations have shown little regard for the Brandt report. As a matter of fact, most of the donor countries have reduced bilateral aid programs or kept them static. A few countries like Sweden and Canada have dramatically increased aid allocations, but these have not been adequate to compensate for lower commitments by the major countries. In an era of high inflation, high deficits, high unemployment, and the seeming ingratitude of some developing nations, development assistance is not a politically popular issue for most of the traditional donor countries.[3] The end result of the decreased assistance was a dramatic diminution of developing countries' capability to implement policies that were formulated without internally generated revenues for their realization.

But regardless of the form and the amount of development assistance that is given to the developing countries, a crucial factor for its effectiveness will still be the administrative capability of the bureaucracies of these countries to implement government policies. There is a need in almost all developing countries to establish or strengthen implementation capability to better manage the aid they receive. In general, the public servants in the developing countries lack administrative ability and managerial skill. Goodman and Love (1979:xii) argued that intensive project investment in developing countries has failed to anticipate the impact on development goals for two reasons: (1) the lack of viable policies, coupled with poor management, has wasted valuable resources, which led to counterproductive disharmony and tension; and (2) planning and project development take place within a social and economic environment that molds and limits the actions of implementing agencies.

The international lending institutions should rethink their policies and try to tie loans to countries' administrative environments because good projects and poor policy formulation and implementation don't make sense. Therefore, there is a need to do more administrative capability assessment prior to loan approval and/or disbursement. The pressure on developing countries to develop project formulation has not always taken the total administrative environment into consideration. In addition, two of the major lending institutions, the World Bank and the International Monetary Fund, often work at cross purposes. The reason is that the bank's bias is for development, the IMF's for financial stabilization. As a result, the developing countries are caught between two competing bureaucracies.

Usually changes occur in a policy during implementation. Berman (1980) differentiates between programmed and adoptive implementation, arguing that only under certain limited conditions should we expect policies to remain static during implementation. For implementation to be successful the goals of policies must be clearly and realistically stated. The problem in the implementation of policies in developing countries arises because policymakers make unrealistic assumptions about their administrative processes. This almost invariably requires many adjustments in the policies during the process of implementation. Jones (1984:165) views implementation as a process of interaction between the setting of goals and the actions geared to achieving them. However, such necessary interaction is often inhibited in developing countries because of the fragmented nature of the bureaucracy. There is often an absence of adequate horizontal integration between its units. In a recent work, John D. Montgomery pointed out that the most important elements of project management are policy continuity and stability. He stated that clearly identified goals by authoritative sources in the government provide guidance of great potential value in the confused immediate environment in which development projects operate (1988:66).

III. CENTRALIZED STRUCTURES OF BUREAUCRACIES

The second major problem of policy implementation in developing countries is the centralization and fragmentation of their administrative structures. While the United States is moving rapidly into a "postliterary" condition,[4] most developing countries are still coping with a "preliterary" situation. In Brazil, for example, one of the most advanced developing countries, the findings of research conducted some years ago revealed that 12% of the Brazilian civil servants never went to school; 21% did not finish elementary school; 13% went to junior high school but did not graduate; 15% graduated from junior high; and 13% attended a university, but only 2% received a university diploma (Garcia-Zamor 1978:474). Unfortunately, this situation has not changed dramatically over the past 20 years. The low level of formal education of developing countries' civil servants is partly responsible for the excessive centralization of authority in the top echelons of their administrative structures (Garcia-Zamor 1986:74). But the tendency to centralize administration is also a function of (1) the governments' perceived needs to control, (2) their lack of trust of lower-level officials, and (3) perhaps a residual of colonial administrative practice.

In the case of Nigeria, Cohen (1980:75) found out that typically the person heading an office or a department hands out very limited and partial tasks to subordinates. All coordination, planning, supervision, and decision making go to the center or top person in the department. Cohen attributed these features of overcentralization and excessive hierarchy to postcolonial functional-ism (1980:74).

Cheena and Rondinelli (1983:16) define decentralization as possessing four major forms, "deconcentration, delegation to semiautonomous or parastatal agencies, devolution to local gov-ernments and transfer from public to nongovernmental institutions." The two authors illustrate the ambivalence of developing nations concerning decentralization. First, although local govern-ments were delegated "broad powers to perform development planning and management func-tions," "adequate financial resources and qualified personnel to carry them out were often with-held." Second, they observed that local government officials were often reluctant to act independently. They continue to depend on the central government ministry officials for decisions (Cheena and Rondinelli 1983:297).

But in the often informal setting of the developing countries, some degree of implementa-tion initiative can exist even when the administrative structure itself is centralized. Esman (1974:14) stated:

> The style of administration [in the developing world] involves changes within bureaucracy—away from hierarchical command and towards patterns that permit greater initiative and dis-cretion at operating levels—and in relationships between administrators and clients in shaping programs of action that accommodate the objectives of government to clientele needs. In the assistance and guidance role, the administrator is a teacher, experimenter, the negotiator as well as a technician. These new patterns of interaction with clients are a hallmark that was not contemplated in the highly structured efficiency-oriented models of Western administration.

The degree of administrative discretion mentioned by Esman is clearly a non-Weberian pattern of behavior, which can prevail in some cases even when the administrative structures are "formally centralized."

Kenye (1985:4) mentioned the negative consequences of excessive regulations (through centralization and/or control) when accompanied by uncontrolled implementation:

> Planned development in the Third World has increased government intervention in the socio-economic sphere and this, in turn, has led to an increased number of regulations. These exces-sive regulations coupled with greater administrative discretion provide opportunities for cor-ruption, since the regulations can be used to frustrate the public and result in bribery to avoid such frustrations.

In the same vein, Gould and Amaro-Reyes (1983:14) view centralization as one of the fac-tors that encourages bureaucratic corruption in developing countries. They argue that the rigidity of overcentralized decision-making structures and processes tends to delay official action, focus-ing those seeking to expedite transactions to resort to bribes and payoffs as a means of overcom-ing cumbersome policy implementation procedures.

Harris (1965:309) states that politicians in most of the developing nations frequently make important policy decisions without the advice of their civil servants. Moreover, political leaders and party officials interfere to an excessive degree in even the detailed implementation of govern-ment policies and programs because of their lack of confidence in the loyalty of the bureaucrats. Harris thinks that party leaders in West Africa are often suspicious of the sympathies and values of the senior civil servants, and he attributes this suspicion largely to differences in educational, social, or ethnic backgrounds.

The cost of failed policies has always hindered the action of bureaucrats both in developed and developing countries. In the United States the consequences of failure of policy formulation may be personal. The rule used to be that U.S. government employees could not be held personal-ly liable for anything that happened while carrying out official duties—even if they were negligent in the way they did their job. While civil servants may have been sued, they rarely faced any serious consequences. However, in early 1988, the U.S. Supreme Court changed the rules to make civil servants more vulnerable to personal damage suits. If the U.S. Congress does not undo the court's ruling, that lack of immunity will put government officials in the precarious situation of having to make policy decisions while worrying about placing their personal fortunes on the line. In a country where lawsuits are so common place, civil servants will worry about losing their homes and their savings. Top officials, with even more to lose personally, also will fret that their subordinates will hesitate about making decisions.[5]

Bryant (1976:47–48) states that if one wants to maximize equity, decentralization may not be the best administrative route since locally entrenched elites are more ready to claim policy outputs than the lower income groups. There might be other advantages to centralization in developing countries. An obvious one is the elimination of the discretionary lapse between policy formation and policy implementation. Policy makers have a greater awareness of, and sometimes even participate in, the process of implementation. In the centralized systems of developing countries policies are more specific. Plans for implementation are less complicated when clear, unequivocal statements of the decisions regarding policy ends and means are formulated as a basis and stimulus for action. These usually entail precise decisions about objectives. The level of specificity is often impaired by the lack of knowledge of the relevant issues and facts by the civil servants who implement the policies. Contrary to what happens in developed countries where the complexity of the systems keeps policymaking in a very broad context, the developing countries try to eliminate from the start all problems and obstacles that may hinder achievement of the policies' objectives. The interrelationships between policies and budgeting and the role of budgeting in policy implementation are more clearly delineated in developing countries. Accurate forecasts are usually used, and the budgeting system is closely linked to policy formulation so that it serves as an effective instrument of implementation. Because of their lack of large resources and revenues, or in some cases because of pressures from international donors, developing countries tend to develop their budgets on the basis of specific policies. It could be said that 90% of all policies are really made at the time the national budget is being elaborated.

This rarely happens in large developed societies where administrative discretion often tries to adapt policies to local means. There, successful implementation occurs in an evolutionary way. The somewhat vague goals stated in policies are interpreted by administrators in various ways as they make their way down the organizational hierarchy. At the end of the process, what actually is implemented could be quite different from the original policy and in some cases at variance with it.

In most developing countries, the lack of computers accounts for the existence of so many forms to be arduously filled out and approved by countless employees in every dealing with the bureaucracy. Countless signatures are needed on many routine procedures, a fact that delays administrative action and creates so much extra trivial work on the periphery of power that relatively little time remains for the execution of the broader tasks of public policymaking. Because of the above-mentioned lack of computers, the bureaucracies of developing countries are infested with tons of worthless documents, which keep public employees busier with paper than with people. In such a context, public policies often are made in response to red tape instead of to people's needs. However, this is not particular to developing countries. Kaufman (1977) makes the same observation about the American bureaucracy. However, the introduction of system analysis and computers in the public services of developing countries can also create obstacles to policy implementation. Many of these countries acquire computers only to find that their effective use depends upon rationalization of administrative processes, availability of data, and meaningful integration of data. The steps to improve information gathering and analysis capabilities require the establishment or strengthening of central statistical offices, improvement of data collection techniques, and moves toward improvement of the quality of data.

IV. DISTORTION OF THE WEBERIAN MODEL

The third major impediment to public policy implementation in developing countries is the distortion of the Weberian model of bureaucracy.[6] These countries tend to be more resistant to changes. They view Max Weber's bureaucratic model as the most perfected, rational means for framing and controlling human activity. However, with changes taking place in the technological, cultural, social, and economic environment, the model is showing an ever-increasing number of imperfections and gaps. A close look at social history in Western Europe clearly reveals that the evolution of public administration there has been greatly influenced by the development of relatively independent market forces in a relatively competitive society. The Weberian model of public administration is closely linked to the development of a civic society where both administrative procedures and market regulations are bound into a well-defined set of rules and leave their defined places for action.

On the private side (market), interest group associations formed a relatively competitive but strong interest block, with a tendency toward self-regulation between employers and employees, and other involved interest groups. Rising capitalism has continuously formed a homogeneous society where each social group may somehow counterbalance the power of the other, with public administration being a sector of the society that is counter-balanced and controlled by strong civic actors. The logic of the Weberian administration—its clear forms of rules, of action, and of hierarchy—is thus not only guaranteed by mere administrative forces inside the bureaucracy through governmental rules, but also by forces outside the bureaucracy that possess strong bargaining power. But when developed capitalism is so closely related to the Western type of administration and vice versa, what does this mean for an underdeveloped capitalism? Doesn't it necessarily lead to the conclusion that, first, due to the structural heterogeneity in developing countries, administrations are differently and contradictorily shaped, and due to a highly unequal distribution of wealth and power (including unbalanced confrontations between social factors), administrations had to gain other roles and other tasks different from the Weberian ones; and/or, second, that the Western bureaucratic model doesn't fit contemporary needs of most developing countries; and/or third, that a strengthening of the social/economic forces may be a *conditio sine qua non* for an effective public administration in developing countries?

For most developing countries the bureaucratic model of developmentalism was implemented very early by the colonial powers. Most public bureaucracies were established as colonial bureaucracies, as bureaucracies of domination and for the transfer of resources to the north. There were control mechanisms especially against the majority of the autochthonous populations. Social groups that originally were clearly separated by common social organizations and cultures were forced by administrative means to live and work together. Perhaps the domination of the rural sector was most important for the development of a highly centralized bureaucracy, and the historical evolution of private large-scale enterprises with relatively low intensity class struggle hindered the penetration of a more equitable capitalism in those early stages. Development in the colonies was always closely related to the state apparatus. Nobody was able to work against the bureaucracy because it tended to control everything. In the early colonial empires, almost every economic activity was to be approved by the central state. These central states were overtaken after independence and finally transformed into modern administrations in the 1950s and the 1960s under the guidance of international and national foreign institutions. But making these new national administrations more efficient was problematic from the very beginning. The strengthening of these postindependence administrations by Western, Weberian types of instruments seem to have made them even more control-oriented and dominant over the rest of society. Already Riggs (1965:77) observed that a "modernization" of public administration does not necessarily mean higher effectiveness of administrative procedures, but could also lead to more repressive tools in the hands of authoritarian regimes.

Although criticized, modified, or only partly adapted, the Weberian model has nonetheless served as a quasi-general reference for developing countries. But their bureaucracies have not been capable of integrating the necessary changes adapting it to their particular situation. In addition, it is difficult to assess when this espousal of the Weberian concept is sincere or simply motivated by self-serving circumstances. The African scholar Bediako Lamouse-Smith (1974:143) clearly made this point:

> The idea of an impartial public service and servants can be counted among the myths of the Weberian ideal type of bureaucracy. Yet in the post-independence civil services of Africa, one frequently meets complaints especially from top officials, that the impartiality of the civil service is being tampered with by the new political leaders. I would suggest that the real meaning behind this complaint is that when the civil servants feel threatened by the dynamism of the imaginative politician, the concept of impartiality becomes a useful channel of escape.

O.P. Dwivedi (1985) expressed the same doubts about the Weberian approach in developing countries. He stated that while these countries continued to profess such administrative values as the doctrine of ministerial responsibility, political neutrality and anonymity of public servants, and the merit principles in recruitment and promotion, political leaders found that these values were counterproductive if the goal was acceleration of social and economic reforms.

He stated further that when conflicts arise between inherited administrative values (Weber's model) and ends and means used by politicians, politics would emerge as the most important value in the governing of a nation (p. 62). This is especially true in the case of small countries where social pressures could make an outcast of any public servant who try to behave in an impersonal manner in the performance of his official duties (Garcia-Zamor 1977; Garcia-Zamor and Mayo-Smith 1983). Price (1975:27–28) found out that in Ghana the bureaucrat is expected to behave impartially when he is dealing with members of his extended kinship family in the bureaucratic setting but at the same time is expected to use his office in a manner that will enhance the wealth, status, and influence of his group. Furthermore, in many developing countries the primary role of the bureaucracy is to serve and sustain the existing political system. Despite some degree of formal decentralization, there is very little delegation of authority. Usually the hierarchical structures exist only in the organigrams. But in practice, instead of the formal organization pictured in the charts, the bureaucracy in the developing countries functions as an informal organization.

Usually in such instances the bureaucracy is multifunctional. This multifunctionalism tends to cause overlapping of duties in various structures, and not enough specific knowledge of the various problems and possible solutions. On the positive side, multifunctionalism may promote the relative ease of public policy formulation and implementation. The distance from the administrative elite to the lowest bureaucratic official will not seem insurmountable. Communication from one level to the next is more easily accomplished than in the unifunctional Weberian bureaucracy. When the two major obstacles to policy implementation—overcentralization and the distortion of the Weberian model of bureaucracy—diminish, the individual bureaucrat has the opportunity to observe first hand the effects of any administrative decision that he makes. As a result, he is able to perform more effectively and to participate in the development of policy as well as in its implementation. For the bureaucrat so involved, this reduces the frustration that comes from the implementation of a policy that has been formulated without reference to his expertise.

The chapter pointed out three major obstacles to successful public policy implementation in most developing countries: the influence of foreign aid on the performance of the public sector and public policies, the highly centralized administrative structures, and a clear distortion of the Weberian bureaucratic model. It could be safely assumed that in most of these countries, the last two obstacles mentioned—overcentralization and the anamorphosis of the Weberian bureaucratic model—are commonly accepted features of the bureaucracy. Therefore, the ability of the developing countries to implement policies will be adversely affected by the degree of their adherence to these two characteristics, especially when accompanied by the usual constraints that come with foreign aid and the lack of trained personnel.

ENDNOTES

1. This may appear to be a sweeping generalization since there is not sufficient similarity among so-called developed societies with regard to adherence to Weberian bureaucratic norms. Certainly there are very different structural patterns of policy implementation in unitary versus federal systems. Federally generated public policy in the United States tends to follow a fairly decentralized pattern. However, this is largely due to (1) the federal system, (2) a constitutional structure that intentionally fragments authority, and (3) a politically active business sector that possesses a tremendous amount of informal veto power vis-à-vis decisions made by the federal government and/or the state governments. It cannot be said that governmental authority is similarly fragmented (and therefore centralized) in France or the United Kingdom. In addition, the U.S. federal bureaucracy contains a curious admixture of career bureaucrats (who presumably acquired their positions via merit) and politically appointed officials who serve at the pleasure of the chief executive. There is probably less administrative neutrality in the United States than there is in many European bureaucracies. The United States and Europe do not have the same administrative traditions, and the Europeans have tended to develop a corps of professional civil servants where the Weberian bureaucratic norm of "administrative neutrality" is more deeply imbedded.
2. As in the case of the developed societies, all developing countries are not alike. Therefore, it is difficult to offer empirical evidence that will apply to all of them. The basic proposition advanced in this chapter is a highly debatable one and is not equally applicable to all developing countries.
3. The 1988–1989 foreign military and economic assistance bill passed by the U.S. House of Representatives calls for $14.3 billion in foreign aid spending, an increase of $709 million above the previous year. Military assistance was set at $9.053 billion, economic assistance $4.5 billion, and export promotion assistance at $715 billion (*Washington Post* May 26, 1988:A19).
4. A condition where reading and writing have been displaced by television and video as the primary sources of mass entertainment and communication (Brumback 1988).
5. A bill passed by the House Judiciary Committee would give relief to U.S. civil servants, and chances are that Congress will approve it. The measure says that any time a plaintiff has a complaint against a federal employee for some action taken as part of his or her job, the mechanism of the Federal Tort Claims Act comes into play. That means first trying to settle the matter out of court and then suing the United States directly.
6. One may argue that such distortion is understandable and even necessary since Weber's model is clearly a formalistic one that lacks such dimensions as informal lines of authority and communication or concern for the individual worker in the bureaucracy. Weber himself indicated that his model was not meant to apply to all conceivable organizational situations, and that it represented only a broad framework rather than an all-encompassing model complete in every detail (Gordon 1986:185).

REFERENCES

Berman, P. Thinking about programmed and adaptive implementations: matching strategies to situations. In *Why Policies Succeed or Fail* (H.M. Ingram and D. Mann, eds.). Sage Publications, Beverly Hills, CA, 1980.

Brumback, R.A. Teaching administration in post-literate society. *Political Science Teacher 1*(2) (1988).

Bryant, C. *Participation Planning, and Administrative Development in Urban Development Programs.* Agency for International Development, Washington, DC, 1976.

Bryant, C., and White, L.G. *Managing Development in the Third World.* Westview Press, Boulder, CO, 1982.

Cheena, S.G., and Rondinelli, D.A., eds. *Decentralization and Development.* Sage Publications, Beverly Hills, CA, 1983.

Cohen, R. The blessed job in Nigeria. In *Hierarchy and Society: Anthropological Perspectives on Bureaucracy* (G.M. Britan and R. Cohen, eds.). Institute for the Study of Human Issues, Philadelphia, 1980.

Dwivedi, O.P. Ethics and values of public responsibility and accountability. *International Review of Administrative Science LI*(1) (1985).

Esman, M.J. Administrative doctrine and developmental needs. In *The Administration of Change in Africa* (P. Morgan, ed.). Dunellen, New York, 1974.

Garcia-Zamor, J.-C. *The Ecology of Development Administration in Jamaica, Trinidad and Tobago, and Barbados.* Organization of American States, Washington, DC, 1977.

Garcia-Zamor, J.-C. An ecological approach to administrative reform. In *Politics and Administration in Brazil* (J.-C. Garcia-Zamor, ed.). University Press of America, Washington, DC, 1978:469–481).

Garcia-Zamor, J.-C. Can participative planning and management be institutionalized in developing countries? In *Public Participation in Development Planning and Management* (J.-C. Garcia-Zamor, ed.). Westview Press, Boulder, CO, 1985:237–245.

Garcia-Zamor, J.-C. Obstacles to institutional development in Haiti. In *Political, Projects, and People: Institutional Development in Haiti* (D. W. Brinkerhoff and J.-C. Garcia-Zamor, eds.). Praeger Publishers, New York, 1986:63–91.

Garcia-Zamor, J.-C., and Mayo-Smith, I. Administrative reform in Haiti: problems, progress and prospects. *Public Administration and Development 3*(1):39–48 (1983).

Goodman, L., and Love, R. *Management of Developing Projects: An International Case Study Approach.* Pergamon Press, Honolulu, published in cooperation with the East-West Center, 1979.

Gordon, G.J. *Public Administration in America*, 3rd ed. St. Martin's Press, New York, 1986.

Gould, D.J., and Amaro-Reyes, J.A. *The Effects of Corruption on Administrative Performance: Illustrations from Developing Countries.* World Bank, Washington, DC, 1983.

Harris, R.L. The role of the civil servant in West Africa. *Public Administration Review XXV*(14):303–313 (1965).

Independent Commission on International Development Issues. *North-South: A Program for Survival. Report of the Independent Commission on International Development Issues.* M.I.T. Press, Cambridge, MA, 1981.

Jones, C.O. *An Introduction to the Study of Public Policy*, 3rd ed. Brooks/Cole, Monterey, CA, 1984.

Kaufman, H. *Red Tape: Its Designs, Uses and Abuses.* Brookings Institution, Washington, DC, 1977.

Kenye, R.H. Politics, bureaucratic corruption and maladministration in third world. *International Review of Administrative Science LI*(1) (1985).

Koenig, L.A. *An Introduction to Public Policy.* Prentice-Hall, Englewood Cliffs, NJ, 1986.

Lamouse-Smith, B. Complexity and African development administration: a sociological perspective. In *The Administration of Change in Africa* (P. Morgan, ed.). Dunellen, New York, 1974.

Mazmanian, D.A., and Sabatier, P.A. *Implementation and Public Policy.* Scott, Foresman, Glenview, IL, 1983.

Mende, T. *From Aid to Recolonization: Lessons of a Failure.* Pantheon, New York, 1973.

Montgomery, J.D. *Bureaucrats and People. Grassroots Participation in Third World Development.* Johns Hopkins University Press, Baltimore, 1988.

Portney, K.E. *Approaching Public Policy Analysis: An Introduction to Policy and Program Research.* Prentice-Hall, Englewood Cliffs, NJ, 1986.

Pressman, J.L. and Wildavsky, A. *Implementation*, 3rd ed. University of California Press, Berkeley, 1984.

Price, R.M. *Society and Bureaucracy in Contemporary Ghana.* University of California Press, Berkeley, 1975.

Riggs, R.W. Relearning an old lesson: the political context of development administration. *Public Administration Review xxv*(1) (1965).

World Bank. *The World Bank Annual Report.* World Bank, Washington, DC, 1986.

49
Policy Choices

Superoptimizing Across Four Continents

Stuart S. Nagel   *Department of Political Science, University of Illinois at Urbana–Champaign, Urbana, Illinois*

I. INTRODUCTION: BASIC CONCEPTS

Superoptimizing analysis refers to dealing with public policy problems by finding an alternative that enables conservatives, liberals, and other major viewpoints to all come out ahead of their best initial expectations simultaneously. Superoptimum solutions (SOS) in public controversies involve solutions that exceed the best expectations of liberals and conservatives simultaneously. We are primarily concerned with public or governmental controversies, not private controversies between individuals such as marriage, consumers, employment, or other such disputes. We are interested instead in controversies over what statutes, judicial precedents, or administrative regulations should be adopted governing marriage, consumers, employment, or other such relations.

An optimum solution is one that is best on a list of alternatives in achieving a set of goals. A superoptimum solution is one that is simultaneously best on two separate sets of goals. One set is a liberal set, and the second set is a conservative set. The two sets may share many or all of the same goals, but they are likely to differ in terms of the relative weights they give to the same goals.

A. An Example

For example, in the minimum wage controversy, both liberals and conservatives endorse the goal of paying a decent wage and the goal of not overpaying to the point where some workers are unnecessarily laid off because their employers cannot afford the new higher minimum. Liberals, however, give relatively high weight to the first goal and relatively low but positive weight to the second goal, and vice versa for conservatives.

The liberal alternative in the minimum wage controversy might be $4.40 an hour and the conservative alternative might be $4.20 an hour. The liberal alternative would thus score higher on the "decent wage" goal, and the conservative alternative lower. On the goal of "avoiding overpayment," the liberal alternative would score lower, and the conservative alternative higher. This real data would thus provide a classic tradeoff controversy.

The object in this example is to find a solution that is simultaneously better from a liberal perspective than $4.40 an hour and better from a conservative perspective than $4.20 an hour. One such super-optimum solution would be to provide for a minimum wage supplement by the government of 22 cents an hour to each unemployed person who is hired. The worker would receive $4.41 an hour, but the employer would pay only $4.19 an hour.

The liberal labor interests would be getting more than their best expectation of $4.40 an hour, and the conservative business interests would be paying less than their best expectation of $4.20 an hour. The government and taxpayers would be benefitting by virtue of (1) the money saved from otherwise providing public aid to unemployed people, (2) the money added to the gross national product which provides income to others, increases taxes, and an increased base on which to grow in subsequent years, (3) better role models for the children of people who would otherwise be unemployed, and (4) an upgrading of skills if qualifying for the wage subsidy means business has to provide on-the-job training and workers have to participate.

B.   SOS Contrasted with Other Types of Solutions

Solutions to public controversies can be classified in various ways. First there are *superoptimum* solutions in which all sides come out ahead of their initial best expectations, as mentioned above. At the opposite extreme is a *supermalimum* solution in which all sides come out worse than their worst initial expectations. That can be the case in a mutually destructive war, labor strike, or highly expensive litigation. *Pareto-optimum* solutions, in which nobody comes out worse off and at least one side comes out better off, are not a very favorable solution compared to a superoptimum solution. A *paretomalimum* solution would be one in which nobody is better off and at least one side is worse off.

A win-lose solution is one in which what one side wins the other side loses. The net effect is zero when the losses are subtracted from the gains. This is the typical litigation dispute when one ignores the litigation costs.

In a lose-lose solution, both sides are worse off than they were before the dispute began. This may often be the typical litigation dispute, or close to it, when one includes litigation costs. Those costs are often so high that the so-called winner is also a loser. That is also often the case in labor-management disputes that result in a strike, and even more so in international disputes that result in going to war.

The so-called win-win solution sounds at first glance like a solution where everybody comes out ahead. What it typically refers to, though, is an illusion since the parties are only coming out ahead relative to their worst expectations. In this sense, the plaintiff is a winner no matter what the settlement is because the plaintiff could have won nothing if liability had been rejected at trial. Likewise, the defendant is a winner no matter what the settlement is because the defendant could have lost everything the plaintiff was asking for if liability had been established at trial. The parties are only fooling themselves in the same sense as someone who is obviously a loser tells himself he won because he could have done worse.

C.   Ways of Arriving at Superoptimum Solutions

Having a third-party benefactor is one of many ways of arriving at superoptimum solutions. Other ways include (1) expanding the resources available, (2) setting realistically higher goals than what was previously considered the best, (3) having big benefits for one side but only small costs for the other side, (4) combining alternatives that are not mutually exclusive, (5) removing or decreasing the source of the conflict, and (6) developing a package of alternatives that would satisfy both liberal and conservative goals.

One procedure for arriving at superoptimum solutions is to think in terms of what is in the conservative alternative that liberals might like. And likewise, what is in the liberal alternative that conservatives might like. Then think whether it is possible to make a new alternative that will emphasize those two aspects. Another technique is to emphasize the opposite. It involves saying what is in a conservative alternative that liberals especially dislike. What is in the liberal alternative that conservatives especially dislike. Then think about making a new alternative that eliminates those two aspects.

A variation on that is to add new goals. The usual procedure starts with the conservative goals as givens in light of how they justify their current best alternative, and it starts with the liberal goals as givens in light of how they justify their current best alternative. This technique says to think about the goals conservatives tend to endorse that are not currently involved in the controversy, but that could be brought in to justify a new alternative. Likewise, what goals do liberals tend to endorse that are not currently involved in the controversy but that could also be brought in?

For this technique, a good example is the free speech controversy where liberals want virtually unrestricted free speech in order to stimulate creativity and conservatives want restrictions on free speech in order to have more order in the legal system. However, liberals also like due process, equal protection, and right to privacy. That raises questions as to whether it might be permissible to restrict free speech in order to satisfy those constitutional rights, where the restrictions are not so great, but the jeopardy of those other rights might be great. Likewise, conservatives like policies that are good for business. They might therefore readily endorse permissive free speech that relates to advertising, to trying to convince workers that they should not join unions or that relates to lobbying.

One problem with superoptimum solutions is that they look so good that they may cause some people to think they might be some kind of a trap. An example is the Camp David Accords. That example is a classic superoptimum solution where Israel, Egypt, the United States, and everybody involved came out ahead of their original best expectations. According to the *New York Times* for March 26, 1989, however, Israeli intelligence at least at first opposed Anwar Sadat's visit to Israel and the Camp David Accords until close to the signing on the grounds that it all sounded so good, it must be a trap. The Israeli intelligence felt that Israel was being set up for a variation on the Yom Kippur War whereby Israel got into big trouble by relaxing its guard due to the holidays. They viewed this as an attempt to get them to relax their guard again, and then any minute the attack would begin. They were on a more intense alert at the time of the Camp David negotiations than they were at any other time in Israel's history. That nicely illustrates how superoptimum solutions can easily be viewed by people as a trap because they look so good that they are unbelievable. Traditional solutions are not so likely to be viewed as traps, and they are taken more at their face value, which is generally not much.

D. Decision-Aiding Software

Superoptimizing is an approach to public policy analysis. Policy analysis or policy evaluation can be defined as processing a set of goals to be achieved, alternatives available for achieving them, and relations between goals and alternatives in order to arrive at a best alternative, combination, allocation, or predictive decision-rule. Policy analysis can be facilitated by decision-aiding software. Such software involves showing goals on the columns of a table, alternatives on the rows, and relations as words or numbers in the cells. The overall totals can be shown on a column in the far right, with an analysis that can quickly show how the totals would change if there were changes in the goals, alternatives, relations, or other inputs.

That kind of decision-aiding software also facilitates the finding of super optimum solutions. It can quickly determine the liberal and conservative totals for each alternative. It can quickly test to see if a proposed superoptimum solution does score better than the best liberal and conservative alternatives using the liberal and conservative weights. Such software also facilitates finding SOS solutions by enabling one to work with many alternatives and many criteria simultaneously. Each side can thereby give on some criteria which are not so important to it, and receive on other criteria, in order to arrive at solutions where both sides come out ahead of their initial best expectations.

Some of the key literature on decision-aiding software includes Patrick Humphreys and Ayleen Wisudha, *Methods and Tools for Structuring and Analyzing Decision Problems* (London: London School of Economics and Political Science, 1987); Saul Gass et al. (eds.), *Impacts of Microcomputers on Operations Research* (Amsterdam: North-Holland, 1986); and S. Nagel, *Evaluation Analysis with Microcomputers* (Greenwich, CT: JAI Press, 1989).

E. Dispute Resolution and Growth Economics

Another stream of inspiration has come from people in the field of mediation and alternative dispute resolution. Some of that key literature includes Lawrence Susskind and Jeffrey Cruikshank, *Breaking the Impasse*: *Consensual Approaches to Resolving Disputes* (New York: Basic Books, 1987); Stephen Goldberg, Eric Green, and Frank Sander (eds.), *Dispute Resolution* (Boston: Little, Brown, 1984); and S. Nagel and M. Mills, "Microcomputers, P/G%, and Dispute Resolution," *Ohio State Journal on Dispute Resolution* 2:187–223 (1987).

Still another stream of inspiration has come from people who are expansionist thinkers. This includes the conservative economist Arthur Laffer and the liberal economist Robert Reich. They both have in common a belief that policy problems can be resolved by expanding the total pie of resources or other things of value available to be distributed to the disputants. The expansion can come from well-placed subsidies and tax breaks with strings attached to increase national productivity. That kind of thinking can apply to disputes involving black-white, rich-poor, male-female, North-South, urban-rural, and other categories of societal disputants. Some of that key literature includes Ira Magaziner and Robert Reich, *Minding America's Business*: *The Decline and Rise of the American Economy* (New York: Harcourt, Brace, 1982), and Paul Roberts, *The Supply Side Revolution* (Cambridge, MA: Harvard University Press, 1984).

When the idea of superoptimum solutions was first proposed in the 1980s, people thought it was some kind of funny trick to think one could arrive at solutions to public policy problems that could exceed the best expectations of both liberals and conservatives simultaneously. Since then, the ideas have been presented in numerous workshops where skeptical and even cynical participants would divide into groups to try to develop SOS solutions to problems within their subject matter interests. They found that by opening their minds to the possibilities and by following some simple procedures, they could succeed in arriving at reasonable SOS solutions. It is hoped that this research will contribute in the long run to decreasing the glamour and excitement of superoptimum solutions by making such solutions almost a matter of routine thinking. There is joy in creating new ideas, but there is more joy in seeing one's new ideas become commonplace.[1]

II. AFRICA: THE ECONOMICS OF EFFICIENT AND EQUITABLE PRICES

High farm prices are the conservative alternative in this context and low prices are the liberal alternative. The liberal weights involve a 3 for urban desires, a 1 for rural desires, and a 2 for all the other goals. With the liberal weights, the SOS wins 76 to 48 for all the other alternatives. We then go back and put in the conservative weights. The conservative weights give a 2 to all the neutral goals just as liberal weights do, but they do a flip-flop on urban and rural desires. For the conservative in the context, rural desires get a 3 rather than a 1, and urban desires get a 1 rather than a 3. The SOS is a winner even with the conservative weights, although now the high prices do better than they did before, but still not as well as the SOS. (See Table 1.)

Table 1 Pricing Food in Africa and Elsewhere

Alternatives	C* goal: Rural well-being	L goal: Urban well-being	N goal: Adminis. feasibility	N goal: farming methods	N goal: Export	N goal: Import technology	N goal: GNP	N goal: Political feasibility	M total weight	L total weight	C total weight
C: High price	5	1	3	4	4	4	4	1	52 (18)	48 (14)	56 (22)
L: Low price	1	5	3	2	2	2	2	5	44 (18)	48 (22)	40 (14)
N: Compromise	3	3	3	3	3	3	3	3	48 (18)	48 (18)	48 (18)
S: Price supplement	5.1	5.1	3	5	5	5	5	5	76.4 (26.4)	76.4 (26.4)	76.4 (26.4)

*C, conservative; L, liberal; N, neutral; S, SOS.

NOTES:

1. The intermediate totals in parentheses are based on the first three goals. The bottom line totals are based on all the goals, including the indirect effects of the alternatives.

2. The SOS of a price supplement involves farmers receiving 101% of the price they are asking, but urban workers and others paying only 79% which is less than the 80% that they are willing and able to pay.

3. The difference of 22% is made up by food stamps given to the urban workers in return for agreeing to be in programs that upgrade their skills and productivity. The food stamps are used to pay for staple products (like rice or wheat) along with cash. Farmers can then redeem the stamps for cash, provided that they also agree to be in programs that increase their productivity.

4. Food stamps have administrative feasibility for ease in determining that workers and farmers are doing what they are supposed to do in return for the food stamps. They cannot be easily counterfeited. They serve as a check on how much the farmers have sold.

5. By increasing the productivity of farmers and workers, the secondary effects occur of improving farming methods, increasing exports, increasing the importing of new technologies, and increasing the GNP.

6. High prices are not politically feasible because of too much opposition from workers who consume, but do not produce food. The high prices though are acceptable if they can be met by way of price supplements in the form of food stamps.

The neutral perspective is not to give everything a weight of 1, but rather a weight of 2. If the neutrals gave everything a weight of 1, they would be giving neutral goals less weight than either the liberals or the conservatives give them. Thus the neutral picture is rural desires get a weight of 2, and so do urban desires. To the neutral, everything gets a weight of 2. The SOS wins with the neutral weights too. It is super-optimum, because it is out in front over both the conservative and liberal alternatives using both the conservative and liberal weights. It also wins over the compromise. The SOS involves the farmers getting better than high prices and the urbanites paying lower than low prices, with the government providing a supplement like the minimum wage supplement, provided that administrative feasibility is satisfied.

Administrative feasibility involves the use of food stamps. They are given to urban food buyers. They cannot be easily counterfeited. Food buyers give them to retailers, who in turn give them to wholesalers, who in turn give them to farmers, who turn them in for reimbursement. Criterion 8 just talks about political feasibility. There should be a separate criterion for administrative feasibility.

Of special importance is that no farmer gets the supplement unless they agree to adopt more modern farming methods. Otherwise it is just a handout for subsidizing inefficient farming. By adopting more modern farming methods, productivity goes up. Food becomes available for export. Foreign exchange then gets acquired for importing new technology. The new technology increases the GNP, and everybody is better off, including the taxpayers who pay the supplement. They are better off because with the increased GNP, the government could even reduce taxes if it wanted to do so. It could reduce taxes below a 20% level and still have more tax revenue if the GNP base has increased substantially.[2]

On the broader implications of the examples, food pricing illustrates the third party benefactor which can be a very useful SOS perspective for resolving conflicts among ethnic groups, economic classes, labor versus management, landlords versus tenants. Other examples include (1) the landlord-tenant resolution with regard to rent vouchers; (2) labor-management resolution with regard to the minimum wage; (3) rural versus urban; and (4) sellers versus consumers. On the international front, the third-party benefactor can be illustrated by the Camp David Accords.

III.   ASIA: POPULATION CONTROL AND REPRODUCTIVE FREEDOM

A.   Ideology and Technocracy

As of the 1970s, the People's Republic of China was seeking to resolve public policy problems largely by consulting the ideological writings of Karl Marx, Mao Zedong, and their interpreters. As of the 1980s, government agencies in China were seeking to become more professional by way of the introduction of personnel management, financial administration, and other bureaucratic ideas from the West, some of which are actually a throwback to Confucius bureaucracy.

Thus ideology became offset by technocracy. What we were seeing may fit the classic Hegelian and Marxist dialectic of thesis, antithesis, and synthesis. Ideology represented the prevailing thesis in the 1970s, whereby population control might be analyzed by reading Marx and Mao. Technocracy represented the antithesis in the 1980s, whereby population control might be analyzed by reading biological literature.

The 1990s may represent a super-optimum synthesis of the best, not the worst of both possible worlds. It may draw upon the idea of having goal-oriented values from the ideological thesis, as contrasted to rejecting values as being unscientific or not objective. Values and goals may be quite objective in the sense of being provable means to higher goals, or in the sense of proving that certain alternatives are more capable of achieving the goals than others.

The 1990s may also draw upon the idea of empirical proof based on observable conse-

Table 2   Superoptimizing Analysis Applied to the China Excess Population Problem

Alternatives	$C*$ goal: Small families	L goal: Reproductive freedom	N total weights	L total weights	C total weights
C: Strict one-child policy	4	2	12	10	14
L: Flexible on family size	2	4	12	14	10
N: One child with exceptions allowed	3	3	12	12	12
S: Causes of excess children	5	5	20	20	20

*C, conservative; L, liberal; N, neutral; S, SOS.

NOTES:

1. Relevant causes of excess children in the China population context include: (1) the need for adult children to care for their elderly parents, which could be better handled through social security and/or jobs for the elderly; (2) the need for extra children to allow for child mortality, which could be better handled through better child health care; (3) the need for male children in view of their greater value, which could be better handled through providing more opportunities for females; (4) The lack of concern for the cost of sending children to college, which could be better handled through a more vigorous program of recruiting rural children to college.

2. It is not a superoptimum solution to provide monetary rewards and penalties in this context because (1) the monetary rewards for having fewer children enable a family to then have more children; (2) the monetary punishments for having more children stimulate a family to have still more children to provide offsetting income; (3) the monetary rewards and punishments are made meaningless by the simultaneous policies which are increasing prosperity in rural China.

quences, rather than ideological labels of socialism or capitalism. It is empirical proof that also makes sense in terms of deductive consistency with what else is known about the world, rather than mindless technical number-crunching without thinking about how the results might fit common sense. Being technical does not necessarily mean being effective in getting the job done efficiently and equitably, which is what should really count in governmental decision making.

The kind of synthesis which this refers to is a synthesis of goals to be achieved (the ideological element) and systematic methods for determining which alternative or alternatives most achieve those goals (the technical element). The true dialectic is dynamic not only in the sense that a thesis leads to an antithesis which leads to a higher level synthesis. It is also dynamic in the sense that a synthesis does not stagnate, but becomes a subsequent thesis to be re-synthesized by a new antithesis into a still higher level of analysis. There may be policy evaluation methods that are even more effective, efficient, and equitable.

Those are the methods that are hinted at in various places in this paper where superoptimum solutions are explicitly or implicitly mentioned. Such solutions enable conservatives, liberals, and other major viewpoints to all come out ahead of their best initial expectations simultaneously. Traditional optimizing involves finding the best alternative or alternatives in a set. SOS analysis involves finding an alternative that is better than what conservatives previously considered the best and simultaneously better than what liberals previously considered the best, using conservative and liberal values.

B.   Alternatives, Goals, and Relations as Inputs

Table 2 can be used to illustrate what is meant by superoptimizing policy analysis where all major viewpoints can come out ahead of their best initial expectations. The table talks about excess population, rather than about the population problem. This is so because most of China's so-called population problem does not relate to a surplus of people, but rather to a shortage of production. Some of the population problem (at least in the short run) may, however, relate to a strain on China's current resources that can be lessened by lessening the number of consumers.

The alternatives are listed on the rows. The conservative alternative (in the sense of being the most regulatory) is to try to enforce a strict one-child policy. The liberal alternative (in the sense of allowing the most freedom) is to be completely flexible on family size. This is also possibly most in conformity with Marxist ideology which tends to view population control as a capitalistic idea designed to either increase the population of the poor (in order to have a reserve army of unemployed people) or to decrease the population of the poor (out of fear that the poor will overwhelm the middle class). Those two Marxist views tend to nullify each other possibly leading one to the conclusion that there is no Marxist view on population policy. The compromise position between conservative regulation and liberal freedom is to have a one-child policy, but with various exceptions such as allowing a second child if the first is a daughter, or allowing a second child among rural but not urban people.

One of the key goals is small families given the tremendous burden on the Chinese economy and government services of a billion people reproducing at a rate greater than about one child per family. Even one child per family would mean substantial short-run population growth. This would occur because people are living longer in China. If one simplifies the arithmetic by saying that if the 500 million males marry the 500 million females and have one child apiece within the next few years, then the population goes from 1 billion to 1.5 billion. That increase of half a billion is more people than every country of the world currently has except China and India. The rich may not get richer, but the highly populated get even more highly populated. The second key goal is reproductive freedom. Even the conservatives recognize that interfering with reproductive freedom makes for a lot of antagonism toward the government. Thus both goals are endorsed by both conservatives and liberals in China, but Chinese conservatives place relatively more emphasis on small families, and Chinese liberals place relatively more emphasis on reproductive freedom.

The relations between the alternatives and the goals are shown on a scale of 1 to 5 where 5 means highly conducive to the goal, 4 means mildly conducive, 3 means neither conducive nor adverse, 2 means mildly adverse, and 1 means highly adverse to the goal. We have here a classic tradeoff: A strict one-child policy is good on small families, but bad on reproductive freedom; flexibility on family size is good on reproductive freedom, but bad on small families; the compromise alternative is middling on both. Like compromises in general, this compromise is better than the worst on both small families and reproductive freedom. It is clearly not better than the best expectations on either goal.

C.   Finding a Superoptimum Package of Policies

In many public policy problems, the superoptimum solution involves well-placed subsidies and tax breaks. Well-placed *tax breaks* are meaningless in a Communist society. Under Communism, people do not do much direct taxpaying (especially income taxes) the way they do in Western societies. Instead the government is supported by paying people less than they are worth in their government jobs. The difference is a hidden tax. Ironically this fits well the Marxist idea of surplus-value exploitation of labor. It is an easy form of tax to collect, but it does not allow for the use of tax breaks as incentives.

China has tried subsidizing small families by giving monetary rewards to those who have small families, and monetary punishments to those who do not have them. The effect has been almost the opposite of the government's intent. The subsidies to small families have in many instances increased their income so they can now afford to have more children. Having a monetary punishment or reduced salary may even motivate parents to have an additional child to help bring in more income to offset the reduced salary. Also, moving simultaneously toward a more prosperous free market (especially in farm products) has enabled many rural people to now have more children and not be bothered by the withdrawal of subsidies or other monetary punishments.

A kind of superoptimum solution may make a lot more sense for dealing with the China population problem. It could provide small families and reproductive freedom simultaneously. Doing so requires looking to the causes of having additional children and then trying to remove or lessen those causes. One cause is a need to have children who will support parents in their old age. Adopting a more effective social security system helps eliminate or lessen that cause.

Another cause is having additional children as backup because the death rate is so high among rural Chinese children prior to age 5. Various forms of pediatric public health can make a big difference such as giving shots and using effective remedies to prevent life-jeopardizing infant diarrhea and dehydration.

A third cause is the widespread feeling that female children are worthless in terms of bringing honor to the family. One therefore keeps trying until at least one son is born. That cause can be substantially lessened by the new moves in China toward much greater opportunities for women to become lawyers, doctors, and enter other prestigious occupations. In China, women's liberation has facilitated birth control, whereas in the United States birth control has done more to facilitate women's liberation.[3]

The population control problem illustrates getting at the causes of the conflict or the problem in order to arrive at a superoptimum solution. We could mention other relevant examples such as decreasing unwanted pregnancies to get at the abortion problem, or decreasing murder to get at the capital punishment problem. There may be some other examples of getting at the causes. We need to go through all the examples that we have and classify them in terms of what SOS method they use.

IV. EAST EUROPE: COLLECTIVISM AND INDIVIDUALISM

The changes that are occurring in Eastern Europe and in many other regions and nations of the world provide an excellent opportunity to apply systematic policy analysis to determining such basic matters as how to organize the economy, the government, and other social institutions. Population control and land reform are highly important problems, but they may not be as basic as reconstituting a society.

Table 3 analyzes the fundamental issue of socialism versus capitalism in the context of government versus private ownership and operation of the basic means of producing industrial and agricultural products. The essence of socialism in this context is government ownership and operation of factories and farms or at least those larger than the handicraft or garden size, as in the Soviet Union of 1960. The essence of capitalism is private ownership and operation of both factories and farms, as in the United States of 1960. The neutral position or middle way is to have some government and some private ownership-operation, as in Sweden of 1960. The year 1960 is used because that is approximately when the Soviet Union began to change with Nikita Khrushchev. The United States also underwent big changes in the 1960s with John F. Kennedy.

Table 3 refers to government ownership-operation as the liberal or left-wing alternative, as it is in the United States and in world history at least since the time of Karl Marx. The table refers to private ownership-operation as the conservative or right-wing alternative, as it is in the United States, and elsewhere at least since the time of Adam Smith. In recent years in the Soviet Union and in China, those favoring privatization have been referred to as liberals, and those favoring retention of government ownership-operation have been referred to as conservatives. The labels make no difference in this context. The object of Table 3 is to find a superoptimum solution that more than satisfies the goals of both ideologies or groups, regardless of their labels.

Table 3   Government Versus Private Ownership and Operation

Alternatives	C^* goal: High productivity C=3 L=1	L goal: equity C=1 L=3	L goal: Workplace quality C=1 L=3	L goal: Environmental protection C=1 L=3	L goal: Consumer protection C=1 L=3	N total weights	L total weights	C total weights
L: Government ownership and operation	2	4	2	2	2	24	32	16
C: Private ownership and operation	4	2	2	2	2	24	28	20
N: Some govt. and some private	3	3	2	2	2	18	24	18
S: 100% govt. own and 100% private operation	> 3	> 3	> 3	> 3	> 3	> 30	> 39	> 21

*C, conservative; L, liberal; N, neutral; S, SOS.

NOTES:

1. The SOS alternative of contracting out to private operation can even apply to public schools, post offices, and municipal transportation. In former socialistic countries, it can apply also to contracting out government-owned factories and land.

2. The contracting out does not have to be to only one private entrepreneur. The two most qualified lowest bidders can both receive contracts for different geographical areas, sectors of the industry, or other aspects of the contract in order to encourage competition.

The key capitalistic goal is high productivity in terms of income-producing goods substantially above what it costs to produce them. The key socialistic goal is equity in terms of the sharing of ownership, operation, wealth, and income. Other goals that tend to be more socialistic than capitalistic, but are less fundamental consist of (1) workplace quality, including wages, hours, safety, hiring by merit, and worker input; (2) environmental protection, including reduction of air, water, radiation, noise, and other forms of pollution; and (3) consumer protection, including low prices and goods that are durable, safe, and of high quality.

Going down the productivity column, the liberal socialistic alternative does not score so high on productivity for a lack of profit-making incentives and a surplus of bureaucratic interference as the capitalistic alternative, assuming the level of technology is constant. The empirical validity of that statement is at least partially confirmed by noting that the capitalistic countries of Japan and West Germany are more productive than their socialistic counterparts of East Germany and China, although they began at approximately the same level as of 1945 at the end of World War II. Going down the equity column, the liberal socialistic alternative does score relatively high. By definition, it involves at least a nominal collective sharing in the ownership and operation of industry and agriculture, which generally leads to less inequality in wealth and income than capitalism does.

On the goals that relate to the workplace, the environment, and consumers, the socialists traditionally argue that government ownership-operation is more sensitive to those matters because it is less profit oriented. The capitalists traditionally argue that private ownership-operation is more sensitive in competitive marketplaces in order to find quality workers and to increase the quantity of one's consumers. The reality (as contrasted to the theory) is that without alternative incentives or regulations, both government managers and private managers of factories and farms are motivated toward high production at low cost. That kind of motivation leads to cutting back on the expenses of providing workplace quality, environmental protection, and consumer protection. The government factory manager of the Polish steelworks may be just as abusive of labor as the private factory manager for U.S. Steel. Likewise, the government factory managers in the state factories of China may be just as insensitive to consumer safety and durability as their monopolistic counterparts in the American automobile industry.

As for how the superoptimum solution operates, it involves government ownership, but all the factories and farms are rented to private entrepreneurs to develop productive and profitable manufacturing and farming. Each lease is renewable every year, or longer if necessary to get productive tenants. A renewal can be refused if the factory or farm is not being productively developed, or if the entrepreneur is not showing adequate sensitivity to workers, the environment, and consumers.

As for some of the advantages of such an SOS system, it is easier to not renew a lease than it is to issue injunctions, fines, jail sentences, or other negative sanctions. It is also much less expensive than subsidies. The money received for rent can be an important source of tax revenue for the government to provide productive subsidies elsewhere in the economy. Those subsidies can be especially used for encouraging technological innovation-diffusion, the upgrading of skills, and stimulating competition for market share which can be so much more beneficial to society than either socialistic or capitalistic monopolies. The government can more easily demand sensitivity to workers, the environment, and consumers from its renters of factories and farms than it can from itself. There is a conflict of interest in regulating oneself.

This SOS alternative is only available to socialistic countries like the USSR, China, Cuba, North Korea, and others since they already own the factories and land. It would not be economically or politically feasible for capitalistic countries to move from the conservative capitalistic alternative to the SOS solution by acquiring ownership through payment or confiscation. This is an example where socialistic countries are in a position to decide between socialism and capitalism by compromising and winding up with the worst of both possible worlds. That means the relative unproductivity of socialism and the relative inequity of capitalism. The socialistic countries are also in a position to decide between the two basic alternatives by winding up with the best of both possible worlds. That means retaining the equities and social sensitivities of government ownership, while having the high productivity that is associated with profit-seeking entrepreneurial capitalism. It would be difficult to find a better example of compromising versus superoptimizing than the current debate over socialism versus capitalism.[4]

The third problem is the privatization problem. It illustrates how two apparently conflicting approaches can be simultaneously combined with a somewhat imaginative combination that is not a compromise. It is a combination where both sides do better than their best expectations rather than yield substantially to the other side. Other examples are the example of legal services for the poor with volunteers absorbed into the salaried system through a well-organized clearinghouse and training program, and combining private enterprise and state enterprise in American higher education within the same schools as well as in the system.

V. LATIN AMERICA: PRESIDENTS AND PARLIAMENTS

This is the fundamental political science dispute between parliamentary and presidential governments, which is applicable to all countries.

A. The Alternatives

The conservative position is generally to support presidential government because it gives greater stability, which conservatives like. The liberal position is to support parliamentary government largely because it is more responsive and liberals have traditionally been more interested in responsiveness, at least with regard to economic issues (although not necessarily with regard to civil liberties issues). The neutral position is to try to find a middle position, which is not so easy. One can make it easier to remove the president through impeachment, but that has never been done. One can try to give parliamentary government more stability by saying that it takes a two-thirds vote to bring down the prime minister rather than a mere majority vote, but that has never been done. One can have a presidential government with short terms and no provision for reelection to get more responsiveness. One can likewise have long terms for members of parliament in order to get more stability.

B. The Goals

The conservative goal should be referred to as continuity, not as stability. Stability sounds like stagnation. Continuity implies growth, but smooth growth rather than jerky growth. Continuity can imply change, but change in accordance with some kind of predictability based on previously developed trends. The key liberal goal is responsiveness, which is broad enough to include more than just electoral responsiveness. This could be an example of raising one's goals so as to broaden the notion of responsiveness like broadening the notion of unemployment, and also broadening the notion of continuity.

C. The Superoptimum Solution

The SOS is to say that the structure is not especially important as to whether one has a chief executive who is chosen directly by the people, or indirectly by the people through the parliament. What is needed is a Constitutional or statutory commitment on the part of the chief executive and the government in general.

1.   Responsiveness

A responsiveness that goes beyond merely reading the public opinion polls in order to get reelected. Responsiveness in the traditional political context has meant that it is easy to throw the government out of power. That is more a process designed to bring about responsiveness than responsiveness in itself. Responsiveness should mean such things as that the government is sensitive to people who are displaced as a result of new technologies or reduced tariffs, i.e., the government is responsive to their need for new jobs. A government is much more responsive if it sees to it that displaced workers find new jobs even though the president is a president for life and cannot be thrown out of office than would be a government in which the prime minister can be replaced by 10% of the parliament saying they want to get rid of him. Responsiveness should mean that when people are hurting, the government does something about it other than changing prime ministers.

2.   Stability

On the matter of stability, we do not want stability. We want continuity. We want continuous growth. Growth is change, not stability. We want statutes and Constitutional provisions that will require the government, whether it consists of Republicans or Democrats, to engage in policies that guarantee about 6% growth per year. We do have a 1946 Employment Act and a 1970 Humphrey-Hawkins Act that say unemployment should not get above 3% and that inflation should not get above 3%. Such laws mean nothing because they provide no provision for enforcement. Worse, they provide no provision to achieve those goals. They are the same kind of fiat like King Canute asking the waves to stop, which can be done by the Army Corps of Engineers building appropriate dams, but not simply by issuing a "there shalt not be" statement.

D. A Pair of Constitutional Provisions

The SOS thus would be a set of statutes or a pair of statutes (or better yet, a pair of constitutional provisions).

1. Continuous Economic Growth

That would require 6% a year continuous growth. That is a minimum. There is nothing wrong with doing better than that, even if it is jerky like one year 10%, another year 6%, another year 12%. That sounds very unstable, but neither conservatives nor liberals would object to that kind of instability. Nobody is likely to object to having their income be highly unstable with one year $1 million, the next year $20 million. When people talk about instability they mean jumping from positive to negative, or positive to zero, but not from very high positive to positive and back.

2. Upgrading Skills

The second statute or Constitutional right is an obligation to displaced workers to be retrained and/or relocated. This is like two new Constitutional rights. Traditional Constitutional rights have related to free speech, equal protection, and due process. Modern Constitutional rights have related to Social Security, minimum wage, safe workplace, and more recently clean air. What we are proposing is a Constitutional right to economic growth and to be relocated if one is a displaced worker. The word relocated sounds too much like moving a person from one city to another. We are also talking about upgrading skills so one can get a better job without moving to another city. Instead of talking about the right to relocation, we should talk about the right to upgraded work. It is not the right to work. That phase has been ruined by people who use it to mean the right not to be in a union. A problem with the concept of the right to upgraded work is there is nothing in that concept that confines it to displaced workers, although that is not necessarily bad. Perhaps all workers should have a right to upgraded work. But especially those who have no work at all as a result of technological change or tariff reductions. If there were really a meaningful right to economic growth and upgraded work, that kind of SOS would score high on continuity. To emphasize that, we need to talk about continuous economic growth. The upgraded work part especially relates to the responsiveness of government.

E. Making Those Rights Meaningful

A key point is that those rights are not meaningful by merely being stated in statutes or Constitutions. They are also not that meaningful by saying that someone who feels he has been denied one of those rights can sue Congress or the president. They are made meaningful by establishing institutions like the Ministry of International Trade and Industry that has a mandate, a budget, personnel, and subunits that are meaningfully relevant to promoting continuous economic growth. One could establish a separate government agency to enforce the right to upgraded work. The rights become meaningful when you have institutions in place to enforce them, not just words in place in a statute or a Constitution. The courts cannot enforce them. It requires specialized administrative agencies. The courts can enforce due process by reversing convictions that violate due process. The courts can enforce free speech and equal protection by issuing injunctions ordering the police to cease interfering with speakers or marchers, or ordering the schools to cease operating segregated classrooms. The courts have no power to award well-targeted subsidies or tax breaks which are needed for ecnomic growth and upgraded work. That requires appropriate administrative agencies.[5]

The presidential versus parliamentary problem involves raising the goals or redefining the goals, especially redefining responsiveness and stability (see Table 4). Other examples include the Hong Kong labor shortage, concerned with redefining unemployment, and the jury size problem, which concentrates on goals rather than alternatives, but is a different approach than redefining the goals.

The presidential versus parliament issue has recently taken on new importance in certain countries:

1. In *Israel* it is being proposed as a way of getting out of the paralysis of the parliament being controlled by small political parties that can disrupt a parliamentary coalition by withdrawing. With a president chosen at large, there would be an institution that could govern without so much undue influence of small political parties.

2. The issue has come up in *Yugoslavia* whereby the president would be and has been, three people: one Serbian, one Croatian, and one Slovenian or from one of the other republics. They operated roughly like that, although more at the vice president level, for 30 years. It did not hold the country together. What held the country together was the Communist party which collapsed and so did the country.

3. It came up in *France* under DeGaulle, partly for the same reasons as Israel, namely the instability of coalition government in parliament. The instability is different, though, from that in Israel. In Israel the parliament could be destabilized by a political party that has two seats out of more than 100 seats withdrawing its support from the government. In France the destabilization occurred because there were five political parties, each of which had about 20% of the representa-

Table 4 Presidential Versus Parliamentary Government

Alternatives	C^* goal: continuity	L goal: Responsiveness	N total weights	L total weights	C total weights
C: Presidential government	4	2	12	10	14
L: Parliamentary government	2	4	12	14	10
N: Compromise	3	3	12	12	12
S: Right to continuous economic growth, right to upgraded work	5	5	20	20	20

*C, conservative; L, liberal; N, neutral; S, SOS.
NOTES:
1. The first part of the SOS alternative is to provide a constitutional right to continuous economic growth, backed up by appropriate governmental institutions like a ministry of international trade and industry. This alternative is especially related to the goal of upward continuity, rather than stagnating stability.
2. The second part of the SOS alternative is to provide a Constitutional right to upgraded skills, backed by appropriate governmental institutions, including a separate government agency to administer skills-upgrading programs. This alternative is especially related to the goal of responsiveness to the needs of adult voters to be more needed in the economy, rather than the responsiveness that is associated with rapid turnover of government personnel.

tion and one of those relatively big political parties decided it did not like the government, the government would collapse. Both France and Israel have strong public administration people who carry on regardless what is happening with parliament. But they do not make policy the way parliament or a president would. France now has a compromise system in that they still have a prime minister, but they also have a president.

A bigger issue that relates to separation of powers is the independence of the judiciary, although that is not presidential versus parliament. It is all three branches of government. Another bigger issue has to do with the conflict between coordinated government and political parties that cannot get along. Though that does show up more when one has a president of one party and a parliament of another party, as the United States does. That can lead to more paralysis than a parliamentary form of government that keeps changing as a result of the changing coalitions. Thus the idea of presidential government providing some kind of stability and coherence that parliamentary government does not provide is quite untrue in the case of the United States. And it would probably be the same of other countries where it is possible for the president to be of one party and the parliament to be another party.

It has happened in France with Mitterrand as a socialist president and parliament dominated by conservative parties. France does not get as paralyzed as the United States though, because they do not have a true presidential system. It is a compromise, and Mitterrand may not even have any veto power over what parliament passes. He is like an elected Queen Elizabeth II to some extent, although more than that partly because of his personality. The Soviet Union also had both a president and a prime minister but the president was very explicitly a figurehead whereas the French president is supposed to be more vigorous, especially by virtue of national election. The Soviet president was chosen by the parliament largely for ceremonial purposes.

VI.   SOME CONCLUSIONS

A.   SOS Solutions

More approaches to SOS solutions that we do not have time to discuss in any detail include:

1.   *Expanding the total resources*, which is what people tend to think of almost immediately as virtually the only approach.

2.   *Big benefits for one side, low costs for the other.*

3.   The *package of alternatives* with something for everybody which is also a common approach, especially to reaching compromises. The idea is to include in the package what otherwise would appear to be conflicting alternatives. A better way to put it is that the package should add up to more conservative goal achievement and more liberal goal achievement than the original conservative and liberal alternatives could achieve.

4.   *Reducing costs and increasing benefits.*

B.   Why Superoptimize

One point made by the participants in the seminars where materials like these were presented was that developing countries like China and the Philippines cannot afford the luxury of superoptimum solutions. Instad, they should perhaps be satisfied with something substantially less than the superoptimum (that point sometimes implied that superoptimizing was too complicated except for people trained in computer science, mathematics, statistical analysis, operations research, and other sophisticated methodologies).

After making the presentations, though, the consensus generally was that those methodologies are largely irrelevant. They can sometimes be even harmful if they cause paralysis or an overemphasis on unnecessary measurement and data. The prerequisites for superoptimizing analysis are basically to have (1) some knowledge of the key facts relevant to the problem, (2) an awareness of such political concepts as "conservative" and "liberal," (3) an understanding of such decisional concepts as "goals," "alternatives," "relations," "tentative conclusions," and "what-if analysis," and (4) some creativity in developing appropriate superoptimum solutions. That kind of creativity is made easier by having the first three of the four prerequisites above. It is also made easier by having access to case studies like the ones previously discussed so that one can learn from the experiences of other groups or individuals in trying to develop related superoptimum solutions.

The point about now being able to afford the luxury of superoptimum solutions may, however, in fact be the opposite of empirical and normative reality. The United States and other developed countries have less need for superoptimum solutions than developing countries do. The United States can probably go for a whole generation without developing any innovative ideas or coming close to solving any of its policy problems. If that happened, the United States would still have a high quality of life because it has such a well-developed cushion to fall back on. Developing countries, on the other hand, cannot afford to be satisfied with merely getting by. Doing so will put them further behind relative to other countries that are advancing rapidly, including countries that were formerly developing countries like Japan, Korea, Hong Kong, and Singapore.

In that context, superoptimum solutions are like free speech. Sometimes people in developing countries say they cannot afford free speech because it is too divisive. After they become more developed, then they can allow opposition parties and not have one-party systems with presidents-for-life. The reality is that they especially need to have free speech in order to stimulate creative ideas for solving their policy problems. Those problems are much more in need of solutions than the policy problems of well-developed countries.

ENDNOTES

1. For further material on superoptimum solutions where both liberals and conservatives come out ahead of their initial best expectations, see Lawrence Susskind and Jeffrey Cruikshank, *Breaking the Impasse: Consensual Approaches to Resolving Disputes* (Basic Books, 1987); S. Nagel, *Decision-Aiding Software: Skills, Obstacles and Applications* (Macmillan, 1990); and S. Nagel, "Super-Optimum Solutions in Public Controversies," *World Futures Quarterly*, 53–70 (Spring 1989).

2. For literature on agriculture policy and developing nations, see Ross Talbot, *The Four World Food Agencies in Rome* (Ames: Iowa State University Press, 1990); E.C. Pasour, *Agriculture and the State: Market Processes and Bureaucracy* (New York: Holmes and Meier, 1990); and William Browne and Don Hadwiger (eds.), *World Food Policies: Toward Agricultural Interdependence* (Boulder, CO: Lynne Reinner Publishers, 1986).

3. For further details on public policy analysis toward China population problems, see Judith Banister, *China's Changing Population* (Stanford University Press, 1987), and Jean Robinson, "Of Family Policies in China" in Richard Hula and Elaine Anderson (eds.), *The Family and Public Policy* (Greenwood Press, 1991).

4. On privatization in the Soviet Union and Eastern Europe, see Jan Prybyla (ed.), "Privatizing and Marketizing Socialism" (*Annals of the American Academy of Political and Social Science*, 1990); and Richard Noyes (ed.), *Now the Synthesis: Capitalism, Socialism and the New Social Contract* (Holmes & Meier, 1991). This book contains in an appendix an open letter to Mikhail Gorbachev advocating retention of title to collective farms while renting the land for entrepreneurial development. The open letter is signed by Nobel Prize winners Modigliani, Tobin, and Solow, as well as leading economists from throughout the world. On privatization in general, see John Donahue, *The Privatization Decision: Public Ends, Private Means* (Basic Books, 1989), and Randy Ross, *Government and the Private Sector: Who Should Do What* (Crane Russak, 1988).

5. On the matter of presidential versus parliamentary government, see "Concentration of Power versus Dispersion of Powers" in Leslie Lipson, *The Great Issues of Politics* (Prentice Hall, 1989), 255–281; "Parliamentary and Presidential Systems" in Herbert Levine, *Political Issues Debated* (Prentice Hall, 1982), 217–239; "Forestalling Divided Government" and "Fostering Interbranch Collaboration" in James Sundquist, *Constitutional Reform and Effective Government* (Brookings, 1986), 75–104 and 165–205; and "Comparative Public Bureaucracies: Administrative Performance and Political Responsibility" in Ali Farazmand (ed.), *Handbook of Comparative and Development Public Administration* (Marcel Dekker, 1991), 485–710.

50

The Need for a Concept in Executive Personnel Systems and Development

Saudi Arabia as an Illustrative Case

Adnan A. Alshiha   *Department of Urban and Regional Planning, College of Architecture and Planning, King Faisal University, Damman, Eastern Province, Saudi Arabia*

Frank P. Sherwood   *Department of Public Administration, Florida State University, Tallahassee, Florida*

I. INTRODUCTION

As public organizations have become larger and more complex, the concern about their leadership resources has gained increasing attention. The problem is one that does not divide the developing and developed societies. Quality leadership is always in short supply, and the need for systems that will provide for the continued recruitment, development, utilization, and retirement of leadership personnel has achieved greater recognition.

Yet in the rush to deal with these very real and visible problems, there has also been a pronounced tendency toward oversimplification. One such predisposition is to assume that competency requirements at various levels in large, complex organizations do not particularly differ. Thus, a person who can be relied on to carry out orders will be similarly capable of conceptualizing what needs to be done and providing the necessary guidance to others. In fact, things do not work that way. At essentially each level of an organization, there is a demand for a different mix of competences.

A second, very common, oversimplification is to assume that the problem of securing effective leadership performance is essentially one of training. This assumption reveals still another flaw in thinking and practice around the world, namely, that there is a clear understanding of what one does and how he or she does it. Obviously, if what is to be learned can be clearly articulated, there is a reasonable prospect that learning will take place. As the learning goal becomes more ambiguous, the application of knowledge is more problematic. Not only is the research very murky on the factors that make for leadership effectiveness, but the great majority of executive development programs have been launched without the necessary attention to competency needs and possibilities for leaders in a given context. There has been much talk about leaders and their development, but very little has been done to form the base on which an effective executive personnel system can be constructed. Little has changed theoretically since Hoyle, commenting on deficiencies in executive development, wrote that "despite the large volume of literature about development and development administration, there is as yet no generally agreed on statement of the role of the senior administrator" (Hoyle 1974).

If there is any doubt about the expansion of enthusiasm and investment in systems and training for top level officials, evidence abounds of new initiatives. In the Middle East the Arab Institute of Public Administration staged its first executive development seminar in Tunisia in August–September 1987.

It has been reported that three South American nations (Brazil, Argentina, and Uruguay) have established programs for top-level administrators (Lobo 1987). Argentina was scheduled to graduate its first group in December 1988, Brazil has created centers to establish an "administrative elite," and Uruguay has started a nine-month program for top-level officials. In expressing his approval of these developments, Lobo (1987:85) said:

> Whatever the outcome of these meetings, there is sufficient evidence to conclude that the key to more effective public service is a new breed of leaders. There will always be need for better planners, better finance specialists, better diplomats and better managers as a whole. However, we must provide a new leadership capable of understanding and dealing with a kind of state which is infinitely more complex in all its dimensions than it used to be.

In Australia and New Zealand reforms of the executive personnel systems have been part of a larger effort to reduce inflexibilities in the bureaucratic process and to provide a much higher degree of freedom to manage. In the Australian national government a senior executive service (SES) was established in 1984 as a centerpiece of the effort to induce higher productivity and performance. A 1983 statement of the government's intentions to reform the Australian public service declared it would focus on "developing a senior executive service free of political patronage which places greater emphasis on management ability, appraisal of performance, and flexibility of deployment in accordance with government priorities" (*Reforming the Australian Public Service* 1983:9). In 1988, the Australian public service commissioner, charged with administering the SES noted that the prime minister had stated to parliament in September 1987 that there would be "a new emphasis on the development of management skills in senior executives" (Enfield 1988). The commissioner himself said:

> The demands on SES officers, which flow from these changes, are substantial. As well changes in the thinking and attitudes of SES officers have been necessary to cope with reforms to administrative law, and with the introduction of equal employment opportunity and industrial democracy . . . SES officers now need to be better managers of people, money and resources. They need to be more entrepreneurial and to think and act more like managers in the private sector. They need to give more attention to the motivation and leadership of their staff. And at the same time they need to maintain the high quality of their policy advice (Enfield 1988:5–6).

The establishment of an SES in the national government was preceded by one in the state of Victoria. SES systems are being considered in other Australian states, most significantly in New South Wales. A senior executive service was also established as part of major reforms of the bureaucracy in New Zealand. Indeed, it was a major part of the dramatic overhaul of New Zealand administrative machinery provided in the State Sector Act 1988, which took effect on April 1, 1988. The act states that the reason for establishing an SES is:

> "to provide and maintain for Public Service a group of senior executives who—(a) Have the ability to manage, at the most senior level, Departments of the Public Service; and (b) By reason of their training and approach to management in the Public Service, shall constitute a unifying force at the most senior levels of the Public Service; and (c) Shall comprise the senior executive service of the Public Service" (State Sector Act 1988:23–24).

While the movement to establish executive personnel systems and development programs is obviously proceeding at a rapid pace, questions must be raised on whether the framers of these undertakings have confronted the problems that have bedeviled efforts in the past. Broad-gauge, effective leaders are needed now, just as they have been in the past. The existence of a need, however, does not necessarily suggest the capacity to specify, summon, and utilize the resources required for satisfaction of that need. As has been pointed out, the very ambiguity that surrounds the whole question of leadership suggests how easy it is to over simplify and to make assumptions that do not have a base in reality.

II. SEARCHING FOR A CONCEPT OF THE EXECUTIVE

It is because of these kinds of issues that the research reported in this essay was undertaken. Saudi Arabia is one of the rapidly developing nations of the world and has achieved immense progress in the last several decades. In the course of these events, there has been a bureaucratic rationalization of its governmental processes. It now boasts a large and complex national government, one that shares with others around the world a need for effective leadership.

Like other modernizing governments, Saudi Arabia has developed an increasing interest in securing the necessary leadership resources for its expanding and complex society. Its Institute of Public Administration, acclaimed for the scale and quality of its programs, has long offered courses in executive development. Yet even this highly respected institution has had difficulty attracting the "real" executives of Saudi Arabia to its programs. Inevitably, the question must be raised whether present strategies are, in fact, meeting the need to identify, develop, and nourish the people who must be recognized as critical to the success of a society.

Inquiry into these issues does not begin, however, with executive development programs. The process of understanding requires a scrutiny of events and circumstances that long predate the establishment of any particular form of training. It was the recognition of this reality that prompted an examination of the Saudi Arabian executive population: who they are, what they do, how they see themselves. In this context, Saudi Arabia can be considered a surrogate for many of the world's societies. It is highly likely that the characteristics of the executive population in this Middle Eastern nation will be found in many other developing nations around the world.

One clear discovery, to be discussed in detail below, was that people at or near the top of government in Saudi Arabia are very much aware that they have tasks and obligations that reach well beyond the more routinized burdens of the middle manager. Yet they have not really begun to internalize the concept of a quite separate organizational role, which, in the U.S. literature, has come to bear the label executive. As a result, incumbents of these positions experience the realities of being an executive but behave as if they were order takers, still residing at middle management levels of the hierarchy.

A. Origins in the United States

The notion of the executive is a relatively new one and seems particularly to have been embraced in the United States. It has been far more common to speak of the "higher civil service," a perspective that does little more than add a hierarchical descriptor to denote status within the career system. Also, the administrative class in the British tradition involves quite a different orientation. It is person-focused, whereas the executive concept is concerned with role. A young man enters the administrative class at about age 25 and makes a career of government service, rising through the ranks and perhaps achieving the status of Sir Humphrey in the British television series "Yes, Minister." In terms of executive theory, on the other hand, the fact that Minister Hacker and Permanent Secretary Humphrey arrived at their present set of responsibilities by different routes does not in any way detract from the reality that they now share a unique set of leadership responsibilities.

1.   Relationship to Separation of Powers Doctrine

While there is little virtue in dwelling extensively on the word executive and its origins, it is important to recognize that it has been a core concept in separation of powers theory, upon which the U.S. government is based. The *Oxford Universal Dictionary on Historical Principles* (1964) notes that the noun executive refers "essentially to a branch of government," and a second definition is of a person in whom the supreme executive magistracy of a country or state is vested. The president of the United States is chief executive of the nation, with responsibility for leading the branch of government that is obligated to "execute" the laws. In this classic sense the word executive certainly conveys the idea of a special niche within the organization and perhaps best suggests the dimensions of a unique and important set of leadership roles within organizations.

2.   Wilson's Use of the Word Executive

In his classic essay "The Study of Administration," Woodrow Wilson found the word executive a helpful one to explain his concerns for administrative performance in the U.S. government (Wilson 1887, 1976). He observed that the U.S. Constitution had little to say about the organizational responsibilities of the presidency, "the greatest of the purely executive offices" (Wilson 1976: 276). He couched his argument for greater attention to administration in the following terms:

> The object of administrative study is to reduce *executive* methods from the confusion and costliness of empirical experiment and set them upon foundations laid deep in stable principle. . . . We are now rectifying methods of reappointment; we must go on to adjust *executive* functions more fitly and to prescribe better methods of *executive* organization and action [italics added] (Wilson 1976:275).

B.   Chester Barnard: Still the Resource for Understanding

In many respects, however, it was an American, Chester Barnard, who provided the intellectual dimension to the word executive in respect to management institutions. His *Functions of the Executive*, published in 1938, developed an immediate following, but it was literally a generation before the full range of his ideas gained a substantial acceptance (Barnard 1938). In the U.S. government, for example, it was only in the decade of the 1960s that the idea of the executive became firmly implanted in personnel practices and processes. An executive assignment system was created in 1967, followed by the creation of a federal executive institute in 1968. Earlier, in the 1950s, the proposal of the Second Hoover Commission to establish an executive personnel system carried the label Senior Civil Service.

1.   The Executive Is Not a Manager

Barnard declares that an executive is *not* a manager. Executives, as he sees it, are a step removed from the operating system of the managers. Asked how he made decisions, one corporate executive is alleged to have said, "I don't make decisions. I create the environment in which decisions are made." Bernard (1938:216) makes much the same point, in arguing for the specialty of the executive role:

The executive functions serve to maintain a system of cooperative effort. They are impersonal. The functions are not, as so frequently stated, to manage a group of persons. I do not think a correct understanding of executive work can be had if this narrower, convenient, but strictly speaking erroneous, conception obtains. It is not even quite correct to say that the executive functions are to manage the system of cooperative efforts. As a whole it is managed by itself, not by the executive organization, which is a part of it.

2.   Attributes of Executives

His discussion of the characteristics needed by executives further suggests the unique tasks in which he expects such people to engage. Barnard identifies four attributes to which he would give priority in selection of executives:

1.   Ability to sense the whole of the system and to understand the harmony of its parts.
2.   Feel the infinite complexity of organizations.
3.   Possess a sense of responsibility, which is dominated by the needs of the organization.
4.   Feel a loyalty that involves a willingness to subjugate one's own needs to those of the organization.

3.   Functions of Executives

Finally, Barnard (1938) posits three basic functions in which executives must engage and that, in effect, define the role.

1.   Formulate the purpose and objectives of the organization. While such formulation is conceived as a function of the executive, Barnard did not conceive it as the responsibility of any single individual. He observed, "No single executive can under any conditions accomplish this function . . . the critical aspect of this function is the assignment of responsibility" (p. 231). Continuing, Barnard wrote, "The function of formulating purposes and objectives and providing for their redefinition is one which needs sensitive systems of communication, experience in interpretation, imagination, and delegation of responsibility" (p. 233).

2.   Promote the securing of essential efforts needed for organization success. While this function may seem an obvious need in any organization, Barnard's detailing of the burdens reveals how difficult is its accomplishment. In effect, he wrote that there are two sides to fulfilling the organization's responsibility: (a) making sure that the work is directed to the appropriate goals, and (b) providing a set of rewards and incentives to the organization members that will be sufficient to secure maximal contributions from them.

He described appropriateness of goals as involving the question of effectiveness. Thus an organization is effective to the degree that it pursues and accomplishes the goals that are most relevant to its mission and larger purpose. "The executive process," he wrote, "even when narrowed to the aspect of effectiveness of organization and the technologies of organization, is one of integration of the whole, of finding the effective balance between the local and broad considerations, between the general and specific requirements" (p. 238). It is clear that Barnard saw the executive as making a special contribution to the organization both by continued reexamination of priorities and by insisting that efforts be directed toward those priorities.

The securing of an appropriate balance of inducements to secure the full commitment of members to the work of the organization was conceived by Barnard as an issue of efficiency. His use of the word, obviously, differed dramatically from standard definitions. While he was not thinking in mechanistic terms, he did honor the idea of a relationship between input and output, as shown in this comment: "maintenance of an equilibrium of organization activities through the satisfaction of the motives of individuals sufficient to induce these activities" (p. 240). An efficient organization over the long run, then, is one that makes sure the rewards are sufficient to cause people to want to stay and to contribute to the best of their ability. In many respects, this concept of efficiency puts high emphasis on the importance of human resources and suggests the critical responsibility of the executive in this area.

3.   Provide a system of communication. Again, the function appears almost elementary, but it is certainly more than writing memos and giving speeches. The first part of Barnard's book is devoted to developing a concept of organizations, and in the last analysis, he regarded an organization as essentially a system of communications. To be sure, there are many forces that either promote or inhibit communications, but the reality, in Barnard's terms, is that organizations are human, interacting systems. Fundamentally, the executive must be constantly attentive to organization strategies that will facilitate cooperation and collaboration and also recognize that getting the right people into the right spots is an important element in effective communications.

Because Chester Barnard's ideas continue to epitomize current orientations toward the executive role, they must be regarded as a foundation for inquiry. It is essentially in his terms that perceptions of the responsibility of top officials must be examined, that the premises of executive personnel systems must be reviewed, and that the relevance and potential contributions of executive development programs must be evaluated.

III.   THE SAUDI ARABIA CASE

A.   Background Information

Saudi Arabia is an ideal representative of a substantial number of developing countries for two principal reasons: (1) it is a mix of a traditional society and a modern one, and (2) the public sector represents a large percentage of the economy, even though there is a free-market system. It is a relatively new state, established in 1932. During the early stages of its development, there was no central administrative body and no modern administrative mechanism with which to manage the country. In the period since 1932 two major factors have influenced its administrative development: (1) the nonconstitutional monarchy as the essence of the political system, and (2) oil revenues.

1.   Prevailing Assumptions

The prevailing assumption has been that executive work can be performed by anyone who is loyal and sincere. Top officials in the early stages of the nation's development were required mainly to provide information and to carry out orders. The process was one-way communication, not interaction and discussion. It was so personalized that many government decisions were made by the king.

The establishment of the Council of Ministers in 1953 marked a real turning point in the administrative development of Saudi Arabia and has led to a continuing increase of rational decision-making processes. However, there has not been a clarification of the difference between the roles of top officials (who should be performing executive functions) and those of middle and lower management. The personnel system makes a distinction between the upper levels (grades 11 to 15) and lower ones only in terms of salaries, fringe benefits, and appointment procedures. Further, all are subject to the same administrative procedures. Thus, there is no executive personnel system in Saudi Arabia, and the absence of such a system has perhaps contributed to the lack of understanding of the executive role and its uniqueness.

2.   Conservative Introduction of Change

Saudi Arabia's relatively short history as a modern nation-state and its commitment to preserving tradition has inevitably affected all aspects of its administrative system. Changes have been introduced conservatively, in order not to disturb traditional social values. Reforms that vary from formal modern education to new administrative rules and regulation have at times been delayed in order to honor the traditional perspective. The effect of this orientation was particularly evident in the early stages of the nation's development when there was a severe shortage of qualified Saudi personnel. This deficit forced the government to fill even high-level administrative positions with non-Saudis. When a few Saudis had acquired a minimum of education, the government was quick to appoint them to high positions, even though their education did not necessarily translate into needed executive competences.

The shortage of qualified personnel continues to be a problem. Now, however, the lack is not one of quantity. There is a substantial number of people with significant education, but degrees do not necessarily qualify one for executive responsibility. Academic qualifications are only one criterion for assessing leadership capacity. In the Saudi public bureaucracy, though, education is assigned a heavy weight in the selection process. Thus there is still a problem of securing quality people at the top levels to deal with an increased complexity of problems and issues.

B.   Nature of the Study in Saudi Arabia

A field study was conducted in Saudi Arabia to determine whether the concepts of executive, executive personnel system, and executive development had taken root among current leaders of the government (Alshiha 1987). The research was conducted through the medium of interviews and questionnaires, with the target population those in the position of general administrator and higher. Such positions are usually graded between 11 and 15 in the civil service and are considered high status.

The central ministries possess the majority of the executives in government service because centralization is still the general mode. As a result, it was convenient and reasonable to restrict the study to the central ministries in the capital city of Riyadh. The number of questionnaires returned (129) was about 50% of the number distributed (260). Given all the forces operating in this situation, the return was considered sufficient to provide important insights on the attitudes of the executive population. Interviews were held with 16 senior officials who were in a particularly good position to reflect on the role of the executive in the Saudi system.

C.   Study Findings

The study findings showed that the concept of the executive has relatively few roots in Saudi Arabia, which is not surprising. Even the concept of rational authority is still a relatively new idea. The concepts of role, system, and development for executives have not yet been assigned much importance, even though the data show the Saudi executive population is fairly young and highly educated. As the awareness of the need for change has grown, the conflict between what ought to be and what is becomes more apparent. Top officials continue to concentrate on the work that is appropriate to middle management: present, specific, internal, and routine administrative tasks. At the same time, most of them expressed the belief that such activities should not consume their time.

1.   Recognition of Importance of Policy-Making Responsibility

Forty-seven percent of respondents, for example, felt that policy making is the most important responsibility of the Saudi executive, and engagement in routine was seen as significant to only

Table 1 Most Important Role of Saudi Executives

Role	Frequency	Percent
Policy making	61	47.3
Controlling	35	27.1
Communicating	23	17.8
Relations with other agencies	4	3.1
Routine tasks	6	4.1
Total	129	100.0

4.1% of the respondents (Table 1). But when they were asked which function required the most of their time, 38.8% indicated it was directing and 38% replied organizing. Planning was reported by 18.6% as consuming the largest amount of time, and 4.7% said their most consuming activity was representation (Table 2). Thus the routine of the administrative process consumes a major portion of the Saudi executives' effort and attention. While the data in Table 1 suggest that Saudi executives have a practical understanding of what must be done at the leadership level, it is obvious from their reports on time use that they are faced with difficulties in constructing their work day to accommodate such imperatives. Strict rules and regulations greatly restrict the freedom of even topmost officials to establish new patterns of behavior.

Despite the fact that the major investment in directing and organizing suggests a heavy menu of day-to-day, repetitive activity, the top leaders in Saudi Arabia do not think of themselves as extensively engaged in routine. The majority (56.5%) see their jobs as diversified to some extent, and more than a third (35.6%) view them as ever changing (Table 3). Only 10 of the 129 respondents (7.8%) classified their jobs as routine.

Table 2 Functions That Require Most of an Executive's Time

Function	Frequency	Percent
Planning	24	18.6
Organizing	49	38.0
Directing	50	38.8
Representing	6	4.7
Total	129	100.00

Table 3 Executives' Classification of Their Work

Responses	Frequency	Percent
Routine style	10	7.8
Diversified to some extent	73	56.6
Always changing	46	35.6
Total	129	100.0

Table 4   Reasons That Executives Become Involved in Routine Work

Reasons	Frequency	Percent
Does not delegate for fear the subordinate will take charge	61	47.3
Likes to be in center of things	30	23.4
System requires him to be involved	33	25.8
Distrusts subordinates	13	10.2
Total	129	100.0

2.   Intrusion of Cultural Factors in Dictating Behavior

Obviously, the problem of getting a grip on the role and responsibility of the executive in Saudi Arabia goes deeper than system demands for conformity. There is, in the culture of the bureaucracy, an assumption that a leader who delegates his authority is revealing that he is not in charge. Thus, when asked what causes them to become involved in routine work, 40.6% of the respondents reported that they do not delegate because of the fear that the subordinate will usurp power (Table 4). It is also evident that any prospect for realignment of duties between middle managers and executives is inhibited by the attitudes of the executives themselves. Three-fourths of them expressed either (1) a fear of the potential power of the subordinate, (2) a distrust of the subordinate, or (3) a desire to be at the center of things. This occurs in spite of the fact that there appears to be a general belief on the part of the respondents that lower-level managers can do the routine work to which everyone currently appears to direct much of their time.

System demands for conformity through rules can be exploited by a leader in various ways. Regulations and tight control have the potential to enhance influence and control. Al-Tawail (1986:55) noted that

> exploitation of official positions and authority for personal gain manifests itself as a behavioral problem in numerous forms, such as use of official property for personal purposes, misuse of public funds, and illegal financial rewards received in return for special treatment, practices which are contrary to administrative norms, social values and ethics.

The attitude and behavior of executives shaped in this way creates an administrative environment of mistrust. Since the executive either is using the system or is afraid that someone else is, he concentrates his efforts and attention on watching and controlling all administrative procedures, even small details, so as to protect himself.

3.   Responsibility Focused on the Superior

Because of the absence of a competitive environment, many executives feel responsible only to their superiors, and not to situational or environmental demands. It is therefore not surprising that only 4.7% of the respondents believed that decisions of top officials were based on the influence of the public and only 7.8% thought that interaction with other organizations had an effect on decisions (Table 5). These are very low compared to the 49.6% who reported that decisions resulted from the demands of the hierarchical leadership. The dominant role that bureaucracy plays in the political system has created a situation in which it is difficult to identify the interests of the public.

The Saudi Arabian economy has expanded so rapidly that much bureaucratic effort has been directed toward maintenance and immediate service tasks, typically undertaken with little preplanning or preparation. As a result, the majority of the respondents (51.9%) identified strategic

Table 5   Basis for Decision Making in Top Positions

Basis	Frequency	Percent
Routine work	34	26.4
Public influence	6	4.7
Interaction with other organizations	10	7.8
Political leadership	64	49.6
Other (public interest, what situation requires, all the above)	15	11.6
Total	129	100.0

planning as the most difficult part of their job (Table 6). This result is not surprising for a system that has caused its executives to think in terms of immediate requirements and to respond to orders from above. Of other difficulties executives face on the job, controlling, with a response of 17.1%, lagged far behind strategic planning as a problem. The emphasis on controlling does, of course, imply that a substantial number of respondents have not yet diverged from a rules and procedures orientation. It can be hypothesized, though, that the difficulties of controlling are outcomes of a rapidly changing and complex system in which feelings of responsibility by the executive have actually out-distanced reality. The failure to delegate the routine to lower and middle management could exacerbate the feeling at higher levels that things are out of control.

IV. CONCLUSION

The perceptions and experiences of Saudi executives are very similar to their peers in other countries. They recognize that those at the top have a special responsibility to see that the organization is directed and moving toward goals that are appropriate for its environmental imperatives. Yet they, like others, find it very difficult to discharge such responsibilities. It is not surprising that an overwhelming number of respondents specified that the toughest part of the job was strategic planning.

While it is very likely that most Saudi executives have a good sense of what they should be doing, there is little support for reaching out in new directions. The hierarchical system itself is a

Table 6   Executives' Responses Concerning the Most Difficult Parts of the Executive Job

Responses	Frequency	Percent
Strategy planning	67	51.9
Controlling	22	17.1
Delegation	8	6.2
Time management	15	11.6
Relations with other organizations	7	5.4
Communication	9	7.0
Other	1	0.8
Total	129	100.0

great restraint on the expression of initiative and difference. The perception that decisions are made largely in terms of hierarchical influence is an important indicator of the limits placed on the individual executive. Further, one does not live in such an environment of hierarchical norms without being affected by it. The present leaders have a great deal of "unlearning" to do, in order to become comfortable with a more chaotic, less predictable, and change-oriented bureaucracy.

The extent of the difficulties that must be confronted is seen most strikingly in the implicit rejection of the basic thesis of Chester Barnard that executives should not manage. Clearly, what Saudi executives are doing is managing. They spend the greater part of their time on directing and organizing activities, and there are few decipherable distinctions between them and lower-level managers. The managerial role appears to be much honored; that of the executive (in Barnard's terms) tends to be ignored. Nor is it likely that a realignment of responsibilities so as to provide opportunities to work at the executive level will come easily. Fully three-fourths of the respondents in the study indicated personal feelings that would substantially block any major delegation efforts.

It should not be assumed that these references to Saudi executives suggest that they are in any substantial way different from their colleagues in other countries. The overwhelming predisposition is for executives to manage—in effect, to do the same things as their subordinates at somewhat higher status and pay. Barnard's essential point that executives assume institutional responsibilities beyond the day-to-day seems generally to have been lost in the rush to proclaim systems and programs that will infuse a new cast of characters without engaging in the hard work of conceptualizing the role of the executive. Only with a clear sense of role can systems and development programs be articulated that will meet a generally recognized need, namely, to provide the world's nations with the best possible leadership resources.

REFERENCES

Alshiha, A. Executive development in Saudi Arabia: the concepts and perspectives. Unpublished doctoral dissertation, Florida State University, Tallahassee, 1987.

Al-Tawail, M. *Public Administration in the Kingdom of Saudi Arabia.* Institute of Public Administration, Riyadh, Saudi Arabia, 1986.

Barnard, C. *Functions of the Executive.* Harvard University Press, Cambridge, MA, 1938.

Enfield, J.D. Speech to the Australian Government Senior Executives' Association. June 2, 1988:4–6.

Hoyle, A.R. some deficiencies in training for senior administrators. *International Review of Administrative Sciences* 40:329–334 (1974).

Lobo, L.C.D. In *The Changing Nature of the Public Service*: *Implications for Education and Training* (K. Kernaghan, ed.). International Institute of Administrative Sciences, Brussels, 1987:77–86.

Oxford Universal Dictionary on Historical Principles. Clarendon Press, Oxford, England (3rd ed. rev. with agenda), 1964:658.

Reforming the Australian Public Service: *A Statement of the Government's Intentions.* Australian Government Publishing House, Canberra, 1983.

State Sector Act 1988, Government of New Zealand. Y.R. Ward, Government Printer, Wellington, New Zealand, 1988.

Wilson, W. The study of administration. *Political Science Quarterly* 2:197–222 (1887).

Wilson, W. I. *Public Administration*: *Cases and Concepts* (R. Stillman, ed.). Houghton Mifflin, Boston, 1976:269–281.

51

The State, Government Bureaucracies, and Their Alternatives

Milton J. Esman   *Department of Government, Cornell University, Ithaca, New York*

I. INTRODUCTION

The three decades following World War II witnessed the high point in the expansion of the modern state. State planning and economic management, it was confidently believed, could ensure steady, uninterrupted economic growth, while the welfare state could underwrite material security and expanded social services for all. This was an era of unprecedented faith in the beneficent role of activist government. It was a universal phenomenon, whether measured by the share of the economy managed and allocated by government or by the proportion of the labor force in public employment. Confidence in the state and in a large public sector in the economy was even more pronounced among the elites of the "developing," newly independent third world societies than among attentive publics in the industrialized countries that were practicing Keynesian economics and expanding their welfare programs. In the socialist states the economy was owned and managed and all economic and social institutions were operated by government in the name of the working class.

II. BUREAUCRACY AND BIG GOVERNMENT

The main operating agents of all these states were their large bureaucratic structures. Whether formally government departments or quasi-government corporations, they functioned similarly and according to the same logic of hierarchy and formal rules. The deficiencies and dysfunctions of bureaucracy were widely recognized—and lamented—by scholars, while bureaucrats were fair game in all these societies for frustrated politicians. The remedies that were proposed—enhancement of skills, improvement of informational and financial management technologies, realignment and rationalization of functions, better incentives through material rewards or by humanizing management and fostering employee participation, more representative recruitment—all were targeted at the high-priority and admittedly difficult task of improving the performance of state bureaucracies, including responsiveness to political control, efficiency in resource use, effectiveness in service delivery, and satisfaction of the public, the intended beneficiaries of their efforts. The implicit assumption was that once government became active in any sector, it must operate through bureaucratic agencies. Therefore the core of academic public administration concerned the behavior of state bureaucracies, while administrative reform was mostly a matter of improving their performance. Dependence of the activist state on its bureaucratic instruments was also incorporated into the conventional wisdom of political thought.

The inevitable reaction against the activist state surfaced as a political challenge in the mid-1970s. The leveling off of economic growth, aggravated by the oil crisis of 1973, triggered taxpayer revolts among the expanded middle classes in Europe and North America, convinced that the high taxes on their earnings were being swallowed up by swollen, unproductive state bureaucracies. They and the welfare states over which they presided were charged with distributing overgenerous welfare largesse to undeserving malingerers in league with arrogant labor unions that were using their muscle to extract an excessive, unearned share of the social product.

III. THE NEOLIBERAL REACTION

This mood of disaffection provided a fresh and welcome constituency for business elites and a resurgent neoliberal and antistate ideology that infused new life into what had seemed to be an outmoded, laissez faire, free market approach to public policy. The well-financed neoliberals launched aggressive, wide-ranging attacks on the interventionist state. Government regulation, they urged, had intruded into every corner of social and economic life, abusing individual rights by arbitrary, meddlesome, and collectivist rules imposed by uninformed, power-hungry bureaucrats accountable to no authority but themselves. The excessive taxes that sustained these unproductive and often corrupt bureaucratic structures stifled economic initiative, while misallocating funds in unproductive subsidies to dying industries and in wasteful, welfare-type expenditures. Along with the labor unions, big government and its parasitical bureaucracies, they argued, were the main problem; they needed to be reined in and in many cases dismantled. A generation that had become accustomed to to ever-rising living standards responded sympathetically to this explanation of the current economic malaise. Its credibility further reduced by chronic price inflation, the activist state ceased expanding and began to retrench.

Beginning in the late 1970s, neoliberals became the universal tone setters for government. Their ascendency was reflected in Margaret Thatcher's unexpected capture of the leadership of the British Conservative Party and her triumph in the general election of 1979. This was followed shortly by the stunning victory in 1980 of Ronald Reagan, a devout convert to the neoliberal creed. Their simple goal was to roll back the interventionist welfare state, to strip it of resources by massive tax cuts, especially for high income individuals and corporations, to restore macro-economic management as far as possible to market forces, and to reduce to a minimum government regulation of economic activity in the interest of business incentives and economic efficiency. State-owned enterprises were to be privatized, divested to private ownership and management. Subsidies to maintain employment in noncompetitive, declining industries and enterprises would be eliminated, social services cut back, welfare entitlements restrained, and labor unions weakened.

The attack on the state reached the third world through the bilateral and multilateral foreign aid agencies, strongly influenced by the British and especially the U.S. government, now in the hands of committed neoliberals whose sense of mission transcended their own state boundaries. Many third world countries had suffered from the contraction of export markets for their primary products in the wake of the international economic slowdown of the late 1970s. To maintain import levels, especially for the urban middle classes, they had contracted heavy debts from commercial banks which they were no longer able to service. Evidence of crude corruption and of gross economic mismanagement were everywhere apparent, including overvalued exchange rates, subsidies for consumption of semiluxuries as well as of necessities, and support for incompetently managed, money-losing enterprises. Together, these produced unsustainable drains on these weak economies, inhibiting production, especially in agriculture. In response to desperate pleas for assistance, the prevailing foreign aid prescriptions, following the neoliberal paradigm, were marketization, deregulation, and privatization, to allow the markets to allocate, stimulate, and discipline economic activity rather than the state and its incompetent, self-serving politicians and bureaucratic agencies. "Policy dialogues" were held and "structural adjustment" loans awarded to impecunious third world governments on condition that they undertake reforms of this type. Neoliberals were persuaded that big government and state bureaucracy had betrayed the third world even more than they had failed the industrialized countries. Most third world leaders in the absence of alternatives, complied with these strictures, less from conviction than from dire necessity. The neoliberal paradigm has retained its intellectual and policy hegemony during the balance of the 20th century.

IV. SOCIALIST NEOLIBERALISM

Prior to the collapse of the Soviet Union in 1991 and the discrediting of socialist economic management, several of the Eastern European countries had attempted to relax centralized bureaucratic management of their economies and allow greater freedom for private enterprise and market processes. Even the Soviet Union under Gorbachev made some gestures in this direction under the label of *perestroika.* The successors of Mao Zedong, beginning in the late 1970s, moved decisively toward market incentives in all sectors of the Chinese economy except heavy industry, despite the opposition of entrenched officialdom and party ideologues. The result in increased production was so spectacular as to energize the entire Chinese economy; the momentum led to the encouragement of foreign investment on a large scale, capitalizing on a well-educated but disciplined, low-wage labor force and the appeal of the potentially enormous Chinese domestic market. The benefits were widely diffused, with substantial gains in living standards. By the 1990s, though the Chinese Communist Party retained undisputed control of government, China had for all practical purposes abandoned the socialist economic model, including bureaucratic management of the economy.

V. GLOBALIZATION OF THE NEOLIBERAL PARADIGM

The prevailing trend is one of globalized market capitalism featuring the transnational mobility of investment capital, large-scale labor migration, and increasingly free passage of goods and services across state boundaries. The dominant institution of the new economy is the large transnational corporation. Because of this evolving global regime, governments have lost some of the control they once exercised or claimed to exercise over their domestic economic affairs, and find themselves required to offer conducive conditions for private enterprise in order to attract job-creating foreign investment. Yet, despite the cheers of some free-market zealots, this has not presaged the demise of the modern state or seriously diminished the need for government services or government regulation, whether provided by state bureaucracies or by other institutions.

During the 1980s the World Bank attempted, through structural adjustment loans, to impose the neoliberal model on third world member states that asked it for assistance to overcome the effects of excessive indebtedness and fiscal bankruptcy. This model called for sharply cutting back the role of government in their economies and for fiscal retrenchment which usually entailed contracting public employment and reducing public services, including education, food subsidies, health, and agricultural extension. These reduced public services adversely impacted low-income families. By the mid-1990s, the Bank had concluded that an effective market economy requires a network of efficient public services including a legal order, law enforcement, sound economic policies and efficient tax collection machinery, plus an infrastructure of public works, schools, and agricultural research and extension, all of them administered by a well-compensated, merit-based civil service.

These lessons had been emphasized by their experiences with post-Communist Russia and the successor states of the former Soviet Empire. For the current neoliberal regime of economic globalization, government remains a necessity, inter alia to protect their citizens from some of the abuses of unrestrained market competition. Since government services must be administered, the principal question is not whether but how. If not by familiar bureaucratic methods, then how?

VI. PERSISTENCE OF THE MODERN STATE

Though its activities, especially in the economic realm, have been contracting during the past quarter century, the modern state remains a formidable presence. Despite the reveries of some neoliberal ideologues and their libertarian allies, the state is nowhere in danger of withering way. The combined intellectual assault on the state by economic conservatives on the right (because it intrudes on private property rights, abridges economic freedom, and distorts economic efficiency) and by their unlikely allies on the countercultural left (because the state and its dehumanizing bureaucracies are believed to be inherently violent exploiters of mankind and of the natural environment) has failed to displace its essential functions. These include national and domestic security; management of international political and economic relations; the building, operation, and maintenance of the physical infrastructure; provision of education, health, and welfare services; protection of natural resources; and management of macroeconomic policy in the interest of growth, stability, employment, and distributional equity. These regulatory, promotional, service, and distributional activities are performed by all modern governments, varying more with their capabilities than with their ideologies. All these activities have to be administered.

How these numerous activities that remain within the purview of the state are to be carried out is our main concern. This depends partly on the values to which individual regimes are committed. The enhancement and maintenance of the power of political elites is surely one such value, along with the availability of the patronage which sustains that power. Ideology is an autonomous variable in determining what the state should should do and how. Both the deployment of power and the force of ideology are conditioned by the constitutional structure of the state and by conventions that prescribe appropriate relations with society. Subordinate to these macropolitical concerns are questions about the relative priority allotted to economic efficiency, individual security, social equity, and responsiveness to public preferences. These often competing values are manifest in the choice of government activities, the design of specific programs, and selection of alternative methods of implementation.

In recent years, in response to economic stagnation, the imperatives of economic efficiency and growth have been displacing individual security, social equity, and indeed responsiveness to public preferences in the policies and programs of governments everywhere. In many third world countries state subsidies for consumption have been eliminated, raising the price of foodstuffs, urban transportation, and other necessities for the urban poor; in the United States tax rates on high incomes have been drastically lowered and welfare services to the poor cut back, further skewing the distribution of income in the dubious hope that this would provide incentives to the wealthy to invest their additional surpluses and thereby stimulate economic growth.

Notwithstanding the general tendency to curb the state, governments everywhere remain responsible for large areas of human concern. What has become increasingly evident, however, is that there are multiple means by which the state can undertake these activities and that this widening range of options has important implications for the study and practice of public administration. A review of these options may be useful to demonstrate the instrumental alternatives available for managing the activities of government.

VII. IMPROVING BUREAUCRATIC MANAGEMENT

The conventional method is that of of direct operation by government through bureaucratic channels. This is how governments are normally organized to conduct business with the public. Bureaucratic structures maximize control from the top, thereby enhancing the power of state elites and the patronage available to them. Since bureaucratic accountability tends to be hierarchical and upward looking, it is weak on responsiveness to public expressions of need, convenience, and preferences. And while bureaucratic agencies may appropriate power from their nominal superiors and use that power to exploit the public, sometimes for their own material benefit, the rules that normally govern their behavior tend also to limit their discretion and thereby provide some measure of predictability and security to the public. The principal burden assumed by academic public administration and management science has been to find ways to extract greater productivity from the resources committed to bureaucratic operations.

More recently, neoclassical economists have found a way—when they are unable to realize their preferred option, transferring government programs to the market—to exorcise the bugbear of bureaucratic monopoly by introducing "market surrogates" into bureaucratic operations. The intention is to require government agencies to compete against one another to attract customers, rewarding those that perform most effectively according to this criterion. Requiring pension funds to compete for subscribers or public schools to compete for students are instances of this policy. The current Chinese experiment with subjecting industrial enterprises to market competition and discipline is a version of the technique of market surrogates applied to economic operations that remain essentially governmental and bureaucratic in their structure but that are expected to be toned up by the necessity of competitive survival and the promise of material rewards for those that compete successfully. The challenge of market surrogates is to reconcile the centralized rules and standardized procedures inherent in bureaucratic operations with the freedom of operation required for successful market competition.

VIII. CONTRACTING FOR SERVICES

Contracting is an important alternative to direct operations. Policies and goals are set and enforced by government, but operations are conducted by individuals and firms outside government. Instead of building and maintaining roads by government departments, these tasks are carried out by contractors selected competitively. Similar procedures can apply to health services, schooling, the management of pension funds, the operation of prisons and hospitals, refuse collection, and the provision of military supplies and equipment. Instead of performing these economic and social services by government-owned and bureaucratically managed institutions, government sees that these activities are performed by engaging private profit-seeking or voluntary nonprofit organizations. Government provides the financing, sets terms and conditions, and arranges for the actual performance of these services by outside contractors.

Though government regulations may apply, employment and management in these contracting firms are not direct responsibilities of government. Chinese farmers on land provided by government contract with the state for the production and delivery of grain at a fixed price; several U.S. states now contract for their prison operations; hospitals owned by cooperatives or religious bodies contract with government to deliver medical and health services financed by public funds.

Since government is often the sole source of funding and the main or exclusive consumer, these are not market-driven private enterprise operations as that concept is normally understood. But the contract method provides flexibility in employment practices, in financial management, and in operational methods plus incentives to competitive performance that are seldom available in the standard procedures of bureaucratic agencies. This is not to say that the contract method is trouble free. Contracts must be monitored continuously for quantity and standards of output and other indicators of compliance, because of the tendency for profit-seeking contractors to cut corners in the interest of higher profits. Government agencies responsible for contract monitoring may lose control of their contractors or be suborned by them, conspicuous cases being the scandals in U.S. military procurement. Both government and the public are thus short-changed. Alternatively government monitors may exercise such detailed and intrusive scrutiny as to vitiate the initiative and flexibility of contracting firms to the point that they differ little from standard government operations. There is nothing new in the contracting system, especially in North America and Europe, and its possibilities are being seriously explored in the ex-Socialist and third world countries.

These methods and the the managerial implications of government contracting have not, however, been a central concern of students of public administration.

IX. REGULATION

One step removed from contracting is regulation, traditionally the domain of lawyers and more recently of economists, rather than students of public administration. Without producing or even financing goods or services, government prescribes the conditions—prices, employee or consumer safety, environmental protection—under which they may legally be produced or sold and establishes enforcement machinery. This machinery is expected to be a lesser burden on government's administrative capacities and resources than direct operation. As part of the recent neoliberal reaction against the state, there has been a movement toward deregulation intended to stimulate economic initiative by relieving producers of the onerous burdens of bureaucratic constraints. Privatization may, however, create the need for fresh regulation to protect the public interest from the abuses of market operations, including the tendency to monopoly.

By a softer form of regulation, governments attempt to substitute inducements for enforcement. It exerts its will be offering incentives, usually financial, for individuals or organizations to behave in ways preferred by government. The costs to government are not in the form of enforcement machinery, but in fiscal subsidies or tax concessions. Instead, for example, of providing banking services to the public, government supervises the operations of private banks to protect depositors—direct regulation; instead of providing loans to small businesses, it provides financial guarantees for small business loans from private banks, incentives, or soft regulation. By regulation, the state can achieve compliance without the burden of direct operation, assuming that the necessary organizational capabilities exist or can be called forth within society to perform these functions and that regulated interests do not succeed in gaining undue influence over the regulatory agencies. Instead of direct enforcement of pollution standards, the U.S. government now authorizes firms that exceed present standards to sell pollution rights to firms that fail to meet the standards, providing a market in pollution rights and financial incentives that reward compliance with the standards set by government. This version of soft regulation provides some flexibility to polluters and relieves government of much of the burden of direct enforcement. Government is not out of the picture; it merely asserts its authority in different ways.

X. VOLUNTARY ORGANIZATIONS

Another form of management is through nongovernmental, voluntary organizations. There is considerable scope for voluntary association in all societies, as groups with common interests prefer to control and manage independently activities that reflect their collective needs. Recent research has demonstrated its special utility in the rural areas of third world countries. There, water users' associations, service cooperatives, community health centers, and credit unions release latent managerial or resource-mobilizing capacities where governments lack the organizational or financial capabilities or the political will to provide services directly. In many societies hospitals, educational institutions, social insurance enterprises, and producer and consumer cooperatives operate on a nonprofit basis independently of the state. These groups may be federated regionally or nationally to achieve benefits of scale and to pressure governments for favorable treatment. They may also, for some purposes, function as government contractors, ranging from the provision of health services for a government-financed social insurance scheme to the grading of produce for marketing and export. The critical point is that their management is accountable to their membership, not to political or bureaucratic superiors in government.

XI. "REINVENTING GOVERNMENT"

The demise and discrediting of socialist economies, of centrally planned economic management, and of statist models of public policy have generated enthusiastic prescriptions for what must remain of government after privatization-marketization-deregulation. These prescriptions would reform government operations by the adoption of practices that have long been associated with large scale private firms. While they have been inspired by US experience, their proponents among management gurus have not hesitated to advocate them for cross-cultural application as well.

"Reinventing" has four dimensions: (1) downsizing to eliminate superfluous staff; (2) the introduction of advanced processing technologies, especially micro computers to speed operations and base administrative decisions on more timely, accurate information; (3) converting public administrators into quasi-entrepreneurs, expected to regard the public as customers and to adapt government operations to their specific circumstances and convenience; and (4) revising the incentive structure of government staff to provide cash awards for outstanding service, rewarding innovative behavior rather than mindless conformity to bureaucratic regulations and precedents.

A version of reinventing is "performance-based organization." For PBOs, quantitative performance targets are established, executives are selected on the basis of merit and proven managerial success from inside or outside government; they are released from the constraints of standard government personnel, financial, and procurement procedures and rewarded financially for meeting or exceeding performance targets, or discharged and replaced if they fall short. They are to be treated like heads of operating subsidiaries of large private corporations.

Experience with reinventing has been mixed and inconclusive. It will be especially interesting to learn how far it is possible, consistent with the rule of law, to endow government officials with discretion to adapt their operations to the demands, preferences, and convenience of "customers," demands that may be in conflict with one another, without abridging provisions of law and the requirements of equity among members of the public. Unlike private enterprises, most government operations are committed to goals other than instrumental efficiency and cost-effectiveness and they function in a legal and political environment that may impose limitations on entrepreneurship and on their ability to deviate from standardized rules and procedures and from bureaucratic workways. Management improvement, upgrading the capacities and the productivity of government employees, providing them with more efficient equipment, increasing their responsiveness to the needs of the diverse publics they serve have been and must continue to be a preoccupation of program managers and senior government staff. Whether and how far the recent attention to "reinventing government" will contribute to administrative reform remains to be seen.

XII. ORGANIZATIONAL NETWORKS

Modern societies are characterized by organizational complexity; the more dynamic the society, the more pluralistic its organizational life. This has led to the formation of organizational networks to perform services required by society. Joining in these networks may be one or more government agencies, voluntary nongovernmental organizations, private enterprises, and local government units. In irrigated agriculture, government may construct and manage the dams and main channels, but water users associations maintain the secondary and tertiary channels and allocate water, while local authorities assess and collect user fees. Government may set the price for crops and provide research and extension services, while financing is managed by a credit union and private firms provide production inputs, processing and marketing, and local governments maintain the feeder roads that are essential to commercial farming. In industrialized, urbanized societies, hospital and health insurance may be sponsored and financed by government which sets payment schedules and prescribes quality standards for service. At the same time, hospital care is provided by nongovernment voluntary associations which contract with private medical practitioners, while local government takes responsibility for health education and environmental sanitation.

Fewer and fewer public services are now provided by a single government department or even by the coordinated efforts of several government agencies. Instead, the objective is to mobilize managerial energies and commitment from diverse elements in society, government sharing with other components of society financial and managerial responsibility for seeing that appropriate services are available. The power that is imputed to government monopoly may prove to be illusory, as many socialist and third world elites discovered during the 1980s. The sharing of responsibility through service networks relieves overloaded governments of financial and managerial burdens that they cannot handle well, while capitalizing on underutilized capabilities elsewhere in society. Where government monopoly has been the norm, positive initiatives may be needed to stimulate the autonomous organizational energies that are latent in all societies, initially, perhaps by divesting some governmental activities to voluntary, private, or local government control. The function of enlightened government is to take care that needed services are available, not to undertake all such activities directly through official agencies. The resultant instrumentalities constitute service networks. The main managerial challenge of networks is the coordination of their diverse components where specific interests may not always be congruent with those of government or of their partners.

The argument of this chapter is that the current decade has witnessed, in virtually all countries regardless of political ideology or stage of development, a notable retrenchment in the activities undertaken by the state. The state remains and will remain a major actor in the lives of citizens, but it has ceased to accumulate additional functions. Governments have been innovating and discovering alternative methods of impacting on society that are less costly and more effective than the the conventional method of direct administration through bureaucratic channels. These alternatives, including contracting, regulation, devolution, and the shaping of service networks are not new discoveries. They have long been employed in the industrialized West, but they are less familiar in third world countries with colonial traditions of direct administration and in postsocialist polities where governments, until recently, claimed a monopoly of legitimate social organization. Though institutionally underdeveloped, these societies contain latent capacities for autonomous social organization that governments need to encourage and draw into networks of public administration. Recent experience in China demonstrates how quickly such latent capacities can be mobilized. The political consequence is likely to be a greater measure of societal pluralism than has previously been tolerated by most third world elites, many of whom, however, are learning to live with such pluralism because of the impressive economic advantages it yields.

XIII. REORIENTING ACADEMIC PUBLIC ADMINISTRATION

The study of public administration has been preoccupied with bureaucratic operations, with identifying its properties, cataloguing its dysfunctions, prescribing principles and practices for extracting more efficient, cost-effective, and responsive performance from its bureaucratic agencies. The highly touted campaign to "reinvent government" and to feature "performance-based organization" are variants of this central tradition. As many government-related programs will continue to be implemented by direct operations and administered along bureaucratic lines, this attention is not misdirected, nor is its relevance diminished by the recent academic focus on public policy, since all policies must somehow be administered. But it is unbalanced and incomplete. Contracting procedures, their possibilities and limitations, have been neglected; the techniques and consequences of regulation have been abandoned to lawyers and economists; opportunities and implications of devolution and the shaping of service networks have only begun to be explored.

It must be evident even from a cursory examination of what governments do that bureaucratic management represents only one of several resources available to discharge the responsibilities that governments undertake. Program design need not begin and end with standard bureaucratic structures that extend their unbroken hierarchies from headquarters in the capital city to individual citizens on the ground. There are viable alternatives and, above all, combinations of the methods outlined in this paper by which the state can accomplish its goals at substantially less cost, though with some possible loss of control that may nevertheless be compensated by enhanced flexibility, timeliness, and responsiveness to public preferences. The task of the practitioner is to design programs of action that incorporate all these possibilities and then to innovate techniques of management that break out of the grip of bureaucratic operations that concentrate on the management of a single organization. Practitioners are then confronted with a wider, more complex array of choices and with a far more sophisticated, less rigidly structured managerial environment. These expanded choices call for coordinating and political skills that may be in short supply and may not be matched by increased rewards.

The task of academic public administration is to transcend its classical preoccupation with conventional bureaucratic structures and procedures while avoiding the opposite extreme of demonizing bureaucracy or dismissing it as irrelevant and outdated. The need is to examine empirically experience with alternative and complementary methods of program management and service delivery, and to clarify for practitioners the range of choices available to them and the implications of these choices for such values as control, equity, responsiveness, efficiency, and cost. We are not likely to witness the realization of the neoliberal vision of the minimal state. Because government is undeniably useful, it will continue to maintain a prominent and active presence everywhere. But its armory is far more diverse than most practitioners or students of public administration have been inclined to recognize. The challenge to academic public administration is to explore, analyze, explain, and evaluate the specific potentials and limitations of each of these institutional options as they apply to the main activities of the modern state.

52
Administrative Corruption

Incidence, Causes, and Remedial Strategies

David J. Gould†   *Graduate School of Public and International Affairs, University of Pittsburgh, Pittsburgh, Pennsylvania*

I. INTRODUCTION

Economic and social development of nations is stymied by the plague of systemic bureaucratic corruption—the institutionalized private-regarding use and abuse of public resources by civil servants. Corruption is a live issue throughout the world. In Africa for instance, many leaders came to power on a popular platform aiming to "do something" about corruption. Most regime adversaries cite persistent corruption as a principal justification for their opposition. However, regime change—even in those cases when accompanied by radically shifted ideological claims—has had little impact on the underlying problem.

To some extent all governments have made attempts—be they sincere or cynical—to control or combat corruption. Virtually all heads of government denounce corruption and call for laws to control it. Yet with few exceptions these laws are flouted or selectively enforced. In many countries in Southeast Africa, Latin America, and the Middle East, corruption is endemic. In Africa corruption is the rule rather than the exception. In an attempt to better understand the phenomenon, this chapter analyzes the nature, incidence, and effects of administrative corruption. It goes on to examine briefly the negative consequences of systemic administrative corruption for economic, social and political development. It then analyzes the causes of administrative corruption, and provides some measure of explanation for the phenomenon. Finally, the chapter examines the types of attempted remedies which governments have mounted to combat or control corruption.

II. DEFINITIONS AND NATURE OF CORRUPTION

Administrative corruption was defined above as the institutionalized personal abuse of public resources by civil servants.

Corruption has no single definition. It varies from region to region and remains largely contextual. In China, the term corruption in general terms spells all types of irregularities and con-

---

†Deceased.

notes bribery, extortion, expropriation of public money, favoritism, nepotism, and factionalism (Lui 1979). Because of the difficulty involved in finding a generalizable definition, some students of the topic preferred to categorize the nature of corruption, thereby substituting corruption for its causes. Heidenheimer (1970) categorized the nature of corruption into three groups: (1) market-centered orientation, (2) public-centered approach, and (3) public office-centered perspective. Universally there are two divergent views on the definition of corruption—the moralists and the functionalists.

A. Moralists

The most frequent way to look at corruption is as an "immoral, unethical" phenomenon. Corruption in this view is a set of aberrations from moral standards of society, resulting in loss of respect for and confidence in duly constituted authority. Myrdal characterizes corruption as "selfish and improper conduct" (Myrdal 1969). Nye put it succinctly: "Corruption is behavior which deviates from the formal duties of a public role (elective or appointive) because of private-regarding (personal, close family, private clique) wealth or status gains, or violates rules against the exercise of certain types of private-regarding influence" (Nye 1967:417).

While powerfully evocative, the moralist approach has limitations:

1.   It tends to individualize a societal phenomenon. If corruption is essentially a problem of "bad" incumbents, the easy solution is to reform them, or, if that fails, to replace them with other, morally upright people. But the new, "moral" replacements are likely to find themselves drawn into the same institutionalized practices. This approach doesn't deal with the extent to which administrative corruption may be a societal problem. By ignoring systemic causes, moralist "solutions" make the underlying conditions worse.

2.   It tends to dichotomize "what is good and what is bad." Yet any society's definition of what is corrupt is relative and evolves over time. In a culturally pluralistic, multiethnic country, where central institutions have little general legitimacy, societal institutions may have great difficulty articulating widely acceptable norms. For example, blood or regional loyalty to family and/or clan is an undergirding moral principle that guides most Africans (Hyden 1983). However, this principle is openly contradicted by the Weberian norms one finds in most African laws governing civil service recruitment, personnel advancement, and avoiding corruption or the appearance of corruption in dealing with family members. In order for *Gesellschaft* norms to win out over *Gemeinschaft* norms, it is necessary for those advocating the former to make an overwhelmingly convincing case to those guided by the latter. Making this case requires fairly irreproachable conduct on their part. If the only way people from a disaffected group or region can feed their children is to violate a norm that for most either appears abstract or hypocritical (i.e., widely violated by groups in power), it is hard to call such behavior immoral. Indeed, in certain extreme circumstances—living in a country characterized by systemic, inequitable corruption—"the individual may have no choice left but to seek a solution in active corruption in order to defend his rights" (Catholic bishops of Zaire in 1978, quoted in Gould and Amaro-Reyes 1983:12).

3.   Even if central, norm-defining institutions have widespread legitimacy, in many instances the legal system has not succeeded in identifying corrupt actions with precision. For example, in most countries, laws prohibit public officials from owning businesses. Sometimes they go so far as to deny "close family members" this right. However, even in the unusual cases where the close family members are specified (i.e., spouse, child), the ways of getting around this, such as by involving perhaps another equally close "brother" or "sister," are legion.

In short, the moralist arguments are weak in that they take little account of societal context, nor do they examine the gap between the formal norms and the underlying practice-girded norms (Caiden and Caiden 1977).

B. Functionalists

Another way of looking at corruption is in terms of the actual function that it plays in socioeconomic development. Functionalists examine the utilitarian consequences, whatever the morality involved, of certain corrupt behaviors. "Revisionists" among them (so called because they critique the earlier view that corruption is absolutely harmful) find corruption to be useful in certain circumstances:

1. Bloated, inequitable, statist bureaucracy blocks private investment. Therefore, corruption sets up a crude kind of "economic efficiency." It impels better choices by rewarding willingness and ability to raise money and pay bribes. In this sense, it improves, albeit selectively, the quality and responsiveness of public services. It cuts red tape, offers incentives, and funnels capital to entrepreneurs; it substitutes for a public works or welfare system. It flourishes as a substitute for the market system, that is, when the market is not allowed to function, nature abhors a vacuum, and corruption fills it (Leff 1979).

2. Politically, corruption is said to promote political development. It can strengthen political parties and enhance national integration by permitting historically "out" groups to buy their way into the system. It is said to offer an acceptable alternative to violence. In a sense, it increases public participation in public policy (Gould 1980:3–4; Klitgaard 1988:30).

3. Pragmatically, political and bureaucratic leaders may see a "national interest" in actively pursuing, or tolerating a certain degree of, administrative corruption. The reason is that countermeasures may be prohibitively expensive and in any case chronically underpaid workers may stay motivated if they earn salary supplements through corruption. Knowing that corruption is systemic and that most if not all civil servants benefit from it in that system, a regime can "save public funds" by foregoing salary increases (Klitgaard 1988).

It can be recognized that in societies characterized by inefficient economic systems, political departicipation, and organizational slowness, corruption can create a kind of efficiency. "If the prevailing system is bad, then corruption may be good" (Klitgaard 1988:33). On the other hand, lest we lower our guard, the supposed benefits of corruption need to be carefully analyzed.

1. Private gains obtained through corruption should not be assumed to translate invariably or even as a rule into investments benefiting the public. The case of mounting third world debt has shown the extent to which resources can be siphoned away from productive investments to private needs. The fact that $5 billion is both the amount of Zaire's foreign debt and the amount of President Mobutu's personal fortune is certainly not pure coincidence (Griffith-Jones 1985).

2. Given the "softness of state" prevalent in most African countries, the major challenge is for state authorities to develop policies and programs designed to win popular legitimacy. However, promotion or tolerance of corruption, even as palliative, can only serve to soften the state further (Caiden 1979).

In conclusion, most postfunctional analyses of corruption see it as "functional dysfunction" (Gould and Mukendi 1988). Some forms of corruption may be beneficial, others deleterious. Corruption may be useful in some ways, as in cutting corners, speeding services, or facilitating integration of outgroups, but harmful in others, for example, societally unproductive, morally repugnant, economically distorting, and politically delegitimizing. From this standpoint, corruption's liabilities far outweigh its benefits.

III. INCIDENCE OF CORRUPTION

The evidence of system corruption is strong throughout Africa. There is no need to review the evidence that has been exhaustively developed elsewhere (Ekpo 1979; Lee 1981; Gould and Mukendi 1988). Despite the great variety of corrupt practices, the manifestations of corruption can be grouped into two categories: (1) corruption in the routine course of government business, and (2) corruption in the implementation of substantive government (Gould 1980; Gould and Amaro-Reyes 1983).[1]

IV. EFFECTS OF CORRUPTION

The overwhelmingly negative effects of corruption may be seen in several dimensions.

A. Regime Legitimacy and Political Stability

In administrative systems characterized by systemic corruption, the honest official is the exception and indeed is the object of ridicule if not exclusion. Its overall effect is to lower public respect for and confidence in government in general and in the administrative system in particular. Cynicism, disillusionment, and alienation, if not outright opposition, are frequent results, leading to lowered citizen participation and an undermining of the regime's legitimacy.

The effect of systemic corruption is to provide a seeming degree of stability to a regime, which is able to rely on it in radiating clientelism. All those touched directly or indirectly by the "benefits" of corruption feel a cemented loyalty to the regime and to its institutions. However, by its nature systemic corruption is ultimately destabilizing since it cannot benefit more than a small minority. Too many people are left out, or receive less than they feel they deserve or than others with no more apparent merit. This creates resentment, which, effectively mobilized, can lead to sudden and sometimes violent regime change.

B. Economic Productivity

Administrative corruption may benefit a few people, but the general effect on society's productivity is negative. The general expectation of corruption for the provision of routine governmental services creates not only injustice toward those who cannot or will not pay, but also more generalized inefficiency as bribeless government services are put on the back burner. The drag on productivity created when officials are focusing most of their energy on private-regarding activities, often working against the public interest, is often calculable. Studies in three Asian countries document that because of corrupt procurement practices, governments in developing countries pay from 20% to 100% more than the price they would pay under noncorrupt conditions (Klitgaard 1988:39–40).

C. Economic Rationality

It can be argued that corruption sets up an ersatz market system to the extent that officials, licenses, or services can be sold to the higher bidder. Those who believe in the efficiency of the market mechanism can take comfort in this concept and to that extent find corruption appealing from the economic standpoint. Revisionists are particularly drawn to this argument where, as is often the case, state enterprises, monopolies, and arbitrary and urban-biased government price controls effectively vitiate the market mechanism. The counterargument is to point to the inherent arbitrariness and irrationality of the corruption-driven ersatz market. Its predictability and stability are compromised by worry about the whims and lasting power of corrupt officials, not to mention the above-noted regime-sapping decline in public confidence. The new market's rationality is constrained by the "money talks" bottom line: the result is that worthy job seekers, project promoters, or service providers are rejected in favor of the highest bidder, no matter how inherently unqualified he/she may be or how economically worthless or wasteful the project.

D. Equity/Justice

Revisionists claim that corruption can result in irrationally unpopular outgroups buying their way in. Although this may occur to some extent, a more serious and inevitable consequence of corruption is a widening of the gap between rich and poor, urban and rural dwellers. Weighing the latter result against the former, certainly the overall impact is one of increased inequity.

V. CAUSES OF CORRUPTION

The causes of administrative corruption include the nature of the postcolonial state, poverty, cultural factors, the nature of the bureaucratic decision-making system in place, and foreign complicity.

A. Nature of the State

Corruption tends to prevail in weak states, soft entities, captured by elites using them for personal enrichment and gain. According to Myrdal (1969), a soft state is characterized among other things by

1. Heavy dependence on outside assistance for setting development agendas and providing resources
2. Widespread social indiscipline and disobedience to public authority
3. Overcentralized government, with opportunities for corruption
4. Rigid bureaucracy, unable to adjust to changing circumstances, and relying on heavy-handed enforcement if not outright coercion

Against this background the government is often perceived by the population as an enemy of the people. Using the African context, Keith Hart noted that "Many [West] African governments represent in themselves the single greatest threat to their citizens, treat the rule of law with contempt, and multiply hastily hatched public schemes designed principally to advance their own private and collective enrichment" (Hart 1982:104).

Often the continuation of such characteristics nearly 30 years into the postcolonial era is attributed in part at least to the colonial legacy of a strong authoritarian, nonparticipatory state. This authoritarian heritage contributes to postcolonial corruption at two levels. First, since the colonial state was conducted by and for foreigners, native citizens developed an attitude of irresponsibility, ultimately coming to thwart government in any way they could. Corruption against the colonial state became almost a patriotic gesture, a step toward sabotaging colonial rule (Werlin 1979). Second, the continuation of authoritarian state patterns—in which government enjoys unquestioned authority over citizens—gives the rulers virtual impunity from any checks, balances, or controls on their untrammelled plundering.

In developing countries, the state has other propensities which contribute to institutionalizing corruption. They include the following:

1. Heavy dependence on import of foreign manufactured and luxury goods as well as foodstuffs, with control over the foreign-currency and customs choke-point decisions squarely in the hands of the "bureaucratic bourgeoisie" (Markowitz 1977).

2. Persistence of colonial-style administrative structures, oriented toward law and order rather than consultation and participation (Gould 1985).

3. The questionable reliability of bureaucrats to the public interest in the face of the ruling party's capture of political and bureaucratic power is another factor contributing to institutional weakness. Loyalty and subservience to the chief executive become the prime requisites for

a successful career and as hedge against insecurity. Patrimonialism, patronage, and clientelism become the norm in the public service, as public norms are subordinated to particularistic norms.

4.   The expanded role of the state in the economy: The state has acquired a virtual monopoly over virtually all sectors of socioeconomic development. The expansion of the state sector in the 1960s and 1970s was led by the creation of thousands of state enterprise in Africa alone. As Jagannathan (1986) noted, the wider the extent of government control of the economy, the more pervasive are the tendencies for corruption.

B.   Poverty and Low Pay

In the third world one of the chief causes of corruption is due to poverty and low, inequitable pay scales. Pay scales throughout Africa have remained poorly structured since colonial times and failed to keep pace with inflation. The buying power of a civil service salary, which might have been adequate 20 years ago, is in most countries sorely inadequate. The prevailing wage scale fails to provide the average civil servant with the means to feed, house, and clothe his/her family. The government worker is required to turn to other means—typically involving corruption—for survival's sake. This is all the more so in countries under IBRD-IMF "structural adjustment" programs, which inevitably insist on civil service raises as a condition for continued external support. Gaps between top officers' pay and that of subordinates creates gross inequities. Subordinates who work hard but do not earn a living wage are unlikely to care deeply about the state and instead become preoccupied with surviving—no matter how. A study of Zairian conditions some 10 years ago revealed that 92% of civil servants were earning less that the *minimum vital*, as determined in a World Bank study that had calculated the average family size to be six, a gross underestimation (Gould 1980). In such conditions, the temptation to use one's public position to extract *haricots pour les enfants*, as corruption is called in Zaire, is difficult to resist.

C.   Cultural Factors

Some analysts of administrative corruption argue that it is the outgrowth of lineage-loyal culture norms and behavioral patterns prevalent in the Third World in general and in Africa in particular. These norms and patterns are assumed to be in conflict with "modern" impersonal values, producing "ambivalence" in Merton's terms, that is, normative expectations of attitudes, beliefs, and behaviors that are incompatible with social statuses and demands (Merton 1967). Ekpo's analysis of corruption in contemporary Nigeria traces its origins to traditional gift-giving practices (Ekpo 1979).

Furthermore, when states are soft, governments weak, national leader's credibility questioned, and citizen allegiance to national interests low, parochial and ethnic ties become the principal avenue for defense of one's interest. One's kinspeople can protect one from police harassment. Ethnic solidarity can help to cover up officials in difficulty. Ethnic brothers and sisters are indulgent and supportive of corruption patterns of fellow kinspeople in power. Moreover, the external family system creates pressure on officials to seek extralegal income in order to attend to family demands (Gould and Mukendi 1988).

D.   Organizational Factors

Among organizational factors creating favorable conditions for corruption are:

1.   *The exclusive pattern of the decision-making process.* The highly centralized state structures and the absence of any meaningful checks and balances on untrammeled power con-

centrate decision-making authority at the top. Away from the light of day, top officials are unconstrained from pursuing private-regarding as opposed to public goals.

2. *Slowness of the policy process.* The high degree of centralization noted above leads to a bureaucratic mentality, wherein every even minor governmental step is "backed up," requiring cumbersome written documentation for the record. Slowdown efforts by bureaucrats can be deliberate in order to induce potential clients to pay "speed-up money" to officials manning key choke points. These funds may be passed up the line to higher-level officials. Patterns of corruption thus become institutionalized. The result is to reinforce bureaucratic centralism and to resist streamlining and reform.

3. *Poor control and accountability systems.* Some degree of autonomous parliamentary, judicial, or even media oversight gives the modern state the means of reviewing or auditing governmental acts, thus providing safeguards against arbitrary or private-regarding decision making. However, few developing countries have a high-power, high-prestige, independent corps of auditors and inspectors. In the few countries where governments have established inspectorate corps, they are further handicapped by the following constraints: attaching the corps to the finance ministry, thus removing nonfinancial decisions from direct control; heterogenous background and inadequate training and equipment; and incongruence between legal system and societal demands: In some countries only a few citizens have access to the laws. In very many cases, some of these laws are clearly inadequate and tend to reflect colonial needs and realities, not those of an independent country. Such laws tend in any case to not be enforced in practice.

E.   Outside Influence and Support

Outside actors often contribute directly or indirectly to corruption. For instance, foreign corporations in developing countries as a rule are more interested in making an investment smoothly, winning a contract, and getting things done expeditiously, than in "good government." Indeed, if "good government" means that rational, objective criteria will be used as a basis for decisions on contracts and public investments, then corporations accustomed to getting their way by bribery may be truly alarmed by it. Efforts by multinational corporations to affect both their parent nations' foreign policy and political change within third-world countries have been extensively documented (U.S. Senate 1973–76). The exhaustive U.S. Senate study cited publishes literally thousands of documents showing illegal, corrupt payments made by the United States-based multinational corporations to public officials throughout the world. This is regrettable, since long-term stability interests would be served by "weighing in" to support strong-teethed laws against corruption rather than by systematically flouting them.

French journalist Pierre Péan has placed the issue in stark perspective:

> There can be no corrupt officials without those who corrupt them. Certain tropical or equatorial elites bear significant responsibility for their countries' suffering. However what about our industrialists, faithfully supported by our governments, who sell to the third world these "white elephants," useless factories, cement cathedrals, roads that go nowhere, projects whose only purpose is to make business for the North and bribes in the South? (Péan 1988: back cover, our translation).

Western business interests are by no means alone in aiding and abetting local corruption. As Gunnar Myrdal noted 20 years ago, Western donors often interpret their political interests in such a way as to prefer dealing with the "devil that we know" to the unknown (Myrdal 1968). Few ambassadors or resident representatives of international organizations will openly dare to raise the issue of corruption with a host government. It is much more expeditious to live with the regime in place, especially when the regime votes one's way in the United Nations, provides military bases on good terms, and/or in other ways proves supportive of one's national interests (Gould 1979b).

VI.   CONTROL OF CORRUPTION/REMEDIES

The principal remedies for corruption that have been tried or proposed in several countries include the following: (1) commissions of inquiry; (2) purges and wars against discipline; (3) codes of ethics and leadership; (4) a freer press; (5) tougher laws and enforcement; (6) anticorruption agencies; and (7) systemic structural and policy changes.

A.   Commissions of Inquiry

A common response to charges of corruption has been to appoint special committees, "commissions of inquiry." According to Williams, they "have proved a major growth industry" (1987:198).

   In the words of Riley, commissions of inquiry are appointed when one of the three conditions applies: "firstly, when a 'scandal' becomes public . . . ; secondly, when a change of government takes place and political advantage can be gained, and, thirdly when serious financial loss or inefficiency is known about by senior figures (and to a certain extent a process of face-saving has to take place)" (in Clarke 1983:195–196). There is, however, an inherent limitation: *quis custodet custodiens*—who will watch over the watchers? "Corruption inquiries . . . always concern other people. Corrupt political leaders almost never instigate inquiries into their own affairs unless they are certain to produce a cosmetic exoneration" (Williams 1987:198).

B.   Purges and Wars on Indiscipline

Some regimes in Africa especially come in not with a whimper but with a bang. Master Sergeant Samuel Doe summarily executed his predecessor and several members of the cabinet upon taking power in Liberia in 1979. Flight Lieutenant Jerry Rawlings executed three former heads of state in Ghana when he took over the same year. An example of campaign directed against corruption was General Murtala Mohammed's "Operation Purge the Nation," launched upon his overthrow of General Gowon in Nigeria in 1975. He purged the civil service departments of 11,000 civil servants, including half the heads of civil service departments. Mohammed's actions were widely popular, as reflected in the following editorial comment at the time: "Corruption, indiscipline and needless arrogance not only abound in the Nigerian civil service; it has become an abode for mediocrity, laziness, apathy, avoidable narrow-mindedness, nepotism, favoritism and tribalism on a stupendous and incredible scale" (Williams 1987:109).

   Such dramatic steps against corruption in Nigeria were of course visible, but had little long-lasting effect. The proof is that General Mohammed was assassinated in 1976 and two additional coups took place since 1975, one led by General Buhari in 1983 and another by General Babaginda in 1986, both of which were designed to overcome corruption and indiscipline. What Aina (1982) has called "structural formalism" came to characterize governmental attempts to deal with corruption. Policies are solemnly enunciated. Some measures are announced and a few are taken, and then nothing.

C.   Codes of Ethics and of Leadership

Certain governments, notably those in East Africa, opted for adoption of "leadership codes," by which high standards of behavior are set for senior political and bureaucratic officials (Williams

1987:110). Sometimes these codes establish a registry for such officials to record all property and business interests and to report all relevant transactions. According to Shivji (1976), however, Tanzanian President Nyerere had difficulty getting the code adopted in his party and cabinet, and it was imperfectly implemented if not sabotaged through transferring property and business interests "into the names of relatives and friends" (Williams 1987:111). Zambia's Leadership Code is a most impressive document to read; however, according to Williams, there have "never been any prosecutions under its provisions" (Williams 1987:111). Failing to provide consistent enforcement tools detracts fatally from such codes' power to set standards and change.

D. A Freer Press

A vigilant, well-supported, freely inquiring press provides a means for the public to monitor governmental activities including ascertaining the extent of corruption in higher places. In several countries, alert newspaper professionals have helped to "break" major scandals. In his study of anticorruption measures in Indonesia, Leslie Palmier singled out the role of the printed press for uncovering official corruption (1985:224–225). Few African countries have a press whose editorialists or journalists feel free to critique the regime in place. Most newspapers are essentially "house organs" whose mandate is to glorify the regime. There are occasional exceptions, such as *Le Politicien* of Dakar and *La Gazette* of Cotonou.

E. Tougher Laws and Enforcement

The temptation is great for governments faced with massive complaints about corruption to pass tough laws outlawing corruption in its various forms and establishing significant enforcement mechanisms. The most common case involves ritualistic prohibitions on soliciting or receiving bribes as a condition of providing a public service. A few governments go so far as to prohibit pursuit of business activities by civil servants. Occasionally there are explicit antinepotistic provisions.

Most laws proscribing various forms of corruption are at worst self-enforcing, or at best rely on prosecutorial agencies that are themselves *suspect*. In addition to the laws themselves, effective control measures should include the following:

1. A staff of investigators, armed with sufficient authority and means of getting around.
2. Sufficient prosecutors, with adequate authority and other resources to arrest and bring deserving cases to trial.
3. A court system sufficiently unblocked and impermeable to pressure as to assure impartial application of the laws and justice.

As the case of Hong Kong shows, even with an impressive British armature of laws anticipating a large variety of corrupt practices, numerous investigators and prosecutors, and a court system disposed to try cases expeditiously, it has proven difficult to properly investigate, catch, bring to trial, and convict those accused of corruption. How much more difficult is the task if the laws are not accompanied by provisions for implementation? (Palmier in Clarke 1983; Lee 1981).

F. Anticorruption Agencies

Some governments have reacted to the public outcry over the scourge of corruption by creating agencies charged with investigating and prosecuting allegations of corrupt practices. The Liberian "Force to Combat Corruption" and the Nigerian "Public Complaints Commission" provide some examples of this phenomenon. Such agencies are not completely useless; a certain number of complaints are received and dealt with, and some evildoers are apprehended and prosecuted (Omale 1981). However, in practice these offices have had limited success. The constraints have proven numerous:

1.   The bureaucracy's discretionary power has been repeatedly upheld in the face of complaints of arbitrariness (Omale, 1981). Other agencies' resentment of the "upstart" nature of the new agency creates difficulties in functioning, in communicating, and particularly in obtaining adequate cooperation and information from the agencies being investigated.

2.   Investigative officers have been constrained by resource scarcity and by their few numbers versus the enormity of the task before them (Gould and Amaro-Reyes 1983).

3.   The Office of the President has the power to call a stop to any current investigation and to orient ongoing investigations (Omale 1981). The chilling effect of such measures is clear.

4.   The protections afforded to citizens who denounce corruption need to be fully assured. Without protection, few citizens are going to take it upon themselves to accuse "big fish." Little wonder that most of the complaints registered involve "little fish."

5.   The safeguards against the investigators themselves becoming "contaminated" by contact with corruption are often inadequate.

These findings reflect inherent weaknesses in the agency form of anticorruption effort.

G.   Systemic Structural and Policy Changes

Public policy has been defined as whatever a public entity decides to do, or not to do, about a particular problem. To the extent that few less developed countries (LDCs) and even fewer African governments have done anything explicit and decisive to counter corruption, public policy to date has been one of frustration. The same can be said of donor agencies, bilateral and multilateral, that annually provide billions in aid, seldom attaching conditions requiring government measures to fight corruption.

Why has so little been done against corruption? The policy forces militating in favor of corruption, and that resist efforts to restrict it, are those that undergird all public policy in any country. They include economic ownership patterns, dominant ideology, social class dominance, political institution's control, bureaucratic patterns, and cultural sway (Gould 1979a: Ch. 2). It can be presumed that where systemic corruption exists, the institutionalized practice has behind it a whole array of economic, political, social, ideological, and cultural supports, both at home and abroad. Donor agencies that choose to ignore or downplay corruption, that work with host government despite widespread and broadly available evidence that they are systemically corrupt, do so out of four possible motivations:

1.   Condescension ("They are only foreigners, it's not our problem.")
2.   Cynicism ("Let them steal each other blind, what do you expect?")
3.   Ignorance ("Corruption? Here? Really?" or "Corruption, maybe it isn't so bad?")
4.   Pragmatism ("It's true they're corrupt, but we support their government and if they get picky and make a fuss, we will have less 'clout' with them.") (Myrdal 1968; Gould 1979a).

However, both presently or potentially constructive forces within host governments and donor agencies may be educable about corruption's liabilities and about the worthiness of attempts to combat it by developing anticorruption policies (ACPs). Governments need to be shown that they can reduce corruption and survive. They need to see that the tradeoff between reformed, clean, efficient government and maintenance of patronage clientelistic-based corruption can be resolved in favor of ACPs. What are the conditions under which policy change is possible with regard to corruption? The answer would appear to lie in a judicious combination of external pressure for strengthened anticorruption efforts (in the form of firm, evidence-based, supportive advice and, if need be, as conditions of future aid) allied with mobilized internal support for reform.

Specific policies worthy of consideration for strengthening anticorruption efforts include the following:

1. Reform the personnel system. In a government of whose budget civil servant salaries represent 75–80%, doing something to enhance their productivity, to reduce their cost, and to diminish their drain on the taxpayers' hard-earned money should be a priority. Specifically, the following ACPs can be considered: (1) Job analysis and audit: The declaration of job vacancies could be based on analysis of real requirements. Holders of jobs with real content and expectations could be more motivated to produce than those holding sinecures. (2) Selection: The selection process could be based on merit and professional standards—including a clean past record—rather than on an existing system of recommendations, political clientelism, and nepotism prevailing in many countries. Those selected in this way are more likely to be honest than the old way. (3) Salaries: The salary system could be changed so that salaries provide a "living wage," thus reducing the "economic incentive" for civil servants to engage in corruption. Special salary incentive payment supplements might be extended to those in sensitive positions as an inducement to avoid corruption (Palmier 1983). Here is an area where the cooperation of foreign donors may be quite useful. The extreme step of salary supplements may be worth taking in the context of the generalized improvement of personnel management resulting from the measures proposed in this section. The promise of a more efficient, less corrupt personnel system would certainly be worth donors' interest. (4) Incentives and sanctions: A performance assessment and evaluation system would give employees a positive incentive to maintain high standards. Sanctions, if enacted and implemented, would dissuade potentially corrupt employees from engaging in corruption.

2. Strengthen the integrity of the auditing function. The auditing function is among the most promising for reducing corruption, yet the most susceptible to corruption. *"Quis custodiat custodiens?"* Reforms designed to heighten the value of this function, insulate it from politics, police its exercise, and make its chief officers into an elite, technically trained, and high-level corps are needed.

3. Strengthen the integrity of the governmental bidding function. The government contracting and bidding function may be held by several ministries; in some countries it is centralized, and/or subject to review, in one or two key ministries, such as finance and/or plan. Like the auditing function, the government bid review function is, in systematically corrupt administrative systems, generally at the core of the system.

4. Decentralize and "participatize" governmental systems. The more broadly citizens participate in government, especially at levels of plan preparation and service delivery, the more "daylight will shine in," and the more difficult it will be for authoritarian, centralized government institutions to act corruptly (Gould 1985).

5. Upgrade laws. The search for contradictions, weaknesses, and loopholes in the present legal system, often the result of an undigested colonial legacy, needs to be intensified.

6. Strengthen court and prosecutorial system. The anticorruption efforts of Burkina Faso in the mid-1980s, carried out primarily through "revolutionary popular tribunals," show that it is possible for laws to be strengthened and the powers of investigatory and prosecutorial authorities reinforced to deal with corruption. Of course, Spartan behavior in high places and strong political commitment from the ruling group greatly facilitate this goal.

7. Strengthen existing anticorruption strategies and forces and create new ones. Thought and effort need to be invested in studying the existing anticorruption forces, analyzing their weaknesses, and proposing ways of beefing them up.

VII. CONCLUSION

Several remedies for combatting corruption have been tried. None, however, will stand a significant chance of taking hold without a degree of commitment by the regime in power. The commitment may be "sincere," it may be based on fear, and/or it may be based on externally imposed conditions. The important things are that the government be *motivated* to do something, that it takes a first step, and that the measures taken be designed in the light of comparative experience.

ENDNOTE

1. For a complete listing of the categories cited, see Gould (1980:123–149), Appendices A and B.

REFERENCES

Aina, S.D. Bureaucratic corruption in Nigeria: the continuing search for causes and cures. *International Review of Administrative Sciences 48*(1) (1982).

Caiden, G., and Caiden, N. Administrative corruption. *Public Administration Review 37*(3) (1977).

Caiden, G. Public maladministration and bureaucratic corruption. In *Fraud, Waste and Abuse in Government: Causes, Consequences and Cures* (J.B. McKinney and M. Johnston, eds.). Prentice-Hall, Englewood Cliffs, NJ, 1986.

Clarke, M., ed. *Corruption: Causes, Consequences and Control.* St. Martin's Press, New York, 1983.

Dumont, R. *L'Afrique Noire Est Mal Partie (False Start for Africa)* (trans. P.N. Ott). Andre Deutsch, London, 1966.

Eisenstadt, S.N., and Lemarchand, R. *Political Clientelism, Patronage and Development.* Sage, Beverly Hills, CA, 1981.

Ekpo, M.U., ed. *Bureaucractic Corruption in Sub-Saharan Africa: Toward a Search for Causes and Consequences.* University Press of America, Washington, DC, 1979.

Gould, D.J. *Law and the Administrative Process: Analytic Frameworks for Understanding Public Policymaking.* University Press of America, Washington, DC, 1979a.

Gould, D.J. The problem of seepage in international development assistance. *Civilisations Brussels, 39/3* (1979b).

Gould, D.J. *Bureaucratic Corruption and Underdevelopment in the Third World: The Case of Zaire.* Pergamon, New York, 1980.

Gould, D.J. Popular participation in African development planning. In *Popular Participation in Development Management: The Case of Africa and Asia* (J.-C. Garcia-Zamor, ed.). Westview Press, Boulder, CO, 1985.

Gould, D.J., and Amaro-Reyes, J. The effects of corruption on administrative performance: illustrations from developing countries. Staff working paper no. 580, Management and Development Series no. 7, World Bank, Washington, DC, 1983.

Gould, D.J., and Mukendi, B.T. Bureaucratic corruption in Africa: causes, consequences and remedies. *International Journal of Public Administration* Fall (1988).

Griffith-Jones. S. Proposals to manage the debt problem. *Development Policy Review 3*(2) (1985).

Hart, K. *The Political Economy of West African Agriculture.* Cambridge University Press, Cambridge, 1982.

Heidenheimer, A.J., ed. *Political Corruption: Readings in Comparative Analysis.* Holt, Rinehart and Winston, New York, 1970.

Hyden, G. *No Shortcuts to Progress: African Development Management in Perspective.* University of California Press, Berkeley, 1983.

Jagannathan, N.V. Corruption, delivery systems and property rights. *World Development 14*(1):127–132 (1986).

Klitgaard, R. *Controlling Corruption.* University of California Press, Berkeley, 1988.

Lee, P.L. (Rahman, A.J.R.), ed. *Corruption and Its Control in Hong Kong.* Chinese University Press, Hong Kong, 1981.

Leff, N.H. Economic development through bureaucratic corruption. In *Bureaucratic Corruption in Sub-Saharan Africa: Toward a Search for Causes and Consequences* (M.U. Ekpo, ed.). University Press of America, Washington, DC, 1979.

LeVine, V.T. *Political Corruption: The Ghana Case.* Hoover Institution Press, Stanford, CA., 1974.

Leys, C. What is the problem about corruption? In *Bureaucratic Corruption in Sub-Saharan Africa: Toward a Search for Causes and Consequences* (M.U. Ekpo, ed.). University Press of America, Washington, DC, 1979.

Lui, A.Y.C. *Corruption in China During the Early Ch'ing Period: 1644 to 1660.* University of Hong Kong, Center of Asian Studies, Hong Kong, 1979.

Markowitz, I.L. *Power and Class in Africa: An Introduction to Change and Conflict in African Politics.* Prentice-Hall, Englewood Cliffs, NJ, 1977.

McKinney, J.B., and Johnston, M. *Fraud, Waste and Abuse in Government: Causes, Consequences and Cures.* Institute for the Study of Human Issues, Philadelphia, 1986.

Medard, J.-F. Public corruption in Africa: a comparative perspective. *Corruption and Reform 1*(2) (1986).

Merton, R.K. *Social Theory and Social Structure.* Free Press, New York, 1967.

Mpinga-Kasenda and Gould, D. *Les Réformes Administratives au Zaire, 1973–1974.* Presses Universitaires du Zaire, Kinshasa, 1975.

Myrdal, G. *Asian Drama,* vol. 2. Twentieth Century Fund, New York, 1968.

Myrdal, G. *The Challenge of World Poverty.* Vintage, New York, 1969.

Noonan, J. *Bribes.* Macmillan, New York, 1984.

Nye, J.S. Corruption and political development: a cost-benefit analysis. In *Bureaucratic Corruption in Sub-Saharan Africa: Toward a Search for Causes and Consequences* (M.U. Ekpo, ed.). University Press of America, Washington, DC, 1979.

Omale, I.I. *When Nigerians Complain: An Assessment of the Rationale for the Functions of the Public Complaints Commission.* Ph.D. dissertation, University of Pittsburgh, Pittsburgh, 1981.

Palmier, L. Bureaucratic corruption and its remedies. In *Corruption: Causes, Consequences and Control* (M. Clarke, ed.). St. Martin's Press, New York, 1983.

Palmier, L. *The Control of Bureaucratic Corruption: Cases Studies in Asia.* Allied, New Delhi, 1985.

Péan, P. *L'Argent Noir: Corruption et Sous-Développement.* Fayard, Paris, 1988.

Riley, S. "The Land of Waving Palms": political economy, corruption inquiries and politics in Sierra Leone. In *Corruption: Causes, Consequences and Control* (M. Clarke, ed.). St. Martin's Press, New York, 1983.

Rogow, A., and Lasswell, H. *Power, Corruption, and Rectitude.* Prentice-Hall, Englewood Cliffs, NJ, 1963.

Rose Ackerman, S. *Corruption: A Study in Political Economy.* Academic Press, New York, 1978.

Shivji, I. *Class Struggles in Tanzania.* Heinemann, London, 1976.

U.S. Senate, Committee on Foreign Relations, Hearings before the Subcommittee on Multinational Corporations, 93rd and 94th Congress, Multinational Corporations and US Foreign Policy, Parts I–XIV, 1973–76.

Upper Volta: after the rhetoric. *Africa Confidential 25*(2):5–7 (1984).

Werlin, H. The roots of corruption: the Ghanaian equity. In *Corruption in Sub-Saharan Africa: Toward a Search for Causes and Consequences* (M.U. Ekpo, ed.). University Press of America, Washington, DC, 1979.

Werner, S. New directions in the study of administrative corruption. *Public Administration Review 43*(March–April) (1983).

Williams, R. *Political Corruption in Africa.* Gower, Brookfield, VT, 1987.

Young, C. *Ideology and Development in Africa.* Yale University Press, New Haven, CT, 1983.

53

Public Service Ethics and Professionalism

A Primer for Public Officials

Ali Farazmand   *School of Public Administration, Florida Atlantic University,
Fort Lauderdale, Florida*

I. INTRODUCTION

Public service represents one of the oldest, most highly prized, most widespread and celebrated values in the history of humankind. In traditional societies, little distinction was made between voluntary service for the good of the community and remunerated work performed on a professional contractual basis. A fusion of the roles of government and governed, direct participation in the affairs of state, and the growth, in this manner, of a political culture and administrative skills were favoured by conditions of relative stability and the presence of a leisured class imbued with a strong commitment to the polity's well-being. This situation, however, was transformed with the emergence of vast multinational kingdoms and empires from China to Persia to Rome.

In modern times, the rise of the administrative state, from the 19th century onwards, also led to a vast expansion of the public service. It has been accompanied by bureaucratization which, as Max Weber observed, profoundly revolutionized organizational structures and values. Ironically, those values have lately come into conflict with the long cherished claims of democratic citizenship and participative government. Professionalization of the public service has changed the nature of public organizations by implanting deeply the instrumental rationality that has dominated societies around the globe. This dominance, however, has been more pronounced in the Western countries than in developing nations.

Rationalism and positivism have been part of Western cultures for almost 200 years, whereas normative values are still dominant in most developing countries. However, globalization and cultural convergence, on the one hand, and counterpressures from below against this rampant instrumental rationality, on the other, are changing this situation. The result has been a clash of major values underlying the administrative and political systems around the world.

The rise of mixed economies after World War II and decolonization gave a boost to the administrative state. Eventually, however, the fall of the Union of Soviet Socialist Republics resulted in a reconsideration of societal, organizational, and economic principles. As the dominant economic system, capitalism appears to have risen to the top, with the United States and some European States as leaders in this new global environment.

Capitalist ideology advances the supremacy of the marketplace, together with the benefits of private enterprise and administrative rationality. However, this new trend has been accompanied by pressures from below from citizens who seek empowerment, smaller government, less governmental intrusion into their private lives and democratization of the policy process. The result has been a clash of citizenship values, on the one hand, and the professional administrative values, on the other. Consequently, public service has been badly damaged in terms of institutional capacity, quality of performance, and public image. Resolving this conflict requires the reconciliation of administrative and citizenship ethics.

II.   CRISIS IN THE PUBLIC SERVICE IMAGE

It is through integration of these conflicting values that the image of the public service can be revived and enhanced. This paper addresses this and other issues for discussion and policy recommendations. First, a number of factors contributing to the decline of the image of the public service are discussed. Then, several perspectives are presented on administrative ethics. This is followed by a discussion of professionalization in the public service and its implications for public service ethics. Subsequently, a discussion of public administrators as guardians of the public trust is presented. Finally, some guiding ethical principles are outlined, followed by an annex with some ethical issues, whose policy implications could be explored and debated. Many factors have contributed to the rise and expansion of the modern administrative state. Over the years, the role of government has grown dramatically. It soon became the engine of national growth, of private sector development, of the provision of public services, and of the protection of individual rights. Professionalization of the public service has been a common feature of both capitalism and socialism.

In capitalist countries, mixed economies arose, blurring the boundaries between the two sectors. The values of the public and private sectors also merged to an extent. Still, public service values and commitment remained strong. These professional administrative values displaced those of the earlier political machine systems, which prevailed in many countries during the nineteenth and early twentieth centuries—thus the professionalization of the civil service which followed, resulted in the separation of politics and administration. The politics-administration dichotomy was a dominant philosophy of the administrative state and of the public service. However, despite the improvements in public service delivery which it provided, it also introduced another dilemma in the form of the dichotomy of politics and administration.

The dichotomy put professional administrators in a position of vulnerability, enjoining them to abstain from public policy making and not to engage in activities in the domain of politics, however defined. The democratic values of responsiveness, responsibility, and accountability became major political values, which were perceived to be in conflict with the administrative values of professionalism, efficiency, and effectiveness. Consequently, the administrative state and the public service came under attack from an array of crusaders for democracy. These antipublic service, antibureaucracy, and antigovernment forces have had ideological, political, social, and economic underpinnings, whose exploration goes beyond the limitations of this paper. A severe decline of the public service followed in terms both of institutional capacity and the image it presented in the United States and around the world. The result has been a major crisis of public service professionalism.

III.   ADMINISTRATIVE ETHICS MOVEMENT

Rampant political jobbery and economic corruption have provided much of the impetus for the development of modern public administration and the professionalization of the civil service. Thus, in the United States of America, the 1883 Civil Service Reform Act "actually was the full equivalent of a constitutional amendment, even though there was no way to describe it as such." And as Frederickson put it recently, "The contemporary government ethics movement appears to have essentially the same purpose as the reform movement a century ago—to reduce government corruption." Never before have ethics been so important. The significance of ethics in governance and the public service is high for several reasons. First, the level of corruption in government has increased dramatically. Taking bribes by public officials—mostly political—is a pervasive phenomenon around the world, and the business sector is a major conduit for this practice. Small and big "scams" have resulted in the conviction of numerous officials. Corruption has been a pervasive and enduring public issue. Second, increasingly, "people do not equivocate on government corruption. It is wrong and they are against it." Third, government corruption is a policy issue with strong "carrying capacity". It has reached saturation level. Fourth, matters of government ethics are being increasingly institutionalized. Fifth, ethics cut across all policy fields: business, medical, social service, insurance, social security, the military, economic, scientific, etc.

The growing global concern for administrative ethics has been manifest in at least three areas: academia, legislation and institution-building. Judicial aspects have also been reflected in cases reaching the courts and the decisions rendered. Considerable research and writing on administrative ethics have appeared in the form of scholarly books published during the past 20 years.

Institutional and legislative concerns for ethics have been expressed in many organizational and legal measures adopted to combat corruption, safeguard the integrity of public service and promote professional conduct based on sound ethical grounds. Almost all public organizations and associations of public service appear to have adopted codes of ethics. Institutional arrangements, such as offices to prevent or control unethical conduct, appear everywhere. It is a global phenomenon.

Eight major themes and perspectives appear to have emerged in recent publications on administrative ethics and accountability.

1. *Citizenship and democratic theory*, with an emphasis on the renewal of civic virtue. This theme views public servants as virtuous citizens and as guardians of community interests. Virtuous citizenship is important for democratic governance and administration. Loyalty to democratic values, responsiveness, responsibility and moral conduct are virtues of democratic citizenship. Civility, tolerance, respect for equality and for citizens' rights, as well as obligations are key values in democratic citizenship.

2. *Virtue ethics*, with an emphasis on good character in public service and administration. It is an extension of the first. Character is the focus of study and practice in administrative ethics: the most critical problem is the scarcity of men and women of good character in positions of leadership—whether public, private, educational, or religious. For too long, the management orthodoxy has taken as axiomatic the proposition that good systems will produce good people. However, it is clear that a just society depends more on the moral trustworthiness of its citizens and leaders than upon structures and systems. Costly ethical failures of organizational leaders have caused irreparable damage to public trust and to societal interests. As a personal attribute, virtue is a character trait that inclines us towards ethical conduct. Ethics has ancient origins. For Aristotle, moral virtue comes about as a result of habit, whence its name *ethike* is a derivative of *ethos* (habit). From this it also follows that none of the moral virtues arise in us by nature. Therefore, to Aristotle and all those following this perspective, administrative ethics are cognitive and learned values. But the social environment in which public administrators operate affects the cognitive values acquired or learned. Contemporary writers commonly associate the quest for excellence with the practice of virtue. This perspective has significant implications for modern public administration in that virtuous administrators can be trained and developed through ethical precept for public service. Therefore, unethical behaviour may be considered as a form of corruption, for corruption is the absence of civic virtue.

3. *Foundation thought and constitutional tradition*, insisting on the public officials' ethical obligation to uphold such major values enshrined in constitutions as freedom, liberty, equali-

ty, due process, justice, etc. This perspective also values efficiency in the measure that the ethical and political values of democracy are upheld. It is as central to the theme of public interest as procedural versus substantive justice and seeks to maximize the salutary influence of personal interest and to control the adverse effects of popular passions.

4. *Ethics as education*, with an emphasis on the study of ethics in the public administration curriculum and training public servants for an honourable career. This perspective has a grounding on the educational development of public administrators and highlights community service. Ethics is education in that it transforms officials by moulding their attitudes, behaviour and perception of others. It is through self-development that social administrative ethics are also promoted. Ethics as education is both external learning and internalization of moral values.

5. *The organizational context of ethics*, with a focus on efficiency and effectiveness, but also on the normative values of fairness, justice, and moral conduct: organizations and their members must not be moral only where it is efficient to do so; they must be efficient only where it is moral to do so. Efficiency at any cost is not acceptable, but efficiency with moral and ethical conduct is imperative. Organizational structures reflect value choices and ethical commitments made by those who design organizations. They protect such ethical values as fairness, justice, honesty, accountability, and respect for rights, but may also impede them through built-in bureau pathologies. Structures and procedures may be viewed as mechanisms for pursuing ethical outcomes. Procedural justice is considered as a way to deal with the arbitrariness, tyranny, and injustice that may arise in the exercise of administrative discretion. Thus, discretion should be checked by means of judicial and other institutions. In public administration, a clash between ethics and organizational culture may occur. Critics argue that bureaucratic culture corrupts society through lack of human-centred norms. The manipulative role of power holders degenerates into a system of totalitarianism, in which organizational ethical values are compromised.

6. *Philosophical theory and perspectives*, with a focus on rejecting positivism and postpositivist perspectives in public administration. Rejecting the neutrality argument, this perspective highlights the public servants' active role in upholding and promoting agreed-upon values of the community as public interests. Administrative ethics, therefore, identify professionalism with active moral conduct. The role of professionalism and of professional administrators is emphasized in administrative ethics.

7. *Ethics as consequence or utilitarianism*, with a focus on the outcome of conduct and behaviour in public administration. In a major break with classical thought, Machiavelli argued (*The Prince*) that acts should be judged as good or bad depending on their consequences, rather than on their intentions or the characteristics of their actors. Following this line of argument, John Stuart Mill (1806–1873) wrote (*Utilitarianism*) that "All action is for the sake of some end, and rules of action it seems natural to pursue must take their whole character and colour from the end to which they are subservient. To be good, actions must be means to something admitted to be good, . . . such as health or pleasure."

8. *Ethics as principle*, with an emphasis on categorical imperatives in which absolute right is pursued. Immanuel Kant (1724–1804) approached the question of ethics from a very different angle than Machiavelli or Mill. Kant outlines his categorical imperative as the ultimate basis for ethical action or inaction.

IV. PROFESSIONALISM AND ADMINISTRATIVE ETHICS

From these theoretical perspectives, one can discern implications for modern public administration in which rationality-based organizational and normative values converge with virtuous citizenship.

Max Weber once observed that the modern state administration was bureaucratized everywhere. Both capitalist and socialist States and their administrative systems have gone through bureaucratization, and professionalization. Professionalization of public administration has been characterized by an adherence to the merit system, to task specialization, to systems of checks and balances, and to the organizational values of efficiency, economy and effectiveness achieved through political neutrality. It has also meant adherence to professional standards, values, criteria and ethics rather than political or other criteria.

Thus, generally speaking, the professionalization of public administration and the administrative state present two contrasting perspectives: professionalization introduces task performance, efficiency, effectiveness, objectivity, integrity, identity, and cohesion. It also serves as a bulwark against political corruption and other substandard behaviors in the public service. Its value as a corrective has been recognized. However, the clash between professional civil service values, on the one hand, and the political values of responsiveness, responsibility, and accountability to citizens, on the other, has been a major source of tension between professional career bureaucrats and politicians, elected or appointed. The conflict between professional and political values has captured much of the recent literature in public administration and political science around the globe. Are they really contradictory or complementary?

Two opposing perspectives prevail on this question. The one against professional discretion and participation in policy making asserts that such participation is undemocratic because non-elected, appointed bureaucrats cannot be held accountable to members of the electorate. This perspective also contends that democratic values of responsiveness and responsibility are lost as professional bureaucrats play a part in policy decisions. It is increasingly difficult not to hold professional experts accountable, since only they understand the minutiae of the knowledge they possess. The counter-argument for professional values asserts that professional standards serve the broad public interest. Therefore, they are responsive to societal needs. Accountability is achieved through organizational, professional and personal mechanisms of checks and balances. In addition, legislative, judicial and other means of oversight are exercised over them.

A third theoretical approach consists in combining professional and democratic values in the public service. Therefore, to be a sound administrator it is essential to perform with high ethical values and to promote efficiency and effectiveness, but also responsiveness, responsibility and fairness or justice. Discretion must be exercised under multiple systems of checks and balances, but also with personal and professional integrity and prudence (practical wisdom). Therefore, to be a professional is not enough. One must also be a responsible and responsive administrator. This requires ethical education and training at all levels.

Professional public administrators may be seen as the guardians of the administrative state. They provide stability and continuity in governance, even in the midst of paralyzing political crises, upheavals and revolutions. It is an established fact that bureaucracy has survived political changes for more than three millennia. Public administrators play an active role in the formulation of public policies. But their impact on the pace, style, tone and quality of policy implementation is immense. They may be viewed as guardians of the public trust.

However, to many concerned citizens, experts and political authorities around the world, this assertion also raises a very fundamental question. Who then guards the guardians? This is also a central issue in public management. As Victor Thompson noted some time ago, the increasing specialization of subordinate employees has created a severe imbalance between formal hierarchical authority and the responsibility of high-level administrative elites, on the one hand, and their actual capacity to manage, on the other.

Accountability in the public service is very important because there are many aspects of administrative work that are open to corruption and subversion of the public interest. At the same time, there are aspects of professionalism that make it difficult to attain an acceptable level of accountability. The difficulty in attaining administrative accountability makes administrative ethics particularly important. Ethics is a form of self-discipline, an inner check on the conduct of public servants. Accountability is also an organizational and political concern. It touches on issues of liability, as well as ethical matters. To deal with these two issues of worldwide concern, it is worth considering the question why some public administrators abuse their trust and act in ways considered to be contrary to the public interest and in violation of the public trust.

V. GUARDIANS OF THE PUBLIC TRUST

Generally speaking, there are three categories of factors that impel public administrators to violate the public trust. These are misrepresentation of the public interest, corruption, and subversion.

A. Misrepresentation of the Public Interest

Several factors at work shape public servants' concepts of the public interest. Most of the high-ranking administrative appointees are drawn disproportionately from upper and upper middle class backgrounds. This makes the bureaucracy socially unrepresentative. The social and economic class basis of the civil service is critical because it colors perceptions of how people live, what their problems are, and what they want and need.

Excessive specialization is yet another source of misrepresentation of the public interest. Professional public administrators—like those who perform specialized functions—may develop a narrow outlook concerning the public interest, by either exaggerating the importance of what they do or by downgrading the work of others. Professional lawyers, medical doctors, and scientists are examples of this. Critics have even argued that bureaucracies and bureaucrats tend to develop *bureau ideologies* that frequently distort their view of public needs. This is because all officials exhibit relatively strong loyalty to the organization controlling their job security, prospects, and promotion.

Lastly, misrepresentation may flow from close relationships of public organizations with particular clientele: health, agriculture, the environment, and urban development are cases in point. Public administrators working in such agencies may mistakenly consider the interest groups with which they deal to be truly representative of the population as a whole. The concept of "iron triangles" refers to a phenomenon that has become pervasive in the United States and many other nations. Among the most powerful iron triangles found in the realm of public policy is the military-industrial complex (MIC). In a typical iron triangle, an informal alliance is formed among interest groups, administrative/bureaucratic elites, and legislative committee members (political elites). It functions outside the formal structure and process of the bureaucracy and government, with no records taken or references made. The business, bureaucratic and political elites dominate the policy process, producing tunnel vision and a corresponding lack of transparency and accountability in the transaction of public business.

B. Corruption

Corruption may be viewed as betrayal of the public trust, and is a worldwide phenomenon. It has contributed to the current crisis in the public service image. It is beyond the scope of this paper to discuss its many dimensions, consequences, and causes. Suffice it to say that definitions of corruption vary from culture to culture. What is legal and legitimate in the United States may be considered corrupt in other cultures. There are numerous forms of corruption, including bribery and kickbacks, which have become institutionalized in some political regimes. Other forms of corruption have become so pervasive as to be virtually accepted as normal, including nepotism, favouritism, patronage and the selling or exchange of office for personal gain. Corruption tarnishes the image of the public service and deligitimizes the role of government; in all its forms it violates the public trust and civilized values. The pervasiveness of corruption in the public service makes it imperative to develop ways to guard the guardians.

C. Subversion

Subversion is another reason why public administrators need to be watched and controlled. Public administrators may engage in subversive activities for a variety of reasons: extreme discontent or fear of job loss, resort to clandestine activities in cooperation with antigovernment forces or organizations, corruption, and so on.

Important though it is, the task of guarding the guardians presents a number of problems:

1. *Special expertise and information.*   Public administrators are often experts at what they do. The expertise and specialized information they possess puts them in an advantageous position, which is not matched by outsiders, specially common citizens, but even politicians. This technical, specialized expertise and information are the bases of administrative and organizational decisions, and often beyond the ability of outsiders and those charged with oversight to fathom.

2. *Full-time status.*   Simply stated, the full-time status of public administrators makes it difficult for outsiders, who have many other things to do, to hold them accountable.

3. *Job security and other protections.*   Most public administrators enjoy job security, and any adverse organizational action against them is subject to due process, civil service protection procedures and so on. Discipline and dismissals are difficult, though not impossible. Many small and petty administrative infractions can over time lead to a significant adverse impact on public service image and credibility, as well as on organizational productivity, performance, and service quality.

4. *The law of countercontrol.*   According to Anthony Downs, it takes a bureaucracy to control bureaucracy. The law of countercontrol has several manifestations in different parts of the world. It leads to duplication, waste and the proliferation of bureaucratic organizations for control purposes, a practice which obscures the cardinal purpose of public service, which is to serve the citizens and to protect their interest.

5. *Coordination problems.*   Such problems make accountability difficult for many reasons. For example, separation of powers in the United States between the Executive, Congress, and Judiciary has been a source of difficulties in securing accountability. Analogous examples may be found elsewhere in the world. It is often difficult to hold an agency or administrator accountable, when many organizations and officials are involved in implementation without proper coordination and control.

6. *Fragmentation of organizational functions and structures.*   This is another obstacle in securing administrative accountability. Fragmentation and overlapping functions and responsibilities cause confusion. Accountability is lost because no one seems to be responsible, where everyone is responsible. Blames are shifted from one source to another.

7. *The large size and scope of public administration.*   Almost everywhere in the world, the size, missions, and scope of public administration are extremely broad. Often the structures, rules, procedures and the number of employees employed complicates the task of holding public administrators accountable.

Yet, despite these major obstacles, a number of means have been used to secure accountability in public service and thus to guard the guardians. Codes of professional ethics and education constitute one broad category. A complementary approach encompasses political, legal, cultural, and other institutional arrangements, which are explored below.

VI.   ACHIEVING ACCOUNTABILITY

Administrative accountability in the public service can be achieved through a number of formal means.

A.   Managerial/Organizational

This approach is applied worldwide and is a universal means of achieving accountability in all kinds of organizations. It has several major tenets or values that cut across all organizations and the prevailing culture in societies. These universal organizational values are efficiency, economy, effectiveness, and control. The first three are values of instrumental rationality, while the fourth is both a normative and a rational imperative of organizational accountability. Organizational unity is important for maximization of these values, and several means are used to secure it.

Firstly, hierarchy, authority, and responsibility need to be clearly defined and assigned. Overlapping functions should be reduced; lines of hierarchical authority should be clear and comprehensive. Plural agency heads/leadership tend to divide subordinates' loyalties and to obscure responsibility.

Subordination also is necessary for organizational unity, effectiveness, and accountability. Insubordination is seldom tolerated and is punishable by dismissal. Lastly, the span of control is an effective means of organizational accountability. Essentially a part of the orthodox, classical management and organization theory, a narrow span of control has been viewed as an important principle of accountability.

Organizational loyalty is expected of all members and is assured in many ways: these include socialization into the organizational milieu; occupational specialization makes it difficult for employees to find equivalent positions elsewhere; and dependence on organizations, through pension schemes or indeed conflict-of-interest regulations close the revolving door. Such countries as the United States have legislative regulations that tend to be comprehensive on these matters. Formal disciplinary systems enforce accountability and subordination. They are designed to identify the types of proper conduct and to prevent abuse of agency authority and property.

Disciplinary systems have often been criticized as largely ineffective. Public accountability should seek to enforce much higher standards of behavior, an approach that is professional and legal or constitutional in nature. Audits are strong deterrents to corruption or other abuses of public trust. Audits can also be internal or external, and it may be desirable to employ external as well as internal audits. In many public organizations, both are required.

B.   Political Means

The political approach takes a different road in stressing the need to develop an external means of accountability in public administration. This is frequently done through political control of personnel systems by using patronage appointments. However, other important means are also applied effectively and are familiar to most systems:

1.   Legislative oversight, which can be achieved by means of legislative requirement for the ratification of the appointment of agency heads, legislative investigations and auditing.

2.   Budgetary control, which means the power of the purse, an extremely important legislative check on executive power.

3.   Rotation in office in order to reduce the risk of misrepresentation of public interest, amassment of power or empire-building by key administrators. This is an ancient personnel practice going back to Persia and Rome. Its utility is recognized for a number of reasons around the world. The 1978 Civil Service Reform Act of the United States created the Senior Executive Ser-

vice to enable the federal civil servants to move from one agency to another. Political executives are routinely rotated from office to office, or out of office, when a new political boss arrives.

4.   Representation and public participation as a means of broadening the composition of public service and encouraging diversity, which may bring administrative values closer to the general public, thus reflecting citizens' perspectives and preferences.

5.   Whistleblowing is a widely known practice, with its benefits and costs. The use of hot liens and other confidential channels may be safer for public administrators, protecting them from reprisals. Leaks to the press, exposure to the public and the media, reporting to higher authority, resignation in protest, and exposure are some means of whistleblowing. Some countries have passed legislation protecting whistleblowers.

6.   "Sunshine laws," which require open public dealings as important means of securing accountability and proper conduct of public officials. Today, most American states and local governments have adopted sunshine laws.

7.   Conflict of interest, which is similar to the organizational and managerial approach.

C. Legal Approach

This is a judicial approach to administrative accountability. Administrative liability is one issue; another is a strong and personally internalized incentive to protect the constitutional rights of individual citizens.

D. Cultural Approach

This is another means of achieving accountability in public service. It requires inclusion of significant ethical components in the educational curricula for children and adults. Ethical education can be carried out through religious and secular institutions. Religious institutions and values can be used as major guiding principles in public service conduct. For example, in Islam, like in other religions, there is a high value attached to being a public servant and to proper behavior in personal and public life.

E. Ethics Institutional Approach

A number of institutions can be created and empowered to promote and enforce ethical behavior and accountability. For example, programs for whistleblowing, ethics hot lines, ethics boards and commissions, ethics education programs for elected, politically appointed, and administrative officials, agency ethics officers, financial and conflict-of-interest disclosure systems, and professional codes of ethics are typically found in modern governments. Australia, Canada, the United States, the United Kingdom, Iran, India, and many developing countries have most or all of these institutions in place.

VII. GUIDING PRINCIPLES IN PUBLIC SERVICE ETHICS

Administrative ethics has been enhanced by professionalization in the administrative state. While public service ethics and accountability remain major concerns, the incidence of corruption and unethical behavior is mostly found to be on the political side of the public service. Political executives are often at the apex of public organizations and, as elites, they tend to be key players in most scandals. Professionalism in public administration has helped in curbing political corruption around the world.

Acting as guardians of the public trust, professional administrators are in a central position to revive and enhance the image of the public service. This is a major challenge, which entails a conscious effort of advocacy and enforcement. The following paragraphs present a list of principles that can guide public administrators in promoting the above goals. These principles or precepts are identified as dos and don'ts.

Ethical education.   Ethical education is a must and should be part of all educational systems at all levels. However, education and training in administrative ethics are most essential for public service careers anywhere in the world. They must include both personal and administrative ethics. Civic virtues, virtuous citizenship, respect for others, protection of individual rights and other ethical values should be internalized by public servants. Advice to top executives should also include the following: Set the example and tone for the entire organization by emphasizing education and training in ethics, by thinking and behaving ethically. Advice to public employees: Educate yourself with ethical and moral principles and act ethically; do not compromise on principles; disobey unconstitutional, immoral, illegal, and unethical orders and expose them through the appropriate channels; find appropriate ways to do it.

Preservation of professional and personal integrity.   Professional values should prevail over organizational or personal orders of superiors deemed questionable. Responsible professionalism is an essential component of administrative behavior. This requires self-regulation, knowledge, self-control, a degree of autonomy and personal independence, and subordination of private interests to the public interest and public trust.

Prudence.   The exercise of prudence, which means practical wisdom, was emphasized by two great Persian thinkers of the Middle Ages—Ibn-e-Cina and Nizam-ul-Mulk. Every society has its own thinkers of this calibre. Prudence requires self-control, discretionary decisions based on knowledge, expertise, and ethical judgment.

Public spirit.   Private interests should be subordinate to public, community interests. In making decisions or acting as an administrator, think of the public trust, and citizens' interests first, then think of yourself. Develop civic virtue, act virtuously and promote virtuous citizenship by being a virtuous citizen and acting as a virtuous administrator.

Avoidance of all problems causing public service crises.   Some of these problems are beyond one's control as an administrator, but those values and factors that deter public service corruption and compromise should be adhered to.

Be a responsible administrator.   Act with restraint, discretion, and freedom. Be an example to others. If you cannot continue to perform your duties properly, resign and expose those who make it impossible for you to perform ethically and professionally.

Promotion of the common good.   Devote your time, expertise, and knowledge to building community values and defending the rights of the poor as well as of the affluent. It is the public interest and trust that you must serve at all times with integrity.

Be competent and fair.   Competence comes with training, skills development, and knowledge. It is extremely important to apply competence with fairness, equity, and justice in administrative positions. Efficiency and effectiveness are important organizational and managerial values, but they must be blended with fairness, equity and justice. It is this blend of ethical and professional values that makes professional ethics in public administration possible and desirable.

Follow and enforce the professional code of ethics.   Codes of ethics in public administration are written and unwritten collections or systems of laws, rules, regulations, and norms that guide public service conduct. They are statements of ideals, canons of action consonant with those ideals and binding means of enforcing behavior within the boundaries established by the code. Opponents of codes of ethics argue that one should resist moralizing everything, that rigid codification of right or wrong is dysfunctional, and that bureaucratic neutrality considers it immoral to pass moral judgements on public organizations. Proponents of codes of ethics cite the objectivity and the positive value added through code of ethics enforcement. Some codes of ethics carry sanctions for unethical behaviors while others are more aspirational or guides to public servants.

Establish and affirm professional identity as a public servant, as a professional, as a keeper of public trust and as an ethical person. Resist all forms of corruption.

Avoid unethical dilemmas as much as possible but, if caught in the middle, seek advice and exercise prudence. Most ethical dilemmas can be handled with prudence.

Act morally and ethically with a sound character and responsible judgment. Value and promote the image of the public service.

Combat corruption at any level and at all times. Establish and use commissions of inquiry; wage war on undiscipline, and show moral leadership. Also use scholarly research and the confidential approaches mentioned earlier.

Develop and internalize a sense of total quality management (TQM):   Promote the idea of doing things right the first time and prevent the costly error of duplicating or repeating poor quality work. Do not cheat on your work, internalize work ethics, and develop a sense of motivation for public interest and self-actualization.

View citizens as valued human beings and as community members, not merely as consumers or customers in the marketplace. Discourage an overly biased corporate ideology, which tends to promote corruption and unethical behavior. Markets are not alternatives to public service. Rather, sound governance, public service, and responsible citizenship are sine qua non of a business-friendly environment, the smooth operation of markets, effective democracy, and social peace.

VIII.   ISSUES IN ADMINISTRATIVE ETHICS

Public administrators face significant ethical issues on a daily basis. Some of these issues are strictly organizational, while others are broader societal issues concerning ethics and accountability. Both categories need to be reviewed by public administrators using ethical principles as their guide. The following is a list intended to generate discussion at the meeting:

Recruitment and selection
Employee drug screening and ethics
Alcoholism
Disciplinary action/termination
Salaries, wages, and benefits packages
Discrimination on any basis
Downsizing
Who should go first under cutback programs?
Sexual harassment in the workplace
Work force diversity
Right to strike
Political activities of public employees
Organizational changes affecting employees
Employee fitness programs
Censorship
Private use of employee time and expertise
Patronage vs. merit systems
Whistleblowing
Future employability of employees
Private conduct vs. public conduct

Conflicts between political and career appointees
Covering for the boss
Hierarchical orders
Conflict of interests
Bribery and small scams
Influence wielding
Nepotism and patronage
Ethics of privatization
Morale and productivity
Politicization of the civil service
Merit system erosion
Use of public property for private use
Race, color, convictions, and gender
Fairness, equity, justice, efficiency, and effectiveness

54

Improving Ethical Behavior in Public Organizations

A Practical Approach

Behrooz Kalantari   *Public Administration Program, Savannah State University, Savannah, Georgia*

I. INTRODUCTION

Public disenchantment with government officials is not a new phenomenon in the United States; it is part of the American political culture. However, new developments, including coverups and scandals involving government officials, have severely eroded the public's trust in government institutions. According to a recent survey on business ethics, a majority of public employees believe that ethical violations are common practice at work. (Ward 1998:4). On the other hand, government is expected to be the source of democratic values and guardian of high morals. Therefore, the main task for public managers is to develop a balance between the reality of public organizations and the public's high expectations from them.

Due to the pervasive nature of public employees' behavior, ignoring the impact of their decisions on the larger audience will likely be detrimental to society (McBribe 1990; Lozano 1996:233). It follows that such disregard for ethical considerations might seriously effect the civic morality of individual citizens (Donahue 1989:127). In addition, it negatively affects the level of efficiency of public service as well. Therefore, the main focus of this paper is the development of new strategies to help human resource managers to deal effectively with ethical questions in the next millennium.

Public employees' behavior depend on many factors, including their environment, organizational context, and personal values. They determine the general orientation towards action. In an ideal situation, government employees promote high standards of ethical conduct in public service rather than their own personal interests (Jennings 1985). Problems arise when officials at different levels of public organizations use public resources to satisfy their own personal needs, wishes, and priorities. Therefore, the notion of behavioral control becomes essential in the management of public organizations.

One of the major problems of the status of ethics in public administration emanates from the lack of common agreement on the nature of ethics and thus the lack of a paradigm to provide common understanding of ethics in the field of public administration (Denhardt 1988:1). However, regardless of the ambiguity of its context, there is general agreement that ethics "are prescribed by the values, norms, traditions, and culture of any community, or by consensus among members of the community in specific instances" (Cooper 1991:6).

II. DECISION-MAKING PROCESSES

Public organizations are the aggregate manifestations of the decision-making systems that seek to accomplish specific goals in order to serve social needs. Therefore, the importance of individual decisions has a significant impact on the overall function of the system (depending on the rank and power of the individual decision maker). Early theories of public administration, due to a lack of understanding of different dimensions of organizational life, did not recognize the important role that individual values and perceptions play in the daily decision-making process.

There are several models to explain the decision-making process in organizations. One of the most publicized decision-making models is the rational model which was influenced by Herber Simon. He believed that decision making is at the heart of any organization and emphasizes the importance of rational decision making in organizational efficiency (Simon 1957:38).

Simon believed that facts and values should be separated and organizations should concentrate on factual data in the decision-making process in order to make more rational decisions. However, he argues that in reality decisions are not rational and that due to our human limitations, we make decisions which fall within a "bounded rationality" zone (Simon 1957). According to Simon, only when organizational decisions fall within a certain range, the employee accepts and carries out that decision, he calls it the "area of acceptability" (Simon 1957:133).

Chester Barnard calls the same area as "zone of indifference" (Barnard 1938:168). Both he and Simon believed that replacing individual values with organizational values would maximize efficiency. On the other hand, Robert Dahl disagrees with their approach and indicates that in an organizational setting, decision making involves a mixture of values and facts which cannot be separated (Dahl 1947).

Economic theories approach the decision-making process from a utilitarian perspective. They argue that in any decision-making process, the decision maker makes a cost-benefit analysis to reach a decision. According to this school of thought, although individuals make decisions to maximize their own benefit (because they are rational beings), in the final analysis they contribute to social welfare and their decisions are beneficial to society. Therefore, their decisions are moral (Bentham 1789; Mill 1861; Rashdall 1907; Sidgwick 1907; Moore 1912). This argument might be legitimate for private sector employees, but it cannot be applied to the public sector. It can even be argued that in the public sector, employees' attendance to their own personal needs might be detrimental to the public's needs. Therefore, the major difficulty with this model is the context of its applicability. It might explain the individual profit motive in a business oriented environment which ultimately contributes to the welfare of the whole society. However, this model fails to explain how a decision maker in a public setting is able to benefit society when he/she tries to satisfy his/her own values.

Although Herbert Kaufman did not directly deal with individual values and ethical issues, he introduced a new perspective on the way we look at the way organization's function. He emphasized the importance of personal and environmental factors in the decision-making process through his open-system theory. Kaufman's theory explains many factors which influence the individual's decision-making process (Kaufman 1960). His study of the forest service clearly indicates how individuals can draw from their own past experiences to make decisions. In addition, it explains how they can be influenced by their peers and their social values as well (Kaufman 1960). Consequently, the decision-making process cannot be a simple rational and scientific process and is influenced by many factors, including the personal values and priorities of the decision maker.

It can be argued that a wide spectrum of ethics violations might occur during the decision-making process. Public employees can encounter a variety of ethical problems, including the conscience dilemma of conducting an immoral act or an overt violation of the rules and regulations (Lawrence 1990).

III. WHAT IS ETHICS IN GOVERNMENT?

Although there is no consensus on the definition of ethics, it is related to an individual's conscience by which he/she will be directed to reach a fair decision on the basis of organizational values (Domick 1941). In a philosophical sense, ethics obligates employees to choose between good and evil and directs them to act morally. Ethics originate from the idea that there are certain moral principles that are common to all humans. Therefore, there is a difference between morals and ethics. In general, moral standards depend on the consensus view of what is a right and what is a wrong action in a society. Therefore, there is no specific universal code of morality.

Morals are defined as those actions which are considered "right behavior" in any society. In other words, "a moral judgment often and centrally serves as a kind of injunction, spoken aloud or in one's heart, to others, or to oneself, to behave or not to behave in a certain way" (Bennet 1993:458). Ethics is the process by which we search for moral standards (DeGeorge 1982:12).

Ethics are related to morals as the right behavior which is examined and reflected upon. In other words, ethics are the practical application of moral ideas. Therefore, it is clear that ethical standards focus on individual judgment, action, and analysis of the employee's perception of right and wrong (Leys 1968; Golembiewski 1969; Hart 1974; Henry 1989; Cooper 1986). The terms morals and ethics are often used interchangeably.

Some argue in favor of moral relativism, indicating that an action might be acceptable in one setting which cannot be acceptable in another. Although there is some validity to that theory, there are certain basic moral values which have universal acceptability and are shared by most human organizations. Cross-cultural empirical research indicates that public ethical values are broadly shared within the international community. (Lewis and Gilman 1996:619)

Problems arise when organizational values are undermined by individual value systems. Therefore, no matter how encompassing the rules and regulations are, the human factor is always involved in implementing decisions. This fact is more evident when individual employees delegate more responsibility, authority, and formal power to lower level decision makers (Mosher 134).

IV. ETHICS AND INDIVIDUAL DECISIONS

In order to understand the ethical dimensions of the decision-making process, first one needs to define the limit and scope of ethical concern. The main focus is the area beyond the existing rules and regulations of organizations. It concerns the gray area of employee discretion in carrying out the functions of organizations (zone of discretion). In other words, the focus is on the area where personal ethics and professional ethics are in conflict with one another. The question is how can organizations ensure that professional ethics supersede the personal values. (Cooper 1992:48–49).

There are two main approaches in dealing with administrative ethics. One is "structural approach" (formal-legal), which concentrates on organizational rules and regulations to uphold ethical norms. The other is the "normative approach" which emphasizes the significance of devel-

oping an ethical culture in organizations and goes beyond the normal imposition of structural limitations. (Lewis and Gillman 1996:560). The latter approach holds that it is not possible to cover
every conceivable situation in employees' daily performance of duties. (Harrington 1996:379).
Therefore, it advocates the development of an ethical culture in organizations to promote ethical
behavior. In a practical sense, it is very difficult to monitor this area because the moral choices of
each individual vary depending on the individual's responsibilities within the organization.
(Lozano 1996:230). In addition, organizations cannot control personal values.

More importantly, employees can use organizational rules and regulations to carry out their
wishes, giving the appearance of compliance while in reality, abusing their privileges. Results of
a recent survey of several government employees indicate that although ethical misconduct is
common in public institutions, "all government employees have the same basic level of understanding when it comes to organizational ethics" (Sadri and Rood 1997:1113). Therefore, those
employees who commit unethical behavior would not perceive their decisions as being immoral
or unethical and try to find justification for their actions based on their own moral value. In order
to deal with this zone of discretion, guidelines and ethic codes have been developed to set parameters for employees' behavior and control their abuse of power.

V. ESTABLISHMENT OF CODES OF ETHICS

In order to control individuals from making arbitrary decisions and to provide some form of
accountability in organizations, many public agencies have developed ethic codes. A code of
ethics is the expression of the norms and values of organizations and represents the way things
should be accomplished in organizations. In other words, it provides a framework within which
organizations are supposed to operate.

Although the perceptions of the nature of ethics may vary between cultural and ethnic
groups, "there tends to be broad agreement within national communities on what is right and what
is wrong" (Hartman 1996:11). Codes of ethics provide important cues as to the importance of
general guidelines concerning issues such as honour, integrity, and responsibility. They provide a
comprehensive system of norms and procedures. The ultimate goal of a code of ethics is to internalize the values of organizations. Codes are often criticized for being vague and abstract and not
applicable to specific situations. In addition, codes of ethics lack a compliance mechanism
because they do not have operational enforcement structures and procedures.

Recent research shows that "enforcement of the ethical standard is key to maintaining an ethical work force. The standards lose their credibility unless enforcement is consistent" (Sadri and
Rood 1997:1112). Therefore, it is difficult to provide the public with reliable assurances for the
applicability of the code of ethics (Cooper 1992:144). In a real sense, due to the voluntary nature
of the codes of ethics, they are usually perceived by some as superficial and weak with no real practical meaning. Therefore, codes of conduct and other measures do not effectively deal with the
underlying problem of violating moral laws (Cox and Buck 1994). Due to the lack of other alternatives to guarantee moral quality in our public institutions, ethics education programs are the most
important means to promote professional behavior on the part of government officials.

VI. EDUCATION AND TRAINING

Ethics training is a "professional process by which public servants learn and inculcate ethics, standards of conduct and public service values" (Washington 1997:17). An alternative to deal with the
ethical aspects of public life is educating the employees on moral issues by creating sensitivity
toward them and raising their levels of professionalism (Howell 1982; Crable 1978; Day 1991).

Although it is hard to come up with universal codes of ethics, it is important to personalize them and make them practical and sensitize employees about the consequences of their decisions. For example, fairness, equality, justice, and other values can be communicated through special training and provide examples for the employees to follow.

There is a long standing belief in American society which argues that ethics should always precede power and hold influence over it. Therefore, training should be part of employees' formal education as well as their orientation program. If we approach public administration as a profession, it implies that we deal with a specific area of expertise and value construct which guides the actions of members of the profession. It is within this construct that public administrators should be socialized and trained.

There is a great deal of controversy concerning ethics training. Some argue that changing moral values should not be a legitimate goal in organizations (Callahan and Bok 1980), and some call into question the effectiveness of morals and ethics training (Walton and Warwick 1973; Thompson 1990). However, others are in favor of attempting to develop sound moral and universal standards which can be used to extract moral judgments (Lee 1990; Hume 1948).

Although most ethics training programs are not very successful (Thompson 1990:91), one of the reasons for their failure has been the methods by which training is conducted. It is also often argued that ethics training is ineffective because employees are already aware of the value, but they don't comply. If that was true, training would not change a person's behavior (Walton and Warwick 1973). Here, the main argument is that we simply cannot set moral standards for employees because question of morals are directly related to the question of emotions and passion (Ayer 1950; Stevenson 1944). Therefore, reasoning cannot establish morality. In other words, morals cannot be taught.

According to Kant "moral judgements can be derived from seemingly dispassionate logical reasoning" (Kant 1989:23). It is important to realize that when an employees disregard moral issues and base decisions on personal moral standards, they rely on their own reasoning to reach this decision. Therefore, as long as they engage in analysing their actions through reasonable means, their decisions are not based on emotions, but reason. As a result, we are dealing with a faulty decision-making process which can be changed through logical means including proper training.

Therefore, the purpose of training does not have to be changing the moral values of the individual per se, but to provide individuals with proper tools to evaluate their actions in an organizational context. The main goal should be to develop an understanding for organizational values (virtues) and the ability to visualize the effect of his/her actions on others. Kohlberg argues that "teaching of virtue is the asking of questions and the pointing of the way, not the giving of answers. Moral education is leading the people upward, not putting into the mind of knowledge that was not there" (Kohlberg 1981:30). In other words, we do not teach employees new values, but teach them to make sense of their own values and enable them to reach a universal understanding of the consequences of their own behavior in favor of organizational goals.

VII.   HOW TO CONDUCT ETHICAL TRAINING

As indicated earlier, in order for training to be useful, it has to be as practical as possible. In other words, it should provide practical steps to re-enforce desirable outcomes for achieving organizational goals. One of the problems with most trainings is that employees learn what it is that they are not supposed to do in specific cases, but are not equipped with proper decision-making skills in order to deal with ethical dilemmas (Rice and Drellinger 1990:103). In order to develop effective training, several elements should be taken into consideration including the development of "a decision model for manager that includes a consideration of the ethical ramifications of decisions"

(Hall 1993:237). Therefore, developing some skills such as listening, critical thinking, and moral reasoning are critical in enabling decision makers to grasp the nature and cause of ethical dilemmas and evaluate the effects of their decisions (Piper et al. 1993:119).

It is important to realize that training should be tailored around the needs of each public institution. In addition, political expectations of ethical administration should be included in the training process. Therefore, the development of a training model is extremely crucial in the success of the training process. It is important that "ethical concepts, principles, and theories are introduced early, in order to provide an analytical framework" for training employees. (Madsen 1989:33).

In the final analysis the training program should bring employees into closer contact with their own value system and make them understand the consequences of their actions in relation to others. It is more helpful "to draw upon a collective conscience to discourage wrong doing and encourage the affirmative aspects of ethics" (Donahue 1989:119). Successful training depends on the development of sensitivity to needs and to understanding one's obligations to others.

VIII. CONCLUSION

A major dilemma in managing organizations is balancing social, democratic, and human values with individual discretion. In its extreme manifestation, the individual decision-maker is already aware of the laws and regulations, but he/she perceives them as obstacles in the decision-making process. Therefore, individual employees learn how to deal with ethical dilemmas and make decisions in line with organizational goals. Although the effectiveness of ethical standards are in question, professional and institutional ethical standards could provide an effective guideline for the resolution of ethical dilemmas.

The first step in solving ethical problems in organizations is determining the extent of the problems and pin pointing the roots of those problems. Therefore, for the study of organizational needs, culture, and environment, a training program should be designed. Training should take into consideration the ethical needs of the organization with specific and feasible solutions in mind. Solutions should be specific and practical, aimed at unethical practices in organizations. Creating a feedback mechanism is very critical in evaluating and assessing the usefulness of the training programs. It is critical that training should precede actual job occupancy as part of the orientation program for new employees. In addition, ethical training should be an indispensable part of formal education at the college level. This approach makes ethical training part of the professional training and enhances its legitimacy and significance in the eyes of the employees. Moreover, frequent in-service training is a useful tool to refresh employees' knowledge and communicate new ways to deal with current problems. In other words, ethical training should be an on-going process in any organization.

In order to maintain a high level of sensitivity toward ethical issues, creating a supporting condition for the implementation of ethical values is also very important. A significant factor in determining the success of any training program is the support and commitment of the highest management level to improving ethical conditions. Furthermore, close attention to employees' compensation plans, working conditions, and job security is vital to sustain a healthy ethical environment.

REFERENCES

Ayer, A.J. (1950). Language. In *Truth, and Logic*. London: Victor Gollanez Ltd.
Bennet, J. (1993). The necessity of moral judgements. *Ethics 103*:458–472.

Bentham, J. (1789). *An Introduction to the Principles of Morals and legislation.* Oxford: Clarendon Press.

Bowman, A., and Kearney, R. (1993). *State and Local Government.* Boston: Houghton Mifflin.

Callahan, D. (1980). Goals in the teaching of ethics. In D. Callaham and S. Bok (eds.), *Ethics Teaching in Higher Education.* New York: Plenum Press.

Cooper, T.L. (1990). *The Responsible Administrator.* San Francisco: Jossey-Bass.

Cooper, T.L. (1991). *An Ethic of Citizenship for Public Administration.* Englewood Cliffs, NJ: Prentice Hall.

Cooper, R.G.L. (1992). Professionals in business: where do they look for help in dealing with ethical issues? *Business and Professional Ethics Journal 11*:41–56.

Cox, R.W. III, Buck, S.J., Morgan, B.N. (1994). *Public Administration in Theory and Practice.* Englewood Cliffs, NJ: Printice Hall.

Cradl, R.E. (1978). Ethical code, accountability and argumentation. *Quarterly Journal of Speech 64*:23–32.

Dahl, R.A. (1947). The science of public administration. *Public Administration Review 7*(Winter):1–11.

Denhardt, K. (1988). *The Ethics of Public Sector.* Westport, CT: Greenwood Press.

Donahue, A. (1989). *Ethics in Politics and Government.* New York: H.W. Wilson.

Domick, F. (1941). *Public Administration*, 5th ed. New York: Macmillan.

Denhart, K.G. (1988). *The Ethics of Public Service: Resolving Moral Dilemmas in Public Organizations.* New York: Greenwood Press.

DeGeorge, R.T. (1982). *Business Effects.* New York: Macmillan.

Devlin, P. (1965). *The Enforcement of Morals.* Cary, NC: Oxford University Press.

Day, L. (1991). *Ethics in Media Communications: Cases and Controversies.* Belmont, CA: Wadsworth.

Donahue, M. (1989). *Ethics in Politics and Government.* New York: H.W. Wilson.

Hall, W.D. (1993). *Making the Right Decision: Ethics for Managers.* New York: John Wiley & Sons.

Harrington, L.K. (1996). Ethics and public policy analysis: shareholders' interests and regulatory policy. *Journal of Business Ethics 15*:373–382.

Hartman, D.J. (1996). Audit of ethics in government. *International Journal of Government Auditing 23*(2):11–12.

Hume, D. (1948). Inquiry concerning the principles of morals. In H. Aikend (ed.), *Hume's Moral and Political Philosophy.* New York: Macmillan.

Hunt and Tripok (1993). Universal ethics code. *Public Relations Review 19*:5.

Jennings, B. (1985). *Representation and Responsibility.* Philadelphia: Plenum Press.

Kant, I. (1989). *Fundamental Principles of Metaphysics of Morals.* (Thomas K. Abbott trans.) New York: Macmillan.

Kaufman, H. (1960). *The Forest Ranger.* Baltimore: John Hopkins University Press.

Kohlberg, L. (1984). *Essays on Moral Development*, Vol. II. San Francisco: Harper and Row.

Kohlberg, L. (1981). *Essays on Moral Development*, Vol. I. San Francisco: Harper and Row.

Lee, D.S. (1990). Moral education and the teaching of public administration ethics. *International Journal of Public Administration 13*(1, 2):360–390.

Lewis, C.W., and Gillman, S.C. (1996). Public service ethics: a global dialogue. *Public Administration Review 56*(6):517–524.

Ley, W.R. (1941). *Ethics and Social Policy.* New York: Macmillan.

Lindblom, C.E. (1957). The science of middling through. *Public Administration Review 19*(Spring):79–88.

Lozano, J.M. (1996). Ethics and management: a controversial issue. *Journal of Business Ethics 15*:227–236.

Madsen, P. (1989). An ounce of prevention: designing ethics training programs. *Human Resources Professional* September/October:33–45.

Mill, J.S. (1861). Utilitarianism. *Fraser's Magazine* (October, November, December issues).

McBribe, A. (1990). Ethics in Congress, agenda and action. *George Washington Law Review 58*:231–314.

Moore, G.E. (1912). *Ethics.* London: Oxford University Press.

Mark, L. (1990). Legislative ethics. *Maine Law Review 42*:215–234.

Piper, T.R., Gentile, M.C. and Parks, S.D. (1993). *Can Ethics Be Taught.* Boston: Harvard Business School.

Rashdall, H. (1907). *Theory of Good and Evil.* Oxford: Clarendon Press.

Rice, D., and Drellinger, C. (1990). Rights and wrongs of ethics training. *Training and Development Journal* May:75–93.

Rohr, J. (1989). *Ethics for Bureaucrats.* New York: Marcel Dekker.

Sadri, A., and Rood, T.L. (1997). Ethics in government: a survey of misuse of position for personal gain and its implications for developing acquisition strategy. *Journal of Business Ethics 15*(11):1107–1116.

Sigwick, H. (1907). *Methods of Ethics.* London: Macmillan.

Simon, H.A. (1957). *Administrative Behavior: A Study of Decision-Making Process in Administrative Organizations*, 2nd ed. New York: Free Press.

Stevenson, C. (1993). *Ethics and Language.* New Haven, CT: Yale University Press.

Thompson, B.L. (1990). Ethics training enters the real world. *Training* October:82–94.

Walton, R.E., and Warwick, D.P. (1973). The ethics of organizational development. *Journal of Applied Behavioral Science 9*(6):681–698.

Ward, J. (1998): Survey finds government worker's ethics lacking. *American City and County 113*(5):4–5.

Washington, S. (1997). Management of government ethics. *OECD Observer 204*(Feb/March):15–17.

55
Ethical Issues in the Use of the Internet

Jean-Claude Garcia-Zamor   *School of Policy and Management, Florida International University, North Miami, Florida*

I. INTRODUCTION

At its beginning in 1969, the Internet was a technology-and-communications network for the U.S. Defense Department and for university researchers. By 1996 it had grown into a colossus connecting 52 million of the world's 234 million computers. It serves as everything from a personal playground to an information superhighway for businesses. The formation of a global network society—a world in which people, businesses, and institutions are linked by interconnected computers—is fast becoming a reality. At the present time, only 1% of the world's population is using a personal computer, and even a smaller number are connected to the Internet. But some estimates predict that the world will have at least 1 billion cybercitizens connected to the Internet by the year 2008. However, there are serious concerns over privacy, government regulation, taxation, and whether some countries will ever keep pace with the early starters like the United States. So high is the concern over online privacy in the United States that 82 separate bills are pending in the U.S. Congress regarding privacy online. Similar legislation is either pending or already law in various countries around the world (Sagan 1998:45–46).

The age of technology and computers brings with it unparalleled dilemmas in the industrialized societies, especially in the United States. Three related ethical issues will be discussed in this chapter: cryptology, advertising, and ecommerce on the Internet. These three issues will have great implications in the application of administrative ethics in the more advanced countries. But they also will affect the way the process of development administration will be carried out in the third world countries. As a matter of fact, this technology is making the concept of the "global village" more of a reality. After discussing some ethical problems involved with cryptology and advertising on the Internet, the difficulties of government regulations of these new technologies will be examined. Finally, their impact on development administration will be reviewed.

II. CRYPTOGRAPHY

The issue of cryptography, once a subject only spies and the military had any interest in, has become a hot topic because of its use on the Internet. The dilemma is one of security and privacy versus law enforcement and national security. Encryption policy is both essential for the growth of Internet commerce and vital for protection of privacy in the information age. As the battle is fought, questions of morality and ethics are seldom discussed. In the global world of computers, regulations are being established which must coincide with the establishment of global ethics.

Cryptography is the practice of coding messages so that they can only be read by the intended receiver. In the computer world, it is the scrambling of a message which can only be decrypted if the receiver has the encryption key.

The technology to encrypt messages on the Internet has been around for many years, but it has just within the past few years become an issue. One reason is that more and more sensitive transactions are occurring via the Internet. The problem is that people are increasingly entrusting information to computer—everything from confidential medical records to business plans to money itself. Something needs to be done to provide security so that these data will be protected from eavesdroppers, thieves, and saboteurs. Without encryption, anyone can read these messages and use them for illegal and unethical purposes. For one to read an encrypted message, one must either have the key or be able to decode the encryption.

The strength of the cryptography determines how easy it is to decode. The higher the bits in the key, the harder it is to crack. For instance, a 56-bit key is theoretically 65,000 times harder to crack than a 40-bit key. This is significant because as technology becomes more efficient, these codes become easier to crack with simple computers. In recent attacks on 40-bit exportable cryptography, any attacker with a moderate amount of computer power has been able to decrypt captured messages without access to an encryption key (Garfinkel 1996).

The argument for strong encryption in the business world is convincing. If people can gain unauthorized access to the kinds of information that are being transmitted, the result could be massive fraud and theft. The economic benefit of strong cryptography to business is therefore great.

The first argument that the U.S. government has against cryptography is that of national security. The export of strong cryptography to countries outside the United States has been banned because the government is afraid that the technology will be used against this country. The United States would no longer be able to decode certain information from other countries to which it currently has access. As explained by Simson L. Garfinkel, the author of the book *PGP: Pretty Good Privacy*, "The Government classifies encryption software as munitions, because foreign countries can use such programs to hide their communications during times of war" (1996:15(N) and 23(L)) The result is that only weak cryptography systems are being made by U.S. manufacturers. Although they could sell strong encryption packages to customers within the United States, it is not cost effective to manufacture two different products (Garfinkel 1996). Since software companies do not like to release two versions of their products, they offer a weaker version that is approved for export.

The second dilemma that cryptography presents to the government is one of law enforcement. Like the postal service and telephone system, there are times when illegal communication occurs and law enforcement officials feel they must have access to control it. Not only is there the potential for theft and fraud, but for child pornography, terrorism, drug deals, etc. Law enforcement officials believe that with access to messages sent via the Internet, they can gather evidence regarding many criminal acts.

The government has proposed a system called a key escrow which would allow them access to encrypted information. The system they propose would allow people and companies to purchase and use strong cryptography as long as the key was held by a third party. This key would be available if the company lost access to their key or it could be used by law enforcement individuals if they first obtained a warrant.

There seem to be two main arguments against this system. The first is the fear of the government having access to private information. The idea of Big Brother having the ability to watch every Internet transaction is frightening to many people. Phil Zimmerman, who developed the

Pretty Good Privacy (PGP) cryptography program, feels that people should have the freedom "to whisper something in someone's ear a thousand miles away" (Garfinkel 1996).

The second reason follows the first closely. It is that there is a fear that law officials could misuse the information they access. There is a feeling of general mistrust of the government. As writer Gary H. Anthes puts it, "It boils down to whom you fear more: drug dealers, pedophiles and terrorists or the U.S. government" (1995:66).

Most information recently published on this subject seems to be against government regulation of cryptography. In general, this appears to be because most people are acting under the theory of *egoism*. If cryptography is not regulated, businesses can expand and become faster and more efficient. This would mean larger profits.

In determining a solution to the government's dilemma in dealing with cryptography, one should first separate industry from the individual computer user. In the case of business and industry, the ethical theory of *utilitarianism* should be applied. The reason is that the issues here are of theft and fraud. They do not directly affect personal safety. Will cryptography eliminate misuse on the Internet, or will it enable businesses to circumvent the government? To solve this dilemma, government and business and industry must address these issues collectively. The solution lies in a system that can afford secure communications while allowing justified investigations.

Many people believe that the right to privacy is addressed in the Constitution of the United States. It is, however, more an issue of conventional morality. There are fewer laws encroaching on privacy. Think of the many states that used to have laws against certain sexual acts, even when they occurred in private between consenting adults. Though there are still some states that have these laws, they are seldom enforced. On the other hand, technology has allowed more glimpses into private lives than ever before. The ability to gain personal knowledge through the Internet must be brought into the open for discussion. Should the use of technology follow morality, or should morality be dictated by technological capabilities?

In addition, moral principle need to be applied when discussing privacy versus public safety issues. Freedom of speech does not allow for certain illegal discussion. Some examples of this would be soliciting for prostitution, threatening individuals, giving enemy nations classified information and distributing child pornography. These same laws need to be enforced even when the communication is taking place via the Internet. To allow these communications to occur because of the privacy of one individual is to violate the principles of respect for the rest.

Lastly, if the United States can educate law enforcement officials on ethical behavior, perhaps the mistrust that is now perceived toward these public officials would be alleviated. If they could be trusted to do their jobs according to *duty ethics*, the idea of a key escrow system would not be so scary.

The government regulation of cryptography is a hot subject. The decisions made about it will affect big businesses to government agencies to the personal computer user. In an age where technology is developed at such a rapid rate, time must be taken to develop ethical and moral standards that will protect the users. It is also important because in the rush to compete globally and gain larger profits, there must be respect for individuals. By applying ethical theories, government can help to insure this protection through regulation without harming the inevitable flow of information via the Internet.

III. ADVERTISING ON THE INTERNET

The Internet is rapidly becoming a marketplace where business is conducted. It provides users with advertising, a place to research products, chat rooms to discuss these products, and in many cases the consumer can even buy the product online. Though the Internet is not considered a mass medium, it will be in the near future. The number of people using it is growing at an unprecedented rate. Advertising and sales on the Internet, while providing increasing benefits to both businesses and consumers, are presenting ethical dilemmas as well. In this section, methods of advertising on the Internet will be explored as well as possible problems and issues as the technology and commercialism of the system grows.

The Internet provides a new medium for advertising products. As with television, radio, and print media, the Internet must be able to produce revenue in order to survive. Advertising has provided a method of generating revenue in other forms of mass media, so naturally companies have looked to this newest medium to advertise their products as well. There are several ways that a company may advertise on the Internet. Some of the most common forms include banners, commercial homepages, yellow pages, spamming/junk mail, push-oriented technology, and chat rooms.

Banners, like many forms of traditional advertising try to capture the customer's attention. Banners are typically found at the top of common websites. The difference between a traditional attention-grabbing advertisements and banners are that with one click, the user can gain even more information about the product if they are interested in it. Something called hypertext is used on the Internet to let the user know that they can get additional information simply by clicking on the highlighted text, usually differentiated by a different-color type. The hypertext links the user to another website which contains more information promoting the product.

Popular websites, like search engines and news magazines, sell banner space on their pages. Advertisers may buy banner space at different sites according to their audience, as well. A good example is a cruise line that buys banner space at America On Line's (AOL) Travel Reservation site. Different banners are alternated so that a user may see a different ad each time they open that particular page. Currently, this costs the advertiser 2¢ to 5¢ each time their banner is viewed (Advertising on the Internet 1998).

Another method of advertising is the *commercial homepage*. Most national companies now have a website where their products are promoted. Everything from soda companies, to stock brokers, to universities now have homepages. These are web sites that are set up to promote and provide information about different products. They are primarily set up for consumers who want information about a specific brand product or who are browsing for a particular type of product (Electronic Billboards 1998). For instance, a person who wants information about Florida International University can go straight to FIU's homepage, or a person wanting information about state universities in Florida could browse or search for "Florida state universities" and see that FIU has a homepage.

Yellow pages are now available on the Internet. These business directories can be found for specific localities or worldwide. Yellow pages are usually businesses listed by category which have links to homepages. They also may have phone numbers and addresses. Although the index may be free for businesses, yellow pages often sell banner space to make them profitable (Electronic Billboards 1998).

Like regular mail, advertisers may also send information directly to your email box. This can be done through bulk email and by "spamming." Advertisers can create or buy a list of potential customers and send promotional material straight to those Internet addresses. Spamming is a method of setting up an automatic reply so that the user receives an advertisement every time the user sends email to a specific site. This method of unsolicited promotion or junk mail is frowned upon by most Internet users, but there are no general regulations against it. Some servers prohibit its use by their customers, however (SuperNet 1998).

According to Mitch Wagner (1997a), one of the newest technologies which has advertising potential is push-oriented technology. If users want information about a product or service, they simply make a request via email and the information is automatically sent to their email address.

This allows customers to request information without having to search for it. It is also advanta-geous to the advertiser because they take a more aggressive approach to reaching consumers. Rather than waiting for a user to find and browse the commercial homepage or website, the adver-tiser takes an active role in getting the information to the user. Another advantage is that updated information can automatically be sent to the user and outdated information replaced. Currently, the system is being used mostly for software distribution and information dissemination, but the potential is there to expand the uses for any vendor on the Internet. For example, Wagner (1997b) shows how Ford Motor Company is using it to send distributors information updates to help them sell cars.

One of the most useful ways that businesses can advertise is by word of mouth. The Internet provides its own forums for sharing information between users. Products often receive endorse-ments from users or paid promoters (Electronic Billboard 1998). The users can email friends or lists of people to get the word out. They can also enter chat rooms which allow people to interact electronically via their computers. Chat rooms are very popular on the Internet. Often they are set up by category or interest groups. A person wishing to buy a car, for instance, might enter a chat room on automobiles. More specifically, she/he could enter a room on a make, model, or style of car. They might find others who either have or are considering buying the same car. This allows people to compare notes and receive information from other consumers who are perfect strangers but have similar interests or areas of expertise.

Services like Compunet Services Inc. are available to help advertisers maximize the use of all of the forms of promotion on the Internet. They assert that online advertising "is very cost effective, it offers exposure on a global scale, it is available 24 hours a day and has millions of users." Many such companies currently exist and the market for advertising sales is rapidly increasing (SuperNet 1998).

Another of the advantages of advertising on the Internet is the ability to sell the product online. Companies can advertise their products to users, provide in depth and relevant information about the product, and actually close the sale on the computer. Many industries are adding online sales to their current means of making their products accessible to consumers. A user can buy items such as airline tickets, groceries, and even cars online. And although some industries feel as though they cannot replace their human sales staff with a computer, there is definitely potential for this to occur in the not so distant future.

Most industries use credit cards for money transactions. In the future, however, there may be other methods of electronic commerce. Although this chapter will not go into depth about this topic, it is important to know that new technologies are being developed to make commerce on the Internet easier and more secure (Advertising on the Internet 1998).

One U.S. government estimate predicts that e-commerce will grow into the trillions of dol-lars annually by 2008. A good example of ecommerce performance is Intel Corporation, which sells computer chips through a website. Intel is aiming for more than $1 billion in Internet sales in 1998. That comes after the company after the company discovered that an online effort to support large, existing accounts created an efficient new way to sell to thousands of customers who previ-ously were too small to command the attention of a human salesperson. Over the Web, Intel is interacting with small players and conducting tiny transactions with sufficient customer support at a cost low enough to sustain a new, profitable market. Ecommerce can also have shockingly low overhead costs. Dell Computers reports that in every sale that the company makes over the Web, no employee is involved until an electronic order arrives at the factory, where a custom personal computer is assembled and shipped in a matter of hours (Sagan 1998:46).

Another good example of what is being sold on the Internet is airline tickets. There are sev-eral airline reservation services offered through different servers on the World Wide Web. Ameri-ca On Line's service, for example, allows a user to type in their personal profile, including dates of travel and preferred airlines, and then lists available flights and costs. The user may buy the ticket by giving his or her credit card information.

Although many customers are already using on-line reservation services rather than travel agents, there are concerns about what can and cannot currently be offered on-line. According to Wagner (1997c), some airline deals are not available to users on the Internet. As the demand grows, and more customers use their computers to book their flights, the airlines will save money by advertising online and more deals will become available. Many customers are already using online reservation services rather than travel agents.

A good example of an industry that is struggling with what services to provide on the Internet is life insurance. According to a survey by Computer Sciences Corp (CSC) consumers prefer not to buy insurance on the Internet. Insurance relies on salespeople to get the customer to think about buying the product. Few people actually seek out information on life insurance. According to Hoffman (1997), other arguments against online sales include that the information is too complex and that underwriters require medical information. Although these concerns may be valid today, in the future consumers can anticipate solutions which will make this type of interaction possible. Imagine advertising more like television, user-friendly information to explain the complexities, and the ability of the user to access verified medical records from a physician at the click of a button.

Another reason that many businesses are still wary of advertising on the Web is that they question whether they can reach enough people through the Internet to make a profit. Although the advertising may be inexpensive, building the information data bases, security, and increasing the general infrastructure of their system can become quite costly. According to Kathleen Gow (1997), there are other concerns such as legal questions, limited development tools, taxes, and audit trails.

Also, the Internet is not yet considered a mass medium. McGrath (1997) reports that "more than 15 million North American households had some form of on-line access. In the year 2000, the projection is that North America will have 38 million on-line households." McGrath further reports that "analysts believe the critical mass to be about 30 million households, which suggests that the Web will become a true mass medium about the year 2000." Even if these figures are off, it is safe to assume that the Internet will, in the near future, be a major source for reaching substantial volumes of people.

IV. ETHICAL ISSUES AND DIFFICULTIES REGULATING THE INTERNET

With the incredible rate of increase in the use of the Internet come several ethical dilemmas. As with any new technology, it is hard to predict all of the ramifications and issues that may arise. There are some that are already evident and need to be addressed, however. These ethical issues include freedom of speech, regulating advertising and sales, access, and the human element.

Although many Internet users want quick and easy access to information about products and services, they do not necessarily like the idea of online advertising. There is a general sentiment against regulations on the Internet, however, which means that they do not necessarily agree with banning businesses from advertising. This attitude is based upon the right to free speech which has been championed by computer users since the Internet was first used (Electronic Billboards 1998). Currently, there are plenty of guidelines available for advertisers, but as of yet, few requirements. Part of the reason that this works so well is that unlike other media, the Internet is interactive. If users are unhappy with a product, service, or company, they have the potential to reach out to other customers worldwide and share their experience. It would not be worth it for a company to risk censure by a disgruntled customer who could potentially "talk" to thousands of other users (Electronic Billboards 1998).

The American Marketing Association has a code of ethics for marketing on the Internet which addresses some of these issues. Their proscribed guidelines are as follows:

1. Support of professional ethics to avoid harm by protecting the rights of privacy, ownership, and access.
2. Adherence to all applicable laws and regulations with no use of Internet marketing that would be illegal if conducted by mail, telephone, fax, or other media.
3. Awareness of changes in regulations related to Internet marketing.
4. Effective communication to organizational members on risks and policies related to Internet marketing, when appropriate.
5. Organizational commitment to ethical Internet practices communicated to employees, customers, and relevant stakeholders.

They further assert that "Internet marketers must assess the risks and take responsibility for the consequences of their activities" (Houghton Mifflin Interactive 1998). They are warning advertisers to keep high ethical standards or risk very public criticism.

Many industries are taking these guidelines a step further and are trying to clarify the current laws and regulations in regard to the Internet. A good example of this is the law profession. As Professors Catherine Lanctot and James Maule at Villanova University Law School report, "The state of the law . . . remains unsettled, and, as noted, the United States Supreme Court has recently signaled a willingness to permit greater state regulation of lawyer advertising . . . therefore, lawyers should assume that the advertising rules apply to any communications made on the Internet for the purpose of obtaining clients" (1998). They go on to suggest that solicitation regulations apply to a lawyer's homepage, direct email, discussions that take place on-line, bulletin boards, Internet newsgroups, etc. (1998).

The interests of privacy and growth of a new digital economy can be reconciled. Existing technology could allow customers to make electronic purchases while controlling the release of information about what they are saying. Although in the United States a law proposed by the FBI would mandate an electronic peephole in all encryption programs so that government agents can read all files in some other countries, people are experimenting with solutions to some of these consumer concerns. In Sweden, for example, where 40% of the population has Internet access, the following three issues have been tied to expanding ecommerce:

1. Consumers must be able to make secure payments, meaning that their funds cannot be stolen.
2. They must be able to send secure messages, meaning that their orders and preferences are not shared with others without their approval.
3. Secure logistics must be able to reliably deliver goods and services ordered on line (Sagan 1998:47).

It is clear that at some point, government will ultimately need to address these issues on a broader basis. One of the questions this raises is, "Which government?" It goes beyond state versus federal regulation. The Internet is a worldwide medium. Eventually there will have to be a global regulating body to address ethical issues such as these.

Another concern is that of access. One of the benefits to advertisers is that the majority of Internet users are affluent. According to a survey conducted by Neilsen Research and CommerceNet in 1995, "On average, WWW users are upscale (25 percent have income over $80K), professional (50 percent are managerial or professional) and educated (64 percent have at least college degrees)" (Elbel 1998). As Karen Coyle stated in her seminar on the Ethics of the Internet,

"There is very little commercial incentive to provide information to low income or minority segments of our society—the profit margin is just too low. So we are more likely to have information that benefits car owners than public transit users" (Advertising on the Internet 1998). If the Internet is to become an economic and commercial force, there must be access for all segments of society. In the future, perhaps computers will be as common as televisions in every home, but affordability should be more of a concern as technological advances continue to speed through our society.

The last ethical issue to be addressed in this chapter is that of the human element. Since the first computers were introduced, there has been a fear that they would one day be able to think for themselves and eventually replace the more fragile human being. Computers have come a long way toward that, but are still nowhere near taking over, yet. They are, however, replacing the jobs of many humans. From travel agents, to car salespeople, to cashiers, the trend toward electronic interactive advertising is eliminating the need for human interaction. Even the advent of expert systems is eliminating the need for human experts. Computers are being programmed with the beliefs and perceptions of experts so that the machines may then emulate their decision-making process to determine the most profitable course of action. Once the computer is fed the knowledge, it eliminates the need for the person.

The main predicament that these ethical issues indicate is that the Internet is so new, and so rapidly growing and changing, that society has not kept abreast of these questions. For public administrators to lead the people into the future, they must be aware of these issues. They must be able to address the needs and concerns of the people using these systems. They must also be ready to make difficult decisions regarding a future where physical boundaries become meaningless and the dissemination of information and communication become even more free than they are in the United States today. The Internet as a market place has incredible potential if we can make sure it is used properly by all.

INTERNET SOURCES

http://condor.depaul.edu/ethics/belohlav.html
http://id-ad.com/www/stats.html
http://www.ca-probate.com/comm_net.htm
http://www.cni.org/projects/advertising/www/adpaper.html
http://www.csn.net/~felbel/jmemail.html
http://www.csnet.com/whatinet.htm
http://www.dla.vcop.edu/~kec/ethics.html
http://www.duke.edu/~lrnble/rel185/
http://www.duke.edu/~nmk/project.html
http://www.hminet.com/hmco/college/PridFerr/ethics.html
http://www.jup.com/tracks/advertising
http://www.law.vill.edu/vcilp/MacCrate/mcle/lanctot.htm
http://www.webcom.com/~lewrose/home.html

REFERENCES

Gow, K. (1997). Risk vs. opportunity. *Computerworld Premier 100*, 14–20.
Hoffman, T. (1997). Net not ideal for selling insurance, survey finds. *Computerworld* Feb. 17, 59–61.
McGrath, P. (1997). The Web: infotopia or marketplace? *Newsweek* Jan. 27, 82–84.

Sagan, P. (1998). The new buzz in IT. On-line commerce takes business by storm. *Report on the 1998 Annual Meeting of the World Economic Forum. The View from Davos.* Geneva, Switzerland.

Stone, B. (1997). HAL et al.: how smart is artificial intelligence? *Newsweek* March 3, 10.

Time. (1998). Feb. 9, 20.

Wagner, M. (1997a). Ford pushes net data. *Computerworld* Feb. 24, 71–73.

Wagner, M. (1997b). Net isn't always the ticket. *Computerworld* Feb. 3, 57–58.

Wagner, M. (1997c). Technology lets Web sites get "pushy." *Computerworld* Jan. 6, 55–57.

56

Emerging Challenges in Healthcare Administrative Ethics

A Global Perspective

Carole L. Jurkiewicz   *Public Administration Institute, Louisiana State University, Baton Rouge, Louisiana*

I. INTRODUCTION

There is arguably no other industry that so intimately touches every aspect of our lives as does the delivery of health care. From the broadest dimensions of quality standards, marketing strategy, regulatory control, and fiscal decision making to a particular instance of patient-provider contact, ethical considerations are inextricably bound to every aspect of health care. Given the intimate nature of the services provided, the ethical implications of health care administration naturally encompass both those receiving the services and those providing them.

While previous studies have identified strong individual standards of ethical performance among healthcare executives (Jurkiewicz and Thompson 1999a), the demands of organizational and career success frequently require healthcare executives to compromise these standards (Jurkiewicz and Thompson 1999b). Evidence of this appalling circumstance can be found in the vastly increasing numbers of healthcare fraud investigations and the perception that practices such as falsifying records, kickbacks, and misleading advertising have become commonplace (Strongin 1997). Testimony during the 1997 U.S. federal investigation of Columbia/HCA detailed specific examples of the intense pressure executives regularly face to maximize profits and compromise personal standards (Vladeck 1998).

This chapter offers a global perspective on the ethical challenges faced by health care administrators. It presents findings from a survey of health care executives in the United States and their counterparts in five other modernized countries. The patterns of contrast and comparison that emerge offer a perspective of health care management ethics within a cultural context. Unethical behavior appears to be no less pervasive outside the U.S. system, though it does take different forms. The first section outlines the ethical dimensions of health care administration in the United States. The second compares the challenges faced by healthcare executives in and outside the United States. The chapter concludes with a discussion of these findings, and the basis for action they suggest in enhancing the ethicality of health care administration globally.

II.   FROM REVERENCE TO REPROBATE

Health care executives and the system they represent have historically stood as the embodiment of strong social values. They, along with the direct care givers, epitomized the values of altruism, allegiance, and valor. It was a profession generally viewed as a calling rather than a job, not unlike those individuals drawn to religious service. With the introduction of managed care and a definition of success based as least as much on efficiency and financial stability as on patient satisfaction, the revered position of health care executive has turned into something quite the contrary. In fact, the description of a health care executive has itself shifted, from one qualified solely by his or her medical expertise to one sought after for their business acumen as well. The respect afforded them as representatives of a morally elite corps has been weakened by the widespread recognition that the business of health care is, from a strictly financial standpoint, indistinguishable from all others.

The drive to increase revenues translates into competition for patients, which in turn has contributed to a culture of competition. This competitive stance has prompted action by regulatory agencies and empowered the public to question the motivation behind a variety of health care initiatives. The patient/managed care relationship is increasingly being viewed as a customer/merchandiser exchange (Reinhardt 1998). Knowing the viability of health care institutions depends upon a stream of clients, the public has become increasingly demanding and less easily satisfied (Neumann 1997). Providers have responded by trying to attract patients by meeting public demands for enhanced access, streamlined reimbursement processes, and coverage for preventive care. Whereas the nature of service delivery had heretofore been dictated by the provider, the public now holds considerable sway over determinations of service and schedule offerings. An artifact of this altered health care environment has been the increasing sophistication of its consumers; the public in general is now much more self-directed in comparing and evaluating the quality of care. In addition to becoming more savvy and better educated, the public is also less trusting of the health care system in general. This cycle of lessening trust has fueled growing regulations along with a momentous shift in judicial law that expands the opportunities for individuals to directly sue managed care organizations. As this spiral continues to unfurl one can predict a successive erosion in the esteem with which the profession has traditionally been held.

Amidst this evolving view of health care stripped of its heroic ideal, the health care executive stands at the bow. Competitive pressures, negotiated contracts, capitation, funding constraints, discounted fees, and increased regulatory oversight are pushing from one side, while on the other boards of directors and key executives demand ever higher levels of profitability (Mowll 1998). The health care executive is expected not only to do more with less, but to do it better than before. Profits, competitive strategy, and market dominance are all competing with patient care as end goals for the institution (Levit 1996).

To many administrators such dilemmas are defined more as practical problems than ethical ones. There is a belief that training in strategic management, goal setting, and financial accounting should be preparation enough to resolve these conflicting demands. Yet, at its core, the resolution is rooted in, and advances, a systems of values and principles. How these dilemmas are resolved communicates more forcefully than mission statements the true nature of the institution. To prospective clients, employees, and the public in general, the values demonstrated through executive decision-making position the organization along a continuum of integrity. Beyond the institution itself, the values implicit in these decisions contribute to an increase or decrease in the public's perception of trustworthiness in the industry as a whole. Thus, inextricably bound to issues of fiscal stability, shifting client demand, quality control, political strategy, and regulatory and environmental responsibility, are executive ethics (Ehlen and Sprenger 1998).

III. THE ETHICAL CHALLENGE

Given the central role they play in directing the nature and quality of our health care experience, as well as our trust in the industry in general, the ethical standards of health care executives directly and indirectly affect everyone. In addition to the unobservable effects of this type of service, individuals are affected in very tangible ways: over one-seventh of all the money spent each year in the United States is spent on health care (Jacobs 1995). Ethics permeates the day-to-day and critical aspects of health care administration (Ehlen and Sprenger 1998) both in and outside the United States. Immanent to the nature of the services provided, even the most unambiguous and rote decisions have ethical implications for those receiving as well as those providing the services, implications which extend to the broader industry and society as a whole (Darr 1995; Balda 1994). Biological and technological advances, regulatory pressures, fiscal constraints, advocate demands, and concentrated decision-making authority elevate the ethical issues inherent in healthcare administration to a level of criticality unparalleled outside the industry.

That executives hold the greatest influence over the ethical conduct of the organization and those employed there has been firmly established (e.g., Jurkiewicz and Massey 1998). They are generally attributed with setting the moral tone, and are seen as personally responsible for the set of ethics or norms that govern behavior. While they do not directly monopolize the creation of an organizational culture, the fact that they have the power to punish or reward certain behaviors affords them a clear advantage in developing value systems and codes of behavior (Morgan 1986). Even if an executive's official position is one of organizational amorality, their behavior nonetheless defines and influences their organization's ethical framework. While the structure of organizations allows for a diverse range of evaluative rules and standards among the people employed there, success within the organization is defined by adherence to its overriding ethic. The ability to establish these ethical parameters and reward those who follow in formation is the exclusive purview of the executive. Organizational strategy, thus, reflects the personal values and ethical aspirations of its executives, and in so doing defines the milieu in which the actions of health care executives are inseparable from ethical considerations.

From a broad perspective, the ethical dimensions of healthcare administration encompass fiduciary duties, conflicts of interest, code enforcement, confidentiality, consent, public reporting, resource allocation, accreditation, risk assessment, human resource management, legal and biomedical issues, experimental procedures, marketing, death, dying, and beyond—to the business of organ donation. The ethical challenges facing the U.S. health care industry and the health care executives that direct them have been enumerated elsewhere (Jurkiewicz and Thompson 1999a, b). To what extent do the ethical challenges faced in the U.S. system differ from those in other industrialized countries? The findings from a recent survey are intriguing indeed, and suggest both cultural differences in perception, and global similarities in practice.

IV. VIEWS FROM THE EXECUTIVE SUITE

Senior and midlevel health care executives were surveyed for their perspective on ethical challenges in the workplace. Two hundred seven U.S. executives responded, as did 153 from Australia, Bahamas, England, Mexico, and Taiwan. Male and female respondents comprised a variety of age and ethnic groups. While the U.S. and non-U.S. responses were distinguishable from one another due to the distinct time periods in which the surveys were distributed, the non-U.S. responses were not traced to specific countries. Promises of anonymity and confidentiality took precedence to assure honest answers. Thus, non-U.S. responses were received and analyzed as a collective group. The five tables report key findings from this anonymous survey. Tables 1 and 4 required yes

Table 1 Have You Ever Experienced a Conflict Between What Was Expected of You as an Efficient, Effective Employee and What Was Expected of You as an Ethical Person

	U.S. (N = 166)	Non-U.S. (N = 13)
Yes	62%	16%
No	38%	84%

or no responses; all others were open-ended questions. Not all respondents answered every question, and many open-ended questions elicited more than one discrete item per respondent. Thus, the percentages on open-ended questions are not expected to total 100. The number of responses per question are included.

Table 1 details a substantial difference of perspective between the U.S. and non-U.S. health care executives. When asked whether they had ever experienced a conflict between what was expected of them as an efficient and effective employee and what was expected of them as an ethical person, the U.S. respondents said yes nearly four times as often as did the non-U.S. group. U.S. executives seem to perceive a much greater conflict in this regard. Whether too much or too little is expected of them in terms of ethical standards is not evident. The disparity stands in contrast to non-U.S. respondents who, it may be extrapolated, operate under a more synchronized set of expectations. Be they uniformly low, high, or moderate, dissonance exists at a much lower level for this group compared to U.S. executives. This level of integration may likely stem from a more homogeneous set of values dominant both within and outside the organization. Previous research would suggest that this balance results in much less stress for health care executives outside the United States and, further, likely higher ratings of job satisfaction (Jurkiewicz, et al. 1998).

Against an arbitrary standard of ethical behavior, it is not possible to say whether the U.S. or non-U.S. executives would rank higher. Such a qualitative argument cannot be developed based upon the present data. Yet when placed within the context of previously reported data (Jurkiewicz and Thompson 1999a), suppositions may be made. In that study, health care executives in the United States frequently reported they were forced to lower their personal ethical standards in order to achieve organizational and/or career success. Non-U.S. executives, overall, do not appear to experience this type of conflict. Do the personal standards of non-U.S. and U.S. health care executives differ from one another, or does the disparity exist between organizational standards? This is an intriguing question and the answer could hold significant promise in advancing ethical decision making in health care administration globally.

The results reported in Table 2 indicate a dramatic difference between the rank of individuals with whom U.S. and non-U.S. executives have personal conflict. Nearly 100% of non-U.S. respondents acknowledge conflicts between themselves and others above them in the organizational hierarchy, compared with less than half of the U.S. respondents. Since respondents were senior and midlevel executives, conflicts with those of higher rank would be fewer in number by virtue of the smaller number of individuals holding those positions. U.S. executives, on the other hand, are much more likely to have conflict with those ranked lower than themselves. This would potentially constitute a much larger volume of conflict. Further explicative of this difference is the relative degree of conflict generated by externally imposed constraints—laws, governmental regulations, and societal mores. Non-U.S. executives in the sample were about five times more likely to report ethical conflict in this area than were their U.S. counterparts.

Table 2 Conflicts Between Your Organization's Interests and Your Personal Ethics Occur Most Often When Dealing With Whom

	U.S. (N = 207)	Non-U.S. (N = 153)
Executive management	47%	92%
Supervisors	70%	45%
Peers	38%	45%
Staff	35%	12%
Partnering organizations/competitors	39%	25%
Law/government/society	13%	64%
Suppliers/vendors	51%	58%
Volunteers	32%	4%
Boards of directors	65%	0%

V. AREAS OF ETHICAL CONFLICT

As Table 3 illustrates, the areas in which conflict between personal and organizational ethics arises also differs between the two groups. Conflicts of interest for non-U.S. executives appear to revolve around issues of honesty. Honesty in communication, contracts, and agreements was cited by nearly 100% of these respondents as being areas in which conflict is likely to arise. While honesty is demonstrably important to U.S. executives as well, law breaking and personnel issues appear to command their attention. In conjunction with Table 2, it is apparent that non-U.S. executives experience their superiors as less honest, and U.S. executives experience their subordinates as less fair or just, than either group desires. Even though the respondents held key management roles in their organizations, it appears they lack a cogent strategy to effect change in this regard. Resolving these ethical conflicts, it is thus suggested, requires a systemic initiative encompassing both policy and performance.

Regarding hierarchical sources of conflict, differences between the two groups are both illuminating and puzzling. The results suggest that role expectations or responsibilities are sources of conflict that supersede individual differences. It is possible that these expectations are rooted in cultural norms regarding acquiescence to authority. Whether it is expected or an anomaly to question the decisions made by those with higher organizational authority, norms such as these are

Table 3 In What Areas Do These Conflicts of Interest Between Your Organization's Interests and Your Personal Ethics Arise?

	U.S. (N = 206)	Non-U.S. (N = 152)
Honesty in communication	78%	93%
Giving gifts and bonuses	14%	7%
Fairness and discrimination	83%	62%
Miscellaneous law breaking	100%	48%
Honest in contracts and agreements	91%	98%
Firings and layoffs	84%	27%
Pricing practices	13%	8%

important corollaries in predicting the effect of organizational structure and processes on ethical behavior. While more stringent authoritative controls within organizations are perceived to exist outside as opposed to inside the United States, employees of most industrialized nations participate in an evolving global culture that embraces flattened hierarchies and maintains that trust is earned rather than decreed. If this is accurate, a desire for greater honesty and openness, particularly by those ranked higher within the organization, would be expected. At the same time, data from U.S. executives suggest they expect those below them in the rankings to balance this desire for empowerment with a sense of individual responsibility.

The 2:1 ratio of U.S. to non-U.S. executives who report conflicts related to gifts and bonuses is also worthy of note. Many of the early case studies developed in the United States to aid discussions of organizational ethics revolved around the experiences of U.S. companies in offering or not offering "gifts" to secure international business. Such gifts in the U.S. culture are perceived as bribes and, as such, as unethical and unfair inducements to gain economic advantage. The recent scandal regarding gifts to members of the International Olympic Committee to influence site selection on behalf of Salt Lake City, Utah, led to a widespread cultural conflict of the ethics of gift giving in such circumstances. The findings in this survey demonstrate the continued importance of the issue for U.S. executives. The differences could reflect cultural perceptions or the effect of sensitization to the issue through education and media exposure. If the latter is true, it points to the importance of these avenues of influence in shifting ethical beliefs.

U.S. executives appear divided between those who view some general business practices in their organizations to be unethical, and those who do not. In contrast, nearly three-fourths of the non-U.S. executives see nothing unethical in the general business practices of their institutions. The findings reported in Table 4 are consistent with those reported earlier in evidencing a lack of dissonance between non-U.S. executives' personal and organizational ethics. Caution is necessary when interpreting these findings to avoid concluding that non-U.S. executives work in a more ethical environment. Such a supposition is not supported here. It could be that the ethical standards under which they work are higher, on a particular scale, than are those under which U.S. executives work. Or, it could be that non-U.S. standards on this scale are lower than in the United States, and that non-U.S. executives see no problem in abiding by these directives. While either of this scenarios are possible, when viewed in conjunction with the findings reported in Table 5, another explanation presents itself.

About the same number of non-U.S. health care executives who stated they did not perceive any general business practices to be unethical, cited certain unethical practices they would eliminate if they could. U.S. executives, on the other hand, demonstrated greater consistency in this regard. The same proportion as those responding in the affirmative in Table 4 cited lack of informed consent by patients, undermining coworkers, and budget improprieties for political ends as important concerns. Executives outside the United States listed overcharging those best able to pay, falsifying forms, and political favouritism as their least desirable business practices. Given that a majority of non-U.S. executives cited unethical practices they would like to change, though only a minority said such practices existed, either the question was unclear or there was reluctance

Table 4 Business Practices in Which Your Organization Engages That You Think Are Unethical

	U.S. (N = 207)	Non-U.S. (N = 153)
No	59%	73%
Yes	41%	27%

Table 5   Unethical Practices Within Your Organization That You Would Eliminate if You Could

	U.S. (N = 123)	Non-U.S. (N = 101)
Falsifying forms for financial reasons	56%	68%
Lack of informed consent between org. and patient	16%	44%
Privacy/confidentiality violations	29%	0%
Gratuities accepted that influence decisions	5%	0%
Lying to clients	29%	17%
Hiring and personnel matters	41%	4%
Overcharging those able to pay more	65%	88%
Covertly undermining coworkers	6%	35%
Budget improprieties for political reasons	36%	54%
Political favoritism	7%	67%
Preferential treatment w/o medical reason	44%	53%
Rivalry between professionals at patients' expense	10%	12%
Unnecessary procedures done to make money	50%	50%
Discrimination	26%	2%

to identify behavior as a widespread business practice. U.S. respondents did not indicate there was a difference between the two. This information may serve to guide future researchers in designing surveys for both groups. The types of unethical issues identified here are in accord with the earlier findings of cultural differences. Again, non-U.S. executives demonstrate honesty is a key issue, particularly regarding those above them in the hierarchy. Responses from U.S. executives also support other findings reported here regarding ethical conflict with those below them on the organizational hierarchy.

The legal and personnel-related ethical conflicts of U.S. executives connote a problem of ambiguity. Given that external constraints per se offer relatively little cause for conflict within this group, the finding that firings and layoffs, fairness and discrimination, and miscellaneous law breaking by those generally ranked lower on the hierarchy, indicates something further. Perhaps the practice of interpreting tort law and applying it broadly to employer/employee relationships offers the potential for conflict. The increasingly relaxed labor laws in the United States that endow employees greater freedoms in seeking redress for perceived inequities may also be a profound source of stress. The increase in quantity and size of monetary settlements for this type of litigation in the United States is believed to stem from the ambiguity of the many new personnel laws that have yet to be thoroughly tested in court. That the size of monetary judgments in such cases are large would understandably lead to greater stress on the part of executives in dealing with these types of issues.

The pattern of unethical activity evident in this set of responses is that they are all acts of commission, as opposed to omission. This is a widely documented phenomenon wherein instances of ethical infractions committed through intent are seen as more wrong, while those infractions that result from lack of action are generally excused. Thus, ignoring problems, overlooking certain policies and behaviors, and not voicing objections to known wrongs are generally considered ethical because the negative consequences that result were not intended. In such situations, not doing something is viewed as more ethical than doing something, even though the lack of action may result in greater harm. Reframing ethical issues in terms of their consequences rather than their deliberativeness may serve to emphasize that equally egregious harms can result from inaction as well as action. This is an important and revealing point about all executives in this study.

Collectively, the responses show a significant degree of ethical conflict experienced or perceived by health care executives in the day-to-day administration of their responsibilities. Sources of conflict appear to occur across international boundaries. Given the remarkably high response rate (40% for U.S. and 47% for non-U.S. health care executives) to this survey, the intimate nature of the information provided by respondents, and their reported desire to change specific policies and practices in their organizations that they regard as unethical, a discussion of ethics in the administration of health care seems urgently needed. Broadening the discussion to include global experiences can provide an objective look at the influence of organizational structure and process on executive behavior not possible with a more parochial approach.

VI. WHERE TO GO FROM HERE

This perspective provides a timely and disconcerting picture of ethics in the field of health care administration. The developing scenario includes ongoing violations of personal ethical standards, as well as community expectations and legal precepts in the United States, and calls for increased honesty and fairness, and less politicization in countries around the globe. The question of whether ethical behavior can be equated with economic rationality (Maitland 1997) introduces some interesting paradoxes here. If executives are compromising their personal ethical standards for the sake of economic advantage, and if elevating their ethical behavior to match their personal codes of conduct is believed to be detrimental to financial success, the market discipline hypothesis is hardly confirmed. While compelling, the argument for ethical and economic rationality presumes individuals can choose from a variety of different service providers. This is not the case as mergers and consolidations result in fewer and larger health care providers. Maitland (1997) implicitly presupposes that ethically antithetical behavior produces economic disadvantages. Yet the ethical norm includes behavior which would appear unethical if compared against a equivocal standard, but would not appear abnormal if such behavior were widespread (Jurkiewicz and Thompson 1999a). Essentially, as the contructivist argument would suggest, the method by which we observe predetermines the nature of the conclusions that will be drawn. This is an especially important point as we look for ways to objectively measure, and influence, ethical behavior in health care administration.

A caution in extrapolating these findings may be that those responding to this survey were spurred to do so by the intensity of ethical conflict experienced at their jobs, and that those who didn't respond did not experience the same level of intensity, the effect being that the respondents are atypical of the rest of the population. In the event this is the case, the 40% and 47% response rates would suggest, in and of themselves, that this type of behavior exists at alarming levels.

VII. DESIRE TO IMPROVE

As strong as some of the differences may be, health care executives in this study are uniform in one respect: the desire for conditions to improve in their organizations. Both suggest a surprisingly widespread convention of operation along with a moral judgment of its wrongfulness. That such behavior continues to occur in the face of such strong opposition to it, suggests the source is beyond the executives' span of control. It appears that however strong the individual drive is to do something "right," the need to maintain one's source of income as well as one's position in the organization overrides that desire and leads to wrongdoing. If that is the case, ethics training or intervention focused on the individual is likely misplaced. They already appear to have a sense of what's right, and only require an environment that doesn't demand less.

The ethical dilemmas facing health care executives are arguably more complex than those in any other enterprise as they are simultaneously enmeshed in several different accountability relationships. Viewing their accountability as a pendulum, one sees the swing in one direction toward boards of directors and top executives and in the opposite direction toward the patient. It is an either/or choice that cannot, as the structure is currently configured, blend the two stakeholders. The conflictual pulls can be acute, particularly if the executive entered the field of health care with an ethic of service. Health care executives must reconcile responsiveness, merit, diversity, rights, fiscal responsibility, and efficiency—expectations that are multiple, diverse, conflicting, and themselves changing. Health care executives are called upon to accommodate expectations from several different legitimate sources and be answerable for their actions under whichever accountability relationships are relevant. They must also be able to shift their accountability standards as needed, obey directives, comply with external mandates, exercise discretion responsibly, and be responsive to external stakeholders. As a matter of course they operate under hierarchical, legal, professional, and ethical domains of accountability. Infractions industrywide have historically been reacted to by adding another level of accountability as a safeguard measure, rather than by reassessing the web of existing accountability relationships. Perhaps that is what's needed now: an objective evaluation of the system in which health care executives operate, and how the system itself may be unwittingly eliciting and rewarding behaviors it does not ethically want.

One of the key elements revealed from this study revolves around the apparent incongruence between individual and organizational expectations. It is a conflict of interest wherein duty to oneself and duty to the organization are contraindicative. Characteristic of conflicts of influence is the ease with which the individual incrementally shifts toward excusing ethical infractions that, taken out of context, would stand as monumental lapses in judgment. Financial and competitive pressures entice health care executives to redefine ethical dilemmas as procedural problems. The fast pace of mergers, consolidations, and restructuring accelerates the diffusion of responsibility and information. Lack of a clear system of accountability is a common feature of organizations whose administrators seem divorced from ethical considerations (Jurkiewicz 1999). It is thus imperative that equal or greater effort be exerted in balancing the drive to enhance financial viability with a preeminent concern for the patient in making administrative decisions.

The conflict in administrative ethics is at the same stage biomedical ethics was 20 years ago. From the occasional news story or journal articles will evolve conferences, forums, research centers, and journals. Just as the maturation of biomedical ethics moved from posing questions to seeking solutions, so too is the movement in administrative ethics. The approach adopted in that domain will serve the administrative realm as well: provide a protected forum in which these issues can be discussed openly, the resulting dialogue establishing a consensus of best ethical practices along with methods to enforce them. Toward this end, the effects of sector-specific constraints, competition, governing bodies, fiscal concerns, and client expectations on ethical standards and performance need to be measured. The important step now is to build a body of literature upon which effective interventions can reveal themselves. The unrelenting pace of change demands we move from asking the questions to attempting the answers.

REFERENCES

Balda, J.B. (1994). The liability of nonprofits to donors. *Nonprofit Management and Leadership*, 5, 67–83.

Darr, K. (1995). *Ethics in Health Service Management.* Baltimore: Health Professions Press.

Ehlen, J., and Sprenger, G. (1998). Ethics and decision making in health care. *Journal of Health Care Management, 43*(3), 219–221.

Jacobs, L.R. (1995). America's supply state: health reform and technology. *Health Affairs, 14*(2), 143–157.

Jurkiewicz, C.L. (1999). The phantom code of ethics and public sector reform. (Under review).

Jurkiewicz, C.L., and Massey, T.K. Jr. (1998). The influence of ethical reasoning on leader effectiveness: an empirical study of nonprofit executives. *Nonprofit Management and Leadership, 9*(2).

Jurkiewicz, C.L., Massey, T.K. Jr., and Brown, R.G. (1998). Motivation in public and private organizations: a comparative study. *Public Productivity and Management Review, 21*(3).

Jurkiewicz, C.L., and Thompson, C.R. (1999a). An empirical inquiry into the ethical standards of health care administrators. *Public Integrity, 1*(1), 41–53.

Jurkiewicz, C.L., and Thompson, C.R. (1999b). Conflicts of interest: organizational vs. individual ethics in health care administration. *Journal of Health and Human Services Administration* (forthcoming).

Levit, K. (1996). Health care spending in 1994: slowest in decades. *Health Affairs, 15*(3), 130–144.

Maitland, I. (1997). Virtuous markets: the market as school of the virtues. *Business Ethics Quarterly, 7*(1), 17–31.

Mowll, C.A. (1998). Assessing the effects of increased managed care on hospitals. *Journal of Health Care Management, 43*(1), 68–78.

Neumann, P.J. (1997). Should health insurance cover IVF? Issues and options. *Journal of Health Policy, Politics, and Law, 22*(5), 1215–1239.

Strongin, R. (1997). *Health Care Fraud and Restoring Trust.* Washington: National Health Policy Forum.

Weiss, H.M. (1977). Subordinate imitation of supervisory behavior: the role of modeling in organizational socialization. *Organizational Behavior and Human Performance, 19*, 89–105.

57

Bureaucratic Links Between Administration and Politics

Fred W. Riggs *Department of Political Science, University of Hawaii at Mano, Honolulu, Hawaii*

I. INTRODUCTION

Comparative public administration can scarcely be studied in a meaningful way without taking politics into account. Similarly, of course, comparative politics requires attention to administrative aspects. The myth of a dichotomy between politics and administration has hampered the study of both aspects of governance as a coherent and unified process. The purpose of this essay is to suggest a framework for comparative analysis in which the links between administration and politics can be better understood.

Such framework requires a focus on bureaucracy. No doubt originally rulers created bureaucracies to serve them as instruments of administration, to implement their policies. However, as soon as anyone received an appointment to serve as a public official, that person discovered that the position conveyed power and created political interests. It is not an exaggeration to think of bureaucracy as a class, and as a class that has both pronounced interests and the power to protect them. However, by definition, bureaucracy is only part of a larger system of governance. We can only understand how bureaucrats behave (politically and administratively) when we take that larger system into account.

The history of the word *bureaucracy* reflects the changing role of public officials in different systems of government. It was coined in the eighteenth century to refer to a state dominated by appointed officials (Albrow 1970; Riggs 1979). I shall use *bureaucratic polity* for this concept, which is an essential one in this essay. In popular usage, *bureaucrat* became a term of derision. Needless to say, that sense of the word is ruled out of the present discourse. However, in technical usage the word soon came to mean a ruling class composed of public officials—a similar evolution changed the meaning of "aristocracy" from a type of polity to the name of a class. Then the meaning of "bureaucracy" evolved further until it came to mean the class of appointed officials, or the positions they occupy, whether or not they exercise power. Those who think of bureaucrats as politically "neutral" administrators have carried the idea another step, conceiving of public officials as a kind of powerless apparatus, devoid of self-interest or power.

The myth of a dichotomy between administration and politics rests, in general, on this construction of the word: it postulates a politically neutral "state apparatus," that is, the bureaucracy, which merely implements the policies adopted by a ruling group, whether it consists of a "class," in the Marxist view, or of constitutionally prescribed "political" institutions.

In the American context the dichotomy led to another twist: only careerists—those with long-term tenure—were seen as politically "neutral" and hence as "bureaucrats," whereas transients—holding public office for a limited period of time—were redefined as "political" appointees, and hence not bureaucrats. This peculiar usage could be sustained only by a perverse semantic twist in which "political" was assigned a narrow meaning, referring just to partisan orientations: an action was termed "political" only when it had implications for a political party. Clearly, however, most political action is nonpartisan, involving efforts by a wide variety of individuals and groups to influence the allocation of resources—to determine who gets what, how, and when, as Harold Lasswell wrote—and all appointed officials (transient and careerist) have such political interests. A minority of them are also involved in partisan activities.

Bureaucrats whose long-term careers are at stake clearly have much more to gain or lose in the conduct of government than do transients who shift, without much trauma, to nongovernmental roles. Hence we must conclude that supposedly "nonpolitical" careerists in fact have the strongest motivation to play "bureaucratic politics," whereas the political roles of transient bureaucrats, who can as readily step out of as into governmental roles, are more partisan and personal.

Since most bureaucrats in nonpresidentialist regimes are, in fact, careerists, this narrowed sense of the word seems, on its face, to be reasonable. It permits an equation between careerists—who do need to avoid partisanship in America in order to keep their jobs—and the idea that "bureaucrats" can be "nonpolitical." Sadly, the notion of "bureaucracy" is narrowed even more when the word is used to refer only to civil servants, excluding military officers, or just to intermediate-level officials, excluding both the few at the top and the many at the bottom.

To understand the functions and powers of bureaucracy in a global and comparative context, however, we cannot accept any of these arbitrary limitations. Here I must use "bureaucracy," generically, to refer to *all appointed officials regardless of their tenure in office, their civil/military status, or their rank.* When it is important to distinguish between different kinds of officials, we can easily do so by means of modifiers or other terms, such as civil servants versus military personnel, careerists versus transients, or office holders in various levels, ranks, or classes. Although bureaucratic features can also be found in private organizations, here I shall restrict the term to governmental bureaucracies, and almost always to those working in an executive branch, excluding the staff of legislatures, courts, and other autonomous governmental bodies.

To summarize, public bureaucracies (as defined above) always perform both administrative and political (including nonpartisan) roles. In order to understand how their administrative functions are performed, we need to consider their political roles, and conversely, to understand their political functions we need to think about their administrative roles also. Accordingly, we need to study the institutional factors that affect the motivation and capacity of public officials both to engage in political action and administrative tasks. I shall first discuss three intrabureaucratic variables—tenure, income, and interdependence—that affect bureaucratic performance. Then I shall look at the extra-bureaucratic institutional context of bureaucracy, going from the traditional to the modern, including the Third World.

This emphasis on institutional variables does not imply that social, economic, cultural, geographic, and historical variables are not also important. However, in contemporary research on comparative administration and politics, they have already been studied a great deal at the expense of institutional analysis. Moreover, it is difficult to generalize globally about these variables: because of their infinite variability they are best studied, I think, in specific time/place contexts, as they are in interdisciplinary area studies programs.

II. BUREAUCRATIC VARIABLES

The interest and ability of bureaucrats to govern, to perform both administrative and political functions, depends on their tenure, income, and interdependence.

A. Tenure

Tenure involves an expectation of long-term employment. According to the dictionary, tenure may mean permanence of position. Although often used today in a more specific sense to refer to academic tenure, the term applies in general to all bureaucratic posts. Bureaucrats who hold their positions for indefinite periods of time not only acquire administrative competence from deep experience, but because they have a long-term interest in the preservation of their positions, perquisites, and income, they are both motivated and able to use their offices for political (usually nonpartisan) purposes.

By contrast, transients who enter public service expecting to leave in a few years are likely to be ambivalent, their commitment to bureaucratic values competing with alternative orientations based on their past life and future prospects in the private sector. Their bureaucratic interests, per se, are essentially ephemeral. We may also expect their administrative capabilities to be inferior to those of careerists. Since they must leave public service after a short time in office, they have little opportunity to organize themselves for bureaucratically oriented political action and they may well focus their ambition on post-employment opportunities. Their political interests, therefore, are less bureaucratic than those of careerists and are more likely to be personal or ideological. Bureaucratic politics, therefore, is primarily a function of careerism, of tenured officials.

Among careerists, we need to distinguish between those whose appointments rest on patronage and those recruited and promoted in the context of a "merit" system, that is, procedures whereby the capacity of candidates for appointment is carefully evaluated and promotions are given on the basis of performance. In broad historical terms, most careerists have held their tenure outside of any merit system.

In traditional kingdoms and empires rulers were able to appoint whomever they chose, for whatever reasons, to posts in their bureaucracies. As long as officials loyally served their masters and developed minimal levels of competence—or at least appeared to do so—they were allowed to keep their posts.[1] In the American case the original patronage appointees of the Federalists expected to hold their posts indefinitely, that is, to have tenure (White 1948). It was only after the spoils system had institutionalized transiency that the reformers coupled the reinstitutionalization of tenure with the merit system.

When bureaucratic tenure is rooted in a merit system, public officials gain expertise that permits them not only to fulfill administrative goals but also to struggle effectively for their bureaucratic interests. Moreover, bureaucracies following a merit system become more interdependent, as explained below. Consequently, merit based bureaucracies are more motivated and able to act collectively in support of their class interests than are patronage-based bureaucracies.

In general, premodern bureaucracies were based on patronage and modern bureaucracies involve the use of a merit system. An important and conspicuous exception is provided by the Chinese imperial mandarinate, whose members gained their positions (for the most part) only after passing tough competitive written examinations. Actually, the Chinese model was historically influential in the development of modern Western bureaucracies,[2] and it remains important in those that encourage a class of higher level officials to rotate assignments between different government programs and at various levels.

Such officials acquire an overall perception of government and its problems that permits them to be referred to quite appropriately as "mandarins."[3] In the American case, by contrast, because of a different recruitment and promotion system, expertise translates itself into a strong commitment to the specific programs in which officials hold their tenure. It is more precise to refer to such officials as "functionaries," rather than as mandarins. This distinction helps us understand differences between the dynamics of bureaucratic politics and administration in the industrialized democracies. It may be less important in contemporary third world contexts.

Both mandarins and functionaries are strongly motivated to engage in nonpartisan politics, that is, politics designed first of all to safeguard their own positions and income. To the degree that their access to these benefits is controlled by extrabureaucratic institutions, however, their security and advancement depend on how well they perform their assigned administrative functions. When extrabureaucratic controlling institutions decline or collapse, bureaucrats gain power but administer less well.

In traditional monarchies or empires, the erosion of extrabureaucratic controls normally led to the corruption and fragmentation of patronage-based bureaucracies without entailing the overthrow of ruling families whose titular sovereignty was needed to legitimize bureaucratic power. By contrast, in the twentieth century, the interlocking character of merit-based bureaucracy has led to the creation of many bureaucratic polities, that is, systems in which officials (mainly military officers) have seized direct power, via coups, whenever modern institutions of constitutional government fail to cope with mounting problems. Under these conditions, bureaucratic self-interest dictates the maintenance of the bureaucratic system, but without external controls, officials are able to use and abuse their offices with few restraints. Predictably, then, the quality of public administration suffers and bureaucratic abuses proliferate.

B. Income

Full-time salaried officials are so prevalent in the modern world that we tend to assume that this is the normal situation in all bureaucracies. However, in premodern bureaucracies it was normal for officials to receive only a small part of their total income from official stipends or grants. In large measure their offices entitled them to functions from which they could directly generate personal income. The role of "publican" in New Testament times is well known—these were officials of the Roman Empire who collected taxes, retaining a more or less large share for themselves. Such tax farming was so lucrative that people were willing to buy the positions. Indeed, sale of office has been widely practiced.[4] Even in the Chinese Empire where recruitment to the bureaucracy was normally governed rather strictly by means of public examinations, the sale of office was practiced from time to time.[5] Clearly, by implication, offices could be sold only if they provided lucrative means of income that would more than cover the cost of buying a post. In fact, in the Chinese as in most traditional bureaucracies, it was necessary to pay officials or give them gifts in exchange for services rendered—just as in private professional life a doctor or lawyer is paid a fee for his assistance.

We lack a familiar term for the unofficial, nonsalary income of officials. However, we may well appropriate "prebend" for this purpose. According to its dictionary definition, a prebend is a stipend drawn from a special endowment—as for the support of a clergyman. Max Weber used the term in his classic discussion of premodern bureaucracy: "We wish to speak of '*prebend*' . . . wherever the lord assigns to the official rent payments for life . . . they are goods permanently set aside for the economic assurance of the office" (Weber 1946:207). In my discussion of the contemporary "prismatic" model I extended this idea to situations where various income sources controlled directly by the officials concerned supplement their official salaries.[6]

In the contemporary world prebendary income for officials can be found in all third world countries where public revenues are inadequate to cover salaries at a sufficiently high level to enable bureaucrats to sustain what they regard as a proper standard of living. In those countries where bureaucracy constitutes the ruling class—that is, "bureaucratic polities"—the capacity of officials to exploit their offices for personal gain becomes virtually unlimited. Much of the literature on "bribery" and "corruption" treats this phenomenon as aberrant and immoral. Clearly it does violate the expectations of official behavior applicable in affluent industrialized countries where public revenues are adequate to pay reasonably competitive salaries to public officials and it is normal for them to live on this official income. However, in societies where traditional bureaucratic practices are well remembered, and where a "formalistic" dichotomy between what is officially prescribed and what is actually practiced prevails, it is scarcely surprising if the real (prebendary) income of many if not most public officials should far exceed their formally prescribed salary levels.

A common assumption about full-time salaried bureaucracy is that it renders individual officials helpless in their struggle against centralized state power: they must do as they are told in order to retain their income. Certainly, centrally financed bureaucracies are far less likely to disintegrate into atomistic bureaucratic politics of the sort familiar in traditional societies, leading ultimately to feudalism.

However, there is a political price to be paid. Salaried officials are more likely to act collectively. They cannot so easily splinter off individualistically, as semisalaried prebendaries can do. Moreover, salaried officials become fully dependent on the state and this gives them an uncompromising interest in the fiscal viability of government. As full-time tenured employees who have acquired the technical competence needed in both civil and military matters to sustain the state, their capacity to exercise collective power is greatly enhanced.

Normally, under the control of civilian extrabureaucratic political institutions, officials use their power potential to secure legislative authority and budgetary support for their programs. However, when these extrabureaucratic institutions fail to work successfully, the opportunity arises for organized groups of bureaucrats (normally military officers) to seize power and establish regimes more congenial to their interests. Although the bureaucratic polities that result from such events may degenerate in the direction of "sultanism,"[7] most military rulers recognize that to stay in power and avoid future coups, they must provide a minimal level of governmental competence—at least they need to assure the revenues (whether from internal sources or foreign grants and loans) required to fund the heavy burden of official salaries.

It is possible, however, for these polities to limit their financial burdens by permitting the development of prebendal practices—notably all kinds of bribery, influence peddling, and payoffs, which permit "salaried" officials to enjoy a life style much higher than what their official stipends could support. The financial expectations of full-time salaried officials overload the resources of poor countries, contributing to the breakdowns that lead bureaucrats, seeking to safeguard or enhance their prequisites and uneasy about prevailing conditions, to conspire and seize power.

C. Interdependence

In the simplest bureaucracies each official may be authorized to perform many functions, but with growing differentiation of roles, interdependence between officials and bureaus increases. Modern bureaucracies, by contrast with traditional ones, are highly interdependent. The collection and distribution of revenues, above all, is separated from policy-implementing functions. Military and civil offices are clearly separated, and a wide range of welfare services is organized independently of those dedicated to the maintenance of public order. Organizationwide tasks are established in "staff" agencies, which interlock with programmatic "line" functions.

Broadly speaking, the interdependence of components in modern bureaucracies can be explained as a result of the increasing interdependence of all roles in contemporary industrialized and technologically sophisticated society. However, more specifically, it is linked to the development of the merit system in career services and the dependence of public officials on salaries for full-time work, as explained above. The merit system is typically associated with professionalization, which makes individual specialists increasingly dependent on complementary roles. As for salaries, they cannot be paid reliably without coordinated services for collecting, paying, accounting, auditing, etc. Moreover, reliance on salaries as one's sole source of income implies dependence on the system that generates payrolls.

All of this is quite familiar to observers of contemporary government in all countries, but we need imagination to reconstruct the essential simplicity of traditional bureaucracies in which most functions of government were consolidated under the control of individual officials at all levels, enabling them to "go it alone" when centralized control waned. Although the transformation of relatively undifferentiated bureaucracies into highly differentiated interdependent ones in modern times has not affected the class interest of bureaucrats, it has transformed their options. In order to understand this transformation we need to consider the various types of extrabureaucratic institutions of governance with which bureaucracies interact.

III.   EXTRABUREAUCRATIC INSTITUTIONS

By definition, bureaucracies do not stand alone. They are created by someone else—originally by monarchic rulers and today, usually, by constitutionally rooted governing bodies. These authoritative institutions, however, vary in their viability—some collapsing more readily and often than others—and in their capacity to control the agents who are officially charged with the duty of carrying out their instructions. These extrabureaucratic institutions provide the context within which we can understand how bureaucratic roles are performed.

When military officers rule a country, we know that these extrabureaucratic civilian institutions have failed: in the resulting power vacuum, appointed public officials become the ruling class. In traditional societies such a process resulted in feudalism, a system in which officeholding became hereditary. In our times, the interdependence of modern bureaucracy makes feudalism impracticable. Instead, bureaucracies retain their coherence as a system of interdependent roles, but since they lack formal institutions for self-government, the only way to come to power within a bureaucratic polity is to seize it by a coup d'état. Although some civil servants typically participate in such coups, their reliance on violence means that they must be directed by military officers.

In this essay I shall assume that the administrative performance of appointed officials (i.e., bureaucrats) is related to their political power. However, the nature of this relationship is complex. It is never easy for extrabureaucratic institutions to maintain effective control over bureaucracy, and often enough they fail. Such failures can be attributed both to their own internal failures and to the growing power of bureaucracy. Broadly speaking, the administrative effectiveness of bureaucracy is optimized when its power position is balanced with that of extrabureaucratic institutions. This means that when bureaucratic power radically exceeds that of the extrabureaucratic institutions (or diminishes excessively) administrative performance levels decline.

This view conflicts with the widely accepted myth that politics and administration can and should be divorced—that public officials should not exercise power but should follow politically neutral administrative public service norms and, by contrast, that the politically dominant extrabureaucratic institutions ought to monopolize the shaping of public policies. That myth has been widely disseminated in the third world, especially since World War II, primarily under American influence. Instead of achieving its intended goal of enhancing administrative capabilities, I believe it has, quite perversely, proven counterproductive because it has encouraged the unbalanced growth of bureaucratic power at the expense of the capacity of extrabureaucratic institutions to monitor and control public bureaucracies. Ultimately, therefore, it has tended to undermine rather than to enhance the administrative capabilities of struggling third world regimes.

When we ask why this myth should have become so widely accepted the answer is paradoxical. It is paradoxical because, although many American political scientists have long argued against the dichotomy between politics and administration, the myth persists in everyday life and even permeates much of the research and teaching that is carried on under the name of comparative (or development) administration.[8]

IV. TRADITIONAL INSTITUTIONAL FRAMEWORK

The monarchs who created bureaucracies more than 2000 years ago to serve their administrative (especially military) needs immediately confronted a formidable task, that is, how to counterbalance the growing power of their own appointed officials. Not surprisingly, hereditary rulers often failed, and their "servants" usurped power, reducing titular masters to the role of puppets. However, they could not do so by means of a coup d'état, the typical modern basis for creating a bureaucratic polity. Instead, given their relatively undifferentiated structure and prebendary support base, bureaucracies often dissolved into amorphous or even atomistic self-serving cells that simply undercut the power of monarchs and the administrative capabilities of their regimes.

Bureaucratic power sometimes produced "feudalism" in which officeholders appropriated their titles, converting them into family possessions. This led to an extreme localization of power as the authority of kings and emperors became purely symbolic.[9] Under the Byzantine Empire, by contrast, bureaucratic power did not become hereditary but it became so corrupt that officials used it with impunity to protect their expedient interests at the expense of imperial power.[10]

An alternative scenario evolved in the Middle East. Here, starting with Abbasid caliphs of Baghdad in the eighth century, the rulers chose personal slaves to serve as bureaucrats—they had no personal rights and could not transmit their roles to their children.[11] In the Egyptian case, ultimately—during the Mameluke dynasties, from 1250 to 1517—enfranchised slave officials serving in the sultans's entourage usurped the authority of their rulers. They were able to seize power by assassinating and replacing sultans, a process that became institutionalized over a period of two and a half centuries.[12]

The most successful traditional bureaucratic empire was the Chinese, whose emperors established a counterbureaucracy, the Censorate, designed to monitor and control officials with operational responsibilities. They also relied on a large imperial establishment based on the harem, a horde of eunuchs, and palace favorites recruited by direct patronage.[13] The Confucianist merit system, sponsored by Chinese emperors in order to guarantee a supply of obedient public servants, eventually armed the bureaucracy with a cohesive force that enabled it both to triumph over its imperial masters, and to retain its integrity as a coordinated ruling class. Nevertheless, it always needed imperial legitimation in order to safeguard its own interests. Even so, the bureaucratic system collapsed from time to time, contributing to dynastic failure and intervals of anarchy.

V. MODERN POLITIES

The replacement of royal sovereignty with new self-governing institutions based on the principle of popular sovereignty, as represented through political parties in elected assemblies, and by responsible heads of government, greatly enhanced the capacity of extrabureaucratic institutions to control officials, and also permitted a vast expansion of differentiated bureaucratic functions with an interdependent structure staffed by tenured and salaried personnel.

We are easily confused by the varieties of modern polities because we lack a collective term for the set of institutions designed to implement popular sovereignty: namely, an electoral system, an elected assembly, and a party system. For convenience I refer to this composite set of extrabureaucratic institutions as a *constitutive system*. The relevant sense of constitutive has this dictionary definition: "having power to institute, establish or enact." The term was selected because it resonates with such related words as constitution, constituents, and constituency (Riggs 1969:243–246).

A. Single-Party Regimes

Some critics have argued that single-party authoritarian regimes are "modern" yet lack a constitutive system. However, if we do not define "party system" rigidly by insisting that it must have more than one party, the objection does not hold. As I understand a party system, it is the system formally responsible for nominating and electing officials to public office. As such, it may contain only one party, or it may contain two or more parties. Clearly in countries like the former Soviet Union and China today, the Communist Party does perform this function. Moreover, there are elected assemblies and "elections," even when voters have no option but to support a single candidate for office. Consequently these regimes do have a constitutive system.

The significant point is that when a constitutive system contains only one party, that party is able to manage the elections and dominate the assembly. Moreover, as in all modern polities, the constitutive system is able to control the public bureaucracy, primarily by means of party groups of committees established to monitor the performance of key elements in the state "apparatus." Clearly this effort is not always successful, as seen in the rise of collusive "family circles" (Fainsod 1963).[14] Moreover, the curtailment or abolition of private organizations typical in such polities dictates a mammoth expansion of bureaucratic functions, thereby greatly increasing the difficulties involved in controlling the bureaucracy. Mikhail Gorbachov's *perestroika* reflects a current attempt to ameliorate these problems in the Soviet Union by curtailing the extent of central domination over bureaucratic behavior. The goal is simultaneously to enhance the performance levels of public administration and to transfer some functions to an embryonic "private sector," subject to market rather than direct political controls.

B. Open Constitutive Systems

More responsiveness to public opinion and openness to dissent is achieved in polities whose constitutive system contains a competitive party system—one with two or more parties. No doubt critics will complain that to the degree such polities permit private capitalism, economic power becomes unequally distributed and great inequities can result. However, it also seems apparent that without a vigorous private sector, the economic basis for support of a multiparty system and a powerful elected assembly cannot exist. "Open constitutive systems"—as we may call those containing multiparty systems—are able to control their bureaucracies just as well as the "closed constitutive systems" that have only one party.

However, the way such controls are exercised varies significantly depending on the way the chief executive (or head of government) is chosen. In parliamentary systems the norm involves selection, via the elected assembly, of a governing cabinet under the leadership of a prime minister. By contrast, in presidentialist systems, based on the principle of "separation of powers," we find independent election of a president and an assembly, each with a fixed term of office.

The term *presidentialist* is used to make an important distinction: since parliamentary systems often also have "presidents," whether directly or indirectly elected, we need to distinguish clearly between "presidentialist" systems, based on the separation of powers, and other kinds of "presidential" systems. Moreover, *presidential* is often used in discussions of the role of the president, rather than the constitutional system as a whole. Whether or not the head of state is called a president seems to have no particular importance, and this concept is therefore not used here. What is important is the distinction between two ideal types of open constitutive system: the parliamentary and the presidentialist. No doubt there are numerous varieties of each, and increasingly also hybrids, such as we find in the French Fifth Republic. Because of its historical significance the American regime is treated as a prototype for presidentialism, but comparative analysis of other presidentialist systems is needed to demonstrate its general properties. Because the bureaucratic role under parliamentarism and presidentialism is strikingly different, I shall discuss each in turn.

VI. PARLIAMENTARY REGIMES

In parliamentary regimes, authority is concentrated in a cabinet whose members have been elected by the parliament and are responsible to it. Since they normally stand or fall as a collectivity, the system creates powerful motives for members to reach agreements among themselves before presenting government policies to parliament. A parliamentary cabinet, therefore, is a very potent directorate for the bureaucracy—representing the combined power of an elected assembly, party leaders, and a coordinated executive body.

Parliamentary regimes need bureaucratic support, of course, and they find, for the most part, that they can rely on career officials to help them govern. Because they have tenure and assured income, these officials can be expected to give priority to their governmental responsibilities with minimal extragovernmental commitments. Typically such bureaucracies have an elite (mandarin) class whose members monopolize higher bureaucratic posts and rotate between departments, thereby acquiring a generalist (cross-cutting) sense of the state as a whole rather than a specialized (corner-based) knowledge within particular program or policy domains. Such mandarins have the broad outlook needed to help a cabinet govern effectively. No doubt they also have their own interests and they exercise substantial political power as "advisers" to the cabinet, but it is difficult for them to push autonomous policies on their own.

Few, if any, higher officials in parliamentary regimes are transients. No doubt there are many reasons for this. Highly qualified outsiders, for example, are unlikely to find public office attractive when no assurances of tenure can be offered, since the duration of a cabinet is continuously open to termination by a nonconfidence vote in parliament. By contrast, career officers are quite ready to accept temporary "political" appointments provided they can be sure of returning to permanent positions in the bureaucracy following a cabinet change. Moreover, as long as direct contacts between career officers and parliament can be inhabited, there is little reason for cabinet members to distrust the careerists whom they select to serve as staff members. By contrast, the external connections of transients—where they come from and where they will go later on—may be seen as far more dysfunctional.

Perhaps above all, since cabinet members themselves are powerful elected politicians, there is little need for transient bureaucrats to staff top governmental positions. This point becomes clearer when we look at the extreme contrast that can be found between parliamentary systems (where cabinet members are elected politicians) and bureaucratic polities (where they are all career officials). Presidentialist systems, by contrast, cannot compose their cabinets of elected politicians or of career officers. Consequently they are compelled to recruit transients, not only to the top levels but also to many subordinate positions, as we shall soon see.

In view of the reliance placed by parliamentary cabinets on career bureaucrats (mandarins), it is understandable that these officials should exercise great influence over public policies, especially by "advising" (manipulating) their "masters."[15] Nevertheless, when we compare these regimes to traditional monarchies, we see that their capacity to hold bureaucracies accountable is far greater. Even so, they cannot monopolize power, and bureaucrats inevitably exercise a great deal of effective political influence.

Parliamentary regimes evolved, for the most part, out of monarchies in which bureaucracies were well established prior to the development of representative institutions. This is not to say that they were "merit" systems, based on objective examinations for recruitment and promotion, but parliamentarism did emerge in contexts where a state apparatus of appointed career officials already existed. As the new constitutive systems emerged, it was easier to maintain existing bureaucracies than to transform or replace them in any radical way. The replacement of patronage by merit systems in the bureaucracy appears to have been a function of industrialization more than of democratization.

Both monarchic and parliamentary regimes have always been well aware of the risks involved in bureaucratic power. As new institutions for representative government took shape, pains were taken to make sure not only that bureaucracy would remain under control but even that the control structures would be strengthened. No doubt such efforts were not uniformly successful, as we may infer from the fact that the original meaning of "bureaucracy," a word coined in 18th-century France, was a polity dominated by appointed officials.

Efforts to maintain control over bureaucracy take various forms. On the European continent, in a civil law context, we find a highly legalistic environment in which official conduct is continuously monitored with the help of complex rules and procedures of "administrative law." In Great Britain, by contrast, with its common law traditions, greater reliance is placed on a privileged class of generalist administrators, recruited by examination from the most prestigious (upper-class) universities, who are rotated between various departments and ministries. Their personal loyalty to the "constitutional" (limited) monarchy is counted on to reinforce their accountability to parliamentary institutions and legal constraints.

Except for the United States, the more stable Western democracies studied by comparativists are almost universally parliamentary. Not surprisingly, therefore, parliamentary bureaucratic politics provides the norm against which presidentialist systems, such as we find in the United States, are seen as unique, exceptional, and possibly perverse[16]. The myth of a dichotomy between politics and administration that has its roots in the presidentialist need to use transient bureaucrats simply makes no sense in other kinds of regimes.

VII. PRESIDENTIALIST SYSTEMS

The dichotomy myth also makes no real sense in presidentialist systems but, based on the narrow construction of "politics" to mean "partisan politics," it helps to rationalize the transient/careerist dichotomy. Moreover, because of the prevalence of "iron triangles" that link bureaus to congressional committees and interest groups, there can exist under presidentialism a powerful incentive for bureaucrats to administer well in order to assure continuing support for their programs. This dynamism provides a functional equivalent to the market system and makes the politically neutral teachings of behaviorism and business management theory seem especially relevant and attractive to public administrators.

Nevertheless, the problems involved in trying to provide integrated direction and management under the leadership of the chief executive in a presidentialist system are far greater than those found in parliamentarism. The fundamental problem arises from the need to use transients both at the cabinet level and in many other high public offices. Although transients, precisely because they will soon leave government service, are unable to constitute an organized political threat to the regime, their lack of experience in government, their divided loyalties, and their essentially anarchic and unfocused sense of direction present any president with a stupendous political/managerial problem.

Admittedly, the views advanced here are based mainly on the U.S. experience. The existence of some 30 polities in the third world that have attempted to establish presidentialist regimes needs to be fully taken into account in a proper comparative study of presidentialism. However, I cannot do so here for several reasons.

First, substantively, since all of these regimes have experienced at least one breakdown and military (bureaucratic) rule, we cannot rely on them for evidence about the possibilities for sustained control over the bureaucracy in a presidentialist system. Only the United States has successfully maintained such a control system since it was launched over 200 years ago. A second reason is less substantial: there is simply no time or room in this chapter for a broad comparative analysis of presidentialist systems.[17]

To understand the peculiar features of bureaucratic politics and administration under presidentialism, as revealed in the American case, we need to consider four essential features: (1) a cabinet composed of transients, (2) a vast congressional agenda, (3) a bland, decentralized two-party system, and (4) the need for judicial review.[18] No doubt the presence of these features is well known, and nothing new will be said about them here. However, their links to the core presidentialist feature (separation of powers) and to the dynamics of bureaucratic politics and administration in America are less well understood. My purpose, therefore, is to explain some of these linkages.

A. Cabinet Members

Cabinet members cannot be drawn from Congress without undermining the independent authority of the president. This rule is strengthened by, though it does no depend on, Article I, section 5 of the Constitution, which states that "No Person holding any Office under the United States shall be a Member of either House during his Continuance in Office" (the Constitution of the Fifth Republic has a similar rule, but French elected politicians may hold cabinet posts by surrendering their parliamentary seats). Moreover, American cabinet members cannot safely be recruited from career officials without jeopardizing the independence and leadership capabilities of the President.

If neither elected politicians nor career officers can staff a cabinet, the only remaining option for the president is to select outsiders, that is, transients, to head government departments. They necessarily lack the inside knowledge and experience of careerists. Moreover, since they cannot count on remaining in government service after the current president leaves office, conflicts of interest arise based on cross currents between an official's duties and his or her former and prospective employers in the private sector.

Although transients hold cabinet posts in a presidentialist regime can exercise more power, individually, than any bureaucrats do in parliamentary regimes, their real power is inherently less than that of the elected politicians who serve in parliamentary cabinets. Moreover, their collective power, as a "cabinet," is far less because they do not have to act collegially to keep the government in power. Instead, each cabinet member is cross-pressured by the countervailing interests of the bureaucracy under her or his authority, relevant congressional and interest group forces, and the pulls of the presidency. As a result, presidentialist cabinets are necessarily fissured and noncollegial. They cannot count on the partisan, legislative, and public support that enables parliamentary cabinets both to govern and to act jointly so as to retain their majority in the assembly.

To compensate for the unavoidable divisiveness of a presidentialist cabinet, presidents must recruit even more transients to help them coordinate the whole bureaucratic machinery. From this necessity has evolved the large and complex Executive Office of the President in the United States plus a host of transient employees scattered throughout the bureaucracy. One recent report claims there were some 3000 "non-career employees in the executive branch" in 1984 (Pfiffner 1987).

From its inception the American bureaucracy has included many transients. No doubt, initially, under the Federalists, they often retained their positions after new presidents came to office, but they had not been recruited through a "merit"system, nor did they have legal assurance of tenure in office. From the time of the Jacksonians until the 1880s, frequent rotation in office became normal, although some valued officials were able to retain their positions. Subsequently, starting with the Pendleton Act, career officers began to replace transients in many positions although they never supplanted them.[19]

Although the vast majority of federal officials are now careerists, the American bureaucracy as a whole has always contained a mixture of transients and careerists. The myth of a dichotomy between politics and administration powerfully legitimized the efforts of civil service reformers to extend the career services. The use of "bureaucracy" to mean only career civil servants also strengthened this campaign because it (falsely) implied that public officials are politically neutral, lacking their own class and self-interest. They are, of course, politically interested, but nonpartisan. In recent years, especially under the Reagan administration, the number of transients has grown so much that there is a rising demand for new limits. Consequently, criticisms of the dichotomy myth can be attacked as retrogressive because, by blunting the distinction between political appointees and (supposedly nonpolitical) careerists, they seem to favor the recrudescence of patronage and spoils.

B. The Congressional Agenda

The need to employ transients at the highest levels of bureaucracy to help the president integrate a severely dispersed bureaucratic power structure becomes more understandable when we consider the implications of the congressional agenda. Because of the separation of powers, this agenda is necessarily vast—unlike the agenda of parliaments, which need do little more than accept or reject programs presented to them by the government of the day. A huge agenda necessitates the delegation of real power to specialized standing committees, and also the development of an elaborate congressional bureaucracy. Given the presidentialist separation of powers, therefore, the authority for most public policies, programs, and budgets rests with congressional committees and subcommittees rather than with Congress in plenary session.

As a result, American bureaucrats have to be accountable to dispersed power centers in Congress—as well as to the president and the courts. This is the root cause of the strongly centrifugal forces within the career bureaucracy. It anchors the "iron triangles"—which link bureaucrats with Congressional committees and interest groups—and poses a fundamental and typically presidentialist problem of the urgent need for policy integration. As noted above, a cabinet staffed by transients who must, acting independently, secure congressional support for their programs cannot perform these coordinative functions. Consequently, presidents need to create their own countervailing forces. They can scarcely rely for this purpose, on careerists who are strongly committed to their own programs. They must therefore develop an integrative executive office staffed by personally recruited transients.

C. A Bland, Decentralized Two-Party System

In parliamentary regimes it is possible for a strongly committed party with its own dedicated membership and constituency to exercise real power even though it holds only a minority of seats in the parliament. This fact promotes the development of highly centralized, policy-oriented, multifunctional political parties. By contrast, in a viable presidentialist system, parties must be loose coalitions designed to secure a popular national majority in presidential elections. Consequently they eschew sharp stands on really controversial issues that might antagonize many voters. They are, therefore, necessarily "bland": they cannot produce well-focused and integrated public programs, nor can they form sufficiently coherent policy guidelines to unify a bureaucratized cabinet. Indeed, the party-in-Congress has perilous relations with the party-in-the-administration.

To win congressional and local elections, moreover, parties must be locally responsive. This means that a successful party must often contradict itself in many localities. It can win nationally only by aggregating local majorities. Thus it must be loosely organized and highly decentralized. Successful American parties are not "weak" insofar as they do hold vast coalitions together for successful national campaigns, but they have to be both bland and highly localized.

Because of these properties, American parties cannot guide either the legislature or the executive on most policy issues. Instead, the heavy burden of policy direction falls directly on each president, transients in the cabinet and Executive Office, and the members of Congress. They cannot expect a political party, as such, to offer coherent guidelines, nor can they rely for advice on career officials whose primary allegiance is to their own programs. This reinforces the considerations mentioned above, which compel presidents to recruit their own personal staff and executive officers (mainly transients, often old friends) to provide integrated policy direction for the whole bureaucracy. As members of Congress find their work load mounting, they also add to their personal and committee staffs, composed mainly of transients. It is doubly misleading to refer to these transient bureaucrats as "political appointees." They are not accountable to a political party but belong to the personal entourage of the president and the members of Congress who employ them. Moreover, the term suggests a false dichotomy, that careerists are "nonpolitical," thereby unconsciously reinforcing the myth of separation between politics and administration.

The need for volunteers to help run costly national electoral campaigns also motivates a "spoils" system, which intensifies the pressure to appoint transients throughout the bureaucracy. Because presidentialist parties have to be decentralized, they generate widely dispersed demands for "pork barrel" projects and, correspondingly, for "political" appointments. With transients in control at the center, it is difficult to bar the selection of transients in the hinterlands.

Because presidentialist parties also have to be bland, they cannot make focused demands for specific programs and policies. The rise of interest groups and lobbies, therefore, is directly proportional to the blandness of party programs. This accounts for the importance of lobbyists in a presidentialist system as links between congressional committees and careerists in the bureaucracy. The basic dynamics of presidentialist parties, therefore, contribute simultaneously to the incidence of both party-oriented transients and program-oriented careerists in government service.

D. Judicial Review

In order to umpire the unavoidable disputes and boundary problems that arise from the separation of powers, a powerful court system is needed. However, when courts exercise the power of judicial review, they become arbiters of rules and procedures to such an extent that bureaucrats must continuously consider the legal consequences of their acts and the possible unconstitutionality of the laws they implement. This means that, in addition to their responsiveness to the president and Congress, they must continually orient themselves to past and impending court decisions—a factor that, again, reinforces the extreme dispersal of bureaucratic power and often the timidity of public officials.[20]

E. Bureaucratic Politics Under Presidentialism

On the basis of the American example, then, we may conclude that the basic dynamics of a presidentialist system based on the separation of powers leads to a highly dispersed pattern of bureaucratic politics. This pattern has fundamental administrative and political consequences that are interlocked. These consequences, however, have significantly different implications for careerists and transients.

Career officials realize that their personal success requires them to satisfy the expectations and demands of specific interest groups and concerned members of Congress. These groups and their congressional allies, in turn, know that their needs will be best served by well-qualified officials whose long-term experience and training enable them to administer well. The careerists, accordingly, know that their own self-interests will be best served by good administration of their programs.

Although these careerists are strongly motivated by program politics, they must also be nonpartisan in order to protect their careers when chief executives change. It serves their interests, therefore, to claim to be "nonpolitical."[21] Moreover, to achieve their administrative goals, they are more likely to be helped by the management tools developed in private enterprise than by any kind of sophisticated political analysis of their roles. While acting politically, they need to adopt a non-political posture.

By contrast, the political/administrative motives of transients are more fuzzy and ambivalent. On the one hand, they are motivated to serve those who appoint them: knowing that they have no tenure, they realize they can be summarily discharged at any time. However, this very knowledge also leads them to consider the options open to them in private employment, how best to utilize their experience and connections in government after they leave the public service. Accordingly, their inclination to master the massively complex problems of governmental integration and to serve the general public interest in accordance with presidential guidelines wars with their own long-term personal ambitions and financial interests (Riggs 1988a). Ironically, therefore, the political interest of "political appointees" is much less clearly focused and bureaucratically oriented than is that of the careerists.

If this account is correct, a presidentialist system can provide the political motives for high levels of administrative performance in selected governmental programs. At the same time, it disperses power and dilutes real executive power: a popularly elected president is vested with high authority and great expectations but, because of his necessary reliance on transients, he is severely handicapped in his ability to deliver on those expectations. A system that depends so much on the services of transients is highly vulnerable: it is likely to collapse and to be replaced by a bureaucratic tyranny run by careerists, mainly military officers—as we shall soon see.

VIII.   BUREAUCRATIC POWER IN THE THIRD WORLD

According to statistics collected in 1965 (see Tables 1 and 2) some 57 third world regimes out of a total of 141 (about 40%) had lost power at least once in military coups—100% of the 33 with presidentialist constitutions have experienced at least one breakdown and episode of military rule. More recent figures would not significantly change this finding. Since military officers form part of every country's bureaucracy, the phenomenon has a lot to do with bureaucratic politics—and administration.

Although some may claim that the first modern coup d'état was staged by Napoleon Bonaparte on the 18th Brumaire (November 9, 1799), in its typically contemporary form coups are a

Table 1   The Fate of the 32 Contemporary Monarchies

20 (63%) have lost power since 1920
9 (45%) lost power to coups
11 (55%) lost power for others reasons
12 (38%) remain in power

Source: Riggs (1985).

Table 2   The Fate of New States with Constitutive Systems

109 total of new states with constitutive systems
    48 (44%) new states lost power in coups
    61 (66%) have retained their constitutive systems

Single-party regimes

34 total
    29 (85%) have retained power as of 1985
        17 (59%) originated in resistance movements
        12 (41%) did not originate in resistance movements
     5 (15%) were overthrown by coups

Parliamentary regimes

42 total
    29 (69%) were still in power in 1985
    13 (31%) lost power to coups

Presidentialist regimes

33 total
    33 (100%) were overthrown at least once
    30 (91%) were overthrown by coups
      21 (70%) pre-1920 regimes
       9 (30%) post-1920 regimes
     3 (9%) were overthrown by different (noncoup) means

Summary

5 out of 34 (15%) single-party regimes broke down
43 out of 75 (57%) open states lost to coups

Source: Riggs (1985).

distinctive phenomenon in third world countries. As noted above, although bureaucracies in traditional empires and kingdoms were often able to appropriate power from their rulers, it was unusual for them to displace them. Napoleon's project resembles modern coups in that it was launched at a time when the first French Republic was collapsing. It resembles the traditional Mamluke pattern[12] when Napoleon crowned himself emperor on December 2, 1804, with the help of a captive pope.[22] Modern coups, by contrast, produce "presidents" who have to legitimize their authority by reference to the myth of popular rather than divine sovereignty.

No doubt, from an historian's point of view, the explanation of a coup require that a large number of interdependent variables be taken into account: They constitute a unique configuration in each individual case. However, from the point of view of comparative politics and administration, it is useful to focus on two closely linked variables that seem to play an important part in any general theoretical explanation. The first concerns the role of public bureaucracy and the second involves the viability, or should we say fragility, of regimes. Let me take up each separately.

A. Bureaucratic Power

Virtually all of the new states that were liberated from imperial rule after World War II inherited a well-established and modernized public bureaucracy. By contrast, most of them did not inherit an institutionalized constitutive system. However, there were significant differences among the states concerning the viability of these systems: some were simply much more fragile than others.

Those that were more fragile soon found themselves in the awkward position of being unable to control their own bureaucracies, hence unable to govern. In a situation of political crisis and collapsing public administration, groups of public officials came to the conclusion that it was necessary for them to seize power in order to prevent complete anarchy. Since there is no constitutionally legitimate formula in any country whereby appointed officials select their own leader, the only remaining road to power involves violence or the threat of violence. Exceptionally, desperate civilian leaders called on career officers to rule—as in Burma in 1958. Even there, after parliamentary government was restored, General Ne Win returned to power by a coup in 1962. Usually, then, a bureaucratic cabal, headed by military officers, seizes control of a collapsing regime.

The enhancement of bureaucratic power by coup is a logical extension of the process of bureaucratic indigenization that preceded independence in many new states. We must remember that the colonial bureaucracies created to implement imperial rule were never staffed exclusively by expatriates—to save money, local personnel typically filled a large number of subordinate positions. Depending on the policies of their imperial masters, indigenous officials had already replaced expatriates in many posts prior to independence, a process that was rapidly completed after liberation. Indeed, the demand for promotions by frustrated subordinates within colonial bureaucracies became one of the most important forces behind the independence movements. The political/administrative role of bureaucracy in the new states, therefore, reflects a tension between the forces involved in the creation of new extrabureaucratic constitutive systems and those acting to indigenize the existing bureaucratic machinery of government.

We may, nevertheless, distinguish between the older and the newer states of the third world. Those that were liberated in the twentieth century, notably after World War II, in Asia and Africa, had relatively "modern" bureaucracies in which some kind of merit system had been developed. By contrast, those that secured their independence in the 19th century, particularly in the Americas, inherited a patronage-based premodern type of bureaucracy. Let me hypothesize that it was easier for extrabureaucratic constitutive systems to retain control over patronage-based than over merit-based bureaucracies. This would explain why, in Latin America, the incidence of coups increased as merit systems, especially in the military services, grew. The exceptional case is that of the United States.[18,23]

B. Traditional Monarchies

The traditional form of extrabureaucratic institution was monarchic. In traditional monarchies, as I use this term, kings actually rule—they are not mere figureheads. No doubt, under feudal or quasi-feudal conditions, hereditary officials did deprive them of real power, and the throne became an empty title. In modern times, some monarchies persist after surrendering power to new political institutions based on the notion of popular sovereignty. These constitutional monarchies should be classed as parliamentary regimes—Thailand is an exceptional case inasmuch as the monarchy surrendered power to a bureaucratic polity in which power was seized by public officials (Riggs 1966). We cannot generalize about the political role of "monarchy" if all these cases are included—but when we restrict the notion to regimes in which a king really rules then it becomes a useful concept.

Many monarchies were replaced by new imperial authorities when they were conquered by the Western powers or Japan. Even when these powers had democratic constitutional governments at home, the format of imperial conquest and exploitation was essentially traditional in character. Ultimately, neither the new imperialism nor the old monarchies could survive the forces released in the twentieth century by the global spread of capitalism and industrialism.

The pervasive power of these forces is well known and needs no further comment here. However, we need to note that the legitimacy of traditional kingships found in conquered countries was undermined by conquest, even when they were formally retained under indirect rule. Moreover, the sacred and hierarchic roots of legitimacy for traditional monarchies were destroyed by the secularism and egalitarian norms that spread with Western influence.

The most dramatic manifestation of the end of traditionalism involved the collapse of the Western empires. Liberation movements based on the new norms of egalitarianism and secularism simply overpowered the war-weakened metropolitan powers. Most, but not all, of the remaining traditional monarchies have now also succumbed. About 20 independent non-Western traditional monarchies that survived until World War I have by now lost their powers (see Table 1). Of these, almost half surrendered power to their own bureaucracies following a coup d'état. Exceptionally, the Iranian monarchy fell before a revolutionary movement that was motivated more by traditionalism than by Western secularism.

According to my analysis as of 1985, 12 traditional monarchies still remained in power. An important reason for their survival was probably the existence of natural resources, notably oil deposits, which permitted them to secure so much foreign exchange that they could run their governments without need to tax their people: Saudi Arabia, Kuwait, and Brunei, for example. A few, like Bhutan, are sufficiently remote from the outside world to protect their ancient institutions. To administer their domains, however, all these surviving monarchies have expanded their bureaucracies and, unless revolutions intervene, may eventually experience a fate like that of Thailand in 1932 when activists within its bureaucracy seized power.

C. Constitutional Models

Far more interestingly and importantly, the new states usually borrowed constitutional regimes from their former imperial masters, or they organized single-party authoritarian regimes based on the Soviet (Bolshevik) model. In all these cases a constitutive system had been established as the popularly based ruling institution. However, in almost half of these states these institutions collapsed after an initial "vestibule" period during which they struggled to govern and keep the bureaucracy under control.

According to my 1985 data (see Table 2) there were then 109 new states, of which 48 (44%) had succumbed at least once to a coup d'état—many had succumbed more often. In these 48 states, therefore, the bureaucracy had displaced its constitutive system. There were 61 states (56%) by contrast, that had retained their constitutive systems and were able to sustain, however precariously, a balance of power with their public bureaucracies.

As the figures in Table 2 show, the success ratio of the different kinds of constitutive system varies greatly: of 34 single-party authoritarian regimes, only five (15%) succumbed to coups, whereas of 75 with open (i.e., multiparty) constitutive systems, 43 (57%) succumbed to coups. No doubt it is easier for authoritarian regimes that ban opposition parties and suppress their opponents to sustain their control over the machinery of government than it is for polities based on the protection of minority rights and civil liberties.

An additional factor should be taken into account, however: 17 (59%) of the surviving single-party regimes originated in resistance movements that fought liberation wars. They often received advice and assistance from the Soviet Union and they followed the Bolshevik model of party organization within a revolutionary front. However, when we consider that 12 (41%) of the surviving single-party regimes obtained their independence by peaceful negotiation, we cannot attribute success merely to the mode of liberation.

D. Open Polities

This point can also be analyzed by reference to the history of the open constitutive systems: in general, the presidentialist regimes originated after a revolutionary war, whereas most parliamentary regimes came into existence by negotiation. In these countries, however, revolutionary origin appears to have a negative relation to postrevolutionary survival. Actually, the differences between the fates of presidentialist and parliamentary regimes is quite striking and deserves closer analysis.

Of 33 new states that adopted a presidentialist constitution, at least 30 (91%) have experienced coups—and the remaining three have succumbed for other reasons. By contrast, of the 42 states coded as basically parliamentary in structure, only 13 (31%) have been displaced by military coups. (As the Fijian case suggests, that number would be somewhat higher today.) Could such a radical difference be accounted for by external factors? Since most of the presidentialist cases can be found in Latin America, it is easy to think that the geography, culture, economic conditions, or discordant relations with the United States could account for the differences. No doubt U.S. influence or intervention is also involved in the non-Latin cases, notably the Philippines, South Vietnam, South Korea, and Liberia. Even so, the statistical contrast is suggestive and compels us to consider the possibility that presidentialist systems are inherently difficult to sustain. If so, even a weak premodern bureaucracy might well find itself compelled by the failures of a government to try, in its own self-interest, to fill the "vacuum." If we are to understand the political role of bureaucracies and its relation to the viability of extrabureaucratic (constitutive) systems, then we need to pay attention to the design of these systems and the typical problems they create, especially as they relate to the control and direction of bureaucracies.

E. Presidentialist Regimes

Because of its disastrous record, it is particularly relevant to analyze the presidentialist model. American political scientists, when studying the American polity, have tended to accept its Constitution as a given and while they study its specific problems in great depth, they usually accept the system as a whole as essentially viable simply because it has lasted for over 200 years. Comparativists, while studying political phenomena outside the United States, have often also accepted the American model as a good one that might well be exported to other countries. When it fails elsewhere, they tend to attribute such failure to nonsystemic factors—economic, social, geographic, cultural, etc.

My data suggest that we should at least consider an alternative perspective, one suggesting that presidentialism is an essentially fragile formula. Instead of asking why others fail, should we not ask why the U.S. presidentialist constitution has not collapsed?[23] This is not the place for a survey of all the essential weaknesses in the presidentialist model. However, one of these weaknesses is especially relevant to the focus of this essay: namely, the need for transients to staff the highest offices of the bureaucracy.

If careerists are allowed to occupy these top positions, the balance of power is upset and the president becomes merely a figurehead for the bureaucracy. Recognizing this possibility, however, presidents who seek to enhance their power by appointing transients to top positions encounter another difficulty: unless they are very shrewd and careful, the transients, because of their inexperience and conflicting interests, may serve them poorly. Thus presidents run the risk of cronyism and familism. Not only does this lead to a decline in administrative capabilities, but it discredits the regime and provokes resistance, both by careerists in the bureaucracy and by an increasingly alienated populace.

Other dilemmas encountered in the design of presidentialist regimes are also critical, especially the danger of a deadlock between the president and Congress. Although, as in the Philippine case, a president may seek to resolve such a deadlock by usurping power and ruling by martial law and edict, the far more usual scenario involves a coup in which a group of military officers, fearing a complete collapse of governing functions and hence also disaster for the bureaucracy, decides to step in, overturn the government and the constitution, and rule by fiat.[24] Although such disasters have also occurred in parliamentary regimes, they are much less frequent. This suggests the need for a parallel study of the structures and processes that enable parliamentary regimes, more often than presidentialist ones, both to sustain a relatively open society and at the same time to maintain sufficient control over their public bureaucracies to assure an adequate level of administrative performance.

IX. CONCLUSION

Although the foregoing survey of the political/administrative role of bureaucracy in many different kinds of regimes has been cursory, it may be adequate to support the general proposition that all bureaucracies have their own political interests and power enough to protect them. However, the way in which they do this has a major impact on their administrative performance, ranging from one extreme, in bureaucratic polities, where their role as a ruling class enables them to flout administrative values, to another extreme where, in balance with a well-established constitutive system, they find that the best way to assure their own self-interest is to administer well.

Ironically, when they are so motivated, especially in presidentialist systems, it seems to be expedient for career officers to deny their own political interests and activities and to pretend that they are completely nonpolitical. The myth of a dichotomy between politics and administration that can emerge out of this situation has led, I believe, to a grave distortion in the study of American public administration, and this distortion has had damaging consequences when extended to other countries where, unintentionally, it has provided tools for strengthening bureaucracy without a parallel development of equivalent power in the countervailing extrabureaucratic institutions of government.

NOTES

1. "The Prefect, by the way he implements the Emperor's instructions, can execute a policy in direct contravention of those instructions-and no one dare inform the Emperor in such a case" (Carney 1971, Book II:103).

2. An explanation of the Chinese ("mandarin") background of the Indian Civil Service and, through it, the British civil service system can be found in Teng (1943).

3. "If through some miracle a group of mandarins from the [Chinese] Imperial court could come to Paris . . . they would have to adjust to modern technology and democratic procedures, but otherwise they could act like genuine French mandarins" (Dogan 1975:4).

4. Max Weber provides an illuminating analysis of the political tensions between traditional rulers and bureaucrats involved in tax-farming and the purchase of office. "The mode of tax-farming or the transfer of taxes," he writes, "can thus vary widely, according to the distribution of power between the lord and the tenant [official]" (Weber 1946:206). Concerning Hapsburg rule in Spain and the Spanish Indies, we read that "In the seventeenth century there were very few posts which were not granted at

one time or another, without much regard to the capacity of the applicants, in return for cash payments" (Parry 1953:1). "The Spanish Crown in the sixteenth-century sold offices more openly than the English but less freely than the French" (Parry 1953:3). Details on the French experience can be found in Swart (1949). The main incentives for the sale of public office were financial: "In an age when government finance, no less than custom, made the payment to most officials of adequate salaries quite out of the question, a system of payment by prequisites was inevitable" (Parry 1953:2). The availability of such prequisites made candidates willing to pay for them. For embattled rulers, as a result, "The sale of colonial offices had become a regular and important source of revenue" (Parry 1953:4). Of course, there were also political considerations. Parry tells us that "Viceroys and governors, if allowed to appoint the holders of such offices, might use their patronage to create private factions. They could not do so if the offices were sold, with proper safeguards, at public auction" (Parry 1953:2). Thus the controlled sale of office tended to centralize control and contain the growth of regional bureaucratic power. Ultimately, however, the system failed because, as Parry reports, "In actual money the system must have cost the Crown far more, in the end, than it brought in in purchase prices. The cost in other ways— the lowering of standards and of morale throughout the service, the creeping paralysis of administration, the loss of confidence in royal justice—cannot be computed." Apparently it contributed much to the collapse of the Hapsburgs (Parry 1953:73).

5. During the Sung dynasty "the sale of office . . . was not allowed to approach the proportions once reached in the Han, and later under the Manchus, when its prevalence seriously damaged the morale of the service" (Kracke 1953:76).

6. "The prebendal basis, characteristic of traditional bureaucracies . . . requires each official to procure a large part of his income for himself, as from fees, gifts, rents, tributes or other payments not directly allocated or distributed to him by a central treasury" (Riggs 1964:44).

7. The term "sultanism" has been proposed by Linz. Following Max Weber's lead, Linz identifies a form of traditional authority in which the ruler "exercises his power without restraint at his own discretion and above all unencumbered by rules or by any commitment to an ideology or value system" (Linz 1975:259).

8. Elsewhere I have tried to explain the rise and persistence of the dichotomy myth in American politics and scholarship (Riggs 1988b). Although the immediate causes for the rise of the myth were inherent in the political reform movement that tried to stem the "spoils" system that overburdened the American bureaucracy with transients, the ultimate cause involves the dynamics of presidentialism, which necessitates the employment of transients in the public bureaucracy. Viewed in this context, the dichotomy myth became a useful weapon in the struggle to achieve a balance between careerists and transients in American public administration.

9. Coulborn (1956), on the basis of comparative analysis, reconstructs a scenario in which feudalism rises on the ashes of collapsed bureaucratic empires. Among its features are hereditary office-holders who may or may not possess fiefs. European feudal lords (bureaucrats?) appropriated their fiefs as family possessions, while in the Japanese case landless but hereditary officeholders (*samurai*) became more numerous, as the great lords (*daimyo*) consolidated their control over large fiefs. "The feudal class, including both enfeoffed vassals and landless salaried retainers, was on the way to becoming a hereditary bureaucracy" (Reischauer 1956:35).

10. Bureaucratic politics in fifth century Byzantium relied on three interlocking perquisites of office: *praescriptio fori*, or the right of an agency to try cases involving accusations against it; *sportulae*, or the fees and tips exacted by officials in exchange for their services; and *suffragium*, the rules governing the purchase and ownership of office. These rules made the Byzantine bureaucracy a self-governing body able to defy the imperial authority (Carney 1971, Book II:106–111).

11. Such a system prevailed in the Ottoman Empire, in which, according to S.N. Eisenstadt, "The personal subservience and the social autonomy of the bureaucracy were insured by the system of having it composed mostly of members who were the sultan's personal slaves, and had been recruited from alien elements." Eisenstadt's monumental work and extensive bibliography provide a starting point for anyone interested in studying the bureaucracies that developed in traditional monarchies and empires (Eisenstadt 1963). Concerning the origin of the slave official system, Lane-Poole tells us that:

From the time when the Arabs came in contact with the Turks on the Oxus and brought them under the rule, Turkish slaves had been highly prized in Muslim households. Their physical strength and beauty, their courage, and their fidelity had won the trust of the great emirs, and especially of the caliphs, who believed they could rely more safely upon the devotion of these purchased foreigners than upon their own jealous Arabs.

When those in the caliph's service had shown their talent and loyalty, they were often emancipated and appointed to government offices, especially in the palace and as governors of provinces (Lane-Poole 1968:59,60).

12. Details can be found in Lane-Poole:

The annals of mamluke dominion are full of instances of a great lord reducing the authority of the reigning sultan to a shadow, and then stepping over his murdered body to the throne. Most of these sultans died violent deaths at the hands of rival emirs, and the safety of the ruler . . . depended mainly upon the numbers and courage of his guard. . . . A coalition would be formed among a certain number of disaffected nobles, with the support of some of the officers of the household or of the guard and their retainers would mass in the approaches to the royal presence, while a trusted cup-bearer or other officer, whose duties permitted him access to the king's person, would strike the fatal blow; and the conspirators would forthwith elect one of their number to succeed to the vacant throne (Lane-Poole 1968:244–245).

The word *mamluk*, according to Lane-Poole, means "owned" or "belonging to" and was "applied to white male slaves captured in war or purchased in the market" (1968:242). A recent and somewhat opinionated account is given by Glub (1973). A short but useful summary of the Mameluke dynasties is contained in the Egypt entry in the *Encyclopedia Britannica.*

13. "The Censorate was destined . . . to develop elaborate procedures for checking on the day-to-day operations of all the central governmental agencies; in later dynasties this system covered the whole empire" (Kracke 1953:442). According to Weber, a constant struggle prevailed in the Chinese empire between the literati bureaucrats and the palace establishment but "in the long run and again and again the literati won out" (Weber 1946:442).

14. Under the heading "Party Organization and Controls at the Oblast Level," Fainsod (1963:62–92) gives exceptional insight, based on documents captured by the German army, into the mechanisms whereby the Communist party sought (not always successfully) to control the conduct of bureaucrats in the state apparatus.

15. In England, we are told, "higher civil servants determine not only how policies should be effected, but also, to a very significant extent, which should be effected" (Chapman 1970:153). Similarly, in Canada, "even officials who claim total administrative detachment in fact play politically significant roles" (Campbell and Szablowski 1979:210).

16. For example, we are told that in the normal (i.e., parliamentary) model, relations between civil servants and legislators are "mediated" by cabinet members, whereas in America one finds the "end-run model," that is, the "extreme case of direct linkage" between officials and legislators (Aberbach et al. 1981:233–235).

17. A round table on Comparative Presidentialism was held at the world congress of the International Political Science Association in August 1988, and plans have been made for panels on this theme at future conferences of the American Society for Public Administration, American Political Science Association, and International Sociological Association.

18. The "essential" features are those that are needed in order for a presidentialist system not to break down and lead to military rule. A provisional effort to identify such essential or "paraconstitutional" features is offered in Riggs (1988c).

19. Information on the patronage system initiated by the founding fathers is given in White (1948). President Andrew Jackson "did not introduce the spoils system," according to White, but he "did introduce *rotation* into the federal system. . . ." However, as rotation in office mounted, partisanship in office grew (White 1954:4–5). Although the Pendleton Act firmly established career services in the U.S. fed-

eral government, it did so very cautiously, placing only about 10% of federal positions in the new "classified civil service," and these were mainly very subordinate posts (Van Riper 1984:105). Subsequently, of course, the percentage of careerists greatly increased, but transients never disappeared.

20. Dwight Waldo thinks of "the judicial functions and apparatus as constitutionally privileged and functionally specialized instruments of public administration" (Waldo 1987:5). Rosenbloom (1987) summarizes recent developments and offers a good bibliography. A detailed discussion of problems involved in judicial review of acts by government agencies can be found in Ball (1984:227–257). Ball's symposium, as a whole, reviews the multiplicity of controls imposed over federal bureaucrats in America.

21. No doubt the "nonpolitical" label also serves the interests of careerists in other ways. Peters, for example, notes that "For administrators, this presumed separation of administration and politics allows them to engage in politics without the bother of being held accountable politically for the outcomes of their actions" (Peters 1978:137).

22. The Mamluk usurpers, in 1250, of the title of sultan clearly felt a need for legitimation by the sacred authority of the caliph. An opportunity arose when the first great Mamluk sultan, Beybars—a successful general who had assassinated and replaced his predecessor, Kutuz, in 1260—"invited an exiled representative of the extinguished 'Abbasid caliphate to come to Cairo [in 1261], where he enthroned him with splendid pomp as the rightful pontiff of Islam . . . and received from him the gold-embroidered black turban, the purple robe, and the gold chain and anklets, which denoted the duly appointed and spiritually recognized sovereign of the caliph's realm" (Lane-Poole 1968:264–265). A line of powerless caliphs remained in Cairo subsequently until 1538, when the caliphate was assumed by the Ottoman sultans. Throughout this period these caliphs obediently legitimized the rule of Mamluk sultans as they came to power, whether by inheritance or, more importantly, by a coup.

   An apparently successful modern example of monarchist usurpation might be found in Iran, where Reza Khan Pahlavi, an army officer, seized power in 1921. Four years later he ousted the Qajar shah and launched a new dynasty. This maneuver seemed to have succeeded when his son, Muhammad Reza Shah Pahlavi, succeeded him in 1941, following British and Soviet intervention during World War II. No doubt he would have lost power during the premiership of Mohammad Mossadeq (1951–1953) had not the American CIA helped him to topple Mossadeq from power. In historical perspective, his success was short-lived for, as everyone knows, the monarchy came to an end in 1979 in the face of an Islamic fundamentalist revolution spearheaded by the Ayatollah Ruhollah Khomeini.

   In 1912, following the collapse of the Manchu Dynasty in China, a presidentialist republic was established with General Yuan Shih-kai as President. Impatient with Congress and republican ideas, Yuan tried, without success, to start a new Imperial dynasty. Colonel Jean-Bedel Bokassa, who seized power in the Central African Republic on January 1, 1966, had himself crowned emperor in December 4, 1977. On September 20, 1979, he was deposed by the former president, David Dacko, with French military assistance. These episodes suggest that once the monarchic idea had been discredited, it was futile for coup leaders to try to resurrect the formula.

23. In Riggs (1988c) I have speculated about a half dozen fundamental problems in presidentialist systems and tried to suggest some of the American governmental practices that enabled this regime to survive.

24. Elsewhere I have tried to explain the typical scenario of a coup d'état and its underlying bureaucratic dynamics (Riggs 1981).

REFERENCES

Aberbach, J.D., Putnam, R.D., and Rockman, B.A. *Bureaucrats and Politicians in Western Democracies.* Harvard University Press, Cambridge, MA, 1981.

Albrow, M. *Bureaucracy.* Praeger, New York, 1970.

Ball, H. *Federal Administrative Agencies, Essays on Power and Politics.* Prentice-Hall, Englewood Cliffs, NJ, 1984.

Campbell, C., and Szablowski, G.J. *The Superbureaucrats.* Macmillan, Toronto, 1979.

Carney, T.F. *Bureaucracy in Traditional Society.* Coronado Press, Lawrence, KS, 1971.

Chapman, R.A. *The Higher Civil Service in Britain.* Constable, London, 1970.

Coulborn, R. A comparative study of feudalism. In *Feudalism in History* (R. Coulborn, ed.). Princeton University Press, Princeton, NJ, 1956.

Dogan, M. The political power of the western mandarins. In *The Mandarins of Western Europe: The Political Role of Top Civil Servants* (M. Dogan, ed.). Wiley, New York, 1975.

Eisenstadt, S.N. *The Political Systems of Empires.* Free Press of Glencoe, London, 1963.

Encyclopedia Britannica. Egypt. History: Mohammedan Period. *Encyclopedia Britannica*, Vol. 8, pp. 86–90.

Fainsod, M. *Smolensk Under Soviet Rule.* Vintage, New York, 1963.

Glub, J. *Soldiers of Fortune: The Story of the Mamlukes.* Stein and Day, New York, 1973.

Kracke, E.A. *Civil Service in Early Sung China, 960–1067.* Harvard University Press, Cambridge, MA, 1953.

Lane-Poole, S. *A History of Egypt in the Middle Ages.* Methuen, London, 1901. Republished by Frank Cass, London, 1968.

Linz, J. Totalitarian and authoritarian regimes. In *Handbook of Political Science* (F.I. Greenstein and N.W. Polsby, eds.), Vol. 3. Addison-Wesley, 1975:175–411.

Parry, J.H. *The Sale of Public Office in the Spanish Indies Under the Hapsburgs.* Ibero-American 37, University of California Press, Berkeley, 1953.

Peters, B.G. *The Politics of Bureaucracy: A Comparative Perspective.* Longman, New York, 1978.

Pfiffner, J.P. Political appointees and career executives. *Public Administration Review 47*:57–65 (1987).

Reischauer, E.O. Japanese feudalism. In *Feudalism in History* (R. Coulborn, ed.). Princeton University Press, Princeton, NJ, 1956, pp. 26–48.

Riggs, F.W. *Administration in Developing Countries: The Theory of Prismatic Society.* Houghton Mifflin, Boston, 1964.

Riggs, F.W. *Thailand: The Modernization of a Bureaucratic Polity.* East-West Center Press, Honolulu, 1966.

Riggs, F.W. The structures of government and administration reform. In *Political and Administrative Development* (R. Braibanti, ed.). Duke University Press, Durham, NC, 1969:220–324.

Riggs, F.W. Shifting meanings of the term "bureaucracy." *International Social Science Journal 32*:563–584 (1979).

Riggs, F.W. Cabinet ministers and coup groups. *International Political Science Review 2*:159–188 (1981).

Riggs, F.W. Bureaucratic power and administrative change. *Administrative Change* (Jaipur) *9*(2):105–158 (1985).

Riggs, F.W. Bureaucratic politics in the US: benchmarks for comparison. *Governance 1*(4):343–379 (1988a).

Riggs, F.W. The interdependence of politics and administration. *Philippine Journal of Public Administration 31*(4):418–438 (1988b).

Riggs, F.W. Survival of presidentialism in America. *International Political Science Review 9*(4):247–278 (1988c).

Rosenbloom, D. Public administrators and the judiciary. *Public Administration Review 47*(1):75–83 (1987).

Swart, K.W. *Sale of Offices in the Seventeenth Century.* Nijhoff's-Gravenhage, Netherlands, 1949.

Teng, S.-Y. Chinese influence on the Western examination system. *Harvard Journal of Asiatic Studies 7*:267–312 (1943).

Van Riper, P.P. *History of the United States Civil Service.* Row, Peterson, Evanston, IL, 1984.

Waldo, D. A theory of public administration means in our time a theory of politics also. Lecture at annual meeting of the American Political Science Association, Chicago, 1987.

Weber, M. *From Max Weber: Essays in Sociology* (trans. H.H. Gerth and C.W. Mills). Oxford University Press, New York, 1946:206.

White, L.D. *The Federalists: A Study in Administrative History, 1789–1801.* Free Press, New York, 1948.

White, L.D. *The Jacksonians: A Study in Administrative History, 1829–1861.* Macmillan, New York, 1954.

58

The Strategic Environment of Public Managers in Developing Countries

John D. Montgomery   *John F. Kennedy School of Government, Harvard University, Cambridge, Massachusestts*

I. INTRODUCTION

Managers concerned with public purposes must deal with problems *external* to their organization as well as more obvious *internal* issues like motivating employees, monitoring a performance, and pursuing efficiency through the prudent allocation of resources. Indeed, they need the support, or at least the neutrality, of a whole network of outsiders to achieve their major internal goals. That is their external "strategic environment"; it may be especially important in preindustrial countries, where, in the long run, development policies depend for their success on the behavior of the public, and not just that of a particular government agency or a few corporate actors.

For purposes of this discussion, the "external environment" will be defined to include (1) relationships with political leaders, both national and local; (2) negotiations and transactions with other administrative units whose collaboration is desired for programmatic reasons; and (3) links to the general public or to special publics and informal groups that are affected by the programs being administered. Dealing with these elements in the external environment is considered a "strategic" function of management because it requires long-term continuities of purpose and relationships, and because it involves discretionary actions that may not be viewed as a formal part of an organization's mission.

This chapter will describe these three major aspects of the strategic environment. In doing so, it will draw on the actual experience of government officials in 37 countries in Africa, Asia, Europe, and the Americans in dealing with those external actors.[1] These managers include both administrators in central agencies and rural development project officers.[2]

The data on which this analysis draws consist of 4534 events that were reported by managers who were asked to describe the most recent incidents in their own direct experience or observation that constituted "effective" or "ineffective" management. The incidents themselves are random in the sense that they were presented as the "most recent" or "next most recent" events of their type rather than having been singled out as especially important or dramatic incidents.[3] They thus constitute a data base of typical experiences rather than flowing from heuristic models of behavior. This base was gathered over a period of about a decade, incorporating experiences in Asia and Africa as well as a small comparative sample from North America and Europe.[4] The events come from respondents at all levels of career management, from public, parastatal, and private institutions, and managers working in central as well as rural assignments.[5] Except where the findings vary according to these categories, the events are treated as a group, without differentiation among managerial levels or types of organizations.

The experiences permit us to classify behavior in all three categories of strategic management, including political, administrative, and public relations.

II. POLITICAL ENVIRONMENT

Democratic theory posits that bureaucrats are to be controlled by elected politicians, including legislators and executives. Both branches of government are expected to participate in providing policy guidance and, along with the judiciary, in establishing procedural and substantive safeguards that are supposed to protect the public against arbitrary behavior on the part of administrators, professional politicians are expected to mediate both substantive and procedural controls established in administrative organizations. They exercise substantive controls by enacting and proclaiming policies. And they are also said to influence procedures both directly and by permitting the public to participate in setting or criticizing them. They provide linkages to interest groups that impress their demands upon the administrative system; they take an active role in defining the public interest that managers are expected to respect and serve; and they oversee the procedures governments set up to insure the accountability of public servants (Gruber 1987:17–24). In mature polities, public managers may also be expected to control themselves through the ethics of their profession (Friedrich 1940:6), but the politician is also on hand to ensure that these ethical restraints function effectively.

How well does this model of the political environment describe conditions in developing countries? If these controls significantly affect bureaucratic behavior, that fact should be observed in the managers' experience with political figures. And if policy trickles down from politicians to public managers, there should be frequent interactions between the two groups at the top, and a flow of information and guidance toward the bottom.

This model of behavior applies to developing countries in at least one respect: The traditional line of demarcation between "political" and "administrative" officials is still observed in newly independent countries. Most of them have succeeded in maintaining the neutrality of the civil service, and public managers do see their careers as distinct from those of politicians (Montgomery 1986). But the behavioral part of the model does not fit reality very well in those countries. The intertwining of these two sets of careers does not necessarily affirm the "control" thesis described above, though the transactions between the two are strong and significant features of the strategic environment of public management.

Nor does the relationship conform to an alternative model, that of spoils and patronage. The work of the two groups is distinct enough to challenge the frequent condemnation of the civil service in developing countries as hopelessly "politicized" (Hyden 1983). Indeed, the interactions between the two are relatively infrequent in this sample of experience. As in the case of democratic polities, it is more appropriate to treat the political environment in which these managers work as one that calls for pragmatic, functional responses and initiatives than of control, and it is one of practical exchanges rather than political patronage. Nor do these relationships seem to take place predominantly at top levels or indeed to involve major policies at all.

There were only 210 incidents in this entire sample in which managerial events involved a relationship with politicians. Three times as many of these reports came from managers working in rural areas as from those located in central ministries. Thus most of the incidents involved local, rather than national, politicians. Rural managers, of course, did not have some interactions with national politicians (24 incidents), but they had five times as much to do with local political leaders. These interactions dealt more with problems of internal management than with major project goals. Although many instances of the former had negative consequences, politicians were also able to contribute to developmental objectives in a surprisingly high number of cases. These relationships sometimes appeared as "interference" with internal management, but they contributed to managerial objectives as well. Both sets of circumstances will be considered more fully as the incidents themselves are presented.

A. Effects on Internal Management

The most frequent characteristic of politician-manager relationships came in the form of political "interference" with internal procedural activities, that is, with questions of staffing, discipline, and internal regulations. This result was even more striking among the *national* managers we studied in Africa (17 of the 42 "political environment" incidents from that group concerned internal administrative matters) than among the *rural development* managers, most of whom came from Asia (37 of their corresponding 156 incidents).

When *national* politicians were mentioned in these incidents, it was usually to set hours or conditions of work, to protect favorite employees from disciplinary action, to influence personnel assignment, or to insist on preferential treatment for their protegés. Here are some examples of such events, in which managers had transactions with politicians.

> My organization was losing money because we had to employ too many unproductive workers. The minister looked only at the political fallout and did not realize that these organizations could collapse from overstaffing.

> When our association elected some members of the opposition party to the managing committee, we ran into trouble.

The agenda for *local* politicians who became involved in project operations was different: they wanted to participate in contract negotiations, influence a siting decision, emplace a local loyalist in a project office, or see to it that farmer organizations were properly linked to their political ambitions.

> I wanted to have the area surveyed and the construction design approved before we started an irrigation project, but the politicians ordered it constructed right away so they could claim credit for it.

> A conflict broke out between an MP and the area administrator. I called a meeting to work out an agreement that permitted the two to coexist without wrecking my project.

Most of the incidents that involved internal operations had negative consequences for the organization's objectives.

B. Contributions to Project Goals

Not all the omens are bad when political negotiations enter into the life of the manager, however: there were also events that revealed positive contributions from politicians, especially from local figures. There were 43 cases in which politicians used their influence to create new opportunities for the beneficiaries of a project, or where some obstacles were removed through their intervention. But these instances rarely involved top-down policy guidance. Rather, they involved lateral negotiations. Local politicians tended to be more helpful than national ones. In 32 cases, local political leaders were reported as having contributed to the rural development goals associated with a project, and only three such cases involved national politicians. Among managers working in central ministries, only four cases re presented contributions that politicians made to administer goals. These are some of the positive influences described in the events gathered from rural development managers:

> Politicians helped us secure support and voluntary labor from their constituencies in connection with the Mahveli project.

> It took the President himself to bring about a resolution of a problem posed by legal resistance to the release of lands for a resettlement project which had been held up for 10 years after the settlers had already planted the coconut trees on which their livelihood would depend.

> Village leaders were trying to hold up implementation of a cooperative project, but the members were able to get political support than enabled them to continue.

When the politicians did have a positive effect, it was because of their ability to increase the opportunities for local self-improvement that the development projects were seeking to bring about.

There were also, of course, contrary effects on project goals, but they were fewer in number. In 30 instances, political leaders—primarily (26 cases) at the local level)—detracted from project efficiency or denied an opportunity the project's beneficiaries might otherwise have enjoyed. Typical examples of these situations are:

> An MP came along and told our people not to make the 25% contribution they were expected to offer for the construction of shallow wells, on the ground that people in a neighboring area were getting their water free from another agency.

> We were trying to organize a youth complex for unemployed people, but the party required that we confine membership to their own followers. Since very few of them were unemployed, we were unable to reach our goal.

Only where politicians influenced the opportunity-generating capacity of a project did these relationships have a positive effect. In the managers' overall experience with politicians, there were more negative cases than positive ones. It seems only fair to add, however, that the positive instances were often more important than the negative ones, many of which, indeed, will seem trivial to most readers. For example, there were 38 occasions on which politicians requested favors for themselves or their followers, and 28 other instances when the politician's actions produced confusion on the part of the staff and thus interfered with project operations. What effect these intrusions had on the eventual outcomes of the projects was probably insignificant, especially in the context of the total influence of local political leaders. At the national level, the politician's role seemed intentionally neutral. Occasions consisted largely of cases where politicians reviewed administrative operations or tried to change priorities. Such consequences occurred in only 16 cases (see Table 1 for details).

The balance between "positive" and "negative" influences of politicians in the managers' perception of their relationships can be inferred from the fact that 191 of the cases were classified by the respondents themselves as representing an ineffective performance on their part, and only

Table 1 Incidents Defining the "Political" Environment

Nature of incident	SADCC sample	IRD sample	Other data	Total
Internal operations	17	37	1	55
Contribution to goals	4	35	4	43
Detraction from goal	0	26	4	30
Requests for favors	10	28	0	38
Source of oconfusion	4	22	2	28
Changes in priorities	7	8	1	16
Total	42	156	12	210

19 as "effective" management. Of the "negative" influences, the largest number (53) came from internal interferences, followed by requests for favors (35), and activities that seemed to reduce the opportunities the projects were intended to provide.

III. ADMINISTRATIVE ENVIRONMENT

Organizational loyalty is sometimes thought of as a kind of bureaucratic deformity because it tends to place the immediate mission ahead of the public welfare. Administrators afflicted with that syndrome are blamed for becoming so attached to institutional obligations that they are unwilling to subordinate their short-term goals to the common purposes, especially if they are expected to cooperate with other agencies. Bureaucrats in this condition are described as being at war with each other almost every time their organizations come into contact; there are celebrated cases in which collaboration among different agencies, even when obviously in the national interest, failed because of an apparent conflict with the organizations' interests (Wohlstetter 1962).

Once again, the model fits reality imperfectly. This affliction was fairly rare in the managerial experiences observed in this study. The sample included 254 incidents involving managers' relations with other administrative organizations. Obviously, managers deal with other managers much more than they do with politicians. What is less obvious is the nature of these relationships: most of them concerned managers' expectations of performance on the part of other agencies, and, lamentably, most of these expectations were disappointed. A second category of relationships reveals problems of overlapping jurisdictions that inhibited the clarity of organizational missions. Third came the hierarchical relationships with other units within their own institution, which challenged their discretion in dealing with immediate problems. Finally there were problems of communications, the transmission of information necessary for them to accomplish their objectives. In each category, examples of successful and ineffective managerial performance occurred. But there is no Hobbesian war of each against all. Ineffectiveness has to be explained in other ways.

A. Expected Collaboration with Other Agencies

Although anticipated cooperation from other agencies was a major source of disappointment to operating managers, there were exceptions, and something can be learned from them. The coordinated operations coded in this sample produced 71 success stories, and 65 failures. Coordination is difficult but possible.

In programs in which more than one agency was assigned functions that were mutually reinforcing, or where cooperation was developed out of necessity, managers often benefited from the presence of other agencies in their domain of responsibility. For example, in establishing farmers' cooperatives where insurance guarantees were required, several different organizations would have to collaborate in program design and implementation, and reports of their efforts were usually positive. And projects involving water, forestry, and agriculture inputs turned out to fulfill expectations about as often as they disappointed them; in addition, there were plenty of instances in which seeds and other inputs were delivered satisfactorily in integrated rural development schemes, or where agencies involved in introducing large-scale construction projects were able to cooperate in getting data and working out designs. A major impetus to collaboration was the crisis situation: an emergency of any kind seemed to stimulate cooperative behavior among independent agencies jointly responsible for development operations.

The disappointments arose when routine operations were left to proceed along sectoral lines without any coordinating mechanisms being set in place, or when international donors dropped out or changed roles.

Some of the failures may prove instructive to project designers: when different agencies were expected to share the operating costs of integrated operations, public-sector managers were rarely able to do so effectively. In contrast, managers from private companies or parastatal organizations, spurred on by economic discipline, usually worked out an appropriate form of cost-sharing.

Another contrast appears when projects involving construction or production (the three incidents in this category were all successful) are compared with situations requiring the joint use of existing resources (only three cases appeared, and all resulted in disappointment). Perhaps managers can cooperate more effectively in creating public goods than in sharing them.

B.   Overlapping Jurisdictions

The next most important issue appeared in 49 cases: overlapping or confused jurisdictions. Only 10 were resolved successfully. Most of the incidents in this category dealt with uncertainties of mission and with conflicts caused by organizational rivalries or inadequate program design.

Confused mission assignments occurred in 22 cases, of which 17 had to be coded as having unsuccessful outcomes. Local experts in a rice production scheme, for example, were unable to function on the basis of the kinds of directions the managers received from project headquarters; in another case, ministries assigned to cooperate a project could not distinguish among their roles. In only five of the instances in which such confusion occurred was the manager able to resolve disputes between two agencies, or to set up a procedure whereby the participating organizations were able to find ways of working together.

Other cases of confused jurisdictions occurred when managers were required to report to two or more different supervising units. There were six such instances, some of which involved decentralized offices of an organization whose directives conflicted with those coming from the same central headquarters. In one situation, a coordinator intervened in the chain of command to give directions to a subordinate of the manager who was in charge of the project. In two similar cases, international donors took it upon themselves to give instructions to line officers working for a government agency on a project receiving foreign aid.

Attempts to deal with these problems by reorganizing the participating units succeeded in one case, which involved an effort to coordinate science policy by consolidating independent agencies and reassigning their functions and responsibilities; however, in seven other instances, reorganization only complicated the work of subordinate managers, at least in the short run. Most of the unsuccessful instances generated from this study involved attempts to merge family planning and health activities, which apparently exacerbated professional rivalries and confused priorities among field offices.

C.   Hierarchical Relationships

Relationships with higher levels within the same organization were involved in 31 cases, of which about half (16) represented situations in which the relationships within the hierarchy affected managerial operations positively or negatively. Four categories of situations appeared in these cases: those in which the higher levels were placed in a position where they were expected to support the subordinate units, or where they neglected to do so; those involving supervision and span of control; cases where policy clarity and direction were involved; and those in which personal relationships were the key to the outcome.

Support from higher levels often occurred when superiors in central offices were able to confirm a position taken by subordinate managers in dealing with other organizations (five cases), but there were also disappointed expectations, most of which involved failure to deliver promised resources (four cases). One ambiguous outcome was coded positively when the manager was able to obtain the needed resources from local authorities after his own agency let him down.

In every case where problems of supervision appeared, they seemed to be the result of overworked staff who were unable to monitor field activities adequately for want of time. There were three such cases, but it is noteworthy that in four others, the solution was resolved by a reorganization or by delegation of authority.

Personal relationships speeded up action in one case, and were responsible for timid and unsatisfactory career decisions in another.

D.   Communications Problems

Since communications across administrative boundaries often lie at the heart of these relationships, we coded separately the situations in which information about policies or mutual problems was referred to as having been exchanged or withheld. We found 31 such cases, of which only three could be regarded as positive. In all of these cases, communications were an important part of the problem. It appears to be almost a universal problem: only among American public managers could communications be rated satisfactory; elsewhere, and for African managers in particular, the only times communication among different agencies was noted at all, the outcomes were unfavorable.[6]

This finding must be regarded cautiously: use of data of this type for such purposes may be of limited generalizability, since we could not include instances in which information was taken for granted, that is, where managers got just the right amount of it. Nor was it possible to tell when they got too much of it to be able to function effectively. Both conditions would be observable realities, but to explore them adequately would require additional data gathering.

But what we were able to learn about communications problems from these incidents suggests some tentative hypotheses at least about the areas in which difficulties seemed to occur. The four areas in which we coded the 31 cases were problems of mutuality and multidirectional flow of information; the completeness and accuracy of information needed for managerial operations; the timeliness of its delivery; and the form in which it was delivered.

Failure to notify all parties concerned with a given activity occurred in 10 cases; in only two was a manager able to take action because he had been given information he was not expecting. In both of these situations the results were positive, and in all of those in which an affected party was omitted from the line of communications, the outcome was unfavorable. Ignorance does not promise bliss among managers.

Incompleteness in communications occurs often enough to suggest the need to review the contents as well as the procedures followed in management information systems. There were seven situations in which information was inaccurate or deficient in ways that affected the outcome of a managerial function, including one in which a budget was inaccurately prepared as a result, and one in which international negotiations were hampered by a manager who had failed to get enough information about the subject of an aid proposal. In three cases, however, good information averted unfortunate consequences, including one situation in which the manager set up a new communications procedure in order to improve knowledge inputs he though others needed.

Timeliness was the issue in seven more cases, of which six were coded as ineffective managerial behavior because the information required for a certain action did not arrive when the decision had to be made. In only one situation was there a positive outcome: foreseeing a potential cost if things went as planned, one manager interceded in an ongoing situation and supplied information that averted the problem.

Good or bad form in communications was less frequently observed than might be expected from the amount of attention devoted to the subject in the management literature and in training programs: there were only two such cases, one of which was positive. A manager perceived that a serious altercation would follow if a certain communication went forward, and rephrased the document in such a way as to defuse the situation. The negative case was one in which a communication took place by phone with no written confirmation, as a result of which no action was taken.

E. Implications for Design

Although relationships among administrators as reported in these incidents usually had unfavorable consequences, the exceptions show the extent to which managers an gain by engaging in constructive negotiations with each other.

The cases now at hand could be desegregated further to show the conditions associated with success or failure. For example, managers of field projects resolved problems of overlapping jurisdiction themselves in more than half the cases where they arose; private-sector managers seemed better off than their counterparts in the public sector, having encountered cooperation from other actors in more than half the cases in which they expected it; and in spite of the normal center-field distrust that is said to prevail in rural development projects, when it came to a crunch, higher levels supported their operating managers in most of the cases in which other agencies were involved. It may come as no surprise to note that center-field support was especially noticeable among American managers, suggesting the solidarity that can be developed in stable line organizations.

The worst performance in resolving interorganizational relationships was at the national level in the SADCC data. Rural development managers in developed countries were much more successful than these in dealing with these issues (see Table 2).

One of the most common problems of interorganizational relationships is overlapping jurisdiction. Such conflicts were much more serious in the field than in central offices. Resolution of those problems depended more on local initiatives among the manager themselves than on support from political leaders or from higher administrative authority. Once again, issues of lateral cooperation are especially serious in the less developed countries, but they are dealt with more effectively at rural than national levels.

Communications problems like those described in the previous section (that is, cases that describe a need for information about policy issues) are more serious at central than at field levels, perhaps because rural development managers expect to be on their own. These aspects of interorganizational relations can be relieved by a good communications environment. American public managers enjoy a more satisfactory situation than do their private-sector counterparts, and they are also better off in this respect than their colleagues in other countries, whether the issue is delivering and receiving information or providing support where administrative relationships become tense (see Table 2).

Table 2 Incidents Defining the "Administrative" Environment

Nature of incident	SADCC sample		IRD sample		Other data		Total
	Pos.	Neg.	Pos.	Neg.	Pos.	Neg.	
Expected cooperation	6	10	42	39	23	16	136
Overlapping jurisdiction	6	10	4	26	0	3	49
Higher-level support	2	2	8	8	7	5	32
Communications	0	11	0	0	3	23	37
Total	14	33	54	73	33	47	254

IV. PUBLIC ENVIRONMENT

Prevailing models drawn from Europe and the United States suggest that bureaucrats at the bottom of the hierarchy tend to have more discretion in dealing with the public than those at the upper levels. This discretion arises from both their more numerous interactions with it (Aberbach et al. 1981:210) and the absence of doctrine of instructions for dealing with the public at large (Wilson 1968; Lipsky 1980). Data from Africa and Asia support both findings.

It is also argued that upper-level managers interact more frequently with policymakers than do those at the bottom of the hierarchy, especially in regimes (such as Britain, the Netherlands, and Sweden) where bureaucrats and politicians share a mutual responsibility for national policy (Aberbach et al. 1981:236–237). In regimes such as the United States, Germany, and Italy, where the responsibility is divided, managers have more contact with the interest-articulating sectors of the polity.

This finding is only indirectly supported by evidence of the public environment as encountered in Asia and Africa. The greater frequency of public contact at lower levels of the bureaucracy in developing countries (i.e., rural offices) is inversely related to the importance of those relationships for policymaking.

The general public is not a major natural constituency of most public managers in this sample of experience. The data show that their work seldom brings them into direct contact. it is the "special publics"—the organized groups of clients or users—that demand most of the attention of desk-born bureaucrats, especially those engaged in rural operations. As already suggested, the managerial environment includes a hefty dose of relationships with political leaders, especially in rural posts, and it is apparently through them that managers deal with the public.

This finding is suggested by evidence of two kinds: the frequency with which managers identify relationships with the public, and the rather trivial nature of the substantive issues that arise when such relations do occur.

Of the 116 incidents in our sample that show a relationship between managers and the public, only 36 could be described as referring to the general public. Both centrally located managers (12 incidents) and field officials (24 incidents) have such relationships, and the overall outcomes are positive (19) just about as often as they are negative (17).

It would also appear that officials in central ministries have fewer of these "public relations" problems than project managers working in rural areas, and from the incidents themselves it is obvious that such problems are not perceived as being especially serious there. There are frequent situations in which the rural project manager has to provide instruction to the public (in matters such as family planning, nutritional guidance, and community action), or in which managers are responding to individual complaints or, in a few cases, trying to enlist public support for a policy they are trying to implement. Typical incidents read like this:

> A man who looked very poor asked a colleague of mine for help. Not only did she not help him, but also shouted at him saying that he could go anywhere he wanted and that she was not afraid of him.

> My community services officer organized the closure of a squatters camp at the instance of a community group. He did so without provoking a disturbance from the men who used the facility.

> A group of miscreants were disturbing the deep tubewell scheme. The IRDP officials called a meeting which the village Youth Welfare society attended, and they voluntarily took on the task of protecting the crop at night.

Much more of the time and attention of public managers was taken up by "special publics," which they were expected to organize into user groups (nine incidents). In cases where they were already organized, they were expected to deal with them as part of their routine responsibilities (71 incidents). In the overwhelming number of cases, experiences with special publics occurred in the work of rural development managers, with only eight such incidents being reported by central officials.

But the incidents themselves, though not policy related, were sometimes quite important to project success. Some organizing tasks called for unusual degrees of leadership. There were frequent reports of efforts to organize village youth, and as many more describing conflicts among the new organizations, or between them and local administrative bodies with which their functions seemed to overlap. Nearly all (seven) of the relatively few cases in which managers were called upon to organize special publics were described in a positive context.

Similarly, managerial experiences in dealing with existing public organizations were more often positive than not (36 to 17). Disappointments included situations in which government bodies failed to provide the support the managers had promised or were unable to sustain activities they had inaugurated. One particularly painful incident involved both situations:

> Upon completion of the five year project, the state government wanted the Social Welfare group to continue implementing it. But it did not release funds in time to retain the employees required, and nobody was prepared to take over because there was no machinery at the district level. In the end, though, the work was done by unofficial volunteers in spite of the inconvenience of having none of the required transport.

There are several other cases in which volunteers were able to sustain an operation that was deemed valuable to local citizens, and in at least one instance they were able to carry out duties for which the government was unable to provide qualified staff:

> In my Thana the cooperative members were trained to vaccinate the livestock and they were able to vaccinate a large part of the cattle population: a function that would have been impossible for just our one livestock officer to perform.

Of special interest is the fact that voluntary organizations, especially those with international connections, were useful in all cases where they were encountered, even though (or perhaps because) they would occasionally work outside the rules and regulations that were supposed to prevail in local operations. There were 18 such incidents, all occurring in the rural sector, and all coded as positive. Voluntary organizations created by religious groups, or by groups of local employers or business men, were welcome additions to the resources available to rural development managers.

In sum, the strategic environment of local managers includes a much greater prevalence of public relations activities, in an operational sense, than that of officials working out of central ministries and agencies. But the general public is not a major factor in their official lives at either level, apart from dealing with complaints and isolated requests. Special publics, like farmers' organizations, youth groups, and charitable volunteer agencies, constitute an important part of the constituency of rural development administrators (see Table 3).

V. CONCLUSION: PROFILES OF THE STRATEGIC ENVIRONMENT

The extent to which career managers, both national and local, are shown here to concern themselves with the external environment may be a surprise to many readers. In particular, evidence suggests that the greatest exposure these managers have occurs among those who are assigned to duty at the village level. Of the 1200 events reported by managers of rural development projects,

Table 3   Incidents Defining the "Public" Environment

Nature of incident	Total	IRD	SADCC	Positive	Negative
Organizing special publics	9	6	3	7	9
Dealing with Special publics	53	48	5	36	17
General public relations	36	12	14	19	17
Voluntary organizations	18	18	0	18	0
Total	116	84	22	80	43

we were able to code 873 references to an administrative, political, or public relations issue.[7] In contrast, of the 2500 events in the sample of national-level managers we found only 112 such references.

This decline in attention to the external environment as managers are promoted to positions in the capital is reversed after managers reach the very top of the organizational apex. A study of the diaries of permanent secretaries in Southern Africa showed that of the 482 activities reported in their weekly summaries, 36% involved functions that brought them into some relationship with outside groups. In a still larger sample of managers who occupied positions as bureau and division chiefs, there were 1171 entries, of which 40% showed similar preoccupations (Montgomery 1986:220). Closer examination of these entries helped explain why: the largest single category of such events involved some kind of international relationship, and next in line was negotiating with other groups for the purpose of coordinating their activities—both functions being almost the exclusive prerogative of managers at the top of the system.

Much of our existing expertise about management derives from the intensive study of the managerial behavior that are associated with internal affairs like task performance, both in connection with routine, repetitive chores and in dealing with crises. Similarly, much of our knowledge of the strategic environment has come from a few careful case studies of decision making in small groups. Neither of these approaches provides the basis for mapping the external environment as a whole. This preliminary study, although based on incidents gathered for training purposes, gives a useful perspective on the proportion and importance of external activities.[8] The data permit us to suggest how the external environment of management could be mapped in any given country on the basis of current experience.

If the sets of data used in this study were to be aggregated, the gross profile of the strategic environment of management in these developing countries of Africa and Asia would look something like this:

I.   Relationships with political leaders (210 incidents)
    A.   Effects on internal management (55)
    B.   Effects on project goals (73)
    C.   Requests for favors (38)
    D.   Sources of confusion (28)
    E.   Changes in priorities (16)
II. Transactions with other administrative units (254)
    A.   Collaboration (136)
    B.   Overlapping jurisdiction (49)
    C.   Hierarchical inks (32)
    D.   Systems communications (37)

The practical value of such knowledge, assuming that it can be developed more fully by more extensive and more directed data-gathering exercises,[9] would come from its potential influence on managerial performance through improved training procedures and better organizational designs.

Some of the training implications are already obvious. That the external environment has strategic significance for public managers is demonstrated both by the frequency of their interactions with other actors and by the somewhat unexpected nature of those interactions. It does not deserve the neglect it receives in training programs, and what training there is tends to miss the practical needs of managers.

The politician's role is encountered not so much in the abstract exercise of democratic controls as in the temptation to participate for personal reasons in organizational decisions and activities, a condition for which managers should be prepared before their on-the-job training starts. At the same time, the potential of these relationships for the accomplishment of project goals is almost certainly overlooked in the conventional training of public managers especially that scheduled at the beginning of their careers. And while it may be obvious that managers should be "sensitive" to public wants and attitudes, a fact that is also amply demonstrated in these incidents, those engaged in developing training programs need to consider how they can make use of indigenous experience to enhance such sensitivity in the classroom. Finally, and less obviously, it is a fact that managers at the higher levels of an organization are likely to be involved in negotiations with interest groups and "special publics" rather than with the public at large, an aspect of strategic management that is ignored in most inservice training efforts.

Career development in developing countries needs to take account of these findings about the external environment. Many newly independent countries follow the colonial pattern, which means starting the careers of their newest civil service recruits at the village level, by assigning them to either rural development or general ("district") administrative duties, then promoting them to the center. Such career lines need to take into account of the S-curve that characterizes the course of public relations at different levels of an organization. The preliminary findings presented here suggest that it is important for managers *at the very beginning* of their careers to prepare themselves to deal with the public, including organized subgroups of it, and especially in situations where their work calls for them to influence local communities or participating citizen groups. In contrast, it is important for managers at higher levels to gain skills in dealing with their administrative counterparts in other organizations and at higher levels in their own institutions.

Project designers should also take note of the evidence provided here that getting too many parallel organizations in the loop of activities is a recipe for trouble in the field. Interorganizational issues present some of the most important problems managers face in working out of remote offices. Shared responsibilities among agencies need to be made part of organizational design rather than being left to the ingenuity of practicing managers. Although the academic literature has tended to be skeptical of the recent fad calling for the integration of regional rural development services, the experiences reported here suggest that the alternative is worse. Integration is clearly a difficult art form, but failure to provide coordinating mechanisms among interdependent services calls for the exercise of skills that are even more difficult to acquire (Ruttan 1984; Honadle and Van Sant 1985; Cohen 1987).

It is not to be expected that all managers will confront the relationships described here in the same proportion everywhere, irrespective of the country or the sector of activity in which they are working. But that fact should only encourage further applications of this approach, it should be possible to construct profiles of the external strategic environment in any situation, once data like those generated in this analysis become available. The proportion of problems arising out of transactions with politicians, administrators, or the public will certainly be different from one situation to another, but the consistency that is now known to characterize the patterns of behavior among African managers (Montgomery 1987) suggests that prototypes of managerial situations can provide useful guidance to those concerned with improving managerial performance.

In addition to these practical considerations, one or two recurrent problems in political theory can also be illuminated by examining the nature of the responsibilities public officials exercise in these different contexts. For example, the extent to which regimes differ in their capacity to subject managerial activities to the disciplines of responsible government is largely unknown. Answering such questions will extend our understanding of basic constitutional questions that have fascinated political philosophers since the time of Aristotle. Disaggregating data like the SADCC and IRD studies to permit country comparisons would help establish the differences in control mechanisms that actually guide bureaucratic behavior in different regimes.

Fortunately for those of us who enjoy the unrelenting effort of mankind to understand and control government, resolving such questions one by one will leave enough challenges behind to keep our successors busy for a long time to come.

ACKNOWLEDGMENTS

My research assistant at the Kennedy School of Government at Harvard University, Mr. G. P. Shukla, performed the special coding of data required to prepare this article. I am grateful as well to my colleagues Michael O'Hare and Marc Lindenberg for helpful suggestions on an early draft.

NOTES

1. Nine of these countries were in the southern part of Africa (see note 2); the participating managers there were mostly situated in the capital cities. Eleven Asian countries provided the rural data (most of which came from Bangladesh, India, and Pakistan; the other Asian examples came from managers from various Asian countries who were in training in the subcontinent). The Asian participants were assigned as rural development project mangers. The sample also includes responses from managers in 19 industrialized countries in the Americas and Europe, all of whom were working in large cities.

2. The data base of incidents described in this chapter comes from two sources. The first, described here as the SADCC studies, incorporates about 2500 events gathered as part of a research project sponsored by the Southern Africa Development Coordinating Conference during the summer of 1984. The countries participating in the original study were Angola, Botswana, Lesotho, Malawi, Mozambique, Swaziland, Tanzania, Zambia, and Zimbabwe, to which an American sample and additional data from Britain, France, Germany, and several other countries were added. The tables in this chapter distinguish between the original SADCC data, the IRD (integrated rural development) data described below, and the "other" respondents from industrial countries, which are included in the tables only for the sake of comparison. The procedures and survey instrument used in these countries were identical, and the results reflect differences in managerial environment rather than the instrument used in gathering data. The respondents in these studies were for the most part officials who were working in central ministries and agencies. The second set of data (the IRD study) consists of 1200 events gathered in Asia (largely in the subcontinent), to which were added another 275 events generated in Africa from the same instrument. Since the findings from the two regions are essentially the same, the numbers are not presented separately in this paper. Most of the respondents in this second set were managers of integrated rural

development projects. These two data sets permit us to examine the working environment of both "central" and "rural" managers working in developing countries.

3. The method employed in this study was derived from the "critical incident" procedure, which was developed during World War II in order to determine whether and how training and organizational changes could improve the performance of combat pilots. It has since been employed thousands of times for purposes of studying human performance in different situations, private, professional, military, and civilian. The seminal article on this experience is by John C. Flanagan (1954). For a recent bibliography on the subject, see Grace Fivars (1980). This method should not be confused with survey techniques, which are intended to elicit information about opinions. When such polls are used to generate conclusions characterizing large groups, they have to rely on statistical sampling techniques to prevent distortion. In the critical incident method, it is the most recent experience of the respondents that is to be gathered, so randomness is a by-product of the experience reported, the incidents and not the respondents constitute the universe to be analyzed. In the SADCC study, the respondents were asked by the training authorities of their own governments to participate in the survey. Since the invitations were extended by a central staff agency, the entire cadre of active managers was accessible for assignment. In the IRD study, the survey forms were administered to rural development managers who were already participating in training programs.

4. The total includes 2062 from the SADCC project, 1788 from the integrated rural development project, 587 from managers made available at the Harvard Business School including private and public executives mostly from the United States and Europe, and 97 from U.S. public-sector managers participating in a Harvard University executive training program at the Kennedy School of Government.

5. These subclassifications of respondents were about equal as to hierarchical level, as coded from their administrative titles. Most of the SADCC and IRD data came from the public sector, and most of the American and European data from the private sector. They produced only slight variations in terms of the strategic environment, however, and are therefore presented separately only where the differences are significant.

6. Successful communications may not have been reported in this exercise; however, not all of the preconditions to effective behavior may be noted at all by the managers involved. The contrast mentioned in this paragraph between positive and negative incidents in communications may therefore be overstated.

7. This total should not be added up to generate percentage figures of whole and parts, since in some instances a single event reported several such relationships.

8. The SADCC study was intended to identify training needs of African managers, and to distinguish between skills that were region-wide and thus could be served by regional institutions, as contrasted with those that were nation-specific and would be best provided in-country. The IRD study was designed to contrast the managerial problems of "integrated," as contrasted with "sector-specific," rural development projects.

9. It should be emphasized that these managerial events were gathered for other purposes than to map the strategic environment; the profile drawn here may be taken as a first cut, based on a large number of mini-cases of "effective" and "ineffective" managerial behavior, which were then disaggregated to identify categories of actors. Research directed specifically at questions of political guidance, control mechanisms, and public relations would provide a richer, more detailed harvest of information, though there is no particular reason to expect the resultant findings would be very different in their general configuration.

REFERENCES

Aberbach, J.D., Putnam, R.D., and Rockman, B.A. *Bureaucrats and Politicians in Western Democracies.* Harvard University Press, Cambridge, MA, 1981.

Cohen, J.M. *Integrated Rural Development, The Ethiopian Experience and the Debate.* Scandinavian Institute of African Studies, Uppsala, 1987.

Fivars, G. *The Critical Incident Technique: A Bibliography.* American Institutes for Research, Palo Alto, Calif., 1980.

Flanagan, J.C. The critical incident technique. *Psychological Bulletin, 51*(3):335 (1954).

Friedrich, C.J. Public policy and the nature of administrative responsibility. in *Public Policy 1940* (C.J. Friedrich and E.S. Mason, eds.). Harvard University Press, Cambridge, MA, 1940.

Gruber, J.E. *Controlling Bureaucracies: Dilemmas in Democratic Governance.* University of California Press, Berkeley, 1987.

Honadle, G., and Van Sant, J. *Implementation and Sustainability: Lessons from Integrated Rural Development.* Kumarian Press, West Hartford, CT, 1985.

Hyden, G. *No Shortcuts to Progress: African Development Management in Perspective.* University of California Press, Berkeley, 1983.

Lipsky, M. *Street Level Bureaucracy, Dilemmas of the Individual in Public Services.* Russell Sage Foundation, New York, 1980.

Montgomery, J.D. Life at the apex: the functions of permanent secretaries in nine Southern African countries. *Public Administration and Development* 6(3):211 (1986).

Montgomery, J.D. Probing managerial behavior, image and reality in Southern Africa. *World Development* 15(7):911 (1987).

Ruttan, V.M. Integrated rural development: a historical perspective. *World Development XII*:4 (1984).

Wilson, J.Q. The bureaucracy problem. *Public Interest* 6:4 (1967).

Wilson, J.Q. *Varieties of Police Behavior, The Management of Law and Order in Eight Communities.* Harvard University Press, Cambridge, MA, 1968.

Wohlstetter, R. *Pearl Harbor, Warning and Decision.* Stanford University Press, Stanford, CA, 1962.

59

The Achievement Crisis

Management of the Unforeseen

Joseph W. Eaton   *Graduate School of Public and International Affairs, University of Pittsburgh, Pittsburgh, Pennsylvania*

I.   DOES NOTHING EVER GO JUST RIGHT?

We are all surrounded by alleged experts in making future-oriented decisions—politicians, administrators, business managers, and human service professionals. Many of us rely on managers of mutual funds to invest our money so that in the future, our assets will gain in value and/or earn high dividends. We want our physicians to keep us healthy or to minimize future health hazards. Politicians promise to reduce crime.

Achievement, like a job promotion, is likely to be associated with two types of outcome:

1.   *Foreseen* outcomes, like purchase a bigger home. The family will have more space. Children experience more privacy and luxury. But they also must adjust to living in a new neighborhood, where they no longer live close to those who were their friends.

2.   *Unforeseen* outcomes, which could not be guarded against. They may be positive, in that the children find better friends than in the old neighborhood. But the wife may meet a neighbor with whom she falls in love, leading to a contested divorce over custody of the children. The big new house has to be sold at a loss, to pay the divorce attorneys and court costs.

When scientific achievement are under consideration, such as the discovery of a new therapeutic drug, the Food and Drug Administration requires a lengthy and thorough testing for side effects on animal and human subjects. A new drug will be approved for being dispensed only under medical supervision. This precaution makes it highly likely that its use is restricted to when its therapeutic potential (achievement) is much greater than its negative side effects. But patients with unusual medical conditions or allergies will have negative reactions. Epidemiological studies estimate that in the United States the number exceeds 2 million annually, with in excess of 100, 000 fatalities, (Lazarou et al. 1998).

The process of forecasting is more complex when psychological, social or political achievements are involved. Qualitative or normative considerations affect how the "crystal ball" outcome is interpreted. There often are no agreed upon guidelines of what is an is achievement.

Successes in planned future oriented social actions are always limited. Race relations in the United States were seen as significantly "advanced" when urban schools were ordered to integrate. But in large U.S. cities like Washington and Detroit, public schools are now more segregated than before integration-oriented busing was adopted. Whites and black middle-class families have moved into the suburbs or send their children to private school.

To sum up, planned social interventions are commonplace. They are undertaken in the expectation that the new situation will be more favorable than the status quo. Since no one can learn enough about the multiple variables which affect the future, unforeseen outcomes are inevitable. They tend to be under-reported in the media or people repress them, since they feel guilty about them.

In traditional societies such guilt and fear of future-oriented achievement have given rise to such superstitions as the "evil eye." Amulets are worn against bad luck. Boasting is taboo, at the risk of offending evil spirits who are always believed to be as ready to bring about a more unhappy state of affairs.

In modern societies, a rapidly increasing proportion of the work force is engaged in future oriented planning. Attorneys draw up wills to keep Federal death taxes to a minimum and to prevent siblings suing each other over the distribution of their parental estate. More and more Americans employ financial consultants, accountants, psychologists, physicians, and consult phone "psychics." Daily newspapers and news broadcasts devote much of their space to data an analysis on the basis of which future events are forecasts. "Will the Republicans lose control of Congress in the November 2000 election?" "Will the Social Security Trust Fund run out of cash in 2025?"

II.   ANATOMY OF THE ACHIEVEMENT CRISIS

Achievements like atoms, have positive, negative, and neutral charges. Winning a big lottery ticket is positively valued. Most winners accept as reasonable (neutral) the fact that they have to pay a tax on their winnings. But will the news of the sudden wealth turn members of their family into a target of a kidnap gang?

The analysis of future events is facilitated by a systematic application of seven social psychological variables:

Benefit-loss balance
Halo creation and the deflation process
Multiple roles and their accommodation
Multiple social values and their accommodation
The planning process and available resources
External dimensions
Positive and negative recruitment processes

A.   Benefit-Loss Balance

Disappointments arise in part when differing perceptions are found among the participants in an achievement event. Most common are disputes concerning what would be an equitable distribution of the benefits. It is often difficult for collaborators to agree on a formula for reallocating the additional resources, privileges, and opportunities.

Sacrifice and opportunity costs are inherent in many achievement triumphs. In upwardly mobile poor families, the parents deprive themselves of even modest comforts to save money so they might send at least one of their children to a university. After graduation, how will this child—now an adult—apportion the gains from his new status between himself and the parents?

The latter may never have mastered the English language. The first-generation American is likely to want to buy an expensive home in a prestige suburb, but he will need to consider the alternative of living more modestly for an other decade in order to help younger siblings who now need help to pay for their higher education.

During a period of national liberation struggle, personal priorities such as making money in a business give way to patriotic agitation. While the revolution is in process it is not wise to discuss how the hoped-for gains of success will be apportioned after freedom is won. Factionalism is best to avoid discussing "who will be invited to work in the government" or "who will receive a government contract to furnish important supplies."

When publishing his detailed field study of Polish education, Joseph R. Fiszman referred to the psychic opportunity cost of scholars, dedicated employees, or anyone active in advancing a public cause. They must allocate time and energy that could otherwise be used to advance their personal and family priorities (Fiszman 1972): "To Gale and Sula In compensation for all the time they missed their father and the promises made but rarely kept."

The benefit-loss balance calls attention to an interesting social fact. In an emergency, money, time—and even one's health—are contributed freely to a good cause. There is no thought of meticulous bookkeeping, of who does what to achieve a shared goal. No overtime payments are demanded.

Achievement crises can be minimized by taking note of the "cost benefit" dimension. This strategy was well illustrated by the passage of the G.I. Bill of Rights. After World War I, the soldiers who fought and were injured in the vicious trench warfare of Europe often had reason to become resentful veterans. After discharge, those without employable skills, had to peddle apples in the street or depend on charity of their family or church.

This postvictory crisis was largely avoided after World War II. With more than 15 million Americans in uniform, earning lower than marketplace wages, the Defense Department realized that after victory, these war heroes had no chance to accumulate capital to help them readjust to civilian life. Veterans were given legal entitlements to obtain loans and grants to study, to start a business and to buy a home. All but a small proportion adjusted well to becoming civilians.

At the global planning level, after Hitler attacked the Soviet Union the Allies offered the Communists unconditional support including food, medical supplies, and technology. The overwhelming American economic and military power was not used to exact reasonable agreements about postwar borders. Stalin was not asked to commit his government to withdraw from the Baltic states and Poland after they would be liberated from German occupation by Soviet troops supplied by Western aid. While the war was being waged, such issues were evaded in the interest of the Allied unity against the common enemy. However, the subsequent cold war rift might have been reduced by more advanced planning to prevent Soviet expansion into the territory of previously free East European nations.

B. Halo Creation and the Deflation Process

Unrealistic and often fictitious qualities are attributed to political leaders. The alleged economic genius of Ronald Reagan and the fictitious military qualifications of Abdul Nasser were engineered by extensive media campaigns. Shortcomings were ignored or censored from being noted publicly. Their "superman" image was reinforced by a network of protocol and ceremonials that helped to turn a normal human being into an awesome "Mr. President" or "Comrade Chairman." Even President Franklin D. Roosevelt referred to Stalin, the world's most ruthless mass murderer, as "Uncle Joe," the allegedly wise and heroic leader of Russia's valiant resistance against Nazi Germany.

Politicians are not alone in being the object of halo creation. Nearly all children are viewed as being above average by those who love them. The immigrant parent who manages to help a son go through medical school will even explain a B grade in pathology as a sign of near genius. After all, "our boy never went to an Ivy League school and he had to help out at home." The belief of the family in the exceptional talent of the son contributes to their willingness to help him and his readiness to exert the extra effort to succeed in medical school.

Once the young physician graduates, both he and his parents are likely to face reality. With a mere average school transcript he may have to settle for an internship at a community hospital. He will become an average doctor making a good living, but he will have to correct the charismatic fiction of being a near genius. He will risk being accused of malpractice if he accepts responsibility for medical problems outside his range of training and experience.

The unfrocking of charisma frees its followers to make decisions on their own. Policies which did not work well will be more readily recognized and the corrected. If a corporate chief executive officer is fired, lower-echelon experts are more likely to be able get a hearing of their previously suppressed divergent strategies. Children of strong parents will begin to strike out on their own once they begin to recognize that their parents are not always making decisions that have optimum consequences.

Charisma building and its exposure have become the object of a powerful industry—advertising and public relations. In election campaigns, 30-second television spots focus on the allegedly unusual qualities of the candidate, while her opposition will remind the viewer of her alleged deficits. Advertising succeeded in making many consumers believe that Bayer aspirin is better than the less expensive versions. But because of side effects, hospitals are more inclined to use Tylenol to counteract minor pain symptoms.

The halo inflation dimension is difficult to prevent, except through the strict enforcement of laws to require truth in advertising. Scientific research often is undertaken to differentiate between widespread belief about problem solving and the actual limitations of such recommended solutions. Women and minorities are able to enter occupations which previously were denied to them, but an achievement crisis is waiting in the wings if affirmative-action programs ignore the reality of certain personal limitations in performance, which all professionals must learn to accept.

Halo correction procedures are commonplace. For public figures, much of it is done by investigative reporters. Processed foods in the United States must list their fat, cholesterol, and other content. Physicians need to pass qualifications examinations and be recertified from time to time on the basis of passing technical examinations. Patients with serious medical problems can get a second opinion which is usually reimbursed by their health insurance. When such procedures are absent, as in the case of judges appointed for life or university professors with tenure, incompetence is more difficult to deal with. The incompetent are able continue to exercise authority even when they fail to keep up with the expertise and objectivity which were allegedly present at the time of their appointment.

Habits are useful in enabling people to deal with routine matters efficiently, like getting enough sleep every night. But there are unusual situations, where prudent modifications are functional to deal with unusual situations. Overtime hours will have to be worked to get a job done within a deadline to avoid a contractual penalty for missing a completion deadline.

C. Multiple Roles and Their Accommodation

All human beings go through life performing culturally accepted and expected role models. We are children to our parents, parents to our own offspring, subordinates to managers at work, and a boss to those who subject to our supervision. As members of an army reserve unit, we be drafted with almost no notice to serve in a U.S. military mission, without being able to be with our wife on the 10th wedding anniversary.

As members of a religious group, race (skin color) affinity category, or sex we are subject to normative behavior expectation (social roles). We are debtors, who have a mortgage on our home. It has to be paid each month, even if we lose our job. We have close childhood friends, with whom it would be fun to spend a vacation, but this is also the only time the family can be together for a longer period of time. There are finite limits to how much time and emotional energy we can devote to each of these social roles.

General Eisenhower sported a mistress when commanding the Allied armies in Europe, while his wife in the United States was battling an alcoholic addiction. When the war was over, he had to make a choice. It was Mamie, the mother of his children, who went with him to become president of Columbia University and to serve as his First Lady in the White House.

The demands of competing social roles turn many an achievement situation into a crisis. Married couples work together to build up a family estate to provide for their retirement and the welfare of their children. No books are kept of how many hours each partner devotes to the common cause. But if one or both of them want to end the marriage, sizable family assets end up being transferred by the parsimonious couple who wanted to leave their children with a good estate to the two divorce attorney teams. Their savings are transferred to help the attorneys to send *their* children to a good university.

Role conflicts are built into many occupations. Physicians, attorneys, accountants and other specialists, including plumbers and butlers have to deal with the following types of conflicting expectations:

1.   We want to maximize our earning by getting as much work as we can handle and charging as much as the market will bear. We want to do well for the family.

2.   We want clients have to trust our integrity and believe that no unnecessary services or procedures are being recommended. Our billings rarely can be checked, but they should nevertheless be accurate and without padding.

Priority assigned to multiple and competing roles change after each major achievement. A child who completes her university education will take a job much lower in social status than that of the people whom she may have met when living at home. She will be uncertain how much financial support to expect from her parents. She may meet a wonderful man who is already married. Shall she encourage the breakup of his marriage?

At the international or macro level, the Dr. Robert Oppenheimer controversy dramatized the role conflict issue inherent in public achievement situations. This distinguished physicist was the chief architect of the atom bomb, which probably saved millions of casualties—American, Japanese, and people in the occupied Asian nations like China, from which Japan retreated without a battle.

After Japan's surrender Dr. Oppenheimer's intellect and scientific concern turned to a new challenge: How can the world community live with "the bomb"? His preoccupation with nuclear disarmament options now led to attacks on his "patriotism." He was allowed to retain the role of chairman of the Atomic Energy Commission, but denied a security clearance. Over 40 years would pass before his views were embraced by the U.S. Department of Defense and the Department of State.

His Soviet counterpart experienced an even more serious achievement crisis. Andrei Sakharov was treated as an anti-Soviet pariah once the Soviet Union was enabled by the team of technicians he had organized to build atomic weapons. He and his wife were mistreated by the secret police and exiled from their home until a dramatic reversal of policy by Mikhail Gorbachov in 1987, who freed him from exile and persecution.

Many of these of these achievement-related social role priorities can be anticipated by reviewing how a successful will impact on the multiple roles of those involved in a planned program to change the status quo.

D.   Multiple Social Values and Their Accommodation

Most people are influenced by social values including religious principles, nationalist aspirations, and family expectations. Ideological differences can be played down temporarily during a crisis in the interest of maintaining unity, as in the case of World War II. Then the United States and the Soviet Union fought together against Nazi Germany, Italy, and Japan. But after winning the war, the military achievement was quickly replaced by a bitter "cold war" for supremacy between "Communism" and "free enterprise capitalism."

France, Italy, Turkey, and Israel have parliaments factionalized by multiple parties, each with different ideological and/or religious platforms. They can only be governed by a multiple-party coalition. Policies have to compromised if instability and unrest are to be curbed. The armed forces of Turkey forced the breakup of a government headed by a Muslim fundamentalist Welfare party, when the prime minister began to appoint too many Islamic fundamentalists to key positions in the government.

Social values impact many human decisions. School choice for children—parochial, public, or secular-private—reflects such ideological variations. Religious beliefs affect the acceptance or rejection of birth control devices and the decision of how to deal with an unwanted pregnancy. Conservative politicians tend to advocate that wages should be taxed but earnings from profits be exempt. The upwardly mobile child of an immigrant family often has to confront the conflict of values of two worlds. Shall he marry a woman to match the cultural heritage of the parents? Or shall he marry into a more Americanized majority-group family, where his children will be assimilated to become better integrated in the majority culture? Many religious "conversions" reflect such status considerations.

Most people learn to handle such value-based achievement crises; others are driven to a psychotherapist's couch in an effort to obtain professional help to manage their difficulty in conforming to their multiple normative expectations. A religious conversion may override hedonistic values. Acceptance of Islam by prison inmates is often associated with remarkable changes in behavior. The newfound faith often enables them to give up reliance on addictive drugs and to adopt a highly disciplined life style. But conversion can also take place for pro-forma reasons, like a wife adopting the religion of her husband, without necessarily changing her belief system.

Social value differences always crop up when people work together. The editors of the 900-year-anniversary history volume of the village of Theilheim, Germany, chose to include a list of the owners of all 112 homes in 1850 and those registered as owners in 1988. This comparison enabled to authors to document a tragic event. In 1850, Theilheim had been a center of Jewish life. Almost half of the villagers were Jewish. None of their descendants remained in 1988. In 1942, the remaining 40 German citizens who were Jewish were deported by the Gestapo to extermination camps (Theilheim 1994). Today Theilheim remains what the Nazis called "judenrein." But there are a significant number of villagers who wish this tragedy could have been prevented. It is no longer hidden from their children.

Social value differences can be accommodated in two ways:

1.   *Dominance and suppression* of persons who share values different from those in control. Serbian was the language of instruction in the public schools of the Kosovo province of Yugoslavia, although 90% of the population use Albanian as their mother tongue. Under UN protection, Albanian is now taught. In Saudi Arabia, Sharia laws are imposed although they increasingly conflict with the values of educated Saudis. They believe that men and women should have full equality.

2.   *Tolerance of alternative values.* In Switzerland "ethnic cleansing" atrocities were inhibited by a mutual toleration policy of different ethnic, religious, and language groups. German-, French-, and Italian-speaking areas have been unified since 1848, within a confederation that reserves much legislative, executive, and judicious autonomy to its 22 cantons (states).

When religious wars devastated Europe, the Ottoman Empire had adopted the "**Millet**" toleration system. As early as in the 14th and 15th century, in areas conquered by the Ottoman Turks, Christians, Jews, and well-defined nationalities were granted a high degree of judicial and administrative authority to regulate marriage, divorce, inheritance, and other personal status issues for their members (Gibb and Bowen 1957).

E. The Planning Process and Available Resources

Planning is a process of collecting information about the past and the present to make two types of forecasts:

1. What is likely to happen at a given time in the future—a day, a month, years, or decades—if nothing is done to change the status quo, such as traffic from point A to B?

2. What is likely to happen if a given future-oriented action is taken, such as building a new road or subway?

The capacity to plan to influence the future on the basis of a body of data differentiates the way most people in modern societies live from the more fatalistic outlook of our forebears. In the past, and in much of the third world, future making is seen as an activity reserved to God, luck, or the will of an all-powerful ruler. The ideology of fatalism is widespread, competing with the more activist orientation that it is within the power of human beings to influence what will happen in the foreseeable future.

Future-oriented planning is increasingly being mandated. In the United States it is almost impossible to obtain a building permit, without an approved detailed architectural plan how the building is to be constructed. Businesses looking for venture capital are expected to construct a plan for the use of new capital. Physicians make treatment plans. Researchers formulate a detailed design to guide their use of funds to investigate a problem. Third-world and the socialist nations produce long-range social and economic development plans, most often in five-year intervals.

Planners must always consider the presence of externalities. Industrialization is nearly always associated with environmental pollution. Young villagers migrate to overcrowded cities, where AIDS infections have become endemic, reversing the improvement of life expectancy generated by the improvement in the quality of drinking water.

Planning projects are likely to be activated when elections loom or a new party comes to dominate the government. Between November 1992 through March 1993 after the election of President Clinton, at least seven major documents were commissioned within the federal government to reassess water quality and use issues (Roger 1993). Few were implemented.

Future-oriented planning must deal with the differences in short-term and long-range planning processes. The risk of unanticipated factors is smallest when plans are made for the next day, week, or year. More information about the past and present is available to make forecasts for the future than when plans have to be made for many years or several decades.

In traditional societies, customs enshrined in nostalgic traditions are thought to be the "best" guidelines for the future. This outlook fails to fit the realities of modern life. The centers of ancient cities, like Bankok, Cairo, and Jerusalem, "just grew" without prior town planning. In our modern, automobile-centered world, they are now afflicted with chronic traffic jams and a sewage system with insufficient capacity to drain the increasing volume of waste generated by their inhabitants.

Planning has become an inherent part of modern living, with rapid growth of pertinent information which can be stored and analyzed with the help of computers. But there also is a limit on the volume of data which can be taken into account. The U.S. Bureau of the Budget has to act in weeks or a few months, lest the year for which they are budgeting has begun. Time is a limiting factor. Nevertheless, we have more control over our environment than our parents or grandparents. Imperfections have always been part of the planning process, but because of the ease of generating data, we also know much more about what is *not* working well than our forefathers had to admit to themselves.

F. The Externality Dimension

All plans are affected by what economists call externalities—favorable or unfavorable factors in another system not subject to control of the planners.

World War II freed the United States from a devastating economic depression. It brought women and blacks into skilled jobs from which prejudice and union rules had excluded them. But these gross inequities were not what brought the United States to mobilize 15 million men and women to fight all over the world against the Japanese, the Germans, and the Italians. Wars were not precipitated to right domestic wrongs; wars were the externality which in 1865 led to the Emancipation Declaration and in 1941 to a further reduction of institutional racism and sexism.

The United Nations was established to maintain peace, but disinterest or the veto power of one or more of the five permanent members of its Security Council have prevented forceful and decisive intervention in Yugoslavia, Rwanda, Cambodia, Afghanistan, and other trouble spots. One of the externalities is probably the fact that Russia is reported to be owed in excess $6 billion, which Iraq cannot repay until the economic boycott is lifted.

Some externalities can be estimated in advance and be included in the planning process. We can insure our home against being damaged by an earthquake, but not against destruction by nuclear war. An employee may advance his career by conscientious performance of his job. But he also needs to protect himself against externalities that would terminate his employment, such as new invention or a corporate merger. He needs to maintain professional contacts with alternate employers or acquire additional skills that would enable him to earn a living should his present post be terminated.

The concept **externality** reflects a professional bias among some economists who assert the questionable theory that **most** factors of a complex system—like an economic boom—can be forecast, provided we could command the time and the resources to collect all the pertinent data. This assumption is highly questionable. We lack the knowledge, the time and the capacity to handle all the relevant data, even if they were available. Before going to a restaurant, we can compare locations and prices of a few close enough to reach at suppertime. But we have no way of ascertaining in which restaurant the chief cook is at home sick and therefore unable to insure the restaurant's usual level of quality.

Planners must accept being approximators. We can bias the future by intervening along some dimensions under our partial control, such as allocating money and manpower to achieve a given objective. This is not enough to prophesy, but it reduces the uncertainty of our lives when compared to the realities with which prior generations had to contend with.

G.   Positive and Negative Recruitment Capability

The proportion of well-qualified and highly motivated employees is an important dimension of its capacity to perform its mission. How many executives are backed up by subordinates qualified to replace them? Or is an enterprise short in human talent so that many key posts have to be staffed by inept, corrupt, or disinterested personnel?

Progressive companies, like Microsoft, through an impressive record of positive recruitment, are able to attract many well-qualified employees. Senior officials are offered attractive working conditions and compensation packages, including stock options. The U.S. Peace Corps also has this type of recruitment capability. Applicants are screened for their idealism and technical qualifications. Positions are left vacant if no qualified volunteer is available.

Negative recruitment factors will begin to infect an agency when insecure persons, fearful of competition from more recently trained and more energetic junior employees, are allowed to surround themselves with "yes" people. Their more talented subordinates will look elsewhere to develop their career. Employees whom no competing agency is ready to offer a better job will gradually fill more and more of the upper-echelon vacancies. They tend to be among the less talented in the pertinent labor supply. The organization men, who know how to adjust to the whims of charismatic leaders, rarely have the qualities to succeed them. They tend to lack the sense of autonomy and confidence to make decisions on their own.

Negative recruitment often occurs after an election victory or a revolution. Setting off a car bomb is not suitable preparation for becoming Minister of the Interior. Nor are retired generals necessarily well qualified to be personnel managers of a large corporation, whose employees are not subject to military discipline. In private enterprise, managers must negotiate with the labor union and handle egocentric scientific workers, who are likely to question a management decision which conflicts with their views.

U.S. World War II veterans enjoy a 5% advantage over nonveterans in competitive examinations for civil service jobs. This small preference is not likely to result in negative recruitment. But what if the credit for past national service were to be 25% of the score? Many underqualified veterans would get jobs in place of fully qualified personnel whose scores reflect their actual performance in the examination. Such dysfunctional preferences are quite common in organizations where loyalty to a leader or to an ideology is rated very high, as in religious organizations.

In the federal system, this achievement crisis risk has been addressed by strictly limiting the number of "political" positions. Most federal posts are now governed by civil service regulations. But in some state and local jurisdictions, the "spoils system" is still commonplace. Many a leader elected with a large majority finds himself defeated by being obligated to honor too many political "debts" when staffing his administration.

III. ACHIEVEMENT CRISIS MINIMIZATION

Achievement crises cannot be evaded, but much can be done to minimize their negative impact. Insurance can be purchased against a negative event like theft, fire, or earthquake. Environmental-impact statements are now required by Congress before major construction projects will be authorized. The statements estimate the risks, negative side effects, and costs of dealing with them.

There also are such programs as liability insurance. Successful professionals are prone to being sued for damages because it is known that they have "deep pockets"—enough money. But there is no insurance against social and psychological problems our era. Racial inequities, pervasive poverty among minorities, and high crime rates reflect deeply rooted social-system variables which require more than money to be reduced to more tolerable proportions.

Technical problems are handled more easily. In the U.S. federal government, the Legislative Reorganization Act of 1970 and the Technology Assessment Act of 1972 both stress the need for early identification of possible complications that may result from the enactment of new legislation. More and more impact statements are being asked for. Data are being assembled on budget and on inflation when a new project is proposed (Renfro 1977). The Congressional Budget Office, the General Accounting Office, and the Congressional Research Service of the Library of Congress continue to be called upon by Congress. Their reports may be considered prior to voting on future-oriented programs which do not become ideologically divisive.

The uncertainty aspect is all too often reviewed only by narrowly specialized managers. Lawyers will rightfully call attention to the need to enact a new laws to handle the probable consequences of what is being anticipated. Engineers will demand doubling of the safety margin of skyscraper cross beams. But they all need to extend their planning beyond their own field of expertise. The social-economic system variables reviewed in this article are likely to affect the how any future-oriented plan will work out.

IV. UTOPIA: A MODEL WITHOUT ACHIEVEMENT CRISIS

The achievement crisis model is emotionally hard to live with. It contradicts the optimism that somewhere there is a perfection on the horizon. We all have experience with problem solving. We often realize that there were side effects, but we generally learn to live with them. We accept that some stocks in which we invest decline in value. What is more difficult is to accept the reality that every achievement will expose us to new challenges. Some are welcome but others are not. No one can live to a 100 without some deteriorating wear and tear that reduces the quality of life. There are no permanent "fixes" in the real world.

This "imperfection" theory contradicts the Utopia model espoused by many different social movements. Orthodox Marxists as well as persons with deep religious Jewish, Christian, or other beliefs have their version of paradise, a model of ultimate perfection. In the Marxian version of near paradise, man was viewed to be its creator. A "dictatorship of the proletariat" was seen to be essential to overcome capitalistic exploiters and counterrevolutionaries. This was to be the price of achieving a classless society of free and good people. Oppressive aspects of the government would then wither away. Labor would cease to be a dehumanized commodity. Each person would give service in accordance with his abilities and receive benefits as needed.

More than 80 years have passed since the 1917 Russian Revolution. After more than seven decades, the Soviet Communist Party had to confront the reality in 1988 that the "new Soviet man" was too uncommon to have much of an impact. The system collapsed because of its internal contradictions. Its leadership had lost faith that Marxism is a workable model.

Religious people trust in God. Traditions vary widely on how this supernatural paradise is allegedly operated. The range is from the hedonistic pleasures of the Germanic Valhalla to more spiritual versions avowed by religious Jews and Christians: The dead will be resurrected. Mankind will live in a permanent spiritual grace when God decides the time has come for the appearance of a new savior, the Messiah, Ha-Mashiach.

By contrast, the social science view of reality seems confused and emotionally barren. The idea of inevitable progress has to be dismissed for lack of evidence. The best that can be said about the achievement crisis view of cyclical social change is that it helps to make life interesting. At birth we stand condemned to growing up in a non-Utopian milieu, learning to solve most problems within a range of what people can live with.

In our era of rapidly changing technology and incremental volume of scientific knowledge, Alvin Toffler (1972) calls attention to the "shattering stress and disorientation that we induce in individuals by subjecting them to too much change in too short a time." He coined the concept "future shock" to describe a sickness from which allegedly large numbers already suffer. But these victims of rapid change are a minority compared to those who enjoy the freedom of nontraditional life styles to express personal preferences. Consumers may sometimes feel distressed by "overchoice," but much of the time, choice making in a suburban mall is fun.

Poverty has been close to abolished in the Scandinavian nations and in Holland, Switzerland, Germany, and the Arab oil nations. But none of these societies would claim to have attained a "Utopian" state. The sociological critique of Utopia can be summed up in the following proposition about its instability: ***Utopias are intellectual abstractions which can be temporarily and partially approximated but never realized.*** Planned social change, more realistically conceived, is both an achievement and a crisis-prone activity. Benefits will always be partial. For most people this is good enough, much of the time.

V. THE "NO-PLANNING" OPTION

There is a social version of the Heisenberg law in physics: As the volume of reliable and valid data used in planning a project increases, the time and expense of the planning process also grow. Problem-solving efforts will be excessively delayed unless an optimum path is compromised. "Guesstimates" and less than thorough study of all possible externalities will have to be included in the planning process.

There are limits to crisis prevention efforts. The preparation of forecasts cannot be allowed to become so time-consuming as to prevent or delay the timely initiation of problem solving. In the emergency room of a hospital, guessstimated decision must often be made to proceed with the implementation of a plan well before all feasible details can be checked. Futuristic planning includes the risk of error, contingency, and opportunity cost. The only realistic goal is their minimization and their counteraction at a later stage, when an unanticipated achievement crisis begins to become apparent.

Inaction, in the name of "we still do not have all of the data," has often been used as a tactic for maintaining the status quo. **Not planning for the future** also is a policy. Its consequences need to be compared to alternate models of timely intervention.

In most American presidential campaigns both parties tend to be deliberately vague in spelling out how they would pay for their vision of the future. They avoid spelling out how their new or updated public programs would be paid for without a federal tax increase. This contrived vagueness is an achievement crisis prevention strategy. In politics there is opportunity to make promises. Voters want to believe such fairy tales, but it would become politically risky to discuss the cost in new taxes or in reducing appropriations to popular programs in order to free resources for new ones.

VI. SUMMARY

Insufficient planning is commonplace. Side effects are inherent in any future-oriented program. Some of them can be forecast on the basis of existing knowledge. But in the minds of many, they emerge as seemingly "unanticipated" consequences of purposive social actions (Merton 1930). Econometricians denigrate these realities as "static" with the implication that with added knowledge, more and more of them can be included in mathematical models of future economic developments. Their optimism is questioned widely by psychologists and sociologists, who include the nonrational aspects of both individuals and of the social systems in their frame of reference.

Negatively perceived side effects can, however, be minimized by applying the conceptual scheme of seven socioeconomic aspects of the planning process. This is being well illustrated by the protracted negotiations between Israelis and Palestinians. For both a peace treaty will be an achievement crisis. The more than eighty years of periodic armed struggle to resolve conflicting aspirations through armed struggle has been counterproductive, especially for the Arab world. Compromises on the table are being reviewed by the negotiators in terms of the following projected consequences for the future:

1.   Systematic examination of the balance of costs and sacrifices which can be sustained during the achievement period. It will need to be modified during the postachievement situation. At all times the planning process will need to meet standards of equity of the multiple interest factions among the people who helped bring about the achievement.

2.   In most achievement situations there are persons with leadership responsibilities. They may have charismatic qualities, but in the long run, the halo of their avowed qualifications will be discounted. When this process is too long delayed, the leaders are likely to be allowed to function in the management of situations beyond their capabilities. This contingency is what makes dictatorships such a dangerous mode of governance.

3.   Priorities among the multiple social roles of each participant must be helped to be rearranged after an achievement situation. This often means new patterns of division of labor among the persons who worked in unison to complete a project. The achievement crisis can be minimized to the degree that the relative priority pyramid of multiple personal roles of each participant during the postachievement phase are allowed to be modified to meet new aspirations.

4.   A political climate must be encouraged within which social value differences can be expressed and mediated, especially if they were suppressed during the achievement struggle period. Agreement about common "objectives" tends to be exaggerated during the period of emergency when different persons and groups sacrifice to achieve a common goal. This temporary unity must be allowed to give way to expressions of previously suppressed normative differences.

5.   The achievement crisis is affected by the presence or absence of future-oriented planning processes. The degree of uncertainty can be reduced significantly by planning for a variety of plausible outcomes. But planning is not equivalent to prophecy. In the real world, hardship and reverses, not just victory and achievement, need to be anticipated. Planned objectives sometimes need to be changed in midstream, especially when significant miscalculations were made about the required resources in money, materials, and personnel.

6.   In every plan, externalities can be expected to have an impact beyond the jurisdiction of the administrators. The achievement crisis can be minimized by identifying them and by counteracting their probable impact. This may mean coalition building with interest groups that had originally been ignored.

7.   Planners must avoid the selection of personnel in an organization on the basis of irrelevant criteria, unrelated to the requirements of each position. If these criteria are violated, negative recruitment decisions will erode the capacity of an organization to handle its responsibilities in an optimum fashion.

When achievement crises are anticipated, individuals engaged in planning for their own or other people's future will modify the Utopian expectations that are the substance of which daydreams are built. They will be alert to the reality of problem solving. A degree of uncertainty and risk will always be part of the equation. There are side effects to anything people eat, experience, or think about. Nor is there any social program which abolishes the uncertainty element of the human condition.

REFERENCES

Fiszman, J.R. (1972). *Revolution and Tradition in People's Poland: Education and Socialization.* Princeton, NJ: Princeton University Press.

Gibb, H.A.R., and Bowen, H. (1957). *Islamic Society and the West: A Study of the Impact of Western Civilization on the Near East.* London: Oxford University Press.

Merton, R.K. (1936). Unanticipated consequences of purposive social action. *American Sociological Review, 1,* 894–904.

Lazarou, J., Pomeranz, P.H., and Corey, P.N. (1998). Incidence of adverse drug reactions of hospitalized patients: meta analysis of prospective studies. *Journal of the American Medical Association, 279,* 1200–1205.

Renfro, W.L. (1977). *Forecasting and Futures Research in Congress: Background and Prospects.* Washington: Library of Congress, Congressional Research Service, 77–169 SP, CB 1 60 CB 1 60 B, Aug. 24, 1977, pp. 13–14.

Rogers, P. (1993). *America's Water: Federal Roles and Responsibilities,* Cambridge, MA: MIT Press. 202–203.

Festgemeinsschaft "900 Jahre Theilheim." (1994). *900 Jahre Theilheim mit Daechheim, 1094–1994,* 65–71. Wuerzburg, Germany: Fraenkische Gesellschaftdruckerei und Verlag, GMBH.

Toffler, A. (1972). *Future Shock.* New York: Random House.

60

The Politics of Administrative Reform

Public Bureaucracies as Agents of Change in Great Britain and the United States

David L. Dillman   *Department of Political Science, Abilene Christian University,*
Abilene, Texas

I. INTRODUCTION

The reform movements in Great Britain and the United States which resulted in the creation of career civil service systems marked the beginning of a long history of reform. In both countries, the civil service has been repeatedly condemned, reformed, and condemned. Indeed, each successive round of condemnation and reform typically points out a vice and remedy contrary to or at least distinctly different from that earlier essayed. Civil service reform from this perspective is essentially a political debate between individuals and groups holding alternative notions of the nature of responsible government. Reform from this perspective is a complex web of reactions to changing political values, responses to political pressures, and initiatives from groups within and external to bureaucracy.

Most analyses of administrative reforms focus on pressures coming from actors outside the bureaucracies—interest groups, legislatures, elected executives—to change administrative procedures or structures to conform to new values or to secure power. Bureaucratic actors are sometimes ignored, cast as disinterested bystanders in reform efforts. At other times, it is argued that neutral civil servants pursue administrative changes that are strictly managerial or technical in hopes of achieving greater efficiency and effectiveness.

Perhaps most frequently, bureaucrats are portrayed as self-interested participants in the reform process, alternatively resisting or supporting administrative reforms depending upon the reforms' impact. Public choice economists such as James Buchanan argue that public administrators can be expected to only pursue their own self-interests (1975). Peter Wilenski (1979:358) has observed that "it is not only that administrators are reluctant to change processes and procedures with which they have grown familiar, but rather that those groups who stand to lose their privileged position become aware of this danger and fight to retain it." Michael Gordon (1971:43) has noticed that bureaucrats are "predisposed above all toward routine processing, toward reconciliation of diverse opinions, and toward a notion of harmony tantamount to an almost unswerving bias in favor of the status quo." Civil servants, then, are cast typically in the role of either nonparticipants, apolitical technicians, or active resistors of administrative change.

This chapter will focus on the role of American and British civil servants in the dynamics of the administrative reform process. Are bureaucrats mostly bystanders or do they sometimes lead reform efforts? Do administrators always inhibit change or do they ever initiate and guide reform processes? Are they always self-interested or do they ever pursue changes which promote a broader good?

II.   CIVIL SERVANTS AT THE CREATION

The creation of civil services in Great Britain and the United States was set in motion by multiple forces and events: political and social pressures, intellectual trends, and external events. Certainly, mass publics, interest groups, reform associations, political parties, legislatures, and heads of government were important participants in the creation. Just as clearly, within the whirlpool of 19th-century forces and events in Britain, administrators, too, "played an important part in presiding over and guiding administrative developments already in train" (Chapman and Greenaway 1980:227). By the 1830s the practice of removing public officials for partisan purposes was on the way out, as was the practice of political assessments. Indeed, in larger departments promotions were made from lower offices, pass examinations were being implemented, and permanent tenure was the normal practice (Eaton 1880:182–183). These developments were encouraged by department heads who hoped to reap the benefits of continuity and experience.

By midcentury, public officials and reformers were focusing on patronage as the source of "official delays, official evasions of difficulty, and official indisposition to improvement" (Northcote and Trevelyan 1854). That such complaints were not unanimous throughout the civil service is an indication that some departments were reasonably competent. Departments such as the Admiralty were setting quite high examination standards while others, such as the Home Office, were administering weak pass exams or none at all. Thus, while reformers were attempting to unify the civil service departments under a system of competitive academic examinations, it is clear that many bureaucratic leaders out of necessity were already setting higher standards and seeking to implement them.

Among the reformers were Sir Stafford Northcote, a civil servant at the Board of Trade, and Sir Charles Trevelyan, a Permanent Secretary to the Treasury. With persistence and skill, they were able to link the concepts of open competitive examinations, division of labor between intellectual and mechanical tasks, and promotion by merit to the aspirations of liberal social and political reformers such as Gladstone (Chapman and Greenaway 1980:218). Northcote and Trevelyan (1854) not only wrote the report that set out the basic features of the British civil service for the succeeding 100 years, but Northcote campaigned tirelessly for reform seeking support from every important segment of the community (Titlow 1979:68–88). During the 16 years between the issuance of the Northcote-Trevelyan Report in 1854 and its acceptance by Gladstone's Order in Council in 1870, civil servants, like Northcote and Trevelyan, were central figures in guiding the reform's development and securing its acceptance.

Similarly, in the United States public officials presided over the creation of a career civil service in 1883. This is not to argue that bureaucrats single-handedly initiated the reform effort. But while Thomas Jenckes was leading reformers in a moral crusade to make government more representative of middle-class morality and business competence, some top public officials were unilaterally implementing administrative change designed to secure more competent workers and protection from spoils politics (Van Riper 1958:66; White 1958:270; Hoogenboom 1961:41–45).

Where the spoils politics of the nineteenth century was taking a toll on the provision of public services, "the burden of administrative work was carried on by a nucleus of permanent clerks who knew what had to be done" (White 1956:374) and who were relied upon by department heads. Thus, "responsible officials recognized the need for skilled employees—a need which has increased as government functions multiplied and became more complex" (Hoogenboom 1961:69). For example, Secretary of the Treasury Boutwell, whom most reformers regarded as an enemy, was in 1870 the first official to administer a competitive examination in the Treasury Department in order to secure competent workers. Likewise, Silas W. Burt, a civil servant in the New York Customhouse, was an articulate, politically astute advocate for the concepts embodied in the Civil Service Reform Act of 1833. Burt did not originate the idea that competitive examinations be administered to new entrants at the lowest grades by a board of examiners, but he took advantage of his position to successfully implement these concepts as the rules of the Customhouse by 1879 (Hoogenboom 1961:172–173). As early as 1853 the Classification Act was supported by the bureaucracy itself; administrative work required a minimal level of competence and systematization.

These brief histories of the creation of civil services in Britain and America suggest, contrary to the prevalent view that officials are always barriers to change, that some key civil servants were early and consistent advocates of reform. Rather than being bystanders, many public officials were active leaders in the reform efforts, encouraging and guiding the development of new administrative structures and processes.

III. AMERICAN CIVIL SERVANTS AND THE CSRA

Administrative reforms in the 20th century, of course, were driven by different forces than in earlier periods—forces that to a large degree have been reactions to 19th-century reforms. During the 1970s in the United States, frustrations with economic and social policy led to wide public discontent with the civil service. Furthermore, American politicians of all stripes were suspicious of a civil service thought to be powerful enough to redirect or stifle their political agendas. Presidential candidate Jimmy Carter was no exception, making civil service reform a key component of his 1976 campaign. While citing the need to increase governmental productivity, clearly, just as important to the future president was the desire to assert political leadership over a bureaucracy believed to be overburdened by "neutral protectionism" and "legalistic complexity" (Newland 1976:529–537).

Within the bureaucracy, many senior career civil servants complained about work governed by an overly centralized system constrained by self-defeating rules. Many career officials with supervisory responsibilities argued that the system weakened their ability to manage. A tangle of rules and procedures made it difficult to reward outstanding performance or to penalize poor performance, thus holding employees accountable. Career and political executives alike agreed that congressionally imposed pay caps and pay compression at the top levels provided little material incentive to excel. Civil Service Commission (CSC) executives were concerned about the system's deficient management practices and weak executive training and development programs. They also held a long-standing concern about the lack of opportunities for career officials to advance to senior levels in the civil service brought on by growth in the numbers of political appointees in top positions. In addition, the CSC hoped to bring order to the multiplicity of hiring authorities in the supergrades and more control over the total numbers in the executive cadre.[1]

President Carter was well prepared when he presented his Civil Service Reform Act (CSRA) to Congress in March 1978. In mid-1977 the Federal Personnel Management Project, composed of nine task forces and close to 150 people, had been organized to begin the process of developing the reform package and garnering support from the executive agencies and Congress. The project was headed by Dwight Ink, a respected federal career executive, and the task forces were composed largely of career executives. Thus, the Personnel Management Project institutionalized the bureaucracy's access to the reform process.

Career officials in the Civil Service Commission had been working at least since the mid-1950s on proposals to create a corps of professional, governmentwide managers in the federal service.[2] Indeed, the Senior Executive Service Task Force (a work group of the Federal Personnel Management Project), which was composed of three career civil servants, had little to do since a well-developed plan already existed.[3] A top civil servant noted, regarding the Carter reform package, that "the whole damn thing was conceived by the civil servants. . . . The proposals were developed by people in the trenches like me and people who work for me who are career civil servants. They're the ones who have seen what is wrong with the system and proposed what should be done to fix it" (Lynn and Vaden 1979:334). Comparing the original Senior Executive Service (SES) recommendations of the CSC's career staff with the Carter administration's proposals to Congress reveals surprisingly few changes.

This is not to say that there was unanimity among career officials. Many civil servants were skeptical that objective performance evaluation was possible, believing that personal favoritism and political bias could never be entirely eliminated. Many executives agreed with one bureaucrat's view that the SES "is an obvious attempt to politicize the civil service system. Nothing more and nothing less" (Lynn and Vaden 1980:105). The consequences of politicization, many critics warned, would be a civil service in which technical knowledge and expertise suffered and "yes men" would be substituted for "constructively critical and politically neutral professionals" (Rosen 1978:302). While senior civil servants, especially personnel professionals, played a significant role in the development and adoption of the 1978 CSRA, large numbers of career bureaucrats found the reforms wanting. Indeed, less than a year after the adoption of the SES, Lynn and Vaden (1979:341) concluded that "there does not appear to be a great mandate of support for the Carter proposals."

Evaluation of the CSRA found continued widespread dissatisfaction and discontent (Ingraham and Ban 1984; Pearce and Perry 1983; Bowman 1982). One immediate reaction, for example, was the creation in 1980 of the Senior Executive Association to represent the interests of SES members. In addition, there was an exodus of senior executives from the SES and government.

How does one reconcile the key roles bureaucrats had in shaping the 1978 reforms and the harsh reactions to it during its implementation? First, it is possible that those personnel professionals who shaped the reforms were guided by flawed managerial and organizational assumptions (Thayer 1987). Second, evaluation studies suggest that career officials originally were supportive of the SES *concept* but quickly become disillusioned when political realities intruded. Specifically, monetary incentives such as bonuses and awards were reduced in numbers and pay raises were capped. In addition, the numbers of career SES members decreased while the numbers of noncareer SES members and Schedule C employees increased (GAO 1987). Third and similarly, senior executives did not see a linkage between performance and pay, awards, or other personnel actions (Pearce et al. 1985).

Critics typically point to the failure or partial adoption of reforms as evidence that a hostile bureaucracy has sabotaged reform efforts. While the record of the CSRA indicates that "it has not achieved most of what it apparently intended to do" (Ingraham 1984:276), clearly the reasons for this policy failure are many and complex. They include the lack of program clarity, the failure to resolve inconsistencies and to define new roles, budgetary and personnel cutbacks, the attempt to transfer wholesale to the public sector motivational techniques that were currently popular in the private sector, and the changing political environment and presidential priorities of the 1980s. In some agencies implementation of the major provisions of the CSRA faced opposition; in other agencies implementation occurred on schedule with career officials facilitating the changes.

IV. THE FULTON REFORMS AND BRITISH CIVIL SERVANTS

In the years after World War II in Britain, the massive societal and economic changes that were under way had important consequences for the civil service. Britain's economic decline and loss of empire raised doubts about the competence of the bureaucracy. The democratization taking place in education placed pressure on the civil service to become more open. In a governmental system that had become more complex the traditional conventions of ministerial responsibility and bureaucratic anonymity were often breached. Finally, the bureaucracy was attacked from both the left and right for its perceived power to protect the status quo. Britain's Harold Wilson expressed Labour's skepticism of the civil service by complaining that "whoever is in office, the Whigs are in power" (Balogh 1959:111–112). Likewise, the Conservative leader Margaret Thatcher later came to the prime minister's office suspicious of the centrist, consensus politics of the bureaucracy (Ridley 1983:36).

The clamor of British academics, journalists, politicians, and public opinion against the civil service reached a crescendo in the late 1950s and early 1960s. Criticisms were aimed at the skills (or lack thereof) and character of administrators, the class structure of the service, the bureaucracy's lack of political responsiveness, and the power of the Treasury. The Labour government that came to power in 1964 provided a catalyst that brought together the myriad pressures and actors for a burst of reforming activity.

It is important to note that outsiders did not have a monopoly on criticisms of the bureaucracy. Many top civil servants in the early 1960s were taking the unusual step of publicly chastising the civil service and calling for change. For example, an assistant secretary at the Ministry of Defense warned in 1964 that management should be taken more seriously in the civil service (Nairne 1964:113–122). Others, like R.G.S. Brown (1965:327), a principal in the administrative class, called upon his peers to develop a better problem-solving attitude by recruiting more specialists, training administrators in the use of management techniques and in their substantive areas, and breaking down the communication barriers between administrators and experts.

Civil service staff associations, particularly those representing professional, technical, executive, and clerical classes, also generated pressures for reform. In testimony to the Fulton Committee, for example, the Institution of Professional Civil Servants (IPCS) complained that "management and administration at the higher levels are still almost exclusively the monopoly of the Administrative Class" and called for the abolition of class divisions (Fulton Committee Report Vol. 5, 1968:286). In addition, the early postwar years witnessed a number of departmental committee inquiries and informal inquiries investigating the need for administrative change.

Accepting the recommendation of the House of Commons Estimates Committee, Prime Minister Harold Wilson established the Fulton Committee in early 1966. The committee was composed of 12 members, including two permanent secretaries and several others with civil service experience, and a small staff of civil servants, including a principal in the Treasury who served as the committee's secretary. Its findings were undoubtedly influenced by the mood of the country, the thinking of the new labour government, and a plethora of critical literature. Indeed, taken as a whole, its findings, reported in 1968, were basically a compilation of then fashionable criticisms.

To address the problems attributed to the civil service the Fulton Committee made 158 distinct recommendations. Significantly, many of the committee's recommendations "merely confirmed developments which were going ahead in the Civil Service quite independently of [the Fulton] enquiry" (Editorial 1968:368). For example, the Treasury had already embarked upon several reorganizations in the early 1960s. In 1963 a Centre for Administrative Studies was established which, among other activities, started a short course on economics for assistant principals. In addition, efforts were made in some technical departments to move specialists to top posts, although the success of these efforts may be questioned. Even the committee's "proposal for 'one class' was first considered within the service [in 1943], long before it was publicly discussed" (Chapman and Greenaway 1980:161). It is clear that senior civil servants provided not only guidance but, in certain specifics, the stimulus for reform.

While immediate reaction to the Fulton Report was mixed, ranging form enthusiastic support to vitriolic denigration, many senior civil servants opposed the characterization of the civil service as amateurish and were skeptical of recommendations for greater specialization and wider use of management techniques. Undoubtedly speaking for the Treasury and many higher civil servants, Lord Simey, a member of the committee, noted that while modern quantitative techniques are needed, they do not "supersede the importance of the fundamental qualities of judgement [and] decisiveness, and the ability to understand how the reshaping of values may be embodied in and implemented by public polity" (Fulton Committee Report Vol. 1, 1968:102). Likewise, Lord Helsby (1968), former head of the Home Civil Service, denounced the report and asserted that it had a "rather imperfect understanding" of what a professional is in the British government.

Even the response of staff associations was muted in tone, pledging to study the report's proposals, but disappointed that the committee found it necessary to caricature the civil service. Among the civil service unions there was general support for the creation of a new civil service department, the Civil Service College, and proposals for better promotion opportunities. Yet there was also deep skepticism about the proposed abolition of classes among unions representing administrative and clerical classes.

Prime Minister Wilson accepted the Fulton Report's major recommendations and began implementing those recommendations that the primary participants found acceptable. A Civil Service Department and Civil Service College were soon established. The proposal for the abolition of classes, the most controversial recommendation of all, was ceremoniously accepted then delegated to the civil service officials and unions to be implemented privately. The politicians' concern to appear to respond to popular demands for reform had been accomplished. As the pressures of more immediate constituent and policy concerns took over, the detailed implementation of the reforms was left to the civil servants.

It is the view of many critics that the civil service sabotaged the Fulton reforms, specifically, that the unions and Treasury officials worked to prevent the changes Fulton prescribed. In a 1980 version of this critique, Lord Crowther-Hunt and Peter Kellner (1980) claimed that administrative class civil servants exerted power to block key Fulton proposals. The new Civil Service Department, they argued, was staffed by the same Treasury amateurs who always had been responsible for the civil service. Likewise, the abolition of classes was accepted in principle, but civil service mandarins cleverly maintained a de facto class structure that preserved their power. Increased selection of late entrants, in-and-outers, and specialists at higher levels was proclaimed a fact by the career officials without any substantive change. Thus, according to Kellner and Crowther-Hunt (1980), the old administrative class simply carried out those proposals that it wanted and ignored the others.

Another version of the bureaucracy's role in reform is possible. To discuss, develop, and implement the details of the Fulton Report, a joint committee composed of higher civil servants and union officials was established. A key figure was Sir William Armstrong (later Lord) who, as Joint Permanent Secretary at the Treasury responsible for management prior to and during the Fulton deliberation, and permanent secretary of the new Civil Service Department and head of the Home of Civil Service after Fulton, had been involved in each stage of the reform debate. He had presented evidence on behalf of the Treasury to the Fulton Committee, had been privy to discussions with committee members during work on the report, and had advised Prime Minister Wilson on implementation matters. As chairman of the joint committee, Armstrong had reservations about the unified grading structure, believing that such a structure would create staffing problems.

Thus, the joint committee asserted that "the introduction of the new structure is far too great an undertaking to be completed in a single heave. It will therefore be necessary to approach the task in stages" (Joint Committee on the National Whitley Council 1969:24). Changes were made incrementally to remove the horizontal barriers to mobility between classes and the vertical barriers to promotion of specialists into the top administrative positions. But the changes fell short of the Fulton recommendations and were, interestingly enough, similar to what the Treasury had recommended to the Fulton Committee.

Between the cup of those Fulton recommendations accepted by the Parliament and the lip of the recommendations ultimately implemented by the bureaucracy were many intervening factors. The disappointment that many reformers experienced in the Fulton case can be explained in part by the complex interaction of union and official self-interest, the lack of clear principles and goals to guide reform, competing perspectives, and the lack of parliamentary-political intervention at the implementation stage. In short, it may be argued that the Fulton proposals were never implemented in full because there never developed a clear political consensus that these were the correct proposals.

V. BUREAUCRATS AND RESPONSIBLE GOVERNMENT

While there is truth to the observation that civil servants often act as conservators of the status quo, the sketches of administrative reform in this chapter suggest a slightly different equation. For example, both the SES and major components of the Fulton Report were the culmination of administrative initiatives. The Carter administration's proposal for a Senior Executive Service was the progeny of many years of work by the Civil Service Commission. Career officials developed the technical details and helped advocate the reform agenda within Congress and the executive agencies. Similarly, many of the Fulton Committee recommendations, "although thought by some people outside the administrative system to be original solutions to problems of contemporary concern, had already been under consideration years before within the civil service itself" (Chapman and Greenaway 1980:216). In each instance the respective bureaucracies were attempting to find solutions to longstanding administrative deficiencies. This is not to say that political and social pressures did not stimulate and provide the context for reform. Nor is it to suggest that administrative solutions do not have larger societal or political implications. However, it is to stress that career officials, on occasion, may provide innovative leadership in the reform process.

Furthermore, even when administrative reforms have emanated from actors outside the bureaucracy, civil servants have been leaders in encouraging, guiding, and implementing administrative change. Career bureaucrats "are not necessarily dedicated to maintenance of the status quo, but often review programs and procedures to improve their effectiveness" and seek support of political leadership to carry out their proposals (Greenberg 1978:16). Sir Charles Trevelyan and Silas W. Burt seem to have played this role. In the 20th century, Dwight Ink and William Armstrong exemplified civil servants who positively guided the development and adoption of administrative reforms. These and other civil servants in the United States and Britain were what Chapman and Greenaway call "creative reformers." "But their creativity often lay less in initiating change or producing their own original ideas than in making use of good ideas from wherever they happened to come" (Chapman and Greenaway 1980:219).

The role of the civil service in the administrative reform process cannot be easily categorized. In the cases studied here, the public administrators cannot be said to have opposed change; they were, however, cautious and conservative. Yet their conservatism was positive rather than reactionary, prudent rather than rigid. The bureaucracy serves to accommodate a wide spectrum of interests, facilitate consensus among groups within and external to the bureaucracies, and instigate change in order to preserve and enhance the strengths of the administrative apparatus. By subscribing to incremental, consensual reform behavior, the civil services of Britain and the United States are a reflection of the liberal democracies in which they reside. They play a role that is more stable and accommodating than many of its critics desire, yet more positive and creative than others concede.

ENDNOTES

1. For early thinking of the CSC staff, see Personnel Management Project, Task Force Report on Senior Executive System (1977a), and Personnel Management Project, Task Force on Executive Personnel (1977b).
2. The senior civil service concept had been introduced as early as 1935 by the Commission of Inquiry on Public Service Personnel.
3. Noted during an interview with a reform participant, Washington, DC, 1981.

REFERENCES

Balogh, T. (1959). The apotheosis of the dilettante. In H. Thomas (ed.), *The Establishment.* London: Anthony Blond Ltd.

Bowman, J.S. (1982). A symposium on civil service reform. *Review of Public Personnel Administration 2,* entire issue.

Brown, R.G.S. (1965). Organization theory and civil service reform. *Public Administration 43,* 325–335.

Buchanan, J.M. (1975). *The Limits of Liberty: Between Anarchy and Leviathan.* Chicago: University of Chicago Press.

Chapman, R.A., and Greenaway, J.R. (1980). *The Dynamics of Administrative Reform.* London: Croom Helm.

Eaton, D.B. (1880). *Civil Service in Great Britain. A History of Abuses and Reforms and Their Bearing Upon American Politics.* New York: Harper and Brothers.

Editorial: Reforming the bureaucracy. (1968). *Public Administration 46,* 367–374.

Fulton Committee Report. (1968). Committee on the civil service. *The Civil Service 3638,* Vols. 1–5.

General Accounting Office, United States. (1987). Federal employees, trends in career and noncareer employee appointments in the executive branch. GAO/GGD-87-96FS.

Gordon, M.R. (1971). Civil servants, politicians, and parties. *Comparative Politics 4,* 29–58.

Greenberg, S.H. (1978). The senior executive service. *Bureaucrat 7,* 16–22.

Helsby, L. (1968). The Fulton report. *Listener 80,* 859–860.

Hoogenboom, A. (1961). *Outlawing the Spoils.* Urbana, IL: University of Illinois Press.

Ingraham, P.W., and Ban, C. (1984). *Legislating Bureaucratic Change: The Civil Service Reform Act of 1978.* Albany, NY: State University of New York Press.

Ingraham, P.W. (1984). Civil service reform and public policy: do we know how to judge success or failure? In P.W. Ingraham and C. Ban (eds.), *Legislating Bureaucratic Change.* Albany, NY: State University of New York Press.

Joint Committee on the National Whitley Council. (1969). *Developments on Fulton.* London.

Kellner, P., and Crowther-Hunt, L. (1980). *The Civil Servants.* London: Macdonald General Books.

Lynn, N.B., and Vaden, R.E. (1979). Bureaucratic response to civil service reform. *Public Administration Review 34,* 333–343.

Lynn, N.B., and Vaden, R.E. (1980). Federal executives, initial reactions to change. *Administration and Society 12,* 101–120.

Nairne, P.S. (1964). Management and administrative class. *Public Administration 42,* 113–122.

Newland, C.A. (1976). Public personnel administration: Legalistic reform vs. effectiveness, efficiency, and economy. *Public Administration Review 36,* 529–537.

Northcote, S., and Trevelyan, C. (1854). *Report on the Organization of the Permanent Civil Service.* C. 1713. Great Britain.

Pearce, J.L., and Perry, J.L. (1983). Federal merit pay: a longitudinal analysis. *Public Administration Review 43*, 315–325.

Pearce, J.L., Stevenson, W.B., and Perry, J.L. (1985). Managerial compensation based on organizational performance: a time series analysis of the effects of merit pay. *Academy of Management 28*, 261–278.

Personnel Management Project. Task Force on Executive Personnel. (1977a). *Initial Option Paper.* Washington, DC: U. S. Civil Service Commission.

Personnel Management Project. Task Force Report on Senior Executive Service. (1977b). *Final Report*, Vol. II, Appendix II. Washington, DC: U.S. Civil Service Commission.

Ridley, F.F. (1983). The British civil service and politics: principles in question and traditions in flux. *Parliamentary Affairs 36*, 28–48.

Rosen, B. (1978). Merit and the president's plan for changing the civil service system. *Public Administration Review 38*, 301–304.

Thayer, F.C. (1987). Performance appraisal and merit pay systems: the disasters multiply. *Review of Public Personnel Administration 7*, 36–53.

Titlow, R.E. (1979). *Americans Import Merit.* Washington, DC: University Press of America.

Van Riper, P.P. (1958). *History of the United States Civil Service.* Evanston, IL: Row, Peterson.

White, L.D. (1956). *The Jacksonians.* New York: Macmillan.

White, L.D. (1958). *The Republican Era: 1869–1901.* New York: Macmillan.

Wilenski, P. (1979). Political problems of administrative responsibility and reform. *Australian Journal of Public Administration 38*, 347–360.

61

Media and the Bureaucracy in the United States

Behrooz Kalantari   *Department of Public Administration, Savannah State University, Savannah, Georgia*

I. INTRODUCTION

The main objective of this study is to highlight certain characteristics about the dominant entertainment media and their relation to society, culture, politics, and bureaucracy in the United States. Other considerations, including differences among various media outlets, citizens' own predispositions and perceptions on certain issues, and other factors which can influence the relations among the media, public, and political institutions are not given attention. Therefore, the focus of attention is on the role of media in society.

The role of media on society and its impact on politics has been an important topic in the study of political communication. It is crucial to concentrate on the ways and means by which the mass media use their capabilities and opportunities to influence the formation and implementation of public policy in the United States. Although it is difficult to assume a great degree of uniformity among different media networks, there are some characteristics which can be attributed to the most dominant media. Some members of the media are more even-handed than others in dissemination of information to the public (public radio and television fall within this category). The emphasis of this study is on the entertainment media.

Due to the nature of the media and the mechanism of its operation, the most effective way for the media to affect the political decision-making process is through influencing the public. This is accomplished through altering and shaping the public's perception toward politics or political organizations. Individual citizens usually receive their information about public affairs from two major sources: the mass media and interpersonal communication. However, the importance of media is prevalent because "the content of most politically relevant information, as well as of conversation about politics, is dependent on information obtained from the media."[1] Therefore, the media have become the single most important source for disseminating information in society.

It can be argued that the national media networks developed and evolved into an entity which independently shapes the reality inside and outside the United States. Although there is considerable difference among different communications media in their relationship with the environment and the public, they all share several important attributes. They create, demonstrate, and portray reality through "the use of symbols or interpretation of the most abstract form of concepts in society."[2]

Newspapers were the first mass medium to reach many people. They started during the

1830s and were followed by the mass circulation of national magazines by the turn of the 20th century. Shortly after that, in the beginning of the 20th century, movies reached the public; and in 1906 voice communication was sent through the radio signals and captured the imagination of millions of people.[3] Television effectively entered the race in the 1950s.

The most important attribute of the mass media is its ability to create images which contribute to better understanding of reality and enhancement of its scope. It can:

> enlighten, comfort, uplift, and inspire. They are the basic coinage of all culture, the essential units on which civilization rests. Respect for words are two sides of the same coin, and that coin is the currency that will enable the media to make a decisive contribution to world culture.[4]

Studies on the behavior of American voters indicate that most voters receive their information on political events from the mass media.[5]

Among the communications media, studies show that "television news and newspapers are major sources of information" for the voters.[6] Particularly, television uses "verbal and nonverbal symbols, sound, and visual imagery" to communicate its messages.[7] The television medium has an advantage of being more accessible to the public than other media. Therefore, television has turned into the most powerful tool to influence and shape the people's attitude and beliefs concerning political and social events.[8]

II. MEDIA AND CREATION OF IMAGES

Many criticisms have been launched against the media concerning the way they carry their functions as an institution which is trusted to convey political and social events in a value-free and neutral manner. The media have often been condemned for their bias in creating negative images of reality and even working against the social fabric of society. For example, the media are held responsible for the deterioration of the family values in the United States.

As opposed to the ideal world, in which the media are only a medium of transmitting information, the media are not value-free agents; they play and advocate certain social and political values and priorities in society.[9] Regardless of its rise and fall in public's perception, the media still remain the major force in shaping the attitudes and perceptions of the people and their political leaders. This is often accomplished through the exploitation and manipulation of the dominant political culture of society.

III. SIGNIFICANCE OF POLITICAL CULTURE

Political culture is not a new concept and has been used by ancient civilizations. According to Kincaid, "Greeks believed that . . . regimes are basically products of character, chance, and circumstance."[10] Modern usage of the concept is very common in the literature under different terms such as national character, tradition, ideological orientation, etc.[11] Some political science scholars refer to the concept of political culture as a "common belief" among the people in a community. They believe that it provides the citizens with a perception of their role in society and "how the government ought to be conducted and what it should try to do."[12] Gabriel Almond used the concept of "political culture" for the first time and believed that "every political system is embedded in a particular pattern of orientations to political action."[13] The collective orientations are referred to each society's political culture. The orientations can be cognitive (knowledge of the system), affective (feeling toward the system), and evaluative (opinion and judgment about the political system).[14]

Lucian Pye argues that "political systems are held together by a sense of collective identity and thus are based upon sentiments of loyalty which evoke parochial attachment to unique historical experience."[15] He perceives the political culture as a "subjective understanding on behalf of the individuals."[16] According to Hunt, political culture reflects "the values, expectations, and implicit rules that expressed and shaped collective intentions and actions."[17] Therefore, it can be argued that political culture as an important concept is deeply rooted in the human political history and plays a significant role in determining the success or failure of a polity.[18]

One of the main characteristics of political culture is its changing nature which is due to the change of citizens' perception and expectations about government and politics. These changes in perception take place mostly through the exchange of information between the citizens and their environment. In this process of change and exchange of information, the mass media play the most prominent role in creating new images and expectations:

> The images conjured up and projected by the media help to shape and reshape the images held by the audiences. In other words, the public imagination is in part the imaginary experiences afforded by the popular media.[19]

Although the pattern of change is usually slow and differs from one society to another, acquisition of information is vital to the images that they hold and expectations that they develop concerning the proper role of their political systems. There is no preconceived agenda or code of conduct for interpreting the news or information by the media; they usually interpret the events according to their own personal beliefs and for the benefit of their sponsor organizations. Perhaps, the profit motive is the strongest force which shapes the way information is processed and presented to the public. Therefore, in some instances, media can easily overlook the most important part of the news and present the public with a sensational view of the events.[20]

IV. MEDIA'S MOTIVES AND CHARACTERISTICS

People with different political orientations have blamed the media for its bias.[21] In reality, the underlying purpose of the media is to attract more audiences and increase its popularity and profit. It is widely believed that "the product of the news media, the content of which is not designed primarily to serve the purchaser . . . but is to please a third party-the advertiser."[22] On the other hand, it is important to realize that in production and presentation of political events, many individuals are involved, which makes it a very complex process. This is due to the fact that almost everyone in the production process tries to mold and shape the reality according to his/her own value system and present it to the public. Therefore, a piece of information can be interpreted differently from one person to another, depending on who has been producing and reporting it. Consequently, the media are not neutral observers or reporters of the news and information, but participants in and interpreters of the information. Members of the media see themselves not only as representing the public interest but also as the determinant of what the public should hear, think, and decide concerning an issue, with their own interests in mind.[23]

Entertainment has become the major focus for the media by giving priority to those pieces of information which can amuse the public regardless of its quality. Therefore, in order to make the news more presentable to the public, they trivialize it and, in some instances, undermine important aspects of its content.[24] For example, analysis of the media's treatment of the 1996 presidential election indicate that they "trivialized and cheapened the campaign" and ignored the issues of the election.[25] Therefore, most of the mass media treated the presidential election as a race between opposing groups rather than how politics affects the public.[26] For the media, the most important aspect is "selectivity" of information to match their own standards of newsworthiness, which determines what kinds of information should be disseminated to the public. Members of media

> not only are more subjective in determining whether a story will make it into the news, but in deciding what sort of "slant" it will be given and how much coverage it will receive. Even the wire services have succumbed, running (or not running) stories that, in the past, would have gotten the reporters and editors responsible fired. The worst example of bias and selectivity are seen on network television programs, which have come to value entertainment more than the news.[27]

As a result, the public cannot grasp the magnitude of many important issues because it gets cluttered and wrapped up with unrelated but amusing information. This phenomenon is often called "entertainmentization" of information. Consequently, the "lines between politics, news, and entertainment" eventually get blurred and it is hard to separate news from entertainment.[28]

The other characteristic of the media which is often investigated is its negative and cynical approach in interpreting the issues and information.[29] In other words, mass media have a tendency to portray the negative aspects of reality and news and overlook the positive. The underlying reason for media's negativity is its obsession with its profit motive. Therefore, since negativity sells, there is no reason to be positive about things.[30] They see themselves as agents of public sensationalism and arousal rather than just neutral channels of information for the people. Media reporters want to make the public listen and pay attention by emotionalizing the issues in order to attract more customers, more advertisers, higher ratings, and higher profits.

In order for the media to justify its negativity and cynicism, it is important to find a villain to put the blame on and maximize its profit making objective. The most logical choice and often used potential villains in society are the public institutions and politics in general. Perhaps, the underlying reason for media's choice is the United States' political culture, which is generally cynical about politics. Therefore, the media effectively seize the opportunity and materialize on that. For example, "media coverage of political corruption confirms public's belief in the fallibility of politicians."[31] However, for the media establishment, this negativity and cynicism is usually perceived differently. They call it "adversarial journalism," which is often praised by its practitioners and promoted through the profession.[32]

V.   SETTING THE PUBLIC AGENDA

It is difficult to investigate the media's ultimate effects on individual citizen's behavior. However, as was indicated earlier, the media are an important source of political socialization in every society. Therefore, it has a powerful effect on people's perception of reality in evaluating and processing the relevant facts and information about political events. In practice, the popular or entertainment media constantly send messages that tell us "who we are—or ought to be—within the context of the larger community and what values and institutions we should adhere to, as members of that community."[33] In other words, the media set the public's agenda by determining what is important and what is not relevant to their everyday life.[34]

Perhaps, the issue of agenda setting by the media is the most critical issue concerning the political decision-making process. In the political arena, there are many agendas which can be followed and "just as there are many more issues, concerns, and conflicts than government can address, there are many more potential stories that the media can report."[35] Media influences the political agenda by emphasizing certain issues while ignoring others, which gives prominence to some issues at the expense of others.[36] Therefore, policy makers have to watch for the negative effects of the media coverage on the public concerning their policies.[37] Moreover, they have to be cognizant of the fact that negative media coverage can also influence some undecided legislators as well.[38] Consequently, in the final analysis, the media determine the outcome of political decisions and the direction of political issues.[39]

VI.   MEDIA, POLITICS, AND BUREAUCRACY

The media's negativity and self-centered view of social and political events have caused profound distrust by the public toward their political institutions and have severely questioned their legitimacy.[40] The ultimate result of this popular distrust and doubt about government's conduct is a sense of national despair and lack of confidence in political institutions and political leaders, which in the final analysis are the guardians of public trust.[41]

In this court of public opinion in which media is the prosecutor, judge, and decision maker, politicians are in an awkward situation. On the one hand, they are part of the political establishment which has been blamed for all societal faults. On the other hand, they understand the power of the media and their need to influence and shape the public opinion in their favor.[42] Therefore, they try to gain access to the media by making themselves presentable and disassociate themselves from political institutions and political establishment.[43] They project the image of being outsiders, and have nothing to do with real politics in Washington and political organizations. Consequently, politicians, in order to please the media and win their favor, instead of defending the government and politics which are constantly under attack, point at bureaucracy and other government institutions as real villains.

Although in the long run politicians themselves will be hurt for bashing the government, their immediate concern is getting as much popularity as they can and get elected to a political office. Ultimately, the bureaucracy and other institutions of government, with little influence and access to the media, get victimized and condemned without proper investigation in their operation. Ideally, no person or institution should be assumed guilty or innocent for its conduct, and there should be a balanced and fair treatment in reaching any verdict, but in reality this does not take place.[44] The main problem with the media game is to legitimize its position on issues which usually are not fully analyzed; ultimately, the public is left out misinformed and misguided. Due to the Constitutional guarantees and importance of freedom of expression in society, it is hard to conceive of much legal restriction on the media's behavior. However, consideration of imposition of some ethical standards on the media's conduct and behavior could be a major improvement.[45]

VII.   CONCLUSION

Everyone in the media and in the political arena is striving to influence the public for his own personal or organizational gain. Therefore, in this competitive game for public's attention, the gatekeepers, who are the media persons, have the upper hand. They are able to influence the political culture, determine the life and career of politicians, change national priorities, and provide support for their choices.[46] Consequently, the media have gained a great deal of power in determining the outcome of political decisions and the public's perception on bureaucracy.

In this game of power and influence, the real losers are those who do not have adequate access to the media and are the targets of media attacks. The most obvious victim is the government in general, and the bureaucracy in particular. It only makes sense that the media, with such power and influence, be held responsible for their behavior in dealing with the public's political life.

It is hard to impose any specific value and responsibility on the media. However, there are standards of fairness and morality, which are compatible with the democratic values in society and can provide guidance in determining the behavior of the media. Considering the fact that 80% of the media is controlled by 50 major corporations in the United States, perhaps corporate values should loosen their grip on those institutions which are supposed to serve the public interest.[47]

ENDNOTES

1. Silva, Lenart. *Shaping Political Attitude: The Impact of Interpersonal Communication and Mass Media.* Thousand Oaks, CA: Sage Publications, 1994:4.
2. Edelman, Murray. *The Symbolic Use of Politics.* Urbana: University of Illinois Press, 1967:5.
3. Swanson, David L. In Robert L. Savage and Dan Nimmo (eds.), *Politics in Familiar Contexts: Projecting Politics Through Popular Media.* New Jersey: Alex Publishing Corporation, 1990:8–12.
4. Johnson, Paul. The Media and Truth: Is There a Moral Duty? *Current,* December 1992:4.
5. Weaver, David H. What Voters Learn from Media. *Annals of the American Academy of Political and Social Science,* July 1996, *546*:34.
6. Chaffee, Steven, and Stacy Frank. How Americans Get Political Information: Print Versus Broadcast News. *Annals of the American Academy of Political and Social Science,* July 1996, *546*:48.
7. Nimmo, Dan, and J.E. Combs. *Mediated Political Realities.* New York: Longman, 1990:27.
8. Schewellin, Michael. CNN: Television for the Global Village: World Leaders Watch Each Other on the Tube. *World Press Review,* December 1990:34.
9. Weaver, Paul. Newspaper News and Television News. In Aspen Institute (ed.), *Television as a Social Force.* New York: Praeger, 1975:81–96.
10. Kincaid, John. *Political Culture, Public Policy and American States.* Philadelphia: Institute for the Study of Human Issues, 1982:2.
11. Martindale, Don. The Sociology of National Character. *Annals of the American Academy of Political and Social Studies.* March 1967:30–36.
12. Beer, Samuel H. The Analysis of Political System. In S. Beer and A.B. Ulam (eds.), *Patterns of Government.* New York: Random House, 1962:32.
13. Almond, Gabriel A. Comparative Political Systems. *Journal of Politics* 1956; *18*(3), 396.
14. Parson, Talcott and Shills, E. *Toward a General Theory of Action.* Cambridge, MA: Harvard University Press, 1954:13.
15. Pye, Lucian W. *Asian Power and Politics.* Cambridge, MA: The Belknap Press of Harvard University Press, 1985:125.
16. Pye, Lucian W. *Politics, Personality, and Nation Building: Burma's Search for Identity.* New Haven, CT: Yale University Press, 1962:12.
17. Hunt, Lynn. *Politics, Culture and Class in the French Revolution.* Berkeley: University of California Press, 1984:610.
18. Almond, Gabriel. The Intellectual History of the Civic Culture Concept. In G. Almond and S. Verba (eds.), *Civic Culture Revisited.* Boston: Little, Brown, 1980:1.
19. Savage, Robert L., and Nimmo, D. *Politics in Familiar Contexts: Projecting Politics Through Popular Media.* New Jersey: Alex Publishing Corporation, 1990:6.
20. Jamieson, Kathleen. *Atlanta Constitution.* Sept. 15, 1994:A13:1.
21. Newcomb, Horace, and Alley, R. In *The Producer's Medium.* H. Newcomb and R. Alley (eds.) New York: Oxford, 1983; Michael Parenti. *Make-Believe Media.* New York: St. Martin's Press, 1992; William Rusher. *The Coming Battle for the Media.* New York: Morrow, 1988; Michael Jay Robinson. Just How Liberal Is the News. *Public Opinion,* February/March 1983:55–60.
22. Bagdikian, Ben H. *The Media Monopoly.* Boston: Beacon Press, 1992:207.
23. Lester, Elli. Manufactured Silence and the Politics of Media Research: A Consideration of the Propaganda Model. *Journal of Communication Inquiry,* 1992; *16*(1), 45–56.
24. Parenti, *op. cit.,* 1992:178.
25. Grossberger, Lewis. Cutting on the Bias. *Media Week* 1996, *6*(43), 46.

26. McCarthy, Abigail. The Media vs. The People: Please Tell Us What We Need to Know. *Commonweal* 1996, *123*(4), 8.
27. Novak, Robert. Political Correctness Has No Place in the Newsroom. *USA Today.* March 1995:45.
28. Freedom Media Studies Center. *The Homestretch: New Politics, New Media, New Voters?* New York: Columbia University Press, 1992:99–100.
29. Weaver, Paul H. *New York Times*, July 29, 1994:A27:2.
30. Robinson, Michael Jay. Just How Liberal Is the News. *Public Opinion.* February/March 1983:55–60.
31. Wines, Michael. Corruption Lite, Democracy's Junk Food. *New York Times*, January 12, 1997:E1.
32. Ansolabehere, Stephen, et al. *The Media Game.* New York: Macmillan, 1983:221.
33. Savage and Nimmo, *op. cit.*, 1990:3.
34. Page, Benjamin I., and Shapiro, R.Y. What Moves Public Opinion. *American Political Science Review*, 1987; *81*:40.
35. Nelson, Barbara J. The Agenda-Setting Function of the Media: Child Abuse. In Doris A. Garber (ed.), *Media Power in Politics.* Washington: Congressional Quarterly, 1990:84.
36. Trumbo, Craig. Longitudinal Modeling of Public Issues. *Journalism and Mass Communication.* Monograph No. 152, August 1995:50.
37. Adams, William C. Marrying the Functions: The Importance of Media Relations in Public Affairs. *Public Relations Quarterly*, 1995; *40*(3), 10.
38. Iyengar, S., and Kinder, D.R. *News That Matters.* Chicago: University of Chicago Press, 1987.
39. Roberts D.F., and Bachen, C.M. Mass Communication Effects. *Annual Review of Psychology*, 1981:350; Schmul, Robert. Putting a National Spin on Politics. *Chicago Tribune*, December 18, 1994:4, 3:2.
40. Robinson, Michael J. Public Affairs Television and the Growth of Political Malaise. *American Political Science Review*, 1976; *70*:425–430.
41. Seymour, Martin L., and Schneider, William. *The Confidence Gap.* New York: Free Press, 1983.
42. Nimmo, Dan, and Combs, J. *The Political Pundits.* New York: Praeger, 1992.
43. Hattersley, Roy. Society that Bites Off Less Than It Can Chew. *Guardian*, 1994; 21:1, 3.
44. Davis, Richard. *The Press and American Politics: The New Mediator.* New York: Longman, 1992.
45. Kennamer, J. David, ed. *Public Opinion, the Press and Public Policy.* New York: Praeger, 1992.
46. Linsky, Martin. *Impact: How the Press Affects Federal Policymaking.* New York: W.W. Norton, 1986.
47. Parenti, Michael. The Myth of a Liberal Media. *The Humanist.* January/February 1995; *55*(1):7.

62

Bureaucracy, Agrarian Reforms, and Regime Enhancement

The Case of Iran*

Ali Farazmand   *School of Public Administration, Florida Atlantic University, Fort Lauderdale, Florida*

I.   INTRODUCTION

Public bureaucracies play significant roles in societies. As instruments of power, they are strong forces used by ruling powers to govern and to enhance regime maintenance[1] yet the political role of public bureaucracies has remained underresearched and, as scholars like Waldo and Riggs acknowledge, very little is known about their political role.[2,3]

This chapter examines the political and administrative roles of a large public bureaucracy—the Ministry of Agriculture and Rural Development (MARD)—in Iran during the 1960s and the 1970s. It also examines some of the major impacts of the revolution of 1978–79 on this bureaucracy and its politics. The purpose is to explain how the MARD helped maintain and enhance the Pahlavi regime under the Shah, how it transformed the rural socioeconomic system of feudalism into capitalism, what impacts these roles had on Iranian society both politically and economically, what happened to the MARD after the revolution of 1978–79, and, finally, what changes have taken place in the postrevolutionary agrarian policy under the Islamic republic.

In the 1960s the MARD was crucial in implementing a number of agricultural and rural reforms, including land reform, and in changing the socioeconomic and politicoadministrative structures of rural Iran, where about 75% of the nation's population resided. The MARD was also crucial to the survival and maintenance of the Pahlavi regime and in furthering its economic interests. Currently, it is instrumental in dealing with agricultural, developmental, and rural problems under the Islamic republic.

This chapter is based on data and information collected for a dissertation case study conducted during 1980–82 and a research paper during a four-month visit to Iran in 1983 as well as more recent data collected in the late 1990s. Information included interviews (over 100) conducted with a number of officials and others in Iran and the United States, a large number of Iranian

---

*Reprinted, in part, from *Intl. J. Pub. Admin.*, *12*(1), 1989, with updates.

and U.S. government documents, and numerous scholarly works and other secondary materials. Finally, the personal observations and experiences of the author (POEA) as a former client of several agencies, a public administrator, and a researcher in Iran, are also incorporated.

II. THE POLITICAL AND SOCIOECONOMIC ENVIRONMENTS

Formally, Iran was a constitutional monarchy until 1979; in reality it was absolute monarchy, and the separation of power was a farce. The parliament was a rubber stamp and conformed to the Shah's dictates.[4–6] The political elite was only a "second stratum,"[7] translating the Shah's dictates to the bureaucracy for implementation.[7,8] The Shah's status became absolute during 1953, when a successful CIA-led military coup returned him to the throne after a serious challenge led by the then popular premier, Dr. Mosaddegh. Several other challenges were suppressed after 1953 by the Pahlavi regime, and the Shah exercised absolute rule with the support of the United States and other allies.[7,9–12]

Socioeconomically, rural Iran was predominantly feudal until the 1960s. The landed aristocracy, including the Shah's family, dominated the country. While 75% of the nation's population lived in rural areas, less than 0.3% owned and controlled the 50,000 villages of Iran. The biggest force was the Shah himself, who owned more than 2000 of the best villages taken forcibly by his father, Reza Khan. Sharecropping was prevalent, and the peasants lived in a virtual serfdom.[8,11,13–17] The attitude of the peasantry toward the state was negative, since they saw its organizations, especially its rural police (*Gendarmerie*), as an instrument enforcing feudal power.[5,14]

The politicoadministrative and managerial functions in rural Iran before the 1960s were carried out by the aristocracy's representatives and the administrative units controlled by the local elite. The Shah and his state had little, if any, direct control over these areas and their populations.[14,16] After 1953, economic power in Iran was controlled by the royal family, international monopolies, and their agents. During the 1960s and 1970s, feudalism was transformed into a system of capitalism, which became an integral part of the international capital.[8,11,13–17] To preserve the regime, the Shah used strategies of coercion, reform, and cooptation in dealing with opposition and dissent.[4,8] The MARD played a major role in accomplishing this and other objectives.

III. THE POWER POSITION OF THE MARD

The power of the MARD was enhanced by the wide discretion given to it by the regime. It was actively involved in policy and politics by (1) allocating resources in agricultural and rural areas, (2) policy formulation and presentation, (3) assuming more functions in competition with other public organizations, and (4) its technical expertise. The MARD was the primary implementer of the policies and reforms of the 1960s and 1970s aimed at restructuring rural Iran to serve the country and the regime economically and politically. This made it one of the most powerful institutions in society. The Shah identified the regime with state power, and tolerated no challenge to this power.[5,8,18,19]

Members of the bureaucratic elite in Iran were also members of the political and economic elites and served in several powerful roles simultaneously.[7,8,20] They were "quasi-politicians" and "quasi-administrators,"[21] who played "tri-active" roles in society: as administrators, as politicians, and as businessmen.[9] Additionally, field administrators of the MARD were actually "the little kings" and "stability-maximizers."[11,22] But Anthony Down's "climbers" and "conservers"[23] were found at all levels of the bureaucracy where they were actively involved in system transformation and regime enhancement during the reform period of the 1960s.

IV. REFORMS OF THE 1960S AND THE MARD

After 1953, several factors forced the Shah to pursue socioeconomic reforms to broaden political support and buy regime legitimacy. They included the limited support of the aristocracy, the possibility of peasant rebellion against both the regime and the aristocracy, the nature of feudalism as an obstacle to economic development, the need for state control over the rural areas for regime maintenance, and the pressures of the Kennedy administration.[11,13,24–27]

In 1962, the Shah declared the so-called White Revolution composed of 12 reform points, at the heart of which was land reform.[28] Implementation of the three stages of the land reform took more than 10 years and was more conservative than revolutionary.[8,20,24,29] As Keddie stated, the reform represented "more regularization of the existing situation than any profound reform."[24] There were many exclusions in the law and numerous bureaucratic obstacles. Mechanized and semi-mechanized lands, for example, were excluded. As a result, huge numbers of rural peasants were driven off their lands because the landlords either registered the lands as excluded or transferred them to their children. This process was supported by the MARD's organizational inaction.[8,30]

In 1972, when the government announced the completion of the reform, fewer than 10,000 of the 50,000 villages had been partially *sold* to the peasants. Land reform was followed by a number of rural and agricultural reform policies declared by the Shah during the early 1970s. The primary responsibility for implementing these reforms was given to the MARD.[6,8,11]

The Ministry of Agriculture was one of the smallest civilian bureaucracies until 1962. During the 1960s and 1970s it grew in size, budget, and power so rapidly that it became one of the most powerful bureaucracies in Iran.

A. The Politics of Reforms

Over one-half of the 12 points of reform were directed at the peasants. The rationale and objectives were political, economic, and social. As stated in the law, land reform was aimed at abolishing the feudal system in rural Iran.[28] This involved a number of more specific objectives: (1) destroying the landed aristocracy; (2) creating a new class of allies for the regime and the Shah; (3) developing modern capitalist mechanisms in agricultural and rural areas, along the lines of the world market; and (4) demonstrating to the world that Iran was "modern" and worthy of foreign aid.[16,17,20,22]

Strong evidence shows that the Shah's main purpose was to gain massive peasant support (even temporarily) beyond the "small traditional ruling classes."[17] This was done by promising them land, silencing the urban intelligentsia who opposed both the regime and feudalism, and appointing some of the members of the intelligentsia as project officers, a step urged by the American government. All of these were intended to gain legitimacy and broaden the support for the regime among the peasants, workers, and the commercial-bureaucratic middle classes.[17,20,27] After 1953, the Shah's only political support was the army and the royalists, and the rest of the population seemed to be against him; there was also a possibility of peasant revolt.[7,8,10]

The rationale was clearly stated by Premier Amini (who was favored by the Kennedy administration): "We must not allow the people's anger to rise. It would sweep us all away, the Shah and the Aminis."[24] The architect of the reforms, Amini's minister of agriculture, Arsanjani, similarly stated, "one can no longer continue with this system from the middle ages. . . . That has now confronted us with the choice of 'red' or 'white' revolution. If the country remains in its present situation, it will explode."[11] Thus, the Shah declared a "white revolution" and received support from the peasantry at the state-organized Peasant Congress in January 1963.[17,31] In this way the reform programs served "system preservation"[23] and weakened the "opportunity for superclass challengers."[11]

Moreover, the reforms enhanced regime maintenance through the bureaucratization of Iran, which extended the state control over rural areas and replaced the feudal power.[8] Finally, they furthered the economic interests of the Shah and his regime by establishing a capitalist economy monopolized and controlled by the royal family. But the power of the landed aristocracy was not eliminated; it was incorporated into the ruling class and became one of the major bases of the regime and its state.[6,8,29,32] Such transformation took several centuries in Europe,[33] but there was no indigenous evolution from feudalism to capitalism in Iran, no agricultural or industrial revolution.[14,34] The result, instead, was a negative development and a loss in agricultural independence.[6,8,12]

V. ACHIEVEMENTS AND FAILURES OF THE MARD

The MARD was very effective in changing the socioeconomic structure of Iran and in system maintenance. In brief, the major organizational achievements of the MARD included the abolishment of feudalism, the establishment and promotion of capitalism in rural areas, the bureaucratization of rural Iran, and the establishment of state power in those areas.[6,8,20,32] The MARD also weakened the possibility of a peasant revolt.

On the negative side, the MARD failed to replace the old, independent economic system with another independent economic system. The MARD also failed to promote the agricultural sector. indeed, the self-sufficient (even exporting) agriculture of Iran was replaced by an 80% dependence on foreign imports. The contribution of agriculture to the industrial sector and the GNP declined, and its surplus generation fell drastically.[6,8,19,35,36] Moreover, the MARD failed to promote rural development; it promoted an exodus to major cities. This happened as a result of the rural displacement, partial and unequal implementation of reforms, bureaucratic corruption and repression, and the widening gap between rich and poor. These migrants (9 million) ultimately fueled the revolution in the streets in 1978–79. Thus, while the MARD played an effective role in enhancing regime maintenance, it planted the seeds of system destruction at the same time.[4,6,8,19,20]

Most of the aforementioned failures should be attributed to the nature of the regime, which called for reform "but sought preservation of the ongoing" political and economic relations.[6,8,20]

VI. MANAGEMENT OF CHANGE, DEVELOPMENT, AND SYSTEM MAINTENANCE/ENHANCEMENT

Several characteristics explain the political strategy of the regime and the organizational behavior of the MARD in implementing reforms and in managing change during the 1960s and 1970s.

First, through organizational fragmentation and duplication, agricultural and rural reforms were implemented by several competing agencies and organizations, including the Ministry of the Interior. Some of these organizations (e.g., Land Reform, Rural Cooperatives, Natural Resources) were created during the 1960s and consolidated with the Ministry of Agricultural in the mid-1970s, to form the MARD. This strategy prevented power concentration in a single agency. But it resulted in waste and duplication, which were encouraged by the political system, for they were functional to regime maintenance by providing employment and cooptation.[6,8,11]

Second, organizational consolidation and further centralization were pursued forcefully in the 1970s. The purpose was to achieve more political coordination and tighten organizational control established through rural bureaucratization in the 1960s.

Third, through a regionalization process, the MARD divided the country into agricultural regions (poles) crossing provincial lines. This created legal and authority conflicts as the MARD assumed more political and administrative functions within the regions (poles) and undermined the authority and power of the district, local, and provincial governors.[8] This policy process demonstrated the increasing organizational power of the MARD in society, and provided various mechanisms of control that facilitated state-corporate partnership strategies and regime maintenance/enhancement.[8,11]

Fourth, most of the agricultural plans, programs, and projects were carried out and managed by public-private partnership strategies. The MARD subsidized many such projects, including several large-scale agribusinesses (joint ventures with foreign firms), royal farm and agroindustrial corporations, rural development enterprises, etc. These strategies developed capitalism in rural Iran.[8,11]

Fifth, tremendous organizational growth took place in several ways and was facilitated by special authority granted to the MARD by the regime. Highly educated technical and nontechnical personnel were recruited both from within the country and from abroad. The MARD also hired a large number of college graduates for political reasons.[37] The budget of the MARD also grew rapidly, making it a very attractive organization for careerists. It was also used for political cooptation.[7,19] Professionally, the organization developed to the highest level of technology and human resource training, and an increasing number of agricultural/technical colleges and institutions served it across the country.

Sixth, security clearance was a must for every recruit, compensation was attractive, and opportunities for corruption were available through purchases, contracts, and other sources. Organizational professionalization and politicization along with appointment of ambitious, politically loyal "climbers" to key positions were among the personnel approaches used by the MARD. This provided a professionally competent and politically loyal bureaucracy, which had a tremendous amount of power.[4,6,8,13,20]

Seventh, one of the 12 points of the reforms of the 1960s was the "administrative revolution," but it was "forgotten" soon. And, as Bill put it, "this revolution exist[ed] on paper only".[20]

The administrative reform failed to materialize because the political system encouraged many bureaucratic pathologies such as corruption, duplication, overcentralization, red tape, and the like, all of which were functional to regime enhancement by providing means of employment, cooptation, and control.[7,8,20] The administrative reform also failed because it "was undertaken for its own sake."[38] Another reason for failure was the negative public attitude toward the regime. As Cottam stated: "Any regime considered by its attentive public to be an American creation or at least a dependency, will be fundamentally fragile."[10] An American adviser, Frank Sherwood, added: "We built roads to nowhere just to keep people busy and to have some legitimacy in paying them." One of the major achievements of the reform was position classification, which, according to Sherwood, contributed to "to organization rigidity and inflexibility."[39] This facilitated political control and served regime maintenance.

Eighth, the MARD was highly politicized by the following means: partisan political appointment, partisan activities, Shah-worshiping, ideology, and activities of the security organization (SAVAK).[8,40–42] While these means of politicalization helped the regime maintenance process, they also helped sow the seeds for a challenge to the system.

VII. BUREAUCRACY AND THE REVOLUTION

Until the revolution of 1978–79, several forms of regime challenging were carried out directly or indirectly by public employees.

A. Regime Challenging

The regime challenging process evolved principally outside the bureaucracy, but it drew part of its forces from the middle and lower echelons of the bureaucracy during the violent months of the fall of 1978 and winter of 1979. As political repression intensified, these forces became more active. The majority of MARD personnel, like the members of other public organizations, joined the revolution.[8,42] Even some regime maintainers seem to have changed positions and taken part in the process.[8,42,43]

The majority of the regime challengers in the bureaucracy were professional and technical personnel—who were alienated from and frustrated by the system and the regime, the lower echelon bureaucrats and clerks—who had suffered the most in the bureaucracy, and the young college graduates—who were also part of the intelligentsia critical of the system.[5,20]

Regime challenging within the bureaucracy took several forms: (1) refusal to believe official statements; (2) whistle-blowing; (3) silent resistance; (4) rigorous application of merit system and opposition to favoritism, patronage, and discrimination in administrative behavior;[5,20] (5) noncooperation;[42] (6) disobedience by experienced senior bureaucrats; (7) adherence to religious laws, especially by the followers of Ayatollah Khomeini, who was seen by Iranians as a noncompromising leader opposing the regime; and (8) strikes, which became the most effective means of regime challenging. Only in late 1978 did the MARD's internal regime challengers join the general strikes and take part in the revolution. Other members of the bureaucracy then followed suit.[8,42]

B. The Revolution of 1978–79

The Iranian revolution of 1978–79 was a general popular uprising with the participation of all levels of the citizenry. Its aim was to eliminate the monarchy, the regime of the Pahlavi and the Shah, and to change fundamentally the economic and social system of Iran.[10,18,30,44]

The revolution was also directed against the bureaucratic machine of the government, which, as a power instrument, had the primary function of maintaining the regime and enhancing its economic and political interests.[4,8,11,20,44,45]

Although the main blow to the regime was delivered by the revolutionary forces in urban areas, rural participation in the revolution was also significant, both directly and indirectly. Most of the 9 million proletarianized rural migrants ultimately fueled the revolution on the streets of the cities and became active participants in politics. As struggles spread into the countryside, most of the remaining rural population fought against both the regime and its local supporters, the large landowners and the remaining feudal lords.[8,30,46] The peasant struggle against the feudal lords continued in 1979 and intensified during 1980–81.[46]

It was a popular expectation among the general populace that the bureaucratic "machine of the regime" would be smashed or at least reorganized in a way as to be accountable and responsive to the public.[46] Unless changed and controlled, the "old bureaucracy could pose a serious threat to the revolution, its gains and its people."[47] A detailed analysis of the major impacts of the revolution on Iranian bureaucracy and civil service is made by the author elsewhere.[8] The following is a brief account of some of the major impacts pertaining to the MARD, with an examination of the postrevolutionary agrarian policies of the Islamic Republic.

Since 1979, several conflicting and contradictory changes have taken place in society, which have affected the MARD, and in land and other agricultural policies, which shape the state-peasant relations.

C. Organizational/Structural Changes

Three major phases characterize the changing status of the MARD in particular and the bureaucracy in general in postrevolutionary Iran: (1) the status quo; (2) debureaucratization; and (3) rebureaucratization.

1. Status Quo (1979)

During 1979, under the provisional administration of Mehdi Bazargan, no fundamental changes took place in either the socioeconomic or the administrative systems of Iran. While the monarchy and the Pahlavi regime were abolished, the structure of the bureaucracy remained unchanged. However, there were forces in society that sought fundamental changes in the country, including the abolishment of the old bureaucracy.[48] But Premier Bazargan seemed to be opposed to those changes, repeatedly stated in public that "we wanted rain but received flood," complaining about the "unrealistic demands of the people."[49] Overall, less than 5% of the key administrators—mainly the regime maintainers—lost their jobs, and a policy of "wait-and-see" seemed to be prevalent in the bureaucracy as the old administrative rules and procedures were ignored and new laws were yet to be prepared.[48]

2. Debureaucratization (1979–1982)

During this second phase of the revolution, numerous political events took place in Iran, a subject that is beyond the scope of this chapter. In short, it was a period of "life-and-death situations for the Islamic Republic."[50] The phenomenon of debureaucratization started when "the people, disenchanted with and distrustful of the bureaucracy, began forming voluntary mass organizations of their own" to provide public services and help themselves throughout the country.[50,51] A large number of these grass-roots organizations took over many administrative functions of the bureaucracy in rural and urban areas. These organizations replaced, temporarily to a great extent, many bureaucratic organizations and provided uncomplicated services.

The most important of these organizations included the Reconstruction Crusade (*Jehad-e-Sazandegi*), a huge multipurpose cooperative mass organization covering almost all villages of Iran; the Economic Mobilization (*Basij-e-Eghtesadi*), for distribution of rationed goods and services (as a result of the Iraqi invasion and the war); the neighborhood committees (*komitehs*), which distributed rationed coupons and administered a number of neighborhood affairs (located in mosques, in operation tasks); the Housing Foundation (*Bonyand-e-Maskan*), which provided low-income housing by giving people loans (through banks) and pieces of land taken away from large landlords; the Islamic Societies (*Anjumans*); and the Seven-Member Boards (*Heiathay-e-Haft Nafare*), which were responsible for redistribution of lands among landless peasants. As one administrator of the MARD put it, "these organizations, especially the *Jehad-e-Sazandegi*, accomplished numerous development projects such as building public baths, bridges, roads, small dams, rural electrification, and the like." And, one peasant stated, "the Jehad-e-Sazandegi has been the 'shining ring' of the Islamic Republic," a statement widely supported by many others.[52]

Changes within the bureaucracy included growth in size because of the nationalization of major agro-industrial enterprises, banks, and other organizations, and politicization and Islamization of the bureaucracy. This expansion exceeded the 15–20% of public employees who lost their jobs through purges and other personnel actions. One of the most important changes in the bureaucracy was democratization of the administrative system. Organizational democracy was promoted by the growth of the Employees Councils (*Showrahs*) and Committees (*Komiteh*), group decision making, and legislative oversight mechanisms.[52,53] Permanent religious representation at the top of every agency was also a form of control over the bureaucracy. Commenting on the committees and councils, one high-level administrator noted that they were innovative and they promoted democratic ideas in our system. But many committee members lacked managerial experience and administrative skills. It was not uncommon to see anarchy, but organizational democracy was prevalent."[53] Direct public access to high officials of the bureaucracy was also made easy. An example of this was the case of the then Minister of the MARD, Esfahani who "simply sat on the floor of his office, listened to peasants, and handled their problems."[53] This trend toward debureaucratization began to reverse towards the end of 1982, as changes in the power structure of the government and the institutions of the state became more apparent.

3. Rebureaucratization

The trend toward rebureaucratization started in late 1982 and has continued since. Among the major events in this new phase have been a shift of power within the government toward moderate-right, political stabilization, increased diplomatic relations with Western countries, and institutionalization of power in society. The ruling power has been exercised by the "moderate-right groups, mainly religious, which represent the fundamentalists and the Bazar, large landowners, and industrialists".[4]

As part of the postrevolutionary institutionalization of power, the parliament (*Majlis*) ratified administration-sponsored bills to include the aforementioned grass-roots organizations and thousands of their local and regional offices in the centralized bureaucracy. By mid-1983, the Revolutionary Guards Organization and the *Jehad-e-Sazandegi* organization had already become separate ministries. The argument of Premier Mousavi and other supporters of this policy is that it would reduce duplication and waste, and would result in increased efficiency, better coordination, and uniformity in policy implementation.[54] The opponents, on the other hand, have charged that this policy promotes "state bureaucratization of the society, inhibits citizens' initiative, especially in rural areas, and takes away their independence, thus making them dependent on the central government."[55]

In April 1983, the Vice-Minister of the MARD told the author that, while some of these concerns were legitimate, the institutionalization policy was necessary to improve administrative performance and security. He favored, however, decentralization of the administrative system. A reorganization plan for the MARD was submitted to and approved by the parliament in 1983. The plan called for centralization of policymaking at the center and decentralization of policy implementation at the provincial and local levels.[56]

While the Ministry of *Jehad-e-Sazandegi* has been established as a separate bureaucracy, numerous independent rural organizations have been consolidated with the MARD, and its power position in society has been increased. As part of the rebureaucratization of society, standardization and routinization of administrative processes have been pursued, and there has been a return to the bureaucratic practices of the old regime. Once again, agricultural and land disputes are being referred to the Ministry of Justice, which still applies to many of the old laws. This seems to have had significant negative impacts on the attitudes of citizens, especially in rural areas.[57]

While organizational consolidation, centralization, and bureaucratization have advanced, privatization of some of the formerly nationalized agro-industries and businesses has been pursued as a new government policy. A conclusion of this study is that a major purpose of the rebureaucratization of postrevolutionary Iran is system maintenance and enhancement of the Islamic Republic. This view is reinforced by the current agrarian/rural policies of the government.

D. Agrarian and Rural Policy

Until 1983, one of the popular government policies was to reverse the rural exodus by encouraging migrants to return to the countryside, by supporting the rural independent cooperative organizations, and by emphasizing rural revitalization and agricultural independence. This policy was highly favorable to the rural population, and seemed to be "effective in returning hundreds of thousands of former peasants back to villages."[58] A financial incentive plan provided as much as 200,000 Tumans ($22,000) to able individuals returning to agricultural practice; they would also receive land, subsidies, and long-term, low-interest loans from the government.[59] This policy was reinforced by the effective "operations of the Jehad-e-Sazandegi and by other independent rural organizations such as the large multipurpose Cooperatives formed and run by farmers throughout the country."[59] The constitutionally formed, independent village Islamic Societies (*Anjumans*)[60] also provided support for a policy of "agricultural development and self-sufficiency by 1990."[61]

In short, an egalitarian policy was pronounced (land belongs to the peasant who tills it), pursued, and "achieved a major success in returning many people back to villages and in raising agricultural production."[47,61] Three major factors seem to have contributed to this policy success: (1) the relative independence of peasant organizations; (2) the government support, however inconsistent, including free electricity to rural households and legal support of the Revolutionary Courts;[62] and (3) the land reforms.

Land reforms has been one of the most important popular demands of the rural people, and two major plans for land reforms have been offered. The most egalitarian plan was the Esfahani Bill (1980), which drew strong opposition from the landed class and their supporters, including some conservative religious leaders, and was killed in the parliament. If approved, "it would abolish large landholding, and promote an independent cooperative system as the primary form of agricultural organization. . . . It was one of the most egalitarian land reforms in Iranian history."[63]

Following the Esfahani Bill, a much less radical land reform bill for redistribution of *selected* land among landless peasants was approved by the cabinet and the parliament. This legislation authorized the formation of an elected "Seven-member Board" (*Heyat-e-Haft-nafare*) in each district to identify and redistribute among landless peasants the lands taken away from large landowners and feudal lords, many of whom had fled from the country.[64] Despite continued harassment and even assassination of some members of these boards by armed agents of landowners across the country, the plan seems to have been relatively effective and popular among peasants.[65]

This policy trend and the debureaucratization process appeared to change toward the end of 1982. While the independence of peasant organizations has been taken away by bureaucratization, their grievances are referred to the judicial bureaucracy, and government support has also gradually shifted in favor of large landownership. Evidence suggests that even feudalism has been promoted once again in some rural areas.[66] Implementation of the land reform has been slowed down, abandoned entirely in many areas, and conflicts and clashes between peasants and agents of the reviving large landowners continue to rise. This is because the power of the landowners is being restored as they are encouraged to return to their businesses and their security is being assured by the government. Many of these landowners and feudalists had either fled the country or changed their residency during the revolution in order to escape the peasants' revenge. As one parliamentary deputy put it:

> . . . they were afraid to go back to the villages because of their atrocities, plunders and illegal acquisition of lands. When the revolution took place, rural people found the revolutionary organizations on their side and decided to get rid of the feudals and their representatives. But now a lot of these people are disappointed and discouraged because the same feudals are returning to the villages. The government should not let the old system start all over again. The country depends on these farmers.[67]

Many of the lands distributed since 1980 among landless peasants have been claimed once again by returning landowners *(Malekin)*, and some of these lands have been returned to the landlords by the local governments.[67] The MARD and the Ministry of Justice, which still applies many of the old laws, have supported this policy and have been its major implementing institutions. In May 1983, the author saw this policy enforced. The case involved a farmer who was asking the Vice Minister of the MARD for the title to the land given to him after the revolution. Vice Minister Zali responded negatively and referred the peasant to the Ministry of Justice. "The MARD no longer deals with disputes over the agricultural lands." While the revolutionary court had told the farmer to remain on the farm, the Ministry of Justice had ordered him to evacuate the land and the house and return them to evacuate the land and the house and return them to the former landowner.[67,68]

There have even been attempts since 1983 to abolish the new land reform law, but this policy initiative has evoked strong resistance from many peasants and some members of the revolutionary clergy.[69] Supporters of large landholding have even pushed "to nullify the limited law of land reform of the 1960s."[69] The supporters "have used, as a basis for their argument, the Ayatullah Khomeini's general opposition to the Shah's reform measures during 1963."[70] While this proposal has not received legislative support, it has "reinforced the reversed trend of favoring large landowners in Iran."[71] Sharecropping is in practice in some areas again. As a consequence, rural migration to urban areas has been on the rise, and it is expected that this rural exodus will continue. Since 1983, this problem has been acknowledged by even the revolutionary leaders and the administrative officials at the MARD, "but little has been done to stop it other than asking peasants not to leave the countryside."[72]

VIII. CONCLUSIONS

The Ministry of Agriculture and Rural Development (MARD) played a significant role in Iranian society under the Shah. Socioeconomically, it transformed rural feudalism into capitalism. Politically, the MARD established a firm control over rural Iran through rural bureaucratization, and helped maintain the Shah's regime and enhance its interests economically and politically for two decades. The MARD failed, however, to play a significant role in agricultural and rural development of Iran. Indeed, its organizational behavior had major negative impacts on rural Iran, producing increased agricultural dependence on foreign imports (up to 80%) as well as rural exodus. The displaced and proletarianized rural population took active part in the revolution of 1978–79 in the countryside and in the streets of the major cities.

The revolution was against the state bureaucracy as much as it was against the Shah and his regime. Several attempts were made to debureaucratize and democratize the administrative system of Iran during the early years of the revolution, and major policy steps were taken to promote an egalitarian system of agriculture, encourage independent rural peasant organizations, and promote rural development. This state-peasant relationship was broadened by several supportive government policy measures, including the relatively progressive land reform. Nevertheless, the recent policy trends toward rebureaucratization of rural Iran, reviving large landownership, and abandoning the land reform seem to have had major negative impacts on state-peasant relationships and discouraging implications for agricultural development in Iran.

Agricultural output has dropped sharply, foreign imports of necessary foods have increased to almost 80% (the level before the revolution), and huge rural migration to urban areas is underway again. The MARD has been playing a major role in implementation of these policies. This study expects that the newly created Ministry of *Jehad-e-Sazandegi* (a rival bureaucracy to the MARD) will either be consolidated with the MARD and thus strengthen this bureaucracy even further, or take over the MARD, which will result in the same outcome.

One of the conclusions of this study is that not only has the Iranian bureaucracy not been abolished by the Revolution, it has survived and prevailed. It exercises a great deal of power and is being used for system enhancement as well as public administration under the Islamic Republic. This trend will likely continue despite the public's disenchantment and rural exodus.

In addition to the issues discussed earlier, several other factors seem to have contributed to public dissatisfaction. They include the war, which has been draining the financial and human resources of the country; the black market and the high inflation rate; the shortage of some basic foods and necessities; the application of many of the laws and rules of the old regime; and the appearance of many pathological behaviors of the bureaucracy such as corruption, nepotism, and red tape, to name but a few. These problems have often been acknowledged even by officials, including the powerful religious/political leaders like the then Speaker of the Parliament, Hojjatulislam Hashemi Rafsanjani,[73] Prime Minister Mousavi,[74] and the then Interior Minister, Nategh-e-Nuri.[75] Other reports about the general public dissatisfaction with the bureaucracy have appeared in the major daily newspapers such as *Kayhan*, *Ettalaaat*, and *Islamic Republic*.[76]

Two approaches could reduce public dissatisfaction with the bureaucracy, improve the state-peasant relationship, and promote agricultural/rural development. One possibility is for the government to encourage and support, both financially and technically, the independent peasant organizations. Along with a comprehensive land reform, various types of cooperative systems can be supported by the government to promote independent democratic activities among rural people. This would likely stop rural exodus, decrease the public's dependence on the bureaucracy, reduce the size of the bureaucratic administration, and promote the peasants' initiative and responsibility. Such steps would broaden political and economic support for the government. Self-management and democratic administration would also promote economic and rural development. Thus, instead of rebureaucratizing society, the new government could, and should, pursue a debureaucratization.

The second possibility rests on the need for major reforms in the structure and process of Iran's administrative system. The postrevolutionary administrative system was expected to be responsive to the public demands, be democratic and representative of nationalities and ethnic backgrounds. Corruption and other bureaucratic pathologies should be reduced, if not eliminated. A substantial change in the administrative, labor, and judicial laws also seems necessary to avoid public dissatisfaction. The administrative system, moreover, needs to be developed professionally, and a merit system should be applied in the bureaucracy. Every political system is concerned with regime maintenance, but overemphasis on this will, the author believes, hinder creativity, development, and organizational performance.

IX. UPDATE ON THE 1990S

Since publication of the first edition in 1991, there have been many changes in Iranian public administration and bureaucracy. The earlier trend of rebureaucratization slowed down in the 1990s, a decade which should be characterized by structural and process reforms in Iranian governance, administration, politics, and economics. Many of these changes and reforms have come about as a result of the stabilization of the new republic as well as the fact that postrevolutionary environment requires new thinking and new measures in adaptation to the domestic, regional, and international/global environments of politics, economics, and administration.

Administratively, the 1990s was a period of many reforms under two reform-oriented presidents: Hashemi Rafsanjani and Mohammad Khatami; both devoted to the reconstruction of the postrevolutionary Iranian economy, political process, and public administration. A key feature of these reforms has been the massive privatization policy that began under President Rafsanjani and continued slowly until the midterm of Khatami's presidency, when proposed as part of his proposed Third Five-Year Development Plan (2000–2005) and his comprehensive program of massive privatization with a scope beyond most governments have undertaken or considered in the world. It is unlikely that such an extreme plan of economic and administrative change will take place, as the Guardian Council, a high governance body overseeing legislative action, vetoed the

Parliament approval of the program for being unconstitutional. It is likely that a compromise will be reached through revision of the program.

Iran has already used contracting out as a major public-private partnership scheme in building and implementing massive number of developmental projects in industry, commerce, and infrastructure development since the end of defensive war against Iraq. With privatization implementation, public-private sector restructuring will take place in favor of private sector, which is being drawn increasingly into the traps of the globalizing transworld corporations receiving concessions from the new administration of Kahatami, who is trying to gain the attention and cooperation of the Western powers and multinational corporations for investments in Iran. This would mean abandoning some of the earlier nationalistic policies of Iran in developing and sustaining a strong independent national policy and governance structure that does not succumb to global superpower and the transworld corporations. The International Monetary Fund and the World Bank's conditions for international aid—namely, structural adjustment, including privatization—have been taken for granted by the new administration, a mistake that might cost independent Iran direly in the future. However, it remains to be seen how the legislature and the Guardian Council will react to these structural changes that can threaten Iranian domestic and foreign policies.

Downsizing, deregulation, and privatization affect Iranian public administration severely, but what is needed at the same time is a clear plan of administrative reform and of organizational and managerial development that would improve public administration performance. This plan is still missing.

X. POSTSCRIPT

Since the end of the defensive war against Iraq, and since publication of the first edition of this book, there has been considerable changes in Iranian agrarian and rural policy. Although migration has never stopped, its pace has slowed down. Many factors contribute to rural migration to urban areas, including change of career by younger generation, urban amenities, and others. Structural conditions have improved in rural Iran, and government support for peasants in fiscal distress have helped alleviate some of the problems Iranian farmers have faced. In fact, the face of rural Iran has changed dramatically, as I observed in my visit to Iran in 1994, after more than 10 years since 1983, and more have been noticed during my last two visits, in 1998 and 1999.

Construction of new roads and highways have connected urban centers to remote areas deep into mountains, facilitating communications and transportation. Bridges, public schools, colleges, technical institutes, and new urban developments have spiraled throughout Iran. Electricity, television coverage, and other opportunities have reached the remotest areas of the countryside. Yet, major cities are swelling with population and pollution, which has caused serious deterioration of quality of life. The above postrevolutionary achievements must be put in the context of international economic boycotts by the United States and Western Europe. Only recently have economic and political relationships begun to improve, and are growing, with European countries, but the United States is still pressuring Iran with stubbornness and irrationality, hoping with futility to bring Iran to her knees, a policy that has failed for 20 years since the revolution.

Another point to keep in mind is that Iran has been hosting for almost 20 years about 4 million refugees from her neighboring Afghanistan and Iraq. Although their number has now been reduced to about 2.5 million, these refugees have been spread throughout Iranian society, enjoying the benefits of public goods and privileges to which Iranian citizens are entitled. Their presence has been a heavy burden on the Iranian economy and social and cultural services, including education, recreation, transportation, and employment. Iran has also suffered from a heavy burden on fighting a gigantic route of drug trafficking from Afghanistan. Both financially and militarily, Iran has been engaged in heavy battles with these international outlaws whose ultimate destination is Europe and the United States, but Iran has paid heavy costs for intercepting them almost on daily basis. Yet, no international assistance has come to Iran on either the refugee or drug fighting problems.

While a lot has been achieved in rural Iran, there still a lot more need to be done, such as development of small industries, agricultural development projects, improvements in seeds and other crop development—Iran is heavily engaged in this already—and other projects that would not only keep rural population, but also improve their life standards by bringing many educational, technological, recreational, cultural, and other urban amenities to rural areas. Recent legislation approved the consolidation of the two rival ministries of Agriculture and Jihad-e-Sazandege.

ENDNOTES

1. Blau, P., and Meyer, M. Why Study Bureaucracy? In *Current Issues in Public Administration* (F. Lane, ed.), 3rd ed. St. Martin's Press, New York, 1986, pp. 5–14.
2. Waldo, D. *The Enterprise of Public Administration.* Novato, CA: Chandler-Sharp, 1980.
3. Riggs, F. The Unity of Politics and Administration: Implications for Developments. Paper presented at *The National Conference of the American Society for Public Administration*, Anaheim, CA, April 13–16, 1986.
4. Bill, J., and Leiden, C. *The Middle East: Politics and Power.* Allyn and Bacon, Boston, 1974.
5. Binder, L. *Iran: Political Development in a Changing Society.* University of California Press, Los Angeles, 1962.
6. Halliday, F. *Iran: Dictatorship and Development.* Penguin Books, New York, 1979.
7. Zonis, M. The Political Elite of Iran: Second Stratum? In *Political Elite and Political Development in the Middle East* (F. Tackau, ed.). John Wiley and Sons, New York, 1975.
8. Farazmand, A. Bureaucratic Politics Under the Shah: Development or System-Maintenance? Ph.D. dissertation, Maxwell School Citizenship and Public Affairs, Syracuse University, Syracuse, NY, 1982, pp. 70–107. Also see Chapter 55 of this volume.
9. Albert, D.H., ed. *Tell the American People: Perspectives on the Iranian Revolution.* Movement for a New Society, Philadelphia, 1980.
10. Cottam, R. Goodby to America's Shah. *Foreign Policy 34* (Spring 1979).
11. Helmut, R. Land Reform and Agribusiness in Iran. *MERIP Reports 43*, Middle East Research and Information Project, December 1975.
12. Sharan, P. *Government and Politics of Persia.* Metropolitan Publisher, India, 1983.
13. Keddie, N. The Iranian Power Structure and Social Change: 1800–1969: An Overview. *International Journal of Middle East Studies* 2:3–20 (1971).
14. Keddie, N. *Historical Obstacles to Agrarian Change in Iran.* Claremont Asian Studies, No. 8, September 1960.
15. Lambton, A. *Landlord and Peasant in Persia.* Clarendon Press, 1953.
16. Lambton, A. *The Persian Land Reform, 1962–1966.* Clarendon Press, Oxford, 1969.
17. Platt, K. *Land Reform in Iran.* U.S. Department of State-AID, Washington, DC, June 1970, SR/LR-18.
18. Bill, J. Iran and the Crisis of '78. *Foreign Affairs 57*:323–342 (1978–79).
19. Graham, R. *Iran: The Illusion of Power.* St. Martin's press, New York, 1979.
20. Bill, J. *The Politics of Iran: Groups, Classes and Modernization.* Charles E. Merrill, Columbus, OH, 1972.
21. Riggs, F. *Administration in Developing Countries: The Theory of Prismatic Society.* Houghton-Mifflin Company, Boston, 1964.
22. Fesler, J. The Political Role of Field Administration. In *Papers in Comparative Public Administration* (F. Heady and S. L. Stokes, eds.). Institute of Public Administration, University of Michigan, Ann Arbor, 1962:118–120.

23. Downs, A. *Inside Bureaucracy.* Little, Brown, Boston, 1965.
24. Keddie, N. The Iranian Village Before and After Land Reform. *Journal of Contemporary History* 3:69–91 (1968).
25. Saikal, A. *The Rise and Fall of the Shah*, Princeton University Press, Princeton, NJ, 1980:18.
26. United Nations, Iran Employment Service Organization. *Inter-Regional Labor Clearance.* Technical Report 2, IRA/70/018, Declassified Confidential, ILO, Geneva, 1975.
27. U.S. Department of State. Iran: Recommendations re Iran's Third Five-Year Plan. *Declassified Documents Quarterly 4*:123 (1978).
28. Government of Iran, Ministry of Information. *Basic Facts About Iran.* Tehran, 1974.
29. Claude, A. Introducing a Cooperative in Shah Abad: A Conflict Ridden Village in Iran. In *Cooperative and Planned Change in Asian Rural Communities: Case Studies and Diaries*, Vol. VI of *Rural Institutions and Planned Change* (Inayattullah, ed.). United Nations Institute for Social Development, Geneva, 1970.
30. Hooglund, E. Rural Participation in the Revolution. MERIP Reports 87. Middle East Research and Information Project, May 1980.
31. Inayatullah, United Nations, RISD. *Cooperatives and Development in Asia: A Study of Cooperatives in Fourteen Rural Communities of Iran, Pakistan and Ceylon.* RISD Series of Rural Institutions and Planned Change, Geneva, Vol. VII, 1972:78.
32. Weinbaum, M.G. Agricultural Policy and Development Politics in Iran. *Middle East Journal 31*:434–451 (1977).
33. Etzioni-Halevy, E. *Bureaucracy and Democracy: A Political Dilemma.* Routledge and Kegan Paul, Boston, 1983.
34. Ashraf, A. Historical Obstacles to the Development of a Bourgeoisie in Iran. *Iranian Studies 2*:54–79 (1969).
35. Caldwell, J.A. *Iran: A Report.* Morgan Guaranty Trust Company, New York, April 9, 1975.
36. Kurtzig, M. USDA: Economic Research Service, Iran's Imports of U.S. Farm Products Soar in Fiscal 1975. *Foreign Agriculture XIII*:2–4 (1975).
37. Interviews with several senior career and political officials of the MARD, Tehran, 1981, 1983.
38. Gorvine. In *Administrative Problems in Pakistan* (G. Birkhead, ed.). Syracuse University Press, Syracuse, NY, 1966: 186.
39. Sherwood, F. Learning from the Iran Experience. *Public Administration Review 40*:415 (1980).
40. Shah's speech of March 2, 1975. Ministry of Information and Tourism pamphlet, pp. 11–13.
41. Karanjia, R.K. *The Mind of a Monarch*, London, 1977:236.
42. Personal interviews held with 22 officials of the MARD, Tehran, January 12–14, 1981, March 1983.
43. Interviews with three former bureaucratic elites in Tehran, March 1983.
44. Keddie, A.N. Oil, Economic Policy and Social Conflict in Iran. *Race and Class, XXI*, 1979.
45. Farazmand, A. The Impacts of the Revolution of 1978–1979 on Iranian Bureaucracy and Civil Service. *International Journal of Public Administration*, Fall 1987.
46. Personal interviews of the author with 20 administrators of the MARD and with a number of rural people in five villages in the province of Gilan, March 1983.
47. Interview with a professor of Tehran University, Tehran, March 1983.
48. Interviews with several administrators at the MARD, and with a professor of Tehran University, March–April 1983.
49. Public radio speeches of Premier Bazargan during the early months of 1979.
50. Personal interview with a professor of Tehran University, May 1983.
51. Statement was made by an administrator at the MARD.
52. Interviews with several administrators at the MARD, and with a professor of Tehran University, March–April 1983; also, conversations with a number of peasants in five villages in the Gilan Province, March–April 1983.
53. Interviews with several members of the Parliament (*Majlis*), and with a professor of Tehran University, April 1983.
54. Radio broadcasts of Parliamentary debates during the months of April and May 1983. Also, personal

interviews with two Parliamentary members, and with an official of the Office of the Prime Minister, Tehran, May 1983.

55. Interviews with two Parliament deputies and with a professor of Tehran University, May 1983.

56. Personal interviews with the Vice Minister and three high career executives of the MARD, Tehran, May 1983. Also, see *A Look at the New Reorganization Plan of the MARD*, publication #6 in Farsi (Persian), Tehran, Government of the Islamic Republic of Iran, MARD, dated February 1983.

57. The official argument for this policy is that the judicial branch, which now replaces the Revolutionary Courts, should resolve the disputes between the landowners and peasants. The critics argue that the judicial bureaucracy must be reorganized and corrected first, and their laws be changed. Interviews with three higher civil servants at the MARD in Tehran and interviews with five farmers at the MARD in Tehran and Rasht, April 1983. Also, personal observations at the Office of the Prime Minister, April 1983.

58. Personal interviews with several civil servants at the MARD; also, conversations with several peasants in one of the villages of Gilan Province, March 1983.

59. Interviews with several farmers who benefited from such incentives, Rasht, Gilan, March–April 1983.

60. As will be explained later, these Societies have become increasingly bureaucratized since 1983.

61. Interviews with several administrators at the MARD, and with several peasants in five villages in Gilan, March, April 1983.

62. Inconsistencies were observed "when Revolutionary Judges sometimes ruled against peasants regardless of monumental undisputable evidence. This happened wherever and whenever the Judges were influenced by the local/regional feudal landowners." Inconsistency was also observed when the government supported some landowners in their violent clashes with peasants. This happened in several places, including, for example, in the village of Shekalgurab, where the Revolutionary Guards were ordered to support the local landowner, Brarjan, who had oppressed the peasants for more than 40 years and had organized a violent attack on the village people. "We had a local revolution here, which drew national media and press attention," stated a local teacher and farmer, in Shekalgurab, March 1983. This author has known these peasants and Brarjan since childhood, and has followed this particular case since the revolution.

63. Personal interview, Tehran, May 1983. Also, interviews with three administrators at the MARD and with several educated farmers in Foumenat in the Gilan Province, March and April 1983.

64. Many of these feudal landowners were either related to the royal family or were among the so-called "thousand families" who constituted national, provincial and local economic and political elites of Iran. As mentioned before, the Shah was the largest feudalist in Iran; he owned more than 2,000 best villages forcibly gained by his father, Reza Khan.

65. Interviews with more than 15 administrators of the MARD in Tehran and Rasht, March–April and May 1983. Also, conversations with a number of rural people in several villages in Gilan, March, April 1983. Bloody clashes seemed to be a common and expected occurrence between the organized armed agents of feudal landowners and the peasants in Gorgan, Gilan and other rural areas. For example, members of the distributing board were assassinated at night in Kerman, Azarbayejan, and Gilan provinces during 1982 and 1983.

66. Also, interviews with two professors of Tehran University and with an agricultural expert at the MARD, Tehran, May 1983.

67. Interview held with a member of the Parliament (*Majlis*), Tehran, April 1983.

68. Cases of returning landowners and the revival of feudalism in Iran are many. The cited case of Shekalgurab, involving the Chorbani family vs. Brarjan, is only one example.

69. Interview with a high level agricultural expert at the MARD, May 1983; also parliamentary debates broadcast on radio during the months of May, June, and July of 1983.

70. Although Ayatullah Khomeini expressed general opposition to the Shah's white revolution, he never spoke specifically against the land reforms.

71. As one farmer put it, "we don't have much support from the government, the Malek (landowner) and his agents are back and act boldly. . . . The black market is in charge and we only suffer. There is no incentive or hope to stay in rural area," Tehran, May 1983.

72. Interview with a high-level agricultural expert at the MARD; also, parliamentary debates broadcast on radio during the months of May, June and July of 1983. Moreover, several conversations with rural people in five villages in Gilan-Foumenat, May 1983. Personal observations of the author also supported this trend.

73. See *Daily Kayhan*, *Air Edition*, September 14, 1983.

74. See *New York Times*, October 28, 1985.

75. See *Daily Ettlaat*, January 8, 12, 1984. The Minister reported a major bribery problem in the Tehran Municipal Administration.

76. *Kayhan*, *Air Edition*, April 13, 1983; *Ettlaat*, *Ibid.*; *Islamic Republic*, February 1, 1983. For a detailed discussion on the public dissatisfaction with the bureaucracy, see Farazmand, "The Impacts of the Revolution," Chapter 76 of this volume.

63
Bureaucracy and Debureaucratization

Demetrios Argyriades   *R. F. Wagner Graduate School of Public Service, New York University, New York, New York*

I. INTRODUCTION

Observing the evolution of public administration over the past two centuries, what is really striking is the metamorphoses in social institutions produced by shifting paradigms of state and public service, the scope and role of government, and—in the last analysis—changing conceptions of Man. It would indeed be plausible to argue, paraphrasing the poet Paul Valéry, that all new great departures in government and public administration necessarily imply a different model of man.[1]

In the 210 years that have elapsed since the days of the French Revolution, the world has seen the rise of radical ideologies, especially the emergence, apotheosis, and then decline of statism and bureaucratic centralism. To older forms of government, whose intellectual origins go back to the Middle Ages, the Jacobin philosophy of the French Revolution opposed another model. In light of this new model, the notion of autonomous self-ruling collectivities standing between the State and the individual citizen had very little place. Decentralization could be described at best as delegation of power to groups, associations or local government entities established by the state. To all intents and purposes, it represented a limited and voluntary devolution of responsibility, which an all-powerful central government could revoke at will.

Nourished both by the liberal doctrines of the Enlightenment and by the tide of romantic nationalism that followed, the concept of the state that emerged from the French Revolution left little room for rights or idiosyncracies whose source lay in tradition. Barely disguised, its oligarchic tendencies become apparent during the interwar years, which also marked the apogee both of the nation-state and centralization, particularly in Europe. A forceful and extreme expression of *étatisme*, the well-known Fascist motto proclaimed: "All for the State, nothing against the State, nothing outside the State" (Schneider 1969:207).

In Germany, the leveling of hitherto distinctive, traditionally autonomous territorial entities culminated in the *Anschluss*, which saw the incorporation of independent Austria in the Third Reich. Its record on minorities was probably the worst ever recorded in history. But few of the nation-states that sprung from the dismemberment of Europe's old empires looked kindly upon the presence of diverse, long-established religious, ethnic, cultural, or otherwise distinctive subgroups within their boundaries. Few respected and protected the rights of those minorities under their jurisdiction, in spite of treaty provisions enjoining them to do so.

There can be little doubt that the defeat of Fascism discredited not merely state-engineered repression, but totalitarian government practices in general. The new surge of concern for individual needs, the tenor of pronouncements such as the Universal Declaration of Human Rights[2] contributed decisively to the decline of management ideologies, whose authoritarian overtones were unmistakable and traceable in part to the scientific claims of classical management doctrines.

A new intellectual climate more tolerant of pluralism has further sapped the force of dogmatism and *étatisme* that for a long time served as powerful props of bureaucratic centralism. The demystification of the State in large parts of the world has gradually opened the way for a reexamination of bureaucratic theory in a new light. However, other factors have also been at work contributing decisively to change in this direction. Perhaps foremost among them is the corrosive impact of public education and technological progress on attitudes and values that, in the past two centuries, gave credence and support to authoritarian hierarchical structures.

II. THE BUREAUCRATIC MODEL IN RETROSPECT AND PROSPECT

The bureaucratic model, such as we know it today, is very much the product of eighteenth century thought. Its intellectual roots, of course, go further still to Rome and to Byzantium.[3] Pyramidal and fused, designed to enforce control and unity of direction, it was, in fact, the outgrowth of a long gestation process punctuated by major reforms. Those reforms had commonalities in spite of many differences. They laid the foundations of administrative systems in Europe, North America, and other parts of the world.

In retrospect, this movement has been credited with a degree of deliberateness and singleness of purpose that, in fact, was seldom present. The motives and the forces were complex in most cases. Administrative reform and institution-building during the nineteenth and early twentieth centuries were not isolated phenomena. They partook of wider trends, which progressively transformed the economy and societies of Europe, North America, Japan, and other countries. Bureaucratization—the confluence of those currents—extended far beyond the public service domain. It reached and touched most fields of social organization.

The bureaucratic model was manifestly a composite of many diverse elements. The model represented an early response to the emerging problems of complexity and scale in government, the quest for cost-effective service delivery, but also for objectivity, legality, and integrity in the discharge of the functions of public management.

The basis of it all was a certain conception of Man and a belief in Reason. Related to this concept was stress on formal structure, as the manifestation of reason and right order in human organization. Such emphasis on structure, in turn, reflected a new world view, a vision of the universe as a machine that worked with the perfection of a precision instrument.

Fascination with machines—like our own romance with computers—was as widespread in the eighteenth and nineteenth centuries as it was understandable. It was, after all, the invention of the steam engine that triggered and propelled the industrial revolution in Europe and America. Machines not only changed the nature of the productive process. They also profoundly affected human relations and, ultimately, altered the distribution of power in society at large.

Machines became a metaphor for speed, predictability, accuracy and efficiency. Their merits illustrated the technical superiority of bureaucratic systems over all other forms of organization. "The fully developed bureaucratic mechanism compares with other organizations exactly as does the machine with non-mechanical modes of production" (Gerth and Mills 1957:214)

To clarify this point, Max Weber elaborated on those distinctive traits of bureaucratic systems which, in his mind, accounted for their triumph: "Precision, speed, unambiguity, knowledge of the files, continuity, discretion, unity, strict subordination, reduction of friction and of material and personal costs—these are raised to the optimum point in the strictly bureaucratic administration and especially its monocratic form" (Gerth and Mills 1957:254).

In retrospect, Max Weber's testimony notwithstanding, it would appear that the much vaunted qualities of the bureaucratic machine model were only in a small part responsible for its success. More critical a factor in this regard was its consonance and congruence with the prevailing values system. Bureaucratization, in almost every case, coincided with the decline of patrimonial states based on prescriptive rights. It formed an integral part of the manifold transition from feudal aristocracy to capitalist democracy and from a chiefly agrarian to a predominantly urban industrial society.

In government organization and in the private sector, this period of transition was an age of reconstruction and institution building on an unprecedented scale. It witnessed the development of public education, the rise and proliferation of new professions in almost every field. One of the great accomplishments of this remarkable era—from the 1780s to World War I approximately—was, without any doubt, the reform and reconstruction of the profession of government. The values and the principles on which it was established were in fact, in many cases, none other than the puritan work ethic, allied to a firm belief in the moral ascendancy of learning.

The notion that society would be better served through the creation of a permanent cadre of career officials recruited and promoted solely on the basis of merit was not exactly new. Born in China,[4] it also found expression in Plato's *Republic* and *Laws*. The novelty introduced by 19th-century reforms was the equation of knowledge with virtue and the meaning invested in knowledge.[5]

Graham Wallas, Weber's contemporary, who hailed the merit system as "the one great political invention of nineteenth century England," discerned in its establishment the catalytic influence of a new approach to government. He wrote: "The conception was gaining ground that it is upon serious and continuous thought and not upon opinion that the power to carry out our purposes in politics or elsewhere must ultimately depend" (Wallas 1948:249).

Given the certainty of knowledge—as distinct from mere opinions—the bureaucratic model appeared to satisfy the essential preconditions for value-maximizing rational choices. It placed at the disposal of the decision makers a set of rules and tools best calculated to give them full control of all the relevant data in undiluted form. The underlying assumption that public administration was fundamentally a technique encouraged the belief that, given sound techniques and rightly fashioned structures, the right decisions would follow.

The primacy of technique was one of the main facets of bureaucratic doctrine. The notion that techniques, like machines, are value-free added substance to the view that the civil service profession in a bureaucratic state was also inherently neutral. Belief in the neutrality of the civil service profession was only partly grounded on the scientific claims advanced, at the turn of the century, on both sides of the Atlantic, on behalf of the new discipline of public administration. It also drew inspiration from *étatisme*, a forceful affirmation of the overriding claims of a transcendant state. It can be fairly asserted that state ideology and the professionalization of the public service both powerfully reinforced the centripetal tendencies inherent in the nature of bureaucratic systems.

After World War I, the emerging quest for unity and standardization added momentum to the centralization of civil service management. This movement drew support at once from growing concern for cost containment in the wake of the rapid expansion of public service complements and the parallel development of civil service unions. Beginning in the 1920s, the establishment and strengthening of central management agencies continued unabated after World War II, becoming in this process one of the most abiding features and commonest concerns of civil service reform.

The prominence accorded to central planning, coordination and control in civil service management attests to the tenacity of administrative doctrines that constitute the legacy of the nineteenth century thought and yet have strongly influenced administrative reform almost to our own days.

With minimal variations, those doctrines brought to light the strong, manifold quest for professional identity. This quest was made apparent both in the marked distinction between political posts and the civil service proper and in the tightly knit common career structures that often had the effect of buffering officialdom from external pressures. From Britain in the 1920s to France in the 1950s and 1960s, from Sir Warren Fisher to Roger Grégoire, professional identity, significantly grounded on the perceived neutrality of administrative functions, and common service of a transcendant State were major guiding lights in civil service reform. A measure of autonomy and centralization in civil service management appeared as the logical corollaries of this approach.

The civil service systems developed in this manner exemplified the view that permanent appointments and a career structure afforded the best safeguards not only of continuity, consistency, and efficiency, but also against the dangers of favoritism and arbitrariness.

As already stated, there was really nothing new in this approach. It harked back to the values that prompted the reforms of civil service systems in Europe and America during the nineteenth century. Those reforms were motivated partly by the quest for probity, economy, and efficiency, but also in many countries by the conviction that the civil service should be truly public domain and that the state—because it is the state—should be a model employer.

The equal opportunity model employer concept, which, allied to professionalism, provided the foundation for most of the Western bureaucracies, has also been a source of inspiration during the postwar drive for institution building in the new states and the construction of international organizations within the United Nations system and beyond.

III.   FROM DOGMATISM AND CLOSURE TO AN OPEN-SYSTEMS APPROACH

In light of the ubiquity of this approach, and in light also of the vigor and tenacity of bureaucratic doctrines well into the 1950s and 1960s, the subsequent departures in civil service policy have been nothing less than spectacular. There may be many reasons for this dramatic change whose multiple dimensions we are only now beginning to comprehend. In general, it seems that while the erstwhile quest for global central planning and integration has not been totally abandoned, the persistent powerful pulls in the direction of plurality and diversification have won the upper hand (Caiden 1988:331 et seq.). In this and other ways, we are witnessing the passage from a closed-systems theory to an open-systems approach in public management.

Essentially, the former rested on the belief that civil service standards could best be set, its policies established and problems solved by reference to a universal model constructed on the basis of a coherent body of scientific knowledge, but also of an ideology highlighting the significance of service to the state. The latter, by contrast, conceded the impossibility of adequately encompassing the volatile, prismatic, and differentiated reality of modern administration into a single conceptual framework. It readily admits to the existence of constraints in government's capacity to cope and deal effectively with all the problems of scale and complexity in modern administration. It also recognizes that there are limitations in seeking to combine the principles of tenure and of career structures with the changing political orientation of governments, the rapid transformation of socioeconomic conditions and technological progress.

In a more general manner, an open system's theory views organizations as complex and polymorphous, often fragmented entities in constant interaction with their external environment through shifting, permeable boundaries. The primacy now accorded to the external environment, as a critical determinant of organizational behavior and the perceived centrality of power in coping with the challenges presented by the environment have produced a shift of focus and a change of approach in organizational decision-making. They have induced a new, more pragmatic, less dogmatic, relativistic approach to problem-solving in the context of public management.

Contemporary literature often conveys the impression that the intervening changes are here to stay, representing, so to speak, the fruit of an advance in knowledge and research akin to scientific discovery and innovation. What we may overlook is the pervasive influence of ideological currents, that represent reactions to shifting circumstances.

Specifically, there is reason to believe that the recent transformations in organizational outlook are in large part the outcome of the escalating crises, which shook the mood of optimism of the early postwar decades. The multiple political and economic crises of the last 25 years revealed for all to see the vulnerability of a social equilibrium and economic prosperity, which were thought to have been based on lasting foundations. The advent of dictatorships in certain states and student and labor unrest in others undermined the credibility of the institutional framework. Events in Eastern Europe, the emergence of Kleptocracies and "soft states", the failure of many countries to keep their competitive edge, and growing indebtedness in others, all these in different ways occasioned a reordering of national priorities, accompanied at times by pressures for retrenchment in light of perceived scarcity.

These escalating crises and the failure of the ambitious technocratic schemes of the past were largely instrumental in shaking public confidence and causing disaffection with the administrative state. President Reagan's remark that government was not the solution to our problems, but rather itself the problem[6] expressed this mood of diffidence which marked a whole decade. This, of course, might well go away, not unlike the sense of doom which the financial crisis had brought and that has yielded now to an equally misplaced state of collective euphoria.

Recent attacks on "bureaucracy" and continuing disaffection with the administrative state run counter to the fact that bureaucratic structures have in the past two centuries served as the foremost vehicle of social, economic, and constitutional progress. An instrument of change, indeed in many cases the spearhead of reform, those structures have themselves been transformed, over time, by the conscious or involuntary incorporation of values and ideas that they had generated for export to the environment. Conceivably, we are witnessing a crisis brought about by multiple antinomies produced within the system as a result of this rapid feedback process.

Developed in the wake of the Age of Enlightenment, bureaucratic structures were designed with strictly limited purposes in mind. One such primary objective was the rule of law and protection against arbitrariness. Another was defense against domestic unrest or the threat of external aggression.[7] It would be fair to argue that, more than other values, legality, objectivity and accountability presided in the shaping of bureaucratic structures in European countries, at any rate. How, fashioned in this manner, such basically conservative, control-oriented structures could yet be made to minister the goals and needs of change is a seeming paradox.

The answer to this paradox lies partly in those values that constitute the legacy of the Age of Enlightenment and added to the pressures for administrative reform. Max Weber rightly observed that bureaucratic administration was the exercise of control on the basis of knowledge.[8] During the 19th century, belief in the value of knowledge went hand in hand with faith in the inevitability and boundlessness of Progress. Tennyson's "In Memoriam" gave eloquent expression to this belief and the Eiffel Tower, constructed as a centennial monument to the French Revolution, became a soaring tribute to the achievements of human creativity.[9]

The conscious quest for excellence, implicit in the principle of *detur digniori* and the pursuit of knowledge, opened avenues to change that tradition and prescription had kept forever closed. They furnished a new basis for the depersonalization and institutionalization of bureaucratic authority, but also for the legitimation of change, reform, and progress.

Through a veritable process of rapid goal succession, bureaucratic administration was turned into an essential vehicle of democratization through social, economic, and political reforms. In some European countries, those goals were forced to yield, for some time at any rate, to irredentist pressures for national fulfillment and territorial aggrandizement.

The goals and priorities that they were made to serve have often marked the structures and operative norms of bureaucratic systems. For instance, the special circumstances of the French

Revolution and its aftermath immensely accentuated the centripetal tendencies inherent in bureaucracy. The threats of foreign invasion, domestic unrest or secession have similarly impacted administrative systems in many another country. The case of Hitler's Germany is the ultimate example of the complete distortion of the nature and purposes of bureaucratic institutions by a corrupt regime bent on the annihilation of its opponents. In Eichmann, it produced the epitome of evil in our century, the blindly obedient servant of a totalitarian state.

In more constructive ways, political democracy and socioeconomic progress have in the past half century profoundly modified the purposes, domains, character and structures of public administration. In Europe, in particular, socioeconomic changes have gradually but steadily attenuated the rigours of an élitist tradition and class differentiation in the civil service. American reluctance to view administration as an élite function accounts for several differences that set the American civil service apart from its European counterparts. It largely explains, for instance, the distinctive policies adopted early on with an accent on training and specialization, which became highly prized in the United States long before they could be accepted in Europe.[10]

Such conditions in America have also smoothed the path of affirmative-action programs. Those programs, in support of women and minorities, have added new dimensions to "representativity," a policy of concern that in the past was essentially limited to low-level functions and tainted by the practice of patronage and spoils in the Jacsonian era (Wildavsky 1988:754).

Long viewed as unacceptable and unnecessary, "representative bureaucracy"[11] has moved into the mainstream of public personnel management not merely in international but also many national organizations. Undoubtedly a departure from "merit" *stricto sensu*, it is yet a concession to pluralism, a sign of recognition of diversification and differentiation both in the public service and in its external environment.

IV. THE DECLINE OF AUTHORITY STRUCTURES

In these and other ways, political democracy, societal transformations, and technological progress have largely modified the pristine structures and values of public administration. A complex process of functional and social differentiation has gradually eroded the rigidities of hierarchical authority structures and further mitigated the old perceived antinomy between structure and change. In many ways, debureaucratization is the many-sided outcome of this cumulative process.

Debureaucratization, in other words, can be viewed as an adaptive process of incremental change in line with the conditions and needs of our postindustrial information society. Though prompted in some cases by pressing financial imperatives in the wake of the global recession, the latest spate of reforms had also unmistakable ideological overtones. In England, in Japan, and in the USA, these reforms signified disenchantment with technocratic models, which do not seem to work (Caiden 1988:332). Likewise, the current literature suggests dissatisfaction with the present state of knowledge in public administration (Timsit 1986; Daneke 1990; Kettl 1990; Waldo 1990; Peter, B.G. & D.J. Savoie, 1994; Frederickson H.G., 1996, 1997; Simon H., 1998; Premfors R., 1998). In the quest for fresh approaches, systems theory may provide a more constructive framework than the engineering models of the past.

This is not an attempt to belittle the substantial contribution of the technocratic movement or the new public management which bears its marks.[12] Rich in metaphors inspired from industrial engineering and economics, they fostered an adherence to conventional orthodoxies and belief in "the one best way," for which the classical schools have been criticized. Nonetheless, they also encouraged the search for and development of useful methodologies, research techniques, and tools that form an integral part of the practice of modern management.

In acknowledging our debt, we must emphasize the part that the classical schools have played in creating a corpus of knowledge, identifying concerns, developing ideas and sets of professional values that, to this day, loom large in the study of public administration (Pugh 1989:2). Likewise, we must concede that to bureaucratic patterns we owe a considerable measure of the successes registered by the administrative State in two particular areas, the progress of the welfare State and the consolidation of what in French is known as *l'état de droit*: that is, the rule of law and protection of the citizen against arbitrary power. Though after World War II especially bureaucracy also served the goals of reconstruction and economic development, it may be fair to argue that it has been best suited to tasks of law enforcement and distributive justice.

Historically, bureaucracy has proved more apt at fostering uniformity and homogeneity, less at coping with diversity. It has been more effective at centralized direction, top-down planning, and control than at concensus-building, participative management, and innovation. Its record of success was founded only in part on its alleged "technical superiority," much vaunted by Max Weber. In the last analysis, what accounted for the effectiveness of bureaucratic structures was their essential congruence with the prevailing values system predicated on acceptance of hierarchical distinctions and deference to authority.

It cannot be overlooked that where bureaucracy flourished, in Europe, Japan, and China, it has derived support from parallel hierarchies and value systems in church organization, the schools and universities, professional associations, the military, the family, and society at large, which all exemplified the virtue of obedience to duly constituted authority. Though often committed to change, bureaucracy drew sustenance from an ingrained belief in a well-ordered universe in which every individual—man, woman and child—was beholden to a station with corresponding duties. Departing from one's station, neglecting the performance of one's assigned tasks was seen as invitation to anarchy and chaos.[13]

For centuries, mythology, religion, and tradition combined to inspire respect for established authority. More recently, however, there has been a decline in creeds and ideologies that in the past had acted as integrative concepts. The demystification of the state, the attenuation of social distinctions, increasing mobility in general, and, last but not least, the changing role and structure of the family have all, in different ways, contributed to lessening the rigors of hierarchical authority structures. They have, by the same token, deprived them of important traditional sources of sustenance.

Other factors have assisted and accelerated this process: the spread of the Internet, the expanding world of learning accompanied, however, by increasing specialization and growing interdependence in almost every sphere. Taken together, these factors have revolutionized the values, structures, and processes of public administration. Thus, the immediacy of response and "suspension of judgment" have largely disappeared from the manifestations of deference to authority. And gone are the mystique, the symbols, and the accoutrements in which its exercise was couched in former times. The differentiation of needs, technologies, skills, and interests has carried in its trail a wide diffusion of power at almost every level. The compact, monocratic, patriarchal, pyramidal structures that constitute the legacy of eighteenth-century thought and of the administrative reforms that it inspired no longer represent the prevalent reality of the contemporary world of public organizations.

Monopoly of knowledge, not mere possession of it, as Weber might have thought, accounted for the effectiveness of bureaucratic power. However, as Wildavsky aptly remarked, this monopoly has gone, driven out by the development of policy analysis.[14]

> All around the country, in think-tanks, consulting firms, universities, state and local governments, congressional staffs, and elsewhere, there are rival teams of analysts who have recently been or expect soon to be in government. They know as much as those in the bureaucracy (or they used to know a much or more). Virtually everything that officials can say based on their expertise can be contradicted with conviction by these analysts in (temporary) exile. Conse-

quently, public officials can no longer say with confidence that their views should carry special weight because they know so much more than their critics (Wildavsky 1988:254).

Dissemination of knowledge and information make bureaucratic secrecy increasingly hard to countenance or to sustain. They generate demands from organizational members but also stakeholders and clients to speak and to be heard. Under such conditions, openness, consultation, and participation are very fast becoming essential daily facets of organizational life and *sine qua non* conditions of effective policy making. No longer can decisions be reached, as in the past, by managers or "experts" acting in isolation, and then communicated to a passive body of underlings. Staff-management relations, but also the conditions of sound policy-planning have changed so much that, in most present-day successful organizations, "Collegial not command structures become the natural basis for organization. Not 'command and control' but conferring and 'networking' become the mandatory modes of getting things done" (Cleveland 1985:188).[15]

V. WHITHER PUBLIC ADMINISTRATION

The rapid transformation of organizational values, structures, and processes is making new demands on managers and gradually changing the nature of public administration as a profession. Considering the drive toward centralization and standardization of more than half a century, the current stress on pragmatism, inclusion, decentralization, and flexibility represents nothing less than a dramatic shift and change of orientation.

The causes for this shift are partly technological and partly ideological. There cannot be any doubt that technological progress, especially in the fields of information, management, telecommunications, and transportation, has created possibilities for geographical dispersion unknown to bureaucratic organizations in the heyday of concentration and centralization. Technological innovation has thus, in this regard, added momentum to the centrifugal pulls that rising educational and living standards have triggered in the North and West especially.

Those intervening changes bring into sharp relief the constant interaction of structure and environment in public organizations. They also point, however, to the centrality of power and to the distribution of power as critical determinants in the evolution of management ideology.

Considering developments in public administration during the past two decades, what comes as no surprise is the degree to which the public service profession has followed, internationally, the oscillating fortunes and mostly fading prominence of the public sector. Once viewed as the steam engine of economic progress, it has been criticized in many different countries as bloated, unproductive, and badly in need of reform.

> It is time to check and reverse the growth of government which shows signs of having grown beyond the consent of the governed.
>   It is my intention to curb the size and influence of the Federal establishment and to demand recognition of the distinction between the powers granted to the Federal government and those reserved to the States or the people (Levine and Rosen 1986:196).

Echoes of those concerns have been heard also in Britain, Australia, New Zealand, Canada, and other countries. Almost throughout the world, in highly industrialized and developing countries alike, the recession of the 1980's and early 1990's triggered pressures for containment and retrenchment of both the size and scope of the public sector (Fry 1988; Argyriades 1986). Thus far, the effects of cutback management have, on the whole been limited. True, the legacy of the crisis and the lean years that followed have brought about a surge of cost consciousness and a new keen awareness of the importance of efficiency in the public sector. Few governments, however, have so far tried to apply productivity criteria in order to limit its growth. This is true of developing countries where the limited potential for privatization and virtually no outlets for university graduates outside the public sector restrict the governments' room to maneuver. But it is even true of the United Kingdom and the United States, two of the foremost proponents of cutback management.[16]

Of course, there have been changes, notably in the direction of privatization and deregulation. Departments have been pressured to give up self-sufficiency and to resort more frequently to private contractors. However, the much heralded decisive reorientation of government has yet to come about. The forces of inertia have once more demonstrated that they can find support in the awesome scale and complexity of modern administration.

In qualitative terms, on the other hand, the effects of cutback management on the public service have not been negligible. Far more than the pursuit of privatization, relentless attacks on "bureaucracy" and the glorification of private enterprise have taken a heavy toll from the public sector. They have thus been conducive to a climate of opinion in which the business schools can barely cope with demand, while public administration, as a field of graduate study, is generally considered as only a second best.

Compared to new opportunities both in the private sector and in the expanding nonprofit service sector, the relative advantage afforded by security in government employment appears severely eroded.[17] Of course, there is far more to current attempts at reform than sheer cutback management. These often touch the core and, in a number of ways, call into question some of the basic values of the public service profession. Hugh Heclo summed up the problem in this remark:

> Even the current terminology of "public management" gives me problems . . . The two labels [of "public manager" and "civil servant"] conjure up rather different images. A public manager is a task-oriented achiever of goals, a civil servant is an official in service to the State and the public. . . . A public manager does a job, duties are defined by the managerial task at hand. A civil servant occupies an office, his duties extend beyond any given task and are derived from a shared concept of office (Heclo 1984:106–107).

In contrast to the past, more technocratic reforms of the 1950s and 1960s, present efforts to revamp and to revitalize the administrative system are profoundly ideological in nature. (B. Guy Peters, 1994) Though coming from the government, they seek to stem its growth and to reduce its role *as a political goal*. Or even when reduction of government activity is not the main concern, a drastic realignment of forces and redistribution of power within the system are seen as the prerequisite for the attainment and consolidation of the reform objectives.[18] More than ever before, the infusion of new values, often in open conflict with long-accepted norms, has been advanced as one of the primordial facets of debureaucratization.

Not surprisingly in the light of continued resource scarcity, cost effectiveness is high in the new scale of values. It is generally conceded that both in the United Kingdom and in the United States[19] the stress on cost effectiveness has produced some good results and promoted nonspectacular but no less important betterments in the "nuts and bolts" of management. It is also broadly agreed that, in these and other countries, the stress on cost effectiveness and the pursuit of economy during the 1980s and 1990s, have prompted government agencies to adopt more businesslike methods in the discharge of their functions.

It has been pointed out, on the other hand, by no less an authority than the former director-general of the Royal Institute of Public Administration, that the process has been carried too far in some respects. According to this view, it has produced an oversimplified, one-sided approach to the functions of top management in the public service. On the plus side, this new stress on financial management initiative may jolt senior civil servants into a more acute awareness of their responsibility for the proper deployment and use of resources in their care. On the minus side, however, there may be a certain danger of sacrificing quality and equity to expediency; a latent risk of fostering an attitude of mind according to which ends justify the means. "To misquote Oscar Wilde, it looks as though to-morrow's Whitehall manager will know the cost of everything, but the value of nothing" (Plowden 1985:408; Metcalf).

More important still, two concepts whose primacy and vitality may have been undermined by the recent wave of reforms are those of the state as a model employer and of the civil service as a strictly neutral profession "committed to rigorous abstention from public identification with party political opinions" (Johnson 1985:415). Security of tenure, neutrality, and anonymity were viewed for close to a century as sine qua non conditions of securing for the State through bonds of lifelong service those "who are in a true sense *aristoi*" (Hughes 1949:72).

For a variety of reasons, political and social, few countries have seen fit to make and mark the break with the career principle in the public service. Increasingly, however, the practice of lateral entry through fixed-term contracts is gaining ground. It is hoped in this way to bring into the service, indeed to the top civil service, new people and ideas and thus to stimulate a fresh, entrepreneurial and more creative approach to public business. (G.B. Reschenthaler and F. Thompson, 1998; L.E. Lynn, 1998)

Improved performance standards have been introduced. Significantly, however, parallel measures to enhance the mobility of executives were coupled with provisions whose net effect has been to increase the potential for political appointments and for political influence on the career development of senior civil servants. In this manner civil service reforms in some countries constitute a slight reversal of a secular trend, which goes back to 1883 and which focused on neutrality. Those measures, emphasizing the need to increase responsiveness and lessen the insulation of the public service, received a powerful boost during the Reagan years (Cayer 1987; Yaeger 1987).

In broadly similar ways, but with varying degrees of efficacy and appropriateness, "managerialism" is seeking to detach the civil service from its traditional moorings. The movement is widespread, observable at once at the national, subnational, and international levels. One aspect of this break with long-established patterns is a deliberate effort, through training, education and other means, to change habits of minds, standards of work and behavior (Caiden 1988:341). Another is diversity and flexibility in matters of selection, recruitment and promotion of public servants. There has been a de-emphasis on consistency and predictability of career patterns, notwithstanding the risk of offending expectations well-established through long practice.[20]

In matters of remuneration, the promise of periodic adjustments in the light of "fair comparisons" with outside occupations has also suffered a setback as a result of pressures for containment of public service costs. The pressures of ideology and rapid random change have caused a double shift to decentralization and diversification of policies and practices on entry-level hiring, employment, motivation, remuneration and deployment of personnel (Ban and Ingraham 1988; OECD 1988). The unity, cohesion, and relative autonomy of the public service have lost a certain measure of the appeal they enjoyed in former years.

VI. TECHNOLOGY, IDEOLOGY, AND DEBUREAUCRATIZATION

Debureaucratization has become an omnibus term to describe a complex trend of change, disaggregation and differentiation in the process of conversion of administrative systems from closed to open systems. It is a global trend with striking commonalities, but also with variations around the world. Several recent congresses of the International Institute of Administrative Sciences brought into sharp relief the range of shared experience in countries which, significantly, count free-enterprise economies, newly industrialized and developing states in their number. More dramatically, however, events in Eastern Europe since 1989 highlight the scope, intensity, and magnitude of change.

Throughout the world today, there is a mounting challenge to centralized, hierarchical, control-oriented structures, which constitute the legacy of nineteenth century thought. The mechanistic models that it produced and that have found expression through the classical management schools die hard, but increasingly are rejected as largely irrelevant to contemporary conditions. "In a climate of social values that stress participation and democracy, bureaucracies with their centralized structures of authority and control are anachronistic" (Pfeffer and Salancik 1978:281).

In large parts of the world, the centrifugal pulls in the direction of debureaucratization are drawing support from renascent ethnic, regional or territorial movements highlighting the decline of the strong integrationist forces and the "melting pot" ideal of the past (Argyriades 1980:176).

More generally, however, rising public expectations, assisted by the spread of education and technological progress are generating pressures for greater devolution, decentralization, more latitude and freedom for differentiation, experimentation, and greater participation of interested groups in public policymaking.

> "More than increasing efficiency, decentralization seeks to bring government *back* and *closer* to the *citizen,* a feature that has made it one of the critical facets of the transition process and administrative reform . . ." (United Nations 2000:7)

It seems that everywhere those centrifugal pulls, supported by political and socioeconomic changes, accelerate a process of disaggregation and differentiation of inherited structures. The compact, monocratic pyramidal organizations of the past are slowly giving way to a plethora of new structures which, in many different ways and with varying degrees of success, endeavour to contain the fluid reality of contemporary public administration.

Advances in the fields of telecommunication and information management are, without any doubt, among the foremost catalysts of this "revolution of structures," with obvious side effects in almost every sphere of social life. In almost every system, the pressures generated by technological progress, the needs and opportunities that it creates are helping to transform old bureaucratic structures and corresponding processes.

The need and the conditions for coalition building and resource mobilization in large, heterogeneous, and often fragmented organizations are also important factors of structural reform. Securing a support base, essential to survival, is not facilitated by the scale and complexity of the activities of modern government. The strains on modern government caused by this growing complexity and scale of operations have brought into sharp focus the problem of *capacity*: how much, in other words, a human organization can comprehend, absorb, process, and accomplish effectively.

The effects of resource scarcity in the wake of the recession of the 1980s and early 1990s have added credibility to calls for massive cuts in government activity. However, notwithstanding the strong conservative backlash in the concurrent invectives on "government bureaucracy," there can be little doubt that pressures for reform and debureaucratization stem from other, more profound and potentially more lasting ideological undercurrents.

In country after country, the *adequacy* of the existing administrative systems has been called into question. The transformation processes and mechanisms for feedback are often found defective. However, even more than the flaws in systems delivery, it is the very bases on which those systems rest that have come under mounting criticism. Debureaucratization responds to a growing sense that several core values of public administration no longer correspond, sufficiently at any rate, to the values and the needs of society at large. This crisis in the values of public administration is visible on many levels. Perhaps most fundamentally, the very notion of public administration as a distinct profession has been called into question (Waldo 1988:929).

Professionalism implies not only an ideology or shared-values system—implicit, for example, in the Hippocratic Oath—and not only a common core of knowledge and technology, but also and most importantly "the exercise of control over practice"[21] on that basis. In many ways, accordingly, professionalism is viewed as inimical to openness and as a factor of closure. At times of rapid change, it is seen as a buffer from reality, insulating public servants from the powerful winds of change.

There is little worth remaining in the old politics-administration dichotomy that Professor Riggs dismissed as an "implausible myth," an "American illusion" (Riggs 1988:343), but that nevertheless provided a point of departure in the long march to professionalization of the public service, notably in the United States. The technocratic doctrines to which it was allied have long lost credibility, as did some of the "tools" constructed by engineers for use by management specialists. But then, at times of scarcity, so have the "human" models developed by sociologists and social psychologists in past more affluent times. The interpenetration of politics and administration is everywhere accepted both as a fact of life and, perhaps, as a condition of survival and success. Everywhere, it has brought in its trail a certain loss of autonomy and particularism that, in the past, had helped forge a distinct identity for the "civil service profession."

Allied to this development, a powerful combination of economic, social and political factors is gradually bringing about a substantial transformation in the operational values of the profession. Whether these will prove lasting or not is difficult to say. For now, at any rate, productivity and effectiveness appear to have been raised to the top of the scale of priorities in the new "managerial" approach. In the tug-of-war between public needs and public wishes, under the pressures of "consumerism,"[22] the growing role in government of lobbies, clienteles, and interest groups may have won the upper hand. How rationality norms and the traditional values of neutrality, objectivity, legality and the quest of the common good have fared is a matter for conjecture. That even in the past, these values and these norms were not always translated into practice is not the issue. What perhaps is more important is the fact that, cast in the mold of societal expectations, civil servants in the past saw themselves as beholden to those principles.

The changing role and image of the public service are certainly outcomes of changing expectations and values in society. The quest for flexibility in policies and structures reflects a very real and deep sense of impermanence, which has become pervasive. It corresponds, in fact, to the prevalent mobility and the discontinuity of change in almost every sphere. Likewise, the value accorded to improvisation—"creative problem solving," as it is often called—bespeaks the growing feeling that rapid adaptation to new social conditions is a sine qua non of survival.

There are obvious limitations and inherent contradictions in this approach. Impatience with rigidities in rules and in procedures is all too often coupled with calls to brush aside important safeguards in areas of vital concern. It is not accidental that the rise of "managerialism"—the primacy accorded to economy and effectiveness in public administration—has largely coincided with renewed attacks on trade unions and attempts to curb their influence. "Let the manager manage" conveys a certain attitude inimical to dialogue, intolerant of dissent and, in the last analysis, incompatible both with democracy and progress.

As a novel approach, the rise of managerialism in public administration has had a certain impact on patterns of selection, appointment and promotion, but also on general attitudes and behaviours in the public service. Indeed, it could be argued that, in a number of cases, it has reopened the back door for a return to favoritism and arbitrariness. Whether this is compatible with improvements to the quality of management in general is at least open to question.

VII. CONCLUSION

Debureaucratization denotes the gradual erosion of organizational models whose roots go back two centuries or further still. Though early portents of this process could be detected in the humanist critiques of the postwar years especially (e.g., McGregor 1960), it was in the 1980s that mounting disaffection with public sector policies added fuel to attacks on bureaucratic structures, where these were found more prevalent (i.e., in the public sector), perhaps on the presumption that they were the corollaries and necessary vehicles of policies that failed.

A process of debunking of administrative legacies, debureaucratization is also nonetheless the rapid piecemeal change occasioned by convulsions in the sociopolitical, economic, and technological spheres. Potentially far-reaching, it has yet to produce convincing alternative models and strategies for action in the public sector especially. Its impact is most visible on bureaucratic structures highlighting, as they did, the importance of authority and grounded, as they were, on the twin principles of hierarchy and specialization.

A sequel of the Enlightenment, bureaucratization, during the 19th century, attempted to remove or to reduce the marks of arbitrariness in governance by cutting off the roots of public administration in history, tradition and prescription. However, rationality which it replaced as the basis of authority served to revitalize those organizational structures as structures of domination and control. By contrast, the cumulative changes of the past few decades have undermined the effectiveness of bureaucratic structures, by altering the nature and purpose of authority on which they had long rested.

The changes in the nature and manifestations of authority which have occurred are potentially as far-reaching for the State and for society, as the Pharisaic movement and the Protestant Reformation—its Calvinist version especially, proved to be for organized religion (Jewish and Christian, respectively). It may be worth recalling that the Calvinist movement portended the divestiture of a priestly ruling class, the displacement of authority from a highly centralized, hierarchically structured organization and decentralization of decision-making power to the local congregations of the faithful.[23]

Not unlike the disenchantment (*Entzauberung*) of the world of faith which, according to Max Weber, the Reformation movement brought to its ultimate conclusion (Weber 1967:116; Giddens 1971:128), the complex manifold trends inherent in the process of debureaucratization have carried one step further the secularization of the world of government. They have fostered the diffusion of political power at all levels and the demystification of the authority of the State. As in the 15th century, the invention of the printing press contributed to spreading the Protestant message and sapping clerical influence, so in our day, the growth of education and the advances of modern technology have brought about the erosion of bureaucratic power, that rested on control of information sources, monopoly of knowledge and mastery of techniques in certain critical areas.[24] Paradoxically, however, this process has been coupled with re-personalization, deconstruction and deinstitutionalization of public power in some cases.

Both in the 15th century and in our day, dissemination of knowledge in an *accessible* form (translation of the Bible into the vernacular had that precise effect) helped undermine the authority of formal organizations, which served as sole purveyors of such important knowledge. The spread of education and broader range of options to which it also led have helped narrow the distance between the power centres and those that they administer. In many intangible ways, this move has been conducive to greater reluctance to accept subordination and dependence on external authority.

In Calvinism, the outcome of this quest for total religious autonomy was what Max Weber termed "unprecedented inner loneliness" (Giddens 1971:128). The quest was predicated on "intense worldly activity" of the individual and a "coherent . . . life of discipline," "not single good works, but a life of good works combined into a unified system." Complete responsibility and self-discipline were the Calvinist alternatives for "the very human Catholic cycle of sin, repentance, atonement, release, followed by renewed sin" (Weber 1967:117).

In our day, the ongoing complex process of gradual emancipation from external controls coincides in many areas with a significant rise in the threshold of overall competence—the level of capacity and skill required for the effective participation of individual citizens in the social, economic, and public life in general. Debureaucratization, the Reformation movement of our times, confronts us with this challenge: it could compound the symptoms of disorganization, indeed ungovernability, passivity, exclusion, marginalization, alienation and lawlessness which can be found all around us—or it could pave the way for a more democratic, more open, self-directed, and self-governed society.

ENDNOTES

1. "All politics," wrote Paul Valéry, "implies a certain idea of Man." See Valéry (1962:103). On this subject, see also Edmund Leach, "Models of Man," in W. Robson (1974:153).
2. General Assembly Resolution 217 (III) of December 10, 1948.
3. On the Roman antecedents of church and state bureaucracies, see A.H.M. Jones (1986), esp. Chapters XI–XIX and XXII–XXIV.
4. See Max Weber, *The Chinese Literati*, in H.H. Gerth and C. Wright Mills (1957:416–442).
5. Of those that eye to eye shall look on knowledge
   Under whose command is Earth and Earth's
   And in whose hand is Nature like an Open Book.
   Compare this view of knowledge in Tennyson's "*In Memoriam*" with that set forth in Proverbs 3–13:
   Happy is the one who finds wisdom,
   The one who gains understanding
   For its fruits are better than silver
   Its yield greater than fine gold
   It is more precious than rubies
   No treasure can match it.
   Knowledge as an end in itself or a means of growth and of spiritual enrichment now gives way to the concept of knowledge as an instrument of power, material enrichment, and social prominence.
6. Quoted by Richard Reeves in the *New York Times* (Sunday, February 9, 1984, Magazine section).
7. A classical example was the prefectoral system developed in the wake of the French Revolution with a view to restoring and reinforcing central authority in rebellious distant provinces as well as to preparing for the wars that were to follow.
8. "Bureaucratic administration," he wrote, "means fundamentally the exercise of control on the basis of knowledge. This is the feature of it which makes it specifically rational" (Weber 1947:339).
9. Régis Debray, *Revolution and the Sacred*. Lecture given on Thursday, November 17, 1988, at New York University in the framework of New York University's bicentennial commemoration of the French Revolution. See Nicole de Montricher, *The Prefect and State Reform in Public Administration*, 78(3)2000:657–678.
10. See The American Constitution and the Administrative State: A Symposium on the Observance of the Bicentennial of the Constitution of the U.S. *Public Administration Review* 47(1) (January/February 1987), passim.
11. Term borrowed from Kingsley (1944).
12. On this subject see William Akin (1977) and Daniel Nelson (1980).
13. William Shakespeare in *Troilus and Cressida*, Act 1, Scene 3:
    The heavens themselves, the planets, and this centre
    Observe degree, priority, and place,

Insisture, course, proportion, season, form,
Office, and custom, in all line of Order . . .
    O! when degree is shak'd,
Which is the ladder to all high designs
The enterprise is sick. How could communities
Degrees in schools, and brotherhoods in cities,
Peaceful commerce from dividable shores,
The primogenity and due of birth,
Prerogative of age, crowns, sceptres, laurels,
But by degree, stand in authentic place?
Take but degree away, untune that string,
And, hark! what discord follows . . .

14. On the uses and misuses of policy analysis, see Richard P. Nathan (1988).
15. According to Y. Dror, on the other hand, "Clear establishment of legal authority . . . is critical in disaster conditions . . . authority to make decisions and activate multiple agencies is vital" (1988:265). See also Dror (1999).
16. "There were 499,000 in 1945, with departments staffed on a full war footing. Mrs. Thatcher this year apparently needs more than Churchill did to win the War: she has 504,000." *The Economist* (31 May 1986), p. 18, quoted in Geoffrey K. Fry (1988:3). See also Demetrios Argyriades (1986:8–10, 30–31); and (1996:60–63).
17. ". . . . in a recent sample of the career members of the Senior Executive Service (the top 6,000 members of the Civil Service), 72 per cent responded 'No' when asked if they would recommend a career in the federal government for their children" (Charles H. Levine and Bernard Rosen 1985:203).
18. For developments in the USSR, see Dawn Oliver (1988:411–428).
19. For comparisons of Britain and the United States, see Paul E. Arnold (1988:726–732); Christopher Pollitt (1990).
20. "The hope and indeed expectation of promotion is . . . something the civil servant . . . lives with throughout his life. The Service is so graded and its salary scales so adjusted that failure to cross a particular promotion bridge at more or less the expected time may well represent a serious set back, not only financially, but socially and personally" (Dunnill 1956:61).
21. See James A. Stever (1987), quoted by Dwight Waldo (1988:930).
22. " 'Consumerism' has . . . become an officially-approved fashion. In hospitals, schools, housing schemes, advice and information services and many other aspects of public administration managers are being exhorted to pay more attention to consumer wishes, offer consumers wider choice, and develop techniques for 'marketing' their particular service" (C. Pollitt, quoted by J. Potter 1988:149).
23. According to S.W. Baron, "Calvin . . . repudiated the idea of a universal monarchy as 'most absurd.' His own experience also taught him that larger states were less manageable than smaller republics and more inclined to increase their wealth by conquest and extortion" (1947:122).
24. "More and more the specialized knowledge of the expert became the foundation for the power position of the officeholder." See H.H. Gerth and W.C. Mills (1957:235). See also G. Timsit and C. Wiener, "Le Modèle Marxiste de l'Administration" in L. Boulet (1980:24).

REFERENCES

Akin, W. *Technology and the American Dream*: *The Technocrat Movement 1900–1941*. University of California Press, Berkeley, 1977.

Argyriades, D. Centralisme Bureaucratique de Décentralisation. In *Science et Action Administratives*: *Melanges Georges Langrod* (L. Boulet, ed.). Editions d'Organisation, Paris, 1980.

Argyriades, D. Reconsidering Bureaucracy as Ideology. In *Strategies for Administrative Reform* (G. Caiden and H. Siedentopf, eds.). D.C. Heath, Lexington, MA, 1982:39–57.

Argyriades, D. The Adaptation of Government to Economic Change. *XXth International Congress of Administrative Sciences*, *Amman*, *Jordan*, 1986.

Argyriades, D. Neutrality and Professionalism in the Public Service. In Democratization and Bureaucratic Neutrality (H.K. Asmerom and E.P. Reis, eds.). Macmillan, London, 1996, 45–77.

Arnold, P.E. Reorganization and Regime in the U.S. and Britain. *Public Administration Review 48*(3): 726–732 (1988).

Ban, C., and Ingraham, P. Retaining Quality Federal Employees: Life After PACE. *Public Administration Review 48*(3):708–716 (1988).

Baron, S.W. *Modern Nationalism and Religion.* Harper & Brothers, New York, 1947.

Boulet, L., ed. *Science et Action Administratives: Mélanges Georges Langrod.* Editions d'Organisation, Paris, 1980.

Caiden, G.E., ed. Symposium on Public Policy and Administrative Reform. *Policy Studies Journal 4*(8), special issue 4 (1982).

Caiden, G.E. The Vitality of Administrative Reform. In *International Review of Administrative Sciences*, Vol. 54, Sage, London, 1988:331–357.

Caiden, G.E., and Siedentopf, H., eds. *Strategies for Administrative Reform.* D.C. Heath, Lexington, MA, 1982.

Cayer, J. Managing Human Resources. In *A Centennial History of the American Administrative State* (R.C. Chandler, ed.). Macmillan, New York, 1987:327–343.

Cleveland, H. The Twilight of Hierarchy: Speculations on the Global Information Society. *Public Administration Review 45*(1):185–195 (1985).

Cobban, A. *The Nation State and National Self-Determination.* Thomas Y. Crowell, New York, 1969.

Daneke, G. A Science of Public Administration. *Public Administration Review, 50*(3):383–392, 1990.

Dror, Y. *Policymaking Under Adversity.* Transaction Books, New Brunswick, NJ, 1986.

Dror, Y. Decisionmaking under Disaster Conditions. In *Managing Disaster: Strategies and Policy Perspectives* (L.K. Comfort, ed.). Duke University Press, Durham, NC, 1988:255–273.

Dror, Y. Enhancing Professionalism in Public Policy Planning in Public Service in Transition: Enhancing its Role, Professionalism, Ethical Values and Standards, United Nations, New York, 1999.

Dunnill, F. *The Civil Service: Some Human Aspects.* Allen & Unwin, London, 1956.

Fry, G.K. The Thatcher Government, the Financial Management Initiative and the New Civil Service. *Public Administration 66*(1):1–20 (1988).

Gerth, H.H., and Mills, W. *From Max Weber: Essays in Sociology.* Routledge & Kegan Paul, London, 1957.

Giddens, A. *Capitalism and Modern Social Theory: An Analysis of the Writings of Marx, Durkheim and Max Weber.* Cambridge University Press, London, 1971.

Hambleton, R. Consumerism, Decentralization and Local Democracy. *Public Administration 66*(2):125–147 (1988).

Heclo, H. A Comment on the Future of the U.S. Civil Service. In *The Higher Civil Service in Europe and Canada* (B.L.R. Smith, ed.). Brookings Institution, Washington, DC, 1984.

Hughes, E. Sir Charles Travelyan and Civil Service Reform. *English Historical Review 64*:72 et seq. (1949).

Johnson, N. Change in the Civil Service: Retrospect and Prospects. *Public Administration 63*(4):415–433 (1985).

Jones, A.H.M. *The Later Roman Empire, 284–602,* Vols. I and II. Johns Hopkins University Press, Baltimore, 1986.

Kettl, D.F. The Perils—and Prospects—of Public Administration. *Public Administration Review 50*(4):411–419, 1990.

Kingsley, D. *Representative Bureaucracy.* Antioch Press, Antioch, OH, 1944.

Levine, C., and Rosen, B. The Federal Government in the Year 2001: Administrative Legacies of the Reagan Years. *Public Administration Review 46*(3):196 et seq. (1986).

Nathan, R.P. *Social Science in Government: Uses and Misuses.* Basic Books, New York, 1988.

Nelson, D. *Frederick W. Taylor and the Rise Scientific Management.* University of Wisconsin Press, Madison, 1980.

OECD. *Public Management Studies: No. 4. Recent Trends in Performance Appraisal and Performance-Related Pay Schemes in the Public Service.* Paris, OECD, 1988.

Oliver, D. "Perestroika" and Public Administration in the USSR. *Public Administration 66*(4):411–428 (1988).

Plowden, W. What Prospects for the Civil Service? *Public Administration* 63(4):393–414 (1985).

Potter, J. Consumerism and the Public Sector: How Well Does the Coat Fit? *Public Administration* 66(2):149–164 (1988).

Pugh, D.L. Professionalism in Public Administration: Problems, Perspectives and the Role of ASPA. *Public Administration Review* 49(1):1–9 (1989).

Riggs, F.W. Bureaucratic Power and Administrative Change. *Administrative Change XI*(2):105–157 (1984).

Riggs, F.W. The Interdependence of Politics and Administration. *Philippine Journal of Public Administration XXXI*(4):418–438 (1987).

Riggs, F.W. Bureaucratic Politics in the U.S.: Benchmarks for Comparison. *Governance: An International Journal of Policy and Administration I*(4):343–379 (1988).

Robson, W.A., ed. *Man and the Social Science.* Sage, Beverly Hills, CA, 1974.

Schneider, H.W. *Making the Fascist State.* Howard Fertig, New York, 1969.

Stever, J.A. *The End of Public Administration: Problems of the Profession in the Post-Progressive Era.* Transnational, New York, 1987.

Timsit, G. *Théorie de l'Administration.* Economica, Paris, 1986.

United Nations. Reforming Civil Service Systems for Development. Report of an international seminar held at Beijing, August 14–24, 1984. United Nations, New York, 1985.

Valéry, P. *History and Politics* (trans. Folliot and Mathews). Panthéon, New York, 1962.

Waldo, D. A Theory of Public Administration Means in Our Time a Theory of Politics Also. In *Public Administration: The State of the Discipline* (N.B. Lynn and A. Wildavsky, eds.). Chatham House Publishers, Chatham, NJ, 1990:73–88.

Waldo, D. The End of Public Administration. *Public Administration Review* 48(5):929–932 (1988).

Wallas, G. *Human Nature in Politics*, 4th ed. Constable, London, 1948.

Weber, M. *The Theory of Economic and Social Organization* (T. Parsons, ed.). Macmillan, New York, 1947.

Weber, W. *The Protestant Ethic and the Spirit of Capitalism.* Unwin University Books, London, 1967.

Wildavsky, A. Ubiquitous Anomie: Public Service in an Era of Ideological Dissensus. *Public Administration Review* 48(4):753–755 (1988).

Yaeger, F. Assessing the Civil Service Reform Acts's Impact on Senior Manager Work Priorities. *Public Administration Review* 47(5):417 et seq. (1987).

Yates, D. *Bureaucratic Democracy.* Harvard University Press, Cambridge, MA, 1982.

Yates, D. *The Politics of Management, Exploring the Inner Workings of Public and Private Organizations.* Jossey-Bass, San Francisco, 1987.

64

Women in Bureaucracies

Equity, Advancement, and Public Policy Strategies

Jeanne-Marie Col   *Department of Economic and Social Affairs, The United Nations, New York, New York*

Dhipavadee Meksawan   *Office of the Civil Service Commission, Royal Government of Thailand, Bangkok, Thailand*

Orapin Sopchokchai   *Department of Social Development, Thailand Development Research Institute, Bangkok, Thailand*

I. INTRODUCTION

Although almost every nation grants women equality under the law, as citizens, as workers, and especially as employees in civil service systems, this legal equality is often not sufficient to ensure that women are able to contribute fully to national development. As recently as 1981, M. J. Anstee, United Nations Assistant Secretary General, stated that "An obvious shortcoming world-wide was the failure to involve women in the development process. This would not happen until there were more women involved in the planning process, in the administration at all levels, and in all sectors" (International Association of Schools and Institutes of Administration, 1981). An increase in women's participation in decision making in the public service is expected to increase overall productivity, to increase public-sector responsiveness to women's needs, and to provide opportunities for women's advancement.

Advocates for the full utilization of work force potential often cite the underutilization of women as an impediment to the fullest development of human resources. Those who advocate bringing greater numbers of women into the work force at all levels, including the highest, recognize the importance of supportive public policy and supportive public policy leaders. The increasing role of women in public bureaucracies illustrates the linkage between administration and politics, and especially between administrative performance and political responsibility. While bringing women into the highest levels of public policymaking requires strong political commitment, women's participation in decision making increases the likelihood of public policies sensitive to the needs of women and the probability of women's consequent regime support.

In increasing the participation of women, public-sector organizations face dual challenges, that is, development and equality. Often being the largest organization in a country, the public service can set the policy of national development, including human resource development, and play the role of model employer for the private sector. Public service organizations also have at least two advantages in bringing about social change: they can place governmental sanctions behind their decisions (for example, a decision such as "equal treatment of minority groups"), and they can call on motives other than the profit motive in developing commitment to a change program such as human resources development (Col and Suzuki, 1987).

Governments, as well as public administration theorists, have often cited the policy advantages of a bureaucracy representative of the diverse persons and interests in a society (Mosher, 1968; Kirkhart, 1971), although demographic trends are also leading to greater diversity. While this representation may be passive in nature, assuming sensitivity to issues through personal identification, representation may also be active through seeking connections to clients. Current trends link demographic representation with bureaucratic trends toward liberation from overly hierarchical command structures and toward increased participation by all employees and clients in decision making (Ingraham and Rosenbloom, 1989). Processes of liberation, participation, and representation indicate structural and behavioral changes that encourage the inclusion, at all levels, of persons and interests previously underrepresented. These trends toward a more humanistic bureaucracy emphasize not only the moral need to respect the expertise and values of all people (Ferguson, 1984) but also the organizational need to fully utilize all available talent for organization development and innovation (Kanter, 1983). Women's opportunities for advancement will increase within this context of human resources development and utilization.

Public policy strategies that seek to ensure the full utilization of women at the highest levels of decision making must address the barriers and opportunities to women's advancement in at least four stages of career development: basic socialization to attitudes and values, education and training, access to entry positions, and factors in work life that contribute to promotion (Col, 1981). In Figure 1 (Col, 1986), these four factors operate as a potentially restrictive pipeline, with passage through each stage necessary for mobility upward through the figure to the highest levels of the bureaucracy. The identification and analysis of the dynamics among these stages rely on sociological, political, and biological analyses. While a biological focus emphasizes the role of women in reproduction and the political focus emphasizes the perceived struggle for power within bureaucracies and societies, the sociological focus emphasizes role orientations and interrelationships among roles within the bureaucracies (Stewart, 1986). Within this sociological perspective, issues of the distribution of opportunities, power, and numbers lead to prescriptions for structural strategies for women's advancement (Kanter, 1977). At each stage, factors are identified that can be enhanced to contribute to women's full and equitable participation in bureaucracies.

Although all four stages are essential for women's upward mobility in public service systems, the stages take on different levels of importance depending upon the politico–administrative–economic system. In particular, the degree of access to educational institutions and the relative need for trained employees illustrate a significant difference in the factors' importance between developing and developed nations. In nations where the educational infrastructure is inadequate for demand and where trained employees are scarce, women are less likely to be educated, but those women who become educated are very likely to gain entry-level positions. In nations with well-developed educational infrastructure, women are more likely to become educated, but less likely to gain entry-level positions appropriate to their educational achievements. In both situations, socialization to gender-stereotyped role expectations (Hess and Ferree, 1987) reduces women's opportunities to pursue educational opportunities and increases prejudice against women's career advancement (Gutek and Larwood, 1987) through lack of positive behavioral, structural, and supportive policies, as reflected in personal, organizational, and public policy norms.

II. CRITICAL STAGES IN WOMEN'S CAREER ADVANCEMENT

Gender expectations based upon cultural and religious values are reflected in the portrayal of women in the media and in role models in the community, as well as through direct teaching in

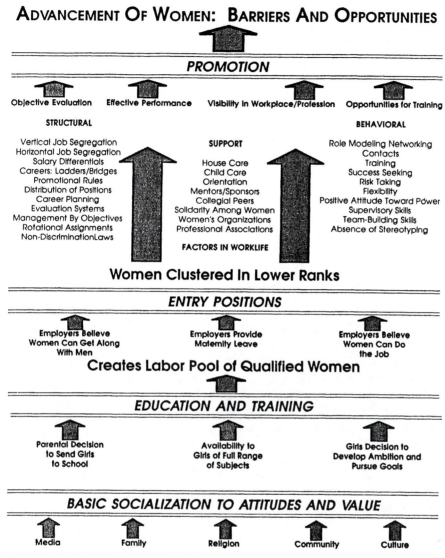

ADVANCEMENT OF WOMEN: BARRIERS AND OPPORTUNITIES

PROMOTION

Objective Evaluation   Effective Performance   Visibility In Workplace/Profession   Opportunities for Training

STRUCTURAL   **BEHAVIORAL**

Vertical Job Segregation	**SUPPORT**	Role Modeling Networking
Horizontal Job Segregation		Contacts
Salary Differentials	House Care	Training
Careers: Ladders/Bridges	Child Care	Success Seeking
Promotional Rules	Orientation	Risk Taking
Distribution of Positions	Mentors/Sponsors	Flexibility
Career Planning	Collegial Peers	Positive Attitude Toward Power
Evaluation Systems	Solidarity Among Women	Supervisory Skills
Management By Objectives	Women's Organizations	Team-Building Skills
Rotational Assignments	Professional Associations	Absence of Stereotyping
Non-DiscriminationLaws		

FACTORS IN WORKLIFE

Women Clustered In Lower Ranks

ENTRY POSITIONS

Employers Believe   Employers Provide   Employers Believe
Women Can Get Along   Maternity Leave   Women Can Do
With Men   the Job

Creates Labor Pool of Qualified Women

EDUCATION AND TRAINING

Parental Decision   Availability to   Girls Decision to
to Send Girls   Girls of Full Range   Develop Ambition and
to School   of Subjects   Pursue Goals

BASIC SOCIALIZATION TO ATTITUDES AND VALUE

Media   Family   Religion   Community   Culture

Figure 1   Barriers and opportunities for women's advancement in the public service.

schools and families. Attitudes that limit parental interest in the accomplishments of their daughters and limit the aspirations of their daughters reduce women's opportunities to enter upward-reaching career ladders. These same attitudes reduce promotional opportunities in bureaucracies. Girls receive positive career direction in wealthier, more educated, and more urban families (Tapales, 1985), and especially where the mother is educated and working (Badri, 1987; Swarup and Sinha, 1986). Girls are also more encouraged to pursue education and careers in nations where women have held leadership positions (Masire, 1986; Swarup and Sinha, 1986).

In virtually every nation, women have a higher illiteracy rate than men (Shaul, 1982). If women do not have access to education, it is impossible for them to move to the highest levels of their employment system. Barriers to women's access to education are financial, structural, and attitudinal. When families have limited resources, they often send only their sons to school (Badri,

1987). When girls are in school, they are seldom offered the full range of subjects, especially math and science (Langkau-Hermann and Sessar-Karpp, 1987). Although they may enter school, the girls often expect low-level jobs in a limited range of fields. This pattern is altered in all-girls schools in which girls are encouraged to pursue all fields and girls assume all leadership positions.

Access to education, however limited, results in some women being prepared for entry-level positions, although mostly in female-dominated bureaucracies, such as social services and education (Col and Suzuki, 1987). Prejudices about women's behavior restrict the hiring and promotion of women. Especially in male-dominated fields, employers doubt that women can do a man's job or that women can get along with men. In addition, employers, husbands, and often the women themselves believe that child-bearing and child-rearing roles, usually socially assigned to women, will encourage women to limit their careers (Tapales, 1985). When women do become educated and gain access to entry-level jobs, they tend to remain clustered in lower ranks in female-dominated bureaucracies.

Access to education, however limited, results in some women being prepared for entry-level positions, although mostly in female-dominated bureaucracies, such as social services and education (Col and Suzuki, 1987). Prejudices about women's behavior restrict the hiring and promotion of women. Especially in male-dominated fields, employers doubt that women can do a man's job or that women can get along with men. In addition, employers, husbands, and often the women themselves believe that child-bearing and child-rearing roles, usually socially assigned to women, will encourage women to limit their careers (Tapales, 1985). When women do become educated and gain access to entry-level jobs, they tend to remain clustered in lower ranks in female-dominated bureaucracies.

Promotional factors can be classified into three categories: structural, behavioral, and supportive. Positive actions and policies in all categories can lead to situations in which women are able to perform effectively, are objectively evaluated, have opportunities for training, and gain positive visibility in their workplace and in their profession. In some nations, women who reach high-level positions are accepted because of the status of their positions or their political connections (Swarup and Sinha, 1986), while in other nations, negative attitudes toward women, based on gender stereotyping, render high-level women without respect and power (Bayes, 1985).

Of the structural factors, the most important are embedded in civil service rules and regulations. Are women assigned to line management positions as frequently as men, or are women usually assigned to staff positions or to "assistant to" positions? Are women posted to a variety of functional responsibilities and geographic locations, in order to gain broad experience, as are the upwardly mobile men? Are women denied positions that require travel or are viewed as dangerous? Do women supervise fewer people? Are there any positions that are denied to women? Do evaluations objectively assess women's styles of managerial and collaborative behavior? Do evaluations separate job performance from irrelevant personal characteristics?

The behavior of both men and women in organizations must be examined. Behavior identified as leading to upward mobility involves success seeking, risk taking, flexibility, responsibility and power seeking, and leading subordinates. These behaviors are substantially outside the subordinate family role often assigned culturally to women (Josefowitz, 1980). Both women and men must adjust their expectations in order to accommodate and even to encourage women to develop managerial interpersonal skills.

Supportive factors include both behavioral and policy issues. In the behavioral sphere, women must seek networking opportunities within organizations and within professional associations. Public policies in the fields of child care, dependent care, house care, and parental leave influence the ease with which women handle the double burden of family responsibilities and work responsibilities. Women need the support of their organizations, their co-workers, and their families if they are to seek a greater role in the work force, especially at the highest level.

III. STRATEGIES FOR WOMEN'S ADVANCEMENT

An international study of women's upward mobility and advancement in public administration and management (Col, 1986), sponsored by the Research Committees on Sex Roles and Politics of the International Political Science Association, explored the sociocultural, economic, political, educational, legal, and organizational factors related to the level of participation of women in administrative policymaking positions and the policies and practices that constrain or enhance women's advancement opportunities. With research carried out from 1984 to 1987, this study, and subsequent enhancements, includes Botswana, Brazil, Bulgaria, China, Finland, the Federal Republic of Germany, Ghana, India, Jordan, Kenya, Malaysia, the Netherlands, Nigeria, the Philippines, the Sudan, Thailand, Turkey, Venezuela, and the United States. These nations include a wide variety of sociocultural, economic, and governmental conditions, which affect the relative importance of women's contributions to national development through participation in public bureaucracies.

In all 19 nations, women are economically active, although the patterns differ according to sector and level. In 1986, China reported 89% of working age women worked for wages, and Jordan reported an increase from 8% in 1979 to 13% in 1985. Although a 1926 law in Turkey allowed women to become civil servants, Turkish women must still have their husbands' permission in order to work. In Jordan, equal pay and equal opportunity for women were granted in 1960 and 1966, respectively. Only in 1967–1968 was discrimination against women in employment declared illegal in Brazil. Nigerian women gained more equal conditions of employment in 1979, when a government circular established women employees' rights to housing, health care, and other fringe benefits. These examples illustrate the slow but steady progress of women's entrance into the work force.

Women's upward mobility still suffers from intentional and legal restrictions in many nations. For example, while the Thai civil service is predominantly female (54%), Thai women are clustered at the lower levels and are legally denied entry to a key position, deputy district officer. Brazilian women are concentrated in ministries such as social service, education, health, and social security. In 1988, Kenya appointed its first woman permanent secretary. On the other hand, Botswana has several women ministers, including the important post of Minister of Foreign Relations. Vertical and horizontal segregation of women characterizes every public service system, although many systems are searching for ways of ensuring more equity for women.

Increased opportunities for women appear to be associated with economic development, political patterns, and urban location. In economic activities, education and skill become more important than physical strength in productive activities. Women play a greater administrative role in urban areas, at least in part because rural areas are generally more traditional and less accepting of female supervision (Swarup and Sinha, 1987). Economic decline and unemployment adversely affect career advancement of women. Stagnating economies and government and private-sector cutbacks in employment disproportionately disadvantage recent and potential entrants into the work force. In Brazil, the overall deterioration of civil servant salaries makes such jobs less desirable to men (Fernandes, 1988), while in Thailand the increasing cost of living has encouraged more families to accept women's employment and contribution to family income as essential to family prosperity (Sophchokchai, 1987). Also, women's opportunities can be affected by political parties (Vertz, 1985), labor unions, and religious institutions. In China, the Communist Party is a major source of cues for socially appropriate attitudes and behavior for women and men (Col, 1988). In the Philippines, precolonial traditions were much more favorable to women than either the Hispanic or American cultures (Tapales, 1985). The coexistence of multiple cultures provides a wider selection of role models. A most crucial policy affecting women's employment involves parental leave and dependent care—that is, their family roles, as expressed by the "double burden" (Leyenaar, 1987; Sinkkonen et al., 1987). Combining family roles and work roles creates role conflict (Tapales, 1985; Ananieva and Razvigorova, 1987). Civil service rules often ignore women's reproductive role, although Brazil's new, yet to be fully implemented, law states that every government agency must provide day care for its employees' children (Fernandes, 1988).

In designing strategies for bringing more women into high-level policymaking positions, governments must focus on two types of issues: pipeline issues and promotion issues. Women will not be available for promotion if they are not educated to skills and ambition that place them in upward-mobility pipelines. If women have been encouraged to develop skills and ambition, then they must be encouraged to move up in their organizations, through beckoning strategies of attitude change, structural change, and supportive policies. At an institutional level, these strategies are often initiated and monitored by a women's machinery, such as a commission, task force, or ministry. For example, in Brazil, a 1985 federal law established the Brazilian National Council for Women's Rights in order to educate women and men, contribute to policy development, establish policy networks, and monitor policy implementation and bureaucratic performance with respect to gender issues (Fernandes, 1988).

The pipeline issues involve attention to the social, economic, and political institutions that shape expectations about appropriate gender roles and opportunities for women. In particular, government must consider the behavioral and attitudinal cues expressed in the media and educational institutions. In addition, government policies must address the financial and social barriers to the identification and preparation of women for contributing to national development. Especially with respect to access to education, governments must examine the cost, availability, and motivational structures in their public service pipelines.

When adequate numbers of women are clustered in the lower ranks of the bureaucracies, government policies must address the issue of barriers and opportunities to women's upward mobility. Major areas for public policy development are civil service rules and regulations concerning parenting, posting, compensation, and training; evaluation systems; career planning and guidance; and training to sensitize both women and men concerning the difficulties to be encountered in integrating previously excluded groups (i.e., women) into the highest levels of policymaking. The clearest method of emphasizing commitment to women's advancement is through positive actions by administrative and political leaders. Because the full integration of women into the highest levels in bureaucracies often challenges widely held assumptions about appropriate roles for women, bureaucratic policies must be supported by strong political commitment to women's advancement.

IV. CONCLUSION

Women's presence in and contribution to bureaucratic performance and national development are affected by many contextual factors such as demographic trends, unemployment trends, and deeply held cultural values. Strategies for increasing women's participation in decision making involve modifying not only bureaucratic structures and behaviors to greater gender sensitivity, but also educational and media policies that strongly influence attitudes toward women's role in society. When women enter the pipeline and are greeted with gender-sensitive personal behavior, organizational upward-mobility policies, and public employment policies, then governments will have the benefit of women's expertise and perspectives at the highest levels of policymaking for national development.

Current trends indicate that governments are developing policies that are gender sensitive. The United Nations Decade for Women globalized the demand for gender-sensitive policies, while economic necessity has facilitated the entry of women into and upward in national work forces. In response to these macro and micro trends, many governments have generated the political will to initiate gender-sensitive policy changes and to monitor the impact of these changes. Bureaucracies have been responsive to global trends and to the practical need for women's expertise and for enhanced employment opportunities for families, especially women-headed households. Governments can overcome gender stereotypes, both within bureaucracies and in societies at large, in order to achieve full utilization of the work force for national development.

V.   RESEARCH UPDATE: UPWARD MOBILITY FACTORS FOR WOMEN'S ADVANCEMENT IN THAILAND CIVIL SERVICE

A.   Introduction

A traditional parable in Thailand compares the people of Thailand to the legs of the elephant with the men in the front "leading" and the women in the back "following." This case study shows that slowly, during the late 20th century, men and women became increasingly equal in the civil service. The Thai Constitution was changed to remove the prohibition against women serving as district directors (the representative of the king and the central government who is closest to the people). And, as indicated in this case study, some ministries were leading the way in promoting women in equal proportion to men. Thus, by the start of the 21st century, it could almost be said that Thai men and women were walking "side by side" (*Kieng Bai, Kieng Lai*).

In 1995, the Royal Civil Service Commission of Thailand with assistance from the United Nations Department of Economic and Social Affairs carried out a study of promotion in the civil service, with special reference to the situation of women. The study is based on statistical analyses and interviews with both female and male incumbents in key positions, particularly those at high levels and those in geographically remote areas. The study focuses on general patterns, career histories, and distinctive success stories. In particular, the study illustrates which factors contribute to promotion of women in certain ministries rather than others. In a review of departmental promotions, the one department that promoted women in equal numbers to high positions utilized strategies such as mentoring, training, and performance comparison.

B.   Background

The Sixth Economic and Social Development Plan (1987–1991) stressed the important role of the government in facilitating social and economic initiatives, such as improvement in the status of women. The plan called for improvement of the efficiency of the public management machinery and placed priority on the development of human resources in the public sector. Listed as one of the targets to be achieved by the end of the Sixth Plan (1991) was the increase of women's representation among the top executive positions from 0.6% at the beginning of the plan to 5% 1991. The long-term Women's Development Master Plan (1982–2001) approved by the cabinet foresees women as a minimum of 30% of officials working in local and national administration and in decision-making positions.

Throughout the 1990s there was a steady increase in women who wanted to serve their country in the civil service at higher and higher levels. In Thailand, as of 1995, women accounted for 55% of the overall civil servants but represented only 30% in the middle-level and less than 10% in the higher executive positions. Within the civil service, female employees outnumbered men in the lowest grades, levels 1 to 3. In contrast, men outnumbered women in level 4 and above. Ninety-eight percent of all female employees are below level 7, with level 11 being the highest and reserved for the 11 permanent secretaries of the ministries and equivalent positions, such as auditor-general and secretary-general of the Office of the Civil Service Commission. Of the 22 permanent secretary positions and equivalent, level 11, the highest permanent official position in the Thai civil service, only one was a woman during the study period (1994–95). At the level of director-general or secretary-general (level 10), there were 5% women, and of the deputy positions (level 9) 8% were women. In state enterprises, men held 87% of the managerial positions.

On the supply side, women outnumbered men at every educational level with the exception of the master's and doctoral, where men greatly outnumbered women. It is said that few organizations are comfortable sending women for advanced degrees, and when women have been sent, these women have, historically, modified their ambitions to accommodate the raising of children. At the same time, women have sometimes refused opportunities for advanced degrees in order to start families. The case studies following illustrate the variety of patterns of women's advancement. In 1994, women made up only 11% of executives at levels 9 to 11; however, the proportion had increased from about 4% in 1981. Only one woman, an auditor-general, held a position at level 11, and she was appointed for about a year in 1995. In 1999, two women held level 11 positions, although women are still proportionately very underrepresented.

Within the Thai public service, there are 14 ministries, 120 departments within those ministries, 76 provinces, and 500 districts within the framework of the central government. The many thousands of villages comprise community-based forums for local activities. In December 1994, the Parliament passed a new law, creating tambon councils and tambon administrative organizations (each unit at the tambon level is composed of 5 to 10 villages). These tambons for purposes of socioeconomic development are legal entities—that is, local self-government. The Thai civil service includes virtually all ministry and department officials at national, provincial, and district levels. The governors of provinces and the directors of districts report to the Department of Local Administration (DOLA) of the Ministry of the Interior (MOI). The Office of the Civil Service Commission has decentralized many personnel functions to the ministries and departments, but retains responsibility for policy guidance, system development, grievances, and ethics.

As can be seen from Table 1, the civil service forms a steep pyramid. There are few promotional opportunities for either men or women; the competition for promotion is very strong. But, one can also note that from 1990 to 1994, there has been an increase in the number of positions at higher levels, with an increase in the absolute number of women promoted to these higher levels.

The Civil Service Act of 1975 is the legal basis for personnel management practices in the Thai civil service. There are no clauses or provisions that can be said to discriminate against women. In examining the written rules and regulations for personnel management, one is led to believe that gender discrimination is nonexistent in the Thai civil service. However, the data reveal bias in the higher levels. As the parable states, women have been considered the "hind legs" of the civil service and have been expected to follow the leadership of men.

Table 1   Number of Women in the Civil Service by Grade, 1990–94

Level	1990		1994	
	Women	Men and women	Women	Men and women
11	0	25	1	28
10	18	274	36	402
9	45	367	200	842
8	492	1928	1440	4994
7	2484	6433	6091	12,289
1–6	NA	NA	181,701	137,529

Source: Royal Civil Service Commission, 1995.

In the civil service, a position is classified into a class and grade level according to its duties and responsibilities. Positions having similar duties and responsibilities form a class. Each class, according to its degree of complexity, is equated to a grade level, of which there are a total of 11. Persons holding positions within the same grade level receive the same pay range. Many classes in the same occupations constitute a class series. Each class series has a written class specification, which is approved by the Civil Service Commission. Class specification is used as the term of reference for job assignments and qualification standard for positionholders. Out of 420 class series specifications there are only two class series that, historically, have specified male gender as one of the requirements for position holders. They are (1) corrections officers for male prisoners, and (2) deputy district directors. Both class series belong to the Ministry of Interior.

Recruitment into civil service is done through competitive examinations open to all that meet the position requirements, which are mainly educational qualifications. The examinations are usually held twice a year. Promotion in service involves three factors: (1) years of service, (2) work experience, and (3) educational background. Within the civil service, rank-in-person predominates over position classification as a basis for promotion and filling of positions in the civil service. Except for the two positions reserved for men, women who possess the required qualifications are eligible to compete in the civil service entrance examination. According to a survey done by the Office of the Civil Service Commission by 1988, about 87% of the applicants who passed the examination were women.

Promotion in the civil service is usually done internally within a department. Cross-promotion between different departments is rare. A person is typically promoted to higher position within the same class series. Seniority is an influencing factor in promotion, and previous work experience in the next-lower level is required. To be eligible for promotion one must possess the qualifications as required of the position which are a combination of (1) years of service, (2) work experiences in related work at the lower level, and (3) educational background. Besides the standard qualification set by the Civil Service Commission, the department or the appointing authority has the power to add other job requirements and criteria such as special training or advanced educational degrees in a specific field as well as certain personal characteristics considered to be appropriate for successful job holders. Since promotion in the civil service is highly competitive, whenever someone is passed over once, they are disadvantaged in future promotions.

"Personal characteristics" are given more emphasis in promotion to higher levels in the civil service. At the lowest levels, the emphasis is primarily on written examinations, whereas by level 7 the selection is based more on interviews, thereby leading to the possibility of more subjective judgments of likely behavior. At the managerial level, the degree of observed assertiveness, decisiveness, and calmness, for example, which may be perceived as gender related, may influence promotion.

Traditionally, the societal image of women in the Thai culture seems to be bounded by two dimensions: as mothers and as wives. This rigid image creates confusion because, in fact, many Thai women work outside the home. Although many men and women still believe that women's primary responsibilities are to serve their husbands and children, women find themselves working because families need two incomes to survive. Although some women raise their children without the contribution of the father, women are not considered "appropriate" heads of households. Therefore, it is not expected for women to be successful in careers outside the home, and especially not more successful than their husbands. A common pattern for women in the civil service is to be married to a man who is in the private sector. The usual explanation involves noting that the private sector pays more, but the public sector is relatively generous in providing maternity leave and security (presumably of greater interest to women). Given the variety of cultural and practical constraints, women themselves often lack the ambition, self-confidence, aggressiveness, and dedication necessary to excel in the world of work.

There is little support from either men or women for women to become leaders through competing with men. The "uncommon" women who dare to break the traditional role of followers, as in the "hindlegs of the elephant," to become leaders who are willing to challenge, to take risks, to make decisions, and to strive for achievement, especially in male-dominated careers, are often condemned by both sexes. Women who reach top positions work very hard to overcome barriers created by both male and female colleagues. These top women are often alienated from their peers. The following case studies illustrate many of these attitudes.

In the 1980s and 1990s, the issue of whether women should be allowed to become deputy district directors (DDDs) was discussed repeatedly by the cabinet and the Parliament. The proposal to nullify the gender-discriminatory cabinet resolution which states that DDDs must be men was initiated by the National Women's Promotion and Coordinating Committee, which cited three main reasons for the nullification: (1) the resolution contravened the UN Convention on Elimination of All Forms of Discrimination Against Women, which had been endorsed and ratified by the Government of Thailand; (2) the long-term women's development master plan (1982–2001) had set a goal for women to be given a minimum of 30% participation in national administration and in decision-making bodies; and (3) there was no justification for the assertion that men are more suitable for the position than women. The role of DDD had evolved from a purely "law and order" role to one focusing on sustainable human development and involving coordination with several other agencies, while requiring the incumbent to be able to play several roles simultaneously. Through 1992, the personnel director of the Department of Local Administration (DOLA) of the Ministry of the Interior (MOI) had continued to assert that the DDD position required both regular inspection trips to remote areas, which would be physically demanding and unsuitable for women, and risky crime suppression work, which would be dangerous. Agreeing with the MOI, the cabinet upheld its previous resolution denying women access to the position of DDD.

This restriction imposed on women had important consequences. The DDD class is the entry level for the career path to top positions in the MOI. The positions of DDD, district director (DD), provincial chief administrator, deputy governor, and governor are all classified within the same class series. The restriction against recruiting women as DDDs automatically deprives them of the opportunity of being appointed DD. The work experience as DDD is the major requirement for being promoted to DD, which is considered as a stepping-stone to all the top positions within the MOI.

In 1993, the Cabinet reconsidered its decision and authorized a partial opening of access for women to this position. The cabinet authorized the creation of a job title of deputy district director/Administration, and opened this position to women. As defined, this position involves office work rather than field work, and essentially replaced the post of district registration officer, many of whom were women and most of whom were shifted to DDD/Administration. These new DDD/Administration incumbents were among the newest, had the least seniority, and were the furthest removed from "acting" as the district officer in "his" absence. Thus, this change had little impact, except to imagine that some day in the future there might be a blurring of the distinction between DDD/Administration and DDD with normal field work responsibilities.

The ministry also began with a "experimental" group of 13 women who were shifted into the DDD-based class series from some other post either within the MOI or within the field service of another ministry. These women were supposed to take on the full roles of DDD and not be limited to "administration." At first, some DDs were reluctant to assign the full range of tasks to these women, but as of 1995, some of these women were gaining the full range of experiences as men who serve as DDs. Both interviews and observations attest to this fact.

Several years ahead of the Ministry of the Interior, the Department of Revenue of the Ministry of Finance had already appointed women as district and provincial revenue directors. For reasons that will be explained below, as early as the mid-1980s, the Revenue Department decided to allow women to compete for positions of district revenue officer (DRO) and provincial revenue officer (PRO), as well as management posts at headquarters. In the districts and provinces, the women who became DROs or PROs were responsible for collecting taxes from "reluctant" tax-payers. These women's duties included traveling to remote areas to enforce tax collection and investigating illegal revenue-related activities. Thus, long before women could be DDDs, women were in the field in remote areas engaged in sensitive and potentially dangerous tasks.

As part of a governmentwide reengineering process, the Government of Thailand is in the process of rethinking its structures and programs in order to improve efficiency and to increase services to the people. This process is exemplified by several government policies. The Tambon Council and Tambon Administrative Organization Act of 1994 increase the autonomy and respon-sibilities of the subdistrict governments in the field of planning social and economic development. This shift implies a change in the role of the DD and DDDs from "control" to "facilitation of development." Thus, through the late 1990s and the beginning of the 21st century, there will be greater emphasis on the "mediating" and "motivating" skills for helping communities to achieve development.

C. Findings: Selected Case Studies

In recent years, some visible shifts in public policy have opened promotion opportunities to women in the Thai civil service. Some successful examples follow.

1. Ministry of the Interior: Department of Local Administration: Governor of Nakorn Nayok Province

In 1993, amid considerable controversy, the Ministry of Interior appointed the first woman gover-nor and first woman vice-governor. Since 1993, the woman governor has received much praise for her work. Charatsri Teepirac was appointed Governor of Nakorn Nayok Province. With a B.A. and M.A. in architecture and a Ph.D. in public administration, she established her career in the Office of the Prime Minister and the Ministry of the Interior. In the Office of the Prime Minister, she began as an architect in the Department of Technical and Economic Cooperation, and by the time she left the department she was a director. In the Ministry of the Interior, she began as director of the Comprehensive Planning Division and is now a governor. In her career, she was active in gen-eral planning for Bangkok and secondary cities. By 1995, she was the leading governor in the campaign against child prostitution, especially through keeping more girls in higher levels in schools. In 1993, she was awarded the "Most Distinguished Civil Servant" award from the king. She added that she was mentored by several key male supervisors, has a supportive husband, and socializes by hosting dinners in her home. By 1994, another woman had been appointed vice-gov-ernor. By 1996, yet another woman had been appointed vice-governor.

2. Ministry of the Interior: Department of Local Administration: Deputy District Director

As part of the Ministry of the Interior experiment in appointing 13 women as DDDs, a woman with a Ph.D. was DDD in general administration in an industrialized district in Samut Prakan Province. With a Ph.D. she was overqualified for the post; men with a Ph.D. are not appointed as DDDs. But as a woman, she realized that she should accept the DDD post in order to be a pioneer and to show that women could do the DDD job very well. When she first took up the post, the DD assigned her only tasks to be accomplished inside the office. After some months, a newly appointed DD, who believed that women should be allowed to try to accomplish all types of functions, assigned her tasks in the community. These tasks included environmental protection and labor relations. Both of these tasks were important because the district includes many factories, with problems of labor-management relations and environmental problems of pollution of air and water.

3. Ministry of the Interior: Department of Local Government: District Director

In January 1996, the MOI appointed the first woman as DD. On February 5, 1996, Prasom Dari-chob, 58, from the Administrative Development Institute, was appointed as DD in Amphawa district of Samut Songkhram Province. She had started her career in the Ministry of Interior in 1963 as inspector-general of Ranong Province, and had recently been director of the Administrative Development Academy, which trains district officers. The director-general of the Department of Local Administration (DOLA) said Prasom's appointment was in line with government policy to promote women's rights and support qualified female officers. Prasom retired in 1998 at age 60.

4. Ministry of Public Health: Physician: Director of a Hospital

In 1995, the Director of the Chiang Rai Hospital was considered a leader in her institution and in the Chiang Rai community. She took charge of this hospital after many years as a successful physician. She noted that when she took charge of the hospital, many physicians were skeptical about how well a hospital would run with a woman in charge. She accomplished three important tasks that established her credibility: (1) she reduced the hospital's budget deficit substantially; (2) she established a new department; and (3) she took part in community activities, both as an individual and by way of encouraging the hospital to be a key stakeholder in community development. At the time of the interview, the head of personnel for the ministry indicated that the Chiang Rai hospital director refused to be posted to the ministry headquarters in Bangkok; the director confirmed this fact. She noted that by serving a specific community that was in great need of a good hospital (there were many HIV/AIDS cases), she felt that she was serving the public in an important function and that she enjoyed being "close" to the people who needed hospital services.

5. Ministry of Public Health: Head, Provincial Medical Center

When this woman took charge of a northern provincial medical services center, she established her credibility through innovative actions. Within a few years, (1) she had developed a widespread nutrition program to iodize salt, in cooperation with the private sector; (2) she had launched a health and sanitation program with the Government of Germany; (3) she had organized weekly staff breakfasts for sharing issues, ideas, and problems (this program became sufficiently institutionalized that the breakfasts took place even when the director was out of town); (4) she had established a mentoring program for young doctors in the province; and (5) she had developed a gender-free title for physicians at the office (the traditional Thai word for doctor referred to men only). Through these actions, she improved service delivery, office morale, staff training, provincial health and nutrition, and the gender climate for women.

6. Ministry of Agriculture: Department of Fisheries: Provincial Officer

When the Department of Fisheries wanted to appoint a woman as a provincial officer, they noted that they needed to a woman who would be appreciated and respected by the province in which she worked. For a province in which one of the largest industries is cultivation and processing of fish, the department appointed a woman with a Ph.D. in diseases of fish. This woman had been serving the department as a technical officer who carried out research and consultation in provinces in which diseases were affecting the fish. In the course of her work, she was sent to Supanburi Province, in which an unknown disease was dramatically reducing the fish yield. In a short time, she was able to identify and eradicate the disease. The people in this province were happy to welcome her as their provincial fisheries officer.

7. Ministry of Agriculture: Department of Fisheries: District Officer

Being very active in Supanburi Province, the Department of Fisheries also sought to appoint a woman as one of the district fisheries officers. At the district level, the most important element of the job is to supervise fishing practices by supporting those whose practices are legal and facilitating the arrest and prosecution of those whose fishing practices are illegal. Illegal fishing practices include killing the fish with an electric charge or a small explosive. The woman chosen as district fisheries officer noted that she often had to patrol the waterways late at night with a police boat in order to arrest the poachers during their criminal activities. Although this work could be considered dangerous, this woman was very brave and had been carrying out these duties for several months. It is useful to note that her children were living with her parents and going to school in Bangkok, and her husband was posted in another province carrying out equally important work for the people's well-being. Because she did not have to worry about the health, education, and safety of her children, she was able to commit herself to a dangerous but important job.

8. Ministry of Mineral Resources: Experienced Geologist

The field of geology is of interest in the study of women's upward mobility because, as of 1995, only 12% of the professional employees were women. In this typically male-dominated field, it is interesting to note that neither of the level 7 women geologists felt that there were serious problems working with male colleagues. Both women indicated that in their secondary and tertiary education, they had been in classes with only men. Thus, they were used to taking initiative, earning respect and behaving collegially with men. Much fieldwork is required of geologists, who sometimes spend as long as a month or two in the wilderness, in the company of an all-male team of colleagues and support personnel. Interestingly, both women indicated that while they did not perceive any problems with male colleagues, they did perceive that the male support personnel who were used to taking orders only from men seemed to find difficulty initially in taking orders from women.

Within the Ministry of Mineral Resources, the experienced woman geologist achieved level 7 through hard work in the field and strategic alliances in the headquarters. In order to participate fully in fieldwork, she and her husband agreed to educate their children in boarding school. This way, she was relatively free to travel to remote areas for weeks and sometimes months at a time to survey geological formations and to explore for mineral resources. At headquarters, she developed cross-speciality competencies by initiating linkages between different mineral resources, and by publishing papers with colleagues in other specialities. In this manner, when positions opened in various specialities, she was able to compete for those promotions based on the cross-speciality papers in which she had participated. She credits her promotions to her assertive acquisition of additional competencies.

9. Ministry of Mineral Resources: Young Geologist

A younger woman geologist had recently completed a Ph.D. on scholarship, thereby taking advantage of the recent decision to allow and even encourage women to go abroad for Ph.D.

degrees. Until the 1980s, it was very rare for Thai women to travel abroad to pursue postgraduate degrees. Now, these women are returning to important jobs in government and private industry. This young geologist took advantage of her extended family, the support of her husband, and the facilities of boarding school in order to combine her work with her family responsibilities. This young woman also enjoyed fieldwork and tolerated the relative lack of respect for women in the field. Both women geologists were pleased that future generations of women might find the field of geology more welcoming to women.

10. Ministry of Finance: Department of Revenue: Level 9 Women at Headquarters

Two women had achieved level 9 status in the Department of Revenue. Their careers are completely different, illustrating two trends: a traditional emphasis on seniority and a more modern emphasis on key skills. Both at headquarters, one worked her way up through the ranks and was nearly ready to retire; the other was in her late 30s but fast-tracked because of skills in languages and practical economics.

The one in her 50s had established a career similar to that of professional, upwardly mobile men in the department. She had held posts of district revenue officer and provincial revenue officer, managing complex field operations and large staffs, and achieved noticeably superior performance in the units that she managed. She led raids on the premises of tax evaders, organized inspections of suspected tax evaders, and coordinated increasingly modern tax administration. She had worked from the grass roots up to the director's office, always devoting herself to high performance management in organizations.

In contrast, the one in her 30s had achieved prominence and promotion through special studies in international taxation treaties, English language studies, and successful completion of special projects deemed impossible by her peers. She was labeled a "high-flyer" and had already made key contributions to tax policy, tax treaties, and issues of taxation in the global economy.

D. Five Factors for Successful Organizational Promotion of Women

In the comparison of five departments, one stands out as having promoted women much more successfully than the others. At the revenue department of the Ministry of Finance, in about 1990, five factors developed to assist women's advancement. While one of these factors pertains to all government departments, the other four factors are unique to the revenue department. The five factors are: (1) national public policy debate; (2) abundant supply of trained and qualified women in the professional specializations for revenue collection; (3) leadership by the director-general of the revenue department; (4) adequate number of qualified and experienced women who lobbied for access to management positions; and (5) the methodology and practice of measuring the performance of organizational units within the department of revenue.

1.   The national policy debate could have influenced all departments within the government. A variety of factors stimulated and influenced this national debate. From the first United Nations Global Conference on Women and Development in Mexico City in 1975, women throughout the world began to discuss women's rights, contraints to women's development—legal and attitudinal—and the paucity of women in decision-making positions in politics and administration, as well as in private sector and civil society. The continued global activities provided a platform for raising issues of "women's rights are human rights" and "the potential contribution of women to sustainable human development." As well, the networking which took place not only

at the official UN meetings but also at the associated forums facilitated the emergence of women's groups in many countries, including Thailand. These groups often took the form of nongovernmental organizations (NGOs) that began to organize women into social, economic, and political interest groups, increasingly able to lobby their national governmental institutions and participate in international events. In Thailand, these NGOs scanned the national scene for flagrant abuses or violations of women's human rights, as well as opportunities and strategies for improving the conditions of women and their influence on policies and practical situations. Beyond the parable of the hind and front legs of the elephant, it is important to remember that Thailand was one of the headquarters for sex tourism, trafficking in women, and with the rise of HIV-AIDS, sexual abuse of young girls. In this policy environment, women's groups were searching for targets of opportunity for improving conditions and policies of concern to women. The role of women in the civil service was one of the many opportunities for promoting women's advancement.

2. Specific to the department of revenue is the abundant supply of trained and qualified women in the professional specializations for revenue collection. In the 1950s and 1960s, many young women in universities decided to specialize in accounting and related subjects. By the 1980s and 1990s, these women were not only qualified but experienced in their profession.

3. Specific also to the department of revenue was the leadership shown by the director-general, who later went on to be promoted to permanent secretary of the Ministry of Finance. The director-general was sensitive to gender issues, and decided to take the lead in promoting women in the department for which he was responsible. Aware of the national policy debate, he believed that he could further the debate by promoting capable women in his department. He realized that women could work in management positions, but he was equally aware that they might face resistance and negative reactions. Thus, at the time he began to promote women to management positions, he provided a mentoring service for the newly appointed women. Within the department's personnel management unit, supervision began to include visiting managerial women in the field (district and provincial levels) and providing networking opportunities among the women.

4. At the time that this director-general was appointed, a significant number of qualified and experienced women began to lobby for appointment to management positions. They quietly circulated the notion that they would be interested in the opportunity, that they believed that they would be successful, and that access to these positions would be in line with trends in national policy.

5. During this same period, the department of revenue developed more sophisticated methodology to measure the performance of organizational units, especially the district and provincial offices. Furthermore, the director-general used the performance reports as a basis for promotion. Thus, the promotion process was specifically gender neutral; both men and women were promoted based on their performance. Fortunately for the department of revenue, the work of the organization, that is, tax collection, is relatively easily measured in quantitative terms. Recognizing which offices increased their revenue collection (and by how much) was a straightforward task. Rewarding the managers of those offices with promotion became automatic. The expectation of reward for recognizable performance further stimulated high-level performance. While other departments may need to make efforts to measure organizational performance, there exists considerable experience in measuring various types of technical, administrative and managerial work in organizations. Based on the experience and "best practice" in the revenue department, one can conclude that women need to be educated and trained, well managed, assertive, visible, and in positions where their performance can be evaluated objectively. The situation further notes that both women's and men's attitudes need to be favorable for women to advance. In the Thai case, changing trends in gender attitudes encouraged women's successful advancement in the revenue department. The UN conferences on women and development, as well as the emerging activism of women's groups and NGOs, facilitated these changes in Thai society.

Table 2 Factors in Promotion of Women in the Thai Civil Service: Necessary, Useful, and Sufficient

	Necessary	Useful	Sufficient	Comments
Conditions	Qualifications generally relate to the job specifications Having had the opportunity to serve in "feeder" (pipeline) positions Ability to pass written examinations up to level 8	Expertise Extra education Extra languages Higher rank/seniority Experience in key posts Hard work (effort) Performance (achievement) Personality (balance between frankness and politeness) Visibility (but subtle) Initiative and problem solving Emphasis/experience in key area of national policy Political connections	Vacancy or unit's willingness to create temporary specialist positions until a vacancy opens up	A combination of several of the "useful" factors seems to be required in order to appear to deserve a promotion as a reward or in order to be seen to be essential to the productivity of the organization.
Comments	These "necessary" conditions seem to be a minimum.	These "useful" factors seem to be the factors most under the control of the individual, as well as the most likely to encourage a unit to create a "temporary specialist" post while waiting for a vacancy.	These "sufficient" conditions seem to be a minimum.	

E.   MYTHS AND REALITIES OF PROMOTION IN THE THAI CIVIL SERVICE

The Thai civil service is characterized by two different classification systems: rank-in-person and position classification. With rank-in-person, the person's rank depends upon seniority and promotion generally based on seniority. With position classification, the person rank adheres not in the person but rather in the particular position to which that the person is appointed based on specific qualifications, experience, and measurable aptitude. While these two systems can be complementary, they can, in particular instances, lead to contradictory personnel recommendations. The current juggling of the two systems leads to some inconsistency in personnel management decisions, although there is increasing emphasis on "putting the right person in the right job." Through analyzing the many comments from the women and men interviewed in this study, it is possible to construct a table delineating conditions that seem to be "necessary," "useful," and "sufficient" for promotion (Table 2). This categorization does not relate to the possibilities for any particular position, but rather refers to the general tendencies in the promotional system at the time of the study.

F.   RECOMMENDATIONS

1.   Promotion

This review of promotion records to all positions of level 7 and above for the years 1993 and 1994 revealed very little data concerning decisions. In the filling of positions of levels 7 to 11, women were seldom in the short lists, and they were seldom chosen to fill the posts. Although each decision is required to have an explanation of criteria and how those criteria were applied in the particular case, very few cases have an explanation more elaborate than the appointee was "more experienced" or "more qualified." This type of vague explanation is nearly useless for auditing personnel decision making for probity, fairness, and "finding the right person for the right job." High-performing women and men will be motivated to achieve more when they are relatively certain that their performance is recognized in the promotion process.

2. Performance Evaluation and Seniority

In a mixed system of rank-in-person and position classification, there is an inherent contradiction between promotion criteria. Rank-in-person assumes emphasis on seniority. Position classification assumes emphasis on performance and its appropriate evaluation and recognition. When the two criteria lead to different promotion results, it is often the director-general of the unit who decides whether to be less controversial and emphasize seniority (clear criteria) or to be more daringly innovative and emphasize performance, about which many people may have differing views concerning measurement. As is shown in this study's departmental comparison, performance criteria tend to lead to promotion of more competent women and men.

3. Organizational Performance Improvement

Based on the experience of the revenue department, one can conclude that accurately measuring the performance of organizational units can lead to merit promotions. This conclusion depends upon the organization understanding its goals and being able to measure the results produced by the various units. The heads of organizational units can be rewarded with promotions, and their potential can be assessed through their management performance. Other staff can learn to work in productive units and adopt a merit-based concept of organizational performance. Thus, one can conclude that organizations will learn to identify goals, measure results, and reward performance for at least three reasons: (1) results orientation; (2) training emerging managers in productive management techniques; and (3) merit promotion, which encourages both men and women to learn and contribute to the success of the organization.

4. Removal of Gender Specifications and Labels

Based on the experience in the provincial medical center, as well as additional anecdotal comments, one can assert the importance of removing gender bias in the labeling of positions in organizations. The director of the provincial medical center developed a gender-free label for physicians at the office (the traditional Thai word for doctor referred to men only). Through these actions, she improved the gender climate for women, and raised morale.

5. Training

A key finding involves the importance of training in gender sensitivity for both women and men. Men need to understand the issues inherent in serving as a "woman manager"; that is, overcoming a tradition of passivity and invisibility, reversing the tendency for women to be the "hind legs of the elephant" and to become more comfortable being side by side with men, and developing an understanding for the dual role of women in the workplace and in the household. In this latter case, men will understand when women are drawn away from work in emergencies, and men will also be able to develop more of a partnership with their wives, sharing family responsibilities. Many of the successful women in these case studies enjoyed the benefit of having a family partnership with supportive husbands. Women, themselves, often undersell their skills and limit themselves to positions that are "helpmate" positions or positions that are lower than those of their husbands or male relatives. Women also benefit from gender sensitivity training. Both men and women need to assess their abilities and personalities in order that the most qualified and interested men and women put themselves forward for promotion to higher positions.

In addition to gender sensitivity training modules, the case studies also identify the importance of further education and skills development. In the area of management, there needs to be a sequence of courses on supervision, management, and high-level executive decision making and judgment. In the area of specific subjects, there needs to be opportunity to enroll in courses to upgrade and update knowledge and perspectives. As long as the organization is clear about the priorities, tasks, and skills needed for accomplishment of those tasks, a training budget is usually money well spent.

A third component of training involves special on-the-job exercises in organizational performance improvement. Using methods such as performance improvement programming (PIP) or strengths-weaknesses-opportunities-threats (SWOT) analysis, people who work together in an office can analyze their work situation and make improvements in their working processes and conditions.

6. Mentoring

Several interviewees, both women and men, mentioned the importance of senior colleagues who helped them to understand their workplace: the social, technical, political, and technological aspects. These senior colleagues answered questions, introduced them to important persons, and reminded them to acquire particular training and to apply to jobs with prospects for upward mobility. Supervisors can be trained to identify and nurture talented subordinates (both directly and indirectly). Directors can include mentoring as one of several criteria in their personal performance appraisal. This criterion can be included systematically throughout the organization. Supervisors can be evaluated on the extent to which they mentor both women and men.

7. Networking

Under the conditions of integrating women into management positions in the civil service, or any other organizations for that matter, it is important to recognize that the first few women in these positions may feel very "lonely at the top." Indeed, they may have few people to talk with about their career strategies, their opportunities, their frustrations, and the various barriers. Directors of organizations can encourage women to establish informal groups to discuss their work and their workplace situations, thereby developing strategies to overcome barriers to improved personal performance, office working conditions, and overall organizational performance.

8. Educational Upgrading Opportunities

From the case studies, one can see that women often have to be better qualified than the men with whom they compete for positions and promotions—for example, the case of the deputy district officer with the Ph.D. and the provincial fisheries Officer with the Ph.D. Education plays an essential role in improved performance and promotion. In the 1990s, there were still few scholarships abroad offered to and/or taken up by women. Given the commitments made by governments at the global conferences on gender and development, the 21st century should see many more women taking advantage of advanced educational opportunities.

G. CONCLUSIONS

The successful promotion of women to high levels in the Thai civil service flows from several "pipeline" factors, as well as the current human capital statistics and current sociocultural issues. These "foundational" pipeline factors are based on access to education and to entry-level jobs. In primary and secondary education, the male/female ratio is almost equal; however, the dropout rate from primary to lower secondary is greater for girls than for boys. The illiteracy rate, although decreasing, continues to be two times greater for women than for men. Career aspirations for women continue to incline generally toward teaching, health professions, and office jobs, primarily clerk and secretarial. At the university level, women represent a relatively low percentage of students in engineering, architecture, geology, medicine, law, and other prestige professions.

Once women are integrated into the civil service, they eventually expect fairness in promotion and advancement. Even where women do not yet expect merit promotion with accurate performance appraisal, directors can see that promoting the best workers, whether they are men or women, enhances organizational performance. The experience of the revenue department in Thailand substantiates this point of view.

In general, promotion becomes especially difficult for women at level 8 (director), when criteria become more subjective. Particular concepts such as leadership, initiative, confidence, or influence are imaged as "male" rather than "female" characteristics, and yet are also defined as requirements for management positions. Although women are now frequently appointed to lower supervisory positions (especially if they supervise women), women's ability to direct the activities of both women and men is still questioned by some people. The civil service regulations allow for promotion to a higher level in rank while waiting for an actual post at that level to become vacant. This device of assigning an officer to "special duties" is used more often for men than women. The specialist positions are created judiciously to provide opportunity for temporary promotion without a specific vacancy available. The women report that at the higher levels promotion almost requires becoming involved in politics, which most of the women find culturally difficult for them. Women also note that they experience fewer opportunities for risk taking and high-performance activities, fewer opportunities for visibility, some negative perceptions of family members and friends, and a special issue of maintaining social status in the community, which high-level men usually accomplish through activities such as drinking, socializing, and playing golf.

The study concludes that women need to be educated and trained, well managed, assertive, visible, and in positions where their performance can be evaluated objectively. The study further notes that both women's and men's attitudes need to be favorable for women to advance.

VIII. METHODOLOGY NOTE

The study team was lead by Col and Dhipavadee, with research specialist Dr. Ronnie Steinberg of Temple University. Dr. Orapin Sophchokchai contributed to the research design and conceptual framework. Several staff, particularly Khun Charnvit and Khun Tassanne of the Thai Civil Service Commission Office, assisted in the fieldwork and statistical analysis.

The study was first conceived in 1987 at a United Nations Interregional Workshop on Women in Public Management. Funding was found in 1992 and the specific study was formulated in 1993. The UN formulation mission, in conjunction with a task force from the Office of the Civil Service Commission (OCSC), interviewed prominent women and men in the civil service from a variety of departments, and reviewed documents concerning the laws and practices of management of the civil service, as well as papers on women and development in Thailand and the few reports on women in management in Thailand. The joint team determined the questions and methodology of the study. In preparation for the actual study, the OCSC gathered basic statistics on the civil service disaggregated by gender. They also made available documents on the structure of the position classification system, and the rules of promotion.

From December 1994 through January 1995, a study team from the United Nations and a task force from the OCSC worked jointly to assess promotion statistics and to carry out structured interviews of a sample of incumbents in selected positions. Gaps in statistics and field data were filled in by further data gathering on promotion records in the selected departments and through structured observations/interviews in the field in March to June 1995, including a two-week visit by UN staff. The final report reflects data from civil service records from 1990 to 1995, and interviews and analysis carried out in early 1995. Also, the team was able to spend one week in a selected district, as a scientific observer of the conditions and operations in a district that had two women deputy district directors and that was engaged in a pilot program of reengineering its operations. This situation permitted relatively realistic observation of day-to-day tasks, performance differences, and especially the "gender climate."

The study focus was women and men in the Thai civil service system, and their status in advancing through the promotional steps from level 1 to level 11 (permanent secretary and equivalents). Of the 22 positions of permanent secretary and equivalent in the Thai civil service, a single woman, who served as auditor-general for about a year (1995) just before retiring, was the only woman up to 1997 who had ever held a level 11 position. Currently, in 1999, there are two women in level 11 positions, including coauthor Dhipavadee Meksawan, who is secretary-general of the Civil Service Commission, after spending seven years as one of four deputies.

The case study methodology involved comparison of women and men in positions dominated by either sex or held equally, within five ministries (fisheries within Agriculture, local administration and community development within Interior, medical science and physicians within Public Health, mineral resources within Science and Technology, and revenue within Finance), with either many or few women in decision-making positions. Incumbents were chosen for interviews both in Bangkok and in areas considered remote, dangerous, and sensitive. As the pyramid of the civil service structure is very steep, interviewees were also chosen at director or deputy level, which are key thresholds for eliminating people from the competition for future promotion.

REFERENCES

Ananieva, N. and Razvigorova, E. (1987). Women in State Administration in the People's Republic of Bulgaria, paper presented at Friedrich Ebert Foundation Conference on Women's Leadership, Bonn.

Badri, A. E. (1987). Women in Public Administration and Management in the Sudan, paper presented at Friedrich Ebert Foundation Conference on Women's Leadership, Bonn.

Bayes, J. (1985). Women in Public Administration in the United States, paper presented at the XIIIth World Congress of the International Political Science Association, Paris.

Col, J.-M. (1981) Women in Public Administration and Management: Trends, Analysis and Training, Report, United Nations, New York.

Col, J.-M. (1986). Factors Affecting Women's Upward-Mobility, paper presented at the Midwest Political Science Association, Chicago.

Col, J.-M. (1988). Policy Development for Increasing the Role of Women in Public Management, United Nations.

Col, J.-M. and Suzuki, I. (1987). Policy Development for Increasing Participation of Women in Public Management: A Training Approach, paper presented at the International Association of Schools and Institutes of Administration, Milan, Italy.

Ferguson, K. E. (1984). *The Feminist Case Against Bureaucracy,* Temple University Press, Philadelphia.

Fernandes, A. M. (1988). Women in Public Administration in Brazil: Upward-Mobility and Career Advancement, unpublished manuscript.

Gutek, B. A. and Larwood, L., eds. (1987). *Women's Career Development,* Sage, Beverly Hills, Calif., 1987.

Hess, B. B. and Ferree, M. M., eds. (1987). *Analyzing Gender: A Handbook of Social Science Research,* Sage, Beverly Hills.

Ingraham, P. and Rosenbloom, D. (1989). The New Public Personnel and the New Public Service, *Public Administration Review 49:2.*

International Association of Schools and Institutes of Administration (IASIA) (1981). *International Perspectives in Public Administration,* Proceedings of the IASIA Round Table, Canberra.

Josefowitz, N. (1980). *Paths to Power,* Addison-Wesley, Reading, Mass.

Kanter, R.M. (1977). *Men and Women of the Corporation,* Basic Books, New York.

Kanter, R.M. *The Change Masters,* Simon and Schuster, New York.

Kirkhart, L. (1971). Toward a New Theory of Public Administration, in *Toward a New Public Administration: The Minnowbrook Perspective* (F. Marini, ed.), Chandler, Scranton, PA.

Langkau-Hermann, M. and Sessar-Karpp, E. (1987). Emerging Careers of Women in the Federal Republic of Germany, paper presented at Friedrich Ebert Foundation Conference on Women's Leadership, Bonn.

Leyenaar, M. H. (1987). Equal Opportunities in Public Administration in the Netherlands, paper presented at Friedrich Ebert Foundation Conference on Women's Leadership, Bonn.

Masire, G. (1986). Women in Administration and Management in Botswana, unpublished manuscript.

Mosher, F. (1968). *Democracy and the Public Service,* Oxford University Press, New York.

Shaul, M.S. (1982). The Status of Women in Local Governments: An International Assessment, *Public Administration Review 42:6.*

Sinkkonen, S., Hanninen-Salmelin, E., and Karento, H. (1987). Women in Leadership Positions in Public Administration in Finland, paper presented at Friedrich Ebert Foundation Conference on Women's Leadership, Bonn.

Sophchokchai, O. (1987) Women in Public Administration and Management in Thailand, unpublished manuscript.

Stewart, D. (1986). Women in Public Administration, paper presented at American Society for Public Administration Conference, Anaheim, CA.

Swarup, H. L. and Sinha, N. (1986). Upward-Mobility and Career Advancement in Public Administration in India, paper presented at Friedrich Ebert Foundation Conference on Women's Leadership, Bonn.

Tapales, P. (1985). Filipino Women in Public Administration: Policy-Making as Political Participation, unpublished manuscript.

Vertz, L. (1985). Women in Government in Venezuela: The Importance of Patronage, Social Class and Socialization, paper presented at the XII World Congress of the International Political Science Association, Paris.

65

Deviant Bureaucracies

Public Administration in Eastern Europe and in the Developing Countries

Kálmán Kulcsár   *Academy of Sciences, Budapest, Hungary*

I. INTRODUCTION

Max Weber had unfolded the ideal type of the bureaucratic organization on the basis of the economic and political processes of the European core and of the continuous rationalization apparently developing within them. He had put the ideal type of the bureaucratic organization within the category of formal rationality, linked to the formal-legal type of dominance; thus it has acquired a historical philosophical content as one of the products and also means of the process of rationalization manifest in history. But just as formal rationality may be separated, or even may get into contradiction with material rationality (as it serves imperfectly, or does not at all serve material rationality in the given case, which incidentally may be different and even contradictory in the different spheres of social activity, such as economy, politics, law, etc.), so the bureaucratic organization may also become dysfunctional in that activity for which it was created, or within its social environment. This dysfunctionality may be manifest in the decrease of the efficiency of the organization, which may go even to extremes, as it had already been suggested by Weber, when he studied what effect the bureaucratic organization would have upon the "technical" productive capacity of the society. Further on, it may be manifest in the "production" of bureaucratic phenomena in the pejorative sense of the term, the inherent nature of which is indisputable within the bureaucratic organization as shown by the results of modern sociological research.

Among the broadly known characteristic features of the Max Weberian ideal type there is the impersonal official, who performs his task *sine ira et studio*, on the basis of his technical training, and whose autocracy is limited by the formal legal norms. This is because, according to Weber, formalism is capable of hindering autocracy with the least effort, just as the content of material utility of the administrative tasks performed in the service of the "subjects" also requires formally treated *rules* (Weber 1987:232). These "rules," however, originate from an external source; after all, a considerable, or even overwhelming, part of the calculable rules determining the work of the bureaucratic office organization comes in principle from an organization occupying a dominant position above the bureaucratic one, from parliament on a national level, and from self-governing bodies on a regional and local level. One of the even theoretically important components of the political system that has evolved in the European core is the *subordination of pub-*

lic administration to legal norms deriving from corporate decisions. However, this situation has become more complicated in reality. Already Weber had indicated the possibility, and the tendency has been clearly outlined that public administration influences, in certain cases situates, and in extreme occasions may even direct corporate decision—in other words, it may get into a dominant position even in the face of the corporate organizations meant to direct it, despite the constitutional regulations. The growing lawmaking of bureaucratically organized public administration is related to this phenomenon. This lawmaking had gradually pushed corporate legislation into the background during the past hundred years, resulting, for instance, in some of the legal norms, or at least a part of them, such as the Acts, passed by the latter one, setting forth the broad objectives, or becoming symbolic ones, the normative content of which was ultimately granted by the regulations elaborated in the organizations of public administration.

A certain change can be sensed even in the public administration of the Western core, in its relationship to the elected bodies, though the influence of public administration starting from "inside" and aiming at the political management typically does not reach the weight of the political objectives received from outside and of the related legal regulation. One may object that the political influence of public administration has been a problem even in Great Britain, where the privileged position of public administration and moreover, according to Dicey's works, even the existence of administrative law has been doubted. "The difficulty with applying the traditional politics [administration distinction to the work of the British higher civil service] lies in the fact that senior civil servants are just as much involved in the political control of their departments, and often, too, in the actual legislative process, as machinery designed to carry out political instructions" (Hill 1972:199). As indicated by the quotation, the participation of the senior civil servant in the legislative process has been effective; moreover, "intervening between the bare bones of Act of Parliament and the decision-making of individual civil servants there is a framework of rules which are described as 'delegated legislation.' In other words, administrative bodies have powers which enable them to legislate" (Hill 1972:61). However, their management by legal norms is not challenged and the weight of their personality does not become dominant in the administrative activity itself.

The bureaucratic organization as an ideal type, as a perfectly working machine in Weber's wording, differs from the ideal type in its real operation because of various factors. Those basic principles upon which the bureaucratic organization is built have never been realized in their totality. Actually the organizational activity is realized through human behavior, and the sociological phenomena deriving from this fact shape the process of the realization of rules based on the above-mentioned principles. The individual, for instance, working in the organization would accept the objectives of the organization in general, and even the influence deriving from the functioning of the entire structure of the organization upon his own behavior, yet he would also follow his own objectives as well as those of the organization, and while accepting the influence of the organization he himself would try to shape organized activity. The complete rational functioning of the bureaucratic organization is restricted by these factors, not speaking about the limitations involved in expertise (which never can be complete), in foresight (which is frequently wrong, particularly in the consequences of decisions), and in the capabilities and characteristics of man performing the organizational activities, and about those objectives that derive also from the conditions of the organization and from the external environmental determination of man working there.

As the bureaucratic organization also lives in a historically developed social environment, its functioning is considerably influenced by the *social content* of the organization itself. The phenomena constituting the social content of the organization partly derive from that already-mentioned fact that organizational activity is realized through human behavior, and partly from the system of relationships between the organization and its social environment and from the changes of these relationships. The social environment has its effect on the place, significance, and functioning of the organization, depending upon its historical, economic, and cultural characteristics, on its political role, and finally on its efficiency within the society.

Weber had referred also to the importance of the environment of bureaucratic administration when he said that such an organization had significant *technical* conditions—he mentioned the technical conditions of contacts, transport, and communications (Weber 1987:231)—but it has become clear from research done since his time [only to mention Selznick (1957:5) or Crozier (1963)] that the effect of the environment is asserted in a broader sense. "Individuals within an administrative organization bring with them certain social commitments and attachments" (Hill 1972:28)—and, I may add, culture, values, norms, etc. alive in the environment.

The often problematic functioning of the organizations of public administration built upon the Western pattern in the developing countries indicates by what modifications the bureaucratic organization, approaching the Weberian ideal type, can be built, if at all (not speaking about its functioning). Leaving along now the level of training, one of the major problems of the public administration of developing societies is the *rationality of the task (objective) in comparison to the environmental conditions.* The rationality of the activities of public administration, as a bureaucratic organization functioning rationally, if it is forced to perform an "economy of shortage"—in other words, it *cannot realize the tasks because of the lack of means*—is inevitably impaired. This "economy of shortage" may be manifest in a relative sense, too, that is, if compared to the set objectives. In this case the organization can only inadequately serve the objectives, not counting with the true conditions, even though the goals may be set by a legal norm.

Rational administration, and rational administrative activity above all, is particularly problematic under such social conditions, which have historically evolved a different type of administration and administrative activity, whereas in the present medium a modern type of bureaucratic administration is needed, which implements legal norms (embodying political ideas) for the solution of tasks. This "bureaucratic administration" is one possible variant of the administrative organization that is called "formal" administration by Fred W. Riggs, After Károly Polányi's "formal" economic concept presuming a price-forming market. "Essential" administration requires just as little the bureaucratic organization working on the basis of legal rules as essential economy does the market, as is pointed out by Riggs (1964:7).

Nowadays the contradiction is that the underdeveloped countries aim at the preservation of certain traditional values besides modernization, but they just as much cannot rely upon traditional administration as upon traditional economy, whereas the bureaucratic type of administration built along the Western pattern is not efficient either, no matter how the latter one is formally developed. It is particularly not efficient when and where this public administration has to perform novel tasks if compared to its Western equivalent. A commonly known example of this is the problematic nature of Indian public administration in the management of state enterprises that are treated as hierarchically subordinated bureaucratic organizations, where their economic operation is made almost impossibly by "administration." The Western model necessarily leads to dysfunctional results because it does not suit these transitory societies, where the promulgated legal norms frequently hardly mean more than pious wishes, where decision making is not delegated because of a multitude of centralized decisions, and where the local authorities are weak. The reason is the too far-fetched nature of the objectives that are supposed to be served by the legal norms and by administration, the lack of the conditions of realization, the resistance of the conditions of the social "medium," and finally, that it is not independent of the "attitude" of the organizations supposed to realize them (Riggs 1964:381, et infra).

Essentially, that feature of the bureaucratic organization that generally challenges the character of a "perfectly functioning machine" also manifests itself in the relationship between the organization and the environment. This "feature" is the clumsiness (occasionally impossibility) of *adaptation to the environment, an inclination to turn away from reality.* Its consequence is that the bureaucratic organization changes when its activity is obviously of dysfunctional effect within the environment (Crozier 1963).

Thus the bureaucratic organization as a formalized one does not function at all with the precision of a machine (even in its original Western European environment), and the rationality of its expert activities can be influenced by a number of factors, yet the statement holds true that no better one has been evolved so far.

Therefore an effectively functioning public administration based on bureaucratic organizations could be interpreted as "deviant" right from the outset if compared to the ideal type, could we find an administration truly corresponding to the ideal type anywhere in reality (which of course would be a conceptual contradiction as it is the conceptual characteristic of the ideal type that it does not manifest itself in each context and detail empirically). Accepting the fact that the public administration of the societies of the Western core constituting the advanced part of the world, growing out from its original European base, which was originally built upon the Weberian ideal type, presents itself as a *pattern* for the modernizing societies together with its dysfunctional phenomena, and occupying a changing position in a changing political system, still the deviant forms of bureaucratic administration can be found in the developing countries and in the East European and East Central European socialist countries in comparison to this pattern in those two respects that I have referred to at the introduction of the present chapter. In other words, if compared to the impersonal nature and primarily external regulation of public administration (which, I repeat, it does not totally exclude its regulation from inside), I would say in brief that the deviance of the bureaucratically organized public administration in the underdeveloped countries—primarily in the Asian and African societies—manifests itself in the *dominance of the role and significance of the official, the administrator*, versus regulated administration, though phenomena of overregulation can also be noted. Further, deviance primarily appears in the *unprecedented growth of the legislative activity of public administration* in the socialist societies that have evolved in the Eastern periphery of Europe, even though the significance of the personality of the official and his set of contacts is also much greater than it is in the core societies. However, the social content of deviance does not derive primarily from the mere divergence from the ideal type, from the "pattern"—thus it cannot be covered by ethnocentrism, or by its phenomena, but by the fact that the divergence multiplies the dysfunctional consequences of public administration while its social effectiveness decreases.

II. DEVELOPING COUNTRIES

Writing about the public administration of developing countries, Fred W. Riggs noted that though formal organizations of administration similar to the European one have appeared in Asia, Africa, and Latin America,

> yet, somehow, closer inspection of these institutions convinces us that they do not work in the same way, or that they perform unusual social and political functions. Perhaps the explanation may be found if we note that the new market and administrative systems have *displaced* but not replaced the traditional systems. In other words, even though the market has invaded the village, it may not have fully eliminated the old redistributive system (Riggs 1964:12).

In these countries one of the characteristics of modernization is the existence of overlapping institutions and effects, which means that "the new formal apparatus, like the administrative bureau, gives an illusory impression of autonomousness, whereas in fact it is deeply enmeshed in, and cross-influenced by, remnants of older traditional social, economic, religious, and political systems" (Riggs 1964:15).

Besides the market, another source of the "deviant" bureaucratic type of public administration that has evolved in the developing countries is the traditional economy (Polanyi). Together with the existence or remains of the substantive economy (Polanyi), they by themselves limit the effectiveness of formal administration linked to the market. And the traditional values and modes of activity also restrict the realization of the legal norms made in a formally legal way (Kulcsár 1987a:109–121).

According to Riggs, one of the characteristics of substantive administration is that the administrative organization does not implement a policy deriving from "outside," from the environment of the organization, from the activities of some political body, which is received in the shape of legal norms (as it would derive from the Weberian ideal type), but either such a set of political objectives and regulation is missing, or, even if lately it has existed formally, "the incumbents may become powerful enough to influence policy formation as much as the politicians to whom they are nominally responsible" (Riggs 1964:14).

The most important element of the deviant bureaucracy of the developing countries is this personal dominance, which directly derives from the functioning of substantive administration. This personal dominance appears in selection, where personal contacts, often patron-client relations, or even family ties are dominant, in the functioning of public administration, where calculable legality is pushed behind the discretion of the official who can be influenced, and even in the organizational hierarchy itself, which means an unnecessarily multiplied grading, decreasing effectiveness, and, finally, where not objective expertise but the relations of authority and personality distribute power and shape the forms of behavior.

However, yet another factor should be mentioned among the ones maintaining the features of substantive administration even with that bureaucratic organization that is apparently a modern one by formal considerations. It is already commonly known that colonial power had quite a significant role in the survival of traditional political culture, which could strengthen its own autocratic rule with the elements and instruments of traditional political culture too (see for instance Pye 1985). An essentially similar phenomenon had taken place in colonial administration also, just because of its dependence upon the traditional political culture. By analyzing the British Indian administration, C. P Bhambhri has stated, among others, that it had two special components: elitism and the loyalty to the masters (Bhambhri 1972:4). These two components are expressly the characteristics of substantive administration. And one could quote a series of such statements that emphasize the role of the official as an individual in the British colonial administration. It was not accidental that Lord Curzon, the one-time British viceroy (who made efforts to introduce modern principles into the British Indian public administration), emphasized that the key to India was lying on the desk of every young British official and that officials' character, abilities, sense of duty, etc. would determine how lasting British rule would be in India (Dilks 1969:31). (In this he essentially repeated Macaulay's views.) If British administration was built much more upon suitable people than on legal norms, then it actually gave a new lease on life to the traditions of substantive administration, just as it strengthened the significance of traditional legal norms and the organization implementing law with the help of indirect rule (see for instance Morris and Read 1972:11–14; Seidman 1978:38). In fact, the penetration of the division of labor of modern economy into the traditional society of the colonies did not necessarily mean the disappearance of the traditional legal order. Empirical surveys prove that "the subsumption of formerly precapitalist producers within capitalist relations of production does not necessarily imply a complete transformation of precapitalist legal forms envisaged as mere simple concepts; but it entails a profound transformation of these forms as concrete concepts to the extent that subsumption constitutes change in the mode of production" (Snyder 1981:296). Similarly, the elements of traditional administration did not disappear either.

Some components of the traditional legal system, however, have survived *after indepen-*

dence just as much as discretional public administration relatively less caring for rules. It is true that the principle of judicial review generally survived in the face of its decisions, at least in the earlier British colonies, but this was frequently functioning just as discretionally as public administration was. (Significant examples are quoted by Seidman 1978:236–238.)

This is now the special situation evolved, when public administration has become a bureaucratic one, in so far as its structure has become *formally* such, with a particularly large number of hierarchical grades, but its bureaucratic phenomena have also multiplied in the pejorative sense of the word, partly because of its growing independence from law, and partly because of the lack of necessary expertise. The latter factor is a particularly important one, because if the personal element becomes dominant in public administration (or retains its original dominance), then the components of the principle of "only good men make good government" that endow the significance of qualifications, suitability, impartiality, etc. would be revalued. Thus the growing independence from law and the inadequate quality of the staff of public administration ultimately do not only produce a deviant bureaucracy, but public administration can then only be of decreasing efficiency. And to show that this is not only relevant in countries of British colonial past, it is sufficient to quote the example of Ethiopia: "The fact that law does not tell each Ethiopian administrator what precisely he is expected to do creates a certain amount of insecurity among bureaucrats, but this insecurity is more than counterbalanced by the traditional attitude that administration is an exercise of privilege rather than a matter of skill, ability and training" (Brietzke 1981:210).

The dominance of the public administrator as an individual against the legal norms is not only created or enhanced by the lack of such norms, but by the opposite as well, namely, the *relative overregulation*, particularly if regulation is far from the real opportunities. This relative overregulation ultimately results in the individual failure of the administrators in a public administration containing the dominance of individuals. After all, the legal norms that cannot be implemented at all, or only to a minor extent, result in discretion independent from the legal norms. On the other hand, the difference between the objectives and principles set in the legal norms and reality, which cannot be bridged over by public administration, manifests itself as the failure of public administration and its employees. Therefore, the more dominant the personal element of public administration is, the more responsibility it takes on itself for the lack of the realization of legal norms that cannot be implemented, and this strengthens further the dominance of the personal element in public administration.

Regulation, however, has been necessarily growing in the earlier colonial societies during the past decades, no matter how much the discretional nature of colonial administration has been preserved. In fact, the majority of these countries have launched some kind of conscious policy of development in the postindependence decades. Though the ideological foundations of such a development policy could greatly differ from one another—extending from socialistic trends to those expressing various fundamentalist objectives—yet lawmaking has had a prominent role in each (at least, after some time and when certain illusions—the illusion of a society without law—got dispersed). Such a changed position of public administration was worded by Bhambhri in the following:

> . . . from limited government we have moved to the era of "Big Government". . . . Though "Big Government" is a universal phenomenon, but in the developing countries it assumes special significance. The backwardness of centuries has to be removed by the efforts of the government. It is impossible for anyone to delineate clearly what a government should do or not do in the sphere of nation-building in the underdeveloped country. Development is a total activity, and ignoring any sector shall create imbalances. And this total developmental activity cannot be undertaken by anyone else except public authorities. . . . "Big Government" assumes "Big Bureaucracy." It is a truism to say that the greater the area of public policy, the greater is the role of implementation and service agencies (Bhambhri 1972:8–9).

Either in the more modest objectives of developmental policy, or—and this is more frequent—legal regulation serving the building of a planned economy and society upon some ideological foundation, *regulation bears the signs of modernization, whereas the behavior of public administration*—particularly regarding the dominance of the administrator—is of traditional nature. Thus the contradictions inevitably come to the surface. In the *present* condition of Indian public administration, for instance, originally organized by the British, congruence between the norms and actual behavior is missing, and the orientation of the lower-level officials in particular toward those administrative norms that contain the office rules, the maintenance of authority based on hierarchy, and the guarantee of impersonality is of a low standard. Other researchers have identified a low level of orientation toward norms safeguarding a rational administration even among senior officials, and from such findings the conclusion derives that the "bureaucratic" structure is more developed. In other words, the relevant rules are more elaborate than their appearance in actual behavior (Panadiker and Kshirager 1971).

Though according to some data such a contradiction does not only occur in the public administration of developing countries—an American survey indicated, for instance, that a considerable number of the employees of public administration are characterized by authoritative inclinations as contrasted to the democratic principles (Wynia 1974)—yet this contradiction as a characteristic feature is alive primarily in the public administration of developing countries. The already-mentioned situation—namely, that the organization of public administration is incapable of implementing the products of overambitious legislation—keeps alive and even strengthens a further traditional feature. This trait is linked to one of the characteristics of traditional legal systems, to the *punitive outlook* (Kulcsár 1987 c:32–33), but it has been alive also in the public administration of developing countries because of the same cultural linkages of the features of political and legal culture. According to Seidman, this "bureaucratic punishment-orientation results from ideology and structure. Administrators see punishment as the only available conformity-inducing measure. Administrators usually deal only with rules that they believe express custom. That suggests punitive sanctions" (Seidman 1978:242). In Seidman's interpretation the social effect of punitive sanction is by all means limited, but it is particularly so in the developmental process, since punishment may strengthen the existing, but may lead less to change, particularly not to the change of behavior deriving from the social environment in a way required by the government. [Actually, this phenomenon became quite clear for me when I analyzed the failure of the changes "forced" by penal law under the conditions of the Stalinist political system in the socialist society (see Kulcsár 1961:273 et infra).]

Thus such a form of deviant bureaucracy has evolved under special social circumstances and specific legal and administrative traditions. In such a situation, public administration, intending to follow the modern bureaucratic pattern, is supposed to solve the tasks occurring in the process of modernization, but partly these tasks cannot be solved on the basis of the legal norms wording ambitious objectives, which should be followed by public administration but which are usually set far apart from reality and cannot be solved by such an organization of public administration that bears signs of bureaucratic organization. In reality, the basic characteristics of the traditional, substantive administration live in them, retaining in particular the dominance of the administrator as a personality and his right to discretional decision making.

III. SOCIALIST SOCIETIES

Another form of deviant bureaucracy evolved in the socialist societies that developed at the Eastern periphery of Europe, under the conditions of the so-called Stalinist political system created in the 1930s in the Soviet Union, on the soil of centralized compulsory plans wishing to eliminate the market economy. This type of bureaucracy was adopted by the European countries following the Soviet model after World War II. The public administration of these countries was much closer to the one evolved in the Western center by the end of World War II, and their administrative traditions were also largely different from those of the underdeveloped countries, as parallel to the development of market economy the Weberian model had occupied the place of the so-called substantive administration already at an early phase of modernization, and they had other differences also from the Russian traditions. Yet *some elements of substantive administration had still been maintained by special social factors*, though to a different extent in each country. In the Hungarian and Polish societies, for instance, where the gentry and the traditions of administrative autonomy had survived for a long time, expert objective knowledge was pushed into the background compared to the knowledge of dominance, or more generally, compared to the dominant political position almost until World War II.

Following World War II, however, it was not substantive economy that had grown into market economy, but attempts were made to *eliminate market economy and the values and forms of behavior linked to the market, to enterprise, and even to the economy artificially by deliberate measures deriving from ideological requirements* in these societies. As mentioned, the efforts toward eliminating market economy were accompanied by an experiment to create a new society based on special ideological premises. And the measures aiming at the creation of the new society were based on an ideologically shaped, ambitious set of objectives put in legal norms. As a large part of the East European and East Central European societies had been yet in the first phase of modernization, and these countries were lagging behind those of the European core with respect to their economic and cultural advancement, efforts toward the creation of a new society had to be launched on the *soil of poverty*, and that also in a way that these societies should reach such a level of development by the renewed takeoff of modernization, which could jointly mean the second phase of modernization *and* an advanced social setup, which would differ from the main line of the Western center. It should be added that traits of the economy of shortage had been alive in these societies because of their historical belatedness, and with a broken-down economy consequent upon the war situation, when the majority of these societies started to follow an unsuitable model and set ambitious objectives for themselves, the economy of shortage had become characteristic of them (see Kornai 1981). Moreover, shortage had grown even relatively in the context of the objectives and reality and with respect to the distance between them.

All these circumstances had produced the second form of deviant bureaucracy in public administration just as in the economy, namely, *rule-creating bureaucracy instead of the rule-observing one.* Such a situation was created in which the *legislative* nature of public administration had been strengthened as well as its law-implementing character, and even in the implementation of law the rules made by public administration itself were dominant.

The exclusion of the market, or its restriction to a very small sphere, the introduction of the system of centrally issued plans by the nationalization or collectivization of the productive and distributory organizations, had *turned economic activity also into public administration.* If the commodity and monetary relations do not assert themselves in keeping with the order of market values, or do not assert themselves at all, then the organization of production, the shaping of the price of individual products—and voluntarily at that, disregarding the costs—distribution, etc. all become administrative activities. Moreover, the organizations effectively producing and distributing get articulated within the system of organizations of the society as units directly managed by administration, behaving in many cases as administrative organizations and occasionally even as authorities. It is only one sign of this economy turned administration that in these countries the disputes of economic organizations had not been (and in some countries are still not being) decided by law courts, but by arbitration committees of administrative nature specifically created for the purpose and directly serving the interests of economic management. This in itself has led to the organizational growth of public organization accompanied by the enhancement of bureaucratic lawmaking.

The socialist societies evolved at the Eastern periphery of Europe have created a special paternalism by centrally ordered economic plans and have strengthened those paternalistic elements that had characterized the political culture of this region anyhow (Kulcsár 1987b).

However, in the case of paternalistic economic and political management, the dominance of the bureaucratic coordination of the society is an inevitable outcome. Moreover, bureaucratic coordination—as analyzed by János Kornai (Kornai 1984:16)—may survive central management; it can be present with greater endurance than the system of paternalist relationships. More precisely, the gradual dismantling of central management, as it began in Hungary from 1968 onward, does not necessarily weaken bureaucratic coordination in a tempo that suits transformation. One reason, of course, is the contradictory, occasionally retrograde, slow nature of transformation itself. János Kornai (1984:20) writes the following in connection with this issue:

> Bureaucracy stretches a net of rules against the stream of social micro-process. If the net is too coarse, then all sorts of irregularities can slip through it. Counter-measure: the net should be woven more fine. This can be called the *inclination of the bureaucracy towards self-fulfillment*: *it is inclined to complement general regulation anew by increasingly concrete and more detailed rules.*

This is how it came about that "the inclination of the bureaucracy towards self-fulfillment" manifested itself in the massive growth of the multitude of indirect regulators simultaneously to the introduction of economic reform, to the transformation of the system of centrally ordered plans. For example, 228 different regulatory elements influenced the changes of profit of the enterprises in 1982. It is not difficult to find examples for such a kind of lawmaking that already embodies the internal logic of the bureaucratic organization. This is a logic that makes itself independent of the socioeconomic environment and its changes to some extent. In fact, such legal norms function practically without any feedback; more exactly, the feedback—if the ineffectiveness of the earlier regulation reached the administrative organization somehow—would set off new lawmaking.

Bureaucratic lawmaking is also a manifestation of those legal norms that do not intend to regulate primarily the activities of citizens or people, but organizational activity, and frequently they lay down the *procedural* aspects of their own activities when they are issued by the different organizations. Incidentally such bureaucratic lawmaking is the inevitable consequence of the economy of shortage. Shortage is accompanied by the distribution of the "shortage goods," and this regulation creates the organizations of distribution on the one hand, and regulating the distribution and behavior demand from those "queuing" on the other. For instance, in the eastern region of Europe the motorcar is not a commodity but a centrally distributed article of shortage, the price of which is independent of its real use value, for which one has to stand in queue; it can be acquired by allocation of the organization especially created for the purpose, and even the second-hand sale is regulated up to a certain period of time. But it is true that these regulations are being violated to the extent that the network of regulation is attempted to be "woven more fine." The more marked the shortage is, the more regulation increases. After all, if an organization created for performing a given task cannot essentially do it, or only with decreased social effectiveness, then its activities would inevitably get distorted and become dysfunctional, and instead of solving the task of "how," self-regulation of the activity appears as a substitute.

The impossibility of the realization of ambitious objectives mostly worded on the level of acts artificially enhances shortage, as *instead of* the realization of the usually ideologically founded objectives and the solution of tasks—since it is impossible to realize them—the organizations for their realization appear. Subsequently, these organizations *narrow* the theoretically set objectives and tasks to such an extent by their regulating activity to allow their realization and solution in some way. This phenomenon can be noticed in the socialist societies living at the Eastern periphery of Europe, though the context and the dimensions may vary in the fields of free medical care, low-rent flats built and distributed by the state, schooling, etc.

A further characteristics is that the *weight of the administrator* appears also in this form of deviant bureaucracy, as the significance of personal contacts survives behind overregulation just because regulation is excessive. Actually, regulation generally allows for discretion, regarded to be exceptional and retained only for certain cases, which, however, formally legalizes the administrator's behavior diverting from the rule. In Hungary, for instance, the rules of the distribution of flats minutely qualify legitimate claims, including the procedure of the administrative organ and the involvement of the public as well; yet with reference to central interests etc., administrative disposition over a part of the flats is practically uncontrollable. Essentially, a similar discretion is the outcome of overregulation as well. A mass of contradictory legal regulation has been created just because of the multilayered and departmental nature of regulation primarily in the field of the economy, such that their observance makes profitable economic activity impossible. If only the ministerial orders and higher-level legal norms are considered, then it turns out that 59.7% of the legal norms promulgated in Hungary between 1945 and 1987 were made on the ministerial level. And if the ministerial directives and instructions, which are formally not legal rules yet are of normative nature (circulars, etc.) are also considered, then lawmaking on the level of administration would be of much higher proportion. Consequently, it is the spontaneous processes of the economy that create those "rules" for organizations and individuals that effectively conduct their behavior, but that differ from, and occasionally oppose, the relevant legal norms. As the violation of legal norms also becomes a practically general feature, the administrator has a chance to identify the violation of law discretionally, more precisely for calling the "chosen" violator to account, usually not because of the concrete violation of law, but by referring to it.

Ultimately, the second form of deviant bureaucracy produces phenomena in the activities of administration similar to the first one, as the most important "result" of both is the *weakening of the performance and social effectiveness of public administration.*

REFERENCES

Bhambhri, C.P. *Administrators in a Changing Society.* National, New Delhi, 1972.
Brietzke, P.H. *Law, Development, and the Ethiopian Revolution.* Brucknell University Press, Toronto, 1981.
Crozier, M. *La Phénomène Bureaucratique.* Editions du Seuil, Paris, 1963.
Dilks, D. *Curzon in India,* Vols. I, II. London, 1979.
Hill, M.J. *The Sociology of Public Administration.* Weidenfeld and Nicholson, London, 1972.
Kornai, J. *The Economy of Shortage.* Amsterdam, 1981.
Kornai, J. *Büurokrataikus és piaci koordináció [Bureaucratic and Market Coordination].* Akadémiai Kiadó, Budapest, 1984.
Kulcsár, K. *A job nevelö szerepe a szocialista társadalomban [The Educational Role of Law in the Socialist Society].* Közgazdasági és Jogi Könyvkiadó, Budapest, 1961.
Kulcsár, K. The social context of bureaucracy. In *Politics and Public Administration in Hungary* (G. Szoboszlay, ed.). Akadémiai Kiadó, Budapest, 1985.
Kulcsár, K. *Modernization and Law. Theses and Thoughts.* Institute of Sociology, HAS, Budapest, 1987a.
Kulcsár, K. *Politikai és Jogszociológia [Political and Legal Sociology].* Kossuth Könyvkiadó, Budapest, 1987b.
Kulcsár, K. Political culture—legal culture. Paper presented at the 13th World Congress on Philosophy of Law and Social Philosophy, August 20–26, 1987, Kobe, Japan, 1987c.
Kulcsár, K. Forced adaptation and law-making. A functional aspect of comparative law. In *Comparative Law,* Waseda University, Tokyo, 1988.
Morris, H.F., and Read, J.S. *Indirect Rule and the Search for Justice.* Oxford University Press, Oxford, 1972.

Panadiker, V.P. and Kshiragar, S.S. Bureaucracy in India: An empirical study. *Indian Journal of Public Administration 2* (1971).

Pye, L.W. *Asian Power and Politics. The Cultural Dimensions of Authority.* Harvard University Press, Cambridge, MA, 1985.

Riggs, F.W. *Administration in Developing Countries.* Houghton-Mifflin, Boston, 1964.

Seidman, R.B. *The State, Law and Development.* St. Martin's Press, New York, 1978.

Selznick, P. *Leadership in Administration.* Harper and Row, New York, 1957.

Snyder, F.G. *Capitalism and Legal Change. An African Transformation.* Academic Press, New York, 1981.

Weber, M. *Gazdaság és Társadalom. A megértö szociológia alapvonalai.* [The Hungarian translation was made on the basis of the 5th ed. of *Wirtschaft und Gesellschaft. Grundriss der verstehenden Soziologie*, I Halbband, 1976.] Közgazdasági és Jogi Könyvkiadó, Budapest, 1987.

Wynia, B.L. Federal bureaucrat's attitudes toward a democratic ideology. *Public Administration Review* March–April (1974).

66

Greek Bureaucracy and Public Administration

The Persistent Failure of Reform

Constantine P. Danopoulos   *Department of Political Science, San Jose State University, San Jose, California*

Andrew C. Danopoulos   *College of Social Sciences, University of California at Davis, Davis, California*

I. INTRODUCTION

Administrative reform, i.e., "the artificial inducement of administrative transformation against resistance" (Caiden 1969:1), has been a much talked about subject by Greek political leaders of almost all ideological dispositions for many decades. In his 1952 *Report on the Greek Economic Problem*, the minister of finance Kyriakos Varvaressos bluntly stated that "we must not expect any real improvement in the country's situation, as long as we do not deal with the fundamental problem of the inadequacy of its administrative machine" (cited in Argyriades 1968:345). Fifteen or so years later George Papadopoulos (1968), head of the military regime (1967–1974), referred to Greece's bureaucracy as "an unbridled organ that has all but ceased being servant of the public." A similar line was struck by Constantine Karamanlis, head of the civilian government that succeeded the fallen Junta, who stated that one of his government's major goals would be to modernize the nation's administrative system by strengthening its "moral," "human," "material," and "structural" bases (Shinn 1985:238). Finally, the socialists under Andreas Papandreou in their 1981 preelection literature identified favoritism, and excessive centralization as the main culprits of administrative inadequacy and promised to place bureaucratic reform high on their list of priorities (Pasok 1981:103–105).

A number of reform efforts have been undertaken since the early 1950s and even before to streamline and professionalize Greece's administrative apparatus, and to improve its effectiveness and capacity for innovation. The latter can be defined as "the generation, acceptance, and implementation of new ideas, processes and products or services," and is considered a salient characteristic of modern bureaucratic organizations (Thompson 1969:5). By all accounts these efforts have not come to fruition and Greece's bureaucracy possesses few of the characteristics associated with developed or rationalist administration, i.e., organizational complexity, high degree of specialization and professionalism, political neutrality, accountability to the legitimate authorities of the state, and responsiveness to the needs of the citizenry (Heady 1979:168–170). In 1985, Apostolos Lazaris, the socialists' minister responsible for the bureaucracy, expressing government as well as public disaffection with resistance to reform referred to the nation's administrative apparatus as "that eternal problem," and characterized relations between the public and the bureaucracy as those between "opponents" (Athens News Agency 1985). A public opinion survey conducted in November 1998, revealed that despite numerous reform efforts, "inefficiency and corruption" continue to pervade "every aspect of the state machinery" (Odyssey 1998:20).

This essay will seek to outline the various efforts of administrative reform in Greece, and to identify and analyze the reasons for the failure of those efforts.

II. HISTORY OF BUREAUCRATIC REFORM

The emergence and evolution of the modern state has been attributed a response to a function of socioeconomic developments such as societal growth, complexity, industrialization, urbanization, and the corresponding demands for public services. Richard Rose attributes the growth and expansion of the modern state and its many social groups and organizations in terms of three categories of functions: defining, such as tax collection, administration of justice, defense, and foreign affairs, without which the state would cease to exist; resource mobilization, denoting state assistance to key economic structures within a society as industry, agriculture, and transportation; and social programs aimed at providing direct benefits to citizens, otherwise known as distribution or redistribution of wealth (cited in Peters 1978:17). Modern bureaucratic structures are at the very heart of the modern state. Indeed, as Fritz Morstein Marx (1967) clearly demonstrates, it would be unreal to perceive any type of national development in which the bureaucracy would not be playing a leading role. Underscoring the importance of modern administration Samuel Krislov (1974:40–41) states: "Bureaucracies are the late bloomers of modern political structure. They grew silently in the underbrush—seldom noticed, little analyzed. . . . They are not loved and respected, but rather tolerated and depended on." It is therefore no accident that the source of modern bureaucracies, at least in the European context, can be traced to the emergence of nationalism and the growth of the centralized, monarchical, absolutist state and its successors over the last four centuries.

A. Birth and Growth of Bureaucracy in Greece: The Early Years

Greek politics and bureaucracy were based on European prototypes adopted on a wholesale basis by the nation's political leadership, beginning with the late 1820s when the country came into existence as a semi-independent entity. Early attempts to forge a modern French-modeled bureaucratic structure in Greece failed. The new country possessed all the characteristics of a traditional agrarian society and its independence was only marginal. The Ottoman Empire—from which Greece gained independence following a protracted struggle—was a corporatist entity. The only contact between the subject people and the Muslim authorities came when the latter came to either collect, taxes or draft people for compulsory and unpaid labor. These much-detested practices encouraged individualism, localism, and the existence of brigandage. Subject people distrusted authority and instead sought the protection of local primates and chieftains—practices that continued in the decades following independence.

As though parochialism and distrust were not enough, the new nation faced other insurmountable difficulties. Its small size, rocky terrain, lack of an economic infrastructure, a largely illiterate population, and an economy based on subsistence farming were some of the many ills that plagued it. To these one must add the overwhelming influence of the "great powers," the early adoption of parliamentarian institutions, and the conflict between the indigenous and Europeanized elites. The administrative apparatus which was established was a highly centralized structure based on "a wholesale and indiscriminate adoption of foreign prototypes," especially France's (Diamandouros 1972:300). Little regard was paid to the differences in culture, economic and social disparities, and historical experiences. Thus, Greece's bureaucracy during the years following independence "did not reflect sufficiently the nature of the Greek society" (Argyriades 1965:298). The civil service became the dumping ground which accommodated thousands who could not find employment in the desperately poor economy and a source of patronage offered by politicians to their constituents in exchange for political support. Absence of a tenure system, low pay, and lack of prestige sufficed to keep the elites away from the ranks of the bureaucracy, all of which rendered the civil servants pawns in the hands of their elected patrons. Keith R. Legg and John M. Roberts (1997:167) are correct when they observe that "the Greek bureucracy could not control the political sector; it was instead used by the political elites."

By the 1870s the bulk of the country's budget was utilized to keep up a huge, highly centralized and grossly ineffective bureaucracy (Dertilis 1977:138–140; Mouzelis 1978:37). From the outside, Greece's administrative structure gave the appearance of modern organization, when in reality it possessed none of the characteristics associated with rationalist administrative institutions.

B. Transition Period

The 1880s ushered Greece into a new period. A new generation of leaders emerged more aware of the need to modernize the country's archaic economic infrastructure. A devastating vine disease in France allowed Greek currant exports to rise dramatically, becoming a lucrative source of foreign exchange. To this should also be added the international crisis which forced financiers to turn the Greece and other Balkan countries to invest their capital. The modernizing-oriented Tricoupis administration took advantage of these and began laying the groundwork for an economic infrastructure. Though subsequent reduction in currant sales and withdrawal of foreign capital caused the failure of these development efforts, they nonetheless generated an urge for social and economic change.

The reform-minded Tricoupis administration sought to revamp the nation's administrative apparatus. He established a mechanism to punish and even expel civil servants guilty of graft and other unethical practices; forbade the transfer of bureaucrats from one ministry, bureau, or office to another before they had met promotion requirements; tied promotion to the level of education; and mandated an examination as prerequisite to employment in the civil service. But the prime minister's reform effort to neutralize and reorganize the bureaucracy failed due to the same clientelistic and cultural traits which carried over in to the new era. Tricoupis' political rivals abolished all relevant legislation when they took power some years later (Argyriades 1968:343–344; Tsoucalas 1977:108–109).

The rise to power of still a new generation of leaders in the 1910s, headed by Eleftherios Venizelos, and the emergence of a small but energetic entrepreneurial class gave development a shot in the arm. As a result of World War I, in which Greece participated, the size of the country increased as did its productive population and gross national product. Greece had entered a transition period which, in spite of reverses in the early to mid-1920s and late 1930s, the devastation of World War II, and the civil war that followed, continued at a slow but steady pace. American economic and military assistance, beginning in 1947, ushered Greece in to a period of healthy economic growth, excessive urbanization, and dramatic increases in per-capita income, literacy, and consumption rates.

New effort was undertaken by Venizelos in the 1910s and 1920s and by succeeding governments to revamp the nation's bureaucracy without overwhelming success. A series of laws were passed in the 1910s designed to modernize Greece's administrative apparatus which included the introduction of a tenure system aimed at neutralizing the civil service and other reforms in many ways similar to those introduced earlier by Tricoupis. Additional safeguards were introduced in 1951, through the introduction of a Civil Service Code, which created a permanent commission responsible for overseeing all facets of administration including recruitment, promotion, retirement, grading, pay, discipline, rights, and duties of administrative personnel (Argyriades 1965:299).

In spite of these efforts the clientelistic practices continued unabated. The bureaucracy grew in numbers and consumed an ever larger slice of the national budget. Keith Legg (1977:291) observes that "the growth of bureaucracy was unrelated to necessity [and] the proportion of state employees to the population as a whole was startling compared to the far more advanced European democracies." The majority of these civil servants possessed little training, and many could not read and write. C.A. Munkman (1958:261), an employee of the American economic mission to Greece, characterized the Greek administrative apparatus as "inefficient and archaic" with "a lot of dead wood" in its ranks.

C. The Postwar Years

While some token efforts were made in the 1950s, the poor reputation of the bureaucracy, and nepotism on the part of the governing conservative political forces which stuffed the civil service with people considered safe, extremely detailed laws, and remoteness from the masses created a "paralyzing effect" and encouraged the "shelving of responsibility." Greece's administrative machine, Langrod (1964:33) concluded, "represents a mosaic of not quite coordinated components isolated from one another, and each consisting of a separate fortress, firmly entrenched against any extraneous attempts at reform." In other words, as Beck and Fainsod (1963:233–300) have argued, progress toward industrialization does not necessarily bring about a corresponding emergence of bureaucratic development.

On Langrod's recommendations, the George Papandreou (1964–65) government proceeded to adopt a series of reforms aimed at improving Greece's administrative apparatus. These included greater emphasis on technical and administrative training, trimming out unnecessary personnel, and decentralization. But when the military took over in 1967 it moved quickly to scrape these steps, most of which had not been fully implemented, denouncing them as Communist inspired. The new rulers denounced the bureaucracy's ineffectiveness, attacked on the corrupt and canvasing practices of the politicians, and made administrative reform—along with economic development, educational reform, the creation of a harmonious and balanced society, and the development of a healthy political life—their five modernizing objectives. But the colonel's nepotistic practices, repression, threats of dismissal, failure to issue clear directives, failure to respond to the needs and recommendations of the civil service, and the planting of informants in the ranks of the civil service rendered the bureaucracy a passive observant. The military rulers were even less successful in their efforts to transform and modernize the nation's administrative apparatus than their predecessors (Danopoulos 1988).

Following the restoration of civilian rule, the conservative Karamanlis/Rallis cabinets (1974–1981) made some feeble attempts of their own, to be followed by a more ambitious efforts by the succeeding socialist governments of Andreas Papandreou (1981–89). Papandreou's administrative reform legislation contained many of the proposals made by his father's government in the mid-1960s, with additional ones as well. The socialists concentrated their effort toward establishing "a more open [civil service] system concerning recruitment, appointments, transfers, and promotions" (Shinn 1985:238). In addition, a uniform salary scale grading and rating system, decentralization and other measures were proposed aimed at reducing the bureaucracies heavy-handness and increase its responsiveness to public needs. The latter included simplification of procedures and establishment of a bureau of public grievances aimed at discouraging the shelving of responsibility and improving interagency communication and coordination. Finally, a School of Public Administration was established in 1985, based on the British and French models, to train high civil servants as well as prospective ones by offering "practical knowledge" in place of "theoretical knowledge" offered by existing university curricula (Athens News Agency 1985). When the conservatives came back to power in 1990, they passed a new and "comprehensive law on administrative reform" (Sotiropoulos 1993:43).

Pasok's return to power in 1993, and the replacement of the ailing Papandreou by the modernist Costas Simitis, set the stage for another wave of administrative reforms. Under pressure from the European Union (EU), the new socialist leader announced on November 1, 1996, that "modernization of public administration [constituted] a top priority issue" in his reform agenda (*Bulletin* 1996:2). The main thrust of Simitis' efforts aim to improve the bureaucracy's capacity to respond "to the needs of the public." Toward this goal, the government adopted a two-track policy. One, to upgrade autonomy and responsibility so that ministries will no longer be in the business of merely "issuing certificates, but drafting and implementing policy." The prime minister hopes to establish a "one-stop shop" allowing the citizen to deal with one single servant "for a variety of administrative issues, such as applying for a pension, or getting a driver's licence, rather than visiting of services to collect taxes" (*Bulletin* 1998:2). The other would improve the technical and technological skills of civil servants so that they can respond to the needs of the citizenry. To help insure performance, the government decided that "civil servants must be evaluated, and set forth a set of "performance indices" (*Bulletin* 1998:2). Finally, to assist citizens air their grievances, Simitis set up an ombudsman's office and appointed Nikiforos Diamandouros, one of Greece's most distinguished social scientists, to head the office. The ombudsman's task is to "help restore the balance between the individual and the state" (Gilson 1998:20).

Though well intended and thoroughly thought out, these new measures have done little to increase the Greek bureaucracy's efficiency, responsiveness, efficacy, and innovative capabilities, and to alleviate public complaints and demands for bureaucratic reform. Fallen prey to the same insidious habits, and responding to the necessity to pay back political debts and place their own people in key posts after decades of conservative rule, the socialists followed many of the old nepotistic practices that they had so vehemently denounced while in opposition. According to sources cited by Dimitri A. Sotiropoulos, "In November 1985 there were approximately 224,000 more employees working for the wider public sector than in December 1980." In the first two years following their return to power in 1991, the New Democracy government added 60,000 more civil servants (Sotiropoulos 1993:44). Despite the fact that the Simitis government has managed to arrest the rate of growth, the total number of public employees (full and part time) is approximately 600,000. This means that about 28% of the total work force are employed by the government sector, giving Greece the dubious distinction of having one of the world's largest bureaucracies in proportion to the country's total population of nearly 10 million inhabitants.

III. ANALYZING THE FAILURE TO REFORM

Greek political leaders of all ideological dispositions, although blaming each other, agree that the bureaucracy remains the single most important impediment in the country's path toward development. Public opinion polls consistently confirm this and express concern regarding Greece's ability to compete effectively within the EU.

By all accounts, the performance of Greek public administration has and continues to be less than "satisficing," which Marsh and Simon (1958:40) define as attaining a satisfactory degree of performance within given conditions. In spite of many efforts to reform, Greece's administrative apparatus displays most of the characteristics associated with the bureaucracies of developing or changing societies which include: imitative rather than indigenous patterns of public adminis-tration, deficiency in skilled manpower, emphasis on orientations that are other than productive, widespread discrepancy between form and reality, and a measure of generous operational auton-omy (Heady 1979:271–275). Why have attempts to bring about a developed bureaucratic machine capable of innovation not produced the anticipated results?

Bureaucracies are societal organizations consisting of individual members of the society. Individual attitudes influence societal behavior, but societal norms, factors, and adaptations also impact on individual behavior (Armstrong 1973:15–23). Societal organizations, including bureaucracies, in turn, are influenced by societal or ecological and individual factors, as well as internal dynamics and organizational norms present in all organizational settings. Though interre-lated, societal, individual, and organizational norms and attitudes can be held responsible for the consistent failure of administrative reform in Greece. Let us examine each one separately.

A. Societal Considerations

There is widespread agreement in the literature that general societal dimensions, historical antecedents, and the political culture of a society explain that society's "orientation" toward administration and affect the attitudes, behavior, norms, and characteristics of its bureaucratic structure. For societal outlooks, particularly a country's political culture, "either support or poten-tially undermine the effectiveness of administrative structures" (Peters 1978:41) and may also help or undermine reform efforts (Caiden 1969:168–190).

These so-called ecological factors have a telling impact on the degree of "acceptability" a bureaucracy enjoys and the potential utility of reform. Acceptability and other key organizational imperatives such as willingness on the part of the public to accept bureaucratic impersonality and universality of rules have been used as a basis to array political cultures along a continuum from underdeveloped to rationalist or modern. The greater the degree of acceptance and rule universal-ity the more developed a culture, and vice versa (Riggs 1966:225–255). Similarly, the more devel-oped a society, the higher the level of professionalization, and vice versa. A political system and its political culture pass through a process of development from traditional to transition before reaching an advanced stage referred to as developed. This process, and especially the transition phase of it, constitute the norm in the so called developing or changing societies of the third world (Riggs 1964).

The traditional society (which nowadays exists only in a few isolated parts of the world) is characterized by ascription, minimal urbanization, low mobility, lack of education, subsistence agrarian economy, parochial political culture, low empathy, and a political system that performs very few functions (Palmer 1985:44–45). Administration, to the extent it exists, performs minimal functions such as to collect taxes and enlist people for compulsory and unpaid labor. Nonprofes-sional criteria as kinship and patronage, as opposed to achievement, discipline, and ability, are used as bases for appointment, promotion, and advancement.

In contrast, transitional societies are characterized by weak political institutions, lack of regime legitimacy, weak civil society, fragmented social organizations, unevenly developed economies, individualism, and ethnic and class cleavages. Developing societies seek simultane-ously to develop economic infrastructures, differentiate their economies, and meet the rising expectations of their people—all with poor and often overstretched resources. The bureaucratic structures of these societies—which by and large tend to be replicas of prototypes in developed countries—are called upon to accomplish these monumental tasks.

Lacking expertise and other ingredients associated with modern bureaucratic organizations, the administrative structures of these states are further handicapped by lack of rule universality and acceptability of administration. Taking their cues from the social milieu, the bureaucracies of developing societies are permeated by formalism, lack of public service ethos, apparent rationality in the pattern of organization, and general reliance on traditional criteria of decision making. Bureaucratic rules provide only a point of departure for bargaining and negotiation in all public–civil service relations (Riggs 1964:200–202; Eisenstadt 1959:302–320). In other words, societal dimensions in traditional as well as developing societies are permeated by an environment where reform is talked about, but the objective conditions for implementation are not exactly present. Society itself is not any more prepared to accept reform than the bureaucracy itself, especially if reform means changes in existing norms and limitations in the lives of the citizenry.

The genesis, evolution, and character of administration in Greece to today from the late 1820s when the country became independent, exemplify the traditional transition scheme outlined above. The first 50 years of independence seem to correspond with the traditional phase of societopoliticoadministrative culture. The decades from 1880 on portray a process of transition characterized by a substantial enlargement of the role of the state in the economic and social life of the country. The transition phase is still going on. Historical antecedents, lack of an indigenous bureaucratic culture, economic difficulties, geographical factors, foreign interference, and cultural attitudes, to name only some, can be said to have influenced Greek political culture. Sotiropoulos (1993:51) is on the mark when he observes the country's civil society is weak, and attributes it to the fact that "voluntary associations are sparse and social organizations are sanctioned by the state." These are responsible for the low degree of acceptability of bureaucracy and universality of rules, and in turn contributed to the consistent failure of administrative reform in Greece.

B. Individual Perceptions

Closely connected with the above are individual attitudes and behavior. Taking cues from the lack of civil society, Adamantia Pollis advances the Greek "concept of self" and analyzes its political and societal implications. Unlike in the West, where the concept of individualism explains a person's place and his relatedness to others and to society, in the Greek context individualism, Pollis (1965:31–32) argues, is "irrelevant" and individual relatedness is determined by membership in groupings such as family, village, and local church. Values such as justice, equality, fairness, and uniform laws are highly regarded in the West and their application is carried out independent of personal relationships. In Greece, on the other hand, "objectivity and impartiality deflect from the of one's personal obligations the virtues to strive for are subjectivity and partiality." As a result the individual suspects political authority, is reserved and cautious in his dealings with government, and takes actions designed to evade state policies, laws, and regulations. The administrative apparatus, being part of the state, is viewed in the same manner (Diamandouros 1983:45).

Greece's formalistic, rigid, and in many ways anachronistic educational system reinforces these attitudes. Until the socialist government pushed through a series of forms, educational curricula emphasized memorization as opposed to understanding and critical interpretation, theoretical but not practical and technical knowledge, conformity and no innovation, and abstract perfection in the place of rational and step-by-step approach problem solving. These, and especially the latter, lead to an all-or-nothing notion that somehow there is a magic and perfect solutions to every problem. Absence of critical thinking, on the other hand, propagates easy acceptance of plans (especially foreign-born ones) designed to remedy such problems. But when they do not produce magic and instant results, such plans are abandoned as quickly as they were adopted. With such individual attitudes prevailing it should come as no surprise that administrative reform in Greece has had a very difficult time.

C. Institutional Imperatives

Being products of this environment, Greek civil servants are not immune to societal and individual norms and behavior patterns. However, there are additional institutional/organizational dimensions that also impede reform. Social organizations, including bureaucracies, carve out their own territory and create their own environment. Set procedures, continuity, and avoidance of controversy and exposure are very much part of organizational life. Reform often means disruption of existing patterns of conduct, uncertainty, dislocation, scrutiny, and pressure to learn new roles and modes of conduct. As a result, civil servants usually "emerge as emotional defenders of a given order of things [and] do not drift naturally into the camp of change" (Marx 1963:87–94). Greek bureaucrats are no exception to these organizational imperatives.

Caiden (1969:144–156) identifies four methods of introducing and implementing administrative reform: (1) imposed through political revolution; (2) introduced to remedy organizational rigidity (reform from within); (3) through the legal system; and (4) through changes in attitudes. The history of administrative reform in Greece indicates that, with the possible and partial exception of Venizelos' efforts which could said to been generated by the 1909 military coup, all attempts to revamp the nation's administrative apparatus have taken the legal route. Various governments adopted West European prototypes and/or sketched out plans with little input from the civil servants themselves. The low prestige and acceptance of bureaucracies, coupled with lack of sophisticated management, knowledge and training, extremely detailed regulations, fear of reprisals, and absence of group consciousness in the civil service, have relegated the Greek bureaucracy to a passive and often apathetic observer in discussions, debates, and plans aimed at administrative reform. But for reform measures to be relevant and to succeed, those directly affected (bureaucrats) must have a hand in their planning and execution. "The struggle for reform," Caimen (1969:183) observes, "can not be clothed in ideological garb or carried out by national sentiment. Administrative reform is a personal matter between people who have to work together all day and every day and carry on whether the reforms are successful or not."

IV. A PARTING WORD

The consistent failure of administrative reform in Greece should not be considered an aberration. For "even in the most favorable circumstances reform is a tricky business" (Caimen 1969:186) and, as the preceding discussion reveals, conditions in Greece have been less than favorable. Societal, individual, and institutional dimensions have mitigated against the success of reform, as have frequent and often abrupt governmental changes and lack of political will to fully implement such measures. But at the end lasting reform "cannot depend on the superiority of power or the coercion of nonbelievers. Ultimately, those who resist reforms have to be won over in spirit as well as in body" (Caiden 1969:154), which is easier said than done.

In recent years, many commentators have expressed the fear that membership in the EU will eventually lead to loss of national identity, language, and "Greekness." It would be a heavenly gift if contemporary Greeks resisted cultural, linguistic, and ethnic assimilation, but availed themselves to the technological, managerial, and administrative know-how their more developed European partners can offer. Membership in the EU may give Greeks the opportunity to become acquainted and absorb national administrative cultures, techniques, and modes of conduct and slowly adapt rather copy them in a wholesale and indiscriminate manner as was the case in the past. In the end, successful administrative reform in Greece may ultimately be based on foreign-born prototypes that failed so dismally in the past. Only time will tell.

REFERENCES

Argyriades, D.C. (1965). Some aspects of civil service reorganization in Greece. *International Review of Administrative Service 314*:297–309

Argyriades, D.C. (1968). The ecology of Greek administration: some factors affecting the development of the Greek civil service. In J.C. Peristiany (ed.), *Contributions to Mediterranean Sociology*, 339–349. The Hague: Mouton.

Armstrong, J.A. (1973). *The European Administrative Elite*. Princeton, NJ: Princeton University Press

Athens News Agency. (1985). Interview with Apostolos Lazaris, Minister of State (Feb. 5).

Beck, C. (1963). Bureaucracy and political development in Eastern Europe. In J. LaPalambara (ed.), *Bureaucracy and Political Development*, 268–300. Princeton, NJ: Princeton University Press

Bulletin. (1996). Simitis announces public administration reforms. (Nov. 2):1–2.

Bulletin. (1998). PM attends session targetting reform of public administration. (Dec. 3):1–2

Caiden, G.E. (1969). *Administrative Reform.* Chicago: Aldine.

Danopoulos, C.P. (1988). The military and bureaucracy in Greece 1967–1974. *Public Administration and Development*, 8(2):219–231

Dertilis, G. (1977). *Koinonikos Metaschimatismos Kai Stratiotiki Epemvasi, 1890–1909*. Athens: Exandas.

Diamandouros, P.N. (1972). The formation of the modern Greek state: 1821–1828. Unpublished Ph.D. dissertation, Columbia University, New York

Diamandouros, P.N. (1983). Greek political culture in transition: historical origins, evolution, current trends. In R. Clogg (ed.), *Greece in the 1890s.* London: Macmillan.

Eisenstadt, S.N. (1963). Bureaucracy and political development. In J. LaPalombara (ed.), *Bureaucracy and Political Development*, 96–116. Princeton, NJ: Princeton University Press

Gilson, G. (1998). Greece's new ombudsman: the people's champion. *Odyssey* (Nov./Dec.):20.

Heady, F. (1979). *Public Administration: A Comparative Perspective*, 2nd ed. New York: Marcel Dekker

Krislov, S. (1974). *Representative Bureaucracy.* Englewood Cliffs, NJ: Prentice-Hall.

Langrod, G. (1964). *Reorganization of Public Administration in Greece.* Paris: Organization for Economic Co-operation and Development

Legg, K.R. (1977). The nature of the modern Greek state. In J.T.A. Koumoulides (ed.), *Greece in Transition.* London: Zeno Booksellers and Publishers.

Legg, K.R., and Roberts, J.M. (1997). *Modern Greece: A Civilization on the Periphery.* Boulder, CO. Westview Press

March, J.G., and Simon, H. (1958). *Organizations.* New York: Wiley.

Marx, F.M. (1973). The higher civil service as an action group in Western political development. In J. LaPalombara (ed.), *Bureaucracy and Political Development*, 62–95. Princeton, NJ: Princeton University Press

Mouzelis, N. (1978). *Neo-Elliniki Koinonia: Opseis Ipanaptyxis.* Athens: Exandas.

Munkman, C.A. (1958). *American Aid to Greece—A Report on the First Ten Years.* New York: Praeger

Palmer, M. (1985). *Dilemmas of Political Development*, 3rd ed. Itasca, IL: F.E. Peacock Publishers.

Papadopoulos, G. (1968). *To Pistevo Mas*, Vol 1. Athens: Government Printing Office

Pasok. (1981). *Diakyrixi Kyvernitikis Drastiriotitas—Symvoleo me ton Lao.* Athens: Panellinio Socialistiko Kinima.

Peters, B.G. (1978). *The Politics of Bureaucracy–A Comparative Perspective.* New York: Longman

Pollis, A. (1965). Political Implications of the modern Greek concept of self. *British Journal of Sociology*, XVI: 29–47.

Riggs, F.W. (1964). *Administration in Developing Countries: The Theory of Prismatic Society.* Boston: Houghton-Mifflin

Riggs, F.W. (1966). Administrative development: an elusive concept. In J.D. Montgomery and W.J. Siffin (eds.), *Approaches to Development—Politics, Administration and Change*, 225–256. New York: McGraw-Hill.

Shinn, R.S. (1985). *Government and Politics, Greece: A Country Study*, 223–286. Washington: American University

Sotiropoulos, D.A. (1993). A colossues with feet of clay: the state in post-authoritarian Greece. In H.J. Psomiades and S.B. Thomadakis (eds.), *Greece, the New Europe, and the Changing International Order*, 43–56. New York: Pella.

Thompson, V.A. (1969). *Bureaucracy and Innovation.* University, AL: University of Alabama Press.

67

Running the Bureaucratic State

Administration in France

David Wilsford   *Institute for American Universities, Aix-en-Provence, France*

I. INTRODUCTION

In all advanced Western democracies, bureaucratic expertise influences policymaking in several important ways: First, because of the specialized skills that they bring to the job through their training or their long tenure in office, bureaucrats are able to give advice that channels the thinking of political officials about the viability of options and alternatives and about what constitutes a problem in the first place. Important political decisions about problems, options, and alternatives are thereby shaped. Second, carrying out the specific tasks that serve to implement policy depends upon the capacities of bureaucratic organizations. Third, more than ever, in a complex and technical world, political decisions about policy—decisions that depend on the building of at least temporary coalitions of widely diverse politicians and other policy actors—are characterized by vagueness and generality. The open space of politically approved policies must then be filled in by specific details that are the bureaucracy's responsibility to generate. Bureaucratic discretion in the implementation of public policy is consequently often very great (see Nadel and Rourke 1975).

   In France, I will argue in this chapter, these characteristics assume their fullest forms. First, the advice that French high functionaries give to political officials tends to carry more weight, due to the more specialized and homogeneous training that they receive in the *grandes écoles* and the legitimacy afforded this specialized training process by French society. Political officials in France who are recipients of expert bureaucratic advice are also more likely to be receptive to it, in the sense that many of these political officials are themselves issued from the same *grandes écoles* and have been members of the same *grands corps*. Of course, ideological and other political differences in France are extremely important. But in certain crucial areas, such as the legitimacy and extent of state intervention in the economy and the society, important consensus characterizes the thinking of high civil servants and politicians from all sides. Finally, vast domains of public policy in France are autonomously regulated by bureaucratic decree. Curiously, however, this powerful administration also exhibits an important weakness: It is particularly vulnerable to direct action, or forms of extreme protest that occur outside of normal politics.[1]

II. SOURCES OF THE FRENCH ADMINISTRATION

The rise of modern French administration begins in the Middle Ages and continues through the Renaissance with the Crown's struggles to subdue and control from the core a periphery that was often rebellious and always remote. The *intendants* were early agents of this administration. They were sent out from the center to the periphery to rule in the name of the crown. These *intendants* were early precursors to today's prefects.

The Crown's activities also gave rise to the growth of early bureaucracy and centralization—in the armies, in finance, and in an array of interventionist techniques such as grants of monopoly, credits, and subsidies that were used to push nascent industries in the directions the Crown saw fit. As Tocqueville argued, the Revolution and Napoleon's subsequent rule by no means razed the administrative edifice. Rather, the centralization of the administration was furthered. Napoleon, moreover, established the first *grande école*—Polytechnique—to provide him with the technical corps necessary to his vast projects. Napoleon also took the rationality of the Enlightenment, which has always informed the outlook of French administration, to new heights through the Code Napoléon, the metric system, and numerous administrative innovations (Vedel 1966).

The cadre of *hauts fonctionnaires*, or high civil servants, serves as the focal point of the French administrative system. They are the several hundred or so highly trained experts in engineering, law, and administrative science who work in constant association with the top politicians who head the ministries and compose the government (sometimes through their service in ministerial *cabinets*, the top personal staffs of the ministers). These *hauts fonctionnaires* also head the ministerial line agencies (called *directions*). They often come from similar socioeconomic backgrounds, and we will see subsequently that they have been trained in highly specialized fields in a small number of elite state graduate schools (called *grandes écoles*). Common background and common training give the *hauts fonctionnaires* a common vision of the role of the state, the capacities of its administration, and the problems and options that they face. It informs their view of what constitutes legitimate demands on the state and of what constitutes legitimate action for the state.

At the system level, crucial features distinguish the French administration from its American counterpart. The first difference is in the conception of public interest that drives high civil servants. The French are idealist whereas the Americans are realist. Of course, in France there is much bureaucratic play that clearly seeks the self-interested, sometimes highly politicized goals of the actors involved. The politicization of the bureaucracy is another common theme. But much more than its American counterpart, the French bureaucratic corps see itself as—and society sees it as—the enlightened interpreter of the *volonté générale*.

This bureaucratic mission means that French high functionaries feel that they act with the authority to perform a special duty. This duty involves the constant definition and defense of the general interest in the face of all who would assert particular or partisan interests contrary to the interests of the whole, or of France. This sense of mission is not unlike the preaching, teaching, and proselytizing of a religious order. The order in French bureaucratic politics is the *grand corps*. Its training grounds are the *grandes écoles*. The mission gives high functionaries in France the perception that the state has an interest that is both definable and defendable. It also shapes their understanding of where interests lie, which of these are compatible with the state's interest, and what types of conduct by decision makers and outside groups are appropriate to this administrative-political universe:

> The ideology which justifies [the monopoly of the state] is that of the general interest. The [French] administration has in effect succeeded in taking over the general interest for itself. No one can incarnate the general interest in the place of the administration except perhaps the political power at the very top. Legitimacy is always on the side of the administration. Individuals, groups, collectivities and political representatives—with the exception of those who are part of the government, and even then—are always suspected of partiality. Thanks to this ideology, the administration can impose its vocabulary, its own mode of reasoning and its competence on the rest of society (Crozier 1974:24).

A second difference is in the structure of the bureaucratic corps in France. The *grandes écoles* feed into the *grand corps* and form an administrative technocracy that is much more cohesive in its values and norms than its American counterpart. Two *grandes écoles* dominate the education of future high functionaries—and not incidentally that of future high executives and scientists in French industry—and they feed into a limited number of top corps. The *Ecole National d'Administration* trains those who enter the *Inspection des Finances*, the *Conseil d'Etat*, and the *Cour des Comptes*. *Polytechnique* trains those who will join the *Corps des Mines* or *Ponts et Chaussés*. Both schools emphasize a curriculum of rational science, the one administrative science, the other natural and engineering science, which orients problem solving toward activist interventionism and a belief in the value of systematic analysis and the powers of reason and intelligence in confronting problems of all kinds (Bodiguel and Quermonne 1983).[2] This "corps phenomenon" in France is characterized by an insular separation from the outside world (especially from civil society, and even, sometimes, from duly elected politicians), a maintenance of prestige through a strict limiting of numbers, a cultivation of an attitude of special privilege and duty, and a profound internalization of an ideology of public service in the general interest (Birnbaum 1978:70–73).

Emphatically, however, neither its training nor its specialization means that the high civil service constitutes a homogeneous, single-minded corps. Nor do high civil servants hold to a narrow range of political opinion, although there does often tend to be some preponderance toward conservatism. Yet in comparison to the United States, or any other country with a fragmented, dispersed bureaucracy, the significance of the French administration to the choices of the French state and the policies it undertakes, as well as to its patterns of interaction with all segments of society, is clear.

III. REVISIONIST VIEWS OF THE FRENCH ADMINISTRATION

Naturally, the reality of the French administration often departs from the image and ideology it fosters. From inside the ministries, in particular, one cannot fail to be impressed with the battles that rage between agencies, between *hauts fonctionnaires*, between politicians and civil servants, between Matignon (the prime minister's office) and the Elysée (the president's). The penetration of administration by politics and politicians and the penetration of politics by administrative technocrats are important problems that have been treated extensively (Baecque and Quermonne 1982), although seldom resolved fully. The autonomy of the administration from politics is another important problem. Pointing out bureaucratic dependency, division, and internal conflict is often played up as revisionist analysis, and there is merit to it. But surely such features of modern bureaucratic and political life can be taken as common to practically all administrations and to practically all (democratic) political systems.

The ideal-typical Rousseauian view of the strong state emphasizes the state's proper independence and autonomy in defining and defending the general will. This view is supported by the dominance of a highly sophisticated juridical tradition in French administrative science. This tradition places great emphasis on the study of formal rules and procedures. One influential critic of the conventional view of the French state, Suleiman (1974), argued, however, that this view was misleading and that the scholarly emphasis on the study of formal rules and procedures was misplaced. For Suleiman, the "sacrosanct state" constituted neither a good description of French administration nor a good prescription. Suleiman showed that the French administration was not homogeneous or nonpartisan, but rather was made up of cross-cutting, conflicting interests. *Hauts fonctionnaires* are not impartial servants of infallible, uniform legal structure. Their views and goals conflict across ministries and *directions* (the line agencies), between *directions* and ministerial *cabinets* (the top personal staffs of the ministers), and between *grands corps*. One locus of constant combat, for example, lies between the finance and other ministries.

The permeability of the French administration to outside interests is another way of looking at unified versus heterogeneous state structures in France and has also proven influential as a critique of the Rousseauian—Colbert view. Meynaud (e.g., 1957) and Ehrmann (e.g., 1957) argued that technocrats split between horizontal and vertical administrations and between the finance ministry and all others. The problem cuts two ways: First, does the technocrat deal from a superior position with underfinanced and poorly (technically) trained interest groups? Does this harm the representative capacities of the administration? Second, do interest group pressures and *pantouflage* (or the "slipping back and forth" between high bureaucratic and high private sector positions) cloud the technocrats' vision of the general will, or public interest? In other words, are high civil servants captured by the very interests they are supposed to administer?[3]

IV. OVERARCHING UNITY OF THE FRENCH ADMINISTRATION

This debate over technocracy characterized much of the French economic planning process throughout the 1950s and 1960s. Ellul (1964) was one particularly influential critic of the supposed fusion—and collusion—of public and private interest in one technocracy.[4] Despite all of these important lines of criticism, however, the French administration is unified in crucial overarching respects. We have seen that it is unified in its training, in its schools, in its perception of rational professionalism, in its view of the world, and in its role in defining and defending *la volonté générale* and the public interest of France. "I want to create a corporation not of Jesuits who have their sovereign in Rome," wrote Napoleon, "but of Jesuits who have no other ambition than that of being useful and no other interest but the public interest" (Lozère 1833:163, cited in Suleiman 1978:97). Explaining the mission for which the *Ecole Nationale de l'Administration* was established, Debré wrote in 1946:

> The training—one need not hide this—also has a moral objective. It is not one of the missions of the school to play politics or to impose a particular doctrine. But the school must teach its future civil servants "*le sens de l'Etat*," it must make them understand the responsibilities of the Administration, make them taste the grandeur and accept the servitudes of the métier (Debré 1946:24–25).

Suleiman (1977) has argued, to be sure, that the French administration is less technocratic than its reputation. Rather, the *grands corps* prize general skills instead of technical specialization. Polyvalence is essential. The well-trained *haut fonctionnaire* is one who can grasp rapidly the essentials of any problem. They are also able therefore to move from sector to sector. Suleiman calls them "generalists of technique." In fact, the skills of the *haut fonctionnaire* are administrative ones. The generalists of technique form an administrative technocracy that directs other technocracies. These high administrators naturally conflict over questions of turf, but they are surprisingly cohesive on questions of policy and in their modes of analysis and accepted routines of problem solving. They are also solidary in maintaining what is for them a mutually beneficial administrative system. As Bon and Burnier (1971:107) argued:

> The technocrat fixes the goals and the means of the technician's work. He is in a position to effect a synthesis of the results obtained, to choose between different options, and to define priorities. Nine times out of ten, he is incapable of taking the place of any of the technicians whose skill he relies on. The technocratic culture is not a technical culture. It integrates the principal results of administrative, financial, industrial and other techniques in order to be able to utilize them as a factor in policymaking.

Or, as one entering class at Polytechnique was told: "The scientific training you receive will not give you the knowledge in any branch that the specialists have, but it will give you the aptitudes and the methods such as to allow you to be on top of everything."

Perhaps a telling indication of the French administration's importance in the society, economy, and in politics is that "administration" is normally spelled with a capital letter when referring to the state civil service, even when occurring in the middle of a sentence. *Toujours est-il, bien entendu, que c'est la faute de l'Administration.*[5] These overarching sources of unity—and of objects of blame—contrast directly with the extreme fragmentation of the American administration.

Further, the doctrine of the administration in France regarding the search for the public interest pushes civil servants to greater activism than their American counterparts, who, if anything, are lulled into inactivity by the American realist conception of the public interest as arising from an interplay of all affected interests. Consequently, the major prescription for bureaucratic behavior in the United States is to give everyone a fair hearing (Nadel and Rourke 1975:414ff). The French are far more informed by the idealist model, wherein the public interest reposes in a higher law or higher state. This is close to Rousseau's *volonté générale* as opposed to *les volontés particulières*. The whole of the *volonté générale* is always greater than the sum of *les volontés particulières*. High administrators are admonished to assess the public interest and pursue it independently of factions, groups, or even well-meaning but ill-informed politicians. The problem of accountability that arises is partially resolved through informal internal controls on bureaucratic behavior. For example, no matter how lofty the bureaucrat's perception of his role, he will always be tied in part to his perceptions of public opinion and important social and political demands. Internalized values and professional norms also serve in part to check bureaucratic behavior. In France these are based upon the highly developed rational educational process. But of course these methods are imperfect at best.

In clear contrast to the *grands corps* of France, there is no cohesive, uniform elite that governs in the United States. The French elite is held together not in the absence of disputes within its various segments, but by overarching social and educational homogeneity (Birnbaum 1978). Day-to-day consensus of individual French decision makers is very, very far from perfect, but for the big picture—what are society's goals and responsibilities—those who make up the French elite are strikingly uniform in their view of what constitutes proper tasks for the state and proper demands from civil society. This consensus extends to the properness of methods used to communicate demands from society to the state.

Le droit administratif in France, the *hauts fonctionnaires*, and their *grandes écoles* clearly constitute a powerful ensemble of discipline, science, doctrine and profession. Future high-ranking civil servants go through a rigorous and highly developed training and socialization process in a limited number of advanced state schools (such as ENA or Polytechnique). Entrance is strictly limited and rigidly controlled through competitive examination. In administrative sciences, the number of classic texts is great, their codification advanced, their sophistication remarkable, and their authors illustrious.[6]

Some will argue that important cracks are appearing in the once overarching French reliance on centralization and state intervention—which has characterized the French administration at least since the fourteenth century (Nef 1957). Two recent examples provide compelling but far from sufficient evidence for this proposition. The first is the measures decentralizing certain areas of local governance from Paris and the prefects to individual localities undertaken by the socialist governments from 1981 to 1984. There is no doubt that some important decisions formerly reserved to the central authorities may now be made by municipal and regional councils, as well as some—but limited—raising of revenues. But these decision areas are still rather narrow, the all-important raising of revenues is also limited, and, perhaps most important, it is still too early to assess the long-term effects of these changes.

Second, the whole philosophy of privatization and deregulation that the 1986 Chirac government borrowed from Thatcher and Reagan seriously questions the traditional French reliance on state intervention and overarching control of the economy and society. Again, it is far too early to assess the long-term effects of the privatization of such large firms as Saint-Gobain, the banks, or the television network TF1, or the deregulation of currency exchange, the stock market, and investment. In particular, insofar as these changes may redound to the detriment of the French economy in future cyclical downturns, support for them may dwindle rapidly. In any case, Chirac's interpretation of his March 16, 1986, election victory as a mandate for change in these areas was a grave misinterpretation of what the electorate knew very well it was doing, that is, voting against socialists rather than for conservatives. In any case, Mitterand's socialist governments from 1983 to 1986 had already turned from an all-encompassing reliance on state intervention and state control for the solution to vexing economic and social problems to a liberalization and withdrawing of the state from many domains, ranging from currency regulation to enterprise management to social welfare programs (Wilsford 1988b).

Reliance on the state in the face of vexing problems was often embodied in the mechanism of public ownership of enterprises and important industrial sectors, such as mining, steel, or shipbuilding. That the French have been "taking the state back out" is indisputable. This movement probably comes about as a result of a 10-year *conjoncture de crise économique* in which the French economy performed poorly and state intervention was seldom successful in turning industries or firms around, much less making them more internationally competitive. In fact, the French state has realized that its traditional interventionist techniques do not always work, and it has moved *just as actively* toward withdrawing from areas that it previously controlled closely, or permitting, under supervision, more liberty than before.

Although perhaps few French would think about in this way, state intervention of a different sort will probably prove to have been crucial in a long-term economic turnaround. Especially important has been the cutting of vast subsidies to the traditional "smokestack" industries that had been draining the public treasure for many years. Mining, steel, and shipbuilding suffered in particular. Economic crisis and international interdependence sometimes give the state increased leverage or opportunities over entrenched groups, even while serving as important constraints on what the state can do internationally and domestically. All of this suggests that the degree to which a state intervenes and the different methods it uses—ownership, regulation, laissez-faire—are variables that may, precisely, vary from one period to another, given the tools and traditions at the disposal of the state and given the circumstances involved at any one time.

In addition to persistent and consistent activism, the French state is characterized by one final feature of overarching unity, the finance ministry. The *Inspection des Finances* is one of the most prestigious and most powerful of any of the *grands corps*. "Any time even a single franc is involved, the guys from the finance ministry always have something to say about it," complained one high civil servant from another ministry. Even groups recognize that insofar as public expenditures or public revenues may be involved in programs of interest to them, the finance ministry will always have to be consulted. More often than not, the views of finance prevail over those of other ministries in cases of conflict.

V. PATTERNS OF POLICY MAKING IN THE FRENCH ADMINISTRATIVE STATE

In France, the state's relations with many groups from civil society have long exhibited certain characteristics associated with what American political science currently calls neocorporatism. Neocorporatism as a modern version of corporatism is a way of actively arranging the representation of interests in civil society to the state. Neocorporatism differs from traditional corporatism, however, in permitting, even prescribing, much liberty to civil society, and in denying vigorously the historical totalitarianism of many corporatist regimes, such as Mussolini's Italy or Hitler's Germany. In neocorporatism, the number of groups granted official representative status is limited, and these are also given privileges by the state over their interest sectors. But the freedom of any other group to form or to act politically is not affected (Schmitter 1974).

Indeed, in France, it is the state that determines who is a legitimate partner in the search for the public interest. The French state therefore formally recognizes and confers official status upon many groups, and it often subsidizes their activities with both money grants and nonmonetary benefits, such as equipment and office space. There are of course many reasons that the state favors a host of interest groups. It does so in part to ensure their cooperation in the implementation of policies, in part because of the pervasive ideology of national solidarity. This ideology holds that the state *should* help groups to organize members and pursue goals by providing resources to the groups. The state, in this view, is a facilitator of the public good. The state's role here is not unlike the tradition of the German state and the importance it places on the state's responsibilities for keeping essential social partnerships healthy. Bériot (1985) estimates that two-thirds of all groups in France receive outside financial support. Eighty percent of this support comes in the form of subsidies from the national and local government. The French state also has withdrawn subsidies from groups—ranging from medical associations to labor unions—whose activities it did not like. The prevalence and active management of subsidies to groups, as a tool for structuring the representation of interest sectors, is a particularly corporatist aspect of the relations between groups and the French state.

The French state also actively seeks to institutionalize its relations with groups, another characteristic compatible with and essential to neo-corporatism. *Structure* is a concept important to understanding the French administrative spirit. It goes far toward explaining the French approach to power and organization, and an emphasis on problem solving with *structures* is found among French groups generally. "*Les structures*" are made up of rules and people who use the rules to manage specific tasks and the demands of other people. In France, very little can be done outside of a *structure*. "*Il faut créer de nouvelles structures*" to resolve such and such a problem. "*On va créer une structure*" to respond to such and such a demand. In its own way, the spirit of French administration and organization is very activist, but never ad hoc. Routine and formal capacity are prized; spontaneity is not. Further, French administrators need interlocutors to participate in these structures. Without them, curiously, a dialogue is not possible. Without dialogue, solidarity and openness are clearly shown to be fake.

But neo-corporatism is not an entirely accurate characterization of a pattern of relationships that gives so much to the state and so little to the groups, as is so frequently the case in the French political system. Indeed, the state needs the cooperation of some groups for the smooth implementation of various public policies. But in France, the state has been able to structure the channels of influence in such a way that it can often choose to hear what it wishes to hear. This dominance of the French state over interests is based first in the strong, relatively unified character of its administration, and second in the fragmentation of many important interest sectors. Thus while the strong state necessary to the arranging of neo-corporatism does obtain in France, it is of equally primary importance that there are very few peak associations in France. An innate fragmentation—both ideological and nonideological—characterizes many interest sectors, from the medical professions to industrial workers. Moreover, through its ability to designate more than one group as simultaneously representative of the interests of any one sector, the French state *ensures* that competing groups will in effect cancel each other out. This strategy is often used by the French state when its interests so dictate.

The French state's powers and the organizational fragmentation of interests enable the administration to "consult" different interests as policy is formulated, giving the appearance of substantive input into decision making, commonly referred to as *concertation*. François Bloch-Lainé, one of the most respected high civil servants of the postwar French administration, gave a classic and encompassing definition of *concertation* as applied to the economy: "It is a pattern of relations in which representatives of the state and representatives from firms and groups meet in an organized, ongoing fashion to exchange information, assess performance compared to forecasts, and make decisions together or formulate advice for the government" (Bloch-Lainé 1964).

But the consultation implied by *concertation* is often superficial, for it enables the state to simultaneously find support for its own view while ignoring or diffusing opposition. Indisputably, both substantive and symbolic consultation occur. Substantive consultation occurs especially when it serves the state's interests—and it does so in a host of areas. But symbolic consultation assumes greater importance in French policymaking than in many other advanced democracies.

Typically, the process of *concertation* is initiated by a high-level civil servant or by a minister by sending a series of *notes d'orientations*, or preliminary proposals, to various groups that are likely to be concerned by the measures that are envisioned. These will serve as the texts for negotiations over the specifics of these measures. These *notes d'orientations* constitute the first phase of *concertation*. The administration expects its interlocuters to study these texts and then—in a second phase of *concertation*—come together with it to discuss differences and shortcomings before final publication of the relevant decrees in the *Journal officiel*. This second phase begins with written evaluations of the preliminary proposals by the groups. Formal meetings then take place between *hauts fonctionnaries* and group representatives to hammer out common ground, or a *synthèse globale*.

Often, of course, groups oppose reforms sought by the administration. Consultation meetings then sometimes break off, are rescheduled and canceled again numerous times. Reforms are then frequently decreed and implemented anyway. Groups often pursue studied variations of cooperation in this consultation process. A strategy some groups adopt is to "never leave a seat at the [consultation] table empty." These groups recognize that their input is often meaningless, but argue that the administration is so important to them that they cannot afford to bypass any opportunity, however symbolic, for contact. A second strategy is to "leave the seat empty as an express sign of protest." Some groups that adopt this strategy out of frustration often then come back to the table subsequently, recognizing the validity of the first argument. A third strategy is to attend the consultation meeting in order to walk out noisily in protest once the meeting is convened.

In France, ministers and bureaucrats enjoy great discretion in deciding who to consult and who to listen to among the consulted. The French state structures interest-group activity and policy outcomes by opening or closing policymaking arenas to different participants. One interest-group leader complained that too often formal consultation is just that: formal but not substantive. This leader cited the example of discussing a proposed measure in a ministerial committee meeting and then seeing the final text of the measure printed the next day in the *Journal officiel* (Wilson 1983:900). According to another leader: "Of course, we and other[s] were invited to the ministry. But in the end, and even during the discussions, the outcome was clear. The government had already made up its mind and 'listened' only to those groups which shared the government position." Access does not necessarily equal influence. Consultation is often no more than a symbolic benefit to the groups.

Suleiman's respondents (1974:333 ff) argued that consultation served an informative and persuasive function—*from* the administration *to* interest groups: "My job is to explain and to inform. . . . Contacts [with interest groups] are necessary. But I think I can say that we always manage to have our view prevail," argued one director. Another reported: "We always consult. it doesn't mean that we listen, but we consult. We don't always reveal our intentions. We reveal only as much as we think it is necessary to reveal." Thus Suleiman argued that one important function of consultation was the opportunity it gives the administration to present interest groups with *faits accomplis*, that is, decisions it has made before consultation.

Consultation tends therefore to occur late in the administrative decision-making process, in contrast to the American practice of early consultation as proposals are formulated (Chubb 1983). Suleiman (1974:335–336) described a typical policy process: The preparation of texts, whether laws, decrees or reforms, begins in secrecy within a small administrative group. Gradually, the initial group seeks the agreement and cooperation of other groups within the ministry and then from other ministries. Once a final text is agreed upon by the administration, interest groups are approached and informed of the proposed policy. A closed approach is essential, one director reported to Suleiman, "because otherwise there will be opposition over every provision and the text will never get drawn up" (1974:335–336). Another director commented, "We ask for [interest groups'] advice only after we have a completely prepared text. And we do this just to make sure that we haven't made some colossal error" (1974:336).

The emphasis on "texts" is another common feature of the French administrative process. In France, high civil servants often deal with groups' opposition by pointing to the "text." This conveniently removes direct responsibility from the civil servant, for he or she merely "administers" (*gérer* in French) a text that has previously been duly negotiated and approved. *On gère les textes* in the French administrative vocabulary. This approach neatly cuts off other avenues of possible recourse to the groups.

Consequently, in the face of the French administration's high-handedness, direct action assumes great importance in the relations between many organized interests and the French state. Direct action—such as walkouts, boycotts, demonstrations, or strikes—is quite common to French interest-group activities, while it is relatively absent from a more open system such as the American. Even such supposedly pacific groups as physicians or hospital interns are quite willing to exit traditional political channels and engage in demonstrations and strikes. The frequent resort to various forms of direct action indicates the highly reactive posture that the French state forces upon organized groups. In the United States, strikes and other forms of direct actions are rare, because groups can almost always exploit the dispersed structure of the American state.[7]

Some direct action in France seems relatively minor, particularly if it takes the form of a simple walkout from a meeting or speech. Other direct action, such as strikes or demonstrations, sometimes assumes great importance. Nuisance activities such as walkouts enhance the polemic style of French politics and cut off avenues for political and negotiating dialogue. Some groups may register appeals with the Council of State protesting administrative rulings, but judicial avenues in France are seldom very productive. Certainly they are not in the short term, for even if the Council of State were to agree with the appeal, the point is often moot as its case backlog runs anywhere from three to five years. Boycotts are therefore frequently used to express opposition to administrative requirements or reforms. Sometimes these boycotts are extraordinarily effective in an administrative system that prides itself on the symbolism of participation and consultation. That symbolism is an important source of legitimacy for what is in fact a relatively closed and often heavy-handed administration.

The effectiveness of demonstrations and strikes depends on many variables, among which are cohesiveness of the movement and how widespread its support is. Groups ranging all the way from students to physicians in France have undertaken both successful and unsuccessful demonstrations and strikes. They have occurred under both conservative and socialist rule. They have been used throughout the Fourth and the Fifth Republics.

VI. CONCLUSION: THE FRENCH ADMINISTRATION IS STRONG BUT ALSO VULNERABLE

The French state's structure gives civil servants and their political leaders certain advantages in day-to-day decision making that severely handicap outside groups, like students, teachers, physicians, workers, or many others who are concerned (Wilsford 1988a). For example, in France, the government controls the legislative process through its proposal and decree powers. This government is headed by a strong executive. The government alone determines the legislative agenda and gives approval to bureaucratic decrees. The legislature is very weak. Above all, we have seen throughout this chapter that the French state is also aided by its elite bureaucratic corps. Its members are trained in the best higher educational institutions—the *grandes écoles*—at state expense. Most top officials—both from the left and from the right—are graduates of these schools and started their careers in the bureaucratic corps. Finally, the French judicial system is very weak. It does not provide alternative avenues of protest for those who disagree with laws or administrative rulings, as the American court system does. Limited judicial access and limited judicial powers give the state greater autonomy in its relations with civil society. And of course the state sometimes abuses this autonomy. For example, Malik Oussékine, a French student, was severely beaten by state police during the Latin Quarter demonstrations of December 1986. He later died from those injuries. Or André Dogué, a physician, was also beaten by riot police during an otherwise peaceful demonstration of medical associations at the Invalides in 1980.

Despite the recent "minimal" state fad in France (Sorman 1984), bureaucrats, politicians, and interest-group leaders share a common view of the role of the state, its mission, and its options. This chapter has argued that this tradition of state power underpins an active, interventionist state, which does not hesitate to use its strategic position to structure interest representation in either pluralist or corporatist ways. The French state recognizes groups, thus sanctioning them. But it may also withdraw recognition. The state, too, subsidizes many groups. These funds provide the crucial resources for offices, personnel, equipment, research, all indispensable to organizing and articulating interests. The state may also withdraw subsidies—it has done so in the past—making organization and articulation of interests more difficult. State authorities in France also enjoy great discretion in deciding who to consult and who to listen to among the consulted. The state may do all of these things to open and close policymaking arenas. The French state orchestrates policymaking far more than its American counterpart. With relative ease, the French state may induce wider participation ("pluralism") by involving more interest groups. Or it may constrain participation in policymaking ("neocorporatism") by closing out interest groups.

Because outside input into administrative decision making tends to occur late in the French policymaking process, in contrast to the American pattern of early consultation with concerned groups as proposals are formulated, warning signals of possible or probable opposition and violence are often ignored. The closed policy-making process in France avoids the problems of opposition and delay, but it is also dangerously vulnerable to protest. Paradoxically, the strong French state is sometimes weak indeed.

In comparative perspective, the French state and its administration could be compared to other states and their administrations along two dimensions. The first dimension is one of permeability of the state to many diverse interests coming from civil society and ranges from extreme openness to extreme closedness. Along this variable, the French state is less permeable to interest group pressures than other democratic states such as the United States, Britain, Germany, or Sweden. France is probably similar in this respect to Japan. The French state is more permeable, however, to group pressures than a host of nondemocratic states, ranging from Chile to Russia.

The second dimension of useful comparison is that of the capacity of the state to execute its will. The success of the state in imposing innovations and reforms on recalcitrant groups from civil society is one of the best tests of the state's strength. The French state could be considered stronger according to this criteria than the United States, Britain, or Germany, perhaps equally as strong as Japan, and clearly weaker than Russia. We have noted one important weakness of the French state, however, that comes out of its strength: the vulnerability to extreme forms of protest.

In important ways, the strong state tradition in France that we have explored in this chapter is similar to the tradition of Americanism that Hartz (1955) identified in the United States. They both serve as overriding factors of consensus in otherwise extremely plural societies. The French state's ideology protects the state's interests. These are sometimes perceived as those of functionaries or as those of privileged groups in the economy or the society. But just as often, or perhaps more often, the state's interests are *perceived* as the amalgam or distillation of the interests of all, the community, the whole of which is France. This whole is far greater than its parts. The state ideology protects the role of the functionary, and it protects the centralization of the system. But it does not protect political institutions such as those that make up the regime type. To the contrary, the regime type is highly vulnerable in France to passing crises and humors. A succession of political regime changes ranging across all types litters the landscape of France's political history.

Indeed, there is such high politicization over issues and between political parties in France, charged by an all encompassing and violent polemic, that it is difficult for the institutions of a political regime type to become anchored solidly in French political culture. There has never been a political consensus in France, which like Americanism in the United States could serve to bind elements together in agreement over the modalities and institutions of governance and change. In France, the strong state bound a fractious society together. The strong state itself was all that warring elements could agree upon, each hoping it would serve its own purposes. There has been in France, perhaps, an *administrative consensus.*

The overall relations between society and the state in France are characterized by what may be termed state-dominated pluralism. The state itself is administratively dominated. In a system of extreme pluralism of groups, the focal point of both policymaking and interest-group activity is found in the bureaucratic departments. This gives the French state, through its bureaucratic institutions, more capability for control over interest group activity than is found in the "neutral" state of American pluralist theory, wherein policy outcomes are sometimes characterized as the "sum of vectors" pushing in upon the state from society.

Of course, in state-dominated pluralism, the state and its structures are by no means homogeneous. Despite the tone of this chapter, the "strong" state is of course by no means all-powerful. Centers of power compete within the vast French bureaucracy. Perhaps some groups can play opposing centers of power off one another, thus enhancing their own maneuverability in the bureaucratic universe. But we have also noted that the finance ministry is an important source of uniformity in this universe. Finally, even when the French state seems all-powerful, it will not necessarily make the right decisions as a consequence. Sometimes it will, and sometimes it will not. The strength of the state cannot protect it from errors of judgment.

The French state is strong in part because it eliminates much access to alternative arenas of policymaking and influence, such as powerful legislature or judiciary. When groups cannot play conflictual interests within the bureaucracy against each other, they have little other recourse but to exit the political system altogether. This feature points to the French state's high vulnerability to direct action—walkouts, boycotts, demonstrations, strikes—and other forms of sometimes violent protest. The state in state-dominated pluralism is more effective at policymaking than its American pluralist counterpart, although it may not necessarily be more right and it is clearly ineffective at absorbing protest.

ENDNOTES

1. All translations from the French are mine; all unattributed quotations in this chapter come from personal interviews.
2. This driving, overarching ethos of the French administration comes through even in the most casual

reading of Baecque (1973), Baecque and Quermonne (1982), Gournay (1978), Quermonne (1983), and Bodiguel and Quermonne (1983), even as each of them addresses the forces of fragmentation and conflict that weaken and cast suspicion on the administrative mission.

3. Ehrmann and Meynaud engaged in a detailed exchange about these questions in a series of scholarly articles and books that lasted until at least 1963. The two citations here are among the earliest examples in this exchange. Space does not permit us to consider others.

4. Gilpin (1968) describes the appeal of French political leaders and *hauts fonctionnaires* to technique and scientific reason in defense of controversial projects, such as the nuclear *force de frappe*, the Concorde supersonic transport plane, or uranium enrichment plants (see also Hall 1986:176–180).

5. Trans.: Of course, you know, it's the bureaucracy's fault.

6. For a small but revealing sample, one has simply to thumb through Rigaud and Delcros (1984), Braibant (1984), Gournay (1978), or the incomparable and unsurpassed Vedel (1966).

7. Kitschelt (1986) also suggests the systematic structuring of interest-group activities as a function of political "opportunity structures" facing the groups. Looked at this way, the French political system and the predominant role it assigns to the administration offer the groups few opportunities for meaningful input inside the normal administrative process. By contrast, American groups are offered an array of varied opportunities to penetrate the administrative-political system.

REFERENCES

de Baecque, F. *L'Administration centrale de France*. Armand Colin, Paris.

de Baecque, F., and Quermonne, J.-L. *Administration et politique sous la Cinquième République*. Presses de la Foundation Nationale des Sciences Politiques, Paris, 1982.

Bériot, L. *Le Bazar de la solidarité*. J.-C. Lattès, Paris, 1985.

Birnbaum, P. *La classe dirigeante française*. Presses Universitaires de France, Paris, 1978.

Bloch-Lainé, F. *A la recherche d'une économie concertée*, 3rd ed. Editions de l'Epargne, Paris, 1964.

Bodiguel, J.-L., and Quermonne, J.-L. *La haute fonction publique sous la Ve République*. Presses Universitaires de France, Paris, 1983.

Bon, F., and Burnier, M.-A. *Les Nouveaux inteliectuels*. Paris, 1971.

Braibant, G. *Le droit administratif français*. Presses de la Fondation Nationale des Sciences Politiques et Dalloz, Paris, 1984.

Chubb, J. *Interest Groups and the Bureaucracy*. Stanford University Press, Stanford, CA, 1983.

Crozier, M. *Le phénomène bureaucratique*. Seuil, Paris, 1963.

Crozier, M. La centralisation. In *Où va l'Administration française?* (M. Crozier, ed.). Editions d'Organisations, Paris, 1974.

Debré, M. *Réforme de la fonction publique*. Imprimerie Nationale, Paris, 1946.

Ehrmann, H.W. *Organized Business in France*. Princeton University Press, Princeton, NJ, 1957.

Ellul, J. *The Technological Society*. Knopf, New York, 1964.

Gilpin, R. *France in the Age of the Scientific State*. Princeton University Press, Princeton, NJ, 1968.

Gournay, B. *Introduction à la science administrative*. Presses de la Fondation Nationale des Sciences Politiques, Paris, 1978.

Hall, P.A. *Governing the Economy: The Politics of State Intervention in Britain and France*. Oxford University Press, New York, 1986.

Hartz, L. *The Liberal Tradition in America*. Harcourt Brace Jovanovich, New York, 1955.

Kitschelt, H. Political Opportunity Structures and Political Protest: Anti-Nuclear Movements in Four Democracies. *British Journal of Political Science* 16 (1986).

Lozère, P. *Opinions de Napoléon*. Firmin Didot Frères, Paris, 1833.

Meynaud, J. Les groups d'intérêt et l'administration en France. *Revue Française de Science Politique* 7(3):588 (1957).

Nadel, M.Y., and Rourke, F.E. Bureaucracies. In *Handbook of Political Science*, Vol. 5 (F.I. Greenstein and N.W. Polsby, eds.). Addison-Wesley, Reading, MA, 1975.

Nef, J. *Industry and Government in France and England 1540–1640*. Great Seal Books, Ithaca, NY, 1957.

Quermonne, J.-L. *Le gouvernement de la France sous la Ve République*, 2nd ed. Dalloz, Paris, 1983.

Rigaud, J., and Delcros, X. *Les institutions administratives françaises: Les structures.* Presses de la Fondation Nationale des Sciences Politiques et Dalloz, Paris, 1984.

Schmitter, P. Still the century of corporatism? *Review of Politics* (1974).

Sorman, G. *La solution libérale.* Grasset, Paris, 1984.

Suleiman, E.N. *Politics, Power and Bureaucracy: The Administrative Elite in France.* Princeton University Press, Princeton, NJ, 1974.

Suleiman, E.N. The myth of technical expertise: selection, organization and leadership. *Comparative Politics 10*:137–158 (1977).

Suleiman, E.N. Higher education in France: a two-track system. *West European Politics 1*:97–114 (1978).

Vedel, G. *Traité de science administrative.* Mouton, Paris, 1966.

Wilsford, D. Tactical advantages versus administrative heterogeneity: the strengths and the limits of the French state. *Comparative Political Studies 21*:1 (1988a).

Wilsford, D. The Private/Public Paradox: Privatization as an Instrument of State Control in France. Presented to the Midwest Political Science Association, Chicago (1988b).

Wilson, F.L. French interest group politics: pluralist or neocorporatist? *American Political Science Review*, December (1983).

68

Challenges to Privatization in Developing Countries

A New Look

William Kurtz and Robert B. Cunningham *Department of Political Science, The University of Tennessee, Knoxville, Tennessee*

Yaser M. Adwan *Social Security Corporation, Amman, Jordan*

I. INTRODUCTION

"Privatization" means moving from greater to lesser public sector involvement in the production or delivery of goods and services. Reducing government ownership of a cement plant from 51% to 21%, liquidating the assets of a government-owned wood-processing factory, allowing competition along bus routes, contracting for sanitation services, or selling the national airline exemplify privatization. The privatization concept has trickled down to the developing nations (Berg 1987; Moe 1987; Young 1987). Not only Britain, France, and the United States, but also Turkey, Sri Lanka, Tanzania, Malaysia, Bangladesh, and most developing countries are shedding national assets in pursuit of ideology, effective organizational performance, or budget relief (Aylen 1987; *Christian Science Monitor* 1987; *Economist* 1985; Hamlin and Lyons 1996; Jomo 1995; Young 1987).

But is privatization the optimal economic development strategy for every situation? Are there conditions under which public sector provision of goods and services might be more appropriate than relegating the task to the private sector? A number of sources (Aylen 1987; Ayub and Hegstad 1987; *Economist* 1985; Kohli and Sood 1987; Pliatzky 1988) have taken a financial approach to the question of economic growth, arguing that either public or private sector ownership can achieve an efficient use of resources. An available capital market, transparent transactions and subsidies, a market environment, managerial incentives, financial autonomy and accountability, and audit capability, if present, contribute to economic growth, whether the producers are private or public.

These desirable financial conditions cannot be legislated into existence. Institutional support and political will are causally prior to financial factors. Given the usual situation where political will and institutional/cultural support for economic growth as primary values are not presently strong, what is an appropriate national development strategy? This chapter offers a brief evaluation of recent privatization efforts and guidelines for achieving increased effectiveness and legitimacy in providing goods and services under public sector control. Combining traditional values with postmodern approaches to governance may increase economic effectiveness and enhance regime legitimacy, thus contributing to a climate supportive of the financial conditions which contribute to economic growth.

II. WHY PRIVATIZATION?

Under competitive market conditions the private organization is believed to provide products or services at a lower cost than the public organization.[1] A key underlying assumption is that a more or less free market where perfect competition, or something reasonably resembling perfect competition, describes the economy (Gianaris 1996). In such an economy, producers and consumers have equal access to information, resources, and products. Factor prices and customer preferences are the only constraints. Both the nation as a whole and individual consumers are believed to be the winners in a free market. Producers are forced to innovate on a continuous basis in order to maintain or create a competitive advantage over alternative suppliers of the product, for profit is possible only under a condition of market disequilibrium (Gilad 1984).

Many scholars offer evidence that privatization aids in the development process (Jayasankaran 1995). By eliminating state monopolies, goods and services can be produced more efficiently. Since many public services are monopolies, the common belief is that the public sector will always tend toward inefficiency since it has no competition, cannot go bankrupt, and lacks an incentive to excel (*Economist* 1985).

A developing nation may have many motivations behind its decision to privatize public services. Internal motivations include spiraling costs of subsidizing public sector enterprises; keeping tax rates down by profiting from the sale of enterprises; an expanding public bureaucracy; or general dissatisfaction with the performance of public organizations (Adam et al. 1992; Cowan 1990). External motivations for privatization revolve around two aspects of one central issue: debt. Many developing nations have enormous debt and expect privatization to raise revenue to relieve this burden (Marber 1997). The IMF, the World Bank, and the United States may pressure developing nations to privatize in order to receive aid or loans (Knight 1992). External pressure helps induce nations to sell or restructure public enterprises.

III. FACTORS IMPEDING COMPETITIVE MARKETS IN DEVELOPING NATIONS

The argument that private enterprise delivers goods and services efficiently and effectively assumes clear institutional boundaries between public and private sectors and an absence of collusion among producers. These assumptions sometimes hold in developed nations, but in developing nations markets often operate poorly due to (1) a lack of institutional boundaries between public and private sectors, (2) informal collusion among producers, and (3) interconnectedness among elites.

A. Institutional Boundaries

Most developing nations have a limited constitutional history and minimal delineation between private and public sectors (Berg 1987; Manasan 1988). After a country's colonial experience, the newly independent state had a substantial task in meeting the expectations of citizens (Cowan 1990). Private and public are blurred in the minds of many citizens, and the sanctity of private property does not strike a responsive chord in the public consciousness, as it can in the West. The softness of legal protections for private investment increases the risks to potential entrepreneurs, who fear market interference by the government either in the form of direct takeover, or legislation which affects factor and product prices, or arbitrary implementation by state officials. Especially at risk are ethnic or religious minorities—evidenced by Indonesian violence against their ethnic Chinese citizens in 1998.

Despite the fact that a market economy may not exist fully in developing countries, privatization is often used as a tool for economic development (Pelikan 1997). The collapse of the Soviet Union, and Russia's headlong rush to private ownership of property, created a situation in which rules, laws, and implementers lacked widespread understanding or legitimacy among the public. Not only are institutional boundaries between public and private difficult to discern, in many cases they may not exist. Property rights are prerequisite to private enterprise (Hill and Karner 1996), and must be formalized so that property can be exchanged (deSoto 1996). In some former communist states which have moved rapidly from state ownership to private ownership without institutional regulation of property, legitimacy and legality are major concerns. Who owns resources, who ends up with resources, how they are distributed, and who is involved in this process are all questions that have yet to be answered when assets are quickly rushed from public to private ownership.

Some governments in developing nations have inconsistent economic policies, randomly adjusting their philosophies and imposing frequently changing, and often contradictory, regulations (*Economist* 1985; Georgakopoulos et al. 1987; Kohli and Sood 1987). Such an environment of governmental interference discourages entrepreneurial behavior. Investments must have higher rate of return on capital to achieve profitability, which means higher production costs. The lack of legally based, culturally understood institutional boundaries between public and private have direct impact on product prices.

B. Informal Collusion Among Producers

Producers, while perhaps giving lip service to the free market system, act to constrain the operation of that market, for in a perfect market the marginal profit is zero, as each producer expands production to capture the last bit of demand (Hardin 1977; Olson 1965). Aside from innovation, only by restraining market effects can profits be made. Therefore, collusion among sellers is a tendency in all open markets, and is particularly likely to occur in developing nations where sellers are few and can communicate easily with each other. The smaller the number of sellers, the easier the communication, the easier the collusion, and the greater the likelihood of higher product prices and production inefficiencies.[2]

Small and developing countries have limited internal markets, therefore few producers of nonagricultural items. The producers of nonagricultural products find it easy to communicate to protect their common interest, which is high prices. Therefore, in a small nation the market, left to its own devices, often will not act efficiently because of its small size, which can support few producers.[3]

C. Interconnectedness Among Elites

The tendency toward oligopoly or monopoly is exaggerated in countries where elites are interconnected, as is often found in developing nations. Connectedness may reflect family ties, a regional or ethnic bond, attendance at the same high school or university, a common cultural experience such as membership in a revolutionary political movement, or simply an economic recognition that unless the rich and politically powerful stick together they may go down together.[4] Outsiders have difficulty obtaining information, as veiled relationships between established businesses and government officials serve to restrict information availability. The personal contacts between governmental officials and elites lead to differential access to information, to the disadvantage of newcomers and racial or ethnic minorities (Addison and Demery 1987; Halliday 1979; Berg 1987). Tacit agreements to stay out of markets, and third-party hints or suggestions discouraging those considering entry, can often inhibit entrepreneurs who would otherwise be willing and able to enter. Interconnected elites result in high prices.

IV. GOVERNMENT INTRUSION INTO THE MARKET

An alternative to private oligopoly is public enterprise. Public enterprise refers to any government-owned or government-controlled unit that produces or sells goods to the public. This is the business component of the public sector, acting as both a producer and trader in goods and services (Cowan 1990; El-Naggar 1989). Public enterprises may be wholly owned by the state; owned partially by state and partially by private investors; owned by government but managed privately; or they may provide services directly. Government entry into the market as partial or full owner can occur for any of the following reasons: national security, national interest, or to satisfy public or lender opinion.

A. National Security

Nations which lack an institutionalized process for changing regime leaders on a regular basis face the risk of external attack or internal insurrection as the means of political change. Understandably, a nation's leadership wants to maintain itself in office. Access to financial resources is an important means for instigating regime overthrow. To be involved in manufacturing is a source of wealth, wealth which can be used as a base for opposition to the existing regime. Naturally, any regime will be concerned about this; and the privilege of producing/selling may be permitted only to "safe" businesspeople presumed loyal to the regime (Keddie 1985). Favoring friends widens elite support for the regime while keeping the enterprise in private hands (Addison and Demery 1982). Such private enterprise does not contribute to efficiency.

Alternatively, the enterprise may be located in the public sector, which is by definition under regime control, although perhaps more subject to a wider range of political influences than would be the case under private control (Georgakopoulos et al. 1987). Usually, public distribution will best meet the requirement of national security and internal stability. National security can be used as a blanket justification to cover various actions far from the usual meaning of that term.[5]

B. National Interest

Under the guise of "national interest," capital assets can be transferred to or from the government (Bozeman 1988). "National interest" is more open-ended than national security (Aberbach and Rockman 1988; Staats 1988) for "the national interest" has no objective content, and can be interpreted in whatever manner desired by the regime. National *security* usually justifies transferring the assets from the private sector to the public sector. National *interest* may move assets from either sector to the other. The reasoning is often ad hoc rather than based upon a consistent plan, policy, or rationale (Key and Thompson 1986). Prices are artificial and knowledge of the market is limited. Few people know the value of the enterprise to be sold or bought, and information about the sale is closely held to discourage potential purchasers/sellers.[6] The asset is often bought from or sold to those persons having close connections to the governing authorities. Since in developing nations the persons having sufficient financial means to buy or sell significant capital assets are few, potential buyers are known to political leaders.

Enterprises bought by the government may reward the seller with a high price; companies sold by the government may go for a price below the market value (*Economist* 1985). The terms and conditions of sale are not always publicly disclosed (Ayub and Hegstad 1987; Pliatzky 1988).

C.   Satisfying Public or Lender Opinion

Privatizing can create a negative public image for the government, but may be necessary in order to gain the favor of international lending agencies. Quite often, in order to receive aid from international organizations or Western nations where privatization is currently a consuming passion, developing nations are pressured to privatize (*Economist* 1985; Klein 1982; Knight 1992). Divestiture occurs to ensure outside financial support. If assets are divested at a low price, the impression of a government giveaway is communicated (Bailey 1987; Starr 1987). If the assets command a high price, the impression is left that public administrators do not comprehend the value of the resources they manage. The government takes the risk of alienating local public opinion. While a negative image of privatization often does exist, in some countries privatization efforts might be used to increase public confidence in government. Many nations seek to increase indigenous ownership of property (Ramanadham 1989). In other instances, privatization may be used to end skepticism of poorly run or corrupt government enterprise. The rationale depends on the country's political culture and history.

V.   SOCIAL AND POLITICAL INFLUENCE IN PUBLIC ENTERPRISES

Public enterprises are highly susceptible to costly, perhaps illegal, practices. The public official managing a government enterprise is pressured in purchasing, marketing, and employment decisions. Influential citizens can benefit by selling products to the public enterprise at a high price, purchasing goods and services from the public enterprise at a low price, and placing persons loyal to themselves in significant positions in the employ of the organization. Even high-minded, scrupulously honest political figures can hamper the profitability of the enterprise by demanding that the organization market the product below production cost for the publicly produced good (Georgakopoulos et al. 1987). Given these factors, it is difficult to determine whether a publicly owned or operated organization is performing efficiently. Profit and loss statements convey limited, and perhaps distorted, information. According to Ayub and Hegstad (1987), it would be better to let the market operate freely and then use the profits to finance the desired social objectives.

Considering market size, lack of institutional boundaries, informal collusion of producers, interconnectedness among elites, and social networking structures that circumvent state regulations, neither the open market nor government regulation/ownership leads necessarily to an efficient economic system.

VI.   PRIVATE CONTROL VERSUS PUBLIC CONTROL

Should the government (1) take a free market, hands-off approach, allowing producers collude to keep prices high, (2) play a limited role by acting as an overseer; or (3) get into the business of producing the goods/service? If the goods/service is in high demand, with a sizable market and a reasonably large number of suppliers, the market system can control prices. In noncompetitive markets the influence on prices of public versus private ownership is not known, and noneconomic factors come into play.

For developing nations, extensive government involvement in producing goods and services may not constitute an optimal policy from an economic perspective. However, considering the societal constraints within which the economic activity of the country is conducted, government involvement in the economy is understandable if the alternatives are collusive elites and/or regime instability.[9] For example, labor regulations in Arab oil-producing countries restrict the number of expatriate employees to less than 25% of each firm. This policy is intended to safeguard a country's social and political system. Thus, manpower shortages may cause inefficiency in both the public and the private sectors. The competition for skilled and managerial manpower is severe (Muna 1980:20). Public control can provide security and equity, but often with low efficiency. The government may be unable to afford the luxury of equity. If the private sector alternative is rejected due to non-competitive market conditions or regime instability, what can be done to achieve effective public management/regulation of societal goods and services?

VII.   ENHANCING PUBLIC SECTOR EFFECTIVENESS

Effective management can increase the efficiency of either private or public organizations (Jomo 1995). Thus, efficiency gains cannot be attributed simply to a change in ownership. If government is to be involved in the economy, success depends on strong commitment to the administrative sector from the political elite (Adwan 1986; Cook and Kirkpatrick 1995). The challenge to administrative effectiveness comes (1) externally—organization members must cope effectively with traditional social pressures, and (2) internally—innovation and creativity must be demanded from the public service.

First, traditional loyalties mandate preference in hiring and promotion for in-group persons (Berg 1987; Cunningham and Sarayrah 1993; Muna 1980:75). This obstacle to organizational effectiveness must be met by effective management and commitment within the government organization and by support for the integrity of the organization by outside political forces.[10] Denying unearned favors to kin and cohorts will require that controlling authorities expend political capital.[11] Standing firm in order to build an effective organization will pay dividends in the short run in terms of morale among public administrators, and over the long run will engender confidence in the regime from the wider public.

Public managers must reject the in-group loyalties often present in developing nations (*Economist* 1986). Elites must identify those components of the public sector which are critical to the economic life of the country and ensure that values appropriate to efficiency are not corrupted in those organizations by in-group favoritism. Interference by political leaders represents the external challenge to organizational effectiveness.

Second, there is an internal challenge. The strategic planning/strategic management literature emphasizes that under conditions of change and environmental uncertainty, managers must take risks and innovate in order to maintain organizational effectiveness (Branson 1985; Donaldson 1985; Stevenson and Gumpert 1985). New ways must be sought to address old problems. Many countries of the developing world now have middle- and upper-level administrators who hold administrative values considered appropriate for operating an efficient administrative system (Park 1987). Following achievement values from the Weberian model is not enough. Effective executives in innovative organizations push the decision point to the lowest reasonable decision level (Branson 1985; Martin 1993). Devolving authority results in both better policy and more effective implementation. Midlevel officials see the problems and opportunities first-hand. Competent middle managers, supported by superiors, can render the decision acceptable to the antagonist. In an effective organization competent subordinates enhance a superior's reputation.

Innovation and devolved authority, insulated from the pressures of traditional loyalties by unswerving political support at the highest levels, are an effective alternative to privatization. In developing nations it is standard practice to bring any undesired outcome to the highest point of appeal possible, thus clogging the decision system and spreading lethargy at the lower levels of the organization (Adwan and Al-Kayed 1988). With the combination of a clear policy statement by an innovative organization head, the support of relevant political leadership for the organization head in pursuing policy based on sound economic principles (Shaikh 1987), devolving decisions to the lowest point, and training middle managers in interpersonal skills (Fisher and Ury 1987) and allowing them to make mistakes (McCormack 1984), the morale of the agency and its performance should be raised. As a result, the communications channels to the top are reasonably clear, and the executive can turn attention to the larger problem of coping with the environment rather than facing a constant stream of supplicants for favors.

Innovation, devolving authority, and involving lower-level employees—undergirded by political support—is necessary to engender organizational effectiveness. This alternative cannot guarantee success. Public administrators, even those with a predisposition to innovation and decentralization, are subject to cultural pressures and have the same temptations as other citizens (Walsh 1979). Attentiveness by political elites, organization openness, an ethos that making mistakes is permitted, and indoctrination in the bargaining strategies of Fisher and Ury's (1987) *Getting to Yes* will enhance the probability of success.

The recommendations for effective public enterprise management are compatible with the normative position taken by postmodern public administration scholars such as Fox and Miller (1996), McSwite (1998), and Wamsley and Wolf (1996). The next section links public enterprise effectiveness in developing nations to postmodern public administration theory.

VIII. POSTMODERN ALTERNATIVES FOR PUBLIC SERVICE MANAGEMENT

Substantial scholarship in the fields of public administration and political development deals with the problem of legitimacy. Legitimacy has implications for political stability and administrative effectiveness. If legitimacy is an issue for a stable, economically prosperous nation such as the United States, the question of legitimacy raises stronger questions in developing nations. The Weberian model of cold efficiency, and its late twentieth century face of technicism (McSwite 1996), *presumes* legitimacy. Technicism seeks efficiency, and emphasizes the non-human element in economic and social processes. This ideology may appeal to a developing state seeking rapid growth through *laissez faire* economics.

Technicism in public service provision means bureaucracy, leaving important public decisions to appointed officials. Bureaucracy, whether market driven and customer based, or classic top-down, incorporates a technicist mindset—division of labor, chain of command, technical precision, efficiency. Technicism and market economics gnaw away at legitimacy, for citizens come to perceive their leaders as isolated, arbitrary, and distant. Traditional decision-making processes in developing countries involve interpersonal relations and discourse. Perhaps regime legitimacy can be achieved by pursuing another path—serving citizens through dialogue and discourse rather than technicism.

Dialogue and discourse weave together partial and temporal truths through a process of ongoing communication which is iterative and focused, seeking to meet common needs and wants rather than to achieve a narrowly defined efficiency. Governance by discourse addresses specific problems with concrete solutions (Cunningham and Sarayrah 1993:Ch. 17). This collaborative pragmatism encourages an active citizenry and permits public service provision to reflect a communally understood truth (McSwite 1997). Over time, a governance process built around the principles of dialogue, iterative decision making, temporal truths, and subjectivity strengthen the nation (McSwite 1996).

In the Middle East and Africa, the term for this process is *Wasta*; in China, *Guanxi*. It is called *Wa* in Japan, and *Inhwa* in Korea. *Wasta* exists in many cultures and specifically refers to either the act or the person who mediates and intercedes between two interested or grieving parties. *Wasta* dominates many basic functions of government, including specific rules and statutes. In service provision, *Wasta* expands the range of possible outcomes beyond the realm of bureaucratic alternatives, allowing governments to reflect social relations and norms. When governments accommodate *Wasta* in moderation, they become legitimate in the eyes of the citizenry (Cunningham and Sarayah 1993).

Wa and *Inhwa* are complementary concepts. *Wa* refers to the Japanese tradition of group loyalty, consensus building, and trust. Group relationships are superior to all others, and individual relationships typically serve only to bring groups together (Alston 1989). Contracts and official decisions are typically viewed as fluid and subject to change. *Inhwa* focuses on the individual, linking unequals and focusing on the harmony between them. *Inhwa* contracts and decisions, highly affective and emotional, stress loyalty by subordinates and nurturing by superiors (Alston 1989). *Inhwa* also stresses the ability to change as conditions change, and to be sensitive to those conditions.

Guanxi is a typically Chinese approach to decision making and the distribution of resources. *Guanxi* refers to either a relationship or the people with whom the connection is made. Originally developed to cope with shortages of necessities, *Guanxi* refers to reciprocal obligations, full commitment, and equity (Hwang 1987; Alston 1989; Brunner et al. 1990; Bian 1994; Luo 1997). As with *Wasta*, the *Guanxi* acknowledges that rules and statutes exist, but the *Guanxi* works around them or expands their meaning. For instance, in employment decisions, it has been documented that each decision is made on a case by case basis. Rules governing qualifications certainly exist, but one's *Guanxi*, and communications with the *Guanxi*, determine hiring and/or transfer requests (Bian 1994).

In *Guanxi*, personal affiliations are more important than group affiliation or legal standards (Luo 1997). As a result, Chinese citizens rely more on personal contacts than they do on impartial bureaucratic justice to get things done. Choosing the informal structure indicates a certain level of legitimacy for *Guanxi* decision making that may not exist with bureaucratic decision making. *Guanxi* supersedes free market forces while still encouraging development via the effective allocation of resources (Brunner et al. 1990). It circumvents the traditional, bureaucratically determined lines of authority and decision making, thereby placing resources where they are needed and guaranteeing reciprocity and fairness. These exchanges should favor the weaker member (Alston 1989), thereby enhancing a fair and equitable distribution of resources (Hwang 1987). *Guanxi* incorporates the virtue of flexibility and change due to the individual nature of the relationship. If one's position changes, so does the interpersonal relationship.

These methods work outside the legal structure and open the possibility for abuse. However, they do extend decision making beyond the bureaucratic unit, while stressing fluidity and change. These alternative decision-making structures raise two related concerns. First, they involve superior/subordinate relationships. Second, there are no legal limits to the scope of their powers. Although detrimental to provision of services when left unchecked, the power of interpersonal relationships shows promise for enhancing effectiveness and legitimacy when engaged in responsibly.

Wa and *Inhwa* tend to work within the legal structure, simply aiding those in selected groups or relationships. They celebrate the Confucian quality of nurturing (Alston 1989). *Guanxi* has shown promise as an alternative service delivery structure. Whether *Guanxi* works around the rules or breaks the rules is in the eye of the beholder. Bureaucracy and hierarchy have proven useful for repetitive tasks, but few governments of developing nations have achieved consensus on standard operating procedures. Rather than try to import the modern bureaucratic organization, perhaps it would be useful for developing countries to augment bureaucracy by adopting other means for decision making and resource allocation.

Central to postmodern thought is the absence of a "one best way" to allocate resources and make decisions. The characteristics of collaborative decision making are fairly universal, and can be seen in the notion of "campfire" decision making. Campfire decision making involves dialogue among the parties involved, leading to a commitment to the decisions made (Cunningham and Adwan 1991). Compatible with the postmodern tradition, campfire decision making would bring local and indigenous values into the decision-making and resource allocation processes. Including indigenous values lessens conflict between technology and culture (Cunningham and Sarayah 1994). Postmodern decision-making structures borrow the ideas of indigenous values, communication, and flexibility from the informal structures such as *Wasta* and *Guanxi*.

IX. CONCLUSION

The revenue from sales of public enterprises in developing countries rose from about $2 billion to nearly $40 billion in 1994 (Poole 1996). Are these enterprises enhancing the productivity and lowering the external debt of the host nation? Or is the revenue from such sales gobbled up by current account shortfalls, leaving the nation poorer for the long run (*Economist* 1998)? A World Bank study has concluded that privatization has had little impact on efficiency and economic growth (Cook and Kirkpatrick 1994). Workers in privatized industries may be better off, but efficiency has not necessarily gained. Privatization is merely a means to an end, not the end. Perhaps an effective public organization should be considered as an alternative to private sector provision of public services.

Innovation, insulation, involvement, responsibility, and devolving authority—the public sector answer to privatization—require the commitment of substantial social and political resources by the decisional elite. This program should commence with the most significant agencies, then spread only as fast as political commitment and managerial resources allow. Each of the components must be present, for without devolving authority, innovation will not be effectively implemented; without innovation, devolving authority has no direction; without insulation, neither devolving nor innovation can be implemented; and without responsibility, the actions of the public sector lack legitimacy. If the developing nation's leadership is unwilling to commit to these reforms, perhaps privatization is the appropriate course of action.

The above reforms, compatible with contemporary management theory and public administration postmodern thought, represent an alternative to private sector service provision. Perhaps the blending of indigenous values with these current ideas will achieve both legitimacy and efficient service provision.

ENDNOTES

1. This is the argument of the public choice perspective. A summary is presented in Ostrom and Ostrom (1971); a critique is provided by DeGregori (1974).
2. If there are many sellers, the collusion can be effected by government mediation through marketing boards or government-set product prices.
3. Often local producers are protected from foreign competition by import restrictions. The question of whether "natural monopolies" (free-market conditions which militate against more than one producer) occur in these situations is not addressed here.
4. The short article by Bertram Gross (1973) and Philip Selznick's (1949) *TVA and the Grass Roots* are instructive on showing how the ideas and talents of able outsiders are co-opted to strengthen the existing elite structure.

5. Mexico justified keeping an airline in the public sector on the grounds that it was a "strategic" question (*Economist* 1985).
6. Tanzania and Argentina are specific examples here. Other cases are found throughout Latin America and the Arab world. For the case of Tanzania, see *Christian Science Monitor* (1988).
9. Allende (1988) points out the pervasiveness of political considerations in public enterprises.
10. For an extended discussion of this issue see Cunningham (1988), especially Chapter 19.
11. Rosabeth Kanter (1982) argues that innovative private sector middle managers need support from their superiors in order to be effective. Without this climate of job security innovation will not occur.

REFERENCES

Aberbach, J., and Rockman, B. (1988). Mandates or mandarins? Control and discretion in the modern administrative state. *Public Administration Review, 48*:605–611.
Adam, C., Cavendish, W., and Mistry, P. (1992). *Adjusting Privatization.* Portsmouth, NH: Heinemann Educational Books.
Addison, T., and Demery, L. (1987). Alleviating poverty under structural adjustment. *Finance and Development, 24*(4):41–44.
Adwan, Y. (1986). Concepts, approaches, and styles of administrative reform in Arab countries. In Al-Saigh (ed.), *Administrative Reform in the Arab World: Readings.* Amman, Jordan: Arab Organization of Administrative Sciences.
Adwan, Y., and Al-Kayed, Z. (1988). The responsiveness of government officials to public demands: a comparative study. *Asian Affairs, 10*:1–15.
Allende, J. (1988). Toward a theory of state enterprises in less developed countries. *Public Enterprise, 8*:147–163.
Alston, J. (1989). Wa, guanxi, and inhwa: managerial principles in Japan, China, and Korea. *Business Horizons, 32*(2):26–31 (1989).
Aylen, J. (1987). Privatization in developing countries. *Lloyds Bank Review, 193*:15–30.
Ayub, M., and Hegstad, S. (1987). Determinants of public enterprise performance. *Finance and Development, 24*(4):26–29.
Bailey, R. (1987). Uses and misuses of privatization. *Proceedings of the Academy of Political Science, 36*(3):138–152.
Bian, Y. (1994). *Work and Inequality in Urban China.* Albany, NY: State University of New York Press.
Berg, R. (1987). Privatization: developing a pragmatic approach. *Economic Impact, 57*(1):6–11.
Bozeman, R. (1988). Exploring the limits of private sectors: sector boundaries as Maginot Line. *Public Administration Review, 48*:672–674.
Branson, R. (1985). Risk taking. *Journal of General Management, 11*:5–11.
Brunner, J., Chen, J., Sun, C., and Zhou, N. (1989). The role of guanxi in negotiations in the Pacific Basin. *Journal of Global Marketing, 3*(2):7–23.
Christian Science Monitor. (1987). Privatization. May 26:1, 12.
Christian Science Monitor. (1988). Tanzania. May 31:10.
Cook, P., and Kirkpatrick, C. (1995). Privatization policy and performance. In P. Cook and C. Kirkpatrick (eds.), *Privatization Policy and Performance.* New York: Prentice-Hall.
Cowan, G. (1990). *Privatization in the Developing World.* Westport, CT: Greenwood Press.
Cunningham, R. (1988). *The Bank and the Bureau.* New York: Praeger.
Cunningham, R., and Adwan, Y. (1991). Campfire decision-making and strategic management: a politics and leadership approach to economic development. *Public Administration and Development, 11*(5):511–520.
Cunningham, R., and Sarayrah, Y. (1993). *Wasta: The Hidden Force in Middle Eastern Society.* Westport, CT: Praeger.
Cunningham, R., and Sarayrah, Y. (1994). The human factor in technology transfer. *International Journal of Public Administration, 17*(8):1419–1431.
DeGregori, T. (1974). Caveat emptor: a critique of the emerging paradigm of public choice. *Administration and Society, 6*:205–228.

de Soto, H. (1996). The missing ingredient: what poor countries will need to make their markets work. In T. Anderson and P. Hill (eds.), *The Privatization Process*.

Donaldson, L. (1985). Entrepreneurship applied to middle management: a caution. *Journal of General Management*, *10*(Summer):5–20.

Economist. (1985). Privatization: everybody's doing it differently: world survey of the selling of state assets. *297*(Dec. 21):71–86.

Economist. (1986). Argentina. March 8:63.

Economist. (1998). The suffering Gulf. *349*(Oct. 24):41–42.

El-Naggar, S. (1989). Privatization and structural adjustment. In El-Naggar and Said (ed.), *Privatization and Structural Adjustment in the Arab Countries*. Washington: International Monetary Fund.

Fisher, R., and Ury, W. (1987). *Getting to Yes*. New York: Penguin.

Fox, C., and Miller, H. (1995). *Postmodern Public Administration: Toward Discourse*. Thousand Oaks, CA: Sage.

Georgakopoulos, T., Prodomidis, K., and Loizides, J. (1987). Public enterprises in Greece. *Annals of Public and Co-operative Economy*, *58*:351–368.

Gianaris, N. (1996). *Modern Capitalism: Privatization, Ownership and Democracy*. Westport, CT: Praeger.

Gilad, B. (1984). Entrepreneurship: the issue of creativity in the marketplace. *Journal of Creative Behavior*, *18*:151–161.

Gross, B. (1973). An organized society? *Public Administration Review*, *33*:323–327.

Halliday, F. (1979). *Iran: Dictatorship and Development*. New York: Penguin.

Hamlin, R., and Lyons, T. (1996). *Economy Without Walls*. Westport, CT: Praeger.

Hardin, G. (1977). The tragedy of the commons. In G. Hardin and J. Baden (eds.), *Managing the Commons*. San Francisco: W.H. Freeman.

Hill, P., and Karner, M. (1996). Spontaneous privatization in transition economies. In T. Anderson and P. Hill (eds.), *The Privatization Process*. Lanham, MD: Rowman & Littlefield.

Hwang, K. (1987). Face and favor: the Chinese power game. *American Journal of Sociology*, *92*(4):944–974.

Jayasankaran, S. (1995). Privatization pioneer: Malaysia's privatization programme. *Far Eastern Economic Review*, *158*(3):42–44.

Jomo, K. (1995). *Privatizing Malaysia*. Boulder, CO: Westview Press.

Jomo, K. (1995). Malaysia's privatization experience. In P. Cook and C. Kirkpatrick (eds.), *Privatization Policy and Performance*. New York: Prentice Hall.

Kanter, R. (1982). The middle manager as innovator. *Harvard Business Review*, *60*:95–105.

Keddie, N. (1985). Islamic revival in the Middle East: a comparison of Iran and Egypt. In S. Farsoun (ed.), *Arab Society: Continuity and Change*. London: Croom Helm.

Key, J., and Thompson, D. (1986). Privatization: a policy in search of a rationale. *Economic Journal*, *96*:18–32.

Klein, T. (1987). Debt relief for African countries. *Finance and Development*, *24*(4):10–13.

Knight, J. (1992). Public enterprises and industrialization in Africa. In F. Stewart (ed.), *Alternative Development Strategies in Sub Saharan Africa*. New York: St. Marten's Press.

Luo, Y. (1997). Guanxi and performance of foreign-invested enterprises in China: an empirical inquiry. *Management International Review*, *37*(1):51–70.

Manasan, R. (1988). The public enterprise sector in the Philippines: economic contribution and performance, 1975–1984. Paper presented at the annual conference of the Western Governmental Research Association, San Francisco, March 16–19.

Marber, P. (1997). Alleviating motion sickness: transportation privatization trends in developing countries. *Journal of International Affairs*, *50*(2):633–673.

Martin, B. (1993). *The Public Interest? Privatization and Public Sector Reform*. Atlantic Highlands, NJ: Zed Books.

McCormack, M. (1984). *What They Don't Teach You at Harvard Business School*. New York: Bantam.

McSwite, O.C. (1996). Postmodernism, public administration, and the public interest. In G. Wamsley and J. Wolf (eds.), *Refounding Democratic Public Administration*. Thousand Oaks, CA: Sage Publications.

McSwite, O.C. (1997). *Legitimacy in Public Administration*. Thousand Oaks, CA: Sage Publications.

Moe, R. (1987). Exploring the limits of privatization. *Public Administration Review*, *47*:453–460.

Muna, F. (1980). *The Arab Executive*. New York: St. Martin's Press.

Olson, M. (1965). *The Logic of Collective Action.* Cambridge, MA: Harvard University Press.

Ostrom, V., and Ostrom, E. (1971). Public choice: a different approach to the study of public administration. *Public Administration Review, 31*:203–216.

Park, Y. (1987). Evaluating the performance of Korea's government-invested enterprises. *Finance and Development, 24*(2):25–27.

Pelikan, P. (1997). State owned enterprises after socialism: why and how to privatize them rapidly. In T. Haavisto (ed.), *The Transition to a Market Economy.* Brookfield, VT: Edward Elgar Publishers.

Pliatzky, L. (1988). Optimising the role of the public sector: constraints and remedial policies. *Public Policy and Administration, 3*:35–45.

Poole, R. (1996). Privatization for economic development. In T. Anderson and P. Hill (eds.), *The Privatization Process.* Lanham, MD: Rowman & Littlefield.

Ramanadham, V. (1989). *Privatization in Developing Countries.* New York: Routledge.

Selznick, P. (1949). *TVA and the Grass Roots.* Berkeley: University of California Press.

Shaikh, A. (1987). Performance evaluation of public enterprises. *Annals of Public and Cooperative Economy, 58*:396–414.

Starr, P. (1987). The limits of privatization. *Proceedings of the Academy of Political Science, 36*(3):124–137.

Staats, E. (1988). Public service and public interest. *Public Administration Review, 48*:601–605.

Stevenson, H., and Gumpert, D. (1985). The heart of entrepreneurship. *Harvard Business Review, 63*:85–94.

Walsh, A. (1979). *The Public's Business: The Politics and Practices of Government Corporations.* Cambridge, MA: MIT Press.

Young, P. (1987). Privatization around the world. *Proceedings of the Academy of Political Science, 36*(3):190–209.

69

Bureaucracy in Bangladesh

Politics Within and the Influence of Partisan Politics

Habib M. Zafarullah   *School of Social Science, University of New England, Armidale, New South Wales, Australia*

Mohammad Mohabbat Khan   *Bangladesh Public Service Commission, Dhaka, Bangladesh*

I. INTRODUCTION

In the contemporary world, one of the pressing problems in governance concerns the politicization of the public bureaucracy and its effect on administrative performance. Politicization, which can occur at different levels of the administrative structure, relates to (1) intergroup or interagency discord and competition for greater power and influence over the adminstrative system and civil service management (Peters 1995:34–35, 217–218; Self 1972:87–88), and (2) the partisan interference of the political executive in administrative procedures and career practices (recruitment, promotion) either to augment political control or to secure the bureaucracy's compliance and commitment to its policies and programs (Peters 1995:202; Ståhlberg 1987:365).

External influence can reinforce existing intrabureaucratic conflicts or create new patterns of tension. Opposing groups based on academic or professional background, functional classification (generalists vs. specialists), regional ties, recruitment criteria (merit vs. equity), gender, and political orientation/attachment may seek and obtain supporters or advocates within political structures and can resort to tactics to influence reform initiatives to promote their interests within the administrative system. Both ruling and opposition parties may have their points of contact in the bureaucracy and partisan bureaucrats maintain clandestine links with parties providing them with information and advice (Aberbach et al. 1981). A partisan bureaucrat can use legitimate authority and exercise discretion to favor party supporters in obtaining benefits from the administration (Riggs 1969:259).

Politicization can also be equated with patronage. In order to create or tighten its hold on the administrative system or, more generally, to control the bureaucracy, the political leadership may place its favored career officials in strategic positions in the governmental hierarchy or employ outsiders on contract (often retired bureaucrats, business people or academics who have an attachment toward the ruling party). These "superbureaucrats" maintain "close and often collegial links" with the political executive (Campbell and Szablowski 1979:13). The power of the institutionalized career bureaucracy may be curbed or partisan cells within the bureaucracy assisted by the cooptation of party-loyals to advisory bodies in the areas of policy development and program administration (Peters 1995:234–238). Such a strategy may, however, induce conflicts between career civil servants and political appointees and may serve as a catalyst for bureaucratic politics. At lower levels, the ruling party may influence the recruitment process to enable its adherents to gain entry into the civil service (Ståhlberg 1987:366; Jain 1989:364–365). Political interference may also influence the promotion of officials to higher positions; party political considerations then become more important than merit criteria.

Most third world countries at independence inherited well-organized bureaucracies constructed by colonial powers. These were developed along classic Weberian lines, displaying the norms of neutrality, nonpartisanship, meritocracy, and *esprit de corps*, and used as an instrument of government. Over time, due to the absence of effective political institutions and perennial governmental instability, the bureaucracy, because of its organizational coherence, acquired a preeminent position in society and in some countries gradually assumed the role of a ruling elite (Smith 1996:226). On the other hand, taking advantage of its academic grounding, expertise, knowledge, experience and information monopoly, the bureaucracy dominated the policy process. Even after the installation of democratic institutions and launching of pluralist politics, the bureaucracy has remained a proactive actor in policy making and implementation. Its involvement in political decision making has expanded and its autonomy further consolidated, despite deep divisions and intensity of politics within its structure. One functional group pits itself against another to obtain career-aligned benefits or to protect or widen its turf within the administrative structure (Turner and Hulme 1997:69). Ruling regimes, constantly facing the threat of being swept out of office, intrude into the bureaucratic domain to obtain support by patronizing individuals and groups subscribing to its ideology or policies. Partisan interference normally becomes evident after a change of government when the new ruling party engages itself in bureaucrat cleansing—getting rid of those it identifies with its political adversary and putting its own protégés in their place. Politicization then subsumes the entire administrative fabric.

Politics has always enshrouded the bureaucracy in Bangladesh ever since it emerged as an independent nation. Its ramifications have been administration-wide and, in some cases, transcended bureaucratic boundaries. It has had an adverse impact on bureaucratic performance and has affected the credibility of civil servants in serving the public. In this chapter, we examine the extent of politicization in the civil service in Bangladesh, since its inception as an independent state. It seeks to understand the dimensions of bureaucratic politics and to analyze the pattern of relationship between the various actors involved. The focus will be on the intrabureaucratic struggles for 'equitable' share in policy making and administration, political interference in staffing the civil service, and the involvement of career officers in outside partisan politics.

II. BACKGROUND

Like most nations of the third world, Bangladesh was under colonial rule for a long time. British rule, spanning over 200 years, left a distinct political and administrative heritage. A small but powerful group of civil servants, especially recruited and indoctrinated, dominated over a highly centralized administrative structure. They were utilized as instruments of imperial control, ostensibly to bridge the gap between the ruler and the ruled. Generally, they performed two major functions—corrective and revenue administration, with some involvement in judicial affairs (Misra 1970; Khan 1976).

The institutionalization of the bureaucratic system was deliberately planned to stall the development of indigenous political institutions. This was in line with the British imperial policy of suppressing nationalistic movements for self-rule and freedom by the native population. The perpetuation of colonial rule demanded the appointment of senior bureaucrats to key political positions—as governors of provinces, members of legislative councils, or viceregal councillors. Their direct links with the imperial government in London through the viceroy and the Secretary of State for India demonstrated the enormous influence they wielded over political and administrative structures in British India.

However, in spite of the discreet handling of the bureaucracy and moves to resist the persistent agitation of the natives for self-rule by the British rulers, colonial control had to be gradually abated and independence finally granted. Two separate nations—India and Pakistan—were created in 1947. But freedom from colonial rule did not usher in changes in the role or attitude of the bureaucracy. A pattern similar to the one that was obtained in British India characterized the political and administrative system in Pakistan. Within the administrative system, elite civil servants sought to protect themselves as an institution and frustrated major reform efforts that threatened to sever their ties with tradition and break their monopolistic hold over key policy making positions (Khan 1980).

Weak political leadership, dominance of a small capitalist class, and inter- and intraparty feuds on trivial partisan issues contributed to the making and unmaking of fragile coalitions that thwarted political development (Maniruzzaman 1971; Jahan 1972). The political quagmire that followed goaded an ambitious military leadership to seize state power in connivance with the elite civil service. A long period of military-bureaucratic dominance over the state apparatus, ceaseless political repression, economic disparity between regions, and sinister designs to destroy cultural values of the Bengalees[1] were instrumental in the political disintegration of Pakistan and in the emergence of its eastern wing as an independent nation—Bangladesh—in 1971 (LaPorte 1972; Morris-Jones 1972).

III. PROFILE AND CONTEXT OF THE BUREAUCRACY

The public bureaucracy in Bangladesh is still laden with traditions that are colonial in nature. Being still largely elitist in character, bureaucrats, as a social group, are insulated from the rest of society; a wide gap exists between the bureaucracy and the people at large. There is little direct interaction between the bureaucracy and the public. As in colonial days, civil servants manifest a paternalistic attitude toward the people who encounter problems in gaining access to public service.

After almost two decades of pseudodemocratic and authoritarian rule, the major political forces arrived at a consensus on an acceptable system of government. Parliamentary democracy, discarded for one-party presidential rule in the mid-1970s, was restored in 1991. Fair elections produced two representative governments—the Bangladesh Nationalist Party (BNP) government in 1991 and the Awami League (AL) government in 1996—and the parameters of democratic governance were drawn. Parliament was revitalized and its committee system made operative. Civil society began playing a more active role, and economic liberalization programs leased a new life to a dormant private sector. However, due to the weakness of the political leadership and the impotence of extrabureaucratic structures (parliament, party system, and accountability mechanisms), bureaucratic domination remains as effusive as ever, pervading the entire societal fabric. Bureaucrats have taken upon themselves the responsibility of public decision making, and there is no efficacious means of holding them accountable for their actions. The administrative system is characterized by an agglomeration of colonial values, undue formalism, bureaucratic corruption and intransigence, ubiquity of rules and procedures, and the inefficiency syndrome. A highly centralized, top-heavy bureaucratic structure has produced a capricious approach in dealing with administrative matters. Although in recent years, greater emphasis has been put on the idea of decentralization and on its corollary, popular participation in administration, particularly at the subnational levels, these have remained illusory and trapped at the level of rhetoric.

The governmental machinery revolves around the central secretariat—the nerve center for public administration. It consists of a large number of ministries, each under the political control of a minister and manned by career civil servants belonging to one of the 29 functional cadres that make up the Bangladesh Civil Service (BCS). The higher generalist bureaucrats are primarily responsible for the formulation of public policies whose implementation is overseen and controlled by line ministries. A myriad of executive agencies scattered throughout the country undertakes the implementation of public policies and monitors their success or failures (Zafarullah 1998).

Theoretically, the cadres are of equal status with no supremacy of one over the other as in preindependence days, although in practice a deviation from this ideal is apparent. Young people with general education are eligible to enter these cadres at the base level through an open competitive examination conducted by an "independent" constitutional body—the Public Service Commission (PSC). The differentiated career structure of civil servants is primarily based on the rank-in-corps philosophy. The general rule in determining promotions is to take both competence and seniority into account, but exceptions have been galore with political factors serving as primary inputs. A promotion-from-within policy is followed, and the lateral induction of noncareerists into higher ranks is an exception but is increasingly gaining ground.

The civil service is generally managed by members of the generalist (administrative) cadre, which has "a very incomplete understanding of how to manage the forces that drive public administration" (World Bank 1996). The methods applied are archaic, and the approaches used in career planning and constructing staffing and development standards have outlived their existence elsewhere (Zafarullah et al. 1997). The academic standard of the recruitment examination is low compared to the standard at the universities, and there is hardly any scope by which to test a candidate's true aptitude and personality. The country's Constitution provides for equal employment opportunity, but affirmative action plans are also followed in appointing members of disadvantaged groups (Zafarullah and Khan 1983). There are over a million employees in the public sector, of whom over 80,000 are either members of the BCS or are uncadred officers holding higher (class 1) positions; the remaining are lower-level personnel serving in a variety of governmental organization and autonomous bodies (BBS 1997:68). This number is small compared with the population of the country, which is about 120 million. The several cadres may be grouped into four broad categories—generalist (or administrative), financial, functional, technical/professional.

IV. POLITICS WITHIN BUREAUCRACY

A. Politics of Generalist Aggrandizement

The dominance of generalist civil servants in administrative affairs, particularly their occupation of important positions in the bureaucratic hierarchy, has been strongly resented by other groups of civil servants. The nongeneralists felt that after independence the erstwhile dominating tendency of the generalist cadre over other segments of the bureaucracy would end and that a system would emerge wherein equity for all civil servants in terms of career advancement and prospects would be ensured. Technocrats and professionals within the civil service demanded that key positions in public agencies (for instance, Ministries of Health, Flood Control and Irrigation, or autonomous bodies like the Power Development Board) performing functions of a purely technical nature should be staffed by technical BCS personnel only.

The generalist cadre is actually a combination of two different services that existed in Pakistan before 1971—the Civil Service of Pakistan (CSP), which was an all-Pakistan service at the helm of the national bureaucracy, and the East Pakistan Civil Service (EPCS), which was the regional administrative service functioning in the area that is now Bangladesh. The members of the CSP exhibited certain distinctive characteristics that gave the service the appearance of an institutional bureaucracy. They supported the continuation of the imperial heritage, which had led to the British officers' control over key positions in the early years of independent Pakistan. They worked for the maintenance of the generalist tradition and manifested a negative attitude toward politicians, on the one hand, and a paternalistic attitude toward the common people, on the other.

The elite character of the CSP was ensured by reserving important positions for its members, prohibiting the lateral entry of other cadre personnel into its fold, and maintaining a rigorous indoctrination scheme for its members, which contributed to its institutionalization and buoyed its monopolistic control of policy making functions. All these permitted the CSP to fortify itself and protect its parochial interests in the face of some realistic efforts by the political leadership to introduce reforms that, to some extent, would have diluted its power and prestige (Khan 1979).

The EPCS, on the other hand, with a much smaller domain to administer, was a low-rated service vis-à-vis other all-Pakistan (the police service for instance) and central superior services like the foreign, audit and accounts, taxation services, to name a few. Basically, the EPCS was under the administrative control of the CSP as the highest positions in the regional administration were invariably occupied by the latter. Consequently, the prospects for career progression of EPCS officers were severely restricted.

After the independence of Bangladesh, the former officers of the EPCS (hereinafter ex-EPCS) began an organized campaign to project itself as the premier civil service of the country. Their argument was based on the premise that as they had served exclusively in the territory that became Bangladesh, they inherited the sole right to be at the forefront of civil service affairs. This created antagonism and animosity between the erstwhile CSP (hereinafter ex-CSP) and the ex-EPCS. But the former's overall superiority was acknowledged and welcomed by the political leadership, thereby giving its members an upper hand in managing and controlling the administrative apparatus (Zafarullah 1987). Although initially the ex-EPCS was unwilling to accept the hegemony of ex-CSP men,[2] its members softened their stance considering the odds against their claims. Not only did they accept the leadership of ex-CSP officers, they also sided with them to promote their common generalist interests. The ex-CSPs moved fast and tactically formed an alliance with the ex-EPCS group to counter the growing strength of specialist civil servants.

Despite the tension and politics within the bureaucracy, generalist civil servants gradually consolidated their position within the administrative system of the country especially after the organizational changes in the late 1970s. Their continued domination over important public agencies gave them a clear edge over specialists and other functional civil servants in terms of power, position, and status. There were other factors as well that contributed toward the ascendancy and entrenchment of the generalist cadre. These will become evident in course of this discussion.

B. Reforms and Politics

Successive governments since independence made efforts to bring about reform in the machinery of government, particularly in the civil service (Khan 1989). In 1973, the Administrative and Services Reorganization Committee (ASRC) recommended certain basic changes to the inherited civil service system like the creation of a single, classless grading structure by amalgamating the various existing categories of cadres and subcadres. Several measures were outlined to develop an integrated public personnel management system encompassing a rational selection process based on merit, long-term career planning, coordinated institutionalized training, and a promotion system based on merit and seniority (Khan and Zafarullah 1982b). The National Pay Commission

(NPC) devised a new pay structure that sought to narrow the disparity between the existing highest and lowest scales of pay.

The Pay and Services Commission (P&SC), appointed by the first military regime in 1976, followed the ASRC in proposing the amalgamation of all existing services into an "all-purpose" civil service. It also emphasized merit as the principal criterion in recruitment and promotion. Additionally, it proposed the removal of discrepancies among different services by introducing uniform scales of pay and equitable scope for advancement. More importantly, it recommended the creation of a "supercadre" at the top of the hierarchy drawing on personnel from all over the civil service structure.

The second military regime further consolidated the reforms of its predecessor. It appointed a committee in 1982 to propose measures to rationalize the organization and functions of the government and improve efficiency in the civil service. Its recommendations were drastic and included inter alia reduction of the number of public agencies and retrenchment of redundant personnel.

During the initial years of independence, administrative reform efforts of the political regime in power were intended basically to ensure political control over the bureaucracy and make it accountable to the political leadership for its actions. The ASRC recommendations had clearly reflected the regime's intents. In particular, it wanted to do away with the generalist monopoly and create greater opportunities for specialists in governmental affairs. Though the ASRC worked rather closely with influential political leaders in government and was thereby tremendously influenced by the political ideology of the ruling party, its well-worked-out reform plan was inexplicably shelved by the government.

Despite the favorable political climate for reform and a strong political leadership supporting change, by the time the ASRC reported the government had already adopted a go-slow stance on administrative reform (Khan and Zafarullah 1982a). It chose to maintain the *status quo* in the bureaucracy—changes it believed might hamper postwar reconstruction in which generalist civil servants had a major role to play. Any move to weaken their entrenched position at that time would have meant serious disruption in developmental programs.

The report of the NPC was only partially implemented. The recommendations relating to pay and other benefits of higher civil servants remained unattended, largely due to generalist resistance. The report was regarded by the generalist group as a blueprint to undermine its status and prestige because of its proposals to introduce equity in the pay structure (Khan and Zafarullah 1982a).

The failure of the government to reform the bureaucracy was a triumph for the generalist class. It took for granted its power and authority in public administration; its members fancied themselves as a force to be reckoned with. Their assigned duties and responsibilities were so basic and important for running the state machinery that no government, however powerful and popular, could afford to strike at them.

The military takeover in late 1975 further reinforced the generalist domination within the bureaucracy. The regime was reluctant to disrupt the existing relations among the various components of the administrative system. More importantly, it needed the support and cooperation of senior bureaucrats in governing the country. The report of the P&SC was clearly indicative of the regime's grand design. Unlike the ASRC and the NPC, the P&SC was wholly constituted of either retired or serving senior bureaucrats who manifested a conservative outlook toward reform. During the working of the commission, generalist civil servants became unusually restive to influence its recommendations. In the member-secretary of the P&SC who was a serving ex-CSP officer, they had the promoter of their vested interests. Disregarding all norms and ethics, he altered parts of the draft report to accommodate generalist interest vis-à-vis its power and position in the bureaucracy (Khan and Zafarullah 1982a). He was said to have the tacit support of the P&SC

chairman, himself a retired senior generalist. This malicious attempt failed due to the vigilance of other members of the Commission. To what extent generalists can go to preserve their hold in administration is well illustrated by this incident.

The P&SC report was generally acceptable to all segments within the bureaucracy. The initial reaction of both generalists and functionalists (e.g., officers of the accounts, audit, taxation, customs departments) was one of optimism, for they found the proposed civil service structure more equitable and advantageous to their career prospects. Up to a certain level in the administrative hierarchy, members of all services were to have a distinct advantage in entering a super-cadre—the Senior Selection Pool (SSP)—because of the nature of the duties they performed. The specialists were under the impression that they too would have easy access, like their generalist counterparts, into the SSP. But this was not to be, due to the manipulation of the process of constituting the pool and inducting members into it by senior generalists. The government-specified principles were violated in encadring pool members. Instead of selecting them on the basis of performance in specially designed tests conducted by the PSC, the pool was arbitrarily filled by all former CSP officers and senior members of the ex-EPCS. It thus became the exclusive domain of generalists.

The entire process of organizing the SSP was intended to maintain the hegemony of generalist bureaucrats and deliberately depriving members of other services from occupying senior positions in the civil service. In effect, the SSP gave generalists still wider opportunities to control the administrative system. Specialists expressed their resentment and displeasure at the way the original intention of P&SC for creating an open structure at the apex of the bureaucracy had been defied. They took exception to the fact that the SSP was a built-in device to further the interests of generalists and made its protests unequivocal. Its abolition by the second military regime was thus a political response to the tension within the bureaucracy.

Efforts at administrative reform in the new democratic setup have been frustrated by both bureaucratic inertia and political inaction (Zafarullah 1996). The external stimuli for reform generated by the United Nations Development Programme (UNDP) and the World Bank succumbed under stiff generalist resistance and the BNP and AL governments' indifference. The contemplated changes were directed at both the macro- and microlevels of governmental administration and had the potentiality to fabricate a new relationship between the political and bureaucratic structures, improve accountability mechanisms, open up the administration for greater public scrutiny of its operations, raise efficiency and performance, neutralize generalist dominance and, hence, balance the disparities between cadres (UNDP 1993; World Bank 1996). The generalists displayed their usual opposition to any move to strip them of their preeminent position in the administrative apparatus while the specialists were by and large supportive of proposed changes. The BNP government ignored the UNDP plan, and the AL administration ignored the World Bank report. Both, fearful of a backlash from either side of the bureaucratic fence and of increasing existing tensions in the civil service if either plan was adopted, chose to appoint their own reform committees—a clever ploy to postpone reforms. "*Ad hocery*" has had preference over concrete action. In the meantime, the bureaucracy remains ruptured into several clefts, each with its own agenda for self-deification and control over administrative affairs.

C. Politics Between Cadres

Intercadre rivalry began when the cadre system was established in the BCS in 1977 with the altruistic purpose of removing existing staffing discrepancies among various categories of civil servants. It was designed to correct past discrimination by "equalizing incentives" and by broadening the recruitment area for higher executive and policy making positions in the governmental hierarchy (World Bank 1996:131). However, in reality the several cadres are locked in uncompromising asperity. The feud is no longer between the generalists and the nongeneralists, but has spread thick and fast throughout the civil service. The generalists are now at war among themselves ("patriots" vs. "nonpatriots"; see below), the functionalist cadres dispute each other's position, while the specialists are at ceaseless loggerheads with the rest. Noncadred personnel in the civil service are also waging a war against all BCS cadres.

All civil service cadres have their separate or combined associations with trade union attributes, although unionism is proscribed by law (GOB 1979). In fact, to destroy the entrenched position of the generalists, specialists (engineers, medical practitioners, scientists, agriculturists, and other professionals) organized themselves into a cohesive force earlier than their antagonists in the aftermath of the reforms of the 1970s. In promoting their cause, these associations are involved in active lobbying to impress upon the government the "genuineness" of their demands for equitable participation in administration. This infighting within the bureaucracy has been watched by all past (and present) governments without demur. Indeed, they tacitly encouraged the moves of the several conflicting groups by deliberately remaining indifferent. They sought to obtain political capital out of the situation by keeping the bureaucracy divided with vain attempts at curbing its power.

The BCS Central Coordination Council, a conglomerate of several non administrative cadre associations, and the *Prokrichi* (an alliance of physicians, engineers and agriculturists) have forged a coalition to "coordinate their strategies and activities" against the administrative cadre (Ahmed 1996:257). These two apex bodies, supported by their respective constituent associations, operate a Central Action Council to persistently pressure the government to fulfill their demands. To further intensify the pressure especially in the compensation front, members of 15 functionalist cadres have formed a Committee for Realizing the Demand for Eliminating Intercadre Salary Discrimination. The Association of Financial Services (a loose ad hoc coalition of the customs and excise, audit and accounts, and taxation cadres) enlivens itself whenever their mutual interests are at stake. While all these bodies are basically united in their crusade against the generalists, the Bangladesh Noncadre Officers' Association is critical of the BCS in general and is active in promoting the interests of a large majority of employees located throughout the governmental structure. Then, there is an organization of subalterns in government—the *Sramik Karmachari Oikyo Parishad* (SKOP), which is perennially antiestablishment in its orientation and known for its harassment of past regimes with frequent industrial action, the most recent relating to office hours.

The generalist cadre has its own association, with some of its members occupying very senior and strategic positions in the administrative hierarchy. This gives the association the scope to play a decisive, if not a commonly approved, role in civil service management. It single-handedly fights for its cause against all odds and has inherited from its colonial and postcolonial experience a tremendous dexterity to sway over all successive governments, irrespective of their political complexion. This influence is the bone of contention between the nongeneralist bureaucracy and ruling regimes which have demonstrated a remarkable propensity to toe the generalist line.

The principal reasons for the intercadre conflict relate to perceived and real discrimination against members of the nongeneralist cadres in terms of their upward mobility and placement in the highest decision-making positions. The other reasons are the government's nonobjective approach in deciding promotions in the civil service, arbitrary regradation of existing positions (usually reclassified at a higher level), salary disparities, and the constitution of the proposed "economic pool"—a super policy-making cadre. The nongeneralists struggle for parity among the cadres, while the generalists fight to maintain their supremacy in the administrative machine.

Conflicts also stem from the government's wavering attitude toward principles established either by itself or its predecessors. The two democratically elected governments have shown an extraordinary penchant for reversing policies formulated by its political adversary. But, whenever it saw potential benefits deriving from the same policies, it did not hesitate to salvage, normally under pressure by vested interests in the civil service, and have them implemented. The group(s) which profit(s) from them are pleased; others not benefited agitate and create bureaucratic turmoil. Thus, when a report, prepared during the second military regime, recommended new rules for upgrading positions, almost all the nongeneralist cadres benefited (*Independent* 6 January 1998). The rules were annulled by the BNP government when it discovered pay anomalies between cadres on whom the rules were applied and those left out. But instead of correcting the problem, the government allowed the disparities to prevail, thereby intensifying intercadre tensions. The AL government initially remained silent on the issue, but strong lobbying by generalists forced the prime minister to change its position further aggravating the conflict.

What is most disconcerting to the public is the way the conflicting groups threaten each other and resort to actions that have profound implications for the public's image of the bureaucracy, its responsibility, and its performance. Frequent work stoppages, picketing, demonstrations, and street marches, threatening the government with strike action, besieging and terrorizing decision makers at the top level and at times holding them hostage, and clashes with police are some of the methods used by the conflicting groups to put pressure on the government (see issues of *The Independent* and *The Daily Star* between October 1997 and February 1998; *Holiday* 10 June 1997).

D.   Politics of Individual Advancement

At another level of bureaucratic politics, civil servants strive for career advancement or in obtaining extra benefits for themselves by direct intervention. Here, they operate in their individual capacities and not as members of any cadres. However, they may utilize their cadre affiliations or their political connections in promoting their case. *Tadbir* (personal lobbying) becomes a critical factor in achieving their objectives (see Anisuzzaman 1986). This normally happens in gaining extensions after retirement, overseas scholarships, lucrative positions in international organizations, and transfers to government agencies or public corporations of their choice. Individuals interested in a higher position within a cadre can also manipulate the promotion process to gain an advantage over other aspirants. Officers in the central personnel agency (the Ministry of Establishment, for instance) responsible for providing inputs to the process are alleged to be engaged in modifying seniority lists to strengthen their own chances for promotion (*Daily Star* 4 December 1997). This, however, is more of an ethical problem than pure bureaucratic politics.

A source of brewing discontent among midranking and junior officers in the bureaucracy is the system of contractual appointments at the highest level of the civil service hierarchy. The existing 10% quota for filling the important positions of secretaries from outside or by retirees is being exceeded by the government and this is seen by career bureaucrats as a deterrent to their route to the higher echelons of the civil service or in statutory bodies. What annoys them is the arbitrary manner by which retired secretaries are reemployed on contract. In the absence of any rational guidelines, nonobjective criteria and the personal convenience and circumstances of individuals are taken into account rather than the needs of the administration. Thus, contracts vary from a year to three. Some in statutory bodies are also given the rank and status of a state minister—a way of politicizing a public body (*Daily Star* 13 December 1997).

Careerists due for promotion are apparently disturbed being "denied the opportunity of reaching the top." From them come "accusations of unfairness in the evaluation of performance" and the manner by which the contractual appointees are "judged by their political leanings and not quality" (*Holiday* 23 December 1997). Many would suspect this move as a precursor to the abolition of tenure at the top of the civil service, a practise that has been institutionalized in many other civil service systems.

Personal lobbying is also instrumental in obtaining governmental nomination for well-funded scholarships tenable in overseas universities or for positions in international organizations such as the World Bank, International Monetary Fund, the United Nations, or any of its agencies. Higher-ups in the foreign office or the Economic Relations Division (ERD) are the first to know of offers being made to the government by these organizations. If they themselves are interested in these they will go all out to ensure getting their aspired positions; if they are not, they will promote others on ascriptive (as opposed to achievement) factors. Similarly, scholarships are monopolized by nominating officers or their proteges (Siddiqui 1996:78). Such a personal approach breeds misunderstanding both within and among cadres and can be a cause for conflict.

E. Politics Among Departments

Some of the key central coordinating ministries or divisions under them (like Finance, Establishment, Cabinet) have considerable influence over state management. Rules and regulations for conducting the general administration of the country and in particular those relating to public personnel administration are formulated by the Cabinet Division and the Establishment Ministry. Being exclusively staffed by generalists, they manifest a tendency to prepare guidelines and establish procedures that tend to discreetly favor their own kind. The Establishment Ministry and the PSC, an autonomous body, do not see eye to eye on many personnel issues, and frequent tussles between them affect civil service management. This has a telling effect on the morale of the rest of the civil service.

In matters of procurement and supply, the ERD and the ministries of Commerce, Industry and Finance are often tied up in disagreements. Differences of opinion and lack of proper consultation between the Finance Ministry and the planning machinery adversely impact upon national development plans and programs (Khasru 1997). Nation-building activities at the field level involving two or more line ministries often end up in disasters due to interorganizational disputes. The operational freedom of the central bank has been eroded by the continued interference of the Finance Ministry in monetary policy implementation and administration (Baqi 1997). Such eclipsing of one public organization by another more dominant causes skepticism, breeds suspicion, and incites politics.

Although the rules of business in government expressly provide for interdepartmental consultation whenever the need arises (GOB 1996), in practice such consultations are a rarity. The Secretaries Standing Committees serve no useful purpose, as the members (mainly generalists) use them for socialization rather than for sorting interdepartmental problems (Siddiqui 1996:122). Ministers do discuss inter ministerial issues quite frequently at cabinet meetings and send directives to their respective departments for action, but these are not always followed. This is mainly because of the parochial attitude of civil servants, generally dominating the composition of a particular ministry or its affiliate departments/agencies, who tend to emphasize sectarian interests of their own cadres. The obvious result is the suboptimization of goals at the expense of the common goal. The symptoms of such petty politics among departments are malcoordination, mistrust among officials, and divided loyalty.

To extend their dominance over the administrative apparatus, the different cadres strive to have their members placed at the field offices scattered throughout the country through their sponsoring ministries. At the local level, executive officers who belong to the generalist civil service confront the difficult task of obtaining the support and cooperation of the representatives of various functional ministries like agriculture, rural development, and health and family planning. The reason is obvious: the latter, being of the same rank and status as that of the executive officers at that level, are unwilling to accept the authority of generalists officers.

V. INFLUENCE OF PARTISAN POLITICS

Bureaucrats, especially those at the senior levels, have been enmeshed in politics since the days of the War of Independence in 1971. The close association between the top leaders of the AL, the party that led the movement for independence, and those civil servants who had crossed the border and sought refuge in neighboring India in forming the "government-in-exile" (also known as the Mujibnagar government) was one of the most important factors in opening the bureaucracy to direct political influence as well as in enculturing bureaucrats to foster political ambitions.

In organizing the civil administration of the Mujibnagar government, civil servants did play a vital role. As they lacked prior administrative experience, politicians had to depend rather heavily on appointed officials in establishing policy priorities, in maintaining liaison with the Indian government, in organizing campaigns abroad to support the cause of the people fighting at home, and, to some extent, in coordinating the civil aspect of the war against the Pakistani regime. These bureaucrats proclaimed themselves as "patriots" for their "contribution" to the independence movement.

A. Politics of Patriotism

The close rapport between the AL government and the "patriotic" bureaucrats continued after the establishment of the Bangladesh polity in December 1971. This had far-reaching consequences in creating intrabureaucratic tensions and in further politicizing the bureaucracy.

The number of civil servants supporting the Mujibnagar government was small; neither were they senior to those officers who remained inside the country. On the other hand, the latter, who "reluctantly served the Pakistani military junta amid continual harassment" (Zafarullah, 1987), had among their ranks some very senior-ranking and highly experienced officers. The so-called patriot bureaucrats convinced the ruling leadership that they were the ones who should be in command of the civil service in the new nation. They lobbied hard in impressing upon the political leadership that those civil servants who had remained inside the country during the war, irrespective of their feelings toward the cause of independence or attitude toward the Pakistani military regime, were "quislings." The "patriot" bureaucrats not only sought to fulfill their career objectives through such activities but also wanted to remain close to the citadel of power.

Their attempts initially succeeded. The government, sympathetic toward them, rewarded them with accelerated promotions or graded them higher on seniority lists, placed them in key positions, and enhanced their salaries and benefits. This injudicious action of the government to patronize a special group of civil servants at the expense of others sowed the seeds of factionalism within the bureaucracy which, as we have seen, later took different dimensions and engulfed the entire administrative setup. The "patriot" bureaucrats formed their own association, the Mujibnagar Government Officers/Employees Association, to make their presence felt in advancing their vested interests and in collectively giving direct support to the government.

B. Politics of Alienation

The majority of civil servants who became the victims of this imperious governmental action felt aggrieved, and they gradually diverted themselves from being wholly committed to their work. On its part, the political leadership initiated a serious campaign to defame the bureaucracy in general. Haunted by the memories of bureaucratic domination in preindependence days, the political leadership was bent upon curtailing the power of the bureaucracy and bring it under its control. Senior civil servants who were unaccustomed to political control became restive and disillusioned. But there was little they could do at that point of time. Civil service morale fell to a low level, and the War of Independence had left them divided and disorganized.

Within a month of independence a large number of senior civil servants, suspected for their political orientation by the political executive, were forcibly retired under a special presidential order that provided for the dismissal of any officer without the right of appeal. This practice continued until the end of 1974, when arbitrary dismissals became a common feature creating panic in civil service circles (Ahamed 1980). It amounted to direct partisan control of the bureaucracy by a highly prejudiced political clique.

Another move that estranged bureaucrats was the lateral induction of a large number of party sympathizers and supporters to high ranks in the civil service. In many cases these entrants had little or no experience in administrative matters, and instead of providing administrative leadership they only complicated matters and obstructed the normal functioning of the bureaucratic machine. The hiatus between political appointees and career bureaucrats rapidly widened making the implementation of political decisions complex. The net result: administrative efficiency declined, the quality of service delivery dropped substantially, insubordination became an administrative nuisance, and, last but not least, bureaucratic turmoil thrived in an environment of distrust and hostility.

C. Institutionalizing Politics

The AL government's efforts at debureaucratization and maintaining control over the bureaucracy failed. By the end of 1974 social, political, and economic forces created a situation where the government was hard-pressed to maintain its popularity and thereby keeping itself in power. By drastically altering the political paradigm, the ruling party replaced the multiparty parliamentary system with a one-party presidential monolith with all political-administrative powers concentrated in the chief executive. To be effective, such a centralized political system required the support and cooperation of the bureaucracy. This was ensured by integrating the bureaucracy and the only legal political party of the country. High-ranking civil servants were inducted into the highest policy making bodies of the party, appointed governors of administrative units at the subnational levels, and selected for positions normally meant for politicians. The governors were to work under the direct command of the party chairman within an integrated structure where the bureaucracy was to be an important component.

D. "Civilianization" of Military Rule and Bureaucratic Input

After the fall of the AL regime and for over a decade longer, the country was under military rule or its "civilianized" variant. Civil servants, generalists in particular, played a key role in sustaining military rule and in facilitating its gradual "civilianization." Senior bureaucrats were appointed members of presidential advisory councils immediately after the two military takeovers in 1975 and 1982. They were assigned the more important ministerial portfolios because of their "expertise" and "experience" in administration. Also, they were placed on important advisory committees and made members of reform planning bodies. This gave them the power to significantly influence almost all governmental decisions. Senior generalist bureaucrats enthusiastically participated in activities to create and uphold a favorable image for the military rulers and to give their regimes a populist appearance.

The military-bureaucracy relationship was mutually advantageous and reinforcing for both groups. Bureaucrats all along manifested an aversion for politicians. They were allergic to political control and accountability. On the other hand, they were more comfortable in an impersonal and formal work environment but one where they could exercise discretionary powers and where the value system of political structures did not impede bureaucratic norms. Military administration based on a rigid hierarchical system and strict adherence to procedure seemed to appropriately match the bureaucratic way of life. In a similar vein, military hierarchs found it convenient to utilize the bureaucracy to hang on to power. Ostensibly, to close the gaps that existed between them and the people at large, they manifested a concern for the well-being of the common people by taking on a wide array of development programs particularly in the rural areas. Here the bureaucrats came in handy: they supervised, coordinated, and monitored the implementation of these programs. Their feedback was invariably positive, irrespective of the success or failure of such programs whose implementation they oversaw. This feedback was used by the state-owned media to extol the "achievements" of the military regime. The bureaucrats were motivated to lie about the actual situation simply to please the dictators and thereby to gain undue advantage in governance. By supporting military rulers they were, in essence, exposed to partisan politics.

E. Bureaucracy's Antimilitary Stance

Another cross current of the military-bureaucracy relations emerged by the time the military regimes became relatively civilianized. The floating of a political party by the dictators and their transformation as civilian presidents, a series of elections to provide political legitimacy to their regimes, the attempt to construct "democratic" institutions, and the entrenchment of the military in politics and administration completed the formal "military withdrawal" from politics, but the linkages of the civilianized regime with the military endured. After their voluntary retirement from service, senior military officials overnight became politicians by joining and holding key positions in the ruling party hierarchy. The process of inducting military personnel, both serving and retired, into top administrative positions in government departments and public corporations as well as in diplomatic missions abroad gained momentum. Such a situation created dissension among career-conscious civil servants who were averse to the lateral induction of ex-military officers.

A policy of the second civilianized government reserving 10% of all vacant positions in the civil service for military personnel was received by these bureaucrats with serious exception, as it aimed at undermining their career prospects. The powerful association of generalist bureaucrats, whose support contributed toward military rule, now openly voiced its resentment against reservation of positions for ex-military personnel. Career diplomats were equally displeased with the government's placement of an increasing number of military men to ambassadorial positions. Positions of a technical nature, however, were not all that affected by outside intrusion but specialists too had their reservations against the policy. Clearly this phenomenon signified a new pattern in the military-bureaucracy relationship. This, however, became redundant after democratization in the 1990s.

F. Partisan Politics and Politicization

As noted earlier, party politicization had its root during the War of Independence. During the first AL rule (1972–75), partisan influence over the bureaucracy was pervasive and the group it nurtured reciprocated by creating a support base for the regime in the civil service. However, with the advent of prolonged military rule, this group became passive, its presence less conspicuous, and its overbearing sway over civil service management less ominous. On the other hand, the anti-AL bureaucrats gradually became prominent by their close rapport with the military leadership. Many of them replaced AL appointees in key positions in national administration, public sector bodies, and diplomatic missions. After civilianization they began to be identified as pro-BNP bureaucrats, although everyone was not involved in party politics and some adopted a totally neutral stance.

The emergence of the Jatiya Party (JP), the political platform of the second military ruler, did not upset the AL-BNP equation in the civil service, which by now had been clearly divided along party lines. The JP and also the Jamat-e-Islami (a party based on religion) had their sympathizers in the bureaucracy but, for all practical purposes, they supported the BNP faction. As in national politics where politicians frequently change their political colors, partisan bureaucrats often have changed their party allegiance.

However, partisanship, which resulted from overt party influences, remained confined to the internal dynamics of the bureaucracy. It remained latent from the public eye until the butt end of authoritarian rule in 1990. Both the BNP and AL factions in the bureaucracy played a decisive part in overthrowing the military-turned-civilian dictator by withdrawing their support for his regime when popular upsurge against it reached its zenith (Maniruzzaman 1992:207). This event demonstrated that the bureaucracy could not retain its "apolitical" and "neutral" posture or remain aloof from a unique turning point in the nation's political history. The bureaucrats—generalists and nongeneralists alike—wanted to be a part of it, and everyone welcomed their direct political participation in the movement for democracy.

The return of pluralist politics, however, has exposed the bureaucracy to indiscriminate politicization by the ruling party. The BNP, the first to regain power in the new democratic framework, distributed patronage to its cronies without rhyme or reason. The promotion process was subjected to nonmerit criteria to favor partisan bureaucrats, the recruitment to the BCS was manipulated to induct university graduates with BNP orientation, and party loyals were placed in key national institutions (including the universities and "autonomous" bodies) and local bodies. Politicization became a politically contentious issue and debated in public and in parliament. The print media highlighted both ruling-party desecrations and opposition flak.

The opposition reproach, however, lacked credibility. The AL, while condemning the government for utilizing the bureaucracy for sinister political purposes, was itself guilty of influencing its own lackeys in the bureaucracy to frustrate the government's policy initiatives and to further its political agenda. The pro-AL faction's explicit support of the opposition camp to dislodge the government in 1996 was the vertex of direct political involvement of an overzealous partisan clique within the bureaucracy attempting to impress a party close to reclaiming government (for details, see Rashiduzzaman 1997:263). Once in power, the AL leadership moved swiftly to reward such partisanism by distributing patronage at an even greater magnitude than the regime it replaced. The old Mujibnagar Association has been revived. A bureaucratic cabal, close to the prime minister, has virtually taken over the running of the state—managing key departments, often disregarding ministerial advice, and accountable only to the chief executive (Khasru 1998).

On a different plank, political pressure on important functionaries restraining them from performing their officially sanctioned duties has hit at the heart of bureaucrats' time-honored role of objectively pursuing administrative rationalism, regardless of their political orientation. By forcing them to depart from prescribed practice (for an illustration, see *The Daily Star*, 16 February and 6 May 1998), politicians deaccentuate bureaucratic ethics and make a mockery of the notions of accountability, a vital component of democratic governance.

VI. CONCLUSION

The public bureaucracy in Bangladesh is entrapped in parochial individual and group-centered politics. This politics has both an internal and an external dimension. The internal dimension includes those aspects of bureaucratic politics that are pursued by bureaucrats at the microlevel, that is, when they interact with one another either individually or as a group. Here both the protagonists and antagonists are bureaucrats fighting among themselves to maintain their supremacy within the bureaucratic system. The factionalism of yesteryear, based on the politics of "patriotism," has been replaced by a much more intense power- and career-centered intrabureaucracy strife fuelled by intemperate ruling-party interference.

Generalist civil servants have all along fought specialists/functionalists to maintain their dominant position in the public administration of the country, and they have been by and large successful in their efforts. This success can be attributed to a number of factors: an administrative system that is still immersed in traditions; the paternalistic attitude of civil servants performing general administrative functions with wide-ranging power and authority; slow growth and development of democratic traditions due to the infirmity of politicians and the nondevelopment of political institutions due to two military takeovers of state power; and, last but not least, the ramifications of a malevolent military-bureaucracy alliance which enlarged bureaucratic power. A crucial factor that has contributed to the generalist bureaucracy's hold over the civil service even in the face of continuing pressure from their adversaries is the determined leadership provided by some of its senior members who had learned the trade of state management while serving in the erstwhile Pakistani bureaucracy before independence.

The external dimension of bureaucratic politics concerns civil servants' involvement in state politics, which is sometimes direct and conspicuous. In the context of Bangladesh, this type of involvement has been the result of a combination of factors: alienation of groups either opposed to or indifferent to ruling party sentiments, politicization of the higher ranks of the administration, and considerable bureaucratic input in the "civilianization" process of military regimes. The reasons for such involvement, however, have differed regimewise: sometimes the lead came from the other side, and in others, bureaucrats themselves took the initiative. Nevertheless, because of such involvement the political role of bureaucrats has overshadowed their publicly accepted role as neutral, nonpartisan career civil servants.

Neutrality has lost its relevance in the emerging politics-bureaucracy interface. With the ascendancy of the bureaucracy in the business of government, especially in policy making and implementation, it would be naive to assume its higher echelons, if not the entirety of the civil service, to be oblivious to partisan concerns. A bureaucracy unresponsive to the policies of a democratically elected political regime is useless to society and makes a derison of democracy itself, but for the long-term good and to satisfy the majority of the people it cannot afford to be parochial and partisan in its pursuits. If the politics of bureaucracy hurts society in general, it is indeed a problem.

ENDNOTES

1. The people of Bangladesh are Bengalees by ethnic origin. They speak Bangla, derived from Sanskrit, and have a distinct cultural makeup that make them different from the people of (West) Pakistan.
2. At independence there were no Bengalee women representatives in the CSP.

REFERENCES

Aberbach, J., Putnam, R., and Rockman, B. (1981). *Bureaucrats and Politicians in Western Democracies.* Cambridge, MA: Harvard University Press

Ahamed, E. (1989). Dominant bureaucratic elites in Bangladesh. In M.M. Khan and H.M. Zafarullah (eds.), *Politics and Bureaucracy in a New Nation*: *Bangladesh.* Dhaka: Center for Administrative Studies.

Ahmed, N. (1996). The second BNP government in Bangladesh: an appraisal. *Asian Profile 24*(3), 253–265

Anisuzzaman, M. (1986). Administrative culture in Bangladesh: the public-bureaucrat phenomenon. In

M.M. Khan and S.A. Husain (eds.), *Bangladesh Studies: Politics, Administration, Rural Development and Foreign Policy.* Dhaka: Centre for Administrative Studies.

Baqi, A. (1997). Bangladesh bank reels under finance ministry. *Dhaka Courier* 7 November

BBS. (1997). *1996 Statistical Yearbook of Bangladesh.* Dhaka: Bangladesh Bureau of Statistics.

Campbell, C., and Szablowski, G. (1979). *The Superbureaucrats: Structure and Behavior in Central Agencies.* Toronto: Macmillan

Daily Star, The (Internet edition). National daily published in Bangladesh.

GOB (Government of the People's Republic of Bangladesh). (1985). *Civil Employees of the Government of Bangladesh.* Dhaka: Ministry of Establishment, Statistics and Research Branch

GOB. (1996). *Rules of Business.* Dhaka: Cabinet Division, President's Secretariat.

GOB. (1979). *The Government Servants Conduct Rules.* Dhaka: Government Press

Holiday (Internet edition). National weekly published in Bangladesh.

Independent, The. National daily published in Bangladesh

Jahan, R. (1972). *Pakistan: Failure in National Integration.* New York: Columbia University Press.

Jain, R.B. (1989). Bureaucratic politics in the third world: some reflections. In Jain, R.B. (ed.), *Bureaucratic Politics in the Third World.* New Delhi: Gitanjali Publishing House

Khan, M.M. (1980). *Bureaucratic Self-Preservation: Failure of Major Administrative Reform Efforts in the Civil Service of Pakistan.* Dhaka: University of Dhaka.

Khan, M.M. (1979). Civil service of Pakistan as an institution: reasons for resistance to change. *Indian Political Science Review, 13,* 133–153

Khan, M.M. (1989). Resistance to administrative reform in Bangladesh, 1972–1987. *Public Administration and Development, 9,* 301–314.

Khan, M.M., and Zafarullah, H. (1982a). Administrative reform and bureaucratic intransigence in Bangladesh. In G.E. Caiden and H. Siedentopf (eds.), *Strategies for Administrative Reform.* Lexington, MA: Lexington Books

Khan, M.M., and Zafarullah, H. (1982b). Public bureaucracy in Bangladesh. In K.K. Tummala (ed.), *Administrative Systems Abroad.* Washington: University Press of America.

Khasru, A. (1998). Bureaucrats' bonanza. *Holiday,* 23 March

Khasru, A. (1997). Ministerial fights over ADP. *Holiday,* 1 December.

LaPorte, R. Jr. (1972). Pakistan in 1971: disintegration of a nation. *Asian Survey, 12,* 97–108

Maniruzzaman, T. (1971). *The Politics of Development: The Case of Pakistan, 1947–1958.* Dhaka: Green Book House.

Maniruzzman, T. (1992). The fall of the military dictator. *Pacific Affairs, 65*(2), 203–224

Misra, B.B. (1970). *The Administrative History of India 1834–1947.* Bombay: Oxford University Press.

Morris-Jones, W.H. (1972). Pakistan: post-mortem and the roots of Bangladesh. *Political Quarterly, 18,* 187–200

Peters, B. (1995). *The Politics of Bureaucracy.* New York: Longman.

Rashiduzzaman, M. (1997). Political unrest and democracy in Bangladesh. *Asian Survey, 37*(3), 254–268

Riggs, F.W. (1969). The structures of government and administrative reform. In R. Braibanti (ed.), *Political and Administrative Development.* Durham, NC: Duke University Press.

Riggs, F.W. (1964). *Administration in Developing Countries.* Boston: Houghton-Mifflin

Self, P. (1972). *Administrative Theories and Politics.* London: George Allen and Unwin.

Siddiqui, K. (1996). *Towards Good Governance in Bangladesh.* Dhaka: University Press Limited

Smith, B. (1996). *Understanding Third World Politics.* Bloomington: Indiana University Press.

Ståhlberg, K. (1987). The politicization of public administration: notes on the concept, causes and consequences. *International Review of Administrative Sciences, 53,* 363–382

Turner, M. and Hulme, D. (1997). *Governance, Administration and Development.* London: Macmillan.

UNDP. (1993). *Report on Public Administration Sector Study in Bangladesh.* Dhaka: United Nations Development Programme

World Bank. (1996). *Government That Works.* Dhaka: World Bank.

Zafarullah, H. (1998). National administration in Bangladesh: an analysis of organizational arrangements and operating methods. *Asian Journal of Public Administration, 20*(1)

Zafarullah, H. (1987). Public administration in the first decade of Bangladesh. *Asian Survey, 27*(4), 459–476.

Zafarullah, H. (1996). Toward good governance in Bangladesh: external intervention, bureaucratic inertia and political inaction. In M. Alauddin and S. Hasan (eds.), *Bangladesh: Economy People and the Environment*. Brisbane: University of Queensland

Zafarullah, H., and Khan, M.M. (1983). Staffing the higher civil services in Bangladesh: an analysis of recruitment and selection processes. *Public Administration and Development*, *3*, 121–134.

Zafarullah, H., Khan, M.M., and Habibur Rahman, M. (1997). Civil service systems: Bangladesh. Paper presented at the Conference of the Consortium on Comparative Civil Service Systems, Indiana University, Bloomington.

70

Bureaucratization of the Arab World

Incompatible Influences

Jamil E. Jreisat   *Department of Government and International Affairs, Public Administration Program, University of South Florida, Tampa, Florida*

I.   INTRODUCTION

The Arab world is a vast and complex region stretching over southwest Asia and North Africa. Despite the many unifying features that tie the Arab people together, the Arab world is politically fragmented into 21 separate political entities; some of them are ministates with fewer than 2 million citizens. The Arab people have common cultural attributes and values strengthened by common language and religion and stimulated by shared history and collective aspirations. While imperial domination of the Arab world has officially ended, imperial designs and ambitions to control the region continue. Foreign military presence and a considerable influence over policies of certain countries are widely recognized by the Arab people as foreign threats to their lands, sovereignty, and natural resources, particularly oil.

Variations also permeate in geography, politics, economic growth, and social development. In recent years, the region's diversity has become more visible in terms of administrative capacity, organizational sophistication, and citizens' involvement in governance. Vast differences prevail as well in levels of urbanization, literacy, per-capita income, and foreign debt (see Table 1).

During the second half of the 20th century, Arab countries, and most developing countries, pursued a path of development through comprehensive central plans that incorporated policies, projects, and programs formulated by the national governments. These development plans also required the creation of numerous organizational structures to implement proposed policies and objectives. Always, public administration played a central role in the Arab national development. Indeed, it is repeatedly argued that administrative development is a prerequisite of national development (Al-Tayeb 1986; Aba-Al-Khail 1986; El-Fathaly and Chackerian 1983:194). Not surprisingly, therefore, initiating organizations to accomplish the central plans became a common practice. Institutes of public administration, various academic programs in universities focusing on the public sector, training programs for employees, and contracts with foreign consultants—all were associated with developmental programs in the Arab states. Various technical-assistance and financing agreements were concluded between these countries and the World Bank, the United Nations, and several other industrial countries.

After several decades of commitment of resources, Arab states have received mixed reviews of what has been accomplished in terms of comprehensive development or administrative change.

Table 1   The Arab World: Basic Indicators

	Population (millions)	Per capita GNP ($–1995)	External pub. debts (Billions $)	External pub. debt (% of GNP)
Low-income countries				
Somalia*	6.0	290	2.29	236.9
Sudan[†]	26.0	—	—	—
Middle income				
Mauritania	2.3	460	2.46	243.3
Yemen Arab Republic	15.3	260	6.20	155.2
Morocco	26.6	1,110	22.14	71.0
Egypt	57.8	790	34.01	73.3
Tunisia	9.0	1,820	9.90	57.3
Jordan	4.2	1,510	7.94	126.2
Syria	14.1	1,120	21.30	134.8
Lebanon	4.0	2,660	2.96	25.5
Upper middle income				
Algeria	28.0	1,600	32.6	83.1
Oman	2.2	4,820	3.10	29.5
Iraq[†]	18.0	—	—	—
Oil exporters				
Libya	4.0	5,460	—	—
Saudi Arabia	19.0	7,040	—	—
Kuwait	1.7	17,390	—	—
United Arab Emirates	1.7	17,400	—	—
United States (for comparison)	263.1	26,930		

Source: World Bank, *World Development Report 1997* (pp. 214–215, 246–247; three other member states of the Arab League are not listed: Bahrain, Qatar, and Palestine: classification of countries is that of the World Bank).
*Numbers from 1987 World Bank statistics.
[†]Estimates for 1998.

Actually, appraisals of administrative reform in most Arab states reveal unimpressive results. A poor implementation record is attributed, in part, to incongruities of methods and objectives of reform as well as to formidable political obstacles (Jreisat 1997:223–231, 1988:85). Other assessments are even more negative, if not discouraging. One such assessment concludes that bureaucratic performance in several Arab countries (Egypt, Saudi Arabia, and Sudan) offers "little hope that Middle Eastern bureaucracies will serve as positive forces of economic and social development in the region" (Palmer et al. 1987:241). The list of bureaucratic deficiencies incorporates adjectives such as "lethargic, apathetic, arrogant, corrupt, insensitive to the masses, non-innovative, venal and incompetent" (Palmer et al. 1987:241).

Nonetheless, the literature reflects no agreement on cause and effect of bureaucratic ills in the Arab world. Research in comparative administration and comparative development has not produced anything resembling a consensus on what tried-and-tested frameworks are appropriate to carry out analysis, evaluation, and comparison. Some intriguing research orientations, deriving from differing intellectual bases, promise explanatory concepts and an organizing power of data. Despite their common assumptions and some overlapping, these perspectives have attracted various disciplinary research interests, methodologies, and prescriptive conclusions (Honadle and Rosengard 1983).

First is the cultural approach that recognizes culture as determinant of behavioral patterns, which thus shape managerial practices and values. Second is the political-context approach that concentrates on the relationships between political regimes and administrative systems as the key to understanding and to changing public bureaucracies.

II. CULTURE AND ADMINISTRATION

This research tradition is based on the premise that culture, however defined, influences organizations through societal structures such as laws and political systems and through the values, attitudes, behavior, goals, and preferences of participants—citizens, employees, and especially managers (Adler et al. 1986:299). Too many variations of this perspective exist in the literature to permit sufficient review here. Hofstede's (1993) framework, however, provides an example of the school that considers management skills to be culturally specific: a management technique or philosophy that is appropriate in one national culture is not necessarily appropriate in another. Hofstede claims (1993:81) that "there are no such things as universal management theories."

The perception of culture "as the collective mental programming of the mind which distinguishes the members of one human group from another" (Hofstede 1980:21) leads to a sort of cultural determinism where every managerial act or decision is the inevitable consequence of its cultural antecedents. Culture, in Hofstede's meaning of collective mental programming, is difficult to change; it is "what personality to an individual" (1980:21). These conclusions, perhaps overdrawn, consign modernization efforts to failure unless such efforts are in the images of existing cultural norms of the society.

The culture school is open to serious criticisms; Honadle and Rosengard (1983:5) call it "little more than a subtle and sophisticated form of ethnic stereotyping that moves blame for failure off the shoulders of donors and reformers and onto the backs of Third World people." The criticism may not be far-fetched. Executives of multinational corporations viewing expansion in markets of Islamic countries frequently are warned: Be aware of the "Muslim way" of doing things—which cements the idea that managerial attitudes and skills necessary for successful operations in the Muslim world are different from those needed in Europe or America (Wright 1981).

While there is ample evidence of reductionism in Hofstede's thesis, particularly when applied in single-culture studies, his approach remains unique for its organizing power and for its measurement effort. His framework is briefly presented here with an attempt to relate its elements to the Arab countries. Hofstede reduces differences among countries to four underlying value dimensions along which the countries could be positioned. The dimensions represent elements of common structure in the cultural systems. The position of a country on each of the four dimensions is indicated by a score on a range representing the different responses to the four issues, as found in a survey of 116,000 people in 50 countries (Hofstede 1980:83).

A. Collectivism Versus Individualism

Collectivism is a preference for a tightly knit social framework in which individuals can expect their relatives, clan, or other "in-group" to look after them in exchange for unquestioning loyalty. In contrast, individualism refers to a loosely knit social framework wherein individuals are supposed to take care of themselves. On the index measuring individualism from zero to 100, the Arab countries included in the study as a group (Egypt, Iraq, Kuwait, Lebanon, Libya, Saudi Arabia, and United Arab Emirates) are ranked 38. This ranking indicates low individualism and high collectivism in these systems.

Collectivism usually breeds particularistic forms of policy making and decision making processes; therefore "collectivism" becomes a managerial euphemism for favoritism and nepotism in public organizations. Under such conditions, universal rules of merit, equality, and concern for administrative performance are overridden by obligations to family and loyalty to kin group (Ali 1987; Nakib and Palmer 1976; Altuhaih and Fleet 1978; Nyrop 1980). In the Arab world, Nydell (1987:37) points out that "a manager or official is always willing to reconsider a decision, regulation, or problem in view of someone's personal situation. Any regulation can be modified or avoided by someone with enough persuasive influence, particularly if the request is justified on the grounds of unusual personal need."

B. Power Distance

This refers to the acceptance of power in institutions and organizations and how a society handles whatever inequalities occur. People in large power-distance societies accept a hierarchical order more readily than those in a small power-distance society, who strive for equalization and demand justification for power inequalities.

Arab countries included in this study rank near the top (80 on the index, or 44–45 among the 50 countries) in terms of power distance. The more pronounced the inequality of power in the organization, the greater support is given the notion of existing dominant "bureaucratic elites" in Arab systems of government who constitute a privileged class and perpetrate social inequality and stratification (Ayubi 1980) as they concentrate power in their hands (Palmer et al. 1987)

C. Uncertainty Avoidance

Strong uncertainty-avoidance societies maintain rigid codes of belief and behavior and are intolerant toward deviant persons and ideas. This has consequences for the way people build their institutions and organizations.

The Arab states included in this study ranked 68 on the uncertainty avoidance index. Many of the Arab bureaucracies are excessively formalized and codified, with a tendency toward over-centralization. One effect perhaps is the low level of innovativeness in these administrative systems, frequently reported in comparative and development literature (Al-Nimir and Palmer 1974, 1982; Wahba 1983; Nyrop 1980).

The weak capacity for innovation of the Arab bureaucracy is coupled with clerkism in administration. Clerkism is a behavioral trait evidenced in the administrator's preoccupation with small and routine matters to the detriment of overall policies of the organization and in isolation from environmental reality. Clerkism is the phenomenon of an individual in a leadership position operating with the mentality and perspective of a clerk unmindful of the larger questions. Such attitudes have been fostered by and institutionalized during colonial administrations, L. Pye (1969:410) points out; they demanded infinite attention to detail and inhibition of imagination, achieving a remarkable uniformity of the product in the colonies even when major cultural differences prevailed.

D. Masculinity Versus Femininity

Masculinity is measured in terms of preference in society for achievement, heroism, assertiveness, and material success. The opposite, femininity, stands for preference for relationships, modesty, caring for the weak and the quality of life. Surprisingly, considering stereotypes in the West, the Arab countries included in Hofstede's study ranked about in the middle on the index (53). They are exceeded by the United States (62), West Germany (66), and Venezuela (73).

On the status of women in the Arab world, Nydell (1987:53) points out that the degree to which women have been integrated in the workforce varies widely among the countries. In Lebanon, Jordan, Syria, and Egypt, educated women are very active at all levels of society. In Saudi Arabia, Yemen, and the Gulf states, few women have jobs outside the home despite strong support in many quarters for women's education. Consequently, in addition to the issue of equality, some of these societies are deprived of the energies of a major segment of the population in implementing national development policies.

In conclusion, the assumption that culture determines organizational and managerial processes of a society is an overstatement of contextual relationships. Certainly, these relationships are significant but they are not *determining* the bureaucratic structures and functions in the society. In addition to criticisms of the cultural perspective (stated above), culture remains a fluid concept. It is constantly changing through education and information; it is not a monolithic source of influence. In fact, many cultures may coexist in one society. Thus, the extent and the efficacy of cultural norms in shaping managerial processes remain an empirical relationship to be established rather than assumed.

III. POLITICS AND BUREAUCRACY

Cross-national comparisons of public administration have always been concerned with the political context of public organizations. The attainment of conceptual consistency in studying or analyzing the administrative-political relationships has been a subject of articulation since Woodrow Wilson's famous pronouncement in 1887 that administration is not politics, since each is a distinct field of study and learning. Consistent with this conceptualization is Max Weber's view of differing administrative practices prevailing within each of the traditional, charismatic, and legal-rational political orders. Thus, bureaucracy is the form and the process for the functioning of "modern officialdom" in the legal-rational system of authority found in the capitalist-democratic Western systems (Gerth and Mills 1958:196–244).

More recent authors articulated frameworks, mostly as typologies, that compare political regimes and their relationships with other institutions in the society, particularly the bureaucracy. One of these frameworks has been suggested by Esman (1966:71). He considers three political elements as crucial in the processes of nation building and socioeconomic development: (1) a governing elite that moves and guides the modernizing process; (2) a doctrine that legitimizes (in terms of programmed action) the norms, priorities, instruments, and strategies of the governing elites; and (3) a series of instruments through which commitments to action are translated into operating programs. The administrative system is one of those facilitating instruments, along with political organizations, associated interest groups, and mass media. Even when the administrative system is considered in this analysis as an indispensable instrument through which modern governing elites carry out policy, the subordinate position of administration in the political order is unambiguous.

Based on certain common structural and behavioral characteristics, Esman (1966:87) defines five regime types: (1) conservative oligarchies, (2) competitive interest-oriented party systems, (3) dominant mass-party systems, (4) authoritarian military reformers, and (5) Communist totalitarians. The majority of the regimes functioning in developing countries can be placed in one of these types. Not all these regime types are equally capable of organizing and energizing their developing societies to accomplish the developmental tasks, however. The structures, values, power configurations, and styles unique to each regime profoundly affect their capabilities.

Students of comparative politics and development have been compiling and correlating data on a large number of variables for cross-national comparisons and suggesting regime typologies that often are similar and informative about politics and administrative interactions within the larger environment but less valuable in specifying or producing administrative capabilities or standards of performance. In this connection, a germane view is how one conceives the role of bureaucracy and its impact on the development of political systems in developing countries. Riggs (1963) is concerned about the balance between political institutions making policy and bureaucratic structures implementing policy. He sees premature and rapid expansion of bureaucracy creating imbalance and inhibiting political development. Others recognize the problem of imbalance but argue that bureaucracy seems the only hope for developing societies for achieving economic development. Until the desired equilibrium between bureaucratic power and political control is attained, bureaucracy remains the principal initiator of change (La Palombara 1971; Braibanti 1971; Heady 1971).

Similarly, administrative systems in Arab countries cannot be separated from their compelling political contexts. Enormous powers in the hands of kings, presidents, and prime ministers are uniformly centralized, excessive, and mostly unchecked. Consequently, the bureaucratic system acts as the regime's servant rather than as a source of independent professional decision making. Generalizations from what appear to be asymmetrical relationships, however, are misleading and may obscure a highly complex system of interactions that are mutually exploitative and legitimizing. Critics of bureaucracy in the Arab states tend to exaggerate its self-serving tendencies, its influences in shaping societal politics, and its evolution to become a "new privileged class" (Ayubi 1980:450, 461).

But bureaucracy often is blamed for failures not totally of its own or within its domain, such as the lack of progress in areas of political participation or enhancing citizens' role in governing. Serving such objectives in the Arab state would place bureaucracy in contradiction with the wills and desires of the political leaders who rule autocratically and pack government senior posts with relatives and loyalists instead of professionals with neutral competencies. The evaluation needed, therefore, is against performance-based criteria. The deficiency of bureaucracy has to be determined empirically rather than through stereotypical generalizations. Whether bureaucracy is overpowering as in Egypt, overstaffed as in Saudi Arabia and Kuwait, or ill trained as in most Arab states, performance is the most reliable determiner of its quality and worth. Performance of bureaucracy includes rendering general public services and meeting obligations in the area of national development. In this regard, as Esman (1991:145) points out, politics is seen "as less benign and much more threatening" to managerial achievement. Clearly, in managing public policies, Arab leaders have not excelled in making rational choices, in effective use of public resources, or in their deference to citizens' rights and freedoms.

While the cultural and political context frameworks are helpful in explaining mostly environmental influences on bureaucracy, the compelling question remains, What do we learn about bureaucracies of the Arab world through these frameworks? Or more appropriately, What do we want to know about them and why?

The cultural framework underlines ecological factors that influence administrative behavior and action. We find, for example, the particularistic orientation of decision makers in Arab states rooted in the value placed on loyalty to kinfolk and other members of the collectivity to which the individual belongs. Hence, widespread nepotism in public service is not treated as corruption, and frequently there are no attempts to hide it. Such attitudes and practices create far-reaching implications for the prospects of public administration reform.

The political context of Arab regimes is largely dominated by concerns for survival of the political leader and his ruling cohorts. As a result, relations with outside powers have often been a function of inter-Arab regime feuds or schemes for sustaining or augmenting the powers of a ruler or his dynasty. An important factor in these power contests for survival has always been a perpetual search for allies within the Arab states as well as for protection by a dominant foreign power. Thus, major public policy decisions are divorced from citizens needs, demands, or preferences.

Instead of being representative, public policies of the regime primarily strive to accommodate objectives of satisfying external powers that safeguard the regime and preserving the domestic oligarchy that ensures regime's durability. Consequences to public administration are direct and many: (1) public policies generally lack public support; (2) governing the political state continues to be mainly based on factors of political loyalty, patronage, and wholesale corruption rather than professional competence; (3) overall, administrative reform implementation has been rendered ineffectual, autocratic, and marginal (Jreisat 1997:226).

IV. RECONCILING INCOMPATIBILITIES

Bureaucracy in the Arab world, as elsewhere in developing countries, suffers many problems and shortcomings. Arab bureaucracies are likely to be overstaffed with underskilled employees. Public employees are habitually formalistic and rigid in their application of the rules. Not surprising, therefore, administrative reform has been claimed by every Arab state while competent implementation is the glory of none. Is lack of fundamental administrative change caused by ills inherent in the bureaucratic model itself (Thompson 1964:100) or that bureaucracy is hobbled by forces in its environment, particularly the political system? Bureaucracy, the critics claim, is unfit to handle the complex tasks of socioeconomic change in Arab countries because it tends to form a new privileged class, and it completely bureaucratizes politics (Ayubi 1980; Waterbury 1983; Palmer et al. 1987).

But the ills of bureaucracy are not considered inevitable side effects or inherent traits of the bureaucratic model itself. As C. Perrow (1979:7) points out, "bureaucracy is a form of organization superior to all others we know or can hope to afford." In its original formulation, the bureaucratic model provides for reliance upon expertise and skills and for equal treatment of all employees. To attain uniformity in its decisions, bureaucracy keeps records and data on work and output as it sets and enforces rules and regulations that serve legitimate organizational goals. Thus, bureaucracy, as in common wisdom, is supposed to be an instrument of managerial precision, promptness, and efficiency, despite an opposite view held by the public (Jacoby 1973:157).

Why, then, do Arab bureaucracies have immense policy failings and grossly deficient performances? Clearly, there is no one definite explanation. However, over the years, several deep-rooted factors have compounded the negative effects that decreased overall outcomes of bureaucratic actions. These are some of the relevant factors:

1.   The growth of governmental structures to implement development policies and programs resulted in overstaffing of public organizations so that they can meet the requirements of their expanded new roles. The abrupt addition of many inexperienced and ill-trained new recruits contributed to larger government but not necessarily to more competent public management. Moreover, poorly defined and poorly articulated functions and responsibilities permeated the employment hierarchy. Thus, in a significant way, economic and social trends have had disruptive effects on public organizations.

2.   Certain traditional values, when rigidly practiced, tended to create incompatibilities with elements of the rational and impersonal characteristics of bureaucratic management. The Arab culture is described as emphasizing "social solidarity, family loyalty, dominance of authority and rectitude" (Ali 1987:97). As indicated earlier in applying Hofstede's model, the Arab societies ranked high on the indexes of cultural collectivism, power distance, and uncertainty avoidance. Consequently, these cultural norms generate attitudes, values, and customs inconsistent with the impersonal and uniform values of bureaucracy. This is why political leaders are able to permissively subordinate universal rules of bureaucracy to particularistic considerations in the conduct of public affairs.

3.   Arab regimes lag behind the profound changes their societies are undergoing. Instead of managing the transition, muddled political processes have failed to provide meaningful institutionalized participation (Hudson 1977:389). Incumbent regimes have not developed clear, consistent national objectives with worthy strategies to achieve them. Traditional bases of authority have weakened or become inappropriate to the functions of the modern state. Tribal, religious, ethnic, or regional interests cannot substitute for public interest as legitimizing foundations of political actions. At the same time, political leaders grew mistrustful of opposition and regularly increased concentration of powers in their hands, augmenting regime authoritarianism and further weakening public participation in governing. In reaction, Arab bureaucracies have substituted routine work, self-serving behavior, and survival techniques to risk-taking management. Such bureaucratic behavior has been a major obstacle to numerous campaigns for administrative reform, generally decreed by the political leaders. Bureaucrats continued to increase in numbers and learned to patronize and endure conflicting pressures of politics on one side and demands of duty on the other. Thus, avoidance of responsibility, apathy, or inaction became among the survival techniques frequently employed by bureaucrats. No wonder citizens have been generally suspicious and disdainful of public authority, without differentiating between the political and the administrative sides.

4.   The outcomes of administrative development initiatives in the Arab world at large are not commensurate with the extensive investments in institutions and programs designed to build needed administrative capacities. So far, advanced academic education as well as practical training in modern management have made only a small difference in building institutional capacities, solving chronic managerial problems, or responding to pressing managerial needs. Research output is consistently lacking in empirical substance or conceptual sophistication. Development organizations established to provide technical assistance, training, and research for individual countries or for all the Arab states are torn by internal feuds, bursts of poor leadership, and lack of resources. The task of generating administrative knowledge and providing technical assistance is still largely left to foreign consultants, institutions, and publications. Arab developmental institutions simply have not developed sufficiently from within to be able to shoulder the responsibilities thrust upon them.

These and related matters indicate that transformation of the functions of the state requires reconciling many conflicting values and incongruities. Foremost is the issue of control. The Arab central governments have not leaned the lesson of sharing responsibility and control with citizens, local authorities, or the private sector. Nor have these systems even begun to effectively employ modern notions of accountability in managing the state. One can confidently argue that the central government will continue to retain functions such as overall planning, policy formulation, information guidance, organizational coordination, and monitoring. But purely economic responsibilities have to be shared with the private sector and intermediate social organizations in order to stimulate investment of private capital and to apply efficient market mechanisms of production and service. This has to evolve along with processes of gradually converting economic public organizations to authoritative macroregulatory departments with unified functions (IIAS 1997:138).

A reformist strategic plan would have to examine and redesign the relationships with local authorities to enhance their functions and to clarify questions of accountability. Local authorities have not been activated to share in the responsibilities of developing their communities mainly because of dominance by the central government. Many aspects of the relationships between central and local authorities have to be reconsidered. This includes the payment transfer systems and clearer definition of respective powers of central and local governments over finance and decision making in general.

Finally, accountability remains an illusive part of the administrative problem of the Arab state, causing greater inefficiency instead of being a part of the solution. Established forms of accountability have often been portrayed as bureaucratic constraints which limited managerial freedom through procedural rigidity and formalism in operations. Current management reforms are forcing a reassessment of ideas about accountability in government. The traditional reliance on hierarchial forms of accountability had operated to restrict managerial discretion and to enforce procedural compliance rather than to focus attention on results that policies were supposed to achieve (IIAS 1997:73). Today, management reform emphasizes accountability that balances legitimate public goals and functions of public managers toward the organization as well as to the public at large. Administrative reforms will accomplish very little if the processes of accountability in public decision making remain unaffected.

V. CONCLUSION

Analysis of the cultural and political contexts of administration in the Arab societies produces insights about differences and similarities of the overall political and administrative systems, but these have limited impact on the operational dimensions of management. At the same time, all tinkering with managerial problems and issues has a common goal: to improve performance by building administrative capacity for action and reforming dysfunctional administrative structures and behaviors. Thus, descriptive analyses, while necessary to understand the global issues of management and underline relevant nonmanagerial contextual influences, are insufficient for action-oriented reformist initiatives.

Cultural and political analyses indicate that fundamental administrative change is not attained through occasional, precipitous campaigns for reforming one administrative aspect or another. Successful efforts have to be realistically linked to a reliable diagnosis of the problems and the weaknesses of organizational performance, and not simply as perceived at the political level. In brief, it is doubtful that administrative change (reform) will attain its objectives as long as such change (1) is conceived and directed for political ends rather than administrative, professional ones, (2) does not lead to alterations or modifications of regime's operative methods, and (3) continues to exclude inputs from employees and affected citizens from the process.

Administrative reform efforts are continuous. They seek to achieve significant improvement in the performance of agencies through fundamental and planned changes in organizational structure, employee behavior, and the environments. Thus, to attain desired objectives, reform has to be comprehensive, guided by broad principles, and linked to specific strategies that have operational thrust as integral parts. Applying developmental policies in the Arab world—socioeconomic as well as administrative—to achieve desired results requires substantial revisions of conventional methods, providing particular attention to these propositions:

1. Objective methods of research should define and confirm administrative problems rather than political expediency.
2. Broader sources of input to be procured from employees and citizens.
3. Ethical and professional aspects of public service to be accorded higher priority in reform initiatives, and to be emphasized from a human-resource developmental perspective and not only through the usual control and control measures.
4. Political interference in technical-managerial measures to be kept at a minimum.

REFERENCES

Aba-al-Khail, M. (1986). The role of administrative reform in facing economic changes. Speech delivered at the 20th International Congress of Administrative Sciences, Amman Jordan

Adler, N.J. (1986). *International Dimensions of Organizational Behavior.* Boston: Kent Publishing.

Adler, N.J., Doktor, R., and Redding, S.G. (1984). From the Atlantic to the Pacific century: cross-cultural management reviewed. *Yearly Review of Management of the Journal of Management, 122*:295–317

Ari, A. (1987). The Arab executive: a study in values and work orientation. *American-Arab Affairs 19*:94–100.

Al-Nimir, S., and Palmer, M. (1982). Bureaucracy and developments in Saudi Arabia. *Public Administration and Development, 2*(1):93–104

Al-Tayeb, H.E. (1986). Administrative reform in the Arab Wold. Unpublished paper, in Arabic, February 1986.

Altuhaih, S., and Fleet, D.V. (1978). Kuwait management: a study of selected aspects. *Management International Review, 18*(1):13–22

Ayubi, N.M. (1980). *Bureaucracy and Politics in Contemporary Egypt.* London: Ithaca Press.

Braibanti, R. (1971). Administrative reform in the context of political growth. In F.W. Riggs (ed.), *Frontiers of Development Administration*, 227–246. Durham, NC: Duke University Press

El-Fathaly, O., and Chackerian, R. (1983). Administration: the forgotten issue in Arab development. In I. Ibrahin (ed.), *Arab Resources: The Transformation of a Society*, 193–209. London: Croom Helm

Esman, M.J. (1991). *Management Dimension of Development.* West Hartford, CT: Kumarian Press.

Esman, M.J. (1966). The politics of development administration. In J.D. Montgomery and W.J. Siffin (eds.), *Approaches to Development: Politics, Administration and Change.* New York: McGraw-Hill

Gerth, H.H., and Mills, C.W., eds. (1958). *From Max Weber: Essays in Sociology.* New York: Oxford University Press.

Heady, F. (1970). Bureaucracies in developing countries. In F.W. Riggs (ed.), *Frontiers of Development Administration*, 459–485. Durham, NC: Duke University Press

Hofstede, G. (1993). Cultural constraints in management theories. *Academy of Management Executive, 7*(1).

Hofstede, G. (1980). *Culture's Consequences: International Differences in Work-Related Values.* Beverly Hills, CA: Sage

Honadle, G.H., and Rosengard, J.K. (1983). Politics versus culture: an assessment of 14 mini-cases of management improvement in developing countries. Unpublished paper presented at the National Conference of ASPA, New York.

International Institute of Administrative Sciences (IIAS). (1997). *New Challenges for Public Administration in the Twenty-First Century.* Brussels: IIAS

Jacoby, H. (1973). *The Bureaucratization of the World* (trans. E. Kanes). Los Angeles: University of California Press.

Jreisat, J.E. (1997). *Politics Without Process: Administering Development in the Arab World.* Boulder, CO: Lynne Reinner

Jreisat, J.E. (1988). Administrative reform in developing countries: a comparative perspective. *Public Administration and Development, 8*(1):85–97.

Jreisat, J.E. (1986). Introduction. In J.E. Jreisat and Z.R. Ghosheh (eds.), *Administration and Development in the Arab World.* New York: Garland

La Palombara, J. (1971). Alternative strategies for developing administrative capabilities in emerging nations. In F.W. Riggs (ed.), *Frontiers of Development Administration*, 171–226. Durham, NC: Duke University Press.

Nakib, K., and Palmer, M. (1976). Traditionalism and change among Lebanese bureaucrats. *International Review of Administrative Sciences, XLII*(1):15–22

Nydell, M.K. (1987). *Understanding Arabs.* Yarmouth: Intercultural Press.

Palmer, M., Al-Hegelan, A.R., Abdulrahman, M.B., Leila, A., and Yassin, E.S. (1987). Bureaucratic rigidity and economic development in the Middle East: a study of Egypt, the Sudan and Saudi Arabia. *International Review of Administrative Sciences, 53*:241–257

Perrow, C. (1979). *Complex Organizations: A Critical Essay.* Glenview, IL: Scott, Foreman.

Pye, L.W. (1969). Bureaucratic development and the psychology of institutionalization. In R. Braibanti (ed.), *Political and Administrative Development.* Durham, NC: Duke University Press

Riggs, F.W. (1963). Bureaucrats and political development: a paradoxical view. In J. La Palombara (ed.), *Bureaucracy and Political Development*, 120–167. Princeton, NJ: Princeton University Press.

Thompson, V. (1964). Objectives for development administration. *Administrative Science Quarterly, IX*: 91–108

Wahba, M.M. (1983). The Egyptian public sector: the control structure and efficiency considerations. *Public Administration and Development, 3*:27–37.

Waterbury, J. (1983). *The Egypt of Nasser and Sadat.* Princeton, NJ: Princeton University Press

Wright, P. (1981). Organizational behavior in Islamic firms. *Management International Review, 21*(2): 86–94.

71

The State and Bureaucracy

The Turkish Case in Historical Perspective

Metin Heper   *Department of Political Science, Bilkent University, Ankara, Turkey*

I. TURKEY: A POLITY VIRTUALLY SUI GENERIS

When viewed from a comparative perspective, the Ottoman-Turkish polity evinces a "strong state" in a third world context. The Ottoman Empire, the antecedent political formation of the present-day Turkish Republic, had been an "imperial regime," and the system as crystallized during the initial institutionalization pattern (ca. 1300–1600) was a bureaucratic rather than a patrimonial polity.

If after Eisenstadt (1987:175–178) one takes imperial (as well as imperial-feudal) regimes as political systems where center-periphery relationships are characterized by a high level of distinctiveness and autonomy of the centers, the Ottoman polity had been an imperial regime par excellence. In the first place, although it was a "Muslim state," in relative terms, the influence of the religion at least on matters of state was greatly constrained. The temporal power overshadowed the divine one. The Ottoman sultans issued rules and regulations that flouted freely the Islamic precedents (Inalcik 1968–1970:21). Based on the principles of "necessity" and "reason" and summed up by the norm of rationality, a particular outlook was formulated that provided ideals and values for the ruling groups. These ideals and values were inculcated in the military and the civil bureaucracy cadres in the state-run schools and through the roles that these functionaries filled, that is, through organizational socialization (Findley 1982: 158). Called *adab*, this was "a secular and state-oriented tradition" (Findley 1980:9).

Second, in the Ottoman polity one came across a dominant center facing a weak periphery. This was basically due to the fact that the military played a key role in the establishment of the Ottoman Empire. There was an emphasis on purely "political goals" of conquests, territorial expansion, and maintenance of a strategic position in international diplomacy at the expense of an emphasis on the economic strength and expansion of the polity per se through mercantilist policies (such as France and Prussia of the 17th and 18th centuries), let alone an emphasis on the advancement of social groups or the entire population or "society" (such as England of the 18th and 19th centuries).

The types of goals pursued and the success in attaining them helped the Ottoman rulers to maintain their autonomy from the social groups. They obtained ample revenues from war booty. They also forcefully recruited young men from among the non-Muslim families in the conquered areas, converted them to Islam, educated and socialized them through the state-run schools (as already mentioned), employed them as military officials and civil servants, and used them to tax and control the Muslim social groups. These particular arrangements and the lack of a stress on economic goals enabled the rulers to obviate the need to mobilize social groups, and thus to accommodate their political demands; the rulers did not have to grant political territorial rights to the social groups in question. In the process, *Standes* and *parlements* remained alien to the Ottoman scene (Heper 1992).

It follows that not unlike the political experience of continental Western European polities, the Ottomans, too, had a distinctive center, or state, with its own normative system.[1] In the Ottoman case, however, the center was far more autonomous than its European counterparts (Mardin 1969; Heper 1980). The latter were imperial-feudal regimes; the Ottoman polity was an imperial regime. While in continental Europe the normative system of the center including that of the bureaucracy was to some extent interpenetrated by aristocratic and middle-class values (Armstrong 1973:93–103), in the Ottoman Empire the bureaucratic elite were "devoted exclusively to the secular interests of the state" (Inalcik 1964:55); it has been claimed that "they represented no group or class interest, not even their own" (Berkes 1964:62).

It also follows that the Ottoman polity was a bureaucratic polity and not a patrimonial regime if the latter regime is defined, after Eisenstadt (1987:179), as a polity where the center may turn out to be more grandiose than the periphery, but the center is nevertheless structured according to principles that are not greatly different from those prevalent in the periphery. One significant implication of the bureaucratic structuring of the Ottoman polity for the later periods has been that the salience of the state and the high respect for the state had been important dimensions of the Turkish political culture. On this particular point the Turkish political experience has differed sharply from those of many other third world countries. For reasons which we cannot elaborate here,[2] the political actors in many new countries, in particular in those with a colonial background, had been unable to transcend their particularistic orientations and develop a distinct political collective identity. Politics in these countries came to be based primarily on a system of relations linking rulers not with the "public" but only with patrons, associates, clients, supporters, and rivals, who together constituted "the system" (Eisenstadt 1973:14, 49; Heeger 1974:8; Clapham 1986:43, 49, 143).

Given the particular development of the Ottoman-Turkish polity as delineated here, the political and administrative roles that the Ottoman and Turkish bureaucracies have adopted can be placed in perspective if, after Evans et al. (1985), we bring the state "back in" and view it as an alternative mode of political integration and legitimization. The state as conceptualized in this latter approach is a *generalizing* idea. It embodies norms and values formulated by the self-designated "state elite" in the name of general interest. Two complementary characteristics of the state in question derive from its generalizing characteristic: (1) the state is an *integrating* idea: it attempts to unify the disparate elements of society around the norms and values in question; (2) the state is a *legitimating* idea: only that political power that is exercised in line with the said norms and values is legitimate.[3]

The salience in the Ottoman-Turkish political experience of the phenomenon of the state as conceptualized here gave rise to a long-lasting conflict between the "state elite" and the "political elite." For the most part the bureaucratic elite acted, not even doubled, as the state elite.[4] Thus in Turkey the political role of the bureaucracy did not vary, as Heady (1979) and others[5] hypothesized, with the "regime type"; if anything, the reverse was true.

In Turkey democratization of the polity was not an upshot of increased pressures from the weighty social groups; democratization was rather engineered by the state elite themselves. This process was started as part and parcel of defensive modernization strategy of the Ottoman rulers. Its origins go back to the 1860s when the secondary elite *within* the Ottoman bureaucracy wished to participate in the decision-making process. Thus "democratization" of the system was conceived as a means to greater degree of (substantive) rationality on the part of the bureaucratic elite;

these elite aimed at arriving at more intelligent decisions through a clash of ideas. Democratization was not taken as a process that would make possible conciliation of sectional interests.

In the event, the transition to multiparty politics in the 1940s gave rise to a sharp configuration between the state elite and the political elite. The bureaucratic acting as the state elite attempted to carve out a sphere for themselves in which they could act autonomously, and to monitor the activities of the political elite in the area the former left to the latter.

A distinction made at the time by the bureaucratic intelligentsia reflected the division of labor in question. These intelligentsia distinguished "active dynamic politics" (politicians trying to capture political office and *articulating* rather than *aggregating* interests) from "politics in its widest sense" (determination of public policy by the bureaucratic elite on the basis of "rational" criteria). The formula discovered here was the concept of "the requirements of the service [which] could be determined only by the bureaucratic elite." The formula in question was used by the bureaucratic intelligentsia to bolster their attempts to structure a sovereign and autonomous state in the realm of public bureaucracy (Heper 1985a:82). A complementary aspect of politics in Turkey has been that in the eyes of the bureaucratic elite the elected governments were legitimate to the extent to which their activities did not violate the norms and values designated by the bureaucratic elite. All of the three military interventions in Turkey were carried out because the elected governments were perceived as having drifted away from Ataturkism—official ideology clamped upon Turkish polity by the bureaucratic elite (Tachau and Heper 1983).

It is for this reason that, as I have noted elsewhere (Heper 1985b), the dominant (Weberian) paradigm on bureaucracy has been less than satisfactory to explain the political role of the bureaucracy in a country like Turkey because the proponents of the Weberian approach have not entered into an explicit discussion of the role of the state (in the sense it is conceptualized here). Diamant (1970:509–510), for instance, observed that "there is considerable evidence from a variety of developing polities that the nature and form of the legitimacy help shape the organization and functioning of the bureaucracy," but he did not entertain the idea that the state could be an integral part of the "legitimating system." Presthus and Monopoli (1977:176), who even conceived "political culture as well as political structure as a systematic and independent variable that helps explain both the role and ideology of bureaucracies cross-nationality," did not consider the state in conjunction with political culture (Badie and Birnbaum 1983:86–92). Nor did they think that in given cases the impact upon the bureaucracy of the phenomenon of state may be greater than that of the government formed by the elected representatives of the people.

The survey data in Turkey and South Korea showed that the "historical bureaucratic tradition," rather than variations in regime type, may offer the better explanation of the behavior of the public service in some countries, especially where a firmly established tradition of the civil service exists. That study, in which I participated, found that in Turkey, a country considered more polyarchal than South Korea, the bureaucratic elite attributed to themselves a greater degree of substantive rationality (in the Weberian sense) than did their counterparts.[6]

II. OTTOMAN-TURKISH BUREAUCRATS, STATE, AND POLITICS

A. The Ottoman Period (1299–1923)

From the particular perspective suggested here the Ottoman centuries can be divided into three distinct periods. The first period extends from the beginning of the 14th century to the middle of the 16th. The rule during this phase was enlightened despotism, or rule based on carefully delineated state norms. The state was structured in the person of the sultan. The sultan, however, was not a patrimonial ruler. His was not a personal rule, for he was the first servant of the state. At the time, civil servants were expected to be both personally loyal to the sultan and meritorious (Barnett 1964:70). Merit was here conceived in terms of their conformity to the *adab*, that is, the secular and state-oriented, tradition. Theirs were to be substantive rationality; as an extension of the sultan, each official, in his relations with people, was a minisultan himself. As Inalcik (1971:113) noted, "those who were in the service of the sultan or who exercise authority in his name . . . were considered a separate and distinct group above the rest of the population."

From the second part of the 16th up to the 19th century this particular institutionalization pattern underwent significant transformations. The sultans lost their control over the "free-floating resources" and over the polity. In the process, the *adab* tradition of the earlier centuries were eroded. In order to strengthen their claims to absolute authority the sultans increasingly underscored their religious role as caliphs, or the divinely selected and inspired leader of Islam.

As the Ottoman center thus showed characteristics of a patrimonial rather than bureaucratic rule the "meritocracy" tended to be replaced by a system of patronage. Each group within the bureaucracy began to organize itself around one or several ambitious pashas, or higher functionaries. The Ottoman bureaucracy lost its earlier characteristics as the loyal servant of the state; "all state positions, all instruments exercising state-delegated authority" came to be a means for personal gain" (Inalcik 1972:342). Also during this period the local notables gained influence, particularly through their role as tax farmers.

As an integral dimension of the defensive modernization strategy that the Ottomans adapted from the end of the 18th century onward, there were efforts, particularly during the *Tanzimat* (Regulation) period (1839–1876), to reestablish the distinctiveness of the center. Not unlike the rationalist tradition of 18th-century Western Europe, the political conception underlying the *Tanzimat* period was a direct relationship between the state and each of its subjects. There was no place in this particular scheme for a privileged local notable class, not even for their role as intermediaries between the state and the people.

Within the center itself initially, that is, during the first three decades of the 19th century, the goal was to reestablish the primacy of the Sultan not as a personal ruler but, again, as the first servant of the state. The Sultan (Mahmud II, 1808–1839) considered himself "the enlightener of the citizenry. . . . He brought the concept of *adalet* (justice) to the field of legal enactment where it meant the promulgation and judicial execution of rules outside (and later superseding) the 'will' of the Sultan . . . outside the Şeriat (Islamic canon law)" (Berkes 1964:9–95). Mahmud II also took measures to render the civil bureaucracy into a pliable instrument, one with a formal rationality.

With the outset of the *Tanzimat* period, however, the civil bureaucratic elite began to take initiative in the pursuance of the Ottoman modernization program. Their motto of the necessity of "institutions replacing individual rulers" could easily be put into practice in a milieu with a tradition of a distinctive center. The civil bureaucratic elite adopted the secularizing orientation restarted by Mahmud II. *Adap* tradition was revived in its most secular form; the only criterion in promulgating policies and programs was going to be "reason" (Mardin 1962:104). The bureaucratic elite of the time viewed themselves (and no longer the sultan) as the servants of the state. The bureaucratic elite thought that the policies developed by them, and freed from Islamic tradition, would be best for the Empire. The civil bureaucracy aspired to substantive rather than formal rationality.

B.   The Republican Period (1923 to Present)

1.   The Single-Party Years (1923–1950)

Ataturk, founder of the Turkish Republic, nurtured for Turkey a political system in which initially the state would have salience but in time this state would wither away. In Ataturk's view, in the last decades of the Ottoman Empire the sultans had shown signs of drifting to personal rule and had given short shrift to the vital interests of the country.[7] Ataturk thought Turkey needed a state distinct from the person of the rulers.

From 1919 (when he started the Turkish "War of Independence") until 1938 (when he died) Ataturk attempted to institutionalize an impersonal state in Turkey on two planes. First, he tried to depersonalize the day-to-day conduct of public affairs. He was careful to differentiate between the person who occupied a public office from the office itself (Heper 1985:60–61).[8] Second, he was instrumental in developing a republican version of *adab* tradition, later referred to as "Ataturkism."

In Ataturk's view, the natural progress that people would have gone through if left to their devices had been arrested by the personal rule of the sultans. It was thus incumbent upon the new leadership group to restart and accelerate that progress (toward contemporary civilization). Ataturkism was conceived as a means to that end. It was taken as an antidote to the hold of religion, that is, "a nonscientific mentality," on society. Thus, the basic components of Ataturkism were (1) republicanism, or need for an impersonal rule; (2) nationalism, or people themselves generating their own goals; (3) populism, or emphasis on general interest; and (4) secularism, or nation's goals derived from nonreligious precepts.

Ataturk did not have high regard not only for the Ottoman sultans but also for the bureaucracy the republic inherited from the Ottomans. In his opinion the civil servants had remained indifferent to, if not actively undetermined about, the national effort during the Turkish War of Independence (1919–1922). Thus, initially, Ataturk tried to relegate them into a secondary role. At this stage, for him the civil bureaucracy was to be a lesser part of the government. The high degree of centralization effected in each ministry left but little room for bureaucratic initiative.

Later, however, when some elements from the bureaucracy were purged and the products of the new schools offering a Westernized curriculum began to join the civil service, Ataturk began to see the bureaucratic elite as an integral element of the leadership group which was to lead Turkey to "contemporary civilization." Having had the assumption that the people inherently had a potential to develop, Ataturk, however, did not perceive the bureaucracy as an Hegelian "absolute class," or as the sole formulator and guardian of the general interest. It is true that the bureaucratic elite were expected to be loyal to and the promoter of Ataturkism, but Ataturkism as taken by Ataturk was not an ideology in the Shilsian sense, that is, a closed system of thought, but it was a mentality (Ozbudun 1981:87–92), or "non codified ways . . . of reacting to situations" (Linz 1975:266–269).

2.   The Multiparty Years (1945 to the Present)

Despite the essentially instrumental role that Ataturk attributed to civil bureaucracy, even during Ataturk's life time the bureaucratic elite aspired to a much more substantive role. They tried to acquire for themselves such a place in the polity through a reinterpretation of Ataturkism. The bureaucratic elite attempted to legitimate the influential role they wanted to play in what was now formally a Rousseaunist parliamentary democracy by transforming Ataturkism as a mentality into a political manifesto. The principles of Ataturkist thought that were described above as techniques of finding out truth began to be loaded with substantive meanings. For the bureaucratic elite, reformism came to mean preserving and safeguarding whatever institutional transformations were effected in the fabric of the Turkish social and political structure. The institutional transformations in question became ends when they should have been only means (Turhan 1967:71–72).

The formal education offered to the prospective bureaucratic intelligentsia was conducive to reviving the bureaucratic ruling tradition that had first fully developed during the *Tanzimat* era. The school engendered in the bureaucratic elite a willingness to act as a policy initiator and/or policy maker rather than as a policy implementer, and inclination to place emphasis among the decision-making factors on what they thought was best (Heper and Kalaycioglu 1983:190).

Following the transition to multiparty regime in the 1940s the Democratic Party, which captured political office in 1950, came to power with the claim that they represented "the people as against the bureaucracy (read the 'state')." For a long time in the post-1950 period, however, the elitist approach on the part of the bureaucracy did not wane. The bureaucratic elite were unwilling to accept an instrumental role for themselves with popular sovereignty as a fact of life. Thirty-four of the 36 civil servants who held highest bureaucratic posts from 1945 to 1960 agreed (in 1969) that "what Turkey needs more than anything else is experienced and informed people significantly contributing to public policy-making" (Heper 1976:516), and, needless to say, they considered themselves as best fitting that definition. In 1974, among 510 civil servants in eight central ministries, mean scores on a Likert scale (ranging from 1 to 5 with higher scores indicating a higher-ranking one each scale) for "tolerance for a democratic way of life" were 1.48, for "elitism" 3.58, and for "social responsibility" 3.53 (Heper 1977:76). And in 1978, among all the civil servants in the central organizations of three ministries only 16.4% disagreed with the statement that as compared to other citizens civil servants judged the country's interests better (Bozkurt 1980:130).

Not unlike the bureaucratic intelligentsia, the military, too, took democracy at the time as a discourse at a high level of rationality. Not unexpectedly, the rationality in question was defined in terms of the Atatürkist principles loaded with substantive meanings (Heper 1985b:85). When the military intervened in 1960 they adopted the view that political power had fallen into a position hostile to the state's genuine and main institutions, and to Ataturk's reforms, which were considered to be of extraordinary value and importance if Turkey was to occupy a worthy place among the nations of the world as a civilized state (Ahmad 1977:164).

Thus emerged the 1961 Constitution, which stacked the bureaucratic elite against the representatives of the nation. Article 4 of the Constitution stipulated that "the nation shall exercise its sovereignty through the authorized agencies as prescribed by the principles laid down in the Constitution."[9] The principles in question were made explicit by Article 153, according to which no provision of the Constitution was to be interpreted to nullify certain specific laws that were passed during the Ataturk era. The clear intention was to maintain Atatürkist thought as a political manifesto, and to put an end legally to the supremacy of parliament. Among other institutions, the judiciary was given a considerable share in the exercise of sovereignty. The newly created Constitutional Court had the power to test from the perspective noted here the constitutional validity of statutes. The Council of State (the Turkish version of the French *Conseil d'Etat*) was also conceived as a countervailing force against political governments.

In the last analysis, however, these measures provided only a veto power to the bureaucracy, and as such were bound to be ineffective against a government determined to dominate bureaucracy. The 1961 Constitution, while attempting to bring bureaucratic controls over democracy, had at the same time expanded the scope of basic rights and liberties. In this more liberal milieu ideologies of leftist and rightist variety flourished, and competed successfully with Ataturkism (Frey 1975:70). Some members of the bureaucratic intelligentsia, too, joined the bandwagon of ideological polarization in question. Moreover, during the 1970s in particular, the political parties managed to turn many members of the bureaucracy into political party bureaucrats.[10]

The political governments tried to render bureaucracy into a loyal rather than a legal-rational one. Given the fact that in the Ottoman-Turkish polity the state for a long time almost completely dominated civil society, there has been an absence of a constructive involvement in politics by the entrepreneurial middle classes. Consequently, there was in that polity no development in bureaucracy away from substantive rationality as reflected in cameralism and in reason of state, and toward formal rationality, as reflected in narrow specialization in administrative techniques.

In Turkey, to the extent the state-dominated political system was eroded it tended to be replaced by a party-centered, rather than bourgeois, politics (Heper 1985a:100); that is, antistate political parties have functioned as largely autonomous from weighty social groups. Instead, they came to be vehicles of elite conflict. The conflict revolved around "cultural" rather than "functional cleavages." In the ensuing legitimacy crises that has pervaded Turkish politics, always at issue was the nature of substantive rationality on the part of the bureaucracy, and not its replacement by formal rationality.

Consequently, the bureaucracy's reaction to the efforts on the part of the political governments to politicize it was that of resorting to "negative politics," or alienative political involvement. The bureaucracy and political governments became hostile powers. The former began to sabotage the latter's policies. As the bureaucrats could no longer manipulate appointments and promotions and thus keep under control political spoils, they did this through a pathological bureaucratization of the system (Heper 1977:80–82).

When in 1980 the military intervened (for the third time) in Turkish politics, a new chapter began in the political development of that country. In the eyes of the military, the crisis essentially pointed to the one major failure of the system, namely, the almost complete erosion of the dominant state in the absence of intermediary structures with a moderating influence. In Turkey, the intermediary structures in question could be no other than political parties and the bureaucracy. Before long all the political parties were disbanded, and the military attempted the political engineering of encouraging the establishment of brand new political parties, which, it was hoped, would function responsibly as well as responsively (Turan 1988:73–75).

As for the bureaucracy, the first step was to purge the bureaucracy of the "militants." Also, a considerable number of civil servants were "induced" to retire (Heper 1984:66ff). In the post-1980 restructuring of the Turkish political system the military reserved for itself the "mission" of the guardianship of the state.[11] Thus, during the interregnum (1980–1983) there were efforts to render the bureaucracy into a legal-rational institution.

While some steps were being made in that direction, Turkey again made a transition to multiparty politics. The Motherland Party (MP), which formed the new government, attempted to launch a "liberal revolution" in Turkey (Rustow 1985). Turgut Ozal, who led the MP, found the bureaucracy unable to keep pace with, and in any case not sympathetic to, the far-reaching economic transformation he had in mind (Kazdal 1990:190). According to Ozal, the bureaucracy was either too slow, not dynamic, and unresponsive to people's demands, or ideologically too committed to state intervention, not market oriented, and too caught up in bureaucratic maze (Atiyas 1996:304). Ozal arrived at the conclusion that the economy bureaucracy should have program-oriented (substantive) rationality (contribution to policy making based on expert knowledge) and display effectiveness—as noted, characteristics of a rational-productive bureaucrat—as well as neutrality and efficiency—characteristic of a legal-rational bureaucrat (Heper and Sancar 1998:151). More specifically, openness to innovation and "the ability to get things done" were the primary qualities Ozal sought in bureaucrats (Barlas 1994:116).

The Motherland Party adopted a two-pronged policy of (1) debureaucratization of the system and, in particular, (2) turning the upper reaches of what would remain of the bureaucracy into a rational-productive[12] rather than a legal-rational one. The government tried to carry out debureaucratization through sidestepping some age-old ministry bureaucracies and creating more flexible boards directly responsible to the prime minister, through privatization of some of the state economic enterprises, and through decentralization of the government. The rendering of the bureaucracy into a rational-productive one was tried to be effected through appointing to the heads of the critical directorates and agencies technocrats recruited from outside the bureaucratic ranks (Evin 1988:201–207). Many of these outsiders were selected from among professional Turks living in the United States (Kozanoglu 1995:184).

These restructurings of Turkish public bureaucracy as well as the injection into that bureaucracy of experts from outside had favorable consequences: The bureaucracy began to provide more specialized input to public policy making, and public policies were more effectively and quickly implemented (Cemal 1989:148; Atiyas 1996:293; Heper and Sancar 1998:154–158). On the other hand, while all this was achieved, sometimes bureaucratic norms and propriety were overlooked. For instance, an overwhelming number of experts brought to the bureaucracy from outside were the friends of Turgut Ozal's son. That in some cases appointments to the heads of critical agencies were not solely based on an objective assessment of the candidate's level of skill and knowledge had its adverse consequences; though a small minority, some of these outsiders turned out to be complete failures and/or had to resign because of the charges of impropriety (in the handling of public money) made against them (Oktay 1997:203–220). Ozal's strategy of transforming the public bureaucracy had fair amount of patrimonialism (Sunar 1990:756).

The post-Ozal governments in Turkey abandoned the model of recruiting experts from outside and the quality of persons in the top positions seemed to have experienced a decline (Heper and Sancar 1998:157). In this period, there was also an increase in the improper handling of public funds (Evin 1996:52). Moreover, the bureaucracy was further politicized, which resulted in high turnover among the key higher civil servants. As a consequence of these developments, Turkey still carries the burden of a bureaucracy which evinces strong patrimonial characteristics in an era of increased competition among nations.

ENDNOTES

1. Hale (1976:1), in this context, argued that "while economists and sociologists may rank Turkey as a developing country, her post-Renaissance history has more in common with those of certain European countries than, for instance, with that Nigeria, India or Brazil." Also see Mango (1977).
2. See, inter alia, Mansur (1963:4, 23, 26, 28, 75, 80, 130–131, 168–169) and Scott (1970:27, 40–41).
3. For this definition of the state I draw upon Dyson (1980:208–214). Also see Heper (1987:3–6).
4. Below I take up this point at length.
5. Inter alia, Riggs (1963), Fainsod (1963), and Esman (1966).
6. Reported in Heper et al. (1980:81–105).
7. Here he particularly seems to have in mind the last Ottoman sultan, who, in his opinion, collaborated with the enemy when, following World War I, parts of the country were invaded.
8. On how, despite his charismatic qualities, Atatürk shunned personal rule, see Heper (1980–1981).
9. The (previous) 1924 Constitution had simply stated that the nation would exercise its sovereignty through the GNA.
10. The efforts to politicize the bureaucracy started as early as the 1950s, when the Democratic Party came to power. Before the 1970s, however, the civil servants had never been shuffled in such an arbitrary fashion as they were during this decade (Heper 1979–1980:105–106).
11. The particular arrangements in this regard are discussed in Heper (1988:5–10).
12. According to Ilchman (1968:474–479) the common bond that joins rational-productivity bureaucrats derives largely from their legitimatizing source in knowledge, their loyalty to substantive programs, and their value commitment to productivity.

REFERENCES

Ahmad, F. *The Turkish Experiment in Democracy, 1950–1975.* C. Hurst, London, 1977

Armstrong, J.A. *The European Administrative Elite.* Princeton University Press, Princeton, NJ, 1973.

Atiyas, I. Uneven governance and fiscal failure: the adjustment experience in Turkey. In *Governance, Leadership and Communication: Building Constituencies and Fiscal Reform* (L. Frishtack and I. Atiyas, eds.). World Bank, Washington, DC, 1996.

Badie, B., and Birnbaum, P. *The Sociology of the State* (trans. A. Goldhammer). University of Chicago Press, Chicago, 1983.

Barlas. M. *Turgut Ozal' in Anilari.* Genclik, Istanbul, 1994.

Barnett, M. *The Palace School of Muhammed the Conqueror.* Harvard University Press, Cambridge, MA, 1944.

Berkes, N. *The Development of Secularism in Turkey.* McGill University Press, Montreal, 1964

Bozkurt, O. *Memurlar, Turkiye'de Kamu Burokrasisinin Sosyolojik Gorunumu.* Turkiye ve Ortadogu Amme Idaresi Enstitusu, Ankara, 1980.

Clapham, C. *Third World Politics. An Introduction.* Croom Helm, London, 1986

Diamant, A. Bureaucracy in developmental movement regimes. In *Frontiers of Development Administration* (F.W. Riggs, ed.). Duke University Press, Durham, NC, 1970.

Dyson, K.F.H. *The State Tradition in Western Europe. The Study of an Idea and Institution.* Martin Robertson, Oxford, 1980

Eisenstadt, S.N. *Traditional Patrimonialism and Modern Neo-Patrimonialism.* Sage, Beverly Hills, CA, 1973.

Eisenstad, S.N. Strong and weak states: some reconsiderations. In *The State and Public Bureaucracies: A Comparative Perspective* (M. Heper, ed.). Greenwood Press, New York, 1987

Esman, M.J. The politics of development administration. In *Approaches to Development: Politics, Administration and Change* (J.D. Montgomery and W.J. Siffin, eds.). McGraw-Hill, New York, 1966.

Evans P.B., Rueschemeyer, R., and Skocpol, T. *Bringing the State Back In.* Cambridge University Press, Cambridge, 1985

Evin, A. Changing patterns of cleavages before and after 1980. In *State, Democracy and the Military. Turkey in the 1980s* (M. Heper and A. Evin, eds.). Walter de Gruyter, New York, 1988.

Fainsod, M. Bureaucracy and modernization: the Russian and Soviet case. In *Bureaucracy and Political Development* (J. LaPalombara, ed.). Princeton University Press, Princeton, NJ, 1963

Findley, C.V. *Bureaucratic Reform in the Ottoman Empire. The Sublime Porte, 1789–1922.* Princeton University Press, Princeton, NJ, 1980.

Findley, C.V. The advent of ideology in the Islamic Middle East. *Studia Islamica*, Ex Fasciculo, LV (1982).

Frey, F.W. Patterns of elite politics in Turkey. In *Political Elites in the Middle East* (G. Lenczowski, ed.). American Enterprise Institute for Public Policy Research, Washington, DC, 1975.

Hale, W. Modern Turkish politics: an historical introduction. In *Aspects of Modern Turkey* (W. Hale, ed.). Bowker, London, 1976

Heady, F. *Public Administration. A Comparative Perspective*, 2nd ed. Marcel Dekker, New York, 1979.

Heeger, G.A. *The Politics of Underdevelopment.* St. Martin's Press, New York, 1974

Heper, M. Political modernization as reflected in bureaucratic change: the Turkish bureaucracy and a "historical bureaucratic empire" tradition. *International Journal of Middle East Studies*, 7 (1976).

Heper, M. Negative bureaucratic politics in a modernizing context: the Turkish case. *Journal of South Asian and Middle Eastern Studies*, 1 (1977).

Heper, M. Recent instability in Turkish politics: end of a monocentrist polity? *International Journal of Turkish Politics*, 1 (1979–1980).

Heper, M. Center and periphery in the Ottoman Empire with special reference to the nineteenth century. *International Political Science Review*, 1 (1980).

Heper, M. Transformation of charisma into a political paradigm: "Ataturkism" in Turkey. *Journal of the American Institute for the Study of Middle Eastern Civilization*, 1 (1980–1981).

Heper, M. Bureaucrats, politicians, and officers in Turkey: dilemmas of a new political paradigm. In *Modern Turkey. Continuity and Change* (A. Evin, ed.). Leske and Budrich, Opladen, 1984

Heper, M. *The State Tradition in Turkey.* Eothen Press, Walkington, England, 1985a.

Heper, M. The state and public bureaucracies: a comparative and historical perspective. *Comparative Studies in Society and History*, 27 (1985b).

Heper, M. Introduction. In *The State and Public Bureaucracies. A Comparative Perspective* (M. Heper, ed.). Greenwood Press, New York, 1987.

Heper, M. State and society in Turkish political experience. In *State, Democracy and the Military. Turkey in the 1980s* (M. Heper and A. Evin, eds.). Walter de Gruyter, New York, 1988

Heper, M. Extremely "strong state" and democracy: the Turkish case in comparative and historical perspective. In *Democracy and Modernity* (S.N. Eisenstadt, ed.). Brill, Leiden, 1992.

Heper, M., and Kalaycioglu, E. Organizational socialization as reality-testing: the case of the Turkish higher civil servants. *International Journal of Political Education*, 6 (1983).

Heper, M. Kim, C.L. and Pal, S.-T. The role of bureaucracy and regime types: a comparative study of Turkish and South Korean higher civil servants. *Administration and Society, 12* (1980).

Heper, M., and Sancar, S. Is legal-rational bureaucracy a prerequisite for a rational-productive bureaucracy? The case of Turkey. *Administration and Society, 30* (1998).

Ilchman, W.F. Productivity, administrative reform, and antipolitics: dilemmas for developing states. In *Political and Administrative Development* (R. Braibanti, ed.). Duke University Press, Durham, NC, 1969.

Inalcik, H. The nature of traditional society (Turkey). In *Political Modernization in Japan and Turkey* (R.E. Ward and D.A. Rustow, eds.). Princeton University Press, Princeton, NJ, 1964

Inalcik, H. Islam in the Ottoman Empire. *Cultura Turcica, 5–7* (1968–1970).

Inalcik, H. Ottoman methods of conquest, *Archivum Ottomanicum 3* (1971).

Inalcik, H. The Ottoman decline and its effects upon the *reaya* (people). In *Aspects of the Balkans. Continuity and Change* (H. Birnbaum and S. Vryonis Jr., eds.). Mouton, The Hague, 1972.

Kazdal, I. *Siyasi Iktidar ve Ozal Devri.* Ihya, Istanbul, 1990

Kozanoglu, H. 80'lerin Altin Cocuklari. In *Yuzyil Biterken Cumhuriyet Donemi Turkiye Ansiklopedisi.* Iletisim, Istanbul, 1995.

Linz, J. Totalitarian and authoritarian regimes. In *Handbook of Political Science*, Vol. 3: *Macro-Political Theory* (F.I. Greenstein and N.W. Polsby, eds.). Addison-Wesley, Reading, MA, 1975

Mango, A. The state of Turkey. *Middle Eastern Studies, 13* (1977).

Mansur, F. *Process of Independence.* Routledge and Kegan Paul, London, 1962

Mardin, S. *The Genesis of Young Ottoman Thought.* Princeton University Press, Princeton, NJ, 1962.

Mardin, S. Power, civil society, and culture in the Ottoman Empire. *Comparative Studies in Society and History, 11* (1969).

Oktay, C. *Siyasal Sistem ve Burokrasi: Yukselen Istemler Karsisinda Turk Siyasal Sistemi ve Kamu Burokrasisi.* Der Yayinlari, Istanbul, 1997.

Ozbudun, E. The nature of the Kemalist political regime. In *Ataturk: Founder of a Modern State* (A. Kazancigil and E. Ozbudun, eds.). C. Hurst, London, 1981

Presthus, R.V., and Monopoli, W. Bureaucracy in the United States and Canada. *International Journal of Comparative Sociology, 18* (1977).

Riggs, F.W. Bureaucrats and political development: a paradoxical view. In *Bureaucracy and Political Development* (J. LaPalombara, ed.). Princeton University Press, Princeton, NJ, 1963

Rustow, D.A. Turkey's liberal revolution. *Middle East Review, 17* (1985).

Scott, R. Introduction. In *The Politics of New States* (R. Scott, ed.). George Allen and Unwin, London, 1970

Sunar, I. Populism and patronage: the *Demokrat* party and its legacy in Turkey. *Il Politico, 60* (1990).

Tachau, F., and Heper, M. The state, politics, and the military in Turkey. *Comparative Politics, 16* (1983).

Turan, I. Political parties and the party system in post-1983 Turkey. In *State, Democracy and the Military. Turkey in the 1980s* (M. Heper and A. Evin, eds.). Walter de Gruyter, New York, 1988.

Turhan, M. *Garplilasmanin Neresindeyiz?* Yagmur Yayinevi, Istanbul, 1967.

72

Bureaucratic Politics and Political Regimes

A Comparison of Nicaragua, Guatemala and Costa Rica

Greg Andranovich   *Department of Political Science, California State University, Los Angeles, California*

Gerry Riposa   *Department of Political Science, California State University–Long Beach, Long Beach, California*

I. INTRODUCTION

The purpose of this chapter is to examine the relationship between public bureaucracies and political regimes in three Central American nations in various stages of transition. Nicaragua, the region's newest socialist regime, has attempted to implement a redistributive policy agenda while fighting a civil war and the effects of U.S. economic sanctions. Guatemala, the region's paradigm of authoritarianism, recently held free elections and now has a civilian government closely monitored by the armed forces. Costa Rica, the region's oldest democracy and most stable regime, is currently facing a severe economic crisis that is testing the capacity of its bureaucracy and the limits of its political institutions.

The concept of regime transition has achieved greater currency in comparative public administration (e.g., Linz and Stephan 1978; Malloy 1987; Rosenberg 1987; see also Levine 1988). Central to the emphasis on regime transition is the changing of extant party structures and political alliances, particularly how such structures and alliances affect the legitimacy and efficacy of the state. It is at this juncture that public bureaucracies become central to our understanding of the nature of regime transition. In other words, under what conditions do public bureaucracies advance, retard, or preserve current institutions? As Malloy (1987:242) notes, it is on the state bureaucracy and its patron-client politics, not electoral, parliamentary, or programmatic politics, that regime success and survival depend.

The chapter proceeds as follows. First, the context of bureaucratic politics in Central America is provided. Then, the cases of Nicaragua, Guatemala, and Costa Rica are presented and the particular context of transition in each nation is examined through a discussion of the relationship between each nation's public bureaucracy and its political institutions. The chapter concludes with some observations about the role of bureaucratic politics in regime transition in the late 1980s.

II. BUREAUCRATIC POLITICS IN CENTRAL AMERICA

Seligson (1987) has suggested a cyclical pattern to the democratization process in Central America. Further, the alternating military and civilian regimes do not represent the same goals at different stages of the cycle. In general, the cycle has been military rule leading to civilian rule in the 1940s and 1950s followed by military rule in the 1960s and 1970s and returning to civilian rule in the 1980s. The military regimes of the 1960s and 1970s manifest different characteristics from military regimes in the 1930s. Specifically, Seligson (1987:4–6) notes that the latter regimes were not caretaker regimes but rather that these military regimes often articulated explicit development goals of their own and became central to the development process, eliminating previous party structures and political alliances, and establishing their own parties and developing their own patron-client politics. In this way, bureaucratic politics often reflect consensus and dissensus within the military.

More generally, bureaucracies in Central America have relied on *personalismo* rather than on internal expertise or administrative procedures (Sloan 1984). More important for this chapter, Sloan argues that when regime survival is the primary goal of government, the resulting policies do not necessarily aid in the development of the broader society. This observation of Central American bureaucracy suggests the displacement of professional behavior (a technical means) for regime stability (a political end) and centers on what Sederberg (1983:159) terms the ambiguous potential of bureaucracy. Bureaucracies provide a framework for the extraction of resources, the coordination of supplies, population control, and the distribution of benefits. Regimes need these activities to promote regime maintenance and development goals. Hence bureaucracy has explicit linkages to regime success and survival.

This chapter does not address the role of the United States in the process of regime maintenance in Central America, nor the importance of events in one nation on its neighbors (see Grabendorff et al. 1984; Weeks 1986). The economic crises facing many Central American nations in the 1980s after the prices of agricultural products fell relative to finished goods is not detailed here, nor are the roles of such international agencies as the International Monetary Fund, the World Bank, the Inter-American Development Bank, or the Organization of American States. While all are important, a broader discussion of the issues such topics raise is beyond the scope of this chapter.

A. Nicaragua

The triumph of the 18-year Sandinista revolution in 1979 was the result of a crisis of the state's legitimacy under successive Somoza regimes. Two events in the 1970s broadened the support for the ongoing revolution and contributed to the toppling of Anastasio Somoza. The first was the 1972 Managua earthquake and the subsequent mismanagement of reconstruction. The second was the assassination of a major opposition leader (Chamorro) in 1978, which led to widespread support for the Sandinistas. Postrevolution Nicaragua is representative of the dominant party semi-competitive regime type, in that although the Frente Sandinista de Liberacion Nacional (FSLN) is the dominant party, there exists a loyal opposition of about a half dozen parties and an opposition in principle of another half dozen parties and organizations (most reflecting right-wing or business interests) (Close 1988:127).

1. Somoza's National Guard and the Public Bureaucracy

The Somoza regime relied upon the National Guard to control the population and perpetuate its rule (see Millett 1977). Further, under the Somoza regime the public bureaucracy was limited in scope, highly centralized, yet fragmented and often corrupt. Except for the conduct of economic policy through the Central Bank, the activities of the public bureaucracy could be characterized as passive and fragmented (Graham 1987:18–19). Thus, the combination of an ineffective public bureaucracy and a strong National Guard resulted in the creation of a garrison state in Nicaragua.

The strength of the successive Somoza regimes was based in part on their ability to keep the middle class moderately productive in the economy yet excluded from politics (Cerdas 1986:183–184). This balance deteriorated after the 1972 earthquake when Anastasio Somoza installed himself head of the National Emergency Committee and channeled reconstruction monies to himself, his family, and the Guard. At this point the economic middle class, traditionally uninterested in politics, began to talk of the *competencia desleal* and the illegality of the economic profits gained by the Somoza family and their allies (Black 1981:17). The politics of restriction and exclusion, well practiced by the Somoza bureaucracy, were characteristic of the 1970s (Graham 1987:18–20).

2.   Political Institutions After the Revolution

Following their victory, the Sandinistas articulated the goals around which Nicaraguan society would be organized. Although somewhat ambiguous, consensus surrounded the three major themes: (1) a more humane society, (2) the reconstruction of the national economy, and (3) a reduction of class inequalities (Booth 1982:183). While these abstract goals initially drew support across class and ideological lines, opposition soon emerged over the implementation methods of the Sandinista regime.

Given that the Sandinista's political organization was already in place (i.e., through the party apparatus) and its control over the revolutionary army well established, the FSLN was quickly able to consolidate control over the machinery of government through the Governing Junta of National Reconstruction (JGRN). Later, the Sandinista party continued to exercise its predominant control over government as the party's directorate had little trouble in passing its agenda in the newly formed Council of Government, where FSLN party members held a clear majority. Although espousing a fresh approach to establishing a socialist society based on the concepts of "social pluralism and mixed economy," Nicaragua exemplified the tight congruence between party and state witnessed in other socialist systems.

Nevertheless, as Graham (1987:17) points out, revolutionary breakthroughs do not ensure sustained change in the structures and operation of government, much less in the more critical area of reshaping human relations for a more productive and equitable society. What was essential for the Sandinista regime was to develop a coherent bureaucratic strategy to ensure the implementation of their policy agenda. This strategy was grounded in changing the organizational structures and policy processes of the state, and in the recruitment of staff to implement the new programs.

Approximately 18 ministries were established, ranging from economic planning to labor to agriculture (Close 1988:119). To increase the likelihood that the revolutionary agenda would be implemented, FSLN members headed most of the new state agencies. Staffing shortages, however, did require the recall of former Somoza middle and lower-level bureaucrats. To avoid the appearance of merely substituting a centralized bureaucratic state in place of the Somoza garrison state, the Sandinista agenda included both political and administrative mechanisms to devolve decision-making authority.

Organizational restructuring was only a first step in the Sandinista regime's changing of the flow of public policy making. Generally, the Sandinistas sought to establish a new relationship between bureaucracy and society that allowed for local and regional input driven by popular mobilization and participation, and central government decentralization. Examples of successful public mobilization are found in the Ministry of Education's (MED) recruitment of volunteers for its literacy campaign, effective in reducing illiteracy from 50% to 13% (Booth 1986:565). In addition, the Ministry of Health (MINSA) created public health brigades that increased the availability and accessibility of immunization, nutrition, and maternal health care programs (Bossert 1982:265). Booth (1982:186) notes that the Sandinista regime also was partially successful at creating a new administrative culture receptive to public participation and its revolutionary goals through agency newsletters, study groups, and public employee unions.

Note that this process did not necessarily result in acquiescence to FSLN policy. For example, in agricultural policy the Rural Workers Association (ATC) and the Farm and Ranch Workers' Union (UNAG) successfully pressured state officials to cancel a "significant portion of the outstanding debt contracted by grain producers since 1979" (Deere et al. 1985:102). Also, the Agrarian Tribunal, an appeals court for grievances concerning state expropriation of land, reversed about one-third of the lands expropriated in 1984–85 (Luciak 1987:133).

The second part of the Sandinista agenda was the decentralization of ministries, begun in 1982. This decentralization was reflected in a shift from 15 administratively separate departments to six regional and three special zones, creating the foundation for a greater emphasis on integrated regional policy making (Graham 1987:27). Integration was facilitated through regional planning councils in which regional delegates representing the ministries would meet to discuss regional needs and potential policies. These meetings would be presided over by regional government officials, usually FSLN members. Because FSLN members served as both regional delegates and regional government officials, the party followed this same course of decentralization as the state. Later, in 1984, these structural changes were accompanied by greater regional fiscal autonomy, as the central government included regional block funds to help promote decentralized responsibility (Graham 1987:29). By 1985, Nicaragua's bureaucratic policy making process showed signs of moving from strictly functional agencies to an integrated regional policy process that still maintained the close relationship between party and state.

Wilson (1987) notes that this regionalization program has demonstrated uneven results. At the outset, this program was not simply intended to decentralize the presence of the central government; indeed, it was to decentralize decisions concerning resources and policy activities. This process was projected to increase efficiency, but just as important, it was designed to consolidate state legitimacy at the local level through greater public participation. The regionalization program has increased local responsibility in several ways. Municipal councils, chosen at the local level, submit policy proposals to the regional planning council. In addition, they can incur debt for development projects that have the propensity to become financially self-sufficient, such as hotels and restaurants. Projects are prioritized and selected at the regional level, but usually on the criterion of which proposal has the greatest local support (Wilson 1987:52). However, while this decentralization of the state has increased subnational policy making, central government expenditures and resource allocations continue to disproportionately favor the Pacific region, where the capital city of Managua is located.

In Nicaragua under Somoza, the public bureaucracy was a passive agent of the regime. The Sandinista government has tried to change the public bureaucracy's role in society to advance the agenda of the FSLN. This has been accomplished through the inclusion of new access points for policy input from the bottom up rather than through a centralized, top-down decision-making process. In this way, bureaucratic politics has included linkages with the public at the national and subnational levels of the state, and the current regime has been able to consolidate its political support and advance its policy agenda.

B. Guatemala

The existence of a strong, centralized state in Guatemala derives from the Spanish colonial heritage and the example of the Mexican Revolution and subsequent 1917 Constitution (Calvert

1985:101). Guatemala represents a collegial bureaucratic elite regime, a regime usually dominated by the military who exercise political leadership. Guatemala has had a continuous succession of military regimes for most of this century; the single experience with democracy—styled after Roosevelt's New Deal—ended with the United States-backed coup in 1954. The 1954 coup divided the military over the issues of development and nationalism and led to a succession of military regimes reflecting infighting and power consolidation in the 1960s. By 1970, these regimes had developed a politics of their own.

1. The Militarization of Political Institutions

Since 1944 and the overthrow of General Jorge Ubico y Castaneda (1931–1944), there have been 19 different military regimes and one civilian regime that served at the military's pleasure (Calvert 1985). Black (1984) suggests that the regimes of the 1970s were qualitatively different from earlier regimes in that by this time, the military had its own political agenda and was no longer operating in a caretaker mode.

In general, there were three goals characteristic of military regimes in Latin America in the 1960s and 1970s: (1) to defeat insurgent movements, (2) to develop the national economies, and (3) to establish political institutions that would maintain military control (Calvert 1985; see also Adams 1968). Calvert (1985:160) notes that in Guatemala, particularly in the 1970s, the only area in which the regimes were successful was in establishing political institutions; in fact, the success in this area created new and more serious forms of social unrest that threatened the structure of the military and discouraged broad-based foreign investment in Guatemala. The major reason for this was the extreme use of repression; the military expanded the use and forms of repression from combating insurgency to eliminating political opponents. The origins of the expansion of the use and forms of repression can be found in the 1954 United States-backed coup (Nairn and Simon 1986; Trudeau and Schoultz 1986).

The success of the military in developing political institutions also reflects a change in the political economy of Guatemala. Starting with the Arana regime in 1970, the military actively pursued economic objectives important to the officer corps. Senior officers used state power to obtain economic power and became more closely identified with the system of plantation agriculture and, by the mid 1970s, the development of the Northern Development Zone, a resource-rich area stretching across north-central Guatemala (Black 1984:28–29). During this time the military began to institutionalize its control over the public bureaucracy. This occurred in two ways: through the increased numbers of military personnel in government positions at all levels, and through the direct supervision and control of the forms of democracy. In the first instance, military personnel could achieve higher pay levels through positions in the civilian government. At the same time, because of the growing importance of the military in government, the 1960s saw a revitalization of the curricula at the military academy (Escuela Politecnica); topics such as management and administration were added to provide officers with the skills needed to participate in civilian government (Peralta 1982). In quantitative terms, the enrollment at the military academy tripled between 1970 and 1979 (Handy 1984:181).

Three important developments in the direct supervision of democratic forms were the establishment of quasi-party structures by the military, including the running of candidates acceptable to the military in elections (Black 1984); military control over cabinet appointees (Black, 1984); and the establishment of a parallel military government regulating civilian affairs through the National Interinstitutional Coordinator (CIN)—that is, a military zone commander—in each of Guatemala's 22 departments (Trudeau and Schoultz 1986:41–42). It is with this third development that the currently elected civilian regime of Vinicio Cerezo must contend.

Over time, successive military regimes have formalized their control over civilian political institutions in Guatemala. At this same time, the military has internalized the political conflict inherent in development and is not a homogeneous actor in Guatemalan politics (Adams 1968; Peralta 1982; Handy 1986). Over time (particularly between 1970 and 1982), a number of structural and functional fissures have deepened within the armed forces. These have included divisions between new officers trained in the military academy and older officers and between branches of the armed forces, and the use of domestic repression and the powers of the state for private economic gain, particularly in rural areas.

Although the Rios Montt administration lasted only 18 months, Rios Montt realigned political power. The military, particularly through its development of a parallel government and the required registration of all political parties, continues to play the most important role in Guatemalan politics.

2. Public Bureaucracy and Regime Transition

The civilian government of Guatemala today includes 14 ministries along with a president and vice president (U.S. Central Intelligence Agency 1987). These ministries are virtually the same as those in 1979; a major difference is that today the only representative of the military is the Defense Minister, whereas in the past most ministries were headed by members of the armed forces. Often under the military regimes, the president or chief of state also held the post of Defense Minister. Among the more important ministries to the military have been Finance, Public Education, Interior, and Energy and Mines. Military officers have held ambassadorships and have served on ad hoc committees, such as the important Committee of National Reconstruction, set up in the aftermath of the 1976 earthquake to distribute international aid, and linking reconstruction with internal repression (Black 1984:146; Handy 1984:173–174; Plant 1978).

The major political issues in Guatemala today derive from colonial times (land reform and private property rights; official recognition of Indian languages) and the recent succession of military regimes (the role of the military and the police in the political system; Millet 1985). The two most pressing policy issues are development and the investment/debt crisis and the apparent lack of civilian government authority over the military (i.e., the lack of a legitimate civilian legal system; Nairn and Simon 1986).

In Guatemala, the civilian bureaucracy has been a passive agent of the military regimes, particularly since the 1970s. The extent of the subordination of the public bureaucracy is illustrated by the parallel informal government (i.e., CIN supervision and coordination structure) that has relegated the public bureaucracy's role under the current civilian government to one of maintaining the interests of the military, rather than promoting the transition to a more democratic government.

C. Costa Rica

Costa Rica is the only nation in Central America that has experienced regular, Constitutional, orderly regime changes since 1949; Costa Rica also abolished its standing army in 1948 (Booth 1984). In part this stems from the early development of the coffee economy: Like the rest of the region, economic power is concentrated, but unlike the rest of the region, the social relations that were manifested were not coercive between owners and labor. Some of the large estates were subdivided, and this produced a class of medium-size farmers, which subsequently led to active political participation by a broad spectrum of society (Maira 1986). Costa Rican democracy has exhibited openness to the extent that the current economic crisis is in part blamed on the inability of the political institutions to effectively contend with the nation's population growth, imbalances between economic sectors, and the uncontrolled growth of the state itself.

1. Political Institutions

Constitutionally, Costa Rica is a unitary state; the powers of the central government, however, are fragmented. In part this stems from the weakened powers of the presidency and the fact that power is widely distributed within the executive branch (Hughes and Mijeski 1984:89–90). The president has limited control over an executive branch featuring a variety of organizational forms beyond the usual ministries including semiautonomous institutions and commercial enterprises. In all, there are 182 units within the executive branch, 76 of which were created after 1960 (Ameringer 1982:42). Because most of these institutions were created in an ad hoc manner, there is overlap and duplication of function between them. For example, some 40 agencies have responsibility for family assistance and 40 additional agencies for housing assistance (Wesson 1984:222). Further, Costa Rica has been dominated by a single party, the National Liberation Party (PLN), although other parties have contested the PLN and have even elected presidents. Indeed, Costa Rica is the only nation in the region in which opposition parties have not been repressed. An important component of PLN strength is that two of the three major labor confederations are dominated by the PLN, which also includes the majority of public bureaucrats.

2. Public Bureaucracy and Regime Transition

The decentralization of the executive branch has contributed to the economic crisis of the 1980s in the following ways. First, the autonomous institutions have their own budgetary authority, including borrowing authority. These institutions, like the Costa Rican Electrical Institute, can follow their own program regardless of how it affects the policy objectives of the president or the Assembly (Booth 1984:169). In addition, these institutions often have their own agendas and clientele; special-interest politics is characteristic of Costa Rican politics. Second, the state is the largest employer in Costa Rica, and public sector workers have effectively unionized and, through strikes and other work stoppages, have increased the costs of government (Wesson 1984:222). Finally, the protection of civil service regulations has limited presidential control to the extent that public service is hereditary in some sectors, such as insurance (Wesson 1984:222). The structural weakness of the executive means that bureaucratic politics cannot be effectively interrupted and overcome in a time of crisis.

Between 1978 and 1982, under the Carazo administration, there were a series of organizational changes, primarily to coordinate the activities of the vast bureaucracy (Wesson 1984:220). These changes added to the size of government without reforming the weak executive control. Indeed, rather than coordinate among existing agencies, there was further duplication of functions. During this time, public sector employment increased by 10,000 while private-sector employment decreased by 4000 and the public sector accounted for 62% of the internal debt (Wesson 1984:225). In 1982, after seeing corruption in government increase steadily through the 1970s and the nation declared technically bankrupt in 1981, Monge was elected to the presidency on an austerity platform. During this period of crisis there was internal dissension over alternative policy options (e.g., whether to follow International Monetary Fund economic guidelines; how to deal with Nicaragua), which has polarized public opinion and has led to the establishment of a number of right wing organizations and candidates. The current president, NLP's Oscar Arias Sanchez, is facing a situation in which many Costa Ricans are realizing that while they have been forced to sacrifice under the state's austerity program, the special interests have benefited from paying lower wages and receiving government support for export production (Barry and Preusch 1986:191).

In Costa Rica, the public bureaucracy has contributed to the current crisis through the semiautonomous nature of the public bureaucracy and the overly protective civil service. The decentralized nature of power in the Costa Rican state has allowed public bureaucrats to pursue their own agendas to the detriment of governmentwide policy. In this way, bureaucratic politics have retarded the capacity of the regime to address changing public expectations and current economic exigencies in a period of needed transition.

III. LINKING BUREAUCRATIC POLITICS AND POLITICAL REGIMES

Bureaucracies are an integral part of the development process in third world nations, regardless of the type of political regime. Their role is twofold: first, public bureaucracies manage banks, utilities, and commercial development; second, these activities also help promote the legitimacy of the extant regime. In Central America, we have seen that the public bureaucracies, whether efficient or not, have grown in size and represent a new political and economic class. In theory, the bureaucracy is a public servant, yet in practice it plays varying roles in the political processes of regime transition, advancing, retarding, or helping maintain the extant regime. Bureaucratic interests may range from being relatively autonomous from the elected regime to being subordinated to other political institutions, particularly the military.

Our case studies of three Central American nations demonstrate the important role bureaucracies play in regime transition, although these roles are manifested in different ways. Nicaragua's public bureaucracy appears to have contributed to the advancement of the Sandinista policy agenda, whereas in Guatemala the public bureaucracy, operating from a subordinate position, seemingly can only help to maintain the existing military control over the elected regime. Costa Rica, on the other hand, illustrates a bureaucratic framework that has retarded the ability of the regime to address the range of political and economic problems that are currently being experienced.

All three nations are affected by a shortage of monies and technical expertise in the public sector. Consequently they have experienced various inefficiencies, and make bureaucratic capabilities suspect. Yet it appears that Nicaragua's approach—integrating more regional and local decision making—has allowed the Sandinista regime to implement its policy agenda during the transitional period. The Nicaraguan model, dissimilar from conventional Central American bureaucratic models, may indeed hold developmental potential for other third world nations.

REFERENCES

Adams, R.N. The development of the Guatemalan military. *Studies in Comparative International Development*, 4(5):91–110 (1968)

Ameringer, C.D. *Democracy in Costa Rica*. Praeger, New York, 1982.

Barry, J. and Preusch, D. *The Central American Fact Book*. Grove Press, New York, 1986

Black, G. *Triumph of the People*: *The Sandinista Revolution in Nicaragua*. Zed Books, London, 1981.

Black, G. *Garrison Guatemala*. Zed Books, London, 1984

Booth, J. *The End and the Beginning*: *The Nicaraguan Revolution*. Westview Press, Boulder, CO, 1982.

Booth, J. Representative Constitutional democracy in Costa Rica: adaptation to crisis in the turbulent 1980s. In *Central America*: *Crisis and Adaptation* (S.C. Ropp and J.A. Morris, eds.). University of New Mexico Press, Albuquerque, 1984, pp. 153–188

Booth, J. Nicaragua. In *Latin America and Caribbean Contemporary Record*, Vol. IV: *1984–85* (J.W. Hopkins, ed.). Holmes and Meier, New York, 1986, pp. 565–587.

Bossert, T.J. Health care in revolutionary Nicaragua. In *Nicaragua in Revolution* (T. Walker, ed.). Praeger, New York, 1982, pp. 259–272

Calvert, P. *Guatemala: A Nation in Turmoil*. Westview Press, Boulder, CO, 1985.

Cerdas, R. Nicaragua: one step forward, two steps back. In *The Central American Impasse* (G. Di Palma and L. Whitehead, eds.). Croom Helm, London, 1986, pp. 175–194

Close, D. *Nicaragua: Politics, Economics and Society.* Pinter, New York, 1988.

Deere, C.D., Marchetti, P., and Reinhardt, N. The peasantry and the development of Sandinista agrarian policy, 1979–1984. *Latin American Research Review, 20*(3):75–109 (1985)

Grabendorff, W., Krumwiede, H.-W., and Todt, J., eds. *Political Change in Central America: Internal and External Dimensions.* Westview Press, Boulder, CO, 1984.

Graham, L.S. The impact of revolution on the state apparatus. In *Nicaragua: Profiles of the Revolutionary Public Sector* (M.E. Conroy, ed.). Westview Press, Boulder, CO, 1987, pp. 17–37

Handy, J. *Gift of the Devil: A History of Guatemala.* South End Press, Boston, 1984.

Handy, J. Resurgent democracy and the Guatemalan military. *Journal of Latin American Studies, 18*(Nov.):383–408 (1986)

Hughes, S.W., and Mijeski, K.J. *Politics and Public Policy in Latin America.* Westview Press, Boulder, CO, 1984.

Levine, D. Paradigm lost: dependence to democracy. *World Politics, 40*(April):377–394 (1988)

Linz, J., and Stephan, A., eds. *Breakdowns of Democratic Regimes.* Johns Hopkins University Press, Baltimore, 1978.

Luciak, I. National unity and popular hegemony: the dialectics of Sandinista agrarian reform politics. *Journal of Latin American Studies, 19*(May):113–140 (1987)

Maira, L. Authoritarianism in Central America: a comparative perspective. In *The Central American Impasse* (G. Di Palma and L. Whitehead, eds.). Croom Helm, London, 1986, pp. 14–29.

Malloy, J.M. The politics of transition in Latin America. In *Authoritarians and Democrats: Regime Transition in Latin America* (J.M. Malloy and M. Seligson, eds.). University of Pittsburgh Press, Pittsburgh, 1987, pp. 235–258

Millet, R. *Guardians of the Dynasty.* Orbis, New York, 1977.

Millett, R. Guatemala:progress or paralysis. *Current History, 84*(March):109–113, 136 (1985)

Nairn, A., and Simon, J.-M. Bureaucracy of death. *New Republic,* June 30:13–17 (1986).

Peralta, G.A. The process of militarization in the Guatemalan state. *Latin American Research Unit Studies, 5*(Sept.):39–58 (1982)

Plant, R. *Guatemala: Unnatural Disaster.* Latin American Bureau, London, 1978.

Rosenberg, M.B. Obstacles to democracy in Central America. In *Authoritarians and Democrats: Regime Transitions in Latin America* (J.M. Malloy and M.A. Seligson, eds.). University of Pittsburgh Press, Pittsburgh, 1987, pp. 193–215

Sederberg, P.C. *Interpreting Politics,* 3rd ed. Chandler and Sharp, Novato, CA, 1983.

Seligson, M.A. Democratization in Latin America: the current cycle. In *Authoritarians and Democrats: Regime Transitions in Latin America* (J.M. Malloy and M.A. Seligson, eds.). University of Pittsburgh Press, Pittsburgh, 1987, pp. 3–14

Sloan, J.W. *Public Policy in Latin America.* University of Pittsburgh Press, Pittsburgh, 1984.

Trudeau, R., and Schoultz, L. Guatemala. In *Confronting Revolution* (M. Blachman et al., eds.). Pantheon, New York, 1986, pp. 23–49

U.S. Central Intelligence Agency. National Foreign Assessment Center. (1979–1987). *Chiefs of State and Cabinet Members of Foreign Governments.* Government Printing Office, Washington, 1987.

Weeks, J. An Interpretation of the Central American crisis. *Latin American Research Review, 21*(3):31–54 (1986)

Wesson, R. Costa Rica: problems of social democracy. In *Politics, Policies, and Economic Development in Latin America* (R. Wesson, ed.). Hoover Institution Press, Stanford, CA, 1984, pp. 213–233.

Wilson, P.A. A comparative evaluation of regionalization and decentralization. In *Nicaragua: Profiles of the Revolutionary Public Sector* (M.E. Conroy, ed.). Westview Press, Boulder, CO, 1987, pp. 41–58.

73
Evolution and Revolution

Enduring Patterns and the Transformation of
Latin American Bureaucracy

Jack W. Hopkins   *School of Public and Environmental Affairs, and Center for Latin
American and Caribbean Studies, Indiana University, Bloomington, Indiana*

I. INTRODUCTION

In longevity, Latin American bureaucracy has few peers in the Western world. The public administration systems of Latin America have endured, as the quincentennial celebration reminded us,
for over half a millennium. In that 500-year history, Latin American bureaucracy coped with the
exploration and conquest of the Americas, survived the sweeping revolutions and movements for
independence, endured the struggles of nation building, provided the foundation for economic and
social development, and adapted to or was radically transformed by modern revolutions in the
twentieth century.

It is the purpose of this essay to examine the long history of Latin American bureaucracy
from its colonial origins to the recent revolutionary changes in Cuba and Nicaragua with the
objective of identifying common elements and persistent characteristics. The relative permanence
of public administration systems in Latin America since the early 1500s suggests that patterns of
behavior set during the colonial era have been influential on later developments. Thus it is important to trace the evolution of public administration and bureaucracy since its colonial origins.

II. COLONIAL LEGACY

The great longevity of Spanish colonial administration in America—over 300 years—suggests
that the patterns established then would leave a significant imprint on public administration and
government in Latin America. A similar impact resulted from Portuguese colonial administration
in Brazil, although several political events modified the effects in that case. In both situations,
however, it is highly likely that the character and form of colonial administration was formative of
later developments throughout the region.

Spanish colonial administration characteristically divided authority and responsibility; the
system was predicated on a deep distrust of initiative by colonial officials in the Americas. Thus
the Crown prescribed a rigid administrative hierarchy, and a variety of overlapping features were
built in to control the system.

The legal framework of colonial administration in America derived from the Laws of the Indies, which extended down to the minutest detail. Virtually no aspect of political, economic, or social life escaped the coverage of the Laws of the Indies. The sheer volume of proscriptions proved overwhelming to colonial officials and the Crown's subjects alike; overlapping laws and duplication resulted in considerable confusion about the application and pertinency of laws and regulations.

The situation was further complicated by the great distance between colonial administrators in the New World and the Crown and court in Spain and Portugal. That separation, along with the complexity of the laws themselves, fostered an attitude of noncompliance or, at best, minimal compliance on the part of colonial officials. Conscious evasion at times, but also the impossibility of complete compliance and fidelity, was the cause. Thus the frequently used formula *Obedezco pero no cumplo* became a useful administrative device for pledging obedience while not complying with directives from the Crown and the Council of the Indies in Spain.

Fairly rapidly, in spite of the vast extension of the Spanish empire in America, the Crown developed complex and elaborate controls over its colonies in the New World. Very early in the 16th century the *Casa de Contratación* was established to oversee commerce and trade, and in 1524 the *Consejo de Indias* was set up with administrative, legislative, and judicial authority over the colonies.

As these functions and organizations developed, they exercised a supreme oversight on behalf of the Crown, and in practice the administrative, legislative, and judicial functions were melded without regard for separation. Similarly, although the Crown's personal representative, the viceroy, theoretically possessed all power in his domain, in practice he was undercut or bypassed on occasion by other institutions, notably the *audiencia*. This body functioned as a high judicial organ and a court of appeals, and it could communicate independently with the Council of the Indies. In addition, the *audiencia* frequently took on administrative and military authority. In fact, the viceroys and the *audiencia* evolved so that they partially checked each other.

The territorial extent, distance, and complexity of the empire presented problems of control from the start. As the colonial system matured, administration became more institutionalized; the bureaucratic devices to control the empire became more cumbersome as checks and balances were sought by the Crown.

One of the most important control devices was the *residencia*, adopted from the kingdoms of Castile and Aragon. The *residencia* consisted of a comprehensive audit of a colonial official after his term of office was completed. The official was required to remain at his post until the examination was concluded. A similar inspection was the *visita* or *visitación*, which could come at any time. These institutions were intended to maintain the Crown's control over the far-flung empire in America and to rein in the sometimes strong personalities of the viceroys and other colonial officials.

Because the Laws of the Indies were extraordinarily complex and detailed, and because of the centralized nature of the colonial system, administration became ponderous and tedious. The paternalistic system demanded frequent and extremely detailed reports from officials at all levels; these dealt with the minutest aspects of government. The cardinal virtues were order and orthodoxy, and eventually the incredible weight of law and regulation practically immobilized the colonial empire. Bureaucratic requirements smothered local initiative and the empire staggered under the burden.

Although the Crown attempted to reform and modernize the cumbersome structure, its efforts were too late to resuscitate it. The *intendente* system, applied first in the mid 1700s in Cuba, was a belated attempt to bring further control over revenues. The practical effect was to add greater centralization to an empire already choking on control.

Other factors exerted stronger influence toward the eventual disintegration of the system.

The sale of public offices by the Crown only encouraged a cynical, materialistic attitude among officials. Sale of offices led to sale of the functions of government, including justice, so that graft, bribery, and wholesale corruption became endemic to the colonial system of administration. The absence of any form of representative or democratic government that might have served to introduce countervailing controls into the system allowed such practices and styles to continue to the end of the empire. The colonial system was a frail foundation for the development of viable public administration after independence.

The Portuguese colonial system in the New World was, in general, far less rigidly controlled than the Spanish. Portugal's colonial arrangements in Brazil were more haphazard and casual than Spain's elsewhere, and only after 1580 (when Philip II took over Portugal) did the Portuguese system take on characteristics from the Spanish empire. After Portugal threw off Spanish control in 1640, an attempt to organize administration in Brazil was developed. Its ultimate effect, however, was to encourage localism in Brazil as a result of the great land grants made to *donatorios*, who exercised virtually feudalistic power over their domains.

As in the Spanish colonies, the Portuguese system left the way open for widespread corruption in colonial officials, in spite of attempts at reform. The positive effect of the looser Portuguese system of administration, however, was to create a less rigid form of government, with local foundations that could respond more effectively after independence.

III. EVOLUTIONARY CHANGE

The disintegration of the Spanish empire in the Americas left a great political void; national organizations, public institutions, and local governing experience were lacking. There was no strong foundation for viable public administration anywhere in the region. Much the same situation existed in Brazil, in spite of the role of the *donatorios* in providing the basis for at least the rudiments of local government. Further, the transfer of the Portuguese court to Rio de Janeiro in 1808, after Napoleon's invasion of Portugal, smoothed the way to independence. Upon King João's return to Portugal in 1820, his son Pedro remained in Rio, and in 1822 declared Brazil's independence. The country's transition to self-rule was thus moderate and nonviolent and the development of a public administration system was spared the wrenching changes that affected the rest of Latin America.

For most of the newly independent states of Latin America, the transition to independence was characterized by intense competition among local elites in regard to the form of the new governments, in terms of both philosophy and structure. Much of the philosophical debate occurred between liberal and conservative groups over such questions as the role of the Church. But fundamental disagreements over the matter of hierarchy versus individual rights continued to occupy many of the new nations. Likewise, political structure proved difficult to resolve in several countries: the conflict over centralized versus federal government influenced the nature of public administration systems. As Graham (1987a:89) points out, in most of the new states, a conscious attempt was made to bring about a definitive break with Hispanic institutions. Except in Brazil, local elites searched for institutional models in other countries. Various political, structural, and administrative arrangements were borrowed as organizational concepts for the new states.

Generally, the unitary state from French experience was the dominant form throughout most of Latin America; this was accompanied by a central administrative apparatus that steadily evolved to more complex, structurally differentiated systems as the societies developed (Wright 1970). But in much of Latin America, a continuing discrepancy between forms and political realities plague governments as they attempt to implement public policies. As Graham (1987b:94) observes, "bureaucratic complexity at the center does not necessarily imply extensive and well-developed administration farther afield."

Neither do bureaucratic complexity, differentiation, or high levels of training assure effective implementation of public policy. On the contrary, these characteristics may lead to overbureaucratized organizations that suffer premature rigor mortis. In the two revolutionary societies examined below, Cuba and Nicaragua, truly monumental programs have been carried out effectively with the barest minimum of technically trained professionals. Although the Cuban state apparatus has committed several grievous errors in program planning and implementation, at the same time many of its achievements are extraordinary.

It is entirely possible that Guerreiro-Ramos (1970:24–25) may be correct in suggesting that "the intimate association of the bureaucracy with the values and cultures of middle classes is a drawback to the development process. . . . The poor, in advanced nations, the masses in the peripheral countries are unable to get their needs perceived and satisfied by the existing bureaucratic structures." As suggested in another article (Hopkins 1971:357),

> the distinctive cultural traditions and social environment of the Latin American bureaucracy place far more serious barriers in the path of development toward more client orientation and toward broader participatory systems of administration. It is likely that the effectiveness of social intervention by the public bureaucracies under these conditions will vary accordingly.

Recruitment patterns in Latin American bureaucracies, especially in the more industrialized countries (Argentina, Brazil, Venezuela, Chile, and Mexico particularly), also show greater specialization. Increasing numbers of *técnicos* (technical specialists) were employed in government agencies and ministries as more specialized and technical functions were undertaken by the states. But, as in many less developed countries, problems of coordination and control arose in part because of the shortage of administrative specialists, and the shortage was not being filled by Latin American universities and institutes (Wright 1970:6–7).

A related problem stems from the formalistic nature of civil service codes, which, theoretically, emphasize merit as the principal criterion in personnel recruitment, selection, remuneration, and tenure decisions. But, as Wright (1970:9) observes, "Although achievement standards increasingly have been honored in the selection of bureaucratic personnel, they often coexist with criteria of nepotism, friendship, and, most commonly, political affiliation." In Brazil, the *panelinha* serves as a mutual aid grouping of individuals in a particular interest area and promotes group interests in the bureaucracy (Leeds 1964; Daland 1968).

However true this may be as a generalization, there is good reason to doubt the conventional wisdom about complete turnover of senior personnel whenever the presidency changes. Empirical studies in several countries, including Guatemala, Mexico, and Peru, indicate rather that the more common phenomenon is either brief interruption of service or transfer from one ministry to another. The evidence suggests that Latin American bureaucrats tend to be survivors and that their careers, if not completely orderly and stable, are at least long.

Cleaves (1974) notes that "Chilean presidents have had little difficulty gaining the bureaucracy's allegiance. Almost all middle and upper administrative posts are spoils of the new government. Though protected from summary dismissal and salary cuts, the displaced administrators from the previous regime are delegated minor tasks in which they lose almost all influence."

In Guatemala, during the regime of Jacobo Arbenz Guzmán (1951–54), the intellectuals and liberals who held top administrative posts under Juan José Arévalo (1945–51) were replaced by members of the Communist party and militant rural organizers. Organizations were staffed with "politically reliable recruits." Major changes in the allocation of public resources followed. The government of Carlos Castillo Armas (1954–57) maintained most of the new social programs and retained most of the new groups in the bureaucracy, even though often at lower levels (Weaver 1971).

Many studies of bureaucracy and public administration in Latin America conclude that certain characteristics appear to be persistent despite constant reform efforts. Among the frequently cited characteristics are excessive centralization of authority, supervisory instability, legalism, inadequate communication, and incomplete staff management. Weaver's (1973:359) summary observation on the Guatemalan bureaucracy during a period of social change is typical: "Everything rises to the top; the top does not delegate and thus cannot fix responsibility; the operational level exercises effective control by refusing to take action; patrones protect; subordinates express deference and rectitude; compliance, not performance, is the standard for evaluation."

Sloan (1984:248) describes the Latin American bureaucracies as characterized by "*personalismo*, nepotism, job insecurity, high turnover, lack of expertise, inadequate use of expertise when it exists, overcentralization of authority, formalism, stultifying legalism, lack of coordination, and corruption."

In effect, what Weaver termed "pre-modern procedures" seem to be intransigent in much of Latin American bureaucracy. The constant search for a codified basis for administrative action serves mainly to trap the public administration system in inaction and delay. Tuohy (1973) found similar characteristics in Mexico. Even major reform efforts have, in general, affected the situation only moderately. In Peru, for example, the long-running reform program of the National Office for Public Administration Reform and Training (ONRAP) tended to provide services that were "pedestrian, narrow-gauge, and specific, and because its recommendations were typically standardized remedies they were rejected frequently by the recipient" (Hopkins 1973:129). At times, reform efforts foundered because they received weak or lukewarm political support, as in Venezuela (Groves 1979). To avoid the problem of diffuse, systemwide reform efforts, Thurber (1966) saw the "islands of development" strategy as the most effective approach to development administration. That strategy focuses on the identification of elements of strength and potential in a society and then concentration in them of resources and efforts for planned change. The strategy appears to have yielded best results in situations where a more professional approach to problem solving already existed, as in ministries of public health.

Graham (1968) found in Brazil that a basic cause of the lack of success was the failure "to come to terms with the conflict emerging between individual values and the new norms which had been forcibly applied to the administrative system" (Graham 1968:191). Simple imposition of foreign norms, concepts, and techniques frequently was not sufficient to change administrative behavior.

Serious stresses on the public administration systems in Latin America have resulted from what Graham (1987a:96–98) refers to as the "myth of state supremacy." For much of the mid-1900s, promoters of economic development argued for stronger national governments, which would have the technical and administrative capacity to plan and direct the development process. This included not only various centralized staff agencies for budgeting and planning but also a vast decentralized structure made up of a variety of government enterprises, corporations, institutes, credit and development banks, and other institutions in a loosely articulated "independent public subsector" (as it is termed in Peru). This sector typically was allocated a very large portion of the national budget, often without centralized budget control.

In the last quarter of the 20th century, a widespread reaction to the apparent inefficiencies of the public bureaucracy and the independent public subsector has led to efforts to reduce the dominant role of the state in economic planning, direction, and control. All over the region (even in Cuba), private initiative and market concepts are being employed more fully. A deliberate effort to reduce the size and scope of the public sector began in many countries. (Hopkins 1996).

IV. REVOLUTIONARY CHANGE

Several situations in widely separated countries allow us to assess the impact of revolutionary change on public administration systems of Latin America. The most prominent cases in point are Cuba after 1959, Chile during the government of Salvador Allende (1970–73), and Nicaragua following the Sandinista revolution of 1979. In each of these three states, the established system underwent radical alterations that took different forms. It will be instructive to examine the three cases in order to evaluate the extent to which seemingly impervious systems were affected by these radical pressures.

A. Cuba

Typical of many revolutionary societies, Cuba struggled after the revolution of 1959 with the problems of constructing a reliable apparatus to manage the affairs of state. Many of the early postrevolution officials were poorly prepared for public administration careers; many came from socioeconomic groups with little or no management experience. To fill the void left when large numbers of the trained bureaucratic personnel fled Cuba after 1959, untrained people were thrust into responsible administrative positions.

Not surprisingly, one of the most important criteria for selecting bureaucratic personnel was political reliability. Leaders of the revolutionary movement were forced to emphasize reliability when they faced (alleged) sabotage by hostile administrators during the early years of the revolutionary government (Petras 1970). As in Maoist China, stronger weight was put on political purity than on technical competence; the Maoist alternative, "politics takes command," had many analogies in early revolutionary Cuba (Whyte 1973). Thus, some of the normal sources of bureaucratic efficiency were sacrificed for greater political reliability. Several years were to pass before sufficient administrators who were both technically trained and politically reliable began to come from Cuban universities and training institutes.

Partly because of the mass exodus of trained administrators, and partly because of rapid rotation of competent people from one position to another to meet critical needs, the majority of bureaucrats in the early years were generalists with limited specialized competence (Petras 1970:17).

Petras (1970:17) describes the "ambulating bureaucrat" as the characteristic feature of the Cuban bureaucracy. Much of this resulted from the early overwhelming load of immediate problems and tasks that befell the revolutionary government. The ambulatory bureaucrat is "constantly on the move attempting to locate problems and to solve them on the spot. . . . Most bureaucratic activity focuses on specific problems encountered in specific areas." This ad hoc approach to problem solving, however, contributed little to the building of institutional capability in the regular bureaucracy and, indeed, may have complicated institution building. The Cubans refer to this style as *por la libre*, typified by Fidel Castro's own free-wheeling decisionmaking (Harris 1992:78). By the early 1970s, a sort of "democratic centralism" had evolved as part of the gradual institutionalization, but there was always the tendency for this approach to become bureaucratic centralism, and exactly this often occurred. The economic crisis of the late 1960s and the "rectification process" led to the adoption of new organizational principles which were intended to promote democratic centralism, and to strengthen the role of the new professionals in the bureaucracy (Fitzgerald 1990:60–61).

Institution building, in many respects, poses one of the most perplexing of the problems of revolutionary societies. Transforming social and political revolutionaries into competent technicians and administrators who will serve the now-stable state is extraordinarily difficult. Typically, many serious mistakes are committed before a new cadre of leaders becomes available. Even now, 40 years after the revolution, many problems of administration remain.

The inadequate cadre of trained administrators was only one of the problems. Complicating the task of building an effective state apparatus was the rapid collectivization of economic activities in Cuba after 1959. By 1968, virtually 100% of industry, construction, transportation, retail trade, wholesale and foreign trade, banking, and education was collectivized (Mesa-Lago 1970:204). The administrative burden that faced the underdeveloped bureaucracy was enormous. Serious errors in state planning resulted as the inexperienced personnel attempted to cope with the new challenges. In another respect, the dominant power and personality cult that surrounded Fidel Castro was contrary to the whole process of institution building or institutionalization of the revolution. Orderly and consistent policymaking by the bureaucracy was interrupted constantly by the ad hoc decisions of the "Maximum Leader" himself.

The revolution had established its credibility early with the popular sector by a series of steps and policies: agrarian reform, defiance of the United States (including defeat of the Bays of Pigs invasion), rent reductions, wage increases, and others. But undermining that credibility was increasing economic stringency, brought to a head by the eventual loss of Soviet support in the 1980s. Even before the collapse of the Soviet Union, Cuban policy making was characterized by fits and starts that seriously complicated effective institution building. Battles among the ruling elite, the struggle to define Cuba's international role, and disagreement over the appropriate economic model for Cuba made the task of institutionalizing the revolution difficult. A host of specialized agencies and organizations emerged, but often without rational connection with the formal bureaucracy. Juan del Aguila describes the result as a "veritable bureaucratic anarchy." (Aguila, p. 80). In the mid-1980s, Castro declared that the revolution had lost its way, and he attacked practices and institutions that undermined the revolution, including profiteering, *empleomania* (overstaffing), and the complaisant bureaucracy (Padula, 1993, pp. 30–310). Castro's attacks on "bureaucratism" and the privileged position of bureaucratic officials have been a constant in Cuban politics. Many of the problems, as Juan del Aguila observes, stemmed from the regime's "sacrificing economic rationality to political considerations and social mobilization." (Aguila 1984:48). Power was concentrated in the revolutionary elite and the developmental model depended on appeals to sacrifice and obedience. As time passed, clearer lines of responsibility were gradually established among the various administrative and state organs. But the process of institutionalization has not reached the stage where a differentiated bureaucracy can exert substantial influence on major decisions.

Despite substantial opening of certain economic sectors, particularly tourism and mining, to foreign investment, the Cuban economy is still essentially a planned economy and state enterprises continue to dominate. Limited market reforms in the early 1990s, such as free farmers' markets and "dollarization," have not changed that reality. Virtually all final decisions are still made at the top level by party and central planning officials, despite the stated intention to decentralize management for more local, grassroots control. Habel (1991:74) observes that in several parts of the state apparatus "it is the cadres' long training received in the Soviet Union that is dominant." Whether such training fits the current challenges confronting Cuba remains highly problematical. "The Cuban leadership is searching for a middle way to avoid the pitfalls of bureaucratic planning, on the one hand, and the damaging effects of market reforms, on the other" (Habel 1991:167).

Harris (1992:85–86) sees the selection of cadres (the directive leadership of the bureaucracy) to be a critical and necessary element for the democratization of the basic organizational structures, and as yet, selection of directive cadres is under the control of the top leadership. Since 1970, however, the increasing output of training institutes and schools has produced large numbers of better-trained "new professionals" who are slowly replacing some of the old cadres in the bureaucracy, though not without resistance. (Fitzgerald 1990:Ch.5).

Despite all the "rectification" efforts, the Cuban government continues to be plagued by various forms of bureaucratic centralism. This may take the form of undue interference or usurpation by high-level officials in the decisions that have been delegated to lower-level officials or by higher officials' bypassing worker participation in preparing and implementing plans. (Fitzgerald 1990:Ch. 6). The old habits stemming from the highly centralized decisionmaking that was characteristic of the earlier period have been hard to break, even with the intensified rectification efforts and reemphasis on moral incentives that began in 1986. Whether Cuba will be able to achieve a higher level of democratic centralism, given the enormous challenges facing the regime as the 40th anniversary of the revolution approached, remains very problematic.

B. Chile

The free election of Socialist candidate Salvador Allende to the presidency of Chile in 1970 may be classified as revolutionary because Allende was "firmly committed to fundamental transformation of his country's existing socio-economic order" (Valenzuela 1978:41). He rapidly moved to attempt to enact and implement his social and economic program, which included income redistribution, expansion of government programs and services, state control of key industries, and extension of land reform.

Unfortunately, Allende's attempt to radically transform class and property relations in Chile was forced to contend with "a highly polarized society with strong centrifugal tendencies," and his initiatives "were blocked in the rambling bureaucracy and questioned by the courts, the Contraloria, and the Congress" (Valenzuela 1978:59–60). By its very nature, the Chilean bureaucracy was difficult to control and direct into new paths of development. As Cleaves (1974:1) observes, Allende found it necessary to depend somewhat more on unions, political parties, and paramilitary groups to promote his political program. Although the national government was highly centralized geographically in Santiago, a large part of the bureaucracy was composed of "institutionally decentralized" agencies. Before 1970, some 35% of the budget of the national government went to the decentralized agencies, which had responsibility for the regulation of vast areas of Chilean society. The directorates of these agencies were made up in large part of representatives of various interest groups in Chile. Recruitment for government agencies relied heavily on political patronage, so that a very informal political system operated within and alongside an ostensibly formal civil service (Parrish 1971). The difficulty of controlling the bureaucracy was aggravated by the policy of the Central Bank in bypassing normal budgetary procedures and lending large amounts of funds to nationalized industries as well as to other government agencies. As Valenzuela (1978:64) observes, "The already cumbersome and decentralized Chilean public sector became more and more unmanageable." The critical weakness of the Allende government was that it was a minority presidency (Allende received 36.2% of the vote in 1970) and the Congress was dominated by the Christian Democrats and the Right. To control the coalition system, it was necessary to share government patronage with each party organization by means of a complex quota system. At all levels, from ministers down to the lowest officials, "elaborate schemes were instituted to divide up public employment and responsibility" (Valenzuela 1978:65).

In the process, the Allende government suffered seriously in its effectiveness and its ability to assert control. Party cleavages at every level complicated the task of implementing change. Valenzuela (1978:56–66) points out how the fractionalization of parties and the politics of quotas and political appointments caused the loss of governmental authority. Orders from managers who belonged to other parties were simply ignored by workers, and frequently party meetings were necessary to resolve the impasse.

These problems only reinforced the tendencies of the Chilean state bureaucracy toward decentralization and autonomy of sectors. The government increasingly lost a sense of clear direction, and Allende's control of many officials and programs was severely restricted. Traditional decision-making institutions lost much of their authority over policies and programs; the system faced collapse. "In time mobilization would get out of hand, but it was the countermobilization of those who felt threatened in a system which lost authority which finally contributed to the breakdown of Chilean democracy" (Valenzuela 1978:107). "The surprise," Cleaves (1974:321) concludes, "was that Allende, the politician, did not reach a compromise with his opponents (as had his predecessors with theirs) in time to avert a total rejection of his policy accomplishments and the reigning political system."

C. Nicaragua

Following the Sandinista victory in 1979, the new government acted with alacrity to quickly create or reorganize a different state apparatus. In some cases, where the overthrown Somoza regime had simply neglected certain social services, the challenge was to construct virtually from the ground up an apparatus for handling newly established state services. That was a daunting task, as Vanden and Prevost (1993:1) observe:

> When it took power in July 1979, the Sandinista government of Nicaragua did not have any well-developed theory of Marxist democracy on which to draw. Nor did it have fully democratic models on which to base its praxis or on which it could rely for support, sustenance, and encouragement to develop its own democratic Marxism. There were few real-world examples and little support from actual nation states to develop a democratic form of socialism, and even fewer to do so within the specific historic conditions in Nicaragua.

In general, the Sandinista approach to system changes included three major elements: widespread consultation, mass participation, and decentralization. That the Sandinista revolution at base was a popular insurrection favored the development of the first two elements, particularly the participative approach. At the same time, the authoritarian traditions of Nicaragua and its long periods of dictatorial rule ill-equipped the country for rapid democratization. Much of the tension that followed the revolution stemmed from the inherent internal strains between the vanguard Sandinista party (the FSLN), the party that wished to lead the revolutionary transformation of Nicaragua, and its own ideals for democratizing the political system, that is, moving toward pluralism. Two of the fundamental principles of the FSLN, as presented to the people by Carlos Fonseca in the "Historic Principles" were, first, political pluralism and second, popular participation and mobilization (Wright 1995:78–79). As Vanden and Prevost (1993:6) point out, "The Sandinistas hoped to break with the old authoritarian [and bureaucratized] Marxism that had dominated the movement in and outside of Latin America." The real problem in Nicaragua was how to construct a democratic system within socialism. The paradox was that the FSLN, fearful of possible reversion to the sham democracy of *somocista* Nicaragua, kept substantial power for itself.

Previous neglect of social services such as health, education, and welfare programs left a great void of qualified professionals as well as the requisite bureaucratic structure to administer such functions. Thus the Sandinista government faced an enormous need for personnel committed to the revolution's goals. This demanded massive mobilization and popular participation, much of which was promoted from below rather than being imposed from above. The result, as Graham (1987a:20) notes, was "the interjection of considerable pragmatism as people learned administration by doing and responded to the demands articulated from below." "What was most distinctive about the Nicaraguan case," Graham (1987a:18) observes, "was the extent to which the revolutionary government had been able to create a very different state apparatus in a relatively short period of time." Indeed, one of the most fundamental characteristics of the new system was the real participation of common people at the local level. Accordingly, a network of neighborhood organizations developed throughout the country: the Sandinista Defense Committees;

AMNLAE (the women's organization); UNAG, the National Union of Farmers and Ranchers; new labor organizations, and the popular church was encouraged.

Extensive consultation with citizens was carried on in the *Consulta Nacional* with the objective of determining popular attitudes and appropriate structures for the public sector. Thus an enormous number of people became involved in the process at the grass-roots level; much of the initiative came from citizens taking upon themselves the burden of insuring that basic social services were available and accessible. In the process, the very nature of government was changed. However, when the state resumed jurisdiction, this informal citizen participation led to some conflicts with the formal procedures of government (Graham 1987a:20).

The regionalization and decentralization of the Nicaraguan state apparatus were complicated by debates over the appropriate roles for state and party. In the final analysis, the Sandinista leadership rejected the model of parallel state and party organizations from Soviet and East European experience. Instead, the choice was a fusion of state and party roles through dual responsibilities; in this way, the system provided for better articulation between party, state, and society (Graham 1987a:28–29).

Regionalization in Nicaragua resulted principally from central government leadership; there was no strong regional pressure, except from the eastern region, for such changes. Regionalization was seen as a measure to make the newly expanded state apparatus more efficient and to strengthen the municipalities. The regional governments were seen as a means to provide decentralized support to the municipalities throughout the country. Wilson describes the Nicaraguan regionalization as an outstanding example of "participatory, bottom-up planning." In the planning system in Nicaragua, grass-roots participation was not nearly as evident as in the development of the social services functions or in the municipalities where resource allocation is "highly participatory." Nevertheless, some ministries did encourage public meetings and workshops at the zonal level (Wilson 1987:50–54).

In post-1979 Nicaragua, the distinguishing characteristic of public administration was the grass-roots organizations that developed outside the formal state apparatus. This factor provided the spark and the dynamism that made government work under difficult conditions. As Graham (1987a:31) observes, the mass mobilization creased "a new, younger generation of self-taught, activist administrators who were learning to develop a pragmatic, flexible response to the groups closest at hand."

The first free elections after the 1979 revolution were conducted in 1984, and the government was reorganized after the elections. Although its basic structure remained much the same, the president, because of the state of emergency stemming from the contra war, assumed greater power than normal. Because of the war, the system hardly had a good opportunity to prove itself before the next elections of 1990, which ended Sandinista rule.

As a general phenomenon, the Sandinista revolution and its subsequent impact on Nicaraguan public administration are highly significant. So much of Latin American administration and bureaucratic norms has been emulative of other systems. But in Nicaragua, indigenous solutions were sought and developed. What was in the making between 1979 and 1986 was a new state apparatus and, consequently, the initiation for the first time in Latin American experience of an administrative system that was drawing its strength from national experiments rather than from models taken from abroad, be they capitalist or socialist (Graham 1987a:36).

The new government of Violeta Barrios de Chamorro, committed to neoliberal economic reform and backed by the United States and other capitalist governments, faced both a fractious legislature and a rebellious popular sector. As a result, Chamorro turned increasingly to executive powers as a means of bypassing the legislature and reorganizing the government. What residues of the revolutionary transformation will persist after the new administration, elected in 1996, remains to be seen.

V. POLICY IMPLICATIONS

The crucial test of any public bureaucracy comes from its capacity to formulate and implement policies effectively. Faced with the myriad, pressing tasks of economic growth, distribution, and development, Latin American bureaucracies struggle under a nearly impossible burden. Cultural expectations that favor government intervention are well established in Latin America, and governments have long exerted a major role in deciding who gets what, when, and how. But the dynamics of managing growth, distribution, increasing participation, and development have all but overwhelmed the public administration systems. Sloan (1984:247) observes:

> The ability of the government to control this volatile situation is further reduced by the low degree of legitimacy commanded by so many Latin American political systems. Because of this lack of legitimacy, and the political instability that inevitably follows, each social sector demands special protection, special administrative representation, special funds, earmarked taxes, constitutional provisions, and so forth, to assure that, whatever happens politically or economically, their particular social sector will maintain its benefits and security. No group has faith in the honesty, impartiality, and efficiency of the government. These attitudes then contribute to the inability, of the state to rationalize distributive policies in some overall development plan.

The general experience thus far suggests that more indigenous solutions, perhaps deriving from relatively abrupt changes, are more likely to cope effectively with the urgent problems of development than are imported models. Yet under even the best conditions, the weight of the past, economic imperatives, demands for broader participation, and pressures for more equitable distribution combine to confront governments of Latin America with enormously difficult policy choices. The public bureaucracies, in general, are ill equipped to handle the task.

VI. CONCLUSIONS

The infinite variety of bureaucratic types in Latin America complicates the difficulty of broad generalizations on the theme. The need for a "broadly integrative work to coherently and systematically relate and test an array of hypotheses" (Hopkins 1973:134) remains unfulfilled. Although an increasing number of discrete, idiographic studies are available on individual countries, public administration systems, and specific bureaucratic organizations, comprehensive integration of such studies has not been attempted. Perhaps that is an unrealistic goal for the social sciences.

The title of this chapter suggests the concluding generalization. After over 300 years of colonial rule and some 175 years of independent government, the enduring patterns of bureaucracy in Latin America persist except for the few cases were thoroughgoing political and social revolution have occurred. Even in those instances, much of the characteristic core, in terms of bureaucratic style, remains. The tenacity of those features, given the long history of attempted reform, governmental turnovers, foreign influences, and directed attempts at exogenous change, is truly remarkable. The bureaucracies appear to have deeply absorbed and internalized certain characteristics of colonial administration as well as cardinal features of the culture, and these have, in effect, served to transmute attempts at change in a peculiar Latin American mold.

REFERENCES

Aguila, J.M. del *Cuba: Dilemmas of a Revolution.* Westview, Boulder, CO, 1984.
Baloyra, E. and Morris, J.A., eds. *Conflict and Change in Cuba.* University of New Mexico Press, Albuquerque, 1993.

Booth, J.A. *The End and the Beginning: The Nicaraguan Revolution.* Westview Press, Boulder, CO, 1985.

Centro de Estudios Sobre America. *The Cuban Revolution into the 1990s: Cuban Perspectives.* Westview Press, Boulder, CO, 1992.

Cleaves, P.S. *Bureaucratic Politics and Administration in Chile.* University of California Press, Berkeley, 1974.

Conroy, M.E., ed. *Nicaragua: Profiles of the Revolutionary Public Sector.* Westview Press, Boulder, CO, 1987.

Daland, R.T. Development administration and the Brazilian political system. *Western Political Quarterly*, *21*(June):331 (1968).

Fernandez, D., ed. *Cuban Studies Since the Revolution.* University Press of Florida, Gainesville, 1992.

Fitzgerald, F.T. *Managing Socialism: From Old Cadres to New Professionals in Revolutionary Cuba.* Praeger, Westport, CT, 1990.

Graham, L.S. *Civil Service Reform in Brazil: Principles Versus Practice.* University of Texas Press, Austin, 1968.

Graham, L.S. The impact of the revolution on the state apparatus. In *Nicaragua: Profiles of the Revolutionary Public Sector* (M. Conroy, ed.). Westview Press, Boulder, CO, 1987a.

Graham, L.S. Independence and nation building in Latin America. In *Latin America: Perspectives on a Region* (J.W. Hopkins, ed.). Holmes & Meier, New York, 1987.

Groves, R.T. Administrative reform and the politics of reform: the case of Venezuela. *Public Administration Review*, *27*:436–445 (1967).

Guerreiro-Ramos, A. The new ignorance and the future of public administration in Latin America. LADAC paper, April 1970.

Habel, J. *Cuba: The Revolution in Peril.* Verso, London, 1991.

Harris, R.L. Bureaucracy versus democracy in contemporary Cuba: an assessment of thirty years of organizational development. In *Cuba in Transition: Crisis and Transformation.* Westview Press, Boulder, CO, 1992.

Hopkins, J.W. Dialectical organizations in developing systems: barriers in the Latin American case. *Journal of Comparative Administration*, *3*:357 (1971).

Hopkins, J.W. Contemporary research on public administration and bureaucracies in Latin America. *Latin American Research Review*, *9*(Spring):134 (1973).

Hopkins, J.W. Public enterprise management in Latin America. In *Public Enterprise Management: International Case Studies* (A. Farazmand, ed.). Greenwood Press, Westport, CT, 1996.

Leeds, A. Brazilian careers and social structure: an evolutionary model and case history. *American Anthropologist*, *66*(December):1337 (1964).

Mesa-Lago, C. Ideological radicalization and economic policy in Cuba. *Studies in Comparative Economic Development*, *5*(10):204 (1970).

Padula, A. Cuban socialism: thirty years of controversy. In *Conflict and Change in Cuba* (E.A. Baloyra and J.A. Morris, eds.). University of New Mexico Press, Albuquerque, 1993.

Parrish, C.J. Bureaucracy, democracy, and development: some considerations based on the Chilean case. LADAC Occasional Papers, Series 2, No. 1. University of Texas, Institute of Latin American Studies, Austin, 1971.

Perez-Stable, M. "We are the only ones and there is no alternative": vanguard party politics in Cuba, 1975–1991. In *Conflict and Change in Cuba*, University of New Mexico Press, Albuquerque, 1993.

Petras, J.F. Formulating and implementing public policy in a revolutionary setting: the case of Cuba. LADAC paper, April 1970.

Ritter, A.R.M., and Kirk, J.M., eds. *Cuba in the International System: Normalization and Integration.* St. Martin's Press, New York, 1995.

Ruffin, P. *Capitalism and Socialism in Cuba: A Study of Dependency, Development and Underdevelopment.* St. Martin's, New York, 1990.

Sloan, J.W. *Public Policy in Latin America: A Comparative Survey.* University of Pittsburgh Press, Pittsburgh, 1984.

Spalding, R. *Capitalists and Revolution in Nicaragua: Opposition and Accommodation, 1979–1993.* University of North Carolina Press, Chapel Hill, 1994.

Thurber, C.E. Islands of development: a political and social approach to development administration in Latin America. LADAC paper, 1966.

Tuohy, W.S. Centralism and political elite behavior in Mexico. In *Development Administration in Latin America* (C.E. Thurber and L.S. Graham, eds.). Duke University Press, Durham, NC, 1973.

Valenzuela, A. *The Breakdown of Democratic Regimes: Chile.* Johns Hopkins University Press, Baltimore, 1978.

Vanden, H.E., and Prevost, G. *Democracy and Socialism in Sandinista Nicaragua.* Lynne Rienner Publishers, Boulder, CO, 1993.

Walker, T.W., ed. *Nicaragua Without Illusions: Regime Transition and Structural Adjustment in the 1990s.* Scholarly Resources, Wilmington, DE, 1997.

Weaver, J.L. Bureaucracy during a period of social change: the Guatemalan case. LADAC Occasional Papers, Series 2, No. 2, 1971.

Weaver, J.L. Bureaucracy during a period of social change: the case of Guatemala. In *Development Administration in Latin America* (C.E. Thurber and L.S. Graham, eds.). Duke University Press, Durham, NC, 1973.

Whyte, M.K. Bureaucracy and modernization in China: the Maoist critique. *American Sociological Review,* *38*(April):149–163 (1973).

Wilson, P.A. A comparative evaluation of regionalization and decentralization. In *Nicaragua: Profiles of the Revolutionary Public Sector* (M. Conroy, ed.). Westview Press, Boulder, CO, 1987.

Wright, B.E. *Theory in the Practice of the Nicaraguan Revolution.* Ohio University Center for International Studies, Latin American Studies No. 24, Athens, 1995.

Wright, F.J. Bureaucracy and political development: an application of Almond and Powell to Latin America. University of Arizona, Institute of Government Research, Research Series No. 3, Tucson, 1970.

74

Regime Changes, the Bureaucracy, and Political Development

Ledivina V. Cariño　　*College of Public Administration, University of the Philippines,*
Quezon City, Philippines

> Even in case of revolution by force or of occupation by an enemy, the bureaucratic machinery
> will normally continue to function just as it has for the previous legal government.
> 　　　　　　　　　　　　　　　　　　　　　　　　　　　—Weber (1947:338)

I.　INTRODUCTION

The civil service is the arm of the government in implementing its vision for the people under its
jurisdiction. Students of public administration generally regard it to be a neutral, professional institution that can serve any regime. The seeming ease with which the civil service glides from one
government to the next has made the interaction of a regime and the bureaucracy[1] practically a non-
issue in the discipline, discussed only in scattered references in the theoretical literature. Yet even
a cursory reading of administrative case studies and bureaucratic history would suggest that this is
a grave omission, since this relationship varies along several important factors, frequently becomes
conflictual, and is sometimes blamed for the failure of political leaders to transform society.

　　This chapter attempts to fill this gap by taking Weber's statement as its hypothesis. The relationship between a regime and a bureaucracy during a change of government can be marked by
disruption as well as continuity. I contend that continuity has been assumed because public administration (PA) has tended to operate under two limiting perspectives: (1) a liberal view of the role
of the state in society and (2) an evolutionary, "value-neutral" concept of political development.
These have tended to view the bureaucracy as a simple receptacle of regime decisions, uninvolved
in and unaffected by political forces—groups as well as ideas—clashing in the social arena. Suggesting a perspective that can more easily permit PA to deal with one of the key intersection points
of politics and administration—the regime-bureaucracy nexus—is thus the first task of this chapter. Second, I will explore patterns of regime-bureaucracy interaction (RBI). Finally, based on
that, I will make preliminary conclusions on the relationship of RBI and political development and
on bureaucratic tenacity and change.

II.　A BROADER FIELD OF PUBLIC ADMINISTRATION

To make the field of PA both manageable and scientific, "running the Constitution" as opposed to
"framing it" (adapted from Wilson 1887) has been its main preoccupation. Despite an increasing-

ly rich harvest of papers on such subjects as the political bureaucracy and the bureaucracy-democracy connection, the lens continues to be trained on the technical capacity and activities of the administrative system. When other political institutions are discussed, the civil service is usually seen as taking orders from the political leadership or reacting to demands of other groups, rather than as the initiator of the interaction or its active protagonist.

These have long been exposed as fictions. It is well known that the bureaucracy interacts with political institutions and groups other than its presumed boss, the political leadership. Indeed, aware of the power lurking in its expertise, monopoly of information, size, and permanence, the organization has even been uncovered as a possible bureaucracy-for-itself, serving chiefly its own interests rather than those of its superiors—the regime heads, and the people. Nevertheless, despite systematic treatment of other political-administrative issues and numerous case studies to the contrary, the Weberian idea has persisted. Consider Goonatilake: "It is difficult to imagine that the behaviour of a bureaucracy would change in any fundamental manner largely as a result of changing the national political regime" (1975:6).[2] Thus, the field has continued to treat the bureaucracy as a mere administrative instrument, its involvement in politics circumscribed by its subordination to the ordained power holders.

A. Role of the State in Society

This view proceeds from the liberal perspective of the role of the state in society. Under it, the state is a neutral arbiter of demands of relatively equal groups, a contrast to the Marxist position of a capital-dominated state (Held 1983). Although they posit different roles for the state, these two positions look at bureaucracy in similar terms: a willing subject of the political leadership, with no links to other social forces. They also maintain the same ambivalence about its power—at times considering it as a mere implementor of regime decisions, at others recognizing it as potent in its own right.

A third view sees the state as the entity forced to decide on labor-capital conflicts, ethnic clashes, religious riots, and other societal problems.[3] This view continues the liberal assumption of a relatively autonomous state but accepts the Marxist image of a society composed of conflicting groups with unequal economic and political power. The state here practically has the status of a "playing referee," tending to side with the already privileged. However, from time to time, it may align with nondominants because of their strength and militance or the desire to pacify them for the longer-term success of the capitalist enterprise or an ethnic group's continued hegemony.

If this larger perspective is accepted, then the state is not only placed in a turbulent environment but the bureaucracy itself has to be recognized as among the groups involved in the struggle. It may serve dominants or have-nots, be congruent or at variance with the desires of the regime, pursue its own interests or be the conduit of those with other ideas. In contrast to the first two, this view regards bureaucratic autonomy from both the state and society as an empirical question.

B. Political and Administrative Development

Public administration assumes the political context of a liberal democracy under which goals are set by a political leadership directly responsible to the sovereign people through elections. The bureaucracy fulfills its responsibility as it becomes a compliant implementor of regime policies. The leadership hands down the political guide for bureaucratic actions. Meanwhile, the administrative criteria of economy, efficiency, and rationality are expected to be universal and applicable to all bureaucracies.

With the emergence of new states in the late 1940s, Western exportation of the discipline became more vigorous even as many countries abandoned (or never sought) liberal democracy.

The inclusion of "development" as a primary goal did not change the emphasis on technical issues, since the concept was often reduced to a computable factor. The idea of development as "orderly" also engendered an acceptance of a kind of social change where the already privileged maintained their dominance, while only lip service was paid to social justice. This made development administration a technocratic instrument squarely on the side of the status quo.

In time, development administration even appeared to be better suited to authoritarian settings (Nef and Dwivedi 1981). It developed the bureaucracy at the expense of representative institutions, propagated administrative tools adapted from military purposes, neglected the more time-consuming (and more democratic) processes of participation and negotiations, and centered on streamlining machinery and procedures rather than access for and responsiveness to the people.

This was taking place in a receptive social science environment where "political development" was being described in similar terms. A conflict-free political order was expected to preside over rapid social change (Huntington 1968) and the development of the political system seemed unilinear, evolutionary, and irreversible (as criticized by Riggs 1968)—this, while movements for independence, general strikes, coups, and revolutions were taking place all over the world. The study of administration was indifferent to these political currents, as if civil servants simply waited on the sidelines to serve dispassionately the eventual victor.

The concept of "political development" centered, as public administration did, on capacities and performance of political institutions. "Democracy," the dispersion of power, was not at the core of the definition both because it conveyed a bias toward Western political institutions and because many American client-states would thus be excluded (Pye 1966).

It should be obvious that I am not satisfied with the mainstream view of the field and its political environment. Political development for me does not necessarily convey an image of modern institutions—even one including a strong, efficient and capable bureaucracy—if amid concentrated power and a cowed citizenry. Rather it must describe a country that is the focus of the collective commitments of its people, including its civil servants, that is moving toward greater pluralism and popular liberation, that allows for dissent and alternation of power. Democracy is thus very much a part of this concept. A country suffers discontinuities in political development if its pluralist course is cut down by an authoritarian takeover. It may sink further as other dictators grab power or move forward again by restoring democracy.

By the same token, a bureaucracy is adjudged developed as it becomes a responsible democratic institution. The technical side is not obliterated, but it plays a secondary role to political values. Ritualistic compliance with rules, no matter how methodologically expert, is not administrative development. Nor is effective pursuit of antipopular goals.

III. PATTERNS OF REGIME-BUREAUCRACY INTERACTION

The interaction of a political leadership and its civil service takes place in a state presiding over societal conflicts and subject to advances or reversals in political development. Here, a regime's mastery over the bureaucracy is not automatic. Rather, they are in a constant struggle for control. Their relationship takes two main forms: regime ascendancy and bureaucratic subordination, or bureaucratic power-sharing and coequality with the regime.

Regime ascendancy is the legal norm in most countries and is supported by the politics-administration dichotomy. The functional difference between politics and administration and the hierarchical precedence of politics are inarguable (Kirwan 1987). The problem arises when the functions are assigned institutional domains and the norm is assumed to describe an unchanging dominance of the regime over the bureaucracy. Also, because the bureaucracy is assumed to be neutral, values and commitments of its members are regarded as aberrations from the theory and are often ignored. Thus, a new regime's inherited bureaucracy is expected "to normally continue to function as before," whatever its differences with the incumbent government's beliefs, methods, and goals.

The second form, bureaucratic power-sharing, is necessarily short of dominance; otherwise the bureaucracy becomes the political leadership. The civil service manages to achieve some coequality with the regime by getting it to promulgate its proposals or to implement them regardless of formal policy. Some bureaucracies have promoted their goals not so much in dominating the leadership as in "resisting subordination" (Weaver, speaking of post-1944 Guatemala, 1973:359) or in "insulating itself from all but the most drastic changes of political direction" (Siegel, on the Brazilian civil service, 1973:374). In extreme cases, bureaucratic ascendancy may amount to a power grab without formal replacement of the leadership.

The regime-bureaucracy struggle can best be seen during periods of government succession. Since most new regimes are critical of their predecessor's performance, each will attempt to reform and control this inherited organization upon its installation. For its part, the civil service may comply with enthusiasm, resist, or proceed with policies of its own.

The relationship of the regime and the bureaucracy is expected to differ in democratic and authoritarian systems. The matrix below shows four possible interaction patterns. I analyze each cell based on theoretical contributions and actual examples. I hope to show the dynamics of the encounter by citing some struggles of the leadership and the bureaucracy particularly during regime change.

A.   Democracy and Regime Ascendancy

Cell 1 is the legally expected interaction of a political leadership and bureaucracy in a democracy. But simple obedience to law cannot explain the persistence of this model even in Great Britain. While strong public service unions and support of client groups have provided the civil service some power, the latter's control is maintained because of more policy continuity among the British parties than is usually recognized (Navarro 1976; Kingsley 1952).

On the other hand, a bureaucracy may sabotage a new regime that has markedly different goals from the one it replaced. For instance, in the 1940s, the radical Saskatchewan Cooperative Commonwealth Federation (CCF) failed to fulfill its reform agenda as bureaucrats made themselves indispensable to the new governors but continued to implement reactionary policies, even to the extent of changing the intent of CCF's new laws (Lipset 1952). Thus although pre-CCF, the regime-bureaucracy interaction (RBI) exemplified Cell 1, with the CCF, the RBI became that of Cell 2.

A regime-dominant situation does not even require a merit system. The Dominican Republic functions under spoils, reinstituted since 1951 by the dictator Trujillo. Succeeding elected presidents justify this arrangement as more politically correct, as it safeguards their "traditional right" to dismiss political enemies and reward friends. Their contention is supported by many civil servants who had gotten their jobs through patrons and fear to lose them if reform legislators succeed in reinstituting the merit system (Kearney 1986).

Possible Patterns of Regime-Bureaucracy Interaction

Political system	Regime ascendancy	Bureaucratic coprimacy
Democratic	1	2
Authoritarian	3	4

In the case of the Philippines, the ascendancy of the political leadership was maintained through six postindependence regime changes. That civil service was a mixed system—a strong law favoring merit, and political interference in appointments but not in promotions. Bureaucratic subordination had been nurtured by American tutelage, a strong presidency, and staffing by specialists, which has made a combined career in administration and politics quite a rarity.

Bureaucratic subordination has continued through the authoritarian years (1972–1986) and the redemocratizing regime of Corazon Aquino (1986 to date). Her presidency is relatively weaker because of both new constitutional provisions and her personal preference. The civil service is stronger, having more militant employee organizations that are supported by labor, cause-oriented groups, and the senate. However, it remains unable—and unwilling—to contest the leadership for power, appearing to be content with being treated more fairly, rather than gaining more power for itself (Cariño 1988).

Regime dominance may also be fostered by the leadership's strong links with popular forces, making orchestrated resistance to it futile. This is illustrated by Nicaragua's Sandinista government (1979 to date), which took over the civil service left behind by the Somoza dictatorship. It was a particular target of the CIA's infamous manual, which gave precise examples on how government personnel may sabotage the new regime. This has not happened, although there remain traces of workers' "historic vacation" (malingering and absenteeism) (Collins 1982; Borge 1982). The Sandinista regime did not purge personnel, but reorganized the bureaucracy and made it more permeable and subject to popular organizations (Oquist 1986).

B. Democracy and Bureaucratic Coprimacy

Cell 2 depicts a bureaucracy-dominated democracy. This arrangement has been prescribed as a means of safeguarding democracy, particularly in situations where the bureaucracy appears to be the most responsive political institution. For instance, Etzioni-Halevy encourages the bureaucracy to "exempt itself from political control in order to prevent the disruption of the democratic process itself" (1985, p. 92). Otherwise, she avers, the allocation of resources will be based on "open or disguised bribery" of supporters to buy their loyalty. She equates permanent appointments with the bureaucracy's ability to resist partisan pressures.

Not all analysts are as supportive of bureaucratic coprimacy. Etzioni-Halevy herself warns that the power struggle of the civil service and the political leadership is most difficult because it comes at the point of no rules, that is, outside the electoral process where loss or victory is decided by majority vote (Etzioni-Halevy 1985:96–98).

Ideally, a bureaucracy operating in Cell 2 is participatory and nonhierarchical, dealing directly with public interest groups representing racial, gender, and class minorities. Because of its avowed responsiveness, its proponents seem to suggest that it can ignore elected intermediaries between the civil service and the people (Thompson 1983; Harmon 1971).

Yet democracy may not be served by this arrangement. Thompson (1983:246–248) notes that officials may simply play off competing groups against each other or coopt them to legitimize decisions bureaucrats prefer.

Moreover, even a bureaucracy's actions in favor of the poor may not necessarily signal a strong commitment to substantive democracy. Instead, as Poulantzas (1980:146) warns, "They [the bureaucrats] may interpret the theme of democratization of the state not in terms of popular intervention in public affairs but as the restoration of their own role as arbiters standing above social classes."

Bureaucratic coprimacy may result from intrinsic characteristics such as its expertise, permanence, and institutionalization (Weber 1947; Kamenka and Krygier 1979). For instance, the Indian bureaucracy was said to allow reforms to prosper only if they were a "means of increasing their [civil servants'] power or [if] neutral vis-à-vis their existing roles" (Jain 1976:427). This situation has even been generalized to a proposition, drawing from examples in Latin America, that "reforms often strengthened the capacity of the national bureaucracies to dominate their environments" (Parrish 1973:230).

The situation seemed to be different in newly independent Bangladesh at the start of Sheik Mujibur Rahman's regime (1971–1974). Attempting to introduce socialism and reverse bureaucratic dominance under Pakistan, the 1971 constitution had provided for dismissals and demotions at the pleasure of the president. The leadership also removed senior officials' prerequisites and made the pay structure more flat to control conspicuous consumption and provide for equity. The initial result was a "denounced, demoralized and demotivated bureaucracy" (Kahn and Zafarullah 1982:160).

Nevertheless, within a year, the civil service has persuaded the leadership to shelve the reorganization plan. Moreover, Mujib's efforts at decentralization were captured by civil servants who (instead of elected officials) filled local positions and mobilized people in the guise of popular participation. The regime also lost moral authority as it allowed political connections to prevail, and as its redistributive schemes benefited the middle class, which was its backbone of support, instead of the poor as its slogans proclaimed (Islam 1985).

The Mexican system at first glance seems to exemplify a leadership's dominance over the bureaucracy. Since presidents are prohibited from succeeding themselves, every election period results in a wholesale turnover of positions, with the incoming president bringing his own top officials and their aides (Tuohy 1973). However, because the new incumbent is handpicked by his predecessor, the civil service may not be so much replaced as rearranged, with an official named to a new position bringing his old staff with him (Weaver 1973).

This situation allows civil servants to maintain a long-term career in government and to consolidate their power vis-à-vis the transient *politicos*. For instance, Camp reports that bureaucrats withheld information from President Luis Echevarria (1970–1976) on the true potential of Mexican oil reserves "for fear that he would use it irresponsibly" (1985:113). Further bureaucratic capture of the leadership may be manifested in another passage from Camp: "Now, rather than influencing decisions with their advice, *they are making most of their own decisions directly*" (1985:113, my emphasis). This is a situation similar to the CCF experience in Saskatchewan described earlier (Lipset 1952). These suggest that democracy may be precarious in a situation of bureaucratic attempts to share power.

C. Authoritarianism and Regime Ascendancy

Cell 3 marks bureaucratic subordination under an authoritarian leadership. The concentration of power in the ruler gives the bureaucracy (and indeed any other political institution) very little room to maneuver.

The Korean experience under Park Chung Hee (1961–1963) is relevant here. Park ousted the year-old democratic government installed by the students' uprising that had in turn led to the fall of Syngman Rhee, first president of the Republic of Korea. The Park regime immediately "wiped out" the politicians (Cho 1970:133). It seemed more cordial to the civil service, allowing "ideas accumulated under previous governments [to be] presented through the hands of civil servants" (Cho 1970:134). However, any bureaucratic designs for coprimacy were felled by a ruthless purge that removed more than a fourth of the civil servants. Moreover, dishonesty in public office became punishable by death (Cho 1970).

The military government also translated the planning and programming system it had successfully used in the Korean War. That innovation was fought by civil servants because of its strong military underpinnings, the secrecy that surrounded its preparation, and their perception that it would be a control mechanism over them. Such struggle proved futile, since the military regime was supported by the private sector in its new thrusts and methods and in its desire for bureaucratic overhaul.

Within two years, Park felt secure enough to retire his uniform and succeed himself through elections. At that point, he had also managed many changes in the bureaucracy, reserving as much as a fourth of top administrative positions to former military officers, and making merit the basis for career mobility. However, while the civil service lost the battle to preserve its personnel, it had little problem with the regime's conservative stance, pro-American leanings, and rejection of the militant studentry.

The Nazis effected a more radical transformation of the bureaucracy through changes of personnel (permeation of Nazi activists into the service, parallel Nazi-bureaucracy jurisdictions, dismissals, and transfers), replacement of law by discretion, propaganda, and terror. Burin (1952) argues that Weber's hypothesis of bureaucratic tenacity could not apply to Nazification because the charismatic and arbitrary regime was outside the bounds of the rational bureaucratic ethos he had assumed in his analysis.

The fear of violent reprisals by the regime also characterized the Philippine civil service under martial law (1972–1986). With summary dismissals and worse threats hanging over their heads, the personnel consented to distortions and violations of professional standards, leading some to circulate social indicators that made the regime look good, undertake mass mobilization in the guise of people empowerment, or count poll results before election day.

D. Authoritarianism and Bureaucratic Coprimacy

Cell 4 shows authoritarian leadership joined by a bureaucracy assuming less explicitly subordinate roles. Usually, leaders of military and civilian bureaucracies combine in ruling the state. Civilian power in the coalition may increase over time.

In Indonesia under guided democracy (1959–1965), Sukarno maintained a difficult balance between the military and the Communist party, with the civil service perceptibly below the coalition. The military led by General Suharto gained the upper hand following the 1965 Communist massacre. His New Order State (1965 to date) declared all civil servants as members of GOLKAR, the ruling party, formally incorporating them into the leadership. Their power sharing developed less abruptly, but after 20 years, the leadership can be said to be a mix of the military and civil service, heading what Budiman (1988) calls a "bureaucratic-capitalist state." They ran state enterprises, claiming for Indonesians what had previously been an economy dominated by Chinese and Dutch capitalists. Budiman further suggests that bureaucratic power has replaced money capital as the means of production in that country. Entry into power can be enjoyed by nonbureaucrats only if they are allied to military and civilian officials through marriage or other ties.

Another example is Thailand, which has developed as a "bureaucratic polity" since the coup of 1932, one contributory factor to which was the dissatisfaction of civil servants to King Prachathipok's *dullayaparp*, or mass personnel layoffs. In fact, that change of government, led by the military but participated in by civil service officials, has been called "a revolution of the bureaucrats, by the bureaucrats, and for the bureaucrats" (Wongtrangan 1988:49–50). From then on, with the legislature, parties, and interest groups relatively weak, the bureaucracy has been the strongest influence on the executive, whether he be an elected prime minister or one installed by a coup. The extent of capture of the political leadership by the civil service is considerable since the bureaucracy not only resists its control but has itself determined constitutional arrangements. It has such dominance over the Thai National Assembly that it has been called "an adjunct of the bureaucracy" (Samudavanija 1987:75).

Bureaucratic dominance in Cell 4 has been anticipated in the literature for the same intrinsic attributes identified in Cell 2. Hegel adds that the bureaucracy has "*the* most important role" in the state since it provides the rationality without which the decisions of the prince can only be arbitrary (Perez-Diaz 1978: 10, 11). Through that rationality, the bureaucracy can elevate its interests as the universal, "while the general interest is reduced thereby to the status of a special interest" (Marx as cited in Lefebvre 1968: 142).

In other cases, administrative leaders have been recruited into the regime and are not distinguishable from it. High-level bureaucrats were alleged to be party to the coup of 1975 in Bangladesh (Khan and Zafarullah 1982) and to several putsches in Turkey (Dicle 1982). Thus, authoritarian regimes may be welcomed by senior civil servants as a mechanism for augmenting their power.

IV.   THE REGIME-BUREAUCRACY NEXUS AND POLITICAL DEVELOPMENT

I have discussed four possible forms of the regime-bureaucracy interaction and given empirical examples of each. I want to stress here that being the result of tensions and struggles, the type of regime-bureaucracy nexus in any country is probably not completely settled and an ascendant political leadership at a given period may be dominated by its civil service at another.

The cases may not be representative of all regime-bureaucracy interactions, the set of countries discussed being an artifact of availability of materials instead of a random sample. However, although quite truncated, they show the dynamism of the government-bureaucracy encounter during regime transitions, which I hope convinces one that this is an exciting area to analyze. Kurt Lewin has well said that the best way to know how an organization works is to try to change it. Indeed, it may be in the analysis of the regime-bureaucracy nexus that the way a civil service works can be best understood.

Although all new leaderships attempt to dominate the bureaucracy, each civil service has also tried to fight back, thereby making even a clearly regime-dominant situation the result of a struggle rather than passive submission. The cases also show that a bureaucracy can move from being dominant to being dominated, or vice versa, depending on such factors as its awareness and use of its power, the protagonists' links to other political forces, the perceived legitimacy of the regime, the kind of transforming demands it makes, its position in the democratic-authoritarian axis, and its distrust of or acceptance of this inherited institution.

A.   Regime Changes and Democracy

What weapons the new government unleashes upon the bureaucracy can be a mirror of its commitment to democracy. Despite a proclaimed return to democracy, the reputed unfairness of the purge, salary restructuring, and reorganization of the Aquino government has parallels in its inability to prosecute redistributive programs and change the Philippine government's age-old leanings toward the landed class. Mujib's socialism allowed demands of political supporters to override its desire for equity and merit in the civil service, just as its socialism floundered not only because the bureaucracy resisted, but because it provided more benefits to the middle class.

All regimes claim a movement toward democratization. This makes it difficult to decide, except by hindsight, whether irregular successions will lead to democracy or authoritarianism. Yet the way an incumbent government attempts to control and direct the bureaucracy may provide a clue as to its real nature. A leadership secretive to its civil service may presage the exclusion of other sectors from the decision-making process, while opening up the bureaucracy to influences and demands of other political groups suggests a government that will take democratization seriously. Meanwhile, the Korean approach against corruption, though fairly administered, could not mask its authoritarian stamp due to its vehemence and cruelty.

Qualities of the bureaucracy may be devalued as the new regime introduces its new programs. This can cut both ways. The Hitlerian regime had little use for the rationality the bureaucracy could offer, preferring to use arbitrary procedures, terror, and emotions. In the Korean case, Park's reorganization followed lines initially suggested by higher civil servants based on their long tenure and competence. But with growing strength, the regime turned inward and excluded them from involvement in important decisions.

By contrast, the new Nicaraguan process involved less secrecy but remained an assault to a civil service used to monopolizing information. Unlike Korea, the regime turned outward, giving peasants, unions, and other affected groups a say in affairs that used to be the bureaucratic domain, thus resulting in a diminution of its power, as in Korea, but unlike it, through the regime's dispersion of its own power to other sectors.

I have regarded political development as the movement toward democracy and bureaucratic development concomitantly as the improvement of the organization's capacity for responsiveness and accountability. Some analysts, dissatisfied with the unresponsiveness of elected officials, would rather connect the bureaucracy to popular forces directly, ignoring the hierarchical and legal claims of the incumbent government. Yet this presents dangers that should be anticipated.

First, weakening the tie between the leadership and the bureaucracy will not necessarily lead the bureaucracy to seek guidance from more credible groups. Rather, it can regard itself as society's sole guardian. Unchecked, it may elevate, as Marx warns, its special interests as the general interest, and thus use power mainly for its own ends.

Second, the implicit assumption seems to be that the bureaucracy can lead the transformation of society, because of its expertise and close acquaintance with development issues. Trusting the bureaucracy to do that in the hope that it can lead to a realignment of power in the society has not proved viable in the cases I have discussed. Rather it has tended to withhold information or limit the ways other sectors can get it. Thus, the reformer is better advised to work through other social groups with more direct responsibility to the people. The civil service can at best assist in societal transformation, especially if so pressured by the leadership and its publics.

Third, the political leadership, no matter how authoritarian, cannot exist completely out of the pale of public accountability. It has to maintain a semblance of legitimacy and thus will work for some public acceptance no matter how twisted its ends. Thus, it must continue to be the focus of protests and reforms, along with and not as an alternative to pressures on the bureaucracy.

B. Lack of Bureaucratic Continuity

The cases have shown a great variety of ways in which the political leadership and the bureaucracy may relate to each other. Indeed, it would seem easy to dismiss Weber and Goonatilake and assert unequivocally that regime changes are inevitably followed by a break rather than a continuation of the functioning of the bureaucracy. There are many ways in which this assertion may be said to be true.

In normal successions (the replacement of one government by another through constitutionally ordained means), each new regime with a spoils system or some variation of it replaces many government employees with people of its own choice. The rationale is that the new staff are more attuned to the new leaders' ideas and commitments. Even in countries formally under the merit system, an overhaul can be effected not only by replacing civil servants at the apex but by altering structures, and hence, communication lines and networks through which they win, maintain, or accumulate power.

When a new government ousts its predecessor abnormally, the probability of bureaucratic disruption looms larger. The instruments of the delegitimated predecessor become fair game for not only change but abolition, "purification," and "transformation." Such venerated values as security of tenure and professionalism become thrown aside as summary dismissals become the order of the day.

Complementary to, or in place of, purges, governments installed irregularly may change the bureaucracy by making what used to be valued or tolerated no longer acceptable. Ethical behavior is a common target, and incoming governments whose legitimacy is self-proclaimed attempt to win popular acceptance through puritanical measures.

C.   Bureaucratic Tenacity and Its Limits

In the end, was Weber right or wrong? The sense in which he was wrong tends to be clear-cut—regimes do change the bureaucracies they inherit by altering their personnel, structures, and reward systems and thus their relationships to it and to the people.

On the other hand, the hypothesis of continuity is also demonstrated in some ways. For instance, the Philippines has remained regime-ascendant through several normal successions and an authoritarian regime which was even willing to allow bureaucrats entry into the corridors of power. Bureaucratic tenacity was also shown by the Bangladeshi civil service. The Mujib regime's attempt to move from a dominant bureaucracy under Pakistan to a politically controlled civil service after Liberation could not succeed. Indeed, the civil service not only worked for its downfall, but resumed its supremacy in the immediate post-Mujib era. Thus while there are dramatic changes in the bureaucracies and societies I have discussed, there are also important underlying continuities that must be recognized.

The senses in which Weber was right also show, paradoxically, that we should not accept his statement lightly. The bureaucracy can and does persist, unchanged, through various regime changes, including even the violent ones he gave as examples. But it also changes, not in the evolutionary sense in which all things are bound to be modified in the long run, but in abrupt, dramatic, even disruptive ways. And the herald and chief instrument for that discontinuity is change of the political leadership and how it battles—attacks, tames, wins over, negotiates with, loses from—its inherited bureaucracy. That political leadership has to articulate and be serious about the newness of the vision it brings, since, as Lipset said, regime changes do not matter unless the successor government represents a new social movement. Thus, in the first place, the bureaucracy will change only if there is a change of regime, and only if it successfully imbues the bureaucracy with the mission it is pursuing.

The chances of that success are mediated by the battle the bureaucracy undertakes with the new leadership, but are not wholly dependent upon it. Rather the struggle is located in the state and society, and other institutions help or hinder its development. The exclusion of other sectors strengthens the political leadership and enables it to pursue its goals more effectively, but only if it desires the authoritarian path. If the commitment be to democracy, the entry of other political organizations is needed to change the bureaucracy. But their participation may constrain not just the bureaucracy but also the leadership itself. It will tend to push the bureaucracy toward the prescribed arrangement under which channels of accountability are clear, but this movement toward Cell 1 is not in a vacuum, but in the context of legislatures, parties, and popular organizations that are developing also as institutions that limit and harness the bureaucracy and the political leadership as democratic instruments. With active political forces, the struggle can have democratic outcomes. But if the push from them is absent, the political leadership, unaccountable, may control the bureaucracy and try to arrogate all power to itself. Even if the civil servants fight the political leadership to insist on their rights or its accountability, it will not succeed. No civil service can develop democratically against the pressures of the leadership and the society. Indeed, no bureaucracy can be better than the society in which it operates.

ACKNOWLEDGMENTS

The support of the Reflections on Development Program of the Rockefeller Foundation in the writing of this paper is hereby gratefully acknowledged.

ENDNOTES

1. The "government" and the "bureaucracy" together comprise the executive branch. I use the former synonymously with "regime" and "political leadership." It includes elective persons as well as those they appoint to the Cabinet or equivalent posts. "Bureaucracy," "civil service," and "administrative system" denote the civilian state apparatus.
2. Goonatilake's views are instructive because he is otherwise very critical of American-sponsored development administration.
3. Originally, the third view posits the state as an arena of *class* struggle, being espoused principally by neo-Marxists (Held 1983). I am modifying it to encompass the struggle not only of classes but of other groups as well. Classes, though significant, are not the sole bases of divisions in the society. Nevertheless I do not deny that many so-called cultural and political splits have their roots in, or are related to, economic exploitation.

REFERENCES

Borge, T. The second anniversary of the Sandinista revolution. In *Sandinistas Speak* (B. Marcus, ed.). Pathfinder Press, New York, 1982, pp. 127–140.

Budiman, A. The emergence of the bureaucratic capitalist state in Indonesia. In *Reflections on Development in Southeast Asia* (T.G. Lim, ed.). ASEAN Economic Research Unit, Institute of Southeast Asian Studies, Singapore, pp. 110–129.

Burin, F.S. Bureaucracy and national socialism: a reconsideration of Weberian theory. In *Reader in Bureaucracy* (R.K. Merton, A.P. Gray, B. Hockey, and H.C. Selvin, eds.). Free Press, New York, 1952, pp. 33–47.

Camp, R.A. The political technocrat in Mexico and the survival of the political system. *Latin American Research Review*, 20:98–118 (1985).

Cariño, L.V. *Bureaucracy for a Democracy: The Struggle of the Philippine Political Leadership and the Civil Service in the Post-Marcos Period.* College of Public Administration, University of the Philippines, Manila, 1988.

Cho, S.C. Two reforms under the military government in Korea: a comparative analysis. In *Administrative Reforms in Asia* (H.B. Lee and A.G. Samonte, eds.). Eastern Regional Organization for Public Administration, Manila, Philippines, 1970, pp. 125–164.

Collins, J. *What Difference Could a Revolution Make?* Institute for Food and Development Policy, San Francisco, 1982.

Dicle, I.A. Public bureaucracy in Turkey. In *Administrative Systems Abroad* (K. Tummala, ed.). Lanham, New York, 1982, pp. 265–302.

Etzioni-Halevy, E. *Bureaucracy and Democracy: A Political Dilemma*, rev. ed. Routledge and Kegan Paul, Boston, 1985.

Goonatilake, S. Colonial administration to development administration: a transition from a colonial to a neocolonial theme. *Journal of Development Administration (Sri Lanka)*, 5:1–11 (1975).

Harmon, M. Normative theory and public administration: some suggestions for a redefinition of administrative responsibility. In *Toward a New Public Administration: The Minnowbrook Perspective* (F. Marini, ed.). Chandler Publishing, Scranton, PA, 1971, pp. 172–185.

Held, D. *States and Societies*. New York University Press, New York, 1983.

Huntington, S.N. *Political Order in Changing Societies.* Yale University Press, New Haven, CT, 1968.

Islam, S.S. The Role of the state in the economic development of Bangladesh during the Mujib regime (1972–1975). *Journal of Developing Areas*, *19*:185–203 (1985).

Jain, R.B. *Contemporary Issues in Indian Administration.* Vishal Press, New Delhi, 1976.

Kamenka, E., and Krygier, M., eds. *Bureaucracy: The Career of a Concept.* Edward Arnold, London, 1979.

Kearney, R.C. Spoils in the Caribbean: the struggle for merit-based civil service in the Dominican Republic. *Public Administration Review*, *46*:144–151 (1986).

Khan, M., and Zafarullah, H. Public bureaucracy in Bangladesh. In *Administrative Systems Abroad* (K. Tummala, ed.). Lanham, New York, 1982, pp. 158–187.

Kingsley, J.D. The execution of policy. In *Reader in Bureaucracy* (R.K. Merton, A.P. Gray, B. Hockey, and H.C. Selvin, eds.). Free Press, New York, 1952, pp. 216–221.

Kirwan, K.A. Woodrow Wilson and the study of public administration—response to Van Riper. *Administration and Society*, *18*:389–401 (1987).

Lefebvre, H. *The Sociology of Marx.* Pantheon Books, New York, 1968.

Lipset, S.M. Bureaucracy and social change. In *Reader in Bureaucracy* (R.K. Merton, A.P. Gray, B. Hockey, and H.C. Selvin, eds.). Free Press, New York, 1952, pp. 221–252.

Navarro, V. Social class, political power and the state: their implications in medicine, Parts I and II. *Journal of Health Politics, Policy and Law*, *1*:256–284 (1976).

Nef, J., and Dwivedi, O.P. Development theory and administration: a fence around an empty lot? *Indian Journal of Public Administration*, *27*:42–66 (1981).

Oquist, P. El Estado Revolucionario en Nicaragua, Seminar on Planning and Administration of Development in Central America and the Caribbean, sponsored by the Escuela Superior de Administration Publica de Colombia and the Ministry of Foreign Affairs, Bogota, Colombia, 1986.

Parrish, C. Bureaucracy, democracy and development: some considerations based on the Chilean case. In *Development Administration in Latin America* (C.E. Thurber and L.S. Graham, eds.). Duke University Press, Durham, NC, 1973, pp. 229–259.

Perez-Diaz, V. *State, Bureaucracy and Civil Society: A Critical Discussion of the Political Theory of Karl Marx.* Macmillan, New York, 1978.

Poulantzas, N. *State, Power, Socialism.* Verso Edition, London, 1980.

Pye, L.W. *Aspects of Political Development.* Little, Brown, Boston, 1966.

Riggs, F.W. The dialectics of developmental conflict. *Journal of Comparative Political Studies*, *1*:197–226 (1968).

Samudavanija, C.A. The bureaucracy. In *Government and Politics of Thailand* (S. Xuto, ed.). Oxford University Press, Singapore, 1987, pp. 75–109.

Siegel, G.B. Brazil: diffusion and centralization of power. In *Development Administration in Latin America* (C.E. Thurber and L.S. Graham, eds.). Duke University Press, Durham, NC, 1973, pp. 362–381.

Thompson, D.F. Bureaucracy and democracy. In *Democratic Theory and Practice* (G. Duncan, ed.). Cambridge University Press, Cambridge, 1983, pp. 235–250.

Tuohy, W.S. Centralism and political elite behavior in Mexico. In *Development Administration in Latin America* (C.E. Thurber and L.S. Graham, eds.). Duke University Press, Durham, NC, 1973, pp. 260–280.

Weaver, J.L. Bureaucracy during a period of social change: the case of Guatemala. In *Development Administration in Latin America* (C.E. Thurber and L.S. Graham, eds.). Duke University Press, Durham, NC, 1973, pp. 314–361.

Weber, M. *The Theory of Social and Economic Organization* (trans. T. Parsons). Free Press, New York, 1947.

Wilson, W. The study of administration. *Political Science Quarterly*, *2*:197–222 (1887).

Wongtrangan, K. Thai bureaucratic behavior: the impact of dual values on public policies. In *Reflections on Development in Southeast Asia* (T.G. Lim, ed.). ASEAN Economic Research Unit, Institute of Southeast Asian Studies, Singapore, 1988, pp. 49–79.

75

Revolution and Public Service in the Third World

Peter H. Koehn   *Department of Political Science, University of Montana, Missoula, Montana*

I. INTRODUCTION

When I began teaching at then Haile Selassie I University (HSIU) in 1970, the students in my class initially refused to take the study of public administration seriously. Without a revolution, they argued persuasively and nearly unanimously, no significant changes in administration (or in public policy) could be introduced in Ethiopia. "Let us assume, then, that revolution has occurred," I would commence, in order to promote academic discourse. "How should the people's affairs be administered after the revolution?"

Four years later, a military committee (Derg) overthrew Emperor Haile Selassie and embarked on revolutionary change (Koehn 1975:7–21). By now, most of these former HSIU students who have not been arrested, killed, or forced into exile have engaged in postrevolution administration for nearly one-quarter of a century. This chapter is addressed in part to evaluating the results of that experience.

The subject of "public administration after the revolution" frequently confronts students of comparative and development administration. The current history of postrevolution public service includes such diverse and important cases as the People's Republic of China, the Islamic Republic of Iran, Cuba under Fidel Castro, and Ethiopia following the termination of imperial rule. In analyzing these experiences, scholars need meaningful criteria for evaluating public service in postrevolution circumstances. The work of Frantz Fanon, who articulated a theory of third world revolution along with a powerful commitment to the interests of the masses, holds out the prospect of providing a useful critical perspective.

The collection of essays contained in Fanon's (1963) *The Wretched of the Earth* constitutes his most relevant treatment of issues related to postrevolution public service. In this volume, the author sounds a cautionary note concerning political behavior in third world societies following a successful national liberation struggle that parallels the Algerian experience. Guidelines that apply to the organization and conduct of public service in postrevolution circumstances constitute an important part of his work. The central quest is for government devoted to serving the masses (Fanon 1963:198).

The principal ingredients in Fanon's approach can be summarized under four headings: decentralization of authority, posting to the countryside, popular participation, and simplicity of explanation. In the pages that follow, these guidelines are embellished and applied as evaluative criteria. The primary context for analysis is postrevolution Ethiopia. For comparative and illustrative purposes, occasional references also are made to particularly important parallels and variations in the People's Republic of China and the Islamic Republic of Iran. The conclusion evaluates the Ethiopian record, critically assesses Fanon's approach, and returns to the comparative theme.

II. DECENTRALIZATION

Frantz Fanon is a strong proponent of administrative decentralization, a popular concept even among far less radical theorists. In "Spontaneity: Its Strength and Weakness," he warns against the inclination of postindependence leaders to centralize government and impose a rigid administrative framework on the people of the countryside. He takes issue with the claim that "a small dose of dictatorship is needed" in third world countries. According to Fanon (1963:118), the centralized approach to dealing with country people is akin to the colonial system. He insists that it must be replaced by "decentralization in the extreme." This is essential because "it is from the base that forces mount up which supply the summit with its dynamic, and make it possible dialectically for it to leap again" (Fanon 1963:197–198).

A. The Initial Postrevolution Period: The Derg (1974–1977)

Following the overthrow of Emperor Haile Selassie I and the imperial regime, Ethiopia's postrevolution rulers inherited a highly centralized political-administrative system. After a brief period during which the new military leaders created rural and urban development institutions at the grass roots and tentatively introduced decentralization measures, the Derg (ruling military committee) pursued a strategy of recentralizing authority.

The initial decentralization phase encompasses roughly the first two and a half years of Ethiopia's postrevolution political history. During this period, the Derg established local peasant associations and neighborhood urban cooperatives and assigned major development responsibilities to these grassroots institutions and their elected leaders (see Cohen and Koehn 1977:10–13, 16–18, 30–31, 38–39; Brietzke 1982:247). According to John Markakis (1987:266), peasant associations "attained a remarkable degree of self-rule" during the "early and creative phase of the revolution." Urban associations (*kebele*), led by an elected policy committee, assumed responsibility for a broad array of community self-help functions and for resolving local disputes over land and housing (Koehn 1980b:88–92).

The military leadership, nevertheless, encountered entrenched resistance within its own ranks as well as within the bureaucracy to the ideas of decentralizing authority and promoting peasant and worker empowerment. High-level administrators equivocated on the Derg's announced commitment to "decentralized administration" by failing to delegate, engaging in reorganization exercises that had the effect of concentrating bureaucratic authority, and, finally, by reserving broad latitude for central government intervention in local affairs in order to ensure that decentralization would not be "abused" (Cohen and Koehn 1980:279, 296–297; Koehn 1980b:94; Brietzke 1982:299, 302).[1] The Derg also suppressed the budding labor movement (Petras and Morley 1984:21–22). In spite of professed support for the idea of self-government and regional autonomy, moreover, the Derg never implemented "a real measure of devolution, political or social, to major constituent communities within the Abyssinian heritage" (Davidson 1987:11–12; Koehn 1980b:95–96).

B.   The Middle Postrevolution Period: Mengistu Haile Mariam (1977–1991)

Mengistu Haile Mariam's consolidation of power in 1977 introduced the second phase of postrevolution military rule. This period witnessed the official return to centralizing tendencies in Ethiopia. Defeat of the radical intelligentsia heralded unyielding repudiation by the state of proposals calling for decentralization, popular empowerment, meaningful regional autonomy, and an end to the primacy of the bureaucracy and the military (Markakis 1987:264, 270). Furthermore, the Mengistu regime established coopted "higher" institutions that undermined the local policy-making power of peasant associations and *kebele* (Ottaway 1987:32, 36; Koehn 1986:30; Markakis 1987:266–267; Dessalegn Rahmato 1987:163).[2] Ministries endeavored to direct project planning and execution from Addis Ababa—with varying degrees of success (Cohen 1987:162, 237–238). By the early 1980s, "'centralism' had become a key slogan both in the media and in official statements" (Dessalegn Rahmato 1987:164). In 1982, Paul Brietzke (1982:204) concluded that "too many decisions are still made at the top or not made at all in Ethiopia." In Donald Rothchild's assessment (1987:130–131), "among the avowedly 'Marxist' states, no regime is more bureaucratic centralist in formal orientation while being less able to control antagonistic elements in its midst than Lt. Col. Mengistu Haile Mariam's regime in Ethiopia" (also see Rothchild and Olorunsola 1983:8).

The top-down construction and installation of the single Worker's Party of Ethiopia (WPE), the government's embrace of centralized planning, and the official proclamation of the People's Democratic Republic of Ethiopia in September 1987 signaled the culmination of the centralizing trend. Christopher Clapham (1987:155–156, 160) suggests that the WPE achieved a degree of control over local institutions that far exceeded prerevolutionary patterns. The consequences included loss of enthusiasm and legitimacy at the peasant association level and establishment of hierarchical organizations that proved poorly suited to encourage production (Clapham 1988:160; Griffin and Hay 1985:66). Other scholars pointed to the widespread practice of postrevolution interference in administrative affairs by military "advisers" and party cadres as a barrier to effective development administration (Brietzke 1982:201, 204; Cohen and Koehn 1980:296; Keller 1984:9).[3]

C.   The Current Postrevolution Period: Meles Zenawi (1991 to the Present)

After the defeat of Mengistu's forces by the Tigrayan People's Liberation Front (TPLF) in 1991 (see Young 1994), the new government of Ethiopia renounced and reversed many of the previous regime's centralizing policies. Article 9, Section 1 of the *National/Regional Self Governments Establishment Proclamation No. 7 of 1992* provided for devolution to the regional level of

> legislative, executive and judicial powers in respect of *all matters within their geographical areas except* . . . defence, foreign affairs, economic policy, conferring of citizenship, declaration of a state of emergency, deployment of the army . . . , printing of currency, establishing and administering major development establishments, building and administering major communication networks and the like. . . .

In 1993, Meles Zenawi, then President of the Transitional Government of Ethiopia (TGE), expressed commitment to devolving a "large measure" of power to the grass roots in his address to a U.N. Economic Commission for Africa conference on development management (also see Rowe 1994:20). Moreover, he pointed out that the specific approach to devolution adopted by the TGE "recognized and embraced" ethnic diversity (Meles Zenawi 1993:5–7). All of the new regional boundaries created under Article 1 of *Proclamation No. 7 of 1992*, with the exception of the capital city of Addis Ababa, explicitly followed the prevailing geographic distribution of Ethiopia's population by nationality (also see Lyons 1996). Moreover, the Transitional Charter affirmed the right of nationalities and peoples to "determine their own affairs by themselves" and Ethiopia's 1994 Constitution grants each region the right to determine its official language.

The 1994 *Constitution* creates eight rural regions. Most regions, with the notable exception of the consolidated Southern Nations, Nationalities, and People's Region, are dominated by one ethnic group. Vast variations can be found among the eight regions in terms of population and geographic size, natural-resource base, infrastructure, and administrative capacity (see Cohen 1995:11, 23–24). Regions are divided further into zones (about 50 had been established by mid-1995) and *wereda* or districts (approximately 670). Regional administrative bureaus, staffed in part with personnel transferred from line ministries, implement "policies, standards, and national programs formulated at headquarters, as well as projects identified and designed at the field level" (Cohen 1995:10). Grass-roots urban *kebelle* and rural peasant associations continue to provide basic local services and to perform decisive political roles (see Lyons 1996:140–142).

In terms of functional authority, Ethiopia's ethnic-devolution strategy experienced a slow start in practice. Bureaucratic opposition from line-ministry officials played a role in frustrating and delaying major devolution exercises. As of 1995, nationally determined technical standards and policies continued to prevail at regional and local levels (Cohen 1995:10–11, 15–17). Ethiopia's entrenched unintegrated prefectoral system of deconcentrated local government (see Koehn and Cohen 1975) had not yet disappeared. By the end of the decade, however, regional officials in exceptional areas such as Tigray had begun to reinterpret and reorient central policies to fit the local context (Keeley and Scoones, 2000:110–112).

Furthermore, "the center . . . dominates revenue and budget allocations" in Ethiopia. In terms of fiscal decentralization, "the Government has not taken sufficient steps to clarify tax powers," and the center continues to control the most lucrative revenue sources (Cohen 1995:16–18). Growing transfers to the regions are based upon a complex formula that emphasizes equity; they also increasingly rely on block grants. In 1996, regions gained greater control over the allocation of block grants and over their recurrent/capital division. They now retain any budget supluses at the end of the fiscal year (John Cohen, personal communication, 10 April 1996). These developments indicate that Ethiopia gradually is moving toward devolution in the crucial area of fiscal decentralization. However, the prospect of local control over financial resources is constrained because "aid agency projects dominate the capital budget and [agency personnel] are unlikely to agree to local-level budgetary reallocation of their targeted grants and loans" (Cohen 1995:19).

III.   SERVICE IN THE COUNTRYSIDE

The second element in Frantz Fanon's development-administration strategy is straightforward. The interior of the country, which is "unknown," underdeveloped, and increasingly deserted, must receive priority attention. In Fanon's vision, "the interior, the back country, ought to be the most privileged part of the country" (Fanon 1963:118, 185–186).

For the administrative officer (as well as the party leader), this goal necessitates living and working in outlying areas. It also requires the appointment of dynamic and highly qualified district officials. Through constant contact with the rural masses, postrevolution development administrators will be able to awaken the countryside and bring about the growth of peasant consciousness that Fanon (1963:185–187) views as a prerequisite for progress. The rural retention of autonomous and indigenous peasant-association leaders greatly facilitates this task (Migdal 1974:222–223).

In general terms, Ethiopia's postrevolution leaders have been committed to rural-development priorities. The radical land reforms introduced by the Derg in 1975 provide the strongest demonstration of this commitment (see Koehn 1979:57–63). The Mengistu regime's unwilling-ness to set attractive prices for state-controlled grain purchases (Dessalegn Rahmato 1987:172) and its excessive military expenditures constituted the most deeply resented failures to support a rural-oriented development policy.

With regard to Fanon's insistence on service in the countryside, the Ethiopian case provides uneven results. On the positive side, the Derg succeeded in posting a new core of educated and progressive administrators to key field positions within the Ministry of Interior's rural local gov-ernment system (Cohen and Koehn 1980:278), initiated a yearlong "development through coop-eration" campaign (*zemecha*) involving student service in the provinces in 1975, and implement-ed an exceptionally effective literacy campaign. There is little evidence, however, that other central ministries followed Interior's lead or dramatically increased the relative strength of their field staffs—even though the overall size of the civilian bureaucracy grew considerably between 1977 and 1982 (see Clapham 1987:159). In addition, rapid staff turnover turned out to be a char-acteristic outcome of rural projects sponsored by the Ministry of Agriculture (Cohen 1987:162, 178, 235–236).[4]

Although the Derg's brief experiment with the *zemecha* program resembled Mao's Cultural Revolution model of posting to the countryside (see Freedman and Morgan 1982:230–231, 236–237), Ethiopia's military rulers and vested rural interests found students too radical and zeal-ous in pressing for change (Cohen and Koehn 1977:21–22; Brietzke 1982:246) and quickly ended the experiment. Markakis (1987:297n) points out, moreover, that "the young radicals . . . appoint-ed to replace the aristocrats in the provincial administration in 1975 sided with student activists in the agitation that swept the countryside during the development campaign and had to be removed."

Some twenty years later, Meles Zenawi readdressed the issue of service in the countryside by introducing a bold personnel transfer exercise. In 1995, John Cohen (1995:16) found that "225,000 of [Ethiopia's] 275,000 civil servants now serve devolved local governments." In theo-ry, the new cadre of local government employees will no longer be dependent upon the center for technical and operational direction once they have received appropriate training and become responsive to local policy makers.

IV. POPULAR PARTICIPATION

Frantz Fanon is an ardent advocate of a radically participative approach to development. In "The Pitfalls of National Consciousness," he consistently points to the value of involving the people in the planning, management, and execution of projects. The village understands problems that the individual refuses to see (Fanon 1963:188–189, 193, 197, 200–201; also see Honadle 1982:175). Fanon (1963:180) specifically advocates "organizing wholesale and retail cooperatives" along democratic and decentralized lines. Relying upon the same insight that guides much contempo-rary management theory, he argues (1963:193) that:

> The important thing is . . . that the whole people plan and decide even if it takes them twice or three times as long. The fact is that the time taken up by explaining, the time "lost" in treating the worker as a human being, will be caught up in the execution of the plan. People must know where they are going and why.

The overall record of the postrevolution regime in Ethiopia is particularly weak with regard to popular participation in development. Early proclamations gave the members of peasant asso-ciations and urban cooperatives wide latitude for involvement in the planning and execution of community self-help projects. The Derg even moved to make some resources available for such undertakings (see Cohen and Koehn 1977:23, 30–31, 36; Koehn 1980b:88–90; Brietzke 1982:202). By 1977, however, the military rulers already had begun to divert the new rural and urban associations away from tasks of development administration and self-government and to channel their resources and energies into military mobilization activities (Cohen and Koehn 1980:302; Koehn 1980b:93). Christopher Clapham (1988:160–161) reported in 1988 that peasant association leaders regarded collecting taxes and eliminating resistance to change as their two most important functions. By the end of the Mengistu period, association devoted scarce resources and energies to maintaining defense squads, operating jails, assigning target numbers of people for resettlement and forced labor on state farms, and applying penalties for failure to attend meetings.

In dramatic contrast to Fanon's warning (1963:201) that development projects not be "parachuted down from above," Ethiopia's postrevolution leaders insisted upon making major policy decisions at the center and requiring local compliance. Paul Brietzke (1982:200) traces this tutelage approach to the military officer's preference for rigid hierarchical systems that allow little opportunity for local initiative. The principal examples of centrally derived schemes that bred resentment and resistance among the rural populace in Ethiopia are mechanized and highly centralized state farms,[5] producer cooperatives, compulsory purchasing at fixed prices, the north-to-south peasant resettlement program, and the extensive villagization campaign (see Alemneh Dejene 1987:146–147; Dessalegn Rahmato 1987:172; Markakis 1987:267; Ottaway 1987:36). With regard to the last scheme on this list, for instance, John Cohen and Nils-Ivar Isaksson (1987:450–463) reported that

> the villagisation campaign was designed and implemented from the top down. The *Guidelines* were formulated centrally in the National Planning Commission and the Ministry of Agriculture, under the direction of the country's senior government and party leadership.

In light of the complete absence of participation on the part of those affected, it is not surprising that Cohen and Isaksson also discovered, as Fanon foresaw, that many villagers were "uncertain about why they were moved, and . . . about what steps should be taken to deal with their new problems or to take advantage of their new conditions."

According to President Meles, the Transitional Government of Ethiopia "devolved power not just to the various regions but also to the districts and the villages, and we have confidence that when power is devolved to the grass roots, . . . democracy becomes meaningful to the ordinary Ethiopian and . . . the ordinary Ethiopian is empowered" (quoted in Rowe 1994:23). Although the situation varies from region to region, depending on the local political context and the rate of expansion in the administrative and technical capacity of regional and zonal administrators, there is little evidence of movement in the direction of community empowerment under the devolved system (see Young, 1998:200–203; Keeley and Scoones 2000:111–115). In the crucial areas of needs assessment, project identification, and budget and plan formulation, even regional governments are denied decision-making roles. They submit regional priorities to the center, where "recurrent and the capital budgets are formulated by the Ministries of Finance and Planning and Economic Development" (Cohen 1995:18) and approved by a Budget Steering Committee in the Office of the Prime Minister (John Cohen, personal communication, 10 April 1996). Although constituents elected candidates to regional and local-level councils in 1992 and 1995, moreover, the limited evidence available suggests that locally elected officials in most regions of Ethiopia remain "inclined to listen to the advice of central ministry personnel" (Cohen 1995:7–12, 16).

V.   SIMPLICITY OF EXPLANATION

The last major component in Fanon's guidelines for postrevolution public service can best be described as simplicity of explanation. His principal concern is that government officials apply "their theoretical knowledge to the service of the people" (Fanon 1963:113). His essay on "The Pitfalls of National Consciousness" (1963:187, 189) is decidedly antitechnocratic. He regards recourse to technical language that is inaccessible to the masses as "obscuring"—that is, "a mask behind which stands out the much greater business of plunder." According to Fanon, "civil servants and technicians ought not to bury themselves in diagrams and statistics, but rather in the hearts of the people." He concludes that "everything can be explained to the people, on the single condition that you really want them to understand" (also see James 1996:310).

The keys to explanation are political education and organizing (Fanon 1963:180–181), a communal process of self-criticism, communicating in accessible speech (James 1996:310), and ideology. It is essential that development administrators be guided and motivated by an original non-Western ideology that avoids neo-colonialist dependency, embraces human liberation, and does not force the people to follow a predetermined path (see Wright 1986:682; Fanon 1963:167–168; Taiwo 1996:259). Fanon is less than sanguine about prospects that this change will occur in postindependent third world societies, however. In *Toward the African Revolution* (1964:186), he laments that "for my part, the deeper I enter into the cultures and political circles the surer I am that the great danger that threatens Africa is the absence of ideology."

The Ethiopian case indicates that Fanon's pessimism on this score is warranted. The Mengistu regime evidenced little appreciation of the possibility that "socialist transformation is not simply a matter of technical progress directed from above—by the state" (Galli 1986:10; Koehn 1980a:40). The continued emphasis of the Ethiopian state on capital- and energy-intensive agricultural techniques, coupled with heavy fertilizer application (Koehn 1986:230) and escalating indebtedness to Western financial institutions (Hancock 1985:57–58), resulted in the perpetuation of external dependency (Dessalegn Rahmato 1987:176).

Ethiopia's postrevolution military rulers also allowed bureaucratic complexity and administrative specialization to persist without fundamental change (Brietzke 1982:215).[6] Mengistu's regime increasingly embraced Soviet and Eastern European advisers, technology, and equipment, instead of relying exclusively upon Western capitalist approaches and assistance. In a November 1988 interview, Mengistu Haile Marian explicitly rejected the idea of restructuring along the lines of *perestroika* as inappropriate for Ethiopia (Perlez 1988:6). Adherence to pre-*perestroika* Soviet thinking (see Girma Negash and Koehn 1987:21) is certainly not what Fanon had in mind when he stressed the importance of devising an alternative, indigenous ideology.

In contrast to the Mengistu era, Meles Zenawi and the Ethiopian Peoples Revolutionary Democratic Front (EPRDF) have emphasized ethnicity and local culture as bases for interest articulation and political mobilization (also see Lyons 1996:142). This approach possesses inherent potential to embody simplicity of explanation and understanding, indigenously defined paths, and considerable local diversity.

VI. CONCLUSIONS

The need for bureaucracy poses fundamental challenges for postrevolution societies. The development of a self-seeking, privileged state apparatus can swiftly subvert the gains and goals of revolutionary change. Gerald Chaliand (1976:191) warns that "the bureaucracy's tendency to set itself up as omnipotent needs constantly to be thwarted in order to keep popular mobilization going as long as possible." Mao Zedong (see Freedman and Morgan 1982:29–37; Dittmer 1974: 447) and Frantz Fanon shared this understanding.

Fanon's concise reflections on public service are replete with insights for students of development administration in postrevolution circumstances. His warnings against centralization and top-down administrative impositions, the exhortation to serve in the countryside, the insistence on public participation in the planning and execution of development projects, and his emphasis on simplicity of explanation are essential components in an overall strategy of creating government, party, and NGO structures that will remain at the service of the masses.

A. The Ethiopian Case

Postrevolution Ethiopia provides scant evidence of public service in the interests of the masses, although there are areas of improvement relative to the Haile Selassie era. The four major guidelines drawn from Fanon provided a useful basis for critical evaluation. The results suggest that the failure of the Mengistu Haile Mariam regime to adhere to such principles accounts in large part for the poor public-service record encountered in postrevolution Ethiopia. Under Mengistu, the Ethiopian bureaucracy lacked popular legitimacy and operated outside public control (Brietzke 1982:204). This situation is not surprising, viewed from Fanon's perspective, given the ruler's emphasis on centralization of decision-making authority, the absence of effective public participation in development, the regime's lack of priority commitment to service in the countryside, and its preoccupation with technocratic approaches and imported ideology.

Meles Zenawi's moves in the direction of ethnic devolution are particularly interesting in the Ethiopian context and beyond. If fully implemented, this experiment either would provide support for, or undermine, the underlying premise that devolution and community empowerment along nationality lines concomitantly advances local socioeconomic development and defuses separatist inclinations (see Meles Zenawi 1993:5–8).[7]

B. Conceptual Limitations

While Frantz Fanon's work presents a useful starting point for critical assessments of post-revolution public service,[8] it is far from complete. The Ethiopian case suggests that Fanon overlooked at least three vital factors. First, preoccupation with war and repression on the part of a postrevolution regime diverts essential resources from development, makes it even more difficult to place and retain qualified administrative and technical staff in countryside positions (see Rondinelli 1981:618–619), and promotes the exodus of valuable personnel (see Koehn 1991).[9] One outcome is increased external dependency (see Girma Negash and Koehn 1987:22–23, 31).

In addition, Fanon underestimates the importance of nationality sentiments as a motivating force for energizing devolved bureaucratic structures and promoting development. Mobilization along nationality lines is a vital force in the Horn of Africa (see Markakis 1987:272–276; Hyden et al. 1996:33–34) and elsewhere in the world (see, for instance, Rex 1997:470–472). However, instead of recommending ways to harness the potential of nationality identification, Fanon dismisses and decries "autonomist tendencies" along with regionalism and federalism (Fanon 1963:114).

Finally, Fanon does not adequately address the challenging issue of declining bureaucratic motivation (or "revolutionary will") over time (regarding Iran, for instance, compare Farazmand 1987:344 with pp. 357–358). How can a postrevolution society sustain a high level of commitment to public service on the part of its administrative cadre? Fanon's emphasis on developing an original, indigenous ideology is helpful in direction, but fails to take us far enough. What are the critical obstacles to grass-roots liberation and development that such an ideology must address? Can the arousal of traditionalism occur without closing off needed change?[10] Can the mobilizing features of indigenous culture be pruned of elements that obstruct human liberation and social change? How can ideology outweigh the objective position of the state bureaucracy (see Galli 1986:61–62) or overcome the material condition of the rural masses (Markakis 1987:274–275) and lack of class solidarity among the peasantry (Migdal 1974:222–224).

In the end, neither the Ethiopian nor the Iranian case refutes Chaliand's (1976:190) troubling assertion, based upon Chinese revolutionary experience, that "even anti-bureaucratic campaigns themselves are launched and finally controlled by a segment of the bureaucracy." The twin phenomena of the rise of a powerful bureaucratic class that is preoccupied with self-aggrandizement and shorn of ideological commitment and the centralized bureaucratization of revolution, experienced by European socialist countries as well as by third world societies (see Hodges 1981:40–50, 71–75, 181; Farazmand 1987:337–338, 346–347, 355–356; Kraus 1984:207, 210–211; Clapham 1988:8–9; Harding 1981:294–295, 336–337, 357–359; Ma 1996:129, 133, 143, 152, 162), continue to challenge students and practitioners of postrevolution public administration.

ENDNOTES

1. The particular mix of centralization, decentralization, and mass mobilization pursued in the People's Republic of China during the Cultural Revolution is described in Dittmer (1974:466, 469, 477), Conyers (1977:106–109), and Harding (1981:236, 265, 289–295). On the growth of independent, grass-roots organizations (including neighborhood committees and Islamic societies) that delivered local services and performed other public administration functions in the initial postrevolution period in Iran, see Farazmand (1987:342–343). In Iran, as in Ethiopia, "the centralized structure of the civil service remained the same" (Farazmand 1987:353). On the demise of independent workers' councils and the absence of powerful grassroots labor organizations in Iran, see Bayat (1988:52–53).

2. According to Clapham (1988:157–159), the state exercised centralized management and control over peasant associations through bureaucratic officials (specifically district officers) rather than through the hierarchy of the Ethiopian Peasant Association (EPA).

    In some regions, nevertheless, service cooperatives became popular and effective institutions for promoting modest agricultural enterprises. Alemneh Dejene (1987:138, 76–79) describes the activities of a successful producer cooperative at Hureta Hetosa even though he is critical of the government's policy of pushing collective farming through the establishment of producer cooperatives. Griffin and Hay (1985:62, 64–66) argue persuasively that the expansion of cooperative agriculture, focusing on the service cooperative, is an essential rural development strategy in Ethiopia that offers the only alternative to external dependence and the introduction of large-scale projects that exacerbate disparities in income distribution.

    Alemneh Dejene (1987:139) also cites the lack of basic administrative training programs as a major obstacle to managerial competence at the service cooperative level. This point has wider application. For the benefits of decentralization to be realized, moves in that direction must be accompanied by carefully designed and executed training programs (see Hyden et al. 1996:48–49; Koehn and Ojo, 1999:8–9).

3. Fanon (1963:185–186) also cautions against "mingling the party with the government" because the party must retain the vital role of controlling the bureaucratic bourgeoisie. On the decline of concurrent positions as state bureaucrats and party officials in the People's Republic of China, see Harding (1986:24–25). On the ineffective and counterproductive nature of CCP political supervision of the bureaucracy in post-Mao China, see Ma (1996:169–170).

4. Chinese experience indicates that "poor morale has been particularly prevalent at the basic rural levels, where only limited material benefits accompany official posts, and where cadres have often been caught between the conflicting demands of their neighbors and their superiors" (Harding 1981:347).

5. Griffin and Hay (1985:54–56) contend that the inefficiency of state farms was, in part, the result of an "excessively centralized" administrative system whereby "even routine decisions must be referred by the farm manager to higher authority, that is, to the enterprise, corporation or Ministry or perhaps even the Central Planning Supreme Council."

6. For the contrasting situation of China during the Great People's Cultural Revolution, see Dittmer (1974:475) and Conyers (1977:111–112). In the post-Mao period, increased emphasis has been placed upon expert knowledge (see Heady 1984:393–394; Hodges 1981:170–172). Nevertheless, specialists,

and the technical skills and scientific information they possess, continue to be suspect in a bureaucracy "dominated by administrative generalists" (Harding 1981:359). A similar revival of the norm of expertise occurred in the third phase of the Iranian revolution (Farazmand 1987:345). On the connection between reliance upon technocratic expertise and the expansion of bureaucratic power and privilege, see Heady (1984:279–280).

7. For contrasting expectations on the outcome of this approach, see Cohen (1995:5n, citing Samuel P. Huntington) and Walle Engedayehu (1994:180–181, 189).

8. Otwin Marenin (1981:29) argues convincingly that Marxist analysis, to be persuasive, must "develop a more empiricist justification" because the "mere assertion of being right . . . is for practical purposes counterrevolutionary, for it is so easy to discredit."

9. Farazmand (1987:355) makes a similar point in his analysis of the performance of Iranian public institutions in the postrevolution era. Material resources are crucial, according to Migdal (1974:210–213, 222), as inducements for peasant participation in new programs and in generating peasant support for complex goals.

10. Dwivedi and Nef (1982:73–74) raise this issue, but fail to address it in convincing detail. They suggest that fundamentalism, involving the juxtaposition of traditionalism and mass arousal, can provide the basis for a new ideology that is not "anti-developmental in its impact." In contrast, Nigel Gibson (1991:3–4) reads Fanon to argue against the "uncritical appropriation" of tradition.

REFERENCES

Alemneh Dejene. *Peasants, Agrarian Socialism, and Rural Development in Ethiopia*, Westview Press, Boulder, CO, 1987.

Bayat, A. Labor and democracy in post-revolutionary Iran. In *Post-revolutionary Iran* (H. Amirahmadi and M. Parvin, eds.). Westview Press, Boulder, CO, 1988, pp. 41–55.

Brietzke, P.H. *Law, Development, and the Ethiopian Revolution.* Bucknell University Press, Lewisburg, PA, 1982.

Chaliand, G. *Revolution in the Third World; Myths and Prospects.* Viking Press, New York, 1976.

Clapham, C. Revolutionary socialist development in Ethiopia. *African Affairs*, 86:151–165 (1987).

Clapham, C. *Transformation and Continuity in Revolutionary Ethiopia.* Cambridge University Press, Cambridge, 1988.

Cohen, J.M. *Integrated Rural Development; The Ethiopian Experience and the Debate.* Scandinavian Institute of African Studies, Uppsala, Sweden, 1987.

Cohen, J.M. 'Ethnic federalism' in Ethiopia. Development Discussion Paper No. 519, Harvard Institute for International Development, Cambridge, MA, October 1995.

Cohen, J.M., and Isaksson, N.-I. Villagisation in Ethiopia's Arsi region. *Journal of Modern African Societies*, 25:435–464 (1987).

Cohen, J.M., and Koehn, P.H. Rural and urban land reform in Ethiopia. *African Law Studies*, 14:3–62 (1977).

Cohen, J.M., and Koehn, P.H. *Ethiopian Provincial and Municipal Government: Imperial Patterns and Postrevolutionary Changes.* Michigan State University Press, East Lansing, 1980.

Conyers, D. Administration in China: some preliminary observations. *Journal of Administration Overseas*, 16:98–113 (1977).

Davidson, B. Thirty years of liberation struggle. *Africa Today*, 34:5–16 (1987).

Dessalegn Rahmato. The political economy of development in Ethiopia. In *Afro-Marxist Regimes; Ideology and Public Policy* (E.J. Keller and D. Rothchild, eds.). Lynne Rienner, Boulder, CO, 1987, pp. 155–179.

Dittmer, L. Revolution and reconstruction in contemporary Chinese bureaucracy. *Journal of Comparative Administration*, 5:443–486 (1974).

Dwivedi, O.P., and Nef, J. Crises and continuities in development theory and administration: first and third world perspectives. *Public Administration and Development*, 2:59–77 (1982).

Fanon, F. *The Wretched of the Earth.* Grove Press, New York, 1963.

Fanon, F. *Toward the African Revolution (Political Essays).* Monthly Review Press, New York, 1964.

Farazmand, A. The impacts of the revolution of 1978–1979 on the Iranian bureaucracy and civil service. *International Journal of Public Administration*, *10*:337–365 (1987).

Freedman, A., and Morgan, M.C. Controlling bureaucracy in Communist China. In *Administrative Systems Abroad* (K.K. Tummala, ed.). University Press of America, Washington, 1982, pp. 229–264.

Galli, R.E. Amilcar Cabral and rural transformation in Guinea-Bissau: a preliminary critique. *Rural Africana*, *25–26*:55–73 (1986).

Gibson, Nigel. The 30th anniversary of Fanon's *Wretched of the Earth*—a view from the 1990s. Paper presented at the 31st Annual Meeting of the African Studies Association, St. Louis, Nov., 1991.

Girma Negash and Koehn, P. Refugee formation and superpower politics in the Horn of Africa. Paper presented at the 30th Annual Meeting of the African Studies Association, Denver, Nov. 21, 1987.

Griffin, K., and Hay, R. Problems of agricultural development in socialist Ethiopia: an overview and a suggested strategy. *Journal of Peasant Studies*, *13*:37–66 (1985).

Hancock, G. *Ethiopia: The Challenge of Hunger*. Victor Gollancz, London, 1985.

Harding, H. *Organizing China: The Problem of Bureaucracy 1949–1976*. Stanford University Press, Stanford, CA, 1981.

Harding, H. Political developments in Post-Mao China. In *Modernizing China: Post-Mao Reform and Development* (A.D. Barnett and R.N. Clough, eds.). Westview Press, Boulder, CO, 1986, pp. 13–37.

Heady, F. *Public Administration: A Comparative Perspective*, 3rd rev. ed. Marcel Dekker, New York, 1984.

Hodges, D.C. *The Bureaucratization of Socialism*. University of Massachusetts Press, Amherst, 1981.

Honadle, G. Development administration in the eighties: new agendas or old perspectives? *Public Administration Review*, *42*:174–179 (1982).

Hyden, G., Koehn, P., and Saleh, T. The challenge of decentralization in Eritrea. *Journal of African Policy Studies*, *2*:31–51 (1996).

James, J.A. 'Bread and land': Frantz Fanon's 'native intellectual.' In *Fanon: A Critial Reader* (L.R. Gordon, T.D. Sharpley-Whiting, and R.T. White, eds.). Blackwell Publishers, Oxford, 1996, pp. 309–331.

Keeley, J. and Scoones, I. Knowledge, power and politics: the environmental policy-making process in Ethiopia. *Journal of Modern African Studies*, *38*:89–120 (2000).

Keller, E.J. State, party and revolution in Ethiopia. Unpublished paper in the author's possession, 1984.

Koehn, P. Ethiopian politics: military intervention and prospects for further change. *Africa Today*, *22*:7–21 (1975).

Koehn, P. Ethiopia: famine, food production, and changes in the legal order. *African Studies Review*, *22*:51–71 (1979).

Koehn, P. The Ethiopian revolution: events, interpretations, and implications. *Africa Today*, *27*:33–45 (1980a).

Koehn, P. Forecast for political change in Ethiopia: an urban perspective. In *Analyzing Political Change in Africa; Applications of a New Multidimensional Framework* (J.R. Scarritt, ed.). Westview Press, Boulder, CO, 1980b, pp. 74–106.

Koehn, P. Agricultural policy and environmental destruction in Ethiopia and Nigeria. *Rural Africana*, *25–26*:23–53 (1986).

Koehn, P. *Refugees from Revolution: U.S. Policy and Third-World Migration*. Westview Press, Boulder, CO, 1991.

Koehn, P., and Cohen, J.M. Local government in Ethiopia: independence and variability in a deconcentrated system. *Quarterly Journal of Administration*, *9*:369–386 (1975).

Koehn, P.H., and Ojo, J.B. Making aid work in Africa in the new millennium. In *Making Aid Work: Innovative Approaches for Africa at the Turn of the Century* (P.H. Koehn and J.B. Ojo, eds.). Lanham, MD, 1999, pp. 1–14.

Kraus, R. Bureaucratic privilege as an issue in Chinese politics. In *China's Changed Road to Development* (N. Maxwell and B. McFarlane, eds.). Pergamon Press, Oxford, 1984, pp. 203–212.

Lyons, T. Closing the transition: the May 1995 elections in Ethiopia. *Journal of Modern African Studies*, *34*:121–142 (1996).

Ma, S.K. *Administrative Reform in Post-Mao China*. University Press of America, Lanham, MD, 1996.

Marenin, O. Essence and empiricism in African politics. *Journal of Modern African Studies*, *19*:1–30 (1981).

Markakis, J. *National and Class Conflict in the Horn of Africa.* Cambridge University Press, Cambridge, 1987.

Meles Zenawi. Keynote Address presented at the U.N. Economic Commission for Africa Conference on Development Management in Africa, Addis Ababa, 8 March 1993.

Migdal, J.S. *Peasants, Politics, and Revolution; Pressures Toward Political and Social Change in the Third World.* Princeton University Press, Princeton, NJ, 1974.

Ottaway, M. The political economy of development in Ethiopia. In *Afro-Marxist Regimes: Ideology and Public Policy* (E.J. Keller and D. Rothchild, eds.). Lynne Rienner, Boulder, CO, 1987, pp. 25–42.

Perlez., J. Ethiopia's president looks toward better U.S. relations. *New York Times,* Nov. 28, 1988, pp. 1, 6.

Petras, J.F., and Morley, M.H. The Ethiopian military state and Soviet-US involvement in the Horn of Africa. *Review of African Political Economy, 30*:21–31 (1984).

Rex, J. The problematic of multinational and multicultural societies. *Ethnic and Racial Studies, 20*:455–473 (1997).

Rondinelli, D.A. Administrative decentralization and economic development: the Sudan's experiment with devolution. *Journal of Modern African Studies, 19*:595–624 (1981).

Rothchild, D., and Olorunsola, V.A. Managing competing state and ethnic claims. In *State Versus Ethnic Claims: African Policy Dilemmas* (D. Rothchild and V.A. Olorunsola, eds.). Westview Press, Boulder, CO, 1983, pp. 1–24.

Rothchild, D. Hegemony and state softness: some variations in elite responses. In *The African State in Transition* (Z. Ergas, ed.). St. Martin's Press, New York, 1987, pp. 117–143.

Rowe, R. Ethiopia: emerging from a long dark age. *Courier, 145*:16–26 (1994).

Taiwo, O. On the misadventures of national consciousness: a retrospect on Frantz Fanon's gift of prophecy. In *Fanon: A Critical Reader* (L.R. Gordon, J.D. Sharpley-Whiting, and R.T. White, eds.). Blackwell Publishers, Oxford, 1996, pp. 255–270.

Walle Engedayehu. Ethiopia: the politics of ethnic federalism. *Africa Quarterly, 34*:149–192 (1994).

Wright, D. Fanon and Africa: a retrospect. *Journal of Modern African Studies, 24*:679–689 (1986).

Young, J. Peasants and revolution in Ethiopia: Tigray, 1974–1989. Ph.D. dissertation, Simon Fraser University, Burnaby, B.C., Canada, September 1994.

Young, J. Regionalism and democracy in Ethiopia. *Third World Quarterly 19*:191–204 (1998).

76

Bureaucracy and Revolution

The Case of Iran*

Ali Farazmand   *School of Public Administration, Florida Altantic University, Fort Lauderdale, Florida*

I. INTRODUCTION

What are the relationships between a revolution and the bureaucratic machinery of a country? Does a revolution noticeably affect the civil service system? Do popular anti-bureaucratic slogans result in any fundamental changes in the structures, processes, and values of administrative systems after the revolution? An evaluation of the impacts of the revolution of 1978–1979 on Iran's bureaucracy and civil service system may serve to shed some light on these questions. This chapter explains some of the major impacts of this revolution in the Iranian civil service and bureaucracy.

The following discussion is based on information collected in three ways: first, surveys of speeches, radio broadcasts, and newspapers; second, examination of relevant government documents, official statements, and administrative reports; third, direct observation in a number of civilian agencies and organizations as a client, as a consultant, and as a researcher during a 5-month visit to Iran in 1983 and subsequent visits in the late 1990s. Interviews were also conducted with a number of officials and with ordinary citizens.

The Iranian revolution was a general and popular uprising in which all segments of the citizenry participated. Its aim was to eliminate the monarchy—the absolutist regime of the Pahlavi and the Shah—and to change fundamentally the economic and social systems of the society.[1] Furthermore, the revolution was directed against the bureaucratic machinery, which, as a power instrument, had the primary function of maintaining the regime and furthering its interests through constraints and control.[2] Popular expectation was that this bureaucratic machine could be smashed and reorganized in a way as to make it accountable and responsive to public needs. As in other revolutions, the new leaders were faced with the question of what to do with both the military and the bureaucratic segments of the old regime. Unless controlled, they could pose a serious threat to the revolution.[3]

The changes that occurred in the bureaucracy are examined here in terms of structure, process, and attitude in the three phases of the revolution.

---

*Reprinted from *Int'l. J. of Pub. Admin.*, *10*(4):337–365 (1987), with updates.

II.   FIRST PERIOD (1979)

The initial period after the victory of the revolution produced no fundamental change. It began with the establishment of the Provisional Government in February 1979 and ended with the collapse of the administration of Prime Minister Bazargan 8 months later, a result of the militant students' occupation of the American Embassy. This government was mainly secular and interested in maintaining the status quo. It was not clear whether it could change the administrative structure. Complaining about the "unreasonable demands of the people," Bazargan lamented: "We wanted rain, but received a flood."[4]

A.   Structural Impacts on the Civil Service

This period can be characterized by inconsistent, haphazard, and minor change in the civil service. Initiated and carried out mainly from within civil service ranks, these changes were often opposed by the Bazargan administration and resisted by its political appointees.[5]

   While the public sector was enlarged through nationalization of some enterprises, the highly centralized structure of the bureaucracy remained intact.[6] Overall, about 5% of key government personnel lost their jobs. The major criteria for personnel separation were political—SAVAK association, Shah worshipping, leftist ideology, and personal reasons. A few strategically placed members of the bureaucratic elite were also tried and executed by revolutionary courts. The Bazargan administration was opposed to most of these decisions.[7]

   Although the new government had formal authority, the real power was exercised by the newly formed committees and councils in the civil service. These intraorganizations were formed by those who sought major structural changes in the bureaucracy. Their purpose was "to democratize the administrative system."[8]

   Among the organizations that now were abolished by the Revolutionary Council were the Royal Inspectorate Organization, the Royal Court, the Royal Social Service Organization, the SAVAK (Secret Policy), and political *Rastakhiz* Party, and other security and political organizations.

B.   Process and Attitude Impacts

Civil service authorities were often sluggish in performing routine duties, although some sectors such as postal services and communications were very active. Decision-making seemed to be fragmented and contradictory. Implementation was even more difficult since there were no clear-cut goals and objectives and organizational coordination was poor.[8] "Wait-and-see" was the prevalent attitude.

   At the same time, red tape was cut as "rules and regulations were relaxed or ignored, and the activities were carried out by concerned groups".[8] Motivation to serve the society seemed to be strong. The morale of employees appeared high, and a sense of cooperation and revolutionary spirit gained momentum among the middle and lower-level personnel who sought fundamental changes. This was manifested in their demands for major administrative and organizational change.[9]

III.   SECOND PERIOD (1979–1982)

The second period began in November 1979 with the occupation of the American Embassy by militant students, part of the forces that demanded fundamental changes in socioeconomic and political systems in Iran. As a result, Bazargan's provisional administration collapsed and new revolutionary leaders took steps to radicalize the society. As a scholar at Tehran University put it, "These leaders represented both religious and secular sectors and different social levels, but unlike the previous period, the religious leaders took the upper hand."[10] The major events in this period included the presidential and parliamentary elections, the establishment of the Parliament (Majlis), prolific legislation, more nationalization of enterprises, the hostage crisis, the Iraqi invasion and the accompanying war mobilization activities, minority rebellions, several military coups, and other political events. It was a turbulent period of "life and death situations for the Islamic Republic."[11]

A. Structural Impacts on the Bureaucracy and Civil Service

One of the most important changes in the civil service was the growth of the employee council (*Showra*) and committee (Komeeteh) systems, which were active in decision making and implementation. "This system performed many organizational functions, initiated and formulated policy and supervised its execution."[12]

This was a time of a major structural change. As one administrator put it, the movement was toward "democratization of the internal organizational process and the administrative system." But "anarchy and lack of organizational discipline was a common problem," claimed another administrator.[13]

The second, and perhaps the most significant, structural impact of the revolution was the phenomenon of debureaucratization of society. A large number of independent, grass-roots organizations had sprung up in rural and urban areas to deliver public services, engage in developmental projects, and contribute to the defense of the country. Of these organizations, the Neighborhood Committee (*Komeeteh-e-Mahalli*) and Islamic Societies (*Anjuman-e-Islami*) in each village, office, and factory were very active politically and administratively. These organizations seemed to have "virtually replaced many bureaucratic organizations by performing many public administrative functions."[4] It is not clear, however, how effective and efficient these organizations were and for how long they would remain unbureaucratic.

Another impact of the revolution was the new Constitutional requirement of legislative approval for every major policy or for the reorganization of government agencies. Because of the long and intense legislative debates that arose, the Parliament became a fierce battleground for various interest groups. Nevertheless, it "prevailed as the most democratic institution in the country."[14]

Still another significant structural change in the bureaucracy was the legislatively required reorganization of government agencies and organizations, especially at the top. Three major features of this reorganization, which is presently in operation, are (1) the formation of the "Supreme Council" system of leadership at the top of every public agency and organization, (2) the collective decision making of this top leadership body, and (3) the strong permanent representation from the religious leadership, especially from the holy city of Qum (Ghum), where the religious academy is centered and prominent scholars teach Islam as a comprehensive system of politics, administration, etc.[15]

The size of the civil service was also affected. While the number of government employees grew as a result of more nationalization of private institutions, the overall number of public employees was reduced by about 25% as a result of purges during the second period. These purges seemed to be mainly arbitrary and excessive.[15,16]

The establishment of the Administrative Justice office and the politicization of the bureaucracy were among the last structural impacts of this stage of the revolution.[17]

B. The Process and Attitude Impacts

Administrative tasks were more difficult to carry out because of defense mobilization, a freeze on government hiring, and some salary cuts. Combined with skyrocketing inflation, "uncertainty, job insecurity, and political activism were rampant in the civil service. Personnel activities were reduced to an essential minimum."[17,18]

Direct access to public officials, however, became very easy. An example of this was the case of the Minister of Agriculture (Reza Esfahani), who "simply sat on the floor of his office, opened the door, and handled the problems and grievances of the barefoot peasants."[19] This openness and easy access to public officials seemed to have a positive impact on public attitude toward the bureaucracy.

Revolutionary spirit seemed to be the leading attitude among many employees. Most civil servants seemed determined to defend the revolution and its gains. Popular victories in the war front also strongly motivated them to work harder. But, since the merit system was ignored and expertise was not appreciated, professional bureaucrats "felt uneasy, insecure, and uncertain about their futures."[20] And, as another administrator stated, "abuses of excessive power in some agencies were having a negative impact on the attitude of some professional personnel who were loyal to both the revolution and the leadership."[20] The attitude of the public toward the bureaucracy also began to change as time passed and the war continued.

IV. THIRD PERIOD (1983–1994)

This period marks a major shift in the direction of moderation, a relaxation of radical positions in domestic and international affairs, and a standardization of societal arrangements. The containment of terrorism and the military defeat of opposition groups in the society strengthened the trend toward institutionalization, stabilization, and long-term planning. Religious ideology and Islamization of the society were emphasized, and "unity of all Islamic groups and individuals" was repeatedly called for by Ayatullah Khomeini.[21]

Another major feature of this period was the ratification of the first Five-Year Development Plan by the Majlis (parliament). The plan calls for recruiting and training tens of thousands of professionals, experts, and other occupational personnel for development purposes.[22] Universities and colleges were opened, a number of restrictions—such as those on foreign travel—were eased, and gradual development of normal relations with other countries was initiated.

A. Structural Impacts on the Bureaucracy and Civil Service

One major change in the bureaucracy has been the return of the notion of "expertise," and the call for "experts and professionals" in the civil service system. This has resulted in relative job security for the bureaucrats and professionals. The speeches of the leaders of the revolution emphasized the need for experts and professionals to implement the long-term plans and help rebuild an Islamic Iran. The speaker of the majlis, for example, claimed: "We welcome all Iranian experts to help rebuild the country as long as they have no criminal records against the Islamic Republic."[23]

Many of the structural changes that were initiated in the bureaucracy during the second phase, including the reorganization of the administrative system, have remained in force. Perhaps the most significant structural change in the civil service in the third period is the trend toward bureaucratization of a large number of the independent grass-roots organizations that developed during the second phase of the revolution. According to a high-level administrator in the Ministry of Agriculture,

> . . . these organizations have been responsible for the initiation and implementation of numerous development projects in urban and rural areas—construction of roads and bridges, low-income housing, public baths, communications development, rural electrification, etc. They

also contributed to the defense of the nation against the Iraqi invasion, and helped relieve the hardships on the war refugees.[24]

These organizations were formed and staffed by dedicated volunteers to provide various public services. They included the Reconstruction Crusades (*Jehad-e-Sazandegi*); the Mobilization Corps for Defense of the Revolution (*Sepah-e-Basij*); the Seven-Member Board for Land Distribution (*Heiat-e-Haft Nafare*); the Islamic Societies (*Anjumanha*) in the villages, factories, and offices; and the Economic Mobilization Network (*Basij-e-Eghtesadi*).[25]

The Majlis ratified administration-sponsored bills to include these organizations and thousands of their regional and local offices in the government's centralized bureaucracy. The Revolutionary Guards Organization and the Reconstruction Crusade Organization became Ministries by mid 1983, and others have been under consideration. The argument of Premier Mousavi and his supporters was that the consolidation and integration of these organizations into the central administration of the government would help reduce duplication and waste, and would result in increased efficiency, better coordination of governmental activities, and uniformity in policy implementation.[25,26] In a meeting that this author had with the then Vice-Minister of the Ministry of Agriculture, it was disclosed that reorganization and consolidation were government priorities.[27] Opponents of the policy, on the other hand, argue that this move increases rebureaucratization of the society, inhibits innovation and initiative on the part of the citizenry—especially in rural areas—and makes them dependent on the state.[28]

Another change was a return to old bureaucratic practices. For example, land disputes were again being sent by the Ministry of Agriculture to the Ministry of Justice, one of the most controversial institutions of the past, and one that still applies most of the old laws. This practice seems to have had significant adverse impacts on the attitudes of rural citizens toward the state.[29]

The power of the landowners and industrialists was also being restored as they were encouraged to return to their businesses. Many of these landowners had either fled the country or changed their place of residence during and after the revolution in order to avoid the peasants' retaliatory actions against them.[29,30] During a meeting with the vice minister of the Ministry of Agriculture and Rural Development in the spring of 1983, this author witnessed a case of land dispute brought by a farmer. The land that had been given him after the revolution was now being forcefully claimed by the previous owner who had returned to the village. The farmer requested transfer of ownership title. The vice minister responded that the farmer should go to the Ministry of Justice since "the MARD no longer deals with disputes over agricultural lands." While the revolutionary courts had told the farmer to remain on the farm, the Ministry of Justice ordered him to return the land to the previous owner.

Still another structural impact affected the employment of women. In 1983, the government submitted a bill to parliament that called for moving tenured, full-time female employees in the civil service to a part-time basis. It claimed that the foremost role of women is home management and child-rearing, and that their part-time employment would contribute to better employment for males. Women's reactions to this policy were noted in the official newspaper, the *Islamic Republic Daily*, on February 1, 1983. The paper reported that female government employees "are worried about their future, and are concerned lest they will be separated from employment for different reasons and different considerations and their income be cut." This bill was, nevertheless, later passed.

This legislation has made firing female employees easier. It was estimated that about 100,000 women in the civil service are subject to this new law. If implemented, it could have an adverse impact on government operations, and on tens of thousands of families in the country.[31]

Finally, another structural impact on the civil service and the bureaucracy has been the exercise of a great deal of power by the Islamic Societies (*Anjumans*), which had been established earlier in every village, department, and factory. Although their power has been defined by the Islamic Constitution and by the religious authorities as advisory and as overseers of the operations of the bureaucracy, it seems that they have been playing administrative and political roles as well. This structural change is also significant in that these societies have been given strong support by the religious authorities and are called the "ears and eyes" of the Islamic Republic. System maintenance and Islamization seem to be among their major objectives.[32]

B. Process Impacts

The hiring freeze continues in most organizations. Many negative behaviors of the bureaucracy appear to have been revived. According to some, "it is almost impossible to get things done."[33] "Red tape" and low performance seem to be prevalent problems. As one high-level administrator stated, "one has to be extremely patient. You know our bureaucracy, how slow it is and how much deference is required."[34]

As administrative performance has slowed down, public discontent toward the bureaucracy has grown. One could argue that this problem is caused by the revolution, which interrupted the smooth functioning of established institutions. But critics charge that the old bureaucracy was corrupt, inefficient, and repressive. Therefore, a return to the practices and structures of the old bureaucracy would be a major mistake with adverse effects on administrative performance and on the attitudes of citizens toward it. The latter argument is supported by abundant evidence about the Pahlavi bureaucracy as well as interviews conducted in Iran during 1983.[35]

A professor of public administration at Tehran University remarked: "The problems of the bureaucracy are going to increase as more private institutions are nationalized and more independent voluntary organizations are becoming bureaucratized."[36] Routinization of the administrative process continues mainly on the basis of old laws and regulations. This process is accompanied by another problem: Many developmental functions continue to be postponed because of the war and budget constraints. The sharp drop in oil prices in the world market has also had a negative impact on the administrative process.[37]

C. Impacts on Attitudes

Impacts on the attitudes of bureaucrats and of the general public toward the bureaucracy can be observed. The attitudes and morale of the professional bureaucrats appear to have improved. Although still denied many key managerial positions, they seem to be relatively content. "An administrator is an administrator whether it is the Shah's regime or the Islamic Republic; it makes no major difference. His job is to implement decisions made by political officials and those at the top of organizations," stated a senior career executive at the NIRT.[38]

The conflict between the need for a merit system and the desire for religious-political loyalty continues to be prevalent in Iran's civil service. Patronage is prevalent, and evidence of indifference in employee behavior is not difficult to see. As one professional administrator put it, "There is little doubt that the negative bureaucratic values and behavior in the civil service are, and continue to be, major stumbling blocks to individual and societal achievement."[39] When introducing his proposed 24 cabinet members to the Parliament in 1985, Prime Minister Mousavi called for the elimination of government red tape. The *New York Times* reported that "The failure of the previous cabinet to cut red-tape had been mentioned by some members of Iran's powerful business community in opposing a second term for Mr. Mousavi."[40]

The attitude of the general public toward the bureaucracy also seems to be becoming negative. One of the targets of the people's revolution was the old bureaucratic machine. The growth of grass-roots organizations during and after the revolution seemed to be an indication of a need for changing that bureaucracy. Through a nationwide network of "economic mobilization," for example, these and other organizations have distributed rationed food. As one senior official of the Ministry of Economics pointed out, and several middle-class citizens agreed, "without this network, many people would not have been able to obtain basic food items due to the high inflation, the black market, and the so-called 'economic terrorists.' "[41]

Evidence suggests that the underlying reason for the success of these organizations has been public participation in decision making and implementation process. It is not clear, however, whether these organizations will be able to continue to perform successfully without the government's technical and financial support.[42] Nevertheless, evidence suggests that recent government moves to integrate these independent organizations into the centralized bureaucracy have increased negative attitudes of the general public toward the bureaucracy.

Indications of discontent with bureaucratization are several. The daily newspaper, *Keyhan*, reported in 1983 that a 55-year-old worker who had been fired had taken his grievance to the Minister of Labor. He was quoted as saying: "It is almost eight months that I have been coming and going, and so far no result has materialized, and I want the government, which is the protector of the oppressed, to investigate the position of people like me."[43]

The same paper quotes another citizen:

> . . . now some ministries and administrative agencies do not act revolutionary . . . and in my belief, the administration must first plan and then, by establishing an Islamic system and a revolution in the civil service organizations, create a healthy communication between the *administrative system and the client people.* This would result in more trust towards the administration by the people who constitute most of the clients of the ministries and organizations.

There are many people who seem to have given up hope of relief from bureaucratic agencies. For example, after three years of pursuing their cases with the Ministries of Agriculture and Justice, several individuals finally gave up because of the bureaucracy's inaction and insensitivity.[44]

V. SUMMARY AND CONCLUSION

The Iranian bureaucracy and civil service system under the Pahlavi regime was characterized by inefficiency, pervasive corruption, nepotism, rigid centralization, and other bureaupathologies. It did not operate on a merit system, although a merit system was introduced during the 1960s and 1970s.

The revolution of 1978–1979 seemed to be against this bureaucracy as much as it was against the Shah. Most Iranians expected that this system would be reorganized in such a way as to make it accountable to the people. As a result of this expectation and a general distrust of the old bureaucracy, a number of people's organizations sprang up throughout the country during and after the revolution. These groups of volunteers made decisions and took action in regard to various public functions. These grass-roots organizations accomplished numerous community and development projects and contributed to the defense of the country.

In spite of a number of structural changes in the civil service, along with Islamization and further politicization, the impact of the revolution on the bureaucratic machine of the country has not been very significant. Fundamental changes in administrative structure and process have not taken place. Centralization has been forcefully pursued. Despite the establishment of the Islamic Councils, the centralized structure of the civil service has remained the same. The merit system is ignored; religious and political loyalty has become the first principle of personnel action. Political loyalty has been assured, it seems, by a number of judicial, religious, and legislative oversights and control systems. They include, for example, the permanent religious representation at all agencies, the Islamic Societies, or watchdog groups, the presidential and cabinet mechanisms of control over the bureaucracy, various tools of legislative oversight, etc. These mechanisms and political appointments assure system maintenance and leadership control over the bureaucracy.

Many problems of the civil service system, such as corruption, are becoming pervasive again. Corruption has even been acknowledged by government authorities. For example, the then Minister of the Interior, Nategh Nurie, introducing the new Mayor of Tehran in 1984, reported that "unfortunately there are still people in the municipal administration who take bribery."[45]

The extent of the problems of the Iranian bureaucracy can also be seen in the public statements of the former powerful Speaker of the National Assembly (Parliament), Hojjatulislam Hashemi Rafsanjani (the former president):

> If this administrative system is not corrected, it is impossible to get fruitful results from our efforts. Whatever laws we legislate, no matter how good a leadership the Imam exercises, and whatever judgments the judges make, no work can be done effectively. Ladies, gentlemen, sisters, and brothers: this is the administrative system we have. Do not try to use influence and don't violate the rights of others. Sometimes the causes of corruption is the people themselves: not yet gone to the government offices, they try to meet their objective by *parti* [influence wielding]. Administrative works require piety. We cannot consider an expert civil servant without piety as equal to an expert civil servant with piety and moral devotion.[46]

In short, several attempts took place to debureaucratize the administrative system during the early years of the revolution.

As the government became more stabilized and Islamization intensified, however, the processes of rebureaucratization, further centralization, consolidation of the administrative system, and control mechanism have been emphasized for system enhancement. The Iranian bureaucracy has not been abolished by the revolution. On the contrary, it has survived and prevailed as a well-entrenched institution of power. This trend will likely continue in the future despite the public's disenchantment with the bureaucracy.

Several factors may explain public dissatisfaction with the bureaucracy. First, the protracted war against Iraq has been draining the natural, human, and financial resources of the country, limiting the capacity of the public institutions to respond to public demands. Additionally, the number-one priority of the government has been declared to be the war, leaving everything else in lesser importance. Now that the war has ended, much of these resources can be transferred to other purposes. Second, shortages of major food items and other household necessities and a long waiting period have caused dissatisfaction.

Third, the black market has also contributed to public dissatisfaction; its pervasiveness has frustrated many people. As one expert at the Ministry of Economics put it, "the longer the war continues, the worse the black market situation will become. The majority of people can not afford to buy things in the black market with 10 or even 50 times higher than the rationed prices."[47] Fourth, corruption—which was one of the most serious problems of the Pahlavi bureaucracy—is becoming pervasive again. It has become manifest in a variety of forms: bribery, favoritism, *parti bazi* (influence wielding), nepotism, etc.

Fifth, governmentalization of many voluntary, independent organizations has taken control and management of these organizations away from the people (farmers, workers, shopkeepers, professionals, and others), creating disappointment and resentment. As one student of public administration at the University of Tehran put it, "it is a process of rebureaucratization of society that we are witnessing now. The state needs more control and coordination, but people also want to be less dependent on the central bureaucracy where everything moves very slowly."[48]

This rebureaucratization of society seems to have strong advocates within the ruling Islamic Republic Party, including the former Prime Minister Mousavi, who favored a strong centralized administrative system for purposes of control, coordination, and elimination of duplications. But, as Blau and Meyer indicate, "bureaucratization quite often has the opposite effect of producing inefficiency."[49] The problem of bureaucratization is coupled with the recent privatization policy of the government. Since 1983 privatization of many governmental functions and organizations has been pushed, and some public enterprises have been returned to private individuals, many of whose large properties were confiscated during the early years of the revolution. These include big landowners, industrialists, and contractors. There has even been parliamentary discussion about returning lands distributed or sold to peasants during the 1960s and early 1980s to former landowners. The privatization policy does not seem to be contradictory to the rebureaucratization policy. Indeed, they are complimentary and reinforce each other. Government-business partnership strategies have been resumed, and public financing of business continues through subsidies to the returning large landowners and industrialists.

At the same time, grass-roots organizations were bureaucratized, disappointing and discouraging farmers and some workers. This public dissatisfaction was also manifest among some professional groups in the country. The strike of the country's physicians, nurses, and pharmacists in July 1986, protesting state control of their associations, is an example. A letter seeking support from Iranian physicians abroad indicated that 6000 physicians had left the country since 1979 and others were considering this option.

This problem of rebureaucratization and public dissatisfaction is aggravated by the fact that most of the old laws, rules, and regulations remain operative and govern the new organizations joining the administrative system. Most people expected these laws and regulations of the old regime to be abolished. The unreformed Ministry of Justice, which applies the old laws, is one major source of disappointment for many people. While more religious judges are being trained in Qum, most of the old laws continue to govern the judicial system.

One example of the problem is the notorious Article 33 of the old Labor Law under the Pahlavi, which gave absolutely uncontested right to private employers to fire their workers without due process and grievance resolution procedures. That law has remained unchanged under the private sector's pressure despite the frequent protests of the labor movement and opposition from some religious leaders.

Finally, the low morale, lack of pay raises, and fear of arbitrary personnel actions within the bureaucracy also seem to have some negative impacts on the internal operations of the bureaucracy, resulting in administrative behavior dissatisfying to the public.

It is beyond the scope of this chapter to discuss in detail conceivable alternatives to deal with the issue of public dissatisfaction with the bureaucracy. However, two possible approaches could improve public attitude toward the bureaucracy. One possibility is for the government to encourage and support, both financially and technically, the independent, nonprofit, grass-roots organizations. Various types of cooperative systems can be encouraged and supported by the government to promote independent democratic activities among citizens. This would decrease the public's dependence on government bureaucracy, decrease the size of the bureaucratic administration, and promote the people's initiative and responsibility. It would also provide a broader basis of political and economic support for the government in power. Self-management and democratic administration would also promote economic development. So, instead of bureaucratizing society—a phenomenon that took place under the Shah—the new government could, and should, pursue debureaucratization and democratize and develop the administrative system.

The second possibility points to major reforms in the structure and processes of Iran's administrative system. The postrevolutionary administrative system was expected to be responsive to public demands, to be democratic and representative of nationalities and ethnic backgrounds, and to reduce, if not eliminate, corruption and bureaucratic pathologies. Many laws of the old regime cannot be respected by the citizens who staged a revolution. A substantial change in administrative, labor, and judicial laws seems necessary to reform the bureaucracy. The administrative system, moreover, needs to be developed professionally, and a merit system should be applied in the bureaucracy. Every political system is concerned with its maintenance. But overemphasis on system maintenance (or enhancement) at the expense of administrative efficiency and satisfactory public service would, this author believes, hinder employee initiative, creativity, and organizational performance.

These two approaches, if applied, could significantly decrease public dissatisfaction and provide a more democratic, efficient, and responsive administrative system for post-revolutionary Iran.

IV.   UPDATE: STATUS OF THE BUREAUCRACY IN THE 1990S[50]

The decade of the 1990s witnessed some major changes in the Iranian political, economic, and administrative structures. On the political side, the two-term election of President Hashemi Rafsanjani provided a period of continuity in the reinstitutionalization process of governance along with a strong legislative process that supplied laws and regulations for the economy, foreign relations, and administrative system. Gradually, relationship with international community increased and economic growth became a hallmark of this period.

Economic growth of the 1990s, up to the latter part of the decade, was made possible by the emphasis on postwar reconstruction of the economy and, especially, the infrastructure development of the nation. Infrastructure and development projects spiraled all over Iran, in urban and rural areas. Building bridges, roads, highways, public facilities, dams and irrigation systems, housing and urban development projects, colleges and universities, and other industrial and commercial schemes continued throughout the Rafsanjani administrations. Iran experienced high rates of economic growth, and urbanization also grew fast, but rebuilding the defense infrastructure was perhaps a top priority for Iran. As a result, Iran for the first time produced medium-range missiles capable of reaching Israel. Iran's military-industrial system also produced a number of other weapons never owned by Iran, including ammunition, antimissile weapons, helicopters, and more. Iran also strengthened its navy infrastructure to the highest level of its history. The bureaucracy was instrumental in this process of incredible growth and development.

These achievements were attained despite the relentless and brutal economic, political, and military sanctions Iran received from its global adversary, the United States and its European and other collaborators. Iran also met a backbreaking challenge of managing about 4 million refugees from the neighboring countries of Iraq and Afghanistan, plus the relentless pressure of drug traffickers from its eastern borders with Pakistan and Afghanistan whose aim has been to transport the deadly substance to Europe and North America. Once again, just as in the ancient time when Iran stopped the eastern barbarian devastation into Europe, Iranian interception of drug traffickers has saved millions of lives in West, all without appreciation and recognition. Only the United Nations has recognized this strategic struggle Iran has been engaged in and has provided symbolic support for such an effort, which has cost Iran hundreds of millions of dollars per year and numerous losses of its military personnel.

With the rapid economic growth and developmental projects also came corruption and the notion that many development projects began but were never finished. Corruption, common as it is worldwide, also inflicted Iranian government involved in growth activities. Scandals and investigations revealed major corruption cases implicating some of the high officials. An example of this is the former mayor of Tehran whose administration was found by the court of many wrongdoings and corruptions. Although political struggle between the two factions of government was also responsible for his arrest and conviction, there was no doubt that corruption had spread under his administration.

The landslide election of the reform-oriented Mohammad Khatami as the new president of Iran has been a landmark development in Iranian post-revolutionary politics and governance. Since 1998, there has been a continuously intensified struggle between two factions of the government and politics in Iran, with the supporting and opposing forces from both secular and religious bases. This has resulted in a divided government and politics in Iran, causing both opportunities for massive discourse and paralysis of governance in many cases. Both political factions have solid points of credible arguments that make the discourse a fascinating intellectual enterprise in postrevolutionary Iranian politics, governance, and administration.

Administratively, several changes took place in the 1990s. At the center of all administrative changes was the bureaucracy itself. Obviously, one of the major changes was the further growth of the public sector though both the expansion of the Mostazafin Foundation (organization for the oppressed poor) and the increase in number of other regular government agencies. Another development was the huge enterprise of managing the massive reconstruction and infrastructure development programs. This responsibility put a heavy burden on the bureaucracy and administrative system. But partnership with the private sector was sought by the Rafsanjani's administration. Therefore, a third development was the growth of public-private partnerships in development projects and reconstruction and infrastructure development activities. Partnership resulted in initiation and adoption of privatization schemes. Thus, a fourth development, privatization, started out as a policy to transfer governmental functions of running a number of public enterprises to the private sector. But the government was divided on this issue, with traditional conservatives opposing it and reformists in its favor. However, some privatization programs were met severely with the workers' protests in various parts of the country, and government backed down on some projects.

With the election of the President Khatami, privatization has been pursued very comprehensively, vigorously, and sweepingly. There are various, and contradictory, personalities with different ideological orientations within the Khatami administration. Therefore, it is not surprising to see extreme elements pushing massive and sweeping privatization as a policy solution to some of the problems of governance. Khatami's proposed Third Development Plan (2000–2005) had called for a full-fledged privatization that included virtually all public enterprises and a massive number of governmental functions traditionally performed by the government agencies. Surprisingly, the conservatively controlled parliament approved the plan, but the Guardian Council, a higher body of legislative governance, rejected it for being unconstitutional. Either a compromise or rewritten legislation is expected to be the result of this legislative development, because it is unlikely that the legislation ever reaches the High Expediency Council, the highest governance body of the nation; legislation rarely does. Nevertheless, a large number of public enterprise and many governmental functions have already been privatized, with their destinies unknown at this time. While privatization remains as a key policy issue, political and economic liberalization has captured Iranian public opinion, behind which external pressures and influence, especially of the United States and of other Western powers, are at heavy play.

Reform of the bureaucracy and of the entire administrative system can not succeed by simple solutions such as massive and weeping privatization. Privatization is not a panacea; it will cause more problems for the government than ever before. Even the strongest proponents of privatization admit that it has serious negative consequences and that it is one of several alternatives to government reforms. I have argued that privatization is and should be one of the last resort policy options for improving government performance. Launching a serious program of revolutionary reform can and should be the first priority, using a combination of top-down, bottom-up, and institutional approaches of organizational and administrative change and development. This also includes public enterprise management reform in postrevolutionary reform. Another alternative to privatization is transfer of control and management of some enterprise to the cooperative systems and promotion of these self-governing organizations throughout Iran.

They promote self-sufficiency, reduce bureaucratic red tape, and promote democratic governance and administration.

Privatization may reduce temporarily some functions of government, but will increase other functions of governance-monitoring and regulating the economy and industries. It also increases corruption, raise prices, causes disruption in economic development of the country; remember that government is and has always been the engine of infrastructure and national development in both industrialized and developing countries. Contract management, regulatory administration, and social welfare functions can increase governmental responsibility, size, and operations. With privatization, government responsibility to citizens does not disappear; it only increases, as the government is and should be accountable to the public for the actions of newly privatized institutions.

Bureaucracy is a creature few people like. It is difficult to like bureaucracy. It is an easy target for criticism. But is the bureaucracy that even the critical politicians like most. This is an observation that has been made in the West as well as the east. Bureaucracy performs essential political as well as economic as well as social functions in society. It provides order and stability, and its security-military functions are invaluable. Bureaucracy is extremely functional to system maintenance and regime enhancement in all societies. Conservative former President Ronald Reagan of the United States had promised to slash the bureaucracy once elected, but he actually increased significantly the size and budget of the bureaucracy during his tenure of administration.

Why does bureaucracy persist? It does so because it is imperative to the existence and promotion of the capitalist order. Bureaucracy and capitalism go and grow hands in hands, as Max Weber once correctly observed. Market is inherently chaos-oriented and generates disorder, inequality, unfairness, cheating and more, but market also needs a strong state and bureaucracy. Without order market is doomed. Order is provided by bureaucracy, so the accumulation of surplus capital is facilitated without problems, problems that are created by the same market capitalism. The problems are the byproducts of corporate capitalism. With the rise of globalization and globalizing transworld corporations, there will be more inequality, more poverty, more social institutional destruction, more environmental degradation, and more social and economic problems, all of which must be brought under control.

The security and military bureaucracies are on the rise everywhere, including in the United States. But the rise of security and order bureaucracy in postrevolutionary Iran is contrary to the ideals of the revolution, a fact that the political and administrative leaders need to keep in mind. To avoid the social and political consequences of sweeping privatization, of increasing security bureaucracies, and of bureaucratic pathologies, serious reforms of administration and organization are needed to embrace and engage citizens, professional administrators, and institutions of self-governance. By enabling the environment for growth and promotion of nonbureaucratic, self-governing organizations, the postrevolutionary state can promote and improve public administration and social cohesion in Iran. Bureaucracy has survived all political masters and changes, but it is the character of the state and bureaucracy that matters most, its orientation toward serving the broad public interests.

ENDNOTES

1. References concerning the causes of the Iranian Revolution are many. For a small sample, see Cottam, Richard, Goodby to America's Shah, *Foreign Policy 34* (Spring, 1979); Bill, James, Iran and the Crises of '78, *Foreign Affairs 57* (Winter, 1978–79); Keddie, Nikki, Oil, Economic Policy and Social Conflict in Iran, *Race and Class 21* (1979); Helmut, Richard, The America's Shah, The Shahanshah of Iran, *MERIP Reports 40*, New York, Middle East Research and Information Project, 1975; Hooglund, Eric,

Rural Participation in the Revolution, *MERIP Reports 87*, 1980; Halliday, Fred, *Iran: Dictatorship and Development*, Penguin Books, New York, 1979; Graham, Robert, *Iran: The Illusion of Power*, St. Martin's Press, New York, 1979.

2. See, for example, Bill, James, *The Politics of Iran: Groups, Classes, and Modernization*, Charles Merrill, Columbus, Ohio, 1972, Bill, James, and Leiden, Carl, *The Middle East: Politics and Power*, Allyn and Bacon, Boston, 1979; Zonis, Marvin, *The Political Elite of Iran*, Princeton University Press, Princeton, NJ, 1971; Farazmand, Ali, *Bureaucratic Politics Under the Shah: Development or System Maintenance?*, Ph.D. dissertation in public administration, Maxwell School, Syracuse University, 1982.

3. This expectation was expressed by the majority of politicians and citizens interviewed by the author in the spring of 1983.

4. Premier Bazargan repeated this statement several times in radio broadcasts during the early months of 1979. This was further verified through interviews held in Tehran in April 1983 with Parliament members.

5. April 1983 interviews held with several administrators and/or committee members in the civil service. These changes undermined the hierarchical control of the provisional administration. As one administrator put it, "everyone wanted changes in the administrative system, some called for abolition of the bureaucracy, and others called for its reform. But all wanted their paychecks."

6. Interviews with some members of these organizations including the Reconstruction Crusade (*Jehad-e-Sazandegi*), April 1983.

7. Interviews with three officeholders in the State Organization for Employment and Administrative Affairs (SOEAA), April 1983. These opinions were confirmed by conversations held with others formerly with the civil service.

8. Interviews with civil service officials at SOEAA and the National Radio and Television (NIRT), Tehran, April 1983.

9. Interviews held with three administrators at the Ministry of Communication and Postal Services, Tehran, April 1983.

10. Personal interview with a professor of the University of Tehran, May 1983.

11. Interviews with several deputies of the Parliament and with administrators in the Ministry of Agriculture, Tehran, April 1983. Also, information gathered from the National State Radio broadcasts during the same period.

12. Interview with a professor of the University of Tehran, May 1983.

13. Interviews with several administrators at the Ministry of Agriculture and the NIRT, Tehran, April 1983.

14. Interviews with two members of the parliament and three civil servants at the Ministry of Education and the NIRT, April 1983; also, interview with a professor of Tehran University, April 1983.

15. Interviews with several administrators at the NIRT, Ministry of Agriculture, including its then vice minister, and with a Professor of Tehran University, April–May 1983. Also personal conversation of the author, same period.

16. Also, interview held with a higher civil servant at the SOEAA, Tehran, May 1983.

17. Interviews with several civil servants and political appointees at the Ministry of Higher Education and the Ministry of Education, Tehran, April 1983. Also see P. Sharan, *The Government and Politics of Persia*, Metropolitan Publisher, New Delhi, 1983.

18. Statement was made by a civil servant.

19. Interviews with civil servants at the Ministry of Agriculture and Rural Development (MARD), Tehran, April 1983. Also conversations held with farmers in the province of Gilan during the same period.

20. Interviews with several civil servants, administrators and political appointees at the Ministry of Agriculture and Rural Development (MARD), the Ministry of Economics, and the SOEAA, Tehran, April 1983.

21. Interviews with three members of the Parliament and five high civil servants at the Ministry of Agriculture, Tehran, April 1983. Further interviews with four officials of the Organization of *Jehan-e-Sazandegi* (Reconstruction Crusade) in the province of Gilan.

22. Presentation of the economic adviser to Prime Minister Mousavi to the Plan and Budget Organization at the annual meeting of the Association of Iranian Economists in Tehran, May 1983. The author was in attendance at the meeting.

23. Public speeches of the revolutionary leaders—Imami Kashani, Hashemi Rafsanjani, Moghaddass-e-Ardebili, and Mahdavi Kani—at the Friday prayers at Tehran University during March, April, and May 1983. Interviews with three high-level administrators at the NIRT, SOEAA, and the Ministry of Education, Tehran, March 1983. Also, presentation of the new Five-Year Plan made by a member of the Plan and Budget Organization at the annual meeting of the Association of Iranian Economists held in Tehran, May 1983.

24. Interview with a high official (planner and organizational strategist) of the Ministry of Agriculture and Rural Development (MARD), April 1983. Also, additional interviews with a number of urban and rural citizens of Tehran and Northern Iran.

25. Radio broadcasts of the Parliamentary debates during April and May 1983. Also, interviews with members of the Parliament and two personnel officers at the SOEAA during the same period.

26. Also, interviews with an official of the Office of the Prime Minister (OPM), and with a Parliament deputy, May 1983.

27. Interviews with two Parliament deputies in Tehran, May 1983; also an interview held with a professor of Tehran University, May 1983.

28. In the same meeting, a high-level administrative assistant to the minister in "Organization and Strategy" outlined to the author the main features of the recently redesigned organization structure, which was submitted to the Parliament for approval. The reorganization plan called for decentralization of the MARD with policy power for the center and greater administrative decision powers for both the provinces and local government departments.

29. Interviews with three higher civil servants of the Ministry of Agriculture in Tehran, April 1983. Also, five interviews held with the farmers, who brought their complaints to the MARD in Tehran and Rasht during April 1983. Moreover, personal observations at the MARD's Office of the Minister, April 1983.

30. Also, interview with a member of the Parliament in Tehran in April 1983.

31. Interview with an administrator of the Ministry of Labor and Social Affairs, Tehran, March 1983.

32. See Farazmand, A., Public Administration in Iran, in *Public Administration in the Third World* (V. Subramaniam, ed.), Greenwood Press, Westport, Conn., 1990. Also, personal observations of the author at the NIRT and in several rural areas of the Gilan province, where the author gained insights from conversations with the rural people. Moreover, interviews with three middle-level administrators of the Personnel Department of the NIRT and two top administrators at the Ministry of Economics, held in Tehran, May 1983.

33. Conversations with three administrators at the NIRT, Tehran, May 1983.

34. Conversations with an administrator in charge of legal affairs at the NIRT, Tehran, March–May 1983.

35. For a sample of evidence on the aspects of the Pahlavi bureaucracy, see notes 1 and 2. Interview held in Tehran with a professor of Tehran University in April 1983. Also see A. Farazmand, *The State, Bureaucracy, and Revolution in Modern Iran: Agrarian Reform and Regime Politics* (New York: Praeger, 1989).

36. The author was a participant at the meeting where he was a member of the Curriculum Planning and Development Committee for the Public Administration and Business Management programs of the universities of the country.

37. Interviews with two Parliament members, Tehran, April 1983. An interview with a professor of Tehran University, April 1983.

38. Conversations with a high-level administrator of the NIRT, Tehran, May 1983.

39. Observations and interviews at the NIRT, the Ministry of Agriculture, and the Ministry of Finance and Economics. The quoted statement was made by a financial manager at the NIRT during the interview in April 1983.

40. See *The New York Times*, October 28, 1985.

41. The "Economic Terrorists" referred to here are some of the Bazar merchants and other war profiteers who have taken advantage of a wartime economy. It is believed that these merchants created artificial shortages, resulting in a black market economy. Public outrage about this situation caused the resignation of the Minister of Commerce and Trade in 1983.

42. Interviews and observations in Tehran and Rasht, spring 1983.

43. See *Keyhan, Air Edition*, April 13, 1983.

44. Ministry of Agriculture, April 1983. Interviews and conversations with several farmers, and with officials at different levels. Also, conversations with several professionals at the Ministry of Higher Education, May 1983. This author's personal experience was also supportive evidence of this problem. The experience dealt with several agencies, including the NIRT, in which, despite the strong reception of the Agency Head, no cooperation was received from the administrative director regarding the use of this author's professional service in the organization.

45. See *Ettlaat*, Jan. 8 and 12, 1983 (in Farsi).

46. See *Keyhan, Air Edition*, Sept. 14, 1983 (in Farsi).

47. Interviews with a high-level administrator at the Ministry of Economics, Tehran, May 1983.

48. Conversations with a student at the University of Tehran, School of Public and Business Administration, May 1983.

49. See Peter Blau and Marshall Meyer, Why Study Bureaucracy?, in *Current Issues in Public Administration* 3rd ed. (F. Lane, ed.), St. Martin's Press, New York, 1986, p. 6.

50. See Ali Farazmand, "Bureaucracy and Revolution: The case of Islamic Iran: A Theoretical and Empirical Analysis," paper presented at the International Congress on Elucidation of the Islamic/Iranian Revolution, Tehran, October 2–4, 1999, p. 53; Ali Farazmand, "Privatization in Post-Revolutionary Iran," in Ali Farazmand, ed., *Privatization Or Reform: Implications for Public Management* (Westport, CT: Greenwood Press, 2000); "Administrative Reform in Post-Revolutionary Iran," in Ali Farazmand, ed., *Administrative Reform in Developing Nations* (Westport, CT: Greenwood Press, 2000). Also see Ali Farazmand, *Post-Revolutionary Iran: Regime Change, Elite Change, and the Bureaucracy* (forthcoming).

Index